Human Resources Management In Canada

CANADIAN SEVENTH EDITION

GARY DESSLER
Florida International University

NINA D. COLE
Brock University

VIRGINIA L. (GINI) SUTHERLAND
Sir Sandford Fleming College

Prentice Hall Canada Inc.,
Scarborough, Ontario

Canadian Cataloguing in Publication Data

Dessler, Gary 1942-   .
    Human resources management in Canada

Canadian 7th ed.
Canadian 5th ed. by Gary Dessler and Alvin Turner
ISBN 0-13-907528-3

1. Personnel management.   2. Personnel management–Canada.
I. Cole, Nina D.   II. Sutherland, Gini.   III. Title.

HF5549.D64 1998   658.3   C98-931173-2

© 1999 Prentice-Hall Canada Inc., Scarborough, Ontario
A Division of Simon & Schuster/A Viacom Company

Previous editions were published as *Human Resource Management in Canada* © 1992 Prentice-Hall Canada Inc. by Gary Dessler and Alvin Turner; *Personnel Management* © 1984 by Gary Dessler and John F. Duffy.

Publisher: Patrick Ferrier
Acquisitions Editor: Mike Ryan
Developmental Editor: Amber Wallace
Senior Marketing Manager: Ann Byford
Production Editor: Nicole Mellow
Copy Editor: Catharine Haggert

Production Coordinator: Deborah Starks
Permissions/Photo Research: Karen Becker
Cover Design: Alex Li
Cover Image: © Paul Anderson/SIS
Page Layout: Phyllis Seto
Interior Design: Ann France

Original English Language edition published by Prentice-Hall, Inc., Upper Saddle River, New Jersey.
Copyright © 1997, 1994, 1991, 1988, 1984.

1 2 3 4 5   RRD   03 02 01 00 99

Printed and bound in the USA.

Visit the Prentice Hall Canada Web site! Send us your comments, browse our catalogues, and more at **www.phcanada.com**. Or reach us through e-mail at **phcinfo_pubcanada@prenhall.com**.

"HR Leaders Brainstorm the Profession's Future" by Shari Caudron, copyright August 1994. "Preventive Maintenance Techniques for Staying Union Free" by J. F. Rand, copyright June 1980. "Affirmative Action Programs: Have We Forgotten the First Line Supervisor?" by Tove Hanner, copyright June 1979. Used with permission of ACC Communications Inc./ *Personnel Journal* (now known as *Workforce*), Costa Mesa, CA. All rights reserved.

Statistics Canada information is used with the permission of the Minister of Industry, as Minister responsible for Statistics Canada. Information on the availability of the wide range of data from Statistics Canada can be obtained from Statistics Canada's Regional Offices, its World Wide Web site at http://www.statcan.ca, and its toll-free access number 1-800-263-1136.

Dedicated to my son, Derek
G.D.

To Peggy Martin.
N.C.

To Doris, Jim, Nancy, Lynda, and Tom. With thanks for
your support and love, Gini.
G.S.

◆

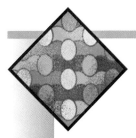

Brief Contents

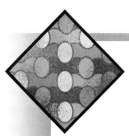

Table of Contents

CBC

CBC

CBC

Chapter 18: Occupational Health and Safety **668**

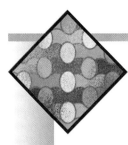

Preface

Human Resources Management in Canada is based on two key premises: 1) that human resources are the most important asset in most Canadian organizations today, something that is being acknowledged by an increasing number of managers across the country; and 2) that the effective management of the employment relationship is a responsibility shared by human resources specialists, all supervisors and managers, and increasingly, employees themselves. A strong foundation in human resources management (HRM) is important for supervisors and managers in every field and employees at every level—not just those working in human resources or industrial relations departments or aspiring to do so in the future. This book was designed to provide students specializing in HRM, those in general business or business administration programs, supervisory/managerial staff, and small business owners with a complete, comprehensive review of essential HRM concepts and techniques in a highly readable and understandable form.

The Canadian seventh edition provides extensive coverage of all essential HRM topics such as job analysis, recruitment, selection, orientation, training, compensation and benefits, performance appraisal, health and safety, and union–management relations. Fostering employee commitment is used as an integrating theme, and quality management and productivity improvement are emphasized throughout and explored thoroughly in chapter 10. Many suggestions regarding practical applications have been included, such as how to implement a harassment policy, develop a job description and legally defensible job specifications, recruit online, handle a selection interview, appraise performance, deal with substance abusers, and handle grievances. Key legislation affecting today's workplaces is covered in full: human rights, employment equity, pay equity, employment/labour standards, labour relations, and occupational health and safety. Since legislation affects virtually every aspect of HRM, legal issues are discussed throughout the book, and suggestions are provided regarding ways to ensure compliance, while simultaneously increasing employee commitment and productivity.

Human Resources Management in Canada, C/7/e, is based largely on the authors' research and teaching experience in HRM, but also incorporates the hands-on experience acquired by the two Canadian authors while previously employed as HR practitioners. Numerous examples are provided, illustrating the ways in which HR managers in Canada are actually applying the principles discussed. The content is enhanced and validated by research findings and the published works of many individuals, cited throughout.

Changes to the Canadian Seventh Edition

Human Resources Management in Canada, C/7/e, has been substantially reorganized, and now includes six sections and nineteen chapters. The following is a brief summary of some of the new and expanded material in each chapter.

PART ONE: HUMAN RESOURCES MANAGEMENT IN PERSPECTIVE

Chapter 1   **Human Resources Management: The Field and Its Environment** Expanded coverage of the HRM responsibilities of all managers, demographic trends, work force diversity and its impact, and technology (including human resources information systems). New material on globalization, trends in the nature of jobs and work, new modes of organizing and managing, and the importance of employee commitment.

Chapter 2   **The Evolving Role of HRM: From Staff Function to Strategic Partner** The history of HRM now appears in this chapter. New material on ethics, social responsibility, the current role of human resources departments, strategic planning, the role of the HR department as a strategic partner, and the impact of effective HRM practices on employee performance and the bottom line. Moved to this chapter is much-expanded coverage of professionalism and auditing the HR system.

Chapter 3 **The Changing Emphasis: From Legal Compliance to Valuing Diversity** Totally reorganized and updated coverage of equality, equal opportunity, and equity. Expanded coverage of bona fide occupational requirements, reasonable accommodation, and harassment. New material on diversity management.

PART TWO: MEETING HUMAN RESOURCES REQUIREMENTS

Chapter 4 **Designing and Analyzing Jobs** Totally reorganized and expanded coverage of organizing work and job design. Expanded coverage of legal compliance issues, job descriptions, and job specifications. Material added on NOC Codes, physical demands analysis, statistically derived job specifications and job analysis in a "jobless" world.

Chapter 5 **Human Resources Planning** New material on the link between HRP and strategic planning, the importance of environmental scanning, and HR programs to balance supply and demand. Expanded coverage of succession planning.

Chapter 6 **Recruitment** New material on constraints, online recruiting, recruiting a more diverse work force, and developing and using application forms. Separate section on recruiting non-permanent staff includes expanded coverage of temporary employees and new material on contract employees and outsourcing/subcontracting.

Chapter 7 **Selection** New material on the legal implications of negligent hiring and wrongful dismissal; constraints on selection; teleconferenced, videoconferenced, and computerized interviews; realistic job previews; and strategies for making hiring decisions. Expanded coverage of reliability and validity, the steps in the selection process, and legal issues (including medical exams and drug testing). Section added on designing and conducting an effective semi-structured interview.

PART THREE: DEVELOPING EFFECTIVE HUMAN RESOURCES

Chapter 8 **Orientation and Training** New material on internet- and intranet-based training, literacy training, diversity training, and improving customer-service skills.

Chapter 9 **Career Development** Chapters on "Management Development "and Career" Management" have been combined. New material on building a learning organization, life-long learning, career planning systems, and roles in career development.

Chapter 10 **Managing Quality and Productivity** Leading-edge material has been added, replacing chapters on the fundamentals of motivation, quality of work life, and non-financial motivation techniques including: HRM and business process reengineering, quality management, ISO 9000/14000, and moving toward empowered jobs. Sections on international participative management programs and making self-directed teams more effective have been expanded.

Chapter 11 **Performance Appraisal** New coverage of computerized performance appraisals, diversity issues and appraisal biases, performance management, 360-degree feedback, quality-based appraisals, and ethical issues.

PART FOUR: COMPENSATION ADMINISTRATION

Chapter 12 **Establishing Pay Plans** New material on laws affecting compensation in Canada, particularly pay equity, skills/competency-based pay, and executive compensation.

Chapter 13 **Pay-for-Performance and Financial Incentives** Expanded coverage of gain-sharing. New material on the use of incentive plans to improve employee performance and morale, and how incentive plans can backfire.

Chapter 14 **Employee Benefits and Services** Updated coverage of government-sponsored benefits, particularly pertaining to workers' compensation, and flexible benefits plans. New material about pay on termination of employment. Expanded coverage of ways to reduce health-care costs and disability claims, particularly in the area of mental health.

PART FIVE: BUILDING EFFECTIVE EMPLOYEE/EMPLOYER RELATIONSHIPS

Chapter 15 **Fair Treatment: The Foundation of Effective Employee Relations** Updated coverage of topics related to employee rights and management rights. New material on electronic eavesdropping and trespassing, employee privacy, and downsizing and morale. Expanded coverage of ways to avoid wrongful dismissal lawsuits and discipline guidelines.

Chapter 16 **The Dynamics of Labour Relations** Totally rewritten chapter. Expanded coverage of the contemporary legal framework, the labour movement in Canada today, the union organizing process, union recognition, and decertification. New material on management's labour relations strategies, the labour relations process, the impact of unionization on HRM, and current challenges confronting the Canadian labour movement.

Chapter 17 **Collective Bargaining and Contract Administration** New material on the collective bargaining process; preparation for negotiations; face-to-face negotiations, including interest-based and mutual gains bargaining; the contract approval process; third-party assistance, including interest arbitration; and building effective labour–management relations. Expanded coverage of contract administration and handling grievances.

Chapter 18 **Occupational Health and Safety** New coverage of WHMIS, workplace violence, AIDS, reducing repetitive strain injuries through ergonomics, and reducing job stress through wellness programs.

PART SIX: INTERNATIONAL ISSUES IN HUMAN RESOURCES MANAGEMENT

Chapter 19 **Managing Human Resources in an International Business** New full chapter on international HRM with coverage of the nature of international business, how intercultural differences impact HR, improving international assignments, selecting international managers, adaptability screening, international compensation, and international performance appraisal and labour relations.

Key Features

Although there are many good HRM texts available in Canada, we are confident that ours stands out among them. Not only is the content extremely current—designed to take readers beyond the year 2000—we have adopted suggestions for improvement provided by students using previous editions, faculty, and reviewers; and included numerous features to improve readability and make the material more practical, meaningful and interesting.

Highlighted Themes

- **Diversity Counts** There is a Diversity Counts box in almost every chapter, which describes some of the issues and challenges involved in managing the diverse work force found in Canadian organizations. Topics range from innovative childcare to ergonomic aids for older workers, outreach recruitment strategies, potential performance appraisal biases, building a family-friendly benefits package, gender differences in dispute resolution, and sending female managers abroad.

- **Information Technology and HR** Examples are provided throughout the book describing how computers are being used, not only for storage, retrieval, and analysis of information, but for a wide range of broader applications, including developing employee skills inventories, recruiting online, computer-assisted selection interviewing, internet-based training, conducting employee attitude surveys, and costing benefits and bargaining proposals.

- **HR and the Responsive Organization** These boxes provide examples that illustrate the ways in which organizations primarily, but not exclusively, in Canada, are responding to their changing environments in order to thrive in their product or service market. Topics range from flattening the hierarchy and decentralizing decision making to integrating HR planning and strategic planning, broadbanding, and mutual gains bargaining.

- **Building Employee Commitment** These boxes provide examples of techniques organizations are using to increase the commitment of their employees, such as employee empowerment, actively encouraging promotion from within, instituting value-based hiring practices, and providing long-time employment without guarantees.

- **Small Business Applications** Recognizing that small businesses are playing an increasingly important role in the Canadian economy, and are a major source of employment, suggestions are provided to assist those in smaller businesses, with limited time and resources, to implement effective HRM policies and procedures. Concrete, practical hints are included for activities ranging from writing job descriptions to administering selection tests, interviewing applicants, checking references, setting up a training program, developing a pay plan, and outsourcing benefits.

- **Global HRM** Recognizing the increasing impact of globalization, topics highlighted in the Global HRM boxes range from protecting human rights on an international basis to global job rotation and management development, extending participative decision making abroad, and issues in compensating expatriate employees.

Additional Features

- *Chapter Outlines* Each chapter begins with a chapter outline that highlights key topic areas.

- *Learning Outcomes* Specific learning goals are also defined on each chapter-opening page.

- *Key Terms* Key terms appear in boldface within the text, are defined in the margins, and are listed at the end of the chapter.

- *Current Examples* Numerous real-world examples of HRM policies, procedures, and practices at a wide variety of organizations, ranging from small service providers to huge global corporations, can be found throughout the text.

- *Full-colour Figures, Tables and Photographs* Throughout each chapter, key concepts and applications are illustrated with strong, full-colour visual materials.

- *Weblinks* Helpful Internet sites are provided throughout the text and are easily identifiable by the Weblinks icon shown here.

- *End-of-Chapter Summaries* At the end of each chapter, the summary reviews key points and links the critical content.

- *End-of-Chapter Discussion Questions and Exercises* Each chapter contains a set of discussion questions, as well as both group and individual exercises, that stimulate critical thinking and discussion, and provide an opportunity to review key principles and develop some hands-on skills.

- *Running Case* A running case on the Carter Cleaning Company illustrates the types of HRM challenges confronted by small-business owners and front-line supervisors, and is accompanied by critical-thinking questions, which provide an opportunity to discuss and apply the text material.

- *Case Incident* A different case incident can be found at the end of each chapter. These cases present current HRM issues in a real-life setting, and are followed by questions designed to stimulate discussion and promote the use of problem-solving skills.

- *Human Resources Management Simulation* There is a section at the end of almost every chapter, which provides a direct link to experiential exercises and role plays in Prentice Hall Canada's *Human Resources Management Simulation* by Phillip G. Day (013-922659-1).

- *CBC Video Cases* To underscore the practical, real-world orientation of this book, fourteen video cases have been included, based on CBC programs. They provide an additional bridge between the course material and ongoing Canadian events.

- *Take It to the Net* Each chapter ends with the address of the Companion Web site for *Human Resources Management in Canada,* C/7/e— **www.prenticehall. ca/dessler**. Visit this site to access online experiential exercises, Weblinks, Netnews, and more.

- *Notes and References* This section includes references from academic and practitioner journals and books, historical information, as well as personal observations and experiences of the authors.

Supplements

Human Resources Management in Canada, Canadian seventh edition, is accompanied by a complete supplements package.

- **Instructor's Manual with Video Guide** (013-999061-5) This comprehensive guide contains a detailed lecture outline of each chapter, descriptions of the discussion boxes, answers to discussion questions, a review of the application exercises, and helpful video case notes.

- **The Test Item File** (013-999079-8) The test item file contains over 1 500 multiple-choice, true/false, and short essay questions. Each question is rated by level of difficulty and includes a text page reference. It is available in both printed and electronic formats.

- **Prentice Hall Custom Test** (013-999087-9) This powerful computerized testing package merges the Test Item File with a state-of-the-art software package in the Windows platform. With the Prentice Hall Custom Test's user-friendly test-creating abilities, you can create tailor-made, error-free tests quickly and easily. The Custom Test allows you to create an exam, administer it traditionally or online, and evaluate and track student's results—all with the click of the mouse.

- **Transparency Resource Package** (013-999095-X) Over 100 transparency masters highlighting key concepts featured in the text are available in printed format and electronically in PowerPoint 4.0.

- **Prentice Hall Canada/CBC Video Library** Prentice Hall Canada and the CBC have worked together to bring you fourteen segments from the CBC series *Venture* and *The National Magazine*. Designed specifically to complement the text, this case collection is an excellent tool for bringing students in contact with the world outside the classroom. These programs have extremely high production quality and have been chosen to relate directly to chapter content. Please contact your Prentice Hall Canada sales representative for details.

- **Companion Website** For a multitude of practice questions, experiential exercises, key terms and concepts, Weblinks to related sites, Netnews (Internet Newsgroups), Netsearch, CBC video case updates and more, check out the *Human Resources Management in Canada,* C/7/e, Companion Website at **www.prenticehall.ca/dessler**.

Acknowledgments

The manuscript was reviewed at various stages of its development by a number of peers across Canada, and we wish to thank those who shared their insights and constructive criticism. Among them are Gordon Barnard, Durham College; Phillip Day, Sir Sandford Fleming College; Edward G. Fisher, University of Alberta; Jane Guzar, Mohawk College; Kristi Harrison, Centennial College; Beverly Linnell, Southern Alberta Institute of Technology; Shirley Richards, Humber College; Jennifer Singh, Seneca College; and Eileen B. Stewart, British Columbia Institute of Technology.

At Prentice Hall Canada, we are very grateful for the support and dedicated efforts of Amber Wallace, as well as Pat Ferrier, Catharine Haggert, Nicole Mellow, and Mike Ryan.

Special thanks are extended to the research assistants who helped to obtain Canadian material and provided ongoing assistance and support: Tim Arnold, Lynda Phillips, and Wendy Thompson.

On a personal note, we thank our family members and friends who provided advice, moral support, and encouragement, without whom this book would never have been completed: Derek and Claudia; Len; Doris, Jim, Nancy, and Tom.

Gary Dessler
Florida International University

Nina D. Cole
Brock University

Virginia L. (Gini) Sutherland
Sir Sandford Fleming College

Photo Credits

companion **Website...**

Your Internet companion to the most exciting, state-of-the-art educational tools on the Web!

The Prentice Hall Canada Companion Website is easy to navigate and is organized to correspond to the chapters in this textbook. The Companion Website is comprised of four distinct, functional features:

1) **Customized Online Resources**

2) **Online Study Guide**

3) **Reference Material**

4) **Communication**

Explore the four areas in this Companion Website. Students and distance learners will discover resources for indepth study, research and communication, empowering them in their quest for greater knowledge and maximizing their potential for success in the course.

A NEW WAY TO DELIVER EDUCATIONAL CONTENT

1) Customized Online Resources

Our Companion Websites provide instructors and students with a range of options to access, view, and exchange content.

- **Syllabus Builder** provides *instructors* with the option to create online classes and construct an online syllabus linked to specific modules in the Companion Website.

- **Mailing lists** enable *instructors* and *students* to receive customized promotional literature.

- **Preferences** enable *students* to customize the sending of results to various recipients, and also to customize how the material is sent, e.g., as html, text, or as an attachment.

- **Help** includes an evaluation of the user's system and a tune-up area that makes updating browsers and plug-ins easier. This new feature will enhance the user's experience with Companion Websites.

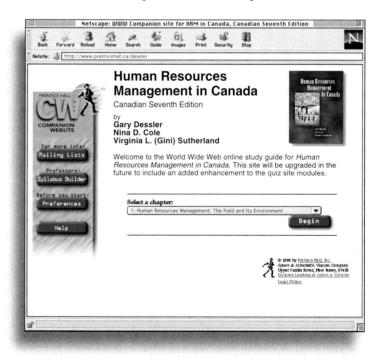

2) Online Study Guide

Interactive Study Guide modules form the core of the student learning experience in the Companion Website. These modules are categorized according to their functionality:

- True-False
- Multiple Choice
- Experiential Exercises

The True-False and Multiple Choice modules provide students with the ability to send answers to our grader and receive instant feedback on their progress through our Results Reporter. Coaching comments and references back to the textbook ensure that students take advantage of all resources available to enhance their learning experience.

3) Reference Material

Reference material broadens text coverage with up-to-date resources for learning. **Web Destinations** provide a directory of Web sites relevant to the subject matter in each chapter. **Net News (Internet Newsgroups)** are a fundamental source of information about a discipline, containing a wealth of brief, opinionated postings. **Net Search** simplifies key term search using Internet search engines.

4) Communication

Companion Websites contain the communication tools necessary to deliver courses in a **Distance Learning** environment. **Message Board** allows users to post messages and check back periodically for responses. **Live Chat** allows users to discuss course topics in real time, and enables professors to host online classes.

Communication facilities of Companion Websites provide a key element for distributed learning environments. There are two types of communication facilities currently in use in Companion Websites:

- **Message Board** – this module takes advantage of browser technology providing the users of each Companion Website with a national news group to post and reply to relevant course topics.

- **Live Chat** – enables instructor-led group activities in real time. Using our chat client, instructors can display Website content while students participate in the discussion.

Companion Websites are currently available for:

- Starke: Contemporary Management in Canada
- Kotler: Principles of Marketing
- Evans: Marketing Essentials

Note: **CW '99** content will vary slightly from site to site depending on discipline requirements.

The Companion Websites can be found at:

www.prenticehall.ca/dessler

PRENTICE HALL CANADA

1870 Birchmount Road
Scarborough, Ontario M1P 2J7

To order:
Call: 1-800-567-3800
Fax: 1-800-263-7733

For samples:
Call: 1-800-850-5813
Fax: (416) 299-2539
E-mail: phcinfo_pubcanada
@prenhall.com

Chapter 1

Human Resources Management: The Field and Its Environment

Chapter Outline

- ◆ **Introduction to Human Resources Management**
- ◆ **Internal Environmental Influences**
- ◆ **External Environmental Influences**
- ◆ **Tomorrow's HR Today**

Learning Outcomes

After studying this chapter, you should be able to:

Define human resources management and *describe* its objectives.

Discuss the human resources management responsibilities of all managers.

Explain the role of the human resources department.

Discuss the impact of organizational culture and climate on human resources management.

Describe the external environmental factors affecting human resources management policies and practices, and explain their impact.

Describe the new modes of organizing and managing that have emerged and *explain* the importance of employee commitment.

Introduction to Human Resources Management

What Is Human Resources Management?

human resources management (HRM)
The activities, policies, and practices involved in obtaining, developing, utilizing, evaluating, maintaining, and retaining the appropriate number and skill mix of employees to accomplish the organization's objectives.

Human resources management (HRM) refers to the management of people in organizations. It comprises the activities, policies, and practices involved in obtaining, developing, utilizing, evaluating, maintaining, and retaining the appropriate number and skill mix of employees to accomplish the organization's objectives. The goal of HRM is to maximize employees' contributions in order to achieve optimal productivity and effectiveness, while simultaneously attaining individual objectives (such as having a challenging job and obtaining recognition), and societal objectives (such as legal compliance and demonstrating social responsibility).[1]

Objectives of Human Resources Management

The objectives of HRM include:

- assisting the organization in attracting the quality and quantity of candidates required, in light of the organization's strategic and operational goals, staffing needs, and desired culture
- helping to create a climate in which employees are encouraged to develop and utilize their skills to the fullest
- helping to maintain performance standards and increase productivity through orientation, training, development, job design, effective communication, and performance appraisal
- helping to establish and maintain a harmonious working relationship with employees
- helping to create and maintain a safe and healthy work environment
- developing programs to meet the economic, psychological, and social needs of the employees
- helping the organization to retain productive employees
- ensuring that the organization is in compliance with provincial/territorial and federal laws affecting the workplace (such as human rights, employment equity, occupational health and safety, employment standards, and labour relations legislation).

In many firms, senior managers have come to the realization that human resources are the organization's most important asset. In order to survive, remain competitive, grow, and diversify, an organization must ensure that the interests and goals of its human resources are managed carefully. As noted by one leader in the HR field:[2]

Yesterday the company with the access to the most capital or the latest technology had the best competitive advantage. Today, companies that offer products with the highest quality are the ones with a leg up on the competition. But, the only thing that will uphold a company's advantage tomorrow is the calibre of people in the organization.

Many studies have shown that people are more committed to their jobs when their participation is valued and encouraged. Here, a group of assembly-line workers in a Tokyo Nissan factory participate in a worker productivity session attended by managers and supervisors.

Rather than addressing organizational goals as separate and distinct from those of employees, they should be seen as compatible and mutually inclusive. A win-win situation results when this occurs. As demonstrated conclusively in a recent award-winning study, investment in sound HRM programs and practices contributes to greater financial performance and productivity, as well as reduced turnover.[3]

Why Is Human Resources Management Important to All Managers?

Managers at all levels must concern themselves with HRM, since they all meet their goals through the efforts of others, which requires the effective management of people. Every supervisor and manager has responsibilities related to a wide range of HRM activities. These include analyzing jobs, planning labour needs, selecting employees, orienting and training employees, managing compensation, communicating (which includes counselling and disciplining), and maintaining employee commitment. They also include ensuring fair treatment; appraising performance; ensuring employee health and safety; building and maintaining good employee/labour relations; handling complaints and grievances; and ensuring compliance with human rights, occupational health and safety, labour relations, and other legislation affecting the workplace. Regardless of field of expertise, from accounting to production control, learning about employee rights, employer responsibilities, and effective HRM practices can provide all managers with knowledge that will enable them to perform more effectively.

This book is designed to provide information that will assist individuals who are currently working in a human resources department, or planning to do so in the future, those currently working in a supervisory or managerial capacity in another department, as well as those who are planning (or hoping) to assume such responsibilities in the future. As one company president summed up:[4]

> *For many years it has been said that capital is the bottleneck for a developing industry. I don't think this any longer holds true. I think it's the work force and the company's inability to recruit and maintain a good work force that does constitute the bottleneck for production. I don't know of any major project backed by good ideas, vigour, and enthusiasm that has been stopped by a shortage of cash. I do know of industries whose growth has been partly stopped or hampered because they can't maintain an efficient and enthusiastic labour force, and I think this will hold true even more in the future. . . .*

At no time in history has that statement been more valid than it is today. As we'll discuss in a moment, such factors as increasing work force diversity; trends in technology; increasing government involvement in the employer-employee relationship; and globalization, have triggered an avalanche of change, one that many firms have not survived. In such an environment, the future belongs to those managers who can best manage change; but to manage change, they must have committed employees who do their jobs as if they own the company. Throughout this book, we'll demonstrate that sound HRM practices and policies can play a crucial role in fostering such employee commitment and enabling organizations to better respond to change.

www.io.org/~pmi/p5.html
Gateway to Hot HR Sites

Current Human Resources Management Functions

authority
The right to make decisions, direct the work of others, and give orders.

line authority
Authorization given to managers to direct the work of those reporting to them and make decisions about operational issues.

Most firms today, except for very small businesses, have a human resources (HR) department, headed by a human resources professional. To understand how the duties of this individual and other HR department staff relate to the HRM duties of managers throughout the rest of the organization, it is helpful to distinguish among line, staff, and functional authority.

Authority is the right to make decisions, direct the work of others, and give orders.

Line authority authorizes managers to direct the work of those reporting to them and make decisions about operational issues, and may be exercised only over employees in a manager's direct chain of command. Human resources professionals,

line manager
An individual who is in charge of an aspect of operations directly linked to the organization's product(s) or service(s).

staff authority
The authority to assist, counsel, advise, or provide service to others, but not to direct or control their activities.

staff manager
The person in charge of a function or department that is not directly linked to the organization's product(s) or service(s), but rather provides assistance and support.

functional authority
Authorization to make final decisions on issues affecting other departments or aspects of operations. The HR department is generally given functional authority for highly technical activities, such as compensation and benefits administration, and activities for which centralization enhances efficiency and effectiveness, such as recruitment.

for example, have line authority within the HR department and often in such service areas as the lunchroom or cafeteria.

Individuals known as **line managers** are in charge of an aspect of operations directly linked to the organization's product(s) or service(s). Hotel managers, directors of patient care, retail store managers, and managers of production and sales are generally line managers.

Staff authority, in contrast to line authority, authorizes managers to *assist*, *counsel*, *advise*, or provide service to others, but does not include the right to direct or control. Such authority is derived from acquired expertise and knowledge. Individuals with staff authority must rely primarily upon their ability to think strategically, their reputation, and their powers of persuasion to gain the confidence and respect of other managers. Human resources professionals, for example, are responsible for advising other managers on issues ranging from selection and training to grievance handling and disciplinary action, but cannot give those managers direct orders.

Managers in charge of functions or departments that are not directly linked to the organization's product(s) or service(s), but which provide assistance and support, are known as **staff managers**. HR managers, accounting managers, and managers of information support services are generally staff managers.

Functional authority involves authorization to make final decisions on issues affecting other departments or aspects of operations. The HR department is generally given functional authority for highly technical activities, such as compensation and benefits administration, and activities for which centralization enhances efficiency and effectiveness, such as recruitment. Having each department manager make decisions about pay structures, benefits, or recruitment methods could lead to inequities and excessive costs, and would be highly inefficient. The delegation of functional authority to the HR department to handle such matters ensures control (including consistent application and legal compliance), cost-efficiency, and uniformity.

Human Resources Management Responsibilities of All Managers

According to one expert, "The direct handling of people is, and always has been, an integral part of every . . . manager's responsibility, from president down to the lowest-level supervisor."[5]

In small organizations, managers may carry out all of their HRM duties unassisted. But as the organization grows, they often need the assistance, specialized knowledge, and advice of a separate human resources staff.[6]

Organization size and complexity are generally major factors in senior management's decision to establish a HR department. As an organization grows, effectively managing human resources and ensuring legal compliance becomes more of a burden. Once department managers and first-line supervisors find that HRM activities interfere with their other responsibilities, the benefits of delegating some of their HRM tasks to a separate HR department are generally seen to exceed the costs of establishing such an entity.

The Role of the Human Resources Department

Once a HR department has been created, it is the unit that has overall responsibility for HRM programs and activities. The primary role of the HR department is to ensure that the organization's human resources are utilized effectively and managed in compliance with company policies and procedures, government legislation, and, in unionized settings, collective agreement(s). All managers should be familiar with the role of the HR department to effectively utilize the department's assistance and services.

HR department staff are involved in five distinct types of activities: formulating policies and procedures, offering advice, providing services, monitoring to ensure compliance, and serving as a consultant and change agent.

Formulating Policies and Procedures The head of the HR department usually plays a leadership role in initiating and formulating HR policies and procedures that are consistent with overall organizational objectives. They must also be compatible with current economic conditions, collective bargaining trends, and applicable employment legislation. Often, though, the actual formulation of HR policies and procedures for approval by senior management is a cooperative endeavour among managers, nonmanagerial employees, and HR department staff. A **policy** is a predetermined guide to thinking, established to provide direction in decision making. Policies are extremely important because they define the organization's position on given issues; communicate management's expectations of employees; articulate acceptable/unacceptable behaviour; ensure consistency in the treatment of employees and continuity and predictability in the course of action; and serve as standards against which performance can be measured. As illustrated in **Figure 1.1**, HR **procedures** specify a prescribed sequence of steps to be followed when implementing HR policies.

policy
A predetermined guide to thinking, established to provide direction in decision making.

procedure
A prescribed sequence of steps to be followed when implementing organizational policies.

Figure 1.1
Sample HR Policy and Procedure

Source: Johnson & Johnson Medical Products. Used with permission.

Johnson & Johnson

MEDICAL PRODUCTS
Peterborough, Ontario K9J 7B9

Corporate Policy & Procedure

Policy No.: A-2.4
Page: 1 of 2
Date: Jan 1992
Sup: New

Human Resources
Section 2–Personnel Administration

Employee Complaint Resolution Procedure

I.   Policy

It is the policy of Johnson & Johnson Medical Products to provide all employees with a procedure for discussing job-related matters such as treatment or conditions of work, job dissatisfaction, suggestions, complaints, misunderstanding, and grievances; and to facilitate the prompt handling of employee concerns. This procedure is intended to cover employee relations issues in a broad sense including concerns about supervision, interpretation of Personnel policies, and other employee questions about any aspect of the operation of Johnson & Johnson Medical Products. The following guidelines are intended to ensure the effectiveness and credibility of this procedure.

II. General

Employees should be encouraged to discuss their concerns, and complaints with their immediate supervisor. In addition, an employee may raise concerns with the Human Resources department without the knowledge of their immediate supervisor. It is the function of the Human Resources department to receive complaints and, as necessary, to act as the employees' spokesperson in resolving inequities, if they exist. No restrictions should prevent employees from bringing their concerns to anyone within the Corporation.

Figure1.1
(continued)

Human Resources will act promptly to resolve any situation which deviates from the conditions established in the Corporate Policy and Procedure Manual and established company practices. If the employee is being treated unfairly, management will correct the situation. When the complaint results from a misunderstanding, management will completely explain the reason for their position.

An employee may also use this system to voice concern about any practice, policy or event which may be acting against the company's best interests, or to question conditions that appear improper or unfair.

III. Communication

Employees should be reminded periodically of this procedure and their ability to use it.

IV. Procedure

a) As a first step, the employee is encouraged to discuss the concern with their supervisor.

b) If dissatisfied with the supervisor's response, the employee is encouraged to discuss the concern with the supervisor's manager.

c) If the concern is still unresolved, the employee should contact the Human Resources department. If the employee feels it would not be appropriate or tactful to discuss the concern with the supervisor or the supervisor's manager first, the employee should immediately contact the Human Resources department.

d) A member of the Human Resources department will discuss the concern as quickly as possible, investigate if necessary, and recommend resolution procedures as appropriate.

V. Confidentiality

a) Concerns and/or complaints will be handled confidentially. If a problem cannot be resolved confidentially, the employee must give explicit approval before any further action is taken.

All complaints will be resolved in keeping with the policies and practices of Johnson & Johnson Medical Products.

b) There will be no retaliation against employees who use this procedure.

To maximize effectiveness, HR policies and procedures should be put in writing. Often, they are compiled in a policy manual or made available online, so that they are readily accessible. This helps to ensure that the same information is communicated to all employees, and that there is consistency in employee treatment. In addition, it means that many questions or concerns can be resolved without HR department staff assistance.

Offering Advice   In order to cope with increasingly complex HR issues and the ever-changing work environment, managers at all levels frequently turn to the HR department staff for expert advice and counsel. Members of the HR department are expected to be completely familiar with employment legislation, HR policies and procedures, collective agreements, past practices, and the outcome of recent arbitration hearings and court decisions, so they can provide sound guidance and suggested solutions.

Providing Services   The HR department generally provides services in the following areas on an ongoing basis: maintenance of HR records, recruitment, selection, orientation, training and development, compensation and benefits administration, employee counselling, and labour relations.

Monitoring to Ensure Compliance   The HR department staff are generally responsible for monitoring to ensure compliance with established HR policies and procedures. They may analyze data pertaining to absenteeism and turnover or accident rates, for example, to identify problems with policy implementation or failures to comply with specified procedures.

In addition, the HR department staff members play a major role in ensuring compliance with employment legislation. For example, the HR department staff are generally responsible for collecting and analyzing recruitment, selection, and promotion data to monitor compliance with human rights and employment equity legislation. They also assess salary and benefits data to monitor compliance with employment standards and pay equity requirements, and examine grievance issues to monitor compliance with health and safety and/or labour relations legislation.

Serving as Consultant and Change Agent   In most firms, HR department staff serve as in-house consultants to the managers of other departments. Sometimes, HR department staff will recommend using outside consultants for assistance in solving HR issues or handling specialized assignments, such as executive recruitment and job evaluation. Outsourcing is another option that is becoming more widely used.

Outsourcing is the practice of contracting with outside vendors to handle specified functions on a permanent basis. Many firms provide counselling services through experts in employee assistance plans, for example. In a recent survey of 927 firms, the Wyatt Company found that 32 percent of employers outsource some or all of the administration of HR and benefit programs to third party administrators (TPAs). Jacques Martineau, partner of one of Canada's eminent actuarial benefits and compensation firms, Montreal's Martineau Provencher, recently identified three outsourcing trends: pension and benefits administration; workers' compensation administration; and, although rare at present, the entire HR function.[7] One of his firm's clients is Avenor Inc., which has outsourced its pension and benefits administration. According to James Marchant, Vice-President of HR at Avenor, "Outsourcing allowed us to get out of the low value-added administrative work and become more strategic. We now focus on health and safety, leadership development, total compensation, and employee/labour relations."[8]

In addition, HR specialists are expected to be "change agents" by providing senior management with "up-to-date information on current trends and new methods of solving problems"[9] to help the organization increase its efficiency and effectiveness. By constantly monitoring the internal and external environments, HR specialists can help the organization to be proactive when appropriate, rather than always being reactive. Being **proactive** means that HRM problems are anticipated and corrective action begins before the problem occurs, as compared to being **reactive**, which means responding to an already-existing problem. Implementing an employment equity program on a voluntary basis in light of the changing composition of the work force is an example of a proactive strategy. Awaiting legislative requirements prior to implementation of such a program is an example of reactive HRM.

Structure of the Human Resources Department

Figure 1.2 illustrates the typical structure of the HR function in a medium-sized organization (employing 200 to 400 workers). As indicated, the manager of human resources usually reports to the chief executive officer (CEO), and plays a generalist role. Support staff typically perform a wide variety of activities, includ-

**www.hronline.com/forums/
index.html**
HR Network (HRNET)

outsourcing
The practice of contracting with outside vendors to handle specified functions on a permanent basis.

proactive
Anticipating problems and taking corrective action before a problem occurs.

reactive
Responding to an already-existing problem (such as "putting out fires").

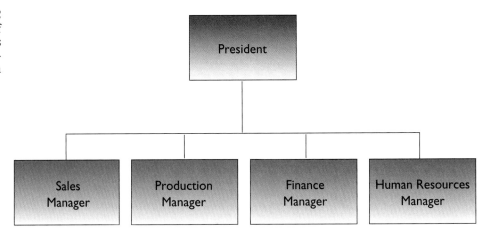

Figure 1.2
Typical Structure of the Human Resources Function in a Medium-Sized Organization

ing maintaining HR records, assisting with recruitment and selection, and ensuring legal compliance.

As demands on the department grow, it increases in importance and complexity. **Figure 1.3** illustrates the subdepartments and hierarchy of jobs within a typical, large-sized manufacturing firm, structured by areas of specialization. When the HR department head plays a major role in the organization's strategic planning and related processes, and the HR department makes a major contribution to the firm, the title vice-president of human resources (or labour relations in a unionized setting) is often used. Those reporting to the department head typically include the following:

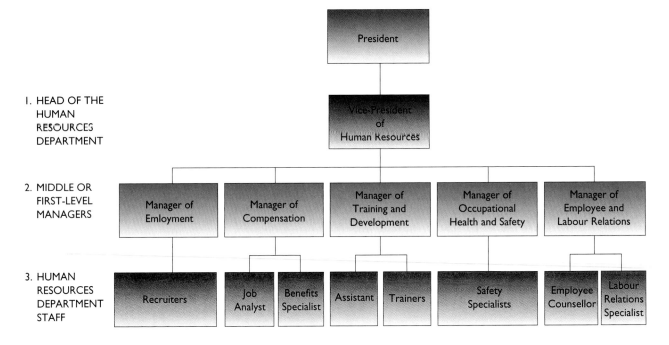

Figure 1.3
Typical Structure of the Human Resources Department in a Large-Sized Manufacturing Firm

- manager of employment (responsible for human resources planning, recruitment, selection, and performance appraisals)
- manager of compensation (responsible for base pay, incentives, and benefits administration)
- manager of training and development (responsible for orientation, training, management development, and career planning)
- manager of occupational health and safety, and
- manager of employee and labour relations (responsible for communications, counselling, contract administration and collective bargaining activities).

Activity managers may be supported by an assortment of specialists, assistants, and secretaries. In large firms, it is the specialists who actually perform such activities as recruitment and training. Community college and university graduates often start their HRM careers in specialist positions.

Human Resources Management: A Cooperative Effort

Regardless of the size of the HR department, in practice, good HRM is a joint, cooperative effort, with HR specialists and other managers working together. As indicated in **Table 1.1**, in some areas, such as wage and salary policy development and job evaluation, the HR department plays the major role. In others, such as interviewing and handling disciplinary action, the duties are split more evenly with individuals in other departments.

TABLE 1.1 Division of Responsibilities for HR Activities

HR ACTIVITY	COMPANY HAS ACTIVITY	(NO. OF COS.)	RESPONSIBILITY FOR THE ACTIVITY IS ASSIGNED TO:[1] HR DEPT. ONLY	HR AND OTHER DEPT(S).	OTHER DEPT(S). ONLY
Interviewing	99%	(681)	37%	61%	2%
HR record-keeping/information systems	99	(680)	77	22	1
Vacation/leave processing	99	(680)	51	35	14
Insurance benefits administration	99	(677)	87	8	5
Orientation	99	(675)	61	37	2
Wage/salary adjustment processing	99	(674)	77	22	1
Workers' compensation administration	98	(672)	73	15	12
Promotion/transfer/separation processing	98	(672)	71	28	1
Disciplinary procedures	98	(671)	43	55	2
Payroll administration	98	(669)	25	25	50
Recruiting	98	(668)	73	25	2
Job descriptions	97	(666)	62	35	2
Employment insurance	97	(666)	82	11	7
Wage/salary policy development	97	(665)	80	18	2
Performance appraisal, management	97	(665)	47	44	8
Performance appraisal, nonmanagement	97	(663)	47	45	8
Employment equity	97	(662)	87	11	2
Administrative services	97	(662)	15	16	69
Purchasing	95	(654)	3	7	90
Maintenance/janitorial services	95	(653)	10	5	85
Safety programs/compliance	95	(650)	46	33	20
Job evaluation	94	(647)	70	28	2
Security measures	94	(646)	22	22	57

TABLE 1.1 (continued)

HR ACTIVITY	COMPANY HAS ACTIVITY	(NO. OF COS.)	HR DEPT. ONLY	HR AND OTHER DEPT(S).	OTHER DEPT(S). ONLY
				RESPONSIBILITY FOR THE ACTIVITY IS ASSIGNED TO:[1]	
Training, nonmanagement	94%	(641)	21%	51%	28%
Supervisory training	94	(641)	48	44	8
Exit interviews	93	(639)	86	13	1
Complaint procedures	92	(633)	54	44	2
Job analysis	91	(626)	75	23	3
Employee communications/publications	91	(624)	43	37	21
Award/recognition programs	91	(624)	66	29	5
Pension/retirement plan administration	90	(618)	73	18	8
Public/media relations	89	(612)	17	17	66
Travel/transportation services	89	(608)	9	14	77
Management development	88	(604)	49	44	6
Community service	88	(601)	30	31	39
Business insurance/risk management	88	(600)	12	17	72
Recreation/social programs	86	(590)	61	30	9
Tuition aid/scholarships	86	(590)	83	12	4
Human resources forecasting/planning	85	(580)	58	37	5
Pre-employment testing	80	(551)	85	12	3
Executive compensation	80	(548)	55	26	19
Relocation	75	(512)	75	20	5
Office/clerical services	73	(502)	16	22	62
Organization development	73	(498)	46	44	10
Career planning/development	72	(489)	51	45	5
Food service/cafeteria	70	(478)	36	6	58
Employee assistance plan/counselling	69	(472)	83	14	4
Incentive pay plans	69	(472)	50	38	12
College/university recruiting	67	(462)	79	17	4
Productivity/motivation programs	67	(461)	26	61	13
Medical services	61	(414)	73	12	15
Suggestion systems	60	(408)	46	35	19
Health/wellness program	58	(400)	78	14	8
Outplacement	58	(396)	91	8	1
Attitude surveys	55	(374)	81	16	3
Savings plan administration	53	(364)	71	21	8
Preretirement counselling	52	(356)	90	4	5
Union/labour relations	50	(344)	71	27	2
Library	44	(301)	21	9	70
Profit sharing plan administration	39	(273)	59	23	18
Flexible benefits plan administration	36	(245)	87	11	3
Stock plan administration	33	(227)	57	20	23
Flexible spending account administration	29	(197)	83	11	6
Childcare centre	10	(67)	36	9	55

[1]Percentages are based on companies providing data on where responsibility for the activitiy is assigned. Percentages may not add up to 100 due to rounding.

Source: "Personnel Activities: Line-Staff Assignments," Bureau of National Affairs, *Bulletin to Management* (September 1, 1988), p. 2.

Contemporary Challenges in Human Resources Management

Internal and external environmental influences play a major role in HRM. Organizational climate and culture, for example, help to shape HR policies and practices, which, in turn, have an impact on the quality of candidates that a firm can attract, as well as its ability to retain desired workers. The economic environment, labour market conditions, and unions also play a role in determining the quality and variety of employees that can be attracted and retained. There are a number of external challenges, however, that are dramatically changing the environment of HRM, and requiring it to play an ever-more crucial role in organizations. These challenges include demographic trends and increasing work force diversity, trends in technology, increasing government involvement in the employer-employee relationship, globalization, and changes in the nature of jobs and work. After briefly describing the ongoing internal and external influences, we will focus on the external challenges that are having the most significant impact on HRM in Canada today.

Internal Environmental Influences

How a firm deals with the following two internal environmental influences has a major impact on its ability to meet its objectives.

Organizational Culture

organizational culture
The core values, beliefs, and assumptions that are widely shared by members of an organization.

Organizational culture consists of the core values, beliefs, and assumptions that are widely shared by members of an organization. It serves a variety of purposes:

- communicating "what the organization believes in" and "what the organization stands for"
- providing employees with a sense of direction and a sense of what is expected of them in terms of behaviour (norms)
- shaping employees' attitudes about themselves, the organization, and their roles
- creating a sense of identity, orderliness, and consistency
- fostering employee loyalty and commitment.

Culture is often conveyed through an organization's mission statement, as well as stories, myths, symbols, and ceremonies:[10]

> *At Mary Kay Cosmetics Inc. of Canada, the biblical commandment "Do unto others what you would have them do unto you" is taken seriously. There are such personal touches as birthday cards, wedding gifts, and employee picnics. Employees are also expected to help one another to get work done. This demonstration of caring and concern leads employees to feel they can count on their colleagues, not only for work-related assistance, but also with other aspects of their lives.*

employee assistance program (EAP)
A company-sponsored program to help employees cope with personal problems that are interfering with or have the potential to interfere with their job performance, as well as issues affecting their well-being and/or that of their families.

HR managers play an important role in assisting senior management to create and maintain the type of organizational culture desired. Genuine concern and caring about employees can be conveyed by thorough orientation and training programs, strategies encouraging communication flow in all directions, and having an **employee assistance program (EAP)**, a topic to which we'll return in chapter 14. In organizations in which customers or clients are truly valued, employees who provide exemplary service are recognized and rewarded, and there is follow up to ensure customer/client satisfaction.

Having a positive culture earns critical acclaim. Firms such as 3M, Hewlett-Packard, and Bank of Montreal have gained a reputation, not only for the quality of their products and services, but also for positive relationships with their employees and customers/clients.

Organizational Climate

organizational climate
The prevailing atmosphere that exists in an organization and its impact on employees.

Organizational climate refers to the prevailing atmosphere that exists in an organization and its impact on employees. Organizations have personalities, just like people. They can be friendly or unfriendly, open or secretive, rigid or flexible, innovative or stagnant. The major factors influencing climate are management's leadership style, HR policies and practices, and amount and style of communication. The type of climate that exists is generally reflected in the level of employee motivation, job satisfaction, performance, and productivity, and thus has a direct impact on organizational profits and/or ongoing viability.

HR managers play a key role in assisting senior management to establish and maintain a positive organizational climate. They can help to develop policies and organizational structures, for example, that encourage a spirit of teamwork and co-operation within and among business units in working toward common objectives, which can have very positive consequences:[11]

> *In the early 1990s when most other companies were cutting staff to stay afloat, Federal Express Canada Ltd. lived up to its policy of making every effort to avoid layoffs, even though the firm was losing about $1 million a month. Instead, they turned to employees for solutions. Resulting suggestions included cutting costs by using more ground transportation, improving productivity by reducing the number of hours per transaction, raising margins by developing international markets, and increasing efficiency by using more technology. Tapping into employee expertise paid off dramatically. According to Jon Slangerup, Vice President and General Manager, "We turned the company around. Since then, we have increased the number of employees by 20 percent, and Canada is now the most profitable division in the entire company."*

intrapreneur
An employee who is an innovator because he or she has been given the freedom to create new products, services, and/or production methods. Intrapreneuring means creating and maintaining the innovation and flexibility of a small-business environment within a large organization.

When organizations fail to make adjustments in their climate to keep up with environmental changes, difficulties are often experienced. The bureaucratic climate at IBM, characterized by centralized decision-making, hierarchy of command, job security, and a strict promote-from-within policy, has been identified as a key factor in the firm's recent difficulties in maintaining a competitive position on both domestic and foreign fronts. Louis Gerstner addressed this when he took over as Chief Executive Officer (CEO) in 1993. To revamp the climate, he is working to encourage cooperation among divisions and build teamwork and trust. His aim is to eliminate unnecessary bureaucracy and infuse the firm with **intrapreneurs.**[12]

External Environmental Influences

The external environmental factors described on the following pages have a direct or indirect influence on HRM. To be effective, HR managers must monitor the environment on an ongoing basis; assess the impact of any changes; and be proactive in implementing policies and programs to deal with such challenges.

Economic Environment

The economic environment has a major impact on business in general, and the management of human resources in particular. Economic conditions affect supply and demand for products and services, which in turn affect the number and types of employees required, as well as an employer's ability to pay wages and provide benefits. When there is a recession, for example, employers are often forced to downsize by offering attractive early retirement and early leave programs, or by laying off and terminating employees. As an alternative, some firms reduce pay and benefits in order to retain workers.

Figure 1.4 shows the fluctuations in Canadian unemployment rates from 1980 to June 1995. When the economy is healthy, companies often hire more workers, as demand for products and services increases. Consequently, unemployment rates fall, and there is more competition for qualified employees. Conversely, during a downturn, unemployment rates rise, and employers are often overwhelmed with applicants when vacancies are advertised.

productivity
The ratio of an organization's outputs (goods and services) to its inputs (people, capital, energy, and materials).

As illustrated in **Figure 1.5**, **productivity** refers to the ratio of an organization's outputs (goods and services) to its inputs (people, capital, energy, and

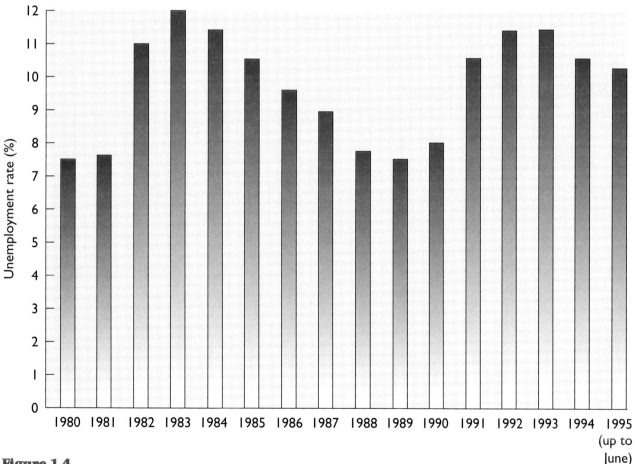

Figure 1.4
Canadian Unemployment Rates (1980–1995)

Source: Statistics Canada, *Labour Force Annual Averages (1996)*, Catalogue No. 71-220. Reproduced by Authority of the Ministry of Industry, 1998.

Figure 1.5
Productivity Ratio

$$\text{Productivity} = \frac{\text{Outputs (Goods and Services)}}{\text{Inputs (People, Capital, Energy, Materials)}}$$

materials).[13] To improve productivity, managers must find ways to produce more outputs with current input levels or to use fewer resources to produce current output levels.

In most organizations today, productivity improvement is essential for long-term success. Through productivity gains, managers can reduce costs, conserve scarce resources, and increase profits. This leads to a win-win situation, since higher profits often result in better compensation and improved working conditions, thereby enhancing the employees' quality of work life and their motivation to further improve productivity.

Canada's relatively low productivity levels and high labour costs are of grave concern, since competition with foreign companies has become increasingly important. The North American Free Trade Agreement (NAFTA), created to establish free trade between Canada, the United States, and Mexico, combined with the continuing liberalization of trade under the multi-nation General Agreement on Tariffs and Trade (GATT), means that Canada's economic success increasingly depends on the ability of Canadian employers to meet international quality and productivity standards. This applies to firms selling products and services in the domestic market, in which foreign competition is increasingly a factor, as well as those with international markets.

Labour Market Conditions

labour market
The geographic area from which an organization recruits employees and where individuals seek employment.

The **labour market** is the geographic area from which an organization recruits employees and where individuals seek employment. In other words, it is the area in which the forces of supply and demand interact. The labour market is often different for various employee groups within an organization. While clerical and technical employees are generally recruited locally, the labour market for senior management and highly specialized personnel is often national or even international in scope.

One measure of an organization's effectiveness is its ability to compete successfully for high calibre human resources. Many factors motivate candidates to seek employment with a particular organization, including type of business/industry, reputation, opportunities for advancement, compensation, job security, and working conditions.

Location and climate and other aspects of a firm's physical surroundings, such as housing, commuting, and living costs, can help or hinder a firm's ability to attract and retain employees. Recent population shifts to the West Coast and small towns and rural areas can be attributed, at least in part, to the desire of individuals to work and live in what they perceive to be a more desirable physical environment. Such shifts alter the demand for and supply of individuals in local labour markets, a factor that firms must always take into account when deciding where to establish a new venture, expand, or downsize.

Because the labour market is not controlled or influenced by any one factor, it is unstructured and often unpredictable. Nevertheless, organizations must constantly monitor and track trends affecting supply and demand of human resources. By doing so, they can gather information about the prevailing pay rates for employees with particular talents or skills, and estimate how difficult it is likely to be to attract and recruit staff.

Labour market conditions should also be monitored to determine present and emerging trends, such as the changing composition of the labour force, as well as changing values and expectations, so that policies and programs can be adapted and/or designed in order to recognize and take advantage of these trends.

Labour Unions

labour union
An officially-recognized association of employees who have joined together for the purpose of presenting a united front or collective voice in dealing with management to secure and further the social and economic interests and well-being of the membership.

Labour unions are organizations of individuals who have joined together for the purpose of presenting a united front or collective voice in dealing with management, to secure and further the social and economic interests and well-being of their membership. Although both an internal and external challenge, we have listed unions as an external factor because they become an additional party in the relationship between the company and employees. Once a union has been certified to represent a specific group of employees, the union negotiates terms and conditions of employment with management, rather than individual employees. The company is required by law to recognize the union and bargain with it in good faith.

In Canada, unions remain a powerful influence. While union membership has declined slightly, it still represents about 34.1 percent of the nonagricultural paid work force; unlike in the United States, where union membership has fallen six percent since 1983 to 15.8 percent of the work force.[14]

Labour unions exert a significant influence on organizations in several ways. When dealing with unionized employees, management has less discretion and flexibility in implementing and administering HR policies, procedures, and practices, since a negotiated collective agreement governs most terms and conditions of employment, including wages and benefits, working conditions, and job security. Often, organizations with a mix of unionized and nonunionized employees institute a policy (whether officially or unofficially) to ensure that similar or even slightly better terms and conditions of employment are provided to nonunionized staff to encourage them to retain their nonunion status.

Labour unions also influence the HR policies and practices in nonunionized organizations wishing to remain union-free. Such organizations monitor bargaining activities in their community and industry, and ensure that their employees are provided with terms and conditions of employment equal to or better than those being negotiated by unions.

When some or all of an organization's employees are unionized, the HR department is responsible for helping to develop sound HR policies and practices that will promote good union-management relations, and create and maintain a harmonious working environment. Knowledge of collective bargaining, contract administration, and pertinent labour relations legislation becomes imperative.

Demographic Trends and Increasing Work Force Diversity

demographics
The characteristics of the work force, which include age, sex, marital status, and education level.

diversity
Any attribute that humans are likely to use to tell themselves, "that person is different from me" and thus includes such factors as race, gender, age, values, and cultural norms.

Demographics refers to the characteristics of the work force, which include age, sex, marital status, and education level.[15] Demographic changes occur slowly and are well measured, which means they are known in advance. As will be discussed further in chapter 3, the fact that Canada's labour force is becoming increasingly diverse is one of the major challenges confronting HR managers today. **Diversity** refers to ". . . any attribute that humans are likely to use to tell themselves, 'that person is different from me'" and thus includes such factors as race, gender, age, values, and cultural norms.[16]

Population Growth   The single most important factor governing the size and composition of the labour force is population growth. The Canadian labour force totalled about 12.6 million people in 1995 and is expected to grow by less than 1 percent annually until the year 2016.[17] As will be discussed below, this means that the average age of the work force is changing rather dramatically.

Canada admits more immigrants per capita than any other country, which also has significant implications for the labour force, as does the fact that there has been a dramatic shift in immigration patterns. Prior to 1966, at least 90 percent of the immigrants who came to Canada were from Europe.[18] As highlighted in **Figure 1.6**, as of 1993 that figure was 17 percent.

By 2001, most people entering the work force will be women, visible minorities, Aboriginal people, and persons with disabilities.[19] We will discuss each of these groups on the following pages, along with some of the challenges and opportunities presented by the increasing availability of members of these four groups.

Age The **baby boomers**, born between 1946 and 1964, began crowding into the labour market in the late 1960s. This led to a domination of the work force by this generation until the 1980s. The sheer number of "boomers" helped to expand the economy and made it easier for HR departments to focus on issues such as cost containment, since recruitment and selection, while important, were not the most critical problems. Individuals in the "population bulge" are currently experiencing greater competition for advancement. This challenges managers to find new strategies for forging career paths, such as lateral moves, to keep this group motivated and satisfied. As can be seen in **Figure 1.7**, the baby boomers are rapidly advancing towards middle age. Since life expectancies are continuing to increase, and the baby boomers have had much lower fertility rates than their predecessors, the average age of the population is increasing substantially. According to Statistics Canada, between 1993 and 2015, older age groups, 45–54 and 55–64, will grow dramatically, by 155 and 194 percent respectively. In contrast, the youth population, aged 15 to 24, will increase by only five percent.[20] Providing pension and social security benefits for the baby boomers when they reach retirement

baby boomers
Individuals born between 1946 and 1964.

Figure 1.6
Immigrants to Canada, by Region of Origin, 1992 and 1993

Source: Statistics Canada, Adapted from *Report on the Demographic Situation in Canada (1994)*, Catalogue No. 91-209, Table 27. Reproduced by authority of the Ministry of Industry, 1998.

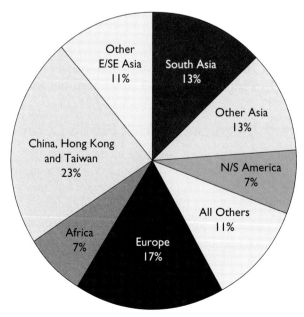

Figure 1.7
**Population Projections
for Canada**

Source: Statistics Canada,
*Current Demographic Analysis:
Fertility in Canada—From Baby
Boom to Baby Bust*, Catalogue
No. 91-524E (Ottawa,
November 1984.) Reproduced
with permission of the
Minister of Supply and
Services Canada, 1991.

(Under Assumption of Fertility Rate of 1.5)
% Distribution of Population by Age Group

	0–14	15–64	65+	Mean Age
2001	17.2	70.2	16.6	38.2
2011	15.2	70.5	14.3	40.8
2021	14.3	66.7	19.0	43.2
2051	13.0	61.2	25.8	46.2

www.hr2000.com
HR Online

sandwich generation
A term referring to individuals who have responsibilities for rearing young dependents, as well as assisting elderly relatives who are no longer capable of functioning totally independently.

early in the next century will present a very serious problem for employers and governments, given the smaller labour force available to support the retirees. Long-range planning will be required to find viable solutions.

Early in the new millennium, this demographic trend will culminate in a complete reversal of the traditional labour force pattern. Many organizations with a primary interest in the younger age group, such as retail establishments and fast-food chains, can expect the population from which they gain customers and part-time workers to shrink dramatically. Some employers are already undertaking initiatives to attract older workers, especially those who have taken early retirement, by offering job sharing and expanding the number of part-time hours available. McDonald's, for example, is actively recruiting seniors,[21] as well as directing advertising efforts to appeal to the seniors' market.

HR specialists must remember that many HR policies that attract and motivate a predominantly young work force are not appropriate for an aging one, due to differing values and priorities. Furthermore, having workers of diverse ages may create a need to bridge the generation gap. Young managers may have difficulty gaining the respect of those reporting to them who are older than they are, or in exerting their authority. In addition, because of differing values, employees may have difficulty understanding and communicating with those from another generation.

The aging of the population has had another impact. Many middle-aged employees are caught in the **sandwich generation**, with responsibilities for rearing young dependents as well as assisting elderly relatives who are no longer capable of functioning totally independently. Strategies for dealing with the aging of the work force and assisting employees to balance work and family responsibilities revealed in a survey of 400 HR practitioners include:

- using retirees on special projects (42%)
- hiring retirees as consultants (39%)
- having retiree job banks (6%)
- reducing early-retirement incentives (32%)
- allowing gradual retirement (3%) and rehearsal retirement (2%)
- offering wellness programs (43%)
- instituting pension benefits for part-time workers (18%)
- providing eldercare information and referral (20%), and
- eldercare counselling (5%).[22]

Education The level of education of the Canadian labour force is increasing at a significant rate. Currently, more than three out of four Canadians aged 20 to 24 have at least completed high school.[23] In addition, more Canadians are pursuing higher education through a variety of institutions, including trade schools, community colleges, and universities. Adult Canadians are returning to evening part-time studies in record numbers,[24] a trend that many firms encourage through tuition-assistance programs. More and more organizations are arranging for in-house programs, not just for skills training, but also academic upgrading. Some even make it possible to complete a master's degree on site![25]

Another trend in education is the growth in the number of cooperative-education programs, designed to enable students to gain work experience while still attending school. There are now more than 50 000 students in co-op programs in a wide range of disciplines at over 140 universities, colleges, and other institutions.[26]

Given the better educated labour force and their higher expectations, HR managers are expected to try to ensure that the talents and capabilities of employees are fully utilized and opportunities are provided for career growth. In today's economic climate, this is not always possible. Many college and university graduates find themselves working in jobs that do not fully utilize their skills and knowledge. In fact, thousands of well-qualified people are underemployed.[27] Improving the quality of work life is therefore more important than ever.

While the good news is that many Canadians are highly educated, the bad news is that there is a widening gap between the educated and uneducated. About four million Canadians are still **functionally illiterate**; unable to read, write, calculate, or solve problems at a level that enables them to function independently or perform routine technical tasks. What is worse, about 40 percent of this group are younger than 45, which means they are in their prime career years. Not only does this reduce the overall productivity levels in organizations, but it may also be a major contributor to safety violations and accidents.[28] One study found that 16 percent of adult Canadians have limited reading skills and cannot handle most daily demands without assistance.[29] A frightening reality is that inadequate reading and writing skills has replaced lack of experience as the major reason for rejecting entry-level candidates.[30] If they are hired, their limited literacy hampers their ability to upgrade their skills.

A related problem confronting organizations is technological illiteracy. A few firms have been proactive in addressing these issues. For example, IBM Canada has spent more than $60 million since 1982 working with Canadian educational institutions to help improve technological skills.[31]

functionally illiterate
Unable to read, write, calculate, or solve problems at a level required for independent functioning or the performance of routine technical tasks.

Visible and Ethnic Minorities   The proportion of visible and ethnic minorities entering the Canadian labour market is growing, in jobs ranging from general labour to technical, professional, and skilled trades. It is estimated that by 2006, 19 percent of the total Canadian population will be visible minorities.[32] Ethnic diversity is also increasing, according to census data. Between 1986 and 1991, there was a 20 percent increase in the proportion of the population indicating that they were neither French nor British in origin. In 1991, more than 4 million Canadian residents (15 percent of the population) had a first language other than French or English. Of these, approximately 380 000 could speak neither of Canada's official languages: 28 percent speaking Chinese as a first language, 15 percent Italian, and 11 percent Portuguese.[33]

HR specialists must ensure that policies and programs are developed in their organizations to accommodate and celebrate the diverse cultural characteristics of visible and ethnic minority employees, something that requires much more than ensuring compliance with human rights legislation.

Women   The number of women in the Canadian work force has increased dramatically in the past fifteen years, and indications are that the number will continue to grow. Currently, women make up approximately 45 percent of the Canadian labour force, and the average woman works a total of 30 to 45 years. By the year 2000, women's participation rate in the work force is expected to match men's. One study projects that by the year 2005, 85 percent of Canadian women between the ages of 25 and 54 will be in the labour force.[34] Factors contributing to the dramatic increase in female participation rate include smaller family size, increased divorce rate, the need and desire for dual family incomes, increased educational level, and the availability of more flexible working hours and part-time jobs.

The continued movement of women into management positions has implications for both career development and recruiting programs.

However, there is still strong evidence that women are underutilized in the Canadian work force.[35] For example, a 1994 study of 423 organizations reported that 30 percent of first-line supervisors were female, whereas only 17 percent of middle managers and eight percent of executives were women.[36]

Of particular significance to employers is the increasing number of women in the work force with dependent children. Organizations such as Warner-Lambert Canada, Apple Canada, Bell Canada, and the Royal Bank are making a determined effort to accommodate working women and shared parenting responsibilities by providing family-friendly benefits, such as alternative career paths for women, extended leaves for parenting, flexible work schedules, and opportunities for job sharing and telecommuting. The Bank of Montreal has a "Work and Life program," which offers flexible working arrangements to both men and women. At present, 35 percent of the 4 500 employees taking advantage of the program are men. While surveys of international and Canadian firms have found that about three-quarters of employers surveyed offer at least one family-friendly benefit, more than 60 percent of the respondents reported that they were not convinced that top management believed that family-friendly policies and benefits made good business sense.[37]

Francophones   Although truly a cultural mosaic (multilingual and multiracial), Canada is officially bilingual. It is the only major industrialized country with two official languages. There are large French-speaking populations in the provinces of Ontario and New Brunswick, and Quebec is predominantly French-speaking. Organizations operating in these provinces, particularly in Quebec, must ensure that their policies, procedures, and practices conform to the requirements of relevant employment legislation, as well as meeting the expectations of all of their employees. Furthermore, although organizations functioning in French are found predominantly in Quebec and parts of New Brunswick, many firms in both private and public sectors must be able to serve their clientele in both French and English.

Aboriginal Peoples   For members of the First Peoples, (North American Indians, Inuits, and Métis) obtaining jobs and advancing in the workplace are both difficult. The 1995 federal Human Rights Commission report indicated that while First Peoples represented about 3.0 percent of the available work force, only 1.1 percent of people employed in federally-regulated organizations were Aboriginal persons. Aboriginal peoples were underrepresented in all regions, including those with large Aboriginal populations, due to low employment and disproportionately high termination rates.[38] In addition, there are dramatic income disparities between the general population and First Peoples.[39]

Persons with Disabilities   According to one estimate, there are approximately 2.3 million working-age adults with disabilities in Canada, of whom 56 percent are in the work force.[40] Prejudice is still a serious barrier to employment for persons with disabilities. Despite the fact that human rights legislation in every Canadian jurisdiction prohibits discrimination against individuals with disabilities, and that studies show that there are no performance differences in terms of productivity, attendance, and average tenure between employees who classify themselves as disabled and those who do not,[41] persons with disabilities experience high rates of unemployment and underemployment.

Values Differences   HR managers must be extremely aware that related to the work force diversity described above are significant value differences about the overall importance of work, what aspects or characteristics of a job are most important, tolerance of discipline in terms of hours and pace of work, and attitudes toward authority. Employees increasingly expect to exercise more freedom from management control, and are more demanding and questioning. More people are seeking challenging jobs and defining success in terms of personal self-expression and fulfillment of potential on the job. Workers are also seeking a better balance in life between work and other interests, including family, and value free time more than they did in earlier decades.[42] It is important that policies and practices be adapted to embrace the diversity of the dominant values represented in an organization's work force.

Overall Impact of Increased Diversity   The increasing diversity of the Canadian labour force is currently placing tremendous demands on HRM, and will continue to do so.[43] The shortage of workers aged 25 to 34, combined with the aging work force, means that early retirement may be discouraged in the future and mandatory retirement at age sixty-five, which is currently legal in many Canadian jurisdictions, may become a policy of the past. In addition, career opportunities in management for workers in the 35 to 44 age cohort may be constrained by the abundance of more experienced members of the 45 to 54 age cohort. To retain valuable employees, lateral career moves and other alternatives to promotion will need to be explored as avenues of growth and challenge. The large number of baby-boom women in the labour force is pressuring employers to ensure equity with respect to employment and advancement opportunities, as well as compensation. The upswing in the number of dual-career couples will force more employers to establish family-friendly benefits. They may provide childcare facilities on or near company premises, as VanCity has done (described in the Diversity Counts box), or offer child- and eldercare referral services; and must accommodate the travel, scheduling, and moving needs of dual-career employees.

Technology

It is mainly through technological innovation that firms develop new products and services and/or improve existing ones in order to remain competitive; and gain the productivity and quality needed for competitive advantage.

Manufacturing advances, such as robotics and computer-aided design/computer-aided manufacturing (CAD/CAM), have eliminated many blue-collar jobs, replacing them with fewer but more highly-skilled jobs. When robots were introduced in the automobile industry, for instance, there was a major decrease in the demand for welders and painters, but a new demand for technicians who could program, install, and service automated equipment.[44] Due to computer technology, similar changes have been occurring in the nature of office work. Optical scanners, computerized x-ray scanners, and Magnetic Resonance Imagery (MRI)

Diversity Counts
Innovative Childcare at VanCity

In October of 1995, VanCity Credit Union partnered with community-based Citygate Preschool Children's Centre, and purchased one emergency childcare space and six priority spaces for its employees.

The centre, operated by the YWCA, is located near VanCity's head office in Vancouver. Employees with children aged three to five can reserve space for up to two working days per week, to a maximum of six days per month. The service is available from 7:45 a.m. to 6:00 p.m. Employees using the service pay $10 per day. Van City pays the balance, about $25 per day.

Although the program was originally intended to provide substitute care when an employee's regular arrangement was unavailable, VanCity expanded the program to accommodate needs that arose due to job demands, and employees are now benefitting from the service in a variety of circumstances. For example, space can be reserved for children of employees who have to travel a long distance to attend training programs at head office, thereby disrupting their regular childcare arrangements.◆

Source: Nora Spinks, "Adventure in Innovative Childcare," *Canadian HR Reporter* (April 8, 1996), p.12. Copyright MPL Communications Inc., Reproduced by permission of *Canadian HR Reporter*, 133 Richmond Street West, Toronto, Ontario M5H 3M8.

Computer-aided manufacturing processes are revolutionizing work in dozens of industries. These techniques require better trained and more committed employees.

www.avantech.ca
HR Technology

are technological advances that have caused major occupational changes in the medical field. The overall impact of technological advances in almost every field is that labour-intensive blue-collar and clerical jobs have been decreasing, while technical, managerial, and professional jobs are on the increase. This shift in employment opportunities has many implications for organizations: Jobs and organization structures are being redesigned, new incentive and compensation plans instituted, revised job descriptions written, and new programs instituted for employee selection, evaluation, and training/retraining—all with the help of HR specialists.

Unfortunately, the training of the Canadian labour force has not kept pace with the rate of technological change and innovation. Consequently, there is a scarcity of skills in certain fields. Many Canadian high-tech firms, such as COM-DEV, Siemans Electric and Gennum Corp., bemoan the fact that it often takes months, sometimes even a year or more, to find qualified people,[45] despite the fact that there are currently approximately 1.4 million Canadians seeking employment.

While much of the impact of information technology has been positive, it has also led to some organizational problems. For many employees, it has created anxiety, tension, resentment, and alienation. Unions have consistently expressed concerns about job displacement and health hazards, such as those related to video display terminals. All of these issues must be addressed through effective HRM practices such as information sharing, counselling, ergonomic refitting, job redesign, and training.

Information technology has also hastened what experts call the "fall of hierarchy," or promotion of egalitarianism. Power and authority are spread more evenly among all employees. For example, with "distributed computing," every employee with a personal computer on his or her desk can tap into the firm's computer network and obtain needed information. As one manager at Goodyear Tire and Rubber Company explains: "It used to be, if you wanted information, you had to go up, over, and down through the organization. Now you just tap in. That's what broke down the hierarchy. It's not why we bought computers, but it's what they did."[46] Expecting employees to make more decisions has implications for selection, training, and compensation.

Questions concerning data control, accuracy, right to privacy, and ethics are at the core of a growing controversy brought about by the new information technologies. Sophisticated computerized control systems are used to monitor employee speed, accuracy, and efficiency in some firms, including Bell Canada. While supporters claim that such systems improve productivity and the objectivity and consistency of performance measurement; computerized control systems have been linked to decreased privacy and job satisfaction, and increased stress.[47]

Human Resources Information Systems Information technology has major implications for HR departments. Many firms now have a **Human Resources Information System (HRIS)** to store detailed information on employees, HR policies and procedures, government laws and regulations, collective agreements, etc. Computer applications include salary and benefits administration; tracking statistics on absenteeism, grievances, and health and safety; collecting data for government statistical reporting and employment equity purposes; advertising jobs and recruiting candidates; and communicating with employees. According to a survey conducted in 1993, to which individuals at 502 organizations from across Canada responded, computer utilization ranges from 96.3 percent in payroll management to 12.1 percent in career planning.[48] In the Information Technology and HR boxes throughout this text, we will describe how computers are being used, not only for storage, retrieval, and analysis of information, but for broader applications, including basic report production, long-range forecasting and strategic planning, and evaluation of HR policies and practices. Having a HRIS enables a firm to perform tasks that would be difficult, if not impossible, to do manually. At Edmonton's Public School Board, for example, a computer-driven telephone system has automated teacher absence reporting, and handles 600 to 800 placements per day.[49]

Having an HRIS makes information available and retrievable in a timely manner, and contributes to the organization's efficiency and effectiveness:[50]

> *As explained by Tom Armour, Director of Compensation, Benefits and Systems at Hewlett-Packard (Canada) Limited, "Technology means we can deliver services to our employees and managers with fewer resources, and at less cost than 10 years ago." Ten years ago, Armour's office was drowning in paper. "When we needed to communicate an internal policy or service we'd throw an 80-page manual at employees. We'd pay serious dollars to an ad agency for a glossy benefits brochure that we might have to use white-out on a month later, because of legislative changes." Today, the HR Department can place an information package on compensation in employees' hands in three days, "as opposed to three months."*

Just as HR issues have been increasingly recognized as critical factors in strategic planning decisions, a well-designed HRIS with the ability to quantify, analyze, and model change can serve as a major management tool. However, the more computerized the organization becomes, the more intense the need to create better ways to ensure security of the confidential stored HR data. Shell Canada is one organization that has dealt with all of these issues, as described in the Information Technology and HR box.

Human Resources Information System (HRIS)
A computerized system used to collect, record, store, analyze, and retrieve data pertaining to an organization's human resources.

Information Technology and HR
Intranet Technology at Shell Canada

Calgary-based Shell Canada is taking advantage of intranet technology (the ability to set up an internet within the organization) to view and control a wide variety of personal information and HR data.

Working with IBM Canada Ltd. and IBM partner Lansa Canada, Shell's HR and Information and Computing (I&C) teams have developed a new Employee Services System/Management Access System (ESS/MAS). This system empowers employees and managers by providing online access and control to information traditionally managed by HR department personnel.

Prior to the implementation, there were several factors that had to be taken into consideration. First, the system had to provide access to 3 700 employees across Canada. To accomplish this goal, the company wanted to use its existing IT and network infrastructure to provide reasonable access and response times and to minimize IT administration and support, especially for remote sites. Security was another issue. In addition, the solution had to be easy for employees to use with minimal training and it had to be bilingual.

Shell had recently implemented the HR/Payroll module of the J.D. Edwards (JDE) system on its AS/400 Advanced Series computers. Since 90 percent of the data required by ESS/MAS already existed in JDE, the development team decided to implement an AS/400-based Web solution with a different front end, linking the JDE data on the AS/400 to an intranet solution. The application was deployed Canada-wide with full transaction security and protection of AS/400 data.

"Based on the existing back-end infrastructure, we focused on selecting tools for the AS/400 to give everyone online access," said Ed Teron, Shell Canada's IT Project Manager. "We wanted an option that we could put in place quickly, but that could be extended to other projects."

Using Lansa software for the AS/400 and I/Net software, Lansa Canada and Shell designed and built a secure system that worked almost entirely within the existing environment.

"The system is easy to maintain and the JDE-based HR/Payroll module required absolutely no modification for this project," said Teron. "The brains behind this design is the data transformation function which enables ESS/MAS to be completely buffered from the JDE system. If JDE functions and data change, then most of our changes, if any are required at all, are done in the transformation portion of the system."

The system's ESS portion allows English- and French-speaking employees to view their own personal data, job history records, benefits, pension information, and payroll details. They can update information such as their own home address, telephone number, marital status, or emergency contact. Using electronic forms and email linked to Shell's HP Open/Mail environment, they can also request updates to benefits and pension plans.

Using the MAS, managers can access basic employee information such as name, address, job history, training records, and emergency contacts for individuals reporting to them directly or indirectly. They can also search for types of employees and jobs within the organization. An electronic personnel update function enables managers to submit changes to employee information via email. Managers can also use the system to enter and approve inputs to the corporate salary administration program on an annual basis.

"With this intranet solution, we have enabled our employees to be better informed and thus improve their decision-making abilities," said Debbie Hutchings, Shell's HR Systems Coordinator. "At the same time, we have reduced the reliance of employees on HR staff for general inquiries, reduced HR administration costs, and increased the opportunity for more value-added work by HR staff."

Source: Lori Allan, "Intranet Fits HR in a Nut Shell," *Computing Canada* (June 23, 1997), p.48.

Government

Various laws enacted by governments have had and will continue to have a dramatic impact on the employer-employee relationship in Canada. In one recent survey, 70 percent of the HR specialists responding cited changing regulatory requirements as a major factor altering their work environment.[51]

The legal framework for employment includes constitutional law, particularly the Charter of Rights and Freedoms; acts of parliaments; **common law**, which is the accumulation of judicial precedents that do not derive from specific pieces of legislation; and **contract law**, which governs collective agreements and individual employment contracts. Such laws impose specific requirements and constraints on management policies, procedures, and practices.

common law
The accumulation of judicial precedents that do not derive from specific pieces of legislation.

contract law
Legislation that governs collective agreements and individual employment contracts.

Some of the employment-related legislation is aimed at prohibiting discrimination in various aspects and terms and conditions of employment, such as human rights, employment equity, and pay equity. Other laws require employers to meet certain obligations, such as occupational health and safety, employment standards, and labour relations. Still others make various payments mandatory, such as Workers' Compensation, Employment Insurance, and the Canada/Quebec Pension Plans.

To avoid flooding the courts with complaints and the prosecution of relatively minor infractions, the government in each jurisdiction creates special regulatory bodies to enforce compliance with the law and aid in its interpretation. Such bodies, which include human rights commissions and ministries of labour, develop legally-binding rules, called **regulations**, and evaluate complaints.

regulations
Legally binding rules established by the special regulatory bodies created to enforce compliance with the law and aid in its interpretation.

All of the laws mentioned above and their regulations, which will be discussed in detail later in this book, have important implications for HR managers. First, they must stay abreast of the laws. Since the decisions of courts and quasi-judicial bodies (such as human rights tribunals and labour relations boards) affect interpretation, and legislation itself changes frequently, keeping abreast of legislative developments is a major ongoing responsibility for HR managers. Often, the HR department staff play a major role in helping other managers to remain current by circulating reading material or holding seminars. Second, HR managers must develop and administer policies and practices that ensure compliance to avoid loss of government contracts, suits by affected employees or regulatory bodies, fines, and bad publicity. Finally, they must try to ensure that compliance does not interfere with the efficient and effective accomplishment of their other responsibilities. This means finding ways to comply with regulatory requirements with as little cost and disruption as possible. For example, the Workplace Hazardous Materials Information System legislation (which will be discussed in chapter 18) requires that all employees handling hazardous substances (which includes those using liquid paper correction fluid!) receive training. Many firms have developed manuals, videotapes, and self-administered quizzes, such that employees can study independently at home or at work during off-peak times, and submit their completed quizzes for evaluation and verification of training completion.

One of the factors that makes the laws affecting employment in Canada so challenging is the different jurisdictions involved. Employment Insurance and the Canada Pension Plan are federal laws that apply to all employers and employees in Canada, with one exception—the Quebec Pension Plan applies to employers and employees in the province of Quebec. Other legislation varies from one jurisdiction to another. The Canada Labour Code and Canadian Human Rights Act (federal legislation) apply only to those sectors of the economy regulated by the federal government, which represents about 10 percent of the Canadian work force, including federal government departments and agencies, federal Crown corporations, chartered banks, airlines, national railways, the Canadian armed forces, shipping companies and ports, the insurance and communications industries, and certain interprovincial and international operations. Each province and territory has its own human rights, employment standards, labour relations, health and safety, and workers' compensation legislation. While there is some commonality across jurisdictions, there is also considerable variation. Minimum wage, overtime pay requirements, vacation entitlement, and grounds protected under human rights legislation, for example, vary from one province/territory to another. Furthermore, some jurisdictions have pay and employment equity legislation; others do not. Since virtually every aspect of HRM is affected by legal and/or judicial influences, legislative issues will be discussed in almost every chapter of this text.

Globalization

globalization
The tendency of firms to extend their sales or manufacturing to new markets abroad.

Globalization refers to the tendency of firms to extend their sales or manufacturing to new markets abroad. For businesses everywhere, the rate of globalization in the past few years has been nothing short of phenomenal.

While about 80 percent of Canada's exports still go to the United States, currently Canada has approximately 200 international trading partners.[52] As one international business expert puts it, "the bottom line is that the growing integration of the world economy into a single, huge marketplace is increasing the intensity of competition in a wide range of manufacturing and service industries."[53]

Production is becoming globalized, too, as firms around the world put manufacturing facilities where they will be most advantageous. There are increasing numbers of **multinational corporations**, firms that conduct a large part of business outside the country in which they are headquartered and that locate a significant percentage of their physical facilities and human resources in other countries. Many organizations are locating new plants in areas where wages and other operating costs are lower. For example, Hewlett-Packard's computers are assembled in Mexico, and 3M, the manufacturer of Scotch tape, chemicals, and electrical accessories, has located one of its newest plants in India.[54]

multinational corporation
A firm that conducts a large part of business outside the country in which it is headquartered and that locates a significant percentage of its physical facilities and human resources in other countries.

While cheaper labour is one reason for transferring operations abroad, another is to tap what *Fortune* calls "a vast new supply of skilled labour around the world."[55] Many multinational firms set up manufacturing plants abroad, not only to establish beachheads in promising markets, but also to utilize that country's professionals and engineers. For example, Asea Brown Boveri (a $30-billion-a-year Swiss/Swedish builder of transportation and electric generation systems) already has 25 000 new employees in former Communist countries and has shifted many jobs from Western to Eastern Europe.

This globalization of markets and manufacturing has vastly increased international competition. Throughout the world, organizations that formerly competed only with local or national firms—from airlines to automobile makers to banks—are now facing an onslaught of foreign competitors.

From tapping the global labour force to formulating selection, training, and compensation policies for expatriate employees, managing globalization will continue to be a major HR challenge in the years to come.

Trends in the Nature of Jobs and Work

Major changes have been occurring in the nature of jobs and work, in part as a response to a number of the environmental challenges already discussed.

telecommuting
The use of microcomputers, networks, and other communications technology, such as fax machines, to perform work in the home that is traditionally done in the workplace.

Telecommuting   **Telecommuting** is the use of microcomputers, networks, and other communications technology, such as fax machines, to perform work in the home that is traditionally done in the workplace. Canadian firms with telecommuting policies include the Royal Bank, the Bank of Montreal, Bell Canada, and Digital Equipment of Canada Ltd. Generally, some attendance in the office is required to maintain contacts and attend meetings.

As will be explained in detail in chapter 10, not all jobs can be done on a remote basis. For that reason, most telecommuters are information workers, such as writers, computer programmers, and accountants.

In choosing telecommuters, organizations need to ensure that people are selected who have been with the firm for some time, have the psychological characteristics to work at home, and are self-motivated.[56]

contingent employees
Individuals hired to deal with temporary increases in an organization's workload or to perform specialized tasks for which current employees are lacking time and/or expertise.

Use of Contingent Employees   Many firms are using more **contingent employees**, including temporary workers, part-time workers, and freelancers, to effectively handle vacation and leave coverage, peak-period demands, extra workload, and specialized tasks or assignments, without committing themselves to providing permanent employment or benefits. Some predictions suggest that contingent workers will make up approximately 50 percent of the work force by the year 2000.[57]

Using placement agencies such as Olsten or Kelly Services to obtain temporary employees means that organizations can obtain employees who have been screened and trained, upon little advance notice. The fact that the number of people employed by temporary-help agencies in Canada increases annually is an indicator of their value to employers.

There are more part-time workers in Canada now than ever before: 2.1 million as of 1993.[58] Twenty-six percent of employed women work part-time, primarily in the sales and service industries.[59] This increase in part-time workers has resulted in more concern about pay and benefits inequities.

Freelancers are a new breed of employees who work directly for the employer through contract arrangements. Often they are contracted to provide specialized services one or two days a week on a permanent basis.

The use of contingent workers is not restricted to clerical jobs. Many come from the executive suite or middle management—specialists in their fields—including marketing and advertising executives, human resources professionals, project managers, accountants, writers, graphic designers, and lawyers.[60] In fact, it is estimated that professionals currently comprise about 20 percent of the total contingent work force.[61]

small business
A firm with fewer than 50 employees, generally characterized by individual or small group ownership, owner involvement in the management of the company, and operations restricted to a particular geographical area (although customers may be geographically dispersed).

Small Businesses   **Small businesses,** classified as firms with fewer than 50 employees, whether sole proprietorships, partnerships or corporations, are a large and increasingly important part of the Canadian economy. Generally characterized by individual or small group ownership, owner involvement in the management of the company, and operations restricted to a particular geographical area (although customers may be geographically dispersed), recent Statistics Canada figures indicate that small businesses account for 98 percent of all enterprises and slightly less than one-fifth of all business revenue.[62]

Small businesses are typically run by **entrepreneurs** who are willing to accept the personal financial risks involved, knowing that they will benefit directly from the success of their enterprise. Many large corporations began as a small business venture. For example, Steven Jobs and Steve Wozniak began making personal computers in Wozniak's garage. From this meagre beginning, Apple Computer evolved.

Unfortunately, not all small business owners enjoy such success. The risk of failure is high. In fact, according to a recent edition of CBC's *National Magazine* (October 8, 1996), more than one-half of new business ventures fail during the first year.

Many of those who are self-employed work in the service sector, which will be discussed next. While only about 15 percent of the work force is self-employed, self-employment accounted for approximately 25 percent of the overall employment growth in 1994. Three-quarters of this growth was attributable to women.[63]

A Service Society As can be seen in **Figure 1.8**, employment trends in Canada have been experiencing dramatic change. There has been an ongoing decrease in jobs in the **primary sector**, which includes agriculture, fishing and trapping, forestry, and mining. In fact, this sector now represents only one job in twenty.

**Figure 1.8
Employment Trends**

Source: Statistics Canada, *Labour Force Annual Averages (1996)*, Catalogue No. 71-220, Page A50. Reproduced by authority of the Ministry of Industry, 1998.

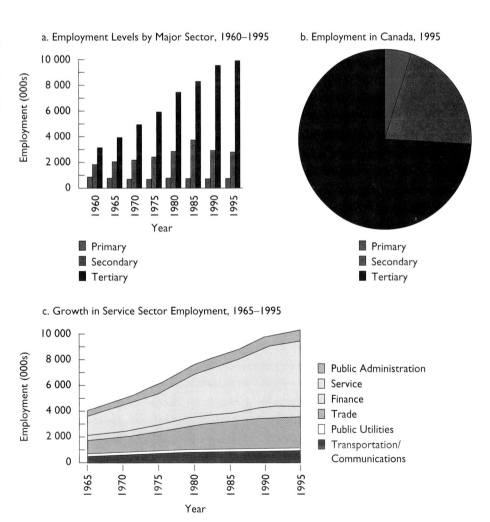

a. Employment Levels by Major Sector, 1960–1995

b. Employment in Canada, 1995

c. Growth in Service Sector Employment, 1965–1995

secondary sector
Manufacturing and construction.

tertiary or service sector
Public administration, personal and business services, finance, trade, public utilities, and transportation/communications.

www.comcheq.ca
Comcheq Payroll Services

knowledge worker
An employee who transforms information into a product or service, whose responsibilities include planning, problem solving, and decision making.

human capital
The knowledge, education, training, skills, and expertise of a firm's workers.

While the **secondary sector** (manufacturing and construction) grew from 1960 to 1985, between 1985 and 1995 employment in those industries dropped by over 25 percent, which represents almost 1 000 000 jobs. In common with trends in Western Europe and the United States, the sector of the Canadian economy accounting for the greatest growth in recent decades is the **tertiary or service sector**, which includes public administration, personal and business services, finance, trade, public utilities, and transportation/communications. In 1995, three of every four jobs in Canada were in this sector.[64]

While much of this growth is attributable to rapid technological change, particularly in telecommunications and computer applications, part is due to the outsourcing of particular activities by primary and secondary sector firms to decrease costs and increase efficiency. Subcontracted functions range from building maintenance to provision of security, cafeteria management and laundry services; to payroll and training and development.

Since all jobs in this sector involve the provision of service, often in person, but increasingly through the design, installation, and maintenance of service-providing technologies (such as automated banking machines and cable television), effectively managing and motivating human resources is critical. Although there are some lesser-skilled jobs (in housekeeping and food services, for example), many service-sector jobs demand **knowledge workers**, employees who transform information into a product or service, whose responsibilities include planning, problem solving, and decision making.

Knowledge Work and Human Capital Management expert Peter Drucker has said that the typical business will soon bear little resemblance to that of 30 years ago: "[it] will be knowledge-based, an organization composed largely of specialists who direct and discipline their own performance through organized feedback from colleagues, customers and headquarters. For this reason, it will be what I call an information-based organization."[65] As a result, the distinguishing characteristic of companies today and tomorrow, according to many experts, is the growing emphasis on **human capital**—the knowledge, education, training, skills, and expertise of a firm's workers—at the expense of physical capital like equipment, machinery, and the physical plant.[66] Jobs today demand a level of expertise far beyond that required of most workers 20 or 30 years ago, which means that human capital is quickly replacing machines as the basis for most firms' success.

Furthermore, it is not unusual for more than one quarter of sales to come from products less than five years old. As a result, "innovating—creating new products, new services, new ways of turning out goods more cheaply, has become the most urgent concern of corporations everywhere."[67]

For managers, the challenge of fostering intellectual or human capital lies in the fact that knowledge workers must be managed differently than workers of previous generations. New HRM systems and skills are required to select and train such employees, encourage self-discipline, win employee commitment, and spark their creativity. According to a recent Conference Board of Canada report,[68]

> *Traditional management systems that rely on top-down control and value employees more for their hands than their brains are increasingly seen as archaic. It is no longer possible to rely simply on those at the top of the organization; leaders must tap into the skills and ideas of all employees.*

3M is one organization that has learned how to encourage creativity and access the skills and ideas of all of its employees:[69]

Although there are currently 65 000 different products, to make sure that it doesn't rest on its laurels, there is a corporate policy that 30 percent of its annual revenues must come from products that are less than four years old.

Over the years, 3M has mastered the art of motivating employees to come up with new and useful ideas. Every 3M employee must take courses on risktaking, handling change, and assuming responsibility for his or her job. Scientists and engineers are actively encouraged to form small groups to come up with new ideas and launch new products. If they can't obtain funding from the managers of their own business units, they can seek money from other business groups. If that fails, they can appeal to a panel of scientists from across the firm to obtain a "Genesis Grant," which provides up to $50 000 in funding. Three Canadian groups have recently obtained such grants.

3M has a long history of success with innovations that initially seemed useless, but later went on to earn millions of dollars. For example, 3M executives tried to end the Thinsulate project at least five times. Innovators within 3M persisted, however, and the light, waterproof, synthetic fibre is now used in sporting goods, shoes, and car doors. In short, Thinsulate has become a wildly successful product, but it only saw the light of day because the firm offered ways for creative employees to bring it to the market.

Tomorrow's HR Today

New Management Practices

In the organizations that have successfully responded to the dramatic changes occurring in their internal and external environments, new modes of organizing and managing have emerged. For example:

bureaucratic structure (bureaucracy)
A pyramid-shaped organization, characterized by a hierarchical structure and many levels of management.

The traditional, **bureaucratic structure**, characterized by a pyramid shape and hierarchies with many levels of management, *is being replaced by new organizational forms,* generally emphasizing cross-functional teams and improved communication flow, with corresponding de-emphasis on "sticking to the chain of command" to get decisions made.[70]

Flatter organizations are the norm. Instead of firms with seven to ten or more layers of management, flat organizations with just three or four levels are starting to prevail. At Celestica Inc., a subsidiary of IBM Canada Ltd., which manufactures computer electronics, there are only two levels of management beneath President Eugene Polistuk. Management only comprises about five percent of the firm's total staffing—and that's for 1 500 people and $1.4 billion business.[71]

Since managers have more people reporting to them in flat structures, they cannot supervise their employees as closely. At 3M's plant in Brockville, Ontario, workers on the shop floor conduct the entire recruitment and selection process, from initial interviewing to testing. The small worker teams of six to eight people also handle quality control, logistics, scheduling, and shipping and receiving.[72] Babcock & Wilcox is another firm which has recognized the importance of employee **empowerment**. The strategies used are described in the Building Employee Commitment box.

empowerment
Providing workers with the skills and authority to make decisions that would traditionally be made by managers.

Building Employee Commitment

Employee Empowerment at Babcock & Wilcox

As a management theory, empowerment is increasingly in vogue: The premise is that higher levels of employee involvement will yield better business decisions, increase customer service, and have a positive impact on the bottom line.

However, achieving empowerment often demands major changes in the ways in which employees are managed, a prospect that can be rather frightening to some. According to Ron Speight, HR Manager at Babcock & Wilcox, what makes the notion of empowerment so intimidating is that it calls for a dramatic departure from traditional, top-down approaches to management, and that calls for a whole new way of running a business. "It's a process of changing attitudes—from senior management level, right down to the grass roots of the organization. It's about changing mindsets, the way people think, the traditions, the historical practices of the organization—really changing the very culture of the organization."

Babcock & Wilcox (B&W), a manufacturer of steam-generating products for industry and utility use, located in Cambridge, Ontario, is one of a growing number of organizations that has recognized the value of getting employees more involved in business operations.

B&W first began grappling with the implications of employee empowerment when it launched a total quality management (TQM) initiative in 1991. An integral part of that initiative was to get employees more involved in problem solving and decision making. Ron Speight remembers that there was tremendous scepticism on the part of employees at first and that some middle managers felt threatened by the process.

To gain support for its new vision, B&W initiated extensive training. A four-and-a-half-day session, addressing such key issues as leadership and continuous improvement, was developed for all supervisors and managers. A series of "Talk with the Top" brown bag luncheons, at which employees could talk with department heads about TQM were also held. Such an open communications environment helped to underscore the company's commitment to its new direction, according to Speight.

Several other initiatives helped to propel the empowerment process. The first was an employee survey, coordinated by Fran Gregory, Manager of Public Relations and Communication. The results clearly indicated that the employees wanted to get more involved, but didn't know how.

At the same time, senior managers came to realize that they could benefit from employee involvement, but that their own management styles were preventing input. "We sometimes bit off more than we could chew," says Speight, "and we were trying to do too much ourselves. It took us a while to realize that we were an obstacle."

This revelation compelled senior managers to look for ways to involve employees in day-to-day business matters. Cross-functional teams were established to address a number of issues, including the development of an employment equity program, an employee assistance program, and a workplace harassment policy.

In addition, three teams were established to help the firm achieve its vision, each of which is headed by a group of senior managers and draws in different employees, depending on the project being tackled. The Communications Team focuses on information sharing to help support the vision. Members of this team helped with the implementation of the employee survey and communication of the results, for example. The Action Team identifies other steps that the firm must take to make the vision a reality. The Review Team monitors the company's overall progress towards goal achievement.

Another significant change at B&W lies in its new efforts to recognize employee contributions and celebrate success. "One of the ways we're nurturing the process is through the implementation of an employee recognition program," says Fran Gregory. "We're recognizing employees for their continuous improvement, both on an individual basis and on a team basis." A "steam spirit" award has been established to recognize team initiatives that help improve the organization, and there is a comparable award recognizing individual contributions.

B&W also celebrates overall corporate success. When major business contracts are signed, evening gatherings for employees are held, complete with beer, wine, and hors d'oeuvres.

Taking a multi-faceted approach has established empowerment as a cultural norm at B&W. According to Speight, "[our] actions were designed to demonstrate clearly to employees that we are serious about this, that senior management is committed. That was a big hurdle. I think people in the organization now believe that we're serious. This is not a flash in the pan."

Source: Claudine Kapel, "Shooting for the Moon," *Human Resources Professional* 9, no. 1 (January 1993), pp. 17–20.

Experts argue in favour of *turning the typical organization upside down*. They say today's organizations should put customers/clients on top and emphasize that every move the company makes should be toward satisfying customer needs. To accomplish this goal, front-line employees—the reception-area clerks at the Holiday Inn, customer service representatives at Canada Trust, flight attendants on Canadian Airlines, and assemblers at GM Canada—must be given the authority to respond quickly to customer/client needs. The main purpose of managers in such "upside down" organizations is to assist the front-line staff by ensuring that they have the resources that they need to do their jobs effectively.

boundaryless organization structure
A structure in which relationships (typically joint ventures) are formed with customers, suppliers, and/or competitors, to pool resources for mutual benefit or encourage cooperation in an uncertain environment.

Boundaryless organization structures are emerging. In this type of structure, relationships (typically joint ventures) are formed with customers, suppliers, and/or competitors, to pool resources for mutual benefit or encourage cooperation in an uncertain environment. Pooling resources for mutual benefit was the goal when Canadian manufacturing firm Milltronics Ltd., based in Peterborough, Ontario, signed an agreement with Sir Sandford Fleming College. The College and Milltronics planned to launch a new training program designed to give them a competitive edge in the international market. A training coordinator, jointly hired and funded, is working full time at Milltronics.[73]

Work is increasingly organized around teams and processes rather than specialized functions. Over 40 percent of those responding to a recent Conference Board of Canada survey indicated that team-based activity was widespread.[74] Teams are certainly the key to success at Celestica Inc. and the Markham, Ontario plant of Ford Electronics Manufacturing Corporation, both winners of the 1993 Canada Awards for Business in the category of Total Quality.[75] While self-managed teams are not yet common, both Celestica[76] and Xerox Canada[77] have recognized their value and are implementing them.

The bases of power are changing in today's organizations. According to management theorist Rosabeth Moss Kanter, position, title, and authority are no longer adequate tools for managers to rely on to get their jobs done. Instead, "success depends increasingly on tapping into sources of good ideas, figuring out whose collaboration is needed to act on those ideas, and working with both to produce results. In short, the new managerial work implies very different ways of obtaining and using power."[78]

Managers no longer manage. Yesterday's managers knew that the president or owners gave them the authority to command and control employees. Today, most managers realize that reliance on formal authority is increasingly a thing of the past. According to Peter Drucker, managers have to learn to manage in situations in which they do not have command authority, and "are neither controlled nor controlling."[79] Yesterday's managers thought of themselves as a "manager" or "boss." Today's managers increasingly think of themselves as a "sponsor," "team leader," or "internal consultant."

Managers today must build commitment. Building adaptive, client-focused or customer-responsive organizations means that eliciting employees' commitment and self-control is more important than ever. Jack Welch, former CEO of General Electric, put it this way: "The only way I see to get more productivity is by getting people involved and excited about their jobs. You can't afford to have anyone walk through a gate of a factory or into an office who is not giving 120 percent."[80]

The HR and the Responsive Organization box provides an example of how one firm—Asea Brown Boveri—is putting changes like all of those described above into practice.

HR and the Responsive Organization

Asea Brown Boveri (ABB)

Zurich-based electrical equipment maker Asea Brown Boveri (ABB) is one good example of a firm that "dis-organized itself to compete in the fast-moving global market of the next ten years." ABB did four things to make itself super-responsive: it organized around mini-units, empowered its workers, flattened its hierarchy, and eliminated central staff. How did ABB do it?

First, within two years of taking over this $30 billion firm, Chair Percy Barnevik "de-organized" its 215 000 employees into 5 000 minicompanies, each averaging only about 50 workers. For example, the ABB hydropower unit in Finland is a highly customer-focused little business, one in which employees' efforts are all centred on its local (Finnish) customers. Each of ABB's 50-person units is run by its own manager and three or four lieutenants. Such small units are very manageable: It's a lot easier to keep track of what everyone is doing when there are only 50 people than when there are 1 000, let alone 5 000 or 10 000.

Next, to speed up decision making, the 5 000 minicompanies are autonomous and empowered. Their employees have the authority to make most of their own business decisions without checking first with top management.

For example, if a customer has a complaint about a $50 000 machine, a minicompany employee has the authority to approve a replacement on the spot, rather than having to wait for reviews by several levels of management. Giving employees this much authority means, by the way, that ABB's 5 000 businesses must be staffed, as management expert Tom Peters puts it, by "high-performance team members," highly skilled employees with the capacity and commitment to make those big decisions.

Next, in a break with most big firms, ABB's 215 000-employee organization has only three management levels (compared to the seven or eight a comparably-sized company might have). There is a 13-member top-management executive committee based in Zurich. Below this is a 250-member executive level that includes country managers and executives in charge of groups of businesses. The third level consists of the 5 000 minicompany managers and their management teams. By flattening the hierarchy or chain of command, and letting lower-level employees make their own on-the-spot decisions, ABB enables its employees to respond more quickly to customers' needs and competitors' moves.

Fourth, since decision making was pushed down to front-line ABB employees, ABB was able to eliminate most of headquarters' staff advisers. For example, when Barnevik became CEO in 1980, he found 2 000 people working at headquarters, basically reviewing and analyzing (and slowing down) the decisions of the firm's lower-level employees. Within a few months, Barnevik reduced the staff to 200—and he reduced it even further in later years. As ABB acquired other companies, Barnevik took the same approach. For example, when Finland's Stromberg Company was acquired, he reduced its headquarters' staff from 880 to 25. Similarly, he reduced staffing at German ABB headquarters in Mannheim from 1 600 to 100.

Responsiveness is the net effect of all this reorganization: a lean, flat organization staffed with highly committed employees who are organized into small, empowered teams, each able to respond quickly to competitors' moves and customers' needs with no need to wait for approval from headquarters.

Source: Tom Peters, *Liberation Management* (New York: Alfred Knopf, 1992), p. 9.

The Plan of This Book

This book is premised on two beliefs. First, we believe that HRM is the responsibility of *every* manager—not just those in the HR department. Throughout this book, we have therefore included practical suggestions designed to help all managers carry out their day-to-day responsibilities more effectively. The second belief is that, given the need for a self-disciplined work force and responsive organization in order to thrive in these fast-changing times, HR programs should contribute to building and maintaining employee commitment. Thus, we have provided numerous examples to illustrate the ways in which HR activities can help foster employee commitment.

This book is divided into six sections. In the remainder of part one, we'll first discuss the increasing importance of the HR function and its evolving role in strategic decision making. Then we'll present the rights of employees and obligations of managers pertaining to equal opportunity and equity, and what is involved in truly embracing and valuing diversity. In part two, we'll cover four critical aspects of HRM: designing and analyzing jobs, human resources planning, recruitment, and selection. The focus of part three will be on developing effective human resources through orientation and training, career development, managing quality and productivity, and performance appraisal. In part four, all aspects of compensation administration will be explored, from establishing pay plans, to the issues involved in pay-for-performance strategies and use of financial incentives, to employee benefits and services. Part five will describe ways to build effective employee/employer relationships in both union and nonunion settings, and will delve into topics such as fair treatment, the dynamics of labour relations, union organizing, collective bargaining, contract administration, and occupational health and safety. In part six, we'll examine international issues in HRM.

Chapter Review

Summary

1. Human resources management (HRM) refers to the management of people in organizations. It comprises the activities, policies, and practices involved in obtaining, developing, utilizing, evaluating, maintaining, and retaining the appropriate number and skill mix of employees to accomplish the organization's objectives. HRM is important to all managers, since they must meet their goals through the efforts of others, which requires the effective management of people.

2. Line authority authorizes managers to direct the work of those reporting to them and make decisions about production, and may be exercised only over those in a manager's direct chain of command. Line managers are in charge of an aspect of operations directly linked to the organization's products or services. Staff authority involves authorization to assist, counsel, advise, or provide service to others. Staff managers—those responsible for service departments, such as HRM and accounting—possess such authority. Functional authority involves the right to make final decisions on issues affecting other departments. The HR department typically has functional authority for highly technical activities, such as compensation and benefits administration, and activities for which centralization enhances efficiency and effectiveness, such as recruitment.

3. Every supervisor and manager is responsible for HRM. In firms in which there is an HR department, the role of the HR staff involves formulating and administering policies and procedures; offering advice to managers throughout the firm; providing services in areas such as staffing, orientation, training, and labour relations; helping to ensure compliance with policies and procedures, collective agreements, and legislation; and serving as a consultant and change agent.

4. The size and sophistication of the HR department and specific functional areas therein is linked to the size and complexity of the organization.

5. Internal environmental factors influencing HRM include the organizational culture, which consists of the core values, beliefs, and assumptions that are widely shared by members of the organization; and the climate, which is the prevailing atmosphere. It is linked to management's leadership style, HR policies and practices, and amount and style of communication.

6. There are a number of external factors which have an impact on HRM, including economic factors, labour market conditions, labour unions, demographic trends and increasing work force diversity, technology, government, globalization, and trends in the nature of jobs and work.

7. In order to respond to such challenges, new modes of managing and organizing have evolved. The traditional pyramid-shaped organization is giving way to new organizational forms; flatter organizations are becoming the norm; and employees are being empowered to make more decisions. Upside-down organizations and boundaryless organization structures are becoming more common; work is increasingly organized around teams and processes; the bases of power are changing; and team leaders are replacing managers. Building employee commitment has become critical to organizational survival and success.

Key Terms

authority	contingent employees	entrepreneur
baby boomers	contract law	functional authority
boundaryless	demographics	functionally illiterate
organization structure	diversity	globalization
bureaucratic structure	employee assistance	human capital
(bureaucracy)	program (EAP)	Human Resources Information System (HRIS)
common law	empowerment	

human resources management	organizational climate	sandwich generation
intrapreneur	organizational culture	secondary sector
knowledge worker	outsourcing	small business
labour market	policy	staff authority
labour union	primary sector	staff manager
line authority	proactive	telecommuting
line manager	procedure	tertiary or service sector
multinational corporation	productivity	
	reactive	
	regulations	

Discussion Questions and Exercises

1. In your own words, define human resources management and describe its objectives.

2. Differentiate among line, staff, and functional authority.

3. Explain why all managers are HR managers, and provide three examples illustrating how HRM concepts and techniques can be beneficial to all managers.

4. Describe the role of the HR department.

5. Describe the two major internal environmental influences on HRM.

6. Explain how changing demographics and increasing work force diversity have had an impact on the organization in which you are working or one in which you have worked.

7. Describe the impact of three of the external environmental challenges presented in this chapter, other than changing demographics and increasing work force diversity.

8. In this chapter, a number of emerging forms of organizing and managing were briefly presented. Based on personal experience or information gleaned through reading or discussion with others, cite three examples of organizations that have restructured or adopted a new approach to management. Describe the changes made and explain the impact.

9. Explain why employee commitment is critical in organizations today.

Application Exercises

RUNNING CASE: Carter Cleaning Company

Introduction

The main theme of this book is that human resources management—activities like recruitment, selection, training, and rewarding employees—is not just the job of a central HR department, but rather the responsibility of every manager. Perhaps nowhere is this more apparent than in a typical small service business. The owner/manager usually has no HR staff on whom to rely. However, the success of his or her enterprise (not to mention his or her family's peace of mind) often depends largely on the effectiveness of the processes through which employees are recruited, hired, trained, evaluated, and rewarded. Therefore, to help illustrate the HRM responsibilities of all managers and ways in which they can be handled effectively, we have included an ongoing saga—a continuing case, based on a small business in central Canada. In the segment of the case at the end of each chapter, the main character—Jennifer Carter—will be confronted with HR challenges that must be resolved by applying the concepts and techniques discussed in that particular chapter.

In order to answer questions arising in the incidents at the end of subsequent chapters, the following background information is required:

Carter Cleaning Centres   Jennifer Carter graduated with a degree in Business Administration from Northern University in June 1994, and, after considering several job offers, decided to do what she had really always planned—go into business with her father, Jack.

Jack Carter opened his first laundromat in 1980 and his second in 1982. The main attraction to him of these coin laundry businesses was that they were capital- rather than labour-intensive. Once the investment in machinery was made, the laundromat could be operated with just one unskilled attendant and none of the labour problems one normally associates with being in the retail service business. The attractiveness of operating with virtually no skilled labour notwithstanding, in 1986 Jack decided to expand the services in each of his laundromats to include the dry cleaning and pressing of clothes. He embarked, in other words, on a strategy of related diversification, in that he added new services that were related to and consistent with the existing coin laundry facilities. His decision was based in part on the fact that he wanted to better utilize the unused space in the rather large stores he currently had under lease, and partly because he was, as he put it, "tired of sending out the dry cleaning and pressing work that came in from our coin laundry clients to a dry cleaner five miles away, who then took most of what should have been our profits." To reflect the expanded line of services, he renamed his two stores "Carter Cleaning Centres." Sufficiently satisfied with their performance, he opened four more similar facilities over the next five years. Each centre had its own on-site manager and seven employees, on average, and annual revenues of about $400 000. It was this six-store chain of cleaning centres that Jennifer joined upon graduation.

Her understanding with her father was that she would serve as a troubleshooter/consultant to him, with the aim of learning the business, and incorporating modern management concepts and techniques to resolve problems and facilitate growth.

Questions

1. How important is effective human resources management in a small business such as Carter Cleaning? Why?

2. What internal and external environmental challenges is Jennifer likely to confront? How will they affect the business?

CASE INCIDENT: HR Systems Inc.

Lou Wally and Stan Smith founded HR Systems Inc. three years ago in Calgary, to provide three types of HR services to firms in the area.

Their first and most profitable market is small businesses. Instead of hiring a full-time person to develop employee handbooks, HR policy manuals, performance appraisal systems, job analysis questionnaires, job descriptions and specifications, compensation plans, etc., it is more cost-effective for many small firms to contract with HR Systems Inc. to do so.

The second service is the provision of an Employee Assistance Program (EAP) to participating companies for a reasonable fee.

The third service involves extensive management consulting activities, including outplacement, executive recruitment, small business development, training and development, and problem analysis/correction/follow-up.

Lou and Stan are quite informal in their own management style. Lou is a trained psychologist and wants to have a solid working team. Stan, although telling everyone outwardly that this is what he wants, is from another school of thought. He doesn't like or trust visible minorities and believes in hierarchical management. He expects employees to be creative in their work groups but to "do as they're told or else!" The implication is that if employees don't have their noses to the grindstone or disagree with his approach, they should pack up their belongings and go.

Lou and Stan fill the positions of Executive Vice President and President, respectively. The Company comprises approximately 20 employees and several temporary contractors. The Program Managers are all male. The newest hires have been females—in both professional and secretarial positions, who are paid well below the prevailing wage rates. There are no Aboriginal persons or visible minority group members, and there have been no efforts to hire any.

As stated, both Lou and Stan are informal. They believe in Friday afternoon staff meetings that include wine, beer, and racist and dirty jokes. Some of the women in this relatively new and growing company have indicated to Lou that they feel rather uncomfortable in the staff meetings, and would prefer not to attend. Stan has made it clear that attendance is mandatory.

The Program Manager for the Employee Assistance Program is a former salesperson, who has little background or experience in the field. His performance in obtaining new clients is poor and he does not appear to have an appreciation for professional confidentiality. For example, on two separate occasions he reported the personal difficulties specific employees were experiencing to management personnel at their firms. Although his efforts were well intentioned (he was seeking authorization for increased services due to some extreme personal circumstances), the damage was done.

There are interpersonal problems among the various work groups and the company is rife with rumours. The employees are becoming increasingly concerned about their hard-earned credibility in a relatively small business community. Several of the professionals on staff are very angry that the owners do not practice the very management styles they are teaching and selling. Staff are also afraid that the company might be experiencing financial problems, since cheques have been delayed and two employee paycheques bounced. This is of grave concern to several of the employees who are the sole support of their families.

Recognizing that there are a few problems in the firm, the two owners have just hired you as the Human Resources Manager, and given you responsibility for "getting things back on track."

Questions

1. Describe the organizational climate at Personnel Systems Inc.
2. As the new HR manager, which internal and external environmental factors would you be particularly concerned about? Why?
3. Explain the contributions you feel you will be able to make to the organization.
4. How would you recommend that the remaining problems be addressed?

Source: Based on a case developed by Sharon Craig, while employed as a faculty member at Sir Sandford Fleming College, Peterborough, Ontario.

Human Resources Management Simulation

As explained in this chapter, government legislation has a major impact on HRM activities. Section 1 in part 3 of the simulation deals with legislation. The owners of Acme Metal Stamping Ltd. are committed to establishing an employee relations atmosphere that supports the rights and needs of employees. To this end, it is imperative that the Human Resources Manager and other managerial personnel stay abreast of current employment legislation and evaluate its impact. Exercise 12 requires the preparation of a list of current provincial employment legislation, an explanation of the HR functions primarily affected by each, and a brief description of the effect of each on management's ability to manage.

Video Case

First Downsizing, Now Outsourcing

Having barely adjusted to downsizing and its HR implications, employers and employees are now having to deal with outsourcing, which has become an important new trend in the Canadian economy. Like much workplace restructuring, outsourcing has eliminated some jobs and created others.

In the past, smaller companies often subcontracted functions that were not economical for them to perform. Larger corporations tended to conduct all activities "in house" to maintain control of quality and costs. Today, however, more companies of every size are considering outsourcing as a viable, efficient option.

Traditionally, only legal, security, and cleaning services were outsourced. Now, any activity that can be accomplished better and cheaper by a specialist is outsourced. Companies can then concentrate on doing what they do well. Computerized functions were some of the first operations to be outsourced. Some organizations, such as Roy Thomson Hall (Toronto), have found it difficult to keep up with the rapid changes in computer technology: adaptation costs were too high, their staffing was inadequate, and/or current employees lacked the required skills. For them, outsourcing computerized functions was clearly an appropriate response.

Outsourcing is often accompanied by restructuring, which can create new positions, often in management, (as was the case at Prudential Insurance Company), and eliminate others (as at Consumers Distributing warehouse operations). In some instances, outsourcing has been responsible for a substantial company growth rate—20 percent in some manufacturing operations, according to the Canadian Manufacturers' Association.

Outsourcing is not always the answer. However, it can be a positive move, as long as those doing the work can meet the technological and cost expectations of the company hiring them.

Questions

1. Describe the advantages and disadvantages of outsourcing.
2. What does outsourcing mean to the current employees of companies deciding to subcontract their work?
3. How can companies deciding to outsource some of their functions protect the job security of their current employees?

4. What role should unions play in outsourcing decisions, if any?

5. What implications does outsourcing have for an organization's human resources department?

Video Resource: CBC, *Venture,* "Outsourcing," September 18, 1994.

Take It to the Net

Check out our Companion Website at

www.prenticehall.ca/dessler

for a multitude of practice questions, key terms and concepts, Weblinks to related sites, newsgroups, CBC video updates, and more.

Notes

1. Joyce D. Ross, "A Definition of Human Resources Management," *Personnel Journal* (October 1982), pp. 781–3.
2. Shari Caudron, "HR Leaders Brainstorm the Profession's Future," *Personnel Journal* 73 (August 1994), p. 54.
3. Mark A. Huselid, "Documenting HR's Effect on Company Performance," *HR Magazine* 39, no. 1 (January 1994), pp. 79–85.
4. Quoted in Fred K. Foulkes, "The Expanding Role of the Personnel Function," *Harvard Business Review* (March–April 1975), pp. 71–84.
5. See Robert Saltonstall, "Who's Who in Personnel Administration," *Harvard Business Review* 33 (July–August 1955), pp. 75–83, reprinted in Paul Pigors, Charles Meyers, and F.P. Malm, *Management of Human Resources* (New York: McGraw-Hill, 1969), pp. 61–73.
6. Saltonstall, "Who's Who," p. 63.
7. Quoted in Doug Burn, "Outsourcing: Transforming the Role of Human Resources Professionals," *Human Resources Professional* 14, no. 1 (February–March 1997), pp. 26–33.
8. Quoted in Burn, "Outsourcing," p. 28.
9. Fred K. Foulkes and Henry Morgan, "Organizing and Staffing the Personnel Function," *Harvard Business Review* 56 (May–June 1977), p. 149.
10. Eva Innes, Robert L. Perry, and Jim Lyon, *The Financial Post Selects the 100 Best Companies to Work for in Canada* (Toronto: Collins, 1986), pp. 250–1.
11. Quoted in Ken Mark, "No More Pink Slips," *Human Resources Professional* 17, no. 8 (November 1996), p. 22.
12. Patricia Sellers and David Kirkpatrick, "Can This Man Save IBM?" *Fortune* (April 19, 1993), pp. 63–7.
13. William B. Werther, Jr., William A. Ruch, and Lynne McClure, *Productivity Through People* (St. Paul: West Publishing, 1986), pp. 3–5.
14. Aaron Bernstein, "Why America Needs Unions But not the Kind It Has Now," *Business Week* (May 23, 1994), p. 70.
15. Sylvia Ostry and Mahmood A. Zaidi, *Labour Economics in Canada*, 2nd ed. (Toronto: MacMillan of Canada, 1972).
16. Gerald Ferris, Dwight Frink, and M. Carmen Galang, "Diversity in the Workplace: The Human Resources Management Challenge," *Human Resource Planning* 16, no. 1, p. 42.
17. E.B. Akeyeampong, "The Labour Market: Year End Review," *Perspectives on Labour and Income* (Ottawa: Statistics Canada, Spring 1995), Cat. No. 75-001E.
18. J. Dumas and A. Bélanger, "Report on the Demographic Situation in Canada, 1994" (Ottawa: Statistics Canada, Ministry of Industry, Science and Technology, 1994), Cat. No. 91-209E.
19. R. Lattimer, "Managing Work Force Diversity: Problems Similar in Canada and U.S.," *Towers Perrin Focus* (Spring 1993), pp. 9–10.
20. Earl Miller, "Capitalizing on Older Workers," *Canadian HR Reporter* 10, no. 12 (June 16, 1997), p. 14. Copyright MPL Communications Inc.
21. Anthony Redwood, "Human Resources in the 1990s," *Business Horizons* (January/February 1990), pp. 6–12.
22. *Workforce 2000* (Toronto: Hudson Institute Canada and Towers Perrin, 1993).
23. J. Gartley, "Earnings of Canadians," (Ottawa: Statistics Canada, Ministry of Industry, Science and Technology, 1994), Cat. No. 96-317E.
24. *Maclean's* (August 9, 1982), p. 30.
25. This information is based on the personal experience of one of the authors.
26. "Graduates With Work: Students Are Confident About Work in the New Economy," *Maclean's* (June 27, 1994), pp. 34–6.
27. B. McKenna, "Rough Road Ahead for Unemployed Youth," *The Globe and Mail*, (January 14, 1993), p. B1.
28. Morton Ritts, "What If Johnny Still Can't Read?" *Canadian Business* (May, 1986), pp. 54–7, 124.
29. G. Montigny, K. Kelly, and S. Jones, "Adult Literacy in Canada: Results of a National Study, Part I," (Ottawa: Statistics Canada, Labour and Household Surveys Division, Ministry of Industry, Science and Technology, 1991), pp. 1–46.

30. *Workforce 2000.*

31. Anita K. Ross, "IBM Canada's Involvement in Education," *Canadian Business Review* 17, no. 3 (Autumn 1990), pp. 21–3.

32. C. Taylor, "Building A Case for Business Diversity," *Canadian Business Review* 22, no. 1 (Spring 1995), pp. 12–5.

33. B. Harrison and L. Marmar, "Languages in Canada," (Ottawa: Statistics Canada, 1994), Cat. No. 96-313E, p. 42.

34. "In the Long Run: Good Reasons for Hope," *Financial Times* (March 26, 1984), pp. 21–5.

35. "Equity Works Best," (Toronto: Ontario Women's Directorate).

36. M.K. Foster and B.J. Orser, "A Marketing Perspective on Women in Management: An Exploratory Study," *Canadian Journal of Administrative Sciences* 11, no. 4 (1994), p. 339.

37. Sheryl Fmolkin, "Family Matters: A Funny Thing Happened on Corporate Canada's Way to Improving Productivity," *Benefits Canada Magazine* (May 1995), p. 19.

38. "Women, Visible Minorities See Improvement in Workplace; Pay Gap Between Sexes Still Vexes, *Canadian HR Reporter* (April 8, 1996) p. 4. Copyright MPL Communications Inc.

39. "Schooling, Work, and Related Activities, Income, Expenses and Mobility," (Ottawa: Statistics Canada, 1996), Cat. No. 89-534.

40. "Selected Characteristics of Persons With Disabilities Residing in Households," (Ottawa: Statistics Canada, 1994), Cat. No. 88-555.

41. Susan Goff Condon, "Hiring the Handicapped Confronts Cultural Uneasiness," *Personnel Journal* 66 (April 1987), p. 68.

42. V.V. Murray, "Organization and Administration of the Human Resources Management Function" in *Human Resource Management in Canada* (Scarborough, ON: Prentice-Hall Canada Inc., 1990), p.15, 38.

43. This section is based on Charles Greer, *Strategy and Human Resources* (Englewood Cliffs, NJ: Prentice-Hall, 1995), pp. 49–52.

44. Elizabeth McGregor, "Emerging Careers," *Occupational Outlook Quarterly* 34 (Fall 1990), p. 22.

45. Patricia Orwen, "The Scarcity of Skills: With Unemployment So High, Why Are Thousands of Jobs Going Unfilled?" *The Toronto Star* (July 17, 1993), p. D1.

46. Thomas Steward, "Welcome to the Revolution," *Fortune* (December 13, 1993), p. 72.

47. Marco A. Monsalve and Arlene Triplett, "Maximizing New Technology," *HR Magazine* (March 1990), pp. 85–7.

48. Donald Belfall, "HRIS Snapshot: The Canadian Landscape," *Human Resources Professional* 11, no. 1 (January/February 1994), pp.12–3.

49. Trisha McCallum, "Embracing The Chip," *Human Resources Professional* 13, no. 2 (April 1996), pp. 13–6.

50. Quoted in McCallum, "Embracing the Chip," p. 13.

51. G. Betcherman, K. McMullen, N. Leckie, and C. Caron, *The Canadian Workplace in Transition* (Kingston, ON: IRC Press, Queen's University, 1994).

52. Andrew Purvis, "Super Exporter," *Time* (April 28, 1997), pp. 34–8.

53. Charles W. Hill, *International Business* (Burr Ridge, IL: Irwin, 1994), p. 6.

54. Brian O'Reilly, "Your New Global Workforce," *Fortune* (December 14, 1992), pp. 52–66.

55. O'Reilly, "Your New Global Workforce," pp. 52–66.

56. Trisha McCallum, "Telecommuting," *Human Resources Professional* 14, no. 2 (April/May, 1997), pp. 45–9.

57. Jaclyn Fierman, "The Contingency Work Force," *Fortune* 129 (January 24, 1994), pp. 30–6.

58. Fierman, "The Contingency Work Force," pp. 25–30.

59. "Women in the Labour Force" (Ottawa: Statistics Canada, 1994), Cat. No. 75-507E, pp. 5–10.

60. Heather Hodgman, "The Next Office Temp Could Be You," *Human Resources Professional* 12 no. 3 (May 1995), pp. 16–8.

61. Fierman, "The Contingency Work Force," pp. 30–6.

62. F.A. Starke and R.W. Sexty, *Contemporary Management in Canada* (Toronto: Prentice Hall Canada, 1995), pp. 61520.

63. Akeyeampong, "The Labour Market".

64. "Labour Force Annual Averages" (Ottawa: Statistics Canada, 1996) Cat. No. 71-220-XPB.

65. Peter Drucker, "The Coming of the New Organization," *Harvard Business Review* (January–February 1988), p. 45.

66. Richard Crawford, *In the Era of Human Capital* (New York: Harper, 1991), p. 10.

67. Francis Fukuyama, "Are We at the End of History?" *Fortune* (January 15, 1990), pp. 75–8.

68. Quoted in Claudine Kapel, "Shooting for the Moon" *Human Resources Professional* 9, no. 1 (January 1993), p. 19.

69. Jerry Zeidenberg, "HR and the Innovative Company," *Human Resources Professional* 13, no. 4 (June, 1996), pp. 12–5.

70. This discussion is based on Walter Kiechel III, "How We Will Work in the Year 2000," *Fortune* (May 17, 1993), p. 79.

71. Claudine Kapel, "Quality's Champions," *Human Resources Professional* 11, no. 5 (June/July 1994), pp. 9–13.

72. Zeidenberg, "The Innovative Company," pp. 12–5.

73. "Business, College Join Forces," in News and Views, compiled by Kelly Quinn, *The Human Resources Professional* 13, no. 5 (July/August 1996), p. 19.

74. P. Booth, *Challenge and Change: Embracing the Team Concept* (Ottawa: The Conference Board of Canada, 1994).

75. Kapel, "Quality's Champions," pp. 9–13.

76. "Quality's Champions," p. 12.

77. Claudine Kapel, "Master Copy," *Human Resources Professional* 11, no. 6 (August 1994), pp. 17–8.

78. Rosabeth Moss Kanter, "The New Managerial Work," *Harvard Business Review* (November–December 1989), p. 88.

79. Drucker, "The New Organization," p. 45.

80. Thomas A. Steward, "How GE Keeps Those Ideas Coming," *Fortune* (August 12, 1991), p. 42.

Chapter 2
The Evolving Role of HRM: From Staff Function to Strategic Partner

Chapter Outline

- ◆ **The History of HRM**
- ◆ **Growing Professionalism in HRM**
- ◆ **The Current Role of HR Departments**
- ◆ **Strategic Planning and HRM**
- ◆ **The Role of the HR Department as a Strategic Partner**
- ◆ **Evaluating the HR System**
- ◆ **The Impact of Effective HRM Practices on Employee Performance and the Bottom Line**

Learning Outcomes

After studying this chapter, you should be able to:

Briefly *describe* the history of HRM.

Discuss the growing professionalism of HRM, and *explain* the importance of ethics and social responsibility.

Describe the current role of HR departments.

Describe the nature of strategic planning and *discuss* the role of the HR department as a strategic partner.

Explain why the HR system should be evaluated and *describe* various auditing strategies and techniques used in HRM.

Discuss the impact of effective HRM practices on employee performance and the bottom line.

As a result of all of the challenges discussed in chapter 1, HRM has changed dramatically over time, and has assumed an increasingly important role in organizations. The demands on HR department staff members and expectations regarding the types of assistance they should provide have increased correspondingly. As will be explained in this chapter, the emerging role of the HR department as a strategic partner has been an evolutionary process.

The History of HRM

Human resources management practices have been shaped by society's prevailing beliefs and attitudes about workers and their rights. In general, organizations have not led the way by initiating new directions in HRM; rather, they have reacted to trends.[1]

Table 2.1 outlines the general evolution of management thinking about workers. As can be seen, the general managerial pattern of beliefs has evolved through three distinct stages, each with a different focus: the scientific management model, the human relations model, and the human resources model.[2]

TABLE 2.1 Theories of Management		
SCIENTIFIC MANAGEMENT MODEL	**HUMAN RELATIONS MODEL**	**HUMAN RESOURCES MODEL**
Assumptions	**Assumptions**	**Assumptions**
1. Work is inherently distasteful to most people.	1. People want to feel useful and important.	1. Work is not inherently distasteful. People want to contribute to meaningful goals that they have helped establish.
2. What workers do is less important than what they earn for doing it.	2. People desire to belong and to be recognized as individuals.	2. Most people can exercise far more creative, responsible self-direction and self-control than their present job demands.
3. Few want or can handle work that requires creativity, self-direction, or self-control.	3. These needs are more important than money in motivating people to work.	
Policies	**Policies**	**Policies**
1. A manager's basic task is to closely supervise and control employees.	1. A manager's basic task is to make each worker feel useful and important.	1. A manager's basic task is to make use of "untapped" human resources.
2 A manager must break tasks down into simple, repetitive, easily learned operations.	2. A manager should keep employees informed and listen to their objections to his/her plans.	2. A manager must create an environment in which all members may contribute to the limits of their ability.

(continued)

TABLE 2.1 (continued)

SCIENTIFIC MANAGEMENT MODEL	HUMAN RELATIONS MODEL	HUMAN RESOURCES MODEL
Policies	**Policies**	**Policies**
3. A manager must establish detailed work routines and procedures and enforce these firmly but fairly.	3. A manager should allow employees to exercise some self-control on routine matters.	3. A manager must encourage full participation on important matters, continually broadening employees' self-direction and control.
Expectations	**Expectations**	**Expectations**
1. People can tolerate work if the pay is decent and the boss is fair.	1. Sharing information with employees and involving them in routine decisions will satisfy their basic needs to belong and to feel important.	1. Expanding employee influence, self-direction, and self-control will lead to direct improvements in operating efficiency.
2. If tasks are simple enough and people are closely controlled, they will produce up to standard.	2. Satisfying these needs will improve morale and reduce resistance to formal authority—employees will "willingly cooperate."	2. Work satisfaction may improve as a "by-product" of employees making full use of their resources.

Source: Abridged and adopted from Raymond E., Miles, *Theories of Management*, (McGraw-Hill: New York, 1975). Reprinted with permission of McGraw-Hill.

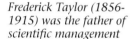

Frederick Taylor (1856-1915) was the father of scientific management

Scientific Management: Concern for Production

scientific management
The process of "scientifically" analyzing manufacturing processes, reducing production costs, and compensating employees based on their performance levels, which evolved from the work of Frederick W. Taylor.

The scientific management movement of the late 1800s and early 1900s had a significant impact on management and the employee-management relationship. Frederick Taylor was the driving force behind **scientific management**, the process of "scientifically" analyzing manufacturing processes, reducing production costs, and compensating employees based on their performance levels.[3] He emphasized systematic job design, task simplification, compensation tied to production, selection of workers with the skills and abilities required to become superior performers, and fit between person and job. He also stressed the need for cooperation, which he felt could be achieved through the use of scientific methods, rules, and procedures that were binding on both workers and managers.

Taylor felt that managers should be responsible for planning, organizing, and determining the best method for performing each job; and workers should focus on what they did best—labouring. He believed that the average worker was basically lazy and motivated primarily by economic gain. On the basis of these assumptions, he advocated achieving operational efficiency by redesigning jobs to maximize productivity, and paying workers a piece rate based on performance, with extra pay for each piece produced in excess of the daily standard. It was his belief that such incentives would lead to higher wages for workers, increased profits for the organization, and harmony in the workplace.

Scientific management, which helped to shape the view that workers were a factor of production who were motivated primarily by money, was widely accepted. It should be noted, though, that not all management theorists in the 1920s and 1930s accepted Taylor's viewpoints. An exception was Mary Parker Follet, a writer ahead of her time, who believed very strongly in self-management; cross-functional cooperation; empowerment; and managers as leaders, not dictators.[4]

The Human Relations Movement: Concern for People

human relations movement
A management philosophy based on the belief that the attitudes and feelings of workers were important and deserved more attention.

Hawthorne Studies
A series of experiments conducted at the Hawthorne Works of the Western Electric Company between 1924 and 1933 that examined factors influencing worker morale and productivity, the conclusions of which had a significant impact on management practices.

The human relations model emerged in the 1920s and 1930s, but was not fully embraced until the 1940s. The primary aim of the **human relations movement** was to consider jobs from an employee's perspective. The human relations advocates believed that the attitudes and feelings of workers were important and deserved more attention. They criticized managers who treated workers as machines.

The driving rationale behind the movement were results from the **Hawthorne Studies**, one of the first cooperative industry/university research efforts, conducted by Elton Mayo, Fritz J. Roethlisberger, and W.J. Dickson. These were a series of experiments conducted at the Hawthorne Works of the Western Electric Company between 1924 and 1933 that examined factors influencing worker morale and productivity. The conclusions had a significant and far-reaching impact on management practices.

The researchers discovered that the effect of the social environment is equal to or greater than that of the physical environment. They learned that workers' feelings, sentiments, emotions, and morale were greatly influenced by such factors as working conditions, supervisory leadership style, and management's philosophy regarding workers. Treating workers with dignity and respect was found to contribute significantly to employee job satisfaction and the attainment of higher productivity levels. The researchers also concluded that economic incentives, considered a key motivator by scientific management proponents, were really of secondary importance to workers.

The researchers found that workers spontaneously formed groups, established group norms, and controlled productivity through various social pressures. Workers who produced in excess of the group's standards were called "ratebusters"; those whose output was unacceptably low were called "chiselers"; and those who complained to a superior were called "squealers." Solid evidence was found to support the position that peer-group pressures influence workers' behaviour.[5]

The human relations approach had wide appeal and was embraced by many organizations. Working conditions in those firms improved substantially. Based on the belief that workers wanted to feel important at work and be recognized as individuals, managerial approaches to worker motivation had a strong social emphasis. To overcome low morale, feelings of alienation, and prevailing poor performance, managers improved the social dynamics of the work environment through such interpersonal strategies as establishing better channels of communication, allowing employees to exercise more self-direction, and treating employees with consideration.

The human relations movement came under severe criticism for overcompensating for the impersonal and dehumanizing effect of scientific management by failing to recognize the importance of structure, standards, procedures, and work rules to control employees' behaviour and guide their conduct to achieve organizational goals. The movement was also criticized for oversimplifying the concept of human motivation and behaviour and failing to recognize the unique beliefs, values, needs, expectations, interests, and abilities of each employee.

The Human Resources Movement: Concern for People and Productivity

human resources movement
A management philosophy focussing on concern for people and productivity.

Human resources management is currently based on the theoretical assumption that employees want to contribute to meaningful goals that they have helped to establish, and can exercise self-direction and self-control to reach the organization's objectives. Arriving at this joint focus on people and productivity involved four evolutional phases.[6]

Phase One In the early 1900s, human resources management, or personnel administration, as it was then called, played a very subservient or nonexistent role in organizations. When a personnel department did exist, it was generally held in low esteem, and located at the bottom of the organization chart. During this period, there were very few laws regulating working conditions and the employee/employer relationship. Organizations focused on maximizing productivity and increasing profits; the human element was generally considered unimportant. During this era, personnel administrators assumed responsibility for hiring and firing, a duty formerly looked after by first-line supervisors; ran the payroll department; and administered benefits. Their job focused largely on ensuring that procedures were followed. As technology in such areas as testing and interviewing began to emerge, personnel departments began to play an expanded role in employee selection, training, and promotion.

Phase Two As the scientific management movement gained momentum, operational efficiency increased. However, since wages generally fell behind productivity growth, workers began to distrust management, and many turned to unions for support. The increase in unionizing activities dramatically influenced the role of personnel departments in organizations. Personnel managers were expected to develop policies and practices that would enable the firm to retain nonunion status, if possible; and if not, to serve as the primary contact for union representatives. The depression of the 1930s also had an important influence on the role of personnel departments. Following the depression, workers sought government intervention to provide some form of financial protection in the case of job loss, and to recognize their rights to form and join unions. Various legislation was enacted, including a minimum wage act, an unemployment insurance program, and protection of workers' rights to belong to unions. Legal compliance was added to the responsibilities of personnel managers.

During the 1940s and 1950s, personnel managers were also involved in dealing with the impact of behavioural theories, particularly those pertaining to motivation. Orientation, performance appraisal, and employee relations responsibilities were added to their portfolio. As a result of their expanding role, the importance of personnel departments began to increase.

Phase Three The third major phase in personnel management was a direct result of the increasing amount of government legislation during the 1960s, 1970s, and 1980s. Laws were passed that affected employees' human rights, wages and benefits, working conditions, and health and safety. The role of personnel departments expanded dramatically. Effective employment policies and practices increased in importance because of societal, governmental, and organizational challenges and objectives, and because of the penalties for failure to meet them. Personnel departments continued to provide expertise in areas such as recruitment, screening, and training, but in an expanded capacity. During the latter part of this era, the term "human resources management" emerged. This change represented a shift in emphasis: Whereas personnel administration emphasized maintenance and administration, the focus of HRM was on corporate contribution, proactive management, and the initiation of change.[7]

Phase Four The fourth phase of HRM is ongoing. Current management thinking holds that workers are motivated primarily by the nature and scope of the job, social influences, the nature of the compensation and incentive systems, organizational culture and climate, management's supervisory style, and individual needs and values. It is widely recognized that employees do not all seek the same rewards from their jobs and that most sincerely want to make a contribution to the organization. In order to harness this drive and determination, organizations must develop strategies to maximize employee performance and potential, such that the goals and aims of both management and employees are achieved. In today's flattened, downsized, and responsive organizations, highly trained and committed employees—not machines—are often a firm's best competitive advantage. The role of HR departments has shifted from protector and screener to planner and change agent.

Growing Professionalism in HRM

profession
A vocation characterized by the existence of a common body of knowledge, requirements and procedures for certification of members, self-regulation, and a code of ethics by which members must abide.

Today, senior HR practitioners must concern themselves with all aspects of HRM and their impact on organizational performance and society as a whole. They must be professionals, in terms of both performance and qualifications.

Every **profession** has four major characteristics:

- the existence of a common body of knowledge, developed through research and experimentation, that is widely communicated through professional literature and exchanged through conferences, seminars, and workshops sponsored by the professional associations
- requirements and procedures for certification of members
- performance standards established by members of the profession rather than by outsiders (self-regulation), and
- a code of ethics by which members must abide.

HRM exhibits all four characteristics.

Professional Associations and Certification

In 1989, more than 2 500 members of the Personnel Association of Ontario (PAO), now the Human Resources Professionals Association of Ontario (HRPAO), received the first professional designation for practitioners in North America.[8] This designation, the Certified Human Resources Professional (CHRP), was granted official recognition by the provincial legislature in 1990. HRPAO, with more than 7 000 members, is still the largest professional association in Canada.

Nearly every province has an association of HR practitioners. The broad objectives of each association are similar:

- providing opportunities for information exchange and cooperation in meeting and solving common problems
- assisting in the provision of training in the field of HR and skills updating, and
- serving as a voice for HR practitioners, especially in response to proposed legislation and legislative reforms.

www.chrpcanada.com
Canadian Council of HR Associations

The provincial associations are affiliated through the Canadian Council of Human Resources Associations (CCHRA), the first national HR organization. Until the incorporation of the CCHRA in 1991, Canada was one of the few countries in the world that did not have collective HR representation at a national level. CCHRA now represents more that 15 000 HR practitioners across the country. Its mission is to provide a collective voice on HR issues, nationally and internationally; establish core standards for the HR profession; and coordinate the portability of HR qualifications.[9]

Other leading professional associations in the HR field include the Canadian Public Personnel Management Association, the Conference Board of Canada, Canadian Management Association, and the International Personnel Management Association. Organizations that represent specialized areas of HRM include the Canadian Compensation Association, Canadian Payroll Association, Canadian Industrial Relations Association, International Foundation of Employee Benefit Plans, Ontario Society for Training & Development, Society of Human Resource Planners, Canadian Association of Human Resource System Professionals Inc., Canada Recruiters' Guild, and Association of Canadian Pension Management. All of these organizations promote the professional growth of their members by sponsoring meetings and workshops, and providing opportunities for contact with other organizations, including government agencies.

Certification involves recognition for having met certain professional standards. For HR practitioners, the certification criteria vary between provinces, but generally include three requirements: membership in good standing and agreement to abide by the association's code of ethics; work experience in the field at a professional/supervisory level for a specified period of time; and completion of an approved program of study. In Ontario, for example, to attain the Certified Human Resources Professional (CHRP) designation, HR practitioners must:

1. Attain credit for eight subjects with a "B" standing or higher (except in Finance and Accounting and Human Resources Research and Information Systems in which a "C" is acceptable). Four of these courses are mandatory, as illustrated in **Figure 2.1**. Candidates must also pass a comprehensive provincial exam.

www.ostd.ca
Ontario Society for Training & Development

certification
Recognition for having met certain professional standards

**Figure 2.1
Human Resources
Professionals
Association of Ontario
(HRPAO) Educational
Program**

Source: Human Resources Professionals Association of Ontario, 1997.

www.hrpao.org
Human Resource Professionals Association of Ontario

The Academic Requirements:
The curriculum is reviewed and kept current by a Board of Examiners. There are 11 courses, divided into Tier I and Tier II. To complete the requirements you must:

1. Become a member of HRPAO; and
2. Complete all four of the Tier I compulsory subjects; and
3. Complete four of the seven Tier II specialty subjects; and
4. Pass the Comprehensive Provincial Examination (CPE).

Tier I—Compulsory Subjects
1. Human Resources Management
2. Organizational Behaviour
3. Finance and Accounting
4. Labour Economics

Tier II—Specialized Subjects
1. Compensation
2. Training and Development
3. Labour Relations
4. Occupational Health & Safety
5. Human Resources Planning
6. Human Resources Research and Information Systems (HRRIS)
7. Designated Elective Course (DEC)—a student may apply for ONE credit in this subject area.

2. Be a member of the Human Resources Professionals Association of Ontario (HRPAO) in good standing

3. Have at least three years' of work experience in the HR field at a professional or supervisory level, and

4. Be sponsored by a CHRP member.

Many colleges and universities have created undergraduate, post-diploma, and graduate programs with specializations in HRM. HR specialists may take the courses required to meet the educational component of their professional designation through educational institutions, or, in some instances, through night classes offered by the provincial association. Although HR associations in each province establish their own educational requirements, there is considerable similarity among programs offered.

Some provincial HR associations require proof of ongoing education to qualify for recertification. For senior practitioners, there is an alternative route to attainment of the CHRP designation in some jurisdictions, including Ontario. The requirements are a significant number of years of experience in the field (ten in Ontario), encompassing a number of areas of HRM, (not a single specialty area), and approval through a peer review process.

Those provinces with associations and certification programs are listed in **Figure 2.2**. One of the first accomplishments of the CCHRA was adoption by member associations of a resolution to recognize the equivalency of provincial HR designations. This means that individuals receiving the CHRP designation in one province are eligible for recognition of their professional status in all member provinces.

**Figure 2.2
Certification Programs
in Human Resources
Management**

Certification in Human Resources Management		Certification in HR Specialties
Canadian Public Personnel Management Association	CPPMA	Canadian Payroll Association: PA – Payroll Administrator
B.C. Human Resources Management Association	CHRP	PS – Payroll Supervisor PM – Payroll Manager
Greater Victoria Human Resources Management Association	CHRP	Canadian Compensation Association: CCP – Certified Compensation
Human Resources Institute of Alberta	CHRP	Professional
Human Resources Management Association of Manitoba	CHRP	CBP – Certified Benefits Professional Ontario Society for Training and Development:
Human Resources Professionals Association of Ontario	CHRP	CTDP – Certified Training and Development Professional

Ethics

ethics
The discipline dealing with what is good or bad, and right or wrong, and with moral duty and obligation.

The professionalization of HRM has created the need for a uniform code of ethics. **Ethics** is the discipline dealing with what is good or bad, and right or wrong, and with moral duty and obligation.

Every day, HR managers must make decisions that have ethical implications. Should an otherwise effective employee be fired for violating certain company regulations? Can or should a manager share personal information about an employee that was gained accidentally, and if so, under what circumstances? Such issues must be dealt with on ethical grounds.

Figure 2.3
Code of Ethics—
Human Resources
Professionals
Association of Ontario

Source: Human Resources
Professionals Association of
Ontario, 1997

Members of the Human Resources Professionals Association of Ontario strive for growth as human resources professionals and commit to the principles of the Code of Ethics to the best of their ability. Human resources professionals shall:

- continue professional growth in human resources management, in support and promotion of the goals, objectives and by-laws of the Association;

- not knowingly violate or cause to be violated, any legislated act, regulation or by-law that relates to the management of human resources;

- demonstrate commitment to such values as respect for human dignity and human rights and promote human development in the workplace, within the profession and society as a whole;

- treat information obtained in the course of business as confidential, and avoid, or disclose, any conflict of interest that might influence personal actions or judgements;

- refrain from inappropriately using their position to secure special privileges, gain or benefit for themselves, their employers or the Association;

- acknowledge an obligation to the employer community to encourage and foster generally accepted codes of moral behaviour; and,

- practice respect and regard for other professional associations.

Professional associations devise codes of ethics to assist their members in handling dilemmas such as those described above. These codes are designed to promote and maintain the highest possible standards of personal and professional conduct among members. Agreement to abide by the code of ethics is one of the requirements to maintain professional status. The Code of Ethics of the Human Resources Professionals Association of Ontario is shown in **Figure 2.3**.

HR professionals are not only concerned with monitoring their own ethics. More and more North American firms are stressing ethical conduct in business. Many have established a code of ethics to govern corporate relations with employees and the public at large, and ensured that all employees are aware of the existence and implications of the code.[10] According to John Belcher, President, Hughes Aircraft of Canada Limited in Calgary, "Consumers are demanding ethical behaviour, and choosing to do business with those companies they perceive as ethical."[11] Increasingly, HR departments are being given a greater role in communicating the organization's values and standards, monitoring compliance with its code of ethics, and enforcing standards throughout the firm. Some organizations, such as Prudential Insurance, have such a commitment to ethics that they have a full-time ethics officer. (To learn more about Prudential's approach to ethics, refer to the HR and the Responsive Organization box.)

HR and the Responsive Organization

Doing the Right Thing at Prudential

Shelley Brown, Ethics Officer at Prudential Insurance Company of America, based in Toronto, believes that the Canadian attitude towards ethics reflects the public's concerns, beyond quality and service, about companies' positions on ethical behaviour, and what they do for employees, customers, and the communities in which they operate.

At Prudential, the impetus behind the ethics program came in 1994 from the president of Canadian operations, Bob McKnight: "My intention was three-fold. First, we looked at what was going on in the industry outside Canada to make sure that we're okay, and that what may be troubling other companies won't trouble us. Next, [it was necessary] to have one part of the company be proactive in this area, with someone from outside the daily operations to see how we are behaving. Lastly, we wanted to give a higher priority to our values of customer focus and being worthy of trust."

Brown, who assumed his current position in 1994, after two years as Director of Human Resources, has a mandate to ensure that all employees act appropriately. He listens to what employees have to say, tracks trends, and establishes policies and procedures.

Since he believes that communication is important in getting the ethical message across to employees and keeping its profile high, Brown writes a monthly column for the company newsletter and visits the regional offices frequently.

Sensitizing employees to ethical issues is not only a preventative measure. An ethical platform can elevate a firm above its competitors, so that it serves as a model for the industry.

Prudential's living benefits program, established in the late 1980s by former president of Canadian operations, Ron Barbaro, is an excellent example. Barbaro realized that the life insurance policies of terminally ill AIDS sufferers could be more usefully applied to support their financial needs while they were still living. Living benefits, a dramatic departure from established practices, is a concept now universally acclaimed and imitated by many insurance companies in North America.

Ethical performance not only inspires consumers to reward companies for exemplary behaviour. Innovative actions like those of Prudential ignite the public's interest and enhance employee pride and commitment. Organizations would be hard pressed to find a better return.

Source: Leslie Goodson, "Doing the Right Thing," *Human Resources Professional* 13 no.1 (February/ March 1996), p.22.

social responsibility
The implied, enforced, or felt obligation of managers, acting in their official capacities, to serve or protect the interests of groups other than themselves.

In recent years, the concept of **social responsibility** has frequently been discussed as a complement to ethics. A company that exercises social responsibility attempts to balance its commitments—not only to its investors, but also to its employees and customers, other businesses, and the community or communities in which it operates. The Body Shop, an early and often-cited example of a socially-responsible firm, proves that businesses can balance profits and principles. Sean Quinn, head of The Body Shop's Social Inventions Department in Toronto, is insistent that being socially responsible does not cost more:[12]

With sales of more than $100 million, The Body Shop is an example of a company that successfully combines profits with principles.

We [the Body Shop] can have sales of $100 million while taking a stand on anti-animal testing, human rights protection, and environmental conservation, the three main criteria against which all our activities are measured. This success demonstrates that profits can be made and principles maintained.

The Current Role of HR Departments

Improving Productivity

As mentioned in chapter 1, productivity improvement is crucial in today's globally-competitive environment. Organizations known for product and service quality strongly believe that employees are the key to their reputation, and that proper attention to employees improves both quality and productivity. A review of management practices in such companies as FedEx Canada, Cadet Uniforms, and CIBC indicates that top-level commitment, employee involvement, and a conscious strategy to encourage innovation are critical for productivity improvement.[13] All of these require the presence of an enlightened and proactive HR department.

The HR department staff play a pivotal role in lowering labour costs, the single largest operating expense in many organizations, particularly in the service sector. Approaches taken include strategies for reducing turnover, absenteeism, and the incidence rate of occupational illnesses and injuries; and adopting more effective recruitment, selection, and training programs. At one international tire manufacturing firm, for example, adopting a behaviour-based interview strategy (which will be described in chapter 7) as the basis for selection of entry-level engineers resulted in savings of $500 000 in three years. These savings were due to lower turnover, lower training costs, and improved capabilities of the engineering staff because of a better fit.[14]

For many firms, instituting tough head-count controls is the first line of attack in terms of lowering labour costs. The HR department generally plays the central role in planning and implementing corporate downsizings like those at IBM, Bell Canada, and the federal government. HR staff often take steps to maintain the morale of the remaining employees. Study after study shows that surviving employees, anxious about the next round of terminations, often suffer stress symptoms, including reduced performance, depression, and proneness to error.[15] After a major downsizing at Apple Canada, mandatory stress-counselling sessions were provided; employees were encouraged to make use of the company-sponsored Employee Assistance Program; managers were encouraged to be more flexible in responding to requests for time off to deal with personal matters; and more people were given the opportunity to do some of their work from home.[16]

Increasing Responsiveness

Making the enterprise more responsive to product innovations and technological change is the basic aim of many of the management strategies listed at the end of chapter 1. Downsizing, flattening the pyramid, empowering employees, and organizing around teams are designed to facilitate communication and make it easier for decisions to be made, so that the organization can respond quickly to its customers' needs and competitors' challenges. The HR department staff play a crucial role in accomplishing these objectives. In the HR and the Responsive Organization boxes throughout the book, numerous examples are provided of ways in which HR practices can help to boost a firm's responsiveness.

Improving Service

Employee behaviour is particularly important in service firms such as banks and retail establishments. If a customer is confronted by a customer service representative

Employees in fast-food establishments are taught how to provide courteous, efficient customer service.

or salesperson who is tactless or unprepared to discuss the pros and cons of the different products or services, or even worse, is downright discourteous, all of the firm's other efforts to attract this customer will have been wasted. Many such organizations have little to differentiate them from their competitors except superior service, and that makes them uniquely dependent on their employees' attitudes and motivation—and thus on effective HRM. As noted by Kevin Scott, Senior Manager of Human Resources at the Bank of Montreal, "In the financial services sector just about everything that's new can be copied by competitors pretty quickly. What distinguishes a company is the "people" business aspects. People are the critical differentiating component...."[17]

Thus, the HR department plays a crucial role in service companies.[18] It has been noted, for instance, that there are "quite a few [employees] who lack the temperament, maturity, social skills and tolerance for frequent contact" that customer service jobs require, and that the first step in avoiding this problem is proper screening and selection.[19] A recent study of service firms highlights the HRM-service link. The researchers found that progressive HR practices, such as facilitating employees' career progress, developing orientation/training programs for new employees, and eliminating conditions on the job that inhibit task performance, appear to improve employees' customer service, as well as the overall quality of that service from the customers' point of view.[20]

The philosophy behind this idea is probably best summed up by Fred Smith, the chairperson and founder of Federal Express, whose philosophy is "people—service—profits." In other words, if progressive HR practices are used to build employee commitment and morale, employees will provide excellent service, which, in turn, will generate profits.

Helping to Build Employee Commitment

Intense global competition and the need for more responsiveness puts a premium on employee commitment. As Jon Slangerup, Vice President and General Manager of Federal Express Canada Ltd., explains:[21]

> *It's a matter of discretionary effort—having employees do things above and beyond the call of duty every single day. To me, that is the difference between a great company and a good one.*

Building employee commitment—creating a synthesis of employee and employer goals so that employees want to do their jobs as if they own the company—takes a multi-part effort, one in which all managers and the HR department staff play a central role. For example, two-way communication fosters commitment, and firms like Federal Express Canada Ltd. and Cadet Uniform Services have had programs that guarantee two-way communication and fair treatment of all employee grievances and disciplinary matters in place for a long time.[22]

High-commitment firms also tend to engage in *actualizing practices,* which aim to ensure their employees have every opportunity to fully use all their skills and gifts at work and become all they can be. HR practices are crucial here, for instance, in establishing career-oriented performance appraisal procedures and open job-posting and job-transfer practices. Convincing employees that the company and all its managers care about them is important, too. For this reason, high-commitment firms like Federal Express and Cadet have adopted no-layoff policies to give employees the security to go the extra mile. They are also very careful about whom they promote into management positions. All aspiring FedEx supervisory candidates must take the firm's multi-step leadership evaluation program to determine if they have the values and skills desired in FedEx managers. Several assessments by superiors and peers are involved, as well as a project supervised by the employee's immediate superior. "It's tough," explains Slangerup, "from beginning to end, it takes from six to twelve months. We're looking for leadership ability and other skills. We want our managers to be coaches and mentors."[23] At Cadet, there is a two-year on-site management training program.[24]

Many firms have recognized the importance of recognition in building commitment and increasing discretionary effort. HR department staff often assume a leadership role in developing recognition programs, such as employee of the month awards. Consumers Gas has adopted a rather unique recognition program, described in the Building Employee Commitment box.

Building Employee Commitment

A Little Recognition Goes A Long Way

Much is made of the potential of discretionary employee efforts, but if the structure and impetus for encouraging commitment and performance above the "call of duty" are not embedded in the corporate culture, such efforts will likely be sporadic at best.

Like many organizations, Consumers Gas in Toronto wanted to become more competitive. Realizing that doing so meant getting the company's 3 700 employees more involved in operations, the firm introduced an innovative program to encourage employee discretionary effort, called Achieving Results Together (ART).

ART is part of a company-wide focus on continuous improvement. According to Jennifer Parr, Director of Organizational Effectiveness, it replaced a system that reinforced a bureaucratic management approach no longer consistent with the company's strategic direction. The old system funneled suggestions through a cumbersome approval process that tended to distance employees from the system, rather than drawing employees and managers closer together.

Under ART, each manager has a budget for spontaneous recognition of employees whose performance exceeds normal job requirements. No approvals are required. Managers reward employees on the spot with tickets for ball games or the theatre or gift certificates. They have complete discretion in tailoring the reward to the recipient and are not required to keep records of the awards or provide a rationale for them. The only restriction, other than remaining within budget, is that cash rewards are not permitted. Managers share information about the program through informal networking and two courses they are required to take, one on management excellence and the other on coaching employee empowerment.

In one situation, a clerical employee, responsible for ordering lunches, beverages, and other items for training sessions, took the initiative to negotiate a better deal from a vendor, reducing company expense by about 25 percent. Her manager rewarded her with a $100 restaurant gift certificate and also recognized her accomplishment at a department meeting.

According to Parr, the total cost of the program is less than that of the suggestion program, even though more people are now receiving recognition. She believes that employees "are doing things on their own" and that managers are not only b more comfortable with the new system, but are offering more praise. There cross-departmental recognition and a growing tendency for employees to nominate other employees for recognition.

Source: Based on George Pearson, "Looking for More Discretionary Effort? A Little Recognition Can Go a Long Way," *Canadian HR Reporter* (July 15, 1996), p.19. Copyright by MPL Communications Inc., Reproduced by permission of *Canadian HR Reporter* 133 Richmond Street West, Toronto, Ontario M5H 3M8.

Developing and Implementing Corporate Strategy

strategy
The company's plan for how it will balance its internal strengths and weaknesses with external opportunities and threats in order to maintain a competitive advantage.

Perhaps the most striking change in the role of the HR department is its growing importance in developing and implementing strategy. Traditionally, **strategy**— the company's plan for how it will balance its internal strengths and weaknesses with external opportunities and threats in order to maintain a competitive advantage—was a job primarily for the company's line managers. Thus, the chief executive officer and senior management team would decide to enter new markets, drop product lines, or embark on a five-year cost-cutting plan, and then more or less leave the human resources implications of the plan (hiring new workers, terminating employees, and arranging for outplacement services, etc.) to be carried out by the HR department staff.

Today, things are very different. Strategies increasingly depend on strengthening organizational responsiveness and building committed work teams, and these put the HR department in a central role. In the words of David Crisp, Vice-President of Human Resources at the Hudson's Bay Company in Toronto,[25]

> *The critical success differentiator today is people. "Best practices" and technology are available to anyone. Financing and customers will go to those companies whose people are fastest into the market with better ideas and better coordination. Our role is to make that possible.*

Thus, it is increasingly common to involve HR department staff in the earliest stages of developing and implementing the firm's strategic plan, rather than simply letting them react to it. In the words of one senior HR practitioner, "I am now a strategic partner with line management and participate in business decisions which bring human resources perspectives to the general management of the company."[26] To explain this statement, we next turn to an examination of strategic planning and a discussion of the strategic role of the HR department.

Strategic Planning and HRM

The Nature of Strategic Planning

corporate-level strategy
Decisions about the portfolio of businesses, that, in total, will comprise the
tior

Managers engage in three levels of strategic decision making in an organization,[27] as illustrated in **Figure 2.4**. Many companies consist of several different businesses. For example, Pepsi, Frito-Lay, and Pizza Hut are all part of PepsiCo. Such companies need a **corporate-level strategy** to identify the portfolio of businesses that, in total, will comprise the organization and the ways in which these will relate to each other.

At the next level down, each of these businesses, such as Pizza Hut, is guided by a **business-level/competitive strategy**, which identifies how it will build and strengthen its long-term competitive position in the marketplace.[28] Such a strategy, for instance, identifies how Pizza Hut will compete with Dominos, or Wal-Mart will compete with Zellers.

res Management in Perspective

**Figure 2.4
Relationships among
Strategies in Multiple-
Business Firms**

Source: James M. Higgins and
Julian W. Vincze, *Strategic
Management Text and Cases*, 5th
ed. (Fort Worth: The Dryden
Press, 1991), p. 263.

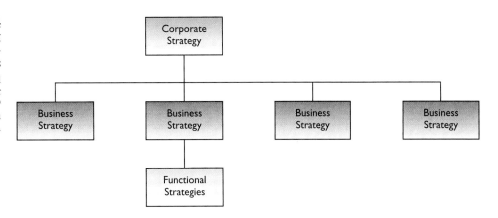

functional strategy
Identification of the basic
courses of action to be pursued by each department or
functional area to help the
business attain its competitive goals.

strategic planning
The corporate-level, organization-wide strategic planning process.

In turn, each business is comprised of various departments, such as manufacturing, sales, and human resources management, each of which has a **functional
strategy** identifying the basic courses of action to be pursued to help the business
attain its competitive goals.

While companies have three types of strategies, the term **strategic planning** is usually reserved for the corporate-level planning process, which applies
organization-wide. Specifically, the strategic plan outlines the overall organizational purposes and goals and how they are to be achieved, given the external opportunities and threats and internal strengths and weaknesses. Deciding whether
to expand into a superstore or continue to operate small local gourmet markets is
a typical strategic planning issue, as is whether to cut costs by amalgamating hospital units and reducing beds or eliminating certain departments and/or services
altogether.

For example, when IBM bought the Lotus software firm in 1995, one goal
was the acquisition of the Lotus Notes networking programs. Sensing the opportunities and threats presented by the Internet's growing popularity and recognizing the firm's relative lack of expertise in networking software, one component of
IBM's strategic plan, developed under the direction of Chairperson, Louis Gerstner, was the decision to diversify by buying Lotus.

In all organizations, the three levels of strategic decision making should be
interrelated and mutually supportive. For example, at the corporate level, IBM's
acquisition of Lotus represented an attempt to reposition the giant corporation to
compete more effectively in the networking era. Having decided to acquire Lotus,
Gerstner and the senior management team then had to make a business-level
strategic decision regarding how to organize IBM's networking business and compete with other firms making similar products. Jim Manzi, the head of Lotus, proposed the merger of Lotus with IBM's other software divisions, under his direction.
This decision was rejected. Gerstner and the senior management team decided to
keep Lotus and its Lotus Notes software separate, and let Manzi leave the firm.

These corporate and business-level strategic decisions, in turn, have shaped
and will continue to shape IBM's functional strategies. For example, IBM's move
into networking has production implications, since it may require phasing out
several hardware manufacturing facilities and consolidating the firm's network
program design facilities in fewer locations. Similarly, IBM's marketing and sales
efforts will no doubt have to be increasingly organized around a networking
sales effort. The HR department will also have to accomplish its share: There will
be facilities to be closed, new ones to be staffed, and network program designers to
be recruited and hired.[29]

Building Competitive Advantage

competitive advantage
Any factors that allow an organization to differentiate its product or service from those of its competitors to increase market share.

cost leadership strategy
The competitive strategy that aims at becoming *the* low-cost supplier of a product or service.

differentiation strategy
The competitive strategy that involves seeking to be unique along dimensions that are widely valued by purchasers of the product or service.

focus strategy
A strategy aimed at serving a narrow target market better than other firms that are competing more broadly, which may involve the use of differentiation, cost leadership, or both.

Every organization tries to achieve a **competitive advantage**, defined as any factors that allow it to differentiate its product or service from those of its competitors to increase market share.[30]

There are a number of different ways in which competitive advantages can be achieved. **Cost leadership**, which means aiming to become *the* low-cost supplier of a product or service, is one. For example, Wal-Mart is a typical industry cost leader, due to its unique satellite-based distribution system and ability to track products from supplier to consumer more effectively than its competitors.

Differentiation is a second competitive strategy. This involves seeking to be unique along dimensions that are widely valued by purchasers of the product or service.[31] Thus, Volvo stresses the safety of its cars, Apple the usability of its computers, Canadian Tire and PetroCan their Canadian identity, President's Choice its reasonably-priced and high-value grocery products, and Mercedes Benz the reliability and quality of its vehicles. Like Mercedes Benz, organizations can usually charge a premium price if they successfully stake out their claim to be substantially different from their competitors in some coveted way.

The aim of the **focus strategy** is to serve a narrow target market better than other firms that are competing more broadly. Achieving this objective may involve using differentiation (such as finding better ways to meet the needs of the target market), a cost-leadership strategy with this particular market, or both. An example of a firm adopting this approach is Porter Paint, which supplies professionals in the house-painting business.

Human Resources as a Competitive Advantage

In today's intensely competitive and globalized marketplace, maintaining a competitive advantage by becoming a cost leader and/or differentiator puts a heavy premium on having a highly committed and competent work force. Many experts emphasize the strategic role that committed employees play in helping organizations to achieve competitive advantage. As one puts it:[32]

> In a growing number of organizations human resources are now viewed as a source of competitive advantage. There is a greater recognition that distinctive competencies are obtained through highly developed employee skills, distinctive organizational cultures, management processes, and systems. This is in contrast to the traditional emphasis on transferable resources such as equipment. . . . Increasingly, it is being recognized that competitive advantage can be obtained with a high quality work force that enables organizations to compete on the basis of market responsiveness, product and service quality, differentiated products, and technological innovation. . . .

An example of an organization that has recognized the importance of its human resources as a source of competitive advantage is Palliser Furniture Ltd. of Winnipeg, a private, family-run business with some 2 000 employees, recognized as the largest furniture manufacturer in Canada:[33]

> While its success is in part attributable to investment in new technology and in-house production of key materials, President Arthur DeFehr stresses the important role played by the firm's human resources. At the new leather plant, self-managed teams of 12 to 15 people construct entire pieces of furniture, using computer-generated designs. These teams have the authority to allocate funds for cross-training and decide who gets it. At present, more than one-third of the workers are multi-skilled. To encourage high productivity and recognize employee contribution,

Palliser has developed a gainsharing plan that allows employees to share financially in productivity improvements.

Strategic Human Resources Management

strategic human resources management
The linking of HRM with strategic goals and objectives in order to improve business performance and develop (an) organizational culture that fosters innovation and flexibility.[36]

HR strategies
The specific actions related to its human resources that the company plans to pursue to achieve its competitive strategy.

The fact that employees are central to achieving competitive advantage has led to the emergence of the field known as **strategic human resources management**,[34] defined as "...the linking of HRM with strategic goals and objectives in order to improve business performance and develop (an) organizational culture that fosters innovation and flexibility...".[35] To be effective as a strategic partner, the HR department needs sophisticated human resources information systems (HRIS), especially in firms with international operations, something that is discussed in detail in the Information Technology and HR box on page 58.

The term "strategic HR" recognizes the HR department's partnership role in the strategic planning process, while the term "**HR strategies**" refers to the specific actions related to its human resources that the company plans to pursue to achieve its aims. One of the primary objectives at both Federal Express Canada Ltd. and Cadet Uniform Services is differentiation through superior customer service. To achieve this goal, their overall HR strategy is aimed at building a committed work force. The specific components of the HR strategy at these two firms include building healthy two-way communication, a rigorous selection process, extensive training, guaranteeing fair treatment and employee security to the greatest extent possible, and instituting various promotion-from-within activities.[37]

HR strategies that fit a cost-leadership orientation emphasize efficient, low-cost production and reinforce adherence to highly-structured procedures. This includes specific job descriptions, job-specific training, careful selection to ensure that employees have the necessary technical qualifications and skills, and a performance appraisal system that weeds out low performers.

The Role of the HR Department as a Strategic Partner

The long history of staff (advisory) authority has left HR departments with a somewhat impoverished reputation. In fact, some people still view HR departments as strictly operational and believe that HR activities are not strategic at all.[38] According to this line of reasoning, HR activities simply "...involve putting out small fires—ensuring that people are paid on the right day; the job advertisement meets the newspaper deadline; a suitable supervisor is recruited for the night shift by the time it goes ahead; and the same manager remembers to observe due process before sacking the new rep who didn't work out."[39]

A more sophisticated (but perhaps no more accurate) view of HR departments is that their role is simply to "fit" HR practices to the company's strategy. In this view, top management crafts a corporate strategy—such as buying Lotus—and the HR department staff are told to create the HR programs required to successfully implement that corporate strategy.[40] As two strategic planning experts have argued, "the human resources management system must be tailored to the demands of business strategy."[41] Their idea here is that "for any particular organizational strategy, there is purportedly a matching HR strategy."[42]

A third view is that the HR department is an equal partner in the strategic planning process. In order to forge the organization's work force into a competitive advantage, the proponents of this viewpoint believe that the HR department staff must be equal partners in both formulation and implementation of the firm's organization-wide and competitive strategies.[43]

www.shrm.org
Society for HR Management

Information Technology and HR:
Boldly Going Where HR Hasn't

Traditionally, human resources staff and systems were isolated from other corporate functions, viewed more as an administrative service than a crucial part of the organization. In some cases, this segmentation led companies to make strategic decisions on future product lines and target markets without knowing whether the human expertise and skills to design and sell the products were actually available. Today, however, things are changing. The HR department is increasingly being viewed as a strategic business partner, contributing to the company's overall mission and profitability.

As companies spread across the globe and become businesses without borders, the role of HR specialists often travels into uncharted territory. Indeed, many organizations are not equipped philosophically or structurally for the evolution that human resources information systems (HRIS) must undergo to meet the challenges of conducting business internationally.

The HRIS must enable all executives, including those responsible for product development, manufacturing, marketing, and finance, to generate an immediate snapshot of the company's existing talent pool. It must also produce a clear picture of the training and career development programs in place, as well as the recruitment tactics being employed in every branch office.

Large corporations, for example, need to empower managers to assemble and disband elite project teams made up of existing employees situated halfway around the world or scattered in a dozen different counties. To do this, the HRIS may have to query several databases and match workers with new projects or business opportunities.

With an integrated and open HRIS in the enterprise, HR managers can make more effective use of employee education and training, design innovative compensation methods, and ensure that the company always has the right people and resources available as different business needs arise.

The HRIS must be able to deal with seemingly basic but essential and potentially complicated responsibilities such as multiple-currency payrolls, multi-country dispersion, diverse jurisdictional tax legislation, and health care benefits and coverage.

Clearly, the HRIS needs to be fully integrated into all departments from the shop-floor to the top-floor in a global enterprise. To achieve this integration and level of HRM capabilities, a secure and robust infrastructure must exist. Internet technology and powerful multi-tiered client/server networks can offer cost-effective solutions, but the networking infrastructure must be open and support traditional PCs and network PCs. Furthermore, the software applications for HR, as well as other functions such as accounting and manufacturing, need to have consistent user interfaces and links to each other so that training will be easy and consistent for staff.

When the HRIS is woven into the fabric of an enterprise system, company executives gain access to powerful analysis and decision-making tools. In addition, HR managers become increasingly involved in the strategic business planning processes, taking on a more important role within the organization.◆

Source: Jean Bryant, "Boldly Going Where HR Hasn't," *Computing Canada* (June 23, 1997), p.48.

Role in Formulating Strategy

Formulating a company's overall strategic plan requires identifying, analyzing, and balancing two sets of forces: the organization's external opportunities and threats on the one hand, and its internal strengths and weaknesses on the other.

This is where strategic HRM comes in. First, HR department staff can play a role in what strategic planners call **environmental scanning**, which involves identifying and analyzing external opportunities and threats that may be crucial to the organization's success. For example, embracing the "high performance or die" model was required at British Columbia-based Fletcher Challenge Canada when international competitors started gobbling up its market share in the pulp and paper industry:[44]

> Fletcher's HR department helped to lead a change process to better align the work of employees with the needs of the organization, given its dramatically changing environment. New initiatives included an improved communications process; the development of a leadership competency model coupled with a new leadership training program; and the introduction of a 360-degree feedback instrument and new performance appraisal system. In addition, Fletcher introduced a new compensation system to establish a better link between on-the-job performance and organizational goals.

In addition, HR managers are often in a unique position to supply information that can be helpful in the strategic planning process. Details regarding a successful incentive plan being used by a competitor, employee opinion survey data eliciting information about customer complaints, and information about pending legislative changes are examples. Furthermore, according to one expert, as a human resources specialist:[45]

> From public information and legitimate recruiting and interview activities, you ought to be able to construct organization charts, staffing levels, and group missions for the various organizational components of each of your major competitors. Your knowledge of how brands are sorted among sales divisions and who reports to whom can give important clues as to a competitor's strategic priorities. You may even know the track record and characteristic behaviour of the executives.

The HR department also participates in the strategy formulation process by supplying information regarding the company's internal strengths and weaknesses. Once weaknesses have been identified, corrective action can be planned and taken. Take Kodak Canada, for example:[46]

> At one end of the scale, with the help of local school boards, the company is providing on-site secondary school credit courses for employees wishing to complete a high school diploma. At the other end, to maintain and improve its competitive position in a business in which complex product technologies and manufacturing processes can change virtually overnight, Kodak's HR development team must scurry to research, source, and evaluate training for each new technology or process as it is introduced. Essentially, they're trying to enhance the skills of all their people and ensure there is a stronger link between business needs and skills delivered.

The strengths and weaknesses of a company's human resources can have a determining effect on the viability of a firm's strategic options. "Situations where HR capabilities serve as a driving force in strategy formulation occur where there are unique [human] capabilities..."[47] In such cases, firms often build their strategy around their HR-based competitive advantage. Take Elaine Minacs, for example, one of six women honoured as 1993 Canadian Woman Entrepreneur of the Year:[48]

> By focusing on her firm's strong suit—customer service, she expanded a business that she started in 1981, in a derelict building in downtown Oshawa, to the Pickering-

based Minacs Group of five companies, with business contracts totalling in the multi-millions. The Employment Centre Ltd., the original business, is now the largest independently-owned employer of temporary and contract personnel in southern Ontario. The trend toward outsourcing constitutes the largest part of Minacs' business. According to Minacs, "We have developed a real expertise in this area—our own training, and training teams focused on customer care."

Role in Executing Strategy

The HR department can also play a pivotal role in the successful execution or implementation of a company's strategic plan. For example, the competitive strategy at Federal Express involves differentiating itself from its competitors by offering superior customer service and guaranteed on-time deliveries. Since basically the same technologies are available to UPS, Purolator, and other competitors, it's the work force at FedEx—its human resources—who provide its crucial competitive advantage. This puts a premium on the firm's HR processes, as discussed earlier, and on the firm's ability to create a highly committed, competent, and customer-oriented work force.[49]

HR departments support strategy implementation in numerous other ways. For example, HR staff are heavily involved in the execution of most firms' downsizing and restructuring strategies through such activities as establishing training and retraining programs, arranging for outplacement services for displaced employees, instituting pay-for-performance plans, and helping to redesign jobs.

HR staff members also play a critical role in strategies to increase organizational effectiveness through better employee–management relations. At SaskPower, the electric utility serving Saskatchewan, the HR department played a key role in improving the relationship between management and the two unions through adoption of a mutual gains approach to bargaining, a topic that will be discussed in more detail in chapter 17.[50]

In some firms, HR's role in executing strategy leads to the creation of an in-house profit centre, engaged in entrepreneurial activities. Such is the case at Ontario's Credit Union Central, described in the HR and the Responsive Organization box.

HR and the Responsive Organization

Creating an In-House HR Profit Centre

Roxanne Henderson, Director of Human Resources at Credit Union Central of Ontario, runs an HR department that is both intrapreneurial and entrepreneurial. The department, known as CCG (Cooperative Consulting Group), has become an "entrepreneur" in the true sense of the word since purchasing a dealership for a human resources information system.

CCG's primary customers are credit unions across Ontario that are members of the Credit Union Central of Ontario (approximately 4 000 employees), Credit Union Central itself (220 employees, including the staff consulting group), and trade associations serving credit unions in Ontario. The business community at large is a secondary market.

"CCG evolved out of an HR and training focus," says Henderson. "Today we are a more 'typical' firm since we offer a full range of services. Still, we retain our core competencies, which are HR-related. Our strategy is to build a portfolio that covers the full employee life-cycle from recruitment through to retirement."

Henderson says the CCG's mandate is very specific: Provide services to members and the business community, but ensure that the department is self-supporting. "It's an absolute given. CCG has to generate a profit."

In addition to being self-supporting, CCG has also been able to reduce the overall operating cost of its parent firm, Credit Union Central, by 47 percent, due to revenue generated from the sale of its products and services.

CCG's entrepreneurial strategies include:

- Putting a price on products and services provided to credit union members that is well below market rate. Prior to this new strategy, member credit unions paid market rate for CCG's services. The introduction of below-market rates has resulted in cost savings of 10 to 30 percent to the credit unions, but has also translated into an increase in the number of HR services the credit unions buy from CCG.

- Expanding its markets to include credit unions in other parts of Canada. Presently, there is a Credit Union Central in every Canadian province. CCG is working with these other companies to share information and reduce the overall cost of the credit union system in Canada. To facilitate this, CCG has created the HR "Best Practices Survey", which benchmarks HR activities, something that had not been undertaken in credit unions previously.

- Expanding its markets to include the United States, where there are an estimated 12 000 credit unions.

- Deciding to invest in other businesses. CCG purchased the Greater Metro Toronto dealership for Vantage Point Software, an HR information system, which, as described above, led to CCG's launch as an entrepreneurial organization.

- Expanding its products and services to meet the HR and management consulting needs of the general business community. Work for these clients is billed at prevailing market rates.

- Actively quantifying results. Clients are guaranteed that they will see "X" bottom-line results.

"We realize our products and services must produce the results we promise our clients," says Henderson. "Our future as a business is riding on our own achievements."

Source: Beverley Cline, "Entrepreneurial HR: A New Mindset," *Human Resources Professional* 14, no.1 (February/March 1997), p. 40.

Examples of the HR Department as a Strategic Partner

Firms like FedEx Canada Ltd., Cadet Uniform Services, Kodak Canada, SaskPower, and Credit Union Central are not the only ones that rely on their HR department staff to perform as partners in the development and execution of their strategic plans. Here are two others:

Colgate-Palmolive Colgate-Palmolive Company is a global manufacturing firm with sales of over $5 billion, that recently received new "marching orders."[51]

After assuming the presidency several years ago, the CEO developed and communicated a new strategic direction for the company, based on what he called his "corporate initiatives." Among other things, the new strategy emphasized concentrating on new products, being the low-cost producer, simplifying businesses and structures, pushing decision making downward, promoting entrepreneurial action, and improving morale and motivation. The aim was to make Colgate a leaner, more responsive competitor in its global markets and focus the company more clearly on health-related products.

Several steps were taken almost at once. Four major businesses were divested, including two sports and recreation companies. A major reorganization took place that eliminated one level of senior management. Additional resources were diverted to new-product development and research and development, and the HR department got a mandate to help Colgate achieve its new goals.

The role of the HR department in strategic management at Colgate-Palmolive is clear from its mandate, which was to develop and execute programs designed to create a corporate culture that would:

- encourage a spirit of teamwork and cooperation within and among business units to work toward common objectives, with an emphasis on identifying, acknowledging, and rewarding individual and unit excellence.
- foster entrepreneurial attitudes among the managers and innovative thinking among all employees
- emphasize the commonality of interest between the employees and shareholders.

To accomplish these goals, numerous HR programs were initiated. For example, the company's executive incentive compensation plan was redesigned to place more emphasis on individual performance and achieving operating targets. Employee benefits were made more flexible and responsive to employees' needs. At the same time, cost controls and employee pay-for-performance plans were instituted and successfully accomplished by effectively communicating both the changes and the reasons for them. The bottom line was that by implementing a number of programs, the HR department helped to refocus employee efforts in a manner that contributed to the execution of Colgate's strategic plan.

3M Canada According to Alan Magrath, Vice President of 3M Canada, headquartered in London, Ontario, "In HR, we're always looking for an innovative way of doing things."[52]

Training people to be creative has enabled 3M to build a $15 billion worldwide business that has made profits for 11 straight years. Moreover, the Canadian arm of the company is pioneering HR practices that are being adopted by the parent company at sites around the globe.

3M Canada's tape manufacturing factory in Brockville, Ontario, is now the model for 3M plants around the world. It was launched in 1993 after a good deal of planning. Eight of the company's manufacturing experts put their heads together and designed their "dream plant." Their ideas included several new concepts for HR practices, from hiring new recruits to the production process.

The factory is operated by small teams of six to eight people, who are expected to work closely together, continuously learn new skills, and innovate. In addition to production work and selection responsibilities, they handle quality control, logistics, scheduling, and shipping and receiving. They are also compensated for their creative efforts—employees split the gains with the firm when they produce an innovation. Awarded more power and responsibility, the employees take pride in the way the factory operates.

Evaluating the HR System

HR audit
An evaluation of the firm's HR activities and the HR department's effectiveness as a strategic partner.

attitude survey
A survey administered to determine employee thoughts and feelings about organizational issues, designed to obtain data about areas of effectiveness and those requiring improvement.

exit interview
A conversation with departing employees to learn their opinions of the employer, managers, policies, and other aspects of employment with the organization, and reason(s) for leaving.

focus group
A group of eight to twelve users of the services of the HR department, who provide in-depth feedback about the HR activities, programs, and services.

records analysis
A review of various organizational records to assess compliance with company policies and procedures, as well as relevant legislative standards; measure the effectiveness of various programs in meeting their stated objectives; and identify areas in which performance improvements are required.

field experiment
A research design that enables the comparison of an experimental and control group, under realistic conditions, to objectively assess the impact and effectiveness of HR programs and activities.

cost-benefit analysis
A comparison of the monetary costs of a particular function with non-monetary benefits gained, such as changes in attitudes or improvement in employee morale.

Just as financial audits are conducted, periodic and systematic evaluations or audits should be conducted to assess how effectively the firm is managing its human resources.[53] Since the entire HR system should be audited, supervisors and managers throughout the organization must be involved, which helps to reinforce the important role all managers play in HRM, and the service and strategic role of HR department staff members.

Comprehensive **HR audits** encompass three areas:

1. The HR department's effectiveness as a strategic partner
2. Organizational compliance with applicable federal, provincial (or territorial), and municipal laws and regulations, and
3. The performance of specific HRM programs and functions.

In addition, area-specific audits may be conducted to evaluate issues of particular concern to management. Such audits may assess the culture of the organization, for example, or the existence of barriers to the advancement of specific employee groups, such as women and visible minorities.

Employee **attitude surveys** are often one component of an HR audit. They provide a means of learning how employees feel about a variety of issues and gaining insight into employee perceptions about the organization's strengths and weaknesses. Typical survey topics include supervision, HR policies and programs, job-related factors, effectiveness of communication strategies, and overall leadership. Survey results provide excellent feedback about how well HR policies and programs are functioning and help to identify areas requiring improvement. When surveys are conducted, it is important that the results are shared with employees. As well, employees should be informed about specific strategies being implemented to address the concerns and correct the problems identified by the survey.

In addition to surveys, organizations use several other research tools to collect data. Interviews with employees and managers can provide specific and detailed information. Many firms conduct **exit interviews** with departing employees to identify any sources of dissatisfaction contributing to their decision to leave. Some organizations use **focus groups** to obtain in-depth information from a small group of employees. These involve an unstructured group discussion with an unbiased facilitator.

A **records analysis** is often included as part of a HR audit. For example, reports pertaining to health and safety, scrap rates, turnover and absenteeism, and grievances are often examined. Internal placement records, selection records, and employee files may also be looked at.

A few firms use **field experiments** to compare an experimental and a control group under realistic conditions. For example, half of the supervisors might be given safety training pertaining to a particular aspect of operations (the experimental group). The supervisors not receiving the training constitute the control group. Several months after training completion, if safety records reveal a significantly lower rate of incidents or accidents among team members of supervisors in the experimental group, this would suggest that the safety training was effective. Due to a number of drawbacks, this technique is not widely used: Those not selected may be dissatisfied and demotivated; participants may feel manipulated; and the results may be confounded by changes in the work environment or discussion about the experiment between members of the two groups.

Whenever possible, audit findings should be translated into quantitative data. A **cost-benefit analysis** compares the monetary costs of a particular function with non-monetary benefits gained, such as changes in attitudes or improvement in employee morale. A **cost-effectiveness analysis** compares the monetary costs and benefits of a particular initiative. For example, the amount spent on health and safety training might be compared to the amount saved due to reduction in equipment damage caused by unsafe practices or decreases in lost-time accidents.[54]

To be meaningful, quantifiable audit results should be compared with some accepted external measure of performance, such as industry norms or research findings. Helpful information can be obtained from Statistics Canada, Labour Canada, the Industrial Accident Prevention Association, business and industry associations, trade associations, consulting firms, and the Conference Board of Canada. Some firms, such as Xerox Canada and the Bank of Montreal, use **benchmarking**, which is a continuous and systematic process of comparing some aspect of organizational performance against data from a firm considered to be superior in that particular area. The Information Technology and HR box presents information about an HR benchmarking network among health-care institutions across Canada. The annual benchmarking survey indicators used by the HR Benchmarking Network are shown in **Figure 2.5**.

Information Technology and HR
HR Benchmarking Network

No sector in Canada has undergone more rapid and fundamental change in recent years than health care. Mergers, consolidations, and other restructuring initiatives have drastically altered the face of health care institutions across the land. Organizations are reorganizing to cut costs and refocus their activities.

The management and staff of these institutions have not been idle in the face of the needed changes. Every function, from patient care to support areas such as finance and information systems, has been re-examining its resource requirements, systems, and practices, with the aim of identifying opportunities to add value to their organizations. HR departments have been no exception.

The Toronto Hospital (TTH) is the largest acute-care health care facility in Canada, with over 7 000 employees at two locations in downtown Toronto. In March of 1994, Clayton Appleton, Vice President of Human Resources at TTH, devised program ideas that could assist HR to meet the "value-added" challenge. One of these was to develop and sponsor a cross-Canada human resources "benchmarking" network and statistical survey for hospitals and health care organizations.

"In the past," comments Appleton, "HR functions in many organizations have been slow to admit that their performance can be measured in the same way as that of operational departments. That attitude has no place in today's HR profession. To survive as a profession, and to become a true strategic partner in the "business" of our organizations, we have to take a critical look at how and why we do things. If you can't measure something, you can't control or improve it. Benchmarking is a step in that direction."

The Human Resources Benchmarking Network was formed with the objective of facilitating and formalizing benchmarking among its members. Its central program, and the main work of the Network members throughout 1995 and early 1996, was the development of an annual statistical survey.

Colin Dawes, Human Resources Manager at TTH, was assigned responsibility for organizing and developing the Network, a natural outgrowth of his involvement in the implementation of the hospital's Human Resources Information System (HRIS). A core group of about 15 institutions from across the country quickly recognized the value of the Network and devoted a great deal of time and effort to bring the idea to fruition.

Care was taken to ensure that the benchmarking program and survey were designed in accordance with accepted benchmarking principles. The focus of the group was on selecting statistical indicators that measured activities representing value-added opportunities in their organizations. To ensure that the indicators selected were appropriate, organizational clients were consulted in the design process, as were HR representatives from across the country. The national nature of the survey posed some special challenges. Several indicators that the core group initially selected had to be reformulated or dropped altogether due to legislative differences between the provinces that would have made inter-provincial comparisons meaningless.

In the end, as shown in **Figure 2.5**, twenty-six indicators were agreed upon, representing the full spectrum of HR activities.

To test the survey instrument, a mini-survey, using eleven indicators, was conducted, covering the period April 1 to September 30, 1995. A report of the results was issued in March of 1996. The first Annual Network Survey was issued and completed in May and June of 1996. Basic statistical results, made available to participating Network members in late summer, were reported for each indicator. Results were broken down further by employee-count, type of institution, province, degree of unionization, and number of beds.

Now that the survey is up and running, the Network has turned its attention to other Network programs and expanding its membership base to include companies outside of the health-care sector.◆

Source: Colin Dawes, "Measuring HR's Pulse," *Human Resources Professional* 13, no. 5 (July/August 1996), pp. 13–5.

Figure 2.5
The Human Resources Benchmarking Network Annual Benchmarking Survey Indicators

Source: Colin Dawes, "Measuring HR's Pulse," *Human Resources Professional* 13, no. 5 (July/August 1996), p. 15.

- External Hire Rate
- Internal Hires to Total Hires Ratio
- Full-time/Part-time Hours Worked Ratio
- RN/RPN Hours Worked Ratio
- Average Time to Fill Position with External Hire
- Average Time to Fill Position with Internal Hire
- Employment Advertising Expense Indicator
- Salary Expense Ratio
- Employee Assistance Program Utilization Rate
- Dental Benefits Claim Expense per Eligible Employee
- Extended Health Benefits Claims Expense per Eligible Employer
- Long Term Disability Claims per Eligible Employee

- Sick Pay Expense Ratio
- Paid Sick Hours per Eligible Employee
- "Final Step" Grievance Rate
- "Final Step" Grievance Resolution Rate
- Health Clinic Employee Visit Indicator
- Health Clinic Service Indicator
- WCB Lost Time Incident Rate
- WCB Lost Work Hours Rate
- WCB New Experimental Experience Rating (NEER) Performance Value
- "Health-related" Redeployment Rate
- Training Offered per Employee
- Training Expense Ratio
- Turnover Rate
- HR "Full-Time Equivalent (FTE)" Indicator

The value to be derived from conducting HR audits lies in making improvements. When using a benchmarking approach, for example, survey results should be used to "peg" an organization's performance relative to that of others, identify any "performance gaps," and suggest possible corrective actions. Outstanding performers on a particular dimension can be contacted to determine how the results were achieved. Strategies for performance improvements can thus be identified and targets set to meet survey benchmarks.[55]

The Impact of Effective HRM Practices on Employee Performance and the Bottom Line

The results of systematic audits and research studies have established that sophisticated and integrated HRM practices have a positive effect on employee performance. Such practices increase knowledge, skills, and abilities; improve motivation; and reduce shirking (employees avoiding work or responsibility due to laziness or selfishness). They also increase retention of productive and competent employees and have a direct and economically significant effect on organizational financial performance. One study of 437 publicly-traded companies demonstrated that firms that effectively manage employee performance through more sophisticated HR practices have higher profits, better cash flows, stronger stock market performance, significant productivity gains, higher sales growth per employee, and lower real growth in number of employees.[56] Empirical studies have also established that 15 percent of the relative profit performance of an organization derives from HR strategy. Furthermore, HR systems can affect a firm's market value by $15 000 to $45 000 per employee; and HR systems can affect the probability of new venture survival by as much as 22 percent.[57]

Chapter Review

Summary

1. The historical development of HRM is linked to scientific management, which focussed on production; the human relations movement, in which the emphasis was on people; and the human resources movement, in which it was recognized that organizational success is linked to both.

2. HRM is now a recognized profession, in that it has a distinct body of knowledge, certification procedures, performance standards established through self-regulation, and a code of ethics.

3. Ethics and social responsibility are of growing importance to organizations.

4. HR departments today play an important role in improving productivity, responsiveness, and customer service; building employee commitment; and developing and implementing corporate strategy.

5. Organizations typically formulate three types of strategies. Corporate strategies identify the mix of businesses in which the firm will engage. Business-level/competitive strategies identify how each of the firm's businesses will compete. Each function or department then has its own functional strategy, identifying how it will contribute to the business strategy.

6. There are three competitive strategies: cost-leadership, differentiation, and focus, all of which require a highly committed and competent work force.

7. Strategic HRM involves linking HRM with strategic goals and objectives to improve business performance and develop an organizational culture that fosters innovation and flexibility.

8. In more and more firms, the HR department is becoming a strategic partner; playing a role in strategy formulation and execution.

9. Just as financial audits are conducted, systematic evaluations or audits should be conducted periodically to assess how effectively the firm is managing its human resources. Comprehensive HR audits encompass three areas: the HR department's effectiveness as a strategic partner; organizational compliance with applicable legislation; and the performance of specific HRM programs and functions.

10. Auditing techniques include attitude surveys, interviews, focus groups, records analysis, and field experiments.

11. Whenever possible, audit findings should be translated into quantitative data. A cost-benefit analysis compares the monetary costs of a particular function with non-monetary benefits gained. A cost-effectiveness analysis compares the monetary costs and benefits of a particular initiative.

12. To be meaningful, audit results should be compared with some accepted measure of performance, such as industry norms or research findings. Benchmarking is a technique used by many firms. It involves a continuous and systematic process of comparing some aspect of organizational performance against data from a firm considered to be superior in that particular area.

13. Systematic audit results and research studies have established a link between effective HR practices, employee performance, and the bottom line.

Key Terms

attitude survey
benchmarking
business-level/
  competitive strategy
certification
competitive advantage
corporate-level strategy
cost leadership strategy
cost-benefit analysis
cost-effectiveness
  analysis
differentiation strategy

environmental scanning
ethics
exit interview
field experiment
focus group
focus strategy
functional strategy
Hawthorne Studies
HR audit
HR strategies
human relations
  movement

human resources
  movement
profession
records analysis
scientific management
social responsibility
strategic human
  resources management
strategic planning
strategy

Discussion Questions and Exercises

1. Describe scientific management and explain its impact on organizations.

2. Explain the importance of the Hawthorne Studies.

3. Describe the forces that shaped the evolution of HRM from personnel management to strategic partner.

4. Explain why HRM is a profession.

5. Describe the types of behaviour and activities that indicate that an organization is both ethical and socially responsible.

6. Describe specific strategies that are used by HR professionals to improve productivity, responsiveness, and customer service; build employee commitment; and develop and implement corporate strategy.

7. Based on inside knowledge, advertising and/or marketing, describe the corporate-level and business-level objectives of a large organization with which you are familiar.

8. Identify the functional strategies of the department or area in which you are currently or were most recently employed.

9. Explain the role of the HR department as a strategic partner.

10. Explain why the HR system should be evaluated and describe four auditing techniques used in HRM.

11. Describe benchmarking and explain its usefulness.

Application Exercises

RUNNING CASE: Carter Cleaning Company

Jennifer's Dilemma

One of the first problems Jennifer faces at Carter Cleaning Centres concerns the inadequacies of the firm's current HRM practices and procedures. Although she hasn't done a formal audit, she notes that there are no written policies, and the practices for recruitment, selection, and training have not been standardized.

As part of her core program of studies at university, Jennifer took several HR courses, which were recognized as credits by the Human Resources Professionals Association of Ontario (HRPAO). Because she found the HR courses quite fascinating, she chose her electives carefully to ensure that when she graduated she would have eight HRPAO credits. She is planning to write the Comprehensive Provincial Exam in September and hopes to attain her professional designation once she acquires experience in the field.

Because of her knowledge of and interest in HRM, Jennifer would like to take over some of the HR responsibilities, but she is a little worried about "stepping on the toes" of the store managers. She knows that her father hasn't really explained her role to the Carter Cleaning employees, and she doesn't want to be seen as "taking over" or "a know-it-all."

Jennifer figures that she and her father should sit down and talk about his vision for the Centres and how she can best assist him.

Questions

1. How should Jennifer and Jack proceed?
2. Explain how a formal HR audit might assist Jennifer and Jack at this time. What systems should be audited?
3. Assuming that Jack agrees that centralization of some HR responsibilities might make sense, what should Jennifer's HR role involve? For which HR activities should the manager at each Centre remain responsible? How should these changes in roles and responsibilities be communicated to the Carter Cleaning staff?

CASE INCIDENT: Jack Nelson's Problem

As a new member of the Board of Directors for a local credit union, Jack Nelson was introduced to all of the employees, starting at the home office. When he was introduced to Ruth, he was curious about her work and asked her to explain its significance and its relationship to the jobs of her coworkers. Ruth really couldn't answer his questions. She explained that she had only been working at the home office for two months. She demonstrated, however, that she knew precisely how to operate the equipment for which she was responsible, and her supervisor commented to Jack that Ruth is an excellent employee.

At one of the branch offices, the supervisor in charge spoke to Jack in confidence, telling him that something was wrong, but she didn't know what. For one thing, she explained, employee turnover was too high. No sooner had one employee been put on the job than another one resigned. With customers to see and loans to be made, she explained, she had little time to work with the new employees as they came and went.

Jack learned that all branch supervisors hire their own employees without communication with the home office or other branches. When an opening arises, the supervisor finds a suitable employee to replace the worker who quit.

After touring the 22 branches and finding similar problems in many of them, Jack wondered what action he should take. The credit union is generally regarded as a well-run institution, and has grown from 27 to 191 employees during the past eight years. The more he thought about the matter, the more puzzled he became. He couldn't quite put his finger on the problem, and didn't know whether or not to report his findings to the president.

Questions

1. What are the major problems in the home and branch offices of the credit union?

2. What do you think is causing these problems?

3. Explain how establishing a human resources department could assist the firm.

4. For what specific functions should the HR department be responsible? What HR responsibilities should the other supervisors and managers have? Why?

Source: Based on Claude S. George, Jr., *Supervisor in Action*, 4th ed., (Englewood Cliffs, NJ: Prentice-Hall, 1985), pp. 307–8. Reprinted by permission.

Human Resources Management Simulation

Exercise 1 in part 1 of the simulation requires preparation for a planning meeting of the management team involved with the new Peterborough plant, at which each manager is expected to submit and discuss an outline of his or her function's objectives for the next six months. Thus, a report is to be compiled, in which objectives pertaining to six key HR activities (recruitment, orientation, job design, development of a performance appraisal system, implementation of health and safety procedures, and development of a discipline procedure) are specified, along with the strategies (action steps) required to accomplish these objectives. A Gantt Chart is to accompany this report, indicating the preliminary timelines established for reaching each objective.

Take It to the Net

Check out our Companion Website at

www.prenticehall.ca/dessler

for a multitude of practice questions, key terms and concepts, Weblinks to related sites, newsgroups, CBC video updates, and more.

Notes

1. V.V. Murray, "Organization and Administration of the Human Resource Management Function," *Human Resource Management in Canada* (Scarborough, ON: Prentice Hall Canada Inc., 1990), p. 15 047.

2. Raymond E. Miles, *Theories of Management* (New York: McGraw Hill, 1975).

3. Frederick W. Taylor, "The Principles of Scientific Management," Jay M. Sharfritz and J. Steven Ott (editors), *Classics

of *Organization Theory,* 2nd ed. (Chicago: The Dorsey Press, 1987), pp. 66–81.

4. D.G. Nickels, J.M. McHugh, S.M. McHugh, and P.D. Berman, *Understanding Canadian Business*, 2nd. ed. (Toronto: Irwin, 1997), p. 220.

5. F.J. Roethlisberger and W.J. Dickson, *Management and the Worker* (Cambridge, MA: Harvard University Press, 1939).

6. This discussion is based on Edward E. Lawler III, "Human Resources Management," *Personnel* (January 1988) pp. 24–5.

7. R. Julian Cattaneo and Andrew J. Templer, "Determining the Effectiveness of Human Resources Management," T.H. Stone (editor), *ASAC: Personnel and Human Resources Division Proceedings* (Halifax: St. Mary's University, June 1988), p. 73.

8. "PAO Gets Designation for HR Practitioners," *Human Resources Management in Canada* 82 (December 1989), p.3.

9. Gary Agnew, "Report from CCHRA President," *Human Resources Professional* 14, no. 1 (February/March 1997), pp. 48–9.

10. Leslie Goodson, "Doing the Right Thing," *Human Resources Professional* 13, no. 1 (February/March 1996), pp. 21–2

11. Quoted in Goodson, "Doing the Right Thing," p. 22.

12. Quoted in Goodson, "Doing the Right Thing," p. 22.

13. Ken Mark, "No More Pink Slips," *Human Resources Professional* 13, no. 8 (November 1996), pp. 21–3; and Claudine Kapel, "Re-Engineering Human Resources," *Human Resources Professional* 12, no. 5 (September 1995), pp. 7–10.

14. David S. Cohen, "Behaviour-Based Interviewing," *Human Resources Professional* 14, no. 2 (April/May 1997), p. 29

15. W. Cascio, "Downsizing? What Do We Know? What Have We Learned?" *The Executive* 7 (1993), pp. 95–104.

16. Shelley Boyes, "Restructuring's Survivors," *Human Resources Professional* 12, no. 4 (July/August 1995), pp. 17–8.

17. Quoted in Beverley Cline, "Entrepreneurial HR: A New Mindset," *Human Resources Professional* 14, no. 1 (February/March 1997), pp. 38–41.

18. See, for example, Benjamin Schneider and David Bowen, "The Service Organization: Human Resources Management is Crucial," *Organizational Dynamics* 21, no. 4 (1993), pp. 39–52.

19. Karl Albrecht and Ron Zemke, *Service America!* (Homewood, IL: Dow Jones-Irwin, 1985), p. 101.

20. Schneider and Bowen, "The Service Organization," pp. 39–52.

21. Quoted in Mark, p. 21.

22. Mark, "No More Pink Slips," pp. 21–3.

23. Quoted in Mark, "No More Pink Slips," p. 22.

24. Mark, "No More Pink Slips," pp. 21–3

25. "Your Voice" *Canadian HR Reporter* (January 16, 1995) p.4. Copyright MPL Communications Inc., Reproduced by permission of *Canadian HR Reporter* 133 Richmond Street West, Toronto, Ontario M5H 3M8.

26. Shari Caudron, "HR Leaders Brainstorm the Profession's Future," *Personnel Journal* 73 (August 1994) p. 54.

27. Patrick Gunnigle and Sara Moore, "Linking Business Strategy and Human Resource Management: Issues and Implications," *Personnel Review* 23, no. 1 (1994), pp. 63–84.

28. Arthur Thompson and A.J. Strikland, *Strategic Management* (Homewood, IL: Irwin, 1992) p. 38.

29. For a description of the need for an effective and integrated strategy see, for example, Erhard Valentin, "Anatomy of a Fatal Business Strategy," *Journal of Management Studies* 31, no. 3 (May 1994), pp. 359–82.

30. Gunnigle and Moore, "Linking Business Strategy," p. 64.

31. Michael Porter, *Competitive Strategy* (New York: The Free Press, 1980), p. 14.

32. Charles Greer, *Strategy and Human Resources* (Englewood Cliffs, NJ: Prentice Hall, 1995), p. 105.

33. D. Roberts, "A Long Way from Cambodia," *The Globe and Mail* (July 5, 1994), p. B18.

34. For a discussion see, for example, Jay Galbraith, "Positioning Human Resource as a Value-Adding Function: The Case of Rockwell International," *Human Resource Management*, 31, no. 4 (Winter 1992), pp. 287–300; and Augustine Lado and Mary Wilson, "Human Resource Systems and Sustained Competitive Advantage: A Competency-Based Perspective," *Academy of Management Review*, 19, no. 4 (1994), pp. 699–727.

35. Catherine Truss and Lynda Gratton, "Strategic Human Resource Management: A Conceptual Approach," *The International Journal of Human Resource Management* 5, no. 3 (September 1994), p. 663.

36. Truss and Gratton, "Strategic Human Resource Management."

37. Mark, "No More Pink Slips," pp. 21–3.

38. For a discussion, see Peter Boxall, "Placing HR Strategy at the Heart of Business Success," *Personnel Management* 26, no. 7 (July 1994), pp. 32–4.

39. Boxall, "Placing HR Strategy," p. 32.

40. Randall Schuler, "Human Resource Management Choices and Organizational Strategy," in Randall Schuler, S.A. Youngblood, and V.L. Huber (editors), *Readings in Personnel and Human Resource Management,* 3rd ed. (St Paul, MN: West Publishing, 1988).

41. For a discussion, see Truss and Gratton, "Strategic Human Resource Management," pp. 670–1.

42. Truss and Gratton, "Strategic Human Resource Management," p. 670.

43. For discussions see, for example, Randall Schuler, Peter Dowling, and Helen DeCieri, "An Integrative Framework of Strategic International Human Resource Management," *Journal of Management,* 19, no. 2 (1993), pp. 419–59; Vida Scarpello, "New Paradigm Approaches in Strategic Human Resource Management," *Group and Organization Management* 19, no. 2 (June 1994), pp. 160–4; and Sharon Peck, "Exploring the Link Between Organizational Strategy and the Employment Relationships: The Role of Human Resources Policies," *Journal of Management Studies* 31, no. 5 (September 1994), pp. 715–36.

44. Claudine Kapel, "High Performance Models," *Human Resources Professional* 11, no. 7 (September 1994), pp. 16–20.

45. William Henn, "What the Strategist Asks from Human Resources," *Human Resource Planning* 8, no. 4 (1985), p. 195; quoted in Greer, *Strategy and Human Resources*, pp. 117–8.

46. Shelley Boyes, "Training a la Mode," *Human Resources Professional* 12, no. 1 (February/March 1995), pp. 13–5.

47. Greer, *Strategy and Human Resources*, p. 116.

48. Tricia McCallum, "The Minacs Touch," *Human Resources Professional* 11, no. 5 (June/July 1994), pp. 21–2.

49. Randall Schuler and Susan Jackson, "Linking Competitive Strategies with Human Resource Management Practices," *Academy of Management Executive* 1, no. 3 (1987), pp. 207–19.

50. Claudine Kapel, "The Feeling's Mutual," *Human Resources Professional* 12, no. 2 (1995), pp. 9–13.

51. The discussion on Colgate-Palmolive is based on Robert Burg and Brian Smith, "Restructuring Compensation and Benefits to Support Strategy," Part I, "Executive Compensation," *Compensation and Benefits Review* (November/December 1987), pp. 15–22.

52. Quoted in Jerry Zeidenberg, "HR and the Innovative Company," *Human Resources Professional* 11, no. 4 (June 1996), p. 12. The discussion on 3M is taken from this article, pp. 12–5.

53. The section on evaluating the HR system is based on two sources, except as noted: G.E. Biles and R.S. Schuler, *Audit Handbook Of Human Resources Management Practices* (Alexandria, VA: American Society for Personnel Administration, 1986); J.J. Phillips "13 Ways to Show You Are Worth It: A Guide to HR Evaluation," *Human Resources Professional* 4, no. 2 (February 1992), pp. 59–63.

54. Excellent information on costing HR activities can be found in: Wayne F. Cascio, *Costing Human Resources: The Financial Impact of Behavior in Organizations*, 3rd ed. (Boston: PWS-Kent, 1991); and Jac Fitz-enz, *How to Measure Human Resources Management*, 2nd ed. (San Francisco: Jossey-Bass, 1995).

55. Colin Dawes, "Measuring HR's Pulse," *Human Resources Professional* 13, no. 5 (July/August 1996), pp. 13–5.

56. Monica Belcourt, "What Gets Measured, Gets Managed," *Human Resources Professional* 13, no. 2 (April 1996), pp. 10–1.

57. Monica Belcourt, "Making A Difference...And Measuring It With the 5 C's," *Human Resources Professional* 13, no. 9 (December 1996/January 1997), pp. 20–4.

Chapter 3

The Changing Emphasis: From Legal Compliance to Valuing Diversity

Chapter Outline

- ◆ **Introduction to the Legal Environment**
- ◆ **Equality**
- ◆ **Equal Opportunity**
- ◆ **Equity**
- ◆ **Impact of Equal Opportunity and Equity on HRM**
- ◆ **Managing Diversity**

Learning Outcomes

After studying this chapter, you should be able to:

Explain the concepts "equal pay for equal work" and "equal pay for work of equal value."

Describe the impact of the Charter of Rights and Freedoms on HRM.

Discuss the grounds of discrimination prohibited under Canadian human rights legislation and *describe* the requirements pertaining to reasonable accommodation.

Discuss the types of behaviour that could constitute harassment and *explain* employers' responsibilities pertaining to harassment.

Describe the human rights enforcement procedures.

Describe the steps involved in employment equity program implementation.

Describe the characteristics of successful diversity management initiatives.

Introduction to the Legal Environment

As discussed in chapter 1, few challenges encountered by HR managers are as overwhelming as those presented by government legislation and regulations. Over the years, primarily due to changing values and societal expectations, the legal requirements pertaining to employee treatment in the workplace have evolved from equality, to equal opportunity, to equity. Today, some proactive organizations are moving beyond legal compliance to voluntary employment equity initiatives and a few have begun to truly value and capitalize on workplace diversity.

The major forms of legislation to be reviewed in this chapter include:

1. **Equality**

   Employment standards legislation is present in the federal jurisdiction and every province/territory. These laws establish minimum entitlements for employees and set some maximum obligations in terms of hours of work per day and/or per week. In most jurisdictions, they also require equality in the pay that men and women performing similar work receive.

2. **Equal Opportunity**

   Equal opportunity legislation makes it illegal to discriminate, even unintentionally, against various groups. Reactive in nature, since it is complaints-driven, the focus of such legislation is on acts which employers should *not* take.

   Included in this category are:

   (a) *The Charter of Rights and Freedoms*, federal legislation that is the cornerstone of equal opportunity, and

   (b) *Human rights legislation*, which is present in every jurisdiction. It prohibits discrimination in all aspects and terms and conditions of employment on the basis of such characteristics as race, colour, national or ethnic origin, and sex.

3. **Equity**

   Equity legislation has the expressed intention of hastening the pace of change for certain groups that, historically, have been disadvantaged in employment. Such laws fall into two categories:

   (a) *Employment equity laws*, which require employers to be proactive in hiring and promoting qualified individuals from four designated groups: women, visible minorities, Aboriginal people, and persons with disabilities, and

   (b) *Pay equity legislation*, which is one component of employment equity, but much narrower in focus. It is aimed at reducing the differences in pay between male-dominated and female-dominated job classes, caused by the undervaluing of work traditionally performed by women.

Discrimination Defined

The word "discrimination" has taken on a negative connotation. When someone is accused of discrimination, it generally means that they are perceived to be acting in an unfair or prejudiced manner. However, definitions of the term in the *Webster's Encyclopedic Dictionary* include "choosing with care," and "good taste, discernment"; in other words, making choices based on perceived differences, which is something people do every day. Deciding at which college or university to take a night-school course, for example, involves discriminating on the basis of such criteria as cost, reputation, and convenience.

What the law prohibits is unfair discrimination—making choices on the basis of perceived but inaccurate differences, to the detriment of specific individuals and/or groups. Standards pertaining to unfair discrimination have changed over time.

discrimination
As used in the context of human rights in employment, a distinction, exclusion, or preference, based on one of the prohibited grounds, that has the effect of nullifying or impairing the right of a person to full and equal recognition and exercise of his or her human rights and freedoms.

It is interesting to note that discrimination is not defined in the Charter of Rights and Freedoms, nor in the human rights legislation in any jurisdiction, except the province of Quebec. Section 10 of the Quebec Charter states:

*Every person has a right to full and equal recognition and exercise of his human rights and freedoms without distinction, exclusion, or preference based on [specific grounds]...****Discrimination exists where such a distinction, exclusion, or preference has the effect of nullifying or impairing such a right****.* [emphasis added]

In the discussion that follows, it will be helpful to keep this definition in mind when the term discrimination is used.

Equality

Employment Standards Legislation

employment (labour) standards legislation
Present in the federal jurisdiction and every province/territory, these laws establish minimum entitlements for employees and set some maximum obligations in terms of hours of work per day and/or per week.

The **employment standards laws**, present in every jurisdiction, specify minimum employer obligations. Those under federal jurisdiction are covered by the *Canada Labour Code*; the ten provinces and two territories each have an employment (or labour) standards act. These laws, which will be discussed in more detail in chapter 12 (Establishing Pay Plans) and chapter 14 (Employee Benefits and Services), establish minimum employee entitlements. They address such issues as wages; paid holidays and vacations; leave for some mix of maternity, parenting, and adoption; bereavement leave; termination notice and overtime pay; and maximum limits regarding hours of work.

equal pay for equal work
The stipulation, specified in the employment (labour) standards or human rights legislation in every Canadian jurisdiction, that an employer cannot pay male and female employees differently if they are performing substantially the same work, requiring the same degree of skill, effort, and responsibility, under similar working conditions.

Every jurisdiction in Canada has legislation incorporating the principle of equal pay for equal work. In most jurisdictions, this entitlement is found in the employment (labour) standards legislation; otherwise, it is in the human rights legislation. In the federal jurisdiction, this principle has been incorporated into the Canada Labour Code since 1971.

Equal pay for equal work specifies that an employer cannot pay male and female employees differently if they are performing substantially the same work, requiring the same degree of skill, effort, and responsibility, under similar working conditions. This principle makes it illegal, for example, for a school board to classify male employees as janitors and female employees doing virtually the same work as housekeepers and provide different wage rates based on these classifications.

Pay differences based on a valid merit or seniority system, or employee productivity are permitted; it is only sex-based discrimination that is prohibited. Enforcement is complaints-based and violators can be fined.

Equal Opportunity

The Charter of Rights and Freedoms

Charter of Rights and Freedoms
Federal law enacted in 1982, which guarantees fundamental freedoms to all Canadians.

The cornerstone of Canada's legislation pertaining to issues of equal opportunity is the *Constitution Act of 1982*, which contains the ***Charter of Rights and Freedoms***. While the Charter applies directly only to the actions of all levels of government (federal, provincial/territorial, and municipal) and agencies under their jurisdiction, because it takes precedence over all other laws (which means that all legislation must meet Charter standards), it is quite far-reaching in scope. There are two notable exceptions to this generalization. The Charter allows laws to infringe on Charter rights if they can be demonstrably justified as reasonable limits in a "free and democratic society." Since "demonstrably justified" and "reasonable" are open to interpretation, many issues challenged under the Charter eventually end up before the Supreme Court, which is the ultimate interpreter of the Charter. The second exception occurs when a legislative body invokes the "notwithstanding" provision, which allows the legislation to be exempted from challenge under the Charter.

The Charter provides the following fundamental rights to every Canadian:

1. Freedom of conscience and religion
2. Freedom of thought, belief, opinion, and expression; including freedom of the press and other media of communication
3. Freedom of peaceful assembly; and
4. Freedom of association.

In addition to these fundamental freedoms, the Charter also provides democratic rights, the right to live and seek employment anywhere in Canada, legal right to due process in criminal proceedings, equality rights, minority language education rights, Canadian multicultural heritage rights, and First People's rights.[1]

At the time the Charter was enacted, it created high expectations on the part of various interest groups, particularly regarding union–management relations. However, the overall impact of the Charter on the industrial relations scene has been relatively modest so far, in part due to the long period of time that cases take to reach the Supreme Court, its final arbiter. In the following sections, we will examine the effects that the Charter has had on HRM and industrial relations.

Charter Content of Particular Interest to HR Managers   Section 2 of the Charter guarantees freedom of association, a very important aspect of industrial relations. Under this section, unions have challenged whether this guarantees that every person should have the right to bargain collectively, strike, and picket.

Section 15—**equality rights**—came into effect on April 17, 1985. In its first paragraph, it guarantees the right to:[2]

> *equal protection and equal benefit of the law without discrimination, and, in particular, without discrimination based on race, national or ethnic origin, colour, religion, sex, age, or mental or physical disability.*

This section, as expected, has caused a flood of litigation.

Examples of Charter Applications   Some of the more prominent issues challenged under the Charter are described briefly below.

The Right to Bargain Collectively and Strike   On April 9, 1987, the Supreme Court of Canada rendered a long-awaited judgment on the impact of the Charter on federal and provincial collective bargaining legislation.

In a 4–2 split decision, the Supreme Court held that Section 2 of the Charter does not include the right to bargain collectively and strike. This judgment was a real blow to the union movement. The court affirmed that Section 2 protects the freedom to establish, belong to, and maintain an association, and to participate in its lawful activities without penalty or reprisal. However, the rights to bargain collectively and strike were determined to be statutory rights created and regulated by the legislature, not fundamental freedoms. Under this ruling, governments can

equality rights
Section 15 of the *Charter of Rights and Freedoms*, which came into effect on April 17, 1985. It guarantees the right to equal protection and equal benefit of the law without discrimination.

pass legislation requiring striking workers to return to work and settle outstanding bargaining issues through final and binding arbitration, generally in the case of "undue public hardship" as when teachers go on strike. A government can also limit unions' ability to negotiate wage and salary increases through wage restraint legislation, such as Ontario's former Social Contract, and impose compulsory arbitration as a means of settling outstanding bargaining issues, rather than granting the right to strike to certain types of workers, such as hospital employees.

The Right to Picket   In another decision, the Supreme Court ruled that the right to picket is not protected under the Charter. Thus, employers can ask for court injunctions to restrict the number of picketers or impose any other reasonable limitation on picketing activity.

Use of Union Dues   On June 27, 1991, the union movement won a historic legal victory pertaining to labour relations legislation,[3] the legality of which was challenged by a community college faculty member from northern Ontario. In a unanimous decision, the Supreme Court of Canada upheld the legality of the Rand formula, which provides for the automatic deduction of union dues from the paycheque of every person in the bargaining unit; as well as the right of unions to spend such dues to support social and political causes and organizations in accordance with the wishes of the membership, as determined by majority vote.

Mandatory Retirement   The Supreme Court has upheld the legality of human rights legislation *that protects only individuals of specified ages from discrimination in employment*, and therefore allows mandatory retirement at the upper age limit. In British Columbia, Saskatchewan, Ontario, Nova Scotia, and Newfoundland, for example, the upper age limit protected under the provincial human rights legislation is sixty-five. The court concluded that the objectives of mandatory retirement were of sufficient significance to justify the limitation of the constitutional right to equality, if a province chose to impose one. In other words, mandatory retirement at that upper age limit, while discriminatory, was judged to be "reasonable and justifiable."

The Supreme Court has also upheld Section 15(c) of the *Canadian Human Rights Act*, which excludes mandatory retirement at "the normal age" from its prohibition on age discrimination. Therefore, federal employment policies requiring that individuals retire at "the normal age" are not discriminatory.

It should be noted that these rulings do not limit the right of a government to prohibit mandatory retirement if it chooses to do so.[4] Alberta, Manitoba, and Quebec have abolished mandatory retirement, as has the federal government for civil servants.

Human Rights Legislation

Every employer in Canada is affected by human rights legislation, which prohibits intentional and unintentional discrimination in their dealings with the public and in their policies pertaining to all aspects and terms and conditions of employment.

Scope   Generally, employment-related laws and regulations are limited in scope; their impact is confined to one or two HRM functions. For example, employment (labour) standards legislation primarily affects the compensation and benefits functions. Other HRM activities, such as recruitment, selection, training, performance appraisal, and labour relations, are largely unaffected.

The human rights legislation; however, is an exception. It is extremely broad in scope, affecting virtually every aspect of HRM: human resources planning, recruitment, selection, training, performance appraisal, and compensation. The way in which employees are treated on the job every day and the climate in which they work are also addressed by this legislation. For this reason, it is critical that all supervisors and managers be thoroughly familiar with the human rights legislation, and their legal obligations and responsibilities specified therein.

human rights legislation
A family of federal and provincial/territorial laws that have a common objective: providing equal opportunity for members of protected groups in a number of areas, including accommodation, contracts, provision of goods and services, and employment.

Overview   Human rights legislation is a family of federal and provincial/territorial laws that have a common objective: providing equal opportunity for members of protected groups in a number of areas, including accommodation, contracts, provision of goods and services, and employment. Our focus is on the provisions related to employment. To review individual provincial and territorial human rights laws would be confusing because of the many but generally minor differences among them, often only in terminology (for example, some provinces use the term "creed," others "religion"). As indicated in **Figure 3.1**, by and large provincial and territorial laws mirror the federal law, and are similar in terms of scope, interpretation, and application. All jurisdictions prohibit discrimination on the grounds of race, religion or creed, colour, marital status, sex, and physical disability. All prohibit age-based discrimination (although the age groups protected differ), and all jurisdictions other than Saskatchewan and Alberta prohibit discrimination on the basis of mental handicap. Discrimination on other

Prohibited Grounds of Discrimination	Federal	Alta.	B.C.	Man.	N.B.	Nfld.	N.S.	Ont.	PEI	Que.	Sask.	N.W.T.	Yukon
Race	♦	♦	♦	♦	♦	♦	♦	♦	♦	♦	♦	♦	♦
Colour	♦	♦	♦	♦	♦	♦	♦	♦	♦	♦	♦	♦	♦
Ethnic or national origin	♦		♦	♦	♦	♦	♦	♦	♦	♦	♦	♦	♦
Creed or religion	♦	♦	♦	♦	♦	♦	♦	♦	♦	♦	♦	♦	♦
Sex	♦	♦	♦	♦	♦	♦	♦	♦	♦	♦	♦	♦	♦
Marital status	♦	♦	♦	♦		♦	♦	♦	♦	♦	♦	♦	♦
Age	♦	18+	19–65	♦	♦	19–65	♦	18–65	♦	♦	18–64	♦	♦
Mental handicap	♦		♦	♦	♦	♦	♦	♦	♦	♦		♦	♦
Physical handicap	♦	♦	♦	♦	♦	♦	♦	♦	♦	♦	♦	♦	♦
Pardoned offence	♦							♦		♦		♦	
Record of criminal conviction			♦							♦			♦
Harassment[1]	♦							♦		♦			♦
Sexual Orientation	♦		♦	♦	♦	♦	♦	♦		♦	♦		♦
Language										♦			

[1] The federal, Ontario, Quebec, and Yukon statutes ban harassment on all proscribed grounds. Manitoba prohibits sexual harassment.

Figure 3.1
Prohibited Grounds of Discrimination in Employment by Jurisdiction
Source: Adapted from *Selected Prohibited Grounds of Discrimination in Employment by Jurisdiction–1996*, (Toronto: Carswell a division of Thomson Canada Limited. Reprinted by permission.

grounds, such as sexual orientation and criminal history, are prohibited in some jurisdictions, but not all. Harassment provisions are currently in effect in Newfoundland, Ontario, Quebec, the Yukon Territories, and the federal jurisdiction.

Human rights legislation permits employers to reward outstanding performers and penalize those who do not meet productivity standards or comply with company rules and regulations. The only stipulation is that rewards and punishments must be based on work-related criteria, not age, sex, or other prohibited ground.

The following discussion will focus on the federal human rights legislation.

The Canadian Human Rights Act

Canadian Human Rights Act
Federal legislation, prohibiting discrimination on a number of grounds. It applies to all federal government agencies and crown corporations and to businesses and industries under federal jurisdiction.

The **Canadian Human Rights Act**, which covers all businesses under federal jurisdiction, was passed by Parliament on July 14, 1977, and took effect in March, 1978. Amended several times since then, it currently specifies that:[5]

All individuals should have an equal opportunity to make for themselves the lives that they are able and wish to have, consistent with their duties and obligations as members of society, without being hindered in or prevented from doing so by discriminatory practices based on race, national or ethnic origin, colour, religion, age, sex, sexual orientation, marital status, family status, disability or conviction for an offence for which a pardon has been granted.

Types of Discrimination Prohibited

intentional discrimination
Deliberately using criteria such as race, religion, sex, or other prohibited grounds when making employment decisions.

Intentional Discrimination Except in specific circumstances, which will be described later, **intentional discrimination** is prohibited. This means that an employer cannot discriminate *directly* by deliberately refusing to hire, train, or promote an individual, for example, on any of the prohibited grounds. It is important to realize that deliberate discrimination is not necessarily overt. In fact, overt (blatant) discrimination is quite rare today. Subtle intentional discrimination can be difficult to prove. For example, if a sixty-year-old applicant is not selected for a job, and is told that there was a better qualified candidate, it is often difficult for the rejected job-seeker to determine if there really was someone who more closely matched the organization's specifications, or if the employer discriminated on the basis of age.

It is also illegal for an employer to engage in intentional discrimination *indirectly*, through another party. This means that an employer cannot ask someone else to discriminate on his or her behalf. For example, an employer cannot request that an employment agency refer only male candidates for consideration as management trainees; or instruct supervisors that women of child-bearing age are to be excluded from consideration for promotions.

It is illegal to discriminate on the basis of age in every jurisdiction in Canada.

Discrimination because of association is another possible type of intentional discrimination, listed specifically as a prohibited ground in six Canadian jurisdictions. It involves the denial of rights because of friendship or other relationship with a protected group member. An example would be the refusal of a firm to promote a highly-qualified white male into senior management on the basis of the assumption that his wife, recently diagnosed with multiple sclerosis, will require too much of his time and attention, and that her needs may restrict his willingness to travel on company business.

Unintentional Discrimination **Unintentional discrimination**, also known as **constructive** or **systemic discrimination**, is the most difficult to detect and combat because it is often hidden. Typically, it is embedded in policies and practices that appear neutral on the surface, and are implemented impartially, but have adverse impact on specific groups of people for reasons that are not job related or required for the safe and efficient operation of the business. Examples are shown in **Figure 3.2**.

Examples of Human Rights Legislation Applications   In order to clarify how the human rights legislation is applied, and the types of discrimination prohibited, a few examples follow.

Race and Colour   It is sometimes difficult to detect which of these two characteristics is the basis of discrimination; often both are involved. Since every jurisdiction in Canada prohibits discrimination on the basis of race, an Ontario example was chosen, which dramatically illustrates the consequences of intentional direct and indirect discrimination:[6]

> *Five former employees of Majestic Electronics Inc., who resigned in late 1986 and early 1987, received a total of almost $300 000 in settlement of a human rights complaint. The Ontario Human Rights Commission investigation found that company president, Curtis Ramsauer, made "bigoted and racist remarks" and ordered that minorities and women be fired from the firm. Four of the complainants, white males who held senior positions at Majestic, were threatened with dismissal when they refused to carry out Ramsauer's orders. The fifth complainant, a woman of East Indian origin, resigned after four days on the job when she was told she would be fired because of her race.*

> *The settlement was the largest ever in a racial discrimination case. Former vice-president of finance, Robert Lee, who earned $90 000 annually, received over $200 000 in lost wages and damages, including compensation for losses he incurred when he was forced to sell his house. The other four complainants each received be-*

unintentional/ constructive/systemic discrimination
Discrimination that is difficult to detect and combat because it is often hidden. Typically, it is embedded in policies and practices that appear neutral on the surface, and are implemented impartially, but have adverse impact on specific groups of people for reasons that are not job related or required for the safe and efficient operation of the business.

**Figure 3.2
Examples of Systemic Discrimination**

Source: Based on material provided by the Ontario Women's Directorate and the Canadian Human Rights Commission.

- minimum height and weight requirements, such as formerly existed for the Canadian armed forces and many police forces, which screened out disproportionate numbers of women and Canadians of Asian origin, who tend to be shorter in stature
- internal hiring policies or word-of-mouth hiring in workplaces that have not embraced diversity
- limited accessibility of buildings and facilities, which pose a barrier to persons with mobility limitations
- culturally-biased or non-job-related employment tests, which discriminate against specific groups
- job evaluation systems that undervalue jobs traditionally held by women
- promotions based exclusively on seniority and experience in firms that have historically been dominated by while males
- lack of explicit anti-harassment guidelines, or an organizational climate in which certain groups feel unwelcome and uncomfortable.

tween $5 781 and $30 587. In addition, Ramsauer was ordered to provide each complainant with a letter of apology and $8 000 in damages. Other terms of the settlement required Majestic to hire qualified women and racial minorities in proportion to the percentage of applications received from those groups. The company was also required to hold semi-annual human rights training programs and include visible minorities and women in any advertising featuring Majestic employees.

Age   The use of age as an employment criterion has been receiving increasing attention. Many employers believe that it is justifiable to specify minimum or maximum ages for certain jobs. In actual fact, evidence is rarely available to support the position that age is an accurate indication of a person's ability to perform a particular type of work:[7]

A 37-year-old man filed a complaint when he was refused employment at Greyhound Lines of Canada Ltd. on the basis of age. The company, which only hired individuals between the ages of 24 and 35 as drivers, justified its position based on the argument that new drivers get the least favourable routes, and must be young enough to cope with the related stress. The Tribunal ruled that there was insufficient evidence to conclude that the inability to cope with stress is related to age.

An important feature of the human rights legislation is that it supersedes the terms of any employment contract or collective agreement:[8]

In the collective agreement between an employer and the Brotherhood of Railway, Airline, and Steamship Clerks, age was used to rank employees hired on the same day on the seniority list. In her complaint against the union, Susan Tanel alleged that the policy resulted in her being denied upgrading from part-time to full-time work on the basis of age. She received compensation in settlement of her complaint. The union and employer, recognizing that their policy was an example of systemic discrimination, and that age is not an appropriate measure of difference in seniority between two employees with equal length of service, no longer apply this or any other age-based seniority policy.

Sex   The Canadian Human Rights Act prohibits discrimination in employment policies and practices on the basis of sex. It is illegal for an employer to allow an individual's sex to influence its recruitment, selection, promotion, training, transfer, or termination policies and practices. Unless there is a justifiable job-related reason, it is also illegal to have separate policies for men and women (for example, specifying that certain jobs are to be performed by men only). Furthermore, employers cannot use or promote tests, standards, and/or other criteria that are biased or discriminate against one sex (or other protected group member), even if unintentionally, unless the employer can prove that such requirements are justifiable:[9]

A woman received $3 500 for lost wages and general damages in settlement of her complaint that a company's height requirement discriminated against women. She was refused an interview for a bus driver job because she did not meet the minimum height requirement of 173 cm (5 feet 8 inches). The case was settled, after conciliation. The company agreed to discontinue its practice of specifying a minimum height for drivers' positions, and has subsequently hired several women shorter than 173 cm. As part of the settlement, the company agreed that the Canadian Human Rights Commission would monitor its driver application records for one year.

As of 1989, in its decision against Canada Safeway Ltd., the Supreme Court of Canada made it clear that discrimination on the basis of the fact that a women is or could become pregnant is a form of sex discrimination and therefore illegal. Prior to that time, it was fairly common to have short-term disability or weekly indemnity insurance plans that excluded pregnancy and related illnesses from coverage. Although the Supreme Court acknowledged that pregnancy is not a sickness or accident, the judges ruled that it is a valid health-related reason for absence from work, and therefore cannot be excluded from benefits plan coverage:[10]

Three women complained that their employer, Canada Safeway Ltd., discriminated against them on the basis of sex, because although the company provided insurance benefits to employees absent from work for medical reasons, pregnancy was excluded from coverage. The company argued on the basis of an earlier Supreme Court decision that although pregnant persons were treated differently from non-pregnant persons, this was not sex discrimination because not all women are or become pregnant. The Court rejected this argument and held that since only women become pregnant, a denial of health benefits to "pregnant people" is tantamount to denying those benefits to women. The Court also noted that for too long society [had] allowed employment practices to impose all the costs of childbirth upon women.

Marital Status Discrimination on the basis of marital status is also illegal:[11]

An airline pilot complained to the Human Rights Commission when he lost his job. He claimed that he was released because he was married and the airline found it more convenient to employ single pilots. When the Human Rights Tribunal substantiated his claim, the company was ordered to pay him $24 487 in lost earnings and general damages.

Family Status In a precedent-setting case regarding family status, the Canadian Human Rights Commission initiated action against the Canada Employment and Immigration Commission (CEIC), now known as Human Resources Development Canada (HRDC):[12]

A complaint was filed by Ina Lang alleging that CEIC denied her application for funding under the Challenge '86 program because the individual she wished to hire to assist her in her childcare business was her daughter. A tribunal found that CEIC had discriminated on the basis of family status, and awarded Ms. Lang $1 000 for hurt feelings. Although the CEIC appealed the decision, the Federal Court of Appeal upheld the tribunal decision.

Pardoned Convicts The Canadian Human Rights Act prohibits discrimination on the basis of conviction for a federal offence for which a pardon has been granted. Applications for pardon may not be submitted until a specified number of years (generally five) following release, parole, or completion of a sentence, and are investigated thoroughly by the RCMP, who verify that applicants have earned the right to have their records "expunged". The purpose is to ensure that individuals who have reformed their ways do not have past indiscretions held against them forever:[13]

A man convicted and pardoned for a drug-related offence applied for a job as a counsellor at a community correctional centre. He had extensive experience working with ex-inmates and the provincial commission on dependency, and was rated as the best candidate for the position. However, Correctional Services rejected him on the basis of his criminal record, arguing that even though he had received a pardon, he still represented a security risk. He appealed to the Canadian Human Rights Commission. Following the Commission's investigation, Correctional Services decided that the applicant's criminal records would not, in fact, inhibit his ability to meet the job requirements, and, satisfied that he was suitable, offered him the position.

It is important to note that the Human Rights Commission *Guide to Screening and Selection in Employment*, included as **appendix 3.1** at the end of this chapter, indicates that it is inappropriate for employers to ask about arrest records. This makes sense, given that being arrested is not necessarily an indication of any wrongdoing. Employers in Ontario and the Northwest Territories, and those under federal jurisdiction elsewhere, cannot ask about conviction records. If information about criminal record is legitimately needed for employment purposes, the question should be phrased: "Have you ever been convicted of a criminal offence for which a pardon has not been granted?" In British Columbia, Quebec, and the Yukon Territories, criminal conviction is a prohibited ground of discrimination, which means that even this question would be illegal. In all Canadian jurisdictions, it is permissible to ask if an applicant is eligible for bonding if being bondable is a job requirement. (Bonding means the firm takes out an insurance policy to pay for any losses caused by employee dishonesty.)

Physical and Mental Handicap   The Canadian Human Rights Act prohibits discrimination in employment policies and practices against an individual on the basis of physical or mental disability, unless accommodation would be impossible (that is, a person who is blind cannot be employed as a truck or bus driver) or accommodating the individual's disability would cause the employer "undue hardship." Many organizations have imposed rigid physical standards for certain jobs. Unless they can prove that these are truly necessary, such standards are not permissible, since they may constitute systemic discrimination. That is why, for example, the Canadian armed forces no longer has specific height and weight requirements. Some employers, such as Johnson and Johnson in Peterborough, Ontario, have conducted physical demands analyses to determine the actual rather than assumed job requirements. Once such analyses, which are described in detail in chapter 4, have been completed, it is much easier for job candidates to identify particular job requirements that might pose problems for them, so that accommodation strategies can be discussed:[14]

> *A man was refused a technician's job because he failed the hearing test administered by the firm. He was tested without his hearing aid. Although he asserted that he could hear well with his hearing aid and could certainly perform the job, the company's medical advisors claimed that the job required normal hearing. After conciliation, the company agreed that the applicant was correct. He was hired as a technician and paid damages of $750.*

Employers in most jurisdictions are also expected to accommodate the needs of individuals with mental disabilities, as this Quebec example illustrates:[15]

www.chra.ca
Accommodating Disabilities

> *A Quebec insurance company was ordered to pay $15 500 for failing to accommodate an employee with depression. The agent, referred to by a Quebec human rights tribunal as Ms. Grenier, was absent from work for nine months due to depression. Thereafter, on the advice of her doctor, she asked if she could work three days a week for two months, prior to returning to full-time employment. The company refused. The tribunal criticized Assurances Générales des Caisses Désjardins for not acknowledging Grenier's depression as a mental disability and dismissing it as a "short-term" problem.*

Sexual Orientation   Since May of 1996, the Canadian Human Rights Act has prohibited discrimination on the basis of sexual orientation (whether an individual is heterosexual, homosexual, or bisexual). A number of other jurisdictions, including Manitoba, Ontario, Quebec, and the Yukon Territories, also prohibit discrimination on this ground.

While the implications are quite clear in terms of most employment issues, such as recruitment, selection, and termination, there are a few benefits administration issues yet to be resolved. Obviously, employers cannot discriminate against a candidate or an employee on the basis of sexual orientation. The question still being resolved is whether the partners of gay men and lesbian women are entitled to be treated as spouses for benefits entitlement purposes. The fact that they have not been formally married does not in itself disqualify such partners. Common-law marriages between heterosexual men and women have legal standing if the partners have been together for at least a year and publicly represented themselves as husband and wife.

In 1995, in a key decision about the provisions of the *Old Age Security Act*, in which a spouse is defined as "a person of the opposite sex...," the Supreme Court of Canada ruled that while the distinction between heterosexual couples and homosexual couples was discriminatory under the Charter, such infringement was "justifiable in a free and democratic society" on the basis that government must be granted some flexibility in deciding which groups are eligible to receive social benefits. Subsequent case law, however, in one major jurisdiction (Ontario), now seems to indicate that provincial human rights legislation, combined with the provisions of the Charter, make it illegal for employers to have group insurance or pension plans that do not extend spousal benefits to same-sex partners.

Until recently, plan sponsors wishing to provide tax-exempt benefits for employees under a private health service plan (PHSP), such as supplementary health insurance or a dental plan, were required to establish a separate plan for same-sex partners. Combining heterosexual and homosexual couples in a single plan meant the loss of the tax-exempt status, since once any benefits were paid for same-sex partners, all benefits paid from the plan were treated as taxable income by Revenue Canada.[16] As of 1997, Revenue Canada decided to broaden its interpretation of a PHSP under the Income Tax Act to include same-sex couples. A problem still remains, though, for pension plan coverage. As yet, Revenue Canada has not amended its position that the definition of "spouse" in a registered pension plan must specify a person of the opposite sex. For now, the only solution seems to be providing same-sex coverage under a separate pension plan.[17]

Specific Human Rights Legislation Issues
Bona Fide Occupational Requirements   Employers are permitted to discriminate if employment preferences are based on a **bona fide occupational qualification (BFOQ)** or a **bona fide occupational requirement (BFOR)**,[18] defined as a justifiable reason for discrimination based on business necessity (i.e., required for the safe and efficient operation of the organization) or a requirement that can be clearly defended as intrinsically required by the tasks an employee is expected to perform. There are some settings in which a BFOR exception to human rights protection is fairly obvious. For example, if a boutique handling ladies' apparel requires its salespersons to model the merchandise, sex is clearly a BFOR. When casting in the theatre, there may be specific roles that justify using age, sex, or national origin as a recruitment and selection criterion.

Where the issue of BFORs gets more complicated is in situations in which the occupational requirement is less obvious. The onus of proof is then placed on the employer.

bona fide occupational qualification (BFOQ) / bona fide occupational requirement (BFOR)
A justifiable reason for discrimination based on business necessity (that is, required for the safe and efficient operation of the organization) or a requirement that can be clearly defended as intrinsically required by the tasks an employee is expected to perform.

There are a number of instances in which BFORs have been established. For example, adherence to the tenets of the Roman Catholic Church has been deemed a BFOR when selecting faculty to teach in a Roman Catholic school.[19] The Royal Canadian Mounted Police has a requirement that guards be of the same sex as prisoners being guarded, which was also ruled to be a BFOR.[20]

However, sex has often not been allowed as a BFOR in what, on the surface, might seem to be reasonable circumstances, such as a male-dominated work site or a workplace that lacked a women's washroom.[21] A 1982 Supreme Court of Canada decision established that mandatory retirement at age sixty for firefighters in Etobicoke, Ontario, was not a BFOR, even though honestly imposed, because there was insufficient evidence that reaching that age impaired ability to perform adequately.[22] In another case, the Canadian Human Rights Commission ruled that visual acuity standards established by VIA Rail were not a BFOR because VIA was unable to justify the objectivity of such standards.[23]

Reasonable Accommodation Employers who believe there is a BFOR for denying employment or assignment to a specific job may encounter the legal principle of **reasonable accommodation**, incorporated in the federal human rights legislation, and that of Manitoba, Ontario, and the Yukon.

The Canadian Human Rights Commission has a guide for employers wishing to accommodate the needs of employees with disabilities. It can be found at the website www.chrc.ca. *Barrier-Free Employers* contains suggestions for accommodating various disabilities and includes a searchable index.

Reasonable accommodation deals with the adjustment of employment policies and practices so that no individual is denied benefits, disadvantaged in employment, or prevented from carrying out the essential components of a job on the basis of prohibited grounds of discrimination. Adjustments to schedules to accommodate religious beliefs or work station redesign to enable an individual with a physical disability to perform a particular task are examples.

Having a disability does not disqualify a person for a job. Indeed, advantages in technology have enabled many people with disabilities to enter the work force and work productively. Here, Nancy Thibeault uses specially designed equipment in her job as telephone operator and receptionist at PAC Corporation.

Employers are expected to accommodate to the point of **undue hardship**, a term for which there is no definitive definition. Relevant considerations may include financial cost, disruption to operations, impact on morale of other employees, and health and safety risks.

Failure to make every reasonable effort to accommodate employees is a violation of the Act:[24]

After becoming a member of the Worldwide Church of God, the complainant, who worked for the Central Alberta Dairy Pool at a milk processing plant, requested unpaid leave for a particular Monday to observe a church holy day. Because Mondays were especially busy days at the plant, his request was refused. When he failed to report for work, he was fired.

The Supreme Court of Canada (1990) ruled that the employer had discriminated on the basis of religion because they failed to accommodate to the point of undue hardship. The court found that since Dairy Pool could cope with employee absences on Mondays due to illness, it could also accommodate a single instance of absence due to religious reasons.

In accommodating unionized employees, the employer and union have a joint (but not equal) responsibility. According to the Supreme Court of Canada (Renaud, 1992) there are two situations in which a union has a duty to accommodate.

The first is one in which the union participated in the formulation of a work rule that has a discriminatory effect on a complainant (that is, there is a provision in the collective agreement that has an adverse impact). In such case, the union shares a joint responsibility. Employers must make every effort to accommodate an employee within the parameters of a collective agreement. However, the union can become involved before the employer has exhausted all options that would not involve amendments to the terms of the collective agreement. The union must be involved in situations in which the accommodation initiative proposed would impact on a collective agreement or bargaining unit employee rights. While the employer is expected to initiate the accommodation process, refusal by the union to consent to reasonable accommodation measures in this type of situation would expose both parties to liability as co-discriminators.

The second situation in which the union has a duty to accommodate is one in which the lack of union support would impede the employer's reasonable efforts to accommodate an employee, even though the union did not participate in the formulation or application of the specific rule or practice that is the source of discrimination.[25]

In some situations, duty to accommodate may be related to testing standards. Employers requiring a high standard of fitness, for example, may face problems developing fair tests. If standards are set too low, people's lives may be endangered; too high a standard may mean losing otherwise highly qualified people—particularly women—to an arbitrary standard:[26]

> *Ms. Meiorin was hired in May 1992 as a forest firefighter in British Columbia and performed well. No physical tests were administered until 1994 because a new test was being designed. As part of that test, Meiorin had to run 2.5 kilometres in 11 minutes or less. While she passed the other physical tests, her best time was 11 minutes, 30 seconds. She was permanently laid off. An arbitrator ruled that her employer was not justified in letting her go and ordered that she be reinstated. Thirty-five percent of female personnel passed the test the first time, compared to 65 to 70 percent of men, an example of systemic discrimination. The arbitrator ruled that the employer had failed to accommodate adversely-affected employees to the point of undue hardship, and expressed doubt that inability to run the race in the specified time "would pose a serious safety risk to herself, fellow employees, or the public at large."*

harassment
A wide range of behaviour that a reasonable person ought to know is unwelcome; however, it also encompasses actions and activities that were once tolerated, ignored, and considered horseplay or innocent flirtation, provided the individual who feels that he or she is being harassed makes it clear that such behaviour is unwelcome and inappropriate and asks that it be discontinued.

Harassment   The federal legislation and that in Ontario, Quebec, and the Yukon, prohibits harassment on all proscribed grounds. Manitoba's legislation bans sexual harassment only. **Harassment** includes a wide range of behaviour that a reasonable person ought to know is unwelcome; however, it also encompasses actions and activities that were once tolerated, ignored, and considered horseplay or innocent flirtation, provided the individual who feels that he or she is being harassed makes it clear that such behaviour is unwelcome and inappropriate and asks that it be discontinued. Examples of the types of behaviour which may constitute harassment are included in **Figure 3.3**. In the case of blatantly inappropriate actions, such as physical assault, one incident may constitute harassment. Generally, however, harassment involves a series of incidents. Protection against harassment extends to incidents occurring at or away from the workplace, during or outside normal working hours, provided such incidents are employment-related.[27] An employer is also responsible for dealing with employee harassment by clients or customers once it has been reported.

Figure 3.3
Examples of
Behaviours That May
Constitute Harassment
Source: Based on material
provided by the Ontario
Women's Directorate and the
Canadian Human Rights
Commission.

- physical assault
- unnecessary physical contact, such as patting, pinching, touching, or punching
- verbal abuse or threats
- unwelcome invitations or requests, whether subtle or explicit, and intimidation
- unwelcome remarks, jokes, innuendos, or taunting about a person's body, attire, age, marital status, ethnic or national origin, religion, etc.
- leering or other gestures
- displaying pornographic, racist, or other offensive or derogatory pictures
- practical jokes that cause awkwardness or embarrassment
- condescension or paternalism that undermines self-respect.

Example of Harassment on the Basis of Ethnic Origin:

A federal department employee filed a complaint with the Canadian Human Rights Commission after she was harassed because of her Italian origin. Several coworkers directed derogatory remarks about Italians toward her and called her names. She complained to her supervisor, who failed to investigate her allegations, merely telling her that such behaviour went on in the office and that she was being overemotional. The commission concluded that the complainant was being harassed. The department agreed to pay the employee $1 200 as compensation for hurt feelings. A memorandum was circulated to all employees reminding them that discriminatory remarks about a person's ethnic origin are a form of harassment and would not be tolerated.[28]

Employer Responsibility   In 1987 (Robichaud v. Treasury Board), the Supreme Court of Canada made it clear that employers and managers have a responsibility to provide a safe and healthy working environment. If harassment is occurring, of which they are aware, or ought to have been aware, they can be charged, as well as the alleged harasser.[29] To reduce liability, employers should establish sound corporate harassment policies, communicate such policies to all employees, enforce the policies in a fair and consistent manner, and take an active role in maintaining a working environment that is free of harassment.

Simply having a policy is not enough, as the following Ontario example illustrates:[30]

General Motors Canada (GM) had a harassment policy, but was still assessed $120 000 in damages for wrongful dismissal of a security supervisor on the basis of his harassment of a female employee who reported to him. The supervisor won his case because GM had not adequately communicated or monitored its harassment policy. It was found that GM had acted arbitrarily in his case because his behaviour was not substantially different from that of other people in the department.

sexual harassment
Harassment on the basis of gender or sexual attractiveness or unattractiveness.

sexual coercion
Harassment of a sexual nature that results in some direct consequence to the worker's employment status or some gain in or loss of tangible job benefits.

Sexual Harassment   The type of harassment that has attracted the most attention in the workplace is **sexual harassment**. According to one noted scholar, sexual harassment can be divided into two categories: sexual coercion and sexual annoyance.[31]

Sexual coercion involves harassment of a sexual nature that results in some direct consequence to the worker's employment status or some gain in or loss of tangible job benefits. Typically, this involves a supervisor using control over employment, pay, performance appraisal results, or promotion, to attempt to coerce an employee to grant sexual favours. If the worker agrees to the request, tangible job benefits follow; if the worker refuses, job benefits are denied.

sexual annoyance
Sexually-related conduct that is hostile, intimidating, or offensive to the employee, but has no direct link to tangible job benefits or loss thereof.

Sexual annoyance is sexually related conduct that is hostile, intimidating, or offensive to the employee, but has no direct link to tangible job benefits or loss thereof. Rather, a "poisoned" work environment is created for the employee, the tolerance of which effectively becomes a term or condition of employment. The following case provides an illustration of this type of harassment, as well as the consequences of management's failure to take corrective action:[32]

> *A woman who put up with 14 years of sexual harassment before quitting her job was awarded nearly $50 000 in damages by an Ontario Human Rights Board of Inquiry. The woman, who worked as a bookkeeper at Levac Supply Ltd., shared a general office area with the office manager, with whom she got along very well initially. After a few months, he became less friendly and began making noises and comments aimed at her, implying that she was working slowly or incompetently. He also began to make personal comments about her size, referring to her and other female employees as "fridge sisters," and making snide comments behind her back. Particularly demeaning to the woman involved were the comments "swish, swish" and "waddle, waddle" when she was wearing nylons. She sometimes yelled at him to "get off her back," but his behaviour continued. While he admitted to "bugging" and "teasing" her, he stated that he had done it simply to "get more productivity" out of her, and that he hadn't realized his comments were upsetting her. The board, however, found that monitoring her productivity was not his job and that his "digs" drove her to tears at times, a fact of which he was well aware. The complainant stated that she had complained about three or four times a year to the head of company operations about the harassment, but no one tried to remedy the situation. The board ruled that the comments, especially the ones which the woman found particularly offensive, implied sexual unattractiveness, and as such, constituted harassment because of sex (gender). The manager was found to have engaged in repeated verbal conduct of a sexual nature, which created an offensive working environment for the victim. Since the head of operations did nothing to stop the harassment, he, the office manager, and the company were ordered to pay her a total of $48 273 in damages.*

A poisoned work environment may exist even if no direct threats or promises are made in exchange for sexual favours.

Harassment Policies An amendment to the Canada Labour Code in 1985 made it mandatory for all organizations operating under federal jurisdiction to develop and implement sexual harassment policies. Many organizations under provincial/territorial or municipal jurisdiction or receiving government funding have a similar legal obligation. Increasingly, however, organizations are developing policies to deal with harassment, whether required to do so by law or not.

As illustrated in **Figure 3.4**, some firms have a policy prohibiting harassment on all grounds, rather than sexual harassment alone. It is important to note, however, that there is a significant difference between implementing a policy designed to prevent harassment in the workplace and a policy uniformly applied without due consideration of the circumstances of the particular case. Complying with the legal obligation to provide a "poison-free" workplace and exercise due diligence after a complaint is lodged does not necessarily require severe discipline in every case. In fact, imposing unduly harsh discipline, in view of the specific circumstances, can lead to a wrongful or constructive dismissal lawsuit, as happened at GM Canada (described earlier). Just as there are numerous types of harassment complaints, there should be varying responses by the employer for inappropriate behaviour that constitutes harassment. Options include counselling, warning, requiring an apology, transfer, suspension, or termination.[33] Tips for managers wishing to implement a harassment policy are included in **Figure 3.5**.

**Figure 3.4
Sample Harassment
Policy**

Source: Sir Sandford Fleming
College, Peterborough,
Ontario. Used with
permission.

**SIR SANDFORD FLEMING COLLEGE
HARASSMENT/DISCRIMINATION PREVENTION POLICY**

Policy No. 3-311	Approved by:	Board of Governors
Page No. 1 of 1	Supersedes:	94-05
		Motion #3

Date Approved: February 4, 1998

Subject: Harassment/Discrimination Prevention

Sir Sandford Fleming College is committed to fostering a work and study environment that is free from discrimination and harassment as enshrined in established provincial and federal statutes. These include, but are not limited to the: Ontario Human Rights Code, Pay Equity Act, Employment Standards Act, and Charter of Rights and Freedoms. These statutes comprise a complex legislative scheme designed to protect the right of every person in Ontario to be free from harassment and discrimination.

The *Ontario Human Rights Code* prohibits discrimination or harassment based on race, ancestry, place of origin, colour, ethnic origin, citizenship, creed, sex, sexual orientation, disability, age, marital status, family status, and record of offenses.

The *Code* requires that a person who has the authority to prevent or discourage harassment and discrimination may be held responsible for failing to do so. All persons in positions of authority have a particular legal duty to be alert to signs of harassment and discrimination in the workplace and/or educational environment. They must take action to address any incidents of which they are aware or ought reasonably to have been aware. This also applies to faculty because of their unique role as managers/facilitators of the learning environment. Decisions made by courts and human rights tribunals in recent years have emphasized this responsibility.

Sir Sandford Fleming College recognizes that a harassment- and discrimination-free work and study environment is essential to effective business practices in today's global market and that the maintenance of such an environment is its legal and social responsibility. Such an environment allows all employees and students to develop to their potential and fosters excellence in educational endeavours for students, staff, faculty, and the community.

**Figure 3.5
Management Tips on
Harassment Policies**

Source: Malcolm MacKillop,
"Dismissal If Necessary; Not
Necessarily Dismissal," *Human
Resources Professional* 13, no. 2
(April 1996), p. 25.

1. Avoid a "Zero Tolerance" approach. Every case has to be decided on its own facts.

2. Have a clear Workplace Harassment Policy that specifically provides for the option of termination of employment where harassment is proven.

3. Provide training sessions to all managers and employees. Providing a copy of your Workplace Harassment policy is a must, and mandatory attendance at the sessions is recommended. Many employers are requiring that all employees sign a copy of the policy and return it to the employer.

4. Monitor the workplace. Supervisors and Managers must be advised of their obligations with respect to monitoring the workplace to prevent a "poisoned workplace" from existing.

5. If a complaint is filed, do a proper investigation. It is absolutely imperative that the accused be given all the details of the complaint and be provided with an opportunity to respond to each allegation.

6. Consider all the relevant factors in determining whether dismissal is appropriate in the circumstances. For instance: what does the complainant want; the nature of the conduct; frequency of the conduct; the position and the length of service of the harasser, adverse effects to the business and the corporate culture.

Court decisions have upheld harassment as just cause for dismissal, when circumstances warrant. For example, the discharge of an employee who sexually harassed his secretary, causing her to file a complaint with the Human Rights Commission was upheld,[34] as was the discharge of a manager who was found guilty of sexually harassing a coworker, even though no complaint was filed with a Human Rights Commission.[35]

Special Programs Section 16(1) of the Canadian Human Rights Act legalizes employment equity initiatives, which are special programs developed by employers to remedy past discrimination and/or prevent future discrimination:[36]

> *It is not a discriminatory practice for a person to adopt or carry out a special program, plan, or arrangement designed to prevent disadvantages that are likely to be suffered by, or to eliminate or reduce disadvantages that are suffered by, any group of individuals when those disadvantages would be or are based on or related to the race, national or ethnic origin, colour, religion, age, sex, marital status, family status or disability of members of that group, by improving opportunities respecting goods, services, facilities, accommodation, or employment in relation to that group.*

Similar wording is found in the human rights legislation in most Canadian jurisdictions.

Employer Retaliation It is a criminal offence to retaliate in any way against those who exercise their rights under human rights legislation. Individuals who file charges, testify, or otherwise participate in any human rights action are protected by law. For example, if a supervisor tries to "get even" with an employee who filed charges, he or she is in violation of the law.

Canadian Human Rights Commission (CHRC)
The federal body responsible for the implementation and enforcement of the Canadian Human Rights Act.

Enforcement The responsibility for enforcement of the Canadian Human Rights Act rests with the **Canadian Human Rights Commission (CHRC)**, the members of which are appointed by the Governor-in-Council. The CHRC consists of a chief commissioner and a deputy chief commissioner, full-time members appointed for a term of not more than seven years; and from three to six part-time members, appointed for a maximum term of three years.

The commission deals with complaints concerning discriminatory practices covered by the Act, and also has the power to issue guidelines regarding its interpretation. Any individual or group may file a complaint with the commission, given that they have reasonable grounds to believe they have been discriminated against. The commission may refuse to accept the complaint for the following reasons:

- if other procedures seem more appropriate
- the complaint seems trivial or to have been filed in bad faith
- more than a year has elapsed since the alleged discrimination took place, or
- it is submitted by someone other than the person who allegedly was discriminated against, unless the alleged victim permits investigation of the claim.

Once the commission accepts the legitimacy of a written complaint, it assumes responsibility for pursuing the investigation and defending the decision reached. This means that the costs are born by the commission, not by the complainant, which makes the process accessible to all employees, regardless of financial means. The commission itself can initiate a complaint if it has reasonable grounds to assume that a party is engaging in a discriminatory practice.

Figure 3.6 outlines the enforcement procedure. After the commission has accepted a complaint, an investigator is appointed to gather the facts. Such investigator has the power to enter an employer's premises, examine records, and interview witnesses. Obstructing an investigation is illegal. Following impartial

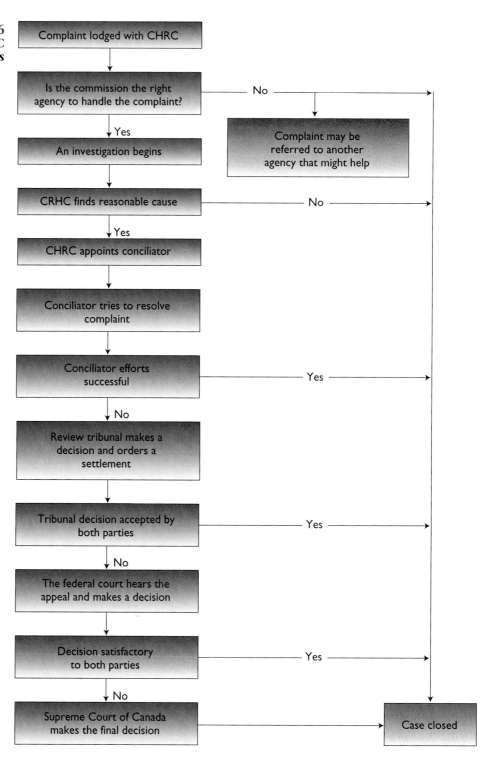

**Figure 3.6
The CHRC
Enforcement Process**

Complaint lodged with CHRC

Is the commission the right agency to handle the complaint? — No — Complaint may be referred to another agency that might help

Yes

An investigation begins

CRHC finds reasonable cause — No

Yes

CHRC appoints conciliator

Conciliator tries to resolve complaint

Conciliator efforts successful — Yes

No

Review tribunal makes a decision and orders a settlement

Tribunal decision accepted by both parties — Yes

No

The federal court hears the appeal and makes a decision

Decision satisfactory to both parties — Yes

No

Supreme Court of Canada makes the final decision — Case closed investigation, a report is submitted to the commission recommending a finding of either substantiation or nonsubstantiation of the allegation. If the allegation is substantiated, a settlement may be arranged in the course of the investigation, or the commission may, after adoption of the investigator's report, appoint a conciliator. Should the parties involved be unable to reach agreement with the assistance of the conciliator, a Human Rights Tribunal consisting of one to three members may be appointed to investigate further.

Remedies for Violations If discrimination is found, there are a number of remedies that can be imposed. The most common is compensation for lost wages. Other financial remedies include compensation for general damages, complainant expenses, and pain and humiliation. The violator is generally asked to restore the rights, opportunities, and privileges denied the victim, such as employment or promotion. A written letter of apology may be required. If a pattern of discrimination is detected, the employer will be ordered to cease such practices and may be required to attend a training session or hold regular human rights workshops, and may even be ordered to develop and implement an employment equity program.

Anyone obstructing an investigation or tribunal, failing to comply with the terms of a settlement, or reducing wages in order to eliminate a discriminatory practice can be found guilty of an offence punishable by a fine and/or jail sentence. The fines range from up to $5 000 for an individual to $50 000 for an employer or employee organization.[37]

Provincial/Territorial Human Rights Enforcement Procedures All of the provinces and both territories have their own human rights commissions, with similar regulations and procedures. If an individual feels discriminated against, he or she has the right to contact a human rights officer, who will investigate the complaint and attempt to reach a settlement that will satisfy all parties. Experience has shown that the majority of cases are settled at this stage. Failing agreement, the case is presented to the Human Rights Commission, the members of which will study the evidence and then submit a report to the minister in charge of administering the legislation. The minister may appoint a Board of Inquiry, which has powers similar to the federal Tribunal. Noncompliance with the course of action decided upon by the Board of Inquiry can result in prosecution in a provincial court of law, resulting in a fine, the maximum amount of which varies by jurisdiction. If an issue has nationwide implications, any provincial court decision may ultimately be appealed to the Supreme Court of Canada.

Equity

www.bloorstreet.com/
300block/aborcan.htm
Aboriginal Links: Canada & U.S.

The Charter of Rights and Freedoms and human rights legislation focus on prohibiting various kinds of discrimination. They are an attempt to create a level playing field in the employment relationship. However, over time it became obvious that there were certain groups for whom this complaints-based, reactive approach was insufficient. Investigation revealed that four identifiable groups—women, Aboriginal people, persons with disabilities, and visible minorities—had been subjected to pervasive patterns of differential treatment by employers, as evidenced by lower pay on average, occupational segregation, higher rates of unemployment, underemployment, and concentration in low status jobs with little potential for career growth.

For example, historically, 60 percent of all women worked in 20 of 500 possible occupational classifications. This is known as **occupational segregation**. Advancement of women and other designated group members into senior management positions has been hindered by the existence of a **glass ceiling**, an "invisible" barrier caused by attitudinal or organizational bias, that limits the advancement opportunities of qualified individuals. The fact that the glass ceiling is still intact was confirmed in a recent study of 776 Canadian firms. In those companies, there is clear evidence of **underutilization** of female employees. Women make up only 5.5 percent of board members and 7.5 percent of officers; 52 percent of the firms have no women among the top twelve officers.[38] There has tended to be a **concentration** of women in certain professions, which have been undervalued and underpaid, such as clerical jobs, non-commission sales positions, and service occupations. The majority of women are still working in traditional occupations—71 percent in teaching, nursing, health-related occupations, clerical, and sales and service occupations.[39] In 1996, average earnings for women working full time was $30 700; the comparable figure for men was $41 800.[40]

The number of young Aboriginal workers has been increasing dramatically during the 1990s; in western Canada they account for a large portion of labour market growth. Despite these facts, many Aboriginal workers are concentrated in low-paying, unstable employment, especially in urban centres.

The unemployment rate for employable persons with disabilities is 20 percent, compared to the national rate of 10 percent. Persons with disabilities face attitudinal barriers, physical demands unrelated to actual job requirements, and inadequate access to the technical and human support systems that would make it possible for them to obtain productive employment. In 1991, eight percent of respondents to a Statistics Canada survey reported that they had been refused employment during the preceding five years because of their disabilities; six percent indicated that they had been dismissed from a job; four percent indicated they had been refused a promotion; and two percent reported being denied access to a training opportunity. Employment income is lower for men and women with disabilities than for their same-gender counterparts at every age.[41]

In the 1991 census, nine percent of adults in Canada were visible minorities.[42] Recent statistics indicate that although visible minorities, 75 percent of whom are immigrants, possess higher educational qualifications, on average, than those who are not visible minorities, they have the highest unemployment rates.[43] Many obtain employment in jobs that do not take full advantage of their skills and qualifications. This is known as **underemployment**. Systemic barriers that have a negative impact on employment opportunities for visible minorities range from culturally-biased aptitude tests, to language-skills demands in excess of job requirements, to lack of recognition of credentials gained elsewhere. Three recent studies also found, however, that racial-minority men earn less than whites, even when they were born and raised in Canada. All three studies accounted for factors that might cause legitimate pay differentials, such as age, occupation, education, experience, and language ability.[44]

A number of jurisdictions passed two categories of legislation after realizing that simply leveling the playing field would not correct these patterns. The first type of legislation, employment equity, is aimed at identifying and eliminating systemic barriers to employment opportunities that adversely affect these four groups. The second, pay equity, focuses on mechanisms to redress the imbalance in pay between male-dominated and female-dominated job classes res[..] the undervaluing of work traditionally performed by women.

Employment Equity

http://info.load-otea. hrdc-drhc.gc.ca/~weeweb/ lege.htm
Federal Employment Equity Law

In 1983, the federal government appointed a royal commission, chaired by Judge Rosalie Abella, to review the employment practices of federal crown and government-owned operations. Its report, tabled in 1984, made recommendations about how the four traditionally disadvantaged groups identified above could be brought into the mainstream of Canada's labour force. The commission recommended that legislation be enacted to cover all federally-regulated employers and urged provincial governments to pass similar legislation. The commission also recommended the use of the term "employment equity" to distinguish Canada's approach from that found in the United States, known as "affirmative action." Affirmative action was often associated with quotas, described later in this chapter, which had become a divisive political issue.[45]

Employment Equity Act
Federal legislation, proclaimed in August of 1987, the intent of which is to remove employment barriers and promote equality for the members of four designated groups: women, visible minorities, Aboriginal people, and persons with disabilities.

Employment Equity Act The federal **Employment Equity Act** was proclaimed in August of 1987. Its intent is to remove employment barriers and promote equality for the members of the four designated groups. The Act requires employers under federal jurisdiction, with more than 100 employees, to develop annual plans setting out specific goals to achieve better representation of the designated group members at all levels of the organization, and timetables for goal implementation. The Act further requires that employers submit an annual report to the Employment Equity Branch of Human Resources Development Canada (HRDC) describing their progress in meeting their self-set goals. These reports, forwarded to the Canadian Human Rights Commission by HRDC, must indicate the representation of members of the designated groups by occupational groups and salary ranges, and information on those hired, promoted, and terminated. Employers are required to retain each plan and all records used to prepare their annual reports for a period of at least three years. Employers who do not comply may be investigated by the Human Rights Commission and, if necessary, prosecuted under the Canadian Human Rights Act. In addition, the Human Rights Commission has the authority to monitor for compliance through the use of random audits.[46]

Federal Contractors Program
A provision of the Employment Equity Act that requires firms with 100 or more employees wishing to bid on federal contracts of $200 000 or more to certify in writing their commitment to employment equity, and to implement an employment equity program as a condition of the bid.

Federal Contractors Program A large number of employers under provincial/territorial jurisdiction are subject to federal employment equity requirements. Under the **Federal Contractors Program**, a provision of the Employment Equity Act, firms with 100 or more employees wishing to bid on federal contracts of $200 000 or more are required to certify in writing their commitment to employment equity and must implement an employment equity program as a condition of the bid. Companies with contracts to provide the federal government with goods or services are subject to random on-site compliance reviews. If such a review reveals that an employer has failed to implement an employment equity program, sanctions are applied, including exclusion of the employer from future government contracts.[47]

One firm that has exhibited exemplary performance under the Federal Contractors Program is Connaught Laboratories, featured in the HR and the Responsive Organization box.

Commitment to Equity at Connaught Laboratories Limited

Connaught Laboratories has been recognized on multiple occasions for its employment equity initiatives under the Federal Contractors Program. In 1993, Connaught took top honours, receiving the federal Vision award.

The fact that the application to the awards program was a joint union-management effort may have contributed to the firm's receipt of this prestigious award. According to Mella Gilheany-O'Neill, Supervisor of Organizational Development, Diversity and Employee Communications, Connaught has made tremendous strides in its efforts to raise awareness of diversity issues as a result of partnership with its union—Local 1701 of the Communications, Energy, and Paperworkers Union.

For example, Connaught has established a joint union-management diversity council that helps to direct initiatives aimed at building awareness of diversity issues in the company. When the council was launched a few years ago, "the union president was very supportive and she joined the council," says Gilheany-O'Neill.

Connaught's initiatives to improve representation of all designated groups include an agreement with the union to allow two six-month work placements per year per designated group to give people from outside the firm an opportunity to acquire work experience.

The initial focus at Connaught was on awareness-building activities, such as articles in the company newsletter under a special diversity logo, cafeteria displays on diversity issues, and the development of a special diversity newsletter that provides updates on the company's demographic statistics. While awareness initiatives will continue, the emphasis at Connaught has now shifted to employee training.

Source: Claudine Kapel, "Variation is the Theme, *Human Resources Professional* 11, no. 3 (April 1994), pp. 10–1.

Employment Equity Programs Mandatory equity programs are virtually nonexistent in provincial and territorial jurisdictions. Quebec has a contract compliance program. A far-reaching, proactive employment equity law enacted in Ontario under an NDP government, which received proclamation on September 1, 1994, was subsequently repealed by the Progressive Conservative government during the fall of 1995. All provincially-regulated employers were covered, including the provincial government and its agencies, except broader public sector employers with fewer than 10 employees; private sector employers with fewer than 50 employees; and police forces covered by the Police Services Act.

Voluntary employment equity programs are legalized under the human rights legislation in most Canadian jurisdictions. Provincial/territorial human rights commissions often provide assistance to employers wishing to implement such initiatives.

Many employers not legally required to implement an employment equity program, such as Sir Sandford Fleming College in Peterborough, Ontario, have done so voluntarily, believing that it makes good business sense. From a practical point of view, employers seldom benefit by excluding people who belong to a

www.ohrc.on.ca
Ontario Human Rights Commission

particular group, such as women or visible minorities, since that limits the labour pool from which to select employees. Being perceived to be discriminatory can also lead to negative public relations for a firm, consumer boycotts, and/or government intervention.

employment equity program
A detailed plan designed to identify and correct existing discrimination, redress past discrimination, and achieve a balanced representation of designated group members in the organization.

The Implementation of Employment Equity An **employment equity program** is designed to identify and correct existing discrimination, redress past discrimination, and achieve a balanced representation of designated group members in the organization. An employment equity program is much more than a formal document prepared by a specialist in HRM. It is a major change-management exercise. Successful implementation requires that employment equity be incorporated in the organization's strategic planning process.[48] A deliberately structured process is involved, tailored to suit the unique needs of the firm, which includes six main steps:

1. Obtaining senior management commitment and support
2. Data collection and analysis
3. An employment systems review
4. Plan development
5. implementation, and
6. A follow-up process encompassing monitoring, evaluation, and revision.

Different groups within an organization should be involved in the implementation process, including senior management, human resources specialists, all other managers and supervisors, and union/nonunion employee representatives.

Step One: Obtaining Senior Management Commitment and Support Senior management's total commitment to employment equity is essential to a program's success. This commitment should be made explicit in the organization's policy statement and supporting documentation; however, senior management must also show visible support throughout the process, and assume overall responsibility and accountability for program results.

Written Policy A written policy, endorsed by senior management, strategically posted throughout the organization or distributed to every employee, is an essential first step. Sir Sandford Fleming College's employment equity policy, shown in **Figure 3.7**, illustrates how such a policy statement can convey senior management's approval of and commitment to the program's development and successful implementation.

Since employees at all levels often have concerns about the implications of employment equity, the policy statement should be supplemented by various communications initiatives. All employees need to know the rationale for the program, types of activities that might be involved, implications for present and future employees, and the names of contact persons. Employees must be assured that information obtained for employment equity purposes will be treated confidentially, published only as aggregate data, and not used for anything else.

Assignment of Staff Responsibility An organization should appoint a senior official to whom overall responsibility and authority for program design and implementation is assigned. Since this individual must have the status and authority necessary to gain the trust and cooperation of managers, supervisors, employees, and union representatives, many firms ensure that he or she has direct access to the chief executive officer. At Canadian National, for example, the Vice-President of Employment Equity reports to the President.[49]

Figure 3.7
Sample Employment
Equity Policy

Source: Sir Sandford Fleming
College, Peterborough,
Ontario. Used with
permission.

SIR SANDFORD FLEMING COLLEGE
POLICY MANUAL

Policy No.   3-310   Approved by: Board of Governors
Page No.   1 of 1   Supersedes: _____

Date Approved: _____
Subject: Employment Equity

The College Has as its goals the hiring, promotion, and professional development of all employees in order to achieve an equitable distribution of women, men, racial and cultural minorities, Aboriginal Peoples, and persons with disabilities throughout the institution, and to eliminate barriers to full and equal participation.

In order for a program to be successful, however, every department manager and supervisor must be assigned accountability and responsibility for program results, since they are the ones who hire, train, interact on a daily basis with, and evaluate employees. One way to accomplish this is to require supervisory and managerial personnel to establish employment equity goals and timetables for their particular area of responsibility and to measure their progress in meeting these targets as part of their performance appraisal process.

Many organizations have found that the best way to build commitment is to form an Employment Equity Committee, with representatives from all levels and areas of the organization. Such committees are generally given responsibility for reviewing policies and practices, making recommendations, and reporting on issues. Ultimate authority, however, usually rests with senior management.

Employers covered by the Employment Equity Act are legally obligated to consult with designated employee representatives, or in unionized settings, the bargaining agent(s). Employee involvement from the beginning helps to build commitment and support.

Communication   Internal communication strategies should be developed that are appropriate for the organization. These might include periodic information sessions, workshops, small group or departmental discussions, poster displays, videos, brochures, newsletters, and memorandums from union officials. Once in place, the employment equity program should be explained at new-employee orientation sessions and in the organization's employee handbook.

Organizations committed to employment equity often wish to communicate this fact externally, as well, in their promotional material, annual report, and recruitment advertising.

stock data
Data that provide a snapshot of the organization at a particular point in time, in terms of how many designated group members are employed, in what occupations, and at what levels and salaries.

flow data
Data tracking designated group members by employment transactions and outcomes.

Step Two: Data Collection and Analysis   The development of an internal work force profile is essential in employment equity planning. Without this data it is impossible to compare internal representation with external work force availability data, set reasonable goals, or measure progress. Profiles must be based on both stock and flow data. **Stock data** provide a snapshot of the organization at a particular point in time, in terms of how many designated group members are employed, in what occupations, and at what levels and salaries. **Flow data** track designated group members by employment transactions and outcomes. This involves determining how many designated group members apply for jobs with the firm, are interviewed, hired, given opportunities for training, promoted, and terminated.

While most information necessary for employment equity planning, such as gender, occupational and career history within the firm, and pay, is available from human resources and payroll files, to obtain data pertaining to the distribution of designated group members a self-identification process is generally used. Under the Employment Equity Act, employers may collect such data, as long as employees voluntarily agree to be identified or identify themselves as designated group members, and the data are only used for employment equity planning and reporting purposes.

Prior to administering a self-identification questionnaire, a climate of trust is essential. Since individuals may fear that self-identification will lead to future discriminatory treatment, a guarantee of confidentiality and an explanation of the importance of the information and ways in which it will be used is critical. The types of information that should be included in the questionnaire are shown in **Figure 3.8**.

Once the self-identification forms have been collected, the data must be organized according to four-digit National Occupational Classification (NOC) groupings, which involves classifying all of the organization's jobs in accordance with the NOC manual developed by Statistics Canada. Once jobs have been classified, a work force profile can be compiled.

The Employment Equity Computerized Reporting System (EECRS), described in the Information Technology and HR box, is available to assist employers complying with federal government requirements. Numerous other software packages have been developed for employment equity data storage and reporting purposes. Virtually all of the Human Resources Information Systems (HRIS) sold in Canada have employment equity modules, along with other applications.[50]

Figure 3.8
Contents of an
Employment Equity
Self-Identification
Questionnaire

Source: Based on *Employment Equity: A Guide for Employers*, (Ottawa: Employment and Immigration Canada, May 1991), Cat. No. LM-143, p. 17.

- an explanation of the organization's employment equity policy, the purpose of the employment equity program, and the need for the information requested
- a guarantee that the information supplied will be kept confidential and only used for employment equity purposes
- self-identification categories, with brief definitions and examples
- space for comments and suggestions
- an indication that the form has been reviewed by the relevant human rights agency, and approved by the bargaining agent(s), where applicable
- the name of the contact person(s) for clarification or further explanation

Information Technology and HR
Employment Equity Reporting

The Employment Equity Computerized Reporting System (EECRS) is a stand-alone system that is well supported technically, user-friendly, and tailored to comply with government reporting requirements. It is used by about 65 percent of federally regulated companies. The software and technical support are free, as is FCPCS (Federal Contractor Program Computer Software).

Source: Linda Gutri, "Training for Equity," *Human Resources Professional* 9, no. 2 (February 1993), p. 14.◆

Data must also be collected on the number of designated group members available in the labour markets from which the organization recruits. As discussed in chapter 1, the labour markets for various positions within the firm may be quite different. While clerical and technical personnel are often recruited locally, the search for managerial and professional employees may be national or international in scope. External labour force availability data may be obtained from Statistics Canada, HRDC, women's directorates in various jurisdictions, and agencies providing specialized assistance to various designated group members.

The comparison of the internal work force profile with external work force availability is called a **utilization analysis**. This type of comparison is necessary in order to determine the degree of underutilization and concentration of designated group members in specific occupations or at particular organizational levels, in proportion to their numbers in the labour market.

Step Three: Employment Systems Review   It is essential that the organization undertake a comprehensive **employment systems review**. Corporate policies and procedures manuals, collective agreements, and informal practices all have to be examined, to determine their impact on designated group members, so that existing intentional or systemic barriers can be eliminated. Typically, employment systems that require review include:

- job classifications and descriptions
- recruitment and selection processes
- performance appraisal systems
- training and development programs
- transfer and promotion procedures
- compensation policies and practices
- discipline and termination procedures, and
- access to assistance, benefits, and facilities.

To assist in identifying systemic barriers, the following questions should be asked about every system under review:[51]

- Is it job related?
- Is it valid? (Is it directly related to job performance?)
- Is it applied consistently?
- Does it have adverse impact on designated group members?
- Is it a business necessity? (Is it necessary for the safe and efficient operation of the business?)
- Does it conform to human rights legislation?

Step Four: Plan Development   Once the work force profile and systems reviews have been completed, the employment equity plan can be prepared.

Goals and Timetables   Goals and timetable are the core of an employment equity program, since they help to ensure that changes in representation become a reality. Goals, ranging from short to long term in duration, should be flexible and tied to reasonable timetables. Goals are not **quotas**.[52] First of all, they are not imposed on the organization. Secondly, they are estimates of the results that experts in the firm have established based on knowledge of the workplace and its employees, the availability of individuals with the skills and abilities required by the firm in the external labour force, and the special measures that are planned.

Quantitative goals should be set, specifying the number or percentage of qualified designated group members to be hired, trained, or promoted into each occupational group within a specified period of time. Qualitative goals, referred to as special measures, should also be included.

Special Measures   There are three types of special measures which should be implemented:

1. **Positive Measures** are initiatives designed to accelerate the entry, development, and promotion of designated group members, aimed at overcoming the residual effects of past discrimination. Providing special training programs or mentoring opportunities to assist designated group members to break the glass ceiling, and targeted recruitment, are examples. Positive measures are intended to hasten the achievement of fair representation of the designated group members in an employer's work force.

2. **Accommodation Measures** are strategies to assist designated group members. Employment policies and practices may have to be adjusted so that no individual is denied benefits, disadvantaged in terms of employment opportunities, or prevented from carrying out the essential duties of the job. Accommodation measures might include job redesign; reassignment of a few job duties; adjusting a work schedule; upgrading facilities; or providing technical, human, or financial support services.

3. **Supportive Measures** are strategies that enable all employees to achieve a better balance between work and other responsibilities and activities. Flexible schedules are an example. They accommodate employees with parenting and eldercare responsibilities; those taking courses on a part-time basis who need to take an occasional day course to complete their degree or diploma requirements; and those who prefer to work long hours early in the week so they can spend Friday afternoons skiing or on the golf course! In northern Canada, some firms have adopted very innovative work schedules so that their First Peoples employees can take part in traditional fishing and hunting activities.

   A tuition advance or reimbursement program is another example. Some firms make the upgrading of skills and knowledge even more accessible by providing allowances for texts and supplies and/or childcare expenses.

Step Five: Implementation   Implementation is the process that transforms goals and timetables and special measures into reality. Implementation strategies will be different in every organization, due to each organization's unique culture and climate. The success of plan implementation is dependent on such factors as senior management commitment, effectiveness of the communication strategies selected, and commitment of lower-level managers and the employment equity committee members. Other factors include the amount of acceptance gained for the special measures planned, and whether or not sufficient resources have been allocated—both financial and human. Those with overall responsibility and accountability for the plan guide the implementation process. The plan should not be seen as "engraved in stone," but rather a document that may need to be modified or revised periodically.

Step Six: Monitoring, Evaluating, and Revising   An effective employment equity program requires a control system so that progress and success, or lack thereof, can be evaluated. Through program monitoring, employers can assess the overall success of equity initiatives aimed at achieving a representative work force and respond to changes in the internal and/or external environment. The monitoring process may involve activities such as a review of flow data on job applications, selection decisions, training, promotions, and terminations. It may also include personal interviews with managers and selected designated group members;

committee review of management progress reports; a review of managerial performance appraisal ratings on employment equity initiatives; and examination of statistical summaries of projected versus actual goal attainment.

Periodic reports (perhaps quarterly) should be issued to update all employees regarding progress and inform them about upcoming special projects or results of completed projects. Outstanding achievements should be given special recognition. This heightens the visibility of the programs and helps to build employee acceptance and management commitment. Annual progress reports should be produced and shared with all employees.

Benefits of Employment Equity   Employment equity makes good business sense, since it contributes to the bottom line. In the words of Robert Rochon, Director of Employment Equity at National Grocers Co. Ltd.:[53]

> *Regardless of any legislative requirement, [employment equity] is a good business decision for us. When you consider the changing face of Canada, it just makes good business sense to reflect the customers that you serve.*

Some of the benefits derived from implementing employment equity include being able to attract and keep the best-qualified employees, which results in greater access to a broader base of skills. Other benefits include higher employee morale due to special measures employed, such as flexible work schedules or job sharing; and improved corporate image in the community.[54]

Impact of Employment Equity   According to the Canadian Human Rights Commission 1995 annual report, employment equity can make a difference:[55]

The representation of women in the federally regulated sector improved, rising from 41.1 percent in 1987 to 44.4 percent in 1994. Although this was slightly below the availability estimate of almost 46 percent, it still represents a substantial increase. Women's presence in senior management grew markedly from only 4.8 percent in 1987 to 12.3 percent in 1994, although this was still less than half of their estimated availability.

Between 1987 and 1994, the total number of visible minority members reported in the federal work force increased by two-thirds, from 29 663 to 49 274. Their representation went from five percent to over eight percent, approaching their labour force availability rate of approximately nine percent.

Unfortunately, Aboriginal people and persons with disabilities did not fare as well. Although the share of the total work force of First Peoples increased from 0.7 percent to 1.1 percent over eight years, this added up to only about one-third of their availability in the Canadian labour force. This group also experienced a disproportionately high termination rate. Although there was an increase in employment of persons with disabilities from 1.6 percent in 1987 to 2.6 percent in 1994, their level of representation still compared very poorly with an available labour force of 6.5 percent. Moreover, much of this increase was a result of an improved rate of self-identification among current employees.

Pay Equity

A study released by Statistics Canada in January of 1997 confirmed that the overall wage gap between men and women remains substantial: women working full time in 1996 took home an average of just 73.4 cents for every dollar earned by their male counterparts.[56] On average, men earn more than women in 513 of 524 occupations. According to Statistics Canada analysts, almost 90 percent of this differential cannot be accounted for by such factors as differences in occupational mix, educational attainment, or experience, and is attributable to "something built into either the work system or the whole labour market."[57] Pay equity legislation is aimed at reducing the "unaccounted for" portion of the wage differential.

pay equity
Providing equal pay to male-dominated job classes and female-dominated job classes of equal value to the employer.

Pay equity, also known as equal pay for work of equal or comparable value, is designed to augment the "equal pay for equal work" legislation mentioned at the beginning of this chapter. In some jurisdictions, such as Ontario, pay equity is covered under separate legislation. For employers under federal jurisdiction, however, pay equity was incorporated into the human rights legislation through an amendment to the Act in 1978. The federal jurisdiction, Quebec, and Ontario have the most comprehensive pay equity legislation, covering virtually all public and private-sector employers. Nova Scotia, Prince Edward Island, Manitoba, and the Yukon have laws that are restricted to the public sector.

As will be explained in detail in chapter 12, pay equity requires an employer to provide equal pay to male-dominated job classes and female-dominated job classes of equal value, on the basis of skill, effort, responsibility, and working conditions. The focus is on eliminating the historical income gap between male-dominated and female-dominated jobs attributable to the undervaluing of work traditionally performed by women. For example, the federal government spent $2.4 million in a pay equity settlement involving 390 federal library science employees (a female-dominated job) who earned less than the male-dominated job of historical researcher, which was found to be of equal value.[58] As this example illustrates, pay equity often requires comparing jobs that are quite different in content. See chapter 12 for details.

The federal pay equity legislation applies to all organizations under federal jurisdiction, regardless of size. It involves a complaint-based system, which means that action is taken once a complaint has been filed by an individual, a group of employees, or a bargaining agent.[59] The largest complaint involving a private company under the federal pay equity law was filed with the CHRC by the two unions at Bell Canada in 1994. Still unresolved at the time of writing, the complaint is based on a 1992 report in which the company and unions documented that 20 000 individuals working as operators, clerks, and salespersons, all female-dominated occupations, earned between $1.80 and $5.00 less per hour than those in male-dominated jobs assessed to be of equal value. One of the unions estimates that a ruling against the company could cost Bell between $400 and $500 million.[60]

Impact of Equal Opportunity and Equity on HRM

Functional Impact

Virtually every HR function is affected by equal opportunity and equity legislation. Human rights legislation applies to all aspects, and terms and conditions of employment. Pay equity affects job evaluation and compensation administration, and employment equity systems reviews involve examination of all policies, procedures, and practices in the workplace. Implementing required changes necessitates much more than document revision. Understanding, acceptance, and commitment are essential, which means that education and communication must be given high priority.

Reverse Discrimination

When organizations decide to adopt a "quota" approach to employment equity, as at the Ontario College of Art, which decided to hire only women for a ten-year

reverse discrimination
Giving preference to designated group members to the extent that nonmembers believe they are being discriminated against.

period to correct a grave imbalance in the ratio of male to female faculty members,[61] or when a specific numerical goal is imposed to overcome past discrimination, as in the case of Canadian National Railways (CN),[62] the employer may be accused of **reverse discrimination**. This involves giving preference to designated group members to the extent that nonmembers believe they are being discriminated against.

In August of 1984, a federal human rights tribunal issued its first decision in Canadian history with regard to a mandatory employment equity program. CN was ordered to hire women for one in four nontraditional or blue-collar jobs in its St. Lawrence region until they held 13 percent of such jobs, the proportion of women in blue-collar jobs in industry in general. At the time, women represented approximately four percent of CN's blue-collar employees. CN was also required to implement a series of special measures, ranging from changing advertising techniques for available jobs to abandoning certain mechanical aptitude tests that had adverse impact on female applicants. This decision was upheld by the Supreme Court of Canada when appealed by CN.

Charges of reverse discrimination place HR managers in a difficult position. On the one hand, they are responsible for eliminating concentration and underutilization resulting from past discriminatory practices. On the other hand, they must also deal with those who feel disadvantaged because of special measures for designated group members. Preferential treatment will always raise questions of fairness; however, the Canadian Human Rights Act and provincial/territorial human rights legislation declare employment equity programs to be nondiscriminatory if they fulfil the spirit of the law.

It is possible to avoid the entire issue of reverse discrimination if the approach taken to employment equity is not one of quotas, the adoption of which by many firms has given affirmative action such a mixed reaction in the United States. Canadian legislation does not require quotas; rather, it specifies that organizations are to establish reasonable goals and timetables, based on external labour force availability data. In fact, Section 33 of the federal Employment Equity Act explicitly provides that neither the CHRC nor the Tribunal may "impose a quota on an employer"; nor can either require the public service "to hire or promote persons without basing the hiring or promotion on selection according to merit."[63] When goals are seen as targets, not quotas, the end result is that a better-qualified candidate who is not a protected group member is never denied an employment-related opportunity. On the contrary, when there are two *equally qualified candidates, based on nondiscriminatory job specifications and selection criteria*, preference will be given to the designated group member. The term "equally qualified" needs to be explained, since it does not necessarily imply identical educational qualifications or years of work experience, but rather possessing the qualifications required to perform the job. Thus, if a job requires two years of previous related experience, the candidate with four years of related experience is no more qualified than the individual with two.

Imperial Oil has adopted a very realistic approach to employment equity, aimed at ensuring fairness for all of its employees, described in the Building Employee Commitment box.

Building Employee Commitment

Imperial Oil's Approach to Employment Equity

A significant aspect of the employment equity efforts at Imperial Oil is that the company has not set quotas for hiring or promoting members of designated groups. Instead, the company measures its progress by monitoring the representation of designated groups in the company's overall statistics for recruitment, promotions, and departures.

"For an organization that's gone from 14 500 employees to 8 400 employees, setting absolute targets is very difficult," says John Crockett, Employment Equity Advisor. "We thought it would be more meaningful to have goals with respect to recruiting, promotion, and attrition. It's like measuring who gets in, who gets ahead, and who leaves."

"Our goal is not to influence the numbers directly, because we feel that's got a lot of problems," says Crockett. "That sets up a negative environment for both white males and members of designated groups. And forcing numbers doesn't deal with the underlying issues that cause the bias in the first place."

For example, after Imperial Oil merged with Texaco Canada in 1990, the company needed to trim its ranks. A financial package was developed for employees who were willing to leave voluntarily. No targets were set as to how many members of the four designated groups the firm wished to retain. However, past experience with corporate downsizings had taught the HR staff that voluntary departure packages generally resulted in a much higher response rate from female than male employees. Since Imperial had not previously published a consolidated list of the different work options for which employees could apply, a factor that might influence departure decisions, the unveiling of the voluntary leave package was synchronized with extensive communication on the company's alternative work arrangement policies.

Several other company initiatives converged within this time frame: a two-hour information session for employees explaining Imperial's revised harassment policy; employee-driven employment systems reviews; and training on diversity issues.

Imperial's overall goal was to demonstrate its commitment to a work environment that supports all employees. The company wanted to avoid creating a situation whereby anyone who opted to leave felt compelled to do so. "If you were a member of a designated group, you'd certainly see that the corporation was undertaking a number of initiatives, on a number of fronts, to create a supportive work environment," says Crockett.

Source: Claudine Kapel, "Variation is the Theme, *Human Resources Professional* 11, no. 3 (April 1994), p. 12.

Managerial Decision Making

Front-line supervisors and other managers may feel a loss of authority in firms that have not done a good job of educating these employees, or have not built responsibility for employment equity results into their performance appraisals.[64] In such cases, to achieve the objectives of the plan, specialists from the HR department may have the final say in hiring and promotion decisions. Since this approach can have a detrimental impact on the quality of the work environment, it should be avoided.[65]

A characteristic of successful employment and pay equity programs is that there is commitment on the part of all managers across the organization. This requires extensive education and training.

The Role of the HR Department

The HR department is generally assigned overall responsibility for legal compliance with human rights legislation and employment equity program results—whether voluntary or legally required—as well as pay equity plan implementation. It is the HR department staff who are expected to keep up-to-date with changing regulations, court decisions, and emerging legal developments.

The HR department staff generally take a leadership role in acquiring information, establishing communication and training strategies, developing programs to ensure company compliance, and government reporting. However, all supervisory and managerial personnel should be assigned responsibility and held accountable for compliance with human rights legislation; collecting accurate information about jobs for pay equity purposes; establishing employment equity goals and timetables, and attaining measurable results within their work area or department.

Managing Diversity

diversity management
Broader and more inclusive in scope than employment equity, it involves a set of activities designed to integrate all members of an organization's multicultural work force and use their diversity to enhance the firm's effectiveness.

Although many people perceive "management of diversity" to be another term for employment equity, the two are very distinct. Managing diversity goes far beyond legal compliance or even implementing an employment equity plan voluntarily. **Diversity management** is broader and more inclusive in scope. It involves a set of activities designed to integrate all members of an organization's multicultural work force and use their diversity to enhance the firm's effectiveness.

As discussed in chapter 1, the ethnocultural profile of Canada has been changing since the 1960s, and will continue to change dramatically over the next twenty years. Canada has seen continued immigration from many lands during the last four decades. Managers at organizations ranging from McDonald's to Holiday Inn, and Bell Canada to Levi Strauss, are learning not only to understand their kaleidoscopic work force but also to manage in diverse work environments. While there are ethical and social responsibility issues involved in embracing diversity, it also makes economic sense, in terms of globalization of world trade and the increasing ethnocultural diversity of Canadian markets.[66]

According to Marie Tellier, Canadian National's Assistant Vice-President of Employment Equity,[67]

The hiring and development and good management of a diverse work force whose values and expectations are different from their managers is no longer an option—it is an economic necessity. By the year 2000, 70 to 80 percent of new arrivals in the work market will be women and non-whites. In this context, diversity management . . . is a necessity imposed by market laws, by competition, and by the need to be the best to survive.

Money talks, and one economic reason for embracing diversity has to do with purchasing power. It is predicted that by 2001, the spending power of Canada's visible minorities will be $300 billion.[68] Employees with different ethnic backgrounds often also possess

Diversity is an asset.

foreign-language skills, knowledge of different cultures and business practices, and may even have established trade links in other nations, which can lead to competitive advantage. Ebco, a manufacturing company in Richmond, British Columbia, for example, was able to tap the networks and skills of its employees to gain business in Germany and Taiwan.[69]

More and more firms, including Digital Equipment and the Bank of Montreal, recognize the moral and economic value of having a work force representative of their clientele. In the words of Edgar Ware, Ethnocultural Business Manager at Digital Equipment of Canada,[70] "We have an obligation to the cultural fabric . . . Digital's plan is to balance diversity in its work force with strategic market segments . . . We want to look like the people we sell to." Doing so not only makes clients more comfortable with the organization, but also may help the firm to identify differences in customer needs or preferences that might otherwise be overlooked. At Levi Strauss, for example, the Dockers line of casual pants, now worth more than $1 billion a year, has been credited to ideas obtained from Argentinean employees.[71]

A third reason for embracing diversity is that visible minorities can help to increase an organization's competitiveness and international savvy in the global business arena. Specifically, cultural diversity can help fine-tune product design, marketing, and ultimately customer satisfaction.[72] A dramatic example is provided in the Diversity Counts box.

Although embracing employee diversity offers opportunities to enhance organizational effectiveness, transforming an organizational culture presents a set of challenges that must be handled properly. Diversity initiatives should be undertaken slowly, since they involve a complex change process. Resistance to change may have to be overcome, along with stereotyped beliefs or prejudices, and employee resentment. The aim is to ensure group cohesiveness, effective communication, retention of outstanding performers, and maximum opportunity for all employees.

Organizations that have been most successful in managing diversity tend to share a number of characteristics, including top management commitment, diversity training programs, inclusive and representative communications, activities to celebrate diversity, support groups or mentoring programs, diversity audits, and management responsibility and accountability.

Diversity Counts
In International Marketing

"Apple Computer might have offended 1.7 billion potential consumers in the growing computer markets of India and the Middle East, had it marketed a piece of seemingly harmless audio software called a 'Moof'," says Santiago Rodriguez, Apple's director of multicultural programs, based in Cupertino, California.

The Moof, which was quickly pulled off the market, was a phonetic combination of a "moo" and a "woof." The "cow-dog" utterance might have been offensive to both Hindus (to whom cows are sacred), and Muslims (to whom dogs are filthy creatures).◆

Source: Jana Schilder, "The Rainbow Connection," *Human Resources Professional* 11, no. 3 (April 1994), pp. 13–4.

Top Management Commitment

As with any major change initiative, unless there is commitment from the top, it is unlikely that other management staff will become champions of diversity. It is no coincidence that organizations that have established themselves as leaders in diversity management, such as the Bank of Montreal, Ebco Industries, and Warner-Lambert Canada, Inc., have had senior-level commitment over an extended period of time.[73]

The fact that many organizations have not yet reached this point is evidenced by the results of a Conference Board of Canada study published in April 1995, which indicated that only six percent of the 466 organizations surveyed included reference to work force diversity in their mission statements, and 86 percent indicated that the HR department was responsible for diversity issues.[74]

Diversity Training Programs

Diversity Training Programs are designed to provide awareness of diversity issues and to educate employees about specific gender and cultural differences and appropriate ways to handle them. Supervisors must be taught strategies to effectively manage and motivate a diverse group of employees. Often, it is appropriate to bring in an outside consulting firm with the requisite expertise to provide the training, at least initially. Renee Bazile-Jones, Partner and Executive Vice President of Omnibus Consulting Inc., says the reason employers hire Omnibus to conduct diversity training seminars for them is because:[75]

> They want to ensure that their employees understand the business case for diversity. Our clients also want employees to understand the bottom-line impact of creating an equitable employment system, its link to valuing diversity, and ramifications on performance . . . Employers also want their employees to identify and eliminate barriers to the achievement of an equitable employment system . . . Our training program creates the link between recognizing and acknowledging differences and the impact on productivity.

To be successful, diversity training must be ongoing, not a one-day workshop. Elements of diversity must be incorporated into all core training programs, based on the needs of specific business units or employee groups.[77]

Specific Strategies

Inclusive and Representative Communications Organizations wishing to incorporate the value of diversity into their corporate culture must ensure that all of their internal communications and external publications convey this message. Inclusive language, such as gender-neutral terms and broad representation in terms of age, gender, race, etc. in company publications are strategies used.

Activities to Celebrate Diversity In addition, diversity must be celebrated in organizational activities. During the Convocation Ceremonies at Sir Sandford Fleming College in Peterborough, Ontario, for example, a traditional First Nations' blessing and tribute play a prominent role.

Support Groups or Mentoring Programs An aim of diversity programs is to ensure that employees encounter a warm organizational climate, not one that is insensitive to their culture or background. To ensure that no one experiences feelings of alienation, isolation, or tokenism, support groups have been established in some firms to provide a nurturing climate and a means for employees who share the same background to find one another.

Some firms, such as Canadian National, have established mentoring programs, through which senior managers identify promising diversity group employees and play a key role in nurturing their career progress. Others have begun mentoring or apprenticeship programs for lower-level employees. Xerox Canada partners with community colleges to provide technical training. The colleges provide students with basic knowledge about electronics and Xerox provides practical work experience. Some of its entry-level jobs have also been restructured so they have fewer technical requirements. Warner-Lambert works with the Scarborough Board of Education's co-op program for students with disabilities to integrate them into the work environment. The school board trains supervisors and coworkers to deal with the students and their individual needs.[77]

diversity audit
An audit to assess the effectiveness of an organization's diversity initiatives.

Diversity Audit To assess the effectiveness of an organization's diversity initiatives, **diversity audits** should be conducted. Evaluation criteria used most often by Canadian firms are increases in awareness of diversity initiatives and acceptance of designated-group member coworkers as measured by employee attitude surveys; recruitment statistics; reduction in turnover among designated-group employees; increases in promotions of designated-group member employees; reduction in the number of harassment complaints; and productivity improvements.[78]

Management Responsibility and Accountability

Just as with employment equity, diversity management initiatives will not receive high priority unless managers and supervisors are held accountable and results are part of their formal assessment.

Managing Diversity in International Businesses

An issue that an increasing number of organizations are having to confront is ensuring that the rights of all of their employees around the world are respected, and that operations outside of Canada meet acceptable labour and human rights standards. As described in the Global HRM box, a few organizations deserve commendation; many others are failing miserably in this regard.[79] Tips for managers wishing to establish a code of conduct for their international operations are included as **Figure 3.9**.

Figure 3.9
Management Tips: On Protection of International Rights

Source: Based on Lynne Sullivan, "Canadian Companies Get a Failing Grade in Protecting International Rights," *Canadian HR Reporter* 10, no. 12 (June 16, 1997), p. 16. Copyright MPL Communications Inc., Reproduced by permission of *Canadian HR Reporter* 133 Richmond Street West, Toronto, Ontario M5H 3M8.

To stand themselves in good stead in terms of attention to labour standards and human rights, companies with international operations should:

- have a corporate code of conduct, which includes labour and human rights issues
- make sure the code applies internationally as well as domestically
- ensure there are adequate enforcement mechanisms, including external audit
- educate key implementers, those advising and assisting implementers, and those responsible for enforcement
- educate the local work force about their rights . . . workers cannot exercise rights of which they are unaware.

Global HRM

Canadian Companies Get a Failing Grade in Protecting International Rights

A report based on a survey by the Canadian Lawyers Association for Human Rights and Canada's International Centre for Human Rights and Democratic Development gives Canadian companies a failing grade for their attention to labour standards and human rights in their international operations.

Of the 43 respondents, 21 have codes of conduct that deal with international operations. All respondents are large companies with operations outside of Canada, including foreign investment, joint ventures, and sourcing or purchasing relationships. Only 18 agreed that "international business has a role to play in promoting international human rights protection and sustainable development"—a curious position in light of business' often-expressed support for "constructive engagement" as a means of promoting better conditions for workers and democratic reforms.

Aside from not having codes at all, the other shortfalls are in the areas of enforcement and education. Furthermore, most companies rely on internal audit; their legal department; or supervisor surveillance, which can't be effective without education. Experience indicates, however, that an external audit, through auditors or community group consultation, is more valuable than all of the above methods.

A few organizations, however, are providing leadership in the protection of international rights. Those singled out for commendation include Ontario Hydro, Levi Strauss, and Reebok.

At the policy level, Ontario Hydro gets credit for comprehensive coverage, including fair wages and working conditions; health and safety standards; freedom of association; and respect for the rights of women, indigenous persons, and tribal people. Hydro also has a policy that it will not knowingly purchase materials or contract services involving violation of rights or social justice.

Levi Strauss stands out for its all-encompassing approach. Long known for its commitment to leadership in business ethics, Levi Strauss has guidelines covering both sourcing and country-of-operations selection. The sourcing guidelines cover environmental, ethical, health and safety, and labour standards, and involve formal "business-partner terms of engagement." These terms include policies for wages and benefits that reflect local law and practices; a refusal to use child, prison, or forced labour; assurances of nondiscrimination; guarantees that there will be no punishment or physical or mental coercion; and freedom of association.

Enforcement practices include detailed questionnaires for business partners, routine and surprise inspections, and contract termination. If Levi believes that a supplier has potential to improve, it will enter into a supervised improvement plan with a time line. Although not mentioned in the report, Levi also implements management training on a global basis, whereby new managers must take courses on management, ethics, and diversity.

Levi reports cancelling contracts with more than 30 suppliers and requiring improvement in more than 100 others. It has also implemented some imaginative solutions. For example, on finding underage workers in an operation in Bangladesh, the company paid the children to return to school and offered them jobs on graduation.

Reebok is another firm with proactive practices, backing up its statement that "human rights is a hallmark of our corporate culture" with initiatives such as a "witness" program, under which human rights activists are given video cameras, computers, and fax machines to engage in their advocacy.

A proponent of constructive engagement, Reebok uses its own people, outside auditors, interviews, and focus groups to superintend code provisions on nondiscrimination, fair wages, child labour, health and safety, and freedom of association.

Only 43 out of 98 firms responded to the survey, something the authors suggest relates to the fact that "Canadian business places a very low priority on communicating its response to issues it confronts in its overseas operation to the non-governmental sector." That may be, or it may be that many surveys get a low response rate. In fact, some non-respondents indicated that they are selective about the surveys in which they participate and others said they didn't have time to respond.

Source: Lynne Sullivan, "Canadian Companies Get a Failing Grade in Protecting International Rights," *Canadian HR Reporter* 10, no. 12 (June 16, 1997), pp. 11, 16. Copyright MPL Communications Inc., Reproduced by permission of *Canadian HR Reporter,* 133 Richmond Street West, Toronto, Ontario M5H 3M8.

Chapter Review

Summary

1. Employment (labour) standards laws exist in every jurisdiction. These laws establish minimum entitlements for employees and set some maximum levels in terms of hours of work per day and/or per week.

2. Every jurisdiction in Canada has incorporated the principle of equal pay for equal work in its employment standards or human rights legislation. Equal pay for equal work specifies that an employer cannot pay male and female employees differently if they are performing substantially the same work, requiring the same degree of skill, effort, and responsibility, under similar working conditions.

3. The Charter of Rights and Freedoms is the cornerstone of Canada's legislation pertaining to equal opportunity. The Charter applies directly only to the actions of all levels of government, and agencies under their jurisdiction, but because it takes precedence over all other laws, it is quite far-reaching in scope. The Supreme Court is the ultimate interpreter of the Charter. Charter issues on which the Supreme Court has ruled which have major implications for HRM include the right to bargain collectively and to strike, the right to picket, use of union dues, and mandatory retirement.

4. Every employer in Canada is affected by human rights legislation, a family of federal and provincial/territorial laws, which prohibit intentional and unintentional discrimination in all terms and conditions of employment. Prohibited grounds of discrimination common across all jurisdictions include race and colour, age, sex, marital status, and family status. Conviction records and having convictions for which pardons have been granted are protected grounds in some jurisdictions, as is sexual orientation. All jurisdictions prohibit discrimination on the basis of physical disability, and most also list mental handicap as a protected ground.

5. Employers are permitted to discriminate if employment preferences are based on bona fide occupational requirements (BFORs). BFORs get complicated in situations in which occupational requirements are not obvious. The onus of proof is then placed on the employer.

6. Employers are expected to make reasonable accommodations to the point of undue hardship. In unionized settings, the union and employer have a joint (but not equal) responsibility for accommodation.

7. Harassment includes a wide range of behaviour that a reasonable person ought to know is unwelcome; however, it also encompasses actions and activities that were once tolerated, ignored, and considered horseplay or innocent flirtation, provided the individual who feels that he or she is being harassed makes it clear that such behaviour is unwelcome and inappropriate, and asks that it be discontinued. Employers and managers have a responsibility to provide a safe and healthy working environment. If harassment is occurring, of which they are aware, or ought to have been aware, they can be charged, as well as the alleged harasser.

8. The type of harassment that has attracted the most attention in the workplace is sexual harassment, which can be divided into two categories: sexual coercion and sexual annoyance. All employers under federal jurisdiction are required by law to develop and implement sexual harassment policies. Many organizations are adopting harassment policies that encompass all of the prohibited grounds of discrimination.

9. There is a human rights commission in each jurisdiction with the authority to receive and investigate complaints, determine their validity, try to achieve a settlement between the parties, and if unsuccessful, to proceed to a board of inquiry or tribunal for resolution. If the allegation is substantiated, there are a wide range of remedies, including compensation for lost wages, general damages, complainant expenses, and pain and humiliation.

10. Federal legislation pertaining to equity includes the Employment Equity Act and Federal Contractors Program. Voluntary employment equity programs are legalized under the human rights legislation in most Canadian jurisdictions.

11. The steps involved in implementing an employment equity program include: obtaining senior management commitment and support, data collection and analysis, an employment systems review, plan development, plan implementation, and a follow-up process encompassing evaluation, monitoring, and revision.

12. Pay equity, also known as equal pay for work of equal or comparable value, requires an employer to provide equal pay to male-dominated job classes and female-dominated job classes of equal value, on the basis of skill, effort, responsibility, and working conditions. The focus is on eliminating the historical income gap between male-dominated and female-dominated jobs attributable to the undervaluing of work traditionally performed by women.

13. Reverse discrimination is an issue that employers can avoid if they establish reasonable goals and timetables, not quotas.

14. Diversity management is much broader and more inclusive than employment equity, involving a set of activities designed to integrate all members of a firm's multicultural work force and use their diversity to enhance organizational effectiveness. Characteristics of successful diversity management programs include top management commitment, diversity training, inclusive and representative communication, activities to celebrate diversity, support groups or mentoring programs, diversity audits, and management responsibility and accountability.

Key Terms

accommodation measures
bona fide occupational qualification (BFOQ)/ bona fide occupational requirement (BFOR)
Canadian Human Rights Act
Canadian Human Rights Commission (CHRC)
Charter of Rights and Freedoms
concentration
discrimination
diversity audit
diversity management
employment (labour) standards legislation
Employment Equity Act
employment equity program
employment systems review
equal pay for equal work
equality rights
Federal Contractors Program
flow data
glass ceiling
harassment
human rights legislation
intentional discrimination
occupational segregation
pay equity
positive measures

quotas
reasonable
  accommodation
reverse discrimination
sexual annoyance
sexual coercion

sexual harassment
stock data
supportive measures
underemployment
underutilization
undue hardship

unintentional/
  constructive/systemic
  discrimination
utilization analysis

Discussion Questions and Exercises

1. Explain what is meant by "equal pay for equal work" and give an example that demonstrates how this concept is applied.
2. Describe the impact of the Charter of Rights and Freedoms on HRM.
3. Differentiate between intentional and unintentional (constructive/systemic) discrimination and provide several examples of each.
4. Explain the grounds of discrimination prohibited under Canadian human rights legislation, giving a specific example for each ground that illustrates the types of activities in which an employer cannot legally engage.
5. Explain "bona fide occupational requirement" and cite three specific examples.
6. Discuss the human rights legislation requirements pertaining to reasonable accommodation. Give five examples of ways in which employers might be expected to accommodate employees.
7. Describe the types of behaviour that could constitute harassment and explain employers' and managers' responsibilities pertaining to harassment.
8. Explain the term "sexual harassment" and describe five types of behaviour that would be considered sexual harassment.
9. Describe the steps involved in the human rights complaint process and list four possible remedies for violations.
10. Describe the steps involved in employment equity program implementation.
11. Explain what is meant by "equal pay for work of equal or comparable value," and give a specific example that illustrates the application of this concept.
12. Differentiate between goals and quotas and explain how employers can avoid the issue of reverse discrimination.
13. Describe the impact of equal opportunity and equity on managers throughout the organization and on HR department staff.
14. Explain how diversity management differs from employment equity and describe the characteristics of successful diversity management initiatives.

Application Exercises

RUNNING CASE: Carter Cleaning Company

Discrimination?

One of the areas about which Jennifer is particularly concerned is legal compliance. She has noted that very little attention has been paid to equality, equal opportunity, and equity issues. Virtually all hiring is handled by each of the centre managers, three of whom are white males and three of whom are white females. None of the managers has received any training on human rights legislative requirements or the types of questions that can and cannot be asked of candidates at job interviews. During her interviews with the managers, Jennifer learned that it is not uncommon for female applicants to be asked questions regarding child-care arrangements or visible minority candidates to be asked about their language skills. White males are not questioned about either of these issues.

Based on discussions with her father, Jennifer has deduced that the rather laid-back attitude toward equality, equal opportunity, and equity issues stems from her father's lack of sophistication regarding legislative requirements, as well as the fact that, as he put it, "Virtually all of our workers are women or visible minorities, anyway, so no one can really come in here and accuse us of being discriminatory, can they?"

Jennifer decided to mull that question over, but before she had time to give it much thought, she was faced with two serious human rights problems. Two women employed in one of the centres privately confided to her that their manager was making unwelcome sexual advances toward them, and one claimed the he had threatened to fire her unless she "socialized" with him after hours. On a fact-finding trip to another centre, a 63-year-old employee complained to her that although he had almost forty years' experience in the business, he was being paid less than people half his age who were doing the very same job.

Jennifer has now written down five questions that she needs to consider.

Questions

1. Is it true, as her father has claimed, that they can't be accused of being discriminatory because they hire mostly women and visible minorities?

2. How should she and her father address the charges of sexual harassment? If the manager is guilty, what should they do?

3. Does the 63-year-old have a complaint for which he can file a charge? Under which legislation? How should his pay issue be addressed?

4. Aside from dealing with the two issues that require her immediate attention, which other HRM matters need to be addressed to ensure that the centres are in total compliance with all legislation pertaining to equality and equal opportunity?

5. Given current demographic trends, should the centres be thinking beyond legal compliance? If so, how?

CASE INCIDENT: Harassment?

Maria has recently been hired as a supervisor in the compensation area of the human resources department, which you manage. She seems to have been accepted by her peers and reporting employees but you have noticed that, for the past three weeks, she has been the last to arrive at staff meetings and always sits as far as possible from Bob, another supervisor.

Yesterday afternoon, you had a very upsetting conversation with Maria. She claimed that for more than a month Bob has been repeatedly asking her to go out with him and that her constant refusals seem to be making the situation worse. Bob has accused her of being unfriendly and suggested that she thinks she is too good for him.

She said that he has never touched her but that he discusses how "sexy" she looks with the other men in the department, who seem embarrassed by the whole situation. Maria also said that Bob's advances are escalating the more she refuses him and that his behaviour is interfering with her job performance to such an extent that she is thinking of resigning.

With Maria's consent, you have just spoken to Bob, who denied her allegations vehemently and believably.

Questions

1. How would you proceed in dealing with this situation?
2. What are your responsibilities to Maria and Bob?
3. If Maria is telling the truth, are you or Bob legally liable in any way? If so, under what conditions?
4. How would you resolve this matter?

Source: Based on a case provided in *Equity Works Best*, a publication of the Ontario Women's Directorate.

Human Resources Management Simulation

Section 1 of part 3 of the simulation deals with legislative issues. Exercise 13 requires a report outlining the rationale behind employment equity legislation and the major requirements of such legislation. The report should also identify measures to ensure equitable treatment of members of the four designated groups that could be implemented immediately as part of the firm's equity in employment policy.

Exercise 14 requires the preparation of a strategy to communicate pertinent information about each of the types of legislation described in this chapter to staff at various levels of the organization, and to gain their acceptance of, and commitment to, the legislative requirements affecting them.

Simulation 4 provides an opportunity to demonstrate, through role playing, the type of corrective action that may be required to ensure a workplace free of harassment and discrimination. The approach taken should be corrective, but educational, aimed at gaining acceptance and cooperation, not mere compliance with company policies and standards.

Video Case

How to Manage in a Cross-Cultural World

With the increase in international business, more and more corporate Canadians are faced with the challenge of surviving and thriving in a cross-cultural environment. Success begins with a basic awareness of cultural differences and an understanding of various cultural norms.

Viewers join a seminar for corporate business people being conducted by Fons Trompenaars, a corporate researcher, on the topic "How to Manage in a Corporate Cross-Cultural World." Fons begins by asking the participants to define what culture means to them, and then directs them to think about how culture affects the ways in which various facets of business are conducted. Distinctive values and norms are also discussed. As Fons and the seminar participants clearly illustrate, in order to conduct business effectively in another country, it is imperative to understand that nation's basic norms and culture. Fons offers a final piece of advice: There are two expressions that work well in any culture, "thank you" and "sorry."

Questions

1. Define culture.
2. Discuss the importance of understanding distinctive cultures when conducting international business.
3. How can the HR department staff help prepare employees to conduct business in a global environment?
4. What implications does the trend toward international business have for recruiting, selecting, and training new employees?

Video Resource: CBC, *Venture*, "Cross Culture," August 6, 1995.

Take It to the Net

Check out our Companion Website at

www.prenticehall.ca/dessler

for a multitude of practice questions, key terms and concepts, Weblinks to related sites, newsgroups, CBC video updates, and more.

Appendix 3.1

A Guide to Screening and Selection in Employment

Subject	Avoid Asking	Preferred	Comment
Name	about name change: whether it was changed by court order, marriage, or other reason maiden name		ask after selection if needed to check on previously held jobs or educational credentials
Address	for addresses outside Canada	ask place and duration of current or recent address	
Age	for birth certificates, baptismal records, or about age in general	ask applicants if they are eligible to work under Canadian laws regarding age restrictions	if precise age required for benefits plans or other legitimate purposes, it can be determined after selection
Sex	males or females to fill in different applications about pregnancy, child-bearing plans, or child-care arrangements	can ask applicant if the attendance requirements can be met	during the interview or after selection, the applicant, for purposes of courtesy, may be asked which of Mr/Mrs/Miss/Ms is preferred

(continued)

Marital Status	whether applicant is single, married, divorced, engaged, separated, widowed, or living common law	if transfer or travel is part of the job, the applicant can be asked if he or she can meet these requirements	
	whether an applicant's spouse is subject to transfer	ask whether there are any circumstances that might prevent completion of a minimum service commitment	information on dependents can be determined after selection if necessary
	about spouse's employment		
Family Status	number of children or dependents	if the applicant would be able to work the required hours and, where applicable, overtime	contacts for emergencies and/or details on dependents can be determined after selection
	about child care arrangements		
National or Ethnic Origin	about birthplace, nationality of ancestors, spouse, or other relatives	since those who are entitled to work in Canada must be citizens, permanent residents, or holders of valid work permits, applicants can be asked if they are legally entitled to work in Canada	documentation of eligibility to work (papers, visas, etc.) can be requested after selection
	whether born in Canada		
	for proof of citizenship		
Military Service	about military service in other countries	inquiry about Canadian military service where employment preference is given to veterans by law	
Language	mother tongue	ask if applicant understands, reads, writes, or speaks languages required for the job	testing or scoring applicants for language proficiency is not permitted unless job related
	where language skills obtained		
Race or Colour	any inquiry into race or colour, including colour of eyes, skin, or hair		
Photographs	for photo to be attached to applications or sent to interviewer before interview		photos for security passes or company files can be taken after selection
Religion	about religious affiliation, church membership, frequency of church attendance		
	if applicant will work a specific religious holiday	explain the required work shift, asking if such a schedule poses problems for the applicant	reasonable accommodation of an employee's religious beliefs is the employer's duty
	for references from clergy or religious leader		
Height and Weight			no inquiry unless there is evidence they are genuine occupational requirements
Disability	for listing of all disabilities, limitations, or health problems	ask if applicant has any condition that could affect ability to do the job	a disability is only relevant to job ability if it:
	whether applicant drinks or uses drugs	ask if applicant has an condition that should be considered in selection	– threatens the safety or property of others
	whether applicant has ever received psychiatric care or been hospitalized for emotional problems		– prevents the applicant from safe and adequate job performance even when reasonable efforts are made to accommodate the disability
	whether applicant has received workers' compensation		

(continued)

Subject	Avoid Asking	Preferred	Comment
Medical Information	if currently under physician's care name of family doctor if receiving counselling or therapy		
Pardoned Conviction	whether an applicant has ever been convicted if an applicant has ever been arrested whether an applicant has a criminal record		
Sexual Orientation	any inquiry about the applicant's sexual orientation		contacts for emergencies and/or details on dependents can be determined after selection
References			the same restrictions that apply to questions asked of applicants apply when asking for employment references

Source: Canadian Human Rights Commission, *A Guide to Screening and Selection in Employment*, (Ottawa: Minister of Supply and Services, 1993). Reproduced with permission of the Minister of Public Works and Government Services Canada, 1998.

Notes

1. *Canadian Charter of Rights and Freedoms*, as part of the Constitution Act of 1982.
2. *Canadian Charter of Rights and Freedoms*, Section 15(1).
3. Personal files of one of the authors. Letter from Fred Upshaw, President, Ontario Public Service Employees Union (July 5, 1991).
4. "Supreme Court Upholds Mandatory Retirement," *Human Resources Management in Canada* 95 (January 1991), pp. 1–2.
5. *Canadian Human Rights Act* (Ottawa: Minister of Public Works and Government Services Canada, 1996) Section 2 (July 1996), p. 1. Reproduced with the permission of the Minister of Public Works and Government Services Canada.
6. "Firm Pays $300000 in Racial Harassment Settlements," *Human Resources Management in Canada* 72 (February 1989), pp. 1–2.
7. *Annual Report of the Canadian Human Rights Commission*, (Ottawa: Government of Canada, 1985), p. 25.
8. *Annual Report of the Canadian Human Rights Commission*, (Ottawa: Government of Canada, 1991), p. 65.
9. *Annual Report of the Canadian Human Rights Commission* (Ottawa: Government of Canada, 1985), p. 25.
10. *Annual Report of the Canadian Human Rights Commission* (Ottawa: Government of Canada, 1989), p. 42.
11. *Annual Report of the Canadian Human Rights Commission* (Ottawa: Government of Canada, 1988), p. 40.
12. *Annual Report of the Canadian Human Rights Commission* (Ottawa: Government of Canada, 1991), p. 71.
13. *Annual Report of the Canadian Human Rights Commission* (Ottawa: Government of Canada, 1981), p. 29.
14. *Annual Report of the Canadian Human Rights Commission* (Ottawa: Government of Canada, 1981), p. 29.
15. "No Insurance Against Discrimination," *Canadian HR Reporter* 10, no. 12 (June 16, 1997), p. 15. Copyright MPL Communications Inc., Reproduced by permission of *Canadian HR Reporter* 133 Richmond Street West, Toronto, Ontario M5H 3M8.
16. Malcolm J. MacKillop, "Should Eligibility for Benefits Be Based on Sexual Orientation," *Human Resources Professional* 12, no. 6 (October 1995), pp. 16–7.
17. "Revenue Canada Okays Same-Sex Coverage," in News and Views, compiled by Carrie O'Grady, *Human Resources Professional* 14, no. 1 (February/March 1997), p. 8.
18. BFOQ and BFOR are used interchangeably. BFOR is used in most Canadian jurisdictions, and BFOQ is more commonly used in the United States. However, decisions of Canadian Courts and Human Rights Tribunals appear to confer the same meaning to both terms.
19. A.P. Aggarwal, *Sex Discrimination: Employment Law and Practices* (Toronto: Butterworths Canada, 1994).
20. H.J. Jain, "Human Rights: Issues in Employment," *Human Resources Management in Canada* (Toronto: Prentice Hall Canada, 1995), p. 50 036.
21. H.J. Jain, "Issues in Employment," p. 50 036.
22. H.J. Jain, "Issues in Employment," pp. 50 034–35.
23. *Human Resources Management in Canada* 95 (January 1991), pp. 6–7.

24. *Annual Report of the Canadian Human Rights Commission* (Ottawa: Government of Canada, 1991), p. 63

25. Barbara G. Humphrey, "Employer/Union Joint Responsibilities," *Human Resources Professional* 13, no. 7 (October 1996), pp. 23–6, 31.

26. Kathy Blair, "Female Firefighter Gets Runaround," *Canadian HR Reporter* 10, no. 11 (May 19, 1997) p. 5. Copyright MPL Communications Inc., Reproduced by permission of *Canadian HR Reporter* 133 Richmond Street West, Toronto, Ontario M5H 3M8.

27. Canadian Human Rights Commission, *Harassment Casebook* (Ottawa: Minister of Supply and Services Canada, 1993), p. 2.

28. Based on Canadian Human Rights Commission, *Harassment Casebook*, pp. 10–1. Reproduced with the permission of the Minister of Public Works and Government Services Canada.

29. Based on Canadian Human Rights Commission, *Harassment Casebook*, p. 3.

30. "Poor Harassment Policy May Cost $120,000," *Human Resources Management in Canada* 145 (March 1995), pp. 7–8.

31. A.P. Aggarwal, *Sexual Harassment in the Workplace,* 2nd ed. (Toronto: Butterworths Canada, 1992), pp. 10–1.

32. "Woman Called 'Swish, Swish and Waddle, Waddle' Wins $50,000 Award," *Human Resources Management in Canada* 95 (January 1991), pp. 7–8.

33. Malcolm MacKillop, "Dismissal If Necessary; Not Necessarily Dismissal," *Human Resources Professional* 13, no. 2 (April 1996), pp. 24–5.

34. Himmelman v. King's-Edgehill School (1985), 7 C.C.E.L. 16 (N.S.S.C.).

35. Tellier v. Bank of Montreal (1987), 17 C.C.E.L. 1 (Ont. Dist. Ct.).

36. *Canadian Human Rights Act* (Ottawa: Minister of Public Works and Government Services Canada, 1996) Section 16(1) (July 1996), pp. 6–7. Reproduced with the permission of the Minister of Public Works and Government Services Canada.

37. *Canadian Human Rights Act*, Section 60 2(a) and 2(b), p. 30.

38. "Glass Ceiling Still Intact," in News and Views, compiled by Carrie O'Grady, *Human Resources Professional* 12, no. 3 (May 1995), p. 22.

39. "Women in the Labour Force," (Ottawa: Statistics Canada, 1994) Cat. No. 75-507E, p. 5.

40. Massimo Commanducci, "Women Make Gains in Wage Equity as Youth Fall Behind, *"Canadian HR Reporter* 11, no. 8 (April 20, 1998), p. 1.

41. "A Portrait of Persons With Disabilities," (Ottawa: Statistics Canada, 1995), Cat. No. 89-542E.

42. Jacquie Miller, (Ottawa Citizen) "Race Affects Earnings, Studies Find," *The Toronto Star* (January 20, 1997) p. A2.

43. J. Badets and T.W.L. Chu, "Canada's Changing Immigrant Population: Focus on Canada," (Ottawa: Statistics Canada, 1994), Cat. No. 96-311E.

44. Miller, "Race Affects Earnings," p. A2.

45. Rosalie Silberman Abella, *Equality in Employment: A Royal Commission Report* (Ottawa: Supply and Services Canada, 1984).

46. *Employment Equity Act and Reporting Requirements* (Ottawa: Employment and Immigration Canada, 1986) and "Employment Equity Audits to Begin," *Canadian HR Reporter* 10, no. 20 (November 17, 1997), p. 8.

47. *Employment Equity Act and Reporting Requirements*.

48. The discussion on the implementation of employment equity is based on *Equity Works Best* and other material provided by the Ontario Women's Directorate, and *Employment Equity: A Guide for Employers* (Ottawa: Employment and Immigration Canada, May 1991), Cat. No. LM-143, pp. 5–91, except as noted.

49. Jennie Constantinides, "Diversity Management," *Human Resources Professional* 7, no. 4 (April 1991), pp. 29–30.

50. Linda Gutri, "Training for Equity," *Human Resources Professional* 9, no. 2 (February 1993), pp. 13–6.

51. *Employment Equity: A Guide for Employers*, p. 19.

52. Mary Beth Currie, "Destined for Equity," *Human Resources Professional* 10, no. 7 (July/August 1993), pp. 7–8.

53. Kelly Toughill, "Firms Back Equity: To Some It's `Good Business Sense' Despite Harris' Vow to Scrap It," *The Toronto Star* (June 21, 1995), p. A2.

54. *Employment Equity: A Guide for Employers*, pp. 5–91.

55. "Women, Visible Minorities See Improvement in Workplace; Pay Gap Between Sexes Still Vexes," *Canadian HR Reporter* 9, no. 7 (April 8, 1996), p. 4. Copyright MPL Communications Inc.

56. Commanducci, "Women Make Gains," p. 1.

57. "Women, Visible Minorities See Improvement in Workplace; Pay Gap Between Sexes Still Vexes," p. 4. Copyright MPL Communications Inc.

58. *Annual Report of the Canadian Human Rights Commission* (Ottawa: Government of Canada, 1991), p. 29.

59. Morley Gunderson and Roberta Edgecombe Robb, "Equal Pay for Work of Equal Value: Canadian Experience," *Advances in Industrial and Labour Relations* 5 (1991), pp. 151–68. See also John G. Kelly, *Pay Equity Management* (Toronto: CCH Canadian Ltd., 1988), pp. 45–54.

60. Canadian Press, "Bell Loses Bid to Block Pay Equity Tribunal," *The Globe and Mail* (February 24, 1997), p. B2.

61. J. Coutts, "OCA to Hire Women for Next 10 Years," *The Toronto Star* (January 9, 1990), p. A13.

62. *Annual Report of the Canadian Human Rights Commission* (Ottawa: Government of Canada, 1985).

63. "Women, Visible Minorities See Improvement in Workplace; Pay Gap Between Sexes Still Vexes," p. 4. Copyright MPL Communications Inc., Reproduced by permission of *Canadian HR Reporter* 133 Richmond Street West, Toronto, Ontario M5H 3M8.

64. Tove Helland Hanner, "Affirmative Action Programs: Have We Forgotten the First Line Supervisor?" *Personnel Journal* (June 1979), pp. 384–9.

65. Hanner, "Affirmative Action Programs," pp. 384–9.

66. Jana Schilder, "The Rainbow Connection," *Human Resources Professional* 11, no. 3 (April 1994), pp. 13–5.

67. Quoted in Constantinides, "Diversity Management," pp. 29–30.

68. Schilder, "The Rainbow Connection," p. 13.

69. Christine L. Taylor, "Dimensions of Diversity in Canadian Business: Building a Business Case for Valuing Ethnocultural Diversity," *The Conference Board of Canada Report* 143-95 (April 1995), p. 3.

70. Quoted in Schilder, "The Rainbow Connection," pp. 13, 15.

71. Alice Cuneo, "Diverse by Design," *Business Week* (October 23, 1992), p. 72.

72. Schilder, "The Rainbow Connection," p. 13.
73. Christine L. Taylor, "Building a Case for Business Diversity," *Canadian Business Review* 22, no. 1 (1995), pp. 12–5.
74. Christine L. Taylor, "Dimensions of Diversity," p. 13.
75. Quoted in Cleta Moyer, "Diversity Management," *Human Resources Professional* 12 no.7 (November 1995), p. 21.
76. Moyer, "Diversity Management," pp. 21–2.
77. Diane Davies, "Equity Equations," *Human Resources Professional* 9 no.5 (May 1993), pp. 15–7.
78. Christine L. Taylor, "Dimensions of Diversity," pp. 16–8.
79. Lynne Sullivan, "Canadian Companies Get A Failing Grade in Protecting International Rights," *Canadian HR Reporter* 10, no. 12 (June 16, 1977), pp. 11, 13.

Chapter 4

Designing and Analyzing Jobs

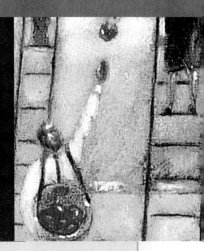

Chapter Outline

- ◆ **Organizing Work**
- ◆ **Job Design**
- ◆ **The Nature of Job Analysis**
- ◆ **Methods of Collecting Job Analysis Information**
- ◆ **Writing Job Descriptions**
- ◆ **Writing Job Specifications**
- ◆ **Job Analysis in a "Jobless" World**

Learning Outcomes

After studying this chapter, you should be able to:

Develop an organization chart.

Explain the industrial engineering, behavioural, and human engineering considerations involved in job design.

Describe the importance of job analysis information.

Describe the basic methods of collecting job analysis information and explain the appropriate use of each.

Conduct a job analysis.

Develop job descriptions and job specifications.

Explain the value of a physical demands analysis and statistically derived job specifications.

Discuss current trends in the nature of jobs and job descriptions.

Organizing Work

An organization is comprised of one or more employees, who perform various tasks. The relationships between people and tasks must be structured in such a way that the organization can achieve its goals in an efficient and effective manner.

organizational structure
The formal relationships among jobs in an organization.

organization chart
A "snapshot" of the firm at a particular point in time, depicting the organization's structure in chart form.

Organizational structure refers to the formal relationships among jobs in an organization. An **organization chart** is often used to depict the structure. As illustrated in **Figure 4.1**, such a chart indicates the types of departments established, the title of each manager's job, and by means of connecting lines, clarifies the chain of command and shows who is accountable to whom. An organization chart presents a "snapshot" of the firm at a particular point in time, but does not provide details about actual communication patterns, degree of supervision, amount of power and authority, or specific duties and responsibilities.

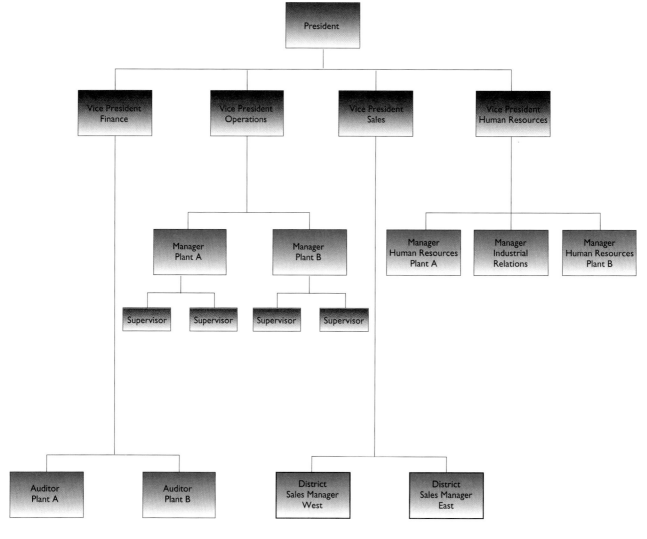

Figure 4.1
A Sample Organization Chart

Designing an organization involves choosing a structure that is appropriate, given the company's strategic goals. There are three basic types of organizational structure, as depicted in **Figure 4.2**: bureaucratic, flat, and boundaryless. As discussed briefly in chapter 1 and as will be explained in more detail later in this chapter, bureaucratic designs are becoming less common; flat structures are increasingly the norm; and boundaryless organizations have started to evolve.

Job Design

job design
The process of systematically organizing work into tasks that are required to perform a specific job.

In any organization, work has to be divided into manageable units and ultimately into jobs that can be performed by employees. **Job design** is the process of systematically organizing work into tasks that are required to perform a specific job. An organization's strategy and structure influence the ways in which jobs are designed. In bureaucratic organizations, for example, since there is a hierarchical division of labour, jobs are generally highly specialized. In addition to organizational objectives and structure, however, effective job design also takes into consideration human and technological factors.

job
A group of related activities and duties, held by a single employee or a number of incumbents.

position
The collection of tasks and responsibilities performed by one person.

A **job** consists of a group of related activities and duties. Ideally, the duties of a job should be clear and distinct from those of other jobs, and involve natural units of work that are similar and related. This helps to minimize conflict and enhance employee performance. A job may be held by a single employee or may have a number of incumbents. The collection of tasks and responsibilities performed by one person is known as a **position**. To clarify, in a department with one supervisor, one clerk, forty assemblers, and three tow-motor operators, there are forty-five positions and four jobs.

Specialization and Industrial Engineering Considerations

The term "job" as it is known today is largely an outgrowth of the efficiency demands of the industrial revolution. As the substitution of machine power for people power became more widespread, experts such as Adam Smith, Charles Babbage, and Frederick Winslow Taylor (the father of scientific management) wrote glowingly about the positive correlation between (1) job specialization, and (2) productivity and efficiency.[1] The popularity of specialized, short-cycle jobs soared—at least among management experts and managers.

work simplification
An approach to job design that involves assigning most of the administrative aspects of work (such as planning and organizing) to supervisory and managerial personnel, while giving lower-level employees narrowly-defined tasks to perform according to methods established and specified by management.

Work simplification evolved from scientific management theory. It is based on the premise that work can be broken down into clearly defined, highly specialized repetitive tasks to maximize efficiency. This approach to job design involves assigning most of the administrative aspects of work (such as planning and organizing) to supervisors and managers, while giving lower-level employees narrowly-defined tasks to perform according to methods established and specified by management.

While work simplification can increase operating efficiency in a stable environment, and may be very appropriate in settings employing individuals who are mentally challenged or lacking in education and training (as in some third-world operations), it is not effective in a changing environment in which customers or clients demand custom-designed products or services of high quality, or one in which employees want challenging work. Moreover, among educated employees, simplified jobs often lead to lower satisfaction, higher rates of absenteeism and turnover, and sometimes lead to a demand for premium pay to compensate for the repetitive nature of the work.

BUREAUCRATIC

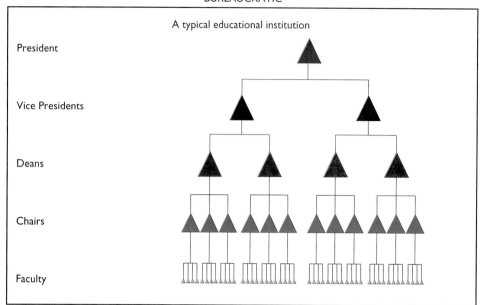

A typical educational institution

President

Vice Presidents

Deans

Chairs

Faculty

- Top-down management approach
- Many levels, and hierarchical communication channels and career paths
- Highly specialized jobs with narrowly defined job descriptions
- Focus on independent performance

FLAT

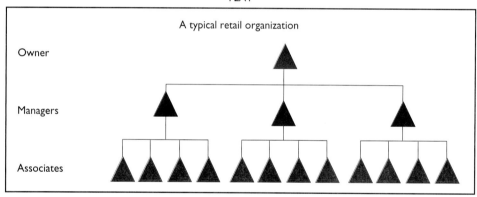

A typical retail organization

Owner

Managers

Associates

- Decentralized management approach
- Few levels and multi-directional communication
- Broadly defined jobs, with general job descriptions
- Emphasis on teams and on customer service

BOUNDARYLESS

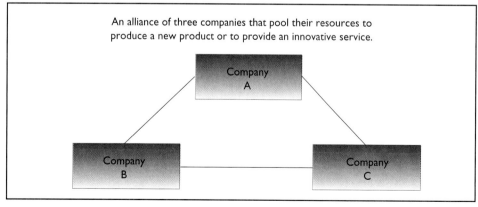

An alliance of three companies that pool their resources to produce a new product or to provide an innovative service.

Company A

Company B

Company C

- Joint ventures with customers, suppliers, and/or competitors
- Emphasis on teams whose members may cross organizational boundaries

Figure 4.2
Bureaucratic, Flat, and Boundaryless Organizational Structures

industrial engineering
A field of study concerned with analyzing work methods; making work cycles more efficient by modifying, combining, rearranging, or eliminating tasks; and establishing time standards.

Another important contribution of scientific management was the study of work. **Industrial engineering**, which evolved with this movement, is concerned with analyzing work methods and establishing time standards to improve efficiency. Industrial engineers systematically identify, analyze, and time the elements of each job's work cycle and determine which, if any, elements can be modified, combined, rearranged, or eliminated to reduce the time needed to complete the cycle.

To establish time standards, industrial engineers measure and record the time required to complete each element in the work cycle, using a stopwatch or work sampling techniques, and then combine these times to determine the total. Adjustments are then made to compensate for differences in skill level, breaks, and interruptions due to such factors as machine maintenance or breakdown. The adjusted time becomes the time standard for that particular work cycle, which serves as an objective basis for evaluating and improving employee performance and determining incentive pay.

Since jobs are created primarily to enable an organization to achieve its objectives, industrial engineering cannot be ignored as a disciplined and objective approach to job design. However, too much emphasis on the concerns of industrial engineering—improving efficiency and simplifying work methods—may result in human considerations being neglected or down-played. What may be improvements in job design and efficiency from an engineering standpoint can sometimes prove to be physiologically or psychologically unsound. For example, an assembly line with its simplified and repetitive tasks embodies the principles of industrial engineering, but may lead to repetitive strain injuries and high turnover and low satisfaction due to the lack of psychological fulfillment. Thus, to be effective, job design must also provide for the satisfaction of human psychological and physiological needs.

Behavioural Considerations

job enlargement (horizontal loading)
A technique to relieve monotony and boredom that involves assigning workers additional tasks at the same level of responsibility to increase the number of tasks they have to perform.

job rotation
Another technique to relieve monotony and employee boredom, which involves systematically moving employees from one job to another.

job enrichment (vertical loading)
Any effort that makes an employee's job more rewarding or satisfying by adding more meaningful tasks and duties.

By the mid-1900s, reacting to what they viewed as the "dehumanizing" aspects of pigeonholing workers into highly repetitive and specialized jobs and other problems associated with overspecialization, various management theorists proposed ways of broadening the numbers of activities in which employees engaged. **Job enlargement** involves assigning workers additional tasks at the same level of responsibility to increase the number of tasks they have to perform. Thus, if the work was assembling chairs, the worker who previously only bolted the seat to the legs might take on the additional tasks of assembling the legs and attaching the back, as well. Also known as horizontal loading, job enlargement reduces monotony and fatigue by expanding the job cycle and drawing on a wider range of employee skills. Another technique to relieve monotony and employee boredom is **job rotation**. This involves systematically moving employees from one job to another. Although the jobs themselves don't change, workers experience more task variety, motivation, and productivity. The company gains by having more versatile, multi-skilled employees, who can cover for one another efficiently.

More recently, psychologist Frederick Herzberg argued that the best way to motivate workers is to build opportunities for challenge and achievement into jobs through **job enrichment**.[2] This is defined as any effort that makes an employee's job more rewarding or satisfying by adding more meaningful tasks and duties. Also known as vertical loading, job enrichment involves increasing autonomy and responsibility by allowing employees to assume a greater role in the decision-making process and become more involved in planning, organizing, directing, and controlling their own work, through such activities as:

- increasing the level of difficulty and responsibility of the job
- assigning workers more authority and control over outcomes
- providing feedback about individual or unit job performance directly to employees
- adding new tasks requiring training, thereby providing an opportunity for growth
- assigning individuals specific tasks or responsibility for performing a whole job rather than only parts of it.

Job design studies explored a new field when behavioural scientists focussed on identifying various job dimensions that would simultaneously improve the efficiency of organizations and satisfaction of employees. One of the best known theories evolving from such research is one advanced by Richard Hackman and Greg Oldham.[3] Their job characteristics model proposes that employee motivation and satisfaction are directly linked to five core characteristics:[4]

1. Skill variety. The degree to which the job requires a person to do different tasks and involves the use of a number of different talents, skills, and abilities.
2. Task identity. The degree to which the job requires completion of a whole and identifiable piece of work, that is, doing a job from beginning to end, with a visible outcome.
3. Task significance. The degree to which the job has a substantial impact on the lives and work of others—both inside and outside the organization.
4. Autonomy. The amount of freedom, independence, and discretion the employee has in terms of scheduling work and determining procedures.
5. Feedback. The degree to which the job provides the employee with clear and direct information about job outcomes and effectiveness of his or her performance.

These core job characteristics create the conditions that enable workers to experience three critical psychological states that are related to a number of beneficial work outcomes:[5]

1. Experienced meaningfulness. The extent to which the employee experiences the work as being important, valuable, and worthwhile.
2. Experienced responsibility. The degree to which the employee feels personally responsible or accountable for the outcome of the work.
3. Knowledge of results. The degree to which the employee understands, on a regular basis, how effectively he or she is performing.

As illustrated in **Figure 4.3**, skill variety, task identity, and task significance are all linked to experienced meaningfulness; autonomy is related to experienced responsibility; and feedback provides knowledge of results.

A job with characteristics that allow an employee to experience all three critical states provides internal rewards that sustain motivation. The benefits to the employer include high-quality performance, higher employee satisfaction, and lower absenteeism and turnover.

As is no doubt quite apparent, the suggestions of Herzberg, and Hackman and Oldham regarding job design and redesign strategies are quite similar. The benefits of job enrichment also include increased motivation, job satisfaction, and performance.

Job enrichment and including the five core dimensions in jobs is not, however, a panacea. Job enrichment programs are more successful in some jobs and settings than in others. Moreover, not all employees want additional responsibility and challenge. Hackman and Oldham stress that the strength of the linkage

Figure 4.3
The Job Characteristics Model

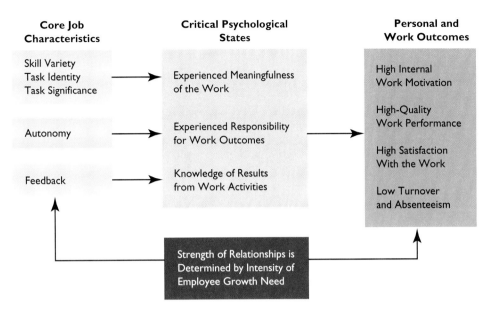

Core Job Characteristics	Critical Psychological States	Personal and Work Outcomes

Skill Variety
Task Identity
Task Significance → Experienced Meaningfulness of the Work

Autonomy → Experienced Responsibility for Work Outcomes

Feedback → Knowledge of Results from Work Activities

High Internal Work Motivation

High-Quality Work Performance

High Satisfaction With the Work

Low Turnover and Absenteeism

Strength of Relationships is Determined by Intensity of Employee Growth Need

among job characteristics, psychological states, and work outcomes is determined by the intensity of an individual employee's need for growth.[6] Some people prefer routine jobs and may resist job redesign efforts. In addition, job redesign efforts almost always fail when employees lack the physical or mental skills, abilities, or education needed to perform the job. Furthermore, neither approach will correct job dissatisfaction problems related to inequitable compensation, inadequate benefits, or lack of job security. Unions have sometimes resisted job enrichment, fearing that management will expect workers to take on more responsibility and challenge without additional compensation. Managers, fearing a loss of authority and control, or worried about possible elimination of supervisory jobs, have also been sources of resistance.

Team-Based Job Design

team-based job designs
Job designs that focus on giving a team, rather than an individual, a whole and meaningful piece of work to do, and empowering team members to decide among themselves how to accomplish the work.

team
A small group of people, with complementary skills, who work toward common goals for which they hold joint responsibility and accountability.

A logical outgrowth of job enrichment and the job characteristics model has been the increasing use of **team-based job designs**, which focus on giving a **team**, rather than an individual, a whole and meaningful piece of work to do. Team members are empowered to decide among themselves how to accomplish the work.[7] Often they are cross-trained, and then rotated to perform different tasks. Team-based designs are best suited to flat and boundaryless organization structures.

General Motors, Saturn Division, is an extremely high-profile operation involving the use of team-based job design. Initiated as a completely new venture within GM, the Saturn car assembly process involves self-managed teams with five to fifteen members. Each team reviews and hires new members, manages its own budget, schedules its work, and makes decisions regarding production and quality concerns.[8]

Human Engineering Considerations

Over time, it became apparent that in addition to considering psychological needs, effective job design must also take physiological needs and health and

human engineering (ergonomics)
An interdisciplinary approach that seeks to integrate and accommodate the physical needs of workers into the design of jobs. It aims to adapt the entire job system—the work, environment, machines, equipment, and processes—to match human characteristics.

safety issues into account. **Human engineering** or **ergonomics**, seeks to integrate and accommodate the physical needs of workers into the design of jobs. It aims to adapt the entire job system—the work, environment, machines, equipment, and processes—to match human characteristics. Doing so results in eliminating or minimizing product defects, damage to equipment, and worker injuries or illnesses caused by poor work design.

In addition to designing jobs and equipment with the aim of minimizing negative physiological effects for all workers, human engineering can aid in meeting the unique requirements of individuals with special needs and adapting jobs for older workers, a topic which is discussed in the Diversity Counts box.

Diversity Counts:
Older Workers Need Ergonomic Aid

Given current demographic trends, when employers think of the workplace of the future, they should be picturing more grey hair, more stiff backs, and more bifocals.

While aging is a relatively individual process that not only affects people at different rates but also varies by body part or function, there are a number of changes that are fairly common:

1. **Muscular strength**—Maximum strength occurs between 25 and 30 years of age. However, the rate of decline in strength appears to be a function of exercise and lifestyle. That is, an active 65-year-old may have 90 percent of his or her maximum strength, whereas a less-fit 40-year-old might have only 80 percent.

2. **Hand function**—As people age, their hands undergo a variety of changes, including a decrease in grip strength and endurance, finger and thumb strength, dexterity, precision, coordination, joint mobility, and sensitivity.

3. **Cardiovascular capacity**—The ability of the heart and lungs to supply blood to the working muscles, to perform light to moderate physically exhausting work, is not grossly age-dependent up to age 65, although capacity for hard, exhausting work is strongly age-dependent, with maximum capacity between ages 20 and 25.

4. **Vision**—Visual capabilities that are affected by aging include the ability to see fine detail sharply (acuity), focus on near and far objects (accommodation), distinguish between light and dark (sensitivity), discriminate certain colours, and judge distance and depth (stereopsis).

5. **Hearing**—Hearing loss with age is caused by a combination of the normal aging process, exposure to noise throughout life, and other factors. It influences ability to detect faint sounds and deal with background noise and multiple sources of noise. Detecting, understanding, and responding to speech sounds, as well as certain frequencies, becomes difficult. The need to listen and detect sounds becomes more demanding and is more tiring and prone to error.

The key for employers when dealing with the effects of their aging work force will be to ensure that jobs that require physical activity are designed with ergonomic principles in mind.

Physical demands, such as manual materials-handling (lifting, pushing, pulling, and carrying), and upper-limb movements (reaching, grasping, pinching, and fingering), will have to be performed using good working postures, and as little force, and as little repetition as possible.

The need for ergonomics interventions to reduce physical demands will be higher than ever before. Items such as mechanical assists for lifting (scissor lift tables, tilters, vacuum lifts) and for assembly (screwguns and adjustable tables) will be essential.

As a result of diminished visual capabilities, performance of employees on assembly and inspection tasks may be greatly reduced. Visual capabilities will influence the lighting levels that are chosen and size of characters for controls and displays. The impact of aging on vision and hearing will need to be considered when dealing with information processing and workplace communication issues.

As Canadian employers fight for competitiveness, the issues of workers' compensation and lost time due to injury top the list of challenges that must be met. Failure to incorporate ergonomic principles into the design of jobs has resulted in almost one-half of all lost-time injuries being caused by repetitive motion or over-exertion. With the effects that aging has on the human body, these rates can only be expected to increase if ergonomics is not considered.

Source: Based on Glenn Harrington, "Older Workers Need Ergonomic Aid," *Canadian HR Reporter* 10, no. 20 (November 17, 1997), p. 20. Copyright MPL Communications Inc., Reproduced by permission of *Canadian HR Reporter*, 133 Richmond Street West, Toronto, Ontario M5H 3M8.◆

The Nature of Job Analysis

Job Analysis Defined

job analysis
The procedure for determining the tasks, duties and responsibilities of each job, and the human attributes (in terms of knowledge skills, and abilities) required to perform it.

Once jobs have been designed or redesigned, an employer's performance-related expectations need to be defined and communicated. This is best accomplished through job analysis, a process by which information about jobs is systematically gathered and organized. **Job analysis** is the procedure firms use to determine the tasks, duties, and responsibilities of each job, and the human attributes (in terms of knowledge, skills, and abilities) required to perform it. In contrast to job design, which reflects subjective opinions about the ideal requirements of a job, job analysis is concerned with objective and verifiable information about the actual requirements. Once this information has been gathered, it is used for developing **job descriptions** (what the job entails) and **job specifications** (what the human requirements are).[9]

Uses of Job Analysis Information

job description
A list of the duties, responsibilities, reporting relationships, and working conditions of a job—one product of a job analysis.

job specification
A list of the "human requirements," that is, the requisite knowledge, skills, and abilities (KSAs) needed to perform the job—another product of a job analysis.

Job analysis is sometimes called the cornerstone of HRM. As illustrated in **Figure 4.4**, the information gathered, evaluated, and summarized through job analysis is the basis for a number of interrelated HRM activities. Having accurate information about jobs and their human requirements, which has been gathered in a gender-neutral, bias-free manner, is essential for legal compliance in each of these areas, as explained below:

Human Resources Planning   Knowing the actual requirements of jobs is essential in order to plan future staffing needs. As will be explained in the next chapter, when this information is combined with knowledge about the skills and qualifications of current employees, it is possible to determine which jobs can be filled

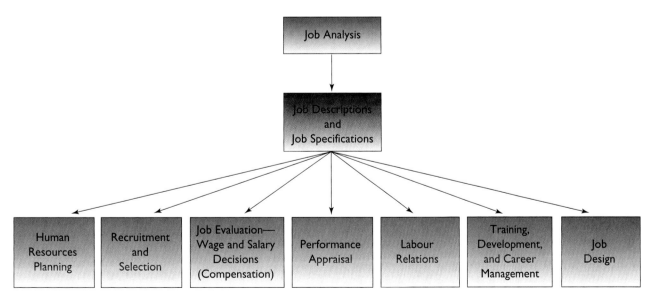

Figure 4.4
Uses of Job Analysis Information

internally and which will require external recruitment. Job analysis information is also extremely helpful in assessing how a firm's employment equity goals can be met most effectively.

Recruitment and Selection The job description and job specification information should be used to decide what sort of people to recruit and hire. Identifying bona fide occupational requirements and ensuring that all activities related to recruitment and selection, such as advertising, screening, and testing, are based on such requirements, is necessary in all Canadian jurisdictions to comply with human rights legislation.

Compensation Job analysis information is also essential for determining the relative value of and appropriate compensation for each job. Job evaluation should be based on the required skills, physical and mental demands, responsibilities, and working conditions—all assessed through job analysis. The relative value of jobs is one of the key factors used to determine appropriate compensation and justify pay differences if challenged under human rights or pay equity legislation. Information about the actual job duties is also necessary to determine whether a job should be classified as exempt or nonexempt for overtime pay and maximum hours purposes, as specified in employment standards legislation.

**www.ipmaac.org/
link-ja.html**
Job Analysis

Performance Appraisal To be legally defensible, the criteria used to assess employee performance must be directly related to the duties and responsibilities identified through job analysis. The standards used must also be justifiable. For many jobs involving routine tasks, especially those of a quantifiable nature, performance standards are determined through job analysis. For more complex jobs, performance standards are often jointly established by employees and their supervisors. To be realistic and achievable, such standards should be based on actual job requirements, as identified through job analysis.

Labour Relations In unionized environments, the job descriptions developed from the job analysis information are generally subject to union approval prior to finalization. Such union-approved job descriptions then become the basis for classifying jobs, and bargaining over wages, performance criteria, and working conditions. Once approved, significant changes to job descriptions may have to be negotiated.

Training, Development, and Career Management By comparing the knowledge, skills, and abilities (KSAs) that employees bring to the job with those that are identified by job analysis, managers can determine the gaps. Training programs can then be designed to bridge these gaps. Having accurate information about jobs also means that employees can prepare for future advancement by identifying gaps between their current KSAs and those specified for the jobs to which they aspire.

Job Design Job analysis is useful for ensuring that all the duties that have to be done have actually been assigned, and identifying areas of overlap. Also, having an accurate description of each job sometimes leads to the identification of unnecessary requirements, areas of conflict or dissatisfaction, and/or health and safety concerns, that can be eliminated through job redesign. Such redesign may increase morale and productivity and ensure compliance with human rights and occupational health and safety legislation.

As explained in the HR and the Responsive Organization box, Canadian Tire is one organization that has recognized the valuable role that job analysis can play.

HR and the Responsive Organization

The Central Role of Job Analysis at Canadian Tire

Since 1987, Canadian Tire has undergone dramatic restructuring. The number of layers in the corporate hierarchy was reduced from ten to five. As part of its overhaul, all major jobs were analyzed and the key "competencies" needed for each—skills, knowledge, values, and behaviours—were identified.

Concurrently, the company defined the "time horizons," or levels of accountability and authority, associated with each job. The time horizon considers to what extent the jobholder must be able to plan into the future to accomplish the job, and to what extent he or she is authorized to make decisions that will determine future direction without approval by a superior.

Employees at the base of the hierarchy work in a time horizon of zero to three months. One level up, managers operate under a time horizon of three months to one year. Above them are directors, whose time horizon is one to two years. Higher still, at the level of vice-president, the time horizon grows exponentially: two to five years. The presidential level is accorded a time horizon of five to ten years.

The emphasis on the job analysis and design process during restructuring served as a major catalyst for the company's subsequent growth and success. The organization was able to establish a meaningful link between overall corporate objectives and strategies for recruiting, training, performance management, and compensation.

Job analysis created an infrastructure for Canadian Tire by defining both the tasks to be performed and the timelines for performing them. Clearly defined roles and responsibilities, in turn, helped to ensure that every level of the hierarchy adds value to the level below, while minimizing unnecessary overlaps and role ambiguity.

Job analysis further paved the way for an effective compensation system. Canadian Tire uses a "skill-based" system that links pay to the complexity of a job.

By constructing a framework to evaluate performance and identify training and development needs, job analysis also supports recruiting. The information gathered helps the organization to determine whether any internal candidates might be suitable for a vacant position. Furthermore, since each job has been carefully defined in terms of contribution to the organization—including the skill and experience needed—the job criteria identify those candidates, whether internal or external, who can actively advance organizational goals.

Canadian Tire has also recognized that job analysis, by defining bona fide occupational requirements, has helped them create a legally-defensible hiring system. The criteria used to evaluate job candidates are directly linked to the effective performance of job duties.

Source: Claudine Kapel, "Giant Steps," *Human Resources Professional,* 9 no. 4 (April, 1993), pp. 13–6.

Steps in Job Analysis

The six steps in doing a job analysis are as follows.

Step 1 Identify the use to which the information will be put, since this will determine the types of data that should be collected and the techniques used. Some data collection techniques—such as interviewing the employee and asking what the job entails and what his or her responsibilities are—are good for writing job descriptions and selecting employees for the job. Other job analysis techniques (like the position analysis questionnaire, described later) do not provide qualitative information for job descriptions, but rather numerical ratings for each job; these can be used to compare jobs to one another for compensation purposes.

process chart
A diagram showing the flow of inputs to and outputs from the job under study.

Step 2 Review relevant background information such as organization charts, process charts, and job descriptions.[10] As explained earlier, organization charts show how the job in question relates to other jobs and where it fits in the overall organization. A **process chart** provides a more detailed understanding of the work flow than is obtainable from the organization chart alone. In its simplest form, a process chart (like the one in **Figure 4.5**) shows the flow of inputs to and outputs from the job under study. (In Figure 4.5 the inventory control clerk is expected to receive inventory from suppliers, take requests for inventory from the two plant managers, provide requested inventory to these managers, and give information to these managers on the status of in-stock inventories.) Finally, the existing job description, if there is one, can provide a starting point for building the revised job description.

Step 3 Select the representative positions and jobs to be analyzed. This is necessary when there are many incumbents in a single job and when a number of similar jobs are to be analyzed, since it would be too time consuming to analyze every position and job.

Step 4 Next, analyze the jobs by collecting data on job activities, required employee behaviours, working conditions, and human traits and abilities needed to perform the job, using one or more of the job analysis techniques explained later this chapter.

**Figure 4.5
Process Chart for
Analyzing a Job's
Work Flow**

Source: Richard I. Henderson, *Compensation Management: Rewarding Performance,* 2nd ed., copyright 1985, p. 158. Reprinted by permission of Prentice-Hall, Englewood Cliffs, NJ.

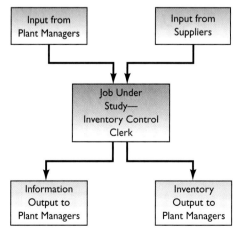

http://harvey.psyc.vt.edu/ja.html
Job Analysis

Step 5 Review the information with job incumbents. The job analysis information should be verified with the worker(s) performing the job and with the immediate supervisor. This will help to confirm that the information is factually correct and complete. By providing an opportunity for review and modification, if necessary, this step can also help gain the employees' acceptance of the job analysis data, as well as the documents derived from this data and subsequent decisions reached.

Step 6 Develop a job description and job specification. A job description and a job specification are the two concrete products of the job analysis. As explained earlier, the *job description* is a written statement that describes the activities and responsibilities of the job, as well as important features of the job such as working conditions and safety hazards. The *job specification* summarizes the personal qualities, traits, skills, and background required. While there may be a separate document describing the human qualifications, job descriptions and specifications are often combined in a single document, generally titled "Job Description."

Methods of Collecting Job Analysis Information

There are various techniques used for collecting information about the duties, responsibilities, and requirements of the job, and the most important ones will be discussed in this section. In practice, when the information is being used for multiple purposes, ranging from developing recruitment criteria to compensation decisions, several techniques may be used in combination.

Who Collects the Job Information? Collecting job analysis data usually involves a joint effort by an HR specialist, the incumbent, and the jobholder's supervisor. The HR specialist (perhaps an HR manager, job analyst, or consultant) might observe and analyze the work being done and then develop a job description and specification. The supervisor and incumbent generally also get involved, perhaps by filling out questionnaires. The supervisor and incumbent typically review and verify the job analyst's conclusions regarding the job's duties, responsibilities, and requirements.

The Interview

Three types of interview are used to collect job analysis data: individual interviews with each employee; group interviews with employees having the same job; and supervisory interviews with one or more supervisors who are thoroughly knowledgeable about the job being analyzed. The group interview is used when a large number of employees are performing similar or identical work, and it can be a quick and inexpensive way of learning about the job. As a rule, the immediate supervisor attends the group session; if not, the supervisor should be interviewed separately to get that person's perspective on the duties and responsibilities of the job.

Whichever interview method is used, the interviewee should fully understand the reason for the interview, since there's a tendency for such interviews to be misconstrued as "efficiency evaluations." When they are, interviewees may not be willing to accurately describe their jobs or those of their employees.

Pros and Cons The interview is probably the most widely used method for determining the duties and responsibilities of a job, and its wide use reflects its advantages. Most important, interviewing allows the incumbent to report activities and behaviour that might not otherwise come to light. For example, important activities that occur only occasionally or informal communication (between, say, a production supervisor and the sales manager) that would not be obvious from the organization chart could be unearthed by a skilled interviewer. The interview also provides an opportunity to explain the need for and functions of job analysis, and it can let the interviewee vent frustrations or views that might otherwise go unnoticed by management. Interviews are also a relatively simple and quick way to collect information.

This technique's major problem is distortion of information, whether due to outright falsification or honest misunderstandings.[11] A job analysis is often used as a prelude to changing a job's pay rate. Knowing that fact, employees tend to exaggerate certain responsibilities while minimizing others. Obtaining valid information can thus be a slow process. Interviewing is also fairly labour-intensive.

Typical Questions   Despite these drawbacks, interviews are widely used. Some typical interview questions include:

Why is the job being performed?

What are the major duties? What percentage of time is spent on each?

What are the major responsibilities?

What types of equipment, machinery, and/or tools are used?

What are the education, experience, skill, and (where applicable) certification and licensing requirements?

What are the basic accountabilities or performance standards that typify the work?

What are the job's physical demands? The emotional and mental demands?

In what physical location(s) is the work performed? What working conditions are involved?

What are the health and safety conditions? To what hazard(s) is there exposure, if any?

Most fruitful interviews follow a structured or checklist format. One such job analysis questionnaire is presented in **Figure 4.6**. It includes a series of detailed questions regarding such matters as the general purpose of the job; responsibilities and duties; education, experience, and skills required; physical and mental demands; and working conditions. A list like this can also be used by a job analyst who collects information by personally observing the work being done or by administering it as a questionnaire, two methods that will be explained shortly.[12]

Interview Guidelines   There are several things a job analyst should keep in mind when conducting a job analysis interview. First, the job analyst and supervisor should work together to identify the employees who know the most about the job, as well as those who might be expected to be the most objective in describing their duties and responsibilities.

Second, the job analyst should establish rapport quickly with the interviewee, by knowing the person's name, speaking in easily understood language, briefly reviewing the purpose of the interview, and explaining how the person came to be chosen.

Third, the analyst should follow a structured guide or checklist, one that lists questions and provides space for answers. This ensures that crucial questions are identified ahead of time, so that complete and accurate information is gathered, and that all interviewers (if there are more than one) glean the same types of data,

Figure 4.6
Job Analysis
Questionnaire
A questionnaire like this
one can be used to
interview job incumbents
or may be filled out by
them.

Source: Douglas Bartley, *Job
Evaluation: Wage and Salary
Administration* (Reading, MA:
Addison-Wesley Publishing
Company, 1981), p. 101–3.

JOB QUESTIONNAIRE
KANE MANUFACTURING COMPANY

NAME _____ JOB TITLE _____

DEPARTMENT _____ JOB NUMBER _____

SUPERVISOR'S NAME _____ SUPERVISOR'S TITLE _____

1. *SUMMARY OF DUTIES:* State briefly, in your own words, your main duties. If you are responsible for filling out reports/records, also complete Section 8.
_____
_____

2. *SPECIAL QUALIFICATIONS:* List any licenses, permits, certifications, etc. required to perform duties assigned to your position.
_____
_____

3. *EQUIPMENT:* List any equipment, machines, or tools (e.g., computer, calculator, motor vehicles, lathes, fork lifts, drill presses, etc.) you normally operate as a part of your position's duties.

EQUIPMENT	*AVERAGE NO. HOURS PER WEEK*
_____	_____
_____	_____
_____	_____

4. *REGULAR DUTIES:* In general terms, describe duties you regularly perform. Please list these duties in descending order of importance and percent of time spent on them per month. List as many duties as possible and attach additional sheets, if necessary.
_____
_____
_____

5. *CONTACTS:* Does your job require any contacts with other department members, other departments, outside companies, or agencies? If yes, please define the duties requiring contacts and *how often.*
_____
_____

6. *SUPERVISION:* Does your position have supervisory responsibilities? ( ) Yes ( ) No. If yes, please fill out a *Supplemental Position Description Questionnaire for Supervisors* and attach it to this form. If you have responsibility for the work of others but do not directly supervise them, please explain.
_____
_____

7. *DECISION MAKING:* Please explain the decisions you make while performing the regular duties of your job.
_____
_____

(continued)

Figure 4.6
(*continued*)

(a) What would be the probable result of your making (a) poor judgment(s) or decision(s), or (b) improper actions?

_____

_____

8. *RESPONSIBILITY FOR RECORDS*: List the reports and files you are required to prepare or maintain. State, in general, for whom each report is intended.

(a)   *REPORT*   *INTENDED FOR*

_____

_____

_____

(b)   *FILES MAINTAINED*

_____

_____

9. *FREQUENCY OF SUPERVISION:* How frequently must you confer with your supervisor or other employees in making decisions or in determining the proper course of action to be taken?

( ) Frequently   ( ) Occasionally   ( ) Seldom   ( ) Never

10. *WORKING CONDITIONS*: Please describe the conditions under which you work—inside, outside, air conditioned area, etc. Be sure to list any disagreeable or unusual working conditions.

_____

_____

11. *JOB REQUIREMENTS*: Please indicate the minimum requirements you believe are necessary to perform satisfactorily in your position.

(a) Education:
   Minimum schooling _____
   Number of years _____
   Specialization or major _____

(b) Experience:
   Type _____
   Number of years _____

(c) Special training:

      TYPE   *NUMBER OF YEARS*

_____

_____

(d) Special Skills:
   Keyboarding: _____ w.p.m.   Shorthand _____ w.p.m.
   Other: _____

12. *ADDITIONAL INFORMATION*: Please provide additional information, not included in any of the previous items, which you feel would be important in a description of your position.

_____

_____

_____

EMPLOYEE'S SIGNATURE _____ DATE: _____

thereby helping to ensure comparability of results. However, leeway should also be permitted by including some open-ended questions like "Was there anything we didn't cover with our questions?"

Fourth, when duties are not performed in a regular manner—for instance, when the incumbent doesn't perform the same tasks or jobs over and over again many times a day—the incumbent should be asked to list his or her duties *in order of importance* and *frequency* of occurrence. This will ensure that crucial activities that occur infrequently—like a nurse's occasional emergency room duties—aren't overlooked.

Finally, after the interview is completed, the data should be reviewed and verified. This is normally done by reviewing the information with both the interviewee and his or her immediate supervisor.

Questionnaires

Having employees fill out questionnaires to describe their job-related duties and responsibilities is another good method of obtaining job analysis information.

The major decision involved is determining how structured the questionnaire should be and what questions to include. Some questionnaires involve structured checklists. Each employee is presented with an inventory of perhaps hundreds of specific duties or tasks (such as "change and splice wire"). The employee is asked to indicate whether or not he or she performs each task and, if so, how much time is normally spent on each. At the other extreme, the questionnaire can be open ended and simply ask the employee to describe the major duties of his or her job. In practice, the best questionnaire often falls between these two extremes. As illustrated in Figure 4.6, a typical job analysis questionnaire might have several open-ended questions (such as "state your main job duties") as well as structured questions (concerning, for instance, job requirements).

Whether structured or unstructured, questionnaires have advantages and disadvantages. A questionnaire is a quick and efficient way of obtaining information from a large number of employees; it's less costly than interviewing hundreds of workers, for instance. However, developing the questionnaire and testing it (perhaps by making sure a representative sample of workers understand the questions) can be an expensive and time-consuming process.

www.acl.lanl.gov
Job Analysis

Observation

Direct observation is especially useful when jobs consist mainly of observable physical activities. Jobs like those of janitor, assembly-line worker, and accounting clerk are examples. On the other hand, observation is usually not appropriate when the job entails a lot of unmeasurable mental activity (lawyer, design engineer). Nor is it useful if the employee engages in important activities that might occur only occasionally, such as year-end reports.

Direct observation and interviewing are often used together. One approach is to observe the worker on the job during a complete work cycle. (The cycle is the time it takes to complete the job; it could be a minute for an assembly-line worker or an hour, a day, or longer for complex jobs.) All the job activities observed are noted. Then, after as much information as possible is accumulated, the incumbent is interviewed, asked to clarify points not understood, and explain what additional activities he or she performs that weren't observed. Another approach is to observe and interview simultaneously, while the jobholder performs his or her tasks.

Participant Diary/Log

diary/log
Daily listings made by employees of every activity in which they engage, along with the time each activity takes.

Another technique involves asking employees to keep a **diary/log** or a list of what they do during the day. Each employee records every activity in which he or she is involved (along with the time) in a log. This can produce a very complete picture of the job, especially when supplemented with subsequent interviews with the employee and his or her supervisor. The employee might, of course, try to exaggerate some activities and underplay others. However, the detailed, chronological nature of the log tends to minimize this problem.

Interviews, questionnaires, observations, and diary/logs are the most popular methods for gathering job analysis data. They all provide realistic information about what job incumbents actually do. The collected data can thus be used for developing job descriptions and job specifications.

Advantages and Disadvantages of the Conventional Data Collection Methods
Interviews, questionnaires, observation, and participant diaries are known as the conventional data collection methods. They are all qualitative in nature. Associated with each are certain advantages and disadvantages, as summarized in **Table 4.1.** By combining two or more conventional techniques, some of the disadvantages can be overcome.

TABLE 4.1 A Summary of General Data Collection Methods for Job Analysis and the Advantages/Disadvantages of Each

METHOD	VARIATIONS	BRIEF DESCRIPTION	ADVANTAGES	DISADVANTAGES
Observations	Structured	• Watch people go about their work; record frequency of behaviours or nature of performance on forms prepared in advance	• Third-party observer has more crdibility than job incumbents, who may have reasons for distorting information • Focuses more on reality than on perceptions	• Observation can influence behaviour of job incumbents • Meaningless for jobs requiring mental effort (in that case, use information processing method) • Not useful for jobs with a long job cycle
	Unstructured	• Watch people go about their work; describe behaviours/ tasks performed		
	Combination	• Part of the form is prepared in advance and is structured; part is unstructured		
Surveys	Structured	• Ask job incumbents/supervisors about work performed using fixed responses	• Relatively inexpensive • Structured surveys lend themselves easily to computer analyses • Good method when survey sample is widely scattered	• Depends on verbal skills of respondents • Does not allow for probing • Tends to focus on perceptions of the job
	Unstructured	• Ask job incumbents/supervisors to write essays to describe work performed		
	Combination	• Part of the survey is structured; part is unstructured		

TABLE 4.1 A Summary of General Data Collection Methods for Job Analysis and the Advantages/Disadvantages of Each (continued)

METHOD	VARIATIONS	BRIEF DESCRIPTION	ADVANTAGES	DISADVANTAGES
Diaries	Structured	• Ask people to record their activities over several days or weeks in a booklet with time increments provided	• Highly detailed informaton can be collected over the entire job cycle • Quite appropriate for jobs with a long job cycle	• Requires the job incumbent's participation and cooperation • Tends to focus on perceptions of the job
	Unstructured	• Ask people to indicate in a booklet over how long a period they work on a task or activity		
	Combination	• Part of the diary is structured; part is unstructured		
Individual Interviews	Structured	• Read questions and/or fixed response choices to job incumbent and supervisor; must be face to face	• More flexible than surveys • Allows for probing to extract information	• Depends heavily on rapport between interviewer and respondent • May suffer from validity/reliability problems
	Unstructured	• Ask questions and/or provide general response choices to job incumbent and supervisor; must be face to face		
	Combination	• Part of the interview is structured; part is unstructured		
Group Interviews	Structured	• Same as structured individual interviews except that more than one job incumbent/supervisor is interviewed	• Groups tend to do better than individuals with open-ended problem solving • Chance that reliability/validity higher than with individuals because group members cross check each other	• Cost more because more people are taken away from their jobs to participate • Like individual interviews, tends to focus on perceptions of the job
	Unstructured	• Same as unstructured individual interviews except that more than one job incumbent/supervisor is interviewed		
	Combination	• Same as combination individual interview except more than one job incumbent/supervisor is interviewed		

Source: William J. Rothewell and H. C. Kazanas, *Strategic Human Resource Planning and Management,* © 1988, pp. 66–68. Reprinted by permission of Prentice Hall, Inc., Englewood Cliffs, New Jersey.

Quantitative Job Analysis Techniques

Although most employers use interviews, questionnaires, observations, and/or diaries/logs for collecting job analysis data, there are many times when these narrative approaches are not appropriate. For example, when the aim is to assign a quantitative value to each job so that they can be compared for pay purposes, a more *quantitative* job analysis approach may be best. The *position analysis questionnaire* and *functional job analysis* are two popular quantitative methods.

position analysis questionnaire (PAQ)
A questionnaire used to collect quantifiable data concerning the duties and responsibilities of various jobs.

Position Analysis Questionnaire The **position analysis questionnaire (PAQ)** is a very structured job analysis questionnaire.[13] The PAQ itself is filled in by a job analyst, a person who should already be acquainted with the particular job to be analyzed. The PAQ contains 194 items, each of which represents a basic element that may or may not play an important role in the job. The job analyst decides whether each item plays a role on the job and, if so, to what extent. In **Figure 4.7**, for example, "written materials" received a rating of 4, indicating that materials such as books, reports, and office notes play a considerable role in this job.

The advantage of the PAQ is that it provides a quantitative score or profile of the job in terms of how that job rates on five basic dimensions: (1) having decision-making/communication/social responsibilities, (2) performing skilled activities, (3) being physically active, (4) operating vehicles/equipment, and (5) processing information. The PAQ's real strength is in classifying jobs. In other words, it allows the assignment of a quantitative score to each job, based on its decision-making, skilled activities, physical activity, vehicle/equipment operation, and information-processing characteristics. The PAQ results can be used to compare jobs to one another;[14] this information can then be used to determine appropriate pay levels.[15]

Functional Job Analysis This quantitative procedure rates each job in terms of the incumbent's responsibilities pertaining to data, people, and things. It also provides detailed information regarding the job's tasks, objectives, and training requirements.[16]

functional job analysis
A quantitative method for classifying jobs based on types and amounts of responsibility for data, people, and things, as well as the extent to which instructions, reasoning, judgment, and verbal facility are necessary for performing assigned tasks. Performance standards and training requirements are also identified.

Functional job analysis rates the job not only on responsibilities pertaining to data, people, and things, but also on the following dimensions: the extent to which specific *instructions, reasoning,* and *judgment* are required to perform the task; the *mathematical ability* required; and the verbal and *language facilities* involved. Functional job analysis also identifies performance standards and training requirements. Performing a job analysis using functional job analysis, therefore, allows the analyst to answer the question, "To do this task and meet these standards, what training does the worker require?"

Figure 4.8 illustrates a completed functional job analysis summary sheet. In this case the job is that of grader (a type of heavy-equipment operator employed in road building). As illustrated, the functional job analysis specifies things, data, people, instructions, reasoning, math, and language ratings. The summary sheet also lists the main tasks in the job, performance standards, and training required.

Figure 4.7
Portions of a Completed Page from the Position Analysis Questionnaire

Source: E.J. McCormick, P.R. Jeanneret, and R.D. Mecham, *Position Analysis Questionnaire.* Copyright 1989 by *Purdue Research Foundation, West Lafayette, Ind.* Reprinted with permission.

INFORMATION INPUT

1 INFORMATION INPUT

	Extent of Use (U)
NA	Does not apply
1	Nominal/very infrequent
2	Occasional
3	Moderate
4	Considerable
5	Very substantial

1.1 Sources of Job Information

Rate each of the following items in terms of the extent to which it is used by the worker as a source of information in performing the job.

1.1.1 Visual Sources of Job Information

1 | 4   Written materials (books, reports, office notes, articles, job instructions, signs, etc.)

2 | 2   Quantitative materials (materials that deal with quantities or amounts, such as graphs, accounts, specifications, tables of numbers, etc.)

3 | 1   Pictorial materials (pictures or picturelike materials used as *sources* of information, for example, drawings, blueprints, diagrams, maps, tracings, photographic films, x-ray films, TV pictures, etc.)

4 | 1   Patterns/related devices (templates, stencils, patterns, etc., used as *sources* of information when *observed* during use; do *not* include here materials described in item 3 above)

5 | 2   Visual displays (dials, gauges, signal lights, radarscopes, speedometers, clocks, etc.)

6 | 5   Measuring devices (rulers, calipers, tire pressure gauges, scales, thickness gauges, pipettes, thermometers, protractors, etc., used to obtain visual information about physical measurements; do *not* include here devices described in item 5 above)

7 | 4   Mechanical devices (tools, equipment, machinery, and other mechanical devices that are *sources* of information when *observed* during use or operation)

8 | 3   Materials in process (parts, materials, objects, etc., that are *sources* of information when being modified, worked on, or otherwise processed, such as bread dough being mixed, workpiece being turned in a lathe, fabric being cut, shoe being resoled, etc.)

9 | 4   Materials *not* in process (parts, materials, objects, etc., not in the process of being changed or modified, that are *sources* of information when being inspected, handled, packaged, distributed, or selected, etc., such as items or materials in inventory, storage, or distribution channels, items being inspected, etc.)

10 | 3   Features of nature (landscapes, fields, geological samples, vegetation, cloud formations, and other features of nature that are observed or inspected to provide information)

11 | 2   Man-made features of environment (structures, buildings, dams, highways, bridges, docks, railroads, and other "man-made" or altered aspects of the indoor or outdoor environment that are *observed* or *inspected* to provide job information; do not consider equipment, machines, etc., that an individual uses in the work, as covered by item 7)

Note: This exhibits 11 of the "information input" questions or elements. Other PAQ pages contain questions regarding mental processes, work output, relationships with others, job context, and other job characteristics.

TASK CODE: GR-08										

WORKER FUNCTION AND ORIENTATION						WORKER INSTRUCTIONS	GENERAL EDUCATIONAL DEVELOPMENT		
THINGS	%	DATA	%	PEOPLE	%		REASONING	MATH	LANGUAGE
3	65	3	25	1	10	3	2	1	3

GOAL: Operates Grader–Output Basic	OBJECTIVE: Backfilling, scarifying, windrowing, cutting firebreak, maintaining haul road, snow removal

TASK: Operates grader manipulating controls to travel forward/back, turn, raise/lower blade, position wheels and blade at correct angles; follows work order, drawing on knowledge and experience, monitoring the performance of the equipment and adapting to the changing situation, constantly alert to the presence and safety of other workers/equipment, in order to perform routine grader tasks such as backfilling, haul road maintenance, snow removal.

(To Perform This Task)

PERFORMANCE STANDARDS	TRAINING CONTENT
DESCRIPTIVE: — Operates equipment properly. — Is alert and attentive. NUMERICAL: — All work meets work order requirements. — No accidents/damage due to improper operating techniques.	FUNCTIONAL: — How to operate grader. — How to do routine grader tasks, such as backfilling, scarifying, windrowing, cutting firebreak, maintaining road, snow removal. SPECIFIC: — Knowledge of specific grader. — Knowledge of work requirements. — Knowledge of specific job site (i.e., layout, soil condition, environment).
(To These Standards)	*(Worker Needs This Training)*

Figure 4.8
Functional Job Analysis Task Statement
Source: Howard Olson, Sidney A. Fine, David C. Myers, and Margarette C. Jennings, "The Use of Functional Job Analysis in Establishing Performance for Heavy Equipment Operators," *Personnel Psychology,* Summer 1981, p. 354.

The National Occupational Classification and Job Analysis

National Occupational Classification (NOC)
A reference tool for writing job descriptions and job specifications. Compiled by the federal government, it contains comprehensive, standardized descriptions of about 25 000 occupations and the requirements for each.

The **National Occupational Classification (NOC)**, compiled by the federal government, is an excellent source of standardized information. It contains comprehensive descriptions of approximately 25 000 occupations and the requirements for each. To illustrate the types of information included, the NOC listing for Specialists in Human Resources is shown in **Figure 4.9**.

Introduced in 1993, the NOC represented a new structure for analyzing and understanding the labour market, reflecting occupational changes that have occurred over the past several decades. It replaced the Canadian Classification and Dictionary of Occupations (CCDO) and the closely-related Standard Occupational Classification (SOC) system devised by Statistics Canada. Each occupational categorization in the NOC is identified by a code number. A two-digit code is assigned at the *major group* level. A third digit is added at the *minor group* level, and a fourth digit is added at the *unit group* level. For example:

Figure 4.9
NOC Job Description for Specialists in Human Resources

Source: Employment and Immigration Canada, *National Occupational Classification*, Cat. No. MP 53-25/1–1992-E (Ottawa: Ministry of Supply and Service, 1992).

Specialists in Human Resources develop, implement, and evaluate human resources and labour relations policies, programs, and procedures and advise managers and employees on personnel matters. Specialists in Human Resources are employed throughout the private and public sectors, or may be self-employed.

Examples of titles classified in this unit group

Business Agent, Labour Union
Classification Officer
Classification Specialist
Compensation Research Analyst
Conciliator
Consultant, Human Resources
Employee Relations Officer

Employment Equity Officer
Human Resources Research Officer
Job Analyst
Labour Relations Officer
Mediator
Union Representative
Wage Analyst

Main duties

Specialists in Human Resources perform some or all of the following duties:

- Develop, implement, and evaluate personnel and labour relations policies, programs, and procedures
- Advise managers and employees on the interpretation of personnel policies, benefit programs, and collective agreements
- Negotiate collective agreements on behalf of employers or workers, and mediate labour disputes and grievances
- Research and prepare occupational classifications, job descriptions, and salary scales
- Administer benefit, employment equity and affirmative action programs, and maintain related record systems
- Coordinate employee performance and appraisal programs
- Research employee benefit and health and safety practices and recommend changes or modifications to existing policies.

Employment requirements

- A university degree or college diploma in a field related to personnel management, such as business administration, industrial relations, commerce, or psychology

or

Completion of a professional development program in personnel administration is required.

- Some experience in a clerical or administrative position related to personnel administration may be required.

Additional information

- Progression to management positions is possible with experience.

Classified elsewhere

- *Human Resources Managers (0112)*
- *Personnel and Recruitment Officers (1223)*
- *Personnel Clerks (1442)*
- *Professional Occupations in Business Services to Management (1122)*
- Training officers and instructors (in 4131 *College and Other Vocational Instructors*)

NOC job descriptions can help employers specify jobs in enough detail to identify a "salesperson—men's clothing."

- Major Group 31—Professional Occupations in Health
- Minor Group 314—Professional Occupations in Therapy and Assessment
- Unit Group 3142—Physiotherapists

These code numbers facilitate the exchange of statistical information about jobs, and are useful for vocational counselling and charting career paths. Since the fourteen NOC Major Group codes are now being used for employment equity reporting purposes, many companies formerly using CCDO and SOC codes have switched to NOC codes.

The two major job-attributes that were used as classification criteria in developing the NOC are skill level and skill type. Other factors, such as industry and occupational mobility, were also taken into consideration.[17] As illustrated in **Figure 4.10**, four skill-level categories are identified in the NOC, describing the educational and training requirements of occupations. Skill type is defined generally as the type of work performed. Ten broad occupational categories (0 to 9) are identified in the NOC, as shown in **Figure 4.11**.

One of the benefits of the former CCDO and the current NOC is that they have helped to promote a greater degree of uniformity in job titles and descriptions used by employers across Canada. This has facilitated the exchange of information about salaries and benefits for compensation administration purposes, and labour supply and demand for human resources planning. Standardized job descriptions also facilitate the movement of workers from areas experiencing high unemployment to those in which there are more job opportunities.

Figure 4.10
NOC Skill Level Criteria

Source: Employment and Immigration Canada, *National Occupational Classification,* 1993. Reproduced with permission of the Minister of Supply and Services Canada, 1998.

	Education/Training	Other
Skill Level A	University degree (Bachelor's, Master's, or postgraduate)	
Skill Level B	Two to three years of post-secondary education at community college, institute of technology, or CEGEP, *or*	Occupations with supervisory responsibilities are assigned to skill level B.
	Two to four years of apprenticeship training *or*	Occupations with significant health and safety responsibilities and registered nursing assistants) are assigned to skill level B.
	Three to four years of secondary school and more than two years of on-the-job training, training courses, or specific work experience	
Skill Level C	One to four years of secondary school education	
	Up to two years of on-the-job training, training courses, or specific work experience	
Skill Level D	Up to two years of secondary school and short work demonstration or on-the-job training	

**Figure 4.11
NOC Skill Type
Categories**

Source: Employment and
Immigration Canada, *National
Occupational Classification*,
1993. Reproduced with
permission of the Ministry of
Supply and Services Canada,
1998.

When the first digit is	... the Skill Type Category is
1	Business, Finance, and Administrative Occupations
2	Natural and Applied Sciences and Related Occupations
3	Health Occupations
4	Occupations in Social Science, Education, Government Service, and Religion
5	Occupations in Art, Culture, Recreation, and Sport
6	Sales and Service Occupations
7	Trades, Transport and Equipment Operators, and Related Occupations
8	Occupations Unique to Primary Industry
9	Occupations Unique to Processing, Manufacturing, and Utilities

When the second digit is	... the Skill Level Category is
1	Skill Level A (Professional Occupations)
2 or 3	Skill Level B (Technical, Paraprofessional, and Skilled Occupations)
4 or 5	Skill Level C (Intermediate Occupations)
6	Skill Level D (Labouring and Elemental Occupations)

Important Note: This applies to all occupations except management occupations. For management, the first digit is "0" and the second digit represents the skill type categories, from 1 to 9, as above.

Writing Job Descriptions

A job description is a written statement of *what* the jobholder actually does, *how* he or she does it, and under *what conditions* the job is performed.

There is no standard format used in writing a job description, but most descriptions contain the following types of information:

1. Job identification
2. Job summary
3. Relationships, responsibilities, and duties
4. Authority of incumbent
5. Standards of performance
6. Working conditions.

As mentioned previously, job specifications may also be included. An example of a partial job description is presented in **Figure 4.12**.

Job Identification

In Figure 4.12, the job identification section contains several types of information.[18] The *job title* specifies the title of the job, such as supervisor of data processing operations, sales manager, or inventory control clerk. (Job titles and descriptions should be kept current, and the NOC can be useful in this regard.) The *job status* section permits quick identification of eligibility for overtime pay. The *job code* permits easy referencing of all jobs. Each job in the organization should be identified with a code. While some firms devise their own coding systems based on wage classification, for example, many use NOC codes to facilitate external comparison and employment equity reporting.

SAMPLE JOB DESCRIPTION

Supervisor of Data Processing Operations	*Exempt*	*1216*
Job Title	Status	Job Code

July 3, 1997	*Olympia, Inc.–Main Office*
Date	Plant/Division

Arthur Allen	*Data Processing–Information Systems*
Written By	Department/Section

Juanita Montgomery	*12*	*736*
Approved By	Grade/Level	Points

Manager of Information Systems	*35 000–Mid 38 500–42 000*
Title of Immediate Supervisor	Pay Range

SUMMARY

Directs the operation of all data processing, data control, and data preparation requirements.

JOB DUTIES

1. Follows broadly-based directives.
   (a) Operates independently.
   (b) Informs Manager of Information Systems of activities through weekly, monthly, and/or quarterly schedules.
2. Selects, trains, and develops employees.
   (a) Develops spirit of cooperation and understanding among work group members.
   (b) Ensures that work group members receive specialized training as necessary in the proper functioning or execution of machines, equipment, systems, procedures, processes, and/or methods.
   (c) Directs training involving teaching, demonstrating, and/or advising users in productive work methods and effective communications with data processing.
3. Reads and analyzes wide variety of instructional and training information.
   (a) Applies latest concepts and ideas to changing organizational requirements.
   (b) Assists in developing and/or updating manuals, procedures, specifications, etc., relative to organizational requirements and needs.
   (c) Assists in the preparation of specifications and related evaluations of supporting software and hardware.
4. Plans, directs, and controls a wide variety of operational assignments by 5 to 7 employees; works closely with other managers, specialists, and technicians within Information Systems as well as with managers in other departments with data needs and with vendors.
   (a) Receives, interprets, develops, and distributes directives ranging from the very simple to the highly complex and technological in nature.
   (b) Establishes and implements annual budget for department.
5. Interacts and communicates with people representing a wide variety of units and organizations.
   (a) Communicates both personally and impersonally, through oral or written directives and memoranda, with all involved parties.
   (b) Attends local meetings of professional organizations in the field of data processing.

The *date* refers to the date the job description was actually written, and *written by* indicates the person who wrote it. There is also space to indicate who *approved* the description. The *immediate supervisor's title* is also shown in the identification section. Space is also provided to show the location of the job in terms of its *plant/division* and *department/section.* Information regarding the job's salary and/or pay scale is sometimes included, as well. If so, *grade/level* indicates the grade or level of the job in the wage or salary classification system, if there is one, and job evaluation points. Finally, the *pay range* space provides the specific pay or pay range of the job. Since pay rates change, many firms omit this information. Providing the grade or level facilitates cross referencing to the collective agreement or salary grid, so that pay information can be easily obtained.

Job Summary

The *job summary* should describe the general nature of the job, listing only its major functions or activities. Thus (as in Figure 4.12), the supervisor of data processing "directs the operation of all data processing, data control, and data preparation requirements." For the job of materials manager, the summary might state that the "materials manager purchases economically, regulates deliveries of, stores, and distributes all material necessary on the production line." For the job of mailroom supervisor, "the mailroom supervisor receives, sorts, and delivers all incoming mail properly, and he or she handles all outgoing mail including the accurate and timely posting of such mail."[19]

Relationships

The *relationships* statement shows the jobholder's relationships with others inside and outside the organization. Figure 4.12 does not include a relationship statement, but one might look like this for a human resources manager:[20]

> *Reports to:* vice-president of employee relations.
>
> *Supervises:* human resources specialist, test administrator, labour relations specialist, and one secretary.
>
> *Works with:* all department managers and senior management team members.
>
> *Outside the company:* employment agencies, executive recruiting firms, union representatives, Human Resources Development Canada (HRDC), and various vendors.[21]

Responsibilities and Duties

This section presents a detailed list of the job's actual responsibilities and duties. As in Figure 4.12, each of the job's major duties should be listed separately, and described in a few sentences. In the figure, for instance, the duty "selects, trains, and develops employees" is further defined as follows: "develops spirit of cooperation and understanding…" "ensures that work group members receive specialized training as necessary…," and "directs training involving teaching, demonstrating, and/or advising…." Typical duties for other jobs might include maintaining balanced and controlled inventories, making accurate postings to accounts payable, maintaining favourable purchase price variances, and repairing production line tools and equipment.

The NOC may be a helpful reference tool when itemizing a job's duties and responsibilities. As shown in Figure 4.9, for example, according to the NOC, a Specialist in Human Resources might be expected to: "develop, implement, and evaluate personnel and labour relations policies, programs and procedures"; "advise managers and employees on the interpretation of personnel policies, benefit programs, and collective agreements"; and "research and prepare occupational classifications, job descriptions, and salary scales."

General statements such as "performs other assignments as required" should be avoided. Most experts state unequivocally that "one item frequently found that should *never* be included in a job description is a 'cop-out clause' like 'other duties, as assigned,'"[22] since this leaves open the nature of the job, and the people needed to staff it, and can be subject to abuse.

While the duties and responsibilities should be described in sufficient detail that training requirements and performance appraisal criteria can be identified, and the qualifications outlined in the job specification can be justified, it is generally possible to make it clear that the incumbent may be asked to perform additional *related* duties, without resorting to such a "cop-out clause." If not, including a statement such as, "The duties and responsibilities outlined above are representative, but not all-inclusive," may meet the firm's need for flexibility without sacrificing the quality and usefulness of the job description.

Authority

This section of a job description should define the limits of the jobholder's authority, including his or her decision-making authority, direct supervision of other employees, and budgetary limitations. For example, the jobholder might have authority to approve purchase requests up to $5 000, grant time off or leaves of absence, discipline department employees, recommend salary increases, and interview and hire new employees.[23]

Standards of Performance

Some job descriptions also contain a *standards of performance* section. This states the standards the employee is expected to achieve in each of the job description's main duties and responsibilities.

Setting standards is never an easy matter. However, most managers soon learn that just telling employees to "do their best" doesn't provide enough guidance to ensure top performance. One straightforward way of setting standards is to finish the statement: "I will be completely satisfied with your work when. . . ." This sentence, if completed for each duty listed in the job description, should result in a usable set of performance standards.[24] Some examples would include the following:

Duty: Accurately Posting Accounts Payable

1. All invoices received are posted within the same working day.
2. All invoices are routed to the proper department managers for approval no later than the day following receipt.
3. No more than three posting errors per month occur on average.
4. Posting ledger is balanced by the end of the third working day of each month.

Duty: Meeting Daily Production Schedule

1. Work group produces no less than 426 units per working day.
2. No more than 2% of units are rejected at the next workstation, on average.
3. Work is completed with no more than 5% overtime per week, on average.

Working Conditions and Physical Environment

The job description will also list the general working conditions involved in the job. These might include information about noise level, temperature, lighting, degree of privacy, frequency of interruptions, hours of work, amount of travel, and hazards to which the incumbent may be exposed.

Job Description Guidelines

Here are some final guidelines for writing job descriptions:[25]

> *Be clear.* The job description should portray the work so well that the duties are clear without reference to other job descriptions.

Indicate scope of authority. Indicate the scope and nature of the work by using phrases such as "for the department" or "as requested by the manager." Include all important relationships.

Be specific. Select the most specific words to show (1) the kind of work, (2) the degree of complexity, (3) the degree of skill required, (4) the extent to which problems are standardized, (5) the extent of the worker's responsibility for each phase of the work, and (6) the degree and type of accountability. Use action words such as *analyze, gather, assemble, plan, devise, infer, deliver, transmit, maintain, supervise,* and *recommend.* Positions at the lower levels of the organization generally have the most detailed explanations of duties and tasks, while higher-level positions tend to have broader responsibility statements, rather than an outline of specific tasks.

Be brief. Short, accurate statements usually best accomplish the purpose.

Recheck. Finally, to check whether the description fulfills the basic requirements, ask, "Will a new employee understand the job if he or she reads the job description?"

Writing Job Descriptions that Comply with Human Rights Legislation   As explained in chapter 3, human rights legislation requires employers to ensure that there is no discrimination on any of the prohibited grounds in any aspect or terms and conditions of employment. When assessing suitability for employment, training program enrolment, and transfers or promotions; and appraising performance, the sole criteria examined should be knowledge, skills, and abilities, as required by the essential duties of the job. While employers are not legally obligated to have job descriptions, it is highly advisable, since failure to develop such descriptions may mean that job duties are never determined, clarified, prioritized, and justified. Essential job duties should be clearly identified in the job description. Indicating the percentage of time spent on each duty and/or listing duties in order of importance are strategies used to differentiate between essential and nonessential tasks and responsibilities.

Even when an employee cannot perform one or more of the essential duties of the job due to reasons related to a prohibited ground, such as a physical disability or religion, an employer is expected to make "reasonable accommodations," unless doing so would present "undue hardship."

Small Business Applications

A Practical Approach

Without the benefit of their own job analysts or (in many cases) their own HR managers, many small business owners face two hurdles when conducting job analyses and writing job descriptions. First (given their need to concentrate on other pressing matters), they often need a more streamlined approach than those provided by questionnaires like the one shown in Figure 4.6. Second, there is always the reasonable fear that in writing up their job descriptions they will inadvertently overlook duties that should be assigned to employees or assign duties to employees that are usually not associated with such positions. What they need here is a sort of encyclopedia listing all the possible positions they might encounter, including a detailed listing of the duties normally assigned to these positions. Such an "encyclopedia" exists, as the National Occupational Classification (NOC) mentioned earlier. The *practical approach to job analysis for small-business owners* presented next is built around this invaluable device.

Step 1. Decide on a Plan.

Developing at least the broad outlines of a corporate plan is the first step. What is sales revenue expected to be next year, and in the next few years? What products will be emphasized? What areas or departments in the company will likely have to be expanded, reduced, or consolidated, given the firm's overall plan? What kinds of new positions will be needed in order to accomplish the strategic plans?

Step 2. Develop an Organization Chart.

Given the plan, the next step should be to develop an organization chart for the firm. A chart should be drawn showing who reports to the owner or CEO and who reports to each of the other managers and supervisors in the firm. Drawing up the organization chart as it is now comes first. Then, depending upon how far in advance planning is being done, a chart showing how the organization should look in the immediate future (say, in two months) and perhaps two or three other charts showing how the organization is likely evolve over the next two or three years can be produced.

Step 3. Use a Job Analysis/Description Questionnaire.

Next, a job analysis questionnaire can be used to determine what the job entails. One of the more comprehensive job analysis questionnaires may be useful (see Figure 4.6, for instance) for collecting job analysis data. A simpler and often satisfactory alternative is to use the job description questionnaire presented in **Figure 4.13**. The information called for should be filled in (using the procedure outlined later) and the supervisors or the employees themselves asked to list their job duties (on the bottom of the page), breaking them into daily duties, periodic duties, and duties performed at irregular intervals. A sample of how one of these duties should be described (**Figure 4.14**) can be distributed to supervisors and/or employees.

Step 4. Obtain a copy of the National Occupational Classification (NOC) for Reference.

Next, standardized examples of the job descriptions needed should be obtained from the *NOC*. A copy can be found in the reference section of the library in most major centres or purchased through the Ministry of Supply and Services in Ottawa.

Step 5. Choose Appropriate Definitions and Copy Them for Reference.

For each department, the NOC job titles and job descriptions that are believed to be appropriate for the enterprise should be chosen and copied for future reference.

Step 6. Put Appropriate NOC Summaries on the Top of the Job Description Form.

The job description should be written next. To facilitate this, the corresponding NOC code(s) and NOC definition(s) should be written under the appropriate headings on the Job Description Form in Figure 4.13. Particularly when (as is usually the case) only one or two NOC definitions apply to the job description being written, the NOC definition will provide a firm foundation for the one being created. It will provide a standardized list and constant reminder of the specific duties that should be included. Including the NOC codes and definitions will also facilitate conversations with the local Human Resource Centre, should this source be used to help find employees for open positions.

Step 7. Complete the Job Description.

An appropriate job summary for the job under consideration can then be written. Next, the job analysis information obtained in step 3, together with the information gathered from the NOC, can be used to create a complete listing of the tasks and duties of each of the jobs. The working conditions section can be completed once all of the tasks and duties have been specified.◆

Figure 4.13
Job Description
Questionnaire

Background Data
for Job Description

Job Title _____   Department _____

Job Number _____   Written by _____

Today's Date _____   Applicable NOC Code(s)_____

I.   Applicable NOC Definition(s):

II.   Job Summary:
     (Summarize the more important or regularly performed tasks)

III.   Reports to:

IV.   Supervises: _____

V.   Job Duties: _____
     *(Briefly describe, for each duty, what employee does and, if possible, how
     employee does it. Show in parentheses at end of each duty the approximate
     percentage of time devoted to it.)*

     A.   Daily Duties:

     B.   Periodic Duties:
          (Indicate whether weekly, monthly, quarterly, etc.)

     C.   Duties Performed at Irregular Intervals:

VI.   Working Conditions:

Figure 4.14
Examples of
Background Data

Example of Job Title: Customer Service Clerk

Example of Job Summary: Answers inquiries and gives directions to customers, authorizes cashing of customers' cheques, records and returns lost charge cards, sorts and reviews new credit applications, and works at the customer-service desk.

Example of One Job Duty: Authorizes cashing of cheques: authorizes cashing of personal or payroll cheques (up to a specified amount) by customers desiring to make payment by cheque. Requests identification, such as driver's licence, from customers, and examines cheque to verify date, amount, signature, and endorsement. Initials cheque and sends customer to cashier.

Writing Job Specifications

Writing the job specification involves examining the duties and responsibilities and answering the question, "What human traits and experience are required to do this job?" Both skill and effort factors should be considered, as well as the human implications of the working conditions. Much of this information can be gleaned from the job analysis questionnaire. The job specification clarifies what kind of person to recruit and for what qualities that person should be tested. As mentioned previously, the job specification may be a separate section on the job description or a separate document entirely; often it is presented on the back of the job description.[26]

Specifications for Trained versus Untrained Employees

Writing job specifications for trained employees might seem relatively straightforward. For example, the specifications for an intermediate-level programming position, accountant, or human resources manager tend to focus primarily on length of previous experience required, educational qualifications, and specialized skills or training needed. However, to comply with human rights legislation, it is imperative that all qualifications listed be justifiable based on actual job duties and responsibilities. Unjustifiably high educational and/or lengthy experience requirements can lead to systemic discrimination. For that reason, many employers are no longer indicating that a degree or diploma is mandatory; rather, they specify that the position calls for a university degree in a specific area, a college diploma in that area, or an equivalent combination of education and work experience.

The job specification for already-trained candidates, such as the financial analysts here at IBM, should indicate clearly that computer literacy is a requirement.

The problems are even more complex when developing job specifications for entry-level positions for which on-the-job training will be provided, since instead of focusing on education or experience, the emphasis is often on physical traits, personality, and/or sensory skills. The actual physical and mental demands of the job become critical. The goal is to identify those personal traits—the human requirements—that are valid predictors of job success. For example, if the job requires detailed manipulation on a circuit-board assembly line, finger dexterity is extremely important, and is something for which candidates should be tested.

Identifying the human requirements for a job is accomplished either through a judgmental approach or statistical analysis.

Job Specifications Based on Judgment

The judgmental approach is based on the educated guesses of job incumbents, supervisors, and human resources managers. The basic procedure here is to ask questions such as "What does it take in terms of education, knowledge, training, and the like to do this job well?" on the job analysis questionnaire.

Based on the information gathered on the job analysis questionnaire, and a careful perusal of the duties and responsibilities listed in the job description, a job specification form, like that shown in **Figure 4.15** should be completed. When filling in human requirements on the job analysis questionnaire and when developing the job specifications, it is important that the actual qualifications of the current incumbent not be confused with the minimum requirements to do the job, since the current jobholder might be under- or overqualified. To avoid overstating or understating qualifications, it is helpful to ask the question, "What minimum qualifications would be required if this job was being filled in the

Figure 4.15
Job Specification Form

Job Specification

Job Title: _____   Job Code: _____

Department: _____   Job Grade: _____

Supervisor's Title: _____   Status: _____

Author: _____   Date: _____

_____

JOB SUMMARY:

SKILL FACTORS:

Education

Experience

Nature of Communication Skills Required
(Oral/Written, Internal/External)

EFFORT FACTORS:

Physical Demands

Mental Demands

WORKING CONDITIONS:

APPROVAL SIGNATURES:

_____   _____
Incumbent   Supervisor

CURRENT DATE: _____   LAST REVIEW DATE: _____

immediate future?" All qualifications listed must be justifiable based on the current job duties and responsibilities.

When developing job specifications, the NOC can provide helpful reference information. Job analysts and vocational counsellors have made judgments regarding the human requirements of all of the occupations included.

To illustrate the types of information and amount of detail that should be provided, a sample job specification for a trust company customer service representative has been included as **Figure 4.16**.

A **physical demands analysis**, which identifies the senses used, and type, frequency, and amount of physical effort involved in the job, is often used to supplement the job specification. A sample form is included as **Figure 4.17**. Having such detailed information is particularly beneficial when determining accommodation requirements.

Job Specifications Based on Statistical Analysis

Basing a job specification on statistical analysis is the most defensible approach, but it is also more difficult. Basically, the aim is to statistically determine the relationship between (1) some *predictor* or human trait such as verbal or written communication skills, keyboarding speed, or finger dexterity and (2) some indicator or *criterion* of job effectiveness (such as performance, as rated by the supervisor). The procedure has five steps: (1) analyze the job and decide how to measure job performance; (2) select personal traits like finger dexterity that are believed to predict successful performance; (3) test job candidates for these traits; (4) measure these candidates' subsequent job performance; and (5) statistically analyze the relationship between the human trait (finger dexterity) and job performance. The objective is to determine whether the former predicts the latter. In this way, the human requirements for performing the job can be statistically ascertained.

This method is more defensible than the judgmental approach, since human rights legislation forbids using traits that could lead to discrimination on a prohibited ground in any employment decisions, unless the employer can prove that there is a bona fide occupational requirement. A statistical validation study provides such proof.

Job Analysis in a "Jobless" World

Over the past few years, the concept of *job* has been changing quite dramatically. As one observer recently put it:

> *The modern world is on the verge of another huge leap in creativity and productivity, but the job is not going to be part of tomorrow's economic reality. There still is and will always be enormous amounts of work to do, but it is not going to be contained in the familiar envelopes we call jobs. In fact, many organizations are today well along the path toward being "de-jobbed."*[27]

Why Companies Are Becoming De-jobbed: The Need for Responsiveness

De-jobbing is ultimately a product of the rapid changes taking place in business today. Organizations need to grapple with a number of revolutionary forces: accelerating product and technological change, globalized competition, deregulation, political instability, demographic changes, and trends toward a service society

Job Specification

Job Title: <u>Customer Service Representative</u> Job Code: <u>CSR.1002173</u>
Location: <u>Main Branch</u> Job Grade: <u>CSR Level 1</u>
Supervisor's Title: <u>Assistant Manager</u> Status: <u>Nonexempt</u>
Author: <u>Renée Cousineau</u> Date: <u>October 06, 1997</u>

JOB SUMMARY:

The incumbent is required to provide courteous, prompt, and efficient customer service in order to achieve a high level of customer satisfaction; identify, resolve, or refer customer banking and account maintenance needs, including the sale of bank products/services to the appropriate trained personnel; carefully handle and balance all cash and related on-line computer entries, in accordance with established Bank Security procedures; and facilitate branch work flow by assisting others with cash counts and preparing customer statements.

SKILL FACTORS:

Education
High School Diploma or an equivalent combination of education and experience. Must have some background in mathematics and accounting. Data entry/keyboarding skills are also required.

Experience
No prior experience is necessary. In-house training will be provided. Working knowledge of the physical handling/counting of cash and procedures for balancing cash and accounting entries would be an asset.

Nature of Communication Skills Required
Excellent oral communication skills are required. The incumbent must be able to communicate courteously and effectively. Excellent interpersonal skills are also mandatory. All functions must be handled with tact and diplomacy.

Customer service delivery involves almost constant contact with the public. External employment-related contacts may include government officials, local business employers and employees, social assistance recipients, and visitors to the community.

EFFORT FACTORS:

Physical Demands
The incumbent is required to stand during the majority of working hours, and spends extended periods in front of a computer monitor. Transferring coins to and from the vault involves a moderate degree of bending, lifting, and carrying.

Mental Demands
Handling customer service functions requires extended periods of mental attention. Entering customer transaction data on the online computer system and handling cash transactions requires concentrated visual attention.

Customer profile information is confidential, which requires moderate discretion.

There is a moderate level of complexity involved in this job. Duties are governed by formal policies and procedures, but dealings with the public require some independent judgment. A supervisor is available at all times to provide consultation and/or authorization.

The consequences of errors are serious, in terms of customer satisfaction and confidence in the bank and its services. Customer Service Representatives are required to balance with 100 percent accuracy at least 80 percent of the days in each month. There is a $30.00 allowance given daily, after which errors are counted against the employee. Employees who do not meet the monthly accuracy standard are subject to disciplinary action.

WORKING CONDITIONS:

The working environment makes few demands on the jobholder. (The incumbent works in a well-lit, well-ventilated, smoke-free, temperature-controlled modern office.) Customer service delivery functions may involve exposure to occasional unpleasant situations and can cause a moderate degree of stress. The incumbent may be scheduled to work on Saturdays and will be required to work overtime on occasion.

APPROVAL SIGNATURES:

_____ _____
Incumbent Supervisor

CURRENT DATE: _____ LAST REVIEW DATE: _____

Figure 4.17
Physical Demands Analysis Form*

Source: Ontario Women's Directorate, *Equity Works Best.* Used with permission.

* Developed by the Ontario Ministry of Labour

Physical Demands Analysis

	Physical Demands		Check if Performed	Weight — Maximum (usual)	*Frequency — 0 Never	1 Seldom	2 Minor	3 Required	4 Major	Comments
Strength	Lifting									
	Carrying									
	Pushing									
	Pulling									
	Fine Finger Movements									
	Handling									
	Gripping									
	Reaching	Above Shoulder								
		Below Shoulder								
	Foot Action	1 Foot								
		2 Feet								
Mobility	Throwing									
	Sitting									
	Standing									
	Walking									
	Running									
	Climbing									
	Bending/Stooping									
	Crouching									
	Kneeling									
	Crawling									
	Twisting									
	Balancing									
Sensory/Perceptual	Hearing	Conversation								
		Other Sounds								
	Vision	Far								
		Near								
		Colour								
		Depth								
	Perception	Spatial								
		Form								
	Feeling									
	Reading									
	Writing									

Human Rights Considerations**
Essential Duties

Non-essential Duties

**Review duties before interview.
Discuss reasonable accommodation at interview.

Frequency (The frequency of maximum weight should be shown without brackets and the frequency of usual weight, within brackets)
0–Not Performed
1–Seldom Performed
2–Minor Daily Activity, Less than 1 Hour
3–Frequent Repetition, for 1–3 Hours Daily
4–Major Job Demand, Maximum ability required.
Frequent Repetition for more than 3 Hours Daily.

and the information age. Forces like these have changed the playing field on which firms compete. Specifically, rapid change has dramatically increased the need for firms to be responsive, flexible, and capable of competing in a global marketplace.

The organizational techniques firms have used to foster responsiveness have helped to blur the meaning of *job* as a set of well-defined and clearly delineated set of responsibilities. Here is a sampling of how these techniques have contributed to this blurring:

Flatter Organizations   Instead of pyramid-shaped organizations with seven or more management layers, flat organizations with just three or four levels are becoming more prevalent. Many firms (including ABB and Celestica Inc., as described in chapter 1) have already cut their management layers from a dozen to six or fewer. As the remaining managers are left with more people reporting to them, they can supervise them less, so every employee's job ends up involving greater breadth and depth of responsibilities.

Work Teams   Work itself is increasingly organized around teams and processes rather than around specialized functions. Over 40 percent of those responding to a recent Conference Board of Canada survey indicated that team-based activity was widespread.[28] Many organizations, such as London Life,[29] Fedex, and Xerox Canada,[30] have introduced self-managed teams. In these organizations, employees' jobs change daily; the effort to avoid having employees view their jobs as a limited and specific set of responsibilities is thus intentional.

In many firms, the widespread use of teams and similar structural mechanisms mean that the boundaries that typically separate organizational functions (like sales and production) and hierarchical levels are reduced and made more permeable. In such firms, responsiveness is fostered by encouraging employees to rid themselves of the "It's not my job" attitude that typically creates walls between one employee area and another. Instead, the focus is on defining the job at hand in terms of the overall best interests of the organization, thereby further de-jobbing the company.

The Boundaryless Organization   As mentioned briefly in chapter 1, boundaryless organization structures are emerging. In this type of structure, relationships (typically joint ventures) are formed with customers, suppliers, and/or competitors, to pool resources for mutual benefit or encourage cooperation in an uncertain environment.

As in team-based organizations, barriers are broken down—in this case between the organization and its suppliers, customers, or competitors, and teams are emphasized. The teams, however, may include employees representing each of the companies involved in the joint venture.

In such structures, jobs are defined in very general terms, since the emphasis is on the overall best interests of the organizations involved.

Reengineering   **Reengineering** is defined as "the fundamental rethinking and radical redesign of business processes to achieve dramatic improvements in critical, contemporary measures of performance, such as cost, quality, service, and speed."[31] In their book, *Reengineering the Corporation,* Michael Hammer and James Champy argue that the principles (like highly specialized divisions of work) that shaped the structure and management of business since the Industrial Revolution should be retired. Instead, the firm should emphasize combining tasks into integrated, unspecialized processes that are then carried out by committed employees.

reengineering
The fundamental rethinking and radical redesign of business processes to achieve dramatic improvement in contemporary measures of performance.

Reengineering is achieved in several ways. Specialized jobs are combined into one so that formerly distinct jobs are integrated and compressed into enlarged, enriched ones.[32] A necessary correlate of combining jobs is that workers make more decisions, since each person's responsibilities are generally broader and deeper after reengineering; supervisory checks and controls are reduced; and, indeed, committed employees largely control their own efforts. Finally, workers become collectively responsible for overall results rather than individually responsible for just their own tasks. As a result, their jobs change dramatically. "They share joint responsibility with their team members for performing the whole process, not just a small piece of it. They not only use a broader range of skills from day to day, they have to be thinking of a far greater picture."[33] Most importantly, "while not every member of the team will be doing exactly the same work ... the lines between [the workers' jobs] blur." And to that extent reengineering also contributes to de-jobbing the enterprise.

The Future of Job Descriptions

Most firms today continue to utilize job descriptions and to rely on jobs as traditionally defined. However, it's clear that more and more firms are moving toward new organizational configurations, ones built around jobs that are broad and that may change every day. As one writer has said, "In such a situation people no longer take their cues from a job description or a supervisor's instructions. Signals come from the changing demands of the project. Workers learn to focus their individual efforts and collective resources on the work that needs doing, changing as that changes. Managers lose their 'jobs,' too. . . ."[34] The HR and the Responsive Organization box below describes some practical HR implications.

HR and the Responsive Organization

Job Analysis, HR, and the De-Jobbed Company

Because job descriptions are (deservedly) so well ingrained in the way that most companies operate, it's unlikely that most firms could (or should) do without them, at least for now. But for the growing number of firms that are shifting to HR systems that don't use job descriptions, what replaces them?

In one firm—British Petroleum's exploration division—the need for flatter organizations and empowered employees inspired management to replace job descriptions with matrices listing skills and skill levels.[1] Senior management wanted to shift employees' attention from a job description/"that's not my job" mentality to one that would motivate employees to obtain the new skills they needed to accomplish their broader responsibilities. The solution was a skills matrix like that shown in **Figure 4.18**. Skills matrices were created for various jobs within two classes of employees, those on a management track, and those whose aims lay elsewhere (such as to stay in engineering). For each job or job family (such as drilling manager), a matrix was prepared. As in Figure 4.18, it identified (1) the basic skills needed for that job and (2) the minimum *level* of each skill required for that job or job family.

Such a matrix shifts employees' focus. The emphasis is no longer on a job description's listing of specific job duties. Instead the focus is on developing the new skills needed for the employees' broader, empowered, and often relatively undefined responsibilities.

The skills matrix appears as a grid. Included but not shown are descriptors for each level of each skill, beginning at the bottom (A) with the lowest level, and increasing with the highest level at the top. For instance, under technical expertise, level A might read, "Is acquiring basic knowledge and has awareness of the key skills," while level H might read, "Conducts and/or supervises complex tasks requiring advanced knowledge of key skills or a thorough working knowledge of a range of key skills."

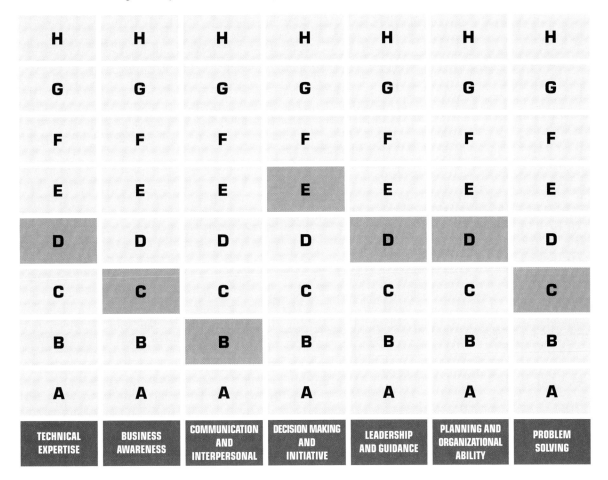

Figure 4.18
The Skills Matrix
The darker boxes indicate the minimum level of skill required for the job.

The skills matrix approach has prompted other HR changes in BP's exploration division. For example, the matrices provide a constant reminder of what skills employees must improve, and the firm's new skill-based pay plan awards raises based on skills improvement. Similarly, performance appraisals now focus more on employee skills, and training emphasizes developing broad skills like leadership and planning—ones that are applicable across a wide range of responsibilities and jobs.

Broader HR issues are also involved when firms de-job. For one thing, ". . . [firms] must find people who can work well without the cue system of job descriptions."[2] This puts a premium on hiring people with the skills and values to handle empowered jobs. As two reengineering experts put it:

For multi-dimensional and changing jobs, companies don't need people to fill a slot, because the slot will be only roughly defined. Companies need people who can figure out what the job takes and do it, people who can create the slot that fits them. Moreover, the slot will keep changing.[3]

There's also a shift from training to education, in other words, from teaching employees the "how" of the job to increasing their insight and understanding regarding its "why." In a rapidly changing industrial environment, the demands for flexibility and responsiveness mean that it's impossible to hire people ". . . who already know everything they're ever going to need to know. . . ."[4] Here, continuing education over the course of the employees' organizational career becomes the norm.◆

1. Milan Moravec and Robert Tucker, "Job Descriptions for the 21st Century," *Personnel Journal* (June 1992), pp. 37–44.
2. William Bridges, "The End of the Job," *Fortune* (September 19, 1994), p. 68.
3. Michael Hammer and James Champy, *Reengineering the Corporation* (New York: Harper Business, 1993), p. 72.
4. Hammer and Champy, *Reengineering*, p. 72.

Chapter Review

Summary

1. Organizational structure refers to the formal relationships among jobs in an organization, and is often depicted is an organization chart. There are three basic types of organizational structures: bureaucratic, flat, and boundaryless.

2. In any organization, work has to be divided into manageable units and ultimately into jobs that can be performed by employees. The process of organizing work into tasks that are required to perform a specific job is known as job design.

3. The term job as it is known today is largely an outgrowth of the efficiency demands of the industrial revolution, which led to work simplification. Industrial engineering, which also evolved at this time, is concerned with analyzing work methods; making work cycles more efficient by modifying, combining, rearranging, or eliminating tasks; and establishing time standards.

4. By the mid-1900s, job enlargement and job rotation evolved as popular strategies to overcome the dehumanizing aspects of highly repetitive and specialized jobs and other problems associated with overspecialization. More recently, job enrichment, based on the premise that the best way to motivate workers is to build opportunities for challenge and achievement into jobs, has become popular.

5. Job design studies explored a new field when behavioural scientists focused on identifying various job dimensions that would simultaneously improve the efficiency of organizations and job satisfaction of employees. One of the best known theories evolving from such research is the job characteristics model, which proposed that employee motivation and satisfaction are directly linked to five core characteristics: skill variety, task identity, task significance, autonomy, and feedback.

6. Over time, it became apparent that in addition to considering psychological needs, effective job design must also take physiological needs and health and safety issues into account. Human engineering, or ergonomics, seeks to integrate and accommodate the physical needs of workers into the design of jobs.

7. Once jobs have been designed or redesigned, an employer's performance-related expectations need to be defined and communicated. This is best accomplished

through job analysis. In contrast to job design, which reflects subjective opinions about the ideal requirements of a job, job analysis is concerned with objective and verifiable information about the actual requirements of a job. Once this information has been gathered, it is used for developing job descriptions (what the job entails) and job specifications (what the human requirements are).

8. Job analysis involves six steps: (1) determine the use to which the information will be put, (2) collect background information, (3) select the representative positions and jobs to be analyzed, (4) collect data, (5) review the information collected with the incumbents and their supervisors, and (6) develop the job descriptions and job specifications.

9. There are four conventional techniques used to gather job analysis data: interviews, questionnaires, direct observation, and participant logs. Quantitative job analysis techniques, useful when classifying jobs for pay purposes is a key aim, include the position analysis questionnaire (PAQ) and functional job analysis (FJA).

10. A job description is a written statement of what the jobholder actually does, how he or she does it, and under what conditions the job is performed. Typical information included is the job identification; a job summary; the relationships, responsibilities and duties; authority of incumbent; standards of performance; and working conditions.

11. The job specification involves examining the duties and responsibilities and answering the question, "What human traits and experience are required to do this job?" Both skill and effort factors should be considered, as well and the human implications of the working conditions. A physical demands analysis is often used to supplement the job specification.

12. De-jobbing is ultimately a product of the rapid changes taking place in business today. As firms try to speed decision making by taking steps like reengineering, individual jobs are becoming broader and much less specialized. Increasingly, firms don't want employees to feel limited by a specific set of responsibilities like those listed in a job description. As a result, more employees are deemphasizing detailed job descriptions, often substituting brief job summaries, perhaps combined with summaries of the skills required for the position.

Key Terms

diary/log
functional job analysis
human engineering
  (ergonomics)
industrial engineering
job
job analysis
job description
job design

job enlargement
job enrichment
job rotation
job specification
National Occupational
  Classification (NOC)
organizational structure
organization chart
physical demands

  analysis
position
position analysis
  questionnaire (PAQ)
process chart
reengineering
team
team-based job design
work simplification

Discussion Questions and Exercises

1. Draw an organization chart to accurately depict the structure of the organization in which you are currently employed or one with which you are thoroughly familiar. Describe the structure depicted and list several advantages and disadvantages associated with such a structure.

2. Explain work simplification. In what situations is this approach to job design appropriate?

3. Differentiate between job enlargement, job rotation, and job enrichment, and provide an example of each.

4. Why isn't it always desirable or appropriate to use job enrichment or include the five core dimensions when designing jobs?

5. What is involved in the human-engineering approach to job design? Why is it becoming increasingly important?

6. We discussed several methods for collecting job analysis data—questionnaires, the position analysis questionnaire, and so on. Compare and contrast these methods, explaining what each is useful for and listing the pros and cons of each.

7. While not legally required, having job descriptions is highly advisable. Why? How can firms ensure that their job specifications are legally defensible?

8. Working individually or in groups, obtain copies of job descriptions for clerical positions at the college or university where you study, or the firm where you work. What types of information do they contain? Do they give you enough information to explain what the job involves and how to do it? How would you improve on the descriptions?

9. Working individually or in groups, use the job analysis questionnaire in this chapter to develop a job description for your professor in this class or your own job. Based on that, use your judgment to develop a job specification. Compare your conclusions with those of other students, groups, or coworkers. Were there any significant differences? What do you think accounted for the differences?

10. Since the president's job in a firm is by nature broader than a factory worker's, is there less need for a job description for the president? Why or why not?

Application Exercises

RUNNING CASE: Carter Cleaning Company

Job Descriptions

Based on her review of the stores, Jennifer concludes that one of the first matters she has to attend to involves developing job descriptions for the store managers.

As Jennifer tells it, her lessons regarding job descriptions in her basic management and HR management courses were insufficient to fully convince her of the pivotal role job descriptions play in the smooth functioning of an enterprise. However, many times during her first few weeks on the job, Jennifer finds herself asking one of the store managers why he or she is violating what Jennifer knows to be recommended company policies and procedures. Repeatedly the answers are either "Because I didn't know it was my job" or "Because I didn't know that was the way we were supposed to do it." Jennifer concludes that a job description, along with a set of standards and procedures that specify what is to be done and how to do it, would go a long way toward alleviating this problem.

In general, each store manager is responsible for directing all store activities in such a way that quality work is produced, customer relations and sales are maximized, and profitability is maintained through effective control of labour, supply, and energy costs. In accomplishing that general aim, each store manager's duties and responsibilities include quality control, store appearance and cleanliness, customer relations, bookkeeping and cash management, cost control and productivity, damage control, pricing, inventory control, spotting and cleaning, machine maintenance, employee safety, hazardous waste removal, human resources administration, and pest control.

The questions that Jennifer has to address follow.

Questions

1. What should be the format and final form of the store manager's job description?

2. Is it practical to specify standards and procedures in the body of the job description, or should these be kept separately?

3. How should Jennifer go about collecting the information required for the standards, procedures, and job description?

CASE INCIDENT: Should Job Descriptions Always Be Followed?

Gisele Renaud, Manager of Product Development, is troubled by the number of complaints she has received recently from the two supervisors reporting to her. Several times, they have complained about problems they are experiencing in terms of employee performance and attitude.

One supervisor told Gisele that she had noticed on several occasions that the performance of five employees reporting to her was at variance with their job description. Specifically, "they were deliberately ignoring the performance standards specified in the job description, and were, in effect, doing their own thing." Initially, she ignored this variance, but since the practice has continued, she indicated to Gisele that she believed something should be done or other employees might decide to follow their example. Gisele firmly believes that there is no point in having job descriptions if they are not followed, but is also concerned that insisting on following the job description might stifle creativity and innovation. She is especially confused because, although she has recently received various compliments about the improved quality of the finished products from some sales and marketing teams, she has also heard negative feedback from one sales team.

The second supervisor told Gisele that various employees have complained to him about the performance standards in the recently revised job descriptions, stating that they were meant for superhumans, not normal human beings.

Questions

1. What should Gisele do?

2. What could account for the variation between employee performance and the standards specified in the job description?

Human Resources Management Simulation

In section 3 of part 1 of the simulation, there are several exercises on job analysis. The first involves preparing a proposal to senior management for analyzing all of the Peterborough jobs, including those of supervisory and technical staff. To be encompassed in the proposal are a description of data collection techniques, the identification of appropriate techniques for various positions, and an explanation

Chapter 5
Human Resources Planning

Chapter Outline

- ◆ The Nature of Human Resources Planning
- ◆ Elements of Effective HRP
- ◆ Forecasting Future Human Resources Needs (Demand)
- ◆ Forecasting Future Human Resources Supply
- ◆ Planning and Implementing HR Programs to Balance Supply and Demand
- ◆ HRP Evaluation

Learning Outcomes

After studying this chapter, you should be able to:

Explain the nature of HRP and *discuss* its importance.

Describe the relationship between HRP and strategic planning and *explain* the importance of environmental scanning.

Describe various quantitative and qualitative techniques used to forecast human resources demand.

Discuss the strategies used to forecast human resources supply.

Describe the ways in which a surplus of human resources can be handled.

Explain how organizations deal with a shortage of human resources.

Describe the HRP evaluation process.

The Nature of Human Resources Planning

Human Resources Planning (HRP) is the process of reviewing human resources requirements to ensure that the organization has the required number of employees, with the necessary skills, to meet its goals.[1] Also known as employment planning, HRP is a proactive process, which both anticipates and influences an organization's future by systematically forecasting the demand for and supply of employees under changing conditions, and developing plans and activities to satisfy these needs.[2] As illustrated in **Figure 5.1**, key steps in the HRP process include forecasting demand for labour, performing an analysis of supply, and planning and implementing HR programs to balance supply and demand. A fundamental HRP decision when demand exceeds supply pertains to whether projected positions

**Figure 5.1
Human Resources
Planning Model**

Step 1:   Forecast Demand for Labour

Considerations	**Techniques Utilized**
• Organizational strategic plans	• Regression analysis
• Organizational tactical plans	• Computerized forecasting techniques
• Economic conditions	• Nominal group technique
• Market and competitive trends	• Delphi technique
• Government and legislative issues	• Managerial judgment
• Social concerns	
• Technological changes	
• Demographic trends	

Step 2:   Analyze Supply

Internal Analysis	**External Analysis**
• Staffing tables	• General economic conditions
• Markov analysis	• Labour market conditions
• Skills inventories	(national and local)
• Management inventories	• Occupational market conditions
• Replacement charts and	
development tracking	
• Replacement summaries	
• Succession planning	

**Step 3:   Implement Human Resources Programs to Balance
          Supply and Demand**

Labour Shortage	**Labour Surplus**
• Overtime	• Hiring freeze
• Hire temporary employees	• Attrition
• Subcontract work	• Buy-outs and early retirement programs
• Recruitment	• Job sharing
• Transfer	• Part-time work
• Promotion	• Work sharing
	• Reduced workweek
	• Alternative jobs within the organization
	• Layoffs (reverse seniority or juniority)
	• Supplemental unemployment
	benefits (SUBs)
	• Termination
	• Severance pay
	• Outplacement assistance

IBM is a recognized leader in the integration of HRP and strategic planning. Within IBM's manufacturing and product development businesses, the corporation's HR department develops a five-year HR strategic plan and a two-year tactical plan based on tentative business goals, formulated after an external environmental analysis and internal analysis of the company's strengths and weaknesses. The importance attributed to the HR department's role in the strategic planning process is highlighted by the fact that no major business decisions are approved until the vice-president of HR concurs with the business plan.[5]

Another organization that has long recognized the importance of integrating HRP and strategic planning is the Saskatchewan Wheat Pool, the largest cooperative in Canada, described in the HR and the Responsive Organization box.

HR and the Responsive Organization

The Integration of HRP and Strategic Planning at Saskatchewan Wheat Pool

During the 1980s, when David Wartman served as Director of HR with Saskatchewan Wheat Pool, the largest cooperative in Canada, his mandate included making the HR division a more effective business partner with the operating divisions. The board of directors and J. Milton Fair, CEO at that time, instituted a strategic planning process that gave HR a chance to work more effectively with their internal customers.

Recognizing that the guidance provided by a mission statement would facilitate divisional planning, the board and senior management worked with an external facilitator to develop guiding principles for the organization. Once there was agreement at that level, the top 100 managers were brought into the discussions in order to achieve a greater level of buy-in.

HR had a dual role in the strategic planning process. Their first responsibility was to develop the HR elements of the corporate environmental scan. The second, as with the operating divisions of the company, was to develop the HR business plan from which the HR budget would flow.

The external scan included identifying the demographic, legislative, and labour market factors in the geographic areas in which there were operations. HR provided data about expected legislative developments, collective agreement provisions (including wage and benefits changes), and trends in working conditions. HR also provided internal data on turnover, training needs, labour relations issues, and other factors important to the operations managers. From these data, all divisions of the company developed their strategic plans. Corporate strategic planning was based on the identification of a "willed future"—where management believed the company should be in the one- to five-year time frame encompassed by the plan.

The next step in the process involved identifying the necessary steps to achieve that willed future. Each operating and service division developed a plan that was brought to a combined board and senior management meeting. Approval of these plans, combined with operating revenue forecasts, provided guidelines for budget preparation. As the HR division became more skilled at the planning process, staff felt the need to ensure integration of HR and operating plans at a more detailed level. With this goal in mind, Wartman initiated a planning conference, to which senior managers of each of their internal customers were invited.

www.phptr.com/ ptrbook/ be_0134464850.html
Human Resources Planning

Following a discussion of the broad HR objectives by the CEO, a round-table session was held. Each of the internal customers addressed his or her primary short-term (one year) and long-term concerns (up to five years). This gave each participant the opportunity to hear the HR priorities of the others and ensure that where there were overlaps, plans would include working together to achieve common objectives. For example, the environmental scan showed that two divisions would be affected by the fact that the Canadian Wheat Board was shifting its export preferences from the Lakehead and St. Lawrence to the West Coast. The HR department's analysis of this shift indicated that cost reductions would be important for the future. Recognizing the need to reduce labour costs, moving from a five-day schedule with overtime pay to a seven-day schedule with shift premiums for the weekend was recommended. This was a significant strategy issue for the terminal elevator division.

The second and third days of the conference enabled HR to develop departmental plans based on assessment of environmental and customer priorities. This exercise involved the full complement of HR staff, divided into their functional units (employee relations, health and safety, staffing/employee development, compensation and benefits, and organization development).

On the final day, HR staff came together to develop their comprehensive plan and ensure that cross-overs between functional areas, such as collective bargaining and compensation, were taken into consideration. Following approval of the plan by the board and senior executive at the annual strategic planning session, the HR budget was developed. Budget approval signalled the beginning of implementation. This did not, however, require slavish adherence to the terms of the plan. Rather, there was constant monitoring and review, resulting in ongoing adjustments based on operational needs of customers or environmental changes.

According to Wartman, over the years, the HR division staff found that they were much more successful in meeting the needs of their customers than before, and that their customers had a better understanding of the constraints under which the HR staff operated.

Source: David Wartman, "Partnering with Business Not New for HR," *Canadian HR Reporter* 10, no. 21 (December 1, 1997), p. 17. Copyright MPL Communications Inc. Reproduced by permission of *Canadian HR Reporter,* 133 Richmond Street West, Toronto, Ontario M5H 3M8.

Failure to integrate HRP and strategic planning can have very serious consequences. For example, according to five Ontario nursing groups, failure of the Health Services Restructuring Commission (HSRC) to consider HRP and funding issues in its recommended restructuring plan for the non-acute care sector will result in deterioration of access to and quality of patient care. The groups say that although the number of patients in non-acute care will increase dramatically in the proposed restructured system, as will the level of illness those patients bring to the system, the level of nursing care in many of the services addressed in the HSRC's discussion paper (released in July of 1997) will decline. Highlights of the nursing groups' brief, *Preserving the Culture of Care in Ontario's Health System,* produced in response to the HSRC's discussion paper, follow:

The [HSRC] paper contains no consideration of staffing ratios and their importance on patient outcomes, nor is there any analysis of the degree to which a properly staffed and skilled non-acute sector would eat into the financial savings from downsizing hospitals.

In their HR planning employers like Burger King and others include close monitoring of trends such as the availability of entry-level labour.

Indeed, in light of the very high proportion of health care costs attributable to staff compensation, the paper is notable for its complete lack of discussion about human resources planning and funding.

Overall, the evidence points to an increased risk of there not being the appropriate mix of caregivers present to head off a crisis before it happens or when a critical incident occurs.

In order to avert this crisis and ensure that HRP issues critical to nursing are addressed, the groups recommend that the HSRC revisit the basic analysis for sizing the non-acute system, and involve primary care providers, such as nurses, in the planning process. As well, they feel that planning for a restructured system should incorporate analysis of the levels of nursing care needed in non-hospital settings and levels of funding for nursing care.[6]

The Importance of Environmental Scanning   As alluded to in the IBM example and explained in the insert on the Saskatchewan Wheat Pool, environmental scanning is a critical component of the HRP and strategic planning processes, since the most successful organizations are prepared for changes before they occur. The external environmental factors most frequently monitored include:

1. Economic conditions (general, regional and local)
2. Market and competitive trends
3. Government and legislative issues, such as new or revised laws and the decisions of courts and quasi-judicial bodies
4. Social concerns related to health care, childcare, and educational priorities
5. Technological changes
6. Demographic trends.

public sector
Government organizations.

quasi-public sector
Publicly supported organizations, such as health-care providers and educational institutions.

As mentioned in chapter 1, economic conditions affect supply and demand for products and services, which in turn affect the number and types of employees required. Over the past few years, for example, many private-sector firms have restructured or downsized. Downsizing used to be relatively rare in the **public** and **quasi-public sectors**. However, due to government cost-cutting strategies, this is no longer the case. The federal government itself has embarked on a plan that will result in approximately 20 000 civil servants being declared surplus.[7] Staffing cuts affect employees at all levels and with all types of skills. Doing more with fewer employees cannot be seen as simply a temporary solution to the recession of the 1990s. More and more firms are trying to reduce their labour costs on a permanent basis in order to remain competitive in an increasingly global market, through such strategies as job redesign, introducing new work practices and team-based structures, and technological innovation. Three-quarters of 53 Canadian CEOs surveyed recently (whose companies employ 350 000) indicated that the trend to leaner workplaces would continue for the next five years. Eighty-eight percent said that their corporate culture had changed in the past five years, most becoming more team-oriented and willing to take risks.[8]

Probably the most significant environmental factor in HRP in Canada today relates to the dramatic changes occurring in the composition of the labour force. A few trends of importance include the following:

- the Canadian labour force totalled about 12.6 million in 1995 and is expected to grow by less than 1 percent annually until the year 2016[9]

- by 2001, most people entering the work force will be women, visible minorities, First Peoples, and persons with disabilities[10]
- by 2015, young workers (15 to 24) will make up a smaller share of the work force than adults twice their age.[11]

As discussed in chapter 1, increasing diversity, the shortage of young workers, and the aging work force all have major implications for such HR activities as recruitment, selection, training, and compensation. Effective HRP involves monitoring such trends, anticipating their impact, and devising strategies to deal with them. The Bank of Montreal, recognizing the importance of fit between employees and customers, has incorporated equal opportunity in its strategic plan, and established a $8-million Possibilities Foundation for visible minority, Aboriginal, and disabled high school students moving on to post-secondary education. Visible minorities, who represent 9.1 percent of the total Canadian work force, now account for 16.1 percent of the bank's work force.[12]

Elements of Effective HRP

Once the human resources implications of the organization's strategic plans have been analyzed, there are four subsequent processes involved in HRP, which will be discussed next.

1. Forecasting future human resources needs (demand)
2. Forecasting availability of internal and external candidates (supply)
3. Planning and implementing HR programs to balance supply and demand
4. Monitoring and evaluating the results.

Forecasting Future Human Resources Needs (Demand)

The Bank of Montreal has taken numerous steps to achieve a more representative work force, including establishing a "Possibilities Foundation."

A key component of HRP is forecasting the number and type of people needed to meet organizational objectives. Managers should consider several factors when forecasting such requirements.[13] From a practical point of view, *the demand for the organization's product or service* is paramount.[14] Thus, in a manufacturing firm, sales are projected first. Then, the volume of production required to meet these sales requirements is determined. Finally, the staff needed to maintain this volume of output is estimated. In addition to this "basic requirement" for staff, several other factors should be considered, including:

1. *Projected turnover* (as a result of resignations or terminations)
2. *Quality and nature* of employees (in relation to what management sees as the changing needs of the organization)
3. *Decisions to upgrade* the quality of products or services or enter into new markets
4. *Technological and administrative changes* resulting in increased productivity
5. The *financial resources* available to each department.

In large organizations, needs forecasting is primarily quantitative in nature and is the responsibility of highly trained specialists. *Quantitative techniques* for determining human resources requirements include trend analysis, ratio analysis, scatter plot analysis, regression analysis, and computerized forecasting. *Qualitative approaches* to forecasting range from sophisticated analytical models to informal expert opinions about future needs,[15] such as a manager deciding that the costs of overtime in his or her department are beginning to outweigh those involved in hiring an additional staff member, and making plans to amend his or her staff complement during the next budget year.

Quantitative Approaches

trend analysis
Study of a firm's past employment levels over a period of years to predict future needs.

Trend Analysis   **Trend analysis** means studying the firm's employment levels over the last five years or so to predict future needs. For example, the number of employees in the firm at the end of each of the last five years might be computed, or perhaps the number in each subgroup (like sales, production, secretarial, and administrative). The purpose is to identify employment trends that might continue into the future.

Trend analysis is valuable as an initial estimate, but employment levels rarely depend solely on the passage of time. Other factors (like changes in sales volume and productivity) will also affect future staffing needs.

ratio analysis
A forecasting technique for determining future staff needs by using ratios between some causal factor (such as sales volume) and number of employees needed.

Ratio Analysis   Another forecasting approach, **ratio analysis,** involves making estimates based on the *ratio* between (1) some causal factor (such as sales volume) and (2) number of employees required (for instance, number of salespeople). For example, suppose a salesperson traditionally generates $500 000 in sales and that in each of the last two years ten salespeople were required to generate $5 million in sales. Also assume that plans call for increasing the firm's sales to $8 million next year and to $10 million two years hence. Then, if the sales revenue–salespeople ratio remains the same, six new salespeople would be required next year (each of whom produces an extra $500 000 in sales). In the following year, an additional four salespeople would be needed to generate the extra $2 million in sales (between next year's $8 million and the following year's $10 million).

Ratio analysis can also be used to help forecast other employee requirements. For example, a salesperson–secretary ratio could be computed to determine how many new secretaries will be needed to support the extra sales staff.

Like trend analysis, ratio analysis assumes that productivity remains about the same—for instance, that each salesperson can't be motivated to produce much more than $500 000 in sales. If sales productivity were to increase or decrease, then the ratio of sales to salespeople would change. A forecast based on historical ratios would then no longer be accurate.

scatter plot
A graphical method used to help identify the relationship between two variables.

The Scatter Plot   A **scatter plot** is another option. Scatter plots can be used to determine whether two factors—a measure of business activity and staffing levels—are related. If they are, then if the measure of business activity is forecast HR requirements can also be estimated.

An example to illustrate follows.[16] Legislative changes to the health-care system require that two 500-bed Toronto hospitals be amalgamated. Both previously had responsibility for acute, chronic, and long-term care. The government's plan is for one facility to specialize in acute care, while the other assumes responsibility for chronic and long-term care. In general, providing acute care requires staffing with Registered Nurses (RNs), while chronic and long-term care facilities can be staffed primarily with Registered Practical Nurses (RPNs).

By the end of the calendar year, 200 beds at Hospital A must be converted from chronic and long-term care beds to facilities for acute patients. At the same time, Hospital A's 200 chronic and long-term patients must be transferred to Hospital B. In a joint meeting, the Directors of Nursing and Human Resources decide that a good starting point in the planning process would be calculating the relationship between hospital size (in terms of number of acute beds) and the number of RNs required. After placing telephone calls to their counterparts at eight hospitals in larger centres across Ontario, including London and Ottawa, they obtain the following information:

Size of Hospital (Number of Acute Beds)	Number of Registered Nurses
200	240
300	260
400	470
500	500
600	620
700	660
800	820
900	860

In order to determine how many RNs would be needed, they use the data obtained to draw the scatter plot shown in **Figure 5.3**, in which hospital size is shown on the horizontal axis and number of RNs is shown on the vertical axis. If the two factors are related, then the points will tend to fall along a straight line, as they do in this case. Carefully drawing a line which minimizes the distances between the line and each of the plotted points permits an estimate of the number of nurses required for hospitals of various sizes. Thus, since Hospital A will now have 500 acute-care beds, the estimated number of RNs needed is 500.

Regression Analysis   **Regression analysis** is a more sophisticated statistical technique that involves the use of a mathematical formula to project future demands based on an established relationship between an organization's employment level (dependent variable) and some measurable factor of output (independent variable) such as revenue, sales, or production level. When there are several dependent and/or independent variables, multiple regression analysis is used.

regression analysis
A statistical technique involving the use of a mathematical formula to project future demands based on an established relationship between an organization's employment level (dependent variable) and some measurable factor of output (independent variable).

**Figure 5.3
Determining the
Relationship Between
Hospital Size and
Number of Nurses**

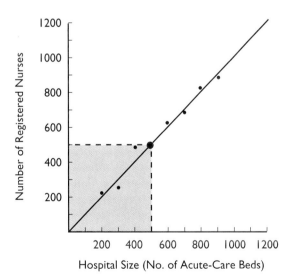

Note: After fitting the line, the number of employees needed, given projected volume, can be extrapolated (projected).

Computerized Forecasting Techniques   Many employers involved in quantitative forecasting use computers and software packages. In such cases, a human resources specialist, working with the first-line supervisor(s) involved, compiles the information needed to develop a **computerized forecast** of human resources requirements.[17] An example of the type of data needed would be direct labour hours to produce one unit of product (a measure of productivity) and three sales projections—minimum, maximum, and probable—for the product line in question. Based on such data, the program generates figures on such things as "average staff levels required to meet product demands" as well as separate forecasts for direct labour (such as assembly workers), indirect labour (support staff, such as secretaries and accounting clerks) and senior staff (such as managers and executives).

With such a system, an employer can quickly translate estimates of projected productivity and sales levels into forecasts of human resources needs, and can easily check the impact of various levels of productivity and sales on human resources requirements.[18]

computerized forecast
The determination of future staffing needs by projecting a firm's sales, volume of production, and the human resources requirements to maintain desired volume of output, using computers and software packages.

Qualitative Approaches

In contrast to quantitative approaches, which rely on statistical formulas, qualitative techniques rely on expert judgements. Two approaches used to gather expert opinions in order to forecast human resources demand (or supply) include the nominal group and Delphi techniques.

nominal group technique
A decision-making technique that involves a group of experts meeting face to face. Steps include independent idea generation, clarification and open discussion, and private assessment.

Nominal Group Technique   The **nominal group technique** involves a group of experts (such as first-line supervisors and managers) meeting face to face. While one of its uses is human resources demand forecasting, it is a technique that can be used to deal with many types of issues and problems, ranging from identifying training needs to determining safety program incentives. The steps involved are as follows:[19]

1. Each member of the group independently writes down his or her ideas on the problem or issue (in this case the causes of demand).
2. Going around the table, each member then presents one idea. This process continues until all ideas have been presented and recorded, typically on a flipchart or chalkboard. No discussion is permitted during this step.
3. Clarification is then sought, as necessary, followed by group discussion and evaluation.
4. Finally, each member is asked to rank the ideas. This is done independently and in silence.

Advantages of this technique include involvement of key decision makers, a future focus, and the fact that the group discussion involved in step 3 can facilitate the exchange of ideas and greater acceptance of results by the participants. Drawbacks include subjectivity and the potential for group pressure to lead to less accurate assessments than could be obtained through other means.

Delphi technique
A judgmental forecasting method used to arrive at a group decision, typically involving outside experts as well as organizational employees. Ideas are exchanged without face-to-face interaction and feedback is provided and used to fine-tune independent judgments until consensus is reached.

The Delphi Technique   While short-term forecasting is usually handled by managers, the **Delphi technique** is useful for long-range forecasting (and other strategic planning issues), since it typically involves the use of outside experts, as well as company employees. Outside experts are often able to be more objective in assessing changes in economic, demographic, governmental, technological, and social conditions and their potential impact. The Delphi technique, a judgmental forecasting method used to arrive at a group decision, involves the following steps:[20]

1. The problem is identified (in this case the causes of demand) and each group member is requested to submit a potential solution by completing a carefully-designed questionnaire. Direct face-to-face contact is not permitted.
2. After each member independently and anonymously completes the initial questionnaire, the results are compiled at a centralized location.
3. Each group member is then given a copy of the results.
4. If there are differences in opinion, each individual uses the feedback from other experts to fine-tune his or her independent assessment.
5. Steps 3 and 4 are repeated as often as necessary until consensus is reached.

As with the nominal group technique, advantages include involvement of key decision makers and a future focus. The Delphi technique, however, permits the group to critically evaluate a wider range of views. Drawbacks include the fact that judgments may not efficiently use objective data, the time and costs involved, and the potential difficulty in integrating diverse opinions.

Managerial Judgment

While managerial judgment is central to qualitative forecasting, it is important to realize that even when using quantitative techniques, managerial judgment plays a large role. It's rare that any historical trend, ratio, or relationship will continue unchanged into the future. Judgment is thus needed to modify the forecast based on anticipated changes. Important factors that may modify the initial forecast of human resources requirements include the following:

1. *Decisions to upgrade the quality of products or services or enter into new markets.* These have implications for the nature of the employees required. Whether the skills of current employees fit with the organization's new products or services will have to be assessed as well.
2. *Technological and administrative changes resulting in increased productivity.* Increased efficiency (in terms of output per hour) could reduce human resources needs. It might come about through installing new equipment or a new financial incentive plan, for instance.
3. *The financial resources available.* For example, a larger budget enables managers to hire more people and pay higher wages. Conversely, a projected budget crunch could mean fewer positions and lower salary offers.

Summarizing Human Resources Requirements

staffing table
A pictorial representation of all jobs within the organization, along with the number of current incumbents and future employment requirements (monthly or yearly) for each.

The end result of the forecasting process is an estimate of short-term and long-range human resources requirements. Long-range plans are, of necessity, general statements of probable needs. Specific numbers are either estimated or omitted.

Short-term plans, although still approximations, are more specific, and often depicted in a **staffing table**. As illustrated in **Figure 5.4**, a staffing table is a pictorial representation of all jobs within the organization, along with the number of current incumbents and future employment requirements (monthly or yearly) for each.

Forecasting Future Human Resources Supply

Short-term and long-range human resources demand forecasts only provide half of the staffing equation by answering the question: "How many employees will we need?" The next major concern is how projected openings will be filled. There are two sources of supply: internal and external. The internal supply consists of present employees who can be transferred or promoted to meet anticipated needs.

Job Title (As on Job Description)	Department	Anticipated Openings by Months of the Year												
		Total	Jan.	Feb.	Mar.	Apr.	May	June	July	Aug.	Sept.	Oct.	Nov.	Dec.
General Manager	Administration	1					1							
Director of Finance	Administration	1												1
Human Resources Officer	Administration	2	1					1						
Collection Clerk	Administration	1		1										
Groundskeeper	Maintenance	4						1	1					2
Service and Maintenance Technician	Maintenance	5	1			2					2			
Water Utility Engineer	Operations	3									2			1
Apprentice Lineperson	Operations	10	6						4					
Water Meter Technician	Operations	1												1
Engineering Technician	Operations	3			2							1		
Field Technician	Operations	8						8						
Senior Programmer/ Analyst	Systems	2				1				1				
Programmer/Operator	Systems	4		2						1			1	
Systems Operator	Systems	5					2						3	
Customer Service Representative	Sales	8	4					3				1		

Springbrook Utilities Commission Staffing Table

Date Compiled: _____

Figure 5.4
A Partial Staffing Table

The external supply consists of people in the labour market not currently working for the organization. Included are those who are employed elsewhere, as well as those who are unemployed.

Forecasting the Supply of Internal Candidates

Before estimating how many external (outside) candidates will need to be recruited and hired, management must first determine how many candidates for projected job openings will likely come from within the organization. Making this determination is the purpose of forecasting the supply of internal candidates.

Estimating the internal supply involves more than merely counting the number of employees. Some firms use the **Markov analysis** technique to track the pattern of employee movements through various jobs and develop a transitional probability matrix for forecasting internal supply by specific categories, such as position and sex. As illustrated in **Figure 5.5**, such an analysis shows the actual number (and percentage) of employees who remain in each job from one year to the next, as well as proportions promoted, demoted, transferred, and leaving the organization. It is these proportions (probabilities) that are used to forecast human resources supply.

Markov analysis
A method of forecasting internal labour supply that involves tracking the pattern of employee movements through various jobs and developing a transitional probability matrix.

Figure 5.5
Hypothetical Markov
Analysis for a
Manufacturing
Operation

1997 → 1998	Plant Manager	Fore-Person	Team Leaders	Production Worker	Exit
Plant Manager (n = 5)	80% / 4				20% / 1
Fore-Person (n = 35)	8% / 3	82% / 28			10% / 4
Team Leader (n = 110)		11% / 12	70% / 77	7% / 8	12% / 13
Production Worker (n = 861)			6% / 52	72% / 620	22% / 189
Projected Supply	7	40	129	628	

Percentages represent transitions (previous year's actuals).
Actual numbers of employees are shown as whole numbers in each block
(projections for 1998 based on current staffing).

In addition to such quantitative data, the skills and capabilities of current employees must be assessed, and skills inventories (either manual or computerized) prepared. From this information, replacement charts and/or summaries and succession plans can be developed.

Skills Inventories **Skills inventories** contain comprehensive information about the capabilities of current employees. Prepared manually or using a computerized system, the type of data gathered for each employee includes name, age, date of employment, current position, present duties and responsibilities, educational background, previous work history, skills, abilities, and interests. Information about current performance and readiness for promotion is generally included as well. Data pertaining to managerial staff is compiled in a **management inventory**. In addition to the information listed above, such inventories also include the number and types of employees supervised, duties of such employees, total budget managed, previous managerial duties and responsibilities, and managerial training received.

To be useful, skills and management inventories must be updated regularly. Failure to do so can lead to present employees being overlooked for job openings. Updating every two years is generally adequate if employees are encouraged to report significant qualifications changes, such as new skills learned and/or courses completed, to the human resources department as they occur.

Manual Systems There are several types of manual systems used to keep track of employees' qualifications. An example of a human resources skills inventory and

skills inventories
Manual or computerized records summarizing employees' education, experience, interests, skills, etc., which are used to identify internal candidates eligible for transfer and/or promotion.

management inventories
Manual or computerized records summarizing the background, qualifications, interests, skills, etc. of management employees, as well as information about managerial responsibilities, duties in current and previous position(s), and management training, used to identify internal candidates eligible for transfer and/or promotion opportunities.

development tracking form is shown in **Figure 5.6**. Such a form may be completed by each employee or filled in by a human resources department member following a face-to-face interview. Once the information has been compiled and recorded, it can be used to determine which current employees are available for and interested in transfer or promotion.

Replacement Charts **Replacement charts** are a visual representation of who will replace whom in the event of a job opening. Many employers use such charts to keep track of potential internal candidates for their most important positions. As can be seen in **Figure 5.7**, such charts typically indicate age and replacement

replacement charts
Visual representations of who will replace whom in the event of a job opening. Likely internal candidates are listed, along with their age, present performance rating, and promotability status.

Figure 5.6
Skills Inventory Form Appropriate for Manual Storage and Retrieval

HUMAN RESOURCES SKILLS INVENTORY AND DEVELOPMENT RECORD			Date: month, year

Department	Area or sub-department	Branch or section	Location

Company service date (month, day, year)	Birthdate (month, day, year)	Job title

Education — Diploma or degree and major field of study

Grade school | High school
6   7   8 | 9 10 11 12 13
College and/or University
1   2   3   4   5

Courses (company sponsored)

Type of course	Subject or course	Year	Type of course	Subject or course	Year

Career and development interests

Are you interested in an alternative type of work? Yes ☐ No ☐	Would you accept transfer to another division? Yes ☐ No ☐	Would you accept lateral moves for further development? Yes ☐ No ☐

If yes, specifically what type?	Comment on any qualifying circumstances

What type of training do you believe you require to:
A) Improve your skills and performance in your present position
B) Improve your experience and abilities for advancement.

Last name

First name

What other assignments do you believe you are qualified to perform now?

Middle name

Languages	Written	Spoken
	☐ ☐	☐ ☐
	☐ ☐	☐ ☐

Societies and organizations   Memberships in community organizations, etc., within last five years. Indicate name of association and office held, if any.

Skills

Type of skill	Certification, if any	Type of skill	Certification, if any

Other significant work experience. (Omit repetitive experiences)

	Location	From yr.	To yr.

Comments: Other significant experience, recreational activities, hobbies, interests, or personal data.

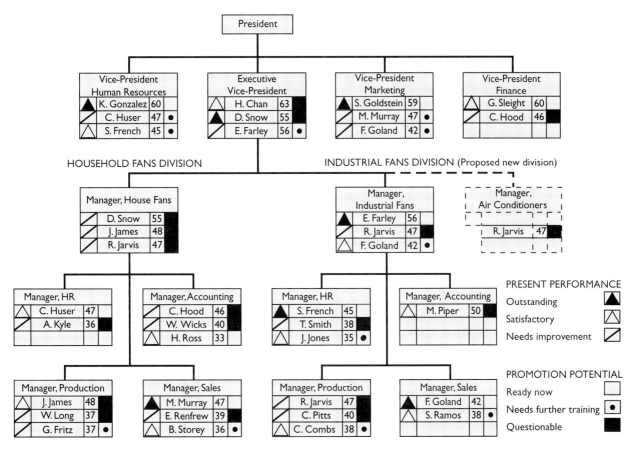

Figure 5.7
Management Replacement Chart

status of potential internal candidates. While age cannot be used as a criterion in making selection or promotion decisions, such information is necessary to project retirement dates, plan lateral moves, etc. Replacement status consists of two variables: present performance and promotability. Information about present performance is gleaned from recent performance appraisals. Future promotability is based on information provided by the employee about future career aspirations, and a subjective assessment by the employee's immediate supervisors of likelihood of future success. To provide a more objective estimate of future potential, this information may be supplemented by results of psychological tests, interviews with human resources specialists, and/or a visit to an assessment centre (which is explained in chapter 7).

replacement summaries
Lists of likely replacements for each position and their relative strengths and weaknesses, as well as information about current position, performance, promotability, age, and experience.

Replacement Summaries While replacement charts provide an excellent quick reference tool, they contain very little information. For that reason, many firms prefer to use **replacement summaries**. Such summaries list likely replacements for each position and their relative strengths and weaknesses, as well as information about current position, performance, promotability, age, and experience. This additional information is extremely helpful for decision makers. Caution must be taken to ensure that there is no discrimination on the basis of age, gender, etc.

Computerized Information Systems   Skills inventories on hundreds or thousands of employees cannot be adequately maintained manually. Many firms, including DuPont Canada and Hewlett-Packard (Canada), computerize this information, and a number of packaged systems are available for accomplishing this task.[21]

In one such system, employees fill out a 12-page booklet in which they describe their background and experience. All this information is transferred to the computer system. When a manager needs a qualified person to fill a position, he or she describes the position (for instance, in terms of the education and skills it requires) and then enters this information into the computer. After scanning its bank of possible candidates, the program presents the manager with a computer printout of qualified candidates.

According to one expert, the basic ingredients of a computerized human resources skills inventory should include the following:

Work experience codes: a list of work experience descriptors, titles, or codes describing jobs within the company so that the individual's present, previous, and desired jobs can be coded.

Product or service knowledge: the employee's level of familiarity with the employer's product lines or services as an indication of where the person might be transferred or promoted.

Industry experience: the person's industry experience, since for certain positions knowledge of key related industries is very useful.

Formal education: the name of each postsecondary educational program completed, the field of study, and degree or diploma granted.

Training courses: those taken or conducted by the employee and, possibly, training courses taught by outside agents like the Canadian Institute of Management.

Language skills: degree of proficiency in languages other than English and/or French.

Relocation limitations: the employee's willingness to relocate and the locales to which he or she would prefer to go.

Career interests: work experience codes to indicate what the employee would like to be doing for the employer in the future. Space can be provided for a brief priority of choices, and a code should be included indicating whether the employee's main qualification for the work he or she wants to do is experience, knowledge, or interest.

Performance appraisals: updated periodically to indicate the employee's achievement on each dimension appraised (leadership ability, motivation, communication skills, and so on) along with a summary of the employee's strengths and deficiencies.[22]

Skills are often included in these types of data banks. Including "training courses completed" might only show what the employee is trained to do, not what he or she has actually shown he or she can do. Including skills such as "remove boiler casings and doors" (number of times performed, date last performed, time spent) enables firms to use the computer to zero in on which employees are competent to accomplish the task that must be done. Skill level can also be included, perhaps ranging from skill level 1 (can lead or instruct others), 2 (can perform the job with minimum supervision), 3 (has some experience; can assist experienced workers), to 4 (has not had opportunity to work on this job).[23] The role of computerized skills inventories and benefits associated with them are discussed in more detail in the Information Technology and HR box.

Succession Planning   Forecasting the availability of inside candidates is particularly important in succession planning. In a nutshell, **succession planning** refers to the plans a company makes to fill its most important executive positions.

www.expertcenter.com
The Expertise Center

succession planning
The process of ensuring a suitable supply of successors for current and future senior or key jobs, so that careers of individuals can be effectively planned and managed.

Information Technology and HR
Computerized Skills Inventories

When filling positions, knowing the job's requirements isn't enough: Managers should also know the skills of possible candidates now employed by the firm. Simply posting the opening on a company bulletin board does not guarantee that every employee will see the posting or will interpret the information appropriately. One way to improve the likelihood that qualified internal candidates will be introduced into the selection process is to have a computerized skills inventory completed and updated regularly by employees. Then the HR department can help to match good internal applicants with job openings.

Both the development of the inventory content and the updating of inventories require significant input from employees. They must believe in the validity of the content of the inventory, and this will happen only if they participate in the development process. If employees have ready access to computers, the inventory can be developed and updated from their workstations. Otherwise, hard-copy memos should request all employees to provide data on their knowledge, skills, and abilities. The range of skills to be listed, the standards that differentiate various skill levels, and the categories to be used should be explained.

Inventories should be regularly updated when an employee has completed a course, seminar, workshop, or assignment that is applicable. If computers are not generally available, employees should be allowed time (20 to 30 minutes) each quarter to update the inventory. Time spent on the updating may be minimized by periodically providing each employee with a hard copy of his or her inventory to mark up before the actual data entry. Skills should be reassessed at least annually at the time of performance appraisals. If an employee has questions about interpretations of skill levels or categories, supervisors or HR department staff should offer assistance. Periodic review of the inventory and the process should occur, and all employees should receive regular training to maintain the validity of the system.

When a vacancy occurs, interviewers specify the parameters of the job based on the skill categories and levels in the job specification. If there is a computerized skills inventory, a list of employees who qualify according to these parameters can easily be generated. This list can be modified based on other factors such as attendance, quality of performance, time in position, and interest of the candidate. Qualified and interested employees can then receive a letter informing them of the opening and inviting them to apply, with a copy to the employee's supervisor.

Expressing interest in a position that offers greater responsibility should be encouraged. Employees who see the company encouraging growth and development are more likely to stay. Developing a skills inventory system with significant employee input, active encouragement to update, and results that keep employees informed of promotional possibilities will enhance organizational commitment and retention.

Straightforward communication with employees is another byproduct of developing a skills inventory process. If an employee is otherwise qualified, is invited to apply, does so, and is then found to have either performance or attendance problems, those hindrances to promotion will be addressed because the process encourages information-sharing. Most employees accept constructive criticism if it is offered in a manner designed to help them progress. Furthermore, by participating in establishing the content and standards of the inventory, employees should have a better understanding of what is expected of them in order to qualify at specified levels and be able to provide valuable job analysis data based on what they actually know about their jobs.◆

In the days when companies were hierarchical and people tended to remain with one employer for years, executive succession was often straightforward. Staff climbed the ladder one rung at a time, and it wasn't unusual for someone to start on the shop floor and end up in the president's office. While that kind of ascent is still possible, employee turnover and flatter structures mean that the lines of succession are no longer so direct.[24] Thus, today, the succession planning process often involves a fairly complicated and integrated series of steps. For example, potential successors for top management might be routed through the top jobs at several key divisions, as well as overseas, and they might be sent through a university, graduate-level, advanced-management program. As a result, a more comprehensive definition of succession planning is that it is the process of ensuring a suitable supply of successors for current and future senior or key jobs arising from business strategy, so that the careers of individuals can be planned and managed to optimize the organization's needs and the individuals' aspirations.[25]

Since succession planning requires balancing the organization's top-management needs with the potential and career aspirations of available candidates, it includes these activities:

> *Analysis* of the demand for managers and professionals by company level, function, and skill.
>
> *Audit* of existing executives and projection of likely future supply from internal and external sources.
>
> *Planning* of individual career paths based on objective estimates of future needs and drawing on reliable performance appraisals and assessments of potential.
>
> *Career counselling* undertaken in the context of a realistic understanding of the future needs of the firm, as well as those of the individual.
>
> *Accelerated promotions*, with development targeted against the future needs of the business.
>
> *Performance-related training and development* to prepare individuals for future roles, as well as current responsibilities.
>
> *Planned strategic recruitment,* not only to fill short-term needs, but also to provide people for development to meet future needs.
>
> The actual activities by which openings are filled.[26]

It should be noted that replacement charts, replacement summaries, and succession plans are considered to be highly confidential in most organizations.

Building Employee Commitment

Replacement and Succession Planning

At General Electric (GE) Canada, replacement and succession planning are an integral component of the overall HR planning process. All salaried employees are encouraged to participate in an accomplishment summary and development review on an annual basis. On one side of a form, employees describe their achievements, strengths, development needs, and career interests. On the flip side, their managers complete a performance appraisal and outline employee development needs and career prospects. The CEO and Vice-President of HR then meets with all the product division managers to review the most "promotable" (Code 1) employees. Up to three backups are identified for each key position, based on degree of readiness. From the annual HR review, the company also identifies the handful of employees with the potential to be officers, the very top echelon in GE's worldwide operations. In addition to job-specific skills, potential executives are expected to have "GE leadership values," which include a dislike for bureaucracy, the self-confidence to empower others, and an understanding of accountability. Potential executives undergo an exhaustive executive assessment interview, conducted by senior HR staff, followed by thorough development planning.

Imperial Oil is another employer that prefers to cultivate its 150 or so executives from within. Superiors essentially prepare succession plans for their employees. A senior management committee, led by the CEO, reviews the top level succession plans for each of Imperial Oil's divisions and major functional positions—about 30–35 posts in all. Senior vice-presidents then review succession plans for the remainder of executive positions. Executives typically begin in an entry-level job, and grow in that discipline for about a decade. As at GE, there is recognition that the attributes that make a successful executive have changed dramatically over the years. In addition to having thorough knowledge, executives must be adept at "dealing with ambiguity" and surviving in unfamiliar territory. Individuals demonstrating potential are exposed to an executive "tester," a different kind of challenge at a management level, typically involving the integration of multiple interests into a single outcome, for example a job combining manufacturing and marketing. According to John Lang, Director of Executive Development and Organization at Imperial Oil, once executives-in-waiting have been identified, a key challenge is to retain them. Doing so means keeping these individuals happy by using them productively today, while channelling their energies into training that will pay dividends in two or three years. Lang's job is to oversee the executive development system, which, like that at GE, includes needs reviews, appraisal forms, and performance ratings.

Source: Stuart Foxman, "Corporate Contenders," *Human Resources Professional* 10, no. 8 (September 1993), pp. 17, 19.

Forecasting the Supply of External (Outside) Candidates

Not every future opening can be filled with present employees. When there are no suitable internal replacements and when openings are for entry-level jobs, there is a need to look at external sources of supply.

Employer growth is primarily responsible for the number of entry-level job openings. While there are some higher-level openings that require such unique talents and skills that they are impossible to fill internally, and some jobs are vacated unexpectedly, a key factor in determining the number of positions that must be filled externally is the effectiveness of organizational training and development and career planning initiatives. If employees are not encouraged to expand their capabilities, they may not be ready to fill vacancies as they arise, and external sources must be tapped.

To project the supply of outside candidates—those not currently employed by the organization, employers assess general economic conditions, national labour market conditions, local labour market conditions, and occupational market conditions.

General Economic Conditions The first step is to forecast general economic conditions and the expected prevailing rate of unemployment. In the short run, the national unemployment rate serves as an approximate measure of how difficult it will be to acquire new employees. In general terms, the lower the rate of unemployment, the smaller the labour supply and the more difficult it will be to recruit employees. It is important to realize, however, that even when unemployment rates are high, some positions will still be difficult to fill, and that unemployment rates vary for different groups, as well as from province to province and from one city to another.

Physiotherapy is a skills-shortage occupation: The demand for physiotherapists exceeds the supply.

National Labour Market Conditions Demographic trends have a significant impact on national labour market conditions. Fortunately for organizations, these trends are known years in advance of their impact. There is a wealth of labour market information available from government and private sources.[27]

Statistics Canada publishes reports on labour force conditions on an annual, monthly, quarterly, and occasional basis. Information is available on: total labour force projections by demographic, geographic, and occupational variables; labour income; census data; and population projections by sex and province. Such data has important implications for organizations:

> *When CAMI Automotive Inc., a joint venture of Suzuki and General Motors, began operation in 1988, a corporate decision was made to include people with disabilities in CAMI's recruitment outreach, since there was recognition that this designated group represents a vast source of untapped potential.* [28] *(The latest figures from Statistics Canada—1991 census data—show that 16 percent of Canadians, or 4.2 million people, have a disability. The unemployment rate for those with severe disabilities was 28 percent, close to three times the national average).* [29]

The Economic Council of Canada has developed a useful tool for forecasting medium-term economic trends called the **Canadian Disaggregated Interdepartmental Econometric Model (CANDIDE)**.[30] It uses over 1 500 regression equations to forecast unemployment and real domestic product (the value of all goods and services produced in Canada, less any increases due to inflation).

Local Labour Market Conditions Local labour markets are affected by many conditions, including community growth rates and attitudes. Anti-business or no-growth attitudes may cause present employers to move elsewhere. The resultant loss of jobs may then force residents to relocate to other areas. In communities experiencing such population declines, it is often impossible to attract new business, since potential employers fear future shortages in the local supply of human resources. The end result is fewer and fewer jobs and more and more people leaving the local labour market—a vicious downward spiral. Conversely, one reason growing cities are attractive to employers is the promise of large future labour markets.

Chambers of Commerce and provincial/local development and planning agencies can be excellent sources of local labour market information.

Occupational Market Conditions In addition to looking at the overall labour market, organizations also generally want to forecast the availability of potential job candidates in specific occupations (engineers, drill press operators, accountants, and so on) for which they will be recruiting. In recent years, for example, there has been an undersupply of computer systems specialists, physiotherapists, and physicians in many parts of the country.

Forecasts for various occupations are available from a number of sources. Human Resources Development Canada (HRDC) publishes both short-term and long-term labour force projections. The short-term projection is published in a report titled **Ford Occupational Imbalance Listing (FOIL)**. This is a quarterly publication estimating labour market demand and supply by occupation. The long-term projection is published in a report titled **Canada Occupational Forecasting Program (COFOR).** This report forecasts demand requirements for over 500 occupational groups on both a national and provincial basis.[31]

Another of HRDC's publications is titled **Canadian Occupational Projection System (COPS).**[32] It projects domestic occupational requirements (demand) and supply, nationally and provincially, for periods of up to ten years. This report is useful for determining whether any projected imbalances will be self-

---

Canadian Disaggregated Interdepartmental Econometric Model (CANDIDE)
A useful tool for forecasting medium-term economic trends developed by the Economic Council of Canada, which uses over 1 500 regression equations to forecast unemployment and real domestic product.

Ford Occupational Imbalance Listing (FOIL)
A quarterly HRDC publication estimating labour market demand and supply by occupation.

Canada Occupational Forecasting Program (COFOR)
HRDC's long-term labour force projection report, which forecasts demand requirements for over 500 occupational groups on both a national and provincial basis.

Canadian Occupational Projection System (COPS)
Another HRDC report, which projects domestic occupational requirements (demand) and supply, nationally and provincially, for periods of up to ten years.

Microelectronics
Simulation Model
(MESIM)
A computerized supplement
to COPS, which integrates
the impact of technological
change on occupational
composition.

correcting or require specific intervention on the part of governments and/or private-sector organizations.

The **Microelectronics Simulation Model (MESIM)**[33], a computerized supplement to COPS, integrates the impact of technological change on occupational composition. Such trends as the increased use of computer-based technology have changed the fundamental nature of jobs and skill requirements. MESIM is able to incorporate these labour market shifts and thus more accurately forecast Canada's occupational composition.

Planning and Implementing HR Programs to Balance Supply and Demand

Once the supply and demand of human resources have been estimated, program planning and implementation commence. To successfully fill positions internally, organizations must manage performance and careers. Performance is managed through effective job design and quality of working life initiatives; establishing performance standards and goals, coaching, measurement and evaluation; and implementing a suitable reward structure (compensation and benefits).

To manage careers effectively, policies and systems must be established for recruitment, selection and placement (including transfer, promotion, retirement, and termination), and training and development. Policies and systems are also required for job analysis, individual employee assessment, replacement and succession planning, and career tracking, as well as career planning and development.[34]

Specific strategies must be formulated to balance supply and demand considerations. As was illustrated in Figure 5.2, there are three possible scenarios:

1. Labour supply exceeds demand (surplus)
2. Labour demand exceeds supply (shortage)
3. Expected demand matches supply.

Labour Surplus

hiring freeze
A common initial response
to an employee surplus.
Openings are filled by reassigning current employees,
and no outsiders are hired.

attrition
The normal separation of
employees from an organization due to resignation,
retirement, or death.

buy-out and early
retirement programs
Strategies used to accelerate
attrition, which involve offering attractive buy-out
(early leave) packages or the
opportunity to retire on full
pension, with an attractive
benefits package.

When the internal supply of employees exceeds the organization's demand, a human resources surplus exists. Most employers initially respond to such a situation by implementing a **hiring freeze**, which means that openings are filled by reassigning current employees, and no outsiders are hired, unless hiring authorization is granted by the CEO due to extenuating circumstances. The surplus is slowly reduced through **attrition**, which is the normal separation of employees from an organization due to resignation, retirement, or death. Attrition is initiated by the employee, not the organization, and although it is a slow method of reducing numbers, it presents the fewest problems. Voluntary departures simply create a vacancy that is not filled, and the staffing level declines without anyone being separated involuntarily. In addition to the time it takes, however, there are some other disadvantages to this approach to downsizing. The greatest drawback relates to the fact that the organization has no control over who stays and who leaves. Thus, valuable high performers may leave, while less-needed or lower-performing employees stay. Other potential problems include the fact that remaining employees may be overburdened with work. Their skills may not match those of the departed employee(s), resulting in decreased or inferior performance, and stagnation may occur due to the lack of new skills and ideas.

Some organizations attempt to accelerate attrition by offering incentives to employees to leave. **Buy-out** and **early retirement programs** are two common examples. Such strategies are used to reduce staffing levels and create internal job openings by offering attractive buy-out (also known as early leave) packages or the opportunity to retire on full pension, with an attractive benefits package, at a relatively early age, often as young as 55. To be successful, buyouts must be handled very carefully. Selection criteria should be established, to ensure that key people who cannot be easily replaced do not leave the firm. A drawback of buyouts and early retirement packages is that they often require a great deal of money upfront. The Quebec government's early retirement program for public employees, for example, will cost a total of nearly $3 billion. Double the number of unionized employees than originally targeted decided to take the package, which means that taxpayers will now pay more than $2 billion to cover its costs.[35] Care must also be taken to ensure that early retirement is voluntary, since forced early retirement is a contravention of human rights legislation, the consequences of which can be extremely costly. In a recent Ontario case, an older worker who was forced to accept early retirement was awarded $250 000 plus benefits.[36]

Reducing the total number of work hours through job sharing and part-time work is an additional strategy used to cope with an employee surplus. **Job sharing** involves dividing the duties of a single position between two or more employees.[37] Reducing full-time positions to *part-time work* is sometimes more effective, especially if there are peak demand periods. Creating a job share position and/or offering part-time employment can be win-win strategies, since layoffs can be avoided. Although the employees involved work fewer hours and thus have less pay, they are still employed, and may enjoy having more free time at their disposal. The organization benefits by retaining good employees.

In 1977, the federal government introduced a **work sharing** scheme, by which employees worked three or four days a week and received unemployment insurance (now called employment insurance) on their nonwork day(s).[38] This was a layoff-avoidance strategy; instead of laying off a few employees, all members of a work group or unit shared part of the layoff. Armco (now Armtec) in Guelph, Ontario, a manufacturer of prefabricated steel buildings, was one organization that used work-sharing arrangements to avoid layoffs and save jobs.

Similar to work sharing, but without a formal arrangement with government regarding employment insurance benefits, is a **reduced workweek**. Employees simply work fewer hours and receive less pay. The organization retains a skilled work force, lessens the financial and emotional impact of a full layoff, and yet manages to reduce production costs. The only potential drawback is that it is sometimes difficult to predict in advance, with any degree of accuracy, how many hours of work should be scheduled each week.

Some organizations with progressive HR policies are able to find *alternative jobs within the organization* for surplus and displaced employees. For example, when Dylex closed its Town and Country stores, more than 500 of the 600 redundant employees in Ontario were placed in other Dylex chain stores.[39]

A **layoff**, the temporary withdrawal of employment to workers for economic or business reasons, is another strategy used to correct an employee surplus. A layoff may only last a few weeks if the purpose is to adjust inventory levels or permit retooling for a new product line, but can last months or even years, if caused by a major change in the business cycle. While unpleasant for both management and workers, layoffs may be required if attrition will be insufficient to reduce employee head count to an acceptable level or if downsizing through attrition will take too long.

In unionized settings, layoffs are typically handled on the basis of **reverse seniority**—the employees hired most recently are the first to be laid off and the last to be recalled. The rights of employees during layoffs and the conditions and

---

job sharing
A strategy that involves dividing the duties of a single position between two or more employees.

work sharing
A layoff-avoidance strategy introduced by the federal government in 1977, by which employees worked three or four days a week and received unemployment insurance (now called employment insurance) on their nonwork day(s).

reduced workweek
A layoff avoidance strategy involving employees working fewer hours and receiving less pay.

layoff
The temporary withdrawal of employment to workers for economic or business reasons, another strategy used to correct an employee surplus.

reverse seniority
The employees hired most recently are the first to be laid off and the last to be recalled.

obligations pertaining to recall are clearly specified in the collective agreement. It is common for re-employment (recall) rights of laid-off employees to be preserved for periods of up to one or two years, providing they do not refuse to return to work if recalled sooner.

When layoffs are expected to be of a short duration, as when plants in the automotive industry shut down for several weeks to change tooling for a new model, juniority may be used instead. If there is a **juniority clause** in the collective agreement, senior workers (those with the greatest length of service) must be offered layoff first. If they accept, they are laid off and collect employment insurance (and organizational benefits), while junior employees retain their jobs. Long-service employees are often quite willing to accept a short-term layoff, since they can have time off for other pursuits, while their take-home pay remains virtually the same since employment insurance cheques don't involve payroll deductions for benefits, union dues, etc. When layoffs are of unknown duration or are expected to be long, long-service employees generally decline to exercise their juniority rights because employment insurance benefits can only be collected for a limited period of time. In such situations, the employees who are lower on the seniority list are laid off.

In nonunion settings, the ability of employees to change jobs and learn new skills, in addition to performance and competencies, is often given more weight than seniority in layoff decisions.

A key advantage of seniority and juniority clauses is objectivity. Using length of service as the basis for layoff and recall decisions is perceived by many to be more fair, since judgment of ability is subjective and favouritism may come into play. Employees themselves can calculate the probability of layoff and recall. There are drawbacks to using seniority as the governing factor, however. Less competent employees receive the same rewards and security as those who are more competent. Talent and effort are ignored. When layoffs occur in reverse seniority order, the payroll is also higher, since those with the most seniority tend to earn more. Also, there is often a disproportionate impact on designated group members, since they are generally more recent hires.

To ease the financial burden of layoffs, some organizations offer **supplemental unemployment benefits (SUBs)**, which increase income levels closer to what an employee would receive if on the job. SUB programs are generally negotiated through collective bargaining. Benefits are payable until the pool of funds set aside has been exhausted.

When employees are no longer required by the organization, the employment relationship may be severed. **Termination** is a broad term that encompasses the permanent separation from the organization for any reason. Since "termination" is often associated with discharge (being fired as a form of disciplinary action), some organizations prefer to use the term "permanent layoff" when employees must be separated due to economic or business reasons.

When the employment relationship is severed due to business necessity, affected employees are often offered severance pay and outplacement assistance. Typically, such benefits are only extended to individuals with acceptable or better performance ratings whose employment is terminated involuntarily.

Severance pay is a lump-sum payment that is given to employees who are being permanently separated, calculated on the basis of salary and years of service. While legally required in certain situations, such as mass layoffs, as will be explained in chapter 15, severance pay is expected when employees are being terminated through no fault of their own. In addition to pay, severance packages often include benefits continuation for a specified period of time. In determining the appropriate severance package, employers should also consider the employee's

juniority clause
A provision in the collective agreement that senior workers (those with the greatest length of service) must be offered layoff first. If they accept, they are laid off and collect employment insurance (and organizational benefits), while junior employees retain their jobs.

supplemental unemployment benefits (SUBs)
A top-up to employment insurance, generally negotiated through collective bargaining, to increase income levels closer to what an employee would receive if on the job.

termination
A broad term that encompasses the permanent separation from the organization for any reason.

severance pay
A lump-sum payment that is given to employees who are being permanently separated, calculated on the basis of salary and years of service.

age and likelihood of obtaining another job. To avoid costly court battles, many employers make reference to "ballpark," "reasonable range," or "reasonable offer" court decisions.[40]

Executives may be protected by a golden parachute clause in their contract of employment, a guarantee by the employer to pay specified compensation and benefits in the case of employee termination due to downsizing or restructuring.

To soften the blow of termination, **outplacement assistance** is often extended. Generally offered by an outside agency, outplacement programs are designed to assist affected employees to find employment elsewhere. Typical aids included to assist affected employees are such services as counselling, job-search skills training, and provision of office space and secretarial services, use of a photocopy and fax machine, and access to long-distance telephone calls. Sometimes letters are sent to other employers or placed in publications such as the *Human Resources Professional* outlining the qualifications of displaced employees and a contact number. Such efforts not only assist the employees affected, but also indicate to the remaining employees and the public that the firm is truly interested in and committed to its human resources.

outplacement assistance
A program designed to assist terminated employees to find employment elsewhere.

www.njhrpg.org/fhomeres. shtml
HR on the Net

Re-evaluating Restructuring   While layoffs and downsizing have certainly been prevalent in Canadian firms in recent years, in many instances, the consequences have not been as positive as anticipated. In a 1994 survey of hundreds of companies, about half reported improved earnings following downsizing, and only a third indicated an improvement in customer service or productivity. Two-thirds stated they had to hire at the same time they were laying off, in order to avoid losing critical skills.[41] Investors generally react negatively to an announcement of layoffs or large-scale work force reductions,[42] and terminations have an extremely negative impact on public perception.

Another cost of downsizing is **survivor sickness**, a range of emotions that can include feelings of betrayal or violation, guilt, and detachment. Study after study shows that remaining employees, anxious about the next round of terminations, often suffer stress symptoms, including depression, proneness to errors, and reduced performance.[43] Some firms, such as Amdahl Canada[44] and Apple Canada,[45] have recognized the existence of survivor sickness, and have taken steps to alleviate it.

This chapter's video case features two companies, Linamar and Sony Music of Canada, that have chosen growth, rather than downsizing, as the way to survive in tough times.

survivor sickness
A range of negative emotions experienced by employees remaining after a major restructuring initiative, which can include feelings of betrayal or violation, guilt and betrayal; and result in stress symptoms, including depression, proneness to errors, and reduced productivity.

Labour Shortage

If the internal supply of human resources cannot fulfil the organization's needs, a human resources shortage exists. Scheduling *overtime* hours is often the initial response. Another short-term solution is to *hire temporary employees*. Employers may also *subcontract work* (if not prohibited by the collective agreement) on a temporary or permanent basis.

As vacancies are created within an organization, opportunities are generally provided for employee transfers and promotions. Performance management, training (and retraining), and career development play a critical role. It should be noted that internal movement does not eliminate a shortage, and *recruitment* will be required. Hopefully, though, resultant vacancies will be for entry-level jobs, which can be more easily filled externally.

A **transfer** involves movement from one job to another that is relatively equal in pay, responsibility, and/or organizational level. Besides improving the

transfer
Movement of an employee from one job to another that is relatively equal in pay, responsibility, and/or organizational level.

utilization of human resources, transfers often broaden an employee's skills and perspectives, thereby making him or her a better candidate for promotion in the future. New technical and interpersonal challenges may lead to increased motivation and satisfaction. Even when minimal new challenges are provided, transfers at least offer some variety, which may enhance job satisfaction.

A **promotion** involves the movement of an employee from one job to another that is higher in pay, responsibility, and/or organizational level. Generally, a promotion is given as recognition of a person's past performance and/or future potential. Promotions are usually based on merit, seniority, or a combination of both.

Merit-based promotions are given as recognition of a person's superior performance in his or her present job. Such promotions should be based on an objective measure of performance, and not personal biases of the decision maker. Promotions based on favouritism result in incompetent people in higher-level, more demanding positions, and resentment among those not selected. Another potential problem with merit-based promotions is the **Peter Principle**, which states that, in a hierarchy, people tend to rise to their level of incompetence.[46] While not universally true, this principle suggests that good performance in one job is not a guarantee of good performance in another. People who are outstanding technically may make very poor managers, for example, because they lack "people" or "team" skills.

In unionized settings, seniority may be the governing factor in promotion and transfer decisions, or the deciding factor in the event of a tie in candidates' skills and abilities. Unions often prefer seniority to be the deciding factor, since length of service is a matter of record and is therefore totally objective. The drawback is that because all workers are not equally capable, the individual who is transferred or promoted may not be the most competent.

promotion
Movement of an employee from one job to another that is higher in pay, responsibility, and/or organizational level, usually based on merit, seniority, or a combination of both.

Peter Principle
The idea that in a hierarchy, people tend to rise to their level of incompetence, a potential problem with merit-based promotions.

Labour Supply Matches Labour Demand

When there is a match between expected supply and demand, organizations replace employees who leave the firm with individuals transferred or promoted from inside or hired from outside. As in shortage situations, performance management, training, and career development play a crucial role.

HRP Evaluation

HRP evaluation
An annual assessment to determine the effectiveness of HRP in meeting management's expectations, which involves determining whether or not goals were reached and reasons for failure, and identifying areas in need of change.

HR planning should be assessed on an annual basis to determine its effectiveness in meeting management's expectations. Since HRP links an organization's HRM activities with its strategic goals and objectives, the strength and adequacy of these linkages should be assessed.[47] This can be done by answering questions such as those in **Figure 5.8**. Whether or not goals were reached and reasons for failure should be determined, and areas in need of change identified.

Specific criteria often assessed include:

- actual staffing levels versus established staffing requirements
- ratio of internal placement to external hiring
- actual internal mobility flow (movement of employees within the organization) versus career development plans
- internal mobility flow versus turnover
- employment equity achievements as compared to established goals and timetables.

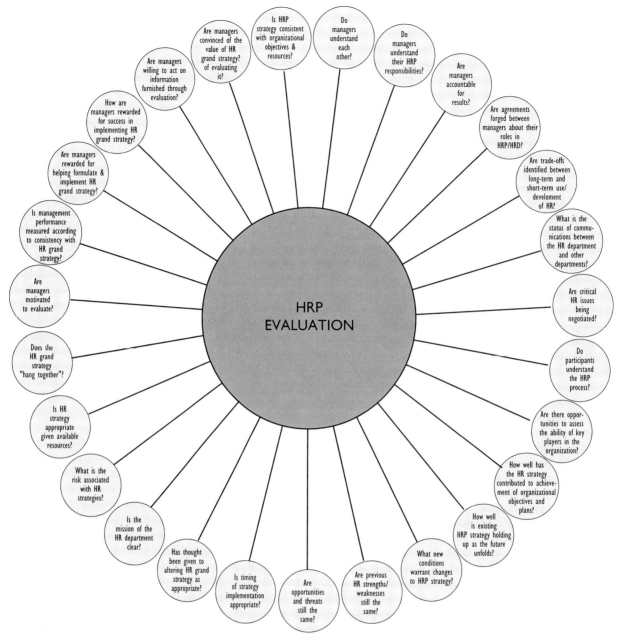

Figure 5.8
A Summary of Reasons for Conducting HRP Evaluation

Source: William J. Rothwell and H.C. Kazana, *Strategic Human Resources Planning and Management,* © 1988, p. 422 Reprinted by permission of Prentice-Hall, Inc., Englewood Cliffs, New Jersey.

Human Resources Accounting

Human resources accounting (HRA) is a process designed to measure the present cost or value of human resources, as well as their future worth to the organization.[48] By putting a dollar value on the organization's most valuable asset—its human resources, HRA provides useful data for HR planning, training and development, and compensation decisions.

human resources accounting (HRA)
A process designed to measure the present cost or value of human resources, as well as their future worth to the organization.

cost models
One type of HRA model that attempts to place a dollar value on human assets based on some kind of cost calculation—acquisition, replacement, or opportunity costs, for example.

value-based models
Another approach to HRA that involves an attempt to evaluate human resources on the basis of their current or future economic value to the organization.

There are two general categories of HRA models: cost and value.[49] The **cost models** attempt to place a dollar value on human assets based on some kind of cost calculation—acquisition, replacement, or opportunity costs, for example. Historical and replacement costs are often computed.

Computing *historical costs* involves computing all of the costs associated with the organization's investment in its human resources. Included are the costs involved in recruiting, acquiring, placing, maintaining, training, and developing employees.

Computing *replacement costs* involves assessing all costs that would be incurred to replace the organization's current work force. The total costs involved in recruiting, selecting, placing, training, and maintaining new employees; vacation and other severance pay entitlement for departing employees; and costs associated with replacing an experienced work force with inexperienced employees, must all be taken into account.

The **value-based models** attempt to evaluate human resources on the basis of their current or future economic value to the organization.

Whatever approach is used, most HRA models involve some degree of subjective assignment of a dollar figure to an employee's services and contributions. While some practitioners and researchers feel that the nature of human assets is such that any attempt to quantify them may be fruitless and unrealistic,[50] having objective and reliable information about the costs of human resources can prove extremely beneficial to HR planners, trainers, compensation administrators, and union–management negotiators.

Chapter Review

Summary

1. Human Resources Planning (HRP) is the process of reviewing human resources requirements to ensure that the organization has the required number of employees, with the necessary skills, to meet its goals.

2. Whether strategic or operational, plans are made and carried out by people. Thus, determining whether or not people will be available is a critical element of both strategic and operational planning processes. HRP and strategic planning become effective when there is a reciprocal and interdependent relationship between them.

3. Environmental scanning is a critical component of the HRP and strategic planning processes. The external environmental factors most frequently monitored include: economic conditions; market and competitive trends; government and legislative issues; social concerns related to health care, childcare, and educational priorities; technological changes; and demographic trends.

4. Once the human resources implications of the organization's strategic plans have been analyzed, there are four subsequent processes involved in HRP: forecasting future human resources needs (demand); forecasting availability of internal and external candidates (supply); planning and implementing HR programs to balance supply and demand; and monitoring and evaluating the results.

5. The end result of the forecasting process is an estimate of short-term and long-range human resources requirements. Long-range plans are general statements of probable needs. Short-term plans, although still approximations, are more specific, and often depicted in a staffing table.

6. Once the supply and demand of human resources have been estimated, program planning and implementation commence. Organizations must manage performance and careers and formulate specific strategies to balance supply and demand considerations.

7. Strategies to deal with a labour surplus include the implementation of a hiring freeze and downsizing through attrition; speeding up attrition through attractive buy-out (early leave) and early retirement programs; reducing hours through job sharing, part-time hours, work sharing or reduced workweeks; finding alternative jobs within the organization for displaced workers; laying off workers on the basis of reverse seniority or juniority; and terminating employment.

8. Scheduling overtime is often the initial response to a human resources shortage. Another short-term solution is to hire temporary employees. Employers may also subcontract work (if not prohibited by the collective agreement) on a temporary or permanent basis. As vacancies are created within an organization, opportunities are generally provided for employee transfers and promotions.

9. When there is a match between expected supply and demand, organizations replace employees who leave the firm with individuals transferred or promoted from inside or hired from outside.

10. HR planning should be assessed on an annual basis to determine its effectiveness in meeting management's expectations. Whether or not goals were reached and reasons for failure should be determined, and areas in need of change identified.

Key Terms

attrition
buy-out and early
  retirement programs
Canada Occupational
  Forecasting Program
  (COFOR)
Canadian Disaggregated
  Interdepartmental
  Econometric Model
  (CANDIDE)
Canadian Occupational
  Projection System
  (COPS)
computerized forecast
cost models
Delphi technique
Ford Occupational
  Imbalance Listing
  (FOIL)

hiring freeze
HRP evaluation
human resources
  accounting (HRA)
job sharing
juniority clause
layoff
management inventories
Markov analysis
Microelectronics
  Simulation Model
  (MESIM)
nominal group technique
outplacement assistance
Peter Principle
promotion
public sector
ratio analysis
reduced workweek

regression analysis
replacement charts
replacement summaries
reverse seniority
scatter plot
severance pay
skills inventories
staffing table
succession planning
supplemental
  unemployment benefits
  (SUBs)
survivor sickness
quasi-pubic sector
termination
transfer
trend analysis
value-based models
work sharing

Discussion Questions and Exercises

1. Explain the nature of human resources planning (HRP) and describe the costs associated with lack of or inadequate human resources planning.

2. Describe the relationship between HRP and strategic planning.

3. Describe various quantitative and qualitative techniques used to forecast human resources demand.

4. Develop a realistic, hypothetical staffing table for a department or organization with which you are familiar.

5. Differentiate between replacement charts and replacement summaries, and explain why replacement summaries are generally preferred.

6. Most employers initially respond to an employee surplus by implementing a hiring freeze and downsizing through attrition. Explain this strategy and discuss its pros and cons.

7. Discuss various layoff-avoidance strategies that can be used to reduce a surplus of human resources.

8. Differentiate between the reverse seniority and juniority approaches to layoff and explain the advantages and disadvantages of each.

9. Explain the role of severance pay and outplacement assistance in employee terminations.
10. Explain how employee transfers can benefit employees and organizations.
11. Differentiate between the seniority and merit-based approaches to promotion and describe the advantages and disadvantages associated with each.

Application Exercises

RUNNING CASE: Carter Cleaning Company
To Plan or Not to Plan?

One aspect of HRM that Jennifer studied at university was HR planning. Her professor in the course emphasized its importance, especially for large organizations. While Carter Cleaning is certainly not large at this time—with only six centres, each staffed by its own on-site manager and seven employees, on average, she wonders if HRP might help to resolve some of their current problems.

At this point, there is only an informal succession plan—both Jennifer and her father are counting on the fact that Jennifer will take over the firm when her father decides to retire.

Carter Cleaning is heavily dependent on their managers—three white males and three white females, and skilled cleaner-spotters and pressers. Employees generally have no more than a high school education (often less). The market for skilled staff is very competitive. Over a typical weekend literally dozens of want ads for experienced pressers or cleaner-spotters can be found in area newspapers. Paid little more than minimum wage, people in these jobs tend to move around a great deal. Virtually all of the incumbents in these positions at the centres are women and/or visible minorities. Turnover (as in the stores of many of their competitors) sometimes approaches 400 percent.

Jennifer is pondering the following questions:

Questions

1. In what ways might HRP benefit Carter Cleaning?
2. Should they decide to proceed with HRP, what steps should Jennifer and her father take?
3. What HRP techniques would be appropriate for them to use?
4. What other issues would have to be addressed to make HRP worthwhile?

CASE INCIDENT: Management Trainees at Nova

It's that time of year again at Nova! Each year, Carl Adams, recruitment officer at head office of the retail chain, visits colleges and universities across Canada to recruit graduates for sales, marketing, human resources, and purchasing management-trainee positions for its twenty-six locations.

In order to predict the number of management trainees required, human resources planning is done each year, based on the budget and forecasted sales. The previous year's plan is also reviewed. There has been virtually no change in the human resources plan over the past ten years.

Natalie Gordon, vice-president of human resources, is feeling rather concerned about what happened last year and wondering how to ensure it doesn't happen again. Based on the HR plan, fifty new management trainees were hired. Unfortunately, six months after they started, the company experienced a drastic drop in sales due to a downturn in the economy, combined with increased foreign competition. Half of the recently hired management trainees had to be laid off.

Carl, who started at Nova as a management trainee when he completed the Business Administration—Human Resources Management Program at Central Community College, has just returned from his first on-campus recruitment campaign, which happened to be at his old alma mater, and reported that his experience was not as pleasant as usual. One of the candidates he interviewed knew someone who had been hired and laid off last year, and indicated that she was rather worried about considering a position with the firm in light of that fact, despite Nova's excellent reputation for promotion from within and overall stability. (Nova, which currently employs over 8 000 employees in its head office and retail stores across the country, has been in business for over seventy years.)

Carl has just finished telling Natalie how embarrassed he was by this candidate's probing questions about job security and how uncomfortable he felt. He ended up simply reassuring the candidate that such a situation could never happen again. Natalie is now wondering how to make Carl's reassurance a reality.

Questions

1. What are the consequences of poor human resources planning at Nova?
2. What problems do you see with Nova's present HRP process?
3. What should Natalie do to more accurately forecast the demand for management trainees for the coming year before Carl does any more on-campus recruiting?

Human Resources Management Simulation

Exercise 10 in the simulation involves devising a succession plan to ensure that each of Acme's managerial and supervisory positions can be filled with a suitable successor in a reasonable period of time. Requirements include providing advice to the Plant Manager on methods of identifying qualified employees and preparing them for promotion, specifying who is responsible for finding eligible employees, and indicating the role of the Human Resources Manager in preparing employees for promotion.

Video Case

Is Downsizing the Answer?

Although the trend in Canadian business has been toward downsizing and lay-offs, downsizing has failed to be as profitable as first predicted. Some companies have focused on growth, with amazing results. Their experience indicates that growth is the way to increase the bottom line.

The idea is to build the business, not shrink it, and control costs, but not by laying employees off. Laid-off employees represent a loss of company culture, history, and knowledge of past mistakes. They might be able to offer valuable advice that could prevent the company from repeating errors and/or help the organization to move in a new direction. Linamar and Sony Music of Canada are two renegade companies that never joined the downsizing race.

Linamar, a Canadian auto parts manufacturer, has focused on growth. The company strives to produce goods faster and better than its competitors. Linamar aims for predictability of products, steady production, increases in export sales, and boosts in productivity levels. Management has recognized that growth is driven by the factory. For that reason, every office employee is given the opportunity to operate the factory machines. The result is positive: Linamar has experienced an increase in sales and work force.

At Sony Music of Canada, president Rick Camilleri decided that the way to increase profits was to spend money. The Sony building was redesigned in order to attract recording artists away from competitors. A feeling of job security has replaced any threat of layoffs. Due to poor quality results experienced in the past, Sony no longer contracts work out. Instead, all products are made at Sony. Work is even accepted from other companies. Orders are filled within twenty-four hours, which supports the company's customer-service orientation.

The message is clear—Investing in future growth pays. A growing company is more responsive and can move ahead of its competitors when opportunities arise. Furthermore, companies that grow have richer shareholders. Linamar stock has risen ten times over the past six years, and Sony stock has tripled in the last three.

Questions

1. Why has downsizing failed to be as profitable as expected?

2. What are companies with a growth mentality, such as Linamar and Sony Music of Canada, doing to increase profits?

3. At Linamar, office staff are given the opportunity to operate factory machines. What are the advantages of this practice for the employees and company?

Video Resource: CBC, *Venture,* "Growth," (April 21, 1996).

Take It to the Net

Check out our Companion Website at

www.prenticehall.ca/dessler

for a multitude of practice questions, key terms and concepts, Weblinks to related sites, newsgroups, CBC video updates, and more.

Notes

1. Naresh C. Agarwal, "Human Resources Planning," *Human Resources Management in Canada* (Toronto: Prentice-Hall Canada Inc., 1983), p. 20 011.

2. James W. Walker, *Human Resource Planning* (New York: McGraw-Hill Book Company, 1980), p. 10.

3. James W. Walker, "Human Resource Planning, 1990s Style," *Human Resource Planning* 13, no. 4 (1990), pp. 229-40.

4. Dave Ulrich, "Strategic and Human Resource Planning: Linking Customers and Employees," *Human Resource Planning* 15, no. 2 (1992), pp. 47–62.

5. "Human Resources Managers Aren't Corporate Nobodies Any More," *Business Week* (December 2, 1985), p. 59.

6. Ruth Featherstone, "Nurses say HR Issues Ignored," *Canadian HR Reporter* 10 no. 21 (December 1, 1997), p. 25. Copyright MPL Communications Inc., Reproduced by permission of *Canadian HR Reporter* 133 Richmond Street West, Toronto, Ontario M5H 3M8.

7. Barrie McKenna, "Axe Falls on Civil Service Jobs," *The Globe and Mail* (May 16, 1995), pp. A1–2.

8. Chris Knight, "Workplaces Getting Leaner, Not Meaner," *Canadian HR Reporter* 10, no. 18 (October 20, 1997), p. 12.

9. E.B. Akeyeampong, "The Labour Market: Year End Review," *Perspectives on Labour and Income* (Ottawa: Statistics Canada, Spring 1995), Cat. No. 75-001E.

10. R. Lattimer, "Managing Workforce Diversity: Problems Similar in Canada and U.S.," *Towers Perrin Focus* (Spring 1993), pp. 9–10.

11. Earl Miller, "Capitalizing on Older Workers," *Canadian HR Reporter* 10, no. 12 (June 16, 1997), p. 14.

12. "Youth Equity at Bank of Montreal," *Canadian HR Reporter* 10, no. 18 (October 20, 1997), p. 12.

13. Herbert G. Heneman, Jr., and George Seitzer, "Manpower Planning and Forecasting in the Firm: An Exploratory Probe," in Elmer Burack and James Walker, *Manpower*

Planning and Programming (Boston: Allyn & Bacon, 1972), pp. 102–20; Sheldon Zedeck and Milton Blood, "Selection and Placement," from *Foundations of Behavioral Science Research in Organizations* (Monterey, CA: Brooks/Cole, 1974), in J. Richard Hackman, Edward Lawler III, and Lyman Porter, *Perspectives on Behavior in Organizations* (New York: McGraw-Hill, 1977), pp. 103–19. For a discussion of equal employment implications of work force planning, see James Ledvinka, "Technical Implications of Equal Employment Law for Manpower Planning," *Personnel Psychology* 28 (Autumn 1975).

14. Roger Hawk, *The Recruitment Function* (New York: American Management Association, 1967). See also Paul Pakchar, "Effective Manpower Planning," *Personnel Journal* 62, no. 10 (October 1983), pp. 826–30.

15. Richard B. Frantzreb, "Human Resource Planning: Forecasting Manpower Needs," *Personnel Journal* 60, no. 11 (November 1981), pp. 850–7. See also John Gridley, "Who Will Be Where When? Forecast the Easy Way," *Personnel Journal* 65 (May 1986), pp. 50–8.

16. Based on an idea in Elmer H. Burack and Robert D. Smith, *Personnel Management: A Human Resource Systems Approach* (St. Paul, MN: West, 1977), pp. 134–5. Reprinted by permission. Copyright 1977 by West Publishing Co. All rights reserved.

17. Glenn Bassett, "Elements of Manpower Forecasting and Scheduling," *Human Resource Management* 12, no. 3 (Fall 1973), pp. 35–43, reprinted in Richard Peterson, Lane Tracy, and Allan Cabelly, *Systematic Management of Human Resources* (Reading, MA: Addison-Wesley, 1979), pp. 135–6.

18. For an example of a computerized system in use at Citibank, see Paul Sheiber, "A Simple Selection System Called 'Job Match,'" *Personnel Journal* 58, no. 1 (January 1979), pp. 26–54.

19. G. Milkovich, A.J. Annoni, and T.A. Mahoney, "The Use of Delphi Procedures in Manpower Forecasting," *Management Science* 19, no. 4 (1972), pp. 381–8.

20. A.L. Delbecq, A.H. Van DelVen, and D.H. Gustafson, *Group Techniques for Program Planning: A Guide to Nominal and Delphi Processes* (Glenview Illinois: Scott Foresman, 1975).

21. For discussions of skill inventories, see, for example, John Lawrie, "Skill Inventories: Pack for the Future," *Personnel Journal* (March 1987), pp. 127–30; John Lawrie, "Skill Inventories: A Developmental Process," *Personnel Journal* (October 1987), pp. 108–10.

22. Alfred Walker, "Management Selection Systems That Meet the Challenge of the 80s," *Personnel Journal* 60, no. 10 (October 1981), pp. 775–80.

23. Amiel Sharon, "Skills Bank Tracks Talent, Not Training," *Personnel Journal* (June 1988), pp. 44–9.

24. Stuart Forman, "Corporate Contenders," *Human Resources Professional* 10, no. 8 (September 1993), pp. 17, 19.

25. This is a modification of a definition found in Peter Wallum, "A Broader View of Succession Planning," *Personnel Management* (September 1993), p. 45.

26. Wallum, "A Broader View," pp. 43–4.

27. Agarwal, "Human Resources Planning," p. 20 039.

28. Sharon Lebrun, "Helping Hands," *Canadian HR Reporter* 10, no. 18 (October 20, 1997), p. 8.

29. Cited in Sharon Lebrun, "Booklets to Connect Disabled With Work," *Canadian HR Reporter* 10, no. 18 (October 20, 1997), p. 8.

30. Pierre Paul Prouly, Luce Bourqualt, and Jean-Francois Manegre, "CANDIDE-COFOR and Forecasting Manpower Needs by Occupation and Industry in Canada" in Larry F. More and Larry Charack (eds), *Manpower Planning for Canadians*, 2nd ed. (Vancouver, BC: Institute of Industrial Relations, University of British Columbia, 1979).

31. Prouly, Bourqualt, and Manegre, "CANDIDE-COFOR."

32. See (1) *Innovations and Jobs in Canada, A Research Report Prepared for the Economic Council of Canada* (Ottawa: Ministry of Supply and Services, 1987), Cat. No. EC22-141/1987; (2) *The Canadian Occupational Projections Systems Issues and Approaches* (Ottawa: Employment and Immigration Canada, January 1983), WH-3-335E.

33. *Human Resource Planning: A Challenge for the 1980s* (Ottawa: Ministry of Supply and Services, 1983), Cat. No. MP43-125/83. See "Innovations and Jobs in Canada," Ch. 4.

34. Walker, *Human Resource Planning.*

35. "Quebec to Pay $3 Billion for Buy-Outs," *Canadian HR Reporter* 10, no. 21 (December 1, 1997), p. 3.

36. Anneli Legault, "Aging Disgracefully," *Human Resources Professional* 10, no. 11 (December 1993), pp. 10–11.

37. David A. Bratton, "Moving Away From Nine to Five," *Canadian Business Review* (Spring 1986), pp. 15–7.

38. Frank Reid, "Combatting Unemployment Through Work Time Reductions," *Canadian Public Policy* 12, no. 2 (1986), pp. 275–85.

39. Linda Gutri, "Survivor Skills," *Human Resources Professional* 9, no. 3 (March 1993), pp. 13–5.

40. Malcolm MacKillop, "Ballpark Justice," *Human Resources Professional* 11, no. 7 (September 1994), pp. 10-1.

41. Margot Gibb-Clark, "Survivors Also Suffer in Downsizing: Expert," *The Globe and Mail* (May 23, 1995), p. B5.

42. D. Worrell, W. Davidson, and V. Sharma, "Layoff Announcements and Shareholder Wealth," *Academy of Management Journal* 34 (1991), pp. 662–78.

43. W. Cascio, "Downsizing? What Do We Know? What Have We Learned?" *The Executive* 7 (1993), pp. 95–104.

44. Gutri, "Survivor Skills," pp. 13-5.

45. Shelley Boyes, "Restructuring Survivors," *Human Resources Professional* 12, no. 4 (July/August 1995), pp. 17–8.

46. Laurence J. Peter and Raymond Hull, *The Peter Principle* (New York: William Morrow, 1969).

47. Walker, *Human Resource Planning*, pp. 355–6.

48. For a comprehensive discussion of human resources accounting, see E.G. Famholtz, *Human Resource Accounting* (San Francisco: Jossey-Bass 1985); H. Das and M. Das, "One More Time: How Do We Place a Value Tag on Our Employees? Some Issues in Human Resource Accounting," *Human Resource Planning* 2, no. 2 (1979), pp. 91–101; W.F. Cascio *Costing Human Resources: The Financial Impact of Behavior in Organizations* (Boston: Kent Publishing, 1985).

49. For a discussion of the various models, see Das and Das, "One More Time, pp. 91–101

50. Das and Das, "One More Time," pp. 91–101.

Chapter 6
Recruitment

Chapter Outline

- ◆ **Introduction**
- ◆ **The Recruitment Process**
- ◆ **Constraints on the Recruitment Process**
- ◆ **Recruiting Within the Organization**
- ◆ **Recruiting Outside the Organization**
- ◆ **Recruiting a More Diverse Work Force**
- ◆ **Developing and Using Application Forms**

Learning Outcomes

After studying this chapter, you should be able to:

Define recruitment and *describe* its purposes.

Explain the recruitment process.

Describe the constraints on recruitment.

Describe the role of job posting, human resources records, and skills inventories in promotion from within.

Describe the methods used for external recruitment and *explain* the appropriate use of each.

Discuss strategies for recruiting a more diverse work force.

Explain the importance of application forms and *design* an application form meeting human rights legislative requirements.

Introduction

recruitment
The process of searching for and attracting an adequate number of qualified job candidates, from whom the organization may select the most appropriate individuals to staff its job requirements.

Recruitment is the process of searching for and attracting an adequate number of qualified job candidates, from whom the organization may select the most appropriate to staff its job requirements. The process begins when the need to fill a position is identified and ends with the receipt of résumés and/or completed application forms. The result is a pool of qualified job seekers from which the individual best matching the job requirements can be selected.

The Purposes of Recruitment

Because the quality of an organization's human resources depends, to a great extent, upon the quality of its recruits, recruitment is a key HR function. Its purposes are to:

- ensure that an adequate pool of candidates is generated at minimum possible cost
- help to increase the success rate of the selection process by eliminating (or at least minimizing) the number of unqualified or poorly qualified applicants[1]
- help to achieve the organization's legal and social obligations regarding the demographic composition of its work force
- attract candidates who not only meet the job requirements, but are also suited to the organization's unique environment and culture.

The Role of the HR Department in the Recruitment Process

As was mentioned in chapter 1, in firms with an HR department, functional authority for the recruitment process is generally delegated to HR staff. In large organizations, in which recruiting is done on an almost continuous basis, there are typically specialists, known as **recruiters**, in the HR department, whose job it is to find and attract capable applicants.

recruiter
A specialist in recruitment, whose job it is to find and attract capable candidates

The Recruitment Process

As illustrated in **Figure 6.1**, there are a number of steps in the recruitment process:

1. Job openings are identified through human resources planning or manager request. Human resources plans play a vital role in the identification process, because they indicate present and future openings and specify which should be filled internally and which externally. Openings do arise unexpectedly, however, in which case the immediate supervisor may have to complete a **human resources requisition form** to obtain authorization to proceed with recruitment and selection.

2. The job requirements are determined. This involves reviewing the job description and the job specification and updating them, if necessary. Manager comments may also prove helpful in identifying requirements, particularly pertaining to personality and fit.

3. Appropriate recruiting sources and methods are chosen. There is no one, best, recruiting technique, and the most appropriate for any given position depend on a number of factors, which will be discussed next.

4. A pool of qualified recruits is generated.

human resources requisition form
A form that must be completed to obtain authorization for recruitment, outlining the position, job specifications, reason for the opening, and date required.

Figure 6.1
An Overview of the Recruitment Process

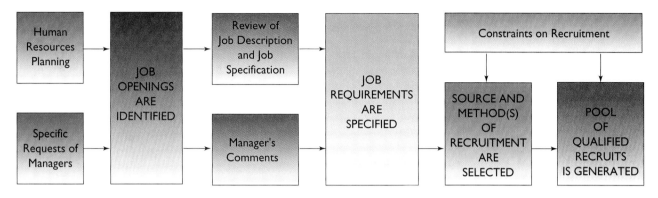

Constraints on the Recruitment Process

In order to be successful, a recruiter must be aware of the constraints affecting the recruitment process. These come from organizational policies and plans, the job requirements, recruiter habits, inducements of competitors, and environmental conditions.

Organizational Policies

Promote-From-Within Policies   Many firms have a promote-from-within policy. Collective agreements often require that jobs be posted internally for a specified period of time before external recruitment can begin, and organizations have adopted a similar policy for their nonunion positions. While there are many advantages to this practice, which will be discussed shortly, having such a policy may mean that a recruiter cannot begin to seek external candidates until the posting period is over, even if he or she is aware that there are no suitable internal candidates.

Compensation Policies   The pay structure and benefits package can pose a constraint, since they influence the attractiveness of the job to potential applicants. Recruiters rarely have the authority to exceed established pay ranges, and may be further constrained by an organizational policy specifying that no one can be hired at a rate higher than the midpoint or other set level within the range.

Employment Status Policies   Some companies have policies restricting the hiring of part-time or temporary employees, which means that only those seeking full-time positions are eligible for consideration as recruits. In other firms, there is a restriction on full-time hiring, which means that recruiters are authorized to hire on a part-time or contract basis only.

International Hiring Policies   Many firms with international operations hire locally whenever possible. Hiring host-country nationals (HCNs) reduces relocation expenses, and minimizes the possibility of family adjustment problems and charges of economic exploitation. In many countries, including Canada, there are legal restrictions on the right to recruit outside the country if there are qualified candidates available within. Moreover, HCNs are more apt to be fluent in the language and to understand and accept local customs and business practices.

In addition to the challenge of recruiting a good performer in an unfamiliar labour market, there is the need to teach the HCN the organization's corporate culture. As well, the organization must provide the technical knowledge required, such that the new employee can operate effectively as a local agent. Many firms have found, though, that providing indoctrination and support systems for an HCN is less onerous than training and supporting a domestic manager on an expatriate assignment.[2]

Organizational Plans

Human Resources Plan The human resources plan provides valuable guidance to recruiters by indicating when and how many candidates will be required for various positions, but may also pose some restrictions, since such plans specify which positions should be filled internally, and which externally.

Employment Equity Plan Whether legally required or voluntarily initiated, if there is an employment equity plan, it must be consulted, since it will specify the organization's goals and timetables pertaining to the hiring of designated group members. To increase the number of qualified candidates from the designated groups, recruiters often use nontraditional (outreach) strategies, a topic that will be explored later in this chapter.

Recruitment Budget The budget established for recruitment also poses some constraints. The costs of telephone calls, travel, advertising, etc. must be taken into consideration. Some positions can be filled very cheaply; others will require extensive advertising, and considerable time and travel. Recruiters have to decide how to allocate their allotted budget dollars in the most effective manner.

Careful human resources planning and forethought by recruiters can minimize expenses. For example, recruiting for several job openings simultaneously can reduce the cost per recruit.

Costs have to be balanced with other considerations, however. For example, relying on three very popular and inexpensive techniques, which will be described later in this chapter (walk-ins, write-ins, and word-of-mouth hiring), can result in systemic discrimination. Also, as will be explained shortly, recruitment method affects the quality of hires and turnover rates.

Job Requirements

The actual requirements of the job for which recruits are being sought poses some constraints. Highly skilled and specialized workers, for example, often have to be hired externally and are generally more difficult to find and attract than unskilled ones. The length of time required, scope of the search area (local, regional, national, or international), amount of compensation required to attract candidates, and recruitment campaign budget are all linked to the job specifications. As explained in the Global HRM box, filling certain high-tech positions may mean seeking recruits from around the world, something that is not easy, given Canada's strict immigration laws.

Global HRM

Bringing Home High-Tech Talent

On May 6, 1997, the Department of Citizenship and Immigration took the unprecedented step of introducing the Software Development Workers Pilot Project, designed to fast track the entry of qualified software professionals to Canada for temporary employment with a Canadian employer. This represents a first step toward Canadian industry's direct participation in the shaping of immigration admission rules to meet its specific needs.

In recognition of the drastic shortage in Canada of software professionals possessing specific skills, the project was developed by Citizenship and Immigration Canada (CIC), in conjunction with Human Resources Development Canada (HRDC), Industry Canada (IC), and the Software Human Resources Council (SHRC), a non-profit, non-governmental body

Seven job descriptions have been designed by the SHRC, CIC, and HRDC and published on SHRC's Web site (www.shrc.ca), setting out specific educational and experience requirements. The positions involved include:

- embedded systems software designer
- software products developer
- MIS software designer
- multimedia software designer
- senior animation effects editor
- software developer—services
- telecommunications software designer.

The expectation is that specific labour market shortages will be addressed without harming the employment opportunities of any newly-graduated Canadian software professionals. The pilot project is by no means an open door for all software professionals. The qualifications are fairly onerous and only foreign workers meeting the duties, skill requirements, and salary guidelines in the relevant category will be fast tracked. All others are subject to the usual immigration validation and screening.

Recruiters are cautioned that careful planning is required to ensure quick processing of the prospective employee's application for temporary employment authorization. Such application is normally made by the foreign worker in the visa office in his or her area of residence. In cases where the worker does not need a visa to travel to Canada, the application may be filed at a Canadian port of entry. It must be accompanied by:

- a job offer or contract of employment coinciding with one of the seven approved job descriptions, listing the job title, duties, wages and working conditions, and length and location of employment;
- a letter from the Canadian employer providing a brief description of the firm, including the date it commenced operations, its business activities, the number of workers employed, and its industry association memberships; and
- a completed Software Development Worker Background Information Form.

Although the pilot project is intended to fill the temporary needs of Canadian employers through the authorization of temporary employment, program hirees can apply for permanent residence at the Canadian consulate in Buffalo, New York, while in Canada. Accordingly, it is possible for temporary entry to continue until landed immigrant status is attained.

The pilot project was originally intended to be in effect for six months only, but has been granted an extension. It does not eliminate any of the legal requirements for entering Canada, such as a medical report (depending on country of residence) and evidence of lack of criminal record.

Further, in some cases, such as those involving citizens of the United States, NAFTA may be more effective for quick and efficient entry of recruits, as the eligibility criteria may be less onerous. Similarly, citizens of signatory countries to the General Agreement on Trade in Services may be more expeditiously processed under the temporary employment provisions of that treaty.

The project has been undergoing review and amendment, so recruiters should keep a close eye on the SHRC website to determine the nature of any changes in eligibility requirements, and details regarding the length of program extension.

Source: Howard D. Greenberg, "Bringing Home High-Tech Talent," *Canadian HR Reporter* 10, no. 17 (October 6, 1997), p. 12. Copyright MPL Communications Inc., Reproduced by permission of *Canadian HR Reporter* 133 Richmond Street West, Toronto, Ontario M5H 3M8.

Recruiter Habits

A recruiter's past successes can lead to habits. Although such habits may eliminate time-consuming deliberations and enhance efficiency, they can also lead to perpetuation of past mistakes or failure to consider more effective alternatives.

Using the same source repeatedly may make it difficult, if not impossible, to reach employment equity goals, and may result in employees who share the same strengths and weaknesses.

Inducements of Competitors

Attracting qualified candidates requires recruiters to market the job and organization. Monetary and non-monetary inducements are used to stimulate interest. The types of inducements being offered by the competition impose a constraint, since recruiters must try to meet the prevailing standards or use alternative inducements to overcome limitations. For example, if a competitor is offering excellent pay as an inducement, and the organization has a far more modest salary range, the recruiter may try to sell the location (in the heart of the beautiful Kawarthas or overlooking the Pacific Ocean) or unique benefits (such as a generous educational subsidy plan, flextime, or childcare facilities).

There is a caution to be noted in the use of inducements, however. The Supreme Court of Canada decision in Queen v. Cognos (1993) makes it clear that employers must take extreme care in describing the nature and existence of an employment opportunity to prospective employees. Representations made must be accurate, not misleading, or the firm can be charged with negligent misrepresentation:[3]

> *Douglas Queen, a Calgary accountant who moved to Ottawa for a job at Cognos Inc., a computer software company, was awarded $67 244 in a wrongful hiring suit. When he was recruited, Mr. Queen was not informed that the financing for the project for which he was being enticed to move to Ottawa had not been finalized. Shortly after being hired, the funding fell through and the responsibilities he thought he would be assuming evaporated.*

Environmental Conditions

As described in detail in chapter 1, external environmental conditions impose a major constraint on many aspects of employment. Changes in the labour market, unemployment rate, economy and legislation, and the recruiting activities of labour-market competitors all affect a recruiter's efforts. Although an environmental scan is an important component of the human resources planning process, the economic environment may change after the human resources plan is finalized. To ensure that the assumptions on which the plan was based are valid at the time of search, recruiters can check three measures:

Leading Economic Indicators   Each month Statistics Canada announces the direction of the leading economic indicators. If these indices signal a sudden downturn or upturn in the economy, recruiting plans may have to be modified.

Want-Ads Index   The volume of want ads in major metropolitan newspapers is monitored and reported as an index by Statistics Canada and the Technical Service Council. An upward trend in this index indicates increased competition for employees who are recruited nationally, such as professionals and managers. To monitor the amount of competition for workers who are usually recruited on a local or regional basis, such as clerical and production employees, the human resources department staff may want to create their own indices to report changes in want-ad volume in the local and regional newspapers. Generally, the more competition there is, the more vigorous and extensive the recruitment campaign must be. A drop in level of competition may narrow the scope of the area of search or make less costly recruitment methods viable.

Actual Activity versus Predicted Activity   Most organizations produce monthly reports in which actual levels of activity (such as sales volume or number of patients admitted) are compared with projections. Since human resources planning is based on predicted activity levels, variations between what was predicted and what is actually occurring may mean that recruiting plans have to be modified.

Recruiting Sources

There are two sources available for recruiting job candidates: internal and external. Although recruiting often brings employment agencies and classified ads to mind, current employees are generally the largest source of recruits. Some surveys have indicated that up to 90 percent of all management positions are filled internally.[4]

Recruiting Within the Organization

Filling open positions with inside candidates has several advantages. Employees see that competence is rewarded and morale and performance may thus be enhanced. Having already been with the firm for some time, inside candidates may be more committed to company goals and less likely to leave. Promotion from within can boost employee commitment and provide managers with a longer-term perspective when making business decisions. It may also be safer to promote employees from within, since the firm is likely to have a more accurate assessment of the person's skills than would otherwise be the case. Inside candidates may also require less orientation and training than outsiders.

Yet promotion from within can also backfire. Employees who apply for jobs and don't get them may become discontented. Informing unsuccessful applicants as to why they were rejected and what remedial actions they might take to be more successful in the future is thus essential.[5] Similarly, many employers require managers to post job openings and interview all inside candidates. Yet, the manager often knows ahead of time exactly whom he or she wants to hire, and requiring that he or she interview all internal applicants is thus a waste of time for all concerned. Groups may also not be as satisfied when their new boss is appointed from within their own ranks as when he or she is a newcomer; sometimes, for instance, it is difficult for the newly chosen leader to adjust to no longer being being "one of the gang."[6]

Perhaps the biggest drawback, however, is "inbreeding." When an entire management team has been brought up through the ranks, there may be a tendency to make decisions "by the book" and to maintain the status quo, when a new and innovative direction is needed. Balancing the benefits of morale and loyalty with the drawback of inbreeding is thus a challenge.

To be effective, promotion from within requires using job posting, human resources records, and skills inventories.[7]

job posting
The process of notifying current employees about vacant positions.

Job Posting   **Job posting** is a process of notifying current employees about vacant positions, generally by placing a form outlining the title, duties (as listed in the job description), qualifications (taken from the job specification), hours of work, pay range, posting date, and closing date (as in **Figure 6.2**) on designated bulletin boards throughout the firm. These bulletin boards may be enclosed in

**Figure 6.2
Sample Job Posting**

Source: Lorann Martinell. Used with permission.

Renfrew County Board of Education

Job Posting Notice

**Secretary
(Special Education)**

This is a full-time position starting November 1, 1998.

Any employee who feels s/he is qualified and wishes to apply, in accordance with the Collective Agreement, must submit an up-to-date resume with attached cover letter to the Director, Human Resources Services, up to and including October 30, 1998.

The secretarial position is responsible for providing secretarial and clerical support services for the Special Education Administrator, Psychologist, and other professional staff and committees. Specifically, this will include setting up, typing, duplicating, and distributing reports, handbooks, policy and procedure manuals, etc.; receiving inquiries by mail, telephone, and in person, from parents, teachers, and other staff; updating student information files; and other related duties.

QUALIFICATIONS: secretarial, clerical training and/or experience; excellent written and oral communication skills; good organizational skills; high ethical standards; and the ability to take initiative.

HOURS: 9:00 a.m. to 5:00 p.m.
                    (40 hrs/week)

DATE POSTED: October 15, 1998

DATE CLOSED: October 30, 1998

A detailed job description is available from the Human Resources Department.

DEDICATED TO EMPLOYMENT EQUITY; QUALIFIED DESIGNATED GROUP MEMBERS ARE ENCOURAGED TO APPLY

Figure 6.3
One Firm's Job Posting
Policy

Source: From the book, *Human Resource Director's Handbook* by Mary F. Cook ©1984. Used by permission of the publisher, Prentice-Hall, Inc., Englewood Cliffs, NJ.

ELIGIBILITY

- All permanent employees who have completed their probationary period are eligible to use the open position listing policy in order to request consideration for a position that would constitute a growth opportunity.
- Employees who have been promoted or transferred, or who have changed jobs for any reason, must wait a six-month period before applying for a different position.

POLICY

- A list of open positions will be communicated to all employees in all facilities. Notices will include information on job title, salary grade, department, supervisor's name and title, location, brief description of the job content, qualifications, and instructions concerning whether or not candidates will be expected to demonstrate their skills during the interview process.
- Basic job qualifications and experience needed to fill the job will be listed on the sheet. Employees should consult with the human resources department if there are questions concerning the promotional opportunities associated with the job.
- Open position lists will remain on bulletin boards for five working days.
- Forms for use in requesting consideration for an open position may be obtained from the human resources department.
- The human resources department will review requests to substantiate the employee's qualifications for the position.
- The hiring manager will review requests for employees inside the company before going outside the company to fill the position.
- It is the responsibility of the employees to notify their managers of their intent to interview for an open position.
- The hiring manager makes the final decision when filling the position; however, the guidelines for filling any open position are based on the employees' ability, qualifications, experience, background, and the skills they possess that will allow them to carry out the job successfully. It is the responsibility of the hiring manager to notify the previous manager of the intent to hire the employee.
- Employees who are aware of a pending opening, and who will be on vacation when the opening occurs, may leave a request with the human resources department for consideration.
- It is the manager's responsibility to ensure that the human resources department has notified all internal applicants that they did or did not get the job before general announcement by the manager of the person who did get the job.
- "Blanket" applications will not be accepted. Employees should apply each time a position they are interested in becomes available.
- Since preselection often occurs, employees should be planning for their career growth by scheduling time with potential managers before posting, to become acquainted with them, and to secure developmental information to be used in acquiring appropriate skills for future consideration.
- There are occasions when jobs will not be listed. Two such examples might be (1) when a job can be filled best by natural progression or is a logical career path for an employee, and (2) when a job is created to provide a development opportunity for a specific high-performance employee.
- In keeping with this policy, managers are encouraged to work with employees in career development in order to assist them in pursuing upward movement in a particular career path or job ladder.

glass and kept locked, so that no unauthorized postings can be placed and postings cannot be removed prior to the closing date. Some firms require that interested employees submit a current résumé to the HR department; others have forms which can be completed.

Job posting can be an effective way of spreading the word about job opportunities to existing employees.

Not all firms use bulletin boards for job postings. Some post jobs in employee publications, have special-announcement handouts, or send out notices by mail. Many firms, such as DuPont Canada, now have computerized job-posting systems, which make information about any vacancies available online or accessible twenty-four hours a day by calling a specific telephone number.

As mentioned earlier, many collective agreements require that all vacant jobs in the bargaining unit be posted for a specified number of days and stipulate that only bargaining unit members will initially be considered. Such requirements help to ensure that members of the bargaining unit receive fair consideration when opportunities for lateral moves and career advancement arise within the local. Many firms have job posting policies covering their nonunion employees as well. An example is presented in **Figure 6.3**. Important guiding principles for such policies are included therein, such as: "All permanent employees...are eligible to use the open position listing policy...to request consideration for a position that would constitute a growth opportunity," and "A list of open positions will be communicated to all employees in all facilities."

As illustrated in **Figure 6.4**, there are advantages and disadvantages to using job postings to facilitate the transfer and promotion of qualified internal candidates. As explained in the Building Employee Commitment box, having a job posting policy is more effective when it is part of a career development program. Employees should be aware of career paths within the organization, and the knowledge, skills, and abilities required to move up the job-progression ladder. The role of job transfers in career growth should also be clarified.

Building Employee Commitment

Promotion from Within

Employees tend to be committed to firms that are committed to them. As explained in chapter 2, two-way communications, guaranteed fair treatment, and job security are some of the things a firm can provide to show that it is indeed committed to its employees. But many employees will ultimately measure their firm's commitment by the degree to which they were able to achieve their career goals. We'll discuss promotion-from-within systems in more detail in chapter 9 (Career Development). However, at this point it's useful to emphasize the fact that internal recruiting and promotion from within can be central to boosting employee commitment.

To build commitment, the promotion-from-within program should be comprehensive. Certainly, firms associated with committed employees—for example, Cadet Uniform Services and Federal Express Canada Ltd.—have promotion-from-within policies. At Federal Express Canada, for instance, about 95 percent of positions are filled internally. But there's more to a successful promotion-from-within program than just a strong policy statement. As we'll see in chapter 9, promotion from within is aided first by careful employee selection. In the words of Arnold Gedmintas, President of Cadet Uniform Services, "We look for people with stable job backgrounds, who are team players, extroverted, and will speak up if they see something is wrong. They have to be willing to learn and have development potential."[1]

Effective promotion from within also depends on other HR actions. The education and training needed to help employees identify and develop their promotion potential must be provided. Career-oriented appraisals are also required, in which the supervisor and employee are charged with linking the latter's past performance, career preferences, and developmental needs in a formal career plan. Finally, a coordinated system for accessing career records and posting job openings is required, one that guarantees all eligible employees will be informed of openings and considered for them.

At Cadet, new jobs are posted internally and everyone can apply. After an interview, successful candidates for management positions undergo a two-year, on-site management training program. At any given time, two to five people are enrolled.

At FedEx Canada, employees moving up the corporate ladder must pass through the Leadership Evaluation and Awareness Process (LEAP). There is also a separate LEAP program for management that requires several assessments by superiors and peers, in addition to completing a project supervised by the employee's immediate supervisor, a process that takes from six to twelve months.

As illustrated by these two examples, internal recruiting and promotion from within can help to build employee commitment. However, a job posting policy alone will not do it.

1. Cited in Ken Mark, "No More Pink Slips," *Human Resources Professional* 13, no. 8 (November 1996), p. 22.

Sources: Gary Dessler, *Winning Commitment* (New York: McGraw-Hill Book Company, 1993), and Ken Mark, "No More Pink Slips," pp. 21–3.

Figure 6.4
Advantages and Disadvantages of Job Posting

Advantages

- Provides equal opportunity for all qualified employees
- Provides every qualified employee with an opportunity to obtain a better job
- Reduces the likelihood of special deals and favouritism
- Demonstrates the organization's commitment to career growth and development
- Communicates to employees the organization's policies and guidelines regarding promotions and transfers

Disadvantages

- Unsuccessful job candidates may become demotivated, demoralized, discontented, and unhappy if feedback is not communicated in a timely and sensitive manner.
- Tensions may rise if it appears that a qualified internal job candidate was passed over for an equally qualified or less qualified external candidate.
- The decision on which candidate to select may be more difficult if there is more than one equally qualified candidate.

Human Resources Records   Human resources records are often consulted to ensure that qualified individuals are notified, in person, of vacant positions. An examination of employee files, including résumés and application forms, may uncover employees who are working in jobs below their education or skill levels; people who already have the requisite knowledge and skills and abilities; or persons with the potential to move into the vacant position if given some additional training.

Skills Inventories   Skills inventories, described in chapter 5, are an even better reference tool. While such inventories may be used instead of job posting, they are more often used as a supplement. Whether computerized or manual, referring to such inventories ensures that qualified internal candidates are identified and considered for transfer or promotion when opportunities arise.

Limitations of Recruiting from Within

It is rarely possible to fill all non-entry-level jobs with current employees. Middle- and upper-level jobs may be vacated unexpectedly, with no internal replacements yet qualified or ready for transfer or promotion; or may require such specialized training and experience that there are no potential internal replacements.

In many firms with a policy of promoting from within, potential external candidates are also considered, to prevent the inbreeding problem described previously. Hiring someone from outside may be preferable to acquire the latest knowledge and expertise or gain new ideas and revitalize the department or organization.

Recruiting Outside the Organization

Unless there is a work-force reduction, even in firms with a promote-from-within policy, a replacement from outside must eventually be found to fill the job left vacant once all eligible employees have been given the opportunity for transfer and/or promotion. In addition, most entry-level positions must be filled by external candidates. The advantages of external recruitment include:

- generation of a larger pool of qualified candidates, which may have a positive impact on the quality of the selection decision (as will be explained in chapter 7)
- availability of a more diverse pool of applicants, which can assist in meeting employment equity goals and timetables
- acquisition of skills or knowledge not currently available within the organization and/or new ideas and creative problem-solving techniques
- elimination of rivalry and competition caused by employees jockeying for transfers and promotions, which can hinder interpersonal and interdepartmental cooperation
- potential cost savings resulting from hiring individuals who already have the skills, rather than providing extensive training.

Planning External Recruitment

When choosing external recruitment method(s), in addition to the constraints mentioned earlier, there are a number of factors that should be taken into consideration: the type of job, the relationship between the method chosen and quality of hire, the yield ratio, and the amount of lead time.

Type of Job   The type of job to be filled has a major impact on the recruitment method selected. This fact is clearly illustrated by the results a comprehensive study of the recruiting practices of 188 North American companies. For managerial positions, 80 percent used newspaper ads, 75 percent used employment agencies, and 65 percent relied on employee referrals. For professional and technical jobs, 75 percent used college or university recruiting, 75 percent also used newspapers and technical journal advertising, and 70 percent used employment agencies. For recruiting sales staff, 80 percent used newspaper ads, 75 percent used referrals, and 65 percent used employment agencies. For office and plant employees, on the other hand, referrals and walk-ins were relied on by 90 percent of the firms responding, while 80 percent used newspaper ads, and 70 percent used public employment agencies (such as Human Resource Centres).[8]

Relationship of Method Chosen and Quality of Hire   Several studies have suggested that the recruitment methods chosen can affect subsequent tenure and job performance.[9] In general, applicants who find employment as walk-ins or through referral by a current employee tend to remain with the organization longer and be higher-quality performers than those recruited through advertising and employment agencies.

Highlights of the results of a study comparing four external recruiting methods follow. The four methods were convention/journal advertising, newspaper advertising, college/university placement offices, and self-initiated walk-ins. They were assessed in terms of employee effectiveness, measured by quality of performance and dependability; absenteeism; satisfaction with supervision; and job involvement.[10]

> *Quality and Dependability*—Applicants who made contact based on their own initiative or in response to convention or professional journal advertising were superior to those recruited through educational institution placement offices and newspaper advertising.

> *Absenteeism*—Those recruited through newspaper ads missed almost twice as many days as did those recruited using any of the other methods.

> *Job Involvement and Satisfaction with Supervision*—Recruits obtained through college/university placement offices reported significantly lower levels of both job involvement and satisfaction with supervision than did employees recruited in other ways.

As mentioned previously, the results of such research must be weighed against employment equity and cost considerations.

yield ratio
The percentage of applicants that proceed to the next stage of the selection process.

Yield Ratios   Yield ratios help to indicate which recruitment methods are the most effective at producing qualified job candidates. A **yield ratio** is the percentage of applicants that proceed to the next stage of the selection process.

A recruiting yield pyramid, such as that shown in **Figure 6.5**, can be devised for each method, by calculating the yield ratio for each step in the selection

**Figure 6.5
Recruiting Yield
Pyramid**

50   New hires
100   Offers made (2 : 1)
150   Candidates interviewed (3 : 2)
200   Candidates invited (4 : 3)
1,200   Leads generated (6 : 1)

process. The firm in this example typically hires fifty entry-level accountants each year through on-campus recruitment at colleges and universities. The firm has calculated that using this method leads to a ratio of offers made to actual new hires of 2 to 1 (about half of the candidates to whom offers are made accept). The firm also knows that the ratio of candidates interviewed to offers made is 3 to 2, while the ratio of candidates invited for interviews to candidates actually interviewed is generally 4 to 3. Finally, the firm knows that the ratio between leads generated and candidates selected for interviews is 6 to 1. In other words, of six leads generated through college/university recruiting efforts, one applicant is invited to attend an interview. Given these ratios, the firm knows that, using this particular recruitment method, 1 200 leads must be generated in order to hire 50 new accountants.

By calculating and comparing yield pyramids for each recruiting method, it is possible to determine which method results in the most new hires for each type of job.

Amount of Lead Time The average number of days from when the company initiates a recruitment method to when the successful candidate begins to work is the **time-lapse data**. Similar to yield ratios, this data is collected for each step in the process.

Let's assume that the accounting company in the above example found the following: six days elapsed between submission of application forms and résumés to invitation for an interview, five days from invitation to actual interview, five days from interview to job offer, six days from job offer to acceptance, and 23 days from acceptance of job offer to commencement of work. These data indicate that, using on-campus recruiting, the firm must initiate recruitment efforts at least forty-five days prior to the anticipated job opening date.

Calculating time-lapse data for each recruitment method means that the amount of lead time available can be taken into account when deciding which strategy or strategies would be most appropriate.

External Recruitment Methods

Walk-Ins Individuals who go to organizations voluntarily to apply for jobs without referral or invitation by the firm are called walk-ins. They are a major, inexpensive source of applicants, particularly for entry-level and unskilled positions. Even when walk-ins drop off a résumé, they are often asked to complete an application form. These applications and résumés are then screened and those considered suitable are kept on file for a period of three to six months and reviewed when a relevant vacancy arises for which external candidates are being considered.

Firms generally treat all walk-ins very courteously and diplomatically. In some organizations, walk-ins are even given a brief interview by a member of the HR department as a public relations gesture.

Write-Ins People who submit unsolicited résumés to organizations are known as write-ins. Such résumés are generally screened by a member of the HR department. If applicants are considered suitable, their résumés are retained on file for a period of three to six months or passed on to the relevant department manager if there is an immediate or upcoming opening for which the applicant is qualified.

Unsolicited résumés are a valuable and inexpensive source of candidates, primarily for managerial, clerical, professional, sales, and technical positions. In many firms, there is a practice of acknowledging the interest of write-in applicants by sending a brief thank-you note.

Some large organizations have started to use computer databases for storing the information found on the résumés and application forms of walk-in and write-in candidates. Whether the original document is paper-based or submitted via email, Web, or fax, it can be scanned and stored on databases for fast, easy access using a few key words.[11]

Employee Referrals Some organizations encourage applications from friends and relatives of current employees by mounting an employee referral campaign. Openings are announced in the company's newsletter or posted on a bulletin board or the intranet, along with a request for referrals. Cash awards or prizes may be offered for referrals that culminate in hirings. At Northern Telecom Canada Ltd. (Nortel), for example, employees who refer recruiters to a successful job candidate receive a $1 600 bonus.[12] Because there are no advertising or agency fees involved, this still represents a low recruiting cost. Other advantages include the fact that employees with hard-to-find job skills may know others in their field; the recruits obtained tend to have a positive, yet realistic impression of the organization; and the candidates referred are of high quality (since employees are generally willing to refer only those in whom they have great confidence). It should be noted, however, that the success of such programs depends largely on the morale of employees.[13]

Employee referral programs are quite popular. Forty percent of the firms responding to one survey said they use some sort of employee referral system and hire about 15 percent of their employees in this manner. Cash awards for referring candidates who are hired was listed as the most common type of referral incentive, the amount of which varied with company size. The cost per hire was uniformly low—far below the cost of an employment agency.[14]

Disadvantages associated with employee referrals include the potential of inbreeding and **nepotism** to cause morale problems, and dissatisfaction of employees whose referral is not hired. Perhaps the biggest drawback of this recruitment strategy, however, is that it may result in systemic discrimination in workplaces that are not diverse, since employees tend to recommend individuals who have backgrounds similar to their own, in terms of race, ethnicity, religion, and so on. To avoid this potential drawback, employers should adopt an employment equity policy; educate their employees about the purpose, importance, and value of diversity; and highlight the organization's commitment to equity in all of their job postings and referral requests.

Educational Institutions Educational institutions are an excellent source of applicants with formal training but relatively little full-time work experience. High schools can provide recruits for clerical and blue-collar jobs. Universities and colleges are excellent sources of applicants for a variety of positions, ranging from police officer to management trainee.

Most Canadian universities and community colleges have placement centres. Organizations provide the placement centre with information about their job openings, which is then posted. When students see postings in which they are interested, they submit an application form and résumé to the placement centre on or before the closing date specified in the posting. The placement centre does not typically do any prescreening, but simply submits to the employer, in a single package, all of the applications received. The employer then selects those applicants who appear to best fit the job specifications and arranges with the placement centre to conduct interviews on campus with those individuals.

Despite the fact that it can be time-consuming and expensive, each year a large number of companies throughout Canada visit selected campuses to conduct

nepotism
A preference for hiring relatives of current employees.

on-campus recruitment activities. In choosing universities or colleges at which to recruit, employers consider such factors as the institution's reputation in critical skills areas, the performance of previous hires from that institution, the reputation of faculty, previous job offer and acceptance rates, the number of potential recruits, the cost involved (due to travel and accommodation expenses), and the ability to meet employment equity goals.[15]

On-campus recruiters seek to accomplish two main tasks: 1) screening candidates to determine which ones are worthy of further consideration; and 2) selling the firm and job to the interviewee.

Most high schools, colleges, and universities have counselling centres. Such centres aid students by providing skills assessment testing and assistance with job-search skills, including résumé preparation and interview strategies. Sometimes they arrange for job fairs, at which employers set up displays outlining the types of job opportunities available.

Cooperative education (co-op) and field placement programs have become increasingly popular in Canada. These programs require students to spend a specified period of time working in organizations as an integral part of their academic program, thereby gaining some hands-on skills in an actual work setting. Co-op programs are now offered in some high schools, as well as in colleges and universities. For the past ten years, for example, Northern Telecom Inc. has offered co-op work terms to high-school students in the Ottawa area, and is planning to begin a similar program in Toronto.[16] Various departments at Woodstock General Hospital in Woodstock, Ontario, ranging from Physiotherapy to Medical Records, have provided opportunities for co-op students from Fanshawe College, Huron Park Secondary School, and Woodstock Collegiate Institute each year for well over fifteen years.[17]

Summer internship programs are part of the recruitment strategy at organizations such as Celestica and Shell Canada.[18] College and/or university students are hired to complete summer projects between their second last and final year of study. Their performance is assessed, and those who are judged to be superior are offered permanent positions following graduation.

Graduates may also be offered internship positions. HR department staff at the Ministry of Natural Resources in Peterborough, Ontario, for example, are currently working with faculty at Sir Sandford Fleming College to develop a six-month internship for graduates of Fleming's Business Administration Program, Human Resources Management Specialization. Graduates will have the opportunity to acquire hands-on skills in various HR functions. Those who prove to be outstanding performers will be considered for full-time employment, as opportunities arise.[19]

Many organizations across Canada have recognized the value of student and graduate internship programs. As explained in the Information Technology and HR box, interns can now be recruited online.

Internship, co-op, and field placement programs can produce a win-win result. The employer is provided with an excellent opportunity to assess the skills and abilities of a potential employee, without incurring any significant costs, while benefitting from fresh ideas brought in by bright, talented, and committed individuals. Because co-op and field placement students and student/graduate interns have been exposed to the organization and its expectations, if hired, they are less likely to leave shortly after hire than recruits with no previous exposure to the firm.[20]

Recognizing these benefits has made internships and co-op programs a major recruitment method in many organizations. Most of the college and university graduates who end up working at Northern Telecom, for example, have done

Information Technology and HR
Finding Interns Online

Recognizing that there are more than half a million young people, many well-qualified graduates with strong academic credentials, who are unemployed or only working part time because they can't find full-time jobs, a group of more than 70 of Canada's largest companies launched Career Edge in October of 1996. This is a national, non-profit, private-sector organization committed to helping Canadian youth gain essential career-related experience through internships. Companies involved include the Toronto-Dominion Bank, Noranda Inc., the Boston Consulting Group, Pan Canadian Petroleum, and Bell Canada.

According to Career Edge President and Chief Operating Officer, Frances Randle, participating firms don't add to their headcount. "Interns can't replace current employees or fill vacancies, but they must have specific job descriptions and be assigned a coach."

Career Edge uses the Internet as its exclusive means of bringing companies and youth together. Interested organizations register with Career Edge and, once approved, are invited to enter information about student internship positions directly on Career Edge's Web site. Prospective interns visit the site, view the available positions and apply directly to the company. Company staff then review the applications and select the candidate(s) to host.

The interns become employees of Career Edge. Host organizations pay $18 024 a year for each intern, of which $15 000 goes to the intern and the balance to taxes and administrative costs. There is no government funding involved.

In early 1997, after four months of operation, 160 interns had been placed, and of those, 18 had been offered full-time employment.◆

Source: "Career Edge: Using the Internet to Give Young People a Start," *Human Resources Professional* 14, no. 2 (April/May 1997), p. 24.

previous internships or co-op work terms. Indeed, Nortel is Canada's largest employer of co-op students and student interns, welcoming about 2 000 each year. In many cases, they are offered jobs even before they complete their programs.[21]

Human Resource Centres Human Resources Development Canada (HRDC) operates over 800 Human Resource Centres across the country. Formerly called Canada Employment Centres (CECs), their purpose is to assist unemployed individuals to find suitable jobs and to help employers locate qualified candidates to meet their needs. There is no cost to either party.

Employers can call and place job postings with the centres, which are then accessed by job seekers via telephone, using the Employment Telemessage system, or online. While used primarily as a source of blue-collar, unskilled, and clerical employees, because there is a National Job Bank that provides a Canada-wide listing of job orders, HRDC can sometimes help employers locate highly-skilled workers who happen to be living in an area of high unemployment and are willing to relocate.

In addition, HRDC now operates the Electronic Labour Exchange (ELE), a computer-based recruitment tool that can match employer job specifications with job-seeker profiles.

HRDC also manages the Employment Insurance program, and offers a variety of other services, ranging from providing information on national labour market conditions, employment insurance, and income security programs, to job-search assistance. They also provide individual and group employment counselling, diagnostic assessment, relocation and travel assistance, and special youth initiatives such as native internships and student business loans. If applicants require additional training or upgrading to help match their skills with jobs available, there are a number of programs to help, ranging from subsidizing wages and training costs for on-the-job training to paying tuition fees and providing income assistance to those attending a community college.[22]

Private Employment Agencies Private employment agencies are quite widespread throughout Canada and are an excellent source of clerical, professional, technical, and managerial employees. They take an employer's request for recruits and then solicit job seekers, relying primarily on advertising and walk-ins/write-ins. Private employment agencies serve two basic functions: expanding the pool of job applicants and performing preliminary interviewing and screening. It should be noted, though, that the amount of service provided varies widely, as does the level of professionalism and the calibre of staff. Some employment agencies carefully screen applicants; others simply provide a stream of applicants and let the client's human resources department staff do the screening. Where agency staff are paid on a commission basis, their desire to earn a commission may occasionally compromise their professionalism, and they may encourage job seekers to accept jobs for which they are neither qualified nor suited.

In most provinces, it is either illegal for private employment agencies to charge applicants a fee for placement, or the fees charged are regulated. Generally, it is the employer who pays the agency fee. It is not uncommon for private employment agencies to charge an employer between 15 and 30 percent of the first year's salary, when an applicant referred by the agency is hired. This percentage may vary depending on the volume of business provided by the client and type of employee sought.

To match the employer's job specifications with the abilities and interests of potential job applicants, agencies may perform a range of functions, including advertising, interviewing, reference checking, and testing for skills, aptitudes, and interests.[23]

There are a number of reasons for an organization to use an employment agency to handle some or all of its recruiting needs. Specific situations in which an agency might be used include the following:

1. The organization does not have an HR department and/or has no one with the requisite time and/or expertise
2. The organization has experienced difficulty in generating a pool of qualified candidates for the position or a similar type of position in the past
3. A particular opening must be filled quickly
4. There is a desire to recruit a greater number of designated group members than the firm has been able to attract on its own
5. The recruitment effort is aimed at reaching individuals who are currently employed and might therefore feel more comfortable answering ads from and dealing with an employment agency.

There are many advantages to using a professionally-operated private employment agency.[24] The agency can save the organization a great deal of time by finding, interviewing, and selecting qualified candidates for referral to the hiring manager; cut down on the number of people for the employer to interview; and help to ensure that only candidates matching the job specifications are interviewed. Agencies failing to do a proper screening job or violating human rights legislative standards earn a bad reputation among human resources professionals and rapidly lose credibility.

To ensure that the agency-employer relationship is positive and to avoid any legal compliance problems, references provided by the agency should be contacted to confirm suitability and professionalism. In addition, it is recommended that organizations do the following:[25]

1. Give the agency an accurate and complete job description. The better the agency understands the job(s) to be filled, the greater the likelihood that a reasonable pool of qualified applicants will be generated.

2. Specify the tools or devices that the agency should use to screen applicants on the firm's behalf. At the very least, find out what devices the agency uses for applicant screening and ensure they meet the firm's standards and expectations.

3. If possible, periodically review data on accepted and rejected candidates. This will serve as a check on the agency's processes and practices.

4. If feasible, develop a long-term relationship with one or two agencies. It may also be advantageous to designate one person in the HR department to serve as the liaison between the firm and agency and/or to have a specific contact at the agency coordinating the firm's recruiting needs.

Executive Search Firms   Employers retain executive search firms to seek out senior-level professional, technical, and managerial employees. Paid a fee by the employer, they are typically used to fill jobs for which the pay range exceeds $40 000 or $50 000. While the percentage of a firm's positions filled by such firms is generally small, they typically include the most critical positions. For executive positions, using an executive search firm may be the firm's only recruitment strategy.

Such firms can be very useful. They often specialize in a particular type of talent, such as executives, sales, technical, or scientific employees. They typically have many contacts and are especially adept at contacting qualified candidates who are employed and not actively looking to change jobs. (That's the reason they have been given the nickname "headhunters"). They can keep the firm's name confidential until late in the search process and save top management time by doing the preliminary work of advertising for the position and screening what could turn out to be hundreds of applicants. The fee paid might actually turn out to be insignificant compared to the cost of company executive time saved.

There are some potential pitfalls, however. Some executive search firms have found that what their clients say they want is not really accurate. It is essential for the employer to explain in detail the type of candidate required—and why. Some headhunters are more salespeople than professionals, and are more interested in persuading the employer to hire a candidate than in finding one who really meets the job specifications. Some firms have also been known to present an unpromising candidate to a client simply to make their one or two other prospects look that much better. When choosing an executive search firm, the following guidelines are recommended by one expert:[26]

1. Make sure the firm chosen is capable of conducting a thorough search. Under the code of ethics of the Association of Executive Recruiting Consultants, a headhunter must wait for a period of two years before approaching a candidate previously placed with an employer to discuss a vacancy with a new client. This means that the headhunter must search in a constantly diminishing labour market. Particularly in the case of large executive search firms, it may become extremely difficult, on occasion, to refer any top-notch candidates, since the best potential recruits may already be working for former clients.

2. Meet and assess the person who will actually be handling the assignment, since the person conducting the search will determine its fate and must be an individual in whose abilities and manner the firm has confidence.

3. Clarify the fees involved. Search firm's fees range from 25 to 50 percent of the annual salary for the position, and are often payable even if the search is terminated by the employer for any reason. Generally, one-third of the fee is payable as a retainer at the outset.

4. Choose a recruiter who is trustworthy. Executive search firms typically learn about their clients' weaknesses, as well as their strengths. It is therefore imperative that the individual who is handling the search can be trusted with what may be privileged information.

5. Check references. Talking to individuals at two or three firms for whom the search firm has recently completed assignments can be extremely helpful.

Some helpful hints for small business owners considering using an executive search firm are provided in the Small Business Applications box.

Small Business Applications

Using Executive Search Firms—When and Why?

There comes a time in the life of most small businesses when it dawns on the owner that his or her managers are not capable of taking the company into the realm of expanded sales or innovative services. A decision must then be made regarding what kinds of people to hire from outside and how this hiring should take place. Should the owner decide what type of person to hire and recruit this person himself or herself? Or should an outside expert be brought in to help with the search?

The heads of most large firms often don't think twice about hiring executive search firms. However, owners of small firms (with their relatively limited funds) may hesitate before committing to a fee that could reach $20 000 to $30 000 for a $60 000 to $70 000 marketing manager. Such hesitation may be short-sighted when the options are actually reviewed.

Engaging in an executive search is not at all like looking for secretaries, supervisors, or data-entry clerks. Recruiting lower-level employees can usually be accomplished easily by contacting the local Human Resource Centre operated by HRDC, placing ads, using relatively low-cost employment agencies, or even by placing a help wanted sign in the front window. However, when seeking a key executive to help run the firm, the chances are high that this person won't be found by placing ads or using most of the other traditional approaches. For one thing, the person being sought is probably already employed and not reading the want ads. Even if a potential candidates does happen to glance at the ads, unless he or she is extremely unhappy at present, there is little likelihood that the ad will spark the effort to embark on a job search.

In other words, there is a danger of ending up with drawer full of résumés from people who are, for one reason or another, out of work or unhappy with their work, and would also be unsuited to the job. It then falls to the small business owner to try to find several gems in this group of résumés and to interview and assess these applicants. This is hardly an attractive proposition, unless the owner happens to be an expert at interviewing and reference checking (and has little else to do).

Thus, there are two potential problems small business owners may encounter when conducting an executive search without assistance. First, as a non-expert, the individual concerned may not even know where to begin: how to write a suitable ad, where to place an ad, where to search, who to contact, how to screen out those who appear to be good on paper but are actually unsuitable candidates, or how to perform adequate reference checking. Second, to be done effectively, the process is generally extremely time-consuming and may divert attention from more important duties. Many business owners find that when they consider the opportunity costs involved with doing their own searches, they are not saving any money at all. For example, the time spent may cost enough in terms of lost sales calls that the company actually comes out behind financially. Often, the question is not whether the small business owner can afford to use an executive search firm, but whether he or she can afford not to.

Advertising Advertising is one of the most often-used recruiting methods. While the media available ranges from television and radio to professional journals, the advantages and disadvantages of which are shown in **Table 6.1**, newspaper advertising seems to be the most popular.[27]

For advertising to bring the desired results, there are two issues that must be addressed: the media to be used, and the construction of the ad.[28] The selection of the best medium—whether it be the local newspaper, a national newspaper, or a technical journal—depends on the type of positions for which the organization is recruiting. Reaching individuals who are employed already and not actively seeking alternate employment requires a different medium than is appropriate to attract those who are unemployed.

To achieve optimum results from an advertisement, the following four-point guide, called *AIDA*, should be kept in mind as the ad is being constructed:

- The ad should attract *attention*. Those ads with borders, a company logo or picture, and that use empty white space effectively stand out. To attract attention, key positions should be advertised in display ads, not lost in the columns of classified ads.
- The ad should develop *interest* in the job. Interest can be created by the nature of the job itself, by pointing out the range of duties and/or the amount of challenge or responsibility involved. Sometimes other aspects of the job, such as its location or working conditions, are useful in attracting interest. To ensure that the individuals attracted are qualified, the job specifications should always be included.
- The ad should create a *desire* for the job. This may be done by capitalizing on the interesting aspects of the job itself and by pointing out any unique benefits or opportunities associated with it, such as the opportunity for career development or travel. Desire may also be created by stressing the employer's commitment to employment equity. The target audience should be kept in mind as the ad is being created.
- The ad should instigate *action*. To prompt action, ads often include a closing date and a statement such as "Call today," "Send your résumé today by fax or email," "Write today for more information," or "Go to the site of our next job fair."

want ad
A recruitment ad describing the job and its specifications, the compensation package, and the hiring employer. The address to which applications and/or résumés should be submitted is also provided.

If constructed properly, advertisements can be an effective instrument for recruiting, as well as for communicating the organization's corporate image to the general public. An ad incorporating the AIDA guidelines is shown in **Figure 6.6**

There are two general types of newspaper advertisements: want ads and blind ads. **Want ads** describe the job and its specifications, the compensation package, and the hiring employer. They also provide the address(es) to which applications and/or résumés should be submitted, often including an email address

TABLE 6.1 Advantages and Disadvantages of Some Major Types of Media

TYPE OF MEDIUM	ADVANTAGES	DISADVANTAGES	WHEN TO USE
Newspapers	Short deadlines. Ad size flexibility. Circulation concentrated in specific geographic areas. Classified sections well organized for easy access by active job seekers.	Easy for prospects to ignore. Considerable competitive clutter. Circulation not specialized—a great number of unwanted readers must be paid for. Poor printing quality.	When it is desirable to limit recruiting to a specific area. When sufficient numbers of prospects are clustered in a specific area. When enough prospects are reading help wanted ads to fill hiring needs.
Magazines	Specialized magazines reach pin-pointed occupation categories. Ad size flexibility. High-quality printing. Prestigious editorial environment. Long life—prospects keep magazines and reread them.	Wide geographic circulation—usually cannot be used to limit recruiting to specific area. Long lead-time for ad placement.	When job is specialized. When time and geographic limitations are not of utmost importance. When involved in ongoing recruiting programs.
Radio and television	Difficult to ignore. Can reach prospects who are not actively looking for a job better than newspapers and magazines. Can be limited to specific geographic areas. Creatively flexible. Can dramatize employment story more effectively than printed ads. Little competitive recruitment clutter.	Only brief, uncomplicated messages are possible. Lack of permanence; prospect cannot refer back to it. (Repeated airings necessary to make impression.) Creation and production of commercials—particularly TV—can be time-consuming and costly. Lack of special-interest selectivity; paying for waste circulation.	In competitive situations when not enough prospects are reading printed ads. When there are multiple job openings and there are enough prospects in specific geographic area. When a large impact is needed quickly. A "blitz" campaign can saturate an area in two weeks or less. Useful to call attention to printed ads.
"Point-of-purchase" (promotional materials at recruiting location)	Calls attention to employment story at a time when prospects can take some type of immediate action. Creative flexibility.	Limited usefulness; prospects must visit a recruiting location before it can be effective.	Posters, banners, brochures, audiovisual presentations at special events such as job fairs, open houses, conventions, as part of an employee referral program, at placement offices, or whenever prospects visit organization facilities.

Source: Adapted from Bernard S. Hodes, "Planning for Recruitment Advertising: Part II," *Personnel Journal* 28, no. 5 (June 1983), p. 499. Reprinted with the permission of *Personnel Journal*, Costa Mesa, CA. All rights reserved.

blind ad
A recruitment ad in which the identity and address of the employer is omitted.

and/or fax number. While the content pertaining to the job, specifications, and compensation is identical in **blind ads**, such ads omit the identity and address of the hiring employer. Potential job candidates are instructed to forward their responses to a post office box number or a newspaper box number. While many job seekers do not like responding to blind ads, since there is always the danger of unknowingly sending a résumé to the firm at which they are currently employed,

Figure 6.6
Newspaper
Recruitment
Advertisement,
Demonstrating AIDA
Principles

Source: Dr. Everett Chalmers
Hospital, Fredericton, New
Brunswick. Reproduced by
permission.

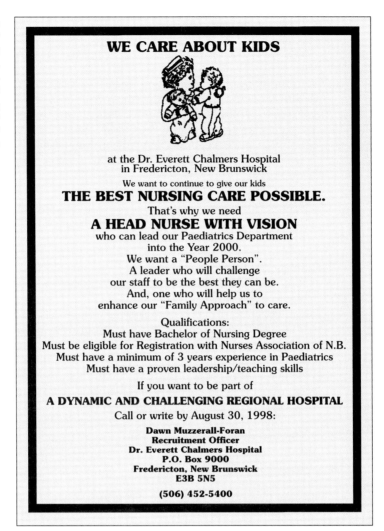

such ads do have some advantages. The opening can remain confidential (which may be necessary if the position is still staffed), countless telephone inquiries may be prevented, and some of the public relations problems associated with disappointed recruits can be avoided.

There are many factors that make advertising a useful recruiting method. Employers can use advertisements to reach and attract potential job applicants from a diverse labour market in as wide or narrow a geographical area as desired. In order to meet employment equity goals and timetables, ads can be placed in publications read by designated group members, such as a minority-language newspaper or the newsletter of a nonprofit agency assisting individuals who have a particular mental or physical disability.

Professional and Trade Associations   Professional and trade associations are often used to find experienced individuals. Many such associations conduct ongoing placement activities on behalf of their members, and most have newsletters or magazines in which organizations can place job advertisements, which are sent to all of their members on a regular basis. Such advertising may attract individuals who hadn't previously thought about changing jobs, as well as those actively seeking employment. Another advantage of this method is that it enables recruiters to target specialists, especially in hard-to-fill technical areas.

Labour Organizations   Some firms, particularly in the construction industry, use union hiring halls as a source of recruits. The union maintains a roster of members, typically skilled tradespersons such as carpenters, pipefitters, welders, plumbers, and electricians, and sends them out on assignment as requests from employers are received. Once the union members have completed their contracted work at one firm, they notify the union of their availability for another assignment.

Military Personnel   The Canadian military may also provide qualified recruits. Individuals leave the forces on a regular basis. Many have been trained in fields in which there tends to be a skills shortage, such as mechanics and pilots; others have received a university or college education, as well as military leadership training, and are potential civilian managerial employees. Thus, military establishments, such as the Royal Military College in Kingston, Ontario, may be an excellent contact for recruiters.

Reservists are also potential recruits. The Canadian Forces Liaison Council (CFLC), formed in 1992, is responsible for promoting the hiring of reservists by civilian employers, the merits of which organizations such as A&P have recognized. After spending a day in the field with militia members at Canadian Forces Base Petawawa, north of Ottawa, Gerald Good, A&P's former President and CEO, was so impressed that he immediately hired several reservists as management trainees.

The Council is also trying to encourage civilian employers to give reservists additional time off for military training without endangering their jobs or seniority. Organizations such as MacMillan Bloedel and Bristol Aerospace have been sold on the value of such leave.[29]

Online Recruiting   Recruiting online is a relatively new business in Canada and one that's growing. Estimates from the United States project that it will be a $5 billion-a-year industry by 2000.[30]

Canadian Airlines recognizes the advantages of online recruiting.

Online recruiting is designed to be simple, efficient, and flexible. It is quite easy to add a career-listings option to an existing Web site. Most job-posting services provide the opportunity for companies to: 1) set limits on the number of applications they will accept, 2) specify the length of time a job is to remain posted, 3) change information, 4) put listings on hold, and 5) reactivate listings at any time.[31] Management tips for selecting an online job-posting service are included in **Figure 6.7**.

A cautionary note is in order. As hinted at in the management tips, Internet-based recruiting services vary greatly. Some offer a "bulletin board," a straightforward chance for organizations to post job openings on the World Wide Web, and to search through electronic résumé banks. Others incorporate online screening and interviewing of candidates.[32] An example of the former is The Monster Board Canada. Long a presence on the World Wide Web, this is Monster Board's first Canada-specific site, now accessed by 50 000 Canadians each month. Companies such as Rolls Royce Canada, Vancouver City Savings Credit Union, and Placer Dome are using this service to advertise for positions ranging from entry level to

Figure 6.7
Management Tips for Selecting an Online Job-Posting Service

Source: "What to Consider When Selecting an Online Job-Posting Service," *Human Resources Professional* 14, no. 2 (April/May 1997), p. 23.

Ready to recruit online? Sandhya Dave, founder and president of HEART (Human Resources Electronic Advertising and Recruiting Tool) Career Connections in Los Altos, California, suggests the following criteria to assess the suitability of a job-posting service.

- **Client control of information**
  The service should have the ability to allow you to control your own data, such as adding and deleting information, and putting on hold and reactivating your postings when you want.

- **Feedback from online service**
  The service can demonstrate through regular reports the effectiveness of your advertising. Knowing how many people have viewed your postings, by position category, gives you an idea of what ads are generating the most visits.

- **Interactivity of site**
  The service offers links to on-screen forms and email addresses that enable respondents to interact with, rather than just view, the site.

- **Accessibility of site**
  The service should offer more than one way to access the Internet other than by the World Wide Web. Options should include using a modem, Telnet site, or other protocols of the Internet, such as Gopher and FTP (File Transfer Protocol).

- **Variety of services and packages**
  The service should offer different packages designated to meet small budgets without sacrificing visibility among the bigger spenders.

- **Quality and quantity of responses**
  The service should demonstrate that, depending on the industry and the type of positions offered, recruiting online will generate more appropriate, though fewer, applications than newspaper ads.

- **Extras**
  The service offers such extras as integrating its job listings site with those detailing information about the city and country—the quality of life, education system, etc.—where the job is located, so the applicant can make an informed decision about applying, and the employer gets a candidate who is more willing to relocate.

www.monster.ca
Monster Board

vice-president of marketing. Located at www.monster.ca, the cost to employers to post a job for 60 days is $150.[33] There are some pitfalls associated with using an Internet career site such as this, of which new users should be aware. As explained in the Information Technology and HR box, some companies are inadvertently guiding people to their competitors because they are unaware of how to use the Internet properly.

An example of a full-service "e-cruiter" is Ottawa-based CareerBridge, which already had 100 mainly high-tech clients at the end of its first year of operations, such as Northern Telecom Ltd., MOSAID Technologies, Lockheed Martin, and DRT Systems. Some of these firms are filling as many as one in three positions via online recruiting. CareerBridge provides software to allow companies to post their job vacancies to its Website. A private email message centre is set up where applicants can send electronic résumés, eliminating the cumbersome paper version. Job hopefuls can be interviewed via email until both parties are ready for a face-to-face meeting. The price of tapping into this technology ranges from $10 000 to $25 000 for a six-month "membership," during which period a company can post as many job openings to the site as it wishes. While the cost seems rather high, the time savings involved make this a very cost-efficient strategy for some firms.[34]

www.careersite.com
www.careernet.org
www.careermosaic.com/cm
Job Postings

CareerBridge completed a virtual career fair for Northern Telecom Ltd. in the fall of 1997. The Nortel job fair took place over two weeks and saw the telecommunications giant advertising dozens of positions online, ranging from research to administration and finance. About 10 000 people accessed the fair, and Nortel received more than 2 000 applications for 30 to 40 jobs. With the stroke of a key, fair organizers could subsequently follow up, alerting candidates that their applications had been received and then instantaneously forwarding résumés to the hiring managers.[35]

There are a number of benefits associated with recruiting on the Web. It is demonstrably quicker to get jobs listed, since the recruiter is not dependent on newspaper or journal advertising deadlines. Online recruiting is cheaper than most print-media advertising, and can also reduce administrative costs, since HR managers can easily deliver job descriptions to Web sites by email, fax, or using an online format. Because there is space online to be much more descriptive without incurring the extra costs associated with print ads, more detailed information is generally provided. This means that there is a greater likelihood of attracting highly qualified candidates, and of unqualified job seekers screening themselves out. The Internet's global reach means that every posting can become international in scope. Recruiters can benefit by reaching pools of potential employees they would never attract otherwise, including Canadians working overseas who wish to return home.[36]

**www.ipmaac.org/
link-empl.html**
Recruiting and Employment

At this point, online recruitment is still focussed largely on computer-related businesses, but the expansion possibilities are limitless, as more and more people become computer literate. According to a survey of 1 882 workers conducted in July of 1997 by two Ottawa-based research firms, the number of workers with direct access to the Internet at work had doubled in each of the previous two years. Six percent of those surveyed in 1995 had access, 11 percent in 1996, and 25 percent in 1997.[37]

Despite high praise for the Internet, no one has yet suggested abandoning traditional recruitment vehicles. At this stage of evolution, using the Web in tandem with other methods, such as private employment agencies and advertising, is a good partnership. This can be seen by the current trend of including a Web site and an email address in print advertising, from which interested candidates can obtain more detailed information.[38] Additionally, companies that place an ad with the *Globe and Mail* now automatically have it posted at the Globe's Career Connect Web site.[39] As before, different strategies will be the most appropriate for different types and levels of positions. In dealing with executives, for example, some of the best candidates may already be happily employed, which means the only way to make them aware of an opportunity is hire a search firm to call them directly.[40] Age may also make a difference in whether to choose the Internet as a recruitment strategy, as explained in the Diversity Counts box.

**careers.theglobeandmail.
com/careerconnect**
Globe and Mail Careers Section

Open House   An increasingly popular recruitment strategy involves holding an open house. Common in retail firms looking to staff a new store from the ground up, open houses have also been the choice of high-tech corporations in an ultra-tight job market, trying to draw out the much-coveted information technology worker.[41] For example, Nortel hosts an open house several times a year. One event, held in June 1996, days after Nortel unveiled its Ottawa expansion plans, attracted 9 000 people, and resulted in the hiring of 200 applicants.[42]

When Canadian Tire hosted its first-ever open house in September of 1997, more than 1 000 job seekers were attracted to its conference centre in Toronto. The company needed to hire for a broad spectrum of positions: finance, information technology, marketing, and logistics. Skilled professionals with a minimum

Diversity Counts
When Recruiting Online

Royal Bank Financial Group is hoping to use its new online recruitment centre, through which job seekers can apply for jobs and submit résumés online, to attract younger workers.

According to Mike Kavanagh, the Manager of Recruitment Strategies, "With young people between the ages of 17 and 34 representing more than 50 percent of all new hires, the bank's recruiting team will increasingly make use of the Internet to post job opportunities and solicit résumés." While the recruitment centre is not designed to recruit younger employees exclusively, the bank is aware of the fact that young people are especially comfortable with Internet technology and more likely to use it in their job search.◆

Source: "Royal Bank Looks for Youth Online," *Canadian HR Reporter* 10, no.19 (November 3, 1997), p. 6. Copyright MPL Communications Inc., Reproduced by permission of *Canadian HR Reporter* 133 Richmond Street West, Toronto, Ontario M5H 3M8.

of three years of experience were invited to drop by. While awaiting their turn for an interview with the hiring manager in their area of expertise, applicants spent time watching a corporate video regaling the firm's attributes, examining the annual report, and reading feature articles chronicling the firm's much-publicized turnaround under CEO Stephen Bachand.[43]

The open house was simply one component of Canadian Tire's recruitment strategy, which included advertising in newspapers and online, as well as taking part in high-tech career fairs. An open house is an excellent strategy if a firm has a lot of hiring needs. An additional benefit is increased department-manager commitment, since they are directly involved. Open houses may also attract more highly qualified candidates than newspaper advertising.[44]

Information Sessions/Career Fairs   Another recruitment strategy, particularly popular with high-technology firms, involves hosting information sessions in communities across the country or hosting a career fair on-site. Recruiters seek to establish an informal, friendly atmosphere by providing refreshments and selecting a relaxed setting. They share information about the organization and its job opportunities with those attending. Top prospects are invited to visit the firm or return at a later date for a more in-depth assessment.

In October 1997, Northern Telecom Ltd. carefully culled 1 000 computer science and engineering students from the best universities across the country. The students were invited to what was billed as one of the largest career fairs ever staged by a North American firm. At the company's sprawling research campus in suburban Nepean, 200 managers from Nortel offices across the country spoke glowingly of career opportunities and answered students' questions. The event, five months in the planning, cost $500 000. Since more than 275 offers were extended as a result, the firm considers it money well spent.[45]

Recruiting Non-Permanent Staff

Seventy-two percent of the respondents to a 1996 Conference Board of Canada survey anticipated an increase in the number of contingent workers over the next five years. Forty-one percent also forecasted a decrease in the number of permanent employees.[46] In these firms, recruiters will spend more time seeking temporary (term, seasonal, casual) and contract workers and less time recruiting permanent staff.

According to a Statistics Canada report released in September 1997, the number of Canadians whose main source of income is from contingency jobs has grown to about 11 percent or 1.3 million workers. The stereotype of contingency work being primarily clerical, manual, or service-oriented is simply not true. Twenty-nine percent of non-permanent employees are from professional and technical fields and six percent are managers and administrators.[47]

Temporary Help Agencies   Temporary help agencies, such as Kelly Services and Office Overload, exist in all major cities in Canada. They do not specialize in providing recruits; instead they are an excellent source of supplemental workers to provide coverage for vacationing, sick, or on-leave employees. Firms also use temporary employees (temps) to handle seasonal work, peak workloads, and special projects for which there are no current employees with time and/or expertise. While most people think of clerical staff when the term "temp" is used, temps are becoming more and more common in legal work, engineering, computer programming, and other jobs requiring advanced professional training.[48] Intercom Management Resources Group is one of many new firms starting up in response to the increasing need for middle- to senior-level specialists for a specific project or term.[49] Temps are agency employees, and reassigned to another employer when their services are no longer required.

Temporary employees provide employers with three major benefits:

1. Temps generally receive less compensation than permanent staff. They do not go on the company payroll or benefits plans. Often, they do not receive any benefits from the agency either, other than the minimum coverage required by law.

2. If a temp performs unsatisfactorily, a substitute can be requested immediately. Generally, a suitable replacement is sent to the firm within one business day.

3. Individuals working as temps who are seeking full-time employment are often highly motivated, knowing that many employers choose full-time employees from the ranks of their top-performing temps. In the event of such a situation, a fee similar to that charged by a private employment agency is paid to the temporary firm, less the amount already paid for the employee's temporary work assignment. Since they can be screened for long-term career potential in an actual work setting, temps can be a low-risk source of permanent employees.

Contract Workers Contract workers, also known as consultants and freelancers, are employees who develop work relationships directly with the employer for a specific type of work or period of time.[50] Sometimes they are contracted to provide specialized services one or two days a week on a permanent basis. PPL Marketing Services, a mid-sized firm in Mississauga, Ontario, with a core staff of some 80 people, uses contract workers on a regular basis—both project-based and permanent. As projects come and go, so do the writers or production people contracted to complete the jobs. PPL also has a senior HR professional on contract, who works for them two days a week, handling critical issues like hiring, exit interviews, and developing salary structures.[51]

Many professionals with specialized skills become contract workers. Included are marketing and advertising executives, human resources professionals, project managers, accountants, writers, and graphic designers,[52] as well as lawyers, physicians, editors, and professors. Some have consciously made a decision to work for themselves; others have been unable to obtain full-time employment in their field of expertise or have found themselves out of a full-time job due to cutbacks. Thus, some wish to remain self-employed; others (such as many adjunct professors at universities and part-time college faculty members) work on a contract basis, hoping to obtain a full-time position eventually. Some firms hire former employees (such as retirees or laid-off workers) on a contract basis. Other organizations learn about potential contract workers through word-of-mouth referrals or advertising.

Because contract workers are not part of the company headcount, managers can rely on their services, while honouring company staffing restrictions aimed at reducing payroll costs.

Contract workers can often be relied upon to be more productive and efficient than in-house employees because they can focus on the task at hand, and not get involved in countless meetings or organizational politics. They can also provide expertise not available in-house or a fresh outsider's perspective. The major drawback of using contract workers is that their commitment to the employer may be somewhat lower than that of permanent staff and the demands and deadlines of their multiple clients may conflict at times.

Outsourcing/Subcontracting As explained in chapter 1, outsourcing or subcontracting is the process by which employers transfer work to another organization specializing in that type of work, which has the ability to perform it more efficiently.

Outsourcing agreements may result in a long-term relationship between the employer and subcontractor, although both parties retain the ability to renew or sever the relationship at their convenience.

While data processing, security, cafeteria services, and housekeeping have been outsourced for many years, companies have recently begun to hire subcontractors to provide services that are important to the business but not within its core capabilities, including research and development, marketing research, and product design. For example, Minacs Group, in addition to its data processing services, runs several mailrooms and marketing departments on behalf of client corporations across the country, and over 100 Minacs staff operate a customer service centre for a large automotive company.[53] A recent survey of 927 firms, conducted by the Wyatt Company, reported that 32 percent of employers outsource some or all of the administration of their human resources and benefits programs.

Improving the Effectiveness of External Recruitment

The determination of who should perform the recruitment function depends mainly on organization size. In large firms, professional HR recruiters are hired and trained. In smaller organizations, recruiting is often one of the responsibilities of the HR generalist. In firms with no HR position, recruitment is generally carried out by all supervisors and managers.

The structure of the firm also has an impact on who performs the function, however. In organizations emphasizing teamwork, such as 3M's plant in Brockville, Ontario, it is the team members who are responsible for this function.[54]

Regardless of who does the recruiting, it is imperative that those responsible have a good understanding of the job specifications and the organization's philosophy and values. Proper training in recruitment strategies and etiquette is also essential.

Recruiters are often the main reason applicants select one organization over another. One study showed that recruiters may have a significant impact on perceived job attractiveness, regard for the job and organization, and intention to accept a job.[55] Thus, choosing personable, enthusiastic, and competent recruiters should improve the effectiveness of an organization's recruitment program.

Recruiting a More Diverse Work Force

Recruiting a diverse work force is not just socially responsible, it's a necessity. As noted previously, the composition of Canada's work force is changing dramatically. Let's quickly review a few trends of significance to recruiters. By 2001, the majority of people entering the work force will be women, visible minorities, Aboriginal people, and persons with disabilities.[56] By 2015, young workers (15 to 24) will make up a smaller share of the work force than adults twice their age.[57]

Also of great significance is the increasing number of women in the work force with dependent children. In 1990, 70 percent of all Canadian couples with children under 19 were dual-earner families. In 1992, 64 percent of married women with children under 16, and 57 percent of married women with children under three were employed.[58] Divorced and separated mothers were even more active in the labour force, with participation rates over 70 percent.[59] As described in the Diversity Counts box, helping such employees to balance work and family responsibilities makes workplaces more attractive and aids in recruitment and retention. The bottom line is that smart employers recognize the need to actively recruit a more diverse work force.

Diversity Counts

Helping Employees Balance Work and Family Makes Workplaces More Attractive

To attract a diverse work force, employers are implementing initiatives that help employees manage their work and family responsibilities more effectively.

People/Family Care Days

Historically, employees had to use their own sick or vacation days to care for sick children. Today, organizations across Canada are recognizing the direct and indirect benefits of replacing traditional sick leave with personal-leave or family-responsibility-leave policies.

The most popular response to emergency or temporary childcare needs is the provision of paid and unpaid time that allows employees to fulfill family responsibilities. The Bank of Montreal's People Care Days; Family Responsibility Leaves at Royal Bank, TD and CIBC; Bell Canada's Family Leave; Hewitt Associates' Dependent Care Days; and Family Sickness Leave at Union Gas are examples.

Childcare Assistance

Some organizations have gone a step further. For example, over five years ago, Royal Bank introduced a childcare information and consultation service. Consultants provide support and assistance to parents to increase the stability of their regular care arrangements and help them establish plans for possible emergencies. Employees receive individual emergency care plans, including referrals to emergency and temporary childcare services.

Emergency Childcare Consortium

The Carleton Board of Education, Ottawa Civic Hospital, Nortel Technologies, County of Carleton Law Association, Ernst & Young (Ottawa Office), and the National Capital Region locals of the Canadian Union of Postal Workers have teamed up to offer more than 10 000 employees and members emergency childcare.

Along with funding from the federal government and the Trillium Foundation, participating organizations contribute to the cost of developing, administering, and evaluating the program. Some participants also pay for all or some of the cost of the care provided, recognizing that the cost of replacing the employee for the same amount of time would be two or three times greater.

After two years of development, the program opened its doors in the fall of 1995. In its first four months of operation, over 200 families received 2 500 hours of care. The average family used the service for 1.7 days per placement during that period. Eighty-eight percent of the care was provided in the child's home.

The service accepts children who are recovering from an illness but is not intended to be used for medical emergencies or when a child is getting ill. Parents are not pressured to go to work if they feel the need to remain home with a sick child. However, if the child is recovering but needs a few days of extra care to regain strength and reduce the risk of recurrence, the program is ideal.

The Future

As public financial support for childcare is reduced, parents will be under greater pressure related to childcare arrangements, and employers will have to become more flexible and responsive in order to attract and retain good employees.

Organizations also need to begin to make investments in creative solutions to assist their employees with the next family care challenge: emergency and temporary eldercare. Today, about one in five adults in the paid labour force is responsible for caring for a senior family member. By 2001, that number will expand to one in three.

Organizations that want to recruit and attract the best will have to respond to changing employee needs and expectations.◆

Source: Nora Spinks, "Adventures in Innovative Childcare," *Canadian HR Reporter* 9, no. 7 (April 8, 1996), pp. 12, 15. Copyright MPL Communications Inc., Reproduced by permission of *Canadian HR Reporter* 133 Richmond Street West, Toronto, Ontario M5H 3M8.

Older Workers as a Source of Candidates

Many employers, recognizing the fact that the work force is aging, are encouraging retirement-age employees to stay with the company or actively recruiting employees who are at or beyond retirement age.[60] There are significant benefits to hiring and retaining older employees. A 1993 study by the American Association of Retired Persons found that older workers have qualities that make them a valuable resource. These include: the highest job satisfaction of any age group; a strong sense of loyalty and organizational commitment; a strong work ethic; good people skills such as patience, empathy, and helpfulness; willingness to work in a variety of roles, including part time; high potential for successful retraining; and a greater likelihood of staying with the firm.[61] Studies have also shown that since older employees are less likely to get work injuries and have lower rates of turnover and absenteeism, their employers benefit from significantly reduced costs.[62]

Recruiting and attracting older workers involves any or all of the methods described earlier, but with one big difference. It generally requires a comprehensive effort before recruiting begins to make the company attractive to older workers. Specifically, organizations should:[63]

- Deal with stereotypical attitudes toward older workers as vigorously as any other form of bias, through education and proactive efforts to eliminate discriminatory practices.

- Check human resources policies, procedures, and practices to ensure that they do not discourage recruitment of seniors or encourage valuable older people to leave. For example, policies promoting early retirement, providing benefits only to full-time employees, and offering no flexibility in benefits or hours of work will impede the recruitment and retention of older workers.

- Develop flexible work options such as part-time positions, job sharing, shorter-than-30-hour workweeks, consulting, seasonal work, reduced hours with reduced pay, flextime, and phased retirement. At Polaroid Corp. and Aetna Insurance, for example, phased-retirement programs retain talented older workers, decrease burnout, and lower costs by prorating benefits payments over gradually reduced work hours. Many of these flexible work options are inducements that will make the workplace more attractive to a wide range of recruits.

- Redesign or create jobs. Manufacturing plants that are geared to robust young males may need modification to accommodate older adults who may have less dexterity and strength. In offices, brighter lighting, firm chairs, and ergonomic work stations may be required to lessen physical stress and fatigue. At Xerox, unionized hourly workers over 55 with 15 years of service, and those over 50 with 20 years of service can bid on jobs at lower stress and lower pay levels if they so desire.[64]

- Invest in training, retraining, career development, and reward systems suitable for older as well as younger workers.

- Offer flexible benefits plans. Allowing employees to pick and choose among benefits options can be attractive to all employees. Older employees may have different preferences, such as longer vacations or continued accrual of pension credits.

Recruiting Designated Group Members

Many of the prescriptions that apply to recruiting older workers also apply to the recruitment of the employment-equity-designated groups—women, visible minorities, Aboriginal people, and persons with disabilities. In other words, employers have to formulate comprehensive plans for attracting such candidates, including overcoming stereotypes and biases; reevaluating human resources policies and practices; developing flexible work options; redesigning jobs; investing in training, retraining, and career development; and offering flexible benefits.

Most of the recruitment strategies discussed previously can be used to attract designated group members, provided it is made clear to all involved in the recruitment process—whether it be employees being asked for referrals or private employment agencies—that the employer is committed to equity and diversity. This can also be stressed in all recruitment advertising. Alternative publications should be considered for advertising—ones targeted to the designated groups—and linkages can be formed with organizations and agencies interested in or specializing in assisting designated group members, both profit and nonprofit. Specific examples follow:

The Canadian Council for Aboriginal Business runs an employment agency called Aboriginal Choice Placement Services for clerical, technical, and engineering positions.

The Bank of Montreal, which is committed to both education and employment equity, recently announced the establishment of an $8-million Possibilities Foundation, as mentioned in chapter 5. This Foundation is aimed at visible minority, Aboriginal, and disabled high school students moving on to post-secondary education. Selected students will be eligible for summer employment and a $1 000 scholarship. Partners in the program include the Halifax Regional School Board, the National Council of Black Educators of Canada, the Black Educators Association, the Canadian Council on Rehabilitation and Work, and the Micmac Native Friendship Centre.[65]

There are two recent publications (produced by a joint effort of Ontario businesses, community service agencies, and government) aimed at ensuring that persons with disabilities are integrated into the workplace. Both are available through the Centre for Management of Community Services, a nonprofit agency that participated in the project. *Opportunity Knocks* is a how-to guide for community agencies to assist them in convincing employers to hire people with disabilities. *It's a Smart Move* targets the corporate sector, and dispels many of the common myths associated with hiring people with disabilities. These include fears that hiring such employees causes WCB premiums to rise and that it's impossible to interview candidates with disabilities without violating human rights legislation. Both publications include case studies of organizations committed to adding persons with disabilities to their work force, such as Canada Trust, McDonald's, CAMI Automotive, Wal-Mart, the Bank of Montreal, and A&P Canada, two of which are highlighted in the HR and the Responsive Organization box. According to the firms interviewed for the employer profiles, there are many advantages to hiring individuals with disabilities, including:[66]

- access to a broader pool of job candidates
- enhanced corporate image
- a more reliable work force
- lower staff turnover
- a work force better prepared to deal with customers or clients with disabilities
- improved staff morale
- better customer service.

Helping Hands at A&P Canada and Canada Trust

A&P Canada aims to provide the highest level of courteous customer service possible. Their employment program to place people with disabilities in the position of courtesy clerk fulfills this objective.

Several dozen people with developmental disabilities are employed through the program, providing a range of services, including price checking, handling perishable product returns, bagging groceries, and carrying groceries to customers' cars. It's up to each store manager whether to opt in or out of the program, which is endorsed by A&P Canada and its union.

Under the guidance of a job coach, provided by local community agencies at no cost, courtesy clerks perform a six-week job placement. Store managers then make their hiring decision, knowing they can rely on free, long-term support from the job coach if needed.

At Canada Trust, call centre employees are required to answer customer inquiries, access data quickly and maintain top-notch customer service. When the firm set up its call centre in London, Ontario, it was competing for the best employees. To expand the pool, it chose to search actively for candidates with disabilities.

Canada Trust works with a nonprofit agency that teaches computer skills to the visually impaired. Braille readers, large print screen options, and voice synthesizers have all expanded the opportunities of persons with visual impairments. Canada Trust employees are up to speed in a minimum amount of time because they arrive having completed a 30-week training program at the agency.

Source: "Helping Hands," excerpts from *Opportunity Knocks and It's a Smart Move*, cited in *Canadian HR Reporter* 10, no. 18 (October 20, 1997), p. 8. Copyright MPL Communications Inc., Reproduced by permission of *Canadian HR Reporter*, 133 Richmond Street West, Toronto, Ontario M5H 3M8.

Developing and Using Application Forms

Purpose of Application Forms

application form
A form completed by applicants for employment designed to collect information about education, prior work record, and job-related skills in a uniform and standardized manner.

Once the organization has a pool of qualified applicants, the selection process can begin. For most employers, completion of an **application form** is the last step in the recruitment process. An application form is a good way to quickly collect verifiable historical data from the candidate. It usually includes information about such areas as education, prior work history, and other job-related skills.

A completed application form provides four types of information.[67] First, it allows the recruiter to make judgments on substantive matters, such as whether the applicant has the education and experience to do the job. Second, conclusions can be drawn about the applicant's previous progress and growth, a trait that is especially important for management candidates. Third, tentative conclusions can be reached regarding the applicant's stability based on previous work record. (Here, however, care must be taken not to assume that an unusual number of job changes necessarily reflects on the applicant's ability; for example, the person's last two employers may have had to lay off large numbers of employees.) Fourth, the recruiter may be able to use the data in the application to predict which candidates will succeed on the job and which will not, a point to which we will return later.

In practice, most organizations need several application forms. For technical and managerial positions, for example, the form may require detailed answers to questions concerning the applicant's education and so on. The form for factory workers might focus on the tools and equipment the applicant has used and the like.

Reasons for Application Forms

Even when detailed résumés have been submitted, most firms also request that a standardized company application form be completed. There are many reasons for this practice:[68]

- Candidate comparison is facilitated because information is collected in a uniform manner.

  - The information that the company requires is requested, not simply that which the candidate wishes to reveal. By asking for work history in reverse chronological order and insisting that dates be provided, for example, gaps in work history may be revealed that are concealed on the candidate's résumé.

  - Candidates are typically asked to complete an application form while on the company premises. Application forms are thus more likely to be samples of the candidates' own work. (It is not uncommon for job applicants to get help, even paid professional assistance, with their résumés.)

  - The way in which an application form is completed reveals information about the candidate's ability to organize his or her thoughts, as well as spelling and grammar skills. This can be extremely important for certain positions, such as secretary, human resources manager, or management trainee.

- Application forms typically ask the candidate to provide written authorization for reference checking. A photocopy of this section of the application form can be faxed or mailed to individuals being asked for references, if so requested. (Many employers today will not give out any reference information until such written authorization has been received.)

- Candidates are asked to sign and date their application form, acknowledging that the information provided is true and accurate, to the best of their knowledge. Next to that affirmation, there is typically a statement about the consequences of lying, such as, "I understand that a false statement may disqualify me from employment, or cause my dismissal." This protects the company somewhat from candidates who falsify their credentials.

- Many application forms today have a section regarding designated group member status, which candidates are asked, but not required, to complete. An example is provided in **Figure 6.8**. As indicated, the information collected is used for employment equity tracking purposes.

Most firms require that a standardized company application form be completed, even if a résumé has been submitted.

Human Rights Legislation and Application Forms

As explained in chapter 3, human rights legislation in every Canadian jurisdiction prohibits discrimination on a number of grounds, including race, religion or creed, colour, marital status, sex, and physical disability. Age-based discrimination is also prohibited (although the age groups protected differ), and all jurisdictions except Saskatchewan and Alberta prohibit discrimination on the basis of mental disability. There are other prohibited grounds, which vary by jurisdiction. Application forms cannot ask questions that would directly or indirectly classify candidates on the basis of any one of the prohibited grounds. Employers with operations in a number of provinces have to ensure that their application forms comply with the human rights code provisions in each.

Figure 6.8
Self-Identification for
Employment Equity
Purposes

Source: Based on *Equity Works Best*, a publication of the Ontario Women's Directorate.

Completion of this section of the application form is considered OPTIONAL and VOLUNTARY.

We are committed to employment equity and outreach recruitment. For purposes of employment equity tracking, we ask that applicants provide us with the following information. All answers will be considered confidential and used only for employment equity data-collection purposes. Eligibility as an applicant will not be affected: All of our selection decisions are based on merit.

Please check the appropriate box(es):

Are you:

❑ Male   ❑ Female

❑ White (Caucasian)

❑ A Visible Minority (Black, Chinese, South Asian, etc.)

❑ Aboriginal (Canadian Indian, Inuit, Métis)

❑ A Person with a Physical or Mental Disability (including learning disabilities)

Please note: This application form has been reviewed and approved by the provincial Human Rights Commission.

Most prohibited questions are fairly easily identifiable—age, date of birth, marital status, etc. Potentially discriminatory information can be revealed, however, by requesting a photograph; asking whether the applicant would prefer to be addressed as Mr./Mrs./Miss/Ms.; requesting a social insurance number; asking for the name, address, and dates of educational institutions attended; and asking questions about workers' compensation claims.

If there are illegal questions on an application form, an unsuccessful candidate may challenge the legality of the entire selection process. In such case, the burden of proof is on the employer. Thus, taking human rights legislative requirements into consideration when designing application forms is imperative. The *Guide to Screening and Selection in Employment* in the appendix to chapter 3 provides helpful hints. Specific guidelines regarding questions that can and cannot be asked on application forms are available through the human rights commissions in each jurisdiction. **Figure 6.9**, a sample application form developed by the Ontario Human Rights Commission, illustrates the types of information that can legally be requested. As indicated in the figure, employers have the right to elicit detailed information about educational qualifications, employment history, and job-related skills—all of the data required to compare candidates to the job specifications.

Using Application Forms to Predict Job Performance

Some firms use application forms to predict which candidates will be successful and which will not, in much the same way that employers use tests for screening.

One approach involves designing a **weighted application blank (WAB)**. Statistical studies are conducted to find the relationship between (1) responses on the application form and (2) measures of success on the job. A scoring system is subsequently developed by weighting the different responses to those particular items. By totalling the scores for each item, it is possible to obtain a composite score for each applicant. It should be noted that there is no difference in appearance between a WAB and a regular application form.

weighted application blank (WAB)
A job application form on which applicant responses have been weighted based on their statistical relationship to measures of job success.

Figure 6.9
Sample Application
Form

Source: Excerpts of the Ontario
Human Rights Commission's
Employment Application Forms,
Interviews, 1992.

APPLICATION FOR EMPLOYMENT

Position being applied for	Date available to begin work

PERSONAL DATA

Last name   Given name(s)

Address	Street	Apt. No.	Home Telephone Number
City	Province	Postal Code	Business Telephone Number

Are you legally eligible to work in Canada?   ☐ Yes   ☐ No

Are you 18 years and more and less than 65 years of age?   ☐ Yes   ☐ No

Are you willing to relocate in Ontario? ☐ Yes ☐ No	Preferred Location

To determine your qualification for employment, please provide below and on the reverse, information related to your academic and other achievements including volunteer work, as well as employment history.
Addition information may be attached on a separate sheet.

EDUCATION

SECONDARY SCHOOL ■	BUSINESS, TRADE OR SECONDARY SCHOOL ■
Highest grade or level completed	Name of course Length of course
Type of certificate or diploma obtained	Licence, certificate or diploma awarded? ☐ Yes ☐ No

COMMUNITY COLLEGE ■	UNIVERSITY ■
Name of Program Length of Program	Length of course Degree awarded ☐ Pass ☐ Yes ☐ No ☐ Honours
Diploma received ☐ Yes ☐ No	Major subject
Other courses, workshops, seminars	Licences, Certificates, Degrees

Work related skills

Describe any of your work related skills, experience, or training that relate to the position being applied for.

Figure 6.9
(continued).

EMPLOYMENT	
Name and Address of present/last employer	Present/Last job title
	Period of employment · Present/Last salary From · To
	Name of Supervisor · Telephone
Type of Business	Reason for leaving
Functions/Responsibilities	
Name and Address of former employer	Last job title
	Period of employment · Last salary From · To
	Name of Supervisor · Telephone
Type of Business	Reason for leaving
Functions/Responsibilities	
Name and Address of former employer	Last job title
	Period of employment · Last salary From · To
	Name of Supervisor · Telephone
Type of Business	Reason for leaving
Functions/Responsibilities	

For employment references we may approach:

Your present/last employer? ☐ Yes ☐ No
Your former employer(s)? ☐ Yes ☐ No
List references if different than above on a separate sheet.

Personal interests and activities (civic, athletic, etc.)

I hereby declare that the foregoing information is true and complete to my knowledge. I understand that a false statement may disqualify me from employment, or cause my dismissal.

Have you attached an additional sheet?
☐ Yes ☐ No

Signature _____ Date _____

As an example, the goal of one study, conducted at a large insurance company, was to determine whether there was a relationship between application form responses and turnover. At the time, the company was experiencing a 48 percent turnover rate among its clerical staff. (In other words, for every two employees hired at the same time, there was about a 50–50 chance that one of them would not remain with the firm for 12 months or longer). The researcher obtained the application forms of about 160 clerical employees from the company's HR files and divided them into two categories: long-tenure and short-tenure employees. After performing various statistical analyses, it became quite apparent that certain responses on the application form were highly related to job tenure. An application form weighted on the basis of this information enabled the firm to predict which applicants would be likely to stay with the firm.[69]

Although studies have shown WABs can be highly valid predictors, and they can be developed fairly easily, such forms are used by relatively few organizations.

Another type of application form that can be used to predict performance is a **biographical information blank (BIB)**, also known as a biodata form. Essentially, it is a more detailed version of an application form, focusing on biographical data found to be predictive of job success. Candidates respond to a series of questions about their background, experiences, and preferences, including willingness to travel and leisure activities. Because biographical questions rarely have right or wrong answers, BIBs are difficult to fake. As with a WAB, responses are scored.

The development of a BIB requires that the items that are valid predictors of job success be identified and that weights be established for different responses to these items. By totaling the scores for each item, it is possible to obtain a composite score for each applicant. BIBs have been found to have moderate validity in predicting job performance.[70]

Chapter Review

Summary

1. Recruitment is the process of searching for and attracting an adequate number of qualified job candidates from whom the organization may select the most appropriate individuals to staff its job requirements.

2. There are a number of steps in the recruitment process. First, job openings are identified through human resources planning or manager request. The job description and job specification are then reviewed to determine the job requirements. Next, appropriate recruiting source and methods are chosen. Using these strategies, a pool of qualified candidates is generated.

3. In order to be successful, a recruiter must be aware of the constraints affecting the recruitment process. These come from organizational policies and plans, the job requirements, recruiter habits, inducements of competitors, and environmental conditions.

4. There are two sources available for recruiting job candidates: internal and external. Although recruiting often brings employment agencies and classified ads to mind, current employees are generally the largest source of recruits. To be effective, promotion from within requires using job posting, human resources records, and skills inventories.

5. Unless there is a work-force reduction, even in firms with a promote-from-within policy, a replacement from outside must eventually be found to fill the job(s) left vacant once all eligible employees have been given the opportunity for transfer and/or promotion. In addition, most entry-level positions must be filled by external candidates.

6. When choosing external recruitment method(s) there are a number of factors that should be taken into consideration: the type of job, the relationship between method chosen and quality of hire, the yield ratio, and the amount of lead time.

7. External recruitment methods include walk-ins, write-ins, employee referrals, educational institutions, Human Resource Centres, private employment agencies, executive search firms, advertising, professional and trade associations, labour organizations, military personnel, online recruiting, hosting an open house, and holding information sessions/career fairs.

8. Strategies for obtaining non-permanent staff include using temporary help agencies, hiring contract workers, and outsourcing/subcontracting.

9. Recruiting a diverse work force is not just socially responsible, it's a necessity. To do so means formulating comprehensive plans to attract a diverse group of candidates, including overcoming stereotypes and biases; reevaluating human resources policies and practices; developing flexible work options; redesigning jobs; investing in training, retraining and career development; and offering flexible benefits.

10. For most employers, completion of a standardized company application form is the last step in the recruitment process. Application forms cannot ask questions that would directly or indirectly classify candidates on the basis of any of the grounds prohibited in human rights legislation.

11. Some firms design weighted application blanks and/or biographical information blanks, and use them to predict which candidates will be successful and which will not.

Key Terms

application form
biographical information
  blank (BIB)
blind ad
human resources
  requisition form

job posting
nepotism
recruiter
recruitment
time-lapse data
want ad

weighted application
  blank (WAB)
yield ratio

Discussion Questions and Exercises

1. Describe the constraints on recruitment.

2. Discuss the advantages and disadvantages of recruiting within the organization.

3. Describe the role of job posting, human resources records, and skills inventories in promotion from within.

4. List the advantages of external recruitment.

5. Explain why the type of job, the relationship between the method chosen and quality of hire, the yield ratio, and the amount of lead time should be taken into consideration when selecting external recruitment methods.

6. Describe the external recruitment methods that would be appropriate for each of the following: factory worker, management trainee, senior engineer with twelve years of experience, senior secretary, Certified Management Accountant, accounts payable clerk, human resources manager, junior buyer, and company president.

7. Working individually or in groups, examine the classified and display ads appearing in the help-wanted section of a recent newspaper. Using the AIDA guidelines presented in this chapter, analyze their effectiveness.

8. Visit the local Human Resource Centre. Come to class prepared to discuss the following questions: How does the job referral service work? What types of jobs seem to be available, predominantly? To what extent would the Centre be a good source of technical, managerial, or professional employees? What other services are offered?

9. Using the yellow pages and local newspapers, determine which employment agencies and professional search firms operate in your area. Do some specialize in particular types of talent?

10. Discuss strategies for recruiting a more diverse work force that are actually being used by firms in your area.

11. Even when detailed résumés have been submitted, most firms also request that a standardized company application form be completed. Why?

12. Working individually or in small groups, design an application form meeting human rights legislative requirements.

Application Exercises

RUNNING CASE: Carter Cleaning Company

Getting Better Applicants

If you were to ask Jennifer and her father what they considered to be their major challenge in running the six cleaning centres, their answer would be immediate and brief: hiring good people. To attract their management staff as well as skilled cleaner-spotters and pressers, they rely primarily on newspaper advertising and word of mouth. Putting a help wanted sign in the front window of the centre with the job opening has generally led to lots of applications but few hires, since most of the applicants lacked the required skills.

There is no promotion-from-within policy. As mentioned previously, virtually all of the employees at the centres, other than the managers, are women and/or visible minorities. Turnover among the experienced pressers and cleaner-spotters sometimes approaches 400 percent.

Jennifer recently spent some time discussing the benefits of HRP with her father and is now focusing on more effective recruitment strategies. Specifically, she is pondering the following:

Questions

1. How could a promote-from-within policy benefit Carter Cleaning? What would be necessary to make such a policy effective?
2. What other external recruitment methods should she and her father consider? Why?
3. How could a more diverse group of applicants be attracted?

CASE INCIDENT: Large Turnovers Are Healthy?

Each year for the past five years, Excellent Transmission Company (ETC) has been experiencing difficulty recruiting qualified candidates for its design and production departments. Management operates on the philosophy that the best job candidates are recent graduates from the automotive engineering programs at community colleges and universities. The management team believes that these individuals are much better prospects than seasoned workers because they offer certain advantages lacking in experienced workers.

New graduates, the managers argue, are usually more innovative, and have newer ideas to offer. They are up-to-date on the latest developments in technology, more energetic and productive, and usually less costly to hire. Further, the ETC managers believe that new graduates are usually more loyal. They are less concerned about internal politics and are less likely to engage in the type of behaviour that will disrupt production.

The ETC management team thinks that large turnover is healthy for the firm. For this reason, almost all job candidates are recruited externally. It is only if the external search is unsuccessful that internal candidates are considered.

Although the company receives many applications each year, ETC is often unable to find the right type of candidate for vacancies which arise.

Questions

1. What are the strengths and weaknesses of the organization's recruitment policy?
2. What are some of the barriers that limit employment and advancement in the firm?
3. As an HR consultant, what changes would you recommend to ETC's recruitment policies and practices? Why?

Human Resources Management Simulation

Section 2 in part 1 of the simulation deals with recruitment, selection, and orientation. The first three steps in exercise 2 are designed to provide some hands-on practice in various aspects of recruitment. First, written recommendations are to be made regarding appropriate recruitment methods for the staff required at the Peterborough plant, ranging from assembly-line workers to engineers. The potential costs of each method are to be compared and assessed as part of the written plan. Once a recruitment strategy has been devised, a newspaper ad is to be designed that will attract qualified candidates for the Maintenance Supervisor position.

Take It to the Net

Check out our Companion Website at

www.prenticehall.ca/dessler

for a multitude of practice questions, key terms and concepts, Weblinks to related sites, newsgroups, CBC video updates, and more.

Notes

1. Robert D. Gatewood and Hubert S. Field, *Human Resource Selection* (Chicago: The Dryden Press, 1990), p. 8.
2. Dan Ondrack, "Global Warning," *Human Resources Professional* 13, no. 3 (May 1996), pp. 27–9.
3. Randall Scott Echlin, "Into the Briar Patch," *Human Resources Professional* 9, no. 3 (March 1993), p. 19.
4. John Campbell and others, *Managerial Behavior, Performance, and Effectiveness* (New York: McGraw-Hill, 1970), p. 23. See also Allan Halcrow, "Recruitment by Any Other Name is Turnover," *Personnel Journal* 56, no. 1 (January 1977), pp. 40–1.
5. David Dahl and Patrick Pinto, "Job Posting, an Industry Survey," *Personnel Journal* 56, no. 1 (January 1977), pp. 40–1.
6. Jeffrey Daum, "Internal Promotion—Psychological Asset or Debit? A Study of the Effects of Leader Origin," *Organizational Behavior and Human Performance* 13 (1975), pp. 404–13.
7. Arthur R. Pell, *Recruiting and Selecting Personnel* (New York: Regents, 1969), pp. 10–2.
8. *Recruiting Practices*, Personnel Policy Forum, Survey No. 462 (Washington, DC: Bureau of National Affairs, August 1979), p. 114; reprinted in Stephen P. Robbins, *Personnel: The Management of Human Resources* (Englewood Cliffs, NJ: Prentice Hall, 1982), p. 115. For another view of this see Phillip Swaroff, Alan Bass, and Lizabeth Barclay, "Recruiting Sources: Another Look," *Journal of Applied Psychology* 70, no. 4 (1985) pp. 720–8. See also David Caldwell and W. Austin Stivey, "The Relationship Between Recruiting Source and Employee Success: An Analysis by Race," *Personnel Psychology* 36, no. 1 (Spring 1983), pp. 67–72.
9. Jean Powell Kirnan, John A. Farley, and Kurt F. Geisinger, "The Relationship Between Recruiting Source, Applicant Quality, and Hire Performance: An Analysis by Sex, Ethnicity, and Age," *Personnel Psychology* 42 no. 2 (Summer 1989), pp. 293–308. See also P.J. Decker and E.T. Cornelius, "A Note on Recruiting Sources and Job Survival Rates, *Journal of Applied Psychology*, 64 (1979), pp. 463–4.

10. James A. Breaugh, "Relations Between Sources and Employee Performance, Absenteeism, and Work Attitudes," *Academy of Management Journal* 24 (March 1981), pp.142–7; R. Wayne Mondy, Robert Noe, and Robert Edwards, "Successful Recruitment: Matching Sources and Methods," *Personnel* (September 1987), pp. 42–6.

11. Al Doran, "Technology Brings HR to Those Who Need It," *Canadian HR Reporter* 10, no. 17 (October 6, 1997), p. 8.

12. John Schofield, "The Nortel Job Machine," *Maclean's* (November 17, 1997), p. 82.

13. Pell, *Recruiting and Selecting Personnel*, p. 13.

14. The study on employment referrals was published by Bernard Hodes Advertising, Dept. 100, 555 Madison Avenue, New York, NY 10022. See also Allan Halcrow, "Employees Are Your Best Recruiters," *Personnel Journal* (November 1988), pp. 43–9. See also Andy Bargerstock and Hank Engel, "Six Ways to Boost Employee Referral Programs," *HR Magazine* 39, no. 12 (December 1994), pp. 72ff.

15. Based on survey results published in the *Personnel Administrator* (Virginia: The American Society for Personnel Adminstration, March 1987).

16. Schofield, "The Nortel Job Machine," pp. 82–3.

17. Based on personal experience of one of the authors.

18. Based on personal conversations with a student and relative of one of the authors.

19. Based on personal experience of one of the authors.

20. Mary E. Scott, "Internships Add Value to College Recruitment," *Personnel Journal* (April 1992), pp. 59–63.

21. Schofield, "The Nortel Job Machine," p. 83.

22. Based on a handout entitled *Checklist of Potential Programs*, obtained from a student, formerly an employee of HRDC, and the HRDC Web site.

23. Harris C. Jain, "Staffing: Recruitment and Selection" in *Human Resources Management in Canada* (Toronto: Prentice-Hall Canada Inc., 1984), p. 25 021.

24. Stephen Rubenfeld and Michael Crino, "Are Employment Agencies Jeopardizing Your Selection Process?" *Personnel* 58 (September/October, 1981), pp. 70–7.

25. Rubenfeld and Crino, "Employment Agencies."

26. John Warcham, *Secrets of a Corporate Headhunter* (New York: Playboy Press, 1981), pp. 213–25.

27. Pell, *Recruiting and Selecting Personnel*, pp. 16–34. See also Barbara Hunger, "How to Choose a Recruitment Advertising Agency," *Personnel Journal* 64, no. 12 (December 1985), pp. 60–2. For an excellent review of ads, see Margaret Magnus, *Personnel Journal*, Vols. 64 and 65, no. 8 (August 1985 and August 1986), and Bob Martin, "Recruitment Ad Ventures," *Personnel Journal* 66 (August 1987), pp. 46–63. For a discussion of how behaviour can influence the initial attraction to an advertisement, see Tom Redman and Brian Mathews, "Advertising for Effective Managerial Recruitment," *Journal of General Management* 18, no. 2 (Winter 1992), pp. 29–42.

28. Pell, *Recruiting and Selecting Personnel*.

29. Paula Romanow, "Business and Reservists," *Human Resources Professional* 12, no. 3 (May 1995), pp. 13–4.

30. Sharon LeBrun, "Is the Future of Recruiting Online?" *Canadian HR Reporter* 10, no. 19 (November 3, 1997), pp. 1, 6. Copyright MPL Communications Inc., Reproduced by permission of *Canadian HR Reporter* 133 Richmond Street West, Toronto, Ontario M5H 3M8.

31. Leslie Goodson, "Recruiting on the Web," *Human Resources Professional* 14, no. 2 (April/May 1997), p. 27.

32. LeBrun, "Future of Recruiting," p. 1.

33. "Monster Board Goes Canadian," *Canadian HR Reporter* 10, no. 19 (November 3, 1997), p. 6.

34. LeBrun, "Future of Recruiting," pp. 1, 6.

35. LeBrun, "Future of Recruiting," pp. 1, 6.

36. Goodson, "Recruiting on the Web," pp. 21, 23.

37. "Employee Use of Internet Doubles," *Canadian HR Reporter* 10, no. 18 (October 20, 1997) p. 3.

38. Goodson, "Recruiting on the Web," p. 27.

39. Al Doran, "HRIS Vendors Catch Up With the Internet," *Canadian HR Reporter* 10, no. 21 (December 1, 1997), p. 14.

40. LeBrun, "Future of Recruiting," p. 6.

41. Sharon LeBrun, "Canadian Tire Opens Its Doors," *Canadian HR Reporter* 10, no. 17 (October 6, 1997), p. 1. Copyright MPL Communications Inc., Reproduced by permission of *Canadian HR Reporter* 133 Richmond Street West, Toronto, Ontario M5H 3M8.

42. Schofield, "The Nortel Job Machine," p. 82.

43. LeBrun, "Canadian Tire Opens Its Doors," pp. 1, 6.

44. LeBrun, "Canadian Tire Opens Its Doors," pp. 1, 6.

45. Schofield, "The Nortel Job Machine," p. 82.

46. Conference Board of Canada, *Contingent Work: Trends, Issues and Challenges for Employers*, February 1997.

47. Ernest B. Akyeampong, "Work Arrangements: 1995 Overview," *Perspectives on Labour and Income* (Ottawa: Statistics Canada, Spring 1997), Cat. No. 75-001-SPE.

48. Linda Dickens, "Part-Time Employees: Workers Whose Time Has Come?" *Employee Relations* 14, no. 2 (1992), pp. 3–12.

49. Heather Hodgman, "The Next Office Temp Could Be You," *Human Resources Professional* 12 no. 3 (May 1995), p. 16.

50. J. Pearce, "Toward an Organizational Behavior of Contract Laborers: Their Psychological Involvement and Effects on Employee Co-Workers," *Academy of Management Journal* 36 (1993), pp. 1082–96.

51. Hodgman, "The Next Office Temp," p. 17.

52. Hodgman, "The Next Office Temp," p. 17.

53. Tricia McCallum, "The Minacs Touch," *Human Resources Professional* 11, no. 5 (June/July 1994), p. 21.

54. Jerry Zeidenberg, "HR and the Innovative Company," *Human Resources Professional* 13, no. 4 (June 1996), p. 14.

55. Michael M. Harris and Laurence S. Fink, "A Field Study of Applicant Reactions to Employment Opportunities: Does the Recruiter Make a Difference? *Personnel Psychology* 40, no. 1 (Winter 1987) p. 781.

56. R. Lattimer, "Managing Work Force Diversity: Problems Similar in Canada and U.S.," *Towers Perrin Focus* (Spring 1993), pp. 9–10.

57. Earl Miller, "Capitalizing on Older Workers," *Canadian HR Reporter* 10, no. 12 (June 16, 1997), p. 14. Copyright MPL Communications Inc., Reproduced by permission of *Canadian HR Reporter*, 133 Richmond Street West, Toronto, Ontario M5H 3M8.

58. Tema Frank, *Canada's Best Employers for Women* (Toronto: Frank Publications, 1994), p. 1.

59. R. Logan and J.A. Bellivieu "Working Mothers: Canadian Social Trends," (Ottawa: Statistics Canada, 1995), Cat. No. 75-001E. pp. 24–8.

60. Robert W. Goddard, "How to Harness America's Gray Power," *Personnel Journal* (May 1987), pp. 33–40.

61. Miller, "Capitalizing," p. 14.
62. Miller, "Capitalizing," p. 14.
63. Miller, "Capitalizing," p. 14, except Xerox example.
64. This example is from Goddard, "How to Harness," pp. 33–40.
65. "Youth Equity at the Bank of Montreal," *Canadian HR Reporter* 10, no. 18 (October 20, 1997) p. 12. Copyright MPL Communications Inc., Reproduced by permission of *Canadian HR Reporter* 133 Richmond Street West, Toronto, Ontario M5H 3M8.
66. Sharon LeBrun, "Booklets to Connect Disabled With Work," *Canadian HR Reporter* 10, no. 18 (October 20, 1997) p. 8. Copyright MPL Communications Inc., Reproduced by permission of *Canadian HR Reporter* 133 Richmond Street West, Toronto, Ontario M5H 3M8.
67. Pell, *Recruiting and Selecting Personnel*, pp. 96–8. See also Wayne Cascio, "Accuracy of Verifiable Biographical Information Blank Responses," *Journal of Applied Psychology* 60, (December 1975), for a discussion of the accuracy of biographical data.
68. This is based in part on "Evaluating Employment Applications" in *Personnel Journal* 63, no. 1 (January 1984), pp. 22–4, which was reprinted from *Supervisor's Newsletter* no. 276 (March 1983).
69. Wayne Cascio, "Turnover, Biographical Data, and Fair Employment," *Journal of Applied Psychology* 61, (October, 1976).
70. C.J. Russell, J. Mattson, S.E. Devlin, & D. Atwater, "Predictive Validity of Biodata Items Generated From Retrospective Life Experience Essays," *Journal of Applied Psychology* 75, (1990), pp. 569–80.

Chapter 7
Selection

Chapter Outline

- ◆ **Introduction**
- ◆ **The Selection Process**
- ◆ **Constraints on the Selection Process**
- ◆ **The Importance of Reliability and Validity**
- ◆ **Steps in the Selection Process**

Learning Outcomes

After studying this chapter, you should be able to:

Define selection and *discuss* its purpose and importance.

Describe the constraints on the selection process.

Define reliability and validity and discuss their importance.

Discuss at least four types of testing used in selection and *describe* the legal and ethical concerns related to medical examinations and drug testing.

Describe the major types of selection interviews and *explain* the problems that can undermine their effectiveness.

Design and *conduct* an effective interview.

Explain the importance of background investigation and reference checking, *describe* strategies to make such checking effective, and *discuss* the legal issues involved.

Describe the supervisor's role in the selection process.

Discuss the importance of selection process evaluation.

Introduction

Selection is the process of choosing individuals with the relevant qualifications to fill existing or projected job openings. Whether considering current employees for a transfer or promotion, or outside candidates for a first-time position with the firm, information about the applicants must be collected and evaluated. Each step in the selection process, from preliminary applicant reception and initial screening to the hiring decision, is performed under legal, organizational, and environmental constraints that protect the interests of both applicant and organization.[1]

Most firms use a sequential selection system involving a series of specific steps. In order to be hired, candidates must successively pass the screening technique involved in each step. Screening instruments typically include interviews, tests, and reference checking. In order for an individual to remain in contention for the position, he or she must meet or exceed the minimum requirements established for each screening technique. At each step, some applicants are rejected.

Purposes and Importance of Selection

The purpose of selection is to choose qualified individuals who possess the necessary skills, knowledge, abilities, personality, interests, and preferences to fill the job opening, who will perform well and fit in with the corporate values and culture. Proper selection is important for three key reasons: company performance, costs, and legal implications.

Company Performance If proper selection was vital during the years when Canada had an economy that was predominantly production-oriented, it is even more important now that the major part of the nation's gross national product is based on the provision of services. Today, the quality of the company's human resources is frequently the single most important factor in determining whether the firm is going to be successful, will realize a satisfactory return on its investment, and will reach the basic objectives specified in its strategic plan.

Cost In recent years, the cost of recruitment and selection has risen substantially. For example, one expert estimates that the total cost of hiring a manager who earns $60 000 a year is about $47 000, once search fees, interviewing time, reference checking, and travel and moving expenses are taken into account.[2] While the cost of hiring non-executive employees is considerably less, it is still enough to warrant an effective selection process. Costs do not end, of course, with the placement of the new employee on the job. Even if an internal candidate is selected, that person will require orientation and training. Often, the cost of training surpasses hiring costs.

Since labour costs make up such a big percentage of overhead expenses in most Canadian organizations (up to 80 or 85 percent in many service organizations, such as hospitals), there are also tremendous costs associated with inappropriate selection decisions.

Much emphasis has been placed on effective training and development and various motivational techniques as means of ensuring that employees make a worthwhile contribution. However, if the wrong employee is selected initially, no training program or motivational strategy—no matter how well conceived and designed—is likely to compensate adequately or offset the original hiring error.

The costs involved in employee training and development make it all the more critical that a great deal of careful attention is focussed on initial selection to ensure that training and development efforts "fall on fertile soil." Furthermore, since most firms believe in promoting from within, a good selection process for vacancies being filled by external applicants will ensure that qualified, promotable employees are brought into the firm.

When an unsuccessful employee must be terminated while on probation, or quits during this time, the recruitment and selection process must begin all over again, and the successor must be properly oriented and trained. These "visible" costs vary widely from job to job, and firm to firm, but there are always costs involved, even for the lowest-level, lowest-paid positions. The "hidden" costs are frequently even higher, including the low quality of work performed by the unsuccessful/unhappy employee while on the job; internal disorganization and disruption the employee may have caused; and customer/client ill will or alienation that may have been generated.

More often than not, really unsatisfactory applicants are screened out and do not get onto the payroll. Those that somehow "slip through" usually reveal their deficiencies and shortcomings early and are terminated during the probationary period. This is not the case, however, with the **marginal or borderline employee**, someone who really is not capable enough to be considered truly satisfactory, and never makes a worthwhile contribution to the firm. Virtually all organizations have some marginal employees on their payroll. In retrospect, these people probably should never have been hired in the first place.

Once marginal employees are on the payroll, it becomes exceedingly difficult to terminate their employment. When they were first hired, their deficiencies and shortcomings may not have been readily apparent; after all, most people are on their very best behaviour while on probation. Typically, it is only after they have been on the job for a while that their limitations become visible.

Frequently, marginal employees are hired by the company when it is in the midst of an expansion program, especially if there is not a formalized selection procedure in place. Under the pressure of the moment, they are not properly screened out. Sometimes an interviewer even realizes that a particular applicant does not really meet all of the critical requirements of the position in question, but does not have the written policy backing (or authority) to insist that selection standards not be compromised. The interviewer may truly believe that with time and training the applicant will develop into a better employee than he or she appears. In reality, this hope is rarely fulfilled. If anything, the marginal applicant usually turns out to be even less satisfactory an employee than expected.

The use of a sequential selection system with a series of steps through which all applicants must proceed, and policies and procedures which ensure that selection standards are never compromised, can help to ensure that unsuitable applicants don't "slip through" and that marginal employees never end up on the company's payroll.[3]

Legal Implications   There are also legal implications associated with ineffective or incompetent selection. As explained in chapter 3, human rights legislation in every jurisdiction in Canada prohibits discrimination in all aspects and terms and conditions of employment, on the grounds of race, religion or creed, colour, marital status, sex, and physical disability. Age-based discrimination is also prohibited in every jurisdiction (although the age groups protected differ), and discrimination on the basis of mental disability is prohibited in most. Discrimination on other grounds, such as sexual orientation and criminal history, is prohibited in some jurisdictions, but not all. Firms must ensure that all of their selection procedures are free of both intentional and systemic discrimination. Failure to do so may result in human rights complaints.

marginal employee
Someone who really is not capable enough to be considered truly satisfactory, and never makes a worthwhile contribution to the firm.

Those organizations required by law to implement an employment equity plan must ensure that all of their employment systems, including selection, are bias-free and do not have an adverse impact on members of the four designated groups—women, visible minorities, Aboriginal Peoples, and persons with disabilities.

Another legal implication is employer liability for negligent or wrongful hiring. Courts are increasingly finding employers liable when employees with unsuitable backgrounds are hired and subsequently engage in criminal activities falling within the scope of their employment. For example, the British Columbia Supreme Court found a children's foundation liable for sexual assaults of an employee upon one of the children in the organization's care.[4]

Finally, there is the legal issue of wrongful dismissal. According to wrongful dismissal case law, employees who are unable to perform a job may be dismissed without any notice or severance. While it is often difficult to prove gross incompetence, companies that satisfy the court's standards (such as warning the employee and giving him or her an opportunity to improve) have been successful. On the other hand, courts typically reject gross incompetence arguments when the employee's poor performance is the result of a flawed selection decision.[5]

Strategies to ensure legal compliance and avoid the negative legal consequences associated with ineffective or incompetent selection will be discussed shortly.

The Role of the HR Department in the Selection Process

While the HR department generally assumes overall responsibility for the selection process, and often does the initial screening, testing, and reference checking, managerial and supervisory staff in all departments have an extremely important role to play. The final hiring decision is generally made by the immediate supervisor. It is therefore critically important that all supervisors and managers understand the purpose and importance of the selection process, as well as the constraints affecting it. They must also be thoroughly trained in the most effective and legally defensible approaches for evaluating applicants and motivated to use them.

The Selection Process

The types of selection instruments and screening devices used vary from one organization to another. Even within a firm, the number of steps in the process and their sequence often varies with type and level of job, as well as source and method of recruitment. **Figure 7.1** illustrates the steps commonly involved. After describing the constraints on the selection process, and discussing the critical importance of validity and reliability, we will discuss each of these steps in turn.

Constraints on the Selection Process

Those involved in the selection process must be aware of the constraints that come with organizational policies and plans, the job requirements, supply challenges, ethics, and legislative requirements.

Organizational Policies and Plans

Strategic Plan   The organization's strategic plan affects the selection process and places major constraints on selection decisions, since the skills and qualifications,

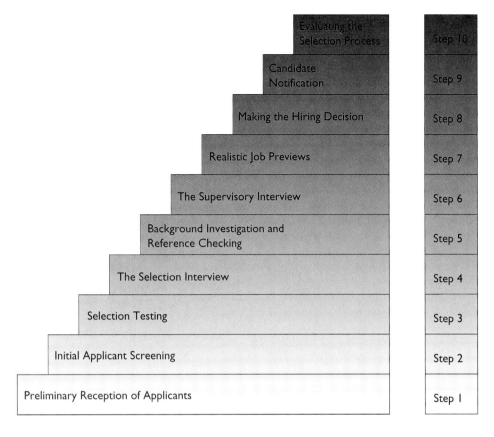

Figure 7.1
Typical Steps in the Selection Process

Evaluating the Selection Process	Step 10
Candidate Notification	Step 9
Making the Hiring Decision	Step 8
Realistic Job Previews	Step 7
The Supervisory Interview	Step 6
Background Investigation and Reference Checking	Step 5
The Selection Interview	Step 4
Selection Testing	Step 3
Initial Applicant Screening	Step 2
Preliminary Reception of Applicants	Step 1

of those chosen must match the organization's strategic requirements. Through selection, the firm attempts to match its intended strategy with characteristics of persons chosen. The characteristics of an organization, such as product lines, services provided, market share, and its priorities, change over time. These changes must be reflected in selection strategies.

Many organizations are now focussing on teamwork skills, for example. In such firms, the entire team may be involved in the selection process. AT 3M's plant in Brockville, Ontario, workers on the shop floor, who work closely together in teams of six or eight, are responsible for choosing new team members. They have been trained to assess applicants in three ways. First, they determine whether recruits have the desired values; next, they conduct some basic paper and pencil testing of problem-solving skills; and finally, teamwork skills are assessed through group exercises.[6] Recognizing that how people get along with each other on the shop floor will have a major impact on the success of plant operation, 3M has the workers decide who they can best work with, right from the start.

Selection Budget All organizations have finite resources. To make the best use of these resources, selection strategies must be cost-effective. The selection process is not an end, it is a means through which the organization achieves its objectives. Without budget limitations, selection procedures could be refined. Without limits, however, employment expenses could be so high that organizational effectiveness would suffer.

Employment Equity Plan Whether legally required or voluntarily initiated, if there is an employment equity plan, it must be taken into consideration when planning the selection process, since selection is one of the major HR activities by which the goals and timetables established by the firm and specified in their employment equity plan can be reached.

The Job Requirements

As explained in chapter 4, it is through job analysis that the organization identifies the duties, responsibilities, and human requirements for each job. By defining bona fide occupational requirements through job analysis and basing selection criteria on these requirements, firms can create a legally-defensible hiring system.[7]

The skills required, mental and physical demands, responsibilities, and working conditions should provide the basis for the information obtained from the applicant, his or her previous employers, and other reference sources, as well as for any employment tests administered. Individuals hired after thorough screening against carefully developed selection criteria, based directly on the job description and job specification, learn their jobs readily, are productive, and generally adjust to their jobs with a minimum of difficulty. As a result, both the individual and organization benefit.

Supply Challenges

selection ratio
The ratio of the number of applicants hired to the total number of applicants.

Although it is desirable to have a large, qualified pool of recruits from which to select applicants, this is not always possible. In fields in which there is a supply shortage, such as physiotherapy, there is often a very small selection ratio. A **selection ratio** is the relationship between the number of applicants hired and the total number of applicants available, calculated as follows:

$$\frac{\text{Number of Applicants Hired}}{\text{Total Number of Applicants}} = \text{Selection Ratio}$$

A small selection ratio, such as 1:2, means that there are very few applicants from which to select. In many instances, a small selection ratio also means a low quality of recruits. If this is the case, it is generally better to start the recruitment process over again, even if it means a hiring delay, rather than taking the risk of hiring an employee who will be a marginal performer at best.

Ethics

Since members of the human resources department have a major impact on the hiring decision, it is important that they have a strong sense of professional ethics.[8] Being offered gifts from a private employment agency wanting the firm's business or being pressured to hire the son or daughter of the company president are examples of ethical dilemmas, that those involved in the selection process may encounter.

Ethical standards pertaining to privacy and confidentiality are also important. The applicant's right to privacy must be balanced against the organization's right to know.

Legislative Requirements

As mentioned earlier, all steps in the selection process must meet human rights and employment equity (where applicable) legislative standards. Organizations must ensure that their selection criteria and screening techniques are justifiable, based on the job requirements, and that none lead to discrimination—whether intentional or systemic.

Legal compliance concerns also require that employers exercise due diligence in employee screening and reference checking. Suggested guidelines for avoiding negative legal consequences, such as human rights complaints, liability for negligent hiring, and unjust discharge suits include:[9]

1. Ensuring that all selection criteria and strategies are based on the job description and job specification. Doing so will enable the employer to prove that a protected group member was denied employment on the basis of legitimate and bona-fide grounds if charged under human rights legislation.

2. Adequately assessing the applicant's ability to meet performance standards or expectations. This will enable the firm to win a wrongful dismissal suit in the case of a new hire discharged due to unsatisfactory performance. If an applicant passes a test given to evaluate his or her abilities in a particular area and is subsequently hired, based, in part, on the test results, and is later discharged due to inadequate skills in that area, the employer would be found liable in a wrongful discharge suit. It is the employer's responsibility to ensure that the candidate possesses the necessary knowledge, skills, or other qualifications to fulfill the job requirements.

3. Carefully scrutinizing all information supplied by each applicant on his or her application form and résumé. To avoid negligent hiring charges, unexplained gaps in employment history should be explored. Any discrepancies between the information provided on paper and that gleaned during interviewing should also be thoroughly investigated. In unjust discharge cases, courts may decide in an employee's favour if the employer had objective information that contradicted the applicant's misrepresentations or embellishments, and ignored it or failed to act upon it.

4. Obtaining written authorization for reference checking from prospective employees, and checking references very carefully. Where justified, based on the job requirements, permission should be obtained for checking credit history, driving record, and/or criminal record. The results of such checking may lead to candidate rejection if the individual's history indicates unsuitability for the job in question. (This requires a delicate balancing of the candidate's legal rights (discussed in chapter 3) and the fear of negligent hiring.)

5. Saving all records and information obtained about the applicant during each stage of the selection process. Having such records, which make it clear that there were bona fide reasons for candidate rejection, is essential for defence against charges of discrimination under human rights or employment equity legislation. Having records that prove that due diligence was exercised in assessing applicant suitability are necessary to defend against charges of wrongful hiring.

6. Rejecting applicants who make false statements on their application forms or résumés. Doing so enables firms to avoid dishonest employees who may have something serious to hide, which could lead to a charge of negligent hiring. Most wrongful dismissal cases involving applicant misrepresentation have been decided in the employer's favour because the misrepresentation resulted in gross incompetence, breach of trust (that is, dishonesty), or both; except in cases in which the employer received both accurate and embellished information, and had objective data that should have enabled him or her to distinguish between the two.

Two critical issues related to legal compliance are reliability and validity, which will be discussed next.

The Importance of Reliability and Validity

Reliability

The degree to which interviews, tests, and other selection procedures yield comparable data over a period of time is known as reliability. **Reliability** is thus concerned with the degree of dependability, consistency, or stability of the measures used.[10] For example, if today a group of interviewers selects three different candidates as their top choices than they did yesterday, their judgments are obviously not reliable. Similarly, a test that results in widely different scores when it (or an equivalent version of the test) is administered to the same individual a few days apart is unreliable.[11]

Reliability also refers to the extent to which two or more methods (such as tests and reference checking) yield the same results or are consistent, as well as the extent to which there is agreement between two or more raters (inter-rater reliability).

When dealing with tests, another measure of reliability taken into account is internal consistency. For example, suppose there are ten items on a vocational interest test, all of which are supposed to measure, in one way or another, the person's interest in working outdoors. To assess internal reliability, after administering the test, the degree to which responses to those ten items vary together is statistically analyzed. (That's one reason why there are often questions which appear rather repetitive on tests).

There are at least four sources of unreliability. First, the selection instrument might do a poor job of *sampling*. For example, one version of a college course test might focus on specific chapters more than the supposedly-equivalent version. Similarly, interview questions may be worded in such a way that they do not do a good job of measuring that which they were supposed to ascertain, such as knowledge about a particular subject. Errors may also result from *chance response tendencies*. For example, a test may be so hard or so boring that the candidate gives up and starts answering questions at random. Third, there might be errors caused by the *conditions* under which the instrument is administered. An interview room with construction noise outside may unnerve a candidate, for example, resulting in far difference performance than if the interview had been conducted in a quiet setting. Finally, there could be *changes within the applicant*. Interview performance after a sleepless night is typically far different than that when a candidate is well rested, for example.

Validity

Validity refers to the accuracy with which a predictor measures what it is supposed to measure. In the context of selection, validity is essentially an indicator of the extent to which data from a selection technique, such as a test or interview, are related to or predictive of subsequent performance on the job.[12] Selection procedures must above all be valid. Without proof of validity, there is no logical or legally permissible reason to continue using the technique to screen job applicants.

To ensure that the selection techniques being used are valid, validation studies should be conducted. There are three distinct types of validity, which will be described next: criterion-related, content, and construct.

Criterion-Related Validity The extent to which a selection tool predicts or significantly correlates with important elements of work behaviour is known as

criterion-related validity
The extent to which a selection tool predicts or significantly correlates with important elements of work behaviour.

criterion-related validity. Correlational methods are generally used to determine the extent of the relationship between predictor information, such as test scores, and criterion data, such as job performance. Correlation coefficients range from 0.00, denoting no relationship, to +1.00 and –1.00, indicating a perfect positive or negative relationship, respectively. The higher the overall validity, the greater the chances of hiring individuals who will be better performers.

Performance on a test, for example, may be compared to actual job performance, in terms of quality and quantity of production, sales volume, supervisory ratings, training outcomes, or other measures of success appropriate for the job. The test has validity to the extent that people with higher test scores are better performers.[13]

There are two distinct types of criterion-related validity: predictive and concurrent. **Predictive validity** is the extent to which predictions about an individual's performance relate to his or her actual behaviour at some future date. To establish the predictive validity of a test, all applicants for a position might be given a test and predictions about their future performance made based on the test scores. Then, some of these applicants would be hired based on existing selection techniques, not the results of the test under study. To validate the test, after those individuals who were tested and subsequently hired have mastered the job, their actual performance, based on ratings of supervisors with whom the test scores have not been shared, would be compared with these predictions. If the test results are shown to be a valid predictor of job performance, the test can be administered to all future candidates for the position.

predictive validity
The extent to which predictions about performance actually relate to subsequent behaviour on the job.

Concurrent validity is the extent to which test scores (or other predictor information) relate to the performance of current employees. Using this technique to validate a test would involve administering the test to a group of current employees and correlating their test scores with some measure of their work performance. If those employees who receive high test scores are also the top performers, then the test is considered valid.[14] The main advantage of this technique is that data on performance of current employees are readily available. A disadvantage is that current incumbents may not be representative of new applicants, who of course are really the ones for whom the test is being developed.[15]

concurrent validity
The extent to which predictor information (such as test scores) relates to the performance of current employees.

Content Validity   When a selection instrument, such as a test, adequately samples the knowledge and skills needed to perform the job, **content validity** is assumed to exist. The closer the content of the selection instrument to actual samples of work or work behaviour, the greater the content validity.[16] For example, asking a candidate for a secretarial position to demonstrate word processing skills, as required on the job, has high content validity.

Ensuring content validity sounds easier that it is in practice. Demonstrating that the tasks a person performs in an interview or test situation are, in fact, a comprehensive and random sample of the tasks performed on the job and that the conditions under which they are performed resemble the work situation is not always easy. Nevertheless, content validity is the most direct and least complicated type of validity to assess. It is generally used to evaluate job-knowledge and skills tests, which will be described later. Unlike the criterion-related methods, content validity is not expressed in correlational terms. Instead, an index that indicates the relationship between the content of the selection instrument and performance on the job is computed from evaluations of a panel of experts.[17]

content validity
The extent to which a selection instrument, such as a test, adequately samples the knowledge and skills needed to perform the job.

Construct Validity   The extent to which a selection tool measures a theoretical construct or trait deemed necessary to perform the job successfully is known as **construct validity**. Intelligence, verbal skills, analytical ability, and leadership skills are all examples of constructs.

construct validity
The extent to which a selection tool measures a theoretical construct or trait deemed necessary to perform the job successfully.

cross-validation
The process of verifying the results obtained from a validation study by administering a test or test battery to a different sample drawn from the same population.

differential validity
Confirmation that the selection tool accurately predicts the performance of all possible employee subgroups, including white males, women, visible minorities, persons with disabilities, and Aboriginal Peoples.

Measuring construct validity requires demonstrating that the psychological trait or attribute is related to satisfactory job performance, as well as showing that the test or other selection tool used accurately measures the psychological trait or attribute.[18]

Regardless of the method used, cross-validation is essential. **Cross-validation** is the process of verifying the results obtained from a validation study by administering a test or test battery to a different sample drawn from the same population.

Experts also recommend that separate validation studies be administered for different subgroups, such as visible minorities and women. If **differential validity** is not assessed, it is possible for a test or other procedure to be a valid predictor of job success for one group (such as white male applicants), but not for all candidates, thereby leading to systemic discrimination. As may be recalled from chapter 3, the issue of differential validity played a significant role in the 1987 landmark decision of the Supreme Court of Canada, upholding a federal human rights tribunal ruling. CN Rail was ordered to cease using the Bennet Mechanical Comprehension Test as a selection tool for entry-level blue-collar jobs in its St. Lawrence region because the test had an adverse impact on female applicants.[19]

The overall effectiveness of a selection program depends on the validity of its components. **Table 7.1** summarizes the results of one study of the validity of various selection tools. Tests with high face validity (that appear valid), such as tests of actual performance, including work sampling, peer evaluations, and assessment centres, rated highest. Indirect evaluations, such as psychological tests or academic performance, rated lower.

Tests with high face validity may also be more acceptable to job candidates. In one study, researchers found strong support for the relationship between perceptions of face validity and organizational attractiveness.[20] In other words, candidates exposed to assessment strategies perceived to be valid were more apt to view the employer favourably, while selection procedures that were perceived to

TABLE 7.1 Validity of Various Selection Devices

PREDICTOR	VALIDITY
Cognitive Ability and Special Aptitude	Moderate
Personality	Low
Interest	Low
Physical Ability	Moderate–High
Biographical Information	Moderate
Interviews	Low
Work Samples	High
Seniority	Low
Peer Evaluations	High
Reference Checks	Low
Academic Performance	Low
Self-Assessments	Moderate
Assessment Centres	High

Source: Neal Schmitt and Raymond Noe, "Personal Selection and Equal Employment Opportunity," in *International Review of Industrial and Organizational Psychology*, eds. Cary L. Cooper and Ivan T. Robertson. Copyright 1986 by John Wiley & Sons, Ltd. Reprinted by permission.

be low in face validity were more likely to be viewed as unfair, and thus targets for complaints and/or legal challenges.

Steps in the Selection Process

In order to gain as reliable and valid a picture as possible of each applicant's potential for success on the job, organizations typically rely on a number of sources of information. As mentioned earlier, the number of steps in the selection process and their sequence varies not only with the organization, but also with recruiting source and method. Reference checking with former employers is not generally a step in the selection of an internal candidate for transfer or promotion, for example. Private employment agencies and executive search firms perform screening, and often do testing and reference checking, which means that the company may only conduct a three-stage selection process: a supervisory interview, realistic job preview, and final hiring decision.

As illustrated in Figures 7.2 and 7.3, both of which reflect the results of a survey of 581 Canadian organizations conducted by James Thacker and Julian Cattaneo of the University of Windsor, the size of the organization and type and level of job also make a difference. **Figure 7.2** summarizes the selection practices of the firms surveyed; **Figure 7.3** shows the major predictors used by the same organizations in selecting individuals for various types of positions.

Figure 7.2
Selection Practices in Canadian Organizations (n=581)

Source: Adapted from J.W. Thacker, and R.J. Cattaneo, "Survey of Personnel Practices in Canadian Organizations," published in *ASAC Proceedings*, June 1987, pp. 56–66. Used by permission of the authors.

Selection Tool	% of Respondents Who Use This Selection Tool in Organizations of		
	Small Size	Medium Size	Large Size
Application Blank	93	94	100
Letters of Reference	76	69	63
Weighted Application Blanks	4	3	5
Biographical Information Blanks	24	25	26
Personality Tests	20	16	28
Aptitude Tests	35	43	57
Honesty Tests	2	0.4	0.8
Interests Inventories	14	10	23

Figure 7.3
Major Predictors Used in Selecting Employees for Different Positions

Source: J.W. Thacker and R.J. Cattaneo, "Survey of Personnel Practices in Canadian Organizations," published in *ASAC Proceedings*, June 1987, pp. 56–66. Used by permission of the authors.

	All % Responding Firms Saying "Yes"			
	Management Staff	White Collar (Professional)	White Collar (Non-Professional)	Blue Collar
Letters of Reference	73.0–80.5	83.5	76.5	48.5
Weighted Application Blanks	60.9–73.9	91.3	78.2	69.6
Biographical Blanks	65.2–79.2	81.9	83.3	70.1
Tests (personality)	68.4–82.5	54.4	50.0	23.7
Assessment Centres	42.3–60.6	22.5	11.3	9.9

Each of the steps commonly involved in the selection process, as identified in Figure 7.1, will now be described.

Step One: Preliminary Reception of Applicants

The selection process is a two-way street. Organizations select employees, and applicants select employers. How initial reception is handled affects an applicant's opinion of the employer.

Initial contact may be made directly with the human resources department, either in person or in writing, or by the exchange of some basic information through the receptionist, such as nature of jobs available, pay rates, and hours of work. Completing an application form is often a key step in this preliminary reception stage.

When the applicant appears in person, a preliminary interview may be granted as a matter of good public relations, especially if there is an opening for which the applicant may be qualified. Such a "courtesy interview" is very brief, but enables a member of the HR department to confirm whether or not the candidate has the "must have" selection criteria and to screen out candidates who are unsuitable or undesirable.

Candidates applying in writing are often sent a polite letter of acknowledgement. If the candidate appears promising, an application form may be enclosed, with the request that it be completed and returned. Some applicants may self-select themselves out of the process at this stage if they realize that they are unqualified or decide they have no desire to work for the firm based on some of the information relayed or the treatment received.

Step Two: Initial Applicant Screening

Initial applicant screening is generally performed by members of the HR department. Application forms and résumés are reviewed. Those candidates not meeting the "must have" selection criteria are eliminated first. Then, the remaining applications are examined and those candidates who most closely match the remaining job specifications are identified and given further consideration.

Step Three: Selection Testing

Selection testing is a common screening device used by organizations for both hiring and promotion purposes. The tests assess specific job-related skills, as well as general intelligence, personality characteristics, mental abilities, interests, and preferences. Tests may involve a demonstration of skills, a simulation, or a written exercise. Testing techniques provide efficient, standardized procedures for screening large numbers of applicants. The use of valid tests can significantly assist in the selection of the most qualified candidate.

The use of tests to assist with hiring and/or promotion decisions has been increasing in recent years, after several decades of decline.[21] Studies have shown that approximately one-third of Canadian organizations use tests for hiring.[22]

In general, testing is more prevalent in larger organizations. In one study, for example, only about 30 percent of employers with fewer than 100 employees reported using tests for hiring, while almost 60 percent of employers with more than 25 000 employees reported doing so.[23] This reflects several things, including the greater need that large firms typically have for efficient, standardized procedures in order to screen high numbers of applicants, and their ability to finance testing programs.

**www.career-doctor.
com/index.htm**
Career Doctor

Fundamental Guidelines to Effective Testing   The Canadian Psychological Association has developed and published comprehensive testing standards, covering such areas as test instrumentation, test use and administration, scoring, and reporting.[24]

Because the field of selection testing involves so many different varieties of tests that purport to measure such diverse attributes of candidates as job performance and honesty, it is important that organizations do a great deal of planning, analysis, and experimentation in order to develop tests that best satisfy their needs.

Basic guidelines[25] for setting up a testing program include:[26]

1. *Use tests as supplements.* Tests should not be used as the only selection technique; instead, they should be used to supplement other techniques, such as interviews and background checks. Tests are not infallible. Even in the best of cases the test score usually accounts for only about 25 percent of the variation in the measure of performance. In addition, tests are often better at telling which candidates will fail than which will succeed.

2. *Validate the tests in the organization.* Both *legal requirements* and *good testing practice* demand that the test be validated in each organization. The fact that the same tests have been proven valid in similar organizations is *not* sufficient.

3. *Analyze all current hiring and promotion standards.* Questions such as: "What proportion of Aboriginal or visible minority applicants are being rejected at each stage of the hiring process?" and "Why are we using this standard—what does it mean in terms of actual behaviour on the job?" should be asked. The burden of proof is always on the organization, which means showing that the predictor (such as intelligence) is related to success or failure on the job.

4. *Keep accurate records.* It is important to keep accurate records of why each applicant was rejected. For purposes of the Human Rights Commission, a general note such as "not sufficiently well-qualified" would not be enough. As objectively as possible, statements should be made explaining why the candidate was rejected. The reasons for rejecting the candidate may be subject to validation at a later date.

5. *Begin a validation program.* If the firm doesn't currently use tests, or uses tests that haven't been validated, a validation study should be started. A predictive validation study is preferable. This requires administering a test to applicants, hiring the applicants without referring to the test scores, and at a later date correlating test scores with their performance on the job.

6. *Use a certified psychologist.* The development, validation, and use of selection standards (including tests) generally require the assistance of a qualified psychologist.

7. *Provide appropriate testing conditions.* Tests should be administered in areas that are reasonably private, quiet, well lighted, and ventilated. All applicants must take tests under the same conditions. Once completed, test results should be held in the strictest confidence and given only to individuals who have a legitimate need for the information and who also have the ability to understand and interpret the scores.

To assess the traits on which job success depends, many firms, such as those that rely on employees' sales skills, administer a skills assessment test before hiring.

Individual Rights of Test Takers and Test Security   Test takers have certain rights to privacy and information under the Canadian Psychological Association's Standards.[27] They have the right to the confidentiality of the test results and the right to informed consent regarding the use of these results. Second, they have the right to expect that only people qualified to interpret the scores will have access to them or that sufficient information will accompany the scores to ensure their appropriate interpretation. Third, they have the right to expect that the test is equally fair to all test takers in the sense of being equally familiar. The tests, in other words, must be secure; no person taking the tests should have prior information concerning the questions or answers.

Types of Tests   A number of the tests commonly used in selection can conveniently be classified according to whether they measure cognitive (thinking) abilities, motor and physical abilities, personality and interests, or achievement.[28] Other potential testing strategies include work sampling, management assessment centres, the miniature job training and evaluation approach, graphology, physical examination, and drug testing.

Tests of Cognitive Abilities   Included in this category are tests of general reasoning ability (intelligence) and tests of specific thinking skills like memory and inductive reasoning.

Intelligence Tests   **Intelligence (IQ) tests** are tests of general intellectual abilities. They measure not a single "intelligence" trait, but rather a number of abilities including memory, vocabulary, verbal fluency, and numerical ability.

Originally, IQ (intelligence quotient) was literally a quotient. The procedure was to divide a child's mental age (as measured by the intelligence test) by his or her chronological age, and then multiply the results by 100. Thus, if an 8-year-old child answered questions as a 10-year-old might, his or her IQ would be 10 divided by 8, times 100, or 125.

For adults, of course, the notion of mental age divided by chronological age wouldn't make sense. For example, we wouldn't necessarily expect a 30-year-old individual to be more intelligent than a 25-year-old one. Therefore, an adult's IQ score is actually a *derived* score. It reflects the extent to which the person is above or below the "average" adult's intelligence score.

Intelligence is often measured with individually administered tests, such as the Stanford-Binet Test or the Wechsler Test. Other IQ tests, such as the Wonderlic, can be administered to groups of people.

Specific Cognitive Abilities   There are also measures of specific thinking skills, such as inductive and deductive reasoning, verbal comprehension, memory, and numerical ability.

Tests in this category are often called **aptitude tests**, since they purport to measure the applicant's aptitudes for the job in question, that is, the applicant's potential to perform the job once given proper training. An example is the test of mechanical comprehension illustrated in **Figure 7.4**. It tests the applicant's understanding of basic mechanical principles. It may therefore reflect a person's aptitude for jobs—like that of machinist or engineer—that require mechanical comprehension. Other tests of mechanical aptitude include the Mechanical Reasoning Test and the SRA Test of Mechanical Aptitude.

Multi-dimensional aptitude tests commonly used in applicant selection include the General Aptitude Test Battery (GATB), Employee Aptitude Survey (EAS), the Flanagan Aptitude Classification Test (FACT), and the Differential Aptitude Test (DAT).

Tests of Motor and Physical Abilities   There are many *motor abilities* a firm might want to measure. These include finger dexterity, manual dexterity, speed of arm movement, and reaction time. The Stromberg Dexterity Test, as illustrated in **Figure 7.5**, is an example. It measures the speed and accuracy of simple judgment, as

---

intelligence (IQ) tests
Tests that measure general intellectual abilities, such as verbal comprehension, inductive reasoning, memory, numerical ability, speed of perception, spatial visualization, and word fluency.

aptitude tests
Tests that measure an individual's aptitude or potential to perform a job, provided he or she is given proper training.

Figure 7.4
Two Problems from
the Test of Mechanical
Comprehension

Source: Reproduced by
permission. Copyright 1967,
1969 by The Psychological
Corporation, New York, NY.
All rights reserved. Author's
note: 1969 is latest copyright
on this test, which is still the
main one used for this
purpose.

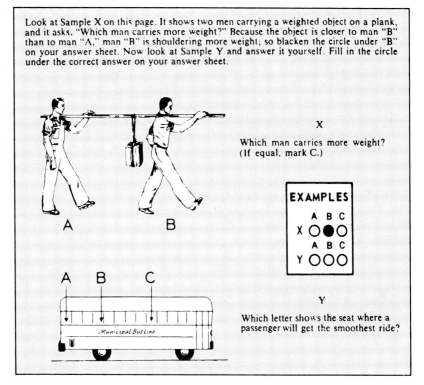

Look at Sample **X** on this page. It shows two men carrying a weighted object on a plank, and it asks, "Which man carries more weight?" Because the object is closer to man "B" than to man "A," man "B" is shouldering more weight; so blacken the circle under "B" on your answer sheet. Now look at Sample **Y** and answer it yourself. Fill in the circle under the correct answer on your answer sheet.

X

Which man carries more weight?
(If equal, mark C.)

EXAMPLES

Y

Which letter shows the seat where a passenger will get the smoothest ride?

Figure 7.5
Minnesota Rate of
Manipulation Test
(top) and Stromberg
Dexterity Test
(bottom)

Source: Educational Test
Bureau and The Psychological
Corporation.

well as the speed of finger, hand, and arm movements. Other tests include the Crawford Small Parts Dexterity Test, the Minnesota Rate of Manipulation Test, and the Purdue Peg Board.

Tests of *physical abilities* may also be required.[29] Physical abilities include static strength (lifting weights), dynamic strength (like pull-ups), body coordination (as in jumping rope), and stamina.[30]

Measuring Personality and Interests   A person's mental and physical abilities are seldom enough to explain his or her job performance. Other factors such as the person's motivation and interpersonal skills are important too. Personality and interests inventories are sometimes used as predictors of such intangibles.

personality tests
Instruments used to measure basic aspects of personality, such as introversion, stability, motivation, neurotic tendency, self-confidence, self-sufficiency, and sociability.

Personality tests can measure basic aspects of an applicant's personality, such as introversion, stability, and motivation. Many of these tests are *projective*. Here an ambiguous stimulus like an ink blot or clouded picture is presented to the person taking the test. He or she is then asked to interpret or react to it. Since the pictures are ambiguous, the person's interpretation must come from within—be projected. He or she supposedly *projects* into the picture his or her own emotional attitudes about life. Thus, a security-oriented person might describe the woman in **Figure 7.6** as "my mother worrying about what I'll do if I lose my job." Examples of personality tests (which are more properly called personality inventories) include the Thematic Apperception Test, the Guilford-Zimmerman Temperament Survey, and the Minnesota Multiphasic Personality Inventory. The Guilford-Zimmerman survey measures personality traits such as emotional stability versus moodiness, and friendliness versus criticalness. The Minnesota Multiphasic Personality Inventory taps traits like hypochondria and paranoia.

Personality tests—particularly the projective type—are the most difficult tests to evaluate and use. An expert must analyze the test taker's interpretations and reactions and infer from them his or her personality. The usefulness of such tests for selection then assumes it is possible to find a relationship between a measurable personality trait (such as introversion) and success on the job.[31]

The difficulties notwithstanding, recent studies confirm that personality tests can help companies hire more effective workers. For example, industrial psychologists often talk in terms of the "Big Five" personality dimensions as they apply to employment testing: extroversion, emotional stability, agreeableness, conscientiousness, and openness to experience.[32] One study focussed on the extent to

Figure 7.6
Sample Picture from Thematic Apperception Test.
How do you interpret this picture?

which these five personality dimensions predicted performance (for instance, in terms of job proficiency and training proficiency) for professionals, police officers, managers, sales workers, and skilled/semiskilled workers. Conscientiousness showed a consistent relationship with all job performance criteria for all the occupations. Extroversion was a valid predictor of performance for the two occupations that involved the most social interaction, namely managers and sales employees. Openness to experience and extroversion predicted training proficiency for all occupations.

A second study confirms the potential usefulness of personality tests in employee selection, while underscoring the importance of careful job analysis. The researchers involved concluded that (under the right circumstances) the predictive power of a personality test can be quite high.[33] However, they also concluded that the full potential of using personality traits in selection will be realized only when careful job analysis becomes the "standard practice for determining which traits are relevant to predicting performance on a given job, and when greater attention is directed to the selection of psychometrically sound and valid personality measures."[34] In summary, personality tests can be useful for helping employers predict which candidates will succeed on the job and which will not. However, validation studies must be carried out very carefully.

interest inventories
Tests that measure the relative strength of an applicant's interest in certain occupations or compare his or her interests with those of other people performing the same kind of work.

Interest inventories measure the relative strength of an applicant's interest in certain occupations or compare a candidate's interests with those of other people performing the same kind of work. Thus, a person taking the Strong-Campbell Inventory would receive a report comparing his or her interests to those of people already in occupations such as accounting, engineering, management, or medical technology.

Interest inventories have many uses. One example is in career planning, since a person will likely do better on jobs that involve activities in which he or she is interested. These tests can also be useful as selection tools. Clearly, if the firm can select people whose interests are roughly the same as those of successful incumbents in the jobs for which it is recruiting, it is more likely that the applicants will be successful in their new jobs.[35]

achievement tests
Tests used to measure knowledge and/or proficiency acquired through education, training, or experience.

Achievement Tests An **achievement test** is basically a measure of what a person has learned. Most of the tests taken in school are achievement tests. They measure knowledge and/or proficiency acquired in areas such as economics, marketing, or human resources management.

Achievement tests are also widely used in employment screening. For example, the Purdue Test for Machinists and Machine Operators tests the job knowledge of experienced machinists with questions like "What is meant by 'tolerance'?" Other tests are available for electricians, welders, carpenters, and so forth. In addition to job knowledge, achievement tests measure the applicant's abilities; a keyboarding test is one example. The use of computers in testing is illustrated in the Information Technology and HR box.

work samples
Actual job tasks used in testing applicants' performance.

Work Sampling for Employee Selection **Work samples** and simulations like assessment centres can be considered tests. However, they differ from most of the tests we've discussed because they focus on measuring job performance directly.[36] Personality and interest inventories, on the other hand, aim to predict job performance by measuring traits such as extroversion or interests.

work sampling technique
A testing method based on measuring performance on actual basic job tasks.

The **work sampling technique** measures how a candidate actually performs some of the job's basic tasks.[37]

There are several advantages to work sampling. Since actual on-the-job tasks are being measured, it is harder for the applicant to fake answers. The work sample

Information Technology and HR
Computer-Interactive Performance Test

Microprocessors and minicomputers have opened up new possibilities for measuring various types of performance and we should briefly review some of these.[1] One expert classifies the uses of computers in selection into four kinds of applications. The first simply uses the computer as a way to administer a currently available printed test. Using the computer in this way facilitates scoring and the compilation of cumulative norms.

A second way in which computers are used today may be called the *adaptive test*. Adaptive tests automatically tailor a sequence of test items to each examinee, contingent on his or her responses to earlier items in the sequence. In tests like these, correct responses generally trigger more difficult items. The effect is to substantially reduce the number of test items needed, since those that are either too easy or hard for the examinee are not administered.

Third, computers are being used to enhance the administration of tests when dynamics are involved, as in tests of perceptual speed. Here the computer can be used to present signals rapidly and sequentially to test the person's perceptual speed. Similarly, a test of short-term memory, where the stimulus can be removed from the display and recall required later, is another example of an application here.

Fourth, computers are being used to measure human capabilities not easily measurable by printed tests. For example, the ability to function under different time pressures, or under different work load conditions, or the ability to concentrate under stress are not easily measured using printed tests. However, computers can measure a person's ability to concentrate as various stimuli are projected on the screen.

For example, a computerized testing procedure was developed for the selection of clerical staff in a large manufacturing company.[2] The eight test components were selected and constructed to represent actual work performed by secretarial employees and to cover typical tasks such as maintaining and developing data bases and spreadsheets, general clerical activities including answering the telephone and filing, and handling travel arrangements. For example, for the word processing test, applicants were given three minutes (monitored by the computer) to type as much of this paper as possible; the computer recorded and corrected the manuscript. For the travel expense form completion task, the applicant needed to access the data base file, use some of the information in it to compute quarterly expenses, and transfer this information to the travel expense form.◆

---

[1] This is based on Edwin A. Fleishman, "Some New Frontiers in Personnel Selection Research," *Personnel Psychology*, no. 4 (Winter 1988), pp. 679–701.

[2] Neal Schmitt et al., "Computer-Based Testing Applied to Selection of Secretarial Applicants," *Personnel Psychology* 46 (1993), pp. 149–65.

---

itself is more clearly relevant to the job for which the firm is recruiting, so in terms of legislative requirements, the firm is on safer ground. Work sampling does not delve into the applicant's personality or psyche, so there's almost no chance of its being viewed as an invasion of privacy. Well-designed work samples also exhibit better validity than do tests designed to predict performance.

The basic procedure[38] is to choose several tasks crucial to performing the job in question and test applicants on each. Their performance on each task is monitored by an observer who indicates on a checklist how well the applicant performs that task. An example follows.

CHECKS KEY BEFORE INSTALLING AGAINST:

_____ shaft	score	3
_____ pulley	score	3
_____ neither	score	1

In developing a work sampling test for maintenance mechanics, experts first list all the possible tasks (such as "install pulleys and belts" and "install and align a motor") that maintenance mechanics would be required to perform. For each task, the experts list the frequency of performance of the task, and the task's relative importance to the overall job of maintenance mechanic. Thus, four crucial tasks here might be installing pulleys and belts, disassembling and installing a gear box, installing and aligning a motor, and pressing a bushing into a sprocket.

Next these four tasks are broken down _into the steps needed to complete them._ Each step, of course, can be performed in a slightly different way. Since some approaches are better than others, the experts give a different weight to different approaches.

This is illustrated in **Figure 7.7**, which shows one of the steps required for installing pulleys and belts: "checks key before installing." As listed on the checklist, different possible approaches here include checking the key against (1) the shaft, or (2) the pulley, or (3) neither. Weights reflecting the worth of each of these approaches are shown on the right of the figure.

Each applicant would be required to perform each of the four tasks. The work is monitored by the test administrator, who watches the applicant and indicates on a checklist like that in Figure 7.7 the approach the applicant used.

Finally, the work sampling test is validated by determining the relationship between the applicants' scores on the work samples and their actual performance on the job. Then, once it is shown that the work sample is a valid predictor of job success, the employer can begin using it for selection.

**management
assessment centre**
A situation in which management candidates are asked to make decisions in hypothetical situations and are scored on their performance. It usually also involves testing and the use of management games.

Management Assessment Centres In a two- to three-day **management assessment centre**, 10 or 12 management candidates perform realistic management tasks (like making presentations) under the observation of expert appraisers; each candidate's management potential is thereby _assessed_ or appraised.[39] The centre itself may be a plain conference room; but it is often a special room with a one-way mirror to facilitate unobtrusive observations. Examples of the simulated exercises included in a typical assessment centre are as follows:

The in-basket. With this exercise, the candidate is faced with an accumulation of reports, memos, notes of incoming phone calls, letters, and other materials collected in the in-basket of the simulated job he or she is to take over. The candidate is asked to take appropriate action on each of these materials. For example, he or she must write letters, notes, or agendas for meetings. The results of the candidate's actions are then reviewed by the trained evaluators.

The leaderless group discussion. A leaderless group is given a discussion question and told to arrive at a group decision. The raters then evaluate each group member's interpersonal skills, acceptance by the group, leadership ability, and individual influence.

Management games. Participants engage in realistic problem solving, usually as members of two or more simulated companies that are competing in the

A management game or simulation is a typical component in a management assessment centre.

marketplace. Decisions might have to be made about matters such as how to advertise and manufacture and how much inventory to keep in stock.

Individual presentations. A participant's communication skills and persuasiveness are evaluated by having the person make an oral presentation on an assigned topic.

Objective tests. All types of paper-and-pencil tests of personality, mental ability, interests, and achievements might also be a part of an assessment centre.

The interview. Most centres also require an interview between at least one of the expert assessors and each participant to evaluate interests, background, past performance, and motivation.

Assessment centres are used increasingly as a selection tool.[40] They were reportedly introduced at the American Telephone & Telegraph Company in the 1950s and are still in use there.

Most studies suggest that assessment centres are useful for predicting success in management jobs.[41] Studies also indicate that assessment centres, insofar as they sample actual, realistic job behaviour, are valid, unbiased selection tools.[42]

The main disadvantage of the assessment centre technique is the high cost involved.[43] The question is whether a centre can do its job less expensively than other selection techniques, and here the evidence is not clear. At least one study suggests that the assessment centre approach is financially efficient.[44] Another researcher, however, concluded that a straightforward review of the participants' HR files did as good a job of predicting which participants would succeed as did their assessment centre evaluations.[45] In another study, a combination of the assessment centre results and an evaluation of the candidate's records was found to be a better predictor than the assessment centre alone.[46]

The Miniature Job Training and Evaluation Approach In this approach, the candidate is trained to perform a sample of the job's tasks and his or her ability to perform these tasks is then measured. The approach assumes that a person who can demonstrate the ability to learn and perform the sample of tasks will be able to learn and perform the job itself.

The approach has advantages and disadvantages. It is "content relevant," testing the applicant with an actual sample of the job rather than just with paper-and-pencil tests. This direct approach may be more acceptable (and fair) to some applicants, such as those for whom English or French is a second language, than the usual paper-and-pencil test. On the other hand, with its emphasis on individual instruction during training, this approach is also a relatively expensive screening device.[47]

polygraph (lie detector) A device that measures physiological changes associated with stress, such as increased perspiration, blood pressure, and heart rate.

The Polygraph and Honesty Testing Some firms use the **polygraph (or "lie detector")** for honesty testing. It should be noted, however, that lie detector tests are not legal as a selection tool in some Canadian jurisdictions, such as Ontario. The polygraph machine is a device that measures physiological changes like increased perspiration. The assumption is that such changes reflect the emotional stress that accompanies lying. The usual procedure is for an applicant or current employee to be attached to the machine with painless electronic probes. He or she is then asked a series of neutral questions by the polygraph expert. These questions might, for instance, confirm that the person's name is John Smith and that he is currently residing in Vancouver.

Once the person's emotional reaction to giving truthful answers to neutral questions has been ascertained, questions like "Have you ever stolen anything without paying for it?" "Have you ever been convicted a crime for which a pardon has not been granted?" can be asked. In theory, at least, the expert can then determine with some accuracy whether or not the applicant is lying.

There are a number of good arguments against the use of polygraph testing. First is the fact that the experience can be demeaning and embarrassing. More important is their questionable accuracy. Estimates about their ability to distinguish between who is lying and who is not range from about 70 to 90 percent. Some emotional people may demonstrate the changes in perspiration, breathing, blood pressure, and pulse rate normally associated with lying, even when telling the truth; while others, accomplished actors, for example, may be able to tell a lie with no discernable physiological changes. Thus, even in jurisdictions in which administering polygraphs is legal, employers often choose other less offensive and more accurate means to assess applicant honesty.

honesty tests
Psychological tests that measure an individual's attitude toward honest versus dishonest behaviours or lack of candour.

Paper-and-pencil **honesty tests** are psychological tests designed to predict job applicants' proneness to dishonesty and other forms of counterproductivity.[48] Most of these tests measure attitudes regarding things like tolerance of others who steal, acceptance of rationalizations for theft, and admission of theft-related activities. Tests include the Phase II profile, the marketing rights to which were recently purchased by Wackenhut Corporation of Coral Gables, Florida, which provides security services to employers. Similar tests are published by London House, Incorporated, and Stanton Corporation.[49]

Several psychologists have expressed concerns about the proliferation of paper-and-pencil honesty tests.[50] Many of the supportive articles have been written by the test publishers themselves, they say. They also argue that additional independent peer review should be conducted before the validity of these devices is accepted.[51]

Even so, several recent studies support the validity of paper-and-pencil honesty tests. One study focused on 111 employees hired by a major retail convenience store chain to work at convenience store or gas station outlet counters.[52] "Shrinkage" was estimated to equal 3% of sales, and internal theft was believed to account for much of this. The researchers found that scores on an honesty test successfully predicted detected theft in this study, as measured by termination for theft. Paper-and-pencil honesty testing may also help companies predict white-collar crime.[53]

There are several reasons to be cautious with any honesty testing program. First, as noted earlier, doubt has been expressed regarding how valid many (or most) paper-and-pencil honesty testing instruments are. Second, on purely humanitarian grounds, one could argue that a rejection (let alone an incorrect rejection) for dishonesty carries with it more stigma than does being rejected for, say, poor mechanical comprehension or even poor sociability. It's true that others may never know why a candidate was rejected. However, the subject, having just taken and "failed" what may have been a fairly obvious "honesty test," may leave the premises feeling that his or her treatment was less than proper. Third, questions and tests in this area pose serious invasion-of-privacy issues, delving as they do into areas such as how the applicant feels about stealing, or whether he or she has ever stolen anything. There are also more legal constraints of which firms should be aware. For instance, honest testing is not legally permissable in many Canadian jurisdictions.[54] Until more widespread evaluations are done, these tests should be used very cautiously and certainly only as supplements to other techniques like reference checking.

www.aspentree.com/ default.asp
Aspentree Software

Figure 7.8
Handwriting Exhibit Used by Graphologist

Source: Reproduced with permission from Kathryn Sackhein, *Handwriting Analysis and the Employee Selection Process* (New York: Quorum Books, 1990), p. 45.

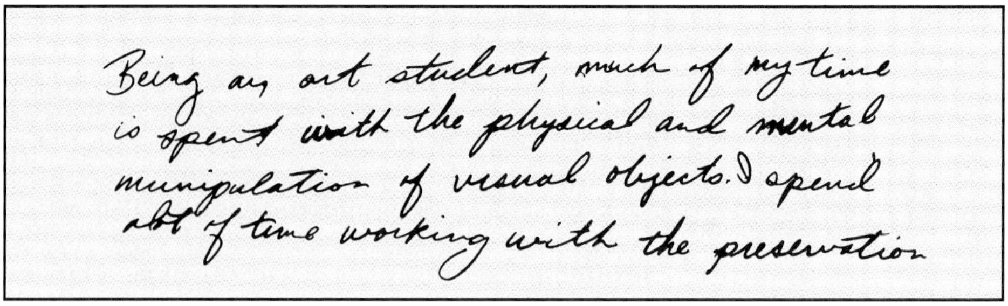

graphology
The use of handwriting analysis to assess an applicant's basic personality traits.

Graphology   The use of **graphology** (handwriting analysis) is based on the assumption that the writer's basic personality traits will be expressed in his or her handwriting.[55] Handwriting analysis thus has some resemblance to projective personality tests.

In graphology, the handwriting analyst studies an applicant's handwriting and signature in order to discover the person's needs, desires, and psychological makeup.[56] According to the graphologist, the writing in **Figure 7.8** exemplifies "uneven pressure, poor rhythm, and uneven baselines." The variation of light and dark lines shows a "lack of control" and is "one strong indicator of the writer's inner disturbance."

While many scientists doubt the validity of handwriting analysis, it should also be noted that the classified sections of international periodicals like the *Economist* still run ads from graphologists offering to aid in an employer's selection process. According to Elaine Charal, Vice-Present of C&M Consultants in Toronto, a firm specializing in assessment and screening, approximately 500 Canadian companies use handwriting analysis to assess job applicants.[57]

Physical Examination   A medical examination may be included in the selection process. There are five main reasons for requiring one. The exam can be used to determine that the applicant qualifies for the *physical requirements* of the position and to discover any *medical limitations* that should be taken into account in placing the applicant. The exam will also establish a *record and baseline* of the applicant's health for the purpose of future insurance or compensation claims. The examination can, by identifying health problems, also reduce *absenteeism and accidents* and, of course, detect *communicable diseases* that may be unknown to the applicant. In large firms, the exam is usually performed by the employer's medical department. Smaller employers retain the services of consulting physicians to perform such exams, which are paid for by the employer.

All medical information should be retained by the examining physican, never placed in employees' HR files. Under human rights legislation, a person with a disability can't be rejected for a job if he or she is otherwise qualified and could perform the job functions with reasonable accommodation. In addition, a medical exam is only permitted during the period between the written job offer and commencement of work. If used, medical exams must be required of all applicants for the job in question.

While an interviewer may ask a candidate if he or she has any disability-related needs that would require accommodation, the focus must be on the type of accommodation the employer might be expected to provide. Companies have no right to request information regarding the nature of a candidate's disability, either from the applicant or the physician performing the medical examination. The physician should only be asked to indicate, in writing, whether or not the applicant is capable of performing the essential job duties, and if not, what type of accommodation might be required.

Drug Testing   The purpose of pre-employment drug testing, which is usually based on urinalysis, is to avoid hiring employees who would pose unnecessary risks to themselves or others; have an attendance problem; and/or perform below expectations.

The legal issues surrounding such testing are somewhat complex. Under human rights legislation, as with any other type of medical examination, pre-employment drug testing is only permitted after a written job offer has been extended. Until recently, it was the policy of most human rights commissions that employers must be able to demonstrate a bona fide occupational requirement in order to justify such testing. Based on the Toronto-Dominion Bank decision, which will be described shortly, it seems that blanket drug testing is not illegal, as long as test results are handled appropriately. Addiction to drugs or alcohol is considered to be a disability under federal human rights legislation, and in many provinces. Thus, to deny or terminate employment on the basis of a positive test could be construed as discrimination on the basis of disability.[58] As with any other disability, employers have a duty to accommodate employees with addiction problems, to the point of undue hardship. In other words, if drug testing is used as a screening device, it can only be used to assess whether or not accommodation might be required, such as referral to the firm's employee assistance program. This was clarified by the recent resolution of a protracted case involving the Toronto Dominion Bank:[59]

> *The Toronto Dominion Bank's drug-testing program was found to be legal under the federal human rights legislation, because potential employees are not denied employment nor current employees dismissed due to drug dependence, but instead are given every possible opportunity to overcome their addiction.*

What complicates the issue even further is the employer's obligations under health and safety legislation and in preventing negligent hiring.[60] Certainly, employers can legally discipline employees for being impaired on the job, with sanctions up to and including discharge. Where there is a bona fide occupational requirement, as in safety-sensitive positions, pre-employment and routine drug testing have been accepted by human rights commissions for a number of years. If an applicant refuses, he or she can be denied employment; a current employee refusing to undergo such testing can be dismissed. For example:[61]

> *An arbitrator upheld Canadian Pacific's decision to discharge a train conductor who refused to submit to a drug test. The individual concerned had been charged by the police with cultivation of marijuana and had a previous conviction for possession. The arbitrator ruled that the employer "was charged with the safe operation of a railroad" and had "a particular obligation to ensure that those employees responsible for the movement of trains perform their duties unimpaired by the effect of drugs."*

Legality notwithstanding, there is widespread opposition to drug testing in the workplace. The Canadian Civil Liberties Association has taken the stance that "no person should be required to share urine with a stranger" as a condition of employment.[62] The issue of invasion of privacy is at the root of much of the controversy. The other source of objection is the questionable accuracy of such testing:

- Urine sampling is considered by many to be an invasion of privacy, as well as degrading and intrusive. While the human rights commissions have adopted the position that if there is to be testing for the use of drugs, the test samples should be analyzed only for the purpose intended, to protect the privacy of the individual,[63] there is nothing to prevent an unscrupulous employer from performing other analyses, such as pregnancy tests for female candidates.

- While breathalyzers and blood tests for alcohol, like those given by police officers on the roadside to drivers suspected of being inebriated, do correlate closely with impairment levels, urine and blood tests for other drugs only indicate whether drug residues are present: They cannot measure impairment, habituation, or addiction.[64]

- Because drug tests cannot indicate whether the individual is impaired at the time the sample is provided, only the use of a substance during preceding days or weeks, the use of drugs during leisure hours may be identified through workplace drug testing, and yet have little or no relevance to the individual's job.[65]

- As with polygraphs, drug tests are not infallible. Some less expensive tests have been known to generate both false negative and false positive results. The accuracy of results is also affected by the professionalism of those processing the samples. In addition, some illegal substances do not register on commonly-used tests.

- The ingredients in a number of legal prescription and nonprescription medications can yield false positive results. Using inexpensive testing, for example, popular over-the-counter pain pills such as Advil and Nuprin can produce positive results for marijuana. To avoid this possibility, and in response to criticism about the highly-personal nature of urine analysis, some employers have turned to hair follicle testing.[66]

Thus, an employer's decision to use drug testing for pre-employment or monitoring purposes involves a delicate balancing of individual right to privacy against risk of liability.[67] Because such tests do not yield data about current impairment or usage level, and may be inaccurate, even an employer's pursuit of a healthy, unimpaired work force and safe working environment do not seem to justify drug testing. The good news is that relatively simple tests that demonstrate the extent of impairment are being developed for manual dexterity and hand-eye coordination, as well as tasks of an intellectual nature.[68] Hopefully, such tests will not only be far more effective in identifying impaired conditions than drug testing, they will also be far less invasive and controversial.

Small Business Applications

Testing

Just because a company is small doesn't mean it shouldn't engage in selection testing. Quite the opposite: hiring one or two mistakes may not be a big problem for a very large firm, but it could cause chaos in a small operation.

A number of tests are so easy to administer, they are particularly good for smaller firms. One is the Wonderlic Personnel Test. This easy-to-use test measures general cognitive ability. In the form of a four-page booklet, it takes less than 15 minutes to administer. The instructions are read to the candidate and then he or she is timed as he or she works

**Figure 7.9
Minimum Scores on
Wonderlic Personnel
Test for Various
Occupations**

Source: Wonderlic Personnel
Test Manual (Northfield, IL:
E.F. Wonderlic & Associates,
Inc., 1983), p. 6.

Position	No. of Questions Answered Correctly in 12 minutes
Administrator	30
Engineer	29
Accountant	28
Programmer	28
Supervisor/Manager	27
Management, Trainee	27
Field Repr. (Sales)	26
Sales Representative	26
Secretary	25
Accounting Clerk	25
Writer, News, etc.	25
Stenographer	24
Cashier	24
Bookkeeper	24
Foreperson	24
Drafting Technician	23
Receptionist	23
Office Worker, General	23
Lineworker, Utility	22
Teller	22
Word Processor	21
Clerk	21
Key Punch Operator	20
Police Officer	20
Skilled Tradesperson	20
File Clerk	19
Maintenance Person	18
Telephone Operator	18
General Labourer	17
Factory Worker, General	17
Skilled Labourer	17
Unskilled Labourer	16
Nurses Aide	15
Custodian	8

through the 50 problems on the two inside sheets. The person's test is then scored by totalling the number of correct answers. The person's score can next be compared to the minimum scores recommended for various occupations (**Figure 7.9**) to determine whether the person achieved the minimally acceptable score for the type of job in question.

A test like this can be useful to help identify people who are not up to the tasks required. However, care must be taken to avoid misuse. In the past, for instance, unnecessarily high cutoff scores were required by some employers for certain jobs, a tactic that, in effect, unfairly discriminated against some designated group members. Similarly, it would probably be neither fair nor wise to choose between two candidates who both exceeded the minimum score for a job by choosing the one with the higher score, since people of lower ability but higher motivation will often outperform those with higher ability but less motivation. Therefore, tests like the Wonderlic are only useful as supplements to a comprehensive screening program. The Wonderlic is available to employers, business owners, and human resources managers with or without previous training in selection testing.[1]

The Predictive Index is another example of a test that is used by large companies, but is equally valuable for small ones, because of its ease of administration and interpretation. The index measures personality traits, drives, and behaviours that are work related—in particular, dominance (ranging from submissive to arrogant), extroversion (ranging from withdrawn to gregarious), and patience (ranging from volatile to lethargic). The Predictive Index test is a two-sided sheet on which candidates or current employees check off the words that best describe them (such as "helpful" or "persistent"). The test is then easily scored with the use of a scoring template.

The Predictive Index provides valuable information about the candidate. For example, for a job involving painstaking attention to details, a candidate who rates toward the careless end of the range would be totally unsuitable. For an exceedingly boring job, preference might be given to candidates who are patient. Each candidate taking the Predictive Index will probably have his or her own unique pattern of responses. However, the Predictive Index program includes 15 standard patterns that are typical. For example, there is the "social interest" pattern, representing a person who is generally unselfish, congenial, persuasive, patient, and fairly unassuming. This is a person who would be good with people and a good interviewer, for instance.

Computerized testing programs like those described earlier in this chapter can be especially useful for small employers. For example, when hiring office help smaller employers typically depend on informal tests of keyboarding and filing. A better way to proceed is to use a program like the Minnesota Clerical Assessment Battery published by Assessment Systems Corp. This program runs on a PC. It includes a keyboarding test, proofreading test, filing test, business vocabulary test, business math test, and clerical knowledge test. It is therefore useful for evaluating the knowledge and skills involved in various office positions, including secretary, clerk, bookkeeper, and filing clerk. Because it is computerized, administration and scoring are simplified and each test can be adapted to the particular position being applied for.[2]

1. Information and tests may be obtained from E.F. Wonderlic and Associates. Inc., 820 Frontage Rd., Northfield. Il 60093. (Telephone: (312) 446-8900).
2. Assessment Systems Corportion may be reached at 2233 University Avenue, Suite 440, St. Paul, MN 55114. (Telephone: (612) 647-9220).

Step Four: The Selection Interview

selection interview
A procedure designed to predict future job performance on the basis of applicants' oral responses to oral inquiries.

The interview is one of the most common and popular devices used for selecting job applicants, used by upward of 99 percent of Canadian companies.[69] Whether candidates are interviewed prior to or following testing varies greatly. The **selection interview** involves a process of two-way communication between the interviewee(s) and the interviewer(s). It can be defined as "… a procedure designed to predict future job performance on the basis of applicants' oral responses to oral inquiries."[70]

Interviews are considered one of the most important aspects of the selection process and generally have a major impact on both job applicants and interviewers. Interviews significantly influence job applicants' views about the job and organization. Interviews enable the employer to fill in any gaps in the information provided on application forms and résumés and supplement the results of any tests administered. They may also reveal entirely new types of information.

A major reason for the selection interview's popularity is that it meets a number of objectives of both interviewer and interviewee. Interviewer objectives include:[71]

- assessing applicants' qualifications
- observing certain aspects of applicants' behaviour, such as communication skills, mannerisms, self-confidence, and interpersonal skills
- gathering information about applicants that will help to predict future performance (such as how well the applicants will perform and how long they will remain in the organization)
- communicating information about the job to the applicants
- promoting the organization and highlighting its attractiveness
- determining how well the applicants would fit into the organization.

Typical objectives of job applicants include:[72]
- presenting a positive image of themselves
- selling their skills and marketing their positive attributes to the interviewer(s)
- collecting information about the job and the organization so that they can make an informed decision about the job, the work environment, and career opportunities.

Types of Interviews   Interviews can be classified in four ways according to (1) degree of structure; (2) purpose; (3) content; and (4) the way the interview is administered. In turn, the main types of interviews used in selection—structured, unstructured, mixed, situational, behavioural, sequential, panel, stress, computerized, and videotaped or videoconferenced—can each be classified in one or more of these four ways.

The Structure of the Interview   First, interviews can be classified according to the degree to which they are structured. In an **unstructured or nondirective interview,** questions are asked as they come to mind. There is generally no set format to follow, and the interview can take various directions. While questions can be specified in advance, they usually are not, and there is seldom a formalized guide for scoring the quality of each answer. Interviewees for the same job thus may or may not be asked the same or similar questions, and the interview's unstructured nature allows the interviewer to ask questions based on the candidate's last statements and to pursue points of interest as they develop. While extremely friendly, unstructured interviews lack reliability.

The interview can also be structured. In the classical **structured or directive interview,** the questions and acceptable responses are specified in advance and the responses are rated for appropriateness of content.[73] In practice, however, most structured interviews do not involve specifying and rating responses in advance. Instead, each candidate is asked a series of pre-determined, job-related questions. Because all applicants are consistently asked the specified questions by the interviewers with whom they meet, structured interviews are generally more valid and reliable than any other interviewing techniques. Structured interviews can also help individuals who may be less comfortable interviewing to ask questions and conduct useful interviews. On the other hand, structured interviews don't always leave the flexibility to pursue points of interest as they develop. The end result may be an interview that seems quite mechanical to all concerned.

Between these two extremes is the **mixed (semi-structured) interview**, which involves a combination of pre-set (structured) questions based on the job description and specification, and a series of candidate-specific questions based on information provided on the application form and/or résumé. The structured questions provide a base of information that allows comparisons between candidates, and the candidate-specific questions make the interview more conversational.

Generally, to ensure that all questions are focused on job-related criteria, even the candidate-specific questions are written down in advance. A realistic

unstructured interview
An unstructured, conversational-style interview. The interviewer pursues points of interest as they come up in response to questions.

structured interview
An interview following a set sequence of questions.

mixed (semi-structured) interview
An interview format that combines the structured and unstructured techniques.

approach that yields comparable answers and in-depth insights, the mixed interview format is extremely popular.

The Purpose of the Interview   Employee-related interviews can also be classified according to their purpose. Thus, as noted earlier, a *selection interview* is a type of interview designed to predict future job performance on the basis of applicants' oral responses to oral inquiries. A **stress interview** is a special type of selection interview in which the applicant is made uncomfortable by a series of sometimes rude questions. The aim is to help identify sensitive applicants and assess degree of tolerance for stress.

In the typical stress interview, the applicant is made uncomfortable by being put on the defensive by a series of frank (and often discourteous) questions from the interviewer. The interviewer might first probe for weaknesses in the applicant's background, such as a job that the applicant left under questionable circumstances. Having identified these, the interviewer can then focus on them, hoping to get the candidate to lose his or her composure. Thus, a candidate for customer relations manager who obligingly mentions having had four jobs in the past two years might be told that frequent job changes reflect irresponsible and immature behaviour. If the applicant then responds with a reasonable explanation of why the job changes were necessary, another topic might be pursued. On the other hand, if the formerly tranquil applicant reacts explosively with anger and disbelief, this might be taken as a symptom of low tolerance for stress.

The stress approach can be a good way to identify hypersensitive applicants who might be expected to overreact to mild criticism with anger and abuse. On the other hand, the stress interview's invasive and ethically-questionable nature demands that the interviewer be both skilled in its use and sure that a thick skin and an ability to handle stress are really required for the job. This is definitely not an approach for amateur interrogators or for those without the skills required to keep the interview under control.

The Content of the Interview   Interviews can also be classified according to the content of their questions. A **situational interview** is one in which the questions focus on the individual's ability to project what his or her behaviour would be in a given situation.[74] The underlying premise is that intentions predict behaviour. For example, a candidate for a supervisor's position might be asked how he or she would respond to an employee coming to work late three days in a row. The interview can be both *structured and situational,* with predetermined questions requiring the candidate to project what his or her behaviour would be. In a structured situational interview the applicant could be evaluated, say, on his or her choice between letting the employee off with a warning versus suspending him or her for one week.

The behavioural interview is gaining in popularity.[75] In a **behavioural interview** a situation is described and interviewees are asked how they have behaved *in the past* in such a situation.[76] Thus, while situational interviews ask interviewees to describe how they *would* react to a situation today or tomorrow, the behavioural interview asks interviewees to describe how they *did* react to situations in the past, giving specific examples.[77] The underlying assumption is that the best predictor of future performance is past performance in similar circumstances.

Finally, *psychological interviews* are interviews, conducted by a psychologist, in which questions are intended to assess personal traits such as dependability.[78] Psychological interviews are often included in assessment centre evaluation.

The interview may use situational, job-related, or behavioural questions and be either structured or unstructured. Psychological interviews generally have a significant unstructured element.

stress interview
An interview in which the applicant is made uncomfortable by a series of often rude questions. This technique helps identify hypersensitive applicants and assess degree of tolerance for stress.

situational interview
A series of job-related questions that focus on how the candidate would behave in a given situation.

behavioural interview
A series of job-related questions that focus on relevant past job-related behaviours.

Administering the Interview   Interviews can also be classified based on how they are administered: one-on-one or by a panel of interviewers; sequentially or all at once; and computerized, audiotaped, videotaped, videoconferenced, teleconferenced, or conducted entirely in person. For example, most interviews are administered *one-on-one*. As the name implies, two people meet alone and one interviews the other by seeking oral responses to oral inquiries. Most selection processes are sequential. In a *sequential interview* the applicant is interviewed by several persons in sequence before a selection decision is made. In an *unstructured sequential interview* each interviewer may look at the applicant from his or her own point of view, ask different questions, and form an independent opinion of the candidate. On the other hand, in a structured sequential or **serialized interview,** each interviewer rates the candidate on a standard evaluation form, and the ratings are compared before the hiring decision is made.[79]

serialized interview
An interview in which the applicant is interviewed sequentially by several persons and each rates the applicant on a standard form.

panel interview
An interview in which a group of interviewers questions the applicant.

A **panel interview** involves the candidate being interviewed simultaneously by a group (or panel) of interviewers (rather than sequentially). The group structure has several advantages. A sequential interview often has candidates cover basically the same ground over and over again with each interviewer. The panel interview, on the other hand, allows each interviewer to pick up on the candidate's answers, much as reporters do in press conferences. This approach may elicit deeper and more meaningful responses than are normally produced by a series of one-on-one interviews. On the other hand, some candidates find panel interviews more stressful and they may actually inhibit responses. An even more stressful variant is the *mass interview*. In a mass interview several candidates are interviewed simultaneously by a panel. Here the panel poses a problem to be solved and then sits back and watches which candidate takes the lead in formulating an answer.

The panel interview provides an effective way of allowing interviewers to follow up on each other's questions.

Increasingly, interviews aren't administered by people at all but are computerized, teleconferenced, or videoconferenced. A **computerized selection interview** is one in which a job candidate's oral and/or computerized responses are obtained in response to computerized oral or written questions and/or situations. The basic idea is generally to present the applicant with a series of questions regarding his or her background, experience, education, skills, knowledge, and work attitudes—specific questions that relate to the job for which the person has applied.[80] In a typical computerized interview, the questions are presented in a multiple-choice format, one at a time, and the applicant is expected to respond to the questions on the computer screen by pressing a key corresponding to his or her desired response. For example, a sample interview question for a person applying for a job as a retail store clerk might be:[81]

computerized selection interview
An interview technique involving a computer, rather than a person. A candidate's oral and/or computerized responses to computer-generated oral or written questions and/or situations are obtained and assessed.

How would your supervisor rate your customer service skills?

A. Outstanding

B. Above average

C. Average

D. Below average

E. Poor

Questions on a computerized interview like this come in rapid sequence and require concentration on the applicant's part.[82] The typical computerized interview then measures the response time to each question. A delay in answering certain questions such as "Can you be trusted?" can flag a potential problem.

Computer-based interviews are generally used to reject totally unacceptable candidates and to select those who will move on to a face-to-face interview.

www.peoplesoft.com
HR Software

They can be very advantageous. Systems like those now online at Great Western Bank of California substantially reduce the amount of time managers devote to inteviewing what often turn out to be unacceptable candidates.[83] Applicants are reportedly more honest with computers than they would be with people, presumably because computers are not judgmental.[84]

The computer can also be sneaky: If an applicant takes longer than average to answer a question like, "Have you ever been caught stealing?" he or she may be summarily screened out or at least questioned more deeply in that area by a human interviewer. Several of the interpersonal interview problems we'll discuss later in this chapter, such as making a snap judgment about the interviewee based

Information Technology and HR
Computer Applications in Interviewing:
The Computer-Aided Interview

When Bonnie Dunn, 20 years old, tried out for a customer service representative's job at Great Western Bank in Chatsworth, California, she faced a lineup of tough customers.

One young woman sputtered contradictory instructions about depositing a cheque and then blew her top when the transaction wasn't handled fast enough. Another customer had an even shorter fuse. "You people are unbelievably slow," he said.

Both tough customers appeared on a computer screen, as part of a 20-minute automated job interview. Ms. Dunn was seated in front of a PC, responding via a colour touch-screen and a microphone. She was tested on making change and sales skills, as well as keeping cool in tense situations.

When applicants sit down facing the computer at Great Western's bank branches, they hear it say, "Welcome to the interactive assessment aid." The computer doesn't understand what applicants say at that point, although it records their comments to be evaluated later. To begin the interview, applicants touch a label on the screen, eliciting an ominous foreword: "We'll be keeping track of how long it takes you and how many mistakes you make. Accuracy is more important than speed."

First, the computer tests the applicant on money skills, asking him or her to cash a cheque for $192.18, including at least three five-dollar bills and two dollars in quarters. Then, when an angry customer appears on the screen, candidates are expected to grab the microphone and mollify him. Later, a bank official who listens to the recorded interviews gives applicants five points for maintaining a friendly tone of voice, plus up to 15 points for apologizing, promising to solve the customer's problem, and, taking a cue from the screen, suggesting that in the future he use the bank's deposit-only line.

The touchy young woman on the screen is tougher. Speaking rapidly, she says she wants to cash a $150 cheque, get $40 in cash, and put $65 in savings and the rest in chequing. As an applicant struggles to sort that out, she quickly adds, "No, it has to be $50 in chequing because I just wrote a cheque this morning." If the applicant then touches a label on the screen that says "?", the woman fumes, "How many times do I have to tell you?"

Great Western reports that its computer-aided interviewing system has been successful. Not only has it dramatically reduced the amount of useless interviewing managers have to do of unacceptable candidates, but candidates hired by the program were reportedly 26% less likely to quit or be fired within 90 days of hiring. (This is partly because the computer tells applicants what the job really involves, something a candidate might be reluctant to ask a person for fear of appearing negative.)◆

Source: This is quoted or paraphrased from William Bulkeley, "Replaced by Technology: Job Interviews," *The Wall Street Journal* (August 22, 1994), pp. B1, B7.

on his or her appearance, are also obviously avoided with this nonpersonal interviewing approach.[85] On the other hand, the mechanical nature of computer-aided interviews can leave applicants with the impression that the prospective employer is rather impersonal. A description of a relatively sophisticated actual computer-based interview is presented in the Information Technology and HR box.

There are some other technology-based alternatives. **Videotaped or audiotaped interviews** involve a combination of in-person and technology-based techniques. First, a traditional face-to-face interview is conducted and taped (with the consent of the interviewee). At the completion of the interview, the job candidate is assessed by the interviewer. The videotape or audiotape is then taken to the company for review by another interviewer or interviewers, including the hiring manager. Those conducting such a review assess the applicant independently, and the assessments are then pooled to arrive at a final candidate evaluation.

There are also two entirely technology-based strategies, which permit "real-time" interviews: **teleconferencing** and **videoconferencing.**

Interest in technology-based alternatives to traditional face-to-face interviews is related to the expansion of national and international markets, satellite or off-site offices, the increasing frequency of home-based employees, increasing competition, and decreasing budgets. All of these factors have contributed to the need for more cost-effective strategies. Alternatives that enable organizations to conduct "long-distance" interviews can save time, money, and effort.[86]

Before considering such interview strategies, employers need to know more about interviewer and applicant comfort level; reliability, validity, and fairness of results; and accessibility. While there has not been a great deal of research to answer such questions, initial indications look promising:[87]

> *In a 1997 study, K.G. Kroeck and K.O. Magnusen assessed videoconferenced college recruitment interviews. They found that while the employers involved preferred face-to-face interviews, they generally believed that they were able to gather appropriate information from the students and to screen out less-qualified candidates. The students participating also preferred traditional interviews, but reported being even more comfortable with the process than the employers did. Both employers and students identified access to a wider pool (of applicants and employers, respectively,) as a major benefit. Interviewer rating errors and patterns were found to be comparable to those in traditional face-to-face interviewers. If anything, the halo effect (the tendency to judge those creating a favourable first impression more positively overall) was reduced.*

> *In another study, conducted by Ellis Associates, a Toronto-based consulting firm, audiotaped and traditional interviews were used in conjunction with one another, and the results compared. It should be noted that all of those involved in the evaluation of candidates had successfully completed an intensive interviewer-training workshop. The evaluations of the seventy interview audiotapes by an independent panel, who did not have any personal contact with the candidates, were almost identical to those of the face-to-face interviewers. In fact, the average total scores for the in-person and audiotaped interview evaluations differed, on average, by only a half point, on a 30-point scale. These results indicate that the evaluations of trained interviewers can provide reliable, fair, and valid information, even when the interviewers do not have direct, face-to-face contact with the candidates.*

> *Aggressive marketing and increased demand mean that even the smallest organization can now easily access video and teleconference services at a reasonable cost. Public videoconference room rentals range from about $60 to $200 per hour for*

videotaped/audiotaped interview
An interview technique that involves both an in-person and technology-based component. A face-to-face interview is conducted and taped. The video or audiotape is then independently assessed by interviewers who have not met the candidate.

videoconferenced/teleconferenced interview
An interview technique that is entirely technology-based. Using a combination of video and audio equipment, or audio equipment alone (in the case of a teleconference), interviews are conducted with candidates who are physically distant from both conference location and interviewer.

each conference site. In some cases, this fee includes the cost of professional guidance, setup, and troubleshooting. In others, the administration fee is extra. The cost of the videoconference itself is generally charged on a per-minute-basis, based on a combination of long-distance telephone rates and the speed of transmission.

One of the larger telecommunications companies advertises a one-hour videoconference between Toronto and Montreal at about $272. A three-way connection between London (Ontario), Toronto and Ottawa would cost about $610.

How Useful Are Interviews?   The ironic thing about interviews is that while they're used by virtually all employers, the statistical evidence regarding their validity is actually very mixed. Much of the earlier research gave selection interviews low marks in terms of reliability and validity.[88] However, recent studies indicate that the key to an interview's usefulness is the manner in which it is administered. Specifically, the following conclusions are warranted based on one recent study of interview validity:

With respect to predicting job performance, situational interviews yield a higher mean validity than do behavioural interviews, which in turn yield a higher mean validity than do psychological interviews.[89]

Structured interviews, regardless of content, are more valid than unstructured interviews for predicting job performance.[90]

Interviewing and the Law   An interview is a selection procedure; interviewers must therefore avoid asking questions that would violate human rights legislation. Questions cannot be asked about candidates' marital status, child care arrangements, ethnic background, and workers' compensation history, for example.

Failing to treat all interviewees in the same manner can also be discriminatory. An interviewer cannot ask only the female applicants for factory positions to demonstrate their lifting abilities, for example, or question female sales applicants about their willingness to travel, but not male candidates. Cutting short an interview based on preconceived notions about the gender or race of the ideal candidate would also be discriminatory.

A helpful phrase to keep in mind when designing interview questions is: "This job requires..." Interviewers who focus on the job description and job specification can gather all of the information required to assess applicants, without infringing on the candidates' legal rights.

Common Interviewing Mistakes   There are several common interviewing mistakes that undermine an interview's usefulness. We'll explain these next, since knowledge of the mistakes is the first step in avoiding them. In the following section, we'll discuss how such errors can be avoided.

Poor Planning   Many selection interviews are simply not carefully planned. With their hectic schedules, HR specialists sometimes conduct interviews without having prepared written questions in advance. Supervisors and managers from other departments often see job applicants relatively infrequently. If inadequately trained in interviewing techniques, they may not know how to plan interviews or understand the importance of doing so.[91]

An interview will be unsuccessful if the interviewer does not have specific selection criteria in mind or has failed to plan strategies for assessing the criteria chosen. Lack of planning often leads to a relatively unstructured interview, in which whatever comes up gets discussed. Since the end result may be little or no cross-candidate job-related information, the less structured the interview is, the less reliable and valid candidate evaluation will be.[92]

Snap Judgments   One of the most consistent findings in the interviewing literature is that interviewers tend to jump to conclusions—make snap judgments—about candidates during the first few minutes of the interview, or even before the interview begins based on test scores or résumé data. For example, one study showed that interviewers' access to candidates' test scores biased the interviewer's assessment of the candidate.[93] Another researcher estimated that in 85 percent of the cases, interviewers had made up their minds about candidates before the interview began on the basis of applicants' application forms and personal appearance. Findings like these underscore that it's important for a candidate to start off on the right foot with the interviewer.

Negative Emphasis   Jumping to conclusions is especially troublesome when the information the interviewer has about the candidate is negative. For example, in one study the researchers found that interviewers who previously received unfavourable reference letters about applicants gave the applicants less credit for past successes and held them more personally responsible for past failures. Furthermore, the interviewers' final decisions to accept or reject applicants were always tied to what they expected of the applicants based on the references, quite aside from their interview performance.[94]

In other words, interviewers seem to have a consistent negative bias. They are generally more influenced by unfavourable than favourable information about the candidate. Also, their impressions are much more likely to change from favourable to unfavourable than vice versa. A common interviewing mistake is to make the interview itself mostly a search for negative information. In a sense, therefore, most interviews are probably loaded against the applicant. An applicant who is initially rated highly could easily end up with a low rating, given the fact that unfavourable information tends to carry more weight in the interview. An interviewee who starts out with a poor rating will find it hard to overcome that first bad impression.[95]

Halo Effect   It is also possible, though, for a positive initial impression to distort an interviewer's rating of a candidate, such that subsequent information is judged with a positive bias. This is known as the halo effect. An applicant who has a pleasant smile and firm handshake, for example, may be judged positively before the interview even begins. Having gained that positive initial impression, the interviewer may not seek contradictory information when listening to the candidate's answers to the questions posed.

Poor Knowledge of the Job   Interviewers who don't know precisely what the job entails and what sort of candidate is best suited for it, usually make their decisions based on incorrect stereotypes about what a good applicant is. They then erroneously match interviewees with their incorrect stereotypes. On the other hand, interviewers who have a clear understanding of what the job entails conduct more effective interviews.

Pressure to Hire   Pressure to hire also undermines an interview's usefulness, since interviewers often lower their standards in such situations. In one study, a group of managers was told to assume that they were behind in their recruiting schedule. A second group was told that they were ahead of schedule. Those "behind" evaluated the same recruits much more highly than did those "ahead."[96]

www.globalx.net&hrd
HRDC—Occupation.Career
Information Branch

contrast or candidate-order error
An error of judgment on the part of the interviewer due to interviewing one or more very good or very bad candidates just before the interview in question.

Contrast (Candidate-Order) Error Contrast or candidate-order error means that the order in which applicants are seen can affect how they are rated. In one study, managers were asked to evaluate a candidate who was "just average" after first evaluating several "unfavourable" candidates. The average candidate was evaluated more favourably than he might otherwise have been, since, in contrast to the unfavourable candidates, the average one looked better than he actually was. In some studies, only a small part of the applicant's rating was based on his or her actual potential. Most of the rating was based on the effect of having followed very favourable or unfavourable candidates.[97]

Influence of Nonverbal Behaviour Interviewers are also influenced by the applicant's nonverbal behaviour. For example, several studies have shown that applicants who demonstrate greater amounts of eye contact, head moving, smiling, and other similar nonverbal behaviours are rated higher. In fact, these nonverbal behaviours often account for more than 80 percent of the applicant's rating.[98] This is of particular concern since nonverbal behaviour is tied to ethnicity and cultural background.

An applicant's attractiveness and gender also play a role.[99] In one study, researchers found that whether attractiveness was a help or a hindrance to job applicants depended on the gender of the applicant and the nature of the job. Attractiveness was consistently an advantage for male applicants seeking white-collar jobs. Yet attractiveness was advantageous for female interviewees only when the job was nonmanagerial. When the position was managerial, there was a tendency for a woman's attractiveness to work against her in terms of recommendation for hiring and suggested starting salary. The following Diversity Counts box provides another example.

Telegraphing Some interviewers are so anxious to fill a job that they help the applicant respond correctly to their questions by *telegraphing* the expected answer.[100] An obvious example might be a question like: "This job calls for handling a lot of stress. You can do that, can't you?"

Diversity Counts
Dressing for the Interview

It will not surprise many women to hear that the way they dress can alter interviewers' selection decisions. In one study, 77 HR managers attending a conference evaluated videotapes of women interviewing for management positions. The women were dressed in one of four styles ranging from a light beige dress in a soft fabric (style 1) to a bright aqua suit with a short belted jacket (style 2) to a beige tailored suit with a blazer jacket (style 3) to "the most masculine" outfit, a dark navy, tailored suit and a white blouse with an angular collar (style 4). A comparison of the hiring recommendations associated with each style suggests that, up to a point, the more masculine the style, the more favourable the hiring recommendations were.

Specifically, applicants received more favourable hiring recommendations as style masculinity increased from style 1 to style 3. However, applicants wearing style 4 (the most masculine style) were turned down. We might surmise the outfit was considered "too masculine" by the interviewers. The findings may not apply to every individual. However, for what it's worth, the researchers suggest that it might be better for women to risk dressing "too masculine" than "too feminine" when applying for management jobs.◆

Source: Sandra Forsythe, Mary Frances Drake, and Charles Cox, "Influence of Applicants' Dress on Interviewers' Selection Decisions," *Journal of Applied Psychology* 70, no. 2 (1985), pp. 374–8.

The telegraphing isn't always so obvious. For example, interviewers' positive first impressions of candidates (from examining application forms and test scores) tend to be linked to use of a more positive interview and vocal style. This can translate into sending subtle cues (like a smile) regarding what answer is being sought.[101]

Too Much/Too Little Talking   Too much or too little guidance on the interviewer's part is another common mistake. Some interviewers let the applicant dominate the interview to the point where too few substantive questions are pursued. At the other extreme, some interviewers stifle the applicant by not giving the person sufficient time to answer questions.[102] The candiate should do 80 percent of the talking.

Playing Attorney or Psychologist   Since the interviewer often plays the role of gatekeeper in determining whether or not the interviewee gets a job, there's sometimes a tendency for interviewers to misuse their power by playing attorney or psychologist. For example, while it's smart to be alert for inconsistencies in applicants' responses, it's important to guard against turning the interview into a game of "gotcha" in which the interviewer derives pleasure from ferreting out and pouncing on interviewees' inconsistencies. Also inappropriate is playing psychologist, probing for hidden meanings in everything the applicants say.[103]

Designing an Effective Interview   Problems like those just described can be avoided by designing and conducting an effective interview, a topic to which we'll now turn.

Since structured situational and behavioural questions are usually the most valid for predicting job performance, conducting an effective interview ideally starts with designing a series of job-related questions that are consistently asked of all applicants for a particular job.[104] Usually a committee of persons familiar with the job develops questions based on the actual job duties and job specification. They then plan a few candidate-specific questions, to allow for probing, and prevent the interview from becoming too mechanical in nature. The procedure consists of the following steps, the first two of which should occur prior to recruitment:[105]

Step 1. Deciding Who Will Be Involved in the Selection Process and Developing Selection Criteria   If a panel interview is being used, the team members should be selected as soon as the job opening is identified, since they will be involved in developing the selection criteria and interview questions. Panels generally consist of three to six members. The immediate supervisor is almost always included, as well as a member of the HR department. The current incumbent (if he or she is leaving the firm on good terms or is being transferred or promoted), peers, reporting employees, and other supervisors with whom the individual would frequently interact, if selected for the job, may also be included on the interview team.

Once selected, the panel members must develop selection criteria. This requires a thorough examination of the job description and job specification. If there is no job description and job specification, or if the information is outdated, job analysis should be performed. This step should occur prior to recruitment, since without accurate information about the job and the essential human qualifications required to perform it, it is impossible to plan an appropriate recruitment campaign, let alone an effective, legally-defensible interview.

Specifying selection criteria involves clarifying and weighting the various pieces of information assembled through perusal of the job description and job specification, and discussion among the interview-team members, especially those most familiar with the job and coworkers.

Step 2. Specifying Musts and Wants and Weighting the Wants

Once agreed upon, the selection criteria should be divided into two categories: musts and wants.[106] This step should also occur prior to recruitment. **Must criteria** are those that are absolutely essential for the job, include a measurable standard of acceptability or are absolute, and can be screened initially on paper. There tend to be relatively few must criteria for any job; often only two: a specific level of education (or an equivalent attained through a combination of education and work experience) and a minimum amount of prior, related work experience. Being a journeyperson in a trade, having a licence to practice, or having a current certificate of competence are other possible must criteria, as long as they are bona fide job requirements. The must criteria should be listed as mandatory on the job posting and in any advertising used. During the initial screening process, candidates whose résumés and/or application forms indicate that they lack even one of the must criteria should be eliminated from the competition. (Note: All must qualifications should be verified for finalist candidates. Applicants may be requested to provide an original transcript, diploma, degree, or certificate, for example, and prior work experience can be confirmed with former employers.)

The **want criteria** are those that have been culled from the must list. They include skills and abilities that are not readily measurable, such as leadership ability, teamwork skills, and enthusiasm; as well as qualifications that are desirable but not critical, such as knowledge of the specific word processing software package used at the firm. A numerical scale can be used to weight these criteria, with 10 being the highest ranking and 1 being the lowest. Those that are critically important (but couldn't be included as musts because they weren't measurable or absolute, or because they couldn't be screened on paper) can be given a weight of 10. Excellent oral communication skills might be an example, if screening for a salesperson. If employment equity considerations are important to the firm, designated group member status, screened on the basis of information provided in the voluntarily-completed section of the application form requesting this information, can be given a weighting of 2 or 3.

Step 3. Determining Assessment Strategies and Developing an Evaluation Form

Once the must and want criteria have been identified, appropriate strategies for learning about each should be identified. For example, word processing skills are best assessed through hands-on testing, rather than interview questions; and oral communication skills can be judged on the basis of interview performance, not the response to a specific question. For some qualifications, especially those that are critically important, the team may decide to use several assessment strategies. For example, each candidate for a team leader position might be asked behavioural questions seeking specific examples of situations in which leadership skills have been demonstrated; such skills might also be assessed through situational questions; references could be questioned carefully about the leadership skills demonstrated at previous places of employment, in school, or as a volunteer; and each candidate's skills might also be assessed through a written test or an assessment centre.

Once all want criteria have been agreed upon and weighted, they become the basis for candidate comparison and evaluation, as illustrated in **Figure 7.10.** During each step of the selection process, including verification of references, information about each of the want criteria should be gathered and recorded. At the end, each candidate can be assessed and given an overall score by adding his or her score on each of the wants. (Note: Using this scoring process, designated

must criteria
Requirements that are absolutely essential for the job, include a measurable standard of acceptability or are absolute, and can be screened initially on paper.

want criteria
Those criteria that have been culled from the must list. They represent qualifications that are not readily measurable or which cannot be screened on paper, as well as those that are highly desirable but not critical.

www.positionwatch.com
Job Information

Worksheet—Comparison of Candidates

Criteria		A Smith		B Brown		C Yuill	
Alternatives							
Must		Info	Go/No	Info	Go/No	Info	Go/No
Education — Office Admin. diploma or equivalent experience (3 years clerical/secretarial experience)		Office Admin. Diploma	Go	Office Admin. Diploma	Go	No Diploma, 1 year related experience	No Go
Experience — At least 2 years' secretarial/clerical experience		3 years' experience	Go	2 years' experience	Go		

Must	Wt.	Info	Sc.	Wt. Sc.	Info	Sc.	Wt. Sc.	Info	Sc.	Wt. Sc.
Keyboarding/Word Processing	10	Word Processing Test	9	90	Word Processing Test	10	100			
Good Oral Communication	9	Interview Assessment	9	81	Interview Assessment	9	81			
Good Spelling/Grammar	9	Test Results	8	72	Test Results	9	81			
Organizational Ability	9	Reference Checking/Simulation/Interview Questions	8	72	Reference Checking/Simulation/Interview Questions	9	81			
Initiative	8	Interview Questions/Simulation/Reference Checking	7	49	Interview Questions/Simulation/Reference Checking	8	64			
High Ethical Standards	7	Interview Questions/Simulation/Reference Checking	7	49	Interview Questions/Simulation/Reference Checking	7	49			
Shorthand Skills (or speed writing)	4	Interview Question & Test Results	4	16	Interview Question & Test Results	0	0			
Designated Group Member; Other than White Female	2	Application Form	2	4	Application Form	0	0			
				448			456			

TOP CANDIDATE

Figure 7.10
Worksheet—Comparison of Candidates for a Secretarial Position

group member status will only become a deciding factor if two candidates are equally qualified. That's what employment equity is supposed to mean!).

Step 4. Developing Structured Interview Questions For those skills, abilities, and qualities that can be assessed through specific questions, structured open-ended questions should be developed. Most of the questions should be situational and behavioural. **Situational questions** pose a hypothetical situation, which could actually occur on the job in question, and ask candidates how they would respond. For example, "What would you do if the machine suddenly began heating up?" **Behavioural questions** request specific examples of past behaviour. For example, "Tell me about a time when you handled a difficult customer. Please be specific." Job-knowledge and worker-requirements questions should also be included. **Job-knowledge questions** assess whether candidates have the basic knowledge needed to perform the job. Often they deal with technical aspects of the job. **Worker-requirements or willingness questions** gauge the applicants' motivation and willingness to perform under prevailing working conditions. Examples include questions about willingness to work shifts, travel, or relocate.

The structured questions will be asked of all candidates, and should be word-processed in advance, with space left between each for interviewer's notes.

Step 5. Developing Candidate-Specific Questions Next, a few open-ended, job-related questions that are candidate-specific should be planned, based on each candidate's résumé and application form. Examples might include: "What specific duties did you perform at SaskPower that would be transferable to the job for which you are applying here?", and "You indicated on your résumé that you were President of the Students' Council when you were in high school. What knowledge or skills did you acquire through this position that would be beneficial in performing the job here?"

The candidate-specific questions should also be word-processed in advance and added to the bottom of the interview questionnaire for each candidate. The questionnaires for each candidate should then be copied for each member of the interview team.

Conducting an Effective Interview Prior to the interviews, each panel member should review the applicants' application forms and résumés, as well as the interview questions planned in advance. Agreement should be reached on the procedure that will be followed. Sometimes each member of the team asks a question in turn; in other situations, only one member of the team asks questions and the others serve as observers. One member of the team should be designated to greet each candidate and introduce him or her to the other team members. A comfortable, quiet, non-stressful setting should be selected. Sitting around a large table in a conference room is much more appropriate and far less stressful than having all panel members seated across from the candidate behind a table or desk, which forms both a physical and psychological barrier.

During the interview, all panel members should keep notes. At the end, candidates should be invited to ask questions and the interviewers should explain the next steps in the selection process. Immediately following each interview, the applicant should be rated by each panel member independently. This information should not be shared until all steps in the selection process, including reference checking, have been completed.

Whether or not time is taken to develop a semi-structured panel interview, there are a number of steps involved in every effective interview:[107]

situational questions
Hypothetical questions designed to elicit from candidates how they would respond to particular work situations.

behavioural questions
Questions requesting specific examples of past job-related behaviour.

job-knowledge questions
Questions that assess whether candidates have the basic knowledge required to perform the job.

worker-requirements or willingness questions
Questions designed to gauge the applicants' motivation and willingness to perform under prevailing working conditions.

Planning the Interview   Interviews must be planned in advance. First, the job description and job specification should be reviewed to establish the skills, knowledge, and other qualifications required of the ideal candidate. Next, each candidate's application form and résumé should be perused, and any areas that are vague or that may indicate strengths or weaknesses should be noted so that questions may be asked about them. Job-related questions, most of which are behavioural and situational, should be written down prior to the interview, with space between each for taking notes.

The location in which the interview will take place should also be planned. Ideally, interviews should be held in a private, comfortable setting, and no telephone calls or interruptions permitted.

The rapport established with a job applicant not only puts the person at ease; it also reflects the company's attitude toward its public.

Establishing Rapport   The main reason for an interview is to find out as much as possible about the candidate's fit with the job specifications, something that is difficult to do if the individual is tense and nervous. The candidate should be greeted in a friendly manner and put at ease. Generally, easy, noncontroversial, questions are asked at the beginning of an interview—perhaps about the weather, ease in finding the interview site, or the candidate's hobbies and interests. A few minutes spent on questions like these can help to reduce the applicant's tension.

As a rule, all applicants—even unsolicited drop-ins—should receive friendly, courteous treatment, not only on humanitarian grounds, but also because the firm's reputation is at stake.

Asking Questions   The questions written in advance should then be asked in order.

Some suggestions to ensure that questioning is effective, include: avoid questions that can be answered "yes" or "no"; don't put words in the applicant's mouth or telegraph the desired answer, by nodding or smiling when the preferred answer is given; don't interrogate the applicant as if he or she is on the witness stand; don't be patronizing, sarcastic, or inattentive; and don't monopolize the interview by rambling, or let the applicant dominate the interview. Do ask open-ended questions; listen to the candidate and encourage the full expression of his or her thoughts; draw out the applicant's opinions and feelings by repeating the person's last comment as a question (such as "You didn't like your last job?"); and ask for specific examples.

Effective interviews require good note taking. Taking notes reduces the likelihood of the interviewer forgetting job-relevant information and subsequently reconstructing forgotten information in accordance with his or her biases and stereotypes. Taking notes thus increases the validity of the interview process.[108]

Closing the Interview   Toward the end of the interview, time should be allocated to answer any questions the candidate may have, and, if appropriate, to advocate the firm and position. While the potential of the job and opportunities at the firm should be discussed with external candidates, in particular, care must be taken not to oversell or misrepresent.

All interviews should be ended on a positive note. The interviewee should be thanked and informed about subsequent steps in the selection process, as well as when he or she will be notified regarding whether or not he or she will be given further consideration.

Reviewing Notes and Evaluating the Candidate   Immediately after each candidate leaves, interview notes should be carefully reviewed and the candidate evaluated against the selection criteria. Delaying judgment until this point can help to prevent the snap-judgment, halo-effect, and negative-emphasis errors.[109]

Since interviews are only one step in the process, no final decision should be reached until all assessments, including reference checking, have been completed.

Small Business Applications

Interview Tips

Many of the points discussed in the section on the selection interview can be combined into a practical interview procedure for a small business. Such a procedure is especially useful when time and resources are scarce, no HR specialist is available, and a quick way to organize the interview process is required. The procedure consists of four steps as follows:

1. Develop selection criteria for the job
2. Determine what basic factors to probe for
3. Use an interview plan
4. Match the candidate with the selection criteria.

Develop Selection Criteria

Even a small business can specify the kind of person who would be best for the job. A quick way to do so is to focus on four basic types of behaviours—*knowledge and experience, motivation, intellectual capacity, and personality,* and ask the following questions:

Knowledge-Experience Factor   What must the candidate know to perform the job? What experience is absolutely necessary to perform the job?

Motivation Factor   What should the person like doing to enjoy this job? Is there anything the person should not dislike? Are there any essential goals or aspirations the person should have? Are there any unusual energy demands on the job? How critical is the person's drive and motivation?

Intellectual Factor   Are there any specific intellectual aptitudes required (mathematics, mechanical, and so on)? How complex are the problems to be solved? What must a person be able to demonstrate he or she can do intellectually? How should the person solve problems (cautiously, deductively, and so on)?

Personality Factor   What are the critical personality qualities needed for success on the job (ability to withstand boredom, decisiveness, stability, and so on)? How must the job incumbent handle stress, pressure, and criticism? What kind of interpersonal behaviour is required in the job up the line, at peer level, down the line, and outside the firm with customers?

Specific Factors to Probe in the Interview

Next, a combination of open-ended questions should be used to probe the candidate's suitability for the job. For example:

Intellectual Factor   Here the interviewer probes such things as complexity of tasks the person has performed, grades in school, and how the person organizes his or her thoughts and communicates.

Motivation Factor   This involves probing such areas as the person's likes and dislikes (for each thing done, what he or she liked or disliked about it), the person's aspirations (including the validity of each goal in terms of the person's reasoning about why he or she chose it), and the person's energy level, perhaps by asking what he or she does on, say, a "typical Tuesday."

Personality Factor   Personality can be assessed by looking for self-defeating patterns of behaviour (aggressiveness, compulsive fidgeting, and so on) and by exploring the person's past interpersonal relationships. Questions can be asked about the person's past interactions (working in a group at school, leading the work team on the last job, and so on). The interviewer should also try to judge the person's behaviour in the interview itself—is the candidate personable? Shy? Outgoing?

Use an Interview Plan

Interviewers should always devise a plan and use it as a guide when developing questions. Significant areas to cover include the candidate's:

- Educational background and qualifications
- Goals and ambitions
- Work experience
- Reasons for applying
- Self-assessment of strengths and weaknesses
- Skills acquired from outside activities that are related to the job.

Following such a plan means developing one or more open-ended questions pertaining to each topic. The job specifications should be kept in mind at all times, as well as the desire to elicit information about four main traits—intelligence, motivation, personality, and knowledge/experience. Particular areas requiring follow up can usually be pursued by asking such questions as "Could you elaborate on that, please?" Notes should be made as each question is answered.

Match Candidate to the Selection Criteria

By following the interview plan, probing for the four factors, and making notes, at the end of the interview it should be possible to summarize the candidate's general strengths and limitations, and draw conclusions about the person's intellectual capacity, knowledge/experience, motivation, and personality. These conclusions should then be compared to the selection criteria. This will provide a rational basis for matching the candidate to the job, one based on an analysis of the traits and aptitudes actually required.◆

Source: Based on John Drake, *Interviewing for Managers: A Complete Guide to Employment Interviewing* (New York: AMA-COM, 1982).

Step Five: Background Investigation and Reference Checking

Use   Most employers try to check and verify the background information and references of job applicants.[110] Estimates of the number of firms checking references exceed 90 percent, with about 80 percent using telephone inquiries.

Most employers at least try to verify an applicant's current position and salary with his or her current employer by telephone (assuming doing so was cleared with the candidate). Others call the applicant's current and previous supervisors to try to discover more about the person's motivation, technical competence, and ability to work with others. **Figure 7.11** is an example of a form used for written reference checking. When reference checking is being done by telephone, questions should be written down in advance.

Recognizing the critical importance of reference checking, but lacking the time or human resources to do a thorough job, some firms use reference-checking services or hire a consultant to perform this task.

Effectiveness Handled correctly, reference checking can be useful. It is an inexpensive and straightforward way of verifying factual information about the applicant, such as current and previous job titles and job duties, current salary range, dates of employment, and reasons for leaving past jobs. As many of the candidate's former employers as possible should be contacted.

Personal references, those attesting to the applicant's character, are usually provided by friends or family. Since their objectivity and candour are questionable, personal references are not commonly checked. Most employers do not put too much weight on letters of reference provided by former employers, either. They are often very general, revealing little useful information about ability to perform the job in question, and are typically extremely positive. Furthermore, sometimes such letters have actually been written by the candidate!

Figure 7.11
Form Requesting
Written Reference
Information
Source: Steven Mitchell Sack, *The Hiring and Firing Book: A Complete Legal Guide for Employers* (New York: Legal Strategies Inc., October 1993).

(COMPANY LETTERHEAD)

To Whom it May Concern:

❏ has been employed by us
_____ ❏ has applied for employment

and given the following information covering employment in your organization. We have been authorized to communicate with you for verification and such reference information as you care to give us.

(Please check if correct or change if incorrect)
Employment dates: _____ _____
Position: _____ _____
Last earning rate: $ _____ per _____ _____
Reason for leaving: _____ _____
Is applicant eligible for rehire _____

_____
Your signature

_____
Title

On the back of this letter we would appreciate any helpful comments you care to make, and will respect your confidence in this matter. The enclosed duplicate is for your own files.

Sincerely yours,

_____
Human Resources Department

Rather than contacting references, educational qualifications are generally most appropriately checked by asking for an original transcript, certificate, diploma, or degree. Photocopies can be altered and therefore should not be accepted.

The use of consumer credit reports by employers as a basis for establishing an applicant's eligibility for employment is fairly restricted in Canada. Such checks must be job related. Positions of trust, such as those that involve the handling of money and financial transactions in banks and other financial institutions, necessitate the use of credit reports, for example. Applicants must agree in writing to a credit report, and have the right to review its contents.

Obtaining Written Permission   Written permission is not only required for credit checking. As a legal protection for all concerned, applicants should be asked to indicate, in writing, their willingness for the firm to check with current and/or former employers and other reference sources, including educational institutions, for an original transcript. There is generally a section on the application form for this purpose. Many employers will not give out any reference information until they have received a copy of such written authorization, by fax or through the mail. Educational institutions generally require written permission and the payment of a small fee prior to issuing a transcript.

Making Reference Checks More Productive   There are several things that can be done to make reference checking more productive.[111] One is to use a structured form to ensure that important questions are not overlooked. Another suggestion is to use the references offered by the applicant as a source for other references who may know of the applicant's performance. Thus, each of the applicant's references might be asked, "Could you please give me the name of another person who might be familiar with the applicant's performance?" In that way, information may be obtained from references who are more objective since they weren't referred directly by the applicant.

Making reference checking productive also requires persistence. The most difficult references to reach are often the ones most reluctant to provide a reference. While this reluctance could be due to a strict company policy on releasing information, it might be because they have nothing positive to say about the applicant.[112]

With the fear of civil litigation increasing, more Canadian companies are ading a "no reference" policy regarding previous employees[113] or are only willing to confirm position held and dates of employment. If complete details cannot be obtained from a firm due to a company's reference-checking policy, the applicant should be asked to identify other information sources, such as individuals working within the firm who might be willing to provide reference data or people who are no longer with the firm. As with all other references, their relevance and impartiality should be taken into account.[114]

A thorough reference audit may be warranted for some positions, particiuarly highly sensitive or critically important ones, rather than just a reference check.[115] A reference audit requires contacting at least two superiors, two peers, and two reporting employees from each job previously held by the candidate, such that a reliable picture of the candidate is gradually formed. For example, the red flags raised by one or two colleagues may be found to be problems that can be traced back through several previous jobs and employers. Of course, some employers have policies that preclude employees (outside the HR department) from providing reference information, and it is always risky to ask candidates to self-select the references. However, such audits can and probably will lead to a more accurate picture of the candidate.

Legal Issues Involved in Obtaining and Providing Reference Information   Failure to check references can lead to negligent or wrongful hiring suits that may involve significant damages. In *Downey v. 502377 Ontario Limited et al.*, the Honourable Justice Keith Gibson rendered a 160-page decision in the first Canadian case to deal with potential liability arising out of failure to do reference checking:[116]

> On September 28, 1984, Bryan Downey went to the Cabaret Restaurant in Toronto. After an altercation in the bar, he was escorted from the tavern and an assault then ensued in the parking lot. Two bouncers, Tony Sotera and Enza Sotera, viciously beat Mr. Downey, leaving him with severe and permanent brain damage that rendered him permanently unemployable and incapable of managing his day-to-day affairs.
>
> While liability was imposed directly against the bouncers, the Court went further and held the employer vicariously liable for failing to properly check the references or criminal backgrounds of the bouncers involved.
>
> The application form for Enza Sotera was missing, and Tony Sotera's application contained false information, which had obviously never been checked. He had also previously been convicted of wounding.
>
> Mr. Justice Gibson awarded damages of over two million dollars against the bar's bouncers, the company that operated the bar, and two shareholders, both of whom were officers of the company.

In providing reference information, the concept of qualified privilege is important. Generally speaking, if comments are made in confidence for a public purpose, without malice, and are honestly believed, the defence of "qualified privilege" exists. Thus, if honest, fair and candid references are given by an individual who is asked to provide confidential information about the performance of a job applicant, then the doctrine of qualified privilege generally protects the reference giver, even if negative information is imparted about the candidate.

However, if a statement is made that is known to be untrue in an attempt to sabotage the employee's chances of finding another job, or is contained in an employment evaluation or performance review, it is likely that malice will destroy the qualified privilege and the Court will not come to the rescue of the reference giver.[117]

Small Business Applications

Reference Checking Policies

Small business owners need to be particularly careful about checking references. As noted earlier, while one or two hiring mistakes may not be disastrous for a very large firm, it can cause chaos in a small one. In fact, the most common employer mistake that leads to liability for negligent or wrongful hiring is inadequately investigating an applicant's background. Furthermore, the more frequently employers check references, the less likely they are to experience problems of absenteeism, tardiness, or poor work quality. Therefore, checking applicants' backgrounds carefully is well worth the time it takes.

Source: Based on James Fenton, Jr. and Kay Lawrimore, "Employment Reference Checking, Firm Size, and Defamation Liability," *Journal of Small Business Management* (October 1992), pp. 88–95.

Step Six: The Supervisory Interview

If the initial selection interview involves a one-on-one interview with a member of the HR department only, rather than a series of sequential interviews or a panel-based interview, the two or three top candidates typically return for a second interview with the immediate supervisor. He or she is generally responsible for making the final selection decision.

There are a number of reasons for this:

- the supervisor tends to know the technical aspects of the job best and is the most qualified to assess the applicants' job knowledge and skills
- the supervisor is typically best equipped to answer any job-specific questions
- the immediate supervisor generally has to work closely with the individual selected and must feel comfortable with that person
- if the supervisor is not committed to the individual selected, he or she can easily set the new hire up for failure
- the individual selected must fit with the current members of the department or team, something which the supervisor is often best able to assess.

When the supervisor recommends hiring an individual, he or she has made a psychological commitment to assist the new employee. If the candidate turns to be unsatisfactory, the supervisor is much more likely to accept some of the responsibility for his or her failure.

Step Seven: Realistic Job Previews

realistic job preview (RJP)
A strategy used to provide applicants with realistic information about the demands of the job, the organization's expectations of the incumbent, and the work environment. Candidates thereby learn about both positive and negative aspects of the job and firm.

The supervisory interview is often supplemented with a **realistic job preview (RJP)**. This is probably the best strategy for creating appropriate expectations about the job.[118] As the name indicates, an RJP presents realistic information about the demands of the job, the organization's expectations of the incumbent, and the work environment. Candidates thereby learn about both positive and negative aspects of the job and firm. RJPs should be tailored to the needs of the organization and can be presented orally; in writing; on videotape; or through a tour, which provides an opportunity to see the job being done, equipment, facilities, and working conditions.

Proponents of RJP believe that applicants who are given realistic information are more likely to remain on the job and be successful, because they will encounter fewer unexpected, unpleasant surprises. Research studies on RJP have reported that realistic job expectations:[119]

- improved employee job satisfaction
- reduced voluntary turnover
- enhanced communication, due to openness and honesty.

While some candidates may choose not to accept employment with the firm after an RJP,[120] those individuals probably wouldn't have remained with the firm long, had they accepted the job offer.

RJPs should never be considered a substitute for in-depth job analysis and continuous monitoring of working conditions. To improve satisfaction and quality of work, the negative aspects of jobs and working conditions should be eliminated whenever possible.[121]

Step Eight: Making the Hiring Decision

To make the hiring decision, information from the multiple predictors used must be combined, and the applicant who is the best fit with the selection criteria identified.

Organizations often use a combination of techniques in the selection process. In the **multiple-hurdle strategy,** an applicant must clear each hurdle before moving on to the next one. This technique is often used to determine who is eligible to move on to the next step in the selection process, such that only those candidates who have cleared all of the previous hurdles remain in contention for the position at the time the hiring decision is being made.

For finalists, firms generally use the **clinical strategy,** which involves making a subjective evaluation of all of the information gleaned about each candidate and arriving at an overall judgment. There is also a **statistical strategy,** which involves combining all of the pieces of information according to a formula, and giving the job to the candidate with the highest score. Although research studies have indicated that the statistical strategy is generally more reliable and valid,[122] most organizations use the clinical strategy.

The validity and reliability of judgments made using the clinical strategy can be improved by using tests which are objectively scored, and devising a candidate rating sheet based on the weighted want criteria.

HR department staff generally play a major role in compiling all of the data. It is the immediate supervisor, however, who is generally responsible for making the final hiring decision.

All information used in making the selection decision should be kept in a competition file, including interview notes, test results, reference checking information, etc. In the event of human rights challenge, negligent hiring charge, or union grievance about the selection decision, such data is critical.

Step Nine: Candidate Notification

Once the selection decision has been made, a job offer should be extended to the successful candidate. Often, the initial offer is made by telephone, but it should be followed up with a written employment offer, in which important terms and conditions of employment, such as starting date, starting salary, probation period, etc. are clearly specified. Two copies of the letter should be sent; one for the successful candidate to sign and return to the firm (provided he or she decides to accept the offer, of course), and the other for the candidate's records.

HR department staff generally handle offers of employment, both the initial offer by telephone and the follow up in writing. Candidates should be given a reasonable length of time to think over the offer, and not be pressured into making an immediate decision. Often, a spouse and/or other family member needs to be included in the candidate's decision-making process.

If there are two candidates who are both excellent, and the second choice would be quite acceptable to all concerned, the runner up is often not notified until after the first-choice candidate has accepted the job offer. Should the first-choice candidate decline the offer, the runner up can then be offered the job.

All finalists not selected should be notified. Sometimes applicants who were not selected for one position may be worthy of consideration for future openings. If so, they should be informed of this fact and their résumés and application forms filed appropriately.

The application form and résumé of the individual hired, along with his or her signed letter of offer, are the first documents placed in his or her HR file.

Step Ten: Evaluating the Selection Process

Evaluating the selection process involves considering a number of questions:

- Are the selection procedures used effective in identifying qualified, capable, productive employees?
- Are the techniques used efficient and worth the costs and trouble?
- Are there ways in which the process could be streamlined or improved?

To answer these questions, feedback is required. Retention data and performance appraisal results can help to identify successes. Feedback on failures is typically ample: complaints from supervisors, poor performance ratings, turnover and/or absenteeism, low employee satisfaction, union grievances or unionization attempts, and even legal challenges.

Constructive feedback can also be obtained by administering a questionnaire to newly hired and newly-transferred or promoted employees, asking for their impressions of the steps involved in the selection process; asking supervisors for information about how easily and how well their recent hires seem to be adapting to the job, team, and organizational culture; and obtaining an informal assessment of the performance of each newly-hired and newly-transferred or promoted employee long before a formal appraisal is due.

In the long run, the utility of the selection procedure must be determined by looking at the quality and productivity of the individuals chosen, as well as the costs incurred in the process. Such costs include out-of-pocket expenses related to testing, interviewing, stationery, postage, etc., as well as the costs associated with the hiring of marginal or unsatisfactory candidates, described earlier in this chapter.

Chapter Review

Summary

1. Selection is the process of choosing individuals with the relevant qualifications to fill existing or projected job openings. The purpose of selection is to choose qualified individuals who possess the necessary skills, knowledge, abilities, personality, interests, and preferences to fill the job opening, who will perform well and fit in with the corporate values and culture.
2. Proper selection is important for three key reasons: the quality of the company's human resources is frequently the single most important factor in company performance and success; there are extremely high costs associated with inappropriate or poor hiring; and there are legal implications related to human rights and employment equity legislation, liability for negligent or wrongful hiring, and wrongful dismissal.
3. There are a number of constraints on the selection process, including the company's strategic plan, selection budget, and employment equity plan; the job requirements; the selection ratio; ethics; and legislative requirements.
4. Reliability, the degree to which selection tools are dependable, consistent, and stable; and validity, which relates to accuracy, are critically important. To satisfy legal requirements, all selection procedures used should be both valid and reliable.
5. The first step in the selection process is the preliminary reception of applicants. The manner in which this is handled makes a major impression on candidates.
6. Human resources department staff typically perform initial applicant screening, which involves perusal of application forms and résumés; elimination of candidates not meeting the "must have" selection criteria; and identification of those most closely meeting the remaining job specifications, worthy of further consideration.

7. The different types of tests used for selection purposes include: intelligence tests, aptitude tests, tests of motor and physical abilities, personality tests, interest inventories, achievement tests, the work-sampling technique, management assessment centres, the miniature job training and evaluation approach, honesty tests, and graphology. Using a polygraph (lie detector) for honesty testing is rather controversial, and is, in fact, illegal in some Canadian jurisdictions. Medical examinations and drug testing are also extremely controversial and are subject to numerous constraints under human rights legislation.

8. The interview is one of the most popular devices used in the selection process. All interviews can be classified according to content, structure, purpose, and method of administration. There are a number of basic types of interviews used for selection purposes: unstructured, structured, mixed, stress, situational, behavioural, serialized, panel, computerized, audiotaped/videotaped, and teleconferenced/videoconferenced.

9. There are a number of potential errors an interviewer can make that undermine the usefulness of the process. These include inadequate planning, making snap judgments, letting unfavourable information bias judgment, being biased by an initial positive impression, not knowing the job requirements, lowering standards under pressure to hire, not allowing for the contrast effect, being unduly influenced by nonverbal behaviour, telegraphing desired responses to the interviewee, talking too much or too little, and playing attorney or psychologist.

10. Designing an effective semi-structured interview involves five key steps, the first two of which should occur prior to recruitment: deciding who will be involved in the selection process and developing selection criteria; specifying musts and wants and weighting the wants; determining assessment strategies and developing an evaluation form; developing structured interview questions; and developing candidate-specific questions.

11. Conducting an effective interview requires planning, establishing rapport, asking open-ended questions, bringing the interview to a close, and finally, reviewing notes and evaluating the candidate.

12. Background investigation and reference checking is extremely important. Written permission for such checking should be obtained from each applicant. While personal references and letters of reference provided by the applicant are not of great value, as many of the candidate's former employers as possible should be contacted. Educational qualifications should also be verified.

13. The immediate supervisor is a key player in selection interviewing, and is generally responsible for making the final selection decision. The supervisory interview is often supplemented with a realistic job preview, an excellent strategy for creating appropriate expectations about the job. Once the selection decision has been made, a job offer is extended to the successful candidate. All finalists not selected should also be notified.

14. Evaluating the selection process involves considering a number of questions, such as: Are the selection procedures used effective in identifying qualified, capable, productive employees? Are the techniques used efficient and worth the costs and trouble? Are there ways in which the process could be streamlined or improved? To answer these questions, feedback is required.

Key Terms

achievement tests	content validity	interest inventories
aptitude tests	contrast or candidate-order error	job-knowledge questions
behavioural interview		management assessment centre
behavioural questions	criterion-related validity	
clinical strategy	cross-validation	marginal employee
computerized selection interview	differential validity	mixed (semi-structured) interview
	graphology	
concurrent validity	honesty tests	multiple-hurdle strategy
construct validity	intelligence (IQ) tests	must criteria

panel interview
personality tests
polygraph (lie detector)
predictive validity
realistic job preview (RJP)
reliability
selection
selection interview
selection ratio
serialized interview

situational interview
situational questions
statistical strategy
stress interview
structured interview
unstructured interview
validity
videoconferenced/
  teleconferenced
  interview

videotaped/audiotaped
  interview
want criteria
work samples
work sampling technique
worker-requirements or
  willingness questions

Discussion Questions and Exercises

1. Briefly describe five constraints on the selection process.

2. Explain what is meant by reliability and validity. What is the difference between them?

3. What should be involved in a) the preliminary reception of applicants? b) the initial screening process?

4. Write a short essay discussing some of the ethical and legal considerations in testing.

5. What types of testing would be appropriate for the following: Supervisor of Data Processing Operations (see job description in Figure 4.12 in chapter 4); secretary; machine operator; draftsperson.

6. Medical examinations and drug testing are extremely controversial and are subject to numerous constraints under human rights legislation. Why?

7. Explain the four basic ways in which interviews can be classified.

8. Design a mixed interview for a position with which you are extremely familiar, basing the candidate-specific questions on your own résumé. Ensure that behavioural, situational, job-knowledge, and worker-requirements questions are included.

9. Briefly discuss five common interviewing mistakes and explain how such errors can be avoided.

10. Background investigation and reference checking is extremely important and should not be omitted. Why?

11. The immediate supervisor is a key player in selection interviewing. Why?

12. Explain the following two statements: Most firms use a multiple-hurdle strategy to narrow down the pool of candidates. The individual to whom the job will be offered is generally chosen using a clinical approach, despite the fact that there is a statistical strategy that is more reliable and valid.

Application Exercises

RUNNING CASE: Carter Cleaning Company
The Selection Process

Jennifer and her father have what the latter describes as an easy but hard job when it comes to screening job applicants. It is easy because for two important jobs—the people who actually do the pressing and those who do the cleaning-spotting—the applicants are easily screened with about 20 minutes of on-the-job testing. As Jennifer points out, "a person either knows how to press clothes fast enough or how to use cleaning chemicals and machines, or he or she doesn't, and we find out very quickly by just trying them out on the job."

On the other hand, applicant screening for the stores can also be frustratingly hard because of the nature of the qualities for which Jennifer would like to screen. Two of the most critical problems facing the firm are employee turnover and lack of honesty. As mentioned previously, Jennifer and her father sorely need to implement practices that will reduce the rate of employee turnover. If it is possible to do this through employee testing and screening techniques, Jennifer would like to know about it because of the management time and money that are now being wasted by the never-ending need to recruit and hire new employees. Of even greater concern to Jennifer and her father is the need to institute new practices to screen out those employees who may be predisposed to steal from the company.

Employee theft is an enormous problem for the Carter Cleaning Centres, and one that is not just limited to employees who handle the cash. For example, the cleaner-spotter and/or presser often open the store themselves, without a manager present, to get the day's work started, and it is not unusual to have one or more of these people steal supplies or "run a route." Running a route means that an employee canvasses his or her neighbourhood to pick up people's clothes for cleaning and then secretly cleans and presses them at the Carter Centre, using the company's supplies, gas, and power. It is also not unusual for an unsupervised person (even one of the managers) to accept a one-hour rush order for cleaning or laundering, quickly clean and press the item, and return it to the customer for payment, without making out a proper ticket for the item or posting the sale. The money in such situations, of course, goes into the person's pocket instead of into the cash register.

The more serious problem concerns the store managers and counter workers who actually have to handle the cash. According to Jack, "you would not believe the creativity employees use to get around the management controls we set up to cut down on employee theft." As one extreme example of this felonious creativity, Jack tells the following story: "To cut down on the amount of money my employees were stealing, I had a small sign printed and placed in front of all our cash registers. The sign said: "Your entire order free if we don't give you a cash register receipt when you pay...Call 962-0734." It was my intention with this sign to force all of our cash-handling employees to ring in customer orders, so that the amounts would be recorded on the cash register tape for our accountants. After all, if all the cash that comes in is recorded in the cash register, then we should have a much better handle on stealing in our stores, right? Well, one of our managers found a diabolical way around this. I came into the store one night and noticed that the cash register that this particular manager was using just didn't look right, although the sign was dutifully placed in front of it. It turned out that every afternoon at about 5:00 p.m. when the other employees left, this character would pull his own cash register out of a box that he hid underneath all our supplies. Customers coming in would notice the sign and of course noted the fact that he was meticulous in ringing up every sale. But unknown to them and to us, for about five months, the sales that came in for about an hour every day went into his cash register, not Carter's. It took us that long to figure out why the cash from that store seemed consistently short."

Given war stories like this, and the fact that there are no formal interviewing procedures being used at present, Jennifer is now pondering the following:

Questions

1. What would be the advantages and disadvantages of routinely administering honesty tests to all employees?
2. What other techniques could the company use to screen out theft-prone employees, and how exactly could these be used?
3. How could effective interviewing help to minimize the turnover and theft problems at the Carter Cleaning Centres?
4. How should references be handled for employees terminated due to theft? Why?

CASE INCIDENT: The Selection Process

Several weeks ago, Marjorie saw an advertisement in the local newspaper for a forklift operator to work in the loading dock area at the ABC Manufacturing Company, the firm at which you are employed as the Manager of Human Resources. She has had seven years of experience in this type of work. Although the thought of having to work on the night shift doesn't particularly appeal to her, her need for additional money and the fact that the job at ABC pays more than she is currently earning prompted her to send in her résumé. She was also impressed by the indication in the ad that employees could qualify for training in more technical areas.

Marjorie was interviewed by Tom, the night shift supervisor, who seemed to have difficulty believing that she had seven years of prior experience. He suggested that she demonstrate her skills by taking a driving test. She complied, even though she was surprised by the request.

Following the test, Tom questioned Marjorie closely about how she would fit into the work environment. He said she would be the only woman working in that area and that the group might not appreciate the constraints on their joking and talking that a woman's presence would cause. He also said that she couldn't expect them to help her out with tasks "just because she is a woman" and asked how her husband would feel about her being out all night. Marjorie assured Tom that this was a normal work setting for her and one that she had learned to handle long ago.

You have just found out about the situation. Apparently, after learning that she was not being offered a job, Marjorie discovered that six men had been hired, none of whom were asked to take a test and none of whom had as much experience as she. She therefore decided to file a complaint with the Human Rights Commission, a copy of which has just landed on your desk.

Questions

1. Based on facts given, do you think Marjorie was treated fairly? Why or why not?
2. There are a number of problems with the current selection process at ABC, including violations of human rights legislation. Explain this statement.
3. As the Human Resources Manager, are you legally liable for Tom's behaviour? Why or why not?
4. In resolving this situation, what issues need to be addressed? How would you address them?

Source: Based on a case provided in *Equity Works Best*, a publication of the Ontario Women's Directorate.

Human Resources Management Simulation

Section 2 of part 1 of the simulation pertains to recruitment, selection, and orientation. Simulation 1 and the last two parts of exercise 2 are designed to provide hands-on skills in various aspects of the selection process.

Part D of exercise 2 requires the design of a plan for screening and interviewing applicants for all of the positions that must be staffed. An important component is specifying who should be involved. Part E of exercise 2 provides the opportunity to create an offer-of-employment letter, outlining terms and conditions of employment. A few hints are in order: 1) A copy of the letter should be signed and returned by the new hire. 2) A signed letter of offer is considered a contract of employment.

The simulation exercise (simulation 1) provides the opportunity to role-play a selection interview for the Maintenance Supervisor position. For the interviewee, this requires preparing answers for anticipated questions and thinking about suitable questions to ask about the job and firm. For the interviewers, requirements include the preparation of interview questions and other selection strategies that will facilitate comparison of the candidate with the selection criteria (based on the job description and job specification). Care must be taken to ensure there are no violations of human rights legislation. The interviewers must also be prepared to sell the job and the firm and answer interviewee questions. Observers involved will be expected to evaluate the performance of both interviewers and interviewee and make specific suggestions regarding improvements.

Video Case

Assessing Attitude and Fit

There is a change in emphasis in today's job market. Education and intelligence are no longer enough. Employers also assess attitude and fit with corporate values and culture.

To explain how this is manifested, the video highlights the steps in the selection process of one employer. As is quite typical today, the Loeb grocery store in Tecumseh, Ontario is swamped with applicants—2 800 applications for 120 positions, most of which are low-paying, part-time jobs. To conduct the initial screening process, Loeb hires an HR consulting firm. As witnessed on video, the first step in the selection process involves initial screening of every application form. The elimination process begins at this point, based on whether or not two references are provided, as requested; desired working hours; and the results of a simple math test. Rose, an employee of the consulting firm, then telephones the employees passing the initial screening process to verify the information on the application form and arrange for an interview, which is designed to uncover specific skill sets and assess suitability for customer-service work. During these interviews, the focus is on behavioural descriptive questions, to unveil communication, leadership, and teamwork skills, as well as dedication and motivation. Following the interview, each candidate is evaluated. Top-ranked candidates are then referred to Loeb for a final interview.

Questions

1. Why are some applicants eliminated during the initial screening process?

2. Describe the primary interview question format that Rose uses. Why is this format effective in determining applicant skills and suitability?

3. What does Rose do immediately following the interview? Why?

4. What is the next step in the selection process for candidates who do well in their interview with Rose?

5. With what guarantee does Rose provide Loeb regarding the candidates that she has referred to them?

Video Resource: CBC *The National Magazine: Friday Survival Guide Part 1* "How to Find and Keep a Job," (February 9, 1996).

Take It to the Net

Check out our Companion Website at

www.prenticehall.ca/dessler

for a multitude of practice questions, key terms and concepts, Weblinks to related sites, newsgroups, CBC video updates, and more.

Appendix 7.1

Guidelines for Interviewees

Here are some hints for excelling in interviews.

The first thing for applicants to understand is that interviews are used primarily to help employers determine what the applicant is like as a person.[1] In other words, information regarding interpersonal skills and the desire to work is of prime importance in the interview, since skills and technical expertise are usually best determined through tests and a careful study of educational and work history. Interviewers will look first for crisp, articulate answers. Specifically, concise responses, full cooperation in answering questions, statements of relevant personal opinions, and the ability to keep to the subject at hand are by far the most important elements in influencing the interviewer's decision. Additionally, there are seven things the applicant should know to get that extra edge in the interview.

First, preparation is essential. Before the interview, the applicant should learn as much as possible about the employer, the job, and the people doing the recruiting. Business periodicals should be consulted regarding what is happening in the employer's field, who the competition is, and how they are doing. Questions such as those listed in **Figure 7.12** should be prepared in advance.

Second, the interviewer's real needs must be uncovered. The applicant should spend as little time as possible answering the interviewer's first questions and as much time as possible getting him or her to describe his or her needs: what the person is looking to get accomplished, and the type of person he or she feels is needed. Open-ended questions such as, "Could you tell me more about that?" may be used.

Third, the applicant should relate him- or herself to the interviewer's needs. Once it is known what type of person the interviewer is looking for and the sorts of

Figure 7.12
Interview Questions to Ask

Source: Based on H. Lee Rust, *Job Search, The Complete Manual for Job Seekers* (New York, AMACOM, 1991), pp. 234–5.

1. What is the first problem that needs the attention of the person you hire?
2. What other problems need attention now?
3. What has been done about any of these to date?
4. How has this job been performed in the past?
5. Why is it now vacant?
6. Do you have a written job description for this position?
7. What are its major responsibilities?
8. What authority would I have? How would you define its scope?
9. What are the company's five-year sales and profit projections?
10. What needs to be done to reach these projections?
11. What are the company's major strengths and weaknesses?
12. What are its strengths and weaknesses in production?
13. What are its strengths and weaknesses in its products or its competitive position?
14. Whom do you identify as your major competitors?
15. What are their strengths and weaknesses?
16. How do you view the future for your industry?
17. Do you have any plans for new products or acquisitions?
18. Might this company be sold or acquired?
19. What is the company's current financial strength?
20. What can you tell me about the individual to whom I would report?
21. What can you tell me about other persons in key positions?
22. What can you tell me about the employees who would be reporting to me?
23. How would you define your management philosophy?
24. Are employees afforded an opportunity for continuing education?
25. What are you looking for in the person who will fill this job?

problems he or she wants solved, the applicant should describe personal accomplishments in terms of the interviewer's needs. He or she may start by saying something like "one of the problem areas you've indicated is important to you is similar to a problem I once faced." He or she should then state the problem, describe the solution, and reveal the results.[2]

Fourth, answering a question should be a three-step process: Pause—think—speak.[3] The applicant should pause to make sure that what the interviewer is driving at is understood, think about how to structure the answer, and then speak.

Fifth, appearance and enthusiasm are important. Appropriate clothing, good grooming, a firm handshake, and the appearance of controlled energy are important.

Sixth, first impressions are important. Applicants should remember that studies of interviews show that in most cases interviewers make up their minds about the applicant during the first minutes of the interview. A good first impression may turn to bad during the interview, but it is unlikely. Bad first impressions are almost impossible to overcome. In fact, once individuals have formed an overall evaluation of another person it is difficult to alter that impression.[4]

Seventh, nonverbal behaviour will communicate more than the actual verbal content of what is said. Here, maintaining eye contact is very important; as is speaking with enthusiasm, nodding to indicate agreement, and remembering to take a moment to frame answers so that they come across as articulate and fluent.

1. James Hollandsworth, Jr., and others, "Relative Contributions of Verbal, Articulative, and Nonverbal Communication to Employment Decisions in the Job Interview Setting," *Personnel Psychology* 32 (Summer 1979), pp. 359–67. See also Sara Rynes and Howard Miller, "Recruiter and Job Influences on Candidates for Employment," *Journal of Applied Psychology* 68, no. 1 (1983), pp. 147–54.
2. Richard Payne, *How to Get a Better Job Quickly* (New York: New American Library, 1979).
3. J. G. Hollandsworth, R. C. Ladinski, and J. H. Russel, "Use of Social Skills Training in the Treatment of Extreme Anxiety of Deficient Verbal Skills," *Journal of Applied Psychology* 11 (1979), pp. 259–69.
4. Robert A. Barron. "Impresson Management by Applicants During Interviews: The Too Much of a Good Thing Effect" R.W. Eder and Gerald R. Ferris, eds. *The Employment Interview: Theory, Research and Practice* (Newburg Park, CA: Sage Publications, 1989) pp. 204–15.

Notes

Notes

1. Robert D. Gatewood and Hubert S. Field. *Human Resources Selection* (Chicago: The Dryden Press, 1990), p. 3
2. Robert E. Sibson, "The High Cost of Hiring," *Nation's Business* (February 1975), p. 85.
3. The section on costs is based on E. Stanton, *Successful Personnel Recruiting and Selection* (New York: AMA-COM, 1977), except as noted.
4. "Employers Liable for Employee's Criminal Acts," *Human Resources Management in Canada* Report Bulletin 150 (Toronto: Prentice Hall Canada, August 1995), pp. 5–6.
5. Steven L. McShane, "Wrongful Dismissal Risks in Employee Selection," *Human Resources Professional* 14, no. 1 (February/March 1997), pp. 20–5.
6. Jerry Zeidenberg, "HR and the Innovative Company," *Human Resources Professional* 13, no. 4 (June 1996), pp. 12–5.
7. Claudine Kapel, "Giant Steps," *Human Resources Professional* 9, no. 4 (April 1993), pp. 13–6.
8. John D. Erdlen, "Ethics and the Employee Relations Function," *Personnel Administrator* (January 1979), pp. 42–3, 68.
9. These guidelines are based on two sources: Steven Mitchell Sack, "Fifteen Steps to Protecting Against the Risk of Negligent Hiring Claims," *Employment Relations Today* (August 1993), pp. 313–20 and Steven L. McShane, "Wrongful Dismissal Risks," pp. 20–5.
10. Gatewood and Field, *Human Resources Selection*, p. 89.
11. Anne Anastasi, *Psychological Patterns* (New York: Macmillan, 1968), reprinted in W. Clay Hamner and Frank Schmidt, *Contemporary Problems in Personnel* (Chicago: St. Claire Press, 1974), pp. 102–9. Discussion of reliability based on Marvin Dunnette, *Personnel Selection and Placement* (Belmont, CA: Wadsworth Publishing Company, Inc., 1966), pp. 29–30.
12. Leona Tyler, *Tests and Measurements* (Englewood Cliffs, NJ: Prentice Hall, 1971), p. 25. More technically, "validity refers to the degree of confidence one can have in inferences drawn from scores, considering the whole process by which the scores are obtained. Stated differently, validity refers to the confidence one has in the meaning attached to scores." (See Robert M. Guion, "Changing Views for Personnel Selection Research," *Personnel Psychology* 40, no. 2 (Summer 1987), p. 208.)
13. Bureau of National Affairs, *Primer of Equal Employment Opportunity* (Washington, DC: BNA, 1978), p. 18. In practice, proving in court the criterion-related validity of paper-and-pencil tests has been difficult.
14. Laurence Siegel and Irving M. Lane, *Personnel and Organizational Psychology Testing* (Homewood, ILL: Richard D. Irwin Inc., 1987), p. 73.
15. Based on J. Tiffin and E. J. McCormick, *Industrial Psychology* (Englewood Cliffs, NJ: Prentice Hall, 1965), pp. 104–5; C. H. Lawshe and M. J. Balma, *Principles of Personnel Testing*, 2nd ed. (New York: McGraw-Hill, 1966).
16. James Ledvinka, *Federal Regulation of Personnel and Human Resource Management* (Boston: Kent, 1982), p. 111.
17. Richard S. Barrett, "Content Validation Form," *Public Personnel Management* 21 (Spring 1992), pp. 41–52.
18. Harris C. Jain, "Staffing: Recruitment and Selection" in *Human Resources Management in Canada* (Scarborough, Ontario: Prentice Hall, 1983), p. 25, 031.
19. Jain, "Staffing: Recruitment and Selection," pp. 50 024-5.
20. James Smither, et al., "Applicant Reactions to Selection Procedures," *Personnel Psychology* 46 (1993), pp. 49–75.
21. Tyler, *Tests and Measurements*, p. 24.
22. Steven Cranshaw, "The Status of Employment Testing in Canada: A Review and Evaluation of Theory and Professional Practice," *Canadian Psychology* 27 (1986), pp. 183–95; James W. Thacker and R. Julian Cattaneo, "The Canadian Personnel Function: Status and Practices," *Proceedings of the Annual Conference Meeting,* Administrative Sciences Association of Canada (Personnel and Human Resources Division) (1987), pp. 56–66.
23. *Personnel Management: Policies and Practices Report No. 22* (Englewood Cliffs, NJ: Prentice-Hall, April 2, 1975).
24. *Guidelines for Educational and Psychological Testing* (Old Chelsea, Quebec: Canadian Psychological Association, 1987).
25. See, for example, Floyd L. Ruch, "The Impact on Employment Procedures of the Supreme Court Decision in the Duke Power Case," *Personnel Journal* 50, no. 4 (October 1971), pp. 777–83; Hubert Field, Gerald Bagley, and Susan Bagley, "Employment Test Validation for Minority and Non-minority Production Workers," *Personnel Psychology* 30, no. 1 (Spring 1977), pp. 37–46; Ledvinka, *Federal Regulations*, p. 110.
26. See Ruch, "The Impact on Employment Procedures," pp. 777–83, in Hamner and Schmidt, *Contemporary Problems in Personnel*, pp. 117–23; Dale Beach, *Personnel* (New York: Macmillan, 1970); Field, Bagley, and Bagley, "Employing Test Validation for Minority and Nonminority Production Workers," pp. 37–46; M. K. Distefano, Jr., Margaret Pryer, and Stella Craig, "Predictive Validity of General Ability Tests with Black and White Psychiatric Attendants," *Person-*

nel Psychology 29, no. 2 (Summer 1976). Also see the Winter 1976 issue of Personnel Psychology 2, no. 4. See also James Norborg, "A Warning Regarding the Simplified Approach to the Evaluation of Test Fairness and Employee Selection Procedures," Personnel Psychology 37, no. 3 (Autumn 1984), pp. 483–6; Charles Johnson, Lawrence Messe, and William Crano, "Predicting Job Performance of Low Income Workers: The Work Opinion Questionnaire," Personnel Psychology 37, no. 2 (Summer 1984), pp. 291–9; Frank Schmidt, Benjamin Ocasio, Joseph Hillery, and John Hunter, "Further Within-Setting Empirical Tests of the Situational Specificity Hypothesis in Personnel Selection," Personnel Psychology 38, no. 3 (Autumn 1985), pp. 509–24.

27. Guidelines for Educational and Psychological Testing.

28. Except as noted, this is based largely on Laurence Siegel and Irving Lane, Personnel and Organizational Psychology (Homewood, IL: Irwin, 1982), pp. 170–85. See also Tyler, Tests and Measurements, pp. 38–79.

29. See, for example, Richard Reilly, Sheldon Zedeck, and Mary Tenopyr, "Validity and Fairness of Physical Ability Tests for Predicting Performance in Craft Jobs," Journal of Applied Psychology 64, no. 3 (June 1970), pp. 262–74. See also Barten Daniel, "Strength and Endurance Testing," Personnel Journal (June 1987), pp. 112–22.

30. Results of meta-analyses in one recent study indicated that isometric strength tests were valid predictors of both supervisory ratings of physical performance and performance on work simulations. See Barry R. Blakley, Miguel Quinones, Marnie Swerdlin Crawford, and I. Ann Jago, "The Validity of Isometric Strength Tests," Personnel Psychology 47 (1994), pp. 247–74.

31. This approach calls for construct validation which, as was pointed out, is extremely difficult to demonstrate.

32. Murray R. Barrick and Michael K. Mount, "The Big Five Personality Dimensions and Job Performance: A Meta-Analysis," Personnel Psychology 44, no. 1, Spring 1991, pp. 1–26. See also Mark Schmit and Ann Marie Ryan, "The Big Five in Personnel Selection: Factor Structure in Applicant and Non-Applicant Populations," Journal of Applied Psychology no. 6 (1993), pp. 966–74; Grant Marshal, et al., "The Five-Factor Model of Personality as a Framework for Personality-Health Research," Journal of Personality and Social Psychology no. 2 (1994), pp. 278–86. For a further discussion of the "big five" personality dimensions see, for example, Deniz Ones, Michael Mount, Murray Barrick, and John Hunter, "Personality and Job Performance: a Critique of the Tett, Jackson, and Rothstein (1991) Meta-Analysis," Personnel Psychology 47, no. 1 (Spring 1994), pp. 147–72.

33. Robert Tett, Douglas Jackson, and Mitchell Rothstein, "Personality Measures as Predictors of Job Performance: A Meta-Analytic Review," Personnel Psychology 44 (1991), p. 732.

34. Tett, Jackson, and Rothstein, "Personality Measures," p 732.

35. For a study describing how matching (1) task and working condition preferences of applicants with (2) actual job and working conditions can be achieved, see Ronald Ash, Edward Levine, and Steven Edgell, "Study of a Matching Approach: The Impact of Ethnicity," Journal of Applied Psychology 64, no. 1 (February 1979), pp. 35–41. For a discussion of how a standard clerical test can be used to screen applicants who will have to use video displays, see Edward Silver and Corwin Bennett, "Modification of the Minnesota Clerical Test to Predict Performance on Video

Display Terminals," Journal of Applied Psychology 72, no. 1 (February 1987), pp. 153–5.

36. Emma D. Dunnette and W. D. Borman, "Personnel Selection and Classification Systems," Annual Review of Psychology 30 (1979), pp. 477–525, quoted in Siegel and Lane, Personnel and Organizational Psychology, pp. 182–3.

37. Paul Wernamont and John T. Campbell, "Signs, Samples, and Criteria," Journal of Applied Psychology 52 (1968), pp. 372–6; James Campion, "Work Sampling for Personnel Selection," Journal of Applied Psychology 56 (1972), pp. 40–4, reprinted in Hamner and Schmidt, Contemporary Problems in Personnel, pp. 168–80; Sidney Gael, Donald Grant, and Richard Ritchie, "Employment Test Validation for Minority and Nonminority Clerks with Work Sample Criteria," Journal of Applied Psychology 60, no. 4 (August 1974); Frank Schmidt and others, "Job Sample vs. Paper and Pencil Trades and Technical Test: Adverse Impact and Examinee Attitudes," Personnel Psychology 30, no. 7 (Summer 1977), pp. 187–98.

38. Siegel and Lane, Personnel and Organizational Psychology, pp. 182–3.

39. Ann Howard, "An Assessment of Assessment Centers," Academy of Management Journal 17 (1974), pp. 115–34; see also Louis Olivas, "Using Assessment Centers for Individual and Organizational Development," Personnel 57 (May–June 1980), pp. 63–7.

40. Development Dimensions, Inc., 1977-1978 Catalog. (Pittsburgh: Development Dimensions Press, 1977), discussed in Wayne F. Cascio and Val Silbey, "Utility of the Assessment Center as a Selection Device," Journal of Applied Psychology 64, no. 4 (April 1979), pp. 107–18.

41. See, for example, Larry Alexander, "An Exploratory Study of the Utilization of Assessment Center Results," Academy of Management Journal 22, no. 1 (March 1970), pp. 152–7.

42. Steven Norton, "The Empirical and Content Validity of Assessment Centers Versus Traditional Methods of Predicting Management Success," Academy of Management Review 20 (July 1977), pp. 442–53. Interestingly, a recent review concludes that assessment centers do predict managerial success, but after an extensive review, "we also assert that we do not know why they work." Richard Klimoski and Mary Brickner, "Why Do Assessment Centers Work? The Puzzle of Assessment Center Validity," Personnel Psychology 40, no. 2 (Summer 1987), pp. 243–60.

43. Cascio and Silbey, "Utility of the Assessment Center as a Selection Device." See also Paul R. Sackett, "Assessment Centers and Content Validity: Some Neglected Issues," Personnel Psychology 40 (Spring 1987), pp. 13–26.

44. David Groce, "A Behavioral Consistency Approach to Decision Making in Employment Selection," Personnel Psychology 34, no. 1 (Spring 1981), pp. 55–64.

45. For an alternative to assessment centers, see Donald Brush and Lyle Schoenfeldt, "Identifying Managerial Potential: An Alternative Assessment Center," Personnel 57 (May–June 1980), pp. 72–3.

46. Philip Lowry, "Selection Methods: Comparison of Assessment Centers with Personnel Records Evaluations," Public Personnel Management 23, no. 3 (Fall 1994), pp. 383–94.

47. Arthur Cosiegel, "The Miniature Job Training and Evaluation Approach: Traditional Findings," Personnel Psychology 36, no. 1 (Spring 1983), pp. 41–56.

48. John Jones and William Terris, "Post-Polygraph Selection Techniques," Recruitment Today (May–June 1989), pp. 25–31.

49. Norma Fritz, "In Focus: Honest Answers—Post Polygraph," *Personnel* (April 1989), p. 8.

50. Bureau of National Affairs, *Bulletin to Management,* September 10, 1987, p. 296.

51. See, for example, Kevin Murphy, "Detecting Infrequent Deception," *Journal of Applied Psychology* 72, no. 4 (November 1987), pp. 611–4, for a discussion of the difficulty of using such tests to provide convincing evidence of deception.

52. John Bernardin and Donna Cooke, "Validity of an Honesty Test in Predicting Theft Among Convenience Store Employees," *Academy of Management Journal* 36, no. 5 (1993), pp. 1097–108.

53. Judith Collins and Frank Schmidt, "Personality, Integrity, and White Collar Crime: A Construct Validity Study," *Personnel Psychology* 46 (1993), pp. 295–311.

54. See Table in James W. Thacker and R.J. Cattaneo, "The Canadian Personnel Function: Status and Practices."

55. Ulrich Sonnemann, *Handwriting Analysis as a Psychodiagnostic Tool* (New York: Grune & Stratton, 1950), pp. 144–5.

56. Sonnemann, *Handwriting Analysis*, pp. 144–5.

57. Camilla Cornell, "The Write Stuff," *Human Resources Professional* 7 no. 6 (June 1991), pp. 15–6.

58. Carole Hoglund, "Mandatory Drug Testing," *Human Resources Professional* 8 no. 1 (January 1992), pp. 21–22.

59. "TD Drug Tests Upheld," *Journal of the Addiction Research Foundation* 23 no. 5 (September/October 1994), p. 3.

60. Hoglund, "Mandatory Drug Testing," pp. 21–2.

61. Hoglund, "Mandatory Drug Testing," p. 22.

62. V. Galt, "Total Ban Sought on Drug Testing by Employers," *The Globe and Mail* (February 22, 1992), p. A6.

63. Hoglund, "Mandatory Drug Testing," p. 21.

64. R.J. McCunney, "Drug Testing: Technical Complications of a Complex Social Issue," in *American Journal of Industrial Medicine* 15, no. 5 (1989), pp. 589–600; discussed in Scott MacDonald, Samantha Wells, and Richard Fry, "The Limitationsof Drug Screening in the Workplace," *International Labor Review* 132, no. 1 (1993), p. 102.

65. For a discussion on this topic see MacDonald et al., "The Limitations of Drug Screening in the Workplace," pp. 105–6.

66. Chris Berka and Courtney Poignand, "Hair Follicle Testing —An Alternative to Urinalysis for Drug Abuse Screening," *Employee Relations Today* (Winter 1991-1992), pp. 405–9.

67. Hoglund, "Mandatory Drug Testing," p. 22.

68. "Catch 22: Under Imperial Oil's Revamped Drug Policy," *Journal of the Addiction Research Foundation* 22, no. 6 (November/December, 1994), p. 12.

69. Tricia McCallum, "The Science of Selection," *Human Resources Professional* 12, no. 3 (May 1995), pp. 9–12.

70. Michael McDaniel, et al., "The Validity of Employment Interviews: A Comprehensive Review and Meta-analysis," *Journal of Applied Psychology* 79, no. 4 (1994), p. 599.

71. James G. Goodale, *The Fine Art of Interviewing* (Englewood Cliffs. NJ: Prentice Hall Inc., 1982) p. 22. See also Robert L. Decker, "The Employment Inverview," *Personnel Administrator* 26 (November 1981) pp. 71–3.

72. Goodale, *The Fine Art of Interviewing*, p. 22.

73. McDaniel, et al., "The Validjty of Employment Interviews," p. 602.

74. McDaniel, et al., "The Validity of Employment Interviews,".p. 601.

75. See, for example, T. Janz, "The Patterned Behavior Description Interview: The Best Profit of the Future in the Past," in eds. R. W. Eder and G. R. Ferris, *The Employment Interview: Theory, Research, and Practice* (Newbury Park, CA: Sage, 1989), pp. 158–68.

76. McDaniel, et al., "The Validity of Employment Interviews," p. 601.

77. See Philip Roth and Jeffrey McMillan, "The Behavior Description Interview," *The CPA Journal* (December 1993), pp. 76–9.

78. See A. M. Ryan and P. R. Sackett, "Exploratory Study of Individual Assessment Practices: Interrater Reliability and Judgments of Assessor Effectiveness," *Journal of Applied Psychology* 74 (1989), pp. 568–79, cited in McDaniel, "The Validity of Employment Interviews," p. 601.

79. Arthur Pell, *Recruiting and Selecting Personnel* (New York: Regents, 1969), p. 119.

80. Douglas Rodgers, "Computer-Aided Interviewing Overcomes First Impressions," *Personnel Journal* (April 1987), pp. 148–52.

81. Rodgers, "Computer-Aided Interviewing," pp. 148–52.

82. Gary Robins, "Dial-an-Interview," *Stores* (June 1994), pp. 34–5.

83. William Bulkeley, "Replaced by Technology: Job Interviews," *The Wall Street Journal,* August 22, 1994, pp. B1, B7.

84. Bulkeley, "Replaced by Technology," pp. B1, B7.

85. For additional information on computer-aided interviewing's benefits, see, for example, Christopher Martin and Denise Nagao, "Some Effects of Computerized Interviewing on Job Applicant Responses," *Journal of Applied Psychology* 74, no. 1 (February 1989), pp. 72–80.

86. Marjory Kerr, "'Long Distance' Interviews Prove Useful," *Canadian HR Reporter* 10, no. 18 (October 20, 1997), pp. 27–8. Copyright MPL Communications Inc., Reproduced by permission of *Canadian HR Reporter*, 133 Richmond St. West, Toronto, Ontario M5H 3M8.

87. Based on Kerr, "Long Distance' Interviews," pp. 27–8..

88. Neal Schmitt, "Social and Situational Determinants of Interview Decisions: Implications for the Employment Interview," *Personnel Psychology* 29 (Spring 1976), pp. 79–101; Lynn Ulrich and Don Trumbo, "The Selection Interview Since 1949," *Psychological Bulletin* 63 (1965), pp. 100–16. See, however, Frank Landy, "The Validity of the Interview in Police Officer Selection," *Journal of Applied Psychology* 61 (1976), pp. 193–8. See also Vincent Loretto, "Effective Interviewing Is Based on More Than Intuition," *Personnel Journal* 65 (December 1986), pp. 101–7; George Dreher et al., "The Role of the Traditional Research Design in Underestimating the Validity of the Employment Interview," *Personnel Psychology* 41, no. 2 (Summer 1988), pp. 315–8; and M. M. Harris, "Reconsidering the Employment Interview: A Review of Recent Literature and Suggestions for Future Research," *Personnel Psychology* 42, 1989, pp. 691–726.

89. This validity discussion and these findings are based on McDaniel, et al., "The Validity of Employment Interviews," pp. 607–10; the validities for situational, job-related, and psychological interviews were (.50), (.39), and (.29), respectively.

90. Mean validities were structured (.44) and unstructured (.33). The researchers note that in this case even the unstructured interviews were relatively structured suggesting that ". . .the validity of most unstructured interviews used in practice may be lower than the validity found in this study." McDaniel et al., "The Validity of Employment Interviews," p. 609.

91. Goodale, *The Fine Art of Interviewing*, p. 26.

92. Goodale, *The Fine Art of Interviewing*, p. 26.

93. McDaniel, et al., "The Validity of Employment Interviews," p. 608.

94. S. W. Constantin, "An Investigation of Information Favorability in the Employment Interview," *Journal of Applied Psychology* 61 (1976), pp. 743–9. It should be noted that a number of the studies discussed in this chapter involve having interviewers evaluate interviews based on written transcripts (rather than face to face) and that a study suggests that this procedure may not be equivalent to having interviewers interview applicants directly. See Charles Gorman, William Grover, and Michael Doherty, "Can We Learn Anything About Interviewing Real People from 'Interviews' of Paper People? A Study of the External Validity Paradigm," *Organizational Behavior and Human Performance* 22, no. 2 (October 1978), pp. 165–92. See also John Binning et al., "Effects of Pre-interview Impressions on Questioning Strategies in Same and Opposite Sex Employment Interviews," *Journal of Applied Psychology* 73, no. 1 (February 1988), pp. 30–7; and Sebastiano Fisicaro, "A Reexamination of the Relation Between Halo Error and Accuracy," *Journal of Applied Psychology* 73, no. 2 (May 1988), pp. 239–46.

95. David Tucker and Patricia Rowe, "Relationship Between Expectancy, Casual Attribution, and Final Hiring Decisions in the Employment Interview," *Journal of Applied Psychology* 64, no. 1 (February 1979), pp. 27–34. See also Robert Dipboye, Gail Fontenelle, and Kathleen Garner, "Effect of Previewing the Application on Interview Process and Outcomes," *Journal of Applied Psychology* 69, no. 1 (February 1984), pp. 118–28.

96. R. E. Carlson, "Selection Interview Decisions: The Effects of Interviewer Experience, Relative Quota Situation, and Applicant Sample on Interview Decisions," *Personnel Psychology* 20 (1967), pp. 259–80.

97. R. E. Carlson, "Effects of Applicant Sample on Ratings of Valid Information in an Employment Setting," *Journal of Applied Psychology* 54 (1970), pp. 217–22.

98. See Arvey and Campion, "The Employment Interview," p. 305.

99. Madelaine Heilmann and Lewis Saruwatari, "When Beauty Is Beastly: The Effects of Appearance and Sex on Evaluation of Job Applicants for Managerial and Nonmanagerial Jobs," *Organizational Behavior and Human Performance* 23 (June 1979), pp. 360–72. See also Tracy McDonald and Milton Hakel, "Effects of Applicant Race, Sex, Suitability, and Answers on Interviewers' Questioning Strategy and Ratings," *Personnel Psychology* 38, no. 2 (Summer 1985), pp. 321–34. See also M. S. Singer and Christine Sewell, "Applicant Age and Selection Interview Decisions: Effect of Information Exposure on Age Discrimination in Personnel Selection," *Personnel Psychology* 42, no. 1 (Spring 1989), pp. 135–54.

100. Arthur Pell, "Nine Interviewing Pitfalls," *Managers* (January 1994), p. 29.

101. Thomas Dougherty, Daniel Turban, and John Callender, "Confirming First Impressions in the Employment Interview: A Field Study of Interviewer Behavior," *Journal of Applied Psychology* 79, no. 5 (1994), p. 663.

102. See Pell, "Nine Interviewing Pitfalls," p. 29; Parth Sarathi, "Making Selection Interviews Effective," *Management and Labor Studies* 18, no. 1 (1993), pp. 5–7.

103. Pell, "Nine Interviewing Pitfalls," p. 30.

104. This section is based on Pursell, Campion, and Gaylord, "Structured Interviewing," and Latham et al., "The Situational Interview." See also Michael A. Campion, Elliott Pursell, and Barbara Brown, "Structured Interviewing," pp. 25–42, and Weekley and Gier, "Reliability and Validity of the Situational Interview," pp. 484–7, except as noted.

105. See also Phillip Lowry, "The Structured Interview: An Alternative to the Assessment Center?" *Public Personnel Management* 23, no. 2 (Summer 1994), pp. 201–15.

106. Steps two and three are based on one of the author's personal experiences, using the Kepner-Tregoe Decision-Making Model.

107. Pell, *Recruiting and Selecting Personnel*, pp. 103–15.

108. Willi H. Wiesner and Robert J. Oppenheimer. "Note-Taking in the Selection Interview: its Effect Upon Predictive Validity and Information Recall." *Proceedings of the Annual Conference Meeting*. Administrative Sciences Association of Canada (Personnel and Human Resources Division) 12 Part 8 (1991) pp. 97–106.

109. William Tullar, Terry Mullins, and Sharon Caldwell, "Effects of Interview Length and Applicant Quality on Interview Decision Time," *Journal of Applied Psychology* 64 (December 1979), pp. 669–74. See also McDonald and Hakel, "Effects of Applicants' Race, Sex, Suitability, and Answers," pp. 321–34.

110. See, for example, George Beason and John Belt, "Verifying the Job Applicant's Background," *Personnel Administration* (November–December 1974), pp. 29–32; Bureau of National Affairs, "Selection Procedures and Personnel Records," *Personnel Policies Forum, No. 114* (September 1976), p. 4. See also Paul Sackett and Michael M. Harris, "Honesty Testing for Personnel Selection: A Review and Critique," *Personnel Psychology* 37, no. 2 (Summer 1985), pp. 221–45.

111. Tiffin and McCormick, *Industrial Psychology*, pp. 78–9.

112. Michael Stamler, "Employment Gaps, References Should be Scrutinized," *Canadian HR Reporter* 9, no. 7 (April 8, 1996) p. 11 Copyright MPL Communications Inc., Reproduced by permission of *Canadian HR Reporter*, 133 Richmond St. West, Toronto, Ontario M5H 3M8.

113. Stamler, "Employment Gaps," pp. 11, 15.

114. Stamler, "Employment Gaps," p. 15.

115. See Howard M. Fischer, "Select the Right Executive," *Personnel Journal* (April 1989), pp. 110–14.

116. Randall Scott Echlin, "References Redux," *Human Resources Professional* 7, no. 8 (September 1991), p. 7.

117. Echlin, "References Redux," pp. 7–8.

118. J.A. Breaugh, "Realistic Job Previews: A Critical Appraisal and Future Research Directions," *Academy of Management Review* 8, no. 4 (1983), pp. 612–9.

119. Patricia Buhler, "Managing in the 90s: Hiring the Right Person for the Job," *Supervision* (July 1992), pp. 21–3.

120. Breaugh, "Realistic Job Previews," pp. 612–9.

121. Bernard L. Dugoni and Daniel R. Ilgen, "Realistic Job Preview and the Adjustment of New Employees," *Academy of Management Journal* (September 1981), p. 590.

122. B. Kleinmutz, "Why We Still Use Our Heads Instead of Formulas: Toward an Integrative Approach," *Psychological Bulletin* 107 (1990), pp. 296–310.

Chapter 8
Orientation and Training

Chapter Outline

- ◆ **Orienting Employees**
- ◆ **The Training Process**
- ◆ **Training Needs Analysis**
- ◆ **Training Techniques**
- ◆ **Training for Special Purposes**
- ◆ **Evaluating the Training Effort**

Learning Outcomes

After studying this chapter, you should be able to:

Explain how to develop an orientation and socialization program.

Describe the basic training process.

Discuss at least two techniques used for assessing training needs.

Explain the pros and cons of at least five training techniques.

Describe how to evaluate the training effort.

Once employees have been recruited and selected, the next step is orientation and training. In this chapter we'll explain that orienting and training employees means providing them with the information and skills they need to successfully perform their new jobs. We'll start with employee orientation.

Orienting Employees

employee orientation
A procedure for providing new employees with basic background information about the firm and the job.

socialization
The ongoing process of instilling in all employees the prevailing attitudes, standards, values, and patterns of behaviour that are expected by the organization.

reality shock
That state that results from the discrepancy between what the new employee expected from his or her new job, and the realities of it.

Employee orientation provides new employees with basic background information about the employer, information they need to perform their jobs satisfactorily, such as what the work hours are. Orientation is actually one component of the employer's new-employee socialization process. **Socialization** is the ongoing process of instilling in all employees the prevailing attitudes, standards, values, and patterns of behaviour that are expected by the organization and its departments.[1]

The new employee's initial orientation, if handled correctly, helps him or her perform better by providing needed information about company rules and practices. It can also help reduce the new employee's first-day jitters and the **reality shock** he or she might otherwise experience (the discrepancy between what the new employee expected from his or her new job, and the realities of it).

Orientation programs range from brief, informal introductions to lengthy, formal programs. In the latter, the new employee is usually given a handbook or printed materials that cover matters like working hours, performance reviews, getting on the payroll, and vacations, as well as a tour of the facilities. As illustrated in **Figure 8.1**, other information typically includes employee benefits, human resources policies, the employee's daily routine, company goals and objectives, company organization and operations, and safety measures and regulations.[2] Note that some courts have found employee handbook contents to represent a contract with the employee. Therefore, disclaimers should be included that make it clear that statements of company policies, benefits, and regulations do not constitute the terms and conditions of an employment contract, either express or implied. Firms should think twice before including statements in the handbook such as "No employee will be fired without just cause" or statements that imply or state that employees have tenure; they could be viewed as legal and binding commitments.

The first part of the orientation is usually performed by the HR specialist, who explains such matters as working hours and vacation. The employee is then introduced to his or her new supervisor. The latter continues the orientation by explaining the exact nature of the job, introducing the person to his or her new colleagues, and familiarizing the new employee with the workplace. An example of a comprehensive orientation program is presented in the Building Employee Commitment box.

In an orientation, the supervisor explains the exact nature of the job, introduces new colleagues, and familiarizes new employees with the workplace.

The Training Process

Introduction: Training and Responsiveness

training
The process of teaching new employees the basic skills/competencies they need to perform their jobs.

Training gives new or present employees the skills/competencies they need to perform their jobs. Training might thus mean showing a machinist how to operate his new machine, a new sssssssalesperson how to sell her firm's product, or a new supervisor how to interview and appraise employees. Whereas training focuses on skills and competencies needed to perform employees' current jobs, *employee and management*

Figure 8.1
Orientation Checklist in a Retail Chain
Source: Strategies for Excellence Inc. Used with permission.

BIG PICTURE

___ Mission, vision, values, principles
___ History of this business
___ Business ethics
___ Customer service philosophy
___ Target market, customer profile
___ Our key customers
___ What makes our business unique
___ Sales philosophy
___ Merchandising philosophy
___ Housekeeping philosophy
___ Our team
___ Trust and respect
___ Sales and revenue goals
___ Structure and size of business
___ Tour of store(s)

PERSONAL ITEMS

___ Payday, how and when
___ Time sheets, reporting
___ Overtime
___ Bonuses and incentives
___ Benefits and paperwork
___ TD1, CPP, EI, etc.
___ Staff discounts
___ Store hours
___ Work schedules and shifts
___ Parking and restrictions
___ Bus transportation and hours
___ Staff lockers, coat rack
___ Breaks and schedules
___ Where to eat
___ Microwave and fridge
___ Dress code, uniforms, grooming
___ What to do if you are late or sick
___ Vacations
___ Personal telephone calls
___ Your personal sales targets

SECURITY AND SAFETY

___ Keys and lock-up procedures
___ Key carrier responsibilities
___ Approved entrances and exits a) store, b) mall
___ Fire alarm box, fire

___ extinguishers, fire drills
___ Smoke detector
___ First aid box
___ Police and ambulance
___ Mall security
___ ID badges and photos
___ Smoking areas
___ Reporting accidents, WCB
___ Shoplifting, shrinkage
___ Fitting rooms
___ Internal theft
___ Lifting and carrying boxes/merchandise
___ Use of drugs and alcohol

INTRODUCTION

___ Owner and manager
___ All full-time and part-time staff
___ Mall security
___ Next-door neighbours
___ Head office staff
___ Delivery staff
___ Suppliers
___ Window dressers
___ Customers

SALES AND ADMINISTRATION

___ Point of sale (P.O.S.) system
___ Ringing up a sale, refund, return, exchange, lay-a-way
___ Telephone etiquette
___ Daily sales summary
___ Inventory listings, philosophy, and storage
___ Packing slips, return slips
___ Breakage or damage reports
___ Shipments: short and long
___ Pricing and prices
___ Markdowns and promotional items
___ Re-ordering
___ Transferring stock between stores
___ Guarantees we offer
___ Housekeeping: washrooms, stock room, fitting rooms
___ Seasonal products, hot items

___ Targets and goals on specific items
___ Target customers
___ Product info sheets, manuals, videos, etc.
___ Features and benefits of products
___ How to approach a customer
___ How to demonstrate a product
___ How to get multiple sales
___ How to handle customer complaints
___ Sales associates' selling responsibilities
___ Test product knowledge, location, and price

MERCHANDISING

___ Philosophy on displaying products
___ Philosophy on window displays
___ Philosophy on signage
___ Seasonal plans
___ Changes: when, how, by whom

COMMUNICATION AND LEARNING

___ Philosophy on communication
___ Philosophy on learning
___ Dealing with constant changes
___ Daily log book
___ Bulletin boards
___ Staff newsletter
___ Customer newsletter
___ Staff meetings
___ Manager availability
___ Ask lots of questions
___ Who to tell? Who needs to know?
___ Telling stories about successes
___ Telling stories about learning opportunities
___ Ask for help
___ Help others
___ Teamwork, buddy system
___ Share new ideas and suggestions
___ The telephone
___ Learning resources

Building Employee Commitment

Orientation and Socialization

In many firms today, orientation goes well beyond providing basic information about such aspects of the job as hours of work. More and more companies are finding that orientation can be used for other purposes, such as familiarizing new employees with the company's cherished goals and values. Orientation thus begins the process of synthesizing the employee's and the company's goals, one big step toward winning the employee's commitment to the firm.

Orientation at the Toyota manufacturing plant in Cambridge, Ontario is a case in point. While it covers traditional topics such as company benefits, it's mostly intended to socialize new employees, that is, to convert Toyota's new employees to the firm's ideology of quality, teamwork, personal development, open communication, and mutual respect.

New manufacturing team members have two days of orientation, which begin by providing basic information on benefits, and the company's health and fitness centres. A plant tour is conducted and the importance of quality and continuous improvement in the manufacturing process is explained. Health and safety issues are another major component of the orientation, along with information on recycling and disposal of hazardous waste. A "meet the managers" session is also included. Employee rules and regulations are discussed and it is stressed that employees can appeal disciplinary action to a board of fellow employees.

It is the orientation material on Toyota's employee relations philosophy that is most directly related to building employee commitment. Toyota's philosophy of teamwork and trust is explained, and beyond that, how systems, procedures, and processes reflect that philosophy. The human resources management function is built around the framework of the company's credo that "people are our most important asset."[1]

Employees thus complete the orientation process with a thorough introduction to Toyota's ideology, in particular its mission of quality and its values of teamwork, kaizen (continuous improvement), and problem solving. That is a big step toward winning new employees' commitment to Toyota and its goals and values.

1. Personal communication with Joe Allan, Toyota Canada, September 19, 1997.

development (explained in chapter 9) is training of a long-term nature. Its aim is to prepare current employees for future jobs with the organization or to solve an organizational problem concerning, for instance, poor interdepartmental communication. The techniques used in both training and development are often the same, however, and the distinction between the two is always somewhat arbitrary.[3]

In fact, training's purposes are broader today than they have been in the past. The training and development function is transforming itself to meet the changing business imperatives of the new millenium. Companies used to emphasize production process training—teaching the technical skills required to perform jobs, such as training assemblers to solder wires or teachers to devise lesson plans.[4] However, training and development programs and their objectives changed in the 1980s and 1990s. Employers had to adapt to rapid technological changes, improve product and service quality, and boost productivity to stay competitive.[5] Improving quality often requires remedial-education training, since quality-improvement programs assume employees can use critical thinking skills, produce charts and graphs, and analyze data.[6] Employees must also use or acquire skills in team building, decision making, and communication. One recent survey found that teamwork is currently the critical training challenge for all employee groups. Leadership, information technology, and the management of change are other important training needs today.[7] As firms become more technologically advanced, employees require training in technological and computer skills (such as desktop publishing and computer-aided design and manufacturing).[8] Also, as increased competition has put a premium on better service, employers have turned increasingly to customer-service training to provide employees with the tools and abilities they need to deal more effectively with customers, such as effective listening skills.

More employers today are also taking advantage of the fact that training can strengthen employee commitment. Few things illustrate a firm's commitment to its employees more than continuing developmental opportunities to better themselves, and such commitment is usually reciprocated. This is one reason why high-commitment firms like Toyota provide about two weeks of training per year for all employees.

In summary, the expansion of training's role reflects the fact that "the game of economic competition has new rules."[9] In particular, it's no longer enough to just be efficient. Thriving today requires that the firm be fast and responsive. It also requires responding to customers' needs for quality, variety, customization, convenience, and timeliness. Meeting these new standards requires a work force that is more than just technically trained. It requires people who are capable of analyzing and solving job-related problems, working productively in teams, and "switching gears" by shifting from job to job as well.

The Ontario Ministry of Economic Development has estimated that by the year 2010, 60 percent of all new jobs will require skills held by only 22 percent of today's workers.[10] Thus training is moving to centre stage as a means of improving employers' competitiveness. The average training investment by Canadian companies has risen from 1.5 percent of payroll in 1990 to almost 2 percent of payroll in 1997.[11] Those with above-average spending include Bell Canada, IBM, the major Canadian banks, companies in the oil and gas industry, and many small businesses. These organizations see training as the key to enhancing their competitive advantage. A 1996 Conference Board of Canada survey found that several of these organizations have set up corporate training centres, which are seen as more effective than universities for managing strategic and cultural shifts. The same survey found that almost half of medium- and large-sized Canadian companies planned to increase spending on training in the year ahead. Decreases in training and development spending were expected by educational and health care organizations.[12]

The Five-Step Training and Development Process

We can conveniently think of a typical training or development program as consisting of five steps, as summarized in **Figure 8.2**. The purpose of the *needs analysis* step is to identify the specific job performance skills needed, to analyze the skills and needs of the prospective trainees, and to develop specific, measurable knowledge and performance objectives. (Managers must make sure that the performance deficiency is amenable to training rather than caused by, say, poor morale due to low salaries.) In the second, *instructional design* step, the actual content of the training program is compiled and produced, including workbooks, exercises, and activities. Next, there may be a third *validation* step, in which the bugs are worked out of the training program by presenting it to a small representative audience. Fourth, the training program is *implemented,* using techniques like those discussed in this and the following chapter (such as on-the-job training and

Figure 8.2.
The Five Steps in the
Training and
Development Process

Source: These are adapted from
Mary D. Carolan, "Today's
Training Basics: Some New
Golden Rules," *HR Focus*
(April 1993), p. 18.

1. NEEDS ANALYSIS

- Identify specific job performance skills needed to improve performance and productivity.
- Analyze the audience to ensure that the program will be suited to their specific levels of education, experience, and skills, as well as their attitudes and personal motivations.
- Use research to develop specific measurable knowledge and performance objectives.

2. INSTRUCTIONAL DESIGN

- Gather instructional objectives, methods, media, description of and sequence of content, examples, exercises, and activities. Organize them into a curriculum that supports adult learning theory and provides a blueprint for program development.
- Make sure all materials, such as video scripts, leaders' guides, and participants' workbooks, complement each other, are written clearly, and blend into unified training geared directly to the stated learning objectives.
- Carefully and professionally handle all program elements—whether reproduced on paper, film, or tape—to guarantee quality and effectiveness.

3. VALIDATION

- Introduce and validate the training before a representative audience. Base final revisions on pilot results to ensure program effectiveness.

4. IMPLEMENTATION

- When applicable, boost success with a train-the-trainer workshop that focusses on presentation-knowledge and skills in addition to training content.

5. EVALUATION AND FOLLOW-UP

- Assess program success according to:
  REACTION—Document the learners' immediate reactions to the training.
  LEARNING—Use feedback devices or pre- and post-tests to measure what learners have actually learned.
  BEHAVIOUR—Note supervisors' reactions to learners' performance following completion of the training. This is one way to measure the degree to which learners apply new skills and knowledge to their jobs.
  RESULTS—Determine the level of improvement in job performance and assess needed maintenance.

programmed learning). Fifth, there should be an *evaluation* and follow-up step in which the program's successes or failures are assessed.

Training and Learning

Training is essentially a learning process. To train employees, therefore, it is useful to know something about how people learn. Some suggestions based on learning theory follow.

First, it is easier for trainees to understand and remember material that is meaningful:[13]

1. At the start of training, provide the trainees with a bird's-eye view of the material to be presented. Knowing the overall picture facilitates learning.
2. Use a variety of familiar examples when presenting material.

3. Organize the material so that it is presented in a logical manner and in meaningful units.

4. Try to use terms and concepts that are already familiar to trainees.

5. Use as many visual aids as possible.

Second, make sure it is easy to transfer new skills and behaviours from the training site to the job site:[14]

1. Maximize the similarity between the training situation and the work situation.

2. Provide adequate training practice.

3. Label or identify each feature of the machine and/or step in the process.

Third, motivate the trainee:[15]

1. People learn best by doing. Try to provide as much realistic practice as possible.

2. Trainees learn best when correct responses are immediately reinforced, perhaps with a quick "well done."

3. Trainees learn best at their own pace. If possible, let trainees pace themselves.

Further strategies for increasing the transfer of training include giving trainees the chance to use their new skills immediately upon their return to work, training managers first and employees second in order to send a message about the importance of the training, and controlling contingencies by planning rewards for trainees who successfully complete and integrate the new training. [16]

Legal Aspects of Training

Under human rights and employment equity legislation, several aspects of employee training programs must be assessed with an eye toward the program's impact on designated group members.[17] For example, having relatively few women or visible minorities selected for the training program may require showing that the admissions procedures are valid—that they predict performance on the job for which the person is being trained.

Similarly, if completing the training program is a prerequisite for promotion, the firm should then be able to show that the training program itself has no adverse impact on women, visible minorities, or other designated group members. In other words, members of protected groups should have as much chance of successfully completing the training as do white males. If they do not, the validity of the training requirements should be demonstrated. For example, it could turn out that the reading level of the training manuals is too high for many visible minority trainees, and that they are thus doing poorly in the program, quite aside from their aptitude for the jobs for which they are being trained. The training program might then be found to be unfairly discriminatory.

Negligent training is another potential problem. *Negligent training* occurs when an employer fails to train adequately, and an employee subsequently harms a third party.[18] Also, employees who are dismissed for poor performance or disciplined for safety infractions may claim that the employer was negligent in that the employee's training was inadequate. Precautions here include:[19]

1. Confirm claims of skill and experience for all applicants.

2. Reduce the risks of harm by extensively training employees who work with dangerous equipment, materials, or processes.

3. Ensure that the training includes procedures to protect third parties' health and safety (including that of other employees).

4. Evaluate the training activity to determine its effectiveness in reducing negligence risks.

Training Needs Analysis

The first step in training is to determine what training, if any, is required. The main task in assessing the training needs of new employees is to determine what the job entails and to break it down into subtasks, each of which is then taught to the new employee. Assessing the training needs of current employees can be more complex, since it involves the added task of deciding whether or not training is the solution. For example, performance may be down because the standards aren't clear or because the person isn't motivated.

Task analysis and performance analysis are the two main techniques for identifying training needs. About 19 percent of employers reporting in one survey said they used **task analysis**—an analysis of the job's requirements—to determine the training required.[20] Task analysis is especially appropriate for determining the training needs of employees who are *new* to their jobs. **Performance analysis** appraises the performance of *current* employees to determine whether training could reduce performance problems such as excess scrap or low output. Other techniques used to identify training needs include supervisors' reports, HR records, management requests, observations, tests of job knowledge, and questionnaire surveys.[21]

Whichever technique is used—task analysis, performance analysis, or some other—employee input is essential. It's often true that no one knows as much about the job as the people actually doing it, so that soliciting employee input is usually wise.[22]

task analysis
A detailed study of a job to identify the skills and competencies it requires so that an appropriate training program may be instituted.

performance analysis
Verifying that there is a performance deficiency and determining whether that deficiency should be rectified through training or through some other means (such as transferring the employee).

Task Analysis: Assessing the Training Needs of New Employees

Task analysis—identifying the broad competencies and specific skills required to perform job-related tasks—is used for determining the training needs of employees who are new to their jobs. Particularly with entry-level workers, it is common to hire inexperienced people and train them.[23] Thus, the aim is to develop the skills and knowledge required for effective performance—like soldering (in the case of an assembly worker) or interviewing (in the case of a supervisor).

The job description and job specification are helpful here. These list the specific duties and skills required on the job and become the basic reference point in determining the training required to perform the job.

Task Analysis Record Form   Some employers supplement the current job description and specification with a task analysis record form. This consolidates information regarding the job's required tasks and skills in a form that's especially helpful for determining training requirements. As illustrated in **Table 8.1**, a task analysis record form contains six types of information:

Column 1, Task List   Here, the job's main tasks and subtasks are listed. For example, if one major task is "Operate paper cutter," subtasks 1.1 through 1.5 might include "Start motor," "Set cutting distance," "Place paper on cutting table," "Push paper up to cutter," and "Grasp safety release with left hand."

Column 2, How Often Performed   Here, the *frequency* with which the task and subtasks are performed is indicated. For example, is it performed only once at the beginning of the shift, or many times, hour after hour?

Column 3, Quantity, Quality Standards   Here, the *standards of performance* for each task and subtask are described. These show the level to be attained by the trainee and should be as specific as possible. They should be expressed in measurable

TABLE 8.1 Task Analysis Record Form

TASK LIST	WHEN AND HOW OFTEN PERFORMED	QUANTITY AND QUALITY OF PERFORMANCE	CONDITIONS UNDER WHICH PERFORMED	COMPETENCIES AND SPECIFIC SKILLS OR KNOWLEDGE REQUIRED	WHERE BEST LEARNED
1. Operate paper cutter	4 times per day		Noisy press room: distractions		
1.1 Start motor					
1.2 Set cutting distance		±tolerance of 0.007 in.		Read gauge	On the job
1.3 Place paper on cutting table		Must be completely even		Lift paper correctly	"
	to prevent uneven cut				
1.4 Push paper up to cutter				Must be even	"
1.5 Grasp safety release with left hand		100% of time, for safety		Essential for safety	On the job but practice first with no
				distractions	
1.6 Grasp cutter release with right hand				Must keep both hands on releases	"
1.7 Simultaneously pull safety release with left hand and cutter release with right hand					
1.8 Wait for cutter to retract		100% of time, for safety		"	"
1.9 Retract paper			retracts	Wait till cutter	"
1.10 Shut off		100% of time, for safety			"
2. Operate printing press					
2.1 Start motor					
.					
.					
.					

Note: Task analysis record form showing some of tasks and subtasks performed by a right-handed printing press operator.

terms like "± tolerance of 0.007 in.," "Twelve units per hour," or "Within two days of receiving the order," for instance.

Column 4, Performance Conditions Here, the *conditions* under which the tasks and subtasks are to be performed are indicated. This is especially important if the conditions are crucial to the training—for example, where the person normally has to work under conditions of turmoil and stress (as in the case of an air traffic controller).

www.chauncey.com/itt/
summary.html
International Standards for Core
Competency Training

Column 5, Competencies and Specific Skills Required This is the heart of the task analysis form. Here the competencies and specific *skills* or *knowledge* required for each of the tasks and subtasks are listed, specifying exactly what knowledge or skills must be taught. Thus, for the subtask "Set cutting distance," the trainee must be taught how to read the gauge. Competencies in coaching and mentoring are becoming critical at the supervisory level.[24]

Column 6, Where Best Learned The decision as to whether the task is learned best *on* or *off the job* is based on several considerations. Safety is one: for example, prospective jet pilots must learn something about the plane off the job in a simulator before actually getting behind the controls.

Performance Analysis: Determining the Training Needs of Current Employees

Performance analysis means verifying whether there is a significant performance deficiency and if so, determining whether that deficiency should be rectified through training or through some other means (such as transferring the employee). The first step is to appraise the employee's performance, since to improve it, the firm must first determine the person's current performance compared to what it should be. Examples of specific performance deficiencies follow:

> "I expect each salesperson to make ten new contacts per week, but John averages only six."
>
> "Other plants our size average no more than two serious accidents per month; we're averaging five."

Distinguishing between *can't do* and *won't do* problems is the heart of performance analysis. First, the firm must determine whether it's a *can't do* problem and, if so, its specific causes: The employees don't know what to do or what the standards are; there are obstacles in the system such as lack of tools or supplies; job aids are needed, such as colour-coded wires that show assemblers which wire goes where; poor selection results in hiring people who haven't the skills to do the job; or training is inadequate. On the other hand, it might be a *won't do* problem. In this case, employees *could* do a good job if they wanted to. The environment has to be changed to allow or encourage employees to improve their performance. For example, the reward system might have to be changed, perhaps by implementing an incentive system.

Setting Training Objectives

Concrete, measurable training objectives should be set after training needs have been analyzed. Training, development, or (more generally) *instructional objectives* are defined as ". . . a description of a performance that learners must be able to exhibit before they will be considered competent."[25] For example:

> *Given a tool kit and a service manual, the technical representative will be able to adjust the registration (black line along paper edges) on this Xerox duplicator within 20 minutes according to the specifications stated in the manual.[26]*

Objectives specify what the trainee should be able to accomplish after successfully completing the training program.[27] They thus provide a focus for the efforts of both the trainee and the trainer, and a benchmark for evaluating the success of the training program.

Training Techniques

After the employees' training needs have been determined, training objectives can be set, and the training program can be designed and implemented. In general, training professionals are trying to provide learning in a more flexible, personalized, and cost-effective manner through increased use of computer-assisted self-study, multimedia, and distance learning.[28] Descriptions of the most popular training techniques follow.

On-The-Job Training

on-the-job training (OJT)
Learning a job while performing it.

On-the-job training (OJT) involves having a person learn a job by actually performing it. Virtually every employee, from mailroom clerk to company president, gets some on-the-job training when he or she joins a firm. In many companies, OJT is the only type of training available. It usually involves assigning new employees to experienced workers or supervisors who then do the actual training.[29]

There are several types of on-the-job training. The most familiar is the *coaching or understudy* method. Here the employee is trained on the job by an experienced worker or the trainee's supervisor. At lower levels, trainees may acquire skills for, say, running a machine by observing the supervisor. But this technique is also widely used at top-management levels. The position of assistant is often used to train and develop the company's future top managers, for instance. *Job rotation*, in which an employee (usually a management trainee) moves from job to job at planned intervals, is another OJT technique. *Special assignments* are another on-the-job training technique designed to give lower-level executives firsthand experience in working on actual problems.

In an assembly plant a newly hired employee receives on-the-job, in-depth training.

Apprenticeship training is a structured process by which individuals become skilled workers through a combination of classroom instruction and on-the-job training.[30] It is widely used to train individuals for many occupations, including electrician and plumber, and it is essentially the type of training new medical interns get during the several years they spend working in hospitals after graduation.

OJT has several advantages. It is relatively inexpensive; trainees learn while producing, and there is no need for expensive off-job facilities like classrooms or programmed learning devices. The method also facilitates learning, since trainees learn by actually doing the job and get quick feedback about the quality of their performance.

However, there are several trainer-related factors that should be kept in mind when designing OJT programs.[31] The trainers themselves should be carefully trained and given the necessary training materials. (Often, instead, an experienced worker is simply told to "go train John.") Experienced workers who are chosen as trainers should be thoroughly trained in the proper methods of instruction—in particular the principles of learning and perhaps the job instruction technique that we address next. A useful step-by-step job instruction approach for giving a new employee on-the-job training follows:

Step 1: Preparation of the Learner

1. Put the learner at ease—relieve the tension.
2. Explain why he or she is being taught.
3. Create interest, encourage questions, find out what the learner already knows about his or her job or other jobs.

4. Explain the why of the whole job and relate it to some job the learner already knows.
5. Place the learner as close to the normal working position as possible.
6. Familiarize the learner with the equipment, materials, tools, and trade terms.

Step 2: Presentation of the Operation

1. Explain quantity and quality requirements.
2. Go through the job at the normal work pace.
3. Go through the job at a slow pace several times, explaining each step. Between operations, explain the difficult parts, or those in which errors are likely to be made.
4. Again, go through the job at a slow pace several times; explain the key points.
5. Have the learner explain the steps as you go through the job at a slow pace.

Step 3: Performance Tryout

1. Have the learner go through the job several times, slowly, explaining each step to you. Correct mistakes and, if necessary, do some of the complicated steps the first few times.
2. The trainer runs the job at the normal pace.
3. Have the learner do the job, gradually building up skill and speed.
4. As soon as the learner demonstrates ability to do the job, let the work begin, but don't abandon him or her.

Step 4: Follow-Up

1. Designate a person to whom the learner should go for help if he or she needs it.
2. Gradually decrease supervision, checking work from time to time against quality and quantity standards.
3. Correct faulty work patterns that begin to creep into the work, and do it before they become a habit. Show why the learned method is superior.
4. Compliment good work; encourage the worker until he or she is able to meet the quality/quantity standards.

Job Instruction Training

job instruction training (JIT)
Listing of each job's basic tasks, along with key points, in order to provide step-by-step training for employees.

Many jobs consist of a logical sequence of steps and are best taught step by step. This step-by-step process is called **job instruction training (JIT).** To begin, all necessary steps in the job are listed, each in its proper sequence. Alongside each step a corresponding "key point" (if any) should be noted. The steps show *what* is to be done, while the key points show *how* it's to be done—and *why*. Here is an example of a job instruction training sheet for teaching a right-handed trainee how to operate a large motorized paper cutter.

Steps	*Key Points*
1. Start motor	None
2. Set cutting distance	Carefully read scale—to prevent wrong-sized cut
3. Place paper on cutting table	Make sure paper is even—to prevent uneven cut
4. Push paper up to cutter	Make sure paper is tight—to prevent uneven cut
5. Grasp safety release with left hand	Do not release left hand—to prevent hand from being caught in cutter
6. Grasp cutter release with right hand	Do not release right hand—to prevent hand from being caught in cutter
7. Simultaneously pull cutter and safety releases	Keep both hands on corresponding releases—to avoid hands being on cutting table

8. Wait for cutter to retract	Keep both hands on releases—to avoid having hands on cutting table
9. Retract paper	Make sure cutter is retracted; keep both hands away from releases
10. Shut off motor	None

Lectures

Lecturing has several advantages. It is a quick and simple way of providing knowledge to large groups of trainees, as when the sales force must be taught the special features of a new product. While written material like books and manuals could be used instead, they may involve considerable printing expense, and they don't permit the give and take of questioning that lectures do.

Some useful guidelines for presenting a lecture follow:[32]

Give listeners signals to help them follow key ideas. For instance, when presenting a list of items, start by saying something like "There are four reasons why the sales reports are necessary. . . . The first . . . the second . . . "

Don't start out on the wrong foot. For instance, don't open with an irrelevant joke or story or by saying something like, "I really don't know why I was asked to speak here today."

Keep your conclusions short. Just summarize the main point or points in one or two succinct sentences.

Be alert to the audience. Watch body language for negative signals like fidgeting and crossed arms.

Maintain eye contact with the trainees in the program. At a minimum, you should look at each section of the audience during the presentation.

Make sure everyone in the room can hear. Use a microphone or talk loudly enough so that people in the last row can hear and, if necessary, repeat questions that come from trainees from the front of the room before answering them.

Control hand gestures. Get in the habit of leaving them hanging naturally rather than letting them drift to the face, then pockets, and so on. Putting hands near the face can block voice projection and also give the impression that the speaker lacks confidence.

Talk from notes rather than from a script. Write out clear, legible notes on large index cards and then use these as an outline rather than memorizing the whole presentation.

Eliminate bad habits. Beware of distracting the listeners by jiggling coins in a pocket or pulling on an earlobe.

Practice. If there is time, make sure to rehearse under conditions similar to those under which the presentation will actually be given.

Audiovisual Techniques

Audiovisual techniques like films, closed-circuit television, audiotapes, and videotapes can be very effective and are widely used.[33] Audiovisuals are more expensive than conventional lectures but offer some advantages. Trainers should consider using them in the following situations:

1. *When there is a need to illustrate how a certain sequence should be followed over time,* such as when teaching wire soldering or telephone repair. The stop action, instant reply, or fast- or slow-motion capabilities of audiovisuals can be useful.

2. *When there is a need to expose trainees to events not easily demonstrable in live lectures,* such as a visual tour of a factory or open-heart surgery.

3. *When the training is going to be used organization-wide* and it is too costly to move the trainers from place to place.

There are three options when it comes to video: buying an existing videotape or film; making one; or having a production company produce the video. Dozens of businesses issue catalogues listing audiovisual programs on topics ranging from applicant interviewing to zoo management.

videoconferencing
Connecting two or more distant groups using audio-visual equipment.

Videoconferencing **Videoconferencing**, where an instructor is televised live to multiple locations, is an increasingly popular way to train employees. It has been defined as ". . . a means of joining two or more distant groups using a combination of audio and visual equipment."[34] Videoconferencing allows people in one location to communicate live with people in another city or country or with groups in several other cities.[35] The communication links are established either by sending specially "compressed" audio and video signals over telephone lines or via satellite.[36]

Given that videoconferencing is by nature visual, interactive, and remote, there are several things that should be kept in mind before getting up in front of the camera. Because the training is remote, it's particularly important to prepare a training guide ahead of time, specifically a manual the learners can use to keep track of the points that the trainer is making. A sampling of other hints would include:[37]

Avoid bright, flashy jewellery, or heavily patterned clothing.

Arrive at least 20 minutes early.

Test all equipment that will be used.

Adjust lights (if necessary and if possible); put lighting in front of participants to avoid shadows.

Have all participants introduce themselves.

Avoid focussing just on one group at one remote site (if there are several) and avoid presenting just to the video camera and not to the in-house participants.

Project the voice and speak clearly; particularly if people at the remote site have a different native language, keep speech free of jargon and needlessly complex words.

Remember that excessive physical movement will cause distortion of the video image where compressed telephone transmission is being used.

Programmed Learning

programmed learning
A systematic method for teaching job skills that involves presenting questions or facts, allowing the person to respond, and giving the learner immediate feedback on the accuracy of his or her answers.

Whether the programmed instruction device is a textbook or a computer, **programmed learning** consists of three functions:

1. Presenting questions, facts, or problems to the learner.
2. Allowing the person to respond.
3. Providing feedback on the accuracy of his or her answers.

A page from a programmed instruction book for learning calculus is presented in **Figure 8.3**. Note how facts and questions are presented. The learner can then respond, and the book contains feedback on the accuracy of his or her answers.

The main advantage of programmed learning is that it reduces training time by about one-third.[38] In terms of the principles of learning listed earlier, programmed instruction can also facilitate learning since it lets trainees learn at their own pace, provides immediate feedback, and (from the learner's point of view) reduces the risk of error. On the other hand, trainees do not learn much more from programmed learning than they would from a traditional textbook. Therefore, the cost of developing the manuals and/or software for programmed instruction has to be weighed against the accelerated but not improved learning that should occur.

Figure 8.3
A Page from a
Programmed Textbook

Source: Daniel Kleppner and
Norman Ramsey, *Quick
Calculus*. Copyright © 1985 by
John Wiley & Sons, Inc.
Reprinted by permission.

Sec. 2   Graphs

17   The most direct way to plot the graph of a function $y = f(x)$ is to make a table of reasonably spaced values of x and of the corresponding values of $y = f(x)$. Then each pair of values (x, y) can be represented by a point as in the previous frame.   A graph of the function is obtained by connecting the points with a smooth curve. Of course, the points on the curve may be only approximate. If we want an accurate plot we just have to be very careful and use many points. (On the other hand, crude plots are pretty good for most purposes.)

Go to 18.

18   As an example, here is a plot of the function $y = 3x^2$. A table of values of x and y is shown and these points are indicated on the graph.

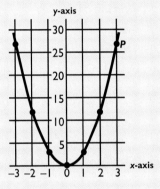

x	y
-3	27
-2	12
-1	3
0	0
1	3
2	12
3	27

To test yourself, encircle below the pair of coordinates that corresponds to the point P indicated in the figure.

[(3,27) | (27,3) | none of these]

Check your answer. If correct, go on to 19. If incorrect study frame 16 once again and then go to 19.

Vestibule or Simulated Training

**vestibule or simulated
training**
Training employees on special off-the-job equipment,
as in airplane pilot training,
whereby training costs and
hazards can be reduced.

Vestibule or **simulated training** is a technique by which trainees learn on the actual or simulated equipment they will use on the job, but are trained off the job. Therefore, it aims to obtain the advantages of on-the-job training without actually putting the trainee on the job. Vestibule training is virtually a necessity when it is too costly or dangerous to train employees on the job. Putting new assembly-line workers right to work could slow production, for instance, and when safety is a concern—as with pilots—vestibule training may be the only practical alternative.

Vestibule training may just place a trainee in a separate room with the equipment he or she will actually be using on the job. However, it often involves the use of equipment simulators. In pilot training, for instance, the main advantages of flight simulators are as follows:[39]

Vestibule training simulates flight conditions at NASA headquarters.

Safety. Crews can practice hazardous flight manoeuvres in a safe, controlled environment.

Learning efficiency. The absence of the conflicting air traffic and radio chatter that exists in real flight situations allows for total concentration on the business of learning how to fly the craft.

Money. The cost of flying a flight simulator is only a fraction of the cost of flying an aircraft. This includes savings on maintenance costs, pilot cost, fuel cost, and the cost of not having the aircraft in regular service.

Computer-Based and Multimedia Training

According to a 1996 Conference Board of Canada survey, 63 percent of respondents used information/communication technologies to enhance training and development.[40] In *computer-based training (CBT)* the trainee uses a computer-based system to interactively increase his or her knowledge or skills. While vestibule or simulated training doesn't necessarily have to rely on computerization, computer-based training almost always involves presenting trainees with computerized simulations and the use of multimedia including video, audio, text, and graphics integrated to help the trainee learn how to do the job.[41]

Multimedia training is most often implemented with CD-ROM technology, but is also available through the Internet and other sources.[42] Interactive multimedia has been found to be more effective for training people than text-based instruction, due to its interactive nature.[43]

A higher percentage of Canadian firms use CBT compared to the United States, primarily because of Canada's geography. CBT is often more cost-effective than traditional training methods requiring instructors and/or trainees to travel long distances to training sites. The Hudson's Bay Company has more that 200 CBT courses available, including merchandising education, product knowledge, and email. When learning to use email, actual mail program screens are used to simulate sending and receiving mail. The program tells learners whether they have completed the screen correctly, and if not, the screen is repeated to allow additional practice.[44] The Liquor Control Board of Ontario uses CBT to teach basic computer skills as well as management and supervisory skills. Hewlett-Packard Canada has an electronic performance support system that provides coaching to employees while on the job.[45]

The most advanced form of simulation is computer-based *virtual reality training*, which requires headsets or goggles, and specially designed computer software. The Repap New Brunswick Inc. paper mill is pioneering the use of virtual reality training in Canada. For them, the biggest benefit of this training is the ability to place people in potentially dangerous situations without actually exposing them to the danger.[46]

CBT programs can be very beneficial. Studies indicate that interactive technologies reduce learning time by an average of 50 percent.[47] Industry Canada estimates that the use of new media applications for training will increase productivity by 0.5 percent over the next ten years, amounting to $2 billion in reduced costs related to travel, accommodation, time away from the job, delivery costs, etc. The new forms of training can also be very cost-effective—while traditional training costs less to develop, new media-based training has a lower cost of delivery over its life span.[48] Other advantages include instructional consistency (computers, unlike human trainers, don't have good days and bad days), mastery of learning (if the trainee doesn't learn it, he or she generally can't move on to the next step in the CBT), increased retention, and increased trainee motivation (resulting from the responsive feedback of the CBT program).

Internet and Intranet-Based Training   Trainers have begun to use the Internet to enhance their own professional development through networking and gaining access to huge databases relevant to their profession, and to deliver training by downloading documents and tutorials.[49] Interactive online education software creates an education network or "virtual campus," which allows students to interact with an instructor and classmates.[50] Transmission costs are negligible compared to videoconferencing, and interactions are free of race, gender, and age discrimination.[51]

While training on the Internet still has some problems, such as slow transmission of video material, intranets (private computer networks within an organization) are a more promising immediate training alternative. Intranets enable trainees to learn what they want, where and when they want, in an interactive manner. For example, IBM employees anywhere in the world can log onto their "Global Campus" through their desktop or laptop computer, whenever it is convenient, and select from over 200 courses.[52] Courses can be updated in one central location much more easily and cost-effectively than CD-ROM and videotaped training material.[53]

Information Technology and HR
Five Levels of Internet-Based Training

Training on the Internet is already a reality and there seems no doubt that firms will soon be relying on the Internet to offer at least some of their training programs. Five levels of Internet-based training are[1]:

1. *General communication.* The Internet facilitates communication between trainers and trainees. Email can be used to distribute course schedules and homework, and trainees can use email for registration purposes and to ask questions. Trainers can organize electronic teleconferencing or "chat" sessions, also called "virtual workshops."

2. *Online reference using hyperlinks.* Trainers can create an entire online library of hyperlinked references. In other words, a user can click on high-lighted text to connect with associated information, such as product manuals, safety manuals, technical documentation, and course catalogues. It is relatively easy to convert material that is already available electronically into a hyperlinked reference. Products are available to convert documents and graphics into a Web format.

3. *Testing, assessment, and surveying.* The Internet can be used to automate the process of sending and receiving tests, test results, and surveys.

4. *Distribution of computer based-training.* Intranets can be used to distribute computer-based training modules, which can be downloaded by employees as needed using a method called File Transfer Protocol. This eliminates the time and expense of disk duplication, packaging, and distribution.

5. *Delivery of multimedia.* The Internet can be used to deliver interactive multimedia in real time over a network. Multimedia delivery on the Net is still slow, but will improve as faster modems become available. Alternatively, company intranets can be used, as they are usually much faster than the Internet.

Many of the benefits of Internet-based training are related to interactivity, or the trainees' ability to respond to or interact with the software training program. The more interaction, the more effective the learning. Overall, many trainers are enthusiastic about using the Internet for training purposes, but others find it difficult to locate what they need in the overwhelming amount of information available on the Net.[2]

1. Based on K. Kruse, "Five Levels of Internet-Based Training," *Training and Development* (February 1997), pp. 60–1.

2. A. Czarnecki, "Harnessing Internet for Training," *Canadian HR Reporter* Special Section "Learning for the Workplace" (May 19, 1997), pp. L21, L25. ◆

Training

It does not pay to spend a lot of time hiring the best employees if the employees hired aren't properly trained. In the book *Made in America,* a group of MIT researchers concluded, for instance, that superior training is one reason Japanese firms have often pulled ahead of North American firms within the same industries. Japanese firms will spend weeks in meticulous training programs developing their workers' expertise, while comparable North American firms often all but ignore the training process.

Because so much is riding on a relatively few employees, it is important that smaller firms carefully train their employees. The concepts and techniques explained in this chapter should help. In addition, some practical procedures for program development follow:

Step 1. Set Training Objectives

First, write down the training objectives. For example, the objective might be to reduce scrap, or to get new employees up to speed within two weeks.

Step 2. Write a Detailed Job Description

A detailed job description is the heart of any training program. It should list the daily and periodic tasks of each job, along with a summary of the steps in each one. Thus, for the job presented in Table 8.1, a main task is "operate paper cutter." The press operator's job description should thus explain how the paper cutter should be operated, including steps such as start motor, set cutting distance, and place paper on cutting table. In other words, the job description should list what is to be done, as well as how to do it.

Step 3. Develop an Abbreviated Task Analysis Record Form

For practical purposes, a small business owner can use an abbreviated task analysis record form containing just four columns. In the first, list *tasks* (including what is to be performed in terms of each of the main tasks, and the steps involved in each task). In column B, list *performance standards* (in terms of quantity, quality, accuracy, and so on). In column C, list *trainable skills* required, things the employee must know or do to perform the task. This column lists specific skills (such as "Keep both hands on releases") to be stressed. In the fourth column, list *aptitudes required.* These are the human aptitudes (such as mechanical comprehension, tolerance for boredom, and so on) that the employee should have to be trainable for the task and for which the employee can be screened ahead of time.

Step 4. Develop A Job Instruction Sheet

Next, a job instruction sheet should be developed. As explained earlier in the chapter, a job instruction training sheet shows the steps in each task, as well as key points for each.

Step 5. Prepare Training Program for the Job

Now all the final training documents and media for the job can be prepared. The training manual for the job should be built around the training sequence, listing steps in each job task and key points.

At a minimum, a training program should include the job description, abbreviated task analysis record form, and job instruction sheet, all collected in a trainer's manual. The latter should also contain a summary of the training program's objectives, the three forms mentioned earlier, and a listing of the trainable skills required. For the trainee, a separate manual might then consist of an introduction to the job, an explanation of how the job fits with other jobs in the plant or office, a job description, and a job instruction sheet.

A decision must be made regarding which media to use in the training program. A simple but effective on-the-job training program using current employees or supervisors as trainers requires only the materials we just described. However, it could turn out that the nature of the job or the number of trainees requires producing or purchasing special audio- or videotapes or films, a slide presentation, or more extensive printed materials.

Many smaller companies are saving on training expenses by entering into cooperative agreements with other firms in their geographic areas. For example, if a company's employees need generic courses (on topics like time management or computer skills, for instance) the firm can probably cut training costs by obtaining training time from an outside supplier as part of a cooperative employers group. Thus, if one firm has eight employees who need time management training and one down the street has a similar need, together they can hire a training supplier to teach a full class of 16 participants, thus sharing the trainer's costs.◆

Source: Bob Filipczak, "Training Consortia: How They Work, How They Don't," *Training* (August 1994), pp. 51–7.

Training for Special Purposes

Training increasingly does more than just prepare employees to perform their jobs effectively. Training for special purposes—dealing with AIDS and adjusting to diversity, for instance—is required too. A sampling of such special-purpose training programs follows.

Literacy Training Techniques

www.nald.ca
Adult Literacy Information Network

Functional illiteracy is a serious problem for many employers. Nearly half of Canadians aged 16 and above have reading skills below international standards. Twenty-two percent have difficulty dealing with printed material, and another 26 percent can deal only with material that is simple and clearly laid out.[54] Yet, as the Canadian economy shifts from goods to services, there is a corresponding need for workers who are more skilled, more literate, and better able to perform at least basic arithmetic skills.

Employers are responding to this problem in two main ways. First, companies are testing prospective employees' basic skills. The second response is to institute basic skills and literacy programs.

One simple approach is to have supervisors focus on basic skills by giving employees writing and speaking exercises. After the exercise has been completed, the supervisor can provide personal feedback.[55] One way to do this is to convert materials used in the employees' jobs into instructional tools. For example, if an employee needs to use a manual to find out how to replace a certain machine part, he or she should be taught how to use an index to locate the relevant section.[56] Another approach is to bring in outside professionals like teachers from a local high school or community college to institute, say, a remedial reading or writing program. Having employees attend adult education or high school evening classes is another option.

Another approach is to use an interactive video disk (IVD). This technique combines the drama of video with the power of microcomputers.[57] An example is

Principles of Alphabet Literacy (PALS). It uses animated video and a computer-stored voice to enable nonreaders to associate sounds with letters and letters with words, and to use the words to create sentences.[58] A second IVD program is called SKILLPAC. This program, subtitled *English for Industry,* was designed mostly for non-native-English speakers. It combines video, audio, and computer technologies to teach language skills in the context of the specific workplace situation in which those skills will be used.[59]

AIDS Education

www.trainingnet.com
8000 training and other
HR events

Many of the estimated 69 000 Canadians infected with the AIDS virus are in the work force, and this creates anxiety for many noninfected employees and a dilemma for their employers.[60] On the one hand, infected individuals must be allowed to remain on their jobs, for both moral and legal reasons. On the other hand, the infected person's coworkers often require some type of training to reduce anxieties and maximize the chances that the employees will be able to work together effectively as a team.

Many firms therefore institute AIDS education programs. The program instituted in the Wellesley, Massachusetts office of Sun Life of Canada, a life insurance company, is typical.[61] Groups of 20 to 30 employees attended 90-minute seminars. In addition to providing detailed information about AIDS, the seminars offered a forum for discussion and questions. Management employees attended three-hour seminars in groups of 10 to 12 people. The seminars covered additional AIDS-related issues, including the need for confidentiality, the potential impact of legislation, and the company's AIDS policy.

There was reportedly little resistance to holding or attending these seminars, in part because the reasons for them were widely communicated in the company's newsletters. Some management employees initially expressed skepticism about devoting so many hours to AIDS education, but after their sessions most reportedly felt differently. Based on pre- and post-seminar questionnaires, the company believes that the seminars were useful in getting employees to learn the facts about AIDS, clearing up misconceptions, and helping to put the personal concerns of many employees to rest.

Training for International Business

As more firms find themselves competing in a global marketplace, they've increasingly had to implement special global training programs. The reasons for doing so range from avoiding lost business due to cultural insensitivity, to improving job satisfaction and retention of overseas staff, to enabling a newly assigned employee to communicate with his or her colleagues abroad.[62]

Many global training programs are prepackaged. They are sold by vendors to employers who have to train one or more of their employees prior to overseas assignments. The following list illustrates the wide range of programs available, as well as what global training courses actually involve:[63]

The Cultural Awareness Program: This is a one-day cultural awareness training program that looks at North American and cross-cultural values and assumptions concerning communication and identity issues.

Executive Etiquette for Global Transactions: This program prepares managers for conducting business globally by training them in the differing etiquette requirements in countries including Germany, Japan, Mexico, Russia, and Saudi Arabia.

Cross-Cultural Technology Transfer: This program shows trainees how cultural values affect one's perceptions of technology and technical learning.

International Protocol and Presentation: This shows trainees the correct way to handle people with tact and diplomacy in countries around the world.

Cross-Cultural Training and Orientation: Topics here include cross-cultural communication and business skills, practical approaches to managing culture shock and adjusting one's lifestyle, stress management, daily life in the host country, spouse's and family's concerns, area studies, and repatriation procedures.

Business Basics for the Foreign Executive: This covers negotiating cross-culturally, working with North American clients, making presentations, writing for North American business, and using the telephone in North America.

Language Programs: Various vendors supply language specialists whose services include translation, interpretation, cross-cultural training, and consulting on language-related needs.

Language Training: Such programs provide language training delivered by certified instructors, usually determined by the learner's needs rather than by the requirements of a predetermined curriculum or textbook.

Specific suggestions for conducting training programs abroad are presented in the Global HRM box.

Global HRM

Training

As firms expand operations abroad, it becomes more important to train foreign nationals. For example, Gillette International brings foreign talent to its Boston headquarters for training in the techniques, policies, and values of the firm before they assume new jobs in their home country.[1]

Training foreign nationals requires more than translating existing programs into other languages. Cultural differences influence both the applicability of training material and the reactions of trainees to the programs. Here are suggestions for conducting training programs abroad:[2]

1. Understand the taboos and turn-ons of the participants' culture. For example, in Japan, risk taking is by and large taboo. Therefore, it may be difficult to get volunteers to participate in a training role-play exercise because doing so is taking a risk. Similarly, in the Middle East, role-plays are games for children, not for adults.

2. Critiquing other people in public is taboo in some Far Eastern cultures. For example, getting a volunteer to be an "observer" in a training discussion or role-play could be difficult because the role of the observer is often to critique the other participants' behaviour.

3. Saving face and not putting people in embarrassing situations is important not just in the Far East. In Middle Eastern countries, East and West Africa, and some European cultures including Spain and Italy, criticizing trainees or making them look foolish is not advisable. In fact, putting them in any activity in which their behaviour will be discussed, debriefed, and/or criticized can create problems.

4. In some cultures it will be difficult to get feedback on a trainer's effectiveness. The trainees may be reluctant to tell the trainer because to do so would be to criticize them and cause loss of face.

5. Make sure to understand how the job that trainees are being trained to do is viewed in their native culture. In Canada, for instance, it's appropriate to tell salespeople to write introductory letters to high-level executives to gain entry to their organizations. In Japan doing so would be highly unusual. Instead, repeated personal visits to drop off business cards are often required.

6. Consider the effects of jet lag and diet changes. For example, while it may be 4:00 P.M. in Toronto where the training is being conducted, the body clocks of participants from France may be set to a more tired 9:00 P.M. Similarly, participants from Japan may expect a rice meal, and all participants fresh from overseas would probably do better with mineral water than soft drinks.◆

1. Jennifer Laabs, "The Global Talent Search," *Personnel Journal* (August 1991), pp. 38–42.
2. Pat McCarthy, "The Art of Training Abroad," *Training and Development Journal* (November 1990), pp. 13–8.

Diversity Training

www.diversityatwork.com/ resource.htm
Diversity Training

With an increasingly diverse work force, many more firms find they have to implement diversity training programs. Diversity training enhances cross-cultural sensitivity among supervisors and nonsupervisors, with the aim of creating more harmonious working relationships among a firm's employees.

Two broad approaches to diversity training are *cross-cultural communication training* and *cultural sensitivity training*. Cross-cultural communication training focusses on workplace cultural etiquette and interpersonal skills. Cultural sensitivity training focusses on sensitizing employees to the views of different cultural groups toward work so that employees from diverse backgrounds can work together more effectively. However, it is necessary to go beyond these approaches in order to gain the extra benefits of a diverse workforce. Diversity training should be seen as a business opportunity and linked to long-term organizational development. All employees should be involved in managing diversity, and diversity initiatives should be planned and supported as any other business opportunity would be.[64]

Diversity training is no panacea, and a poorly conceived program can backfire. Potential negative outcomes include ". . . the possibility of post-training participant discomfort, reinforcement of group stereotypes, perceived disenfranchisement or backlash by white males."[65]

Strictly speaking, it's probably more accurate to talk about diversity-based training programs than about "diversity training." According to one survey of HR directors, specific training programs aimed at offsetting problems associated with a diverse work force included (from most used to least used):

- improving interpersonal skills
- understanding/valuing cultural differences
- improving technical skills
- socializing employees into the corporate culture
- reducing stress
- indoctrinating into the North American work ethic
- mentoring
- improving English proficiency
- improving basic math skills
- improving bilingual skills for English-speaking employees.[66]

Handidactis, a non-profit organization in Montreal, provides sensitivity training to help people deal with those who are disabled, including those with impaired vision or hearing, and individuals who have a physical or mental disability. The first step is to ask the person with the disability if he or she needs anything special to do the job. This step is often overlooked as people jump in to help someone with a disability. This in effect takes away that person's independence, and furthermore the person may not need help. The training also involves discovering what it's like to have a disability, through simulated blindness and speech impediments.[67]

www.training.ibm.com/ ibmedu/announce
IBM Global Campus

An important element of IBM Canada's diversity initiatives is education and training. The process of recognizing, respecting, and valuing differences in the workplace and marketplace does not come automatically, and training helps ensure that all managers and employees understand and incorporate diversity sensitivity and skills in their daily job responsibilities. IBM Canada's diversity training programs started in 1993 with a one-day diversity awareness program that covered all employees. Courses have since been conducted on gender communications and harassment, and diversity messages have been included in annual leadership development programs. Diversity training is comprehensive, starting with awareness for all new employees, and continuing with training for managers that moves beyond awareness to action.

Learning how to recognize and value differences at IBM Canada isn't restricted to the classroom. When employees engage in mentoring or team leadership, they also learn how to increase their personal effectiveness, and unleash synergies that come from diverse workplaces.[68]

Customer-Service Training

It is estimated that by the year 2000, 78 percent of all jobs in Canada will be in the service sector.[69] Thus, more and more companies are finding it necessary to compete based on the quality of their service. It's no longer enough, for instance, to offer a clean room at a decent price when a customer checks into a CP Hotel. To stay competitive, employers like CP Hotels find they have to provide total customer service, from courteous bellhops to easy parking to speedy check-outs.

Many companies are therefore implementing customer-service training programs. The basic aim is to train all employees to treat the company's customers in a courteous and hospitable manner. The saying "The customer is always right" is being emphasized by countless service companies today. However, putting the customer first requires employee customer-service training.

Customer service training at Canadian Pacific Hotels is part of their "Service Plus 2000" program, which includes leadership training as well as front-line service training. The leadership training consists of eleven modules, including coaching, teamwork, and empathy. Trainees write a personal commitment to each module, which becomes part of their individual development-management plan. In this way, all employees are involved in higher service standards. The hotel chain believes that their investment in customer service has provided good returns. Their service ratings are at an all-time high, and employee opinion survey ratings are 10 percent above the norm for the hotel industry.[70]

Training for Teamwork and Empowerment

An increasing number of firms today use work teams and empowerment to improve their effectiveness. They adopt teamwork as a value and then organize work around close-knit work teams empowered to get their jobs done, which means they've been given the authorization and the ability to do their jobs. Both the team approach and worker empowerment are components of what many firms call worker involvement programs. **Worker involvement programs** aim to boost organizational effectiveness by getting employees to participate in the planning, organizing, and general managing of their jobs.

However, many firms find that teamwork doesn't just happen. Instead, employees must be trained to be good team members. That is why firms like Toyota spend considerable time training new employees to be good team members.

Some firms use outdoor training such as Outward Bound programs to build teamwork.[71] Outdoor training usually involves taking a firm's management team

worker involvement programs
Programs that aim to boost organizational effectiveness by getting employees to participate in planning, organizing, and managing their jobs.

out into rugged, mountainous terrain. There they learn team spirit and cooperation and the need to trust and rely on each other by overcoming physical obstacles. As one participant put it, "Every time I climbed over a rock, I needed someone's help."[72] An example of one activity is the "trust fall." Here an employee has to slowly lean back and fall backward from a height of, say, ten feet into the waiting arms of five or ten team members. The idea is to build trust, and particularly trust in one's colleagues.

Not all employees are eager to participate in such activities. Firms such as Outward Bound have potential participants fill out extensive medical evaluations to make sure participants can safely engage in risky outdoor activities. Others feel that the outdoor activities are too contrived to be applicable back at work. However, they do illustrate the lengths to which employers will go to build teamwork.

Empowering employees (either individually or as teams) also almost always requires extensive training. It is rarely enough to just tell group members that they're "empowered" to do all the buying and selling and planning involved in producing, say, the auto component for which they are responsible. Instead extensive training is required to ensure they have the skills to do the job. Similarly, many companies today use work teams or special quality circles to analyze job-related problems and to come up with solutions. (A quality circle is a group of five to ten employees, often a work team, who meet for an hour or two each week during the work day to analyze a problem with their job and to develop solutions.) Employees need to develop the problem-solving and analysis skills required to help the work team be empowered—in this case, to analyze and solve problems. Training in how to use basic statistical analysis tools and basic accounting is an example.

**www.ipmaac.org/
link-trng.html**
Training and Development

Evaluating the Training Effort

After trainees complete their training (or perhaps at planned intervals during the training), the program should be evaluated to see how well its objectives have been met. Thus, if assemblers should be able to solder a junction in 30 seconds, or a photocopier technician repair a machine in 30 minutes, then the program's effectiveness should be measured based on whether these objectives are met. For example, are trainees learning as *much* as they can? Are they learning as *fast* as they can? Is there a *better method* for training them? These are some of the questions answered by properly evaluating training efforts.

According to a recent Conference Board of Canada study, 61 percent of Canadian CEOs demand some measurement of the value of the HR function, most frequently training and development activities.[73] However, fewer than one-third of organizations in a subsequent survey could put a precise figure on their training costs, and only about 16 percent of all training and development activities are subjected to a return-on-investment calculation.[74]

Overall there is little doubt that training and development can be effective. For example, many companies that invested heavily in workplace training have substantially improved their positions. While it may not be just the training, Xerox retrained over 110 000 employees worldwide in the early 1980s and soon regained market share in its industry. General Motors is another firm that has used training to help recapture market share.[75] Formal studies of training programs also substantiate the potential positive impact of such programs. A study conducted in the early 1990s concluded that "firms that establish workplace education programs and reorganize work report noticeable improvements in their workers' abilities and the quality of their products."[76] Another study found that businesses that were operating below their expected labour productivity levels had significant zincreases in productivity growth after implementing new employee training programs.[77] Profitable companies spend the most on training. Those rated as being among the 100 best companies to work for in Canada spend the most per employee on training.[78]

There are two basic issues to address when evaluating a training program. The first is the design of the evaluation study and, in particular, whether controlled experimentation will be used. The second is the training effect to be measured.

controlled experimentation
Formal methods for testing the effectiveness of a training program, preferably with before-and-after tests and a control group.

Controlled experimentation is the best method to use in evaluating a training program. In a controlled experiment, both a training group and a control group (that receives no training) are used. Data (for instance, on quantity of production or quality of soldered junctions) should be obtained both before and after the training effort in the group exposed to training and before and after a corresponding work period in the control group. In this way it is possible to determine the extent to which any change in performance in the training group resulted from the training itself rather than from some organization-wide change like a raise in pay; it is assumed that the latter would have affected employees in both groups equally. In terms of current practices, however, one survey found that something less than half the companies responding attempted to obtain before-and-after measures from trainees; the number of organizations using control groups was negligible.[79]

Training Effects to Measure

Four basic categories of training outcomes can be measured:[80]

1. *Reaction.* First, evaluate trainees' reactions to the program. Did they like the program? Did they think it worthwhile? One expert suggests at least using an evaluation form like the one shown in **Figure 8.4** to evaluate reaction to the training program.[81]

2. *Learning.* Second, test the trainees to determine whether they learned the principles, skills, and facts they were supposed to learn.

3. *Behaviour.* Next ask whether the trainees' behaviour on the job changed because of the training program. For example, are employees in the store's complaint department more courteous toward disgruntled customers than previously?

4. *Results.* Last, but probably most importantly, ask: "What final results were achieved in terms of the training objectives previously set? Did the number of customer complaints about employees drop? Did the reject rate improve? Did scrappage cost decrease? Was turnover reduced? Are production quotas now being met?" and so forth. Improved results are, of course, especially important. The training program may succeed in terms of the reactions from trainees, increased learning, and even changes in behaviour. But if the results are not achieved, then in the final analysis, the training has not achieved its goals. If so, the problem may lie in the training program. For example, training is ineffective when environmental factors are the cause of poor performance.

A 1996 Conference Board of Canada survey found that 84 percent of firms assessed reaction, 42 percent assessed learning, 23 percent assessed behaviour, and only 16 percent assessed results.[82]

Figure 8.4
A Sample Training
Evaluation Form

Purpose: The following items assess the overall value of this training experience:
1. Did you find the quality of this program to be (select one):

_____	_____	_____	_____	_____
Poor	Fair	Average	Good	Outstanding

2. Do you feel that this program was worthwhile in terms of its cost and your time away from normal job duties?
   Yes _____   No _____   Undecided _____
3. Would you recommend this program to your peers?
   Yes _____   No _____   Undecided _____
4. Rate the program for the following qualities

	Poor				Outstanding
	1	2	3	4	5
a. Practical Value	____	____	____	____	____
b. Thoroughness	____	____	____	____	____
c. New ideas gained	____	____	____	____	____
d. Helpful to self-development	____	____	____	____	____
e. Relevance to your job	____	____	____	____	____
f. Efficient use of time	____	____	____	____	____
g. Maintaining your interest	____	____	____	____	____
h. Clear, understandable	____	____	____	____	____

Comments:
5. Check the degree to which the kinds of follow-up to this workshop listed here would be useful:

	Necessary	Desirable	Unnecessary
a. Talking with workshop members to share experiences in applying ideas	____	____	____
b. Opportunity to consult with trainer if a problem arises	____	____	____
c. Advanced workshop in this area	____	____	____
d. Briefing for my supervisors on what I've learned here	____	____	____
e. Other	____	____	____

Chapter Review

Summary

1. Employee orientation provides new employees with the information they need to perform their jobs satisfactorily and is one component of the socialization process.

2. In this chapter we focused on technical skills training for new employees and for present employees whose performance is deficient. For either, uncovering training requirements begins with analyzing the cause of the problem and determining the training that may be needed. It must be determined whether it is a training problem or a more deep-rooted problem like poor selection or low wages.

3. The training process consists of five steps: needs analysis; instructional design; validation; implementation; and evaluation.

4. Some principles of learning theory include: make the material meaningful (by providing a bird's-eye view and familiar examples, organizing the material, splitting it into meaningful chunks, and using familiar terms and visual aids); make provision for transfer of training; and try to motivate the trainee.

5. *Job instruction training* is useful for training on jobs that consist of a logical sequence of steps. *Vestibule training* combines the advantages of on- and off-the-job training.

6. *On-the-job training* is another basic training technique. It might take the form of the understudy method, job rotation, or special assignments and committees. In any case, it should have four steps: preparing the learner, presenting the operation (or nature of the job), doing performance tryouts, and following up. Other training methods include audiovisual techniques, lectures, and computer-assisted instruction.

7. In gauging the effectiveness of a training program, there are four categories of outcomes that can be measured: reaction, learning, behaviour, and results. In some cases where training seems to have failed, it may be because training was not the appropriate solution.

Key Terms

controlled experimentation
employee orientation
job instruction training
  (JIT)
on-the-job training (OJT)
performance analysis

programmed learning
reality shock
socialization
task analysis
training

vestibule or simulated
  training
videoconferencing
worker involvement
  programs

Discussion Questions and Exercises

1. "A well-thought-out orientation program is especially important for employees (like many recent graduates) who have had little or no work experience." Explain why you agree or disagree with this statement.

2. You're the supervisor of a group of employees whose task it is to assemble tuning devices that go into radios. You find that quality is not what it should be and that many of your group's tuning devices have to be brought back and reworked; your own boss says that "You'd better start doing a better job of training your workers."
   a. What are some of the "staffing" factors that could be contributing to this problem?
   b. Explain how you would go about assessing whether it is in fact a training problem.

3. Explain how you would apply our principles of learning in developing a lecture, say, on orientation and training.

4. Pick out some task with which you are familiar—mowing the lawn, tuning a car—and develop a job instruction training sheet for it.

5. Juan Santos is an undergraduate business student majoring in accounting. He has just failed the first accounting course, Accounting 101, and is understandably upset. Explain how you would use performance analysis to identify what, if any, are Juan's training needs.

6. What are some typical on-the-job training techniques? What do you think are some of the main drawbacks of relying on informal on-the-job training for breaking new employees into their jobs?

7. You are to give a short lecture on the subject "Guidelines to Keep in Mind When Presenting a Lecture." Give a five- or ten-minute lecture on the subject making sure, of course, to follow the guidelines as enumerated in this chapter.

8. Working individually or in groups, you are to develop a short programmed learning program on the subject "Guidelines for Giving a More Effective Lecture." Use the example in Figure 8.3 and any other information you may have available to develop your programmed learning program.

9. This chapter points out that one reason for implementing special global training programs is the need to avoid business lost ". . . due to cultural insensitivity." What sort of cultural insensitivity do you think is referred to and how might that translate into lost business? What sort of training program would you recommend to avoid such cultural insensitivity?

10. This chapter presents several examples of how diversity training can backfire such as "the possibility of post-training participant discomfort." How serious do you think potential negative outcomes like these are and what would you do as an HR manager to avoid them?

Application Exercises

RUNNING CASE: Carter Cleaning Company

The New Training Program

At the present time Carter Cleaning has no formal orientation or training policies or procedures, and Jennifer believes this is one reason why the standards to which she and her father would like employees to adhere are generally not followed.

The Carters would prefer that certain practices and procedures be used in dealing with the customers at the front counters. For example, all customers should be greeted with what Jack refers to as a "big hello." Garments they drop off should immediately be inspected for any damage or unusual stains so these can be brought to the customer's attention, lest the customer later return to pick up the garment and erroneously blame the store. The garments are then supposed to be immediately placed together in a nylon sack to separate them from other customers' garments. The ticket also has to be carefully written up, with the customer's name and telephone number and the date precisely and clearly noted on all copies. The counterperson is also supposed to take the opportunity to try to sell the customer additional services such as waterproofing or simply notify the customer that "Now that people are doing their spring cleaning, we're having a special on drapery cleaning all this month." Finally, as the customer leaves, the counterperson is supposed to make a courteous comment like "Have a nice day" or "Drive safely." Each of the other jobs in the stores—pressing, cleaning and spotting, periodically maintaining the coin laundry equipment, and so forth—similarly contain certain steps, procedures, and most important, standards the Carters would prefer to see upheld.

The company has also had other problems, Jennifer feels, because of a lack of adequate employee training and orientation. For example, two new employees became very upset last month when they discovered that they were not paid at the end of the week, on Friday, but instead were paid (as are all Carter employees) on the following Tuesday. The Carters use the extra two days in part to give them time to obtain everyone's hours and compute their pay. The other reason they do it, according to Jack, is that "frankly, when we stay a few days behind in paying employees it helps to ensure that they at least give us a few days' notice before quitting on us. While we are certainly obligated to pay them anything they earn, we find that psychologically they seem to be less likely to just walk out on us Friday evening and not show up Monday morning if they still haven't gotten their pay from the previous week. This way they at least give us a few days' notice so we can find a replacement."

Other matters that could be covered during an orientation, says Jennifer, include company policy regarding paid holidays, lateness and absences, health and hospitalization benefits (there are none, other than provincial health care coverage and workers' compensation) and general matters like the maintenance of a clean and safe work area, personal appearance and cleanliness, time sheets, personal telephone calls and mail, company policies regarding matters like substance abuse, and eating or smoking on the job.

Jennifer believes that implementing orientation and training programs would help to ensure that employees know how to do their jobs the right way. She and her father further believe that it is only when employees understand the right way to do their jobs that there is any hope their jobs will in fact be accomplished the way the Carters want them to be accomplished.

Questions

1. Specifically, what should the Carters cover in their new employee orientation program and how should they present this information?

2. In the human resources management course Jennifer took, the book suggested using a task analysis record form to identify tasks performed by an employee. "Should we use a form like this for the counterperson's job, and if so, what would the filled-in form look like?"

3. Which specific training techniques should Jennifer use to train the pressers, cleaner-spotters, managers, and counterpeople, and why?

CASE INCIDENT: Boeing's New Computer System

In the early 1990s, the Boeing Commercial Airline Group was about to install, in its commercial spare parts department, the largest computing system it had ever developed. The department sells spare parts to commercial airlines. The purpose of the new computer system was to automate many of the department's tasks, including inventory updates, customer inquiry responses, and pricing.

Boeing managers knew that installation of the new computer system would require extensive retraining of its employees. It would affect almost all of the 700 people in the spare parts department, and not just in terms of the technical aspects of using the new computer system. For one thing, the department's offices would become virtually paperless. And perhaps even more scary to the employees was the fact that they would have to spend much more of their day working at their computer terminals. In addition, interpersonal relationships would become more interdependent because each employee would be more reliant on information that others entered accurately onto the computer. Employees had to understand that suddenly they had many more "customers" relying on them—customers who, in fact, were other spare parts department employees.

As the training coordinator put it, "We realized that providing technical training alone wouldn't be enough to ensure a successful implementation." The new system's users would need tools to handle the changes they would experience when the system came online. The training group wanted to make sure that it minimized the stress and confusion that implementation could potentially create. More to the point was that it wanted to make sure all the employees using the new system became "customer-oriented" in terms of providing the information their colleagues/customers in the spare parts department required.

Given the functional diversity of the group, Boeing knew a challenge lay ahead. Half of the group worked in a warehouse and was responsible for shipping, receiving, and storing parts. The other half worked in an office 48 kilometres away. Furthermore, it was a diverse group in terms of educational attainment.

In deciding the nature of the training program, Boeing had a variety of options from which to choose. Because there already was an entire in-house training department, one option was to have it do the training. On the other hand, preparing 700 people in a very short time might require the services of training and development consultants geared to getting a program like this up and running. The training department also had to consider the specific types of training to be used, such as seminars, video instruction, lectures, or books. One firm under consideration was well known for being able to quickly develop large-scale training programs that were generally based around seminars that utilized written and visual material, participative exercises, examples, and lectures.

However, before deciding whether the training program would be managed internally or by a consulting firm, Boeing knew that it had to be clearer about the actual training objectives. For instance, in addition to the purely technical aspects of the training, there was the need to make the employees who used the system more customer-oriented. Employee communication and assertiveness skills possibly had to be developed so that they could make their needs known if there was particular information they wanted from the system that was not being provided by the employees who would now input the data.

Questions

1. What sort of training do you think the spare parts department employees require?

2. How would you go about determining what the specific training objectives should be?

3. Do you think it's advisable for Boeing to go to an outside consulting firm to put together this program, or would you recommend handling it internally?

4. Whether done internally or through the consulting firm, explain how you would go about designing the necessary training program.

Source: This case incident is based on Steve Thieme, "Customer-Service Training Supports Work Systems," *Personnel Journal* 72, no. 4 (1993), pp. 63–5.

Human Resources Management Simulation

Exercise 3 in section 2 of part 1 in the simulation is designed to provide some hands-on practice in designing a standardized new-employee orientation plan. Job-specific variations should be identified and described. Estimated costs are to be included in a written report outlining the components that should be included in Acme's orientation program.

Video Case

Clowns for Managers

Increasingly, organizations are turning to non-traditional forms of training to give them a competitive edge. At the Holiday Inn on King Street in downtown Toronto, senior managers, department heads, and salespeople are learning to be clowns—complete with face paint, big noses, oversize shoes, and clown names like "Montana Mak." At the completion of the training, graduation ceremonies are held, complete with diplomas and introductions of the new clowns to an audience including the media and other hotel employees.

This training has been provided for the last eight years at Holiday Inns in the U.S. At the two most profitable Holiday Inns worldwide, both in Orlando, Florida, the clown training is mandatory.

There are two major benefits from this three-day, $4 000 exercise. The first is enhanced team bonding and staff communication. Second, the training is to enable staff to entertain guests and to promote the hotel by representing it at charity events.

Questions

1. How does this training enhance teamwork and communication amongst trainees?

2. Could a similar approach be used for diversity training or international business training?

3. What specific actions could be taken to evaluate this training?

Video Resource: CBC, *Venture* "Clowns for Managers," November 2, 1996.

Take It to the Net

Check out our Companion Website at

www.prenticehall.ca/dessler

for a multitude of practice questions, key terms and concepts, Weblinks to related sites, newsgroups, CBC video updates, and more.

Notes

1. For a recent discussion of socialization see, for example, Georgia Chao et al., "Organizational Socialization: Its Content and Consequences," *Journal of Applied Psychology* 79, no. 5 (1994), pp. 730–43.

2. Joseph Famularo, *Handbook of Modern Personnel Administration* (New York: McGraw-Hill, 1972), pp. 23.7–23.8. See also Ronald Smith, "Employee Orientation: Ten Steps to Success," *Personnel Journal* 63, no. 12 (December 1984), pp. 46–9.

3. For a discussion of current types of and practices in job skills training, see Harley Frazis, Diane Helz, and Michael Horrigan, "Employer-Provided Training: Results from a New Survey," *Monthly Labor Review* (May 1995), p. 7.

4. See, for example, Carolyn Wiley, "Training for the 90s: How Leading Companies Focus on Quality Improvement, Technological Change, and Customer Service," *Employment Relations Today* (Spring 1993), p. 80.

5. See, for example, our discussion in chapter 1. Also see Wiley, "Training for the 90s," p. 80.

6. The following is based on Wiley, "Training for the 90s," pp. 81–2.

7. Jean-Pascal Souque, *Focus on Competencies: Training and Development Practices, Expenditures, and Trends* Report 177–96, (Ottawa: The Conference Board of Canada, 1996), p. 10.

8. Harley Frazis, Diane Herz, and Michael Horrigan, "Employer-Provided Training: Results from a New Survey," *Monthly Labor Review* (May 1995), pp. 3–17.

9. This is based on Anthony F. Carnevale, "America and the New Economy," *Training and Development Journal* 44, no. 11 (November 1990), pp. 31ff. See also Richard Saggers, "Training Climbs the Corporate Agenda," *Personnel Management* 26, no. 7 (July 1994), pp. 40–5.

10. M. Shostak, "The Promise of New Media Learning", *Canadian HR Reporter* (April 7, 1997), pp. 15, 19.

11. "The Knowledge Worker," *Drake Business Review*, 6(2), 1997, p. 15.

12. J-P Souque, "Focus on Competencies," p. 10.

13. Carnevale, based on Kenneth Wexley and Gary Yukl, *Organizational Behavior and Personnel Psychology* (Homewood, IL: Richard D. Irwin, 1977), pp. 289–95; E. J. McCormick and J. Tiffin, *Industrial Psychology* (Englewood Cliffs, NJ: Prentice-Hall, 1974), pp. 232–340.

14. Wexley and Yukl, *Organizational Behavior,* pp. 289–95.

15. R. E. Silverman, *Learning Theory Applied to Training* (Reading, MA: Addison-Wesley, 1970), Chapter 8; McCormick and Tiffin, *Industrial Psychology,* pp. 239–40.

16. M. Belcourt & P.C. Wright, *Managing Performance Through Training and Development,* (Toronto: Nelson Canada, 1996), pp. 139–66. See also A. M. Saks & R.R. Haccoun, "Easing the Transfer of Training," *Human Resources Professional,* July-August 1996, pp. 8–11.

17. This is based on Kenneth Wexley and Gary Latham, *Developing and Training Human Resources in Organizations* (Glenview, IL: Scott, Foresman, 1981), pp. 22–7.

18. Kenneth Sovereign, *Personnel Law* (Englewood Cliffs, NJ: Prentice-Hall, Inc., 1994), pp. 165–6.

19. These are based on Sovereign, *Personnel Law,* pp. 165–6.

20. Bureau of National Affairs, *Training Employees, Personnel Policies Forum, Survey 88* (Washington, DC: November 1965), p. 5. For further discussion of conducting a needs analysis, see Kenneth Nowack, "A True Training Needs Analysis," *Training and Development Journal* (April 1991), pp. 69–73.

21. B. M. Bass and J. A. Vaughan, "Assessing Training Needs," in Craig Schneier and Richard Beatty, *Personnel Administration Today* (Reading, MA: Addison-Wesley, 1978), p. 311. See also Ronald Ash and Edward Leving, "Job Applicant Training and Work Experience Evaluation: An Empirical Comparison of Four Methods," *Journal of Applied Psycholog* 70, no. 3 (1985), pp. 572–6; John Lawrie, "Break the Training Ritual," *Personnel Journal* 67, no. 4 (April 1988), pp. 95–7; and Theodore Lewis and David Bjorkquist, "Needs Assessment—A Critical Reappraisal," *Performance Improvement Quarterly* 5, no. 4 (1992), pp. 33–54.

22. See, for example, Gean Freeman, "Human Resources Planning—Training Needs Analysis," *Human Resources Planning* 39, no. 3 (Fall 1993), pp. 32–4.

23. McCormick and Tiffin, *Industrial Psychology,* p. 245. See also James C. Georges, "The Hard Realities of Soft Skills Train-

ing," *Personnel Journal.* 68, no. 4 (April 1989), pp. 40–5; Robert H. Buckham, "Applying Role Analysis in the Workplace," *Personnel* 64, no. 2 (February 1987), pp. 63–5; and J. Kevin Ford and Raymond Noe, "Self-Assessed Training Needs: The Effects of Attitudes Towards Training, Management Level, and Function," *Personnel Psychology* 40, no. 1 (Spring 1987), pp. 39–54.

24. J-P Souque, "Focus on Competencies,", p. 5.

25. Richard Camp et al., *Toward a More Organizationally Effective Training Strategy and Practice* (Englewood Cliffs, NJ: Prentice-Hall, 1986), p. 100.

26. J. P. Cicero, "Behavioral Objectives for Technical Training Systems," *Training and Development Journal* 28 (1973), pp. 14–7. See also Larry D. Hales, "Training: A Product of Business Planning," *Training and Development Journal* 40, no. 7 (July 1986), pp. 87–92, and Arnold H. Wensky and Robert Legendre, "Training Incentives," *Personnel Journal* 68, no. 4 (April 1989), pp. 102–8.

27. I. L. Goldstein, *Training: Program Development and Evaluation* (Monterey, CA: Wadsworth, 1974). See also Stephen B. Wehrenberg, "Learning Contracts," *Personnel Journal* 67, no. 9 (September 1988), pp. 100–3; Murray B. Heibert and Norman Smallwood, "Now for a Completely Different Look at Needs Analysis," *Training and Development Journal* 41, no. 5 (May 1987), pp. 75–9; Erica Gordon Sorohan, "We Do; Therefore, We Learn," *Training & Development* (October 1993), pp. 47–55; Melvin LeBlanc, "Learning Objectives Key to Quality Safety," *Occupational Hazards* (January 1994), pp. 127–8.

28. S. Lebrun, "T & D Becoming More Strategic," *Canadian HR Reporter*, February 10, 1997, pp. 1, 2.

29. Wexley and Latham, *Developing and Training,* p. 107.

30. Harley Frazis et al., "Employer-Provided Training," p. 4.

31. "Employer-Provided Training," pp. 107–12. Four steps in on-the-job training based on William Berliner and William McLarney, *Management Practice and Training* (Homewood, IL: Irwin, 1974), pp. 442–3. See also Robert Sullivan and Donald Miklas, "On-the-Job Training That Works," *Training and Development Journal* 39, no. 5 (May 1985), pp. 118–20, and Stephen B. Wehrenberg, "Supervisors as Trainers: The Long-Term Gains of OJT," *Personnel Journal* 66, no. 4 (April 1987), pp. 48–51.

32. Donald F. Michalak and Edwin G. Yager, *Making the Training Process Work* (New York: Harper & Row, 1979), pp. 108–11. See also Richard Wiegand, "Can All Your Trainees Hear You?" *Training and Development Journal* 41, no. 8 (August 1987), pp. 38–43.

33. Wexley and Latham, *Developing and Training,* pp. 131–3. See also Teri O. Grady and Mike Matthews," Video . . . Through the Eyes of the Trainee," *Training* 24, no. 7 (July 1987), pp. 57–62. For a description of the use of computer-based multimedia training, see Erica Schroeder, "Training Takes Off, Using Multimedia," *PC Week*, August 29, 1994, pp. 33–4.

34. Michael Emery and Margaret Schubert, "A Trainer's Guide to Videoconferencing," *Training* (June 1993), p. 60.

35. Emery and Schubert, "A Trainers Guide," p. 60.

36. C. Knight, "Time is Money, and Satellite Training Can Save Both," *Canadian HR Reporter* (September 23, 1996), pp. 1–2.

37. These are based on or quoted from Emery and Schubert, "A Trainer's Guide," p. 61.

38. G. N. Nash, J. P. Muczyk, and F. L. Vettori, "The Role and Practical Effectiveness of Programmmed Instruction," *Personnel Psychology* 24 (1971), pp. 397–418.

39. Wexley and Latham, *Developing and Training,* p. 141. See also Raymond Wlozkowski, "Simulation," *Training and Development Journal* 39, no. 6 (June 1985), pp. 38–43.

40. J-P Souque, "Focus on Competencies," 1996, p. 13.

41. See, for example, Tim Falconer, "No More Pencils, No More Books!" *Canadian Banker* (March/April 1994), pp. 21–5.

42. M. Shostak, "The Promise of New Media Learning," *Canadian HR Reporter*, April 7, 1997. pp. 15, 19.

43. S. Cohen, "A Guide to Multimedia in the Next Millenium," *Training and Development*, August 1997, pp. 33–44.

44. A. Czarnecki, "Interactive Learning Makes Big Dent in Time, Money Requirements for T&D," *Canadian HR Reporter* Special Section "Learning for the Workplace," (November 18, 1996), pp. L30–L31.

45. A. Czarnecki, "Technology-Based Training: Powerful Tool, but not a Panacea," *Canadian HR Reporter* Special Section "Learning in the Workplace," (May 20, 1996), pp. L28–L29.

46. G. Rodden, "Virtual Reality Makes its Pulp and Paper Debut at Repap New Brunswick," *Pulp and Paper Canada*, (May 1996), pp. 8–9.

47. These are summarized in Rockley Miller, "New Training Looms," *Hotel and Motel Management* (April 4, 1994), pp. 26, 30.

48. M. Shostak, "The Promise of New Media Learning," pp. 15, 19.

49. J-P Souque, "Focus on Competencies," p. 15.

50. J. Vardy, "Corporate Training Goes Online," *Financial Post* (May 31, 1995), p. 46.

51. P. D. Munger, "High-Tech Training Delivery Methods: When to Use Them," *Training and Development* (January 1997), pp. 46–7.

52. S. Lebrun, "IBM Moves the Classroom to the Laptop," *Canadian HR Reporter* (January 27, 1997), p. 7. See also M.MacLellan "T&D Pros' Personal Strategies," *Canadian HR Reporter* Special Section "Learning for the Workplace," (May 19, 1997), pp. L17–L20.

53. B. Filipczak, "Training on Intranets: The Hope and The Hype," *Training* (September 1996), pp. 24–32.

54. D. Heyman, "Illiteracy Called Risk to Nation's Progress," *Calgary Herald* (May 6, 1997), p. B3.

55. Ellen Sherman, "Back to Basics to Improve Skills," *Personnel* (July 1989), pp. 22–6.

56. Bureau of National Affairs, *Bulletin to Management* (December 17), 1987, p. 408.

57. Nancy Lynn Bernardon, "Let's Erase Illiteracy from the Workplace," *Personnel* (January 1989), pp. 29–32.

58. Bernardon, "Let's Erase Illiteracy." The PALS course was developed by educator Dr. John Henry Martin.

59. Bernardon, "Let's Erase Illiteracy," p. 32. SKILLPAC was created by the Center for Applied Linguistics and Dr. Arnold Packer, senior research fellow at the Hudson Institute in Indianapolis, Indiana.

60. B. Bell-Rowbotham & K. Ellis, "AIDS in the Workplace," *Benefits Canada* 21, no. 5 (May 1997), pp. 69–74.

61. Jeffrey Mello, "AIDS Education in the Work Place," *Training and Development Journal* (December 1990), pp. 65–70.

62. This is based on Sylvia Odenwald, "A Guide for Global Training," *Training and Development* (July 1993), pp. 22–31.

63. For a full description of these programs as well as the names of the vendors, see Odenwald, "A Guide for Global Training," pp. 24–7.
64. D. Roberts & B. Tsang, "Diversity Management Training Helps Firms Hone Competitive Edge," *Canadian HR Reporter* (June 19, 1995), pp. 17–8.
65. Sara Rynes and Benson Rosen, "What Makes Diversity Programs Work?" *HR Magazine* (October 1994), p. 64. See also Thomas Diamante and Leo Giglio, "Managing a Diverse Workforce: Training as a Cultural Intervention Strategy," *Leadership & Organization Development Journal* 15 no. 2 (1994), pp. 13–7.
66. Willie Hopkins, Karen Sterkel-Powell, and Shirley Hopkins, "Training Priorities for a Diverse Workforce," *Public Personnel Management* 23, no. 3 (Fall 1994), p. 433.
67. C. Knight, "Training of, for and by the Disabled," *Canadian HR Reporter* (June 19, 1995), p. 11.
68. Personal communication with Laurie Harley, Director of Diversity, IBM Canada, October 2, 1997.
69. "Manufacturing Our Future," Canadian Manufacturers Association, 1995.
70. A. Czarnecki, "Customer Service Training: More Than an 'Event'", *Canadian HR Reporter* Special Section "Learning for the Workplace," (May 20, 1996), pp. L4–L6.
71. This is based on Jennifer Laabs, "Team Training Goes Outdoors," *Personnel Journal* (June 1991), pp. 56–63.
72. Laabs, "Team Training," p. 56. See also Shari Caudron, "Teamwork Takes Work," *Personnel Journal* 73, no. 2 (February 1994), pp. 41–9.
73. P. Benimadhu, *Adding Value: The Role of the Human Resources Function*, Report 157-95, (Ottawa: The Conference Board of Canada, 1995).
74. J-P Souque, "Focus on Competencies," p. 8.
75. Carolyn Wiley, "Training for the 1990s," p. 79.
76. Laurie Bassi, "Upgrading the U.S. Workplace: Do Reorganization & Education Help?" *Monthly Labor Review* (May 1995), pp. 37–47.
77. Ann Bartel, "Productivity Gains from the Implementation of Employee Training Programs," *Industrial Relations* 33, no. 4 (October 1994), pp. 411–25.
78. M. Belcourt and P. Wright, *Managing Performance Through Training and Development*, p. 11.
79. R. E. Catalano and D. L. Kirkpatrick, "Evaluating Training Programs—The State of the Art," *Training and Development Journal* 22, no. 5 (May 1968), pp. 2–9. See also J. Kevin Ford and Steven Wroten, "Introducing New Methods for Conducting Training Evaluation and for Linking Training Evaluation to Program Redesign," *Personnel Psychology* 37, no. 4 (Winter 1984), pp. 651–66. See also Basil Paquet et al., "The Bottom Line," *Training and Development Journal* 41, no. 5 (May 1987), pp. 27–33; Harold E. Fisher and Ronald Weinberg, "Make Training Accountable: Assess Its Impact," *Personnel Journal* 67, no. 1 (January 1988), pp. 73–5; and Timothy Baldwin and J. Kevin Ford, "Transfer of Training: A Review and Directions for Future Research," *Personnel Psychology* 41, no. 1 (Spring 1988), pp. 63–105. Anthony Montebello and Maurine Haga, "To Justify Training, Test, Test Again," *Personnel Journal* 73, No. 1 (January 1994), pp. 83–7.
80. Donald Kirkpatrick, "Effective Supervisory Training and Development," Part 3: "Outside Programs," *Personnel* 62, no. 2 (February 1985), pp. 39–42. See also James Bell and Deborah Kerr, "Measuring Training Results: Key to Managerial Commitment," *Training and Development Journal* 41, no. 1 (January 1987), pp. 70–73. Among the reasons training might not pay off on the job are a mismatching of courses and trainee's needs, supervisory slip-ups (with supervisors signing up trainees and then forgetting to have them attend the sessions when the training session is actually given), and no help applying skills on the job. For a discussion, see Ruth Colvin Clark, "Nine Ways to Make Training Pay Off on the Job," *Training* 23, no. 11 (November 1986), pp. 83–7. See also Herman Birnbrauer, "Troubleshooting Your Training Program," *Training and Development Journal* 41, no 9 (September 1987), pp. 18–20; George Bickerstaffe, "Measuring the Gains from Training," *Personnel Management* (November 1993), pp. 48–51; Jim Spoor, "You Can Quantify Training Dollars and Program Value," *HR Focus* (May 1993), p. 3; Jack Trynor, "Is Training a Good Investment?" *Financial Analyst Journal* (September–October 1994), pp. 6–8; and Sarah Dolliver, "The Missing Link: Evaluating Training Programs," *Supervision* (November 1994), pp. 10–2.
81. N.L. Trainer, "Evaluating Training's Four Levels," *Canadian HR Reporter* (January 13, 1997), p. 10.
82. J-P Souque, "Focus on Competencies," 1996, p. 8.

Chapter 9
Career Development

Chapter Outline

Learning Outcomes

After studying this chapter, you should be able to:

Discuss the factors that affect career choices.

Explain how to make a new employee's first assignment more meaningful.

Discuss how to more effectively manage promotions and transfers.

Explain what management development is and why it is important.

Describe on-the-job and off-the-job management development techniques.

Explain how to use HRM techniques to develop a learning organization.

Introduction

career planning and development
The deliberate process through which a person becomes aware of personal career-related attributes and the lifelong series of activities that contribute to his or her career fulfillment.

HRM activities like screening, training, and appraising serve two basic roles in organizations. First, their traditional role has been to staff the organization—to fill its positions with employees who have the requisite interests, abilities, and skills. Increasingly, however, these activities are taking on a second role of ensuring that the long-run interests of the employees are protected by the organization and that, in particular, each employee is encouraged to grow and realize his or her full potential. Referring to *staffing* or *personnel management* as *human resources management* reflects this second role. A basic assumption underlying this role is that the employer has an obligation to utilize employees' abilities to the fullest and to give all employees a chance to grow and to realize their full potential and to develop successful careers.[1] One way this trend is manifesting itself is in the increased emphasis many firms are placing on **career planning and development.** As we reach the turn of the century, career development is becoming widely accepted as a way for organizations to respond to one of the most serious challenges they face, that being keeping their employees motivated and productive in an environment where there are limited opportunities for promotion.[2]

Activities like HR planning, screening, and training play a big role in the career development process. HR planning, for example, can be used not just to forecast open jobs but to identify potential internal candidates and the training they would need to fill these jobs. Similarly, an organization can use its periodic employee appraisals not just for salary decisions, but for identifying the development needs of individual employees and ensuring that these needs are met. All the staffing activities, in other words, can be used to satisfy the needs of both the organization and the individual in such a way that they both gain: the organization from improved performance from a more committed work force and the employee from a richer, more challenging career.[3]

This is illustrated in **Table 9.1**. For example, performance appraisal's traditional

TABLE 9.1 HRM: Traditional versus Career Development Focus

ACTIVITY	TRADITIONAL FOCUS	CAREER DEVELOPMENT FOCUS
Human resources planning	Analyzes jobs, skills, tasks—present and future. Projects needs. Uses statistical data.	Adds information about individual interests, preferences, and the like to data. Provides career path information.
Training and development	Provides opportunities for learning skills, information, and attitudes related to job.	Adds individual growth orientation.
Performance appraisal	Rating and/or rewards.	Adds development plans and individual goal setting.
Recruiting and placement	Matching organization's needs with qualified individuals.	Matches individuals and jobs based on a number of variables, including employees' career interests.
Compensation and benefits	Rewards for time, productivity, talent, and so on.	Adds non-job-related activities to be rewarded, such as United Way leadership positions.

Source: Adapted from Fred L. Otte and Peggy G. Hutcheson, *Helping Employees Manage Careers* (Englewood Cliffs, NJ: Prentice Hall, 1992), p. 10.

focus has been on rating for the purposes of promotion, discipline, and rewards; using it to provide a career development focus means including development plans and individual goal setting. Similarly, HR planning traditionally focusses on job analysis and satisfying the organization's staffing needs; adding a career development focus means including information about individual career interests and preferences as well as career path options.

Before proceeding, it would be useful to define some of the terms we'll be using throughout this chapter.[4] A *career* is a series of work-related positions, paid or unpaid, that helps a person grow in job skills, success, and fulfillment. *Career development* is the lifelong series of activities (such as workshops) that contribute to a person's career exploration, establishment, success, and fulfillment. *Career planning* is the deliberate process through which someone becomes aware of personal skills, interests, knowledge, motivations, and other characteristics; acquires information about opportunities and choices; identifies career-related goals; and establishes action plans to attain specific goals.

**www.cdteam.com/
order.html**
The Career Development Team

Roles in Career Development

As summarized in **Table 9.2**, the individual, the manager, and the organization all have roles in the individual's career development. Ultimately, it is the individual who must accept responsibility for his or her own career; assess interests, skills, and values; seek out career information and resources; and generally take those steps that must be taken to ensure a happy and fulfilling career. This requires an entrepreneurial, goal-oriented approach that requires four key skills: self motivation, independent learning, effective time and money management, and self-promotion.[5] Within the organization the individual's manager plays a role, too. The manager should provide timely and objective performance feedback, offer developmental

---

TABLE 9.2 Roles in Career Development

Individual
- Accept responsibility for your own career.
- Assess your interests, skills, and values.
- Seek out career information and resources.
- Establish goals and career plans.
- Utilize development opportunities.
- Talk with your manager about your career.
- Follow through on realistic career plans.

Manager
- Provide timely performance feedback.
- Provide developmental assignments and support.
- Participate in career development discussions.
- Support employee development plans.

Organization
- Communicate mission, policies, and procedures.
- Provide training and development opportunities.
- Provide career information and career programs.
- Offer a variety of career options.

Source: Fred L. Otte and Peggy G. Hutcheson, *Helping Employees Manage Careers* (Englewood Cliffs, NJ: Prentice Hall, 1992), p. 56.

TABLE 9.3 Four Roles for Managers in Employee Development			
COACH	**APPRAISER**	**ADVISOR**	**REFERRAL AGENT**
Listens	Gives feedback	Generates options	Links employee
Clarifies	Clarifies standards	Helps set goals	to resources/people
Probes	Clarifies job	Recommends/advises	Consults on action
Defines concerns	responsibilities		plan

Source: Fred L. Otte and Peggy G. Hutcheson, *Helping Employees Manage Careers* (Englewood Cliffs, NJ: Prentice Hall, 1992), p. 57.

assignments and support, and participate in career development discussions. The manager acts as a coach, appraiser, advisor, and referral agent, for instance, listening to and clarifying the individual's career plans, giving feedback, generating career options, and linking the employee to organizational resources and career options (**Table 9.3**).

Finally, as we'll also see in this chapter, the employer plays a career development role. For example, the organization should provide career-oriented training and development opportunities, offer career information and career programs, and give employees a variety of career options. Ultimately, as we'll see, employers need not and should not provide such career-oriented activities purely out of altruism. Most employees will ultimately grade their employers on the extent to which the organization allowed them to excel and to become the people they believed they had the potential to become. And that will help determine their commitment to their employers and their overall job satisfaction.[6]

Factors That Affect Career Choices

The first step in planning a career is to learn as much as possible about the person's interests, aptitudes, and skills.

Identify Career Stage

career cycle
The stages through which a person's career evolves.

growth stage
The period from birth to age 14 during which the person develops a self-concept by identifying with and interacting with other people such as family, friends, and teachers.

Each person's career goes through stages, and the current stage will influence the person's knowledge of and preference for various occupations. The main stages of this **career cycle** follow:[7]

Growth Stage The **growth stage** lasts roughly from birth to age 14 and is a period during which the person develops a self-concept by identifying with and interacting with other people such as family, friends, and teachers. Toward the beginning of this period, role-playing is important, and children experiment with different ways of acting; this helps them to form impressions of how other people react to different behaviours and contributes to their developing a unique self-concept or identity. Toward the end of this stage, the adolescent (who by this time has developed preliminary ideas about what his or her interests and abilities are) begins to think realistically about alternative occupations.

exploration stage
The period from around ages 15 to 24 during which a person seriously explores various occupational alternatives, attempting to match these alternatives with his or her interests and abilities.

Exploration Stage The **exploration stage** is the period (roughly from ages 15 to 24) during which a person seriously explores various occupational alternatives. The person attempts to match these alternatives with what he or she has learned about them and about his or her own interests and abilities from school, leisure activities, and work. Tentative broad occupational choices are usually made during the beginning of this period. Toward the end of this period a seemingly appropriate choice is made and the person tries out for a beginning job.

Probably the most important task the person has in this and the preceding stage is that of developing a realistic understanding of his or her abilities and talents. Similarly, the person must make sound educational decisions based on reliable sources of information about occupational alternatives.

establishment stage
The period, roughly from ages 24 to 44, that is the heart of most people's work lives.

Establishment Stage The **establishment stage** spans roughly ages 24 to 44 and is the heart of most people's work lives. During this period, it is hoped that a suitable occupation is found and that the person engages in activities that help him or her earn a permanent place in his or her chosen field. Often, and particularly in the professions, the person locks into a chosen occupation early. But in most cases, this is a period during which the person is continually testing his or her capabilities and ambitions against those of the initial occupational choice.

maintenance stage
The period from about ages 45 to 65 during which the person secures his or her place in the world of work.

Maintenance Stage Between the ages of 45 to 65, many people simply slide from the establishment stage into the **maintenance stage.** During this latter period, the person has typically created a place in the world of work and most efforts are now directed at maintaining that place.

decline stage
The period during which many people are faced with the prospect of having to accept reduced levels of power and responsibility.

Decline Stage As retirement age approaches, there may be a deceleration period in the **decline stage.** Here, many people face the prospect of having to accept reduced levels of power and responsibility, and learn to accept and develop new roles as mentor and confidante for those who are younger. However, it is becoming more common for older workers, despite some decline in physical capabilities, to continue to work until normal retirement age, and beyond. Following retirement, the person finds alternative uses for the time and effort formerly expended on his or her occupation.

Identify Occupational Orientation

Career-counselling expert John Holland says that a person's personality (including values, motives, and needs) is another important determinant of career choices. For example, a person with a strong social orientation might be attracted to careers that entail interpersonal rather than intellectual or physical activities and to occupations such as social work. Based on research with his Vocational Preference Test (VPT), Holland found six basic personality types or orientations.[8]

1. *Realistic orientation.* These people are attracted to occupations that involve physical activities requiring skill, strength, and coordination. Examples include forestry, farming, and agriculture.

2. *Investigative orientation.* Investigative people are attracted to careers that involve cognitive activities (thinking, organizing, understanding) rather than affective activities (feeling, acting, or interpersonal and emotional tasks). Examples include biologist, chemist, and college professor.

3. *Social orientation.* These people are attracted to careers that involve interpersonal rather than intellectual or physical activities. Examples include clinical psychology, foreign service, and social work.

4. *Conventional orientation.* A conventional orientation favours careers that involve structured, rule-regulated activities, as well as careers in which it is expected that the employee subordinate his or her personal needs to those of the organization. Examples include accountants and bankers.

5. *Enterprising orientation.* Verbal activities aimed at influencing others are attractive to enterprising personalities. Examples include managers, lawyers, and public relations executives.

6. *Artistic orientation.* People here are attracted to careers that involve self-expression, artistic creation, expression of emotions, and individualistic activities. Examples include artists, advertising executives, and musicians.

occupational orientation
The theory developed by John Holland that says there are six basic personal orientations that determine the sorts of careers to which people are drawn.

Most people have more than one orientation (they might be social, realistic, and investigative, for example), and Holland believes that the more similar or compatible these orientations are, the less internal conflict or indecision a person will face in making a career choice. In **Table 9.4**, we have summarized some of the occupations that have been found to be the best match for each of these six personal **occupational orientations.**

TABLE 9.4 Occupations Scoring High on Each Occupational Orientation Theme

REALISTIC	INVESTIGATIVE	ARTISTIC	SOCIAL	ENTERPRISING	CONVENTIONAL
Consider these occupations if you score *high* here:					
Agribusiness managers	Biologists	Advertising executives	Auto sales dealers	Agribusiness managers	Accountants
Carpenters	Chemists	Art teachers	Guidance counsellors	Auto sales dealers	Auto sales dealers
Electricians	Engineers	Artists	Home economics teachers	Business education teachers	Bankers
Engineers	Geologists	Broadcasters	Mental health workers	Buyers	Bookkeepers
Farmers	Mathematicians	English teachers	Ministers	Chamber of Commerce executives	Business education teachers
Foresters	Medical technologists	Interior decorators	Physical education teachers	Funeral directors	Credit managers
Highway patrol officers	Physicians	Medical illustrators	Recreation leaders	Life insurance agents	Executive housekeepers
Horticultural workers	Physicists	Ministers	School administrators	Purchasing agents	Food service managers
Industrial arts teachers	Psychologists	Musicians	Social science teachers	Realtors	Tax collectors
Military enlisted personnel	Research and development managers	Photographers	Social workers	Restaurant managers	Mathematics teachers
Military officers	Science teachers	Public relations directors	Special education teachers	Retail clerks	Military enlisted personnel
Vocational agricultural teachers	Sociologists	Reporters	YMCA/YWCA directors	Store managers	Secretaries

Note: for example, if you score high on "realistic," consider a career as a carpenter, engineer, farmer, and so on.

Source: Reproduced by special permission of the publisher, Consulting Psychologists Press, Inc., Palo Alto, CA 94306, from *Manual for the SVIV-SCII,* Fourth Edition, by Jo-Ida C. Hansen and David P. Campbell. © 1985 by the Board of Trustees of Leland Stanford Junior University.

Identify Skills

Successful performance depends not just on motivation but on ability too. Someone may have a conventional orientation, but whether he or she has the skills to be an accountant, banker, or credit manager will largely determine the specific occupation ultimately chosen. Therefore, each individual's skills must be identified.

occupational skills
The skills needed to be successful in a particular occupation. Occupational skills break down into three groups depending on whether they emphasize data, people, or things.

An Exercise   One useful exercise for identifying **occupational skills** is to take a blank piece of paper and write the heading "The Most Enjoyable Occupational Task I Have Had." Then write a short essay that describes the task. Make sure to go into detail about duties and responsibilities and what it was about the task that was enjoyable. Next, on other sheets of paper, do the same thing for two other enjoyable tasks. Now go through the three essays and *underline the skills that were mentioned the most often*. For example, was it putting together and coordinating the school play as part of a job in the principal's office one year? Was it the hours spent in the library doing research when working one summer as an office clerk?[9]

Aptitudes and Special Talents   For career planning purposes, a person's aptitudes (defined in chapter 7) are usually measured with a test battery such as the general aptitude test battery (GATB). This instrument measures various aptitudes including intelligence and mathematical ability. Considerable work has been done to relate aptitudes, such as those measured by the GATB, to specific occupations.

Identify Career Anchor

Edgar Schein says that career planning is a continuing process of discovery—one in which a person slowly develops a clearer occupational self-concept in terms of what his or her talents, abilities, motives, needs, attitudes, and values are. Schein also says that as you learn more about yourself, it becomes apparent that you have a dominant **career anchor**, a concern or value that you will not give up if a choice has to be made. Career anchors, as their name implies, are the pivots around which a person's career swings; a person becomes conscious of them as a result of learning about his or her talents and abilities, motives and needs, and attitudes and values. Based on his research, Schein believes that career anchors are difficult to predict ahead of time because they are evolutionary. Some people may never find out what their career anchors are until they have to make a major choice—such as whether to take the promotion to the headquarters staff or strike out on their own by starting a business. It is at this point that all the person's past work experiences, interests, aptitudes, and orientations converge into a meaningful pattern (or career anchor) that helps show what is personally the most important in driving the person's career choices. Schein identified five career anchors.[10]

career anchor
A concern or value that you will not give up if a choice has to be made.

Technical/Functional Career Anchor   People who have a strong technical/functional career anchor tend to avoid decisions that would drive them toward general management. Instead they make decisions that will enable them to remain and grow in their chosen technical or functional fields.

Managerial Competence as a Career Anchor   Other people show a strong motivation to become managers, and their career experience convinces them that they have the skills and values required to rise to general management positions. A management position of high responsibility is their ultimate goal. Qualifications for these jobs include: (1) analytical competence (ability to identify, analyze, and solve problems under conditions of incomplete information and uncertainty);

(2) interpersonal competence (ability to influence, supervise, lead, manipulate, and control people at all levels); and (3) emotional competence (the capacity to be stimulated by emotional and interpersonal crises rather than exhausted or debilitated by them, and the capacity to bear high levels of responsibility without becoming paralyzed).

Creativity as a Career Anchor People who become successful entrepreneurs have a need to build or create something that is entirely their own product—a product or process that bears their name, a company of their own, or a personal fortune that reflects their accomplishments. For example, one participant in Schein's research became a successful purchaser, restorer, and renter of townhouses in a large city; another built a successful consulting firm.

Autonomy and Independence as Career Anchors Some people seem driven to be on their own, free of the dependence that can arise when a person works in a large organization where promotions, transfers, and salary decisions make them subordinate to others. Many also have a strong technical/functional orientation. However, instead of pursuing this orientation in an organization, they decide to become consultants, working either alone or as part of a relatively small firm. Others become professors of business, freelance writers, and proprietors of a small retail business.

Security as a Career Anchor Some people are mostly concerned with long-run career stability and job security. They seem willing to do what is required to maintain job security, a decent income, and a stable future in the form of a good retirement program and benefits.

For those interested in *geographic security,* maintaining a stable, secure career in familiar surroundings is generally more important than pursuing superior career choices, if choosing the latter means injecting instability or insecurity into their lives by forcing them to pull up roots and move to another city. For others, security means *organizational security.* They are much more willing to let their employers decide what their careers should be.

Identify High-Potential Occupations

Learning about oneself is only half the job of choosing an occupation. People also have to identify those occupations that are right (given their occupational orientations, skills, career anchors, and occupational preferences), as well as those that will be in high demand in the years to come. Investigating occupations can take hours (or perhaps days or weeks) of library research.

There are two basic things that can and should be done to improve career decisions.[11] First, each person must *take charge* of his/her own career by understanding that there are major decisions to be made, which require considerable personal planning and effort. In other words, career choices cannot be left in the hands of others. Each person must decide where she or he wants to go in terms of a career and what job moves and education are required to get there.

Second, each individual must become an effective *diagnostician,* and determine (through career counselling, testing, self-diagnostic books, and so on) what his or her talents or values are, and how these fit with the sorts of careers being considered.[12] In other words, the key to career planning is self-insight.

Career Development and the Responsibilities of the Manager and the Employer

Career Management Guidelines

Along with the employee, the manager and employer both have career management responsibilities. Guidelines here include:

Avoid Reality Shock   Perhaps at no other stage in the person's career is it more important for the employer to be career development-oriented than at the initial entry stage, when the person is recruited, hired, and given a first assignment and boss. This is (or should be) a period of *reality testing* during which his or her initial hopes and goals first confront the reality of organizational life and of the person's talents and needs.

For many first-time workers, this turns out to be a disastrous period, one in which their often naive expectations confront unexpected workplace realities. The young MBA or CA, for example, might come to the first job seeking a challenging, exciting assignment in which to apply the new techniques learned in school and to prove his or her abilities and gain a promotion. In reality, however, the trainee is often turned off by being relegated to an unimportant low-risk job where he or she "can't cause any trouble while being tried out"; or by the harsh realities of interdepartmental conflict and politicking; or by a boss who is neither rewarded for nor trained in the unique mentoring tasks needed to properly supervise new employees.[13] Reality shock (as defined in chapter 8) refers to the results of a period that may occur at the initial career entry when the new employee's high job expectations confront the reality of a boring, unchallenging job.

Provide Challenging Initial Jobs   Most experts agree that one of the most important things is to provide new employees with challenging first jobs. In most organizations, however, providing such jobs seems more the exception than the rule. In one survey of research and development organizations, for example, only 1 of 22 companies had a formal policy of giving challenging first assignments.[14] This imbalance, as one expert has pointed out, is an example of "glaring mismanagement" when one considers the effort and money invested in recruiting, hiring, and training new employees.[15]

Giving an employee responsibility for a major presentation to an important client is one way to front-load entry-level jobs with challenge and to foster employee commitment.

Provide Realistic Job Previews   Providing recruits with realistic previews of what to expect should they be selected to work in the organization—ones that describe both the attractions and also possible pitfalls—can be an effective way of minimizing reality shock and improving their long-term performance. Schein points out that one of the biggest problems new hires and employers encounter during the crucial entry stage is getting accurate information in a "climate of mutual selling."[16] The interviewer (anxious to hook good candidates) and the candidate (anxious to present as favourable an impression as possible) often give and receive unrealistic information. The result is that the interviewer may not form a clear picture of the candidate's career goals, while at the same time the candidate forms an unrealistically favourable image of the organization.[17] Realistic job previews can boost the survival rate among employees who are hired for relatively complex jobs like management trainee, salesperson, or life insurance agent.[18]

Be Demanding   There is often a "Pygmalion effect"[19] in the relationship between a new employee and his or her boss.[20] In other words, the more the supervisor expects and the more confident and supportive he or she is, the better new employees will perform. Therefore, as two experts put it, "Don't assign a new employee to a 'dead wood,' undemanding, or unsupportive supervisor."[21] Instead firms should choose specially trained, high-performing, supportive supervisors who can set high standards for new employees during their critical exploratory first year.

Provide Periodic Developmental Job Rotation and Job Pathing The best way new employees can test themselves and crystallize their career anchors is to try out a variety of challenging jobs. By rotating to jobs in various specializations—from financial analysis to production to human resources, for example—the employee gets an opportunity to assess his or her aptitudes and preferences. At the same time, the organization gets a manager with a broader, multifunctional view of the organization.[22] One extension of this is called **job pathing**, which means selecting carefully sequenced job assignments.[23]

job pathing
Selecting carefully sequenced job assignments to enable employees to test their aptitudes and preferences.

Do Career-Oriented Performance Appraisals Edgar Schein says that supervisors must understand that valid performance appraisal information is, in the long run, more important than protecting the short-term interests of their staff.[24] Therefore a supervisor needs concrete information regarding the employee's potential career path—information, in other words, about the nature of the future work for which he or she is appraising the employee, or which the employee desires.[25]

Provide Career Planning Workshops and Career Planning Workbooks Employers also should take steps to increase their employees' involvement and expertise in planning and developing their own careers. One option here is to organize periodic career planning workshops. A **career planning workshop** has been defined as "a planned learning event in which participants are expected to be actively involved, completing career planning exercises and inventories and participating in career skills practice sessions."[26]

career planning workshop
A planned learning event in which participants are expected to be actively involved in career planning exercises and career skills practice sessions.

Figure 9.1 provides an illustrative agenda for a two-day career planning workshop. Such workshops usually contain a *self-assessment* activity in which individual employees actively analyze their own career interests, skills, and career anchors. There is then an *environmental assessment* phase in which relevant information about the company and its career options and staffing needs is presented. Finally, a career planning workshop typically concludes with goal setting and action planning in which the individual sets career goals and creates a career plan.

A career planning workbook may be distributed to employees either as part of a workshop or as an independent career planning aid. This is "a printed guide that directs its users through a series of assessment exercises, models, discussions, guidelines, and other information to support career planning."[27] It is usually self-paced, so that the employees can complete the exercises at their own pace. As in **Table 9.5**, the career planning workbook normally contains several career self-assessment exercises, as well as information about how to examine career options (such as where to find out more about specific occupations and careers). The workbook may also contain practical career-related information such as how to prepare a résumé. Finally, career planning workbooks usually contain guides for creating a career development action plan. A career planning workbook underlines the employee's responsibility to initiate the career development process, whereas career workshops may reinforce the perception that the employer will do so.[28]

Figure 9.1
Sample Agenda—Two-Day Career Planning Workshop
Source: Fred L. Otte and Peggy G. Hutcheson, *Helping Employees Manage Careers* (Englewood Cliffs, NJ: Prentice Hall, 1992), pp. 22–3.

Before the program—Two weeks prior to the workshop participants receive a letter confirming their participation in the program and package of work to be completed before coming to the workshop. The exercises in this package include skills inventory, values identification, life accomplishments inventory, and a reading describing career direction options.

Day 1

8:30–10:00 Introduction to and Overview of Career Planning

Welcome and Introduction to Program

    Welcome by general manager
    Overview of agenda and outcomes
    Participant introductions (statements of expectations for the program)

Overview of Career Development

    Company's philosophy
    Why career planning is needed
    What career planning is and is not
    Career planning model

10:00–Noon Self-Assessment: Part 1

Individual Self-Assessment: Values

    Values card sort exercise
    Reconciling with values pre-work
    Introduce career planning summary work sheet

Individual Self-Assessment: Skills

    Motivated skills exercise
    Examining life accomplishments (synthesize exercise with pre-work)
    Identifying accomplishment themes
    Preferred work skills (from pre-work inventory)
    Fill in career planning summary work sheet

1:00–3:30 Self Assessment: Part 2

Individual Self-Assessment: Career Anchors

    Career anchoring pattern exercise
    Small group discussions
    Fill in career planning summary work sheet

Individual Self-Assessment: Preferences

    What success means to me
    Skills, knowledge, personal qualities
    Fill in career planning summary work sheet

Individual Self-Assessment: Career Path Pattern

    Synthesize with direction options from pre-work
    Fill in career planning summary work sheet

3:30–4:30 Environmental Assessment

Information About the Company

    Goals, growth areas, expectations, turnover, competition for jobs, skills for the future
    Fill in career planning summary work sheet

Personal Career Profile

    Reality test: how you see self at this point by sharing in group

Day 2

8:30–10:00 Goal Setting

Warm-up Exercise

    Review of where we've been and where we're going
    Setting goals—where do I want to be?

Creating an Ideal Future

    Future skills and accomplishments
    Desired lifestyle
    Life and career goals

10:15–1:30 Environmental Assessment: Part 2

Career Resources in the Company

    Introduce support services and hand out information
    Marketing yourself—what it takes to achieve your goals here

Lunch with Resource People

Describe resource people who will be with the group for lunch and brainstorm questions/issues to be discussed

    Lunch with resource people
    Review lunch discussions

1:30–4:30 Developing career action plans

Making Career Decisions

    Identifying long-range alternatives
    Identifying short-range alternatives

Improving Career Decisions

    Decision styles and ways to enhance them

Creating Your Career Plan

Reconciling your goals with options
Next career steps
Development action plan
Contingency planning

Making It Happen—Making Commitments to Next Steps

Summary and Adjournment

TABLE 9.5 Table of Contents for Short Career Planning Workbook

Chapter 1—Self-Assessment: Taking a Good Look at Yourself
  Introduction
  Accomplishments
  Common Themes
  Assessing Skill Strengths
  Knowledge
  Personal Traits
  Work-Related Values
  Summary
Chapter 2—Examining Career Directions
  Introduction
  Career Directions
  Job Information Resources
  Identifying Organizational and Job Realities
  Resources
  Summary
Chapter 3—Making the Most of a Career Development Discussion
  Introduction
  Preparing a Career Résumé
  Sample Career Résumé
  Preparing for the Career Development Discussion
  Suggestions for an Effective Career Development Discussion
  Summary
  Notes
Chapter 4—Preparing a Career Development Action Plan
  Introduction
  Examining Avenues for Development
  Evaluating Trade-offs
  Preparing a Career Development Strategy
  Afterword

Source: Fred L. Otte and Peggy G. Hutcheson, *Helping Employees Manage Careers* (Englewood Cliffs, NJ: Prentice Hall, 1992), p. 147.

mentoring
The use of an experienced individual (the mentor) to teach and train another person with less knowledge in a given area (the protégé).

Provide Opportunities for Mentoring Mentoring can be defined as "the use of an experienced individual [the mentor] to teach and train someone [the protégé] with less knowledge in a given area."[29] Through individualized attention "the mentor transfers needed information, feedback, and encouragement to the protégé…"[30] and in that way the opportunities for the protégé to optimize his or her career success are improved.

Organizational mentoring may be formal or informal. Informally, of course, middle- and senior-level managers will often voluntarily take up-and-coming employees under their wings, not only to train them, but to give career advice and to help them steer around political pitfalls.

However, many employers also establish formal mentoring programs. Here employers actively encourage mentoring relationships to take place, and may, in fact, pair protégés with potential mentors. Training—perhaps in the form of instructional manuals—may be provided to facilitate the mentoring process and in particular to aid both mentor and protégé in understanding their respective responsibilities in the mentoring relationship.

Managing Promotions and Transfers

Making Promotion Decisions

Employers must decide on what basis to promote employees, and the way these decisions are made will affect the employees' motivation, performance, and commitment.

Decision 1: Is Seniority or Competence the Rule? Probably the most important decision is whether promotion will be based on seniority or competence, or some combination of the two. From the point of view of motivation, promotion based on competence is best. However, the ability to use competence as a sole criterion depends on several things, most notably whether or not a firm is unionized. Union agreements often contain a clause that emphasizes seniority in promotions, such as: "In the advancement of employees to higher paid jobs when ability, merit, and capacity are equal, employees with the highest seniority will be given preference."[31] Although this might seem to leave the door open for giving a person with less seniority, but slightly better ability, the inside track for a job, labour arbitrators have generally held that when clauses such as these are binding only *substantial differences in abilities can be taken into account*. In one case, for example, the arbitrator ruled that seniority should be disregarded only when an employee with less seniority stood "head and shoulders" above the employees with greater seniority.[32] Similarly, many organizations in the public sector are governed by civil service regulations or collective agreements that emphasize seniority rather than competence as the basis for promotion.[33]

Decision 2: How Is Competence Measured? If promotion is to be based on competence, how will competence be defined and measured? Defining and measuring *past* performance is a fairly straightforward matter: The job is defined, standards are set, and one or more appraisal tools are used to record the employee's performance. But promotion also requires predicting the person's *potential;* thus, there must be a valid procedure for predicting a candidate's future performance.

Many employers simply use prior performance as a guide and extrapolate, or assume, that based on the person's prior performance he or she will perform well on the new job. This is the simplest procedure to use.

On the other hand, some employers use tests to evaluate promotable employees[34] and to identify those employees with executive potential.[35] Others use assessment centres to evaluate management potential.

Decision 3: Is the Process Formal or Informal? If promotion decisions are to be based on competence, it is necessary to decide whether the promotion process will be formal or informal. Many employers still depend on an informal system. Here the availability and requirements of open positions are kept secret. Promotion decisions are then made by key managers from among employees they know personally and also from among those who, for one reason or another, have impressed them.[36] The problem is that when employees are not made aware of the jobs that are available, the criteria for promotion, and how promotion decisions are made, the link between performance and promotion is severed. The effectiveness of promotion as a reward is thereby diminished.

For this reason, many employers establish formal, published promotion policies and procedures. Here employees are generally provided with a formal promotion policy statement that describes the criteria by which promotions are awarded. Formal systems often include a job-posting policy. As described in chapter 6, such a policy states that open positions and their requirements will be posted and circulated to all employees. As explained in chapter 5, many employers also compile detailed information about the qualifications of employees in skills inventories, while others use replacement charts or summaries. Computerized information systems can be especially useful for maintaining skills inventories on hundred or thousands of employees. The net effect of such actions is twofold: (1) An employer ensures that all qualified employees are considered for openings; and (2) promotion becomes more closely linked with performance in the minds of employees.

Decision 4: Vertical, Horizontal, or Other?   Finally, employers are increasingly having to deal with the question of how to "promote" employees in an era in which higher-level jobs are less available. On the one hand, layoffs due to mergers have eliminated many of the higher-management positions to which employees might normally aspire, as has the flattening of most organizations.[37] On the other hand, worker empowerment and a related emphasis on technological expertise have created cadres of highly trained professionals, technicians, and first-line workers who aspire to higher-level positions, but find their upward movement blocked by a dearth of openings.

Several options are available here. Some firms have created two parallel career paths, one for managers and another for "individual contributors" such as engineers. In that way individual contributors, such as highly accomplished engineers, can move up to nonsupervisory but still more senior positions such as "senior engineer." These jobs have most of the perks and financial rewards attached to management-track positions at that level.[38]

Another option is to provide career development opportunities for an individual, either by moving the person horizontally or even within the same position he or she currently holds. For instance, a production employee might be moved horizontally to HR in order to give him or her an opportunity to develop new skills and test and challenge aptitudes. And, in a sense, "promotions" are possible even when leaving the person in the same job: for example, some job enrichment is usually possible, and the firm can provide training that increases the opportunity for assuming increased responsibility.[39]

The accompanying Diversity Counts box addresses the question of why women sometimes fail to get to the top of the corporate ladder when it comes to promotions.

Handling Transfers

Reasons for Transfers   As explained in chapter 5, a transfer is a move from one job to another, usually with no change in salary or grade. Employees may seek transfers for personal enrichment, for more interesting jobs, for greater convenience—better hours, location of work, and so on—or for jobs offering greater possibilities for advancement.[40] Employers may transfer a worker in order to vacate a position where he or she is no longer needed, to fill one where he or she is needed, to retain a senior employee (bumping a less senior person when necessary), or more generally to find a better fit for the employee within the firm. Finally, many firms are endeavouring to boost productivity by eliminating management layers. Transfers are thus increasingly a way to give employees, who might have nowhere else to move in their firms, opportunities for diversity of job assignment and, therefore, personal growth.

Effect on Family Life   Many firms have had policies of routinely transferring employees from locale to locale, either to give their employees more exposure to a wide range of jobs or to fill open positions with trained employees. Such easy-transfer

Diversity Counts
In Promotion and Career Management

There is no doubt that women still do not make it to the top of the career ladder in numbers that are in any way proportional to their representation in industry. One Canadian study found that women held only 1.6 percent of jobs at the corporate vice president level and above.[1]

Many explanations have been put forth.[2] Blatant or subtle discrimination, including the belief that "women belong at home and are not committed to careers,"[3] inhibits many managers from taking women as seriously as men. The "old boy network" of informal friendships forged over lunch, at social events, at club meetings, and on the golf course is usually not open to women, although it's often here that promotional decisions are made. A woman who tries to act like "one of the boys" is often considered "too hard or too cold hearted," so that "women aspiring to executive positions have to stay within narrow bands of acceptable behaviour where they may exhibit only certain traditional masculine and feminine qualities, and walking this fine line represents one of the most difficult tasks for executive women."[4] Unlike many men, women are often forced to make the "career versus family" decision, since the responsibilities of raising the children and managing the household still fall disproportionately on women. There may also be a dearth of women mentors, making it more difficult for women to find the role models and managerial mentors and protectors they need to help them guide their careers.

Women and their managers and employers can take a number of steps to enhance female employees' promotional and career prospects. Perhaps the most important task is to vigorously focus on taking the career interests of female employees seriously; in other words, the first step in stripping away the barriers that have impeded women's progress in the past is to accept that there have been and are problems that must be addressed.

Another step is instituting more flexible career tracks so that women who need to take off for several years to raise a family can return and resume their careers. Given the powerful role played by even subtle discrimination, employers also have to take exceptional care to ensure that in all aspects of promotion and career management—from HR and succession planning to performance appraisals and carefully considering candidates for the company's jobs—the process is objective and not subject to hidden biases.

A recent study suggests other steps employers and managers can take. Career encouragement (encouraging female employees to take responsibility for their careers and to map out career plans) appears to increase women's training and development activities, which in turn enhances managerial advancement.[5] Training and development and career encouragement are increased and enhanced by self-confidence, so it is useful to take steps to enhance employees' career self-confidence.

Beyond that there are several things the employee herself can do, say several experts.[6]

Be able and capable: Learn and understand your business.

Be seen as able and capable: Do not let your abilities be discounted or ignored.

Find a mentor and engage in networking.

Train yourself beyond the job and increase your career assets so you will be available when a good job opportunity arises.

Know what you want and prepare to balance and prioritize your life.[7] ◆

1. L. Sullivan, "Room at the Top: Diversity in the Executive Suite," *Canadian HR Reporter*, January 29, 1996, p. 11.
2. Unless otherwise noted this is based on Robert Marrujo and Brian Kleiner, "Why Women Fail to Get to the Top," *Equal Opportunities International* 11, no. 4 (1992), pp. 1–5.
3. Marrujo and Kleiner, "Why Women Fail to Get to the Top."
4. P. Watts, "Lending a Helping Hand," *Executive Female* 12 (1989), pp. 38–40.
5. Phyllis Tharenou, Shane Latimer, and Denise Conroy, "How Do You Make It to the Top? An Examination of Influences on Women's and Men's Managerial Advancement," *Academy of Management Journal* 37, no. 4 (1994), pp. 899–931.
6. These are based on Marrujo and Kleiner, "Why Women Fail to Get to the Top," p. 3; and Ann Morrison, P. White, and Ellen Van Velsor, *Breaking the Glass Ceiling* (Reading, MA: Addison-Wesley Publishing Co., 1987).
7. See also Ronald Burke and Carol McKeen, "Supporting the Career Aspirations of Managerial and Professional Women," *Business and the Contemporary World* (Summer 1993), pp. 69–80.

policies have fallen into disfavour, however. This is partly because of the cost of relocating employees (paying moving expenses, buying back the employee's current home, and perhaps financing his or her next home, for instance) and partly because on the assumption that frequent transfers have a bad effect on an employee's family life.

One study suggests that the latter argument, at least, is without merit.[41] The study compared the experiences of "mobile" families who had moved on the average of once every two years with "stable" families who had lived in their communities for more than eight years. Although mobility was associated with dissatisfaction with social relationships among men and women (for instance, in terms of opportunities to make friends at work and in the community), the major finding was that there were few differences between mobile and stable families. Few families in the mobile group believed moving was easy. However, these families were as satisfied with all aspects of their lives (except social relationships) as were stable families. This study notwithstanding, there is no doubt that employees do resist geographical transfers more today than they did even a few years ago.

Building Employee Commitment

Helping Employees to Self-Actualize

Everyone will come to a point when they will ask whether they have achieved all they wanted to, given their skills, their gifts, and their dreams for themselves, and, if not, then woe to the firm that prevented them from doing so.[1] Few needs are as strong as the need to fulfill one's dreams, to become all one is capable of becoming. Firms that don't cater to this need lose their best employees or drift along with increasingly bitter, unhappy, and uncommitted ones. Psychologist Abraham Maslow said that the ultimate need is "the desire to become more and more what one is, to become anything that one is capable of becoming." Self-actualization, to Maslow, meant that what a man or woman *can* be, he or she *must* be. It refers to the desire for self-fulfillment, namely, to the tendency for the person to become actualized in what he or she is potentially."[2] An important key to winning employees' commitment is thus to help them self-actualize—to become all they can be.[3]

Ironically, many companies not only do not try to fulfill this need, they actively thwart it. As a healthy person matures and approaches adulthood, said noted researcher and author Chris Argyris, he or she moves to a state of increased activity, independence, and stronger interests.[4] The person also becomes capable of behaving in a greater variety of ways and tends to have a much longer time perspective. And as he or she matures from the subordinate role of a child to an equal or superordinate role as an adult, the person also develops more awareness of and control over his or her actions. Often, said Argyris, the typical company with its short-cycle jobs, autocratic supervision, and relative dearth of growth opportunities thwarts these normal maturation changes by forcing employees into dependent, passive, and subordinate roles.

At Maritime Life, headquartered in Halifax, Nova Scotia, each employee has an annual career development account (CDA) of 2.5% of gross pay (eg. $1000 for an employee earning $40 000), which he or she can use to pay for career development. The CDA is often used for books, magazine subscriptions, courses, conferences, and anything else the employee and company agree on. Expenditures must be approved by the corporate training department, and any time off must be approved by the employee's manager. The CDA is one of the most popular benefits with employees. From the company's perspective, it makes employees realize that they are responsible for their own career development.[5] ◆

1. This is based on Gary Dessler, *Winning Commitment* (New York: McGraw-Hill, 1993), chapter 10.
2. Abraham Maslow, "A Theory of Human Motivation," *Psychological Review* 50 (1943), pp. 370–96, reprinted in Michael Matteson and John Ivancevich, *Management Classics* (Santa Monica, CA: Goodyear Publishing Co., 1977), p. 336.
3. Matteson and Ivancevich, *Management Classics*.
4. Chris Argyris, *Integrating the Individual and the Organization* (New York: John Wiley & Sons, 1964).
5. C. Knight, "Career Development: Part of Maritime Life," *Canadian HR Reporter*, (July 14, 1997), p. 1, 11.

Management Development

management development
Any attempt to improve current or future management performance by imparting knowledge, changing attitudes, or increasing skills.

Management development is any attempt to improve managerial performance by imparting knowledge, changing attitudes, or increasing skills. It thus includes in-house programs such as courses, coaching, and rotational assignments; professional programs; and university programs like executive MBA degrees.[42]

The ultimate aim of development programs is, of course, to enhance the future performance of the organization itself. For this reason, the general management development process consists of (1) assessing the company's needs (for instance, to fill future executive openings, or to make the firm more responsive), (2) appraising the managers' performance, and then (3) developing the managers themselves.

Management development is important for several reasons. For one thing, promotion from within is a major source of management talent. One Canadian company dedicated to promoting from within is FedEx. They have improved leadership effectiveness and retention by carefully examining aptitude for managerial success in employees interested in becoming managers through a program called the Leadership Evaluation and Awareness Program (LEAP). LEAP helps employees with managerial aspirations understand the expectations of FedEx leaders, and thus provides an excellent pool of management applicants from which to choose. Management development programs like this facilitate organizational continuity by preparing employees and current managers to smoothly assume higher-level positions. They also help to socialize management trainees by developing in them values and attitudes consistent with those of the firm, and fosters organizational responsiveness by developing the skills that managers need to respond faster to change.[43]

The Changing Nature of Management Development

Some management development programs are company-wide and involve all or most new (or potential) management recruits. Thus, new college or university graduates may join Enormous Corp. and (with two dozen colleagues) become part of the company-wide management development program. Here they may be rotated through a preprogrammed series of departmental assignments and educational experiences that aims to identify their management potential and provide the breadth of experience (in, say, production and finance) that will make the new managers more valuable in their first "real" assignment as group product leaders. Then superior candidates may be slotted onto a "fast track," a development program that prepares them more quickly to assume senior-level appointments.

On the other hand, the management development program may be aimed at filling a specific position, such as CEO, perhaps with one of two potential candidates. When it is an executive position to be filled, the process is usually called succession planning.

As explained in chapter 5, a succession program typically takes place in stages. First, an *organization projection* is made; here each department's management needs are anticipated based on factors like planned expansion or contraction. Next the HR department reviews its *management skills inventories* to identify

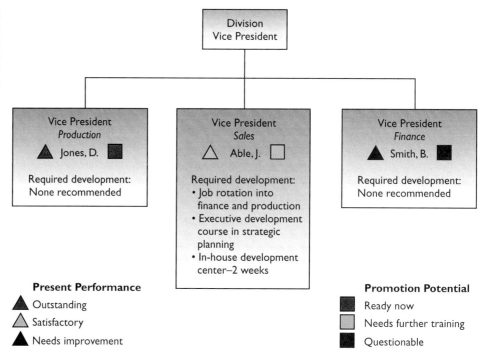

**Figure 9.2
Management
Replacement Chart
Showing Development
Needs of Future
Divisional Vice
President**

Division
Vice President

Vice President
Production

▲ Jones, D. ■

Required development:
None recommended

Vice President
Sales

△ Able, J. ☐

Required development:
• Job rotation into
finance and production
• Executive development
course in strategic
planning
• In-house development
center–2 weeks

Vice President
Finance

▲ Smith, B. ■

Required development:
None recommended

Present Performance

▲ Outstanding
△ Satisfactory
▲ Needs improvement

Promotion Potential

■ Ready now
□ Needs further training
■ Questionable

the management talent now employed. These inventories contain data on things like education and work experience, career preferences, and performance appraisals. Next management *replacement charts* are drawn. These summarize potential candidates for each of the management slots, as well as each person's development needs. As shown in **Figure 9.2**, the development needs for a future division vice president might include *job rotation* (to obtain more experience in the firm's finance and production divisions), *executive development programs* (to provide training in strategic planning), and assignment for two weeks to the employer's *in-house management development centre*.[44]

HR and the Responsive Organization

The Responsive Manager

For the past few years management development's focus has been shifting from preparing managers to fill higher-level slots to preparing them to meet the challenges of managing in a fast-paced environment. Increasingly, therefore, the emphasis is on developing a manager's ability to learn and make decisions under conditions of rapid change.[1]

Two experts put it this way: "As decision makers take on increasing responsibility across their careers, their learning needs move from the arena of task learning to behavioural learning to conceptual or policy-level learning."[2] For example, today's corporate managers are under enormous pressure "to find the strategic opportunities their competitors have yet to find."[3] This means more emphasis on developing their conceptual ability to search for internal strategic opportunities to improve quality, service, and prices. Similarly, all managers—not just those to be posted overseas—have to be well schooled in global economics, foreign markets, and cross-cultural negotiating.[4] And to manage in flatter, more empowered organizations the leader must increasingly become a teacher, coach, and consultant rather than a "boss."[5]

This is causing a corresponding change in the techniques that are emphasized in management development programs. Historically, on-the-job experiences, including on-the-job training, coaching, and rotational assignments, have been far and away the most popular management development techniques.[6] The problem is that these techniques tend to emphasize showing managers current procedures or (at best) getting them to think about how to "do what we're doing today a little better."[7] Today there's a shift toward development techniques that teach managers how to learn and how to develop the competencies they need to cope with change, such as sizing up foreign markets and searching for new strategic opportunities. Special *in-company executive development* programs, *action learning* and *lifelong learning*, are examples to be discussed later.[8]◆

1. Robert Fulmer and Kenneth Graham, "A New Era of Management Education," *Journal of Management Development* 12, no. 3 (1993), pp. 30–8.
2. Fulmer and Graham, "A New Era," p. 33.
3. J. Conger, "The Brave New World of Leadership Training," *Organizational Dynamics*, Vol. 21, no. 3 (1993), p. 49.
4. Conger, " The Brave New World," p. 51.
5. Conger, "The Brave New World," p. 52.
6. Lise Saari, T.R. Johnson, S.D. Mclaughlin, and D. M. Zimmerle, "A Survey of Management Training and Education Practices in U.S. Companies," *Personnel Psychology* (Winter 1988), pp. 731–43.
7. Fulmer and Graham, "A New Era," p. 32.
8. Albert Vicere, Marta Taylor, and Virginia Freeman, "Executive Development in Major Corporations: A Ten-Year Study," *Journal of Management Development* 13, no. 1 (1994), pp. 4–22.

On-the-Job Management Development Techniques

On-the-job training is one of the most popular development methods. Important techniques here include developmental job rotation, the coaching/understudy approach, and action learning.

developmental job rotation
A management training technique that involves moving a trainee from department to department to broaden his or her experience and identify strong and weak points.

Developmental Job Rotation **Developmental job rotation** involves moving management trainees from department to department to broaden their understanding of all parts of the business.[45] The trainee—often a recent college or university graduate—may spend several months in each department; this helps not only to broaden his or her experience, but also to discover the jobs he or she prefers. The person may just be an observer in each department, but more commonly gets fully involved in its operations. The trainee thus learns the department's business by actually doing it, whether it involves sales, production, finance, or some other function.

Job rotation has several other advantages.[46] In addition to providing a well-rounded training experience for each person, it helps avoid stagnation through the constant introduction of new points of view in each department. It also tests the trainee and helps identify the person's strong and weak points. Periodic job changing can also improve interdepartmental cooperation; managers become more understanding of each other's problems, while rotation also widens the trainee's acquaintances among management.

Rotation does have disadvantages. It encourages generalization and tends to be more appropriate for developing general line managers than functional staff experts. Firms also have to be careful not to inadvertently forget a trainee at some deserted outpost.

There are several ways to improve a rotation program's success.[47] The program should be tailored to the needs and capabilities of the individual trainee and not be a standard sequence of steps that all trainees take. The trainee's interests, aptitudes, and career preferences should be considered, along with the employer's needs; the length of time the trainee stays in a job should then be determined by how fast he or she is learning. Furthermore, the managers to whom these people are assigned should themselves be specially trained to provide feedback and to monitor performance in an interested and competent way.

For example, Bell Canada occasionally rotates operating managers and human resources managers to ensure that they remain productive and stimulated. Exposure to unfamiliar areas gives managers an opportunity to expand their knowledge of corporate operations and to learn another area of the company through hands-on experience. [48]

Global HRM

Global Job Rotation and Management

As firms expand multinationally, *developmental job rotation* is taking on a new meaning. At firms like Shell and British Petroleum (BP), rotating managers globally is a primary means through which the firms maintain their flexibility and responsiveness even as they grow to an enormous size.

The rationale for extensive global job rotation is summarized as follows by a Shell senior executive:

> The word summarizing today's business outlook is uncertainty, and the response must be flexibility. For a complex, international, multifunctional organization like the Shell group, the prerequisite for flexibility is a highly skilled, mobile, international body of staff. [1]

The advantage of global job rotation (rotating managers from, say, Sweden to Vancouver, and from Vancouver to Japan) is that it builds a network of informal ties—an information network—that ensures superior cross-border communication and mutual understanding as well as tight inter-unit coordination and control.

Improved communication and understanding stem from the personal relationships that are forged as managers work in the firm's various locations. These activities can also enhance organizational control. When employees from a firm's global locations are rotated or brought together at, say, the Harvard Business School or Europe's INSEAD for a management training program, the aim is more than just teaching basic skills. It is also to build a stronger identification with the company's culture and values. By creating shared values and a consistent view of the firm and its goals, management development activities like these can facilitate communication and ensure that through a sense of shared values and purpose the firm's policies are followed, even with a minimum reliance on more traditional forms of control. [2]◆

1. Quoted in Paul Evans, Yves Doz, and Andre Laurent, *Human Resource Management in International Firms* (New York: St. Martin's Press, 1990), p. 123.
2. Evans et al., *Human Resources Management in International Firms*.

Coaching/Understudy Approach   In the *coaching/understudy approach,* the trainee works directly with the person he or she is to replace; the latter is in turn responsible for the trainee's coaching. Normally, the understudy relieves the executive of certain responsibilities, thereby giving the trainee a chance to learn the job. [49] This helps ensure that the employer will have trained managers to assume key positions when such positions are vacated due to retirement, promotion, transfer, or termination. It also helps guarantee the long-run development of company-bred top managers.

To be effective, the executive has to be a good coach and mentor. His or her motivation to train the replacement will depend on the quality of the relationship between them. Some executives are also better at delegating responsibility, providing reinforcement, and communicating than are others; this also will affect the results.

action learning
A training technique by which management trainees are allowed to work full time analyzing and solving problems in other departments.

Action Learning   **Action learning** releases managers from their regular duties to work full time on projects, analyzing and solving problems in departments other than their own.[50] The trainees meet periodically with a four- or five-person project group, with whom their findings and progress are discussed and debated.

Action learning is similar to and grounded in other development methods. However, with action learning several trainees work together as a project group to compare notes and discuss each other's projects. Action learning often requires cooperation among several employers. For example, an employee from one company might be assigned to a government agency for a research project, while the agency might assign one of its managers to the company.

www.nestadt.com.au/ tract.html
Action Learning

The idea of developing managers this way has pros and cons. It gives trainees real experience with actual problems, and to that extent it can develop skills like problem analysis and planning. Furthermore, working with the others in the group, the trainees can and do find solutions to major problems. The main drawback is that in releasing trainees to work on outside projects, the employer loses, in a sense, the full-time services of a competent manager.

Off-the-Job Management Development Techniques

There are many techniques used to develop managers off the job, perhaps in a conference room at headquarters or off the premises entirely at a university or special seminar. These techniques are addressed next.

case study method
A development method in which the manager is presented with a written description of an organizational problem to diagnose and solve.

The Case Study Method   The **case study method** presents a trainee with a written description of an organizational problem. The person then analyzes the case in private, diagnoses the problem, and presents his or her findings and solutions in a discussion with other trainees.[51] The case method approach is aimed at giving trainees realistic experience in identifying and analyzing complex problems in an environment in which their progress can be subtly guided by a trained discussion leader. Through the class discussion of the case, trainees learn that there are usually many ways to approach and solve complex organizational problems. Trainees also learn that their solutions are often influenced by their own needs and values.

The case method ideally has five main features:[52] (1) the use of actual organizational problems; (2) the maximum possible involvement of participants in stating their views, inquiring into others' views, confronting different views, and making decisions; resulting in (3) a minimal degree of dependence on instructors; who, in turn, (4) hold the position that there are rarely any right or wrong answers, and that cases are incomplete and so is reality; and (5) who still strive to make the case method as engaging as possible through creation of appropriate levels of drama.[53]

Trainees participating in a case-study discussion.

Problems to Avoid   Unfortunately, the case approach often falls far short of its mark.[54] In practice, instructors often dominate group discussions by asking participants questions that they then themselves proceed to answer, through answering specific questions asked by participants and through presenting statements of

Diversity Counts
Do Women Make Better Managers?

Employees often talk today about the need to "shatter the glass ceiling"—the transparent but often impermeable barrier that many women face in trying to move up to the top management levels. The glass ceiling is not a real barrier, of course, but the practical net effect of various prejudices and lack of networking opportunities women face that together make it hard or impossible for women to move up to top management jobs.

While it certainly makes sense to shatter the glass ceiling for equity's sake, there is research that suggests there may be an even better reason to do so, and that is the distinct possibility that, as two researchers conclude, women may simply make better managers these days than do men.[1] Their basic point is that with the trend today toward high-involvement work teams, consensus decision making, and empowerment, the sorts of leadership styles that women already exhibit may be much more appropriate than are men's.

Their conclusion is, of course, based on the assumption that female managers' leadership styles are different than males', and based on their research that appears to be the case. Specifically, their findings indicate that women scored significantly higher than men on all measures of transformational leadership. Transformational leaders "... move followers to go beyond their self-interest to concerns for their group or organization. They help followers develop to higher levels of potential. Such leaders diagnose the needs of their followers and then elevate those needs to initiate and promote development.

They align followers around a common purpose, mission, or vision. They provide a sense of purpose and future orientation . . ." More women than men scored highly on such traditional measures of transformational leadership as encouraging followers to question their old way of doing things or to break with the past, providing simplified emotional appeals to increase awareness and understanding of mutually desired goals, and providing learning opportunities to employees. On the other hand, male managers were more likely to be "transactional"-type leaders, basically by commending followers if they complied or disciplining them if they failed.

Why exactly the male and female managers differed on these leadership measures is not entirely clear. The researchers conclude that the more "... plausible explanation for the observed differences regarding transformational leadership ratings may lie in the tendencies of women to be more nurturing, interested in others, and more socially sensitive."[2] In any case, insofar as it may be such transformational leadership behaviours that are increasingly appropriate in organizations today, it could be that female managers have an edge in exhibiting the sorts of leadership style that "... comprises the most appropriate leadership behaviours to develop followers to achieve their highest levels of potential."[3]◆

---

1. Bernard Bass and Bruce Avolio, "Shatter the Glass Ceiling: Women May Make Better Managers," *Human Resource Management* 33, no. 4 (Winter 1994), pp. 549–60.
2. Bass and Avolio, "Shatter the Glass Ceiling," p. 556.
3. Bass and Avolio, "Shatter the Glass Ceiling," p. 558.

the facts about the case. Instructors also use "mystery to achieve mastery" by intentionally withholding information (for instance, regarding what the company actually did and what its competitors were doing at the time when the case was written) with the aim of maintaining control of the discussion.

There are several things that can be done to make the case approach more effective. If possible, the cases should be actual scenarios from the trainees' own firms. This will help ensure that trainees understand the background of the case, as well as make it easier for trainees to transfer what they learn to their own jobs and situations. Instructors have to guard against dominating the case analysis and make sure that they remain no more than a catalyst or coach. Finally, they must carefully prepare the case discussion and let the participants discuss the case in small groups before class.[55]

management game
A computerized development technique in which teams of managers compete with one another by making decisions regarding realistic but simulated companies.

Management Games In a computerized **management game,** trainees are divided into five- or six-person companies, each of which has to compete with the other in a simulated marketplace. Each company sets a goal (such as "maximize sales") and is told it can make several decisions. For example, the group may be allowed to decide (1) how much to spend on advertising, (2) how much to produce, (3) how much inventory to maintain, and (4) how many of which product to produce. Usually the game itself compresses a two- or three-year period into days, weeks, or months. As in the real world, each company usually can't see what decisions the other firms have made, although these decisions do affect their own sales. For example, if a competitor decides to increase its advertising expenditures, it may end up increasing its sales at the expense of the other firms.[56]

Management games can be good development tools. People learn best by getting involved in the activity itself, and the games can be useful for gaining such involvement. Games are almost always interesting and exciting for the trainees because of their realism and competitiveness. They help trainees develop their problem-solving skills, as well as focus their attention on the need for planning rather than on just putting out fires. The companies also usually elect their own officers and develop their own divisions of work; the games can thus be useful for developing leadership skills and for fostering cooperation and teamwork.

Management games also have their drawbacks. One is that the game can be expensive to develop and implement. Games also usually force the decision makers to choose alternatives from a closed list (for instance, they might have choices of only three levels of production); in real life managers are more often rewarded for creating new, innovative alternatives. On the whole, though, trainees almost always react favourably to a well-run game, and it is a good technique for developing problem-solving and leadership skills.

Outward Bound participants enhancing their leadership skills, team skills, and risk-taking behaviour.

Outside Seminars Many organizations offer special seminars and conferences aimed at providing skill-building training for managers. For example, the Human Resources Professionals Association of Ontario offers a wide variety of seminars on HR topics ranging from "Interviewing Skills for Selection and Appraisal" to "Benchmarking the HR Function" to "HR Applications on the Internet." The seminars range in length from half a day to two days, and are targeted at HR professionals and sometimes other managers as well. Outdoor experiential expeditions, such as those available through the Canadian Outward Bound Wilderness School are sometimes used to enhance leadership skills, team skills, and risk-taking behaviour.[57] Other organizations offering management development services include The Canadian Institute of Management and the International Quality and Productivity Centre.

College/University-Related Programs Colleges and universities provide three types of management development activities. First, many schools provide *executive development programs* in leadership, marketing, human resources management, operations management, and the like. These range from one- to four-day programs to ones lasting one to four months.

The Executive Development Centre at Queen's University in Kingston, Ontario is an example of one of these programs (see **Figure 9.3**). The program uses cases and lectures to provide top-level management talent with the latest management skills, as well as practice in analyzing complex organizational problems.

QUEEN'S EXECUTIVE DEVELOPMENT CENTRE
1.888.EXEC DEV (1.888.393.2338)

Over 800 organizations, including virtually every major Canadian corporation, have profited from executive development programs at Queen's School of Business. Many of our programs are the most popular of their kind in Canada, North America, and the world. We invite *you* to profit from our experience.

QUEEN'S IN-COMPANY PROGRAMS

The expertise of the Queen's Executive Development Centre applied to the particular development needs of clients and their organizations.

QUEEN'S EXECUTIVE PROGRAM

Strategy, operations, and leadership.
April 26 to May 15, 1998
May 17 to June 5, 1998
June 7 to 26, 1998

QUEEN'S MARKETING PROGRAM

Creating competitive advantage through strategic marketing initiatives.
November 16 to 21, 1997
February 15 to 20, 1998

QUEEN'S EXECUTIVE PROGRAM UPDATE

Incorporate the latest developments in management thinking into the Queen's Executive Program organizational models.
June 11, 12, and 13, 1998

QUEEN'S SALES MANAGEMENT PROGRAM

The high-performance sales organization.
November 23 to 28, 1997
February 8 to 13, 1998
April 26 to May 1, 1998

QUEEN'S LEADERSHIP PROGRAM

Using today's most advanced leadership tools and techniques to create a profitable and productive organization.
May 24 to 29, 1998

FINANCE FOR THE NON-FINANCIAL EXECUTIVE

Improve your management decisions.
November 9 to 14, 1997
February 22 to 27, 1998
April 19 to 24, 1998

QUEEN'S STRATEGIC LEADERSHIP PROGRAM

Enhance your skill at leading change through the creation and implementation of imaginative business strategies.
March 29 to April 3, 1998

QUEEN'S INFORMATION TECHNOLOGY PROGRAM

A general management perspective on using information technology to create competitive advantage for your organization.
March 1 to 6, 1998

QUEEN'S OPERATIONS LEADERSHIP PROGRAM

Creating the high-performance workplace through strategic operations initiatives.
November 23 to 28, 1997
February 1 to 6, 1998

QUEEN'S HUMAN RESOURCES PROGRAM

The HR manager as a strategic contributor and business partner in the process of improving organizational performance.
November 2 to 7, 1997

www.bus.sfu.ca/update95/carman.html
Simon Fraser University Career Management Program

Similar programs are available through the University of Toronto, the University of Western Ontario, and many other universities across Canada. Most of these programs take the executives away from their jobs, putting them in university-run learning environments for their entire stay.

Second, many colleges and universities also offer *individualized courses* in areas like business, management, and health care administration. Managers can take these to fill gaps in their backgrounds. Thus, a prospective division manager with a gap in experience with accounting controls might sign up for a two-course sequence in managerial accounting.

Finally, of course, many schools also offer *degree programs* such as the MBA or Executive MBA. The latter is a Master of Business Administration degree program geared especially to middle managers and above, who generally take their courses on weekends and proceed through the program with the same group of colleagues.

The Employer's Contribution   The employer usually plays a role in university-related programs.[58] First, many employers offer *tuition refunds* as an incentive for

**Figure 9.4
Typical Role in a Role-
Playing Exercise**

Source: Norman R. F. Maier
and Gertrude Casselman
Verser, *Psychology in Industrial
Organizations*, 5th ed., p. 190.
Copyright 1982 by Houghton
Mifflin Company. Used by
permission of the publishers.

Walt Marshall—Supervisor of Repair Crew

You are the head of a crew of telephone maintenance workers, each of whom drives a small service truck to and from the various jobs. Every so
often you get a new truck to exchange for an old
one, and you have the problem of deciding to
which of your crew members you should give the
new truck. Often there are hard feelings, since
each seems to feel entitled to the new truck, so
you have a tough time being fair. As a matter of
fact, it usually turns out that whatever you decide
is considered wrong by most of the crew. You now
have to face the issue again because a new truck, a
Chevrolet, has just been allocated to you for assignment.

In order to handle this problem you have decided to put the decision up to the crew. You will
tell them about the new truck and will put the
problem in terms of what would be the fairest
way to assign the truck. Do not take a position
yourself, because you want to do what they think
is most fair.

---

employees to develop job-related skills. Thus, engineers may be encouraged to enroll in technical courses aimed at keeping them abreast of changes in their field.
Supervisors may be encouraged to enroll in programs to develop them for higher-
level management jobs.

Employers are also increasingly granting technical and professional employees extended *sabbaticals*—periods of time off—for attending a college or university
to pursue a higher degree or to upgrade skills.

role playing
A training technique in
which trainees act out the
parts of people in a realistic
management situation.

Role Playing   The aim of **role playing** is to create a realistic situation and then
have the trainees assume the parts (or roles) of specific persons in that situation.[59]

One such role from a famous role-playing exercise called the New Truck
Dilemma is presented in **Figure 9.4**. When combined with the general instructions for the role-playing exercise, roles like these for all of the participants can
trigger a spirited discussion among the role players, particularly when they all
throw themselves into the roles. The idea of the exercise is to solve the problem at
hand and thereby develop trainees' skills in areas like leadership and delegation.

Role playing can be an enjoyable and inexpensive way to develop many new
skills. With the New Truck Dilemma exercise, for instance, participants learn the
importance of fairness in bringing about acceptance of resource allocation decisions. The role players can also give up their inhibitions and experiment with new
ways of acting. For example, a supervisor could experiment with both a consider-
ate and autocratic leadership style, whereas in the real world the person might not
have this harmless way of experimenting. According to Maier, role playing also
trains a person to be aware of and sensitive to the feelings of others.[60]

Role playing has some drawbacks. An exercise can take an hour or more to
complete, only to be deemed a waste of time by participants if the instructor
doesn't prepare a wrap-up explanation of what the participants were to learn.
Some trainees also feel that role playing is childish, while others who may have

had a bad experience with the technique are reluctant to participate at all. Knowing the audience and preparing a wrap-up are thus advisable.

Behaviour Modelling **Behaviour modelling** involves (1) showing trainees the right (or "model") way of doing something, (2) letting each person practice the right way to do it, and then (3) providing feedback regarding each trainee's performance.[61] It has been used, for example, to:

- Train first-line supervisors to handle common supervisor-employee interactions better. This includes giving recognition, disciplining, introducing changes, and improving poor performance.
- Train middle managers to better handle interpersonal situations, for example, performance problems and undesirable work habits.
- Train employees and their supervisors to take and give criticism, ask and give help, and establish mutual trust and respect.

The basic behaviour modelling procedure can be outlined as follows:

1. *Modelling.* First, trainees watch films or videotapes that show model persons behaving effectively in a problem situation. In other words, trainees are shown the right way to behave in a simulated but realistic situation. The film or video might thus show a supervisor effectively disciplining an employee, if teaching how to discipline is the aim of the training program.
2. *Role playing.* Next, the trainees are given roles to play in a simulated situation; here they practice and rehearse the effective behaviours demonstrated by the models.
3. *Social reinforcement.* The trainer provides reinforcement in the form of praise and constructive feedback based on how the trainee performs in the role-playing situation.
4. *Transfer of training.* Finally, trainees are encouraged to apply their new skills when they are back on their jobs.

The Bank of Montreal's Institute for Learning.

In-House Development Centres Some employers have **in-house development centres.** These centres usually combine classroom learning (lectures and seminars, for instance) with other techniques like assessment centres, in-basket exercises, and role playing to help develop employees and other managers.

Two of the best-known centres in Canada are the Bank of Montreal's Institute for Learning and the CIBC's Leadership Centre. Nearly 100 courses are offered at the Institute for Learning, ranging from "Coaching for Performance" to "Consultative Interviewing and Negotiating Strategies" to "Getting Exceptional Results."[62]

Organizational Development **Organizational development (OD)** is a method that is aimed at changing the attitudes, values, and beliefs of employees so that they can identify and implement technical changes such as reorganizations, redesigned facilities, and the like that are required, usually with the aid of an outside *change agent* or consultant.

Action research is the common denominator underlying most OD interventions. It includes (1) gathering data about the organization and its operations and attitudes, with an eye toward solving a particular problem (for example, conflict between the sales and production departments); (2) feeding back these data to the parties (employees) involved; and then (3) having these parties team-plan solutions to the problems. In OD, the participants always get involved in gathering data about themselves and their organization, analyzing these data, and planning solutions based on these analyses.[63] OD efforts include survey feedback and team building, among others.

survey feedback
A method that involves surveying employees' attitudes and providing feedback so that problems can be solved by the managers and employees.

Survey Feedback **Survey feedback** is a method that surveys employees' attitudes and provides feedback to department managers so that problems can be solved by the managers and employees. Attitude surveys such as the one in **Figure 9.5** can be a useful OD technique. The results can be used to compare departments and to underscore dramatically the existence of some problem like low morale, and serve as a basis for discussion among employees for developing alternative solutions. Finally, results of attitude surveys can also be used to follow up on any actions taken to resolve problems to see whether they have been successful in changing the participants' attitudes.

Figure 9.5
Attitude Survey (Excerpt)

Source: Canadian Tire Limited and Organization Studies International Inc. © 1997. Used with permission.

1. How does the kind of work you do influence your *overall attitude* toward your job? It has:
   1. A very favourable influence
   2. A fairly favourable influence
   3. No influence one way or the other
   4. An unfavourable influence
   5. A very unfavourable influence
2. How do you feel about the kind of work you do?
   1. It's exactly the kind of work I like best
   2. I like it very much
   3. I like it, but there is other work I like better
   4. It's OK, there's other work I like better
   5. Don't like it, would prefer some other kind of work
3. How often when you finish a day's work do you feel you've accomplished something really worthwhile?
   1. All the time
   2. Most of the time
   3. About half of the time
   4. Less than half of the time
   5. Rarely
4. I feel my workload is:
   1. Never too heavy
   2. Seldom too heavy
   3. Sometimes too heavy
   4. Often too heavy
   5. Almost always too heavy
5. How do you feel about the amount of work you're expected to do?
   1. Very satisfied
   2. Somewhat satisfied
   3. Neither satisfied nor dissatisfied
   4. Somewhat dissatisfied
   5. Very dissatisfied

(continued)

Figure 9.5
(continued)

6. How does the amount of work you're expected to do influence the way you do your job?
   1. It always allows me to do a good job
   2. It usually allows me to do a good job
   3. It has no effect on how I do my job
   4. It seldom allows me to do a good job
   5. It never allows me to do a good job

7. How do you generally feel about the employees you work with?
   1. They are the best group I could ask for
   2. I work well with them
   3. I have no feelings one way or the other
   4. They are sometimes hard to work with
   5. They are often hard to work with

8. The example my fellow employees set:
   1. Greatly *encourages* me to do my best
   2. *Encourages* me to do my best
   3. Has little effect on me
   4. *Discourages* me from doing my best
   5. Greatly *discourages* me from doing my best

9. Among employees in this unit, there is:
   1. Almost no friction
   2. Little friction
   3. Some friction
   4. Quite a bit of friction
   5. A great deal of friction

10. If Canadian Tire found out an employee was being treated unfairly, it would:
    1. Correct the situation immediately
    2. Probably try to correct the situation
    3. Do very little to correct the situation
    4. Do nothing to correct the situation
    5. Don't know

11. When Canadian Tire makes decisions, how much concern does it show for employee well-being?
    1. A very great deal
    2. Considerable
    3. Some
    4. Little
    5. None

12. How would you describe Canadian Tire as an employer?
    1. Couldn't be much better
    2. Very good
    3. Neither good nor bad
    4. Just another place to work
    5. Couldn't be much worse

(continued)

Figure 9.5

(continued)

13. Does the way your salary increases are determined at Canadian Tire make it worthwhile for you to work especially hard?
    1. It definitely *encourages* hard work
    2. It tends to *encourage* hard work
    3. It makes little difference
    4. It tends to *discourage* hard work
    5. It definitely *discourages* hard work

14. Considering what it costs to live in this area, my pay is:
    1. More than adequate
    2. Adequate
    3. Barely adequate
    4. Inadequate
    5. Very inadequate

15. How many of your needs are satisfied by the pay and benefits you receive?
    1. Almost all of my needs are satisfied
    2. Many of my needs are satisfied
    3. A few of my needs are satisfied
    4. Very few of my needs are satisfied
    5. Almost none of my needs are satisfied

16. For the work I do, my physical working conditions are:
    1. Very good
    2. Relatively good
    3. Neither good or bad
    4. Relatively poor
    5. Very poor

17. How do your physical working conditions influence your *overall attitude* toward your job? They have:
    1. A very favourable influence
    2. A favourable influence
    3. No influence one way or the other
    4. An unfavourable influence
    5. A very unfavourable influence

18. How do you feel about your physical working conditions?
    1. Very satisfied
    2. Well satisfied
    3. Only moderately satisfied
    4. Somewhat dissatisfied
    5. Very dissatisfied

Source: Canadian Tire Ltd. and Organizational Studies International.

team building
Improving the effectiveness of teams through the use of consultants, interviews, and team-building meetings.

Team Building **Team building** refers to a group of OD techniques aimed at improving the effectiveness of teams at work. And, in fact, the characteristic OD stress on action learning—on letting the trainees solve the problem—is perhaps most evident when the OD program is aimed at improving a team's effectiveness. Data concerning the team's performance are collected and then fed back to the members of the group. The participants examine, explain, and analyze the data and develop specific action plans or solutions for solving the team's problems.

The typical team-building program begins with the consultant interviewing each of the group members and the leader prior to the group meeting—asking them what their problems are, how they think the group functions, and what obstacles are in the way of the group's performing better.[64] (Or the consultant may interview the entire group at once, using open-ended questions such as: "What things do you see getting in the way of this group's being a better one?") Sometimes, an attitude survey is used to gather the basic background data for the meetings. The consultant usually categorizes the interview data into themes and presents the themes to the group at the beginning of the meeting. They might include, for example, "Not enough time to get my job done," or "I can't get any cooperation around here." The themes are then ranked by the group in terms of their importance. The most important ones form the agenda for the meeting. The group examines and discusses the issues, examines the underlying causes, and begins work on a solution.

During one of these sessions it is likely that certain nonagenda items will emerge as a result of the participants' interaction. In discussing the theme "I can't get any cooperation around here," for instance, the group might uncover the fact that the manager is not providing enough direction. The manager might be allowing vacuums to develop that are leading to conflict and a breakdown of cooperation. These new items or problems, as well as the agenda items or themes, are generally pursued under the guidance of the consultant. Then steps are formulated to bring about the changes deemed desirable and a follow-up meeting is often scheduled. Here it is determined whether the steps have been implemented successfully.

Notice how the typical team-building intervention relies on the participants themselves doing the research: Information about the group's problems is obtained from the group; members of the group analyze and discuss the data in an atmosphere of cooperation; and, finally, the participants develop solutions or action steps for solving the problems that they themselves have identified.

leadership grid
A matrix that represents different possible leadership styles involving two dimensions—concern for people and concern for production.

Grid training is a formal approach to team building originally designed by Blake and Mouton.[65] Grid training is based on a device called the **leadership grid.** This represents different leadership styles, identifying specifically whether the leader is more concerned with people or with production.

The Grid program is aimed first at developing managers who have a capacity for high levels of both dimensions; they want to get results through committed, cooperative employees. The Grid program assumes that choosing appropriate levels of each dimension for the specific situation makes it easier for a manager to work with employees, superiors, and peers in analyzing group, intergroup, and organizational problems and developing action steps to solve these problems.

Using HRM to Build a Responsive Learning Organization

The former head of strategic planning at Royal Dutch Shell has said, "In the future, the only sustainable competitive advantage may be an organization's ability to learn faster than its competitors."[66] His statement underscores the fact that in a fast-changing world, the last thing a company needs is for new information—

about competitors' actions, customers' preferences, or technological improvements—to be ignored by the company's managers, or lost in a bureaucratic sinkhole of nonactivity. For years, for instance, General Motors seemed oblivious to the competitive and technological advances of its foreign competitors; it finally awoke only when its board decided that too much market share had been lost. On the other hand, firms like Microsoft and General Electric are traditionally quick on their feet, "adept at translating new knowledge into new ways of behaving."[67]

HRM's Role in Building Learning Organizations

learning organization
An organization focussed on creating, acquiring, and transferring knowledge, and at modifying its behaviour to reflect new knowledge and insights.

A number of firms have successfully made the leap into rebuilding themselves as learning organizations. A **learning organization** "... is an organization skilled at creating, acquiring, and transferring knowledge, and at modifying its behaviour to reflect new knowledge and insights."[68] Learning organizations engage in five activities, which we'll discuss next: systematic problem solving; experimentation; learning from experience; learning from others; and transferring knowledge. HR managers can play a crucial role in each.

HRM and Systematic Problem Solving   The learning organization depends on the scientific method rather than on guesswork for diagnosing problems. Employees and managers here don't make decisions based on assumptions; instead they insist on having data and using simple statistical tools to organize data and draw inferences.[69]

Training and development is crucial for fostering such systematic problem-solving skills. Specifically, employees need training in using techniques like interviewing and surveying to generate ideas and collect information; to reach consensus by using special consensus-building techniques; to analyze and display data on special simple statistical charts; and to plan the actions they will take to solve the problem using special planning charts.

HRM and Experimentation   The learning organization also depends on *experimentation,* which means the systematic searching for and testing of new knowledge.[70] It is the role of the HR department and HR managers throughout an organization to formulate incentive plans that ensure that employees who experiment with new processes or products aren't inadvertently punished for trying a new approach. Many organizations have created an over-reliance on the traditional planning process, which involves lengthy periods of analysis before any action is taken. In today's environment, organizations need to learn how to respond quickly with innovative ideas. Spontaneity, creativity, and intuition are required. For example, the management of 3M company supports the development of new products by encouraging research and development staff to use up to 15% of their time to experiment with new product ideas.[71]

HRM and Learning from Experience   Learning organizations also have to "review their successes and failures, assess them systematically, and record the lessons in a form that employees find open and accessible."[72] Training and development plays an important role in facilitating such learning from past experience. For example, case studies and action learning can be used to study and illustrate what has previously been done correctly or incorrectly. Furthermore, companies can also enlist the help of faculty and students at local colleges or universities; they bring fresh perspectives and can view such case studies as opportunities to gain experience and increase their own learning.[73]

HRM and Learning from Others A learning organization is also one that effectively learns from others. Sometimes, in other words, "… the most powerful insights come from looking outside one's immediate environment to gain a new perspective."[74]

Training and development plays a role in obtaining such expertise. For example, employees have to be trained to "cultivate the art of open, attentive listening"[75] in order to gain the fullest understanding of the other company's operations. Employees and managers also must be trained to *benchmark*, the process through which the best industry practices are uncovered, analyzed, adopted, and implemented.[76]

HRM and Transferring Knowledge Finally, learning organizations are adept at transferring knowledge, in other words, spreading knowledge quickly and efficiently throughout the organization.[77]

Training and development plays an important role in cultivating such expertise. For example, in some firms, rotating assignments are used for transferring knowledge. Other companies organize workers into self-managed teams, the members of which must share their knowledge in order to function successfully.

In summary, learning organizations are skilled at creating, acquiring, and transferring knowledge, and at modifying their behaviour to reflect new knowledge and insights. Learning organizations are built on a foundation of systematic problem solving, experimentation, learning from past experience, learning from others, and transferring knowledge. HR managers, particularly training and development staff, play a central role in developing employees' and managers' skills and expertise in each of these areas.[78]

Providing Employees with Lifelong Learning

lifelong learning
Providing extensive continuing training, throughout employees' careers.

Employers can't build learning organizations around managers alone. In today's downsized, flattened, high-tech, and empowered organizations, employers must also depend on their first-line employees to recognize new opportunities, identify problems, and react quickly with analyses and recommendations. As a result, the need has arisen for encouraging **lifelong learning**, in other words, for providing extensive, continuing training from basic remedial skills to advanced decision-making techniques throughout employees' careers.

The experiences at one Canadian Honeywell manufacturing plant provide an example.[79] This plant called its lifelong learning program the Honeywell-Scarborough Learning for Life Initiative. It was "… a concerted effort to upgrade skill and education levels so that employees can meet workplace challenges with confidence."[80]

Honeywell's Lifelong Learning Initiative had several components. It began with adult basic education. Here the company, in partnership with the employees' union, offered courses in English as a second language, basic literacy, numeracy, and computer literacy.

Next, the factory formed a partnership with a local community college. Through that partnership, Honeywell provides college-level courses to all factory employees—hourly, professional, and managerial—giving them the opportunity to earn college diplomas and certificates.[81] This includes a 15-hour "skills for success" program designed to refresh adults in the study habits required to succeed academically. All courses take place at the factory immediately after work.

In addition, job-related training is provided for two hours every other week. These sessions focus on skills specifically important to the job, ". . . such as the principles of just-in-time inventory systems, team effectiveness, interpersonal communication skills, conflict resolution, problem solving, and dealing with a diverse work force."[82]

Executive Development: Key Factors for Success

The idea that there are several key factors for an executive development program's success is illustrated by the results of a survey of executive development practices in 12 leading corporations.[83] This study found a surprisingly high degree of consensus among the 12 firms regarding the characteristics of effective and ineffective executive development processes. In particular, five major success criteria were listed by over 75 percent of the survey participants.

Five Key Factors for Success

These five key factors were as follows:

1. Extensive and visible involvement by the chief executive (CEO) is critical.

In all but one of the companies, extensive and visible involvement by the CEO was described as "essential" and the "single most important determinant" of success for the executive development program. This extensive involvement helped guarantee that the company's executive development process was consistent with the direction the CEO wanted the company to follow. It also lent the process a credibility unachievable in any other way.

2. Corporations with a successful executive development process have a clearly articulated and understood executive development policy and philosophy.

For example, ten of the 12 companies surveyed listed four common objectives of their executive development processes: ensuring that qualified executives would be available to fill current and future assignments; serving as a major vehicle to perpetuate the organization's heritage and shape its culture by communicating its mission, beliefs, values, and management practices; preparing executives to respond to the complex business issues of the changing environment by providing managers with the experience, knowledge, and skills they need in future assignments; and developing a cadre of individuals prepared to assume senior-level general management responsibilities.

3. Successful executive development policies and strategies are directly linked to the corporation's business strategies, objectives, and challenges.

Nine of the 12 companies emphasized that their executive development policies and strategies were consciously linked to the company's business plans and objectives. For example, plans to expand overseas, diversify into new product lines, or consolidate manufacturing operations have implications for management/executive development activities. In the successful programs, the development process was moulded around the company's plans.

4. Successful executive development processes include three main elements: an annual succession planning process; planned on-the-job developmental assignments; and customized, internal, executive education programs supplemented by the selected use of university programs.

First, in all 12 companies succession plans were in place and were actively managed for key positions and individuals. Second, development needs were continually identified (based on these plans), and strategies were developed and implemented to address these development needs. Third, a formal annual planning and review phase was in place to assess each candidate's progress and to review the company's replacement plans.

With respect to on-the-job development, "all the study participants agreed that it was the single most effective developmental tool available to organizations."

The four types of on-the-job experience used most often were: assignment of people to membership on task forces assembled to address specific issues; developmental job rotation experiences lasting from one to two years; overseas assignments; and temporary assignments of relatively short duration.

With respect to executive education, all the companies offered a mix of external university-type programs and customized internal programs. Some of the companies expressed concern about the prohibitive costs of the external programs, although virtually all sent selected employees to them.

5. Executive development is the responsibility of managers throughout the firm rather than of the HR department.

In all but one of the companies in this survey, the role of the HR department was seen as crucial but advisory. HR department staff serve as a resource for all managers regarding the development programs and activities to use and how to use them. However, the actual responsibility for achieving the goals of the executive development program—deciding who will fill future positions, or how to eliminate current managers' shortcomings, for instance—is shared by each and every manager in the organization.

Executive Development in Global Companies

Selecting and developing executives to run the employer's overseas operations presents management with a dilemma. One expert cites "an alarmingly high failure rate when executives are relocated overseas," usually caused by inappropriate selection and poor preplacement development.[84] Yet in an increasingly globalized economy, employers must develop managers for overseas assignments despite these difficulties.

A number of companies have developed and implemented international executive relocation programs that are successful. In addition to the general requirements for successful executive development programs previously listed, preparing and training executives for overseas assignments should also include the following considerations:

www.mentoring-resources. com
Mentoring

1. Choose international-assignment candidates whose educational backgrounds and experiences are appropriate for overseas assignments. As in most other endeavours, the best predictor of future performance is often a person's past performance. In this case the person who has already accumulated a track record of successfully adapting to foreign cultures (perhaps through overseas university or college studies and summer internships) will more likely succeed as an international transferee.

2. Choose those whose personalities and family situations can withstand the cultural changes they will encounter in their new environments. When many executives fail, it is often not because these individuals couldn't adapt but because their spouses or children were unhappy in their new foreign setting. Thus, the person's family situation probably should have more influence on the assignment than it would in a domestic assignment.

3. Brief candidates fully and clearly on all relocation policies. Transferees should be given a realistic preview of what the assignment will entail, including the company's policies regarding matters such as moving expenses, salary differentials, and benefits, such as paid schooling for the employees' children.

4. Give executives and their families comprehensive training in their new company's culture and language. An orientation session should begin with a briefing session, during which the transfer policy is explained in detail to the relocating executive. He or she should also be given a briefing package compiled by the receiving area containing important information about local matters, such as dress codes, shopping, and housing. In addition, an advisor, who

is often the spouse of a recently returned expatriate, should visit the transferee and his or her spouse to explain what sort of emotional issues they are likely to face in the early stages of the move—such as feeling remote from relatives, for instance. The option of attending a two-week language and cultural orientation program offered by a school like Berlitz could also be extended.

5. Provide all relocating executives with a mentor to monitor their overseas careers and help them secure appropriate jobs with the company when they repatriate. This person is usually a high-level supervisor in the expatriate's functional area. The overseas assignee keeps his or her mentor up to date on his or her activities. Similarly, the mentor monitors the expatriate's career while he or she is overseas. Specifically, all job changes and compensation actions involving the expatriate must be reviewed with and supported by the mentor. This helps to avoid the problem of having expatriates feel "lost" overseas, particularly in terms of career progress.

6. Establish a repatriation program that helps returning executives and their families readjust to their professional and personal lives in their home country. For instance, the head of the overseas assignee's department or division could give the transferee a letter stating that the foreign subsidiary guarantees that he or she will be able to return to a job at least at the same level as the one he or she is leaving. As much as a year in advance of the expatriate's scheduled return to headquarters, his or her new job should be arranged by the person's mentor.[85]

Small Business Applications

The president of a smaller enterprise faces both unique advantages and disadvantages when it comes to developing employees for higher-level executive roles. On the negative side, this president has neither resources nor time to develop full-blown executive succession programs or to fund many outside programs like sending potential executives to the Richard Ivey School of Business. Yet at the same time the president of a smaller firm has the advantage of working more closely with and knowing more about each of his or her employees than does the CEO of a bigger, less personal firm.

A relative lack of resources notwithstanding, the smaller firm's president has few needs more important than that of developing senior managers. For most small firms with successful products, it is not a lack of financing that holds them back but a lack of management talent. This is so because all growing firms inevitably reach the point where the entrepreneur/owner can no longer solely make all the decisions. For larger companies, the question of succession planning and executive development is mostly a question of selecting the best of the lot and then developing them: There is usually an adequate supply of talent given these companies' enormous influx of new recruits. For the smaller company, the problem usually is not one of selecting the best of the lot. Instead it's making sure that key positions are filled and that the president will have the foresight to know when to surrender one set of reins over a part of the company's operations.

There are thus four main steps in the smaller company's executive development process:

Step 1. Problem Assessment

The executive development process must begin with an assessment of the company's current problems and the owner's plans for the company's future. Obviously, if the owner/entrepreneur is satisfied with the current size of the firm and has no plans to retire in the near future, no additional management talent may be required.

On the other hand, if plans call for expansion, or current problems seem to be growing out of control, management development/succession planning might be the key.

It often happens, for instance, that as a small company evolves from a mom-and-pop operation to a larger firm, the management system that adequately served the owner in the past is no longer effective. Problems arise as manufacturing orders that were previously profitable now incur overtime costs and excessive waste, and the informal order-writing process can no longer keep up with the volume of orders.

At this point the president must assess the problems in his or her firm, beginning with an analysis of the company's financial statements. Questions he or she should ask include: What is the trend of key financial ratios, such as the ratio of manufacturing costs to sales, or of sales overhead to sales? Are profit margins level, or heading up or down? Are fixed costs remaining about the same, or heading up as a percentage of sales? Next the organization must be analyzed function by function. In sales, is the backlog of orders growing? In manufacturing, are there inventory problems that require attention? In accounting, are the monthly and end-of-year reports produced in a timely fashion? Does the company have a HRM system in place such that as many HR matters as possible—recruitment, testing, selection, training, and so forth—are routinized and carried out in an effective manner? The point is that the owner must assess the problems in his or her firm with an eye toward determining whether and when new management talent is required.

Step 2. Management Audit and Appraisal

One reason management selection and development are so important in small firms is that the "problems" assessed in step 1 are often just symptoms of inadequate management talent. It's simply not possible for the owner/entrepreneur to run a $5 million company the way he or she did when the company was one-tenth the size. Therefore, the lack of adequate management is a depressingly familiar cause for many of the problems in the small growing firm.

The problems found in step 1 can be used as a starting point in conducting a management audit and appraisal of the people now helping manage the firm. One simple and effective way to do this is by evaluating them on the traditional management functions of planning, organizing, staffing, leading, and controlling. For example, within their own areas of responsibility have they instituted plans, policies, and procedures that enable their activities to be carried out efficiently? Have they organized their activities in such a way that their employees have job descriptions and understand what their responsibilities are? In terms of staffing, have they selected competent employees; are their people adequately oriented and trained; and are the pay rates within their group viewed as fair and equitable? In terms of leadership, is the morale in their department satisfactory, and do their people seem to enjoy what they are doing? Are each person's interpersonal relations with other members of the team satisfactory? And in terms of control, has each person recommended and/or instituted a set of reports that provides the information needed to assess adequately how that department is doing?

Step 3. Analysis of Development Needs

The next step is to determine whether any inadequacies uncovered in step 2 can be remedied via some type of development program. At one extreme, the person may not have the potential to grow beyond what he or she is now, and here development may serve no purpose. At the other extreme, the problems uncovered may just reflect a lack of knowledge. For example, sending a bookkeeper/accountant back to school for a course or two in management accounting could alleviate the problem. Another question to answer here is whether the owner/entrepreneur may be responsible for some of the problems, and whether he or she should attend a management development program (or move out of the firm altogether).

Step 4. Identify Replacement Needs

The assessment may uncover a need to recruit and select new management talent. Here, the intellectual, personality, interpersonal, and experience criteria to be used should be determined ahead of time. An on-the-job development program that gives the person the breadth of experience he or she needs to perform the job should also be mapped out.◆

Chapter Review

Summary

1. The key to managing an individual's career is to gain insight into what she or he wants out of a career, as well as his or her talents, limitations, and values, and to assess how they fit with the alternatives being considered.

2. The main stages in a person's career are: growth (roughly birth to age 14), exploration (roughly 15 to 24), establishment (roughly ages 24 to 44, the heart of most people's work lives), maintenance (45 to 65), and decline (preretirement).

3. The first step in planning an individual's career is to learn as much as possible about his or her own interests, aptitudes, and skills. Start by identifying occupational orientation: realistic, investigative, social, conventional, enterprising, and artistic. Then identify their skills and rank them from high to low. Next identify career anchors: technical/functional, managerial, creativity, autonomy, and security. Then ask the person what she or he wants to do.

4. The supervisor plays an important role in the career management process. Important guidelines include: avoid reality shock, be demanding, provide realistic job previews, conduct career-oriented performance appraisals, and provide career planning workshops.

5. In making promotion decisions, firms have to decide between seniority and competence, a formal or informal system, and ways to measure competence.

6. More firms today engage in practices aimed at helping employees "be all they can be," in other words, to self-actualize. Training, job enrichment, and educational opportunities are examples. However, for many employees, self-actualizing boils down to promotions and career progress. Many firms thus institute comprehensive career management/promotion-from-within programs.

7. Management development is aimed at preparing employees for future jobs with the organization, or at solving organization-wide problems concerning, for instance, inadequate interdepartmental communication.

8. On-the-job experience is by far the most popular form of management development. However, the preferred techniques differ by organizational level, with in-house programs being preferred for first-line supervisors and external conferences and seminars more widely used for top executives.

9. Managerial on-the-job training methods include developmental job rotation, coaching, and action learning. Basic off-the-job techniques include case studies, management games, outside seminars, college/university-related programs, role playing, behaviour modelling, and in-house development centres.

10. Organizational development (OD) is an approach to instituting change in which employees themselves play a major role in the change process by providing data, obtaining feedback on problems, and team-planning solutions. Several OD methods including Grid training and survey feedback are described.

11. HRM can contribute to building the learning organization through its impact on: systematic problem solving, experimentation, learning from experience and from others, transferring knowledge, and providing employees with lifelong learning.

12. Successful executive development programs require CEO involvement, a clear development policy, linkage to business strategies, succession planning and development, and managerial responsibility.

Key Terms

action learning
behaviour modelling
career anchor
career cycle
career planning and
    development
career planning workshop
case study method
decline stage
developmental job
    rotation

establishment stage
exploration stage
growth stage
in-house development
    centre
job pathing
leadership grid
learning organization
lifelong learning
maintenance stage

management
    development
management game
mentoring
occupational orientation
occupational skills
organizational
    development (OD)
role playing
survey feedback
team building

Discussion Questions and Exercises

1. Briefly describe each of the stages in a typical career.

2. What is a career anchor? What are the main types of career anchors discussed in this chapter?

3. What are the main types of Holland occupational orientations discussed in this chapter?

4. Describe important sources of information you could use to learn about careers of interest to you.

5. Working individually or in groups, choose three occupations (such as management consultant, HR manager, or salesperson) and use some of the sources described in this chapter to make an assessment of the future demand for this occupation over the next ten years or so. Does this seem like a good occupation to pursue? Why or why not?

6. Working individually or in groups, choose several occupations, such as computer programmer, lawyer, and accountant, and identify as many job openings for these occupations on the Internet as you can. Do you think the Internet is a valuable job search source for these occupations? Why or why not?

7. Discuss the key considerations in a typical small business management development program.

8. Do you think developmental job rotation is a good method to use for developing management trainees? Why or why not?

9. Working individually or in groups, contact a provider of management development seminars such as the Canadian Institute of Management. Obtain copies of their recent listings of seminar offerings. At what levels of managers do they aim their seminar offerings? What seems to be the most popular types of development programs? Why do you think that's the case?

10. Working individually or in groups, develop a series of concrete examples to illustrate how a professor teaching human resources management could use at least eight of the management development techniques described in this chapter in teaching his or her HR course.

Application Exercises

RUNNING CASE: Carter Cleaning Company

Developing Managers

"Management development? Did you say management development? Jennifer, you're my daughter and I love you but I can't believe that with all the problems we're facing here—strong competition, softening economy, 400 percent turnover, employee theft, and supply and waste management cartage costs that are going through the roof—you actually want me to consider setting up some kind of a program that will turn that bunch of deadbeats that we have as managers into nice people. I love you, Jenny, but please let's focus on the problems that we have to get solved today."

Actually, Jennifer was not altogether surprised with her father's reaction, but she did believe that her dad was being more than a little short-sighted. For example, she knew that some successful organizations, like Club Med, had a policy of rotating managers annually to help avoid their getting "stale," and she wondered whether such a program would make sense at Carter. She also felt that some type of simulations might help managers do a better job of dealing with their customers and employees, and she further believed that periodic off-site meetings between her, her father, and the store managers might help to identify and solve problems with the stores. Outside seminars in areas like modern cleaning techniques might also help to boost the current store managers' interest and performance and, of course, there is also the possibility of scheduling potential managers (like a few of the current cleaner-spotters) for management development as well. The company really didn't have much money to spend on matters like this though, and Jennifer knew that to sell the idea to her father she would need a very concrete, tight set of recommendations.

Questions

1. Given a budget of $5 000, what type of management development program can Jennifer formulate for the current store managers? The proposal must include the specific activities (like developmental job rotation) in which the managers should engage over the next four months.
2. Would it be worthwhile for the company to administer an attitude survey of all their employees? Jennifer knows Carter Cleaning isn't a big company, but she is curious as to whether employees would anonymously express their concerns, their likes and dislikes, and perhaps even help identify problems like employee theft that they are encountering on their jobs. If the company does go ahead with the survey, what questions should they ask?

CASE INCIDENT: Reality Shock

Maria Blanco didn't know what to do. After graduating from the University of Ontario in 1995, she'd taken a job with a major Toronto talent agency, thinking she could pursue her first love, entertainment. The agency had a reputation for being like "family," but it turned out that it was like no family she'd ever known. The HR director seemed to go out of his way to diminish the employees' importance by making comments like "If you want to leave, go ahead. I've got another one thousand applicants just like you."

She had spent her first year working in the mailroom and was now trying to figure out whether to leave for another big agency, find a small one, or change careers altogether. "This is not what I got an economics degree for," she thought. Now, in the summer of 1998, she was facing a very tight job market and hadn't been able to save a penny all year. All she knew was that she was miserable.

Questions

1. What would you do now if you were Maria? Why?
2. What could the talent agency have done to avoid problems like this?

Human Resources Management Simulation

Exercise 9 in the simulation provides an opportunity to prepare for a career development interview with a supervisor who wants to be promoted to a manager. The employee has asked for some guidance on what she should do to prepare herself for a promotion. This requires the preparation of an outline of the steps she needs to take to reach her career goals. A succession planning exercise is also provided in exercise 10. It is particularly important to consider how HR staff and the plant manager are going to share responsibility for the development of employees with potential for advancement.

Video Case

Power Presentations

Speaking in public is an essential skill for all managers. However, many people dread this experience, and some consider it a "fate worse than death." Peter Urs Bender is one of the foremost authorities on business presentations. According to Urs Bender, presentations can be made more powerful by breathing deeply to get more oxygen to the brain to aid clear thinking; lowering tone of voice for a more powerful sound; and stepping away from the podium and moving around to let ongoing body language speak. Urs Bender advises speakers not to sip cold water before speaking, as it tightens the throat, and to finish on time. He also advocates planting questions in the audience rather than making statements in self interest such as promoting the speaker's product or service.

Questions

1. List ten situations in which managers have to make presentations.
2. What methods, other than those mentioned above, can be used to handle fear of public speaking?
3. Consult the local telephone directory and list the public speaking clubs or classes available in the area. Call two or three and ask about the services they offer and how to join.

Video Resource: CBC, *Venture*, "Power Presentations," January 28, 1996.

Take It to the Net

Check out our Companion Website at

www.prenticehall.ca/dessler

for a multitude of practice questions, key terms and concepts, Weblinks to related sites, newsgroups, CBC video updates, and more.

Appendix 9.1

Finding the Right Job

Once occupational orientation, skills, and career anchors have been identified, a person must pick out an occupation and make plans for a career. If necessary, he or she must embark on any required training. The next step is to find a job in a desirable company and locale in which to work. Following are techniques for doing so.

Job Search Techniques

Research Perhaps the most direct way of unearthing the desired job is to pick out a desirable geographic area and find out everything about the companies in that area that are appealing. The next step is to determine the people one should contact in those companies to get the desired job. Most public libraries have local directories.

Other general reference material includes the Canadian Key Business Directory, published by Dun & Bradstreet, where the person in each organization who is ultimately responsible for hiring people in the position being sought can be found.

Personal Contacts According to one survey, the most popular way to seek job interviews is to rely on personal contacts such as friends and relatives.[1] A job-seeker should let as many responsible people as possible know that he or she is in the market for a job and specifically what kind of job he or she wants. (But someone who is currently employed probably doesn't want their job search getting back to their current boss; if that is the case, the job-seeker should pick out two or three very close friends and tell them it is absolutely essential that they be discreet in looking for a job for him or her.)

No matter how close friends or relatives are, one should not impose too much on them by shifting the burden of the job search to them. It is sometimes best just to ask them for the name of someone they think should be contacted in the kind of firm desired, and then do the digging.

www.careerkey.com
Career Networking

Answering Advertisements Most experts agree that answering ads is a low-probability way to get a job, and it becomes increasingly less likely that anyone will get a job this way as the level of job increases. It is highly unlikely that as a person moves up in management he or she is going to get a job by simply answering classified ads.

In responding to ads, be sure to create the right impression with the materials that are submitted; check the typing, style, grammar, neatness, and so forth, and check the résumé to make sure it is geared to the job being applied for. In the cover letter, an applicant should be sure to have a paragraph or so which specifically addresses why their background and accomplishments are appropriate to the job being advertised; they must respond clearly to the company's identified needs.[2]

Be very careful in replying to blind ads, however (those with just a post office box). Some executive search firms and companies will run ads even when no mid-level position exists just to gauge the market, and there is always the chance that someone could be trapped into responding to his or her own firm.

Employment Agencies Agencies are especially good at placing people in middle-level jobs but they can be useful for higher-paying jobs as well. Their fees for professional and management jobs are usually paid by the employer. Assuming a person knows the job he or she wants, he or she should review eight or so back issues of the classified ads in the library to identify the agencies that consistently handle these type of positions. The job-seeker should approach three or four initially, preferably in response to specific ads, and avoid signing any contract that gives an agency the exclusive right to place him or her.

Executive Recruiters Executive recruiters are retained by employers to seek out top talent for their clients, and their fees are always paid by the employer. They do not do career counselling, but if a person knows the job he or she wants, it pays to contact a few. Send a résumé and a cover letter summarizing one's job objective in precise terms, including job title and the size of company preferred, work-related accomplishments, current salary, and salary requirements. Firms are listed in the Yellow Pages under "Executive Search Consultants." However, beware, since some firms today call themselves executive search or career consultants but do no job searches: They just charge a (often hefty) fee to help manage a search. Remember that with a search firm the jobseeker never pays a fee.

Career Counsellors Career counsellors will not help anyone find a job per se; rather, they specialize in aptitude testing and career counselling. They are listed in the Yellow Pages under "Career Counselling" or "Vocational Guidance." Their services include psychological testing and interviews with an experienced career counsellor. Check the firm's services, prices, and history as well as the credentials of the assigned counsellor.

Executive Marketing Consultants Executive marketing consultants manage job-hunting campaigns. They generally are not recruiters and do not have jobs to fill. The process may involve months of weekly meetings. Services include résumé and letter writing, interview skill building, and developing a full job-hunting campaign. Before approaching a consultant, though, one should definitely do in-depth self-appraisal (as explained in this chapter) and read books like Richard Bolles's *The Quick Job Hunting Map* and *What Color Is Your Parachute?*

Three or four of these firms should then be checked out (they are listed in the Yellow Pages under "Executive Marketing Consultants") by visiting each and asking: What exactly is your program? How much does each service cost? Are there any extra costs, such as charges for printing and mailing résumés? What does the contract say? After what point will a rebate be provided to a client who is unhappy with the services? The jobseeker should then review his or her notes, check the Better Business Bureau, and decide which of these firms (if any) is for him or her.

Writing A Résumé

A résumé is probably the most important selling document, one that can determine whether an applicant "makes the cut" and gets offered a job interview. Here are some résumé pointers, as offered by employment counsellor Richard Payne and other experts:[3]

Introductory Information Start the résumé with name, address, telephone and fax numbers, and email address (if applicable). Using an office phone/fax number or email address, by the way, can indicate either that (1) the applicant's current employer knows he or she is leaving or (2) the applicant doesn't care whether the current employer finds out. It is usually better to use a home phone/fax number or email address.

Job Objective State the job objective next. This should summarize in one sentence the specific position desired, where one wants to do it (type and size of company), and a special reason an employer might have for wanting the job-seeker to fill the job. For example, "Production manager in a medium-size manufacturing

With more and more companies listing job openings on the Internet just about any serious job hunter should be using this valuable source.

There are many other recruitment services available on the Internet. For example, Monster Board Canada (www.monster.ca) is a bilingual service with thousands of résumés and job ads. Other companies offering recruiting Web sites include Career Site (www.careersite.com/va), Career Net (www.careernet.org), uunet Canada (www.uunet.com/work), Net Jobs (www.netjobs.com:8000), and Careerbridge (www.careerbridge.com).

The Globe and Mail newspaper offers a service called Career Connect (www.theglobeandmail.com/careerconnect). Career Connect is a resource centre for job seekers, who pay to post their résumé at this Web site, and to companies who pay to post notices of job openings. At first the service was used primarily for information technology positions, but now has job seekers and company ads for a wide variety of jobs. There are three ways to submit material to the site. The first is to email the information, which is then cut and pasted into the database at the site. The second is to send a hard copy, which is scanned and reformatted on the Net. The third is to transmit an electronic version of the material (in ASCII format) directly to the database.◆

company in a situation in which strong production scheduling and control experience would be valuable." Always try to put down the most senior title one can expect to secure, keeping in mind the specific job for which one is applying.

Job Scope   Indicate the scope of responsibility in each previous job, starting with the most recent position. For each previous job, write a paragraph that shows the job title, to whom the position reported directly and indirectly, how many people reported to the position (and their job titles), the operational and human resources budgets that were controlled, and what the job entailed (in one sentence).

Accomplishments   Next (and this is very important) indicate the "worth" of the applicant in each of the positions previously held. This is the heart of the résumé. It shows for each previous job: (1) the concrete action taken and why it was taken, and (2) the specific result of the actions—the "payoff." For example, "As production supervisor, I introduced a new process to replace costly hand soldering of component parts. The new process reduced assembly time per unit from 30 to 10 minutes and reduced labour costs by over 60 percent." Use several of these worth statements for each job.

Length   Keep the résumé to two pages or less and list education, and personal background (hobbies, interests, associations) on the last page.

Personal Data   Do not provide personal data regarding age, marital status, or dependents since human rights laws in every Canadian jurisdiction prohibit discrimination based on these factors.

Finally, two last points. First, do not produce an unprofessional résumé: Avoid overcrowded pages, difficult-to-read copies, typographical errors, and other problems of this sort. Second, do not use a make-do résumé—one from several years ago. Produce a new résumé for each job that is applied for, gearing the job objective and worth statements to the job desired.

Make the Résumé Scannable   For many job applications it's important to write a scannable résumé, in other words, one that is electronically readable by a computer system. Many medium- and larger-size firms that do extensive recruiting and hiring now use software to quickly and automatically review large numbers of résumés, screening out those that don't seem to match (often based on the absence of certain key words that the employer is looking for).

There are several guidelines to keep in mind for writing scannable résumés.[4] These can be summarized as follows:

> Use type no smaller than 10 points and no larger than 14 points.
>
> Do not use italicized type, and do not underline words.
>
> Use type styles that work well for résumés and can be scanned as well as read, such as Helvetica, Futura, Optima, Times Roman, New Century Schoolbook, Courier, Univers, and Bookman.
>
> Submit only high-resolution documents. Documents produced on a laser printer work best. Many photocopies and faxes are not clean enough for scanning.
>
> Make sure to present qualifications using powerful key words appropriate to the job or jobs being applied for. For example, trainers might use key words and phrases such as: *computer-based training, interactive video,* and *group facilitator.*

Handling the Interview

Once all the homework is done, the next step is an interview with the person who is responsible for hiring for the job. Here are some suggestions for excelling in an interview to supplement those listed in chapter 7.

Prepare, Prepare, Prepare   First, remember that preparation is essential. Before the interview, learn about the employer, the job, and the people doing the recruiting. At the library, look through business periodicals to find out what is happening in the employer's field. Who is the competition? How are they doing? Check out the Internet to see if the company has a website and scan the contents.

Uncover the Interviewer's Needs   Spend as little time as possible answering the interviewer's first questions and as much time as possible getting the person to describe his or her needs: what the company wants to get accomplished and the type of person needed. Use open-ended questions, such as "Could you tell me more about that?"

Relate Oneself to the Interviewer's Needs   Once it is clear what type of person the interviewer is looking for and the sorts of problems he or she wants solved, the applicant is in a good position to describe his or her own accomplishments in terms of the interviewer's needs. Start by saying something like, "One of the problem areas you've indicated is important to you is similar to a problem I once faced." Then state the problem, describe a solution, and reveal the results.

Think Before Answering   Answering a question should be a three-step process: pause, think, speak. The applicant should pause to make sure he or she understands what the interviewer is driving at, think about how to structure their answer, and then speak. In the answer, the job seeker should emphasize how hiring him or her will help the interviewer solve one or more of their problems.

Make a Good Appearance and Show Enthusiasm   Appropriate clothing, good grooming, a firm handshake, and the appearance of controlled energy are important.

First Impressions Count   Studies of interviews show that in almost 80 percent of the cases, interviewers make up their minds about the applicant during the first few minutes of the interview. A good first impression may turn to bad during the interview, but it is unlikely. Bad first impressions are almost impossible to overcome.

1. Robert Jameson, *The Professional Job Changing System* (Verona, NJ: Performance Dynamics, 1975). See also Kenneth McRae, "Career-Management Planning: A Boon to Managers and Employees," *Personnel* 62, no. 5 (May 1985), pp. 56–60. See also John Wareham, "How to Make a Headhunter Call You," *Across the Board* 32, no. 1 (January 1995), pp. 49–50.
2. The percentage of job seekers who look for work by placing or answering ads has almost doubled since 1970, according to data compiled by the U.S. Bureau of Labor Statistics. See Michelle Harrison Ports, "Trends in Job Search Methods, 1970–92," *Monthly Labor Review* (October 1993), pp. 63–7.
3. Richard Payne, *How to Get a Better Job Quicker* (New York: New American Library, 1987). See also Larry Salters, "Résumé Writing for the 1990s," *Business and Economic Review* 40, no. 3 (April 1994), pp. 11–8.
4. This is based on Erica Gordon Sorohan, "Electrifying a Job Search," *Training and Development* (October 1994), pp. 7–9.

Notes

1. J. Richard Hackman and J. Lloyd Suttle, *Improving Life at Work* (Santa Monica, CA: Goodyear, 1977); see also David Bowen and Edward Lawler, "Total Quality-Oriented Human Resources Management," *Organizational Dynamics* 20, no. 4 (Spring 1992), pp. 29–41.
2. B. Moses, "Employee Career Planning Programs: What's in it for Organizations?" *HR Professional*, September 1985, p. 1.
3. Hackman and Suttle, *Improving Life at Work*, p. 4. For a good discussion of how to maintain a career development process, see Beverly Kaye and Zandy Leibowitz, "Career Development: Don't Let It Fizzle," *HR Magazine* (September 1994), pp. 78–83. See also Robert Bolton and Jeffrey Gold, "Career Management: Matching the Needs of Individuals with the Needs of Organizations," *Personnel Review* 23, no. 1 (1994), pp. 6–24.
4. These are quoted from Fred Otte and Peggy Hutcheson, *Helping Employees Manage Careers* (Englewood Cliffs, NJ: Prentice Hall, 1992), pp. 5–6.
5. K. Gay, "Planning Future Path is Key to a Successful Career," *Financial Post* (July 8, 1995), p. 13.
6. For example, one survey of "baby boomers" concluded that "allowed to excel" was the most frequently mentioned factor in overall job satisfaction in an extensive attitude survey of Canadian supervisors and middle managers between 30 and 45 years old. Judy Rogers, "Baby Boomers and Their Career Expectations," *Canadian Business Review* (Spring 1993), pp. 13–8.
7. Donald Super and others, *Vocational Development: A Framework for Research* (New York: Teachers College Press, 1957), and Edgar Schein, *Career Dynamics: Matching Individual and Organizational Needs* (Reading, MA: Addison-Wesley, 1978).
8. John Holland, *Making Vocational Choices: A Theory of Careers* (Englewood Cliffs, NJ: Prentice Hall, 1973).
9. Richard Bolles, *The Quick Job Hunting Map* (Berkeley, CA: Ten Speed Press, 1979), pp. 5–6.
10. Schein, *Career Dynamics*, pp. 128–29. For a recent description of how to apply career anchor theory in practice, see Thomas Barth, "Career Anchor Theory," *Review of Public Personnel Administration*, Vol. 13, no. 4 (1993), pp. 27–42.
11. Schein, *Career Dynamics*, pp. 252–3.
12. For self-diagnosis books, see, for example, G. A. Ford and G. L. Lippitt, *A Life Planning Workbook* (Fairfax, VA: NTL Learning Resources, 1972).
13. Richard Bolles, *What Color Is Your Parachute?* (Berkeley, CA: Ten Speed Press, 1976), p. 86.
14. Robert Jameson, *The Professional Job Changing System* (Verona, NJ: Performance Dynamics, 1975).
15. Richard Payne, *How to Get a Better Job Quicker* (New York: New American Library, 1987).
16. Personal interview, March 1992.
17. Richard Reilly, Mary Tenopyr, and Steven Sperling, "The Effects of Job Previews on Job Acceptance and Survival Rates of Telephone Operator Candidates," *Journal of Applied Psychology* 64 (1979).
18. Schein, *Career Dynamics*, p. 19.
19. J. Sterling Livingston, "Pygmalion in Management," *Harvard Business Review* 48 (July–August 1969), pp. 81–9.
20. Joel Ross, *Managing Productivity* (Reston, VA: Reston, 1979).
21. Douglas Hall and Francine Hall, "What's New in Career Management?" *Organizational Dynamics* 4 (Summer 1976).
22. H. G. Kaufman, *Obsolescence and Professional Career Development* (New York: AMACOM, 1974).
23. Hall and Hall, "What's New in Career Management?" p. 350.
24. See, for example, Terri Scandurg, "Mentorship and Career Mobility: An Empirical Investigation," *Journal of Organizational Behavior* 13, no. 2 (March 1992), pp. 169–74.
25. Schein, *Career Dynamics*, p. 19. See also Robin Jacobs and Robert Bolton, "Career Analysis: The Missing Link in Managerial Assessment and Development," *Human Resource Management Journa* 3, no. 2 (1994), pp. 55–62.
26. Otte and Hutcheson, *Helping Employees*, pp. 15–6.
27. Otte and Hutcheson, *Helping Employees*, p. 143.
28. B. Moses, "Implementing an Employee Career Development Program - Part Two: Tools to Support Career Development," *HR Professional*, December 1985, pp. 6–10.
29. Timothy Newby and Ashlyn Heide, "The Value of Mentoring," *Performance Improvement Quarterly* 5, no. 4 (1992), pp. 2–15.
30. Newby and Heide, "The Value of Mentoring," p. 2.
31. See for example, Daniel Quinn Mills, *Labor-Management Relations* (New York: McGraw-Hill, 1986), pp. 387–96.

32. James Healy, "The Factor of Ability in Labor Relations," in *Arbitration Today, Proceedings of the Eighth Annual Meeting of the National Academy of Arbitrators,* 1955, pp. 45–54, quoted in Pigors and Meyers, *Personnel Administration,* p. 283.

33. Charles Halaby, "Bureaucratic Promotion Criteria," *Administrative Science Quarterly,* Vol. 23 (September 1978), pp. 466–484.

34. Gary Dessler, *Winning Commitment* (New York: McGraw-Hill, 1993), pp. 144–49.

35. Dessler, *Winning Commitment.*

36. See Joseph Famularo, *Handbook of Modern Personnel Administration* (New York: McGraw-Hill, 1972), p. 17.

37. For a discussion, see Susan Schmidt, "The New Focus for Career Development Programs in Business and Industry," *Journal of Employment Counseling* 31 (March 1994), pp. 22–8.

38. R. Tucker, M. Moravee, and K. Ideus, "Designing a Dual Career-Track System," *Training and Development,* Vol. 6 (1992), pp. 55–8; Schmidt, "The New Focus for Career Development," p. 26.

39. Schmidt, "The New Focus," pp. 25–6.

40. See, for example, Richard Chanick, "Career Growth for Baby Boomers," *Personnel Journal* 71, no. 1 (January 1992), pp. 40–6.

41. Chanick, "Career Growth".

42. Lester A. Digman, "Management Development: Needs and Practices," *Personnel* 57 (July–August 1980), pp. 45–57. See also James Cureton, Alfred Newton, and Dennis Tesolowski, "Finding Out What Managers Need," *Training and Development Journal* 40, no. 5 (May 1986), pp. 106–7, and results of a ten-year survey show an increasingly important role for executive development in building and revitalizing corporate competitiveness. See Albert Vicere, Maria Taylor, and Virginia Freeman, "Executive Development in Major Corporations: A Ten-Year Study," *Journal of Management Development* 13, no. 1 (1994), pp. 4–22.

43. "Why Promoting From Within Works at FedEx," *Ontario Society for Training and Development Update,* November/December 1996, p. 1 & 7; see also "Trends in Corporate Education and Training," Report no. 870 (1986), The Conference Board, 845 Third Avenue, New York, NY 10022.

44. For discussions of the steps in succession planning see, for example, Kenneth Nowack, "The Secrets of Succession," *Training and Development* (November 1994), pp. 49–55, and Donald Brookes, "In Management Succession, Who Moves Up?" *Human Resources* (January/February 1995), pp. 11–3.

45. Dale Yoder et al., *Handbook of Personnel Management and Labor Relations* (New York: McGraw-Hill, 1958), pp. 10–27; for a recent review, see William Rothwell, H. C. Kazanas, and Darla Haines, "Issues and Practices in Management Job Rotation Programs as Perceived by HRD Professionals," *Performance Improvement Quarterly* 5, no. 1 (1992), pp. 49–69.

46. Yoder et al. See also Jack Phillips, "Training Supervisors Outside the Classroom," *Training and Development Journal* 40, no. 2 (February 1986), pp. 46–9.

47. K. Wexley and G. Latham, *Developing and Training Resources in Organizations* (Glenview, IL: Scott, Foresman, 1981), p. 118.

48. R. L. Daft & P.A. Fitzgerald, *Management,* (Toronto: Dryden Canada, 1992).

49. Wexley and Latham, *Developing and Training Resources,* p. 207.

50. This is based on Nancy Fox, "Action Learning Comes to Industry," *Harvard Business Review* 56 (September–October, 1977), pp. 158–68.

51. Wexley and Latham, *Developing and Training Resources,* p. 193.

52. Chris Argyris, "Some Limitations of the Case Method: Experiences in a Management Development Program," *Academy of Management Review* 5, no. 2 (1980), pp. 291–8. For a discussion of the advantages of case studies over traditional methods, see, for example, Eugene Andrews and James Noel, "Adding Life to the Case Study," *Training and Development Journal* 40, no. 2 (February 1986), pp. 28–33.

53. David Rogers, *Business Policy and Planning* (Englewood Cliffs, NJ: Prentice Hall, 1977), pp. 532–3.

54. Argyris, "Some Limitations of the Case Method," pp. 292–5.

55. Rogers, *Business Policy and Planning,* p. 533.

56. For a discussion of management games and also other noncomputerized training and development simulations, see Charlene Marmer Solomon, "Simulation Training Builds Teams Through Experience," *Personnel Journal* (June 1993), pp. 100–5; Kim Slack, "Training for the Real Thing," *Training and Development* (May 1993), pp. 79–89; Bruce Lierman, "How to Develop a Training Simulation," *Training and Development* (February 1994), pp. 50–2.

57. D. McKay-Stokes, "Sleeping in the Snow Together Does Wonders for Morale," *Financial Post* (April 25, 1995), p. 20.

58. Joseph Famularo, *Handbook of Modern Personnel Administration* (New York: McGraw-Hill, 1972), pp. 21.7–21.8. For an interesting discussion of how to design a management game that is both educational and stimulating, see Beverly Loy Taylor, "Around the World in 80 Questions," *Training and Development Journal* 40, no. 3 (March 1986), pp. 67–70.

59. John Hinrichs, "Personnel Testing," in Marvin Dunnette, ed., *Handbook of Industrial and Organizational Psychology* (Chicago: Rand McNally, 1976), p. 855.

60. Norman Maier, Allen Solem, and Ayesha Maier, *The Role Play Technique* (San Diego, CA: University Associates, 1975), pp. 2–3. See also David Swink, "Role-Play Your Way to Learning," *Training and Development* (May 1993), pp. 91–7; Alan Test, "Why I Do Not Like to Role Play," *The American Salesman* (August 1994), pp. 7–20.

61. This section based on Allen Kraut, "Developing Managerial Skill via Modeling Techniques: Some Positive Research Findings—A Symposium," *Personnel Psychology* 29, no. 3 (Autumn 1976), pp. 325–61.

62. *Your Guide to Learning 1997,* The Institute for Learning, The Bank of Montreal.

63. Mark Frohman, Marshall Sashkin, and Michael Kavanagh, "Action Research as Applied to Organization Development," *Organization and Administrative Science* 7 (Spring–Summer 1976), pp. 129–42; Paul Sheibar, "The Seven Deadly Sins of Employee Attitude Surveys," *Personnel* 66, no. 6 (June 1989), pp. 66–71. See also George Gallup, "A Surge in Surveys," *Personnel Journal* 67, no. 8 (August 1988), pp. 42–3.

64. Wendell French and Cecil Bell, Jr., *Organization Development* (Englewood Cliffs, NJ: Prentice Hall, 1978). See also David M. Zakeski, "Reliable Assessments of Organizations," *Personnel Journal* 67, no. 12 (December 1988), pp. 42–4.

65. Robert Blake and Jane Mouton, *The Managerial Grid* (Houston: Gulf, 1964). For an interesting description of the effectiveness of team building in solving a management problem, see, for example, Barry Miller and Ronald Phillips, "Team Building on a Deadline," *Training and Development Journal* 40, no. 3 (March 1986), pp. 54–8.

66. A. DeGeus, "Planning as Learning," *Harvard Business Review* (March/April 1988), p. 71; quoted in Robert/Kenneth Fulmer and Graham, "A New Era in Management Education," *Journal of Management Development*, 12, no. 3 (1993), p. 31.

67. David A. Garvin, "Building a Learning Organization," *Business Credit* (January 1994), p. 20.

68. David A. Garvin, "Building a Learning Organization," *Harvard Business Review* (July–August 1993), p. 80.

69. Garvin, 1994, p. 21.

70. Garvin, 1994, p. 22.

71. M. Crossan, "Improvising at the Office," *The Globe and Mail* (October 3, 1997), p. C1.

72. Garvin, 1994, p. 23.

73. Garvin, 1994.

74. Garvin, 1994.

75. Garvin, 1994, p. 25.

76. Robert C. Camp, *Benchmarking: The Search for Industry Best Practices that Lead to Superior Performance* (Milwaukee: ASQC Quality Press, 1989), p. 12.

77. Garvin, 1994, p. 25.

78. For additional insights into HR and the learning organization, see Charlene Marmer Solomon, "HR Facilitates the Learning Organization Concept," *Personnel Journal* (November 1994), pp. 56–66.

79. This is based on Norman Nopper, "Reinventing the Factory with Lifelong Learning," *Training* (May 1993), pp. 55–7.

80. Nopper, "Reinventing the Factory," p. 56.

81. Nopper, ""Reinventing the Factory."

82. Nopper, "Reinventing the Factory," p. 57. For another example, see Kevin Kelly and Peter Burrows, "Motorola: Training for the Millennium," *Business Week* (March 28, 1994), pp. 158–60, and "Some Nuts and Bolts of Lifelong Learning," *Training* (March 1994), p. 30 (no author cited).

83. Julie A. Fenwick-MacGrath, "Executive Development: Key Factors for Success," *Personnel* (July 1988), pp. 68–72.

84. Paul Blocklyn, "Developing the International Executive," *Personnel* (March 1989), pp. 44–7. See also T. S. Chan, "Developing International Managers: A Partnership Approach," *Journal of Management Development* 13, no. 3 (1994), pp. 38–46.

85. This section based on Blocklyn, "Developing the International Executive." See also "Developing Global Executives," *BNA Bulletin to Management* 44, no. 10, March 11, 1993, pp. 73–4.

Chapter 10
Managing Quality and Productivity

Chapter Outline

- ♦ **Introduction**
- ♦ **Alternative Work Arrangements**
- ♦ **Using Quality Circle Programs**
- ♦ **Quality Management Programs**
- ♦ **Creating Self-Directed Teams**
- ♦ **Business Process Reengineering**

Learning Outcomes

After studying this chapter, you should be able to:

Describe some common alternative work arrangements and list the pros and cons of each.

Explain how quality circles and quality management programs should be set up and managed.

Describe how effective self-directed teams can be created.

Discuss the HR department's role in business process reengineering.

Introduction

Many trends are influencing HR management. Information technology increasingly demands a more sophisticated, better-trained work force. It is estimated that by the year 2000, nearly 80 percent of Canadian jobs will be service jobs, jobs that require empowerment rather than restrictive work rules or supervisory practices. The supply of available labour is growing more slowly than in the past, and the average age of the work force is rising—two more factors that put a premium on using new methods for getting the best out of the work force. Superimposed over all this are changes in work itself, and in the way modern businesses are managed, changes that manifest themselves in a need to depend on employee commitment to provide the responsive and creative solutions that corporate success today requires.

These changes are influencing the HR methods employers use. In particular, employers are increasingly utilizing techniques like quality improvement programs and flexible work arrangements. Programs like these are aimed at eliciting the best that workers can offer by treating them responsibly and by giving them more discretion over their jobs and the opportunity to use their problem-solving skills at work. Some of the most important of these methods are discussed in this chapter. They include such closely related HRM-driven programs as:

Alternative Work Arrangements These generally allow employees to design relatively flexible workdays and/or workweeks for themselves so as to better accommodate their personal needs and preferences.

Quality Circle Programs These involve establishing specially trained work teams that meet periodically (usually weekly) to analyze and solve problems pertaining to their own work areas.

Company-wide Quality Management Programs These programs are designed to improve the quality of the employer's product or services. The basic approach involves a coordinated, company-wide effort built around monitoring customer satisfaction and using employee teams and involvement to continually improve quality.

Self-Directed Teams These are created by empowering work teams to direct their own activities.

Reengineering According to experts Michael Hammer and James Champy, reengineering involves a fundamental rethinking and radical redesign of business processes to achieve improvements in critical measures of performance.

Alternative Work Arrangements

A 1997 Conference Board of Canada survey found that alternative work arrangements are becoming more common. Flexible hours were offered by 64 percent of the 345 organizations surveyed, job sharing by 43 percent, compressed work weeks by 27 percent, and telecommuting by 24 percent.[1]

Flextime

flextime
A plan whereby employees build their workday around a core of midday hours.

Flextime is a plan whereby employees' flexible workdays are built around a core of midday hours, such as 11 A.M. to 2 P.M. Workers determine their own flexible starting and stopping hours. For example, they may opt to work from 7 A.M. to 3 P.M. or from 11 A.M. to 7 P.M. According to a 1997 study by the Canadian Labour

Market and Productivity Centre, based on Statistics Canada data, about 25 percent of the Canadian work force is on a flextime schedule, mainly comprised of professionals, managers, and self-employed persons.[2]

Flextime in Practice   In practice, most employers who use flextime give employees only limited freedom regarding the hours they work. Typical schedules dictate the earliest starting time, latest starting time, and core periods. Employers often hold fairly close to the traditional 9 A.M. to 5 P.M. workday. For example, starting times may be between 7 A.M. and 10 A.M., and core time from 10 A.M. to 3 P.M. The effect of flextime for many employees is to give them about an hour or two leeway before 9 A.M. or after 5 P.M.

Flextime's Pros and Cons   Some flextime programs have been quite successful.[3] Because less time is lost due to tardiness, the ratio of worker-hours worked to worker-hours paid (a measure of productivity) increases. Flextime can also reduce absenteeism and cut down on sick leave being used for personal matters. The hours actually worked seem to be more productive, and there is less slowing down toward the end of the workday. Employees tend to leave early when work is slack and work later when it is heavy. The use of flextime seems to increase employees' receptiveness to changes in other procedures. It also tends to reduce the distinction between managers and workers and requires more delegation of authority by supervisors.

There are some disadvantages. Flextime is complicated to administer and may be impossible to implement where large groups of workers must work interdependently.[4] It also requires time clocks or other time records, which can be disadvantageous from the point of view of employees.

In any event, flextime seems to work. Surveys covering 445 employers (including drug companies, banks, electronics firms, and government agencies) indicate that the percentage of employees reporting flextime-driven productivity increases ranges from 5 percent or 10 percent in some firms to about 95 percent in one airline. On the whole, about 45 percent of employees involved in flextime programs report improved productivity.[5] The failure rate of flextime is also remarkably low, reportedly 8 percent, according to one study.[6]

Conditions for Success   There are several ways to make a flextime program more successful.[7] First, management resistance—particularly at the supervisory level before the program is actually tried—has torpedoed several programs before they became operational. Thus supervisory indoctrination is an important prerequisite to success. Second, flextime is usually more successful with clerical, professional, and managerial jobs, and less so with factory jobs (the nature of which tends to demand interdependence among workers). Third, experience indicates that the greater the flexibility of a flextime program, the greater the benefits (although the disadvantages, of course, multiply as well). Fourth, the way the program is implemented is important; a flextime project director should be appointed to oversee all aspects of the program, and frequent meetings should take place between supervisors and employees to allay their fears and clear up misunderstandings. A pilot study in one department is advisable.[8]

Flextime may be especially valuable for the employer when a work group must share limited resources. For example, computer programmers often spend as much as two-thirds of their time waiting to make computer runs. As one researcher concludes, "because flextime expands the amount of time that the computer is available to the programmer, this allows its usage to be spread over more hours, and the time in queues to make runs and get output back is reduced."[9]

Compressed Workweeks

A number of employers have also switched to a **compressed workweek.** The most common arrangement involves employees working four ten-hour days instead of the more usual five eight-hour days. In Canada, about 10 percent of employers use compressed work weeks, according to a 1997 study by the Canadian Labour Market and Productivity Centre.[10]

Advantages   Compressed workweek plans have been fairly successful as they have several advantages. Productivity seems to increase since there are fewer start-ups and shutdowns. Workers are also more willing to work some evenings and Saturdays as part of these plans. According to one study, 80 percent of the firms with such plans reported that the plan "improves business results"; three-fifths said that production was up and almost two-fifths said that costs were down. Half the firms also reported higher profits. Even the firms not reporting positive results indicated that cost and profit factors at least remained the same. One study suggests that the compressed workweek is generally effective (in terms of reducing paid overtime, reducing absenteeism, and improving efficiency). Furthermore, workers also gain; there is a 20 percent reduction in commuter trips and an additional day off per week. Additional savings (for example, in child care expenses) may also result.[11]

However, there has not been a lot of experience with shortened workweeks, and it is possible that the improvements are short-lived. In one study, for instance, four-day weeks resulted in greater employee satisfaction and productivity and less absenteeism when evaluated after 13 months, but these improvements were not found after 25 months.[12] A recent review of three-day, 38-hour workweeks concluded that compressed workweek schedules have significant positive and long-lasting effects on the organization if handled properly. Regardless of individual differences, those employees who had experienced the 3/38 schedule reacted favourably to it, particularly if they had participated in the decision to implement the new program and if their jobs had been enriched by the schedule change. Fatigue did not appear to be a problem in this survey.[13]

Disadvantages   There are also disadvantages, some of them potentially quite severe. Tardiness, for example, may become a problem. Of more concern is the fact that fatigue was cited by several firms as a principal drawback of the four-day workweek. (Note that fatigue was a main reason for adopting eight-hour days in the first place.)

Other Flexible Work Arrangements

Employers are taking other steps to accommodate their employees' scheduling needs. **Job sharing** is a strategy that allows two or more people to share a single full-time job. For example, two people may share a 40-hour-per-week job, with one working mornings and the other working afternoons. Statistics Canada data indicates that about 10 percent of part-time workers in Canada are job sharing.[14] *Work sharing* refers to a temporary reduction in work-hours by a group of employees during economic hard times as a way of preventing layoffs; thus 400 employees may all agree to work (and get paid for) only 35 hours per week in order to avoid having the firm lay off 30 workers. *Flexiplace,* in which employees are allowed or encouraged to work at home or in a satellite office closer to home, is another example of a flexible work arrangement that is becoming more popular today.

Telecommuting, (which was also defined in chapter 1), is another option. Here employees work at home, usually with their computers and fax machines, using telephone lines to transmit letters, data, and completed work to the office. It is estimated that 6 percent of Canadian workers are telecommuting, according to a 1997 telecommuting survey conducted by KPMG.[15]

For example, IBM Canada has 20 percent of its sales and service workforce telecommuting; Xerox Canada has almost half of its employees working from home, car, or other non-traditional location; and Edmonton Telephone uses information operators who work at home.[16]

Many managers are not comfortable supervising telecommuters, fearing a loss of control. However, according to Jack Nilles, who coined the term "telecommuter," successful telecommuting requires mutual trust being established between an employee and his or her supervisor. To overcome resistance, and ensure they learn the planning and communication skills necessary to build such trust, managers who supervise telecommuters need to be properly prepared and trained.[17]

Benefits of telecommuting range from increases in worker satisfaction to reduced absenteeism.[18] One B.C. firm used telecommuting to enhance customer service when employees agreed to start work at 6 A.M. Pacific time to deal with customers at 9 A.M. Eastern time.[19] Further benefits of telecommuting include decreased real estate costs and increased productivity (due to such factors as commuting time saved, fewer distractions, and ability to take advantage of personal "peak-performance" time).[20]

In order to achieve these benefits, Nora Spinks, president of Work & Family Services, has a number of tips for managers. To ensure the success of telecommuting initiatives, firms should:[21]

- provide prospective teleworkers with training on remote communications and counsel them regarding tax and insurance implications
- make sure prospective telecommuters would not be in violation of a municipal bylaw or condominium rule
- ensure prospective telecommuters have adequate space, lighting, and equipment
- pilot telework arrangements and allow for reversal or change
- start small—two to three days a week maximum
- use technology wisely—telephones, pagers, and computer
- clearly communicate security and confidentiality policies and practices
- communicate expectations regarding such issues as availability during lunch or after regular hours prior to the start of telework
- respect the privacy of teleworkers—don't drop by unannounced
- find ways to include teleworkers in the organizational culture, including meetings and special events.

flexyear
A work arrangement under which employees can choose (at six-month intervals) the number of hours they want to work each month over the next year.

Still other employers, especially in Europe, are switching to a plan they call ***flexyear***. Under this plan, employees can choose (at six-month intervals) the number of hours they want to work each month over the next year. A full-timer, for instance, might be able to work up to 173 hours a month. In a typical flexyear arrangement, an employee who wants to average 110 hours a month might work 150 hours in January (when the children are at school and the company needs extra help to cope with January sales). In February, the employee may work only 70 hours because he or she wants to, say, go skiing.[22]

Mixed Messages about Family-Friendly Alternative Work Arrangements

Although one of the primary reasons for offering alternative work arrangements is to help employees balance their work and family responsibilities, many experts believe that today's high pressure work culture has led to growing expectations for employees to work longer and harder.[23] These conflicting messages led 44 percent of employees in a 1996 flexible workplace survey to say that they were afraid that career advancement would be harmed by taking advantage of flexible work arrangements, and 51 percent said they worried about job security when requesting an alternative work arrangement.[24]

Paradoxically, the survey revealed that employees' fears about taking time for personal needs are resulting in more time off due to stress-related leaves. Insurance carriers report that mental and nervous disability claims rose by 31 percent between 1992 and 1994. The end result is that employee commitment levels are decreasing. Lean workforces often mean that anyone who is not able to attend work is resented because it jeopardizes coworkers' work-family balance. Workers are not complaining because they fear they will be the next ones to be downsized. Until organizations reduce workloads to a level that lets employees lead balanced lives, employee commitment may continue to erode.

Using Quality Circle Programs

quality circle
A group of five to ten specially trained employees who meet on a regular basis to identify and solve problems in their work area.

A **quality circle** (QC) is a group of five to ten specially trained employees who meet for an hour once a week for the purpose of spotting and solving problems in their work area.[25] The circle is usually composed of a work group, people who work together to produce a specific component or provide a specific service.

Steps in Establishing a Quality Circle

The HR department usually plays a central role in establishing a QC program. The four steps in establishing and leading a quality circle are *planning, training, initiating,* and *operating.*

Planning the Circle The planning phase usually takes about one month and typically begins with a top-level executive making the decision to implement the quality circle (QC) technique. This leads to identifying and selecting a consultant who will assist top management in implementing the quality circles in the firm. However, in some cases an in-house *facilitator* will be identified and sent out for special circle methods training. The facilitator then returns to the firm and handles the tasks for which the consultant would otherwise have been responsible.

One of the most important steps in the first phase is selecting the quality circle *steering committee.* The steering committee becomes the group that directs quality circle activities in the organization. The multidisciplinary committee is composed of representatives from the major functional areas of the organization such as production, human resources, quality control, marketing, engineering, finance, as well as union representatives. A participating senior-level representative is necessary to reinforce the company's commitment to the process.

The steering committee has several responsibilities. Perhaps most important, its members establish circle objectives in terms of the kinds of *bottom-line improvements* they would like to see. Yardsticks include reduced errors and enhanced quality, more effective teamwork, and increased attention to problem prevention. At the same time, the steering committee determines issues that are considered outside the charter of the circles—for instance, benefits and salaries, employment practices, policies on discharging employees, personalities, and grievances. The steering committee also chooses the in-house facilitator, the person who will be responsible for daily coordination of the firm's quality circle activities. In most cases the facilitator

www.iqpc.com
International Quality and Productivity Centre

devotes full time to quality circle tasks and is responsible for such specific duties as coordinating the activities of the circles, training leaders for each circle, attending circle meetings and providing expert advice and backup coordination, and maintaining records to reflect circle achievements.

Initial Training   In the second phase, the facilitator and pilot project circle leaders meet (usually with the consultant) to be trained in basic QC philosophy, implementation, and operation. This training typically takes four days and includes various activities. On the first day, for example, the consultant might meet with the leaders to discuss the nature and objectives of quality circles. On the remaining days, trainees use case studies to learn quality circle leadership techniques.

Initiating the Circles   Initiating the pilot program's circles begins with department managers conducting quality circle familiarization meetings with employees, with the facilitator, circle leaders, and (ideally) an executive participating as speakers. Then circle leaders contact each employee to determine circle membership, which is voluntary, and the circles are constituted. The facilitator distributes manuals for circle leaders at this point; they contain an overview of QC principles, as well as an explanation of data collection and problem-solving techniques.

The Circle in Operation   Next, each circle turns to problem solving and analysis. In practice, this involves five steps: problem identification, problem selection, problem analysis, solution recommendations, and solution review by management.

Problem Identification   The problems identified by circle members are often mundane and may not be especially interesting to work groups outside the circle's work area. These problems might include how to keep the area cleaner, how to improve the work group's product quality, or how to speed up the packing of the work group's crates.

Members of a quality circle are responsible for identifying problems, then analyzing them and proposing solutions.

Problem Selection   Next members select the number-one problem on which they wish to focus. Circle members are usually quite familiar with the impediments making it difficult for them to do their jobs. They are thus often in the best position to prioritize problems, although the choice may require the approval of management.

Problem Analysis   In this next step, circle members collect, collate, and analyze data relating to the problem. Group members analyze and solve the problem. A big benefit of quality circles is the sense of satisfaction that members get from being involved in the actual problem analysis process. If they are prohibited from analyzing the problem by an inept leader, they will not only miss this sense of satisfaction but may actually resent (rather than be committed to) implementing the solution. Quality circles are as much a people-building opportunity as a quality-improving one. To derive all the benefits from a circle, the members themselves must be involved in the problem selection, analysis, resolution, and implementation.

Solution Recommendation   The group's recommended solution is then presented to management by group members, with the aid of charts and graphs they prepare themselves. The presentation is usually oral rather than written and more often than not is voluntarily prepared by employees on their own time.

Solution Review and Decision by Management   Quality circles usually operate through the management chain of command. The presentation is made to the individual to whom the supervisor (frequently the circle leader) reports, not to the steering committee or to someone at the executive level. Top managers may be present as observers.

According to one source, from 85 percent to 100 percent of circle suggestions are approved by the manager, often in the presentation meeting itself. Occasionally the manager will need verification of studies done and may even ask a staff person to assist in the verification. In those unusual instances when a manager must decline a recommendation, he or she is trained to explain why it was turned down, so as not to dampen the enthusiasm of the circle members.

There are several predictable problems that quality circles encounter that can be avoided. One is the feeling on the part of the employees that this is "just another program" that will probably evaporate once the initial excitement wears off. Gaining top management's commitment to quality circles is thus crucial for program success. Some employees will complain that the circles are doomed because "management never pays attention to us anyway." Here again, the best solution is to underscore top management's commitment to the quality circle program. Selecting problems outside the circle's areas of expertise is another familiar problem, as when a production group decides to work on a shipping problem. Therefore, circle leaders should be trained to keep their members on track and to caution them to focus on problems within their own area—where they are the experts. Other area's problems can be handed over to the appropriate circle or handed to an interdisciplinary team. Finally, some of the greatest resistance to the circles will come not from the employees but from supervisors, perhaps because they fear that the circles may undermine their traditional authority. This is another reason why top management's commitment is essential—to let supervisors know that the firm takes this program very seriously.

Making Quality Circles More Effective

Studies of quality circle effectiveness generally confirm that it is spotty at best.[26] Many of the so-called studies of QC effectiveness are actually anecdotal case studies, where it is not possible to conclude whether the quality circle program itself created the improvements rather than, say, some parallel changes such as improvements in the firm's financial incentive plan.

Results of more careful experimental studies of quality circles generally indicate that the majority of such programs are successful but that many are not. One study showed some improvement in attitudes, behaviours, and effectiveness but then a decline in each to the initial levels.[27] Results of one recent quality circle study are probably typical. The researcher concluded: "The fact that two of the four circles had actual cost savings ($9 600 and $11 280), none had noticeable quality improvements, all worked on job improvement issues, and three of the four were evaluated as successful by facilitators seems indicative of general quality circle performance."[28] Such spotty results, plus the cost of implementing their circles, prompted many firms to phase out their QC programs. Rather than throw the baby out with the bath water, though, firms can take steps to make their QC programs more effective.

Toward More Effective Quality Circles In general, instituting quality circles without making corresponding changes in management styles and company culture is futile. For example, one research study found that when asked how they liked their quality circle program, participants reportedly used words such as "nuisance," "a joke," and "very unproductive" to describe circle meetings. Participants claimed there were no ideas generated during the sessions, and that the sessions themselves were dull and boring. Most indicated feeling a lack of emotional involvement and claimed they really didn't understand what they were to do or accomplish with the quality circles. An investigation led to the conclusion that the organization's underlying culture was just not conducive to a participative quality circle program.[29]

In a program like this, the bottom-up participation that management wants to encourage must be fostered by a fundamental change in philosophy from top management on down. In other words, managers must make it clear to everyone that they will listen to and act on employees' input, create trust and confidence, and show in concrete ways that they mean what they say about wanting employee input.

The organization mentioned above began to alter its culture by changing some policies that contradicted such a philosophy. For example, the time clock was eliminated. An interdepartmental employee quality circle committee was instituted. This committee in turn established a two-way dialogue between management and workers through regularly scheduled meetings. The basic theme of these meetings was company profitability for survival; it was explained repeatedly that such profitability was the surest route to job security.

As a result of their experience, the consultants to this project suggest the following guidelines for introducing a QC program:

1. Be frank and open with the chief executive officer about the organization's current state of management and employee attitudes.
2. Allow the CEO and senior officials to be models for change in implementing constructive ideas.
3. If possible, make the program voluntary.
4. In the beginning, provide group members with solvable problems. Be prepared to change structures, policies, and procedures. Keep objectives simple.
5. Emphasize that these are not complaint sessions.
6. Communicate and educate every person in the organization about the program. Emphasize that group members need support.
7. Establish a climate of care and feedback.
8. Involve first-line supervisors and make them leaders of the groups whenever possible.
9. Provide additional training to complement quality circle training. Introduce the circles as an ongoing process of good supervision to the supervisors themselves.[30]

Quality Management Programs

Introduction

The Total Quality Management (TQM) movement was started in Japan by Edwards Deming, and is based on the fourteen points shown in **Table 10.1**. The cornerstone of TQM is continuous quality improvement, achieved through teams of empowered, customer-focussed workers solving problems. Many consider TQM to be in serious trouble in Canada, the United States, and Europe. Management consultants McKinsey & Co. estimate that lack of results leads to the demise of two-thirds of TQM programs in their first two years of operation.[31] One expert places TQM initiatives in the U.S. up to ten years behind Japan's, with Canada's slightly behind those in the U.S. Still further behind are the European countries, particularly France and Germany.[32]

TABLE 10.1 Deming's 14 Points of Quality Management

1. Create and publish to all employees a statement of the aims and purposes of the company or other organization. The management must demonstrate constantly their commitment to this statement.
2. Learn the new philosophy, top management, and everybody.
3. Understand the purpose of inspection, for improvement of processes and reduction of cost.
4. End the practice of awarding business based on the price tag alone.
5. Improve constantly and forever the system of production and service.
6. Institute training.
7. Teach and institute leadership.
8. Drive out fear. Create trust. Create a climate for innovation.
9. Optimize toward the aims and purposes of the company the efforts of teams, groups, and staff areas.
10. Eliminate exhortations for the work force.
11a. Eliminate numerical quotas for production. Instead, learn and institute methods for improvement.
11b. Eliminate Management by Objective. Instead, learn the capabilities of processes, and how to improve them.
12. Remove barriers that rob people of pride of workmanship.
13. Encourage education and self-improvement for everyone.
14. Take action to accomplish the transformation.

Source: Reprinted from *Out of the Crisis* by W. Edwards Deming by permission of MIT and the W. Edwards Deming Institute. Published by MIT, Center for Advanced Educational Services, Cambridge, MA 02139. Copyright 1986 by The W. Edwards Deming Institute.

In general, when North American and European companies started to implement TQM in the early 1980s, they assumed they could simply copy the Japanese model. This assumption proved to be unrealistic—TQM is not a "quick fix." However, Deming's concept of quality management is still seen as a key success factor for Canadian companies as they enter the 21st century.

In fact, the most successful quality programs aren't run in isolation but are part of comprehensive, companywide quality improvement programs. Each team's quality improvement projects are conducted within company-wide plans and quality targets and goals; efforts are made to ensure the full support of middle managers; extensive training opportunities are provided; and the culture and reward systems are geared to encouraging employee involvement. Comprehensive quality improvement programs like this go by many names including total quality management (TQM), quality improvement process (QIP), and total quality control (TQC).[33] Regardless of labels, quality management involves a total corporate focus on meeting and often exceeding customers' expectations and significantly reducing the cost resulting from poor quality by shaping a new management system and corporate culture.[34,35]

Many believe that the missing component in quality management outside Japan is effective communication.[36] Companies must build interpersonal communication skills in their management teams that support the problem solving required to achieve quality improvements. Further, commitment by employees to quality initiatives will suffer without visible senior and middle management support. Weston Foods made a commitment to breaking the information barrier between management and shop floor which, over a five year period, resulted in significant improvements in five of Weston's seven operating companies.[37]

Many Canadian companies are now embarking on quality management programs for the second or third time because they believe it is imperative for future

Information Technology and HR
Attitude Surveys

Successful quality management and reengineering initiatives result in improved work flow, better cooperation between departments, and increased supervisory fairness. Many firms rely on attitude surveys to assess the effect of such changes on employee job satisfaction.

Most companies are aware of the need for employee anonymity, the impact of both the design of the questions and their sequence, and the importance of effective communication, including knowing the purpose of the survey before it's conducted and getting feedback to the employees after it's completed. Computerization of surveys can provide anonymity, if there is no audit trail to the user, especially for short answers that are entered rather than written or typed on an identifiable machine.

Survey software packages are available that generate questions for a number of standard topics and can be customized by modifying existing questions or by adding questions. If the survey is computerized, then reports can be generated with ease to provide snapshots of a given period of time, trend analyses, and breakdowns according to various demographics. The firm may be interested in responses by age, sex, job categories, departments, divisions, functions, or geography.

The survey can be conducted by placing microcomputers in several locations convenient for employee use. Employees are advised where the computers will be, for how long, and when the data will be collected (for instance, daily at 5 P.M. for three weeks). The screen should not be viewable by supervisors or passersby. While there may be some risk that employees will take the survey more than once, there are comparable risks with other methods. (For example, who completes the survey mailed to the employee's home?)

Managers may be interested in knowing how they are perceived by their peers and employees. Packages are available that can be customized, which allow the manager to complete a self-assessment tool used to compare self-perceptions to the anonymous opinions of others. This comparison may assist in the development of a more effective manager.

Employees who are leaving the company are often asked their opinions during a formal or informal exit interview. Concerned about future references, employees often state innocuous reasons for leaving, ones known to be acceptable to the company. However, if the exiting employees could respond to computer questions (such as, "If you could change some aspect of supervision, what would it be?" "If you could change some aspect of our benefits, what would it be?") and be assured that answers would not be looked at until several people had responded, more helpful information might be learned.◆

---

success.[38] For example, Cadet Uniform Services in Toronto first introduced TQM in 1982. Although it produced some savings, it didn't really take hold because it was treated as a management program rather than one involving all employees. A few years later, Cadet tried again and included all managers and supervisors, as well as educating all line workers (even translating training literature into six languages) to get them hooked on quality management. Quality improvement teams were set up in each plant. Although the company spent $500 000 over 10 years on quality-related education, the program has resulted in a 99 percent business retention rate due to extremely high customer satisfaction.[39]

Quality Awards Several major awards recognize companies that institute highly effective quality improvement programs. The Deming Prize, named after Dr. W. Edwards Deming and awarded by the Union of Japanese Scientists and Engineers, was the first such award. Miami-based Florida Power & Light Company (FPL),

Florida's largest utility, was the first company outside Japan to win the Deming Prize. Awarded annually (and since 1986 outside Japan), the prize recognizes outstanding achievement in quality control management. In 1987, the U.S. Congress established the Malcolm Baldrige National Quality Award to promote quality awareness, recognize quality achievements of U.S. companies, and publicize successful quality strategies.[40] Firms winning the Baldrige Award have included Cadillac Motor Car Division, Federal Express Corp., and Motorola, Inc.

In Canada, the National Quality Institute (NQI) sponsors the Canada Awards for Excellence, which rewards quality in seven sectors—large manufacturing, small/medium manufacturing, large service, small/medium service, education, government, and health care. The NQI is an independent, not-for-profit organization, which was established in 1992, dedicated to making Canadian companies more competitive in the global marketplace. The quality awards recognize and reward organizations showing outstanding performance based on a comprehensive quality framework. The criteria are leadership, planning, customer focus, people focus, process management, supplier focus, and organizational performance. A team of examiners visits the site of each applicant to verify the information provided. In addition, a random selection of external suppliers and customers of short-listed organizations are contacted.[41]

Features of Two Award-Winning Quality Programs In 1997, the Canada Awards for Excellence went to Brock Telecom Limited of Brockville, Ontario (for the large manufacturing category), and the Orillia Soldiers' Memorial Hospital in Orillia, Ontario (in the health care category).

Brock Telecom Brock Telecom Limited, a wholly owned subsidiary of Northern Telecom, manufactures telecommunications products.[42] Brock Telecom's commitment to quality began in 1987 when its Quality Improvement Program (QIP) was established. Quality initiatives are evident throughout the organization. One of the principles in the company's mission statement is "Excellence in Product and Process Quality." In addition, the seven factors they consider to be critical to their success include "Quality Excellence." Long term strategies for accomplishing the mission include "ensur[ing] human resources are prepared, capable, and empowered to improve and adapt".

Members of Brock Telecom's Leadership Team (directors of all business units and the general manager) demonstrate commitment to quality through participation in formal quality systems, as well as quarterly and annual quality program reviews. The Quality Improvement Team, chaired by a member of the Leadership Team, is responsible for managing and driving quality improvement initiatives. A cornerstone of the QIP is quality education, which provides all employees with quality improvement tools such as Pareto analysis, flowcharting, etc. Members of the Leadership Team are involved in the delivery of quality education.

A 1997 employee survey showed that 91 percent felt that the Brock Telecom was committed to quality improvement; 90 percent believed that process and quality were continually improving to meet customer needs; and 70 percent felt they had a good understanding of the QIP. These high levels of employee awareness are fostered by a number of communication activities, including regular all-employee sessions (six to ten per year), an employee newsletter, focus group sessions, and daily updates presented on TV monitors. Each business unit within the company holds weekly quality meetings. An annual quality review is also conducted, during which results are measured against established targets.

Employee involvement in quality includes participation at all levels, including the QIP steering committee and continuous improvement teams. Seventy percent

www.csa.ca
Canadian Standards Association

www.qcbinc.com
Quality Certification Bureau

of employee suggestions were implemented in 1996, and, together with other employee-driven quality initiatives, produced savings of $3 million that year. The quality recognition program is another principal component of QIP. Peer nominations are made of individuals or teams who exemplify a core value.

The NQI examiners report said that "Brock Telecom recognizes people as being its most valuable resource. . . . A work environment has been created in which there is mutual trust and respect for all individuals. . . . Brock Telecom has created a culture in which responsibility for quality is felt by each and every employee and this strong commitment to quality has generated outstanding results."[43]

Orillia Soldiers' Memorial Hospital (OSMH)   OSMH began formal quality practices in 1992 when it implemented a continuous quality improvement program.[44] The atmosphere of high quality care began with visionary leadership. The Executive Director and the senior management team held bi-weekly reviews of a few key result areas, including customer satisfaction, service quality, and resource management. The senior management team also played an active role in coaching and sponsoring cross-functional quality improvement teams. Other staff developed quality improvement plans for individualized hospital services, participated in self-managed teams, and researched the best practices in the hospital sector.

Over the past several years, 70 new programs and services have been developed in response to community needs. These have been based on information from focus groups and surveys, as well as from patients and their families who serve on advisory councils. Any patient complaint is resolved within four days, and a member of the management team follows up by phone or letter. The success of quality improvement efforts is largely due to staff commitment to patients and to long-term success. Staff participate in the budgeting process and in workflow decisions. Staff ideas and suggestions resulted in half of the $1 million reduction in the hospital's 1996 budget. Quality has changed the organization due to increased communication between departments and a higher degree of respect and trust.

The NQI examiners commented that the OSMH "has taken patient care and concern for the community to a higher level through quality. Staff are completely committed to patients' well-being and feel a tremendous sense of pride in their work. This hospital is a true leader from which both private and public sector organizations can learn a great deal."[45]

Human Resources Management and the Quality Improvement Effort

Many HRM actions can help to ensure a more effective total quality program. Some HRM guidelines based on the experience of award-winning companies are as follows:

- Make sure all teams ensure their efforts are consistent with the firm's goals.
- Do not institute quality circles as separate, parallel organization structures. Simply trying to superimpose quality circles outside the normal chain of command elicits resistance from supervisors, many of whom may make comments like "I don't know what these people are doing—they're not helping me do my job."[46] The teams should, to the greatest extent possible, be composed of natural work units.
- Do not treat the quality improvement program as if it has an end. It is important to emphasize that a quality improvement program that is successful is really a systematic way of doing business, one that has no end.
- Recognize that training is essential. Quality improvement is successful largely because training continually upgrades the problem analysis and statistics skills of even first-line employees. This training is crucial both to

provide the required analytical skills and also to emphasize the firm's commitment to the program.

- Give employees the skills they need to analyze and solve problems; then get them to analyze and solve the problem, and follow up on their suggestions. Whether or not the company achieves its quality goals is, although very important, almost secondary. The new culture that emerges is at the heart of the program.

- Do not focus exclusively on "boosting productivity" or assume that emphasizing quality means that productivity will necessarily fall. In fact, many companies have found that as quality rises, so does productivity.

- Prioritize the organization's needs. It is important to work on only a few needs at once so as not to dilute resources.

- Recognize effort and encourage employees. A main benefit of this type of program is the sense of satisfaction it can foster in employees. This requires encouraging employees to identify and devise countermeasures against problems, and giving them the tools and leeway required to get this job done.

- Reward individual and team efforts in a concrete manner, not necessarily just with money but with rewards like merchandise or pins.

- Remember that the first steps need to be taken by top management: "From the board of directors to every supervisor, management must adopt the principles and language of quality, follow the processes, set examples and guide others. A substantial commitment is necessary for employee education, and for awareness and recognition programs. These programs require reallocation of budgets and personnel, and will take time to produce results but will be worth it."[47]

The HR Department's Role in Quality Awards   HR development and management play a central role in meeting the criteria used for evaluating quality award applicants. Important areas that are evaluated include senior executive leadership (top management's commitment to quality); information and analysis (an adequate system for collecting statistical data on matters such as product or service quality); and strategic quality planning (the adequacy of the firm's planning process and how key quality requirements are integrated into the firm's overall business planning process). Also included are management of quality (for example, rather than viewing design, production, and sales as separate entities, top firms usually recognize the integrated nature of their work so that the departments work together); quality and operational results (to show the firm is achieving continuous improvement in critical operational areas, such as in service quality levels); and customer focus and satisfaction (wherein the examiners look for objective, validated data regarding the applicant's success in satisfying the customer).

Human resources development and management are also critical factors affecting the firm's ability to achieve the full potential of employees in pursuing the firm's quality and performance objectives. The firm's efforts to build and maintain an environment and culture for quality excellence, one conducive to full participation and personal and organizational growth are of great importance.[48]

In practical terms, the extent to which HR management and organizational behaviour techniques (such as enrichment, empowerment, training, and career development) are used to fully tap each employee's potential is very important. For example, employees should be trained to use problem-solving tools and group decision-making skills. The teams and employees should also have enriched and empowered jobs.

www.mgmt14k.com
ISO 14000

www.oceta.on.ca
Ontario Centre for
Environmental Technical
Advancement

HRM and ISO 9000/ISO 14000   HRM practices are also an integral part of companies' efforts to achieve ISO 9000 and ISO 14000 certification. ISO 9000 is the International Organization for Standardization's standard of quality management

TABLE 10.2 ISO 9000 and ISO 14000 Certification Standards

ISO 9001: Quality standards for *design, development, installation, and servicing*; to be used when a supplier's capability to design and supply conforming product needs to be demonstrated. The standard is applicable in situations where design is required and the product requirements are stated principally in performance terms.

ISO 9002: Quality standards for *production, installing, and servicing*; to be used when a supplier's capability to supply conforming product to an established design needs to be demonstrated. The standard is applicable in situations when the specified requirements for a product are stated in terms of an established design or specification and confidence in product conformance can be attained by adequate demonstration of a supplier's capabilities in production, installation, and servicing.

ISO 9003: Quality standards for *final inspection and testing*; to be used when a supplier's capability to detect and control the disposition of any product non-conformity during final inspection and testing needs to be demonstrated. The standard is applicable in situations where the conformance of product to specified requirements can be shown with adequate confidence providing that suppliers' capabilities for inspection and testing conducted on finished product can be satisfactorily demonstrated.

ISO 9000 Series Guidelines:

* ISO 9000-1, 9000-2, 9000-3, 9000-4 provide guidelines for selection and use of the above standards; generic guidelines for the application of the above for suppliers, purchasers, subcontractors, and auditors; guidelines for the application of 9001 for development, supply, and maintenance of software; and guidelines for dependability program management.

* ISO 9004-1, 9004-2, 9004-3, 9004-4, 10005, 10006, 10007 provide guidelines for use in the development and implementation of a comprehensive and effective in-house quality system, with a view to ensuring customer confidence.

ISO 14001: Standards for *environmental management systems* (EMS); to enable an organization to formulate policy and objectives, taking into account legislative requirements and information about significant environmental impacts. The standard applies to environmental aspects that the organization can control and over which it can be expected to have an influence. The standard does not specify environmental performance criteria.

ISO 14000 Series Guidelines:

* ISO 14004 provides guidelines on the development and implementation of EMS and coordination with other management systems. The guidelines are applicable to all organizations interested in developing, implementing, and improving an EMS.

* ISO 14010, 14011, 14012 provide guidelines for environmental auditing (general principles, audit procedures, and qualification criteria for environmental auditors).

Source: The titles and scopes of the ISO 9000 and ISO 14000 series of standards are reproduced with the permission of the Standards Council of Canada (SCC) on behalf of the International Organization for Standardization (ISO). The full text standards may be obtained from the Global Info Centre Canada, 240 Catherine Street, Suite 305, Ottawa, Ontario K2P 2G8.

and quality assurance. ISO 14000 is the standard for environmental management.[49] **Table 10.2** provides the details of each level of certification. In Canada, the National Quality Institute is the body responsible for certifying auditors for ISO certification. Certification usually requires a five-step process: ISO assessment (reviewing the company's quality systems and procedures); quality assurance and policy manual preparation (compiling the specific quality-oriented techniques and policies to be followed); training of employees; documentation of work instructions (documenting each new work procedure, for instance); and registration audit (having the quality system reviewed by a special "registrar" who audits the company's quality efforts).

The HR department plays an important role in providing ongoing support to department managers throughout the firm in the preparation for and management of ISO certification, particularly documentation and training.[50] For example, in one instance:

> Perhaps the most serious problem was that even though a number of people were doing excellent work, they were simply unaware of the physical procedures they were following. Informal on-the-job training that was prevalent in the division was the culprit.[51]

Training for ISO 9000 and ISO 14000 typically covers several things. Specifically, it covers the quality vocabulary associated with the standard, the requirements of each section of the standard, and the training systems quality assurance manuals.[52]

The time commitment and costs involved in obtaining ISO certification can be a burden for small businesses. However, some small businesses are joining together with others to share costs. Some industry and professional associations provide assistance in this regard.[53]

Creating Self-Directed Teams

The Nature of Self-Directed Teams

In the 1950s, psychologist Rensis Likert formulated what would become the classic explanation of cohesive work teams for later generations of organizational experts.[54] First, he said that leadership and other processes of the organization should ensure that each employee will view the experience as one that builds and maintains his or her sense of personal worth and importance.[55] Furthermore, said Likert,

Individuals in most work teams, such as this one at a paper mill, have a high commitment to the group and its work goals, due in part to their shared experiences.

> The most important source of satisfaction for this desire is the response we get from the people we are close to, in whom we are interested, and whose approval and support we are eager to have. The face-to-face groups with whom we spend the bulk of our time are, consequently, the most important to us. [Therefore,] management will make full use of the potential capacities of its human resources only when each person in an organization is a member of one or more effectively functioning work groups that have a high degree of group loyalty.[56]

From a practical point of view, Likert might have added, employees probably tend to develop their first and perhaps most intense commitment to the people in their work groups and to their group's norms and ideals. To many employees the company itself—what it is, where it's going, what its values are—is often little more than an abstraction. But the people with whom they work everyday—the door trim team at Toyota, the menswear group at the Eaton's store, the securities group at Midland Walwyn—are real and worthy of their commitment. They don't want to let their teammates down.

For many firms the ideal situation, as Likert saw, is to organize work around small close-knit teams whose goals are high and whose aims are the same as the firm's. This is what more and more Canadian firms are doing, firms such as Shell Canada, Brock Telecom, 3M Canada, and Norcen Energy Resources Ltd. They and others like them are increasingly organizing the work around small self-contained teams, which are variously labeled self-managed teams, high-performance teams, autonomous work groups or, simply, superteams.[57] Whatever they're called, **self-directed teams** have much in common. Each team generally performs natural sets of interdependent tasks, such as all the steps needed to assemble a car door. They all use consensus decision making to choose their own team members, solve job-related problems, design their own jobs, and schedule their own break time. And their jobs are always enriched in that they do many of the jobs formerly accomplished by supervisors, such as dealing with vendors and monitoring quality. Self-directed teams are also highly trained to solve problems, design jobs, interview candidates, and understand financial reports. They are, therefore, generally *empowered:* They have the training and ability as well as the broad authority to get their jobs done.

> **self-directed teams**
> Highly trained work groups that use consensus decision making and broad authority to self-direct their activities.

A 1994 Conference Board of Canada survey of 109 Canadian organizations using teams found that despite statements indicating a growing reliance on groups or teams, the companies actually exhibited only limited acceptance of management practices essential for optimal team performance.[58] Only one percent of the companies surveyed had eliminated individual merit ratings. None had achieved company-wide acceptance of a change from traditional individual performance appraisal to continuous feedback from the supervisor and many other sources.

Successful team-based organizations have changed from the North American style, individual-based culture to one oriented around groups. To do so involves changing the corporate mindset to adopt beliefs and values that are very different from those held in the past. Communication and collaboration between managers and employees is considered essential, as is executive-level commitment and employee involvement. Surface commitment and lack of cooperation among senior managers are roadblocks to change. Changes in processes, such as reward systems and performance appraisal, signal a commitment to long-term change. Survey respondents indicated that recognition was their preferred form of team reward.

Self-Directed Teams in Action

Consider several examples. At 3M Canada's manufacturing plant in Brockville, Ontario, teams of six to eight workers handle quality control, logistics, scheduling, and shipping and receiving. Work teams also conduct the entire recruitment process, from initial interviews to various forms of testing. Test results are assessed for problem solving and interactive skills to see if the applicant can work as part of a team. A dual focus on groups and creativity is crucial, and team members are expected to continuously learn new skills and to innovate. Every 3M employee must take courses in risk, handling change, and taking responsibility for his or her job. The Brockville plant is now the model for 3M plants throughout the world.[59]

In the early 1990s, Campbell Canada was performing poorly and its future was at stake. Nine Canadian plants had been sold or closed, leaving only two across the country. The company undertook to transform the way workers related to their jobs, and by 1995 the entire Toronto plant had converted to self-managed teams. The following year, total output more than doubled, production costs dropped by just over 30 percent, and productivity went up 37 percent. These results led the U.S. parent company to invest $45 million to modernize production in the Toronto plant. Self-managed teams are considered to have played a crucial role in the turnaround.[60]

In 1993, Shell Canada organized its entire workforce in its new lubricants plant in Brockville, Ontario as self-managing teams responsible for discipline, absenteeism, vacation planning, and training schedules. There are no traditional supervisors, and senior employees are called coordinators. Team members are hired only after completing an elaborate screening process testing technical skills, ability, willingness to learn, and aptitude for teamwork. Forty-six production workers from other plants applied for the new jobs, but only twenty were found to be suitable for the new plant. [61]

At Norcen Energy Resources Ltd. in Calgary, Alberta, a shift from traditional functional departments to cross-functional teams occurred in 1994. The change originated from senior management's vision of an effective culture, but was not undertaken until a process of consultation with employees had been completed. Every Norcen employee is on a team, and there are no managers beneath the VP level. For example, a team composed of geologists, geophysicists, and engineers will focus on one exploration site. Each team elects a leader, and some teams have decided to rotate the leadership role. Team leaders in staff areas such as accounting play an intermediary/liaison role between the team and their VP. Human resources staff provided team training through 1995, using custom-designed workshops covering common purpose, different work styles, feedback skills, and conflict resolution. Teams are responsible for hiring, discipline, and dismissal of their members, but not compensation, as there is a standardized plan across the company. HR department staff now provide ongoing customized consultative assistance to teams. The change was not made without some healthy skepticism, but has been a positive experience overall. [62]

Building Employee Commitment

Empowering Work Teams

Employees tend to be committed to employers who help them actualize at work—in other words, to develop and use their skills and gifts to the maximum. Empowering their work teams and enriching their jobs thus helps employers like Brock Telecom win their employees' commitment.

The Initial Idea

In 1987, the Leadership Team at Brock Telecom realized that the world of manufacturing was rapidly changing and in order to remain competitive, refinements to the company structure and processes would be required. As a result, a quality management program (based on the fourteen-step Crosby total quality management model) was initiated. This represented the beginning of a new culture for Brock Telecom. [1]

The Importance of Teamwork

As part of the quality program, all employees were trained in the quality management process. This provided the employees with the framework and terminology necessary to solve problems from a common level of understanding. It also provided for the natural formation of quality improvement teams. This evolution towards team dynamics, along with effective and open communication, created an atmosphere for continuous improvement, and also increased employee and customer satisfaction.

Milestones

The path toward employee involvement included many milestones, such as the introduction in 1988 of the MRPII system—a fully integrated financial and manufacturing computer system. This system provided the foundation for Brock Telecom to become a first-class manufacturing facility. New levels of trust began to develop between upper management and employees as a result of more open communication. The "open-door" policy at Brock Telecom was rejuvenated and information was shared by all levels. This involved the inclusion in 1989 of union representation at human resources planning meetings and the introduction of regular employee sessions and weekly staff meetings.

The next step in the journey came with the realization in 1992 that some employees lacked the skills necessary to perform their jobs effectively. An in-house training centre was developed to address this issue. The training centre now offers a full range of professional development and job skills training. Every employee has the opportunity to provide input regarding the courses being offered, and in several cases employee teams have been involved in the development and delivery of the curriculum.

Further progress was made through a reengineering initiative in 1994 that eliminated traditional functional organizational barriers. By reorganizing into customer-focussed business units, employee teams were given ownership of complete processes. This resulted in an increased understanding of overall business operations and better customer service. Employees have also been given the opportunity to expand their skills base and business knowledge to complement their new levels of responsibility and subsequently have evolved into cross-trained process teams.

Today

Brock Telecom is characterized by employees who are highly educated and skilled. Between the years 1992 and 1995, for example, Brock Telecom hired over 500 employees, all of whom had post-secondary diplomas or degrees. This reinforces the importance of the common thread that can be seen throughout Brock Telecom's employee involvement history: to run an effective company, management must focus on the needs and capabilities of employees and empower them to work together to improve the business. Empowering employee teams to be directly involved with day-to-day business decisions and operations provides all employees with increased levels of autonomy, while at the same time reducing management overhead. Consequently, Brock Telecom has a direct/indirect labour ratio (the number of production workers compared to the number of support staff) which approaches best-in-class standards. Programs such as the Quality Council, Continuous Improvement, Corrective Action, Cost of Quality, and Recognition are the responsibility of teams comprised of employees from all levels of the organization. In other words, important company initiatives are no longer the sole responsibility of those in upper management, but are the shared responsibility of all employees.

The Next Steps

The core value "Our People Are Our Strength" remains evident as Brock Telecom continues along the employee involvement path. The vision for the future at Brock Telecom is to ensure that all employees continue to receive the training necessary to perform and contribute at the highest possible levels in order to guide, influence, and improve operations.

1. This section based on personal communication from Megan Taylor, Brock Telecom, November 14, 1997.

Making Self-Directed Teams More Effective

There are several factors that contribute to successfully organizing self-directed teams. These include forming a commitment to the principle of teamwork, steeping employees in teamwork terminology and techniques, and fostering employee commitment by enriching the work and empowering the workers.

Three other teamwork success factors deserve emphasis. First, as summarized in **Table 10.3**, insufficient training is consistently listed as the single biggest barrier to effective self-directed teams. *Effective training* usually emphasizes problem solving and communication skills. For example, 83 percent of responding companies with team training teach problem-solving skills. There is also an emphasis on training team members to communicate more effectively and to hold more productive meetings.[63]

Second, *communication* between top management and the teams should be free flowing so the teams can do their jobs. As one study of team-based programs concluded, "These results support the proposition… that employees believe that greater access to information about corporate operations is critical if they are to improve their effectiveness in decision making."[64]

Making self-directed teams more effective also generally requires that the firm's pay plans be refocused around *small-group incentives.*[65] A small-group incentive plan may be defined as "…. a pay method designed to deliver a uniform award, based on the achievement of a single or multiple predetermined goal(s) to all members of a work group who share responsibility for work process and output."[66]

TABLE 10.3 Developing Self-Directed Teams

BARRIERS TO SELF-DIRECTED TEAMS

Barriers	Percentage of Respondents That Mentioned Each
Insufficient training	54
Supervisor resistance	47
Incompatible systems	47
Lack of planning (implementation was too fast)	40
Lack of management support	31
Lack of union support	24

The results are from a 1990 survey by DDI, AQP, and *Industry Week.*

TYPES OF TEAM TRAINING

Type of Training	Percentage of Responding Companies That Offer Each
Problem solving	83
Meeting skills	65
Communication skills	62
Handling conflict	61
SDT (self-directed teams) roles and responsibilities	58
Quality tools and concepts	56
Evaluating team performance	39
Work flow and process analysis	36
Selecting team members	35
Presentation skills	35
Influencing others	29
Budgeting	14

The results are from a 1990 survey by DDI, AQP, and *Industry Week.*

Source: Richard Wellins and Jill George, "The Key to Self-directed Teams," *Training and Development Journal* (April 1991), p. 29.

Global HRM

Extending Participative Decision Making Abroad

While participative self-directed teams may be effective for a company in Canada or the United States, the firm can't necessarily export the approach overseas. There are deep and often irreconcilable cross-cultural differences in values and attitudes from country to country, so that management techniques that work in one country may actually backfire in another.

The findings of one recent study illustrate the problem very well.[1] The study examined how one North American multinational manufacturing company tried to implement participative decision making in its European subsidiaries, and how managers and employees in three European countries reacted to the company's efforts. Specifically, the study sought to ascertain how North American managers differ from their European counterparts regarding such issues as:

- what they think the ideal level of participation should be for their employees
- how they view the benefits of increased participation
- how much participation they feel their employees actually want
- how much participation they think their employees actually have.

The company was hoping to implement participative decision-making programs in Europe that were similar to ones that had been successful in North American, but it got unexpected reactions from European managers and employees. For example, most Dutch managers felt that the prepackaged nature of North American efforts to improve participation by instituting work teams could actually hurt performance and motivation because the teams failed to take individual differences into account. Several Dutch managers stated that the type of programmatic, formalized efforts favoured by the North American parent would not allow managers to encourage participation in ways and at a pace that was consistent with their own styles or the needs of their employees.[2]

British managers had similar reservations about implementing the "North American approach" to team-based participative management. Specifically, they were concerned that the program ignored individual differences in managerial styles and employee abilities. The British managers seemed threatened by the decision-making authority the new work teams would have.

Interestingly, most of the Spanish managers endorsed the idea of self-directed work teams and said they thought it could work in the Spanish plant. But the Spanish managers' stated beliefs were actually somewhat misleading. In fact, Spanish managers reported lower levels of participation among employees than did their Dutch and North American counterparts. In other words, the actual participation was lower—not higher—in the Spanish plants than elsewhere in Europe, although the managers were relatively enthusiastic about participative management.

Overall, the results showed that North American managers have different values and perspectives on employee participation than their counterparts in Britain, the Netherlands, and Spain. They also illustrated some of the problems that can occur from a human resources perspective when a company attempts to push North American values toward participation in European subsidiaries. The company's efforts may be perceived by European managers as being heavy-handed and out of touch with local values.[3] As a result, even when the managers verbally support the parent's efforts, what they actually do may be quite different from what they agreed to. Therefore, before exporting an HR program like self-directed work teams, HR managers should try to accomplish three basic goals:[4]

1. If appropriate, build trust by communicating to local managers that previous corporate HR efforts may have reflected culturally specific beliefs that do not always fit local needs, and that the parent company is committed to developing synergistic policies.

2. Become more aware of the local cultural traditions that may affect attitudes toward participation in decision making.

3. Develop a working partnership with local HR executives to create blended strategies for employee participation that fit the local culture, yet offer something of value to the corporation as a whole. In effect, this will require joint decision making between North American HR executives and their foreign counterparts.◆

1. This is based on Dean McFarlin, Paul Sweeney, and John Cotton, "Attitudes Toward Employee Participation in Decision-making: A Comparison of European and American Managers in a United States Multinational Company," *Human Resource Management* 31, no. 4 (Winter 1992), pp. 363–83.
2. McFarlin et al., "Attitudes Toward Employee Participation," p. 371.
3. McFarlin et al., "Attitudes Toward Employee Participation," p. 378.
4. These are quoted in McFarlin et al., "Attitudes Toward Employee Participation," p. 379.

Business Process Reengineering

What is *reengineering*?

Michael Hammer and James Champy, the fathers of reengineering, define it as "The fundamental rethinking and radical redesign of business processes to achieve dramatic improvements in critical, contemporary measures of performance, such as cost, quality, service, and speed."[67] One of business process reengineering's (BPR) basic assumptions is that the traditional way of organizing departments and processes around very specialized tasks is inherently duplicative, wasteful, and unresponsive to the firm's customers. In reengineering a company and its departments and processes, the reengineers, therefore, need to ask themselves: "Why do we do what we do?" and "Why do we do it the way we do?"

An Example Crossley Carpet Mills Ltd. of Truro, Nova Scotia faced serious problems as free trade and currency fluctuations resulted in U.S. carpet makers increasing their share of the Canadian market from 8.1 percent in 1988 to 41.3 percent in 1991. The company had always emphasized the quality of their carpets, and thus decided to adopt a new strategy focusing on a specialized market niche of high end commercial carpets. Crossley decided to offer woven carpet designs developed in accordance with specific requirements of customers such as contractors and institutions. This represented a philosophical change in the way the company did business—away from increasing its scale of production to a focus on the needs of customers.

Crossley consolidated its ordering and shipping process in Nova Scotia, which reduced delays. This move also reduced overhead, since branch sales offices were closed and sales people began working out of virtual offices in their cars and homes. The company also shortened production runs and moved to a flexible manufacturing operation, which required a radical shift in thinking for many of the employees. Crossley had built a uniquely skilled and committed workforce over the years, which enabled employees to adapt relatively easily to this change.[68]

The Crossley Carpet example illustrates some of the basic characteristics of business process reengineering. In business process reengineering, *workers make more decisions* because large scale manufacturing is replaced by flexible custom-made production. Related to this, *checks and controls are reduced,* and instead there's more emphasis on carefully selecting and training highly-skilled workers. Reengineered processes also tend to take a *case manager approach* to dealing with customers, in that each customer ends up with a single point of contact when checking on the status of an order or request.[69]

The HR Department's Role in Reengineering Processes

In their quest to focus on reorganizing work and eliminating unneeded, duplicative operations, many companies bent on reengineering initially neglected to simultaneously institute new HR practices; they subsequently failed to win the commitment of their managers and employees to their new reengineered jobs.[70] Senior managers now understand that the HR department plays a crucial role in successfully implementing reengineering. Following are some aspects of the HR department's role.

The HR Department's Role in Building Commitment to Reengineering Implementing reengineering successfully means winning employee commitment. As one expert says, "[Reengineering is] about an ongoing, never-ending commitment to doing things better."[71] Even the most brilliant reorganizations and organizational changes can be undermined by recalcitrant employees. Therefore, one key to reengineering is winning people's commitment to the changes and what those changes mean. HR departments, as we've seen, play a big role in winning such commitment through HR practices like value-based hiring, building a sense of community, and installing effective two-way communications practices.

The HR Department's Role in Team Building Business process reengineering generally results in reorganizing the work force from functional departments to process-oriented teams, such as teams of employees working together to process credit requests. As explained in this chapter, the HR department plays a central role in making self-directed teams more effective. For instance, HR department staff provide the required training and ensure that communication between top management and the teams remains open and freely flowing.

The HR Department's Role in Changing the Nature of the Work With reengineering, jobs generally change from specialized tasks to multidimensional generalist work. Not only is each worker usually responsible for a broader, more enriched job, but process team members "... share joint responsibility with their team members for performing the whole process, not just a small piece of it."[72] What this means is that each worker needs to be capable of using a much broader range of skills from day to day; HR department staff play a key role in helping managers to hire high-potential employees and provide them with the training and development they require.

The HR Department's Role in Moving from Controlled to Empowered Jobs People working in a reengineered process are of necessity empowered to perform a broader set of tasks with relatively little supervision.[73] This means that companies that reengineer must use value-based hiring.[74] As two experts put it,

> It is no longer enough merely to look at prospective employees' education, training, and skills; their character *becomes an issue as well. Are they self-starting? Do they have self-discipline? Are they motivated to do what it takes to please a customer?*[75]

The HR Department's Role in Moving from Training to Education Hammer and Champy point out that in companies that reengineer, the emphasis necessarily shifts from training to education. In other words, it's no longer enough to just give employees training that shows them "how" to do the job—such as how to turn the bolt on the left front fender. Instead the new generalist team members need *education:* They need to increase their insight and understanding of how to analyze and solve problems and to understand not just the "how" of the job, but the "why" of it.[76]

The HR Department's Role in Shifting Focus from Activities to Results Reengineering creates work that is measured in terms of its *results*—such as serving customers in a timely manner—rather than in terms of completing an *activity* like taking calls or checking credit. This means that HR department staff need to reevaluate the compensation system. In particular, the reward system should not pay people based just on seniority or "... because another year has passed;"[77] instead, contribution, performance, and results should be the primary bases for determining compensation.[78]

Chapter Review

Summary

1. *Flextime* is a plan whereby employees' flexible workdays are built around a core of midday hours, such as 10 A.M. to 3 P.M. Such plans seem to improve employee attitudes and morale, increase production, and decrease tardiness; however, unavailability of key people at certain times and the difficulty of scheduling activities like meetings can be problems. Flextime and other flexible work arrangements are aimed in part at tapping employees' needs to be treated as responsible human beings, and to that extent they boost quality of work life.

2. A *quality circle* is a group of five to ten specially trained employees who meet for an hour once a week for the purpose of spotting and solving problems in their work area.

3. Steps in establishing a quality circle program include planning, training, initiating, and operating. Problems to be aware of include: poor attitudes such as, "This is just another program," and "Management pays no attention to our ideas"; agendas outside the circle's expertise; problems that are too difficult to handle; and fear on the part of supervisors that they will lose authority and control.

4. Comprehensive company-wide quality improvement programs like that at Brock Telecom basically aim at improving the customer orientation of a firm by appealing to employees' higher-order needs. A framework of objectives or policies is first laid out based on satisfying customers' needs. Then a comprehensive program of training, incentives, continuous improvement teams, and culture modification is carried out to appeal to employees' sense of responsibility. As at Brock Telecom, it's not just the specific techniques (like communication, or training, or incentives) that ensure high performance; the culture of the firm—its basic shared values and attitudes—is important too.

5. *Self-directed teams* carry out interdependent tasks and use consensus decision making to choose the other team members, solve job-related problems, design their own jobs, schedule their own break times, and do much of their own work planning and review. At firms like Brock Telecom, such teams contribute to building commitment by enriching and empowering employees' jobs.

6. Reengineering is the fundamental rethinking and radical redesign of business processes to achieve dramatic improvements in critical, contemporary measures of performance, such as cost, quality, service, and speed. The HR department contributes to reengineering processes by its effect on: building commitment to reengineering; team building; changing the nature of work; empowering jobs; moving from training to education; and shifting focus from activities to results.

Key Terms

compressed workweek   flexyear   quality circle

flextime   job sharing   self-directed teams

    telecommuting

Discussion Questions and Exercises

1. Explain the pros and cons of flextime and the compressed workweek.
2. Explain the steps involved in operating a quality circle.
3. Working individually or in groups, assume that you are a quality circle and that your task is to identify a problem in your "work area" (classroom) and make recommendations on how to solve it. What aspects of the problem identification, solution, and presentation process seems to contribute to improved personal satisfaction and empowerment, if any? Why?
4. What is ISO 9000/ISO 14000? How can HR management contribute to a firm achieving ISO 9000/ISO 14000 status or winning an award like the Deming Prize or NQI Award?
5. Explain how you would set up a company-wide quality improvement program.
6. What steps would you take to institute self-directed work teams?
7. Define "reengineering." Working individually or in groups, develop a brief example of how you would reengineer a familiar process such as class enrollment at the start of a semester.

Application Exercises

RUNNING CASE: Carter Cleaning Company

The Quality Circle Program

As a recent graduate and a person who keeps up with the business press, Jennifer is familiar with the benefits of programs such as quality circles and quality management.

Jack has actually installed a quality program of sorts at Carter, and it has been in place for about five years. Jack holds employee meetings periodically, but particularly when there is a serious problem in a store—such as very poor-quality work or too many breakdowns—he contacts all the employees in that store and meets with them as soon as the store closes. Hourly employees get extra pay for these meetings, and they actually have been fairly useful in helping Jack to identify several problems. Jennifer is now curious as to whether these employee meetings should be formalized and perhaps a formal quality circle program initiated.

Questions

1. Would you recommend a quality circle program to Jennifer? Why? Why not?
2. What other quality management initiatives might Jennifer undertake?
3. Are new work arrangements such as flextime or compressed workweeks practical at Carter? Why or why not?

CASE INCIDENT: Is the Honeymoon Over for Mazda's North American Plant?

It began in the 1980s with great promise: Mazda Motor Corp. was going to build an assembly plant in North America that would eventually provide thousands of high-paying and secure jobs. By 1990, however, conditions had seriously deteriorated and Mazda's honeymoon with North America seemed to have come to an end. Four top North American managers had quit the company since 1988, and Japanese executives had taken the senior posts. The company was on its fourth director of labour relations since hiring began in 1986. Unionized workers were boycotting Mazda's suggestion box, a cornerstone of Japanese-style management. Workers complained of job stress and increased injuries, and absenteeism was running approximately 10 percent, which was higher than in other Japanese plants in North America. But let's start at the beginning, when Mazda began the task of staffing its new plant.

All job candidates applying for assembly jobs went through a five-step screening process that was specifically designed to assess interpersonal skills, aptitude for teamwork, planning skills, and flexibility. This screening process encompassed a lot more than taking a paper-and-pencil test, enduring a few interviews, and providing references. At Mazda, applicants also had to perform tasks that simulated jobs that they might do on the actual factory floor. For example, applicants might bolt fenders onto a car or attach hoses in a simulated engine compartment. This helped Mazda's management to match workers' abilities with specific job requirements, and it also provided applicants with a realistic preview of what they were getting into.

For the initial work force, 10 000 of 100 000 candidates passed the five-step screening process. Of these, only 1 300 were hired. The cost of screening each one of these new employees was about $13 000 per worker.

But new hires didn't just report to the factory floor and join a work team. First, they had to undergo detailed training. That started with a three-week hodgepodge of sessions in which they learned about interpersonal relations, charting quality, stimulating creativity, and the like. This was followed by three days devoted to learning Mazda's philosophy of increasing efficiency through continual improvement. After this basic training came job-specific training. Line workers, for example, spent five to seven more weeks picking up specific technical skills, then another three or four weeks being supervised on the assembly line.

Why did Mazda go to all this expense and effort? The company wanted literate, versatile employees who would accept the company's emphasis on teamwork, loyalty, efficiency, and quality. Moreover, it wanted to weed out any troublemakers. What Mazda got was a work force better educated and nearly a generation younger than the old-line auto workers at most Big Three plants. Mazda also wanted smooth relations with its workers. So it invited the United Auto Workers to organize the plant's employees before operations began. What went wrong? How could all this preparatory work have resulted in a disgruntled work force? The following highlights a few of the causes.

The high turnover among North American managers created instability. North American managers complained about being left out of the information network. Major decisions were controlled by Mazda executives in Japan or local Japanese superiors. Each morning, for instance, North American managers got a "laundry list" from their Japanese "advisor" telling them just what they were supposed to do that day.

Workers' complaints were numerous. They said that the Japanese managers didn't listen to them. They criticized the company's policy of continuous improvement, claiming that this translated into a never-ending push to cut the number of worker-hours spent building each car. To support their argument, they pointed out that other North American companies use 15 percent to 20 percent more workers to produce a similar number of cars. Workers said that even Mazda's team system, which is supposed to give employees more authority and flexibility, is a gimmick. Power was gradually taken away from team leaders; flexibility was a one-way street that management used to control workers; and the team system encouraged workers to pressure each other to keep up the rapid pace.

Japanese executives responded by publicly criticizing workers for lacking dedication. As to high turnover in the management ranks, Japanese executives admit that Mazda's practice of making decisions by consensus often gives the appearance of keeping authority away from its North American executives. But Japanese executives can also claim that the North American workers have just not adapted to Mazda's way of doing business. In spite of worker complaints, management can proudly point to the fact that independent experts give their cars high marks for quality; every bit as high, in fact, as those built in Japan.

Questions

1. Contrast Mazda's selection and training process with those more typically used for manufacturing workers.

2. "Mazda's management doesn't understand the North American worker." Do you agree or disagree with this statement? Discuss.

3. What suggestions, if any, would you make to Mazda's top management regarding its employee practices in North America that might reduce absenteeism, turnover, and improve employee job satisfaction?

Source: Stephen Robbins, *Organizational Behavior* (Englewood Cliffs, NJ: Prentice Hall, 1993), pp. 593–5. Based on W. J. Hampton, "How Does Japan Inc. Pick Its American Workers?," *Business Week* (October 3, 1988), pp. 84–8; G. A. Patterson, "Mazda-UAW's Michigan Honeymoon Is Over," *The Wall Street Journal* (April 17, 1990), p. B1; and J. J. Fucini and S. Fucini, *Working for the Japanese* (New York: Free Press, 1990).

Video Case

ISO 9000

As more and more businesses compete internationally, a world-wide series of quality standards called ISO 9000 is becoming a key marketing tool to access global markets. The program started in Britain and has been used in Europe for some time. ISO registration is fast becoming a necessity to do business in foreign countries, as customers all over the world are requiring their suppliers to be ISO 9000 certified.

The registration process begins with an extensive, detailed documentation of the processes and procedures the company uses to run its business. A growing number of consultants are available to assist with this documentation process and ensure it is prepared in a manner consistent with ISO 9000 guidelines. Then an ISO registrar audits the company to ensure that it is following the processes that have been documented.

There has been criticism of ISO 9000. Critics say the programs only work as well as the consultants who design them. Others point out that many non-ISO registered companies keep track of their business processes too. There are even claims that ISO does not guarantee quality, but rather that the company's paperwork is up to standard, which may or may not be related to the quality of the end product. One European report found that ISO registered companies did not appear to enjoy a competitive advantage over unregistered ones.

Despite these criticisms, ISO 9000 continues to be a cost of doing business in the global marketplace. One only need drive past any industrial area in Canada and see the huge signs on the sides of buildings proclaiming ISO certification.

Questions

1. Why do companies want their suppliers to be ISO 9000 certified?
2. How can companies pass the ISO 9000 audit yet still have low quality products/services?
3. Will the new ISO 14000 series of environmental standards be harder to criticize? Why or why not?

Video Resource: CBC, *Venture,* "ISO 9000," October 8, 1995.

Take It to the Net

Check out our Companion Website at

www.prenticehall.ca/dessler

for a multitude of practice questions, key terms and concepts, Weblinks to related sites, newsgroups, CBC video updates, and more.

Notes

1. N.B. Carlyle, *"Compensation Planning Outlook 1997,"* Conference Board of Canada (1997), p. 10.
2. S. Lebrun, "New Work Styles Gain Converts," *Canadian HR Reporter* (June 2, 1997), p. 16.
3. Donald Peterson, "Flexitime in the United States: The Lessons of Experience," *Personnel* 57 (January–February, 1980), p. 21–37.
4. Stanley Nollen, "Does Flexitime Improve Productivity?" *Harvard Business Review* 56 (September–October 1977), pp. 12–22; Karen Kush and Linda Stroh, "Flextime: Myth or Reality?" *Business Horizons* (September–October 1994), pp. 51–5.
5. Nollen, "Does Flexitime Improve Productivity?"
6. Stanley Nollen and Virginia Martin, *Alternative Work Schedules Part One: Flexitime* (New York: AMACOM, 1978), p. 44.
7. Peterson, "Flexitime in the United States," pp. 29–31.
8. Another problem is that some employers let workers "bank" extra hours by working, say, 45 hours one week so they need work only 35 hours the next week. The problem is that in the 45-hour week the employees should, strictly speaking, be paid an overtime rate for the extra five hours worked. Some employers handle this problem by letting hours worked vary from day to day but requiring each week to be a 40-hour week. Others are experimenting with letting workers accumulate hours and be paid overtime if necessary. See J. C. Swart, "Flexitime's Debit and Credit Option," *Personnel Journal* 58 (January–February 1979), pp. 10–2.

9. David Ralston, David Gustafson, and William Anthony, "Employees May Love Flextime, But What Does It Do to the Organization's Productivity?" *Journal of Applied Psychology* 70, no. 2 (1985), pp. 272–9.
10. S. Lebrun, "New Work Styles," p. 16.
11. Herbert Northrup, "The Twelve Hour Shift in the North American Mini-steel Industry," *Journal of Labor Research* 12, no. 3 (Summer 1991), pp. 261–78; Charlene Marner Solomon, "24-hour Employees," *Personnel Journal* 70, no. 8 (August 1991), pp. 56–63.
12. Northrup, "The Twelve Hour Shift." See also John Ivancevich and Herbert Lyon, "The Shortened Work Week: A Field Experiment," *Journal of Applied Psychology* 62, no. 1 (1977), pp. 34–7.
13. Janina Latack and Lawrence Foster, "Implementation of Compressed Work Schedules: Participation and Job Redesign as Critical Factors for Employee Acceptance," *Personnel Psychology* 38, no. 1 (Spring 1985), pp. 75–92. Interestingly, one way to determine how your employees will react to a 4/40 or flextime work schedule apparently is to ask them ahead of time. One study suggests that thesewill be the reactions that emerge three to six months after commencement of the program. See Randall B. Dunham, Jon L. Pierce, and Maria B. Castaneda, "Alternative Work Schedules: Two Field Quasi-Experiments," *Personnel Psychology* 40, no. 2 (Summer 1987), pp. 215–42.
14. "Job Sharing Benefits for Part-Time Workers," *Canadian HR Reporter* (July 14, 1997), P. 10.

15. *1997 Telecommuting Survey*, KPMG, 1997.
16. J.A. Giibbons, "Telecommuting—the Experiment that Works," *Canadian HR Reporter* (September 9, 1996), p. 16, 17, 22.
17. T. McCallum, "Telecommuting: Managing Work-at-Home Personnel," *Human Resources Professional* (April/May 1997), pp. 45–9.
18. J.A. Gibbons, "Telecommuting—the Experiment that Works," p. 17, 22.
19. K. Robertson, "Business Benefits Often Forgotten in 'Special Case' Attitude to Alternative Work Arrangements," *Canadian HR Reporter* (July 14, 1997), p. 19.
20. T. McCallum, "Managing Work-at-Home Personnel," p. 48.
21. T. McCallum, "Managing Work-at-Home Personnel," p. 49.
22. "After Flexible Hours, Now It's Flexiyear," *International Management* (March 1982), pp. 31–2.
23. This section based on T. Frank, "Workload Puts Bind on Family-Friendly Policies," *Canadian HR Reporter* (September 23, 1996), p. 14.
24. Halifax YWCA, The Maritime Life Assurance Company, & Status of Women Canada, *The Flexible Workplace Study* (1996).
25. This section based on Donald Dewar, *The Quality Circle Guide to Participation Management* (Englewood Cliffs, NJ: Prentice Hall, 1980). See also James Thacker and Mitchel Fields, "Union Involvement in Quality-of-Work Life Efforts: A Longitudinal Investigation," *Personnel Psychology* 40, no. 1 (Spring 1987), pp. 97–112. They conclude that unions' fears of QCs may be misplaced and that after quality-of-work-life involvement, "A majority of the rank and file members who perceived QWL—quality of work life—as successful gave equal credit for the success to both union and management. The rank and file members who perceived QWL as unsuccessful tended to blame management for the lack of success." See also Anat Rafaeli, "Quality Circles and Employee Attitudes," *Personnel Psychology* 38 (Fall 1985), pp. 603–15; Mitchell Lee Marks, Edward Hackett, Philip Mirvis, and James Grady, Jr., "Employee Participation in a Quality Circle Program: Impact on Quality of Work Life, Productivity, and Absenteeism," *Journal of Applied Psychology* 71, no. 1 (February 1986), pp. 61–9, and "Quality Circles: A New Generation," *BNA Bulletin to Management* 38, no. 2 (January 1987), pp. 10–5. See also Preston C. Bottger and Philip Yetton, "Improving Group Performance by Training in Individual Problem Solving," *Journal of Applied Psychology* 72, no. 4 (November 1987), pp. 651–7, and Murray R. Barrick and Ralph Alexander, "A Review of Quality Circle Efficacy and the Existence of Positive-Finding Bias," *Personnel Psychology* 40, no. 3 (Autumn 1987), pp. 579–92.
26. This is based on Everett Adam, Jr., "Quality Circle Performance," *Journal of Management* 17, no. 1 (1991), pp. 25–39.
27. R. W. Griffin, "Consequences of Quality Circles in an Industrial Setting: A Longitudinal Assessment," *Academy of Management Journal* 31, no. 2 (1988), pp. 338–58; reported in Adam, "Quality Circle Performance," p. 27.
28. Adam, "Quality Circle Performance," p. 38.
29. Gopal Pati, Robert Salitore, and Saundra Brady, "What Went Wrong with Quality Circles?" *Personnel Journal* (December 1987), pp. 83–9.
30. Pati Solitaire, and Brady, "What Went Wrong," p. 86.
31. S. Fife, "The Total Quality Muddle," *Report on Business Magazine* (November 1992), pp. 64–73.
32. C. French, "Breaking the Information Barrier," *The Globe & Mail* (October 26, 1993), p. 25.
33. Thomas Berry, *Managing the Total Quality Transformation* (New York: McGraw-Hill, 1991), p. 1.
34. Berry, *Managing the Total Quality Transformation*, p. xv.
35. These are adapted from Berry, *Managing The Total Quality Transformation*, pp. 53–4.
36. "Total Quality Management: The Real Challenge May be Open and Effective Communication Strategy," *Towers Perrin Focus* (Winter 1994), p. 10–1.
37. C. French, "Breaking the Information Barrier," p. 25.
38. C. French, "Breaking the Information Barrier.
39. S. Fife, "The Total Quality Muddle," p. 69.
40. This is based on Shari Caudron, "How Xerox Won the Baldrige," *Personnel Journal* (April 1991), p. 100.
41. National Quality Institute, *The Canadian Quality Criteria,* (1997).
42. This section based on CAE Submission Document, Brock Telecom, 1977.
43. NQI Feedback Report, Brock Telecom, 1997.
44. This section based on personal communication, Glen Penwardern, Executive Director, Orillia Soldiers' Memorial Hospital, November 12, 1997.
45. NQI Feedback Report, Orillia Soldiers' Memorial Hospital, 1997.
46. Private conversation with Wayne Brunetti, Executive Vice President, Florida Power & Light Company.
47. "Building a Quality Improvement Program at Florida Power & Light," *Target* (Fall 1988), p. 8.
48. Joel E. Ross, *Total Quality Management: Text, Cases and Readings* (Delray Beach, FL: St. Lucie Press, 1993), p. 4.
49. Rob Murakami, "How to Implement ISO 9000," *CMA Magazine* (March 1994), p. 18.
50. C. Knight, "HR's Role in ISO 9000," *Canadian HR Reporter* (February 27, 1995), p. 6.
51. Sidney Emmons, "ISO 9001 on a Shoestring," *Quality Progress* (May 1994), p. 50.
52. Rob Murakami, "How to Implement ISO 9000," *CMA Magazine* (March, 1994), p. 18.
53. L.Ramsay, "No Business Too Small for ISO 9000 Certification," *Financial Post* (August 23, 1995), p. 18.
54. The following is adapted from Gary Dessler, *Winning Commitment* (New York: McGraw-Hill, 1993), Chapter 5.
55. Rensis Likert, *New Patterns of Management* (New York: McGraw-Hill, 1961), p. 103.
56. Likert, *New Patterns of Management*, p. 104.
57. See, for example, Brian Dumaine, "Who Needs a Boss?" *Fortune* (May 7, 1990), p. 52; David Hames, "Productivity-Enhancing Work Innovations: Remedies for What Ails Hospitals?" *Hospital & Health Services Administration* 36, no. 4 (Winter 1991), pp. 551–2; see also Shari Caudron, "Are Self-Directed Teams Right for Your Company?" *Personnel Journal* (December 1993), pp. 76–84.
58. This section based on P. Booth, *"Challenge and Change: Embracing the Team Concept,"* Conference Board of Canada (Report #123-94), 1994.
59. J. Zeidenberg, "HR and the Innovative Company," *HR Professional* (June 1996), pp. 12–5.

60. W.G. Nickels, J.M. McHugh, S.M. McHugh, and P.D. Berman *Understanding Canadian Business* (2nd ed.), (Toronto: Irwin, 1997), p. 270.

61. B. Little, "How to Make a Small Smart Factory," *The Globe and Mail* (February 2, 1993), p. B24.

62. Personal communication with Michelle Kline, November 19, 1997.

63. See Richard Wellins and Jill George, "The Key to Self-Directed Teams," *Training and Development Journal* (April 1991), pp. 26–31.

64. Richard Majuka and Timothy Baldwin, "Team-Based Employee Involvement Programs: Effects of Design and Administration," *Personnel Psychology* 44 (1991), p. 806.

65. Sam Johnson, "Work Teams: What's Ahead in Work Design and Rewards Management," *Compensation & Benefits Review* (March–April 1993), pp. 35–41.

66. Johnson, "Work Teams: What's Ahead," p. 39.

67. Michael Hammer and James Champy, *Reengineering the Corporation* (New York: Harper Business, 1994), p. 32.

68. D.W. Conklin, *Reengineering to Compete: Canadian Business in the Global Economy"* (Scarborough: Prentice Hall, 1994), pp. 84–99.

69. For other examples, see David Allen and Robert Nafius, "Dreaming and Doing: Reengineering GTE Telephone Operations," *Planning Review* (March/April 1993), pp. 28–31; D. Brian Harrison and Maurice Pratt, "A Methodology for Reengineering Businesses," *Planning Review* (March/April 1993), pp. 6–11.

70. Hugh Willmott, "Business Process Reengineering and Human Resource Management," *Personnel Review* 3, no. 3 (May 1994), p. 34.

71. James Champy, *Reengineering Management, The Mandate for New Leadership* (Harper Collins, 1995), p. 104.

72. Michael Hammer and James Champy, *Reengineering the Corporation*, p. 68.

73. Hammer and Champy, *Reengineering the Corporation*, p. 70.

74. Hammer and Champy, *Reengineering the Corporation*, p. 71.

75. Hammer and Champy, *Reengineering the Corporation*.

76. Hammer and Champy, *Reengineering the Corporation*.

77. Hammer and Champy, *Reengineering the Corporation*, p. 73.

78. Hammer and Champy, *Reengineering the Corporation*.

Chapter 11

Performance Appraisal

Chapter Outline

Learning Outcomes

After studying this chapter, you should be able to:

Explain why it is important to effectively appraise performance.

Describe eight performance appraisal methods and the pros and cons of each.

Discuss the major problems inhibiting effective performance appraisals.

Discuss 360-degree appraisal from multiple sources.

Conduct a more effective appraisal interview.

Introduction

Virtually all companies have some formal or informal means of appraising their employees' performance. Performance appraisal may be defined as any procedure that involves (1) setting work standards; (2) assessing the employee's actual performance relative to these standards; and (3) providing feedback to the employee with the aim of motivating that person to eliminate performance deficiencies or to continue to perform above par.

Most people have already had some experience with performance appraisals even before their first full-time job. For example, some colleges and universities ask students to rank instructors on scales such as the one in **Figure 11.1**. Do you think this is an effective scale? Do you see any ways to improve it? These are two of the questions you should be in a better position to answer by the end of this chapter.

Figure 11.1
Classroom Teaching Appraisal by Students

Source: Richard I. Miller, *Evaluating Faculty for Promotion and Tenure* (San Francisco: Jossey-Bass Publishers, 1987), pp. 164–5.

Evaluating Faculty for Promotion and Tenure

Classroom Teaching Appraisal by Students

Teacher_____ Course _____

Term_____ Academic Year _____

Thoughtful student appraisal can help improve teaching effectiveness. This questionnaire is designed for that purpose, and your assistance is appreciated. Please do not sign your name.

Use the back of this form for any further comments you might want to express; use numbers 10, 11, and 12 for any additional questions that you might like to add.

Directions: Rate your teacher on each item, giving the highest scores for exceptional performances and the lowest scores for very poor performances. Place in the blank space before each statement the rating that most closely expresses your view.

Exceptional			Moderately Good			Very Poor	Don't Know
7	6	5	4	3	2	1	X

_____ 1. How do you rate the agreement between course objectives and lesson assignments?

_____ 2. How do you rate the planning, organization, and use of class periods?

_____ 3. Are the teaching methods and techniques employed by the teacher appropriate and effective?

_____ 4. How do you rate the competence of the instructor in the subject?

_____ 5. How do you rate the interest of the teacher in the subject?

_____ 6. Does the teacher stimulate and challenge you to think and to question?

_____ 7. Does he or she welcome differing points of view?

_____ 8. Does the teacher have a personal interest in helping you in and out of class?

_____ 9. How would you rate the fairness and effectiveness of the grading policies and procedures of the teacher?

_____ 10. _____

Faculty Evaluation Rating Forms

_____ 11. _____

_____ 12. _____

_____ 13. Considering all the above items, what is your overall rating of this teacher?

_____ 14. How would you rate this teacher in comparison with all others you have had in the college or university?

Why Should Performance Be Appraised?

There are several reasons to appraise performance.[1] First, appraisals provide information upon which *promotion* and *salary decisions* can be made. Second, they provide an opportunity for managers and employees to *review* each employee's work-related behaviour. This in turn enables the manager and employee to develop a plan for correcting any deficiencies the appraisal might have unearthed, and reinforce the things the employee is doing well. Finally, the appraisal should be central to a firm's *career-planning* process because it provides a good opportunity to review each employee's career plans in light of his or her exhibited strengths and weaknesses.

Performance appraisal is particularly important as we head into the 21st century, because employee performance is increasingly critical to business success. Unfortunately, most supervisors and employees are dissatisfied with their performance appraisal programs, because they involve so much personal judgment.[2]

The Supervisor's Role in Appraisal

The supervisor usually does the actual appraising. Therefore, he or she must be familiar with basic appraisal techniques, understand and avoid problems that can cripple an appraisal, and conduct the appraisal fairly.

The HR department serves a policymaking and advisory role. In one survey, for example, about 80 percent of the firms responding said the HR department provides advice and assistance regarding the appraisal tool to use but leaves final decisions on appraisal procedures to operating division heads; in the rest of the firms HR department staff prepare detailed forms and procedures and ensure that all departments use them.[3] HR department staff are responsible, as well, for training supervisors to improve their appraisal skills. Finally, the HR department is also responsible for monitoring the appraisal system's use, and particularly for ensuring that the format and criteria being measured comply with human rights laws and don't become outdated. In one survey, half the employers were in the process of revising their appraisal programs, while others were conducting reviews to see how well their programs were working.[4]

Steps in Appraising Performance

A performance appraisal contains three steps: defining performance expectations, appraising performance, and providing feedback. *Defining performance expectations* means making sure that job duties and job standards are clear to all. *Appraising performance* means comparing an employee's actual performance to the standards that have been set; this usually involves some type of rating form. Third, performance appraisal usually requires one or more *feedback sessions* where the employee's performance and progress are discussed and plans are made for any development that is required.

www.uvm.edu/~uvmppg/ ppg/hr/perfapp.htm
Performance Appraisal Process

Performance Appraisal Problems   When appraisals fail, they do so for reasons that parallel these three steps—defining performance expectations, appraising performance, and providing feedback. Some appraisals fail because employees are not told ahead of time exactly what is expected of them in terms of good performance. Others fail because of problems with the forms or procedures used to actually appraise the performance; a lenient supervisor might rate all employees "high," for instance, although many are actually unsatisfactory. Still other problems arise during the interview-feedback session, which include arguing and poor communications. These and other problems are summarized in **Figure 11.2**. Holding effective appraisals thus begins with defining the job and its performance standards, to which we now turn.

Figure 11.2
Common Performance Evaluation Problems

Source: John E. Oliver, "Performance Appraisals That Fit," *Personnel Journal* 64, no. 6 (June 1985), p. 69.

Problems can occur at any stage in the evaluation process. Some of the pitfalls to avoid in performance appraisals are:

1. *Lack of standards.* Without standards, there can be no objective evaluation of results, only a subjective guess or feeling about performance.

2. *Irrelevant or subjective standards.* Standards should be established by analyzing the job output to ensure that standards are job related.

3. *Unrealistic standards.* Standards are goals with motivating potential. Those that are reasonable but challenging have the most potential to motivate.

4. *Poor measures of performance.* Objectivity and comparison require that progress toward standards or accomplishment of standards be measurable. Examples of measurable standards include quantifiable measures, such as 10 rejects per 1 000 units or 10 sales per 100 calls, as well as qualitative measures, such as projects completed or not completed.

5. *Rater errors.* Rater errors include rater bias or prejudice, halo effect, central tendency, and fear of confrontation.

6. *Poor feedback to employee.* Standards and/or ratings must be communicated to the employee in order for the performance evaluation to be effective.

7. *Negative communications.* The evaluation process is hindered by communication of negative attitudes, such as inflexibility, defensiveness, and a non-developmental approach.

8. *Failure to apply evaluation data.* Failure to use evaluations in human resource decision making and career development negates the primary purpose of performance evaluations. The use and weighting of multiple criteria as well as the frequency of evaluation also present problems.

Defining Performance Expectations

The job description often isn't sufficient to clarify what employees are expected to do, since many descriptions are written not for specific jobs but for groups of jobs. All sales associates in the firm might have the same job description, for instance, although each sales manager may have individual ideas about what his or her sales associates are expected to do. For example, the job description may list duties such as "supervise support staff" and "be responsible for all customer liaison." However, one particular sales associate may be expected to personally sell at least $600 000 worth of products per year by handling the division's two largest accounts; to keep the sales assistants happy; and to keep customers away from company executives.[5]

To operationalize these expectations, develop measurable standards for each. The "personal selling" activity can be measured in terms of how many dollars of sales the associate is to generate personally. "Keeping the sales assistants happy" might be measured in terms of turnover (on the assumption that less than 10 percent of the sales assistants will quit in any given year if morale is high). "Keeping customers away from executives" can be measured with a standard of no more than ten customer complaints per year being the sales associate's target. In general, employees should always know ahead of time how and on what basis they will be appraised.

The Appraisal Itself: Appraisal Methods

The appraisal itself is generally conducted with the aid of a predetermined and formal method like one or more of those described in this section.

Graphic Rating Scale Method

graphic rating scale
A scale that lists a number of traits and a range of performance for each. The employee is then rated by identifying the score that best describes his or her level of performance for each trait.

The **graphic rating scale** is the simplest and most popular technique for appraising performance. **Figure 11.3** shows a typical rating scale. It lists traits (such as quality and reliability) and a range of performance values (from unsatisfactory to outstanding) for each one. The supervisor rates each employee by circling or checking the score that best describes his or her performance for each trait. The assigned values are then totalled.

Instead of appraising generic traits or factors (such as quality and quantity), many firms specify the duties to be appraised. For example, **Figure 11.4**[6] shows an appraisal form for the position of administrative secretary. In this case the job's five main sets of duties have been taken from the job description and prioritized. Importance ratings are indicated as percentages at the top of each of the five categories (word processing, reception, and so on). There is also space on the form for comments, and for evaluation of general performance attributes like reporting for work on time and observing work rules.

Alternation Ranking Method

alternation ranking method
Ranking employees from best to worst on a particular trait.

Ranking employees from best to worst on a trait or traits is another method for evaluating employees. Since it is usually easier to distinguish between the worst and best employees than to rank them, an **alternation ranking method** is most popular. First, list all employees to be rated, and then cross out the names of any not known well enough to rank. Then, on a form such as that in **Figure 11.5**, indicate the employee who is the highest on the characteristic being measured and also the one who is the lowest. Then choose the next highest and the next lowest, alternating between highest and lowest until all the employees to be rated have been ranked.

Paired Comparison Method

paired comparison method
Ranking employees by making a chart of all possible pairs of the employees for each trait and indicating which is the better employee of the pair.

The **paired comparison method** helps make the ranking method more precise. For every trait (quantity of work, quality of work, and so on), every employee is paired with and compared to every other employee.

Suppose there are five employees to be rated. In the paired comparison method a chart is prepared, as in **Figure 11.6**, of all possible pairs of employees *for each trait.* Then for each trait indicate (with a + or −) who is the better employee of the pair. Next the number of times an employee is rated better is added up. In Figure 11.6, employee Maria ranked highest (has the most + marks) for quality of work, while Art was ranked highest for creativity.

Figure 11.3
One Page of a Two-Page Graphic Rating Scale with Space for Comments

Performance Appraisal

Employee Name _____   Title _____

Department _____   Employee Payroll Number _____

Reason for Review: ☐ Annual   ☐ Promotion   ☐ Unsatisfactory Performance

☐ Merit   ☐ End Probation Period   ☐ Other _____

Date employee began present position _____ / _____ / _____

Date of last appraisal _____ / _____ / _____   Scheduled appraisal date _____ / _____ / _____

Instructions: Carefully evaluate employee's work performance in relation to current job requirements. Check rating box to indicate the employee's performance. Indicate N/A if not applicable. Assign points for each rating within the scale and indicate in the corresponding points box. Points will be totalled and averaged for an overall performance score.

RATING IDENTIFICATION

O–Outstanding–Performance is exceptional in all areas and is recognizable as being far superior to others.

V–Very Good–Results clearly exceed most position requirements. Performance is of high quality and is achieved on a consistent basis.

G–Good–Competent and dependable level of performance. Meets performance standards of the job.

I–Improvement Needed–Performance is deficient in certain areas. Improvement is necessary.

U–Unsatisfactory–Results are generally unacceptable and require immediate improvement. No merit increase should be granted to individuals with this rating.

N–Not Rated–Not applicable or too soon to rate.

GENERAL FACTORS	RATING	SCALE	SUPPORTIVE DETAILS OR COMMENTS
1. **Quality–**The accuracy, thoroughness and acceptability of work performed.	O ☐ V ☐ G ☐ I ☐ U ☐	100-90 90-80 80-70 70-60 below 60	Points _____ _____ _____ _____
2. **Productivity–**The quantity and efficiency of work produced in a specified period of time.	O ☐ V ☐ G ☐ I ☐ U ☐	100-90 90-80 80-70 70-60 below 60	Points _____ _____ _____ _____
3. **Job Knowledge–**The practical/technical skills and information used on the job.	O ☐ V ☐ G ☐ I ☐ U ☐	100-90 90-80 80-70 70-60 below 60	Points _____ _____ _____ _____
4. **Reliability–**The extent to which an employee can be relied upon regarding task completion and follow up.	O ☐ V ☐ G ☐ I ☐ U ☐	100-90 90-80 80-70 70-60 below 60	Points _____ _____ _____ _____
5. **Availability–**The extent to which an employee is punctual, observes prescribed work break/meal periods, and the overall attendance record.	O ☐ V ☐ G ☐ I ☐ U ☐	100-90 90-80 80-70 70-60 below 60	Points _____ _____ _____ _____
6. **Independence–**The extent of work performed with little or no supervision.	O ☐ V ☐ G ☐ I ☐ U ☐	100-90 90-80 80-70 70-60 below 60	Points _____ _____ _____ _____

Figure 11.4
Sample Performance Appraisal Form

Source: James Buford, Jr., Bettye Burkhalter, and Grover Jacobs, "Link Job Descriptions to Performance Appraisals," *Personnel Journal* (June 1988), pp. 135–6.

Name _____
Position _____
Rating period from _____ to _____
Rater name _____
Rater title _____
Department _____

Rating Scale Key	
1	Fails to meet job requirements
2	Essentially meets job requirements
3	Fully meets job requirements
4	Meets job requirements with distinction
5	Exceeds job requirements

PART II   Rating Scales for Task Areas

Position: Administrative Secretary
Duties and Responsibilities

A. Word Processing   PCT. (30%)   RATING   1   2   3   4   5

Producing accurate documents in the proper format at 60 wpm from a variety of sources; including oral dictation from dictating machine, shorthand notes or standard formats, transcribes correspondence for general manager; transcribes minutes of meetings; prepares notices, agendas, schedules, and other internal material; prepares surveys for trade associations; compiles operating reports and other reports, including text and tables; prepares copy for trade magazines and newspapers; composes and prepares letters, memoranda, copy, and other documents as needed or on request.

Comments

B. Reception   PCT. (25%)   RATING   1   2   3   4   5

Receiving and recording initial contacts in person or on the telephone and courteously assisting callers or visitors; answers incoming telephone calls, takes message, provides information or routes calls to appropriate individual; greets visitors, provides information or directs to appropriate office or individual; acts as host/hostess and provides incidental services to visitors in waiting status; operates phone mail system; maintains log of callers and visitors.

Comments

C. Scheduling   PCT. (20%)   RATING   1   2   3   4   5

Managing calendar efficiently including arranging appointments, meetings, travel, and similar activities; maintains calendar and makes appointments for general manager, board members, and other staff; prepares requests for reimbursement for official travel; assists with arrangements of annual meeting; makes arrangements for in-service training meetings, including rooms, coffee breaks, and food service when necessary; schedules use of organizational facilities; arranges lodging, travel, and fees for outside speakers and consultants.

Comments

D. Filing and records management   PCT. (15%)   RATING   1   2   3   4   5

Creating and maintaining appropriate filing systems and promptly locating and retrieving needed material upon request; develops space allocation plan and filing system for correspondence, minutes, reports, regulations, and related material; places material into proper location in file; searches for and retrieves material from files; culls, files, and removes material to central location or destroys as needed; maintains and preserves vital records; organizes data from file search into usable format.

Comments

E. General office service   PCT. (10%)   RATING   1   2   3   4   5

Performing related office duties in accordance with acceptable practice and prescribed procedures; processes mail through postage meter, records readings and posts; opens and distributes incoming mail; makes copies of documents; maintains petty cash fund; clips articles from papers and magazines related to the organization; maintains bulletin board.

Comments

(continued)

Figure 11.4
(continued)

PART III Performance Appraisal Form

Does the employee report for and remain at work as required? ❘ yes ❘ no If no, please explain.
Does the employee follow instructions and observe work rules? ❘ yes ❘ no If no, please explain.
Does the employee get along and cooperate with coworkers on the job? ❘ yes ❘ no If no, please explain.
Does the employee have the knowledges, skills, abilities, and other qualifications needed for successful job performance? ❘ yes ❘ no If no, please explain.
Describe any specific actions employee needs to take to improve job performance.
Summarize this employee's overall job performance as determined in your joint discussion.

PART IV Signatures

This report is based on my observation and knowledge of both the employee and the job.	My signature indicates that I have reviewed this appraisal. It does not mean that I agree with the results.
Supervisor ____ Date	
Reviewer ____ Date	Employee ____ Date

Figure 11.5
Alternation Ranking
Scale

ALTERNATION RANKING SCALE

For the Trait: _____

For the trait you are measuring, list all the employees you want to rank. Put the highest-ranking employee's name on line 1. Put the lowest-ranking employee's name on line 20. Then list the next highest ranking on line 2, the next lowest ranking on line 19, and so on. Continue until all names are on the scale.

Highest-ranking employee

1. _____   11. _____
2. _____   12. _____
3. _____   13. _____
4. _____   14. _____
5. _____   15. _____
6. _____   16. _____
7. _____   17. _____
8. _____   18. _____
9. _____   19. _____
10. _____   20. _____

Lowest-ranking employee

Figure 11.6
**Ranking Employees by
the Paired Comparison
Method**

Note: + means "better than,"
− means "worse than." For
each chart, add up the
number of +'s in each column
to get the highest-ranked
employee.

FOR THE TRAIT "QUALITY OF WORK"

Employee Rated:

As Compared to:	A Art	B Maria	C Chuck	D Diane	E José
A Art		+	+	−	−
B Maria	−		−	−	−
C Chuck	−	+		+	−
D Diane	+	+	−		+
E José	+	+	+	−	

↑
Maria Ranks Highest Here

FOR THE TRAIT "CREATIVITY"

Employee Rated:

As Compared to:	A Art	B Maria	C Chuck	D Diane	E José
A Art		−	−	−	−
B Maria	+		−	+	+
C Chuck	+	+		−	+
D Diane	+	−	+		−
E José	+	−	−	+	

↑
Art Ranks Highest Here

Forced Distribution Method

forced distribution method
Similar to grading on a curve; predetermined percentages of ratees are placed in various performance categories.

The **forced distribution method** is similar to grading on a curve. With this method, predetermined percentages of ratees are placed in performance categories. For example, it may be decided to distribute employees as follows:

15% high performers
20% high-average performers
30% average performers
20% low-average performers
15% low performers

As at school, this means not everyone can get an "A" and that one's performance is always rated relative to that of his or her peers. One practical way to do this is to write each employee's name on a separate index card. Then, for each trait being appraised (quality of work, creativity, and so on), place the employee's card in one of the appropriate performance categories. This method has been criticized as demotivating for the considerable proportion of the work force classified as less than average.[7]

Critical Incident Method

critical incident method
Keeping a record of uncommonly good or undesirable examples of an employee's work-related behaviour and reviewing it with the employee at predetermined times.

With the **critical incident method,** the supervisor keeps a log of desirable or undesirable examples or incidents of each employee's work-related behaviour. Then every six months or so, the supervisor and employee meet and discuss the latter's performance using the specific incidents as examples.

This method can always be used to supplement another appraisal technique, and in that role it has several advantages. It provides specific hard facts for explaining the appraisal. It ensures that a manager thinks about the employee's appraisal throughout the year because the incidents must be accumulated; therefore, the rating does not just reflect the employee's most recent performance. Keeping a running list of critical incidents should also provide concrete examples of what an employee can do to eliminate any performance deficiencies.

The critical incident method can be adapted to the specific job expectations laid out for the employee at the beginning of the year. Thus, in the example presented in **Table 11.1**, one of the assistant plant manager's continuing duties is to supervise procurement and to minimize inventory costs. The critical incident shows that the assistant plant manager let inventory storage costs rise 15 percent; this provides a specific example of what performance must be improved in the future.

TABLE 11.1 Examples of Critical Incidents for an Assistant Plant Manager

CONTINUING DUTIES	TARGETS	CRITICAL INCIDENTS
Schedule production for plant	Full utilization of employees and machinery in plant; orders delivered on time	Instituted new production scheduling system; decreased late orders by 10% last month; increased machine utilization in plant by 20% last month
Supervise procurement of raw materials and inventory control	Minimize inventory costs while keeping adequate supplies on hand	Let inventory storage costs rise 15% last month; overordered parts "A" and "B" by 20%; underordered part "C" by 30%
Supervise machinery maintenance	No shutdowns due to faulty machinery	Instituted new preventative maintenance system for plant; prevented a machine breakdown by discovering faulty part

The critical incident method is often used to supplement a ranking technique. It is useful for identifying specific examples of good and poor performance and planning how deficiencies can be corrected. It is not as useful by itself for comparing employees, nor, therefore, for making salary decisions.

Narrative Forms

Some employers use narrative forms to evaluate employees. For example, the form used in **Figure 11.7** presents the Performance Improvement Plan used by one multinational company to evaluate the progress and development of its supervisory employees. The person's supervisor is asked (1) to rate the employee's performance

Figure 11.7
Performance Improvement Plan
Source: Joseph J. Famularo, *Handbook of Personnel Forms, Records, and Reports* (New York: McGraw-Hill, 1982), pp. 216–9.

PERFORMANCE IMPROVEMENT PLAN

Name ———————————————————— Date ————————————

Position Title ————————————————— Dept./Div. ————————

I. PURPOSE AND OBJECTIVE
This form and process is designed to assist the supervisor in analyzing *how* an employee is performing his or her work, that is, the individual skills and knowledge he or she uses in performing the job responsibilities. The primary objective in completing this Performance Analysis and subsequent discussions with the employee is to help the person improve.

II. STEPS IN THE PROCESS
A. Performance Factors and Skills — The individual skills and performance factors represent the major abilities that are required of most employees to perform their jobs. After reading the description of each factor, assign a rating of the employee's skill proficiency using the following guide:

S   —   Strength
SA   —   Satisfactory
N   —   Needs Improvement
NA   —   Not Applicable

Space is provided at the end of this form to write out performance factors/skills considered to be important but not found on this form. However, avoid adding personality traits that do not influence performance.

B. Performance Analysis and Examples — This section provides *specific performance* related examples of observed behaviour. These examples should be stated in terms of what the employee did or said (in completing a task or project) as it relates to the performance factor.

C. Improvement Plan — Specific actions should be listed in this section that will be taken to assist the employee in those areas that require performance improvement. It is suggested that supervisor and employee develop this plan jointly in a discussion session. These actions should focus on activities, tasks, training, expanded job duties, etc., that will afford the employee an opportunity to develop the needed skill. The written Improvement Plan should also state *who* is responsible for completing each step, a *timetable* for completion and a *feedback/followup* process that will monitor the progress

D. Discussion with the Employee — The performance rating and analysis of each factor or skill must be discussed with the employee. The principal focus of this meeting should be on problem solving, i.e., to stimulate the employee to think about the probable causes of the skill or knowledge deficiency and to generate ideas on how to bring about performance improvement in these areas. Working together, supervisor and employee should examine the cause of each deficiency and then jointly develop and agree upon a logical course of action for improvement. The Improvement Plan should be realistic, written down, and followed up in future sessions.

(continued)

Figure 11.7
(continued)

Performance Factors/Skills	Performance Analysis & Examples	Improvement Plan
PLANNING—Forecasting, setting objectives, establishing strategies and courses of action, budgeting, scheduling, programing, and outlining procedures.		
ORGANIZING—Grouping of activities to achieve results, delegating, staffing, and using available resources.		
DIRECTING—Ability to guide and supervise. Stresses the processes of motivating, communicating, and leading.		
CONTROLLING—Developing performance standards, measuring results, and taking corrective action.		
DEVELOPING PEOPLE—Evaluating performance and potential, providing training and development, coaching and counselling, and resolving human resources problems.		
PROBLEM ANALYSIS—Determining pertinent data, differentiating significant from less significant facts, defining interrelationships, and arriving at sound practical solutions.		

(continued)

in terms of standards and (2) to present critical examples and an improvement plan designed to aid the employee in meeting or exceeding these position standards. A summary performance appraisal discussion then focusses on problem solving.[8]

Behaviourally Anchored Rating Scales

behaviourally anchored rating scale (BARS)
An appraisal method that aims at combining the benefits of narratives, critical incidents, and quantified ratings by anchoring a quantified scale with specific narrative examples of good and poor performance.

A **behaviourally anchored rating scale (BARS)** combines the benefits of narratives, critical incidents, and quantified ratings by anchoring a quantified scale with specific behavioural examples of good or poor performance, as in **Figure 11.8**. Its proponents claim that it provides better, more equitable appraisals than do the other tools that have been discussed.[9]

Developing a BARS typically requires five steps:[10]

1. *Generate critical incidents.* Persons who know the job being appraised (jobholders and/or supervisors) are asked to describe specific illustrations (critical incidents) of effective and ineffective performance.

2. *Develop performance dimensions.* These people then cluster the incidents into a smaller set of performance dimensions (say, five or ten). Each cluster (dimension) is then defined.

Figure 11.7
(continued)

Performance Factors/Skills	Performance Analysis & Examples	Improvement Plan
DECISION MAKING— Evaluating and selecting among alternative courses of action quickly and accurately.		
INTERPERSONAL RELATIONS—Effectiveness in relating to others at all organizational levels. Sensitive to the needs of others.		
COMMUNICATION— Ability to get ideas across in a clear and persuasive manner. Skilled in listening to and seeking clarification of other's point of view.		
EMPLOYMENT EQUITY— Supports and implements goals of the firm's employment equity plan.		
JOB KNOWLEDGE—An understanding of the functional components of own job as well as an awareness of work relationships with other areas. Knowledge of one's specialized and technical field of work.		
HEALTH AND SAFETY— Actively promotes and upholds the Corporation's Health & Safety principles, initiates and works for realistic goals.		

3. *Reallocate incidents.* Another group of people who also know the job then reallocate the original critical incidents. They are given the clusters' definitions and the critical incidents and are asked to reassign each incident to the cluster they think it fits best. Typically, a critical incident is retained if some percentage (usually 50 percent to 80 percent) of this second group assigns it to the same cluster as did the group in step 2.

4. *Scale the incidents.* This second group is generally asked to rate the behaviour described in the incident as to how effectively or ineffectively it represents performance on the appropriate dimension (seven- or nine-point scales are typical).

5. *Develop final instrument.* A subset of the incidents (usually six or seven per cluster) is used as *behavioural anchors* for each dimension.

Example   Three researchers developed a BARS for grocery checkout clerks working in a large grocery chain.[11] They collected a number of critical incidents and then clustered them into eight performance dimensions:

KNOWLEDGE AND JUDGMENT

CONSCIENTIOUSNESS

SKILL IN HUMAN RELATIONS

SKILL IN OPERATION OF REGISTER

Figure 11.8
Behaviourally
Anchored Rating Scale

Sales Skills

Skillfully persuading customers to purchase products; using product benefits and opportunities effectively; closing skills; adapting sales techniques appropriately to different customers; effectively overcoming objections to purchasing products.

5 — If a customer insists on a particular brand name, the salesperson perseveres. Although products with this particular brand name are not available, the salesperson does not give up; instead, the salesperson persuades the customer that his or her needs could be better met with another product.

4 — The salesperson treats objections to purchasing the product seriously; works hard to counter the objections with relevant positive arguments regarding the benefits of the product.

3 — When a customer is deciding on which product to purchase, the salesperson tries to sell the product with the highest profit magin.

2 — The salesperson insists on describing more features of the product even though the customer wants to purchase it right now.

When a customer states an objection to purchasing a product, the salesperson ends the conversation, assuming that the prospect must not be interested.
1 —

SKILL IN BAGGING
ORGANIZATIONAL ABILITY OF CHECKSTAND WORK
SKILL IN MONETARY TRANSACTIONS
OBSERVATIONAL ABILITY

They then developed a behaviourally anchored rating scale for one of these dimensions, "knowledge and judgment." Similar to Figure 11.8, it contained a scale (ranging from 1 to 9) for rating performance from "extremely poor" to "extremely good," anchored with specific critical incidents. Thus, in the supermarket example, there was a specific critical incident ("by knowing the price of items, this checker would be expected to look for mismarked and unmarked items"); this helped anchor or specify what was meant by "extremely good" performance. Similarly, there are other critical incident anchors along the performance scale.

Advantages   Developing a BARS can be more time consuming than developing other appraisal tools, such as graphic rating scales. But BARS may also have important advantages.[12]

1. *A more accurate gauge.* People who know the job and its requirements better than anyone else develop BARS. The result should therefore be a good gauge of performance on that job.
2. *Clearer standards.* The critical incidents along the scale help to clarify what is meant by extremely good performance, average performance, and so forth.
3. *Feedback.* The critical incidents may be more useful in providing feedback to appraisees than simply informing them of their performance rating and not providing specific behavioural examples.
4. *Independent dimensions.* Systematically clustering the critical incidents into five or six performance dimensions (such as "knowledge and judgment") should help to make the dimensions more independent of one another. For example, a rater should be less likely to rate an employee high on all dimensions simply because he or she was rated high in "conscientiousness."
5. *Consistency.*[13] BARS evaluations also seem to be relatively consistent and reliable in that different raters' appraisals of the same person tend to be similar.

The Management by Objectives (MBO) Method

management by objectives (MBO)
Involves setting specific measurable goals with each employee and then periodically reviewing the progress made.

Stripped to its essentials, **management by objectives (MBO)** requires the manager to set specific measurable goals with each employee and then periodically discuss his or her progress toward these goals. A modest MBO program can be implemented by a manager by jointly setting goals with employees and periodically providing feedback. However, the term *MBO* almost always refers to a comprehensive, *organization-wide, goal setting and appraisal program* that consists of six main steps:

1. *Set the organization's goals.* Establish an organization-wide plan for next year and set goals.
2. *Set departmental goals.* Here department heads and their superiors jointly set goals for their departments.
3. *Discuss departmental goals.* Department heads discuss the department's goals with all employees in the department (often at a department-wide meeting) and ask them to develop their own individual goals; in other words, how can each employee contribute to the department's attaining its goals?
4. *Define expected results* (set individual goals). Here department heads and employees set short-term performance targets.
5. *Performance reviews: measure the results.* Department heads compare the actual performance of each employee with expected results.
6. *Provide feedback.* Department heads hold periodic performance review meetings with employees to discuss and evaluate the latters' progress in achieving expected results.

One of the foundations of a good Management by Objectives program is open communication, which fosters employee commitment to goals.

Problems to Avoid   There are three problems in using MBO. *Setting unclear, unmeasurable objectives* is the main one. An objective such as "will do a better job of training" is useless. On the other hand, "will have four employees promoted during the year" is a measurable objective.

Second, MBO is *time-consuming.* Taking the time to set objectives, to measure progress, and to provide feedback can take several hours per employee per year, over and above the time already spent doing each person's appraisal.

Third, setting objectives with an employee sometimes turns into a *tug of war,* with the manager pushing for higher goals and the employee pushing for lower ones. Knowing the job and the person's ability is thus important. To motivate performance, the objectives must be fair and attainable. The more a manager knows about the job and the employee's ability, the more confident he or she can be about the standards set.

Mixing the Methods

www.bauschke.com/cpa.htm
Computerized Performance
Appraisal

Most firms combine several appraisal techniques. An example is shown in **Figure 11.9**. This presents a form used to appraise the performance of managers in a large airline. Note that it is basically a graphic rating scale with descriptive phrases included to define the traits being measured. But there is also a section for comments below each trait. This lets the rater jot down several critical incidents. The quantifiable ranking method permits comparisons of employees and is therefore useful for making salary, transfer, and promotion decisions. The critical incidents provide specific examples of good and poor performance.[14]

Some firms utilize computerized approaches, as explained in the Information Technology and HR box.

Information Technology and HR
Computerized Performance Appraisals

More employers are turning to computerized performance appraisal systems today, generally with good results. Several relatively inexpensive performance appraisal software programs are on the market, including Employer Appraiser (Austin-Hayne), Review Writer (Avontos), and Performance Now (Knowledgepoint). All three enable managers to log notes on their employees during the year, and to rate employees on a series of performance traits. Each program generates written text to support every part of the appraisal.[1]

Employee Appraiser, a software package for Windows, provides an illustration of how computerized appraisals are used.[2] It presents the user with a menu of more than a dozen evaluation dimensions, including dependability, initiative, communication, decision making, leadership, judgment, and planning and productivity. Within each dimension are various performance factors, again presented in menu form. For example, under "communication" are separate factors for writing, verbal communication, receptivity to feedback and criticism, listening skills, ability to focus on the desired results, keeping others informed, and openness.

Once the user clicks on a factor, he or she is presented with a relatively sophisticated version of a graphic rating scale. However, instead of numbers, Employee Appraiser uses behaviourally anchored examples. For example, for verbal communication there are six choices, ranging from "presents ideas clearly" to "lacks structure." Once the manager picks the phrase that most accurately describes the worker, Employee Appraiser generates sample text. For example, if Juan's boss chooses "is sometimes unclear," the program might generate the following text: "Juan usually presents his ideas clearly and concisely. However, he sometimes uses terminology that is unclear to others. He would be more effective in his communications if he used less jargon and fewer technical terms."

By the time the manager has moved through all the performance categories and subfactors, Employee Appraiser has generated a solid, detailed written report. The program's built-in text editor or another word processing program can then be used to modify the report and add or delete comments and details.

One of the many useful features of Employee Appraiser is that it includes a log that can be used to collect critical incident events throughout the year so that they're not forgotten. These can then be stored in the Employee Appraiser program and used to provide specific back-up once the final performance appraisal report is printed out.

1. Edward C. Balg, "So You Hate Rating Your Workers?" *Business Week* (August 22, 1994), p. 14.
2. This is based on Peter H. Lewis, "A New Way to Rate Employee Performance More Effectively," *The New York Times* (December 19, 1993), p. 10. Employee Appraiser was developed by the Austin-Hayne Corporation of San Mateo, California. ◆

**Figure 11.9
One Page from a
Typical Management
Appraisal Form**

MAJOR PERFORMANCE STRENGTHS/WEAKNESSES

Read the definitions of each management factor below and choose the ranking which most accurately describes the employee. If, after reading the definition, it is determined that the skill area was not demonstrated because of the nature of the employee's position, indicate as Non-Applicable (N/A). The evaluation on each of the management factors below should relate directly to the employee's actual performance on the job.

PLANNING SKILL – Degree to which incumbent	Ranking Code	(CHECK ONE)	
– Assessed and established priorities of result areas	1	Far exceeds requirements	
– Designed realistic short-and long-range plans.	4	Usually exceeds requirements	
– Formulated feasible timetables.	3	Fully meets requirements	
– Anticipated possible problems and obstacles toward reaching required results.	2	Usually meets requirements	
	5	Fails to meet requirements	

Comments:
_____
_____
_____

ORGANIZING SKILL – Degree to which incumbent	Ranking Code	(CHECK ONE)	
– Grouped activities for optimal use of human and material resources in order to achieve goals.	3	Far exceeds requirements	
	2	Usually exceeds requirements	
– Clearly defined responsibilities and authority limits of employees.	5	Fully meets requirements	
– Minimized confusion and inefficiencies in work operations.	1	Usually meets requirements	
	4	Fails to meet requirements	

Comments:
_____
_____
_____

CONTROLLING SKILL – Degree to which incumbent	Ranking Code	(CHECK ONE)	
– Established appropriate procedures to be kept informed of employee's work progress.	5	Far exceeds requirements	
	4	Usually exceeds requirements	
– Identified deviations in work goal progress.	3	Fully meets requirements	
– Adjusted to deviations in work to ensure that established goals were met.	2	Usually meets requirements	
	1	Fails to meet requirements	

Comments:
_____
_____
_____

Note: This is one page from a multipage form used to appraise managers.

Performance Appraisal: Problems and Solutions

Few of the things a manager does are fraught with more peril than appraising employees' performance. Employees in general tend to be overly optimistic about what their ratings will be, and also know that their raises, career progress, and peace of mind may well hinge on how they are rated. This alone should make it somewhat difficult to rate performance; even more problematic, however, are the numerous structural problems that can cast serious doubt on just how fair the whole process is. In this section we therefore turn to some of the main appraisal problems and how to solve them, as well as to several other pertinent appraisal issues.

Dealing with the Five Main Rating Scale Appraisal Problems

Five main problems can undermine appraisal tools such as graphic rating scales: unclear standards, halo effect, central tendency, leniency or strictness, and bias.

unclear performance standards
An appraisal scale that is too open to interpretation; instead, descriptive phrases that define each trait and what is meant by standards like "good" or "unsatisfactory" should be included.

Unclear Standards   The problem of **unclear standards** is illustrated in **Table 11.2**. Although the graphic rating scale seems objective, it would probably result in unfair appraisals because the traits and degrees of merit are open to interpretation. For example, different supervisors would probably define "good" performance, "fair" performance, and so on differently. The same is true of traits such as "quality of work" or "creativity."

There are several ways to rectify this problem. The best way is to develop and include descriptive phrases that define each trait, as in Figure 11.3. There the form specified what was meant by "outstanding," "superior," and "good" quality of work. This specificity results in appraisals that are more consistent and more easily explained.

halo effect
In performance appraisal, the problem that occurs when a supervisor's rating of an employee on one trait biases the rating of that person on other traits.

Halo Effect   The **halo effect** means that the rating of an employee on one trait (such as "gets along with others") biases the way that person is rated on other traits (such as "quantity of work"). This problem often occurs with employees who are especially friendly (or unfriendly) toward the supervisor. For example, an unfriendly employee will often be rated unsatisfactory for all traits rather than just for the trait "gets along well with others." Being aware of this problem is a major step toward avoiding it. Supervisory training can also alleviate the problem.[15]

central tendency
A tendency to rate all employees the same way, such as rating them all average.

Central Tendency   Many supervisors have a **central tendency** when filling in rating scales. For example, if the rating scale ranges from 1 to 7, they tend to avoid the highs (6 and 7) and lows (1 and 2) and rate most of their employees between 3 and 5. If a graphic rating scale is used, this central tendency could mean that all

TABLE 11.2 A Graphic Rating Scale with Unclear Standards

	EXCELLENT	GOOD	FAIR	POOR
Quality of work				
Quantity of work				
Creativity				
Integrity				

Note: For example, what exactly is meant by "good," "quantity of work," and so forth?

employees are simply rated "average." Such a restriction can distort the evaluations, making them less useful for promotion, salary, or counselling purposes. Ranking employees instead of using a graphic rating scale can avoid this central tendency problem because all employees must be ranked and thus can't all be rated average.

Leniency or Strictness   Some supervisors tend to rate all their employees consistently high (or low), just as some instructors are notoriously high graders and others are not. This **strictness/leniency** problem is especially serious with graphic rating scales, since supervisors aren't necessarily required to avoid giving all their employees high (or low) ratings. On the other hand, when ranking employees, a manager is forced to distinguish between high and low performers. Thus, strictness/leniency is not a problem with the ranking or forced distribution approaches.

strictness/leniency
The problem that occurs when a supervisor has a tendency to rate all employees either high or low.

Diversity Counts
In Performance Appraisal

A recent study illustrates how bias can consciously or subconsciously influence the way one person appraises another. In this study, researchers sought to determine the extent to which pregnancy is a source of bias in performance appraisals.[1] The subjects consisted of a sample of 220 undergraduate students between the ages of 17 and 43 attending a midwestern university.

Two videotapes were prepared of a woman participating in several employment exercises. Each videotape showed three five-minute scenarios in which this woman interacted with another woman. For example, she acted as a customer representative to deal with an irate customer, tried to sell a computer system to a potential customer, and dealt with a problem employee. In each case the performance level of the "employee" was designed to be average or slightly above average. The "employee" was the same in both videotapes and the videotapes were identical except for one difference: The first videotape was made in the "employee's" ninth month of pregnancy, while the second tape was made about five months later. The aim of the study was to investigate whether or not the "employee's" pregnancy influenced the performance appraisal rating she received for dealing with the irate customer, selling the computer system, and dealing with the problem employee. Several groups of student raters then watched either the "pregnant" or "not pregnant" tape. They then rated the "employee" on a five-point graphic rating scale for individual characteristics such as "ability to do the job," "dependability," and "physical mannerisms." For each characteristic the employee was rated from "very poor" (1) to "excellent" (5).

The results of this study suggest that pregnant women may face additional workplace discrimination above and beyond any gender bias that may already exist against women in general. Despite having been exposed to otherwise identical behaviour by the same female "employee," the student raters of this study "with a remarkably high degree of consistency" assigned lower performance ratings to a pregnant woman as opposed to a nonpregnant one.[2] Furthermore, men raters seemed more susceptible to negative influence than did women. Given the fact that many employees still report to a male supervisor and that supervisory ratings are often the determinant of one's advancement, the researchers conclude that any bias that exists could make it even harder for women to have both children and careers. One implication is that raters must be forewarned of such problems and trained to use objectivity in rating employees.

1. Jane Halpert, Midge Wilson, and Julia Hickman, "Pregnancy as a Source of Bias in Performance Appraisals," *Journal of Organizational Behaviour* 14 (1993), pp. 649–63.
2. Halpert et al., "Pregnancy as a Source of Bias," p. 655. ◆

appraisal bias
The tendency to allow individual differences such as age, race, and sex to affect the appraisal ratings these employees receive.

Appraisal Bias Individual differences among ratees in terms of characteristics like age, race, and sex can affect their ratings, often quite apart from each ratee's actual performance.[16] In one study, for instance, researchers found a systematic tendency to evaluate older ratees (over 60 years of age) lower on "performance capacity" and "potential for development" than younger employees.[17] The ratee's race and sex can also affect the person's rating. However, here the **appraisal bias** is not necessarily consistently against designated group members, as it seems to be in the case of older workers. In one study, high-performing females were often rated significantly higher than were high-performing males. Similarly, low-performing blacks were often rated significantly higher than were low-performing whites.[18]

An interesting picture of how age can distort evaluations emerges from a study of registered nurses. When the nurses were 30–39 years old, they and their supervisors each rated the nurses' performance virtually the same. In the 21–29 category, supervisors actually rated nurses higher than they rated themselves. However, for the 40–61 nurse age category, the supervisors rated nurses' performance lower than the nurses rated their own performance. The conclusion here may be that supervisors are tougher in appraising older employees. Specifically, they don't give them as much credit for their success, while attributing any low performance to their lack of ability.[19] A related problem is described in the Diversity Counts box.

An employee's previous performance can also affect the evaluation of his or her current performance.[20] The actual error can take several forms. Sometimes the rater may systematically overestimate improvement by a poor worker or decline by a good worker, for instance. In some situations—especially when the change in behaviour is more gradual—the rater may simply be insensitive to improvement or decline. In any case, it is important when rating performance to do so objectively. Factors such as previous performance, age, or race, should not be allowed to influence results.

How to Avoid Appraisal Problems

There are at least three ways to minimize the impact of appraisal problems such as bias and central tendency. First, raters must be familiar with the problems just discussed. Understanding the problem can help to prevent it.

Second, choose the right appraisal tool. Each tool, such as the graphic rating scale or critical incident method, has its own advantages and disadvantages. For example, the ranking method avoids central tendency but can cause ill feelings when employees' performances are in fact all "high" (**Table 11.3**).

Third, training supervisors to eliminate rating errors such as halo, leniency, and central tendency can help them avoid these problems.[21] In a typical training program, raters are shown a videotape of jobs being performed and are asked to rate the worker. Ratings made by each participant are then placed on a flip chart and the various errors (such as leniency and halo) are explained. For example, if a trainee rated all criteria (such as quality, quantity, and so on) about the same, the trainer might explain that a halo error had occurred. Typically, the trainer gives the correct rating and then illustrates the rating errors the participants made.[22] According to one study, computer-assisted appraisal training improved managers' ability to conduct performance appraisal discussions with their employees.[23]

Rater training is no panacea for reducing rating errors or improving appraisal accuracy. In practice, several factors, including the extent to which pay is tied to performance ratings, union pressure, employee turnover, time constraints, and the need to justify ratings, may be more important than training. This means that improving appraisal accuracy calls for not just training but also reducing outside factors, such as union pressure and time constraints.[24]

TABLE 11.3 Important Advantages and Disadvantages of Appraisal Tools

	ADVANTAGES	DISADVANTAGES
Graphic rating scales	Simple to use; provides a quantitative rating for each employee.	Standards may be unclear; halo effect, central tendency, leniency, bias can also be problems.
Alternation ranking	Simple to use (but not as simple as graphic rating scales). Avoids central tendency and other problems of rating scales.	Can cause disagreements among employees and may be unfair if all employees *are*, in fact, excellent.
Forced distribution method	End up with a predetermined number of people in each group.	Appraisal results depend on the adequacy of the original choice of cutoff points.
Critical incident method	Helps specify what is "right" and "wrong" about the employee's performance; forces supervisor to evaluate employees on an ongoing basis.	Difficult to rate or rank employees relative to one another.
Behaviourally anchored rating scale	Provides behavioural "anchors." BARS is very accurate.	Difficult to develop.
MBO	Tied to jointly-agreed-upon performance objectives.	Time-consuming.

Ethical Issues in Performance Appraisal

Ethics should be the bedrock of a performance appraisal. In fact most managers (and college/university students) understand that an appraiser or professor can "stick to the rules" and conduct a review of one's performance but still fail to provide an honest assessment. As one commentator puts it:

The overall objective of high-ethics performance reviews should be to provide an honest assessment of performance and to mutually develop a plan to improve the individual's effectiveness. That requires that we tell people where they stand and that we be straight with them.[25]

And, of course, it's exactly this type of honest and fruitful appraisal that managers should shoot for. Guidelines for developing an effective appraisal process include the following:[26]

1. Conduct a job analysis to ascertain characteristics (such as "timely project completion") required for successful job performance. Graphically:

   Job Analysis $\rightarrow$ Performance Standards $\rightarrow$ Performance Appraisal

2. Incorporate these characteristics into a rating instrument. (The professional literature recommends rating instruments that are tied to specific job behaviours, that is, BARS.)

3. Make sure that definitive performance standards are provided to all raters and ratees.

4. Use clearly defined individual dimensions of job performance (like "quantity" or "quality") rather than undefined, global measures of job performance (like "overall performance").

5. When using graphic rating scales, avoid abstract trait names (for example, "loyalty," "honesty") unless they can be defined in terms of observable behaviours.

6. Employ subjective supervisory ratings (essays, for instance) as only one component of the overall appraisal process.

7. Train supervisors to use the rating instrument properly. Give instructions on how to apply performance appraisal standards ("outstanding," and so on) when making judgments. Ensure that subjective standards are are not subject to bias.[27]

8. Allow appraisers substantial daily contact with the employee being evaluated.

9. Whenever possible, have more than one appraiser conduct the appraisal and conduct all such appraisals independently. This process can help to cancel out individual errors and biases.

10. Utilize formal appeal mechanisms and a review of ratings by upper-level managers.

11. Document evaluations and reasons for any termination decision.

12. Where appropriate, provide corrective guidance to assist poor performers in improving their performance.

Who Should Do the Appraising?

Who should actually rate an employee's performance? Several options exist.

Appraisal by the Immediate Supervisor   Supervisors' ratings still are the heart of most appraisal systems. Getting a supervisor's appraisal is relatively easy and also makes a great deal of sense. The supervisor should be—and usually is—in the best position to observe and evaluate the performance of employees reporting to him or her and is responsible for their performance.

Using Peer Appraisals   The appraisal of an employee by his or her peers can be effective in predicting future management success. There is a high correlation between peer and supervisor ratings.[28] Peers have more opportunity to observe ratees, and to observe them at more revealing times than supervisors.[29] From a study of military officers, for example, we know that peer ratings were quite accurate in predicting which officers would be promoted and which would not.[30] In

This food service supervisor is conducting a feedback session about an employee's performance during today's major banquet, to keep communications open and build employee commitment.

another study that involved more than 200 industrial managers, peer ratings were similarly useful in predicting who would be promoted.[31] One potential problem is *logrolling*. Here all the peers simply get together to rate each other high.

With more firms using self-managing teams, peer or team appraisals are becoming more popular. At Ciba in Mississauga, Ontario, peer reviews were implemented as part of its transition to self-directed work teams. There was some uneasiness at first, but over time, a trusting relationship developed between coworkers.[32]

Rating Committees   Many employers use rating committees to evaluate employees. These committees are usually composed of the employee's immediate supervisor and three or four other supervisors. Using multiple raters can be advantageous. While there may be a discrepancy in the ratings made by individual supervisors, the composite ratings tend to be more reliable, fair, and valid.[33] Several raters can help cancel out problems like bias and the halo effect on the part of individual raters. Furthermore, when there *are* variations in raters' ratings, they usually stem from the fact that raters often observe different facets of an employee's performance; the appraisal ought to reflect these differences.[34] Even when a committee is not used, it is common to have the appraisal reviewed by the manager immediately above the one who makes the appraisal.

Self-ratings Employees' self-ratings of performance are also sometimes used (generally in conjunction with supervisors' ratings). The basic problem with these is that employees usually rate themselves higher than they are rated by supervisors or peers.[35] In one study, for example, it was found that when asked to rate their own job performances, 40 percent of the employees in jobs of all types placed themselves in the top 10 percent ("one of the best"), while virtually all remaining employees rated themselves either in the top 25 percent ("well above average"), or at least in the top 50 percent ("above average"). Usually no more than one percent or two percent will place themselves in a below-average category, and then almost invariably in the top below-average category. However, self-ratings have been found to correlate more highly with performance measures if employees know that this comparison will be made, and if they are instructed to compare themselves with others.[36]

Supervisors requesting self-appraisals should know that their appraisals and the self-appraisals may accentuate appraiser-appraisee differences, and rigidify positions.[37] Furthermore, even if self-appraisals are not formally requested, each employee will enter the performance review meeting with his or her own self-appraisal in mind, and this will usually be higher than the supervisor's rating.

Appraisal by Employees Traditionally, supervisors feared that being appraised by their employees would undermine their management authority.[38] However, with today's flatter organizations and empowered workers, much managerial authority is a thing of the past, and employees are in a good position to observe managerial performance.[39] Thus, more firms today are letting employees anonymously evaluate their supervisors' performance, a process many call *upward feedback*.[40] When conducted throughout the firm, the process helps top managers diagnose management styles, identify potential "people" problems, and take corrective action with individual managers as required. Such employee ratings are especially valuable when used for developmental rather than evaluative purposes.[41] Managers who receive feedback from employees who identify themselves view the upward appraisal process more positively than do managers who receive anonymous feedback; however, employees (not surprisingly) are more comfortable giving anonymous responses and those who have to identify themselves tend to provide inflated ratings.[42]

360-degree appraisal
A performance appraisal technique that uses multiple raters including peers, employees reporting to the appraisee, supervisors, and customers.

360-Degree Appraisal Many Canadian firms, including B.C. Gas Utility Ltd., Aetna Life Insurance, Scotiabank, Goodyear Canada, and Hallmark Cards, are now using what is called 360-degree appraisal.[43] Here, as shown in **Figure 11.10**, performance information is collected "all around" an employee, from his or her supervisors, employees reporting to the appraisee, peers, and internal or external customers.[44] This feedback was originally used only for training and development purposes,[45] but has rapidly spread to use in the management of performance and pay.[46] The 360-degree approach supports the activities of performance feedback, coaching, leadership development, succession planning, and rewards and recognition.[47]

There are a number of reasons for the rapid growth of 360-degree appraisal despite the significant investment of time required for it to function successfully. Today's flatter organizations mean a more open communication climate conducive to such an approach, and it fits closely with the goals of organizations committed to continuous learning. A multiple-rater system is also more meaningful in today's

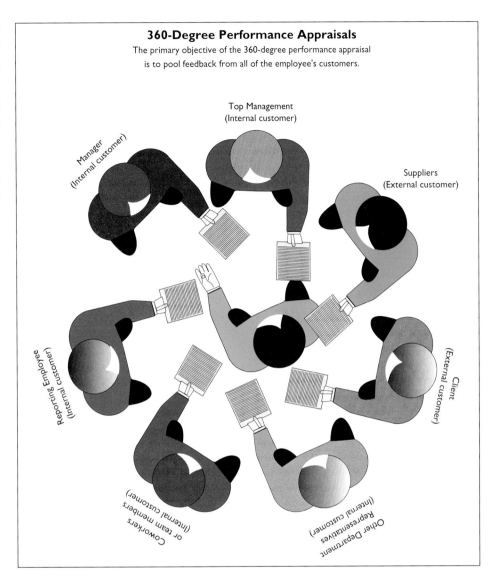

360-Degree Performance Appraisals
The primary objective of the 360-degree performance appraisal
is to pool feedback from all of the employee's customers.

reality of complex jobs, with matrix and team reporting relationships. Further, the widespread lack of confidence in traditional performance appraisals conducted only by a supervisor, and the fear associated with such appraisals on the part of both parties, have reduced the credibility of that approach.[48] A 360-degree appraisal can be perceived as a jury of peers, rather than the supervisor as a single judge, which enhances perceptions of fairness.[49]

Most 360-degree appraisal systems contain several common features. They are usually applied in a confidential and anonymous manner. Appropriate parties—peers, supervisors, employees reporting to the appraisee, and customers, for instance—complete survey questionnaires about an individual. The questionnaires must be custom-designed and linked to the organization's strategic direction, and its vision and values.[50] All this information is then compiled into individualized reports. When the information is being used for self-development purposes only, the report is presented to the person being rated, who then meets with his or her own supervisor (and possibly with their employees) and information pertinent for the purpose of developing a self-improvement plan is shared.[51]

When the information is being used for management of performance or pay, the information is also provided to the ratee's supervisor, and a supportive and facilitative process to follow up is required to ensure the behavioural change required for performance improvement.[52]

Organizations that decide to implement 360-degree appraisal should consider the following advice, which has been generated from organizations that have already done so:[53]

- the organization must be culturally ready for multi-source feedback
- groundwork on vision and values must be completed first
- employees throughout the organization should be involved and consulted on plan design
- the time, effort, expertise, and costs involved must be recognized
- questionnaires and other tools must be customized to fit the organization
- a pilot project should be conducted first
- communication with employees during all phases of design and implementation is critical.

The Appraisal Interview

Types of Interviews

appraisal interview
An interview in which the supervisor and employee review the appraisal and make plans to remedy deficiencies and reinforce strengths.

An appraisal typically culminates in an **appraisal interview.** This is an interview in which the supervisor and employee review the appraisal and make plans to remedy deficiencies and reinforce strengths. There are three basic types of appraisal interviews, each with its own objectives:[54]

Appraisal Interview Type	Appraisal Interview Objective
(1) Performance is satisfactory— Employee is promotable	(1) Make development plans
(2) Satisfactory—Not promotable	(2) Maintain performance
(3) Unsatisfactory—Correctable	(3) Plan correction

If the employee is unsatisfactory and the situation uncorrectable, there is usually no need for any appraisal interview because the person's performance is not correctable anyway. The person's poor performance is either tolerated for now, or he or she is dismissed.

Satisfactory—Promotable   Here the person's performance is satisfactory and there is a promotion ahead. This is the easiest of the three appraisal interviews. The objective is to discuss the person's career plans and to develop a specific action plan for the educational and professional development the person needs to move to the next job.

Satisfactory—Not Promotable   This interview is for employees whose performance is satisfactory but for whom promotion is not possible. Perhaps there is no more room in the company. Some employees are also happy where they are and don't want a promotion.[55] The objective here is not to improve or develop the person but to maintain satisfactory performance.

This is not easy. The best option is usually to find incentives that are important to the person and enough to maintain satisfactory performance. These might include extra time off, a small bonus, additional authority to handle a slightly enlarged job, and reinforcement, perhaps in the form of an occasional "Well done!"

Unsatisfactory—Correctable   When the person's performance is unsatisfactory but correctable, the interview objective is to lay out an action plan (as explained later) for correcting the unsatisfactory performance.

How to Prepare for the Appraisal Interview

www.jps.ab.ca
JPS Management Systems—
Competencies

There are three things to do in preparation for the interview.[56] First, assemble the data. Study the person's job description, compare the employee's performance to the standards, and review the files of the employee's previous appraisals. Next prepare the employee. Give the employee at least a week's notice to review his or her work, read over their job description, analyze problems, and gather questions and comments. Finally, choose the time and place. Find a mutually agreeable time for the interview and allow enough time for the entire interview. Interviews with non-supervisory staff like clerical workers and maintenance people should take no more than an hour. Appraising management employees often takes two or three hours. Be sure the interview is done in a private place where there will be no interruptions by phone calls or visitors.

How to Conduct the Interview

There are four things to keep in mind when conducting an appraisal interview.[57]

1. *Be direct and specific.* Talk in terms of objective work data. Use examples such as absences, tardiness, quality records, inspection reports, scrap or waste, orders processed, productivity records, material used or consumed, timeliness of tasks or projects, control or reduction of costs, numbers of errors, costs compared to budgets, customers' comments, product returns, order processing time, inventory level and accuracy, accident reports, and so on.

2. *Don't get personal.* Don't say "You're too slow in producing those reports." Instead try to compare the person's performance to a standard ("These reports should normally be done within ten days"). Similarly, don't compare the person's performance to that of other people ("He's quicker than you are").

3. *Encourage the person to talk.* Stop and listen to what the person is saying; ask open-ended questions such as "What do you think we can do to improve the situation?" Use a phrase such as "Go on" or "Tell me more." Restate the person's last point as a question, such as, "You don't think you can get the job done?"

4. *Don't tiptoe around.* Don't get personal, but do make sure the person leaves knowing specifically what he or she is doing right *and doing wrong.* Give specific examples, make sure the person understands, and get agreement before he or she leaves on how things will be improved, and by when. Develop an action plan showing steps and expected results as in **Figure 11.11**.

Argumentative behaviour on the part of the manager during a performance appraisal meeting undermines the usefulness of the evaluation process.

How to Handle a Defensive Employee   Defenses are a very important and familiar aspect of our lives. When a person is accused of poor performance, the first reaction will sometimes be *denial.* By denying the fault, the person avoids having to question his or her own competence. Others react to criticism with *anger* and *aggression.* This helps them let off steam and postpones confronting the immediate problem until they are able to cope with it. Still others react to criticism by *retreating* into a shell.

In any event, understanding and dealing with defensiveness is an important appraisal skill. In his book *Effective Psychology for Managers*, psychologist Mortimer Feinberg suggests the following:

1. *Recognize that defensive behaviour is normal.*
2. *Never attack a person's defenses.* Don't try to "explain someone to themselves" by saying things like, "You know the real reason you're using that excuse is that you can't bear to be blamed for anything." Instead try to concentrate on the act itself ("sales are down") rather than on the person ("you're not selling enough").

Figure 11.11
Example of an Action Plan

```
                                    ACTION PLAN

                                                              Date: May 18, 1998


    For: John, Assistant Plant Manager
    Problem: Parts inventory too high
    Objective: Reduce plant parts inventory by 10% in June
```

Action Steps	When	Expected Results
Determine average monthly parts inventory	6/2	Establish a base from which to measure progress
Review ordering quantities and parts usage	6/15	Identify overstock items
Ship excess parts to regional warehouse and scrap obsolete parts	6/20	Clear stock space
Set new ordering quantities for all parts	6/25	Avoid future overstocking
Check records to measure where we are now	7/1	See how close we are to objective

3. *Postpone action.* Sometimes it is best to do nothing at all. People frequently react to sudden threats by instinctively hiding behind their "masks." But, given sufficient time, a more rational reaction takes over.

4. *Recognize human limitations.* Don't expect to be able to solve every problem that comes up, especially the human ones. More important, remember that a supervisor should not try to be a psychologist. Offering employees understanding is one thing; trying to deal with deep psychological problems is another matter entirely.

How to Constructively Criticize an Employee's Performance   When criticism is required, it should be done in a manner that lets the person maintain his or her dignity and sense of worth. Specifically, criticism should be provided constructively in private. Provide examples of critical incidents and specific suggestions of what could be done and why. Avoid a once-a-year "critical broadside" by giving feedback on a daily basis, so that at the formal review there are no surprises. Never say the person is "always" wrong (since no one is ever "always" wrong or right). Finally, criticism should be objective and free of any personal biases.

How to Ensure That the Appraisal Interview Leads to Improved Performance
It is important to clear up job-related problems by setting improvement goals and a schedule for achieving them. In one study the researchers found that whether or not employees expressed satisfaction with their appraisal interview depended mostly on three factors: not feeling threatened during the interview; having an opportunity to present their ideas and feelings and to influence the course of the interview; and having a helpful and constructive supervisor conduct the interview.[58]

However, it is not enough for employees to be satisfied with their appraisal interviews. The main objective is to get them to improve their subsequent performance. Here researchers have found that *clearing up job-related problems* with the appraisee and *setting measurable performance targets and a schedule for achieving them* are the actions that consistently lead to improved performance.

How to Handle a Formal Written Warning   There will be times when an employee's performance is so poor that a formal written warning is required. Such written warnings serve two purposes: (1) They may serve to shake the employee out of his or her bad habits, and (2) they can help the manager defend his or her rating of the employee both to his or her boss and (if needed) to a court or Human Rights Commission. Thus, written warnings should identify the standards under which the employee is judged, make it clear that the employee was aware of the standard, specify any violation of the standard, and indicate that the employee had an opportunity to correct his or her behaviour.

The Role of Appraisals in Managing Performance

Appraisals serve several purposes, including providing information upon which promotion and salary decisions are made. Ideally, however, appraisals should also serve a *managing performance* role, by providing a concrete basis for an analysis of an employee's work-related peformance and the steps that should be taken to maintain or change it. Therefore, this final section provides a discussion of how appraisals can be carried out to better manage employee performance.

Should Appraisals Be Abolished?

www.tka.co.uk/magic/
feature7.htm
Marketing Magic

Many experts feel that traditional appraisals don't help in managing performance and may actually backfire. They argue that most performance appraisal systems neither motivate employees nor guide their development.[59] Furthermore, "… they cause conflict between supervisors and employees and lead to dysfunctional behaviours."[60] The traits measured are often personal in nature and "… Who likes the idea of being evaluated on his or her: honesty, integrity, teamwork, compassion, cooperation [objectivity]…?"[61]

Similarly, proponents of quality management programs (including the late W. Edwards Deming) generally argue in favour of eliminating performance appraisals.[62] They believe that the organization is a system of interrelated parts and that an employee's performance is more a function of factors like training, communication, tools, and supervision than of his or her own motivation.[63] They also suggest that performance appraisals can have unanticipated consequences. Thus, employees might make themselves look better in terms of customer service by continually badgering customers to send in letters of support. Deming particularly argued against forced distribution appraisal systems because of their potential for undermining teamwork.[64]

Criticisms like these appear to be supported by surveys of how managers view appraisal systems. In one study of almost 300 managers, 32 percent rated their performance appraisals as "very ineffective," while only four percent rated them "effective to a large extent."[65] Another survey of 181 manufacturing and service organizations concluded that 11 percent had stopped using annual appraisals, while another 25 percent planned to discontinue them within two years.[66] There's little doubt that most appraisals are viewed with trepidation if not disdain.

CHAPTER 11 ◆ *Performance Appraisal*   **437**

Yet, while these criticisms have merit, it's not practical to eliminate performance appraisals. Managers still need some way to review employees' work-related behaviour. And, although Deming reportedly hated performance reviews, "... he really didn't offer any concrete solution to the problem or an alternative, other than just [to] pay everybody at the same salary."[67] The solution instead is to create performance appraisal systems that make it possible to manage performance in today's team-oriented and quality-oriented environments. Creating more effective appraisals, as described in this chapter, is one way to do this. Others suggest also taking a quality-based approach, which is explained next.

Quality-Based Appraisals for Managing Performance

Quality management programs are organization-wide programs that integrate all functions and processes of the business such that all aspects, including design, planning, production, distribution, and field service are aimed at maximizing customer satisfaction through continuous improvements.[68] Deming said such programs are built on a number of principles, including: ceasing dependence on inspection to achieve quality; aiming for continuous improvement; instituting extensive training on the job; driving out fear so that everyone may work effectively for the company; breaking down barriers between departments; eliminating work standards (quotas) on the factory floor; removing barriers that rob employees of their right to pride of workmanship (in particular, abolishing the annual merit rating and all forms of management by objectives); and instituting a vigorous program of education and self-improvement.[69]

Quality management principles like these can be applied to designing quality-based performance management systems. A *performance management system* can be defined as a performance appraisal system that does not force managers to give false or misleading measurements and instead facilitates open, job-related discussions between the supervisor and the employee.[70] The characteristics of such a system would include:

An appraisal scale that contains relatively few performance categories and avoids a forced distribution.[71]

Objective ways to measure results, avoiding subjective criteria such as teamwork and integrity.[72]

A determination about whether any performance deficiency is a result of (1) employee motivation, (2) inadequate training, or (3) factors (like poor supervision) that are outside the employee's control.

360-degree feedback from a number of different sources, not just supervisors but internal and possibly external "customers" of the employee as well.[73]

Adequate "samples" of work behaviour: "regular observations of their staff members' work behaviours and performance."[74]

An atmosphere of partnership and constructive advice.[75]

A thorough analysis of key external and internal customers' needs and expectations on which to base performance appraisal standards. (For example, if accurately completing the sales slip is important for the accounting department, then the retail sales clerk should be appraised in part on this dimension).

A form for implementing such a quality-based performance management system is shown in **Figure 11.12**. It consists of a performance contract specifying customer expectations and performance goals, as well as an internal customer feedback form.[76]

Figure 11.12
Performance Contract
and Internal Customer
Feedback Forms

Source: David Antonioni,
"Improve the Performance
Management Process before
Discontinuing Performance
Appraisals," *Compensation and
Benefits Review* (May–June
1994), p. 33, 34.

PERFORMANCE CONTRACT

Within the next year, I understand that our organization's objectives are _____

_____ and that the goals of our department are _____ . I also understand that our work unit goals are _____ .

My key internal customers are _____ and their work needs and expectations are _____ .

To make my contribution toward attaining the goals stated above, I understand that I am expected to do the following:

My individual performance goals are _____ .

My goals for improving work methods (process) are _____ .

My goals for improving specific interpersonal work behaviours when I interact with the following _____ are _____ .

I believe these goals are acceptable and attainable. I also understand that I will be evaluated by multiple appraisal sources (supervisor, peers, internal, and, if appropriate, external customers).

Compensation for my work performance will be based on whether my performance was (1) outstanding, (2) fully competent, or (3) unsatisfactory. I understand that the following forms of compensation will be considered: (1) merit award for my individual performance goal attainment, (2) enhancement and utilization of my skills, (3) my work unit's or team's performance (gainsharing), and (4) our organization's performance (profit sharing).

_____   _____

Your signature   Supervisor's signature

(continued)

Chapter Review

Summary

1. People want and need feedback regarding how they are doing, and appraisal provides an opportunity to give them that feedback.
2. Before the appraisal, make sure to clarify the expected performance so that each employee knows what he or she should be shooting for.
3. Performance appraisal tools include the graphic rating scale, alternation ranking method, forced distribution method, BARS, MBO, and critical incident method.
4. Appraisal problems to beware of include unclear standards, halo effect, central tendency, leniency or strictness, and bias.

Figure 11.12
(continued)

INTERNAL CUSTOMER FEEDBACK

As an internal customer of (name)_____ , please give him/her feedback regarding his/her work performance and work behaviours. After you have completed this form, send it to _____ . Your reponses will be tabulated and then discussed with the individual.

To what extent did this individual meet your expectations of work quality in the areas you indicate as important:

	Exceeds	Meets	Doesn't Meet
1. Accuracy of the work you received			
2. Timeliness of the work you received			
3. Dependability of the work you received			
4. Sharing relevant information to help you do your work more efficiently			

In terms of your interactions with this person, please feel free to comment on any of the following:

1. The type of errors and the amount of rework

2. The nature of any work delays

3. Collaborative efforts to improve work or business processes

4. Interpersonal work behaviours

Please list any *new* expectations that you have regarding the work you receive from this person.

Thank you for completing this feedback form. A follow-up interview with you may be established to discuss the feedback, and, if necessary, improvement goals and an action plan will be developed.

5. Most employees probably want a specific explanation or examples regarding why they were appraised high or low, and for this, compiling a record of positive and negative critical incidents can be useful. Even if the firm requires that the appraisal results be summarized in a form such as a graphic rating scale, a list of critical incidents can be useful when the time comes to discuss the appraisal with an employee.

6. The employee should view the appraisal as a fair one, and in this regard there are four actions required: evaluate performance frequently; make sure the rater is familiar with the person's performance; make sure there is agreement between the manager and the employee concerning job duties; and finally, solicit the employee's help when formulating plans for eliminating performance weaknesses.

7. There are three types of appraisal interviews. When performance is unsatisfactory but correctable the objective is to lay out an action plan for correcting performance. For employees whose performance is satisfactory but for whom promotion is not possible, the objective is to maintain satisfactory performance. Finally, the satisfactory—promotable interview has the main objective of discussing the person's career plans and developing a specific action plan for the educational and professional development the person needs to move on to the next job.

8. Preparing for the appraisal interview requires assembling the data, preparing the employee, and choosing the time and place.

9. To bring about constructive change in an employee's behaviour, get the person to talk in the interview. Try silence, use open-ended questions, state questions in terms of a problem, use choice questions to try to understand the feelings underlying what the person is saying, and restate the person's last point as a question.

10. The best way to handle a defensive employee is to proceed very carefully. Specifically, recognize that defensive behaviour is normal, never attack a person's defenses, and postpone actions.

11. The most important objective of an appraisal interview is to clear up job-related problems and set improvement goals and a schedule for achieving them.

12. Appraisals should also ideally serve a performance management role by providing a concrete basis for an analysis of an employee's work-related performance. Creating more effective appraisals, as described in this chapter, is one way to accomplish this. Others suggest taking a quality-based approach. Characteristics of such an approach include: making the appraisal scale as broadly descriptive as possible so that it contains relatively few performance categories and avoids a forced distribution; measuring results objectively; specifically identifying if the performance deficiency is a result of motivation, training, or factors outside the employee's control; using 360-degree feedback; including adequate samples of work behaviour; addressing problems in an atmosphere of partnership and constructive advice; and basing performance standards on an analysis of key external and internal customers' needs and expectations.

Key Terms

360-degree appraisal
alternation ranking
  method
appraisal bias
appraisal interview
behaviourally anchored
  rating scale (BARS)

central tendency
critical incident method
forced distribution
  method
graphic rating scale
halo effect

management by
  objectives (MBO)
paired comparison
method
strictness/leniency
unclear performance
standards

Discussion Questions and Exercises

1. Discuss the pros and cons of at least four performance appraisal tools.

2. Working individually or in groups, develop a graphic rating scale for the following jobs: secretary, engineer, directory assistance operator.

3. Working individually or in groups, evaluate the rating scale in Figure 11.1. Discuss ways to improve it.

4. Explain how the alternation ranking method, the paired comparison method, and the forced distribution method should be used.

5. Working individually or in groups, develop, over the period of a week, a set of critical incidents covering the classroom performance of one of your instructors.

6. Explain, in your own words, how you would go about developing a behaviourally anchored rating scale.

7. Explain the problems to be avoided in appraising performance.

8. Discuss the pros and cons of using different potential raters to appraise a person's performance.
9. Explain the four types of appraisal interview objectives and how they affect the way the interview should be managed.
10. Explain how to conduct an appraisal interview.
11. Answer the question: "How would you get the interviewee to talk during an appraisal interview?"

Application Exercises

RUNNING CASE: Carter Cleaning Company

The Performance Appraisal

After spending several weeks on the job, Jennifer was surprised to discover that her father had not formally evaluated any employee's performance for all the years that he had owned the business. Jack's position was that he had "a hundred higher-priority things to attend to," such as boosting sales and lowering costs, and, in any case, many employees didn't stick around long enough to be appraisable anyway. Furthermore, contended Jack, manual workers such as those doing the pressing and the cleaning did periodically get positive feedback in terms of praise from Jack for a job well done or criticism, also from Jack, if things did not look right during one of his swings through the stores. Similarly, Jack was never shy about telling his managers about store problems so that they, too, got some feedback on where they stood.

This informal feedback notwithstanding, Jennifer believes that a more formal appraisal approach is needed. She believes that there are criteria such as quality, quantity, attendance, and punctuality that should be evaluated periodically even if a worker is paid on piece rate. Furthermore, she feels quite strongly that the managers need to have a list of quality standards for matters, such as store cleanliness, efficiency, safety, and adherence to budget, on which they know they are to be formally evaluated.

Questions

1. Is Jennifer right about the need to evaluate the workers formally? The managers? Why or why not?
2. Develop a performance appraisal method for the workers and managers in each store.

CASE INCIDENT: Appraising the Secretaries at Sweetwater U

Rob Winchester, newly appointed vice president of human resources at Sweetwater University, faced a tough problem shortly after his university career began. Three weeks after he came on board in September, Sweetwater's president, Rob's boss, told Rob that one of his first tasks was to improve the appraisal system used to evaluate secretarial and clerical performance at Sweetwater U. Apparently, the main difficulty was that the performance appraisal was traditionally tied directly to salary increases given at the end of the year. So most administrators were less than accurate when they used the graphic rating forms that were the basis of the clerical staff evaluation. In fact, what usually happened was that each administrator simply rated the clerk or secretary reporting to him or her as "excellent." This cleared the way for all support staff to receive a maximum pay increase every year.

But the current university budget simply did not include enough money to fund another "maximum" annual increase for every staffer. Furthermore, Sweetwater's president felt that the custom of providing invalid feedback to each secretary on his or her year's performance was not productive, so he had asked the new vice president to revise the system. In October, Rob sent a memo to all administrators telling them that in the future no more than half the secretaries reporting to any particular administrator could be appraised as "excellent." This move, in effect, forced each supervisor to begin ranking his or her secretaries for quality of performance. The vice president's memo met widespread resistance immediately—from administrators, who were afraid that many of their secretaries would begin leaving for more lucrative jobs in private industry, and from secretaries, who felt that the new system was unfair and reduced each secretary's chance of receiving a maximum salary increase. A handful of secretaries had begun quietly picketing outside the president's home on the university campus. The picketing, caustic remarks by disgruntled administrators, and rumours of an impending slowdown by the secretaries (there were about 250 on the campus) made Rob Winchester wonder whether he had made the right decision by setting up forced ranking. He knew, however, that there were a few performance appraisal experts in the School of Business, so he decided to set up an appointment with them to discuss the matter.

He met with them the next morning. He explained the situation as he had found it: the present appraisal system had been set up when the university first opened ten years earlier, and the appraisal form had been developed primarily by a committee of secretaries. Under that system, Sweetwater's administrators filled out forms similar to the one shown in Figure 11.3. This once-a-year appraisal (in March) had run into problems almost immediately, since it was apparent from the start that administrators varied widely in their interpretations of job standards, as well as in how conscientiously they filled out the forms and supervised the secretaries. Moreover, at the end of the first year it became obvious to everyone that each secretary's salary increase was tied directly to the March appraisal. For example, those rated "excellent" received the maximum increases, those rated "good" received smaller increases, and those given neither rating received only the standard across-the-board cost-of-living increase. Since universities in general—and Sweetwater U in particular—have paid secretaries somewhat lower salaries than those prevailing in private industry, some secretaries left in a huff that first year. From that time on, most administrators simply rated all secretaries excellent in order to reduce staff turnover, thus ensuring each a maximum increase. In the process, they also avoided the hard feelings aroused by the significant performance differences otherwise highlighted by administrators.

Two Sweetwater experts agreed to consider the problem, and in two weeks they came back to the vice president with the following recommendations. First, the form used to rate the secretaries was grossly insufficient. It was unclear what "excellent" or "quality of work" meant, for example. They recommended instead a form like that in Figure 11.4. In addition, they recommended that the vice president rescind his earlier memo and no longer attempt to force university administrators arbitrarily to rate at least half their secretaries as something less than excellent. The two consultants pointed out that this was, in fact, an unfair procedure since it was quite possible that any particular administrator might have staffers who were all or virtually all excellent—or conceivably, although less likely, all below standard. The experts said that the way to get all the administrators to take the appraisal process more seriously was to stop tying it to salary increases.

In other words, they recommended that every administrator fill out a form like that in Figure 11.4 for each secretary at least once a year and then use this form as the basis of a counselling session. Salary increases would have to be made on some basis other than the performance appraisal, so that administrators would no longer hesitate to fill out the rating forms honestly.

Rob thanked the two experts and went back to his office to ponder their recommendations. Some of the recommendations (such as substituting the new rating form for the old) seemed to make sense. Nevertheless, he still had serious doubts as to the efficacy of any graphic rating form, particularly if he were to decide in favour of his original forced ranking approach. The experts' second recommendation—to stop tying the appraisals to automatic salary increases—made sense but raised at least one very practical problem: If salary increases were not to be based on performance appraisals, on what were they to be based? He began wondering whether the experts' recommendations weren't simply based on ivory tower theorizing.

Questions

1. Do you think that the experts' recommendations will be sufficient to get most of the administrators to fill out the rating forms properly? Why? Why not? What additional actions (if any) do you think will be necessary?

2. Do you think that Vice President Winchester would be better off dropping graphic rating forms, substituting instead one of the other techniques we discussed in this chapter, such as a ranking method?

3. What performance appraisal system would you develop for the secretaries if you were Rob Winchester? Defend your answer.

Human Resources Management Simulation

In Exercise 7, the simulation provides an opportunity to consider two methods of performance appraisal—BARS and narrative (called the "output" method in the simulation)—and decide which one would be appropriate for each of three specific jobs in the plant. The exercise also includes the design of a BARS form. Exercise 8 asks that a presentation be prepared to educate the plant supervisors about the advantages and disadvantages of a more comprehensive performance appraisal system than the one-page form they are currently using. Emphasis needs to be put on how performance appraisal information is needed to perform other HR functions (such as succession planning), to manage the workers on the plant floor, and so on. This preparation should also include some thought about objections that may be raised by the supervisors such as more paperwork, and how these concerns can be addressed. Finally, Simulation 3 provides an excellent opportunity to role play an appraisal interview between the Plant Manager and the Maintenance Supervisor.

Take It to the Net

Check out our Companion Website at

www.prenticehall.ca/dessler

for a multitude of practice questions, key terms and concepts, Weblinks to related sites, newsgroups, CBC video updates, and more.

Notes

1. Kenneth Teel, "Performance Appraisal: Current Trends, Persistent Progress," *Personnel Journal* (April 1980), pp. 296–301. See also Christina Banks and Kevin Murphy, "Toward Narrowing the Research-Practice Gap in Performance Appraisals," *Personnel Psychology* 38, no. 2 (Summer 1985), pp. 335–46. For a description of how to implement an improved performance appraisal system, see, for example, Ted Cocheu, "Performance Appraisal: A Case in Point," *Personnel Journal* 65, no. 9 (September 1986), pp. 48–53; William H. Wagel, "Performance Appraisal with a Difference," *Personnel* 64, no. 2 (February 1987), pp. 4–6; and Jeanette Cleveland et al., "Multiple Uses of Performance Appraisal: Prevalence and Correlates," *Journal of Applied Psychology* 74, no. 1 (February 1989), pp. 130–5; Ian Carlton and Martyn Sloman, "Performance Appraisal in Practice," *Human Resource Management Journal* 2, no. 3 (Spring 1992), pp. 80–94.

2. M. Gibb-Clark, "Employee Appraisals Find Few Friends," *The Globe & Mail* (May 28, 1993), p. B4.

3. Teel, "Performance Appraisal," p. 301. For a good explanation of why sole reliance on appraisal by supervisors may not be a good idea, see Keki Bhote, "Boss Performance Appraisal: A Metric Whose Time Has Gone," *Employment Relations Today* 21, no. 1 (Spring 1994), pp. 1–9.

4. Teel, "Performance Appraisal." See also Martin Friedman, "Ten Steps to Objective Appraisals," *Personnel Journal* 65, no. 6 (June 1986).

5. For a recent discussion see Gary English, "Tuning Up for Performance Management," *Training and Development Journal* (April 1991), pp. 56–60.

6. This is based on James Buford, Jr., Bettye Burkhalter, and Grover Jacobs, "Link Job Descriptions to Performance Appraisals," *Personnel Journal* (June 1988), pp. 132–40.

7. C.L. Hughes, "The Bell-Shaped Curve That Inspires Guerilla Warfare," *Personnel Administrator* (May 1987), pp. 40–1.

8. Commerce Clearing House Editorial Staff, "Performance Appraisal: What Three Companies Are Doing," Chicago, 1985. See also Richard Girard, "Are Performance Appraisals Passé?" *Personnel Journal* 67, no. 8 (August 1988), pp. 89–90, which explains how companies can appraise performance using incidents instead of formal performance appraisals.

9. See, for example, Timothy Keaveny and Anthony McGann, "A Comparison of Behavioral Expectation Scales and Graphic Rating Scales," *Journal of Applied Psychology* 60 (1975), pp. 695–703. See also John Ivancevich, "A Longitudinal Study of Behavioral Expectation Scales: Attitudes and Performance," *Journal of Applied Psychology* (April 1980), pp. 139–46.

10. Based on Donald Schwab, Herbert Heneman III, and Thomas DeCotiis, "Behaviorally Anchored Scales: A Review of the Literature," *Personnel Psychology* 28 (1975), pp. 549–62. For a discussion, see also Uco Wiersma and Gary Latham, "The Practicality of Behavioral Observation Scales, Behavioral Expectations Scales, and Trait Scales," *Personnel Psychology* 30, no. 3 (Autumn 1986), pp. 619–28.

11. Lawrence Fogli, Charles Hulin, and Milton Blood, "Development of First Level Behavioral Job Criteria," *Journal of Applied Psychology* 55 (1971), pp. 3–8. See also Terry Dickenson and Peter Fellinger, "A Comparison of the Behaviorally Anchored Rating and Fixed Standard Scale Formats," *Journal of Applied Psychology* (April 1980), pp. 147–54.

12. Keaveny and McGann, "A Comparison of Behavioral Expectation Scales," pp. 695–703; Schwab, Heneman, and DeCotiis, "Behaviorally Anchored Rating Scales"; and James Goodale and Ronald Burke, "Behaviorally Based Rating Scales Need Not Be Job Specific," *Journal of Applied Psychology* 60 (June 1975).

13. Wayne Cascio and Enzo Valenzi, "Behaviorally Anchored Rating Scales: Effects of Education and Job Experience of Raters and Ratees," *Journal of Applied Psychology* 62, no. 3 (1977), pp. 278–82. See also Gary P. Latham and Kenneth N. Wexley, "Behavioral Observation Scales for Performance Appraisal Purposes," *Personnel Psychology* 30, no. 2 (Summer 1977), pp. 255–68; H. John Bernardin, Kenneth M. Alvares, and C. J. Cranny, "A Recomparison of Behavioral Expectation Scales to Summated Scales," *Journal of Applied Psychology* 61, no. 5 (October 1976), p. 564; Frank E. Saal and Frank J. Landy, "The Mixed Standard Rating Scale: An Evaluation," *Organizational Behavior and Human Performance* 18, no. 1 (February 1977), pp. 19–35; Frank J. Landy et al., "Behaviorally Anchored Scales for Rating the Performance of Police Officers," *Journal of Applied Psychology* 61, no. 6 (December 1976), pp. 750–8; and Kevin R. Murphy and Joseph Constans, "Behavioral Anchors as a Source of Bias in Rating," *Journal of Applied Psychology* 72, no. 4 (November 1987), pp. 573–7.

14. See Martin Levy, "Almost-Perfect Performance Appraisals," *Personnel Journal* 68, no. 4 (April 1989), pp. 76–83, for a good example of how one company fine-tuned its form for individual performance.

15. Teel, "Performance Appraisal," pp. 297–8.

16. For a discussion of this see, for example, Wayne Cascio, *Applied Psychology in Personnel Management* (Reston, VA: Reston, 1978), pp. 337–41. See also T.J. Maurer & M.A. Taylor, "Is Sex by Itself Enough? An Exploration of Gender Bias Issues in Performance Appraisal." *Organizational Behavior and Human Decision Processes*, 60 (1994), pp. 231–51.

17. B. Rosen and T. H. Gerdee, "The Nature of Job Related Age Stereotypes," *Journal of Applied Psychology* 61 (1976), pp. 180–3.

18. William J. Bigoness, "Effect of Applicant's Sex, Race and Performance on Employer's Performance Ratings: Some Additional Findings," *Journal of Applied Psychology* 61 (February 1976). See also Duane Thompson and Toni Thompson, "Task-Based Performance Appraisal for Blue Collar Jobs: Evaluation of Race and Sex Effects," *Journal of Applied Psychology* 70, no. 4 (1985), pp. 747–53.

19. Gerald Ferris, Valerie Yates, David Gilmore, and Kendrith Rowland, "The Influence of Subordinate Age on Performance Ratings and Casual Attributions," *Personnel Psychology* 38, no. 3 (Autumn 1985), pp. 545–57. As another example, see Gregory Dobbins and Jeanne Russell, "The Biasing Effects of Subordinate Likeableness on Leader's Responses to Poor Performers: A Laboratory and Field Study,"

Personnel Psychology 39, no. 4 (Winter 1986), pp. 759–78. See also Michael E. Benedict and Edward Levine, "Delay and Distortion: Passive Influences on Performance Appraisal Effectiveness," *Journal of Applied Psychology* 73, no. 3 (August 1988), pp. 507–14, and James Smither et al., "Effect of Prior Performance Information on Ratings of Present Performance: Contrast Versus Assimilation Revisited," *Journal of Applied Psychology* 73, no. 3 (August 1988), pp. 487–96.

20. Kevin Murphy, William Balzer, Maura Lockhart, and Elaine Eisenman, "Effects of Previous Performance on Evaluations of Present Performance," *Journal of Applied Psychology* 70, no. 1 (1985), pp. 72–84. See also Kevin Williams, Angelo DeNisi, Bruce Meglino, and Thomas Cafferty, "Initial Decisions and Subsequent Performance Ratings," *Journal of Applied Psychology* 71, no. 2 (May 1986), pp. 189–95.

21. W. C. Borman, "Effects of Instruction to Avoid Halo Error in Reliability and Validity of Performance Evaluation Ratings," *Journal of Applied Psychology* 65 (1975), pp. 556–60; Borman points out that since no control group (a group of managers who did not undergo training) was available, it is possible that the observed effects were not due to the short five-minute training experience. G. P. Latham, K. N. Wexley, and E. D. Pursell, "Training Managers to Minimize Rating Errors in the Observation of Behavior," *Journal of Applied Psychology* 60 (1975), pp. 550–5; John Ivancevich, "Longitudinal Study of the Effects of Rater Training on Psychometric Error in Ratings," *Journal of Applied Psychology* 64 (1979), pp. 502–8. For a related discussion, see, for example, Bryan Davis and Michael Mount, "Effectiveness of Performance Appraisal Training Using Computer Assistance Instruction and Behavior Modeling," *Personnel Psychology* 37 (Fall 1984), pp. 439–52.

22. Walter Borman, "Format and Training Effects on Rating Accuracy and Rater Errors," *Journal of Applied Psychology* 64 (August 1979), pp. 410–2, and Jerry Hedge and Michael Cavanagh, "Improving the Accuracy of Performance Evaluations: Comparison of Three Methods of Performance Appraiser Training," *Journal of Applied Psychology* 73, no. 1 (February 1988), pp. 68–73.

23. Davis and Mount, "The Effectiveness of Performance Appraisal Training," pp. 439–52.

24. Dennis Warnke and Robert Billings, "Comparison of Training Methods for Improving the Psychometric Quality of Experimental and Administrative Performance Ratings," *Journal of Applied Psychology* 64 (April 1979), pp. 124–31. See also Timothy Athey and Robert McIntyre, "Effect of Rater Training on Rater Accuracy: Levels of Processing Theory and Social Facilitation Theory Perspectives," *Journal of Applied Psychology* 72, no. 4 (November 1987), pp. 567–72.

25. Larry Axline, "Ethical Considerations of Performance Appraisals," *Management Review* (March 1994), p. 62.

26. Wayne Cascio and H. John Bernardin, "Implications of Performance Appraisal Litigation for Personnel Decisions," *Personnel Psychology* (Summer 1981), pp. 211–2, and Gerald Barrett and Mary Kernan, "Performance Appraisal and Terminations: A Review of Court Decisions Since *Brito* v. *Zia* with Implications for Personnel Practices," *Personnel Psychology* 40, no. 3 (Autumn 1987), pp. 489–504.

27. Barrett and Kernan, "Performance Appraisal and Terminations," p. 501.

28. M.M. Harris & J. Schaubroeck, "A Meta-Analysis of Self-Supervisor, Self-Peer, and Peer-Supervisor Ratings," *Personnel Psychology*, 41 (1988), pp. 43–62.

29. G.P. Latham & K.N. Wexley, *Increasing Productivity Through Performance Appraisal*, (Reading, MA: Addison-Wesley, 1982).

30. R. G. Downey, F. F. Medland, and L. G. Yates, "Evaluation of a Peer Rating System for Predicting Subsequent Promotion of Senior Military Officers," *Journal of Applied Psychology* 61 (April 1976), and Glenn McEvoy and Paul Buller, "User Acceptance of Peer Appraisals in an Industrial Setting," *Personnel Psychology* 40, no. 4 (Winter 1987), pp. 785–98. See also Julie Barclay and Lynn Harland, "Peer Performance Appraisals: The Impact of Rater Competence, Rater Location, and Rating Correctability on Fairness Perceptions," *Group and Organization Management* 20, no. 1 (March 1995), pp. 39–60.

31. Allan Kraut, "Prediction of Managerial Success by Peer and Training Staff Ratings," *Journal of Applied Psychology* 60 (February 1975). See also Michael Mount, "Psychometric Properties of Subordinate Ratings of Managerial Performance," *Personnel Psychology* 37, no. 4 (Winter 1984), pp. 687–702.

32. J. Schilder, "Office Pool Confidential," *Human Resources Professional*, (November 1992), pp. 20–23.

33. Robert Libby and Robert Blashfield, "Performance of a Composite as a Function of the Number of Judges," *Organizational Behavior and Human Performance* 21 (April 1978), pp. 121–9; Walter Borman, "Exploring Upper Limits of Reliability and Validity in Job Performance Ratings," *Journal of Applied Psychology* 63 (April 1978), pp. 135–44; M. M. Harris and J. Schaubroeck, "A Meta-Analysis, pp. 43–62.

34. Walter C. Borman, "The Rating of Individuals in Organizations: An Alternate Approach," *Organizational Behavior and Human Performance* 12 (1974), pp. 105–24.

35. George Thornton III, "Psychometric Properties of Self-appraisal of Job Performance," *Personnel Psychology* 33 (Summer 1980), p. 265; Cathy Anderson, Jack Warner, and Cassie Spencer, "Inflation Bias in Self-assessment Evaluations: Implications for Valid Employee Selection," *Journal of Applied Psychology* 69, no. 4 (November 1984), pp. 574–80. See also Shaul Fox and Yossi Dinur, "Validity of Self-assessment: A Field Evaluation," *Personnel Psychology* 41, no. 3 (Autumn 1988), pp. 581–92; and John W. Lawrie "Your Performance: Appraise It Yourself!" *Personnel* 66, no. 1 (January 1989), pp. 21–33, a good explanation of how self-appraisals can be used at work.

36. P.A. Mabe III & S.G. West "Validity of Self-Evaluation of Ability: A Review and Meta-Analysis." *Journal of Applied Psychology*, 67(3), 1982, pp. 280–296.

37. Herbert Myer, "Self-appraisal of Job Performance," *Personnel Psychology* 33 (Summer 1980), pp. 291–3; Robert Holzbach, "Rater Bias in Performance Ratings: Superior, Self, and Peer Ratings," *Journal of Applied Psychology* 63, no. 5 (October 1978), pp. 579–88. Herbert G. Heneman III, "Comparison of Self and Superior Ratings of Managerial Performance," *Journal of Applied Psychology* 59 (1974), pp. 638–42; Richard J. Klimoski and Manuel London, "Role of the Rater in Performance Appraisal," *Journal of Applied Psychology* 59 (1974), pp. 445–51; Hubert S. Field and William H. Holley, "Employees' Characteristics, Supervisors' Rat-

ings, and Decisions to Discuss Appraisal Results," *Academy of Management Journal* 20, no. 2 (1977), pp. 215–21. See also Robert Steel and Nestor Ovalle II, "Self-appraisal Based Upon Supervisory Feedback," *Personnel Psychology* 37, no. 4 (Winter 1984), pp. 667–85. See also Gloria Shapiro and Gary Dessler, "Are Self-appraisals More Realistic Among Professionals or Nonprofessionals in Health Care?" *Public Personnel Management* 14 (Fall 1985), pp. 285–91; James Russell and Dorothy Goode, "An Analysis of Managers' Reactions to Their Own Performance Appraisal Feedback," *Journal of Applied Psychology* 73, no. 1 (February 1988), pp. 63–7; and Harris and Shaubroeck, "A Meta-Analysis," pp. 43–62.

38. G.P. Latham, D. Skarlicki, D. Irvine & J.P. Seigel, "The Increasing Importance of Performance Appraisals to Employee Effectiveness in Organizational Settings in North America." In C. L. Cooper & I.T. Robertson (eds.) *International Review of Industrial and Organizational Psychology* (Volume 8, 1993, p. 103).

39. H.J. Bernardin & R.W. Beatty "Can Subordinate Appraisals Enhance Managerial Productivity?" *Sloan Management Review* (Summer 1987), pp. 63–73.

40. Manuel London and Arthur Wohlers, "Agreement Between Subordinate and Self-Ratings in Upward Feedback," *Personnel Psychology* 44 (1991), pp. 375–90.

41. London and Wohlers, "Agreement Between Subordinate and Self-Ratings," p. 376.

42. David Antonioni, "The Effects of Feedback Accountability on Upward Appraisal Ratings," *Personnel Psychology* 47 (1994), pp. 349–55.

43. R. Brillinger, "The Many Faces of 360-Degree Feedback," *Canadian HR Reporter* (December 16, 1996), pp. 20–1.

44. Kenneth Nowack, "360-Degree Feedback: The Whole Story," *Training and Development* (January 1993), p. 69. For a description of some of the problems involved in implementing 360-degree feedback see Matthew Budman, "The Rating Game," *Across the Board* 31, no. 2 (February 1994), pp. 35–8.

45. Catherine Romano, "Fear of Feedback," *Management Review* (December 1993), p. 39.

46. M.R. Edwards & A.J. Ewen, "How to Manage Performance and Pay With 360-Degree Feedback," *Compensation and Benefits Review*, 28(3), (May/June 1996), pp. 41–6.

47. R. Brillinger, "The Many Faces," p. 21.

48. R. Brillinger, "The Many Faces," p. 20.

49. J.F. Milliman, R.A. Zawacki, C. Norman, L. Powell and J. Kirksey, "Companies Evaluate Employees from All Perspectives," *Personnel Journal* 73, no. 11, (November 1994), pp. 99–103.

50. R. Brillinger, "The Many Faces," p. 20.

51. See, for instance, Gerry Rich, "Group Reviews—Are You Up To It?" *CMA Magazine* (March 1993), p. 5.

52. R. Brillinger, "The Many Faces," p. 20.

53. R. Brillinger, "The Many Faces," p. 21.

54. See also Jerald Greenberg, "Using Explanations to Manage Impressions of Performance Appraisal Fairness," *Employee Responsibilities and Rights* 4, no. 1 (March 1991), pp. 51–60.

55. Johnson, *The Appraisal Interview Guide,* Chapter 9.

56. Judy Block, *Performance Appraisal on the Job: Making It Work* (New York: Executive Enterprises Publications, 1981), pp. 58–62. See also Terry Lowe, "Eight Ways to Ruin a Performance Review," *Personnel Journal* 65, no. 1 (January 1986).

57. Block, *Performance Appraisal on the Job.*

58. Ronald Burke, William Weitzel, and Tamara Weis, "Characteristics of Effective Employee Performance Review and Development Interviews: Replication and Extension," *Personnel Psychology* 31 (Winter 1978), pp. 903–19. See also Joane Pearce and Lyman Porter, "Employee Response to Formal Performance Appraisal Feedback," *Journal of Applied Psychology* 71, no. 2 (May 1986), pp. 211–8.

59. Edward E. Lawler, III, "Performance Management: The Next Generation," *Compensation and Benefits Review* (May–June 1994), p. 16.

60. Lawler, "Performance Management," p. 16.

61. Dr. M. Michael Markowich, "Response: We Can Make Performance Appraisals Work," *Compensation and Benefits Review* (May–June 1995), p. 25.

62. See, for example, Greg Boudreaux, "Response: What TQM Says About Performance Appraisal," *Compensation and Benefits Review* (May–June 1994), pp. 20–4.

63. Boudreaux, "What TQM Says About Performance Appraisal," p. 21.

64. See, for example, Lawler, "Performance Management: The Next Generation," p. 17.

65. David Antonioni, "Improve the Management Process Before Discontinuing Performance Appraisals," *Compensation and Benefits Review* (May–June 1994), p. 29.

66. Antonioni, "Improve the Performance Management Process."

67. Boudreaux, "Response: What TQM Says About Performance Appraisal," p. 23.

68. Based in part on Joel E. Ross, *Total Quality Management: Text, Cases and Readings* (Delray Beach, FL: Saint Lucie Press, 1993), p. 1.

69. Ross, *Total Quality Management: Text, Cases, and Readings* pp. 2–3, 35–6.

70. Boudreaux, "Response: What TQM Says About Performance Appraisal," p. 23.

71. Lawler, "Performance Management," p. 17.

72. Markowich, "Response: We Can Make Performance Appraisals Work," p. 26.

73. Antonioni, "Improve the Performance Management Process," p. 30.

74. Antonioni, "Improve the Performance Management Process."

75. Antonioni, "Improve the Performance Management Process."

76. See also Clive Fletcher, "Appraisal: An Idea Whose Time Has Gone?" *Personnel Management* (September 1993), pp. 34–7.

Chapter 12
Establishing Pay Plans

Chapter Outline

- ◆ **Basic Aspects of Compensation**
- ◆ **Basic Considerations in Determining Pay Rates**
- ◆ **Establishing Pay Rates**
- ◆ **Current Trends in Compensation**
- ◆ **Pricing Managerial and Professional Jobs**
- ◆ **Current Issues in Compensation Management**

Learning Outcomes

After studying this chapter, you should be able to:

Discuss four basic factors determining pay rates.

Explain in detail each of the five basic steps in establishing pay rates.

Discuss skill/competency-based pay.

Present the pros and cons of job evaluation.

Describe the five basic elements of compensation for managers.

Define pay equity and explain its importance today.

Basic Aspects of Compensation

Compensation at Work

employee compensation
All forms of pay or rewards going to employees and arising from their employment.

Employee compensation refers to all forms of pay or rewards going to employees and arising from their employment,[1] and it has two main components. There are *direct financial payments* in the form of wages, salaries, incentives, commissions, and bonuses, and there are *indirect payments* in the form of financial benefits like employer-paid insurance and vacations.

In turn, there are essentially two ways to base direct financial payments to employees: on increments of time and on performance. Most employees are still paid primarily based on the time they put in on the job. For example, blue-collar workers are usually paid hourly or daily *wages*. Some employees—executive, administrative, and professional—are *salaried*. They are compensated on the basis of a longer period of time (like a week, month, or year), rather than hourly or daily.

The second option is to pay for performance. *Piecework* is an example: it ties compensation directly to the amount of production (or number of "pieces") the worker produces, and is popular as an incentive pay plan. For instance, a worker's hourly wage is divided by the standard number of units he or she is expected to produce in one hour. Then for each unit produced over and above this standard, the worker is paid an incentive. Salespeople's commissions are another example of compensation tied to production (in this case, sales).

In this chapter we will explain how to formulate plans for paying employees a fixed wage or salary; succeeding chapters will cover financial incentives and bonuses, and employee benefits and services.

Psychologists know that people have many needs, only some of which can be satisfied directly with money. Other needs—for achievement, affiliation, power, or self-actualization, for instance—also motivate behaviour but can only be satisfied indirectly (if at all) by money.

Yet even with all our more modern motivation techniques (like job enrichment), there's no doubt that money is still the most important motivator. As two researchers put it:

> *Pay in one form or another is certainly one of the mainsprings of motivation in our society .... The most evangelical human relationist insists it is important, while protesting that other things are too (and are, perhaps in his view, nobler). It would be unnecessary to belabour the point if it were not for a tendency for money drives to slip out of focus in a miasma of other values and other practices. As it is, it must be repeated: Pay is the most important single motivator used in our organized society.[2]*

Basic Considerations in Determining Pay Rates

Four basic considerations influence the formulation of any pay plan: legal, union, policy, and equity.

Legal Considerations in Compensation

There are a number of laws affecting compensation in Canada. These laws vary between the provinces and territories, and there are similar laws at the federal level for employees in interprovincial operations including highway, rail, and air transportation, pipelines, telecommunications, banking, federal crown corporations, and others. Federal government employees are covered under yet another law (Public Service Staff Relations Act). Thus HR managers must pay careful attention to which legislation affects their employees. Further, these laws are constantly changing, and require continual monitoring to ensure compliance. Legislation affecting compensation administration includes:

Employment/Labour Standards Acts (Canada Labour Code)   These laws set minimum standards regarding pay, including minimum wage, maximum hours of work, overtime pay, paid vacation, paid statutory holidays, termination pay, record keeping of pay information, and more. There are variations in some of the minimum standards for students, trainees, domestics, nannies, seasonal agricultural workers, and others. Executive, administrative, and professional employees are generally exempt from the overtime requirements.

Pay Equity Acts   As explained in chapter 3, six provinces enacted pay equity legislation during the 1980s and 1990s: Manitoba, New Brunswick, Nova Scotia, Ontario, Prince Edward Island, and Quebec. These laws apply to public sector employees only, except in Ontario and Quebec, where the laws cover employees in both the public and private sectors. Pay equity laws were enacted to redress the historical undervaluing of "women's work" by providing equal pay for work of equal (or comparable) value performed by men and women. Employers are required to identify male- and female-dominated jobs, and then use a gender neutral job evaluation system based on specific compensable factors (such as skill, effort, responsibility, and working conditions) to evaluate the jobs. Pay for female-dominated jobs that are equivalent in value to male-dominated jobs must be increased to the pay level of the comparable male-dominated job.

Human Rights Acts   As explained in chapter 3, all jurisdictions have enacted human rights laws to protect Canadians from discrimination on a number of grounds in employment and other areas. These grounds differ somewhat between jurisdictions, but most prohibit discrimination on the basis of age, sex, colour, race/ancestry/place of origin, religion/creed, marital/family status, and physical or mental disability.

Canada/Quebec Pension Plan   All employees and their employers must contribute to the Canada/Quebec Pension Plan throughout the employee's working lifetime. Pension benefits based on the employee's average earnings are paid during retirement. Details of these and other benefits are provided in chapter 14.

Other Legislation Affecting Compensation   Each of the 10 provinces, two territories, and the federal government has its own *workers' compensation laws*. The objective of these laws is to provide a prompt, sure, and reasonable income to victims of work-related accidents and illnesses. The *Employment Insurance Act* is aimed at protecting Canadian workers from total economic destitution in the event of termination of employment beyond their control. Employers and employees both contribute to the benefits provided by this act. This act also provides for unemployment compensation—jobless benefits—for workers unemployed through no fault of their own for up to 45 weeks, depending on the unemployment rate in the claimant's region, and other factors.

Union Influences on Compensation Decisions

Unions and labour relations laws also influence how pay plans are designed. The Trades Unions Act (passed by the federal parliament in 1872) and associated legislation and court decisions legalized the labour movement. It gave it legal protection and granted employees the right to organize, to bargain collectively, and to engage in concerted activities for the purpose of collective bargaining or other mutual aid or protection. Historically, the wage rate has been the main issue in collective bargaining. However, other issues including time off with pay, income security (for those in industries with periodic layoffs), cost-of-living adjustment, and various benefits like supplementary health care are also important.[3]

The Canada Labour Relations Board and similar bodies in each of the provinces oversee employer practices and ensure that employees are treated in accordance with their legal rights. Their decisions underscore the need to involve union officials in developing the compensation package.

Union Attitudes Toward Compensation Decisions Several studies shed light on union attitudes toward compensation plans and on commonly held union fears.[4] Many union leaders fear that any system (like a time and motion study) used to evaluate the worth of a job can become a tool for management malpractice. They tend to believe that no one can judge the relative value of jobs better than the workers themselves. And they believe that management's usual method of using several compensable factors (like "degree of responsibility") to evaluate and rank the worth of jobs can be a manipulative device for restricting or lowering the pay of workers. One implication seems to be that the best way to gain the cooperation of union members in evaluating the worth of jobs is to get their active involvement in this process and in assigning fair rates of pay to these jobs. On the other hand, management has to ensure that its prerogatives—such as the right to use the appropriate job evaluation technique to assess the relative worth of jobs—are not surrendered.

Compensation Policies

An employer's compensation policies influence the wages and benefits it pays, since these policies provide important compensation guidelines. One consideration is whether the organization wants to be a leader or a follower regarding pay. For example, one hospital might have a policy of starting nurses at a wage at least 20 percent above the prevailing market wage. Other important policies include the basis for salary increases, promotion and demotion policies, overtime pay policy, and policies regarding probationary pay and leaves for military service, jury duty, and holidays. Compensation policies are usually written by the HR or compensation manager in conjunction with senior management.[5]

Economists have proposed what they call segmented labour markets theories to emphasize that there are high- and low-wage employers.[6] Some employers choose to be leaders regarding pay and some followers, and as a result one U.S. study noted that "A worker who moves from a low- to a high-wage employer within a U.S. city can usually increase his or her pay by over 50 percent with no change in job description." Compensation policies have also been found to have measurable effects on workplace attitudes and behaviours.[7] Not surprisingly, workers receiving high wages are "... less likely to quit, are more satisfied with their pay, and report that they work harder than they have to."[8]

Equity and Its Impact on Pay Rates

The *need for equity* is a crucial factor in determining pay rates, specifically external equity and internal equity. Externally, pay must compare favourably with rates in other organizations or an employer will find it hard to attract and retain qualified employees. Pay rates must also be equitable internally: Each employee should view his or her pay as equitable given other pay rates in the organization. Some firms administer surveys to learn employees' perceptions and feelings about their compensation system. Questions typically addressed include "How satisfied are you with your pay?," "What criteria were used for your recent pay increase?," and "What factors do you believe are used when your pay is determined?"[9]

In practice, the process of establishing pay rates, while ensuring external and internal equity, requires five steps:

1. Conduct a *salary survey* of what other employers are paying for comparable jobs (to help ensure *external equity*).
2. Determine the worth of each job within the organization through *job evaluation* (to ensure *internal equity*).
3. Group similar jobs into *pay grades*.
4. Price each pay grade by using *wage curves*.
5. Fine tune pay rates.

Each of these steps is explained in the next section of this chapter.

Establishing Pay Rates

Step 1. Conduct a Wage/Salary Survey

wage/salary survey
A survey aimed at determining prevailing wage rates. A good salary survey provides specific wage rates for comparable jobs. Formal written questionnaire surveys are the most comprehensive, but telephone surveys and newspaper ads are also sources of information.

benchmark job
A job commonly found in other organizations and/or critical to the firm's operations that is used to anchor the employer's pay scale and acts as a reference point around which other jobs are arranged in order of relative worth.

Compensation or **wage/salary surveys** play a central role in the pricing of jobs. Virtually every employer therefore conducts such surveys for pricing one or more jobs.[10]

An employer may use wage/salary surveys in three ways. First, survey data are used to price **benchmark jobs** that serve as reference points, and are used to anchor the employer's pay scale and around which its other jobs are then slotted based on their relative worth to the firm. (Job evaluation, explained next, is the technique used to determine the relative worth of each job.) Second, 20 percent or more of an employer's positions are usually priced directly in the marketplace, (rather than relative to the firm's benchmark jobs) based on a formal or informal survey of what similar firms are paying for comparable jobs. Finally, surveys also collect data on benefits like insurance, sick leave, and vacation time and so provide a basis on which to make decisions regarding employee benefits.

There are many ways to conduct a salary survey. According to one British study, about 71 percent of the employers questioned rely to some extent on informal communication with other employers as a way of obtaining comparative salary information.[11] Fifty-five percent regularly reviewed newspaper ads as a means of collecting comparative salary information, while 33 percent surveyed employment agencies to determine the wages for at least some of their jobs. About two-thirds of the firms also used commercial or professional surveys conducted by professional and industry associations. Finally, 22 percent of the firms conducted formal questionnaire-type surveys with other employers.

Upward bias can be a problem regardless of the type of compensation survey.[12] While there's no scientific evidence to support the claim, at least one compensation expert argues that the way in which most surveys are constructed, interpreted, and used leads almost invariably to a situation in which firms set higher wages than they might otherwise. For example, "Companies like to compare themselves against well-regarded, high-paying, and high-performing companies," so that baseline salaries tend to be biased upward.[13] Similarly, "Companies that sponsor surveys often do so with an implicit (albeit unstated) objective: to show the company [is now] paying either competitively or somewhat below the market, so as to justify positive corrective action."[14] For these and similar reasons it's probably wise to review survey results with a skeptical eye and to acknowledge that upward bias may exist and perhaps should be adjusted for.

Formal and Informal Surveys by the Employer   Most employers rely heavily on formal or informal surveys of what other employers are paying.[15] Informal telephone surveys are good for collecting data on a relatively small number of easily identified and quickly recognized jobs, such as when a bank's human resources director wants to determine the salary at which a newly open customer service representative's job should be advertised. This informal phone technique is also good for checking discrepancies, such as when the human resources director wants to confirm whether some area banks are really paying such employees 10 percent more than his or her bank. Informal discussions among human resources specialists at regular professional association meetings are other occasions for informal salary surveys.

Perhaps 20 percent to 25 percent of employers use formal questionnaire surveys to collect compensation information from other employers. One page from such a survey is presented in **Figure 12.1**. It is part of a questionnaire that inquires about things like number of employees, overtime policies, starting salaries, and paid vacations. For a salary survey to be useful, it must be specific: Most respondents in one study claimed that job categories were too broad or imprecise, for instance.[16]

Commercial, Professional, and Government Salary Surveys   Many employers also rely on surveys published by various commercial firms, professional associations, or government agencies. For example, Statistics Canada provides monthly data on earnings by: (1) geographic area: national, provincial/territorial, and metropolitan (2) industry: approximately 280 goods-producing (such as construction, clothing, furniture) and service-producing (for example, libraries, finance and insurance, health and social services) industries, and (3) occupation: approximately 25 000 titles in the National Occupational Classification (formerly the Standard Occupational Classification). **Table 12.1** provides an example of earnings data by industry.

The Board of Trade of Metropolitan Toronto conducts and furnishes five compensation surveys annually, covering executives, middle management, professional and supervisory employees, information technology positions, and clerical workers. In all, the surveys include information from over 550 employers in the Toronto region, for 200 positions in 10 industry classifications. Both salary and bonus data are included. A separate survey of employee benefits and employment practices is also conducted. The Economic Research Institute in Vancouver collects and analyzes publicly available salary surveys for more than 4 200 positions in 2 000 industries in nearly 300 cities in North America. These surveys can provide a useful reference for employers making compensation decisions in the cities surveyed.

Private consulting and/or executive recruiting companies like Hay Associates, William M. Mercer, KPMG, and Hewitt Associates annually publish data covering the compensation of senior and middle managers and members of boards of directors. Professional organizations like the Certified General Accountants Association and Professional Engineers Ontario publish surveys of compensation practices among members of their associations.

For many firms, jobs are priced directly based on formal or informal salary surveys. In most cases, though, surveys are used to price benchmark jobs around which other jobs are then slotted based on their relative worth. Determining the relative worth of a job is the purpose of job evaluation, to which we now turn.

Step 2. Determine the Worth of Each Job: Job Evaluation

job evaluation
A systematic comparison to determine the worth of one job relative to another.

Purpose of Job Evaluation   **Job evaluation** is aimed at determining a job's relative worth. It is a formal and systematic comparison of jobs to determine the worth of one job relative to another and eventually results in a wage or salary hierarchy. The basic procedure is to compare the *content of jobs* in relation to one another, for

1. DEMOGRAPHICS (Optional)

SEX ❏¹ M ❏² F
AGE _____ Years (on December 1, 1996)

2. YEAR OF BACHELOR DEGREE

or degree accepted as requirement for registration

┌─────────┐
│ 19 ____ │
└─────────┘

❏ (Check this box & leave year blank if you entered the profession by exam route.)

3. ENGINEERING FIELD/DISCIPLINE

(Check 1 box only)

❏ 01 Areonautical & aerospace
❏ 02 Biomedical, biological
❏ 03 Chemical
❏ 04 Civil
❏ 05 Computer, systems
❏ 06 Electrical, electronics
❏ 07 Environmental
❏ 08 Geological, geotechnical
❏ 09 Mechanical, industrial
❏ 10 Metallurgical, materials, mining
❏ 11 Nuclear
❏ 12 Other (specify) _____

4. HIGHEST DEGREE OBTAINED

(Check 1 box only)

❏ 1 BASc. BEng
❏ 2 MASc, MEng
❏ 3 PhD (Engineering)
❏ 4 MBA
❏ 5 Other (specify) _____

5. OCCUPATIONAL STATUS

❏ 1 Employed full-time (min. 30 hrs/wk) (permanent, salaried)
❏ 2 Employed full-time (min. 30 hrs/wk) (contract, temporary)
❏ 3 Self-employed full-time (owner, principal)
❏ 4 Part-time employee
❏ 5 Unemployed
❏ 6 Retired
❏ 7 Other (specify) _____

6. REGION

(Work location for the majority of the year)

❏ 1 Greater Toronto (includes Oakville, Brampton, Richmond Hill, Ajax)
❏ 2 Greater Ottawa (includes Kanata)
❏ 3 Central Ontario (includes Owen Sound, Orillia, Barrie)
❏ 4 Eastern Ontario (includes Whitby)
❏ 5 Southwestern Ontario (includes Orangeville)
❏ 6 Northern Ontario (Gravenhurst and north)
❏ 7 Out of Province

Instruction:

Please continue to Question #7 if you are a **full-time or self-employed** wage-earner as of December 1, 1996. **If not,** please make sure you have completed the first six questions and #14 and return the questionnaire. Self-employed members complete to question #10 and #14 only.

7. INCOME

(from principal source of employment)

Basic **annual** salary as of Dec. 1, 1996 $_____
**Other cash income received in last
12 months as follows:**
Cash bonus   _____
Profit sharing   _____
Commissions   _____
Overtime payments   _____
Consulting fees   _____
Other (specify)   _____
_____

(exclude deferred profit sharing, car allowance, fringe benefits)
TOTAL INCOME $_____

8. WORK CATEGORY

❏ 1 Largely or entirely engineering
❏ 2 Not purely engineering but associated with or job requirement that you be an engineer
❏ 3 In no way associated with engineering

9. PRINCIPAL FUNCTION

(Check 1 box only)

❏ 01 General management
❏ 02 Engineering management
❏ 03 Administration *(finance, personnel, public relations)*
❏ 04 Computer services/systems
❏ 05 Research & development
❏ 06 Planning
❏ 07 Marketing/sales
❏ 08 Production engineering
❏ 09 Project engineering
❏ 10 Instrumentation/control
❏ 11 Maintenance engineering
❏ 12 Design
❏ 13 Quality assurance
❏ 14 Teaching (university)
❏ 15 Teaching (other)
❏ 16 Environmental/pollution
❏ 17 Health & safety
❏ 18 Other engineering (specify) _____
❏ 19 Other non-engineering (specify) _____

Figure 12.1
Compensation Survey
Source: Professional Engineers Ontario. Used with permission.

10. INDUSTRY SECTOR

(Check 1 box only)

Manufacturing

- ❏ 01   Chemical & pharmaceutical
- ❏ 02   Heavy electrical
- ❏ 03   Electronics, electrical products
- ❏ 04   Machinery (except electrical)
- ❏ 05   Metals
- ❏ 06   Petroleum products
- ❏ 07   Pulp & paper, wood products
- ❏ 08   Aerospace & aircraft products
- ❏ 09   Food, beverages, tobacco
- ❏ 10   Transportation equipment (except aircraft)
- ❏ 11   Other manufacturing (specify) _____

Non-Manufacturing

- ❏ 12   Construction
- ❏ 13   Consulting engineer
- ❏ 14   Consulting, other
- ❏ 15   Mining
- ❏ 16   Electrical utilities
- ❏ 17   Utilities, other
- ❏ 18   Communications services
- ❏ 19   Transportation services
- ❏ 20   Petroleum
- ❏ 21   Data processing
- ❏ 22   Computer systems development
- ❏ 23   Other (services, trade, business, research, professional association, etc.)

Educational & Government (exclude crown corporations)

- ❏ 24   Federal government
- ❏ 25   Provincial government
- ❏ 26   Municipal government
- ❏ 27   Educational Institutions

Instruction: Self-employed members—do not complete questions 11 to 13. Please respond to question 14.

11. RESPONSIBILITY LEVEL

Only engineers working **in engineering** must complete this question (Refer to your anwer for Question #8.)

A ❏ 1   (Use the classification guide
B ❏ 2   presented on the last page
C ❏ 3   if you are unsure of your
D ❏ 4   level.)
E ❏ 5
F ❏ 6

Figure 12.1

(continued)

12. BENEFITS AND WORKING CONDITIONS

Provided by Employer

BENEFIT	YES	NO
Pension	❏ 1	❏ 2
Group Life	❏ 1	❏ 2
Hospitalization	❏ 1	❏ 2
Drug plan	❏ 1	❏ 2
Dental plan	❏ 1	❏ 2
Vision care	❏ 1	❏ 2
Long term disability	❏ 1	❏ 2

Overtime—Are you eligible for paid overtime?

YES ❏ 1   NO ❏ 2

If YES, at what rate?

Straight pay   ❏ 1
Greater than straight pay   ❏ 2
Credit toward time off   ❏ 3
Combination of above   ❏ 4

Working week

Base work week (m,ax. 40 hrs)   _____ (# of hours)
Actual work week   _____ (# of hours)

Collective Agreement—Are your salary and working conditions part of a collective agreement?

YES ❏ 1   NO ❏ 2

13. SIZE OF EMPLOYER ORGANIZATION

(In Canada)

2–25 employees   ❏ 1
26–100 employees   ❏ 2
101–500 employees   ❏ 3
more than 500 employees ❏ 4

14. FUTURE OPTIONS

We are considering the option of conducting this survey on a bi-annual basis (i.e. every 2nd year) starting next year in an effort to avoid a fee increase for this service in future; the Industry/Employer Salary Survey would continue to be conducted annually. Do you support the idea of conducting the membership survey on a bi-annual basis?

❏ 1 Yes   ❏ 2 No   ❏ 3 Undecided

Thank you for your participation.

TABLE 12.1 Statistics Canada Industry Wage Survey

$	1992	1993	1994	1995
All industries[2]	**547.01**	**556.76**	**567.11**	**572.49**
Goods-producing industries	**680.70**	**693.99**	**709.87**	**720.62**
Logging and forestry	697.27	709.99	730.83	732.50
Mining	934.52	946.41	972.67	1 013.75
Crude petroleum and natural gas	1 098.68	1 148.77	1 165.58	1 202.52
Quarries and sand pits	672.02	640.86	669.64	724.13
Manufacturing	652.54	668.95	685.07	693.91
Non-durable goods	619.47	631.49	640.36	650.08
Durable goods	681.62	702.83	723.38	730.08
Food	542.05	560.48	568.74	575.58
Beverages	711.56	755.62	769.65	755.81
Tobacco products	996.97	1 027.06	1 141.55	1 153.45
Rubber products	679.70	689.96	713.30	703.55
Plastic products	561.74	562.31	573.53	576.39
Leather and allied products	396.01	410.33	420.15	435.75
Primary textiles	608.83	631.48	655.56	681.59
Textile products	493.30	492.06	462.14	495.66
Clothing	378.24	375.24	382.74	397.82
Wood	594.90	608.52	619.01	633.74
Furniture and fixtures	498.27	509.30	529.47	529.13
Paper and allied products	828.16	846.78	871.60	900.98
Printing	605.39	618.51	612.83	625.28
Primary metals	831.75	864.33	876.10	896.15
Fabricated metal products	634.24	632.58	648.22	666.67
Machinery	689.32	695.84	721.22	737.18
Transportation equipment	760.62	803.52	845.04	849.45
Electrical and electronic products	728.80	744.12	753.40	736.66
Non-metallic mineral products	695.08	698.31	702.76	719.06
Refined petroleum and coal products	877.55	1 055.05	1 090.97	1 108.76
Chemical and chemical products	768.49	790.88	810.18	803.28
Construction	637.40	639.74	657.87	675.50
Service-producing industries	**506.92**	**516.34**	**524.39**	**528.31**
Transportation and storage	652.99	664.25	675.48	689.24
Communications	679.60	678.49	683.53	697.42
Utilities	905.55	921.10	923.54	937.94
Trade	401.16	409.38	422.14	431.66
Wholesale trade	579.21	590.93	605.56	622.11
Retail trade	320.80	329.65	339.51	342.48
Finance and insurance	626.86	668.49	670.14	687.33
Real estate operators and insurance agencies	520.44	521.78	556.88	558.97
Business services	583.53	586.14	607.24	623.29
Public administration	727.64	746.59	752.88	749.83
Educational services	679.36	685.03	681.92	680.62
Libraries	405.96	422.68	450.63	448.97
Health and social services	485.06	498.45	504.63	503.44
Accommodation, food and beverage	215.84	217.77	227.19	231.80
Amusement and recreation	354.03	357.52	367.26	369.95
Personal services (excluding private households)	305.58	309.44	312.53	322.22

[1] Excludes owners or partners of unincorporated businesses, the self-employed, unpaid family workers, persons working outside Canada, military personnel and casual workers for whom a T4 is not required.

[2] Excludes agriculture, fishing and trapping, private household services, religious organizations and the military

Source: "Estimates of Average Weekly Earnings (including overtime) for All Employees,[1] by Industry, 1992–1995," adapted from "Annual Estimates of Employment, Earnings and Hours, 1984–1996," Statistics Canada Catalogue No. 72F0002XPB. 1997.

Statistics Canada information is used with the permission of the Minister of Industry, as Minister responsible for Statistics Canada. Information on the availability of the wide range of data from Statistics Canada can be obtained from Statistics Canada's Regional Offices, its World Wide Web site at http://www.statcan.ca, and its toll-free access number 1-800-263-1136.

example, in terms of their effort, responsibility, and skills. Once the compensation specialist knows (based on salary survey data and compensation policies) how to price key benchmark jobs and can use job evaluation to determine the worth of all the other jobs in the firm relative to these key jobs, he or she is well on the way to being able to equitably price all the jobs in the organization.

Compensable Factors   There are two basic approaches for comparing jobs. The first one is an intuitive approach. It might be decided that one job is "more important" or "of greater value or worth" than another without digging any deeper into why in terms of specific job-related factors.

As an alternative, jobs can be compared by focusing on certain basic factors they have in common. In compensation management, these basic factors are called **compensable factors.** They are the factors that determine the definition of job content, establish how the jobs compare to each other, and set the compensation paid for each job.

Some employers develop their own compensable factors. However, most use factors that have been popularized by packaged job evaluation systems or by legislation. For example, most of the pay equity acts in Canada focus on four compensable factors—*skill, effort, responsibility,* and *working conditions.* As another example, the job evaluation method popularized by the Hay consulting firm focuses on four compensable factors: *know-how, problem solving, accountability,* and *working conditions.* Often, different job evaluation systems are used for different departments, employee groups, or business units.

Identifying compensable factors plays a pivotal role in job evaluation. All jobs in each employee group, department, or business unit are evaluated *using the same compensable factors.* An employer thus evaluates the same elemental components for each job within the work group, and is then better able to compare jobs—for example, in terms of the degree of skill, effort, responsibility, and working conditions present in each.[17]

compensable factor
A fundamental, compensable element of a job, such as skill, effort, responsibility, and working conditions.

www.crl.com/~clwallis
Compensation Planning Software

Planning and Preparation for Job Evaluation   Job evaluation is mostly a judgmental process, one that demands close cooperation between supervisors, compensation specialists, and the employees and their union representatives. The main steps involved include identifying the need for the program, getting cooperation, and then choosing an evaluation committee; the latter then carries out the actual job evaluation.[18]

Identifying the need for job evaluation should not be difficult. For example, dissatisfaction reflected in high turnover, work stoppages, or arguments may result from the inequities of paying employees different rates for similar jobs.[19] Managers may express uneasiness about the current, informal way of assigning pay rates to jobs, accurately sensing that a more systematic means of assigning pay rates would be more equitable and make it easier to justify compensation practices.

Next, since employees may fear that a systematic evaluation of their jobs may actually reduce their wage rates, *getting employee cooperation* for the evaluation is a second important step. Employees can be told that as a result of the impending job evaluation program, wage rate decisions will no longer be made just by management whim, that job evaluation will provide a mechanism for considering the complaints they have been expressing, and that no present employee's rate will be adversely affected as a result of the job evaluation.[20]

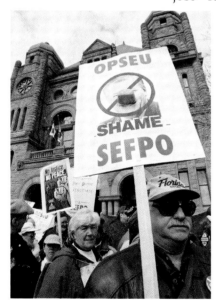

Work stoppages may reflect employee dissatisfaction with pay plans and other forms of compensation such as benefits.

The next step is *choosing a job evaluation committee.* There are two reasons for doing so. First, the committee should bring to bear the points of view of several people who are familiar with the jobs in question, each of whom may have a different perspective regarding the nature of the jobs. Second, assuming the committee is composed at least partly of employees, the committee approach can help ensure greater acceptance by employees of the job evaluation results.

The composition of the committee can be important. The group usually consists of about five members, most of whom are employees. While managers have the right to serve on such committees, their presence can be viewed with suspicion by employees and "it is probably best not to have managerial representatives involved in committee evaluation of nonmanagerial jobs . . . ."[21] However, an HR specialist can usually be justified on the grounds that he or she has a more impartial image than other managers and can provide expert assistance in the job evaluation. One method is to have this person serve in a nonvoting capacity. Union representation is possible. In most cases, though, the union's position is that it is accepting job evaluation only as an initial decision technique and is reserving the right to appeal the actual job pricing decisions through grievance or bargaining channels.[22] Once appointed, each committee member should receive a manual describing the job evaluation process and special instructions and training that explain how to conduct a job evaluation.

The evaluation committee performs three main functions. First, the members usually identify 10 or 15 key benchmark jobs. These will be the first jobs to be evaluated and will serve as the anchors or benchmarks against which the relative importance or value of all other jobs can be compared. Next, the committee may select compensable factors (although the human resources department will usually choose these as part of the process of determining the specific job evaluation technique to be used). Finally, the committee turns to its most important function—actually evaluating the worth of each job. For this, the committee will probably use one of the following job evaluation methods: the ranking method, the job classification method, the point method, or the factor comparison method.

Ranking Method of Job Evaluation The simplest job evaluation method ranks each job relative to all other jobs, usually based on some overall factor like "job difficulty." There are several steps in the job **ranking method.**

ranking method
The simplest method of job evaluation that involves ranking each job relative to all other jobs, usually based on overall difficulty.

1. *Obtain job information.* Job analysis is the first step. Job descriptions for each job are prepared and these are usually the basis on which the rankings are made. (Sometimes job specifications also are prepared, but the job ranking method usually ranks jobs according to "the whole job" rather than a number of compensable factors. Therefore, job specifications—which provide an indication of the demands of the job in terms of problem solving, decision making, and skills, for instance—are not quite as necessary with this method as they are for other job evaluation methods.)

2. *Select raters and jobs to be rated.* It is often not practical to make a single ranking of all jobs in an organization. The more usual procedure is to rank jobs by department or in "clusters" (such as factory workers, clerical workers). This eliminates the need for having to compare directly, say, factory jobs and clerical jobs.

3. *Select compensable factors.* In the ranking method, it is common to use just one factor (such as job difficulty) and to rank jobs on the basis of the whole job. Regardless of the number of factors chosen, it's advisable to explain the definition of the factor(s) to the evaluators carefully so that they evaluate the jobs consistently.

4. *Rank jobs.* Next the jobs are ranked. The simplest way is to give each rater a set of index cards, each of which contains a brief description of a job. These cards are then ranked from lowest to highest. Some managers use an "alternation ranking method" for making the procedure more accurate. Here the committee

members take the cards, and arrange them by first choosing the highest and the lowest, then the next highest and next lowest, and so forth until all the cards have been ranked. Since it is usually easier to choose extremes, this approach facilitates the ranking procedure. A job ranking is illustrated in **Table 12.2**. Jobs in this small health facility are ranked from cleaner up to director of operations. The corresponding pay scales are shown on the right.

5. *Combine ratings.* Usually several raters rank the jobs independently. Then the rating committee (or employer) can simply average the rankings.

Pros and Cons   This is the simplest job evaluation method, as well as the easiest to explain. And it usually takes less time to accomplish than other methods.

Some of its drawbacks derive more from how it's used than from the method itself. For example, there's a tendency to rely too heavily on "guesstimates." Similarly, ranking provides no yardstick for measuring the value of one job relative to another. For example, job no. 4 may in fact be five times "more valuable" than job no. 5, but with the ranking system one only knows that one job ranks higher than the other. Ranking is often used by small organizations that are unable to afford the time or expense of developing a more elaborate system.

Another potential drawback relates to legal compliance requirements. The "whole job" approach to ranking, just described, cannot be used by employers covered by pay equity legislation. Instead, separate rankings must be completed for each of four compensable factors—skill, effort, responsibility, and working conditions—and judgment used to combine the results. Furthermore, jobs must be ranked across clusters or departments, not separately.

Classification (or Grading) Evaluation Method   **Classification** is a simple, widely-used method in which jobs are categorized into groups. The groups are called **classes** if they contain similar jobs, or **grades** if they contain jobs that are similar in difficulty but otherwise different. The federal government's AU (Auditor) job group is an example of a job class because it contains similar jobs such as Auditor, Assessor, and Examiner. On the other hand, the PM (Program Management) job group is an example of a job grade because it contains dissimilar jobs such as Program Consultant (an expert in one government program), Operations Officer (works on special projects), and Agent II (performs complex government benefit entitlement calculations for members of the public).

There are several ways to categorize jobs. One is to draw up *class descriptions* (the analogs of job descriptions) and place jobs into classes based on their correspondence to these descriptions. Another is to draw up a set of classifying rules for each class (for

classification (or grading) method
A method for categorizing jobs into groups.

classes
Jobs are divided into classes based on a set of rules for each class, such as amount of independent judgment, skill, physical effort, and so forth. Classes usually contain similar jobs—such as all secretaries.

grades
A job classification system synonymous with class, although grades often contain *dissimilar* jobs, such as secretaries, mechanics, and firefighters. Grade descriptions are written based on compensable factors listed in the classification system.

Table 12.2 Job Ranking by Olympia Health Care	
RANKING ORDER	**ANNUAL PAY SCALE**
1. Director of Operations	$60 000
2. Head nurse	54 000
3. Accountant	50 000
4. Nurse	40 000
5. Cook	26 000
6. Nurse's aide	24 000
7. Cleaner	20 000

After ranking, it becomes possible to slot additional jobs between those already ranked and to assign an appropriate wage rate.

instance, how much independent judgment, skill, physical effort, and so on, does the class of jobs require?). Then the jobs are categorized according to these rules.

The usual procedure is to choose compensable factors and then develop class or grade descriptions that describe each class in terms of amount or level of compensable factor(s) in jobs. The federal government's classification system, for example, employs different compensable factors for various job groups. The compensable factors for the PM group are knowledge, decision making, operational responsibility, and contacts, whereas the compensable factors for the AS (Administrative Support) job group are knowledge, continuing study, decision making, supervision, and responsibility for contacts. The government is in the process of implementing a universal classification system whereby the same four factors (skill, effort, responsibility, and working conditions) will be used to evaluate all jobs.

grade/group description
Written description of the level of compensable factors required by jobs in each grade. Similar jobs can be combined into grades or classes.

Based on these compensable factors, a **grade/group description** like that in **Figure 12.2** is written. Then the evaluation committee reviews all job descriptions and slots each job into its appropriate class or grade.

The job classification method has several advantages. The main one is that most employers usually end up classifying jobs anyway, regardless of the job evaluation method they use. They do this to avoid having to work with and price an unmanageable number of jobs; with the job classification method all jobs are already grouped

**Figure 12.2
Example of Group
Definition in the
Federal Government**

Source: Human Resources Development Canada, 1997. Used with permission.

GROUP DEFINITION - AUDITING (AU)
The planning, execution, and control of external audit programs; the provision of advice.

Inclusions
Positions included in the group are those that require the application of a comprehensive knowledge of the generally accepted principles of accounting and auditing to the operations of governmental, financial, commercial, and industrial organizations, in the performance of one or more of the following duties:

- The auditing of the accounts and financial records of federal government departments and agencies on behalf of Parliament.

- The auditing of the accounts and financial records of individuals, business enterprises, or provincial or municipal governments to determine their accuracy and adequacy, to establish or verify costs, or to confirm the compliance of transactions with the provisions of statutes, regulations, agreements, or contracts.

- The provision of advice.

- The supervision or direction of any of the above duties.

Exclusions
Positions excluded from the group are those that do not require the application of a comprehensive knowledge of the generally accepted principles of accounting and auditing. Also excluded are all positions requiring the provision of financial management services to federal government departments and agencies, including internal audits, which services are defined in the Financial Administration Group.

Minimum Qualifications
Eligibility for certification as a professional accountant or auditor by a recognized society of accountants, or university graduation with specialization in accounting, business administration, commerce, or finance, and a number of years of auditing experience in which the knowledge equivalent to that of a professional accountant has been acquired.

---

into several classes. The disadvantages are that it is difficult to write the class or grade descriptions, and considerable judgment is required in applying them. Yet many employers (including the Canadian government) use this method with success.

point method
The job evaluation method in which a number of compensable factors are identified and then the degree to which each of these factors is present in the job is determined.

Point Method of Job Evaluation The **point method** is a more quantitative job evaluation technique. It involves identifying (1) several compensable factors, *each having several degrees,* as well as (2) the degree to which each of these factors is present in the job. Thus, assume that there are five degrees of responsibility an employer's jobs could contain. And assume a different number of points is assigned to each degree of each factor. Then, once the evaluation committee determines the degree to which each compensable factor (like "responsibility") is present in the job, the corresponding points for each factor can be added to arrive at a total point value for the job. The result is thus a quantitative point rating for each job. The point method is apparently the most widely used job evaluation method and is explained in detail in the appendix to this chapter.

factor comparison method
A method of ranking jobs according to a variety of skill and difficulty factors, adding up these rankings to arrive at an overall numerical rating for each given job, and then incorporating wage rates.

Factor Comparison Job Evaluation Method The **factor comparison method** is also a quantitative technique and entails deciding which jobs have more of the chosen compensable factors. The method is actually a refinement of the ranking method. With the factor comparison method, each job is ranked several times— once for each compensable factor chosen. For example, jobs might be ranked first in terms of the compensable factor "skill." Then they are ranked according to their "mental requirements," and so forth. These rankings are combined for each job into an overall numerical rating for the job, and then wage rates are incorporated for each factor. This method is also explained in more detail in the appendix to this chapter.

Step 3. Group Similar Jobs into Pay Grades

Once a job evaluation method has been used to determine the relative worth of each job, the committee can turn to the task of assigning pay rates, but members will usually want to first group jobs into pay grades. If the committee used the ranking, point, or factor comparison methods, it could assign pay rates to each individual job.[23] But for a larger employer such a pay plan would be difficult to administer, since there might be different pay rates for hundreds or even thousands of jobs. Even in smaller organizations there is a tendency to try to simplify wage and salary structures as much as possible. Therefore, the committee will probably want to group similar jobs (in terms of their ranking or number of points, for instance) into grades for pay purposes. Then, instead of having to deal with hundreds of pay rates, it might only have to focus on, say, 10 or 12.[24]

pay grade
A pay grade is comprised of jobs of approximately equal value.

A **pay grade** is comprised of jobs of approximately equal value or importance as determined by job evaluation. If the point method was used, the pay grade consists of jobs falling within a range of points. If the ranking plan was used, the grade consists of all jobs that fall within two or three ranks. If the classification system was used, then the jobs are already categorized into classes or grades. If the factor comparison method was used, the grade consists of a specified range of pay rates, as explained in the appendix to this chapter. Ten to sixteen grades per "job cluster" (a cluster is a logical grouping such as factory jobs, clerical jobs, and so on) are common in large organizations.

Step 4. Price Each Pay Grade—Wage Curves

The next step is to assign pay rates to each of the pay grades. (Of course, if jobs were not grouped into pay grades, individual pay rates would have to be assigned

wage curve
A graphic description of the relationship between the value of the job and the average wage paid for this job.

to each job.) Assigning pay rates to each pay grade (or to each job) is usually accomplished with a **wage curve.**

The wage curve depicts graphically the pay rates currently being paid for jobs in each pay grade, relative to the points or rankings assigned to each job or grade by the job evaluation committee. An example of a wage curve is presented in **Figure 12.3**. Note that pay rates are shown on the vertical axis, while the pay grades (in terms of points) are shown along the horizontal axis. The purpose of the wage curve is to show the relationship between (1) the value of the job as determined by one of the job evaluation methods and (2) the current average pay rates for each job or grade.

The pay rates on the graph are traditionally those now paid by the organization. If there is reason to believe that the present pay rates are substantially out of step with the prevailing market pay rates for these jobs, benchmark jobs within each pay grade are chosen and priced via a compensation survey. These new market-based pay rates are then plotted on the wage curve.

There are several steps in pricing jobs with a wage curve using grades. First, *find the average pay for each pay grade,* since each of the pay grades consists of several jobs. Next *plot the pay rates* for each pay grade as was done in Figure 12.3. Then fit a line (called a *wage line*) through the points just plotted. This can be done either freehand or by using a statistical method. Finally, *price jobs.* Wages along the wage line are the target wages or salary rates for the jobs in each pay grade. If the current rates being paid for any of the jobs or grades fall well above or well below the wage line, that rate may be "out of line"; raises or a pay freeze for that job may be in order. The next step, then, is to fine tune the pay rates.

Step 5. Fine Tune Pay Rates

Fine tuning involves correcting out-of-line rates and (usually) developing rate ranges.

rate ranges
A series of steps or levels within a pay grade, usually based upon years of service.

Developing Rate Ranges Most employers do not just pay one rate for all jobs in a particular pay grade. Instead, they develop **rate ranges** for each grade so that there might, for instance, be ten levels or "steps" and ten corresponding pay rates within each pay grade. This approach is illustrated in **Table 12.3**, which shows the pay rates and levels for some of the federal government pay grades. As of the time of this pay schedule, for instance, employees in positions that were classified in grade

Figure 12.3
Plotting a Wage Curve

Note: The average pay rate for jobs in each grade (Grade I, Grade II, Grade III, etc.) are plotted, and the wage curve fitted to the resulting points.

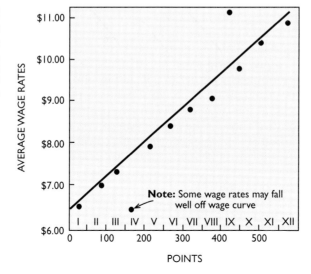

TABLE 12.3 Federal Government Pay Schedules AU.03 – AU.05

	RATE LEVELS WITHIN GRADE				
GRADE	I	2	3	4	5
AU.03	50 243	52 305	54 263	56 123	57 982
AU.04	57 302	59 005	61 141	63 242	65 345
AU.05	63 503	65 636	67 774	69 911	72 047

Source: Human Resources Development Canada, 1997.
Used with permission.

AU.03 could be paid annual salaries between $50 243 and $57 982, depending on the level at which they were hired into the grade, the amount of time they were in the grade, and their merit increases (if any). Another way to depict the rate ranges for each grade is with a *wage structure,* as in **Figure 12.4**. The wage structure graphically depicts the range of pay rates (in this case, per hour) to be paid for each grade.

There are several benefits to using rate ranges for each pay grade. First, the employer can take a more flexible stance with respect to the labour market. For example, it makes it easier to attract experienced, higher-paid employees into a pay

**Figure 12.4
Wage Structure**

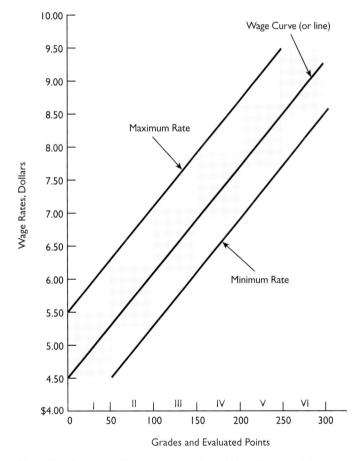

Note: This shows overlapping pay grades and maximum–minimum wage ranges.

grade where the starting salary for the lowest step may be too low to attract such experienced people. Rate ranges also allow employers to provide for performance differences between employees within the same grade or between those with differing seniority. As in Figure 12.4, most employers structure their rate ranges to overlap a bit so that an employee with greater experience or seniority may earn more than an entry-level person in the next higher pay grade.

The rate range is usually built around the wage line or curve. One alternative is to arbitrarily decide on a maximum and minimum rate for each grade, such as 15 percent above and below the wage line. Other employers allow the rate range for each grade to become wider for the higher pay ranges, reflecting the greater demands and performance variability inherent in these more complex jobs.

Correcting Out-of-Line Rates   The wage rate for a job may fall well off the wage line or well outside the rate range for its grade, as shown in Figure 12.3. *This means that the average pay for that job is currently too high or too low*, relative to other jobs in the firm. If a point falls well below the line, a pay raise for the job may be required. If the plot falls well above the wage line, pay cuts or a pay freeze may be required.

Underpaid employees should have their wages raised to the minimum of the rate range for their pay grade, assuming the organization wants to retain the employees and has the funds. This can be done either immediately or in one or two steps.

Pay rates of overpaid employees are often called **red circle**, *flagged*, or *over-rates,* and there are several ways to cope with this problem. One is to freeze the rate paid to employees in this grade until general salary increases bring the other jobs into line with it. A second alternative is to transfer or promote some or all of the employees involved to jobs for which they can legitimately be paid their current pay rates. The third alternative is to freeze the rate for six months, during which time attempts are made to transfer or promote the overpaid employees. If this is not possible then the rate at which these employees are paid is cut to the maximum in the pay range for their grade.

red circle pay rate
A rate of pay that is above the pay range maxiumum.

Current Trends in Compensation

Skill/Competency-Based Pay

Construction workers today are often compensated for their work through the method of skill-based pay, which originated with the guilds of the Middle Ages.

With skill/competency-based pay, employees are paid for the range, depth, and types of skills and knowledge they are capable of using, rather than for the job they currently hold.[25] According to one expert, there are several key differences between skill-based pay (SBP) and job evaluation-driven, job-based pay (JBP):[26]

Competence Testing   With JBP, employees receive the pay attached to their jobs regardless of whether or not they develop the competence needed to perform the job effectively. With SBP, base pay is tied not to the job, but to the employee's skills and competencies.

Effect of Job Change   With JBP, pay usually changes automatically when the employee switches jobs. With SBP that's not necessarily so. Before getting a pay raise, an employee must first demonstrate proficiency at the skills/competencies required by the new job.

Seniority and Other Factors   Pay in JBP systems is often tied to "time in grade" or seniority: In other words, the longer the employee is in the job, the more he or she gets paid, regardless of performance. SBP systems are based on skills, not seniority.

Advancement Opportunities Typically (but not always) there tend to be more opportunities for advancement with SBP plans than with JBP plans because of the company-wide focus on skill building. A corollary to this is that SBP enhances organizational flexibility by making it easier for workers to move from job to job because their skills/ competencies (and thus their pay) may be applicable to more jobs and thus more portable.

In a manufacturing plant setting, workers are sometimes paid based on their attained skill levels. For example, in a three-level plan, level 1 would indicate limited ability, such as knowledge of basic facts and ability to perform simple tasks without direction; level 2 would mean the employee has attained partial proficiency and could, for instance, apply technical principles on the job; and level 3 would mean the employee is fully competent in the area and could, for example, analyze and solve production problems. Typically, employees are continually rotated between different production areas. This system encourages the learning of new skills, and can foster flexibility by encouraging workers to learn multiple skills and willingly switch tasks.

Whether or not skill-based pay results in improved plant productivity is an open question. When used in conjunction with team-building and worker involvement and empowerment programs, it does appear to lead to higher quality as well as lower absenteeism rates and fewer accidents.[27] However, the findings in one firm, which are not conclusive, suggest that productivity was higher at its non-skill-based pay facility.[28]

Ontario Hydro has used competency-based pay for its top 550 executives and corporate officers since 1993. Competence in areas including leadership, team building, and innovation is assessed using behaviourally-based scales that were developed over a lengthy period of time during the first stage of implementation. Competency-based pay was initially developed to assist in placing these employees in broad salary bands (see section on broadbanding below), but is also used for selection, promotion, performance management, and career development. The competency-based pay plan is proving to be more important than ever as Ontario Hydro copes with major political and organizational change, primarily becoming more customer focussed. The need to update competencies by incorporating critical new behaviours related to Hydro's emerging commercial orientation has been identified. Although there are no formal training programs to help executives broaden and enhance their competency levels, company data indicate that this group of senior employees has been handling more complex work at a more mature competency level.

Overall, one recent Canadian survey found that less than 10 percent of employers have implemented skill/competency-based pay, primarily due to difficulties in measuring competency achievement, and because the process of developing competency models is very time consuming.[29]

HR and the Responsive Organization

Broadbanding

The trend today is for employers to reduce their salary grades and ranges from ten or more down to three to five, a process called *broadbanding*. Broadbanding means collapsing salary grades and ranges into just a few wide levels or "bands," each of which then contains a relatively wide range of jobs and salary levels. Thus, instead of having, say, ten salary grades each of which contains a salary range of, say, $15 000, the firm might collapse the ten grades into three broad bands, each with a set of jobs such that the difference between the lowest- and highest-paid jobs might be $40 000 or more. One survey of 61 Canadian employers found that over 20 percent of those organizations responding said they had adopted a broadbanding approach or were considering doing so.[1]

Broadbanding's basic advantage is that it injects greater flexibility into employee compensation.[2] Broadbanding is especially sensible where firms flatten their hierarchies and organize around self-managing teams. The new, broad salary bands can include both supervisors and those reporting to them and can also facilitate moving employees slightly up or down along the pay scale without accompanying promotional raises or demotional pay cuts. For example, ". . . the employee who needs to spend time in a lower-level job to develop a certain skill set can receive higher-than-usual pay for the work, a circumstance considered impossible under traditional pay systems."[3]

Broadbanding also facilitates the sorts of less specialized, boundaryless jobs and organizations being embraced by many firms like General Electric Canada Inc. Less specialization and more participation in cross-departmental processes generally mean enlarged duties or capabilities and more possibilities for alternative career tracks; broader, more inclusive salary bands facilitate this. One expert argues that traditional quantitative evaluation plans actually reward unadaptability.[4] The argument here is that being slotted into a job that is highly routine as defined by a compensable factor such as "know-how" is unlikely to encourage job incumbents to think independently or be flexible. Instead, the tendency may be for workers to concentrate on the specific, routine jobs to which they are assigned and for which they are rewarded.

General Electric Canada Inc. and Ontario Hydro are two organizations that have broadbanded their pay scales. GE Canada was able to restructure nonunion salaried employees into just six broad compensation bands: two for the executive level and four for nonunion salaried employees. Ontario Hydro initially applied broadbanding at the executive level, and is now working toward applying broadbanding at other levels.[5]

Broadbanding a pay system involves several steps. First, as illustrated in **Figure 12.5**, the number of bands is decided upon and each is assigned a salary range. The bands usually have wide salary ranges and also overlap substantially. As a result, there's much more flexibility to move employees from job to job within bands and less need to "promote" them to new grades just to get them higher salaries.

The bands are then typically subdivided into either specific jobs (see **Figure 12.6**) or skill levels (see **Figure 12.7**). For example, a band may consist of a number of jobs

**Figure 12.5
Setting Salary Ranges
for Three Bands**

Source: David Hofrichter, "Broadbanding: A 'Second Generation' Approach," *Compensation & Benefits Review* (Sept–Oct 1993), p. 56.

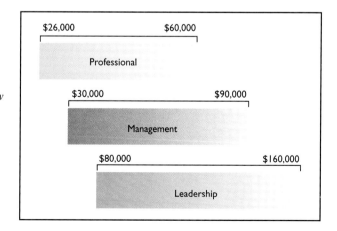

Figure 12.6
Assigning Market Value

Source: David Hofrichter, "Broadbanding: A 'Second Generation' Approach," *Compensation & Benefits Review,* Sept–Oct 1993, pp. 56–7.

Figure 12.7
Positioning Jobs within a Band

Source: David Hofrichter, "Broadbanding: A 'Second Generation' Approach," *Compensation & Benefits Review,* Sept–Oct 1993, pp. 56–7.

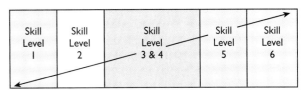

Pay in Relation to Skills

each assigned a market value. More often, bands are sudivided into several skill levels. Ontario Hydro used three skill levels for its executive group: developmental, mature, and expert.[6] With this approach, workers are not paid above market value just for doing a job well or for having seniority. Instead they must increase their competencies such as skills, knowledge, and abilities.[7]◆

1. N. Winter Consulting Inc., *Alternative Compensation Practices*, 1996.
2. David Hofrichter, "Broadbanding: A 'Second Generation' Approach," *Compensation and Benefits Review* (September–October 1993), pp. 53–8. See also Gary Bergel, "Choosing the Right Pay Delivery System to Fit Banding," *Compensation and Benefits Review* 26, no. 4 (July–August 1994), pp. 34–8.
3. Hofrichter "Broadbanding: A 'Second Generation' Approach," p. 55.
4. For example, see Sondra Emerson, "Job Evaluation: A Barrier to Excellence?" *Compensation and Benefits Review* (January–February 1991), pp. 39–51; Nan Weiner, "Job Evaluation Systems: A Critique," *Human Resource Management Review* 1, no. 2 (Summer 1991), pp. 119–32.
5. N. Winter, "Broadbanding: Who's Using It And Why?" *Canadian HR Reporter*, (December 18, 1995) p. 8.
6. Winter "Broadbanding: Who's Using It?
7. Hofrichter, "Broadbanding: A 'A Second Generation' Approach," pp. 53–7.

Why Job Evaluation Plans Are Still Widely Used

Quantitative job evaluation systems, primarily the point plan, are widely used in Canada, partly due to the requirements of pay equity legislation. There are several other reasons for this trend. Proponents argue that individual differences in skill attainment *can* be taken into consideration even when point-type plans are used, since most firms use salary ranges for groups of similar jobs. These salary ranges often reflect differences in the skills attained by, say, different people who may be working on the very same job.[30] Job evaluation advocates also argue that a job description is not necessarily a job restriction, since it's naive to "believe that employees automatically limit their behaviour to what is written on a piece of paper."[31] Furthermore, they say, there's no reason why job evaluation needs to be limited to a specific job. Instead, one could theoretically evaluate the "job" of doing a whole project and from there ascertain the problem solving, accountability, and knowledge that a worker would need to do all the jobs involved in that project. Furthermore, neither skill/competency-based pay nor market-based pay entirely eliminates the need for evaluating the worth of one job relative to others.

Computerized Job Evaluations

As explained more fully in the appendix to this chapter, using a quantitative job evaluation plan such as the point plan can be a fairly time-consuming matter. This is so because accumulating the information about "how much" of each compensable factor the job contains has traditionally been done through an often tedious process in which evaluation committees debate the level of each compensable factor in a job. They then write down their consensus judgments and manually compute each job's point values.

According to one expert, CAJE—computer-aided job evaluation—can dramatically streamline this whole process.[1] Computer-aided job evaluation, she says, can simplify job analysis, help keep job descriptions up to date, increase evaluation objectivity, reduce the time spent in committee meetings, and ease the burden of system maintenance. CAJE "features electronic data entry, computerized checking of questionnaire responses and automated output—not only of job evaluations, but also of a variety of compensation reports."[2] Most CAJE systems have two main components.

There is a structured questionnaire. This contains items such as "enter total number of employees who report functionally to this position." Second, all CAJE systems are built around statistical models, which allow the computer program to price jobs more or less automatically based upon inputted information on such things as prices of benchmark jobs, current pay, and current pay grade midpoints.

Another expert points out that CAJE does not replace but enhances traditional evaluation systems.[3] He says that you still need a traditional job evaluation system to provide "the initial solid analysis of benchmark jobs"—in other words, to identify the relative worth of these benchmark jobs. Then CAJE "streamlines and speeds the job evaluation process for 'non-benchmark' jobs."[4] ◆

1. Sondra O'Neal, "CAJE: Computer-Aided Job Evaluation for the 1990s," *Compensation and Benefits Review* (November–December 1990), pp. 14–9.
2. O'Neal, "CASE."
3. Laurent Dufetel, "Job Evaluation: Still at the Frontier," *Compensation and Benefits Review* (July–August 1991), p. 64.
4. Dufetel, "Job Evaluation."

In the final analysis, their relative ease of use and security are probably the major reasons for the continued widespread use of quantitative plans. Quantitative plans have also recently been facilitated by computerized packages, as explained in the accompanying Information Technology and HR box.

Building Employee Commitment

Compensation Management

Pay plans at well-known and progressive firms such as Saturn Corporation in the United States help illustrate the current trends in job evaluation and compensation management. The compensation plans at Saturn are elements in more comprehensive programs aimed at fostering employee commitment. These elements include value-based hiring, career-oriented appraisals, and extensive employee involvement programs. Compensation therefore tends to reflect the trust with which these firms treat their employees, and the fact that employees are and should be treated as partners in the business.

The compensation policies at Saturn are typical.[1] Saturn's pay plan is built on four principles—salary, trust, few classifications, and pay-for-performance. All Saturn employees are salaried, and there are no time clocks in the facility. Employees go to a keyboard and punch in the number of hours they worked. While there are some checks and balances, the process is basically an honour system. "What it comes down to," said one operating technician, "is a matter of trust."[2]

There are also relatively few job classifications. Virtually all the assembly employees are classified as "operating technicians" as are all nonskilled trades members such as machinists. There are four additional classifications for skilled trades members.

Pay-for-performance is important, too. Under the reward system originally envisioned in the memorandum of agreement between Saturn and the UAW, about 20 percent of each employee's pay was to be "at risk." Specifically, each employee's base compensation was to equal 80 percent of straight-time wages of the average for comparable jobs rates in the U.S. automobile manufacturing industry. Over and above that, a reward system was to be developed that would be based on factors such as achievement of objective productivity targets, individual and work unit performance, quality bonuses, and eventually a "Saturn sharing formula" through which profits were to be shared above a specified level of return to Saturn. At a minimum, therefore, 20 percent of each person's pay was to be at risk, to be earned back if the individual and the company met their productivity goals. Then a profit-sharing formula was to kick in. A slower than expected startup at Saturn forced the firm to reduce the at-risk component to five percent and thus boost the "guaranteed" component of the pay. Under a modified skill-based approach, employees can earn that five percent back by meeting specified training goals (attending training sessions, improving their skills, and so on).

In summary, the trend in firms like Saturn is to:

1. Offer packages of above-average pay combined with incentives and extensive benefits.

2. Build a compensation package that puts a significant portion of pay at risk.

3. Emphasize self-reporting of hours worked rather than devices like time clocks.

4. Build a pay plan that encourages employees to think of themselves as partners. This means that they should have a healthy share of the profits in good years and share in the downturn during bad times.

5. Provide a package of benefits that makes it clear employees are viewed as long-term investments. ◆

1. This is based on Gary Dessler, *Winning Commitment* (New York: McGraw-Hill, 1993), Chapter 9.
2. Personal interview.

A Glimpse into the Future

The evolving practices in firms like Saturn provide a glimpse into the future of compensation management, and that future is now, as far as many firms are concerned. Here's what several compensation experts say can be expected.

First, with an increasing emphasis on flexibility and on empowering employees, in the year 2000 "most traditional job descriptions and hourly employee job classifications will be fed unceremoniously into the paper shredder."[32] Replacing them will be greater latitude for employees to evolve their responsibilities to meet customer needs as they see fit. And there will be an increasing emphasis on paying employees for their competencies rather than just for the job's responsibilities and activities. Measurement systems and rewards will increasingly emphasize paying for results.

Skill-based pay will actually be a return to the compensation methods of the far distant past. Under the apprentice systems that started with the guilds of the

Middle Ages, apprentices had to demonstrate competence at their trade before becoming journeymen, and then masters. So when firms like General Electric condense many jobs into a few broad bands and then base pay differentials on skill levels, they're really returning, to some extent, to the past.[33]

One expert also suggests that as firms like IBM break themselves into small, specialized, and decentralized pieces, the concept of centrally determined compensation plans may become obsolete.[34] He says that at some point managers of decentralized units should get their own salary budgets and then "set pay levels for new hires, determine pay increases, decide when to give raises, and make all other decisions concerning cash compensation for the employees reporting to them."[35]

There will also be a growing emphasis on pay for improved results and on nontraditional pay (also called "alternative rewards"). As summarized in **Figure 12.8**, traditional pay plans based on job descriptions, job evaluations, and salary structures tend to focus, says this expert, on creating order, reinforcing the hierarchy, and directing behaviour.[36] In the future (and, for many firms, now), the emphasis will shift from paying for the job to paying for the employee's contribution. Thus, the focus will shift from creating order and directing behaviour to encouraging involvement and commitment, and to rewarding positive results. Nontraditional or alternative pay plans for doing this include competency or skill-based pay and the sorts of spot awards, team incentives, and gainsharing we'll discuss in chapter 13.

Pricing Managerial and Professional Jobs

www.payroll.ca/english/ english.htm
Payrolls

Developing a compensation plan to pay executive, managerial, and professional employees is similar in many respects to developing a plan for other employees.[37] The basic aims of the plan are the same in that the goal is to attract good employees and maintain their commitment. Furthermore, the basic methods of job evaluation—classifying jobs, ranking them, or assigning points to them, for instance—are about as applicable to managerial and professional jobs as to production and clerical ones.

Figure 12.8
Examples of Traditional and Nontraditional Pay

Source: Sibson & Company, Inc. Reproduced in Charles Cumming, "Will Traditional Salary Administration Survive the Stampede to Alternative Rewards?" *Compensation and Benefits Review* (November–December 1992), p. 45.

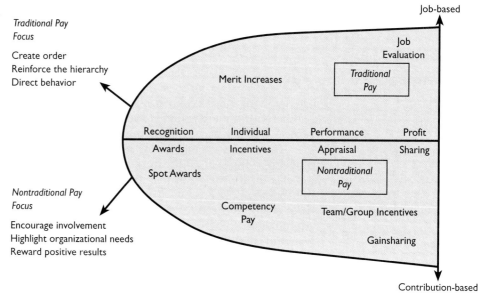

Yet for managerial and professional jobs, job evaluation provides only a partial answer to the question of how to pay these employees. Such jobs tend to emphasize nonquantifiable factors like judgment and problem solving more than do production and clerical jobs. There is also a tendency to pay managers and professionals based on ability—their performance or what they can do—rather than on the basis of static job demands like working conditions. Developing compensation plans for managers and professionals, therefore, tends to be relatively complex, and job evaluation, while still important, usually plays a secondary role to nonsalary issues like bonuses, incentives, and benefits.

Compensating Managers

Basic Compensation Elements   There are five elements in a manager's compensation package: salary, benefits, short-term incentives, long-term incentives, and perquisites.[38]

The amount of salary managers are paid usually depends on the value of the person's work to the organization and how well the person is discharging his or her responsibilities. As with other jobs, the value of the person's work is usually determined through job analysis and salary surveys and the resulting fine tuning of salary levels.

Salary is the cornerstone of executive compensation: It is on this element that the others are layered, with benefits, incentives, and perquisites normally awarded in some proportion to the manager's base pay. *Benefits* (including time off with pay, supplementary health care, employee services, survivor's protection, and retirement coverage) are discussed in chapter 14. *Short-term incentives* are designed to reward managers for attaining short-term (normally annual) goals. *Long-term incentives* are aimed at rewarding the person for long-term performance (in terms of increased market share and the like). Incentives are discussed in chapter 13. *Perquisites* (perks for short) begin where benefits leave off and are usually given to only a select few executives based on organizational level and (possibly) past performance. Perks include the use of company cars, yachts, and executive dining rooms. These benefits are also covered in chapter 14.

Executive compensation tends to emphasize performance incentives more than do other employees' pay plans, since organizational results are likely to reflect the contributions of executives more directly than those of lower-echelon employees. The heavy incentive component of executives' compensation can be illustrated with some examples of the highest-paid Canadian executives.[39] In 1996, for instance, the CEO of Bombardier Inc. earned a salary of $900 000, a short term bonus of $525 420, and other compensation (including stock options) of $17 674 897, for a total of $19 100 317. For the CEO of Thomson Corp., salary was $2 045 400, short term bonus was $3 924 441, and other (including long term) compensation was $5 419 427, making his total compensation for the year $11 389 268. The CEO of BioChem Pharma Inc. earned a salary of $475 218, a bonus of $667 866, and other (including long term) compensation of $8 850 000, for a total of $9 993 104. In general, bonuses today equal 25 percent or more of a typical executive's base salary in many countries, including the United Kingdom, France, the United States, and Germany.[40]

There is considerable disagreement regarding what determines executive pay and, therefore, whether top executives are worth what they are paid. At the lower-management levels (like first-line supervisor), there is no debate; supervisors' pay grades are usually set so that their median salaries are 10 percent to 25 percent above those of the highest-paid workers supervised. And some employers even pay supervisors for scheduled overtime, although labour standards legislation does not require them to do so.[41]

It is at the top-management levels that questions regarding pay abound. It is clear that executive pay varies considerably by country. For example, in 1996, Canadian CEOs on average made 50 percent of what U.S. CEOs did, 96 percent of what Japanese CEOs were paid, and 89 percent of the average British CEO's earnings. Members of Boards of Directors of large Canadian companies are paid an average of $35 000 to $40 000 per year, whereas U.S. companies pay directors an average of $65 700 (U.S.).[42] The traditional wisdom is that a top manager's salary is closely tied to the size of the firm.[43] Yet two experts who tested this idea for the 148 highest-paid executives in the United States concluded that "the level of executive responsibility (as measured by total assets, total sales, total number of shares in the company, total value of the shares, and total corporate profits) is not an important variable in determining executive compensation."[44] Instead, say these experts, an executive's pay is mostly determined by the industry in which he or she works, and the "corporate power structure," since executives who also serve on their firms' boards of directors can heavily influence how much they get paid.

Yet there is conflicting evidence. In one study, for instance, the researcher found that a statistical analysis of the total cash compensation of the chief executive officers of 129 companies showed that they were paid for both responsibility and performance. This researcher found that four compensable factors—company size, profitability, number of employees, and experience—accounted for 83 percent of the differences in pay. Therefore, it appears "that there are rational, acceptable, and abiding principles that govern the total cash compensation of top executives in manufacturing firms."[45]

In any case, shareholder activism is combining with other changes to tighten up the restrictions on what firms pay their top executives.[46] For example, in October 1993 the Ontario Securities Commission approved rules regarding disclosure of executive compensation (salary, bonus, stock options and other compensation) for companies listed on the Toronto Stock Exchange.[47] The chief executive officer's pay must always be disclosed, as well as that of the next four highest paid employees. Further, boards of directors must disclose how they make executive compensation decisions, and hence must act responsibly in reviewing and setting executive pay. That, says one expert, includes determining the key performance requirements of the executive's job; assessing the appropriateness of the firm's current compensation practices; conducting a pay-for-performance survey; and testing shareholder acceptance of the board's pay proposals.[48] A related development for public sector employees was the Ontario government's requirement that, beginning in 1996, public disclosure be made of salaries for provincial government employees earning $100 000 or more.[49] The law also applies to employees in the broader public sector, including hospitals, universities, school boards, crown agencies, and municipalities.

The general trend today is to reduce the relative importance of base salary and boost the importance of short- and long-term executive incentives.[50] The main issue here is identifying the appropriate performance measures for each type of incentive and then determining how to link these to pay. Typical short-term measures of shareholder value include revenue growth and operating profit margin. Long-term shareholder value measures include rate of return above some predetermined base.

Managerial Job Evaluation   Despite questions regarding the rationality of executive pay, job evaluation is still important in pricing executive and managerial jobs in most firms. According to one expert, "the basic approach used by most large companies to ensure some degree of equity among various divisions and departments is to classify all executive and management positions into a series of grades, to which a corresponding series of salary ranges is attached."[51]

As with nonmanagerial jobs, one alternative is to rank the executive and management positions in relation to each other, grouping those of equal value. However, the job classification and point evaluation methods are also used, with compensable factors like position scope, complexity, difficulty, and creative demands.

Compensating Professional Employees

Compensating nonsupervisory professional employees like engineers and scientists presents unique problems.[52] Analytical jobs put a heavy premium on creativity and problem solving, compensable factors not easily compared or measured. Furthermore, the professional's economic impact on the firm is often related only indirectly to the person's actual efforts; for example, the success of an engineer's invention depends on many factors, like how well it is produced and marketed.

The job evaluation methods explained previously can be used for evaluating professional jobs.[53] The compensable factors here tend to focus on problem solving, creativity, job scope, and technical knowledge and expertise. Both the point method and factor comparison methods have been used, although the job classification method seems most popular. Here a series of grade descriptions are written, and each position is slotted into the grade having the most appropriate definition.

Yet, in practice, traditional methods of job evaluation are rarely used for professional jobs since "it is simply not possible to identify factors and degrees of factors which meaningfully differentiate among the values of professional work."[54] "Knowledge and the skill of applying it," as one expert notes, "are extremely difficult to quantify and measure."[55]

As a result, most employers use a market-pricing approach in evaluating professional jobs. They price professional jobs in the marketplace to the best of their ability to establish the values for benchmark jobs. These benchmark jobs and the employer's other professional jobs are then slotted into a salary structure. Specifically, each professional discipline (like mechanical engineering or electrical engineering) usually ends up having four to six grade levels, each of which requires a fairly broad salary range. This approach helps ensure that the employer remains competitive when bidding for professionals whose attainments vary widely and whose potential employers are literally found worldwide.[56]

Current Issues in Compensation Management

The Issue of Pay Equity

The Issue As described in chapter 3, historically, the average pay for Canadian women has been considerably lower than that for men. As **Table 12.4** shows, women's average wages were 46.1 percent of men's average wages in 1967. This "wage gap" of 53.9 percent means that for every dollar earned by a man, a woman earned 46.1 cents. The gap has slowly narrowed to a low of 35.7 percent in 1993, and stood at 37.7 percent in 1994. Some of this gap is due to the fact that women do more part-time work than men, but even when full-year, full-time workers are compared, the gap is 30.2 percent. Moreover, the gap persists even when women have the same qualifications and do the same type of work as men. For example, the 1996 salary survey of the Certified General Accountants Association of Ontario shows that female CGA students make an average of eight percent less that male students, regardless of age, and that fully-qualified female CGAs make less than male CGAs of all ages except for those women aged 26–30, who have the same median salary as males.

Although such factors as differences in hours worked, experience levels, education levels, and level of unionization contribute to the wage gap, systemic

TABLE 12.4				Male/Female Average Earnings Ratio					
YEAR	**FULL-YEAR FULL-TIME WORKERS (a)**			**OTHER WORKERS**			**ALL EARNERS**		
	WOMEN	MEN	EARNINGS RATIO	WOMEN	MEN	EARNINGS RATIO	WOMEN	MEN	EARNINGS RATIO
1967	18 427	31 548	58.4	6 619	13 091	50.6	12 068	26 177	46.1
1969	20 188	34 412	58.7	7 863	17 104	46.0	12 778	27 960	45.7
1971	22 255	37 304	59.7	7 427	14 730	50.4	14 067	30 013	46.9
1972	23 104	38 621	59.8	7 627	14 758	51.7	14 348	31 116	46.1
1973	23 320	39 347	59.3	7 795	14 929	52.2	14 658	31 684	46.3
1974	24 368	40 911	59.6	8 519	15 965	53.4	15 370	32 415	47.4
1975	25 256	41 957	60.2	8 435	16 664	50.6	15 956	33 184	48.1
1976	26 565	44 921	59.1	9 272	17 679	52.4	16 509	35 358	46.7
1977	25 881	41 708	62.1	9 427	15 513	60.8	17 030	33 547	50.8
1978	26 733	42 436	63.0	8 992	15 327	58.7	16 971	33 405	50.8
1979	26 133	41 174	63.5	9 349	16 133	57.9	17 149	33 258	51.6
1980	26 969	41 909	64.4	9 209	14 998	61.4	17 207	33 299	51.7
1981	26 214	41 129	63.7	9 592	15 399	62.3	17 431	32 500	53.6
1982	26 029	40 671	64.0	8 947	14 196	63.0	17 051	30 969	55.1
1983	26 931	41 555	64.8	8 422	13 521	62.3	17 207	31 160	55.2
1984	26 562	40 498	65.6	9 411	13 432	70.1	17 596	30 581	57.5
1985	26 421	40 602	65.1	9 094	12 980	70.1	17 637	31 311	56.3
1986	26 852	40 807	65.8	9 927	13 408	74.0	18 248	31 746	57.5
1987	27 320	41 303	66.1	10 139	13 298	76.2	18 523	32 037	57.8
1988	27 426	41 912	65.4	10 009	13 497	74.2	18 884	32 842	57.5
1989	27 484	41 655	66.0	10 474	14 211	73.7	19 445	32 913	59.1
1990	28 310	41 811	67.7	10 123	14 313	70.7	19 459	32 517	59.8
1991	28 893	41 494	69.6	9 567	13 622	70.2	19 458	31 619	61.5
1992	30 122	41 900	71.9	9 849	12 976	75.9	20 133	31 516	63.9
1993	29 653	41 058	72.2	9 614	12 890	74.6	19 865	30 872	64.3
1994	29 491	42 247	69.8	10 090	12 917	78.1	20 086	32 255	62.3
1995	30 154	41 230	73.1	10 143	13 178	77.0	20 528	31 527	65.1
1996	30 717	41 848	73.4	10 388	13 280	78.2	20 902	32 248	64.8

(a) "Full-year" is defined as 50 to 52 weeks for data prior to 1981 and 49 to 52 weeks for more recent data.

Source: "ªAverage Earnings of Women and Men in Constant (1996) Dollars and Female-to-Male Earnings Ratios, by Work Activity, 1967 to 1996," adapted from "Earnings of Men and Women in 1996," Statistics Canada Catalogue No. 13-217. 1997.
Statistics Canada information is used with the permission of the Minister of Industry, as Minister responsible for Statistics Canada. Information on the availability of the wide range of data from Statistics Canada can be obtained form Statistics Canada's Regional Offices, its World Wide Web site at http://www.statcan.ca, and its toll-free access number 1-800-263-1136.

pay equity
Providing equal pay to male-dominated job classes and female-dominated job classes of equal value to the employer.

discrimination is also present. The purpose of pay equity legislation, which has been introduced in six provinces through the 1980s and 1990s, is to redress systemic gender discrimination in compensation for work performed by employees in female-dominated job classes. Some experts believe that pay equity (called "comparable worth"in the United States) may also become the standard in the United States. **Pay equity** requires that equal wages be paid for jobs of equal value or "worth" to the employer, as determined by gender neutral (that is, free of any bias based on gender) job evaluation techniques. For example, in one Ontario hospital, the female job of ambulance coordinator and the male job of electrician were found to be of comparable value, and the coordinator received a pay equity adjustment of $1.06 per hour.[57] The effect of pay equity on the wage gap is still being assessed, but in Ontario the wage gap narrowed by 9.5 percent between 1987, when the legislation was introduced, and 1993.[58]

Pay Equity and Job Evaluation   The issue of pay equity has important implications for an employer's job evaluation procedures. Most pay equity legislation in Canada requires that every male-dominated job and every female-dominated job be evaluated using four compensable factors (skill, effort, responsibility, and working conditions). In most cases, jobs are then assigned points based on the degree of each factor present in the job, although these factors can also be used with other job evaluation methods. Where a female-dominated job class such as Data Entry Clerk is found to be of equal or comparable value to a more highly paid, male-dominated job such as Boilermaker, then the female-dominated job must be provided with the same compensation (including benefits) as the male-dominated job.

Diversity Counts
In Job Evaluation

Some experts have argued that job evaluation procedures like the point method are inherently unfair to women because they ignore or underestimate the skills associated with the types of jobs often held by women.[1] For example, one expert argues that many of the skills associated with doing jobs such as nursing and teaching go unrecognized because they ". . . mirror traditional duties within the home . . ." and are ignored because it's assumed that they need not be learned on the job or are somehow less important than skills that are based on on-the-job training.[2] As one commentator has noted:

What seems to have occurred is an assumption that because women often exercise such skills [cooking, cleaning, nursing, and sewing, to name a few] at home, they were somehow intrinsic to womanhood and did not need to be [learned] in the same way as typically male skills. Thus the definition of "skill" became molded by male perceptions of what was truly skillful, lower pay for women being the result.[3]

By this line of reasoning, job evaluation procedures like the point method may have an inherent bias against women because they ignore the sorts of skills women may bring to the job, while crediting men for similar skills that need to be learned on the job. For example, while men "typically receive points for dirt and grease that they encounter on the job under a factor designated 'working conditions,' nurses, who deal with vomit and blood on a daily basis, receive no such points."[4] Similarly, male-dominated machinery-based factory jobs typically receive points for noise under the factor "working conditions." They may thus end up with higher evaluations than do female-dominated clerical jobs, in which the workers rarely get credit for concentrating and getting their jobs done amidst the distractions of phones and other interruptions.

Women may even suffer from the fact that much of the training on predominantly female jobs such as clerical jobs is "invisible." As one expert argues:

In contrast to many manufacturing and trade jobs which require a great deal of visible on-the-job training, skills such as typing and stenography are prerequisites for a [clerical] job, and must be learned outside of the employer's presence.[5]

Since these clerical skills may be more likely to go unrecognized, female-dominated jobs (such as clerical jobs), and therefore women, may not receive the points or for that matter the compensation that their skills would otherwise warrant.◆

1. Jennifer Quinn, "Visibility and Value: The Role of Job Evaluation in Assuring Equal Pay for Women," *Law and Policy in International Business* 25, no. 4 (Summer 1994), pp. 1403-44.
2. Quinn, "Visibility and Value," p. 1411.
3. Richard Townsend-Smith, "Sex Discrimination in Employment," *Law Practice & Policy* 148 (1989), p. 15.
4. Quinn, "Visibility and Value," p. 1411.
5. Quinn, "Visibility and Value," p. 1412.

There is also the possibility of bias in the job evaluation plan itself. In particular, some traditional job evaluation point plans "tend to result in higher point totals for jobs traditionally held by males than for those traditionally held by females."[59] For example, the factor "supervisory responsibility" might heavily weight chain-of-command factors such as number of employees supervised and downplay the importance of functional authority or gaining the voluntary cooperation of other employees. The solution here is to rewrite the factor rules in job evaluation plans so as to give more weight to the sorts of activities that female-dominated positions frequently emphasize.[60]

Implications   In the long term, the best way to remove the portion of the wage gap resulting from systemic discrimination is to eliminate male- and female-dominated jobs by ensuring that women have equal access to, and are equally represented in, all jobs. To avoid pay equity problems, questions to ask include:

- Are job duties and responsibilities clearly documented either by a job analysis questionnaire or a job description? Are they reviewed and updated annually?
- Is the pay system clearly documented in a salary administration manual? If not, the credibility and defensibility of pay practices are ripe for challenge.
- When was the pay system last reviewed? If more than three years have passed, serious inequities could exist. Maintenance of pay equity is a requirement of pay equity legislation.
- Are the pay equity laws being monitored and adhered to in each province in which the organization has employees? There are differences in the legislation between jurisdictions.

The Issue of Pay Secrecy

There are two opposing points of view with respect to the question of whether employees should know what other employees in the organization are being paid. The basic argument for "open pay" is that it improves employee motivation, and the thinking here is as follows: If employees believe that greater effort does not result in greater rewards, then, generally speaking, greater effort will not be forthcoming. On the other hand, if employees do see a direct relationship between effort and rewards, then greater effort will result. Proponents of open pay contend that workers who do not know each other's pay cannot easily assess how effort and rewards are related, or whether they are equitably paid, and as a result of this motivation tends to suffer. (They cannot, for example, say "Smith doesn't work hard and so is paid less than Jones, who does work hard.")

The opposing argument is that in practice there are usually real inequities in the pay scale, perhaps because of the need to hire someone "in a hurry," or because of the superior negotiating ability of a particular applicant. And even if the employee in a similar job who is being paid more actually deserves the higher salary because of his or her effort, skill, or experience, it's possible that lower-paid colleagues may convince themselves that they are underpaid relative to the higher-paid individual.

The research findings to this point are sketchy. One study found that managers' satisfaction with their pay increased following their firms' implementation of an open-pay policy.[61] A survey conducted by the U.S. Bureau of National Affairs found that fewer than half the firms responding gave employees access to salary schedules. Those not providing such information indicated, among other things, that "secrecy prevents much quibbling ...," "salary is a delicate matter ...," open pay "could well lead to unnecessary strain and dissatisfaction among managers ...," and "open systems too often create misunderstandings and petty complaints." The

**www.hronline.org/research/
research.htm**
Employers Group

author of this study notes that "whether the inequities result from a growth situation or some other factor, it is clear that some inequities and openness are incompatible."[62] The implication for compensation management seems to be that a policy of open pay can, under the best of conditions, improve employees' satisfaction with their pay and possibly their effort as well. On the other hand, if conditions are not right—and especially if there are any lingering inequities in the employer's pay structure—moving to an open-pay policy is not advisable.

The Issues of Inflation and Salary Compression

salary compression
A situation where longer-term employees' salaries are lower than those for workers entering a firm, due to inflation.

Inflation and how to cope with it has been another important issue in compensation management.[63] **Salary compression** means that longer-term employees' salaries are lower than those for workers entering the firm today, and it is a result of inflation. Its symptoms include (1) higher starting salaries, which compress current employees' salaries; and (2) unionized hourly pay increases that overtake supervisory and nonunion hourly rates.[64]

Dealing with salary compression is a tricky problem.[65] On the one hand, long-term employees should not be treated unfairly or they may become inordinately dissatisfied and possibly leave with their accumulated knowledge and expertise. On the other hand, mediocre performance or lack of assertiveness, rather than salary compression, may in many cases explain the low salaries.

In any case, there are several solutions.[66] As distasteful as it is to many employers to pay employees just for seniority, a program of providing raises based on longevity can be instituted. These raises could be distributed in flat dollar amounts, or as a percentage of base pay, or as a combination of the two. Second, a much more aggressive merit pay program can be installed. This may at least help reduce the morale problems associated with pay compression, since employees know they have the potential for earning higher raises. Third, supervisors can be authorized to recommend "equity" adjustments for selected incumbents who are both highly valued by the organization and also viewed as unfairly victimized by pay compression.

Cost-of-living differentials can help employees cope with the high cost of living in cities such as Tokyo.

Inflation has also put some pension plans in peril.[67] A Canadian executive who retired at the beginning of 1986 had lost over 40 percent of the purchasing power of a fixed-dollar company pension by today, for instance—a frightening state of affairs for retirees whose pensions are not indexed to inflation. While the rate of increase of consumer prices has recently slowed, some fear that inflation is only dormant and that rapid price increases will again occur.

Particularly in periods of high inflation, employers try to cope with inflation's impact in several ways. More employers grant across-the-board salary increases either in lieu of or in addition to performance-based merit increases. Others change their pension plans to index them to inflation so that the value of the pension payments increased along with the rise in the price of goods.[68] The compensation mix is sometimes changed to decrease the emphasis on taxable income like wages and salary and to substitute nontaxable benefits like flexible work hours, dental plans, day-care centres, and group legal and auto insurance plans.[69]

The cost-of-living adjustment (or COLA) clause is sometimes pushed by unions as another way to cope with inflation.[70] The COLA or escalator clause is designed to maintain the purchasing power of the wage rate and operates as follows. Specified increases in the Consumer Price Index trigger increases in the wage rate, with the magnitude of the increase depending on the negotiated COLA formula.[71] The most common formula provides a one-cent per hour wage adjustment for each 0.3 percent or 0.4 percent change in consumer prices.[72] Nonunion employees often then receive a similar adjustment. Periodically, the employer takes a portion of the dollar COLA adjustment and builds it into the employee's base salary, a procedure known as "baking in."[73] COLAs have become less of a concern to unions as inflation has moderated.

The Issue of Cost-of-Living Differentials

Cost-of-living differences between localities have escalated from occasional inconveniences to serious compensation problems. For example, a family of four might live in Halifax for just over $40 000 per year while the same family's annual expenditures in Vancouver would be over $41 500.

Employers are using several methods to handle cost-of-living differentials. The main approach is to give the transferred person a nonrecurring payment, usually in a lump sum or perhaps spread over one to three years.[74] Other employers pay a differential for ongoing costs in addition to a one-time allocation. Other companies simply increase the employee's base salary rate. They give the person an automatic raise equal to the amount by which living costs in the new locale exceed those in the old, in addition to any other promotion-based raise the employee may get.

www.aspm.org
American Society for Payroll Management

Global HRM

The Issue of Compensating Expatriate Employees

The question of cost-of-living differentials has particular relevance to multinational firms. The annual cost of sending a Canadian expatriate manager from Canada to Europe may be quite different compared to the cost of sending him or her to South America or China.

Such wide discrepancies raise the issue of how multinational firms should compensate overseas employees. The issue is particularly important today, in part because of the growing need to staff overseas operations, and in part because of the increasing frequency with which managers and professionals are moved from country to country.

Two basic international compensation policies are popular: home-based and host-based policies.[1]

Under a home-based salary policy, an international transferee's base salary reflects his or her home country's salary structure. Additional allowances are then tacked on for cost-of-living differences and housing and schooling costs, for instance. This is a reasonable approach for short-term assignments and avoids the problem of having to change the employee's base salary every time he or she moves. However, it can result in some difficulty at the host office if, say, employees from several different countries at the same office are all being paid different base salaries for performing essentially the same tasks.

In the host-based plan, the base salary for the international transferee is tied to the host country's salary structure. In other words, the manager from Montreal who is sent to France would have his or her base salary changed to the prevailing base salary for that position in France rather than keep his or her Montreal base salary. Of course, cost-of-living, housing, schooling, and other allowances are tacked on here as well. This approach can cause some consternation to our Montreal manager who might, for instance, see his or her base salary plummet with a transfer to Bangladesh. Conversely, he or she may face the problem of frequent salary fluctuations if he or she moves from country to country fairly often.

There's no one best way to deal with the international compensation problem. One compensation expert suggests a compromise, namely basing the person's new base salary on a percentage of home-country salary plus the higher of a percentage of (1) host-country salary or (2) the amount required in host-country currency to maintain a home-country standard of living in the host location.[2] A recent survey of multinational enterprises suggests that most set expatriates' salaries according to their home-country base pay.[3] Thus, a French manager assigned to Kiev by a Canadian multinational will generally have a base salary that reflects the salary structure in the manager's home country, in this case France. In addition there will be various allowances including cost-of-living, relocation, housing, education, and hardship allowances (the latter for countries with a lower standard of living than Canada, such as China). The multinational employer will also usually pay any extra tax burdens resulting from tax liability over and above that in the manager's home country. As in North America, about one-third of the expatriates' compensation package consists of benefits.◆

1. This is based on Jack Anderson, "Compensating Your Overseas Executives, Part II: Europe in 1992," *Compensation and Benefits Review* (July–August 1990), pp. 29–31.
2. Anderson, "Compensating Your Overseas Executives," p. 31.
3. Richard Hodgetts and Fred Luthans, "U.S. Multinationals' Expatriates' Compensation Strategies," *Compensation and Benefits Review* (January–February 1993), pp. 57–62. See also K. Mark, "Crossing International Pay Lines," *Human Resources Professional* (August/September 1997), pp. 13–6.

Small Business Applications

Developing a pay plan that is internally and externally equitable is as important in a small firm as in a large one. Paying wage rates that are too high for the area may be unnecessarily expensive, and paying less may guarantee poor-quality help and high turnover. Similarly, wage rates that are internally inequitable will reduce morale and cause the president to be badgered mercilessly by employees demanding raises "the same as Joe down the hall." The president who wants to concentrate on major issues like sales would thus do well to institute a rational pay plan as soon as possible.

Developing a Workable Pay Plan

The first step should be to conduct a wage survey. The basic methods for doing so were described earlier in this chapter, but smaller businesses generally depend on less formal methods for collecting this information.

Three sources here can be especially useful. A careful perusal of the classified newspaper ads should yield useful information on wages offered for jobs similar to those which need pricing. Second, the local Human Resources Development Canada (HRDC) office can be a wealth of information, compiling as it does extensive information on pay ranges and averages for many of the jobs listed in the *National Occupational Classification* (This is another reason for using job titles that are consistent with those in the NOC.) The HRDC office can provide information on wages within the local area served by that office, as well as on the broader geographic region served by the group of HDRC offices in adjacent locations. Finally, local employment agencies, always anxious to establish ties that could grow into business relationships, should be able to provide fairly good data regarding pay rates for different jobs.

Next, firms that employ more than 20 employees or so should conduct at least a rudimentary job evaluation. For this, they will first require job descriptions, since these will be the source of data regarding the nature and worth of each job.

It is usually easier to split employees into three groups—managerial/professional, office/clerical, and plant employees. For each of the three groups, determine the compensable factors to be evaluated and then rank or assign points to each job based on the job evaluation.

For each job or class of jobs (such as assemblers), create a pay range. The procedure for doing so was described earlier. However, in general, the midpoint of the range should be the target salary as required by the job evaluation. Then produce a range of about 30 percent around this average, broken into a total of five steps.

Compensation Policies

Compensation policies are important, too. For example, there should be a policy on when and how raises are computed. Many small-business owners make the mistake of appraising employees on their anniversary date, a year after they are hired. The problem here is that the raise for one employee then becomes the standard for the next, as employees have time to compare notes over the space of several weeks or months. This produces a never-ending cycle of appraisals and posturing for ever-higher raises.

The better alternative is to have a policy of once-a-year raises during a standard one-week appraisal period, preferably about four weeks before the budget for next year must be produced. In this way, the administrative headache of conducting these appraisals and awarding raises is dealt with during a one (or two) week period. Furthermore, the total required raise money (which of course has to be computed in advance by the company president) is known more precisely when next year's budget is compiled. Other required compensation policies include amount of holiday and vacation pay (as explained in the next chapter), overtime pay policy, method of pay (weekly, biweekly, monthly), garnishments, and time card or sign-on sheet procedures.

Pay Equity

In provinces with pay equity legislation, all employers with ten or more employees are required to ensure pay equity for their employees. Employers with less than ten employees are exempt. For private sector employers with between 10 and 99 employees, the requirements vary by province. In some cases, the employer must develop and post a pay equity plan. In other cases, the employer must achieve pay equity but is not required to post a plan. However, if there is a complaint in a case where no plan was posted, the employer must be able to identify the steps taken and the calculations made to determine if pay equity adjustments were needed.[1]

A three-stage approach to pay equity can be helpful for smaller employers:

Stage 1: Get a feel for the process of comparing job classes by doing a fast listing of the order of importance of jobs in the organization.

Stage 2: Select the system to be used to compare jobs, then turn the work of comparing jobs over to a subcommittee or job comparison committee that will value jobs and determine comparable jobs.

Stage 3: Review the results and develop a schedule of adjustments.

Many employers with fewer than ten jobs find the ranking system to be the simplest way to evaluate jobs. As explained earlier, the ranking system is acceptable for pay equity purposes if jobs are ranked based on skill, effort, responsibility, and working conditions, without gender bias. Up-to-date descriptions of each job must be used for the evaluation exercise. Next, definitions of the four factors must be carefully prepared. Both physical and mental effort should be included. Factors may be weighted based on their relative importance in the organization. For example, if responsibility is considered to be three times as important as working conditions, and skill and effort to be twice as important as working conditions, the rank awarded to a job for responsibility can be multiplied by three, and the ranks for skill and effort can be multiplied by two.

For paired comparison rankings, each job should be compared to each other job on every factor individually. **Table 12.5a** provides an example of a form for rankings.

TABLE 12.5a Rankings for Skill

JOB CLASS	A	B	C	D	TOTAL TIMES RANKED HIGHEST	WEIGHT	WEIGHTED RESULTS
A-Receptionist	A				1	2	2
B-Owner/Manager	B	B			4	2	8
C-Sales Rep	C	B	C		3	2	6
D-Secretary	D	B	C	D	2	2	4

After conducting the comparisons for each of the four factors, the weighted results for each job on each factor are added to get a final value for each one, as shown in **Table 12.5b**.

TABLE 12.5b Results of Evaluation by Ranking

	SKILL	EFFORT	RESPONSIBILITY	WORKING CONDITIONS	TOTAL
A-Receptionist	2	2	3	4	11
B-Owner/Manager	8	4	12	1	25
C-Sales Rep	6	6	6	2	20
D-Secretary	4	8	9	3	24

Then each female-dominated job can be compared to a male-dominated job of equal or greater value (if one exists) to ascertain whether pay for the female-dominated job needs to be adjusted upward to achieve pay equity.

1. Taken from Ontario Pay Equity Commission, *Implementing Pay Equity in the Workplace*, Revised edition, "Pay Equity in Small Workplaces," 1990.

Chapter Review

Summary

1. There are two bases on which to compensate employees: increments of time and volume of production. The former includes hourly or daily wages and salaries. Basing pay on volume of production ties compensation directly to the amount of production (or number of "pieces" the worker produces).

2. Establishing pay rates involves five steps: conducting a salary survey, evaluating jobs, developing pay grades, using wage curves, and fine tuning pay rates.

3. Job evaluation is aimed at determining the relative worth of a job. It compares jobs to one another based on their content, which is usually defined in terms of compensable factors like skill, effort, responsibility, and working conditions.

4. The ranking method of job evaluation has five steps: (a) obtain job information, (b) select clusters of jobs to be rated, (c) select compensable factors, (d) rank jobs, and (e) combine ratings (of several raters). This is a simple method to use, but there is a tendency to rely too heavily on guesstimates. The classification (or grading) method is a second qualitative approach that categorizes jobs based on a class description or classification rules for each class.

5. The point method of job evaluation requires identifying a number of compensable factors and then determining the degree to which each of these factors is present in the job.

6. The factor comparison method, as explained in the appendix, is a quantitative job evaluation technique that entails deciding which jobs have more of certain compensable factors than others, and using pay rates for each factor.

7. Most managers group similar jobs into wage or pay grades for pay purposes. These are comprised of jobs of approximately equal value or importance as determined by job evaluation.

8. The wage curve (or line) shows the average target wage for each pay grade (or job). It illustrates what the average wage for each grade should be, and whether any present wages or salaries are out of line. Developing a wage curve involves four steps: (a) find the average pay for each pay grade, (b) plot these wage rates for each pay grade, (c) draw the wage line, and (d) price jobs after plotting present wage rates.

9. Developing a compensation plan for executive, managerial, and professional personnel is complicated by the fact that factors like performance and creativity must take precedence over static factors like working conditions. Market rates, performance, and incentives and benefits thus play a much greater role than does job evaluation for these employees.

10. Broadbanding means collapsing salary grades and ranges into just a few wide levels or bands, each of which then contains a relatively wide range of jobs and salary levels.

11. Four main compensation issues discussed were pay equity, pay secrecy, inflation-based salary compression, and cost-of-living differentials.

Key Terms

benchmark job	grade/group description	ranking method
classes	grades	rate ranges
classification (or grading)	job evaluation	red circle pay rate
method	pay equity	salary compression
compensable factor	pay grade	wage curve
employee compensation	point method	wage/salary survey
factor comparison method		

Discussion Questions and Exercises

1. Should job evaluation depend on an appraisal of the jobholder's performance? Why? Why not?

2. What is the relationship between compensable factors and job specifications?

3. What are the pros and cons of the following methods of job evaluation: ranking, classification, factor comparison, point method?

4. In what respect is the factor comparison method similar to the ranking method? How do they differ?

5. Working individually or in groups, conduct salary surveys for the following positions: entry-level accountant, and entry-level chemical engineer. What sources did you use, and what conclusions did you reach? If you were the HR manager for a local engineering firm, what would you recommend that you pay for each job?

6. What are the pros and cons of broadbanding? Would you recommend your current employer (or some other firm you're familiar with) use it? Why or why not?

7. It was recently reported in the news that the average pay for most university presidents ranged around $200 000 per year, but that a few earned closer to $500 000 per year. What would account for such a disparity in the pay of universities' chief executive officers?

Application Exercises

RUNNING CASE: Carter Cleaning Company
The New Pay Plan

Carter Cleaning Centres do not have a formal wage structure nor do they have rate ranges or use compensable factors. Wage rates are based mostly on those prevailing in the surrounding community and are tempered with an attempt on the part of Jack Carter to maintain some semblance of equity between what workers with different responsibilities in the stores are paid.

Needless to say, Carter does not make any formal surveys when determining what his company should pay. He peruses the want ads almost every day and conducts informal surveys among his friends in the local chapter of the laundry and cleaners trade association. While Jack has taken a "seat-of-the-pants" approach to paying employees, his salary schedule has been guided by one basic pay policy. While many of his colleagues adhere to a policy of paying absolutely minimum rates, Jack has always followed a policy of paying his employees about 10 percent above what he feels are the prevailing rates, a policy that he believes reduces turnover while fostering employee loyalty. Of somewhat more concern to Jennifer is that her father has not yet implemented pay equity. Her father's explanation is "We're a small company and it really doesn't apply to us."

Questions

1. Is the company at the point where it should be setting up a formal salary structure complete with a job evaluation? Why or why not?

2. Is Jack Carter's policy of paying 10 percent more than the prevailing rates a sound one, and how could that be determined?

3. Similarly, is Carter's dismissal of pay equity legislation wise and if not, why not?

CASE STUDY: Job Evaluation for Bank Managers

The chairperson of the board of directors of the Canadian Bank has proposed that all managerial positions be included in the bank's job evaluation plan. She has talked with executives in several large business organizations in which such a practice has been found entirely possible and helpful. She proposed this action to the board at its latest meeting. The president asked that no action be taken until she could discuss it with those who would be affected.

Most of the middle-management group appear to be opposed to such a procedure. The president, while trying to remain neutral, has expressed a fear that if salaries are fitted to job evaluation, she will lose her best people. Many department heads and assistants insist that their jobs simply can't be rated on the scale used for lower-level positions. Others argue that no individual or small group can possibly know what their jobs involve. It is also argued that the qualities for which managers are paid are so varied and intangible that no systematic comparison of jobs makes sense.

The HR manager and his staff are united in favouring the idea. The chairperson of the board, through the president, has asked the human resources department to prepare a statement in favour of the development, explaining what it would do and how it would be done.

Question

1. You have been assigned the responsibility for a first draft of this statement to be directed to the rest of the HR staff for discussion. What would your statement say?

Source: Dale Yoder and Paul D. Standohar, *Personnel Management & Industrial Relations* (Englewood Cliffs, NJ: Prentice Hall, 1982), p. 361.

Human Resources Management Simulation

Exercise 11 in the simulation provides an opportunity to consider how pay can be used to affect organizational outcomes such as turnover. A report explaining performance-based pay and skill-based pay is to be prepared, along with recommendations as to which positions should be paid according to each approach. The further issue of whether to adopt a new approach in an already existing plant also needs to be considered. The implications of the presence of a union in the existing plant, and the desire to keep the new plant nonunionized, should be considered carefully in this exercise.

Video Case

How to Get a Raise

Most people get very nervous about asking for a raise. Good preparation can help an employee gain the courage she or he needs in this situation. The most important thing to remember is that this is a negotiation process. The employee should market him- or herself by emphasizing what he or she has contributed to the company. The employee should also show that he or she understands the "big picture" of the company as a whole. It is important to remember NOT to remind the boss of family responsibilities such as children, mortgage payments, etc. The employee should ask for the increase and then be silent and wait for the boss to respond.

The employee must pay attention to the boss' reply. If the response to the request is negative, the employee should stay and determine what results the company needs in order to be able to provide raises, and ask what he or she can do to help achieve the necessary results. This request sends a message that the employee wants to be part of the solution. Also, the employee can ask for compensation other than a base pay increase, such as a car allowance, money to go to conferences to keep up to date on his or her area, a better computer, Internet access, or whatever the employee needs to enhance the value he or she brings to the company.

Questions

1. Why are companies still giving only very small raises (or none) even though the economy has strengthened compared to the early 1990s?

2. Why should an employee not mention his or her financial responsibilities such as children, mortgage payments, elderly parents, etc. when asking for a raise?

3. Talk to three friends or relatives with jobs and ask them what kinds of non-cash compensation they receive and what others they would like to have to help them do a better job.

Video Resource: CBC, *Venture*, "How to Get a Raise," September 7, 1995.

Take It to the Net

Check out our Companion Website at

www.prenticehall.ca/dessler

for a multitude of practice questions, key terms and concepts, Weblinks to related sites, newsgroups, CBC video updates, and more.

Appendix 12.1

Quantitative Job Evaluation Methods

The Factor Comparison Job Evaluation Method

The factor comparison technique is a *quantitative* job evaluation method. It has many variations and appears to be one of the most widely used, the most accurate, and the most complex job evaluation method.

It is actually a refinement of the ranking method and entails deciding which jobs have more of certain compensable factors than others. With the ranking method, each job is generally looked at as an entity and the jobs are ranked in order of importance to the organization. With the factor comparison method each job is ranked *several times—once for each compensable factor chosen*. For example, jobs might be ranked first in terms of the factor "skill." Then they are ranked according to their "mental requirements." Next they are ranked according to their "responsibility," and so forth. Then these rankings are combined for each job into an overall numerical rating for the job. Here are the required steps:

Step 1. Obtain Job Information This method requires a careful, complete job analysis. First, job descriptions are written. Then job specifications are developed, preferably in terms of the compensable factors the committee had decided to use. For the factor comparison method, these compensable factors are usually (1) mental requirements, (2) physical requirements, (3) skill requirements, (4) responsibility, and (5) working conditions. Typical definitions of each of these five factors are presented in **Figure 12.9**.

Step 2. Select Key Benchmark Jobs Next, 15 to 25 key jobs are selected by the job evaluation committee. These jobs have to be representative benchmark jobs, acceptable reference points that represent the full range of jobs to be evaluated.

**Figure 12.9
Sample Definitions of
Five Factors Typically
Used in Factor
Comparison Method**

Source: Jay L. Otis and Richard H. Leukart, *Job Evaluation: A Basis for Sound Wage Administration,* p. 181. ©1954, renewed 1983. Reprinted by permission of Prentice Hall, Englewood Cliffs, NJ.

1. Mental Requirements
Either the possession of and/or the active application of the following:
A. (inherent) Mental traits, such an intelligence, memory, reasoning, facility in verbal expression, ability to get along with people, and imagination.
B. (acquired) General education, such as grammar and arithmetic; or general information as to sports, world events, etc.
C. (acquired) Specialized knowledge such as chemistry, engineering, accounting, advertising, etc.

2. Skill
A. (acquired) Facility in muscular coordination, as in operating machines, repetitive movements, careful coordination, dexterity, assembling, sorting, etc.
B. (acquired) Specific job knowledge necessary to the muscular coordination only; acquired by performance of the work and not to be confused with general education or specialized knowledge. It is very largely training in the interpretation of sensory impressions.
   Examples
   (1) In operating an adding machine, the knowledge of *which key* to depress for a sub-total would be skill.
   (2) In automobile repair, the ability to determine the significance of a certain knock in the motor would be skill.
   (3) In hand-firing a boiler, the ability to determine from the appearance of the firebed how coal should be shovelled over the surface would be skill.

3. Physical Requirements
A. Physical effort, as sitting, standing, walking, climbing, pulling, lifting, etc.; both the amount exercised and the degree of the continuity should be taken into account.
B. Physical status, as strength and eyesight.

4. Responsibilities
A. For raw materials, processed materials, tools, equipment, and property.
B. For money or negotiable securities.
C. For profits or loss, savings, or methods' improvement.
D. For public contact.
E. For records.
F For supervision.
   (1) Primarily the complexity of supervision *given* to employees; the number of employees is a secondary feature. Planning, direction, coordination, instruction, control, and approval characterize this kind of supervision.
   (2) Also, the degree of supervision *received*. If Jobs A and B gave no supervision to employees, but A received much closer immediate supervision than B, then B would be entitled to a higher rating than A in the supervision factor.
      To summarize the four degrees of supervision:
         Highest degree—gives much—gets little
         High degree   —gives much—gets much
         Low degree   —gives none —gets little
         Lowest degree —gives none —gets much

5. Working Conditions
A. Environmental influences such as atmosphere, ventilation, illumination, noise, congestion, fellow workers, etc.
B. Hazards—from the work or its surroundings.
C. Hours.

TABLE 12.6 Ranking Key Jobs by Factors[1]

	MENTAL REQUIREMENTS	PHYSICAL REQUIREMENTS	SKILL REQUIREMENTS	RESPONSIBILITY	WORKING CONDITIONS
Welder	2	1	2	2	1
Crane Operator	3	4	3	3	3
Nurse	1	2	1	1	2
Data Entry Clerk	4	3	4	4	4

[1] 1 is high, 4 is low.

Step 3. Rank Key Jobs by Factors Here evaluators are asked to rank the key jobs on each of the five factors (mental requirements, physical requirements, skill requirements, responsibility, and working conditions). This ranking procedure is based on job descriptions and job specifications. Each committee member usually makes this ranking individually, and then a meeting is held to develop a consensus on each job. The result of this process is a table, as in **Table 12.6**. This shows how each key job ranks on each of the five compensable factors.

Step 4. Distribute Wage Rates by Factors This is where the factor comparison method gets a bit more complicated. In this step the committee members have to divide up the present wage now being paid for each key job, distributing it among the five compensable factors. They do this in accordance with their judgments about the importance to the job of each factor. For example, if the present wage for the job of data entry clerk is $7.25, the evaluators might distribute this wage as follows:

Mental requirements	$1.50
Physical requirements	$2.00
Skill requirements	$2.00
Responsibility	$1.50
Working conditions	$0.25
Total	$7.25

A similar distribution is made for all key jobs.

Step 5. Rank Key Jobs According to Wages Assigned to Each Factor Here each job is ranked factor by factor, but the ranking is based on the wages assigned to each factor. As shown in **Table 12.7**, for example, for the "mental requirements" factor, the nurse job ranks first, while the data entry clerk job ranks last.

Each member of the committee first makes this distribution working independently. Then the committee meets and arrives at a consensus concerning the money to be assigned to each factor for each key job.

Step 6. Compare the Two Sets of Rankings to Screen Out Unusable Key Jobs Now there are two sets of rankings for each key job. One is the original ranking (from step 3). This shows how each job ranks on each of the five compensable factors. The second ranking reflects for each job the wages assigned to each factor. It is now possible to draw up a table like the one in **Table 12.8**.

TABLE 12.7 Ranking Key Jobs by Wage Rates[1]

	HOURLY WAGE	MENTAL REQUIRE-MENTS	PHYSICAL REQUIRE-MENTS	SKILL REQUIRE-MENTS	RESPONSIBILITY	WORKING CONDITIONS
Welder	$13.50	3.00(2)	3.50(1)	3.00(2)	3.00(2)	1.00(1)
Crane Operator	7.75	2.00(3)	1.00(4)	2.25(3)	2.00(3)	0.50(3)
Nurse	15.90	4.00(1)	3.00(2)	4.00(1)	4.00(1)	0.90(2)
Data Entry Clerk	7.25	1.50(4)	2.00(3)	2.00(4)	1.50(4)	0.25(4)

[1] I is high, 4 is low.

TABLE 12.8 Comparison of Factor and Wage Rankings

	MENTAL REQUIRE-MENTS		PHYSICAL REQUIRE-MENTS		SKILL REQUIRE-MENTS		RESPONSIBILITY		WORKING CONDITIONS	
	A[1]	$[2]	A[1]	$[2]	A[1]	$[2]	A[1]	$[2]	A[1]	$[2]
Welder	2	2	1	1	2	2	2	2	1	1
Crane Operator	3	3	4	4	3	3	3	3	3	3
Nurse	1	1	2	2	1	1	1	1	2	2
Data Entry Clerk	4	4	3	3	4	4	4	4	4	4

[1] Amount of each factor based on step 3.
[2] Ratings based on distribution of wages to each factor from step 5.

For each factor, this shows both rankings for each key job. On the left is the ranking from step 3. On the right is the ranking based on wages paid. For each factor, the ranking based on the amount of the factor (from step 3) should be about the same as the ranking based on the wages assigned to the job (step 5). If there's much of a discrepancy, it suggests that the key job might be a fluke, and from this point on, such jobs are no longer used as key jobs. (Many managers don't bother to screen out unusable key jobs. To simplify things, they skip our steps 5 and 6, going instead from step 4 to step 7; this is an acceptable alternative.)

Step 7. Construct the Job-Comparison Scale Once the usable, true key jobs have been identified, the next step is to set up the job-comparison scale (**Table 12.9**). (Note that there's a separate column for each of the five comparable factors.) To develop it, the assigned wage table from step 4 will be needed.

For each of the factors for all key jobs, the job title is written next to the appropriate wage rate. Thus, in the assigned wage table (Table 12.7), the welder job has $3.00 assigned to the factor "mental requirements." Therefore, on the job-comparison scale (Table 12.9) "welder" is written in the "mental requirements" factor column, next to the "$3.00" row. The same procedure is then repeated for all factors for all key jobs.

Step 8. Use the Job-Comparison Scale Now all the other jobs to be evaluated can be slotted, factor by factor, into the job-comparison scale. For example, suppose the job of security guard is to be slotted in. A decision is made as to where the "mental requirements" of the guard job would fit as compared with the "mental requirements" of all the other jobs listed. It might, for example, fit between data entry clerk and crane operator. Similarly, consideration is given to where the "phys-

TABLE 12.9 Job (Factor) Comparison Scale

	MENTAL REQUIREMENTS	PHYSICAL REQUIREMENTS	SKILL REQUIREMENTS	RESPONSIBILITY	WORKING CONDITIONS
.25					Data Entry Clerk
.30					(Security Guard)
.40					
.50					Crane Operator
.60					
.70					
.75					
.80					
.90					Nurse
1.00		Crane Operator			Welder
1.10			(Security Guard)		
1.20					
1.30					
1.40					
1.50	Data Entry Clerk			Data Entry Clerk	
1.60					
1.70	(Security Guard)	(Security Guard)			
1.80					
1.90					
2.00	Crane Operater	Data Entry Clerk	Data Entry Clerk	Crane Operator	
2.25			Crane Operator		
2.40				(Security Guard)	
2.50					
2.80					
3.00	Welder	Nurse	Welder	Welder	
3.20					
3.40					
3.50		Welder			
3.80					
4.00	Nurse		Nurse	Nurse	
4.20					
4.40					
4.60					
4.80					

ical requirements" of the security guard's job fit as compared with the other jobs listed. It might fit between the crane operator and the data entry clerk. The same procedure is repeated for each of the remaining three factors.

An Example Working through an example will help to clarify the factor comparison method. Four key jobs to start will be used to simplify the presentation—there would usually be 15 to 25 key jobs to start with.

Step 1. First, conduct a job analysis.

Step 2. Then select four key jobs: welder, crane operator, nurse, and data entry clerk.

Step 3. Based on the job descriptions and specifications, rank key jobs by factor, as in Table 12.6.

Step 4. Distribute wage rates by factor, as in Table 12.7.

Step 5. Then rank key jobs according to wage rates assigned to each key factor. These rankings are shown in parentheses in Table 12.7.

Step 6. Next compare the two sets of rankings. In each left-hand column (marked A) is the job's ranking from step 3 based on the amount of the compensable factor. In each right-hand column (marked $) is the job's ranking from step 5 based on the wage assigned to that factor, as in Table 12.8.

In this case, there are no differences between any of the pairs of A (amount) and $ (wage) rankings, so all key jobs are usable. If there had been any differences (for example, between the A and $ rankings for the welder job's "mental requirements" factor) that job would have been dropped as a key job.

Step 7. Now construct the job-comparison scale as in Table 12.9. For this, use the wage distributions from step 4. For example, say that in steps 4 and 5, $3.00 was assigned to the "mental requirements" factor of the welder's job. Therefore, "welder" is written on the $3.00 row under the "mental requirements" column as in Table 12.9.

Step 8. Now all the other jobs can be slotted, factor by factor, into the job-comparison scale. No distribution of wages to each of the factors for other jobs is required, just a decision as to where, factor by factor, each of the other jobs should be slotted. This has been done for one other job in the factor comparison scale, shown in parentheses. The same can be done for all other jobs.

A Variation   There are several variations to this basic factor comparison method. One converts the dollar values on the factor comparison chart (Table 12.9) to points. (This can be done by multiplying each of the dollar values by 100, for example.) The main advantage in making this change is that the system would no longer be "locked in" to present wage rates. Instead, each of the jobs would be compared with one another, factor by factor, in terms of a more constant point system.

Pros and Cons   We've presented the factor comparison method at some length because it is (in one form or another) a very widely-used job evaluation method. Its wide use derives from several advantages: First, it is an accurate, systematic, quantifiable method for which detailed step-by-step instructions are available. Second, jobs are compared to other jobs to determine a relative value. Thus, in the job-comparison scale it can be seen that the welder requires more mental ability than a security guard); and one can also determine about how much more mental ability is required—apparently almost twice as much ($3.00 versus $1.70). (This type of calibration is not possible with the ranking or classification methods.) Third, this is also a fairly easy job evaluation system to explain to employees.

Complexity is probably the most serious disadvantage of the factor comparison method. While it is fairly easy to explain the factor comparison scale and its rationale to employees, it is difficult to show them how to build one.

The Point Method of Job Evaluation

The point method is widely used. It requires identifying several compensable factors (like skill and responsibility), each with several degrees, and also the degree to which each of these factors is present in the job. A different number of points is usually assigned for each degree of each factor. So once the degree to which each factor is present in the job is determined, all that remains is to add up the corresponding number of points for each factor and arrive at an overall point value for the job.[1] Here are the steps:

Step 1. Determine Clusters of Jobs to Be Evaluated Because jobs vary widely by department, the same point-rating plan is not usually used for all jobs in the organization. Therefore, the first step is usually to cluster jobs, for example, into shop jobs, clerical jobs, sales jobs, and so forth. Then the committee will generally develop a point plan for one group or cluster at a time.

Step 2. Collect Job Information This means performing a job analysis and writing job descriptions and job specifications.

Step 3. Select Compensable Factors Here select compensable factors, like mental requirements, physical requirements, or skill.

Step 4. Define Compensable Factors Next each compensable factor is carefully defined. This is done to ensure that the evaluation committee members will apply the factors with consistency. Examples of definitions are presented in **Figure 12.10**. The definitions are often drawn up or obtained by the human resources specialist.

Step 5. Define Factor Degrees Next, definitions of several degrees for each factor are prepared so that raters may judge the amount or degree of a factor existing in a job. Thus, the factor "complexity" might have six degrees, ranging from "job is repetitive" through "requires initiative." (Definitions for each degree are shown in Figure 12.10.) The number of degrees usually does not exceed five or six, and

Figure 12.10 Example of One Factor in a Point Factor System

Source: Richard W. Beatty and James R. Beatty, "Job Evaluation," Ronald A. Berk (Ed.) *Performance Assessment: Methods and Applications* (Baltimore: Johns Hopkins University Press, 1986), p. 322.

Example of One Factor in a Point Factor System (Complexity/Problem Solving)

The mental capacity required to perform the given job as expressed in resourcefulness in dealing with unfamiliar problems, interpretation of data, initiation of new ideas, complex data analysis, creative, or developmental work.

Level	Point Value	Description of Characteristics and Measures
0	0	Seldom confronts problems not covered by job routine or organizational policy; analysis of data is negligible. *Benchmark:* General secretary, switchboard operator/receptionist.
1	40	Follows clearly prescribed standard practice and demonstrates straightforward application of readily understood rules and procedures. Analyzes noncomplicated data by established routine. *Benchmark:* Statistical clerk, billing clerk.
2	80	Frequently confronts problems not covered by job routine. Independent judgment exercised in making minor decisions where alternatives are limited and standard policies established. Analysis of standardized data for information of or use by others. *Benchmark:* Social worker, executive secretary.
3	120	Exercises independent judgment in making decisions involving nonroutine problems with general guidance only from higher supervision. Analyzes and evaluates data pertaining to non-routine problems for solution in conjunction with others. *Benchmark:* Nurse, accountant, team leader.
4	160	Uses independent judgment in making decisions that are subject to review in the final stages only. Analyzes and solves nonroutine problems involving evaluation of a wide variety of data as a regular part of job duties. Makes decisions involving procedures. *Benchmark:* Associate director, business manager, park services director.
5	200	Uses independent judgment in making decisions that are not subject to review. Regularly exercises developmental or creative abilities in policy development. *Benchmark:* Executive director.

the actual number depends mostly on judgment. Thus, if all employees either work in a quiet, air-conditioned office or in a noisy, hot factory, then two degrees would probably suffice for the factor "working conditions." It is not necessary to have the same number of degrees for each factor, and degrees should be limited to the number necessary to distinguish among jobs.

Step 6. Determine Relative Values of Factors   The next step is to decide how much weight (or how many total points) to assign to each factor. This is important because for each cluster of jobs some factors are bound to be more important than others. Thus, for executives the "mental requirements" factor would carry far more weight than would "physical requirements." The opposite might be true of factory jobs.

The next step is to determine the relative values or weights that should be assigned to each of the factors. Assigning factor weights is generally done by the evaluation committee. The committee members carefully study factor and degree definitions and then determine the relative value of the factors for the cluster of jobs under consideration. Here is one method for doing this:

First, assign a value of 100% to the highest-ranking factor. Then assign a value to the next highest factor as a percentage of its importance to the first factor, and so forth. For example,

Decision making	100%
Problem solving	85%
Knowledge	60%

Next sum up the total percentage (in this case 100% + 85% + 60% = 245%). Then convert this 245% to a 100% system as follows:

Decision making:	100 ÷ 245 = 40.82 =	40.8%
Problem solving:	85 ÷ 245 = 34.69 =	34.7%
Knowledge:	60 ÷ 245 = 24.49 =	24.5%
Totals		100.0%

Step 7. Assign Point Values to Factors and Degrees   In step 6 total weights were developed for each factor in percentage terms. Now points are assigned to each factor as in **Table 12.10**. For example, suppose it is decided to use a total number of 500 points in the point plan. Then since the factor "decision making" had a weight of 40.8%, it would be assigned a total of 40.8% × 500 = 204 points.

Thus, it was decided to assign 204 points to the decision-making factor. This automatically means that the highest degree for the decision-making factor would also carry 204 points. Then points are assigned to the other degrees for this factor,

TABLE 12.10 Evaluation Points Assigned to Factors and Degrees

	FIRST-DEGREE POINTS	SECOND-DEGREE POINTS	THIRD-DEGREE POINTS	FOURTH-DEGREE POINTS	FIFTH-DEGREE POINTS
Decision making	41	82	123	164	204
Problem solving	35	70	105	140	174
Knowledge	24	48	72	96	123

usually in equal amounts from the lowest to the highest degree. For example, divide 204 by the number of degrees (say, 5); this equals 40.8. Then the lowest degree here would carry about 41 points. The second degree would carry 41 plus 41, or 82 points. The third degree would carry 123 points. The fourth degree would carry 164 points. Finally, the fifth and highest degree would carry 204 points. This step is repeated for each factor (as in Table 12.10).

Step 8. Write the Job Evaluation Manual   Developing a point plan like this usually culminates in a *point manual* or *job evaluation manual*. This simply consolidates the factor and degree definitions and point values into one convenient manual.

Step 9. Rate the Jobs   Once the manual is complete, the actual evaluations can begin. Raters (usually the committee) use the manual to evaluate jobs. Each job, based on its job description and job specification, is evaluated factor by factor to determine the number of points that should be assigned to it. First, committee members determine the degree (first degree, second degree, and so on) to which each factor is present in the job. Then they note the corresponding points (see Table 12.10) that were previously assigned to each of these degrees (in step 7). Finally, they add up the points for all factors, arriving at a total point value for the job. Raters generally start with rating key jobs and obtain consensus on these. Then they rate the rest of the jobs in the cluster.

Pros and Cons   Point systems have their advantages, as their wide use suggests. They involve a quantitative technique that is easily explained to and used by employees. On the other hand, it can be difficult and time consuming to develop a point plan and to effectively train the job evaluation user group. This is one reason many organizations opt for a plan developed and marketed by a consulting firm. In fact, the availability of a number of ready-made plans probably accounts in part for the wide use of point plans in job evaluation.

A study assessing the reliability of four job evaluation methods—ranking, classification, factor comparison, and point—found that ratings from the point method and the job classification method were most consistent, taking overall job evaluation ratings and individual job ratings into account.[2]

1. For a discussion, see, for example, Roger Plachy, The Point Factor Job Evaluation System: A Step-by-Step Guide, Part I," *Compensation and Benefits Review* 19, no. 4 (July–August 1987), pp. 12–27; Roger Plachy, "The Case for Effective Point-Factor Job Evaluation, Viewpoint I," *Compensation and Benefits Review* 19, no. 2 (March–April 1987), pp. 45–8; Roger Plachy, "The Point-Factor Job Evaluation System: A Step-by-Step Guide, Part II," *Compensation and Benefits* Review 19, no. 5 (September–October 1987), pp. 9–24; and Alfred Candrilli and Ronald Armagast, "The Case for Effective Point-Factor Job Evaluation, Viewpoint II," *Compensation and Benefits Review*. 19, no. 2 (March–April 1987), pp. 49–54. See also Robert J. Sahl, "How to Install a Point-Factor Job Evaluation System," *Personnel* 66, no. 3 (March 1989), pp. 38–42.

2. J. B. Cunningham & S. Graham "Assessing the Reliability of Four Job Evaluation Plans," *Canadian Journal of Administrative Sciences* 10 no. 1, (1993), pp. 31-47, 1993.

Notes

1. Thomas Patten, Jr., *Pay: Employee Compensation and Incentive Plans* (New York: Free Press, 1977), p. 1. See also Jerry McAdams, "Why Reward Systems Fail," *Personnel Journal* 67, no. 6 (June 1988), pp. 103–13; James Whitney, "Pay Concepts for the 1990s," Part I, *Compensation and Benefits Review* 20, no. 2 (March–April 1988), pp. 33–44; and James Whitney, "Pay Concepts for the 1990s," Part II, *Compensation and Benefits Review* 20, no. 3 (May–June 1988), pp. 45–50. See also "Aligning Work and Rewards: A Round Table Discussion," *Compensation and Benefits Review* 26, no. 4 (July–August 1994), pp. 47–63 and Marlene Morganstern, "Compensation and the New Employment Relationship," *Compensation and Benefits Review* 27, no. 2 (March 1995), pp. 37–44.

2. Orlando Behling and Chester Schriesheim, *Organizational Behaviour* (Boston: Allyn & Bacon, 1976), p. 233.

3. Richard Henderson, *Compensation Management, (Reston, VA: Reston, 1980)*, pp. 101–27.

4. Edward Hay, "The Attitude of the American Federation of Labour on Job Evaluation," *Personnel Journal* 26 (November 1947), pp. 163–9; Howard James, "Issues in Job Evaluation: The Union's View," *Personnel Journal* 51 (September 1972), pp. 675–9; Henderson, *Compensation Management, (Reuton, VA: Reuton, 1980)* pp. 117–8; Harold Jones, "Union Views on Job Evaluations: 1971 vs. 1978," *Personnel Journal* 58 (February 1979), pp. 80–5.

5. Joseph Famularo, *Handbook of Modern Personnel Administration* (New York: McGraw-Hill, 1972), pp. 27–9. See also Bruce Ellig, "Strategic Pay Planning," *Compensation and Benefits Review* 19, no. 4 (July–August 1987), pp. 28–43; Thomas Robertson, "Fundamental Strategies for Wage and Salary Administration," *Personnel Journal* 65, no. 11 (November 1986), pp. 120–32. One expert cautions against conducting salary surveys based on job title alone. He recommends job-content salary surveys that examine the content of jobs according to the size of each job so that, for instance, the work of the president of IBM and that of a small clone manufacturer would not be inadvertently compared. See Robert Sahl, "Job Content Salary Surveys: Survey Design and Selection Features," *Compensation and Benefits Review* (May–June 1991), pp. 14–21.

6. See David I. Levine, "What Do Wages Buy?" *Administrative Science Quarterly* 38 (1993), pp. 462–83.

7. Levine, "What Do Wages Buy?" pp. 462–5.

8. Levine, "What Do Wages Buy?" p. 462.

9. Vicki Kaman and Jodie Barr, "Employee Attitude Surveys for Strategic Compensation Management," *Compensation and Benefits Review* (January–February 1991), pp. 52–65.

10. "Use of Wage Surveys," *BNA Policy and Practice Series* (Washington, DC: Bureau of National Affairs, 1976), pp. 313–4. In a recent survey of compensation professionals, uses of salary survey data were reported. The surveys were used most often to adjust the salary structure and ranges. Other uses included determining the merit budget, adjusting individual job rates, and maintaining pay leadership. D. W. Belcher, N. Bruce Ferris, and John O'Neill, "How Wage Surveys Are Being Used," *Compensation and Benefits Review* (September–October 1985), pp. 34–51. For further discussion, see, for example, Kent Romanoff, Ken Boehm, and Edward Benson, "Pay Equity: Internal and External Considerations," *Compensation and Benefits Review* 18, no. 3 (May–June 1986), pp. 17–25.

11. Helen Murlis, "Making Sense of Salary Surveys," *Personnel Managemen* 17 (January 1981), pp. 30–3. For an explanation of how market analysis can be used to ensure fair and competitive pay for all jobs in the organization, see, for example, Peter Olney, Jr., "Meeting the Challenge of Comparable Worth," Part 2, *Compensation and Benefits Review* 19, no. 3 (May–June 1987), pp. 45–53.

12. This is based on Frederick W. Cook, "Compensation Surveys Are Biased," *Compensation and Benefits Review* (September–October 1994), pp. 19–22.

13. Cook, "Compensation Surveys Are Biased," p. 19.

14. Cook, "Compensation Surveys Are Biased."

15. Henderson, *Compensation Management*, pp. 260–9.

16. Joan O'Brien and Robert Zawacki, "Salary Surveys: Are They Worth the Effort?" *Personnel*. 62, no. 10 (October 1985), pp. 70–4.

17. Job analysis as discussed in chapter 4 can be a useful source of information on compensable factors, as well as on job descriptions and job specifications. For example, a quantitative job analysis technique like the position analysis questionnaire generates quantitative information on the degree to which the following five basic factors are present in each job: having decision making/communication/social responsibilities, performing skilled activities, being physically active, operating vehicles or equipment, and processing information. As a result, a job analysis technique like the PAQ is actually as (or some say, more) appropriate as a job evaluation technique in that jobs can be quantitatively compared to one another on those five dimensions and their relative worth thus ascertained. Another point worth noting is that a single set of compensable factors may not be adequate for describing all jobs. Many managers, therefore, divide their jobs into job clusters. For example, one organization might have a separate job cluster for factory workers, for clerical workers, and for managerial staff. Similarly, there would then probably be a somewhat different set of compensable factors for each job cluster.

18. A. N. Nash and F. J. Carroll, Jr., "Installation of a Job Evaluation Program," from *Management of Compensation* (Monterey, CA: Brooks/Cole, 1975), reprinted in Craig Schneier and Richard Beatty, *Personnel Administration Today: Readings and Commentary* (Reading, MA: Addison-Wesley, 1978), pp. 417–25; and Henderson, *Compensation Management*, pp. 231–9. According to one survey, about equal percentages of employers use individual interviews, employee questionnaires, or observations by personnel representatives to obtain the actual job evaluation information. See Mary Ellen Lo Bosco, "Job Analysis, Job Evaluation, and Job Classification," *Personnel* 62, no. 5 (May 1985), pp. 70–5. See also Howard Risher, "Job Evaluation: Validity and Reliability," *Compensation and Benefits Review* 21, no. 1 (January–February 1989), pp. 22–36; and David Hahn and Robert Dipboye, "Effects of Training and Information on the Accuracy and Reliability of Job Evaluations," *Journal of Applied Psychology* 73, no. 2 (May 1988), pp. 146–53.

19. See, for example, Donald Petri, "Talking Pay Policy Pays Off," *Supervisory Management* (May 1979), pp. 2–13.

20. As explained later, the practice of red circling is used to delay downward adjustments in pay rates that are presently too high given the newly evaluated jobs. See also E. James Brennan, "Everything You Need to Know About Salary Ranges," *Personnel Journal* 63, no. 3 (March 1984), pp. 10–7.

21. Nash and Carroll, "Installation of a Job Evaluation Program," p. 419.

22. Nash and Carroll, "Installation of a Job Evaluation Program."

23. If the job classification method has been used, then of course the jobs are already classified.

24. David Belcher, *Compensation Administration* (Englewood Cliffs, NJ: Prentice Hall, 1973), pp. 257–76.

25. Gerald Ledford Jr., "Three Case Studies on Skill-Based Pay: An Overview," *Compensation and Benefits Review* (March–April 1991), pp. 11–23.

26. Ledford, "Three Case Studies," p. 12. See also Kathryn Cofsky, "Critical Keys to Competency-Based Pay," *Compensation and Benefits Review* (November–December 1993), pp. 46–52.

27. Kevin Parent and Caroline Weber, "Case Study: Does Paying for Knowledge Pay Off?" *Compensation and Benefits Review* (September–October 1994), pp. 44–50, and Edward Lawler, III, Gerald Ledford, Jr., and Lei Chang, "Who Uses Skill-Based Pay, and Why," *Compensation and Benefits Review* (March–April 1993), pp. 22–6.

28. Parent and Weber, "Does Paying for Knowledge Pay Off?"

29. N. Winter Consulting Inc., *Alternative Compensation Practices*, 1996.

30. This is based on Laurent Dufetel, "Job Evaluation: Still at the Frontier," *Compensation and Benefits Review* (July–August 1991), pp. 53–67.

31. Dufetel, "Job Evaluation," p. 54.

32. Jude Rich, "Meeting the Global Challenge: A Measurement and Reward Program for the Future," *Compensation and Benefits Review* (July–August 1992), p. 27.

33. Rich, "Meeting the Global Challenge," p. 28.

34. A. W. Smith, Jr., "Structuralist Salary Management: A Modest Proposal," *Compensation and Benefits Review* (July–August 1992), pp. 22–5.

35. Smith, "Structural Salary Management," p. 23.

36. Charles Cumming, "Will Traditional Salary Administration Survive the Stampede to Alternative Rewards?" *Compensation and Benefits Review* (November–December 1992), pp. 42–7.

37. Dale Yoder, *Personnel Management and Industrial Relations* (Englewood Cliffs, NJ: Prentice Hall, 1970), pp. 643–5; Famularo, *Handbook of Modern Personnel Administration,* pp. 32.1–32.6 and 30.1–30.8.

38. Bruce Ellig, *Executive Compensation—A Total Pay Perspective* (New York: McGraw-Hill, 1982), pp. 9–10. See also Bryan J. Brooks, "Trends in International Executive Compensation," *Personnel* 64, no. 5 (May 1987), pp. 67–71 and Edwin Lewis, "New Approaches to Executive Pay," *Directors and Boards* 18, no. 3 (Spring 1994), pp. 57–8.

39. *Report on Business Magazine*, July 1997, pp. 70–1.

40. "Executive Pay," *The Wall Street Journal* (April 11, 1996), pp. R16–R170.

41. Ernest C. Miller, "Setting Supervisors' Pay at Pay Differentials," *Compensation Review* 10 (Third Quarter 1978), pp. 13–6.

42. *Report on Business Magazine*, July 1997, p. 70. See also M. Gibb-Clark, "Directors Lag U.S. Pay Levels," *The Globe and Mail* (September 12, 1997), p. B6.

43. Nardash Agarwal, "Determinants of Executive Compensation," *Industrial Relations* 20, no. 1 (Winter 1981), pp. 36–45. See also John A. Fossum and Mary Fitch, "The Effects of Individual and Contextual Attributes on the Sizes of Recommended Salary Increases," *Personnel Psychology* 38, no. 3 (Autumn 1985), pp. 587–602; R. Morissette, *Canadian Jobs and Firm Size: Do Smaller Firms Pay Less?*, Business and Labour Market Analysis Group, Analytical Studies Branch, Statistics Canada, 1991.

44. Kenneth Foster, "Does Executive Pay Make Sense?" *Business Horizons* (September–October 1981), pp. 47–51.

45. Foster, "Does Executive Pay Make Sense?" p. 50.

46. This is based on William White, "Managing the Board Review of Executive Pay," *Compensation and Benefits Review* (November–December 1992), pp. 35–41.

47. K. Howlett. "Pay Rules Signal Changes at OSC," *The Globe and Mail* (October 18, 1993), p. B1.

48. White, "Managing the Board Review," pp. 38–40; see also H. Anthony Hampson, "Tying CEO Pay to Performance: Compensation Committees Must Do Better," *The Business Quarterly* 55, no. 4 (Spring 1991), pp. 18–22.

49. A. Duffy, L. Priest & D. Israealson, "The $100,000-Plus Club," *Toronto Star* (March 30, 1996), p. A2.

50. William White and Raymond Fife, "New Challenges for Executive Compensation in the 1990s," *Compensation and Benefits Review* (January–February 1993), pp. 27–35.

51. Famularo, *Handbook of Modern Personnel Administration,* pp. 32.1–32.6. See also Peter Sherer, et al., "Managerial Salary-Raise Decisions," pp. 27–38.

52. Famularo, *Handbook of Modern Personnel Administration,* pp. 30.1–30.15.

53. Famularo, pp. 30.1–30.5. See also Patric Moran, "Equitable Salary Administration in High-Tech Companies," *Compensation and Benefits Review* 18, no. 5 (September–October 1986), pp. 31–40.

54. Robert Sibson, *Compensation* (New York: AMA-COM, 1981), p. 194.

55. Sibson, *Compensation*.

56. See also Bernisha Bridges, "The Role of Rewards in Motivating Scientific and Technical Personnel: Experience at Egland AFB," *National Productivity Review* (Summer 1993), pp. 337–48.

57. *Ontario Pay Equity Commission Newsletter*, "Pay Equity Nets Gains for Women", p. 4, October 1995.

58. *Ontario Pay Equity Commission Newsletter*, p. 1.

59. Mary Gray, "Pay Equity Through Job Evaluation: A Case Study," *Compensation and Benefits Review* (July-August 1992), p. 46

60. Gray, "Pay Equity Through Job Evaluation," pp. 46–51.

61. Charles M. Futrell, "Effects of Pay Disclosure on Satisfaction for Sales Managers: A Longitudinal Study," *Academy of Management Journa* 21, no. 1 (March 1978), pp. 140–4.

62. Mary G. Miner, "Pay Policies: Secret or Open? and Why?" *Personnel Journal* 53 (February 1974), reprinted in Richard Peterson, Lane Tracy, and Alan Cabelly, *Readings in Systematic Management in Human Resources* (Reading, MA: Addison-Wesley, 1979), pp. 233–9.

63. Margaret Yao, "Inflation Outruns Pay of Middle Managers, Increasing Frustration," *The Wall Street Journal* (June 9, 1981), p. 1. See also, "The Impact of Inflation on Wage and Salary Administration," *Personnel* 58 (November–December 1981), p. 55.

64. This section based on or quoted from "The Impact of Inflation on Wage and Salary Administration," p. 55.

65. Wendell C. Lawther, "Ways to Monitor (and Solve) the Pay Compression Problem," *Personnel* (March 1989), pp. 84–7.

66. Lawther, "Ways to Monitor," p. 87.

67. Robert Dockson and Jack Vance, "Retirement in Peril: Inflation and the Executive Compensation Program," *California Management Review* 24 (Summer 1981), pp. 87–94.

68. Dockson and Vance, "Retirement in Peril."
69. Joan Lindroth, "Inflation, Taxes, and Perks: How Compensation Is Changing," *Personnel Journal* 60 (December 1981), pp. 934–40.
70. Clarence Deitch and David Dilts, "The COLA Clause: An Employer Bargaining Weapon?" *Personnel Journal* 61 (March 1982), pp. 220–3.
71. Patten, *Pay,* p. 181.
72. Deitch and Dilts, "The COLA Clause," p. 221.
73. Patten, *Pay,* p. 182.
74. Rugus Runzheimer, Jr., "How Corporations Are Handling Cost of Living Differentials," *Business Horizons,* Vol. 23 (August 1980), p. 39.

Chapter 13
Pay-for-Performance and Financial Incentives

Chapter Outline

◆ **Money and Motivation: Background and Trends**

◆ **Incentives for Operations Employees**

◆ **Incentives for Managers and Executives**

◆ **Incentives for Salespeople**

◆ **Incentives for Other Professionals**

◆ **Organization-Wide Incentive Plans**

◆ **Developing Effective Incentive Plans**

Learning Outcomes

After studying this chapter, you should be able to:

Discuss how to use piecework, standard hour, and team or group incentive plans.

Explain how to use short-term and long-term incentives for managers and executives.

List the pros and cons of salary plans and commission plans for salespeople.

Discuss three pros and cons of merit pay.

Describe three types of organization-wide incentive plans.

Explain how an incentive plan might backfire and how to avoid such a problem.

Money and Motivation: Background and Trends

www.ftu.edu
Frederick Taylor University

The use of financial incentives—financial rewards paid to workers whose production exceeds some predetermined standard—is not new, but was popularized by Frederick Taylor in the late 1800s. As a supervisory employee of the Midvale Steel Company, Taylor had become concerned with what he called "systematic soldiering"—the tendency of employees to work at the slowest pace possible and produce at the minimum acceptable level. What especially intrigued him was the fact that some of these same workers still had the energy to run home and work on their cabins, even after a hard 12-hour day. Taylor knew that if he could find some way to harness this energy during the workday, huge productivity gains would be achieved.

At this time, primitive piecework systems were already in use, but they were generally ineffective. Workers were paid a piece rate for each piece they produced, based on informally determined quotas. However, rate cutting by employers was flagrant, and the workers knew that if their earnings became excessive, their pay per piece would be cut. As a result, most workers produced just enough to earn a decent wage, but little enough so that their rate per piece would not be reduced.

One of Taylor's great insights was in seeing the need for a standardized, acceptable view of a fair day's work. As he saw it, this fair day's work should depend not on the vague estimates of supervisors but on a careful, formal, scientific process of inspection and observation. It was this need to evaluate each job scientifically that led to the scientific management movement (as described in chapter 2). In turn, scientific management gave way in the Depression-plagued 1930s to the human relations movement and its focus on satisfying workers' social—not just their financial—needs.

Today's emphasis on quality-improvement teams and commitment-building programs is creating a renaissance for financial incentives, pay-for-performance, and variable compensation plans. One California high-technology company gave $100 million in bonuses to its 523 employees in 1996—an average of $76 000 each![1] A 1996 survey by the Conference Board of Canada found that the number of Canadian organizations providing pay-for-performance (pay for individuals or teams based on their achieving quality or quantity goals) increased by an average of 25 percent from 1991 to 1996. **Figure 13.1** illustrates how this trend is occurring at all levels of the organization. The survey also found that 95 percent of the 345 Canadian organizations participating provide pay-for-performance for executives, 77 percent for management and professional staff, and 59 percent to other non-managerial employees.[2] Thus, traditional pay plans are giving way to skill-based plans, and to the sorts of spot awards, team incentives, and gainsharing plans discussed in this chapter.

There are sound competitive reasons for the growing emphasis on such performance-based compensation. For one thing, today's emphasis on cutting costs, restructuring, and boosting performance leads one logically to link pay and performance as Taylor did.

But the growing emphasis on pay-for-performance is also rooted in the trend toward quality-improvement teams and employee commitment programs. The entire thrust of such programs is to treat workers like partners and to get them to think of the business and its goals as their own. It is thus reasonable to pay them more like partners, too, by linking their pay more directly to performance.

Figure 13.1
The Growth of
Pay-for-Performance
Plans in Canada
Source: N.B. Carlyle,
Compensation Planning Outlook
1997, The Conference Board
of Canada, 1996, p. 9.
Reproduced with permission
from the Conference Board of
Canada

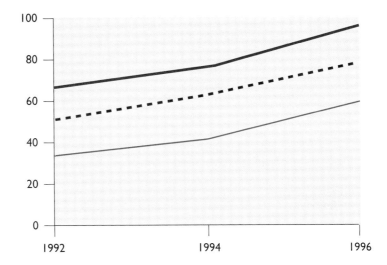

Variable Compensation Plans
(% of organizations reporting payouts)

—— Executive

- - - Management & professionals

—— Non-management

Types of Incentive Plans

spot bonus
A spontaneous incentive
awarded to individuals for
accomplishments not readily
measured by a standard.

There are several types of incentive plans.[3] *Individual incentive programs* give income over and above base salary to individual employees who meet a specific individual performance standard.[4] **Spot bonuses** are awarded, generally to individual employees, for accomplishments that are not readily measured by a standard, such as "to recognize the long hours this employee put in last month," or "to recognize exemplary customer service this week."[5] *Group incentive programs* are like individual incentive plans but give pay over and above base salary to all team members when the group or team collectively meets a specified standard for performance, productivity, or other work-related behaviour.[6] *Profit-sharing plans* are generally organization-wide incentive programs that provide employees with a share of the organization's profits in a specified period.[7] *Gainsharing programs* are organization-wide pay plans designed to reward employees for improvements in organizational productivity. As we'll explain, gainsharing plans generally include employee suggestion systems and focus on reducing labour costs through employee suggestions and participation.[8] **Variable pay** refers to any plan that ties pay to productivity or to some other measure of the firm's profitability.

variable pay
Any plan that ties pay to
productivity or profitability,
usually as one-time lump
sum payments.

For simplicity we will discuss these plans as follows: incentives for operations employees; incentives for managers and executives; incentives for salespeople; incentives primarily for white-collar and professional employees (merit pay); and organization-wide incentives.

Incentives For Operations Employees

Piecework Plans

piecework
A system of pay based on the number of items processed by each individual worker in a unit of time, such as items per hour or items per day.

Several incentive plans are particularly well suited for use with operations employees, such as for those doing production work. **Piecework** is the oldest incentive plan and still the most commonly used. Earnings are tied directly to what the worker produces; the person is paid a *piece rate* for each unit he or she produces. Thus, if Tom Smith gets $0.40 apiece for stamping out door jambs, then he would make $40 for stamping out 100 a day and $80 for stamping out 200.

Developing a workable piece-rate plan requires both job evaluation and (usually) industrial engineering. Job evaluation enables firms to assign an hourly wage rate to the job in question. But the crucial issue in piece-rate planning is the production standard, and this standard is usually developed by industrial engineers. Production standards are stated in terms of a standard number of minutes per unit or a standard number of units per hour. In Tom Smith's case, the job evaluation indicated that his door-jamb stamping job was worth $8 an hour. The industrial engineer determined that 20 jambs per hour was the standard production rate. Therefore, the piece rate (for each door jamb) was $8.00 divided by 20 = $0.40 per door jamb.

straight piecework plan
Under this pay system each worker receives a set payment for each piece produced or processed in a factory or shop.

guaranteed piecework plan
The minimum hourly wage plus an incentive for each piece produced above a set number of pieces per hour.

With a **straight piecework plan,** Tom Smith would be paid on the basis of the number of door jambs he produced; there would be no guaranteed minimum wage. However, after passage of employment/labour standards legislation, it became necessary for most employers to guarantee their workers a minimum wage. With a **guaranteed piecework plan,** Tom Smith would be paid the minimum wage whether or not he stamped out the number of door jambs required to make minimum wage, for example, 11 pieces if minimum wage is $4.40 per hour. But as an incentive he would also be paid at the piece rate of $0.40 for each unit he produced over the number required to make minimum wage.

Piecework generally implies straight piecework, a strict proportionality between results and rewards regardless of the level of output. Thus, in Smith's case, he continues to get $0.40 apiece for stamping out door jambs, even if he stamps out many more than planned, say, 500 per day. On the other hand, certain types of piecework incentive plans call for a sharing of productivity gains between worker and employer such that the worker does not receive full credit for all production above normal.[9]

Advantages and Disadvantages   Piecework incentive plans have several advantages. They are simple to calculate and easily understood by employees. Piece-rate plans appear equitable in principle, and their incentive value can be powerful since rewards are directly tied to performance.

Piecework also has some disadvantages. A main one is its somewhat unsavoury reputation among many employees based on some employers' habits of arbitrarily raising production standards whenever they found their workers earning "excessive" wages. In addition, piece rates are stated in monetary terms (like $0.40 per piece). Thus, when a new job evaluation results in a new hourly wage rate, the piece rate must also be revised; this can be a big clerical chore. Another disadvantage is more subtle; since the piece rate is quoted on a per-piece basis, in workers' minds production standards become tied inseparably to the amount of money earned. When an attempt is made to revise production standards, it meets considerable worker resistance, even if the revision is fully justified.[10]

In fact, the industrial-engineered specificity of piecework plans represents the seeds of piecework's biggest disadvantage these days. Piecework plans tend to be tailor-made for relatively specialized jobs in which employees do basically the same narrow tasks over and over again many times a day. This in turn fosters a certain rigidity: Employees will become preoccupied with producing the number of units needed. They become less willing to concern themselves with meeting quality standards or switching from job to job (since doing so could reduce the person's productivity).[11] Employees tend to be trained to perform only a limited number of tasks. Similarly, attempts to introduce new technology or innovative processes may be more likely to fail, insofar as they require major adjustments to engineered standards and negotiations with employees. Equipment tends not to be as well maintained, since employees are focussing on maximizing each machine's output.

Problems such as these have led some firms to drop their piecework plans (as well as their standard hour plans, discussed next) and to substitute team-based incentive plans or programs such as gainsharing, which we will also discuss.

Standard Hour Plan

standard hour plan
A plan by which a worker is paid a basic hourly rate but is paid an extra percentage of his or her base rate for production exceeding the standard per hour or per day. It is similar to piecework payment but based on a percent premium.

The **standard hour plan** is like the piece-rate plan, with one major difference. With a piece-rate plan the worker is paid a particular rate per each piece that he or she produces. With the standard hour plan the worker is rewarded by a *premium that equals the percent by which his or her performance exceeds the standard*. The plan assumes the worker has a guaranteed base rate.

As an example, suppose the base rate for Smith's job is $8 per hour. (The base rate may, but need not, equal the hourly rate determined by the job evaluation.) And again assume that the production standard for Smith's job is 20 units per hour, or 3 minutes per unit. Suppose that in one day (8 hours) Smith produces 200 door jambs. According to the production standard, this should have taken Smith 10 hours (200 divided by 20 per hour); instead it took him 8 hours. He produced at a rate 25 percent (40 divided by 160) higher than the standard rate. The standard rate would be 8 hours times 20 (units per hour) = 160: Smith actually produced 40 more, or 200. He will, therefore, be paid at a rate 25 percent above his base rate for the day. His base rate was $8 per hour times 8 hours equals $64. So he'll be paid 1.25 times 64 or $80.00 for the day.

The standard hour plan has most of the advantages of the piecework plan and is fairly simple to compute and easy to understand. But the incentive is expressed in units of time instead of in monetary terms (as it is with the piece-rate system). Therefore, there is less tendency on the part of workers to link their production standard with their pay. Furthermore, the clerical job of recomputing piece rates whenever hourly wage rates are reevaluated is avoided.[12]

Team or Group Incentive Plans

team or group incentive plan
A plan in which a production standard is set for a specific work group, and its members are paid incentives if the group exceeds the production standard.

There are several ways to implement **team or group incentive plans.**[13] One is to set work standards for each member of the group and maintain a count of the output of each member. Members are then paid based on one of three formulas: (1) All members receive the pay earned by the highest producer, (2) all members receive the pay earned by the lowest producer, or (3) all members receive payment equal to the average pay earned by the group.

The second approach is to set a production standard based on the final output of the group as a whole; all members then receive the same pay, based on the piece rate that exists for the group's job. The group incentive can be based on either the piece rate or standard hour plan, but the latter is somewhat more prevalent.

A third option is to choose a measurable definition of group performance or productivity that the group can control. For instance, broad criteria such as total labour-hours per final product could be used: piecework's engineered standards are thus not necessarily required here.[14]

There are several reasons to use team incentive plans. Sometimes several jobs are interrelated, as they are on project teams. Here one worker's performance reflects not only his or her own effort but that of coworkers as well; thus, team incentives make sense. Team plans also reinforce group planning and problem solving and help ensure collaboration.[15] In Japan, "the first rule is never reward only one individual." Instead, employees are rewarded as a group in order to reduce jealousy, make group members indebted to one another (as they would be to the group), and encourage a sense of cooperation.[16] There tends to be less bickering among group members over who has "tight" production standards and who has loose ones. Group incentive plans also facilitate on-the-job training, since each member of the group has an interest in getting new members trained as quickly as possible.[17]

A group incentive plan's chief disadvantage is that each worker's rewards are no longer based solely on his or her own effort. To the extent that the person does not see his or her effort leading to the desired reward, a group plan may be less effective at motivating employees than an individual plan. In one study, however, (in which the researchers arranged to pay the group based on the performance of its best member) the group incentive was as effective as an individual one in improving performance.[18]

Incentives for Managers and Executives

www.conferenceboard.ca
Conference Board of Canada

Most employers award their managers and executives a bonus or incentive because of the role managers play in determining divisional and corporate profitability.[19] One survey of 61 Canadian organizations found, for instance, that about 90 percent of companies pay managers and executives annual ("short-term") bonuses.[20] A Conference Board of Canada survey of 345 organizations found that long-term incentive plans (like stock options), which are intended to motivate and reward management for the corporation's long-term growth and prosperity, are used by over 44 percent of Canadian firms.[21] The widespread use of these bonuses may reflect the fact that they can and do pay for themselves by improving management and thus organizational performance.[22]

Short-Term Incentives: The Annual Bonus

annual bonus
Plans that are designed to motivate short-term performance of managers and are tied to company profitability.

Over 80 percent of firms in Canada have **annual bonus** plans aimed at motivating the short-term performance of their managers and executives.[23] Unlike salaries, which rarely decline with reduced performance, short-term incentive bonuses can easily result in an increase or decrease of 25 percent or more in total pay relative to the previous year. There are three basic issues to be considered when awarding short-term incentives: eligibility, fund-size determination, and individual awards.

Eligibility   Eligibility is usually decided in one of three ways. The first criterion is *key position*. Here a job-by-job review is conducted to identify the key jobs (typically only line jobs) that have measurable impact on profitability. The second approach to determining eligibility is to set a *salary-level* cutoff point; all employees earning over that threshold amount are automatically eligible for consideration for short-term incentives. Finally, eligibility can be determined by *salary grade*. This is a refinement of the salary cutoff approach and assumes that all employees at a certain grade or above should be eligible for the short-term incentive program.[24] The simplest approach is just to use salary level as a cutoff.[25] As a rule, bonus eligibility begins somewhere around $40 000 to $50 000.[26]

The size of the bonus is usually greater for top-level executives. Thus, an executive earning $150 000 in salary may be able to earn another 80 percent of his or her salary as a bonus, while a manager in the same firm earning $80 000 can earn only another 30 percent. Similarly, a supervisor might be able to earn up to 15 percent of his or her base salary in bonuses. Average bonuses range from a low of 10 percent to a high of 80 percent or more: a typical company might establish a plan whereby executives could earn 45 percent of base salary, managers 25 percent, and supervisors 12 percent.

How Much to Pay Out (Fund Size)   Next a decision must be made regarding fund size—the total amount of bonus money that will be available—and there are several formulas to do this. Some companies use a *nondeductible formula*. Here a straight percentage (usually of the company's net income) is used to create the short-term incentive fund. Others use a *deductible formula* on the assumption that the short-term incentive fund should begin to accumulate only after the firm has met a specified level of earnings.

Frank Stronach, CEO of Magna Corp, receives very high bonuses in addition to his regular compensation.

In practice, what proportion of profits is usually paid out as bonuses? There are no hard and fast rules, and some firms do not even have a formula for developing the bonus fund.[27] One alternative is to reserve a minimum amount of the profits, say 10 percent for safeguarding stockholders' investments, and then to establish a fund for bonuses equal to 20 percent of the corporate operating profit before taxes in excess of this base amount. Thus, if the operating profits were $100 000, then the management bonus fund might be 20 percent of $90 000, or $18 000.[28] Other illustrative formulas used for determining the executive bonus fund are as follows:

> Ten percent of net income after deducting 5 percent of average capital invested in business.
>
> Twelve and one-half percent of the amount by which net income exceeds 6 percent of stockholders' equity.
>
> Twelve percent of net earnings after deducting 6 percent of net capital.[29]

Determining Individual Awards   The third issue is determining the *individual awards* to be paid. Typically a target bonus is set for each eligible position and adjustments are then made for greater or less than targeted performance. A maximum amount, perhaps double the target bonus, may be set. Performance ratings are obtained for each manager and preliminary bonus estimates are computed. Estimates for the total amount of money to be spent on short-term incentives are thereby made and compared with the bonus fund available. If necessary, the individual estimates are then adjusted.

A related question is whether managers will receive bonuses based on individual performance, team performance, corporate performance, or some combination of these. Keep in mind that there is a difference between a profit-sharing plan and a true, individual incentive bonus. In a profit-sharing plan, each person gets a bonus based on the company's results, regardless of the person's actual effort. With a true individual incentive, it is the manager's individual effort and performance that are rewarded with a bonus.

Here, again, there are no hard and fast rules. Top-level executive bonuses are generally tied to overall corporate results (or divisional results if the executive is, say, the vice president of a major division). The assumption is that corporate results reflect the person's individual performance. However, as one moves further down the chain of command, corporate profits become a less accurate gauge of a manager's contribution. For, say, supervisory staff or the heads of functional departments, the person's performance is a more logical determinant of his or her bonus.

Many experts argue that in most organizations managerial and executive-level bonuses should be tied to both organizational and individual performance, and there are several ways to do this.[30] Perhaps the simplest is the *split-award method,* which breaks the bonus into two parts. Here the manager actually gets two separate bonuses, one based on his or her individual effort and one based on the organization's overall performance. Thus, a manager might be eligible for an individual performance bonus of up to $10 000 but receive an individual performance bonus of only $8 000 at the end of the year, based on his or her individual performance evaluation. In addition, though, the person might also receive a second bonus of $8 000 based on the company's profits for the year. Thus, even if there are no company profits, the high-performing manager would still get an individual performance bonus.

One drawback to this approach is that it pays too much to the marginal performer, who even if his or her own performance is mediocre, at least gets that second, company-based bonus. One way to get around this is to use the *multiplier method.* For example, a manager whose individual performance was "poor" might not even receive a company-performance-based bonus, on the assumption that the bonus should be a *product* of individual *and* corporate performance. When either is very poor, the product is zero.

Whichever approach is used, outstanding performers should get substantially larger awards than do other managers. They are people the company cannot afford to lose, and their performance should always be adequately rewarded by the organization's incentive system. Conversely, marginal or below-average performers should never receive awards that are normal or average, and poor performers should be awarded nothing. The money saved on those people should be given to above-average performers.[31]

Long-Term Incentives

capital accumulation programs
Long-term incentives most often reserved for senior executives. Six popular plans include stock options, book value plans, stock appreciation rights, performance achievement plans, restricted stock plans, and phantom stock plans.

Long-term incentives are intended to motivate and reward top management for the firm's long-term growth and prosperity, and to inject a long-term perspective into executive decisions. If only short-term criteria are used, a manager could, for instance, increase profitability by reducing plant maintenance; this tactic might, of course, catch up with the company over two or three years. Long-term incentives also are intended to encourage executives to stay with the company by giving them the opportunity to accumulate capital (like company stock) based on the firm's long-term success. Long-term incentives or **capital accumulation programs** are most often reserved for senior executives, but have more recently begun to be extended to employees at lower organizational levels.[32]

There are six popular long-term incentive plans (for capital accumulation) in Canada: stock options, book value plans, stock appreciation rights, performance achievement plans, restricted stock plans, and phantom stock plans.[33] The popularity of these plans changes over time due to economic conditions and trends, internal company financial pressures, changing attitudes toward long-term incentives and changes in tax law as well as other factors.

stock option
The right to purchase a stated number of shares of a company stock at today's price at some time in the future.

Stock Options   The **stock option** is by far the most popular long-term incentive in Canada. A stock option is the right to purchase a specific number of shares of company stock at a specific price during a period of time; the executive thus hopes to profit by exercising his or her option to buy the shares in the future but at today's price. The assumption is that the price of the stock will go up, rather than go down or stay the same. If shares provided at an option price of $25 per share are exercised (bought) later for $25 when the market price is $50 per share, a cash gain of $25 per share results if the shares are then sold on the stock market. Often part of the gain is needed to meet income tax liabilities triggered when the options are exercised. Stock options are attractive from a taxation perspective in Canada, as only 75 percent of the gain on exercising the options is taxable. Thus stock option plans are often seen as a cash windfall with no downside risk but unlimited upside potential.[34]

Unfortunately, stock price depends to a significant extent on considerations outside the executive's control, such as general economic conditions and investor sentiment. Stock price is affected relative to the overall stock market by the firm's profitability and growth, and to the extent the executive can affect these factors the stock option can be an incentive. However, in one survey it was found that over half the executives saw little or no relationship between their performance and the value of their stock options.[35]

Book Value Plan   A book value plan is one alternative to stock options. Here managers are permitted to purchase stock at current book value, a value anchored in the value of the company's assets. Executives can earn dividends on the stock they own, and as the company grows the book value of their shares may grow too. When these employees leave the company, they can sell the shares back to the company at the new higher book value.[36] The book value approach avoids the uncertainties of the stock market, emphasizing instead a company's growth. Book value plans are more likely to be used by privately held companies than by publicly traded companies which cannot issue book value stock.

Other Plans   There are several other popular long-term incentive plans. *Stock appreciation rights* (SARs) are usually combined with stock options; they permit the recipient either to exercise the regular stock option (by buying the stock) or to take any appreciation in the stock price in cash, stock, or some combination of these. A *performance achievement plan* awards shares of stock for the achievement of predetermined financial targets, such as profit or growth in earnings per share. A variation on this plan is to provide stock options that are only exercisable after a performance target is achieved. With *restricted stock plans,* shares are usually awarded without cost to the executive but with certain restrictions that are imposed by the employer. For example, there may be a risk of forfeiture if an executive leaves the company before the specified time limit elapses. Finally, under *phantom stock plans* executives receive not shares but "units" that are similar to shares of company stock. Then, at some future time, they receive an amount (usually in cash) equal to the appreciation of the "phantom" stock they own.[37] Some phantom stock plans even provide the full original unit value plus the amount of appreciation.

Whichever long-term plan is used, a main concern today is achieving a "better balance between the personal motives and financial incentives of executives and their fiduciary responsibility to shareholders."[38] The problem is that traditional executive incentives often don't build in any real risk for the executive, and so the executives' and the shareholders' interests could diverge. Often, for instance, options can be exercised with little or no cash outlay by the executive, who then turns around and quickly sells his or her stock. There is, therefore, a growing emphasis on long-term executive incentives that build more executive risk into the formula.[39]

Performance Plans   The need to tie executives' pay more clearly to the firm's performance while building in more risk has led many firms to institute *performance* *plans*. Performance plans "are plans whose payment or value is contingent on financial performance measured against objectives set at the start of a multi-year period."[40] In Canada, these plans are usually limited to three years due to income tax rules. For example, the executive may be granted so-called performance units. These grants are similar to annual bonuses but the measurement period is longer than a year. Thus, the executive might be able to achieve, say, a $100 000 grant, in units valued at $50 per unit, in proportion to his or her success in meeting the assigned financial goals.

Implementing Long-Term Incentives   A study by consultants McKinsey and Company, Inc. suggests that giving managers stock options may be the simplest and wisest route as far as providing long-term incentives for top executives. In the McKinsey study about one-half the companies surveyed had stock options only, and about one-half had performance-based plans in which managers were given cash bonuses for long-term performance.

The results of the McKinsey study indicated that in most cases the return to shareholders of companies with long-term cash performance incentives did not differ significantly from that of companies that had only stock-based incentive plans (like stock options). This was so even though companies that paid cash bonuses had spent more to fund their incentive plans. Their most serious problem in awarding cash bonuses lay in identifying the proper performance measures. The survey concludes that successful long-term incentive plans should (1) use measures of performance that correlate with shareholder wealth creation (that is, return on equity and growth), not earnings-per-share growth; (2) establish valid target levels and communicate them clearly to participants; and (3) provide for target adjustment under certain well-defined circumstances (in other words, the performance standards can be modified if market conditions warrant it).[41]

On the other hand, consultants Watson Wyatt Worldwide suggest that it is not clear that stock options are the best compensation tools for rewarding senior executives because they do not reward strategies that maximize current dividend payouts, or that preserve existing share values in the short term, because executives do not have their own money at risk.[42]

Long-Term Incentives for Overseas Executives   Developing effective long-term incentives for a firm's overseas operations presents some tricky problems, particularly with regard to taxation. For example, extending a Canadian stock option plan to local nationals in a firm's overseas operations could subject them to immediate taxation on the stocks, even though the shares could not be sold because of requirements built into the Canadian-based plan.[43]

The problem extends to executives stationed overseas. For example, it's not unusual for an executive to be taxed up to $70 000 on $140 000 of stock option income if he or she is based in Canada. However, if that person receives the same $140 000 stock option income while stationed overseas, he or she may be subject to both the Canadian tax and a foreign income tax. Therefore, ignoring the overseas country's tax burden could have the effect of either virtually eliminating the incentive value of the stock from the executive's point of view or dramatically boosting the cost of the stock to the company (assuming the company pays the foreign income tax). In any case, firms cannot assume that they can simply export their executives' incentive programs. Instead, they must adapt them to the circumstances by considering various factors including tax treatment, the regulatory environment, and foreign exchange controls.[44]

Incentives for Salespeople

Sales compensation plans have typically relied heavily on incentives (sales commissions), although this varies by industry. In the tobacco industry, for instance, salespeople are usually paid entirely via commissions, while in the transportation equipment industry salespeople tend to be paid a salary. However, the most prevalent approach is to use a combination of salary and commissions to compensate salespeople.[45]

The widespread use of incentives for salespeople is due to three factors: tradition, the unsupervised nature of most sales work, and the assumption that incentives are needed to motivate salespeople. The pros and cons of salary, commission, and combination plans follow.

Salary Plan

www.daily.iastate.edu/
volumes/fall95/95se07/
isu-miller.html
Financial Incentives

In a salary plan salespeople are paid a fixed salary, although there may be occasional incentives in the form of bonuses, sales contest prizes, and the like.[46]

There are several reasons to use straight salary. It works well when the main sales objective is prospecting (finding new clients) or when the salesperson is mostly involved in account servicing, such as developing and executing product training programs for a distributor's sales force or participating in national and local trade shows.[47] Jobs like these are often found in industries that sell technical products. This is one reason why the aerospace and transportation equipment industries have a relatively heavy emphasis on salary plans for their salespeople.

There are advantages to paying salespeople on a straight salary basis. Salespeople know in advance what their income will be, and the employer also has fixed, predictable sales force expenses. Straight salary makes it simple to switch territories or quotas or to reassign salespeople, and it can develop a high degree of loyalty among the sales staff. Commissions tend to shift the salesperson's emphasis to making the sale rather than to prospecting and cultivating long-term customers. A long-term perspective is encouraged by straight salary compensation.

The main disadvantage is that salary plans don't depend on results.[48] In fact, salaries are often tied to seniority rather than to performance, which can be demotivating to potentially high-performing salespeople who see seniority—not performance—being rewarded.

Commission Plan

Commission plans pay salespeople in direct proportion to their sales: they pay for results, and only for results.

The commission plan has several advantages. Salespeople have the greatest possible incentive, and there is a tendency to attract high-performing salespeople who see that effort will clearly lead to rewards. Sales costs are proportional to sales rather than fixed, and the company's selling investment is reduced. The commission basis is also easy to understand and compute.

But the commission plan, too, has drawbacks. Salespeople focus on making a sale and on high-volume items; cultivating dedicated customers and working to push hard-to-sell items may be neglected. Wide variances in income between salespeople may occur; this can lead to a feeling that the plan is inequitable. More serious is the fact that salespeople are encouraged to neglect nonselling duties like servicing small accounts. In addition, pay is often excessive in boom times and very low in recessions.

Combination Plan

Most companies pay their salespeople a combination of salary and commissions, and there is a sizable salary component in most such plans. The most frequent percentage split reported in one study was 80 percent base salary and 20 percent incentives. A close second was a 70/30 split, with a 60/40 split being the third most frequently reported arrangement.[49]

Combination plans provide some of the advantages of both straight salary and straight commission plans, and also some of their disadvantages. Salespeople have a floor to their earnings. Furthermore, the company can direct its salespeople's activities by detailing what services the salary component is being paid for, while the commission component provides a built-in incentive for superior performance.

However, the salary component is not tied to performance, and the employer is therefore trading away some incentive value. Combination plans also tend to become complicated, and misunderstandings can result. This might not be a problem with a simple "salary plus commission" plan, but most plans are not so simple. For example, there is a "commission plus drawing account" plan, whereby a salesperson is paid basically on commissions but can draw on future earnings to get through low sales periods. Similarly, in the "commission plus bonus" plan, salespeople are again paid primarily on the basis of commissions. However, they are also given a small bonus for directed activities like selling slow-moving items.

An example can help illustrate the complexities of the typical combination plan. In one company, for instance, the following three-step formula is applied:

Step 1: Sales volume up to $18 000 a month. Base salary plus 7 percent of gross profits plus 0.5 percent of gross sales.

Step 2: Sales volume from $18 000 to $25 000 a month. Base salary plus 9 percent of gross profits plus 0.5 percent of gross sales.

Step 3: Sales volume over $25 000 a month. Base salary plus 10 percent of gross profits plus 0.5 percent of gross sales.

In all cases, base salary is paid every two weeks, while the earned percentage of gross profits and gross sales is paid monthly.[50]

The sales force also may get various special awards. Trips, home stereos, TVS, VCRs, and video cameras are commonly used as sales prizes. Two Crazy Ladies Inc. of Willowdale, Ontario is in the business of supplying companies with recognition/incentive merchandise. Their most popular items for salespeople are laptop computer briefcases, garment bags, and clothing—particularly leather jackets and golf shirts with a discreet corporate logo.

Incentives for Other Professionals

Merit Pay as an Incentive

merit pay (merit raise)
Any salary increase awarded to an employee based on his or her individual performance.

Merit pay or a **merit raise** is any salary increase that is awarded to an employee based on his or her individual performance. It is different from a bonus in that it represents a continuing increment, whereas the bonus represents a one-time payment. Although the term *merit pay* can apply to the incentive raises given to any employees—office or factory, management or nonmanagement—the term is more often used with respect to white-collar employees and particularly professional, office, and clerical employees.

Merit pay has both advocates and detractors and is the subject of much debate.[51] Advocates argue that only pay or other rewards tied directly to performance can motivate improved performance. They contend that the effect of awarding pay raises across the board (without regard to individual performance) may actually detract from performance by showing employees they'll be rewarded the same regardless of how they perform.

On the other hand, merit pay detractors present good reasons why merit pay can backfire. One is that the usefulness of the merit pay plan depends on the validity of the performance appraisal system, since if performance appraisals are viewed as unfair, so too will the merit pay that is based on them.[52] Similarly, supervisors often tend to minimize differences in employee performance when computing merit raises. They give most employees about the same raise, either because of a reluctance to alienate some employees, or a desire to give everyone a raise that will at least help them stay even with the cost of living. A third problem is that almost every employee thinks he or she is an above-average performer; being paid a below-average merit increase can thus be demoralizing.[53] However, while problems like these can undermine a merit pay plan, there seems little doubt that merit pay can and does improve performance. But it is critical that performance appraisals be carried out effectively.[54]

Merit Pay: Two New Options Traditional merit pay plans have two basic characteristics: (1) merit increases are usually granted to employees at a designated time of the year in the form of a higher base salary (or *raise*), and (2) the merit raise is usually based exclusively on individual performance, although the overall level of company profits may affect the total sum available for merit raises.[55] Two adaptations of merit pay plans are becoming more popular today. One awards merit raises in one lump sum once a year. The other ties awards to both individual and organizational performance.

Lump-sum merit payments are attractive to employers for several reasons. Traditional merit increases are cumulative, while some lump-sum merit payments are not. If the employee's lump-sum merit payments (of, say 5 percent of his or her base salary) is awarded in one lump sum, there is no change in base pay. For example, in a traditional merit pay plan, someone with a salary of $20 000 per year might get a 5 percent increase. This moves the employee to a new base salary of $21 000. If the employee gets another 5 percent increase next year, then the new merit increase of 5 percent is tacked on to the new $21 000 base salary. If the $1 000 merit payment is awarded on a lump-sum basis, base salary remains at $20 000. Another related advantage from the employer's perspective is that lump-sum merit raises can help contain benefit costs, since the level of benefit coverage is usually tied to a person's current base pay.

Lump-sum merit increases can also be more dramatic motivators than traditional merit pay raises. For example, a 5 percent lump-sum merit payment to an employee earning $20 000 is $1 000, as opposed to a traditional weekly increment of $19.25 for 52 weeks. Knowing that base salary levels are not being permanently affected by merit pay decisions can also give management more flexibility (say, in a particularly good year) to award somewhat higher lump-sum merit payments. However, before a firm surrenders the merit raise tool that's often used for raising base salaries, any substantial base salary inequities should be eliminated. That way, weaker performers' salaries are not frozen above higher performers' salaries. The timing of the merit payments may also become more important, since the impact of these payments on the firm's cash flow must now be considered.

Another merit pay option is to award lump-sum merit pay based on both individual and organizational performance. A sample matrix for doing so is presented in **Table 13.1**. In this example the company's performance might be measured by rate of return or sales divided by payroll costs. Company performance

TABLE 13.1 Lump-Sum Award Determination Matrix (an example)

THE EMPLOYEE'S PERFORMANCE (WEIGHT = 0.50)	THE ORGANIZATION'S PERFORMANCE (WEIGHT = 0.50)				
	Outstanding (1.00)	Excellent (0.80)	Commendable (0.60)	Marginal or Acceptable (0.40)	Unacceptable (0.00)
Outstanding (1.00)	1.00	0.90	0.80	0.70	0.50
Excellent (0.80)	0.90	0.80	0.70	0.60	0.40
Commendable (0.60)	0.80	0.70	0.60	0.50	0.30
Acceptable (0.00)	—	—	—	—	—
Unacceptable (0.00)	—	—	—	—	—

Source: John F. Sullivan, "The Future of Merit Pay Programs." *Compensation and Benefits Review* (May–June 1989), p. 29.

Instructions. To determine the dollar value of each employee's incentive award, (1) multiply the employee's annual, straight time wage or salary as of June 30 times his or her maximum incentive award and (2) multiply the resultant product times the appropriate percentage figure from this table. For example, if an employee had an annual salary of $20 000 on June 30 and a maximum incentive award of 7 percent and if her performance and the organization's performance were both "excellent," the employee's award would be $1120: ($20 000 × 0.07 × 0.80 = $1120).

is then weighted equally with the employee's performance, as measured by his or her performance appraisal. Thus, an outstanding performer would still receive a lump-sum award even if the organization's performance were marginal. However, employees with unacceptable performance would receive no lump-sum awards even in a year in which the organization's performance was outstanding. The advantage of this approach is that it forces employees to focus on organizational goals like profitability and improved productivity. The drawback is that it can reduce the motivational value of the reward by reducing the impact of the employee's own performance on the reward.[56]

Incentives for Professional Employees

Stephanie Kwolek, a DuPont scientist, received the company's highest award, the Lavoisier Medal for Technical Achievement.

Professional employees are those whose work involves the application of learned knowledge to the solution of the employer's problems. They include lawyers, doctors, economists, and engineers. Professionals almost always reach their positions through prolonged periods of formal study.[57]

Pay decisions regarding professional employees involve unique problems. One is that for most professionals money has historically been somewhat less important as an incentive than it has been for other employees. This is true partly because professionals tend to be paid well anyway, and partly because they are already driven—by the desire to produce high-calibre work and receive recognition from colleagues.

However, that's not to say that professionals don't want financial incentives. For example, studies in industries like pharmaceuticals and aerospace consistently show that firms with the most productive research and development groups have incentive pay plans for their professionals, usually in the form of bonuses. However, professionals' bonuses tend to represent a relatively small portion of their total pay. The time cycle of the professionals' incen-

Effective merit pay plans are always built on a foundation of fair and accurate appraisals. Some supervisors "grade" more stringently than others, some truly have mostly stars, and others are subject to the traditional rating errors. Comparing the results of various departments or divisions may flag certain problems for closer examination.

After accumulating appraisal data from various departments and/or supervisors, extract the particular area(s) needing review. More than one area at a time can be extracted by sorting the data first by department (in ascending alphabetical order) and then by supervisor's last name (again in ascending alphabetical order).

Then examine statistical averages and variances. Too little variance indicates a central tendency—a supervisor who does not want to distinguish between employees, so all are rated average. Looking at the minimum and maximum scores actually awarded will tell whether or not there is a restricted range—in other words, another indication of little differentiation between employees. Of course, the range may be restricted on the high side (an "easy grader") or the low side. If there is very little difference in ratings, then su-

perior performers are not getting reinforcement and poor performers are not being given clear expectations of what they must do to improve. Penley and Penley point out that small variance indicates "... undifferentiated feedback to the employees."[1]

Also examine the timeliness of appraisals. If the company policy is to appraise the employee on or before the anniversary of hiring date, then that month and day are entered. In another column, enter the date the appraisal was actually done. By subtracting the appraisal date from the hire date, the timeliness of appraisals can be viewed. This is possible because packages such as Lotus 1–2–3 store Gregorian dates based on the number of days since December 31, 1899.[2]

By analyzing the results of the appraisal process, it is possible to see problem areas that demand further training. Cleaning up these problems may well be a prerequisite to initiating an effective incentive plan.◆

1. Larry E. Penley and Yolanda E. Penley, *Human Resources Simulation: Using Lotus 1–2–3* (Carrollton, TX: South-Western Publishing Co., 1988), p. 121.
2. Gregory T. LeBlond and Douglas Ford Cobb, *Using Lotus 1–2–3* (Indianapolis: Que Corporation, 1983), p. 169.

tive plans also tends to be longer than a year, reflecting the long time spent in designing, developing, and marketing a new product.

There are also many nonsalary items professionals must have to do their best work. Not strictly incentives, these range from better equipment and facilities and a supportive management style to support for professional journal publications.

Rewarding Key Contributors

www.dupont.ca/corporate/hr1.htm
DuPont

How do organizations typically reward their key contributors who have had a significant impact on the company's performance? Key contributors are often executives, but they may also be lower-level employees, for example, technical specialists in high technology firms. According to a *Hay Executive and Key Contributor Compensation Survey* of high-technology firms, about 76 percent of the participants reported having some type of formal or informal key-contributor plan. **Figure 13.2** shows that 83 percent of the firms with key-contributor programs used cash in a lump-sum payment to key contributors. About half these firms used some type of stock payment plan (stock options or stock grants). With respect to cash payments, maximum opportunities for individuals ranged from $5 000 to $30 000 (typically $5 000). Other recognition included nonmonetary rewards like automobiles, trips, and

**Figure 13.2
Vehicles Used to
Reward Key
Contributors**

Source: Michael F. Spratt and
Bernadette Steele, "Rewarding
Key Contributors,"
*Compensation and Benefits
Review* (July–August 1985),
p. 30.

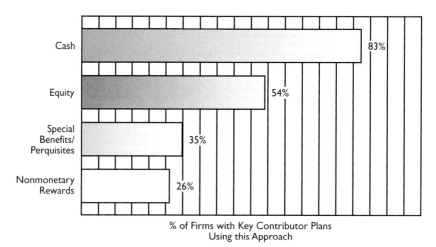

research funding, as well as sabbaticals, public recognition, freedom to choose projects, and "general work-life improvements."[58]

Customer Service Incentive Plans

Firms are also developing merit pay-type plans to reward employees for their contributions to customer service standards. One such program was instituted at the Aetna Life Insurance Company of Canada for call centre employees.

Group benefit sales support employees who provide service to policyholders receive up to 20 percent of their total incentive based on customer satisfaction, assessed using customer surveys. Call centre employees are provided with incentives including movie passes, free pizza lunches, and recognition as "representative of the week/month." Wal-Mart Canada associates who have been commended for good service on customer comment cards receive a large recognition badge to wear in the store. After winning four badges, the associate is recognized with a certificate, and announcements at company meetings and in the company newsletter.

Organization-Wide Incentive Plans

Many employers have incentive plans in which virtually all employees can participate. These include profit-sharing, employee stock ownership, and Scanlon plans.

Profit-Sharing Plans

profit-sharing plan
A plan whereby most or all employees share in the company's profits.

In a **profit-sharing plan,** most or all employees receive a share of the company's profits. Approximately 25 percent to 30 percent of Canadian organizations offer profit-sharing plans.[59] Research on the effectiveness of such plans is sketchy. In one survey, about half the companies believed their profit-sharing plans had been beneficial,[60] but the benefits were not necessarily in terms of increased performance and motivation. Instead such plans may increase each worker's sense of commitment, participation, and partnership. They may also reduce turnover and encourage employee thrift.

There are several types of profit-sharing plans. In cash plans, the most popular, a percentage of profits (usually 15 percent to 20 percent) is distributed as profit shares at regular intervals. One example is Atlas-Graham Industries Limited in Winnipeg. A profit-sharing pool is calculated by deducting two percent of sales from pre-tax profit, and then taking 30 percent of the result. The pool is distributed equally among all employees. Other plans provide cash and deferred benefits. Fisheries Products International Limited in St. John's, Newfoundland, contributes 10 percent of pre-tax income to a profit sharing pool that is divided up, just before Christmas, based on each employee's earnings. The first 75 percent of each employee's share is paid in cash, and the remaining 25 percent is allocated to pension plan improvements.[61]

Profit sharing has perhaps reached its logical conclusion in Japan. Many employees there get a semiannual bonus that reflects the performance of the enterprise. The amount of this bonus is usually the equivalent of five to six months' salary for each employee.[62]

There are also *deferred profit-sharing plans*. Here a predetermined portion of profits is placed in each employee's account under the supervision of a trustee. There is a tax advantage to such plans, since income taxes are deferred, often until the employee retires and is taxed at a lower rate.

Employee Share Purchase/Stock Ownership Plan

employee share purchase/stock ownership plan
A trust is established to hold shares of company stock purchased for or issued to employees. The trust distributes the stock to employees on retirement, separation from service, or as otherwise determined.

Employee share purchase/stock ownership plans (ESOPs) are in place at approximately 25 percent of Canadian organizations.[63] A trust is established to purchase shares of the firm's stock for employees using cash from employee (and sometimes employer) contributions. Employers may also issue treasury shares to the trust instead of paying cash for a purchase on the open market. The trust holds the stock in individual employee accounts and distributes it to employees, often upon retirement or other separation from service. Some plans distribute the stock to employees once a year.

The corporation receives a tax deduction equal to the fair market value of the shares that are purchased by the trustee using employer contributions, but not for any treasury shares issued. The value of the shares purchased with employer contributions, and of any treasury shares issued, is a taxable benefit to the employees in the year of purchase of the shares. This tax treatment can create two problems. First, if the plan requires employees to complete a certain period of service before taking ownership of the shares, and the employee leaves before being eligible for ownership, the employee has paid tax on the value of shares she or he never owns. Therefore, most plans have immediate vesting.[64] Second, if the value of the shares drops, employees may have paid tax on a greater amount than they receive when they eventually sell the shares.

Research suggests that ESOPs do encourage employees to develop a sense of ownership in and commitment to the firm.[65] They do so in part because they provide opportunities for increased financial incentives, create a new sense of ownership, and help to build teamwork. For example, General Printers in Oshawa, Ontario, achieved a dramatic turnaround following the introduction of an ESOP. The firm had been a chronic money-loser, but became profitable the year the plan was introduced, and has remained so in the years since that time. The value of the company has grown 80 percent since the ESOP was introduced, profits are up, spoiled orders are down 50 percent, and far less supervision of employees is required.[66]

General Printers' president, David Fors, far left, credits an employee share ownership plan with the company's turnaround.

Scanlon Plan

Few would argue with the fact that the most powerful way of ensuring commitment is to synchronize the organization's goals with those of its employees:

Scanlon plan
An incentive plan developed
in 1937 by Joseph Scanlon
and designed to encourage
cooperation, involvement,
and sharing of benefits.

to ensure, in other words, that the two sets of goals overlap, and that by pursuing his or her goals, the worker pursues the employer's goals as well. Many techniques have been proposed for obtaining this idyllic state, but few have been implemented as widely or successfully as the **Scanlon plan,** an incentive plan developed in 1937 by Joseph Scanlon, a United Steel Workers Union official.[67]

The Scanlon plan is remarkably progressive, considering that it was developed some 60 years ago. It contains many of the elements associated with commitment-building programs and quality-improvement plans today. The Scanlon plan itself has been refined over the years by organizations such as Scanlon Plan Associates, a nonprofit support group for organizations that have Scanlon plans.

As currently implemented, Scanlon plans have the following basic features.[68] The first is the *philosophy of cooperation* on which it is based. This philosophy assumes that managers and workers have to rid themselves of the "us" and "them" attitudes that normally inhibit employees from developing a sense of ownership in the company. It substitutes instead a climate in which everyone works together because he or she understands that economic rewards are contingent on honest cooperation. A pervasive philosophy of cooperation must therefore exist in the firm for the plan to succeed.[69]

A second feature of the plan is what its practitioners refer to as *identity*. This means that to focus employee involvement, the company's mission or purpose must be clearly articulated and employees must fundamentally understand how the business operates in terms of customers, prices, and costs, for instance.

Competence is a third basic feature. The program today, say three experts, "explicitly recognizes that a Scanlon Plan demands a high level of competence from employees at all levels."[70] The plan therefore assumes that hourly employees can competently perform their jobs as well as identify and implement improvements, and that supervisors have leadership skills for the participative management that is crucial to a Scanlon plan.

The fourth feature of the plan is the *involvement system*.[71] This takes the form of two levels of committees—the departmental level and the executive level. Productivity-improving suggestions are presented by employees to the appropriate departmental-level committees, the members of which transmit the valuable ones to the executive-level committee. The latter group then decides whether to implement the suggestion.

The fifth element of the plan is the *sharing of benefits formula*. Basically, the Scanlon plan assumes that employees should share directly in any extra profits resulting from their cost-cutting suggestions. If a suggestion is implemented and successful, all employees usually share in 75 percent of the savings. For example, assume that the normal monthly ratio of payroll costs to sales is 50 percent. (Thus, if sales are $600 000, payroll costs should be $300 000.) Assume suggestions are implemented and result in payroll costs of $250 000 in a month when sales were $550 000 and payroll costs would otherwise have been $275 000 (50 percent of sales). The saving attributable to these suggestions is $25 000 ($275 000 minus $250 000). Workers would typically share in 75 percent of this ($18 750) while $6 250 would go to the firm. In practice, a portion, usually one-quarter of the $18 750, is set aside for the months in which labour costs exceed the standard.

The Scanlon plan has been quite successful at reducing costs and fostering a sense of sharing and cooperation among employees. In one study, labour costs were cut by 10 percent, and grievances were cut in half after implementation of such a plan.[72]

Yet Scanlon plans do fail, and there are several conditions required for their success. They are usually more effective when there is a relatively small number of participants, generally fewer than 1 000. They are more successful when there are stable product lines and costs, since it is important that the labour costs/sales ratio remain fairly constant. Good supervision and healthy labour relations also seem essential. In addition, it is crucial that there be strong commitment to the plan on the part of management, particularly during the confusing phase-in period.[73]

Gainsharing Plans

gainsharing plan
An incentive plan that engages employees in a common effort to achieve productivity objectives and share the gains.

The Scanlon plan is actually an early version of what today is known as a **gainsharing plan,** an incentive plan that engages many or all employees in a common effort to achieve a company's productivity objectives; any resulting incremental cost-saving gains are shared among employees and the company.[74] In addition to the Scanlon plan, other popular types of gainsharing plans include the Rucker and Improshare plans.

The basic difference among these plans is in the formula used to determine employee bonuses.[75] The Scanlon formula divides payroll expenses by total sales. The Rucker formula uses sales value minus materials and supplies, all divided into payroll expenses. The Improshare plan creates production standards for each department. The Scanlon and Rucker plans include participative management systems using committees. Improshare does not include a participative management component but instead considers participation an outcome of the bonus plan. According to one recent survey, just under 10 percent of Canadian organizations use gainsharing plans.[76]

Steps in Gainsharing Plan   There are eight basic steps in implementing a gainsharing plan.[77] *First,* establish general plan objectives. These might include boosting productivity or reinforcing teamwork, for instance.

Second, define specific performance measures. These usually include productivity measures such as labour or hours or cost per unit produced, loans processed per hour, or total cost per full-time employee. Possible financial measures include profits before interest and taxes, and return on net assets. The *third* step is formulating the funding formula, such as "payroll expenses divided by total sales." This creates the pot of dollars that is shared among participants. (In one study, by the way, an average of 46.7 percent of incremental gains was provided to employees, with the remainder staying with the company.)[78] *Fourth,* determine a method for dividing and distributing the employees' share of the gains among the employees themselves. Typical methods include equal percentage of pay or equal shares, although some plans also try to modify awards to a limited degree based on individual performance. *Fifth,* make the size of the payment meaningful to get participants' attention and motivate their behaviour. One expert suggests a potential of four percent to five percent of pay and a 70 percent to 80 percent chance of achieving the plan's performance objectives as an effective combination. The *sixth* component is to choose the form of payment, which is usually cash but occasionally common stock or deferred cash. *Seventh,* decide how frequently bonuses are to be paid. This in turn depends on the performance measures used: Most financial performance measures tend to be computed annually, while labour productivity measures tend to be computed quarterly or monthly.

The *eighth* and last component is to develop the support or involvement system. The most commonly used systems for fostering a sense of employee involvement include steering committees, update meetings, suggestion systems, coordinators, problem-solving teams, department committees, training programs, newsletters, inside auditors, and outside auditors.

The financial aspects of a gainsharing program can be quite straightforward.[79] Assume a supplier wants to boost quality. Doing so would translate into fewer customer returns, less scrap and rework, and therefore higher profits. Historically,

$1 million in output results in $20 000 (2 percent) scrap, returns, and rework. The company tells its employees that if next month's production results in only 1 percent scrap, returns, and rework, the 1 percent saved would be a gain, to be split 50/50 with the work force, less a small amount for reserve for months in which scrap exceeds 2 percent. Awards are posted monthly but allocated quarterly.[80]

Making the Plan Work   Several factors contribute to a gainsharing plan's successful implementation. While the focus may be on just one goal (like quality), many firms use a "family of measures." For example, one firm chose seven variables (productivity, cost performance, product damage, customer complaints, shipping errors, safety, and attendance) and set specific goals for each (such as zero lost-time accidents, for safety). Then specific monthly bonuses were attached to each goal achieved.[81] Quality, customer service, productivity, and cost represent another familiar family of measures.[82]

   Successful gainsharing programs have several other key ingredients, according to one expert.[83] Management must be committed to implementing and maintaining the gainsharing plan, since managers will have to set and maintain consistent team goals, foster an atmosphere conducive to team effort and cooperation, and reduce adversarial relationships between management and employees. The financial incentive component itself should be simple, and measure and reward performance with a specific set of measurable goals and a clear allocation formula. Employee involvement is required so that the employees who are actually doing the jobs are encouraged to suggest performance improvement ideas. It should also be noted that the partnership between management and employees, as they pursue common goals on which the gainsharing plan's success will depend, requires two-way communication rather than just goal setting and top-down directives.[84]

www.bovino-consulting.com
Gainsharing Consultants

At-Risk Pay Plans

A growing number of firms are implementing new at-risk pay plans. These are sometimes called variable pay plans but are essentially plans that put some portion of the employee's pay at risk, subject to the firm's meeting its financial goals.

   The basic characteristic of all at-risk pay plans is that some portion of the employee's base salary is at risk. At DuPont Canada, for instance, the employee's at-risk pay is four percent. This means each employee will be paid 96 percent of their nominal salary. They can then earn up to 10 percent of that nominal salary based on company performance payable in cash, or company stock. The at-risk approach is aimed, in part, at paying employees like partners. It is actually similar to much more extensive programs in Japan in which the at-risk portion might be 50 percent to 60 percent of a person's yearly pay. To the extent that at-risk pay is part of a more comprehensive program aimed at turning employees into committed partners—a program stressing trust and respect, extensive communications, and participation and opportunities for advancement, for instance—at-risk programs should be successful.

Developing Effective Incentive Plans

Guidelines

There are three major practical considerations in developing an effective incentive plan. First, while there are no hard-and-fast rules, there are some conditions under which straight salary or pay based on time on the job—not on an incentive— makes somewhat more sense:

1. When units of output are difficult to distinguish and measure, straight salary or wages (or perhaps a group incentive plan) is more appropriate.
2. When employees are unable to control quantity of output (such as on machine-paced assembly lines), pay based on time may be more appropriate.
3. When delays in the work are frequent and beyond employees' control, it is impractical to tie workers' pay to their output.
4. Most incentive plans tie pay to the quantity, rather than the quality, of output. When quality is a primary consideration, pay based on time may be more appropriate.
5. Installing an incentive plan often requires an investment in industrial engineering, methods analysis, and computation of unit labour costs. If such precise cost control is not required by competitive conditions, it is probably not worthwhile to develop just to install an incentive plan.

Therefore, in general, it makes more sense to use an incentive plan when:

1. Units of output can be measured.
2. There is a clear relationship between employee effort and quantity of output.
3. The job is standardized, the work flow is regular, and delays are few or consistent.
4. Quality is less important than quantity, or, if quality is important, it is easily measured and controlled.
5. Competitive conditions require that unit labour costs be known and precise.[85]

Second, there are several specific common-sense considerations in establishing any such plan:[86]

1. *Ensure that effort and rewards are directly related.* The incentive plan should reward employees in direct proportion to their increased productivity. Employees must also perceive that they can actually do the tasks required. Thus, the standard has to be attainable, and the necessary tools, equipment, and training must be provided.[87]
2. *Make the plan understandable and easily calculable by the employees.* Employees should be able to calculate easily the rewards they will receive for various levels of effort.
3. *Set effective standards.* This requires several things. The standards should be viewed as fair by employees. They should be set high but be reasonable—there should be about a 50/50 chance of success. And the goal should be specific—this is much more effective than telling someone to "do your best."
4. *Guarantee the standards.* View the standard as a contract with employees. Once the plan is operational, use great caution before decreasing the size of the incentive in any way.[88] Rate cuts have long been the nemesis of incentive plans.
5. *Guarantee an hourly base rate.* Particularly for plant employees, it's usually advisable to guarantee a base rate of pay.[89] Doing so means they'll know that no matter what happens they can at least earn a minimum guaranteed base rate.
6. *Get support for the plan.* Group restrictions can undermine the plan; get the work groups' support for the plan before starting it.

A third and final practical consideration is that financial incentive plans may be best instituted as part of more comprehensive commitment-building programs. Some of the more cogent reasons experts give for being wary of traditional stand-alone pay-for-performance plans can be summarized as follows:

Performance pay can't replace good management. Performance pay is supposed to motivate workers, but lack of motivation is not always the culprit. Ambiguous instructions, lack of clear goals, inadequate employee selection and training, unavailability of tools, and a hostile work force (or management) are just a few of the factors that impede performance. Motivation, in other words, is just one of the elements contributing to effective performance.

Firms get what they pay for. This fact cuts both ways. Psychologists are fond of saying that people often put their effort where they know they'll be rewarded, so a well-designed and functioning incentive plan can help to focus workers' attention on, say, cutting scrap or lowering costs. However, this can backfire. An incentive plan that rewards a group based on how many pieces they produce could lead to rushed production and lower quality. Awarding a plant-wide incentive for reducing accidents may simply reduce the number of reported accidents.

"Pay is not a motivator."[90] Psychologist Frederick Herzberg makes the point that money only buys temporary compliance, and that as soon as the incentive is removed the "motivation" disappears too. He argues that too little money can create an atmosphere in which motivation won't take place. However, he says that adding more and more money won't boost motivation. Instead Herzberg says that employers should provide adequate financial rewards and then build other motivators, like opportunities for achievement and psychological success, into their jobs.

Rewards punish. Many view punishment and reward as two sides of the same coin. Reward has a potentially punitive effect in that, "Do this and you'll get that" is not really very different from "Do this or here's what will happen to you."[91]

Rewards rupture relationships. Incentive plans have the potential for reducing teamwork by encouraging individuals (or individual groups) to blindly pursue financial rewards for themselves. Some performance appraisal systems used for identifying incentive plan winners and losers may then exacerbate the situation, for instance, by forcing employees to be ranked.

Rewards can unduly restrict performance. One expert says that "Excellence pulls in one direction; rewards pull in another. Tell people that their income will depend on their productivity or performance rating, and they will focus on the numbers. Sometimes they will manipulate the schedule for completing tasks or even engage in patently unethical and illegal behavior."[92]

Rewards may undermine responsiveness. Since the employees' primary focus is on achieving some specific goal, like cutting costs, any changes or extraneous distractions mean that achieving that goal will be harder. Incentive plans can, therefore, mediate against change and responsiveness.

Rewards undermine interest and motivation. There is considerable evidence that contingent financial rewards may actually undermine the intrinsic motivation that often results in optimal performance.[93] Two psychologists note, "The research has consistently shown that any contingent payment system tends to undermine intrinsic motivation."[94] The argument is that financial incentives undermine the feeling that the person is doing a good job voluntarily.

There is growing evidence that incentive plans are effective in improving employee morale and contributing to improvements in individual, group, and organizational performance. But it is also clear that not all programs are successful.[95]

Potential pitfalls like those identified above don't mean that financial incentive plans cannot be useful or should not be used. They do suggest, though, that such plans are more effective when implemented as part of a comprehensive management program aimed at bringing out the best in workers by tapping their commitment, self-discipline, and desire to do their jobs well. In general any incentive plan is more apt to succeed if implemented with management support, employee acceptance, and a supportive culture characterized by teamwork, trust, and involvement at all levels.[96] This probably helps to explain why some of the longest-lasting incentive plans, like the Scanlon and Rucker plans, depend heavily on two-way communications and employee involvement in addition to incentive pay. The Building Employee Commitment box later in this chapter presents an example of how one company did this.

Small Business Applications

Several other incentive-plan-improvement guidelines are especially relevant for the small business.

Consider the Current Business Stage of the Company

In designing the incentive plan, consider the firm's life-cycle stage.[1] Small companies experiencing rapid growth usually prefer a broader based profit-sharing plan to the more complicated individual incentive- or gainsharing-type plans. For one thing, profit-sharing plans tend to be simpler and less expensive to implement and require much less planning and administrative paperwork. Furthermore, small firms' employees tend to feel a more direct tie to the company's profitability than do those employed by much larger firms. Similarly, companies in a survival or turnaround situation, or those threatened by takeover, may also opt for less complicated profit-sharing plans. That way top and middle managers can focus all their energies on the crisis rather than on the administrative effort required to implement gainsharing or individualized incentive plans.

Stress Productivity and Quality Measures If Possible

Remember that profitability is not always the same as productivity and that it is usually productivity and quality for which employees should be held accountable, not profitability. The reason is that productivity and quality are controllable, whereas profitability can be influenced by factors like competition and government regulations. As a result, unless it is a simple company-wide profit-sharing plan that is implemented, productivity and/or quality standards should be chosen carefully, focussing on measures that employees can actually control.

Get Employee Input in System Design

It is usually a mistake to implement an incentive plan without input from employees. Therefore, many employers use a program design team composed of selected employees and supervisors. They work with the compensation specialist in the development of the plan, perhaps by explaining idiosyncrasies that need to be taken into consideration or by helping them understand the culture and attitudes in the plant.◆

1. The following are based on Michael J. Cissell, "Designing Effective Reward Systems," *Compensation and Benefits Review* (November–December 1987), pp. 49–56.

Building Employee Commitment

Example of a Total Compensation Program

Progressive firms like Federal Express Canada aim to boost quality and productivity by using innovative incentive plans as part of their commitment-building programs. At Federal Express Canada, quarterly pay reviews and periodic national and local salary surveys are used to maintain salary ranges and pay schedules that are competitive. Internal equity is maintained through the use of job evaluation.

The result is a set of salary ranges such that salaries for each position tend to be equitable relative to other FedEx Canada jobs. At the same time (thanks to the salary surveys), the base salaries are highly competitive as compared with similar jobs in the market. FedEx Canada defines the market as "where we recruit" each pay group. The airline/air freight industry is the primary market for the FedEx Canada pilot and maintenance groups, for instance. The pay rates of FedEx's Canada direct competitors in the air freight industry are compared for the hourly pay group. The management comparison market consists of major national companies, since these jobs are recruited nationally. Usually only salaried employees are hired locally. Therefore, the local market is surveyed for this pay group to determine FedEx Canada's market position.

For virtually all FedEx Canada positions, base salary alone probably makes pay competitive with market rates. However, there is also a heavy emphasis on pay-for-performance. The company is convinced people want to see a relationship between performance and reward, and that their people want to know that when they knock themselves out to reach their part of their 100 percent customer satisfaction goal, their efforts will not go unnoticed. Federal Express Canada, therefore, has as number of pay-for-performance programs.

Merit Program   All employees, salaried and hourly, receive merit increases based on their individual performance. The performance appraisal process at Federal Express Canada provides the vehicle for rating employees' performance, for sharing information aimed at individual development, and for making pay increase recommendations based on sustained performance. To ensure the integrity of the pay-for-performance principle, it is essential that performance appraisals are fair and accurately measure performance.

Star/Superstar Program   All employees with a specified performance rating may be nominated for a Star or Superstar lump-sum bonus. Stars represent the top 10 percent of performers in each division, while Superstars represent the top one percent of performers in the Canadian region.

MBO/MIC and PBO/PIC Programs   These are individual incentive plans for managers and professionals. They were developed to provide management and many salaried employees the opportunity to receive financial rewards for helping attain corporate, departmental, and divisional objectives. The MIC and PIC programs (management incentive compensation and professional incentive compensation) generally reward achievement of divisional and corporate profit goals. The MBO or PBO bonuses (management by objectives and professional by objectives) are tied to individual attainment of people, service, or profit-related goals. Thus, for a regional sales manager, a "people" goal could be an improvement in the person's leadership index score on the firm's annual feedback action survey.[1]

Bravo Zulu Voucher Program   The Bravo Zulu Voucher Program was established so managers could provide immediate rewards to employees for outstanding performance above and beyond the normal requirements of the job. (Bravo Zulu is a title borrowed from the U.S. Navy's semaphore signal for "well done.") Bravo Zulu vouchers can be in the form of a cheque or some other form of reward (such as dinner vouchers or theater tickets). It's estimated that more than 150 000 times a year a Federal Express manager somewhere in the world presents an employee with one of these awards, which average about $50.[2]

Win-Win Program   This program is designed to demonstrate the company's profit-sharing philosophy by financially rewarding superior performance and discretionary team effort. This program provides variable compensation that is in unison with FedEx Canada's long-term compensation strategy. It provides an opportunity for employees of FedEx Canada to actively participate and share in the financial success of the Canadian region.

With the exception of the merit program, all of these pay-for-performance programs are forms of variable compensation. They are paid as one-time lump-sum awards, separate from base pay, thereby enabling the company to reward outstanding performance without permanently increasing its fixed payroll costs. The variability also reflects changes in business conditions and allows Federal Express Canada to react to adverse economic conditions while maintaining its full employment policy.

Beyond this, the other elements of the FedEx Canada commitment-building program should be kept in mind. For example, the firm encourages extensive two-way communication and adheres to guaranteed fair treatment programs. Salary levels are very competitive, and promotion-from-within programs encourage employees to better themselves. Incentives at FedEx Canada are thus just one element in a more comprehensive commitment-building program.◆

1. *Blueprints for Service Quality: The Federal Express Approach*, (New York: AMA Membership Publication Division, 1991), pp. 31–2.
2. *Blueprints for Service Quality*, pp. 34–5.

Chapter Review

Summary

1. The scientific use of financial incentives can be traced back to Frederick Taylor. While such incentives became somewhat less popular during the human relations era, most writers today agree that they can be quite effective.

2. Piecework is the oldest type of incentive plan. Here a worker is paid a piece rate for each unit he or she produces. With a straight piecework plan, workers are paid on the basis of the number of units produced. With a guaranteed piecework plan, each worker receives his or her base rate (such as the minimum wage) regardless of how many units he or she produces.

3. Other useful incentive plans for plant employees include the standard hour plan and group incentive plans. The former rewards workers by a premium that equals the percent by which their performance is above standard. Group incentive plans are useful where the workers' jobs are highly interrelated.

4. Most sales people are paid on some type of salary plus commission (incentive) basis. The trouble with straight commission is that there is a tendency to focus on "big-ticket" or "quick-sell" items and to disregard long-term customer relationships. Management employees are often paid according to a bonus formula that ties the bonus to, for example, increased sales. Stock options are one of the most popular executive incentive plans.

5. Profit sharing and the Scanlon plan are examples of organization-wide incentive plans. The problem with such plans is that the link between a person's efforts and rewards is sometimes unclear. On the other hand, such plans may contribute to developing a sense of commitment among employees. Gainsharing and merit plans are two other popular plans.

6. When incentive plans fail, it is usually because (a) the worker does not believe that effort on his or her part will lead to obtaining the reward, or (b) the reward is not important to the person. Specific incentive plan problems, therefore, include unfair standards, fear of a rate cut, group restrictions, lack of understanding, and lack of required tools or training.

7. Incentive plans are particularly appropriate when units of output are easily measured, employees can control output, the effort–reward relationship is clear, work delays are under employees' control, quality is not paramount, and the organization must know precise labour costs anyway (to stay competitive).

Key Terms

annual bonus
capital accumulation
   programs
employee share purchase/
   stock ownership plan
gainsharing plan

guaranteed piecework plan
merit pay (merit raise)
piecework
profit-sharing plan
Scanlon plan
spot bonus

standard hour plan
stock option
straight piecework plan
team or group
   incentive plan
variable pay

Discussion Questions and Exercises

1. Compare and contrast six types of incentive plans.
2. Explain five reasons why incentive plans fail.
3. Describe the nature of some important management incentives.
4. When and why should a salesperson be paid a salary? A commission? Salary and commission combined?
5. Working individually or in groups, develop an incentive plan for each of the following positions: chemical engineer, plant manager, used-car salesperson. What factors had to be taken into consideration?
6. A university recently instituted a "Teacher Incentive Program" (TIP) for its faculty. Basically, faculty committees within each of the university's colleges were told to award $5 000 raises (not bonuses) to about 40 percent of their faculty members based on how good a job they did teaching undergraduates, and how many they taught per year. What are the potential advantages and pitfalls of such an incentive program? How well do you think it was accepted by the faculty? Do you think it had the desired effect?
7. What is merit pay? Do you think it's a good idea to award employees merit raises? Why or why not?
8. In this chapter we listed a number of reasons experts give for not instituting a pay-for-performance plan in a vacuum (such as "rewards punish"). Do you think these points (or any of them) are valid? Why or why not?
9. What is a Scanlon plan? Based on the information in this book so far, what features of a commitment-building program does the Scanlon plan include?
10. Suppose an instructor decided to award final grades to teams of students in a class, instead of to individuals. What would be the pros and cons of such an approach? Would students like the idea?

Application Exercises

RUNNING CASE: Carter Cleaning Company

The Incentive Plan

The question of whether to pay Carter Cleaning Centre employees an hourly wage or an incentive of some kind has always intrigued Jack Carter. His basic policy has been to pay employees an hourly wage, except that his managers do receive an end-of-year bonus depending, as Jack puts it, "on whether their stores do well or not that year."

He has, however, experimented in one store with incentive plans with mixed results. Jack knows that a presser should press about 25 "tops" (jackets, dresses, blouses) per hour. Most of his pressers do not attain this ideal standard, though. In one instance, a presser named Walt was paid $7 per hour, and Jack noticed that regardless of the amount of work he had to do, Walt always ended up making about

$280 at the end of the week. If it was a holiday week, for instance, and there were a lot of clothes to press, he might average 22 to 23 tops per hour (someone else did pants) and so he'd earn perhaps $300 to $325 and still finish up each day in time to leave by 3:00 p.m. so he could pick up his children at school. But when things were very slow in the store, his productivity would drop to perhaps 12 to 15 pieces an hour, so that at the end of the week he'd still end up earning close to $250 and in fact not go home much earlier than he did when it was busy.

Jack spoke with Walt several times, and while Walt always promised to try to do better, it gradually became apparent to Jack that Walt was simply going to earn his $280 per week no matter what. While Walt never told him so directly, it dawned on Jack that Walt had a family to support and was not about to earn less than his "target" wage regardless of how busy or slow the store was. The problem was that the longer Walt kept pressing each day, the longer the steam boilers and compressors had to be kept on to power his machines, and the fuel charges alone ran close to $5 per hour. Jack clearly needed some way short of firing Walt to solve the problem, since the fuel bills were eating up his profits.

His solution was to tell Walt that instead of an hourly $7 wage he would henceforth pay him $0.40 per item pressed. That way, said Jack to himself, if Walt presses 25 items per hour at $0.40 he will in effect get a small raise. He'll get more items pressed per hour and will therefore be able to shut the machines down earlier.

On the whole, the experiment worked well. Walt generally presses 25 to 35 pieces per hour now. He gets to leave earlier, and with the small increase in pay he generally earns his target wage. Two problems have arisen, though. The quality of Walt's work has dipped a bit, and his manager has to spend a minute or two each hour counting the number of pieces Walt pressed that hour. Otherwise Jack is fairly pleased with the results of his incentive plan and he's wondering whether to extend it to other employees and other stores.

Questions

1. Should this plan, in its present form, be extended to pressers in the other stores?
2. Should other employees be put on a similar plan? Why? Why not?
3. Is there another incentive plan you think would work better for the pressers?
4. A store manager's job is to keep total wages to no more than 30 percent of sales and to maintain the fuel bill and the supply bill at about 9 percent of sales each. Managers can also directly affect sales by ensuring courteous customer service and that the work is done properly. What suggestions would you make to Jennifer and her father for an incentive plan for store managers?

CASE INCIDENT: Sales Quotas

The Superior Floor Covering Company has an incentive program for its sales associates. Incentive earnings are based on the amount of sales in relation to an assigned quota.

The quota is computed each year by management, taking into account the number and type of customers in each sales associate's territory and the previous year's sales records for the company and for its competitors. In the administration of this incentive program, the following problems have arisen. Suggest the solutions you would consider in eliminating these difficulties. Note also the parallels between the problems here and those involving blue-collar, manufacturing incentive plans.

Questions

1. Some of the best sales associates now have too many accounts in the area assigned to them. From the company's point of view, it would be advantageous to reduce the size of the districts covered by each of these representatives and to add several new sales associates who could give more thorough coverage. The outstanding sales associates resent this proposal, however, claiming that it would penalize them for their success.

2. The top-earning sales associates also complain that their base quotas increase each year, reflecting their previous success. This, too, they feel is discrimination against success.

3. Management believes that the company is not acquiring as many new accounts as it should. So-called missionary work, trying to induce a store that has not previously purchased Superior products to become a customer, takes more time and energy than selling old customers. Also, the results of this missionary work may not show up for several years. The present incentive plan gives no credit for this type of work.

4. When business is booming within a sales associate's territory, he or she may receive high bonus earnings even without great effort. When there is a great deal of unemployment in the territory or when competitors decide to lower prices to penetrate this new market, his or her bonus earnings may decline even though sales efforts are at a maximum.

Source: George Strauss and Leonard R. Sayles, *Personnel: The Human Problems of Management,* 4th ed. (Englewood Cliffs, NJ: Prentice Hall, 1980), p. 636. Reprinted by permission.

Video Case

Will You Get a Raise?

For many Canadians, raises were non-existent in the first half of the 1990s. Today, with the exception of employees in high-demand, high-tech jobs, raises are rarely more than the amount needed to keep up with inflation. Consultants are proclaiming that the days of eight percent (or higher) annual increases, common in the 1980s, are over. Companies don't want to be locked into large amounts of base pay.

Variable pay is the new reality in the 1990s. Almost half of Canadian employers offered variable pay by the end of 1995, double the number for 1990. The size of an employee's paycheque now varies depending on whether pre-determined business targets are met. This uncertainty is intended to create a incentive for employees to work hard to attain desired results. The targets can include company budgets/goals for sales and profits, cost cutting, individual or team productivity, and many others. A bonus averaging seven percent to 10 percent of base pay is given at the end of the year if targets are met. If they are not met, no additional compensation is paid to employees. This approach has long been the norm for commissioned salespeople and for senior executives, but is now being pushed down to lower levels of the organization.

In order to determine whether targets are being met, measures of productivity, customer service, and so on, are necessary. This can result in some disruption in the workplace, and a less comfortable environment for employees. Highly motivated, productive employees are the ones who thrive in this atmosphere, and "slackers" who are discovered as a result of the scrutiny process are often not retained. It is clear that the days of automatic pay increases are over, and that incentive compensation linked to performance is here to stay.

Questions

1. What are some of the benefits of incentive pay for companies? For individuals?

2. Talk to three friends or relatives who work for companies with incentive pay. Find out what kind of targets they are required to meet.

3. Under what circumstances might companies revert back to automatic base pay increases for employees?

Video Resource: CBC, *Venture,* "Will You Get a Raise?" April 2, 1995.

Take It to the Net

Check out our Companion Website at

www.prenticehall.ca/dessler

for a multitude of practice questions, key terms and concepts, Weblinks to related sites, newsgroups, CBC video updates, and more.

Notes

1. E.S. Reckard, "$100 Million Bonus to 523 Employees," *Toronto Sun* (December 22, 1996), p. 72.

2. N.B. Carlyle, *Compensation Planning Outlook 1997*, Conference Board of Canada, 1996. pp. 8–9.

3. Except as noted, this section is based on "Non-Traditional Incentive Pay Programs," *Personnel Policies Forum Survey*, no. 148 (May 1991), The Bureau of National Affairs, Inc., Washington, D.C.

4. "Non-Traditional Incentive Pay Programs," p. 3.

5. "Non-Traditional Incentive Pay Programs," p. 9 and A. Czarnecki, "'Spot Awards' Incentives Easily Administered, Flexible, Affordable," *Canadian HR Reporter* (March 13, 1995), p. 15.

6. "Non-Traditional Incentive Pay Programs," p. 13.

7. "Non-Traditional Incentive Pay Programs," p. 19.

8. "Non-Traditional Incentive Pay Programs," p. 24.

9. Richard Henderson, *Compensation Management* (Reston, VA: Reston, 1979), p. 363. For a discussion of the increasing use of incentives for blue-collar employees, see, for example, Richard Henderson, "Contract Concessions: Is the Past Prologue?" *Compensation and Benefits Review* 18, no. 5 (September–October 1986), pp. 17–30. See also A. J. Vogl, "Carrots, Sticks and Self-Deception," *Across-the-Board*, 3–1, No. 1 (January 1994), pp. 39–44.

10. David Belcher, *Compensation Administration* (Englewood Cliffs, NJ: Prentice-Hall, 1973), p. 314.

11. For a discussion of these, see Thomas Wilson, "Is It Time to Eliminate the Piece Rate Incentive System?" *Compensation and Benefits Review* (March–April 1992), pp. 43–9.

12. Measured day work is a third type of individual incentive plan for production workers. See, for example, Mitchell Fein, "Let's Return to MDW for Incentives," *Industrial Engineering* (January 1979), pp. 34–7.

13. Henderson, *Compensation Management*, pp. 367–8. See also David Swinehart, "A Guide for More Productive Team Incentive Programs," *Personnel Journal* 65, no. 7 (July 1986), Anne Saunier and Elizabeth Hawk, "Realizing the Potential of Teams through Team-based Rewards," *Compensation and Benefits Review* (July–August 1994), pp. 24–33, and Shari Caudron, "Tie Individual Pay to Team Success," *Personnel Journal* 73, No. 10 (October 1994), pp. 40–6.

14. Another suggestion is as follows: equal payments to all members on the team; differential payments to team members based on their contributions to the team's performance; and differential payments determined by a ratio of each group member's base pay to the total base pay of the group. See Kathryn Bartol and Laura Hagmann, "Team-based Pay Plans: A Key to Effective Teamwork," *Compensation and Benefits Review* (November–December 1992), pp. 24–9.

15. James Nickel and Sandra O'Neal, "Small Group Incentives: Gainsharing in the Microcosm," *Compensation and Benefits Review* (March–April 1990), p. 24. See also Jane Pickard, "How Incentives Can Drive Teamworking," *Personnel Management* (September 1993), pp. 26–32, and Shari Caudron, "Tie Individual Pay to Team Success," *Personnel Journal* (October 1994), pp. 40–6.

16. Jon P. Alston, "Awarding Bonuses the Japanese Way," *Business Horizons* 25 (September–October 1982), pp. 6–8.

17. See, for example, Peter Daly, "Selecting and Assigning a Group Incentive Plan," *Management Review* (December 1975), pp. 33–45. For an explanation of how to develop a successful group incentive program, see K. Dow Scott and Timothy Cotter, "The Team That Works Together Earns Together," *Personnel Journal* 63 (March 1984), pp. 59–67.

18. Manuel London and Greg Oldham, "A Comparison of Group and Individual Incentive Plans," *Academy of Management Journal* 20, no. 1 (1977), pp. 34–41. Note that the study was carried out under controlled conditions in a laboratory setting. See also Thomas Rollins, "Productivity-Based Group Incentive Plans: Powerful, But Use with Caution," *Compensation and Benefits Review* 21, no. 3 (May–June 1989), pp. 39–50; discusses several popular group incentive plans, including gainsharing, and lists dos and don'ts for using them.

19. W. E. Reum and Sherry Reum, "Employee Stock Owner-ship Plans: Pluses and Minuses," *Harvard Business Review* 55 (July–August 1976), pp. 133–43; Ralph Bavier, "Managerial Bonuses," *Industrial Management* (March– April 1978), pp. 1–5. See also James Thompson, L. Murphy Smith, and Alicia Murray, "Management Performance Incentives: Three Critical Issues," *Compensation and Benefits Review* 18, no. 5 (September–October 1986), pp. 41–7.

20. N. Winter Consulting Inc., *Alternative Compensation Practices*, 1996, p. 5.

21. Carlyle, *Compensation Planning Outlook 1997*, p. 9.

22. S. B. Prasod, "Top Management Compensation and Corporate Performance," *Academy of Management Journal* (September 1974), pp. 554–8; John Bouike, "Performance Bonus Plans: Boom for Managers and Stockholders," *Management Review* (November 1975), pp. 13, 18; "How Pay and Save Grows and Grows," *Forbes* (April 16, 1979), p. 113.

23. Carlyle, *Compensation Planning Outlook*, p. 9.

24. Bruce R. Ellig, "Incentive Plans: Short-Term Design Issues," *Compensation Review* 16, no. 3 (Third Quarter 1984), pp. 26–36.

25. Bruce Ellig, *Executive Compensation—A Total Pay Perspective* (New York: McGraw-Hill, 1982), p. 187.

26. Ellig. *Executive Compensation*.

27. Ellig, *Executive Compensation,* p. 188.

28. See, for example, Bavier, "Managerial Bonuses," pp. 1–5. See also Charles Tharp, "Linking Annual Incentive Awards to Individual Performance," *Compensation and Benefits Review* 17 (November–December 1985), pp. 38–43.

29. Ellig, *Executive Compensation,* p. 189.

30. F. Dean Hildebrand, Jr., "Individual Performance Incentives," *Compensation Review*. 10 (Third Quarter 1978), p. 32.

31. Hildebrand, "Individual Performance Incentives," pp. 28–33.

32. R.M. Kanungo and M. Mendonca, *Compensation: Effective Reward Management* (1997), p. 237.

33. Edward Redling, "The 1981 Tax Act: Boom to Managerial Compensation," *Personnel* 57 (March–April 1982), pp. 26–35.

34. R. Murrill, "Executive Share Ownership," *Watson Wyatt Memorandum*, 11(1), March 1997, p. 11.

35. Belcher, *Compensation Administration,* p. 548; Schechter, "The Tax Reform Act of 1986," p. 23. See also Rein Linney and Charles Marshall, "ISOs vs. NQSOs: The Choice Still Exists," *Compensation and Benefits Review* 19, no. 1 (January–February 1987), pp. 13–25.

36. Basically, book value per share equals the firm's assets minus its prior (basically debt) liabilities, divided by the number of shares. See, for example, John Annas, "Facing Today's Compensation Uncertainties," *Personnel* 33, no. 1 (January–February 1976).

37. Ray Stata and Modesto Maidique, "Bonus System for Balanced Strategy," *Harvard Business Review* 59 (November–December 1980), pp. 156–63; Alfred Rappaport, "Executive Incentives Versus Corporate Growth," *Harvard Business Review* 57 (July–August 1978), pp. 81–8. See also Crystal Graef, "Rendering Long-Term Incentives Less Risky for Executives," *Personnel* 65, no. 9 (September 1988), pp. 80–4.

38. Ira Kay, "Beyond Stock Options: Emerging Practices in Executive Incentive Programs," *Compensation and Benefits Review* (November–December 1991), p. 19.

39. For a discussion see Kay, "Beyond Stock Option," pp. 18–29.

40. Jeffrey Kanter and Matthew Ward, "Long-Term Incentives for Management, Part 4: Performance Plans," *Compensation and Benefits Review* (January–February 1990), p. 36.

41. Murrill, "Executive Share Ownership," p. 5. See also Jude Rich and John Larson, "Why Some Long-Term Incentives Fail," *Compensation Review* 16 (First Quarter 1984), pp. 26–37; Eric Marquardt, "Stock Option Grants: Is Timing Everything?" *Compensation and Benefits Review* 20, no. 5 (September–October 1988), pp. 18–22.

42. Murrill, "Executive Share Ownership," p. 6.

43. Robert Klein, "Compensating Your Overseas Executives, Part 3: Exporting U.S. Stock Option Plans to Expatriates," *Compensation and Benefits Review* (January–February 1991), pp. 27–38.

44. For a discussion see Klein, "Compensating Your Overseas Executives."

45. This section based primarily on John Steinbrink, "How to Pay Your Sales Force," *Harvard Business Review* 57 (July–August 1978), pp. 111–22. See also John Tallitsch and John Moynahan, "Fine-Tuning Sales Compensation Programs," *Compensation and Benefits Review* 26, no. 2 (March–April 1994), pp. 34–7.

46. Straight salary by itself is not, of course, an incentive compensation plan as we use the term in this chapter.

47. Steinbrink, "How to Pay," p. 112.

48. T. H. Patten, "Trends in Pay Practices for Salesmen," *Personnel* 43 (January–February 1968), pp. 54–63. See also Catherine Romano, "Death of a Salesman," *Management Review* 83, no. 9 (September 1994), pp. 10–6.

49. Steinbrink, "How to Pay," p. 115.

50. In the salary plus bonus plan, salespeople are paid a basic salary and are then paid a bonus for carrying out specified activities. For a discussion of how to develop a customer-focused sales compensation plan, see, for example, Mark Blessington, "Designing a Sales Strategy with the Customer in Mind," *Compensation and Benefits Review* (March–April 1992), pp. 30–41.

51. See, for example, Herbert Meyer, "The Pay for Performance Dilemma," *Organizational Dynamics* (Winter 1975), pp. 39–50; Thomas Patten, Jr., "Pay for Performance or Placation?" *Personnel Administrator* 24 (September 1977), pp. 26–9; William Kearney, "Pay for Performance? Not Always," *MSU Business Topics* (Spring 1979), pp. 5–16. See also Hoyt Doyel and Janet Johnson, "Pay Increase Guidelines with Merit," *Personnel Journal* 64 (June 1985), pp. 46–50.

52. Nathan Winstanley, "Are Merit Increases Really Effective?" *Personnel Administrator* 27 (April 1982), pp. 37–41. See also William Seithel and Jeff Emans, "Calculating Merit Increases: A Structured Approach," *Personnel* 60, no. 5 (June 1985), pp. 56–68.

53. James T. Brinks, "Is There Merit in Merit Increases?" *Personnel Administrator* 25 (May 1980), p. 60. See also Dan Gilbert and Glenn Bassett, "Merit Pay Increases are a Mistake," *Compensation and Benefits Review* 26, no. 2 (March–April 1994), pp. 20–5.

54. *Merit Pay: Fitting the Pieces Together,* (Chicago: Commerce Clearing House, 1982).

55. Suzanne Minken, "Does Lump Sum Pay Merit Attention?" *Personnel Journal* (June 1988), pp. 77–83. Two experts suggest using neither straight merit pay nor lump-sum merit pay but rather tying the merit payment to the duration of the impact of the employee's work so that, for instance, the merit raise might last for two or three years. See Jerry Newman and Daniel Fisher, "Strategic Impact Merit Pay," *Compensation and Benefits Review* (July–August 1992), pp. 38–45.

56. John F. Sullivan, "The Future of Merit Pay Programs," *Compensation and Benefits Review* (May–June 1988), pp. 22–30.

57. This section based primarily on Robert Sibson, *Compensation* (New York: AMACOM, 1981), pp. 189–207.

58. Michael Sprat and Bernadette Steele, "Rewarding Key Contributors," *Compensation and Benefits Review* 17 (July–August 1985), pp. 24–37.

59. Carlyle, *Compensation Planning Outlook*, p. 9. See also N. Winter Consulting, Inc. *Alternative Compensation Practices*, p. 5.

60. Bert Metzger and Jerome Colletti, "Does Profit Sharing Pay?" (Evanston, IL: Profit Sharing Research Foundation, 1971), quoted in Belcher, *Compensation Administration,* p. 353. See also D. Keith Denton, "An Employee Ownership Program That Rebuilt Success," *Personnel Journal* 66, no. 3 (March 1987), pp. 114–8 and Edward Shepard, "Profit Sharing and Productivity: Further Evidence from the Chemicals Industry," *Industrial Relations* 33, no. 4 (October 1994), pp. 452–66.

61. D.E. Tyson, *Profit-Sharing in Canada: The Complete Guide to Designing and Implementing Plans That Really Work,* (Toronto: Wiley, 1996), pp. 200–7.

62. Mary O'Connor, "Employee Profit Sharing in Japan," *Personnel Journal* 60 (August 1981), p. 614.

63. Carlyle, *Compensation Planning Outlook*, p. 9.

64. R. Murrill, "Executive Share Ownership," p. 10.

65. Everett Allen, Jr., Joseph Melone, and Jerry Rosenbloom, *Pension Planning* (Homewood, IL: Irwin, 1981), p. 316.

66. S. Lebrun, "ESOP Saves the Day," *Canadian HR Reporter,* November 17, 1987, pp. 1–2. See also William Smith, Harold Lazarus, and Harold Murray Kalkstein, "Employee Stock Ownership Plans: Motivation and Morale Issues," *Compensation and Benefits Review* (September–October 1990), pp. 37–46.

67. Brian Moore and Timothy Ross, *The Scanlon Way to Improved Productivity: A Practical Guide* (New York: Wiley, 1978), p. 2.

68. These are based in part on Steven Markham, K. Dow Scott, and Walter Cox, Jr., "The Evolutionary Development of a Scanlon Plan," *Compensation and Benefits Review* (March–April 1992), pp. 50–6.

69. J. Kenneth White, "The Scanlon Plan: Causes and Correlates of Success," *Academy of Management Journal* 22 (June 1979), pp. 292–312.

70. Markham et al., "The Evolutionary Development of a Scanlon Plan," p. 51.

71. Moore and Ross, *The Scanlon Way,* pp. 1–2.

72. George Sherman, "The Scanlon Plan: Its Capabilities for Productive Improvement," *Personnel Administrator* (July 1976).

73. White, "The Scanlon Plan," pp. 292–312. For a discussion of the Improshare plan, see Roger Kaufman, "The Effects of Improshare on Productivity," *Industrial and Labor Relations Review* 45, no. 2 (1991), pp. 311–22.

74. Barry W. Thomas and Madeline Hess Olson, "Gainsharing: The Design Guarantees Success," *Personnel Journal* (May 1988), pp. 73–9. See also "Aligning Compensation with Quality," *Bulletin to Management, BNA Policy and Practice Series (*April 1, 1993), p. 97.

75. See Theresa A. Welbourne and Louis Gomez Mejia, "Gainsharing Revisited," *Compensation and Benefits Review* (July–August 1988), pp. 19–28.

76. *Alternative Compensation Practices*, p.5.

77. Thomas and Olson, "Gainsharing," pp. 75–6. See also Thomas McGrath, "Gainsharing: Engineering the Human Factor of Productivity," *Industrial Engineering* (September 1993), pp. 61–3, and Paul Rossler and C. Patrick Koelling, "The Effect of Gainsharing on Business Performance at a Paper Mill," and *National Productivity Review* (Summer 1993), pp. 365–82.

78. Carla O'Dell and Jerry McAdams, *People, Performance, and Pay* (American Productivity Center and Carla O'Dell, 1987), p. 42.

79. This is paraphrased from Woodruff Imberman, "Boosting Plant Performance with Gainsharing," *Business Horizons,* (November–December 1992), p. 77.

80. For other examples, see Timothy Ross and Larry Hatcher, "Gainsharing Drives Quality Improvement," *Personnel Journal* (November 1992), pp. 81–9. See also Jerry McAdams, "Employee Involvement and Performance Reward Plans: Design, Implementation, and Results," *Compensation and Benefits Review* 27, no. 2 (March 1995), pp. 45–55.

81. John Belcher, Jr., "Gainsharing and Variable Pay: The State of the Art," *Compensation and Benefits Review* (May–June 1994), pp. 50–60.

82. Robert Masternak, "Gainsharing Boosts Quality and Productivity at a B.F. Goodrich Plant," *National Productivity Review* (Spring 1993), pp. 225–38. See also Susan Hanlon, David Meyer, and Robert Taylor, "Consequences of Gainsharing: A Field Experiment Revisited," *Group & Organization Management* 19, no. 1 (March 1994), pp. 87–111.

83. This is based on Thomas McGrath, "How Three Screw Machine Companies Are Tapping Human Productivity Through Gainsharing," *Employment Relations Today* (Winter 1993/94), pp. 437–46.

84. See, for example, Moore and Ross, *The Scanlon Way to Improved Productivity,* pp. 157–64; Ewing, "Gainsharing Plans," pp. 51–2. For a description of the implementation of a gainsharing plan in health care institutions, see Steven Markham et al., "Gainsharing Experiments in Health Care," *Compensation and Benefits Review* (March–April 1992), pp. 57–64. See also Dwight Willett, "Promoting Quality Through Compensation," *Business Quarterly* (Autumn 1993), pp. 107–11; and Robert Masternak, "Gainsharing: Overcoming Common Myths and Problems to Achieve Dramatic Results," *Employment Relations Today* (Winter 1993/94), pp. 425–36.

85. Belcher, *Compensation Administration,* pp. 309–10.

86. Robert Opsahl and Marvin Dunnette, "The Role of Financial Compensation in Industrial Motivation," *Psychological Bulletin* 66 (1966), pp. 94–118.

87. See, for example, James Gutherie and Edward Cunningham, "Pay for Performance: The Quaker Oats Alternative," *Compensation and Benefits Review* 24, no. 2 (March–April 1992), pp. 18–23.

88. Gary Yukl and Gary Latham, "Consequences of Reinforcement Schedules and Incentives Magnitudes for Employee Performance: Problems Encountered in an Industrial Setting," *Journal of Applied Psychology* 60 (June 1975).

89. Louden and Deagan, *Wage Incentives,* p. 26.

90. The following five points are based on Alfie Kohn, "Why Incentive Plans Cannot Work," *Harvard Business Review* (September–October 1993), pp. 54–63.

91. Kohn, "Why Incentive Plans Cannot Work," p. 58.

92. Kohn, "Why Incentive Plans Cannot Work," p. 58. p. 62.

93. Kohn, "Why Incentive Plans Cannot Work."

94. Edward Deci and Richard Ryan, *Intrinsic Motivation and Self-Determination in Human Behavior* (New York: Plenum Press, 1985), quoted in Kohn, "Why Incentive Plans Cannot Work," p. 62.

95. N. Winter, "Do Alternative Approaches Really Work?" *Canadian HR Reporter* (January 27, 1997), p. 10.

96. Steven Gross and Jeffrey Bacher, "The New Variable Pay Programs: How Some Succeed, Why Some Don't," *Compensation and Benefits Review* (January–February 1993), pp. 55–6; see also George Milkovich and Carolyn Milkovich, "Strengthening the Pay-Performance Relationship: The Research," *Compensation and Benefits Review* (November–December 1992), pp. 53–62; and Jay Schuster and Patricia Zingheim, "The New Variable Pay: Key Design Issues," *Compensation and Benefits Review* (March– April 1993), pp. 27–34.

Chapter 14

Employee Benefits and Services

Chapter Outline

- ◆ **Introduction**
- ◆ **Government-Sponsored Benefits**
- ◆ **Pay for Time Not Worked**
- ◆ **Insurance Benefits**
- ◆ **Retirement Benefits**
- ◆ **Employee Services**
- ◆ **Flexible Benefits Programs**
- ◆ **Benefits Administration**

Learning Outcomes

After studying this chapter, you should be able to:

List and *describe* each of the basic benefits most employers might be expected to offer.

Describe four government-sponsored benefits.

Explain why the cost of insurance benefits is increasing and how employers can reduce these costs.

Describe recent trends in retirement benefits.

Discuss four types of employee services offered by many organizations.

Explain how to set up a flexible benefits program.

Introduction

benefits
Indirect financial payments given to employees. They may include supplementary health and life insurance, vacation, pension, education plans, and discounts on company products, for instance.

Benefits represent an important part of just about every employee's pay; they can be defined as all the indirect financial payments an employee receives for continuing his or her employment with the company.[1] Benefits are generally available to all a firm's employees and include such things as time off with pay, supplementary health and life insurance, and childcare facilities.

Administering benefits today represents an increasingly specialized task. It demands expertise because workers are more financially sophisticated and demanding, and because benefit plans must comply with a number of laws.

Providing and administering benefits represents an increasingly expensive task, too. As shown in **Figure 14.1**, benefits as a percentage of payroll (for public and private sectors combined) are about 41 percent today (compared to about 15 percent in 1953). That translates to around $17 000 in total annual benefits per employee, ranging from a high of $27 066 for the industrial equipment manufacturing industry to a low of $3 954 for the hospitality, tourism, and recreation industries. In terms of the costs of specific benefits, payments for time not worked (vacations, sick days, and so on) represent just over 13 percent of the average employer's payroll. Medical and related benefits (such as supplementary health insurance) account for almost four percent of payroll. Legally required payments (such as for the Canadian/Quebec Pension Plan) represent about 12 percent, while retirement and savings plans and various other benefits account for the remaining benefit dollars. Most employees don't realize the market value and high cost to the employer of their benefits, so prudent employers list the benefits' true costs on each employee's pay stub.

Figure 14.1
Employee Benefits as a Percent of Payroll in 1996

Source: KPMG (1996) *Employee Benefits Costs in Canada*

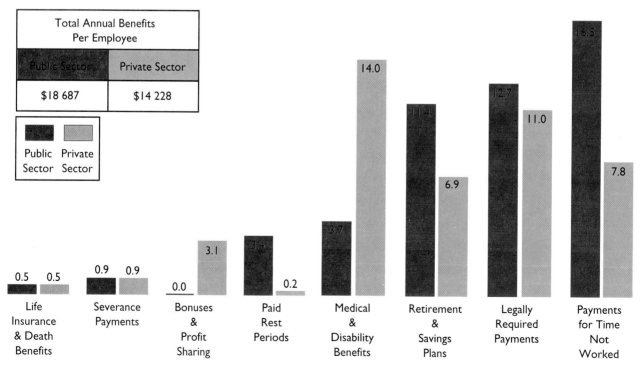

The Benefits Picture Today

Most Canadian companies provide some form of employee benefits.[2] A recent survey conducted by KPMG management consultants found that group life insurance was provided by 99 percent of private sector employers and all public sector employers. About 96 percent of private sector and all public sector organizations provided health and dental care insurance. Just under 50 percent of organizations had some type of employee assistance program; and about 93 percent provided educational subsidies. Most firms also provided retirement benefits. For example, 76 percent of public sector organizations and 70 percent of private sector companies provided some type of pension plan.

There are many benefits and various ways to classify each. For example, the Canada/Quebec Pension Plan is both a government-sponsored benefit and a contribution toward most employees' future retirement income. In the remainder of this chapter we will classify benefits as (1) government-sponsored benefits (2) pay for time not worked, (3) insurance benefits, (4) retirement benefits, and (5) employee services.

Government-Sponsored Benefits

Canada has one of the world's finest collections of social programs to protect its citizens when they can't earn income. Employers and employees provide funding for these plans, along with general tax revenues. In 1996, the average cost to employers for government-sponsored benefits was 12 percent of payroll.[3]

Employment Insurance (EI)

employment insurance
A federal program that provides income benefits if a person is unable to work through no fault of his or her own.

Employment insurance (known as unemployment insurance until 1996) is a federal program providing weekly benefits if a person is unable to work through no fault of his or her own. Approximately 95 percent of Canadian workers are covered by the EI program. It does not apply to workers who are self-employed. EI provides benefits for employees who are laid off, terminated without just cause, or who quit their job for a justifiable reason such as harassment. EI benefits are not payable when an employee is terminated for just cause, for example, theft of company property, or when an employee quits for no good reason. Workers may also be eligible for special EI benefits in cases of illness, injury or quarantine where the employer has no sickness or disability benefits (or once such benefits have been exhausted), and for maternity/parental leaves.

In order to receive benefits, an employee must first have worked a minimum number of hours during a minimum number of weeks called a qualifying period (the number of hours and weeks varies between regions of the country). Then there is a waiting period from the last day of work until benefits begin. The waiting period varies, but is often two weeks. If an employee was provided with severance pay or holiday pay at the time he or she lost his or her job, these payments must run out before the waiting period begins.

The EI benefit is generally 55 percent of average earnings during the last twenty weeks of the qualifying period. The benefit is payable for up to 45 weeks, depending on the regional unemployment rate and other factors. In order to receive EI benefits, individuals must demonstrate that they are actively seeking work. Claimants are encouraged to work part time, as they can earn up to 25 percent of their EI benefit amount before these earnings will be deducted from the benefit. Illness benefits are payable for up to 15 weeks, and maternity/parental leave benefits are payable for up to 25 weeks.

www.hrdc-drhc.gc.ca/isp/ common/home.shtml
Income Security Programs

The EI program is funded by contributions from eligible employees and their employers. Employee contributions are collected by payroll deduction, and employers pay 1.4 times the employee contribution. Employer contributions can be reduced if they provide a wage loss replacement plan for employee sick leave.

As explained in chapter 5, a supplemental unemployment benefit (SUB) plan is an agreement between an employer and the employees (often the result of collective bargaining) for a plan that enables employees who are eligible for EI benefits to receive additional benefits from an SUB fund created by the employer. Such benefits are often found in heavy manufacturing operations, such as the auto and steel industries, where layoffs are common. Some plans also cover employees on sick leave or maternity leave. The purpose of an SUB plan is to supplement EI benefits so that employees can better maintain their standard of living during periods of unemployment by receiving a combined benefit closer to their actual working wage during periods of unemployment. Some SUB plans also provide a lump sum payment to employees who are permanently terminated. The amount of the SUB benefit is usually determined based on length of service and wage rate. Work-sharing programs are a related arrangement where employees work a reduced work week and receive EI benefits for the remainder of the week. SUB plans and work-sharing programs must be approved by the EI Commission.

Canada/Quebec Pension Plan (C/QPP)

Canada/Quebec Pension Plan
Programs that provides three types of benefits: retirement income; survivor or death benefits payable to the employee's dependents regardless of age at time of death; and disability benefits payable to disabled employees and their dependents. Benefits are payable only to those individuals who make contributions to the plans and/or their family members.

The **C/QPP plans** were introduced in 1966 to provide working Canadians with a basic level of financial security upon retirement or disability. Over 30 years later, these benefits do indeed provide a significant part of most Canadians' retirement income. Almost all employed Canadians between the ages of 18 and 65 are covered, including self-employed individuals. Casual and migrant workers are excluded, as well as people who are not earning any employment income such as homemakers. The two plans are similar in contributions, benefits, and rules. The benefits are portable, meaning that pension rights are not affected by changes in job or residence within Canada. Both contributions and benefits are based only on earnings up to the "Year's Maximum Pensionable Earnings" (intended to approximate the average industrial wage) as defined in the legislation. Benefits are adjusted based on inflation each year in line with the consumer price index.

Three types of benefits are provided: retirement pensions, disability pensions, and survivor benefits. The retirement pension is calculated based on the number of years in which contributions were made and the average amount of pensionable earnings in the last three years prior to retirement (a proposal to change this to the last five years is under consideration), with a maximum benefit of 25 percent of average earnings. Plan members can choose to begin receiving benefits at any time between the ages of 60 and 70. Benefits are reduced by 0.5% for each month of early retirement before age 65 and are increased by 0.5 percent for each month of late retirement after age 65.

Plan members who have made contributions for two out of the previous three years (or five out of the prior ten) are eligible for disability benefits, which require a four-month waiting period. Benefits are only paid for severe disabilities that are expected to be permanent or to last for an extended period of time. The disability benefit is 75 percent of the pension benefit earned at the date of disability, plus a flat rate amount per child, payable until the child is 18 (or 25 if attending school). The benefit is payable until recovery, death, or attainment of age 65 (when the C/QPP retirement pension begins). Upon the death of a plan member, a lump sum payment is made to survivors. A monthly pension is also payable to the surviving spouse, based on the pension benefit earned at the date of death, the age of the spouse, and the number of dependent children.

Contributions made by employees (2.925 percent of pensionable earnings in 1997, rising to 4.95 percent in 2003) are matched by employers. The amount of contributions is gradually increasing due to concerns about the ability of these plans to pay benefits to members of the baby-boom generation when they retire.[4]

Workers' Compensation

workers' compensation
Workers' compensation provides income and medical benefits to victims of work-related accidents or illnesses and/or their dependents, regardless of fault.

Workers' compensation laws are aimed at providing sure, prompt income and medical benefits to victims of work-related accidents or illnesses and/or their dependants, regardless of fault. Every province and territory, and the federal jurisdiction, has its own workers' compensation law. These laws impose compulsory collective liability for workplace accidents and work-related illnesses. This means that employees and employers cannot sue each other regarding the costs of workplace accidents or illnesses. Workers' compensation is, in effect, a "no fault" insurance plan to help injured or ill workers get well and return to work. For an injury or illness to be covered by workers' compensation, one must only prove that it arose while the employee was on the job. It does not matter that the employee may have been at fault; if he or she was on the job when the injury or illness occurred, he or she is entitled to workers' compensation. For example, suppose all employees are instructed to wear safety goggles when working at their machines, and one does not and is injured. Workers' compensation benefits will still be provided. The fact that the worker was at fault in no way waives his or her claim to benefits.

Although safety gear is always recommended, failure to wear it does not invalidate an employee's claim for benefits under workers' compensation laws.

Employers collectively pay the full cost of the workers' compensation system, which can be an onerous financial burden for small businesses. The amount of the premiums (called assessments) varies by industry and by actual employer costs. Employer premiums are tax-deductible. Workers' Compensation Boards (Workplace Safety and Insurance Board in Ontario) exist in each jurisdiction to determine and collect assessments from employers, determine rights to compensation, and pay injured workers the amount of benefit to which they are entitled under the legislation in their jurisdiction. Employers and employees have some representation on these Boards, but usually both parties believe they should have more control.

Workers' compensation benefits include payment of expenses for medical treatment and rehabilitation, income benefits during the period of time the worker is unable to work (temporarily or permanently) due to his or her disability (partial or total). Survivor benefits are payable if a work-related death occurs. All benefits are non-taxable. A significant problem can occur with workers' compensation if benefits are set so high (for example, 90 percent of pre-injury net pay), that workers make more money from workers' compensation than when they are working. In 1997, the province of Ontario reduced its benefit level from 90 percent to 85 percent of net pay to provide an incentive for injured or ill workers to return to work.

Controlling Workers' Compensation Costs In most provinces, workers' compensation costs skyrocketed during the 1980s and 1990s. Unfunded liabilities for future pensions across the country reached over $15 billion. Recently, a number of provinces have amended their workers' compensation legislation to reduce benefit levels, limit benefit entitlements for stress-related illnesses and chronic pain, reduce inflation indexing of benefits, and put more emphasis on rehabilitation and return to work. Several provinces followed the lead of Alberta in using sound business principles and practices to streamline the large administrative bureaucracies that had developed and to eliminate unfunded liabilities, while still providing the benefits required by law and generating surplus funds to return to employers.

All parties agree that a renewed focus on accident prevention is the best way to manage workers' compensation costs over the long term. Minimizing the number of workers' compensation claims is an important goal for all employers. While the Workers' Compensation Board pays the claims, the premiums for most employers depend on the number and amount of claims that are paid. Minimizing such claims is thus important.

In practice, there are two main approaches to reducing workers' compensation claims. First, reduce accident- or illness-causing conditions in an organization's facilities by instituting effective safety and health programs and complying with government safety standards. Second, since workers' compensation costs increase the longer an employee is unable to return to work, employers can become involved in instituting rehabilitation programs for injured or ill employees, including physical therapy programs and career counselling to guide such employees into new, less strenuous or stressful jobs to reintegrate recipients back into the work force. Workers are required to cooperate with return to work initiatives such as modified work.[5]

Provincial Health Care Plans

provincial health care plans
Provincial health care plans pay for basic medically-required hospital and medical services with no direct fee to patients.

All provinces and both territories provide basic medical and hospital services with no direct fee to patients. The provinces of British Columbia and Alberta finance their health care plans by requiring monthly premiums to be paid by each resident. These premiums may be subsidized by employers. Ontario, Quebec, Manitoba, Newfoundland, and the Northwest Territories levy a payroll tax to partially fund the cost of their health care plans. Saskatchewan, Prince Edward Island, New Brunswick, Nova Scotia, and the Yukon Territory use general tax revenues to pay for their plans.

The services paid for by these plans include medically required procedures provided by physicians, nurses, and other health care professionals, standard ward hospital accommodation, drugs and medication administered in hospital, laboratory and diagnostic procedures, and hospital facilities such as operating rooms. Some of the services that are not covered by the provincial plans are prescription drugs, dental care, eyeglasses, private-duty nursing, cosmetic surgery, and semi-private or private hospital accommodation.

Pay for Time Not Worked

pay for time not worked
Benefits for time not worked such as vacation and holiday pay, and sick pay.

Pay for time not worked is typically one of an employer's most expensive benefits because of the large amount of time off that many employees receive. Common time-off-with-pay periods include holidays, vacations, sick leave, severance pay, and some leaves of absence. While some of these (such as holidays and vacations) can also be viewed as legally required benefits, the fact is that pay for time not worked is a substantial part of almost every employer's payroll expense. In this section some of the major time-off-with-pay elements will be discussed, specifically: vacation and holiday pay, short term disability/sick pay, leaves of absence, and pay on termination of employment.

Vacations and Holidays

Labour/employment standards legislation sets out a minimum amount of paid vacation that must be provided to employees, usually two weeks per year, but the requirements vary by jurisdiction. The actual number of paid employee vacation days also varies considerably from employer to employer. Even within the same organization the number of vacation days will normally depend on how long the employee has worked at the firm. Thus, a typical vacation policy might call for:

1. Two weeks for the first 5 years of service
2. Three weeks for 6 to 10 years of service
3. Four weeks for 11 to 15 years of service
4. Five weeks for 16 to 25 years of service and
5. Six weeks after 25 years of service.

The average number of annual vacation days is generally greater in European countries.[6] For example, employees in Sweden and Austria can expect 30-day vacations, in France 25 days, and in the United Kingdom, Spain, Norway, Finland, and Belgium 20 to 25 days.

Several practical questions must be addressed in formulating an employer's vacation policies. For example, some vacation plans give the employee his or her regular base rate of pay while on vacation, while others provide for vacation pay based on average earnings (which may include overtime). The statutory minimum accrued vacation time must be paid if an employee leaves before taking it. Consideration must also be given to whether to penalize an employee who takes his or her annual vacation and then resigns before fully earning the vacation time he or she has already taken.

The number of paid holidays similarly varies considerably from one jurisdiction to another, from a minimum of five to a maximum of nine. The most common paid holidays include New Year's Day, Good Friday, Canada Day, Labour Day, Thanksgiving Day, and Christmas Day. Other common holidays include Victoria Day, Rememberance Day, and Boxing Day. Additional holidays may be observed in each province, for example, Saint Jean-Baptiste Day in Quebec.

A number of holiday pay policy issues must also be addressed. For example, provisions must be made for holidays that fall on a Saturday or Sunday: employees are often given the following Monday off when the holiday falls on a Sunday, and Friday off when it falls on a Saturday. Most labour/employment standards legislation also provides for some pay premium—such as time and a half—when employees must work on a holiday.

Short-Term Disability/Sick Leave

short-term disability/sick leave
Plans that provide pay to an employee when he or she is unable to work because of a non-work-related illness or injury.

Short-term disability plans (also known as salary continuation plans) provide a continuation of all or part of an employee's earnings when the employee is absent from work due to non-work-related illness or injury. Usually a medical certificate is required if the absence extends beyond two or three days. These plans often provide full pay for some period of time (often two or three weeks) and then gradually reduce the percentage of earnings paid as the period of absence lengthens. The benefits cease when the employee returns to work or when the employee qualifies for long-term disability. These plans are sometimes provided through an insurance company.

Sick leave plans operate quite differently from short-term disability plans. Most sick leave policies grant full pay for a specified number of permissible sick days—usually up to about 12 per year. The sick days are often accumulated at the rate of, say, one day per month of service. Newfoundland, the Yukon and the federal jurisdiction require sick leave (unpaid). Sick leave pay causes consternation for many employers. The problem is that while many employees use their sick days only when they are legitimately sick, others simply utilize their sick leave as extensions to their vacations, whether they are sick or not. Also, seriously ill or injured employees get no pay once their sick days are used up.

Employers have tried several tactics to eliminate or reduce the problem. Some now buy back unused sick leave at the end of the year by paying their employees a daily equivalent pay for each sick leave day not used. The drawback is that the policy can encourage legitimately sick employees to come to work despite their illness.[7] Others have experimented with holding monthly lotteries in which only employees with perfect monthly attendance are able to participate; those who participate are eligible to win a cash prize. Still others aggressively investigate all absences, for instance, by calling the absent employees at their homes when they are off sick.

Leaves of Absence

All of the provinces and territories, and the federal jurisdiction, require unpaid leaves of absence to be provided to employees in certain circumstances. Some employers provide full or partial pay for all or part of these leaves. Maternity/pregnancy leave is provided in every jurisdiction, and each has one or more of paternity, parental, and adoption leave available as well. The amount of maternity leave is 17 or 18 weeks in each jurisdiction (usually after one year of service), but parental and adoption leaves range from 12 to 34 weeks. Employees who take these leaves of absence are guaranteed their old job or a similar job when they return to work.

Bereavement leave upon the death of a family member is provided for employees in some, but not all, jurisdictions. The amount of time off varies by jurisdiction, and depends on the closeness of the relationship between the employee and the deceased. Bereavement leave is usually unpaid, but in some cases it can be partially or fully paid.

Having a clear procedure for any leave of absence is essential. An application form such as the one in **Figure 14.2** should be the centrepiece of any such procedure. In general, no employee should be given a leave until it's clear what the leave is for. If the leave is for medical or family reasons, medical certification should be obtained from the attending physician or medical practitioner. A form like this also places on record the employee's expected return date and the fact that without an authorized extension his or her employment may be terminated.

While most leaves, including maternity/pregnancy, paternity, parental, adoption, and educational leave are unpaid, it is incorrect to assume that the leave is costless to the employer. For example, one study concluded that the costs associated with recruiting new temporary-replacement workers, training replacement workers, and compensating for the lower level of productivity of these workers could represent a substantial expense over and above what employers would normally pay their full-time employees.[8] An employer may also end up paying group insurance premiums for both the employee who is on leave and the person's temporary replacement.[9]

Pay on Termination of Employment

Employment/labour standards legislation requires that employees whose employment is being terminated by the employer be provided with termination pay when they leave. In most cases, this is pay for time not worked. The amount to be paid varies between jurisdictions and with the circumstances.

Pay in Lieu of Notice An employee must be provided with advance written notice if the employer is going to terminate his or her employment (unless the employee is working on a short-term contract, or is being fired for just cause). The amount of advance notice required increases with the length of employment of the employee (often 1 week per year of employment to a specified maximum), and varies between jurisdictions. Many employers do not provide advance written notice. Instead they ask the employee to cease working immediately and provide the employee with a lump sum equal to their pay for the notice period. This amount is called "pay in lieu of notice."

Figure 14.2
Sample Application
for Leave of Absence

Source: BNA *Bulletin to Management,* September 30, 1993, p. 6.

Name _____ Date of Application _____
Location _____ Department _____

Type of Leave Requested (Check each that applies.)

[　] Medical*　　[　] Educational
[　] Family*　　 [　] Other _____
[　] Military

Start Date (first day of leave) ____　　Return Date (date of return to work) ____

Absence is to be (check each that applies): [　] unpaid
　　　　　　　　　　　　　　　　　　　　　[　] fully paid
　　　　　　　　　　　　　　　　　　　　　[　] partially paid (Please explain.)
　　　　　　　　　　　　　　　　　　　　　　_____
　　　　　　　　　　　　　　　　　　　　　　_____
　　　　　　　　　　　　　　　　　　　　　　_____

Should vacation benefits be used?　　　[　] No
　　　　　　　　　　　　　　　　　　　　[　] Yes (# of hours) ____

Reason for Requested Leave (Explain why leave is necessary.)
_____
_____
_____
_____
_____
_____
_____
_____

*A medical certification is required for medical/family leaves of absence. The health care provider's certification must include:
◇ The date the health condition began;
◇ The expected duration of the condition;
◇ Appropriate medical facts necessary to verify leave requests;
◇ An estimate of the amount of time required to be off work; and
◇ If for a family member's serious health condition, a statement that the employee is needed to care for that family member.
Refer to the Leave of Absence Policy for further certification and reporting requirements.

Employee's Signature _____ Date _____

　　　　I understand that if I do not return from my leave of absence at the expiration
　　　　of this leave, unless an extension has been approved in advance, my
　　　　employment may be terminated.

Supervisor's Signature _____ Date _____

Severance Pay　Employees in Ontario and the federal jurisdiction may be eligible for severance pay in addition to pay in lieu of notice in certain termination situations. In Ontario, employees with five or more years of service may be eligible for severance pay *if* the employer's annual Ontario payroll is $2.5 million or more *or* if the employer is closing down the business and 50 or more employees will be losing their jobs within a six-month period. The amount of the severance pay is one week's pay for each year of employment (maximum 26 weeks). In the federal jurisdiction, employees who have been employed for twelve months or more receive the greater of a) two days wages per year of employment, and b) five days' wages.

Pay for Mass Layoffs The provinces of British Columbia, Manitoba, Ontario, New Brunswick, and Newfoundland require additional pay to be provided when a layoff of 50 or more employees occurs. In Nova Scotia and Saskatchewan, additional pay is required if ten or more employees are being laid off. The amount of additional pay ranges from eight weeks to eighteen weeks, depending on the province and the number of employees being laid off.

Insurance Benefits

Life Insurance

group life insurance
Insurance provided at lower rates for all employees, including new employees, regardless of health or physical condition.

Virtually all employers provide **group life insurance** plans for their employees. As a group, employees can obtain lower rates than if they bought such insurance as individuals. And group plans usually contain a provision for coverage of all employees—including new ones—regardless of health or physical condition.

In most cases the employer pays 100 percent of the base premium, which usually provides life insurance equal to about two years' salary. Additional life insurance coverage is sometimes made available to employees, on an optional, employee-paid basis. Accidental death and dismemberment coverage provides a fixed lump-sum benefit in addition to life insurance benefits when death is accidental. It also provides a range of benefits in case of accidental loss of limbs or sight, and is often paid for by the employer. In some cases the cost of even the base premium is split 50:50 or 80:20 between the employer and employee, respectively. In general, there are three key policy areas to be addressed: the benefits-paid schedule (benefits are usually tied to the annual earnings of the employee); supplemental benefits (continued life insurance coverage after retirement, and so on); and financing (the amount and percent that the employee contributes).[10]

Supplementary Health Care/Medical Insurance

Most employers provide supplementary health care/medical insurance (over and above that provided by provincial health care plans) to their employees. Along with life insurance and long-term disability, these benefits form the cornerstone of almost all benefit programs.[11] Supplementary health care insurance is aimed at providing protection against medical costs arising from accidents or illness occurring from off-the-job causes.

Most supplementary health insurance plans provide insurance at group rates, which are usually lower than individual rates and are generally available to all employees—including new ones—regardless of health or physical condition. Supplementary health care plans also provide major medical coverage to meet medical expenses not covered by government health care plans including prescription drugs, private or semi-private hospital rooms, private duty nursing, physiotherapy, medical supplies, ambulance services, and so on that result from normal health problems or from long-term or serious illnesses

Many employers also sponsor health-related insurance plans covering expenses like vision care, hearing aids, and dental services. In most employer-sponsored dental plans, participants must pay a specified amount of **deductible** dental expenses (typically $25 or $50 each year) before the plan benefits begin. In a majority of cases, the participants in such plans have premiums paid for entirely by their employers.[12]

deductible
The annual amount of health/dental expenses an employee must pay before insurance benefits will be paid.

Reducing Health Benefit Costs Dramatic increases in health care costs are the biggest issue facing benefits managers in Canada today, as shown in **Figure 14.3**. A Conference Board of Canada survey of 401 organizations found that the cost of employer-provided health care benefits rose 26 percent from 1990 to 1994.[13] A KPMG survey of 236 organizations found that the average annual cost per employee for health benefits rose by 75 percent between 1994 and 1996 to over $560 (over $1 000 in manufacturing firms).[14] The main reasons for these increases are increased use of expensive new drugs, rising drug utilization, and "cost cutting" reductions in coverage under provincial health care plans.[15] In a recent development, Quebec has legislated that every employer must provide a drug plan with certain minimum coverage, or else they must cancel all of their other health, accident, sickness, and disability plans.[16]

Many Canadian managers now find controlling and reducing health care costs topping their to-do lists. The focus is usually on prescription drugs, which represent 75 percent of medical benefit costs in Canada.[17] Health Canada estimates that private sector employers' drug costs have increased by 114 percent from 1984 to 1994.[18] As a result, many employers have been changing their medical plans. A study of 150 Canadian organizations by consultants William M. Mercer in 1996 found that three out of four organizations intended to change health care benefits and almost half had made at least one change to drug benefits over the previous three years.[19] These changes so far have reflected the Canadian traditions of freedom of choice and independence of professional clinical judgment, rather than the American style "managed care" approach to diagnosis and treatment.[20]

Figure 14.3
Growth in Employer Health Care Costs
Source: Peter Gorham and Keith Morrallee, "Paying the Pill Bills," *Benefits Canada* (December, 1996), p. 27. Used with permission.

coinsurance
The percentage of expenses (in excess of the deductible) that are paid for by the insurance plan.

The simplest approach to reducing health benefit costs is to increase the amount of health care costs paid by employees. This can be accomplished by increasing employee premiums, increasing deductibles, reducing company **coinsurance** levels, instituting or lowering annual maximums on some services, or even eliminating coverage for spouses, private hospital rooms, and other benefits.[21] In the U.S., smokers pay more for benefits than their non-smoking coworkers, but this has not yet happened in Canada. A positive approach, such as providing rewards for employees in smoking cessation programs, may be more in line with the Canadian tradition of freedom of choice.[22]

Another cost-reduction strategy is to publish a restricted list of the drugs that will be paid for under the plan, to encourage the use of generic rather than more expensive brand-name drugs. New drugs may not be covered if equally effective, cheaper alternatives are available. This approach should be combined with employee education to effectively manage the demand for drugs.

A third approach is health promotion. In-house newsletters can caution workers to take medication properly and advertise programs on weight management, smoking cessation, exercise classes, on-site massage therapists, nutrition counselling, and other wellness programs.[23] After ten years of providing an on-site exercise program for employees, Canada Life Insurance Company found that absenteeism dropped 24 percent for employees who exercised two to three times per week.[24] Husky Injection Molding Systems Ltd. in Bolton, Ontario, believes that their low absenteeism rate of 1.2 percent is due in part to their corporate fitness centre.[25] Employee assistance programs can help to combat alcohol and drug addiction, and provide stress-management counselling. Some companies are developing innovative approaches to creating a healthy work force. In Timmins, Ontario, several local employers have banded together with physicians and pharmacists to develop educational programs to increase wellness of employees. The result has been a greater awareness of drug costs by employees, who now know enough about drug ingredient costs to consider less expensive alternative medication.[26]

An on-site employee fitness centre at Husky Injection Molding Systems in Bolton, Ontrio.

www.benefitslink.com
Benefits Link

A fourth approach is risk assessment programs. Such programs are being used by the Canadian Imperial Bank of Commerce and other companies. A third party conducts a confidential survey of the health history and lifestyle choices of employees in order to identify common health risk factors, such as those associated with heart disease or mental health, so that problem-specific programs can be implemented.[27] Pharmaceutical companies such as Bayer Inc. and Astra Pharma Inc. have moved into the business of helping organizations manage benefit costs.[28]

Another concern is the cost of health benefits provided to retirees. These benefits are more common in large organizations, and typically include life insurance, drugs, and private/semi-private hospital coverage. Some continue coverage to a surviving spouse.[29] A 1996 survey found that 35 percent of employers in the private sector and 50 percent of public sector employers provide retiree benefits.[30] Retiree benefits costs are already exceeding the costs for active employees in some organizations, partly due to encouragement of early retirement during the recent recession/restructuring.[31] As the baby-boom generation retires with increasing life expectancies, these costs will increase rapidly. Employers can cut costs by increasing retiree contributions, reducing coverage levels, increasing deductibles, tightening eligibility requirements, and reducing maximum payouts.[32] A 1994 study found that Canadian employers had an unreported liability of $52 billion for retiree benefits. Since January 1998, Canadian employers have been required to disclose these liabilities in their financial statements.[33]

Long-Term Disability

Long-term disability insurance is aimed at providing income protection or compensation for loss of income due to long-term illness or injury that is not work-related. The disability payments usually begin when normal short-term disability/sick leave is used up and may continue to provide income to age 65 or beyond.[34] The disability benefits usually range from 50 percent to 75 percent of the employee's base pay.

An average disability claim can cost up to $78 000 per injury[35], including production delays, product and material damage due to inexperienced replacement staff, clerical and administrative time, and loss of expertise, on top of the actual benefit payments. Therefore, many employers are taking a preventive approach to managing disability claims, particularly stress-related problems, which account for 25 percent of long-term disability applications. Some are using screening and testing during job interviews to assess each applicant's ability to cope with stress. In many cases, the cost of accommodating an employee's disability can be quite modest. For example, disabled employees unable to type can use a voice recognition system for personal computers, which now costs less than $1 000.[36] Employers are also monitoring claims more closely to look for ways to get the employees back to work faster by using modified work and reduced work weeks. Return-to-work committees can facilitate an earlier return to work by designing rehabilitation programs based on medical reports of physical limitations.

Managing the Cost of AIDS   By now, the fatal nature of AIDS—Acquired Immune Deficiency Syndrome—is unfortunately well known to everyone.[37] However, in addition to the human suffering caused by AIDS, its potential impact on insurance companies and employers' insurance plans must be considered. The average estimated claims payout per AIDS case was about $100 000 in 1994, a considerable sum. As new drugs are developed to prolong the lives of AIDS sufferers, employers' drug costs will increase; however, hospital costs and disability claims costs will be reduced.

The problem is that reining in these costs is hampered by several unique aspects of the AIDS disease. While at the present time it is always terminal, intensive medical intervention is usually necessary for only short periods of time. For most of the time, the need is more custodial and can often be as well administered at home or in non-hospital facilities as inside hospitals. While reduced costs are therefore possible with alternative treatment facilities, some employers' medical plans don't cover them. Such plans are thus self-defeating in requiring more expensive care where it is not needed.

There are psychological barriers that inhibit early diagnosis and more cost-effective treatment. Many AIDS sufferers are reluctant to discuss their illness with their employers for fear of losing their jobs and/or their insurance benefits even though they are legally protected under human rights legislation. At the same time, the reactions of fearful coworkers to AIDS sufferers often further impede open discussions of the problem.

Several North American insurance companies have concluded that the best way to control the cost of AIDS is to rethink the benefits plans with an eye toward providing required care in the least costly way. This often means treating the AIDS sufferer in his or her home and allowing the cost to be paid under the benefits plan (as is not usually allowed now). Thus, the emphasis will increasingly be on *individual case management* (ICM). The plan will be individualized, taking into consideration the patient's ability to care for himself or herself, the availability of others who are able to help in the person's treatment, and the age and condition of the patient. A case history can illustrate this:

> *The patient was admitted to the hospital . . . suffering from a late stage of my-lobacterium intracellular, an opportunistic disease most commonly found among AIDS patients. After six weeks in the hospital, the patient was discharged to an intensive home care routine costing $390 per day. If he had remained in the hospital, the cost would have been $1 100 per day. The attempt at home care lasted only 12 days, at which time the patient's condition degenerated to a point where permanent hospitalization was necessary. Even this modest success with home care resulted in a savings to the plan of $8 520.*[38]

In summary, steps recommended by one expert to help contain the health care benefits costs associated with AIDS are as follows:

Medical plans should be expanded to provide coverage for outpatient services and alternate treatment facilities.

Individual care management, possibly through an employee assistance program (described later in this chapter), should be used to find the most appropriate type of care for each individual.

Employers should not stigmatize those employees who admit they have AIDS.[39]

Mental Health Benefits Costs associated with mental health problems relate to short- and long-term disability, and increased drug usage.[40] Psychiatric disabilities are the fastest growing of all occupational disabilities, with depression being the most common. On any given day, one in every twenty workers is considered depressed. Overall, depression, anxiety, and stress account for 20 percent to 25 percent of disability claims. At the Canadian Imperial Bank of Commerce, short- and long-term disability claims for depression have been growing steadily since 1994, and anti-depressants are one of the most common drug claims. A U.S. study showed that the average time lost per episode of depression is 40 days, meaning that depression accounts for more days off that any other chronic illness. For the employer, the bottom line is that the cost of mental health benefits is substantial. Many companies are trying to help reduce costs with prevention and early intervention programs including psychiatric counselling and peer-support groups.[41]

Retirement Benefits

Pension Plans

pension plans
Plans that provide a fixed sum when employees reach a predetermined retirement age or when they can no longer work due to disability.

defined benefit pension plan
A plan that contains a formula for determining retirement benefits.

defined contribution pension plan
A plan in which the employer's contribution to the employees' retirement fund is specified.

Expenditures for pension plans, at 5.4 percent and 11.4 percent of payroll for the private and public sectors respectively, represents the single most expensive employer-sponsored benefit.[42] Employer-sponsored pension plans are intended to supplement an employee's government-sponsored retirement benefits.

There are many types of **pension plans.**[43] Most fall into two categories—defined benefit pension plans and defined contribution pension plans. A **defined benefit pension plan** contains a formula for determining retirement benefits so that the actual benefits to be received are defined ahead of time. For example, the plan might include a formula that designates a dollar amount or a percentage of annual salary for predicting the individual's eventual pension. A **defined contribution pension plan** specifies what contribution the employer will make to a retirement fund set up for the employee. The defined contribution plan does not define the eventual benefit amount, only the periodic contribution to the plan. In a defined benefit plan, the employee knows ahead of time what his or her retirement benefits will be upon retirement. With a defined contribution plan, the employee cannot be sure of his or her retirement benefits. Those benefits depend on both the amounts contributed to the fund and the retirement fund's investment earnings.

There are two other types of defined contribution plans. Under a group registered retirement savings plan (Group RRSP), employees can have a portion of their compensation, which would otherwise be paid in cash, put into an RRSP by the employer. This results in a pretax reduction in salary, so the employee isn't taxed on those set-aside dollars until after he or she retires (or removes the money from the plan). One attraction of RRSPs is that employees may have a range of investment options for the RRSP funds including mutual funds and bond funds.

Most employers do not match all or a portion of what the employee contributes to the Group RRSP because employer contributions are considered taxable income to employees. Instead, the employer often establishes a **deferred profit sharing plan** (DPSP), and contributes a portion of company profits into the DPSP fund, where an account is set up for each employee. No employee contributions to a DPSP are allowed under Canadian tax law. Group RRSP/DPSP combinations are popular in Canada, because no tax is paid until money is received from the plans at the time of the employee's death or termination of employment (at retirement or otherwise).

It is expected that defined benefit plans will remain in organizations where long tenure is the norm. Defined contribution plans are ideal for a relatively young work force of highly skilled professional and technical people who expect to work with several employers over the course of their careers.[44]

The entire area of pension planning is complicated, partly because of the laws governing pensions. For example, companies want to ensure that their pension contributions are tax deductible and must, therefore, adhere to the Income Tax Act. Each province and the federal jurisdiction also has a law governing employer-sponsored pension plans.

While an employer usually must develop a pension plan to meet the organization's unique needs, there are several key policy issues to consider.[45]

> *Membership requirements.* For example, what is the minimum age or minimum years of service at which employees become eligible for a pension?
>
> *Benefit formula.* This usually ties the pension to the employee's final earnings, or an average of his or her last three or four years' earnings.
>
> *Retirement requirements.* Although 65 is often considered a standard retirement age, employer plans may permit early or late retirement. In companies such as General Motors, for example, only a small proportion of production and office workers retire as late as 65.[46] Partly due to union pressure and partly because early retirement helps open up jobs for younger employees, many employers now encourage early retirement. For example, some plans call for "30 and out." This permits an employee to retire after 30 years of continuous service, regardless of the person's age. In some cases employees can retire with reduced pensions after 20 years of continuous service regardless of the employee's age.[47]
>
> *Funding.* The question of how the plan is to be funded is another key issue. One aspect is whether the plan will be contributory or noncontributory. In the former, contributions to the pension fund are made by both employees and the employer. In a noncontributory fund only the employer contributes.
>
> *Vesting.* Employee **vesting** rights is another critical issue in pension planning. Vesting refers to the money that the employer has placed in the pension fund that cannot be forfeited for any reason. The employees' contributions are always theirs and can never be forfeited. An employee is vested when he or she has met the requirements set out in the plan whereby, upon termination of employment, he or she will receive future benefits based on the contributions made to the plan by the employer on behalf of the employee. In most provinces, pension legislation requires that employer contributions be vested once the employee has

deferred profit-sharing plan
A plan in which a certain amount of company profits is credited to each employee's account, payable at retirement, termination, or death.

vesting
Provision that employer money placed in a pension fund cannot be forfeited for any reason.

completed two years of service. Plans may vest more quickly than required by law. If the employee terminates employment before being vested, he or she may only be entitled to a refund of his or her own contributions, plus interest. Once an employee is vested, all contributions are "locked-in", and cannot be withdrawn by the employee on termination of employment, that is, employees must wait until retirement to receive a pension from the plan. Most plans permit the employee to transfer the amount into a locked-in RRSP (see the next section on portability) but the money cannot be accessed until retirement.

Portability Canadian employers today are being required by pension legislation to make their pensions more "portable" for employees upon termination of employment. This means that employees in defined contribution plans can take the money in their company pension account to a new employer's plan or roll it over into a locked-in RRSP. For defined benefit plans, the lump sum value of the benefit earned can be transferred. **Portability** represents a shift in pension planning away from the idea of a pension serving to keep workers from changing jobs.

Pension law, today's needs for flexible staffing, and the realities of the ongoing corporate restructurings and downsizings are causing more employers to make their pension plans portable. This is often facilitated by switching to defined contribution plans, since defined benefits plans are geared to what the person will receive upon retirement from the firm, although he or she may not see any prospects of staying with the firm until retirement. Other policy options that can reduce the loss of employees' pensions during downsizing include providing extra years of credit in defined benefit plans and extra contributions in defined contribution plans for laid-off workers, and no longer granting lower-percentage cost-of-living adjustments for retirees who have less service or who end employment before retirement.[48]

portability
A provision that employees who change jobs can transfer the lump-sum value of the pension they have earned to a locked-in RRSP or their new employer's pension plan.

Recent Trends

early retirement incentives
Offers to current employees aimed at encouraging them to retire early, perhaps even with the same pensions they would expect if they retired at, say, age 65.

early retirement window
A type of early retirement incentive by which employees are encouraged to retire early, the incentive being liberal pension benefits plus perhaps a cash payment.

Retirement benefits are getting a new twist with so-called **early retirement incentives**—early retirement windows and other voluntary separation arrangements. These are aimed at avoiding dismissals by offering special retirement packages to long-term employees.

Early Retirement Windows Most of these plans take the form of **early retirement window** arrangements in which specific employees (often age 50+) are eligible to participate. The "window" represents the fact that the company opens up (for a limited time only) the chance for an employee to retire earlier than usual. The financial incentive is usually a combination of improved or liberalized pension benefits plus a cash payment. One expert concludes that early retirement has become the method of choice for reducing mid-management and white-collar work forces, with about 13 percent of 362 employers surveyed providing such early retirement windows in one recent year.[49]

Other voluntary separation plans operate more like bonuses for leaving and may apply even to recent hires. The offerings are usually made regardless of age. The financial incentive is typically a cash payment that varies substantially by company but often is in the range of one week's pay per year of service. About one-third of those employees eligible to walk through the early retirement windows typically accept the offer, while about one-fourth of those offered other separation plans do likewise.[50]

Early retirement windows must be used with caution because, unless structured properly, they can be challenged as de facto programs for forcing the discharge of older employees against their will.[51] While it is generally legal to use incentives like early retirement benefits to encourage individuals to choose early retirement, the employee's decision must be voluntary.

www.retireweb.com
Financial Planning for Retirement

Employers must therefore exercise caution in encouraging employees to take early retirement. In particular, the employee's decision to do so must be knowing and voluntary, and the agreement cannot provide for the release of prospective rights or claims, nor be an exchange for consideration that includes benefits to which the employee was already entitled. The employee should be given ample opportunity to think over the agreement and seek advice from legal counsel.[52] The idea of phased-in retirement, whereby employees gradually ease into retirement using reduced work days and shortened work weeks has been in place in Europe for some time. There has been some discussion about this approach in North America, but so far it has not been widely used.[53] The Canadian Auto Workers have negotiated phased retirement plans with Chrysler, Ford, and General Motors, as well as with Air Canada and Canadian Airlines.[54]

Employee Services

While an employer's time off and insurance and retirement benefits account for the main part of its benefits costs, many employers also provide a range of services including personal services (such as counselling), job-related services (such as childcare facilities), and executive perquisites (such as company cars and planes for executives).

Personal Services

First, many companies provide personal services that most employees need at one time or another. These include credit unions, legal services, counselling, and social and recreational opportunities.

Credit Unions   Credit unions are usually separate businesses established with the assistance of the employer. Employees usually become members of a credit union by purchasing a share of the credit union's stock for $5 or $10. Members can then deposit savings that accrue interest at a rate determined by the credit union's board of directors. Perhaps more important to most employees, loan eligibility and the rate of interest paid on the loan are usually more favourable than those found in banks and finance companies.

Counselling Services   Employers are also providing a wider range of counselling services to employees. These include financial counselling (for example, in terms of how to overcome existing indebtedness problems); family counselling (for marital problems and so on); career counselling (in terms of analyzing one's aptitudes and deciding on a career); job placement counselling (for helping terminated or disenchanted employees find new jobs); and preretirement counselling (aimed at preparing retiring employees for what many find is the trauma of retiring). Many employers also make available to employees a full range of legal counselling through legal insurance plans.[55]

employee assistance program (EAP)
A company-sponsored program to help employees cope with personal prolems that are interfering with or have the potential to interfere with their job performance, as well as issues affecting their well-being and/or that of their families.

Employee Assistance Programs (EAPs)   As explained in chapter 1, an **employee assistance plan (EAP)** is a formal employer program that provides employees with counselling and/or treatment programs for problems such as mental health issues, marital/family problems, work/career stress, legal problems, and substance abuse. The number of EAPs in Canada is growing because they are a proactive way for organizations to reduce absentccism and disability costs. There are four basic models in use today.[56] In the *in-house model,* the entire assistance staff is employed by the company. In the *out-of-house model,* the company contracts a vendor to provide employee assistance staff and services in its own offices, the company's offices, or a combination of both. In the *consortium model,* several companies pool their resources to develop a collaborative EAP program. Finally, in the *affiliate model,* a vendor already under contract to the employer subcontracts to a local professional rather than using its own salaried staff. This is usually to service employees in a client company location in which the EAP vendors do not have an office. Key ingredients for ensuring a successful EAP program include:[57]

Specify goals and philosophy. The short- and long-term goals expected to be achieved for both the employee and employer should be specified.

Develop a policy statement. Next, a comprehensive EAP policy statement should be prepared. This should define the purpose of the program, employee eligibility, the roles and responsibility of various personnel in the organization, and procedures for taking advantage of the plan. Recently, employers such as B.C. Hydro and Petro-Canada are linking EAP services with diversity initiatives by providing culturally-sensitive EAP staff.

Ensure professional staffing. Careful consideration should be given to the professional and government licensing requirements as they apply to the people staffing these facilities. If necessary, the services of an experienced person should be retained to assist the firm in drawing up job specifications for the required staff.

Maintain confidential record-keeping systems. Everyone involved with the EAP, including support staff, must understand the importance of confidentiality. Furthermore, files must be locked, access limited and monitored, and identifying information (which might otherwise find itself in an employee's computerized records) kept to a minimum.

Provide supervisory training. While this needn't involve extensive training, supervisors should certainly understand the program's policies, procedures, and services as well as the company's policies regarding confidentiality. And perhaps more important, all supervisors should get some training regarding the outward symptoms of problems like alcoholism as well as how to encourage employees to use the services of the EAP.

Be aware of legal issues. For example, in most jurisdictions counsellors must disclose suspicions of child abuse to an appropriate government agency: In-house counsellors thus put the company in the legal position of having to comply in such an instance. Three ways to safeguard the firm's interests here include retaining legal advice on establishing an EAP, carefully screening the credentials of any staff hired, and obtaining professional liability insurance for the EAP.

Measure effectiveness. An EAP can be evaluated by employee surveys or by external consultants. Tracking costs related to absenteeism, short-term disability, long-term disability, and health care costs can provide valuable evidence of EAP effectiveness. One Canadian study found that short-term disability cases averaged 12.5 days without an EAP and 6.5 days with an EAP.[58]

Other Personal Services   Finally, some employers also provide various social and recreational opportunities for their employees, including company-sponsored athletic events, dances, annual summer picnics, craft activities, and parties.[59] In practice, the benefits offered are limited only by creativity in thinking up new benefits. One study of innovative benefits, for instance, found Canadian companies offering the following benefits, among others:

Lakefront vacations—the company owns lakeshore property and rents cottages and campsites to employees at low rates.

Weight loss program—several companies subsidize costs of weight loss workshops.

Adoption benefit—companies pay amounts of $500 to $1 500 per child for adoption costs.

Company country club—the company maintains a golf course, tennis courts, and football and baseball fields.

Cultural subsidy—the company will pay 33 percent of the cost of tickets to cultural activities such as theater, ballet, museum, and so on up to $100 per year per employee.

Lunch-and-learn program—interested employees can attend lunchtime talks on a variety of subjects, including stress management, weight control, computer literacy, fashion, and travel.

Home assistance—employees may use up to $1 500 of their annual profit-sharing award to save for a down payment on a house or to reduce their down payment, up to a maximum of $15 000.[60]

Job-Related Services

Job-related services aimed directly at helping employees perform their jobs, such as assistance in moving and daycare centres, constitute a second group of services.

Subsidized Childcare   Today large numbers of Canadian women with children under 6 years old are in the work force. Subsidized daycare is one increasingly popular benefit stemming directly from that trend.[61] Many employers simply investigate the daycare facilities in their communities and recommend certain ones to interested employees. But more employers are setting up company-sponsored daycare facilities themselves, both to attract young mothers to the payroll and to reduce absenteeism. Often (as at the IKEA Canada daycare facility in Burlington, Ontario), the centre is a private venture run separately from but paid for by the firm. Where successful, the daycare facility is usually close to the workplace (often in the same building), and the employer provides 50 percent to 75 percent of the operating costs.

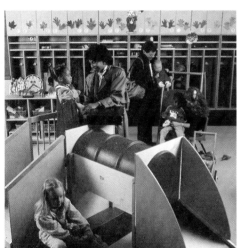

Subsidizing daycare facilities for children of employees has many benefits for the employer, including lower employee absenteeism.

A U.S. survey found that employers can gain considerably by instituting subsidized daycare centres. Increased ability to attract employees, lower absenteeism, improved morale, favourable publicity, and lower turnover are some of the benefits attributed to daycare programs.[62] To make sure the program is worthwhile and that its costs do not get out of hand, however, good planning is needed. This often starts with a questionnaire to survey employees in order to answer such questions as: "What would you be willing to pay for care for one child in a childcare centre near work?" and "Have you missed work during the past six months because you needed to find new care arrangements?" To date the evidence regarding the actual effects of employer-sponsored childcare on employee absenteeism, turnover, productivity, recruitment, or job satisfaction is positive, particularly with respect to reducing obstacles to coming to work and improving workers' attitudes.[63]

Eldercare   With the average age of the Canadian population rising, eldercare is increasingly a concern for many employers and individuals. Eldercare is designed to help employees who must help elderly parents or relatives who are not fully able to care for themselves.[64] Eldercare is expected to become a more common workplace issue than childcare as we move into the 21st century.

From the employer's point of view, eldercare benefits are important for much the same reason as are childcare benefits: the responsibility for caring for an aging relative can and will affect the employee's performance at work.[65] A number of employers are, therefore, instituting eldercare benefits, including flexible hours, long-term care insurance coverage, and company-sponsored eldercare centres.

A typical program could involve:

1. A lunchtime eldercare fair at which community organizations involved with providing services to older people explain to employees the services that are available.

2. Lunchtime information sessions for employees aimed at explaining various aspects of eldercare, such as independent versus dependent living and housing, the aging process, and legal concerns.

3. Distribution of publications listing potential problems associated with eldercare in a question-and-answer format.[66]

Diversity Counts
In Building a Family-Friendly Benefits Package

More and more companies recognize that they need family-friendly benefits to successfully recruit and retain good employees and to maintain high productivity. In a nutshell, family-friendly benefits are benefits options that make it easier for parents of young children to be productive workers. Such benefits are increasingly necessary in a decade in which about two-thirds of the new entrants into the work force will be women and in which about 60 percent of working men have working wives.[1] Many benefits already described in this chapter may in fact be considered family-friendly benefits options; a summary of family-friendly options includes:

1. *Building an on-site or near-site daycare facility.* Some firms, such as Husky Injection Molding Systems Ltd. in Bolton, Ontario, have built such facilities. Although construction costs can range up to $5 000 000, close proximity to the workplace makes such sites very popular with employees.

2. *Partially funding or subsidizing a near-site daycare facility.* Doing so can avoid many of the costs, liabilities, and management problems of on-site centres while providing many of the advantages of a dedicated facility for the firm's employees.

3. *Providing a dependent-care resource and referral service for employees.* With this very popular service employers pay a small per-employee fee to contract with a referral service that provides dependent-care information to employees. The referral service might advise not just on childcare but on eldercare needs and services, too.

4. *Subsidizing dependent-care costs of employees.* Some employers reimburse a percentage of employee dependent-care costs, sometimes up to 100 percent, depending on the company.

5. *Providing, arranging for, or subsidizing temporary and emergency dependent-care.* Breakdowns in childcare arrangements represents one of the most common reasons parents lose time from work.[2] Some employers therefore help employees by reimbursing them for childcare expenses stemming from emergency or nonroutine events; some even provide all or partial payment to fund special activities such as summer camps for older children.

6. *Offering flextime, job sharing, and work-at-home arrangements.* Work arrangements discussed elsewhere in this book such as flexible work schedules can help reduce childcare conflicts and make it easier for employees to do their jobs.

7. *Allowing use of employee leave days for care of sick children.* Many companies now allow extra days of paid sick leave for care of sick dependents. Others let employees use paid vacation time in small increments such as half-days to facilitate taking children to doctors' appointments or caring for sick dependents.

8. *Offering paid and/or extended leave for mothers and/or fathers after the arrival of a child.* Many employers are offering generous paid leave to mothers and fathers after the birth or adoption of a child, or for serious family medical problems.

9. *Allowing new mothers to phase back to work.* In addition to the paid and unpaid leave benefits, some companies let the new mother phase back to work, perhaps by working only partial days or partial weeks at first.[3]◆

1. This is based on Shirley Hand and Robert Zawacki, "Family-Friendly Benefits: More Than a Frill," *HR Magazine* (October 1994), pp. 79–84. See also C. Davenport "Child Care Solutions for a Harried Work World," *Canadian HR Reporter* (April 21, 1997), p. 16.

2. Caroline Eichman, "Surveys Reveal Needs for Work/Family Benefits—By Both Employees and Employers," *Employment Relations Today* (Winter 1992/93), pp. 389–95.

3. For a further discussion see, for example, Douglas Hall and Victoria Parker, "The Role of Workplace Flexibility in Managing Diversity," *Organizational Dynamics* 22, no. 1 (1993), pp. 5–18.

Subsidized Employee Transportation   Some employers also provide subsidized employee transportation.[67] An employer can negotiate with a transit system to provide free year-round transportation to its employees. Other employers just facilitate employee car pooling, perhaps by acting as the central clearing house to identify employees from the same geographic areas who work the same hours.

Food Services   Food services are provided in some form by many employers; they let employees purchase meals, snacks, or coffee, usually at relatively low prices. Most food operations are nonprofit, and, in fact, some firms provide food services below cost. The advantages to the employee are clear, and for the employer the service can ensure that employees do not drift away for long lunch hours. Even employers that do not provide full dining facilities generally make available food services such as coffee wagons or vending machines for the convenience of employees.

Educational Subsidies   Educational subsidies such as tuition refunds have long been a popular benefit for employees seeking to continue or complete their education. Payments range from all tuition and expenses to some percentage of expenses to a flat fee per year of, say, $500 to $600. Some employers have experimented with providing in-house educational programs, such as a Master of Business Administration degree program, in which college/university faculty teach courses on the employer's premises. Other in-house educational programs include remedial work in basic literacy and training for improved supervisory skills. As far as tuition reimbursement programs are concerned, most companies pay for courses directly related to an employee's present job. Many also reimburse tuition for non–job-related courses (such as a secretary taking an accounting class) that pertain to the company business and those that are part of a degree or diploma program.[68]

Executive Perquisites

Perquisites (perks, for short) are usually given to only a few top executives. Perks can range from the substantial to the almost insignificant. A bank chairperson may have a chauffeur-driven limousine, and use of a bank-owned property in the Caribbean. Executives of large companies often use a corporate jet for business travel. At the other extreme, perks may entail little more than the right to use a company car.[69]

A multitude of popular perks falls between these extremes. These include: management loans (which typically enable senior officers to use their stock options); salary guarantees (also known as *golden parachutes*), to protect executives even if their firms are the targets of acquisitions or mergers; financial counselling (to handle top executives' investment programs); and relocation benefits, often including subsidized mortgages, purchase of the executive's current house, and payment for the actual move.[70] A potpourri of other executive perks includes time off with pay (such as sabbaticals), outplacement assistance, company cars, chauffeured limousines, security systems, company planes and yachts, executive dining rooms, physical fitness programs, legal services, tax assistance, liberal expense accounts, club memberships, season tickets, credit cards, and subsidized children's education. Employers have many ways of making their hard-working executives' lives as pleasant as possible!

Indeed, this tendency continues in the face of growing populist sentiment and despite a decade of corporate downsizings, restructurings, and more restrictive tax laws.[71] Some of the most visible status perks such as executive apartments and suites are more rare as are company planes and full-time chauffeurs. However, many companies still provide executives with personal or leased automobiles, supplemental life insurance, and reserved parking spots.

Flexible Benefits Programs

"Variety is the spice of life," the saying goes. This applies very well to company benefits, since the benefits that one worker finds attractive may be unattractive to another. As a result, there is a trend toward **flexible benefits programs** that permit employees to develop individualized benefits packages for themselves by choosing the benefits options they prefer.

Employee Preferences for Various Benefits

Two researchers conducted a study that provides some insight into employee preferences for various benefits.[72] They mailed questionnaires listing seven possible benefit options to 400 employees of a public utility company. Completed questionnaires were received from 149 employees (about 38 percent of those surveyed). The seven benefit options were as follows:

1. A five-day workweek with shorter working days of 7 hours and 35 minutes.
2. A four-day workweek consisting of 9 hours and 30 minutes each day.
3. Ten Fridays off each year with full pay. This includes ten three-day weekends per year in addition to any three-day weekends previously scheduled.
4. Early retirement through accumulating ten days per year until retirement age. The retirement age will be 65 minus the number of accumulated days. Full pay will continue until age 65 is reached.
5. Additional vacation of two weeks per year with full pay, added to the present vacation.
6. A pension increase of $75 per month.
7. Family dental insurance fully paid for by the company.

Finally, employees were also asked to show their relative preference for a pay increase of 5 percent in addition to any general wage increase negotiated.

Results   Two extra weeks of vacation was clearly the most preferred benefit, while the pay increase was second. Overall, the shorter workday was by far the least preferred benefit option.

But this is not the full story; the employee's age, marital status, and sex influenced his or her choice of benefits. For example, younger employees significantly favoured the family dental plan over older employees. Younger employees also showed a greater preference for the four-day work week. As might be expected, preference for the pension option increased significantly with employee age. Married workers showed more preference for the pension increase and for the family dental plan than did single workers. The preference for the family dental plan increased sharply as the number of dependents increased. It should be noted, though, that the survey did not include supplementary health care benefits (which are a major concern to all employees today) as a benefit option.

Because employees do have different preferences for benefits, an increasing number of employers let employees individualize their benefits plans.[73]

The Flexible Benefits Approach

Flexible benefits plans were initially called cafeteria plans because (as in a cafeteria) employees could spend their benefits allowances on a choice of benefits options. The idea is to allow the employee to put together his or her own benefit package, subject to two constraints. First, the employer must carefully limit total cost for each total benefits package. Second, each benefit plan must include certain nonoptional items. These include, for example, Canada/Quebec Pension Plan, workers' compensation, and employment insurance.

Subject to these two constraints, employees can pick and choose from the available options. Thus, a young parent might opt for the company's life and dental insurance plans, while an older employee opts for an improved pension plan. The list of possible options might include many of the benefits discussed in this chapter: vacations, insurance benefits, pension plans, educational services, and so on.

As an example, a flexible plan was instituted at Unilever Canada on January 1, 1996. Unilever employees covered by the plan automatically got core benefits including provincial health care, life insurance of 50 percent of their base pay, business travel accident insurance of three times their base pay, short-term disability that pays 100 percent or 70 percent of base pay (depending on length of service), and long-term disability benefits of 70 percent of base pay that begin after a 26-week absence. In addition, the company also provides flexible benefit credits that the employee can use to pay for extra benefits including medical coverage, dental care, life insurance, and accident insurance. Any leftover credits can be taken in cash or deposited in a health care spending account to pay extra health and dental expenses. Employees may supplement their flexible benefit credits with payroll deduction. Those employees who wish to may opt out of the plan and take their credits as cash (which will constitute taxable income).

Advantages and disadvantages of flexible benefit programs are summarized in **Figure 14.4**.[74] The flexibility is of course the main advantage. Another advantage is long term cost management by limiting the amount provided to employees to buy benefits. One problem is that implementing a flexible benefits plan can involve substantial clerical and administrative costs. Each employee's benefits have to be carefully priced and periodically updated, and even a medium-sized firm would have to computerize the administration of its plan.[75] Although most employees favour flexible benefits, some don't like to spend time choosing among available options, and some choose inappropriate benefits. Various firms have developed computerized games such as one called "FlexSelect." This is a user-friendly interactive program for personal computers that helps employees make choices under a flexible benefits program.[76]

www.benefitsdesign.com
Benefits Design Inc.

**Figure 14.4
Advantages and Disadvantages of Flexible Benefit Programs**

Source: Milkovich and Newman, *Compensation* (Burr Ridge, IL: Irwin, 1996), p. 425.

ADVANTAGES

1. Employees choose packages that best satisfy their unique needs.
2. Flexible benefits help firms meet the *changing* needs of a *changing* work force.
3. Increased involvement of employees and families improves understanding of benefits.
4. Flexible plans make introduction of new benefits less costly. The new option is added merely as one among a wide variety of elements from which to choose.
5. Cost containment—the organization sets the dollar maximum. Employee chooses within that constraint.

DISADVANTAGES

1. Employees make bad choices and find themselves not covered for predictable emergencies.
2. Administrative burdens and expenses increase.
3. Adverse selection—employees pick only benefits they will use. The subsequent high benefit utilization increases its cost.

Although there are only about 150 flexible benefit plans in Canada,[77] they are slowly increasing in popularity. Thus it may be reasonable to assume that the pros outweigh the cons.

Benefits Administration

Whether it is a flexible benefits plan or a more traditional one, benefits administration is a challenge. Even in a relatively small company with 40 to 50 employees, the administrative problems of keeping track of the benefits status of each employee can be a time-consuming task as employees are hired and separated, and as they utilize or want to change their benefits. Even a fairly straightforward problem like keeping track of who is eligible for vacations and when becomes a chore when a lot of employees are involved. As a result, most companies at least make use of some sort of benefits spreadsheet (see the accompanying box) to facilitate tracking benefits. Others use packaged software to update information like vacation eligibility and to trigger, say, a memo to a supervisor when one of the employees in his or her department is overdue for some time off. Another approach is outsourcing benefits administration, including record keeping and administration, and participant communication, to a third party expert. The major advantages are greater efficiency and consistency, and enhanced service.[78]

Keeping Employees Informed

Benefits communication, particularly regarding pension plans, is increasingly important as a large number of people are approaching retirement.[79] Correct information be provided in a timely, clear manner. Pension legislation across Canada specifies what information must be disclosed to plan members and their spouses. Court challenges concerning information on benefits plans are on the rise, as people's awareness of their right to information grows.[80] Increasingly, organizations

Information Technology and HR
Benefits Spreadsheet

Companies want to control benefit costs. One prerequisite is to be fully aware of how much the benefits offered are actually costing the company on an ongoing basis. A benefits spreadsheet will provide this information.

The spreadsheet should list the following, all in separate columns: each employee (by name or number), the job code (to compare benefits by job category); pay rate (annual, monthly, or hourly, since subsequent spreadsheet formulas will then calculate the appropriate rate for the benefit being considered); department (to compare departments or divisions); and each benefit. In order to accu-

rately track current liabilities for benefits accrued but not used, there should be separate columns for liability and use of these benefits.

For example, consider a report on accrued vacations. In the liability column, calculate the accumulation minus use, times current hourly rate of pay. It is this column that will highlight how costly it is to allow employees to accumulate vacation or sick leave from year to year. If an employee accrues at a rate of $10 an hour now but does not use the vacation time until retirement, the cost of those hours could easily double or treble, as his or her pay rises.◆

are utilizing new technology such as online information data bases, interactive voice response systems, Web sites, and benefits call centres to ensure that up-to-date information is provided in a consistent manner. [81] Computers are increasingly being used to inform employees about their benefits and to answer routine questions that might otherwise go unasked or take up a human resources manager's time.[82] Such questions include: "In which option of the medical plan am I enrolled?" "Who are my designated beneficiaries for the life insurance plan?" "If I retire in two years, what will my monthly retirement income be?" and "What is the current balance in my company savings plan?"

At Hewlett-Packard (Canada) Ltd., an electronic pension booklet is available on the company's intranet, and a pension modelling tool can be accessed through the Web. The modelling software allows employees to fill in their personal information to calculate various "what if" scenarios.[83]

Small Business Applications

Benefits Administration Outsourcing for Small Employers

Benefits administration is a complex and time-consuming activity in any organization. For small employers it can be particularly difficult because it often entails finding someone who is knowledgeable enough about benefits to take on this part-time responsibility as well as having enough expertise to perform other duties. One answer to this problem is to consider comprehensive benefit outsourcing.[1]

Claims processing has traditionally been handled by insurance company staff, but most other administrative functions are handled in-house. Some companies are considering more comprehensive benefits outsourcing where record keeping and communication with employees are performed by an outside provider. The Pension Administration Company of Canada in Mississauga, Ontario, is a benefits outsourcing provider for a number of small- and medium-sized clients. It uses a combination of computer technology and advanced telephony to securely and accurately maintain employee records that are easily accessible by the plan sponsor, the plan members, and their insurer(s). The providers also educate, communicate, and interact with plan members. The intent is to provide a single point of contact that offers the right information at the right time, to produce measurable results for employees.

There are four key advantages to small employers who outsource benefits administration:

1. Improved business focus: company staff can focus on their core business activities

2. Greater efficiencies: outsourcing providers have an established technological infrastructure to streamline administration

3. Compliance/consistency: outsourcing providers are responsible for keeping up-to-date with complex operational rules and updating internal systems accordingly

4. Enhanced service: plan members benefit from quicker turnaround on inquiries, and high quality of transactions.

---

1. This section is based on J. Tompkins, "Moving Out: A Look at Comprehensive Benefit Outsourcing," *Canadian HR Reporter* (May 5, 1997), p. 9.

Building Employee Commitment

Example of a Benefits Program

FedEx Canada is a good example of how benefits can help foster high employee commitment.[1]

The firm's retirement benefits are exceptional. Two plans are provided to help the employee prepare for his or her retirement. The pension plan and employee stock ownership plan combine to provide employees with a good income at retirement. The firm offers a defined contribution pension plan to which employees contribute $2\frac{1}{2}$ percent of their earnings and the company contributes 5 percent. The company contributions are vested after two years of employment.

All full-time permanent or part-time employees who have completed at least three consecutive months of employment with Federal Express Canada can also participate in the firm's employee stock purchase plan. This lets them purchase Federal Express stock without commission through payroll deductions in an amount varying from one percent to a maximum of 10 percent of their total salary. These deductions accumulate for a designated period, at the end of which time Federal Express purchases the shares of stock for all participants.

There's more. The firm's tuition refund program lets any permanent employee with six months of continuous service receive financial reimbursement up to a maximum annual amount for his or her continuing education. Employees earn two weeks of vacation after one year with the firm, three weeks after five years, four weeks after ten years, and five weeks of vacation after twenty years with Federal Express Canada.

But for some employees the best is last. Federal Express participates with other airlines that offer interline benefits in a discount travel program. Permanent employees who have completed a minimum of six months of continuous service are eligible to participate. And in a benefit that most employers would find hard to match, permanent employees are eligible to use FedEx's aircraft jump seats for free travel. Permanent employees may travel for personal or business purposes and make their arrangements through the jump seat reservations office in Memphis, which takes the request by phone and confirms it. There is also a computerized system called "Free Bird" that lets employees make the reservations themselves. Then they just have to be at the airport at least two hours prior to the flight, and away they go.◆

1. This is based on Gary Dessler, *Winning Employee Commitment*, (New York: McGraw-Hill Book Company, 1993), Chapter 9; as well as personal communication with Michelle Kerr, FedEx Canada.

Chapter Review

Summary

1. The financial *incentives* we discussed in chapter 13 are usually paid to specific employees whose work is above standard. Employee *benefits,* on the other hand, are available to all employees based on their membership in the organization. We discussed five categories of benefit plans: government-sponsored benefits, pay for time not worked, insurance benefits, retirement benefits, and employee services.

2. Government-sponsored benefits include employment insurance, Canada/Quebec Pension Plan, workers' compensation, and provincial health care plans.

3. Pay for time not worked includes vacation and holiday pay, short-term disability/ sick leave, leaves of absence, and pay on termination of employment.

4. Insurance and accidental death and dismemberment benefits are another type of employee benefit. Most employers provide group life insurance supplementary health care, dental, and long-term disability insurance.

5. There are two basic types of pension plans: defined benefit plans and defined contribution plans. Vesting of employer contributions and portability of pension benefits are two important issues.

6. Most employers also provide benefits in the form of employee services. These include food services, recreational opportunities, legal advice, credit unions, and counselling.

7. Surveys suggest two conclusions regarding employees' preferences for benefits. First, time off (such as two extra weeks' vacation) seems to be the most preferred benefit. Second, the employee's age, marital status, and gender clearly influence his or her choice of benefits. This suggests the need for individualizing the organization's benefit plans.

8. Childcare and eldercare responsibilities are affecting growing numbers of Canadian workers. More and more employers are offering assistance to their employees in these areas.

9. The flexible benefits approach allows the employee to put together his or her own benefit plan, subject to total cost limits and the inclusion of certain nonoptional items. Several firms have introduced flexible plans; they require considerable planning and computer assistance for plan administration.

10. Benefits administration is challenging, and is increasingly being carried out with computers and other new technologies.

Key Terms

benefits
Canada/Quebec
  Pension Plan
coinsurance
deductible
deferred profit-sharing
  plan
defined benefit pension
  plan

defined contribution
  pension plan
early retirement incentives
early retirement window
employee assistance plan
  (EAP)
employment insurance
flexible benefits program
group life insurance

pay for time not worked
pension plans
portability
provincial health care plans
short-term disability/
  sick leave
vesting
workers' compensation

Discussion Questions and Exercises

1. You are applying for a job as a manager and are at the point of negotiating salary and benefits. What questions would you ask your prospective employer concerning benefits? Describe the benefits package you would try to negotiate for yourself.

2. In this chapter we presented findings concerning the preferences by age, marital status, and gender for various benefits. What are these findings and how would you make use of them if you were a human resources manager?

3. What is pension "vesting" and "portability"? Why do you think these are (or aren't) important to a recent university or college graduate?

4. Working individually or in groups, compile a list of the perks available to the following individuals: the head of your local public utilities commission; the president of your college or university; the president of a large company in your area. Do they all have certain perks in common? What do you think accounts for any differences?

5. Working individually or in groups, contact the Workers' Compensation Board and compile a list of their suggestions for reducing workers' compensation costs. What seem to be their main recommendations?

6. You are the HR consultant to a small business with about 40 employees. At the present time they offer only the legal minimum number of days for vacation and paid holidays, and legally mandated benefits. Develop a list of other benefits you believe they should offer, along with your reasons for suggesting them.

Application Exercises

RUNNING CASE: Carter Cleaning Company
The New Benefit Plan

Carter Cleaning Centres have traditionally provided only legislatively-required benefits for their employees. These include participation in provincial health care, employment insurance, Canada Pension Plan, and workers' compensation. The principals of the firm—Jack, Jennifer, and their families—have individual supplementary health and life insurance coverage.

At the present time, Jennifer can see several potential problems with the company's policies regarding benefits and services. First, she wants to do a study to determine whether similar companies' experiences with providing supplementary health and life insurance benefits suggest they enable these firms to reduce employee turnover and perhaps pay lower wages. Jennifer is also concerned with the fact that at the present time the company has no formal policy regarding vacations or paid days off or sick leave. Informally, at least, it is understood that employees get two weeks vacation after one year's work, but in the past the policy regarding paid vacations for days such as New Year's Day and Thanksgiving Day has been very inconsistent. Sometimes employees who had been on the job only two or three weeks were paid fully for one of these holidays, while at other times they weren't. Jennifer knows that this policy must be made more consistent.

She also wonders whether it would be advisable to establish some type of daycare centre for the employees' children. She knows that many of the employees' children either have no place to go during the day (they are preschoolers) or have no place to go after school, and she wonders whether a benefit such as daycare would be in the best interests of the company.

Questions

1. Draw up a policy statement regarding vacations, sick leave, and paid days off for Carter Cleaning Centres.
2. What are the advantages and disadvantages to Carter Cleaning Centres of providing its employees with medical, and life insurance programs?
3. How should Jennifer go about determining whether a daycare centre would be advisable for the company?

CASE INCIDENT: Sick Leave in Spring Valley

A decline in the revenue from property tax, and higher costs for everything from cleaning supplies to wages had brought hard times to the town of Spring Valley. The combination of these factors made it seem impossible for Robert Donizetti, the town clerk, and the budget committee of the town council to provide a balanced budget for the town.

Situated in the Maritimes, Spring Valley has a population of 12 000, a declining one that matched its declining revenue. In casting about for means to finance the small town's operations, Donizetti saw few opportunities for increasing revenue. In the past year one of the town's chief employers, the Acme Manufacturing Company, had been forced to close its local factory, and all parts of the local economy had been affected by the recent business recession. Hence,

Donizetti went carefully over departmental budgets seeking ways to cut costs and eliminate waste.

One area in which Donizetti decided savings could be effected was through policy changes concerning sick leave (currently ten days per year). The town's work force consisted of only about 150 full-time employees, and figures in Donizetti's office showed that sick leave in the past six years averaged 7.34 days per year per employee. Not only was this costly in dollars in terms of Spring Valley's budget, but it also meant a loss of labour efficiency and productivity. Donizetti's statistics showed that female and older employees used more sick leave than males and younger workers. Donizetti prepared the following tables of sick leave averages by age and gender for the budget committee:

Sick Leave in Spring Valley by Gender, 1992–1997		
YEAR	**MALE**	**FEMALE**
1992	6.1	7.9
1993	5.9	7.7
1994	6.4	8.4
1995	6.3	8.7
1996	6.5	8.5
1997	6.8	8.9

Sick Leave in Spring Valley by Age, 1992–1997		
YEAR	**UNDER 30**	**OVER 30**
1992	5.1	6.8
1993	5.3	8.4
1994	5.7	8.1
1995	5.5	7.7
1996	5.8	8.3
1997	5.6	8.6

Spring Valley had not had many labour conflicts. Employee relations were handled through the human resources director, William Danforth, and the Town Employees' Association, whose president was Jessica Blum. With respect to sick leave, the town had, in recent years, agreed to include in it family care, doctor appointments, and emergency time off for such events as funerals.

After a study of the problem, Donizetti recommended that the Town Employees' Association and the human resources department together devise a sick leave incentive program to act as a deterrent to sick leave abuse, and as an equitable plan for the different uses of sick leave.

On June 6 the human resources department presented its proposal. Under its plan, employees would be reimbursed on February 1 of each year for 20 percent of the unused sick leave credits accumulated during the past year. The Town Employees' Association made a counterproposal that included a choice by the employee to consider unused sick leave as vacation time or else to add it to retirement service.

The main point of contention at this stage concerned the percentage of sick leave credit for which an employee might be reimbursed. The town offered no alternative to the 20 percent yearly reimbursement, while the employees demanded that a 100 percent retirement-related incentive be adopted. After several fruitless attempts at negotiation, the two parties agreed to present the problem to a fact finder. His or her findings and suggestions for resolution of the issues would be used as a basis for further negotiations. The fact finder conducted private hearings with both parties and submitted a report on July 15.

Questions

1. Assume that you are the fact finder in the case. Analyze the sick leave problem in Spring Valley and propose a plan that is equitable to both parties.
2. If you were the town manager entrusted with pursuing the best interests of the town, which provisions in the proposal would you accept and which would you attempt to change?
3. Assume that you are the union negotiator. Which provisions would you accept and which would you attempt to change?

Source: Adapted from *Practicing Public Management: A Casebook* by C. Kenneth Meyer et al. Copyright © 1983 by St. Martin's Press, Inc., and used with permission of the publisher.

Human Resources Management Simulation

Exercise 11 in the simulation asks for a report explaining flexible benefits (called "cafeteria-style" benefits in the simulation), and outlining the advantages and disadvantages of this approach. Consider the implications of the union/nonunion composition of the work force, the administrative reality of flexible benefits, and the communication requirements of such a big change in employee benefits. Try to anticipate new benefits employees may want to have added to the plan.

Take It to the Net

Check out our Companion Website at

www.prenticehall.ca/dessler

for a multitude of practice questions, key terms and concepts, Weblinks to related sites, newsgroups, CBC video updates, and more.

Notes

1. Based on Frederick Hills, Thomas Bergmann, and Vida Scarpello, *Compensation Decision Making* (Fort Worth: The Dryden Press, 1994), p. 424. See also L. Kate Beatty, "Pay and Benefits Break Away from Tradition," *HR Magazine* 39, no. 11 (November 1994), pp. 63–8.
2. KPMG, *Employee Benefits Costs in Canada*, 1996, p. 22–3.
3. KPMG, *Employee Benefits Costs in Canada*.
4. M. Hamilton, "Much Ado About Something," *Benefits Canada*, 21(4), p. 67.
5. See, for example, Bialk, "Cutting Workers' Compensation Costs," pp. 95–7. See also H. Amolins "Workers Must Cooperate in Return to Work," *Canadian HR Reporter* (November 3, 1997), p. 8; and C. Knight, "Ontario Businesses Ready for New WCB," *Canadian HR Reporter* (November 17, 1997), p. 9.
6. K. Matthes, "In Pursuit of Leisure: Employees Want More Time Off," *HR Focus*, no. 7 (1992).
7. Miriam Rothman, "Can Alternatives to Sick Pay Plans Reduce Absenteeism?" *Personnel Journal* 60 (October 1981), pp. 788–91; Richard Bunning, "A Prescription for Sick Leave," *Personnel Journal* 67, no. 8 (August 1988), pp. 44–9.
8. Dawn Gunch, "The Family Leave Act: A Financial Burden?" *Personnel Journal* (September 1993), p. 49.
9. See, for example, Kirk Maldonado, "Questions and Answers Regarding the Family and Medical Leave Act of 1993," *Benefits Law Journal* 7, no. 1 (Spring 1994), pp. 73–87. See also Edward Lee Isler, Peter Turza, and John

Seeley, "Impact of the Family and Medical Leave Act on Employee Benefits," *Benefits Law Journal* 7, no. 3 (Autumn 1994), pp. 271–89.

10. Robert E. Sibson, *Wages and Salaries: A Handbook for Line Managers,* (New York: American Management Association, 1967), p. 235.

11. "Employee Benefits in Small Firms," *Bureau of National Affairs Bulletin to Management* (June 27, 1991), pp. 196–7.

12. Rita Jain, "Employer-Sponsored Dental Insurance Eases the Pain," *Monthly Labor Review* (October 1988), p. 18. "Employee Benefits," *Commerce Clearing House Ideas and Trends in Personnel* (January 23, 1991), pp. 9–11.

13. S. Lebrun, "Turning a Blind Eye to Benefits," *Canadian HR Reporter* (February 24, 1997), p. 2.

14. KPMG, *Employee Benefit Costs in Canada* p. 33.

15. F. Holmes, "Shifting the Burden", 21(1), p.41. See also S. Lebrun, "Keeping the Lid on Drug Benefit Costs," *Canadian HR Reporter* (December 16, 1996), p. 12.

16. P. Gorham & K. Morrallee, "Paying the Pill Bills," *Benefits Canada* (December 1996), p. 27.

17. K.Gay, "Companies Target Soaring Benefit Costs," *Financial Post* (October 29, 1994), p. S34. See also S. Lebrun, "Keeping the Lid on Drug Benefit Costs."

18. J. Norton, "Game Plan," *Benefits Canada*, November 1996, p. 29.

19. Lebrun, "Keeping the Lid on Benefit Costs."

20. C. Knight, "Making the Smokers Pay," *Canadian HR Reporter* (May 6, 1996), p. 1.

21. C. Kapel, "Unitel Asks Employees to Share Costs," *Canadian HR Reporter* (June 17, 1996), p. 17.

22. Knight, "Making the Smokers Pay," p. 1.

23. S. Felix, "Healthy Alternative," *Benefits Canada* (February 1997), p. 47.

24. A. Dimon, "Money Well Spent," *Benefits Canada* (April 1997), p. 15.

25. S. Noakes, "A Company That Exercises Together Stays Together," *Financial Post* (March 24, 1995), p. 16.

26. T. McCallum, "Getting a Grip: Business Battles the Health Care Bulge," *Human Resources Professional* (October 1996), p. 13.

27. Dimon, "Money Well Spent," p. 15.

28. Knight, "Managing Health Care Costs," *Canadian HR Reporter* (April 22, 1996), p. 1.

29. K. Gay, "Post-Retirement Benefits Costing Firms a Fortune," *Financial Post* (June 2, 1995), p. 18.

30. KPMG, *Employee Benefits Costs in Canada*, p. ii.

31. Lebrun, "Turning a Blind Eye to Benefits," p. 2.

32. A. Khemani, "Post-Retirement Benefits Liability Grows," *Canadian HR Reporter* (November 4, 1996), p. 17.

33. M. Warren, "Uncovering the Costs," *Benefits Canada* (November 1996), p. 41.

34. A.N. Nash and S.J. Carroll, Jr., "Supplemental Compensation," in *Perspectives on Personnel: Human Resource Management,* in Herbert Heneman III and Donald Schwab, eds. (Homewood, IL: Irwin, 1978), p. 223.

35. M. Cusipag, "A Healthy Approach to Managing Disability Costs," *Human Resources Professional* (June/July 1997), p 13.

36. S.B. Hood, "Repetitive Strain Injury: Preventable Plague of the '90s," *Human Resources Professional* (June/July 1997), p. 29. See also A. Cantor, "Understanding the Costs of Job Accommodation," *Back to Work* (September 1997), p. 5.

37. The following is based on Michael Gomez, "Managing Health Care Costs," Part I, "The Dilemma of AIDS," *Compensation and Benefits Review* (September–October 1988), pp. 23–31; and Nancy Breuer, "AIDS Issues Haven't Gone Away," *Personnel Journal* 71, no. 1 (January 1992), pp. 47–9. See also Kato Keeton, "AIDS Related Attitudes Among Government Employees: Implications for Training Programs," *Review of Public Personnel Administration* (Spring 1993), pp. 65–80; J. McFarland, "Low AIDS Coverage Costs Surprise", *Financial Post* (July 23–5, 1994), p. 6.

38. Quoted from Gomez, "Managing Health Care Costs," p. 28.

39. Gomez, "Managing Health Care Costs," p. 31. See also L. Hartley, "Dealing With HIV/AIDS in the Workplace: Is Your Organization Ready?" *Canadian HR Reporter* (May 20, 1996), pp. 22–3.

40. This is based on S. Felix, "The Gloom Boom," *Benefits Canada* (January 1997), p. 32.

41. Cusipag, "A Healthy Approach to Managing Disability Costs."

42. KPMG, *Employee Benefits Costs in Canada*, p. 21.

43. See, for example, Henderson, *Compensation Management,* pp. 289–90; Famularo, *Handbook*, pp. 37.1–37.9.

44. M. Banks and M. Lowry, "Changing Workforce Requires Rethinking of Pension Plan," *Canadian HR Reporter* (March 10, 1997), p. 17.

45. Sibson, *Wages and Salaries*, p. 234. For an explanation of how to minimize employee benefits litigation related to pension and health benefits claims, see Thomas Piskorski, "Minimizing Employee Benefits Litigation Through Effective Claims Administration Procedures," *Employee Relations Law Journal* 20, no. 3 (Winter 1994/95), pp. 421–31.

46. *The Economist* (August 5, 1978), p. 57.

47. For a discussion of the pros and cons of early retirement, see, for example, Jeffrey Sonnenfelt, "Dealing with the Aging Workforce," *Harvard Business Review* 57 (November–December 1978), pp. 81–92.

48. K. Murray, "How HR Is Making Pensions Portable," *Personnel Journal* (July 1993), p. 43.

49. "Trends," *BNA Bulletin to Management* (May 7, 1992), p. 143.

50. "Plan Design and Experience in Early Retirement Windows and in Other Voluntary Separation Plans," prepared by the staff of Hewitt Associates, 1986. See also Eugene Seibert and Jo Anne Seibert, "Retirement Windows," *Personnel Journal* 68, no. 5 (May 1989), pp. 30–1, examples of wellness program benefits.

51. Marco Colosi, Philip Rosen, and Sara Herrin, "Is Your Early Retirement Package Courting Disaster?" *Personnel Journal* (August 1988), pp. 59–67.

52. See also Eugene Seibert and Jo Anne Seibert, "Look into Window Alternatives," *Personnel Journal* (May 1989), pp. 80–7.

53. L. Ramsay, "Pliant Pension Rules Key to Phased-In Retirement," *Financial Post* (February 9, 1995), p. 19.

54. S. Smolkin, "Bowing Out Gracefully," *Benefits Canada* (October 1996), p. 40.

55. See Henderson, *Compensation Management,* pp. 336–9. See also Lewis Burger, "Group Legal Service Plans: A Benefit Whose Time Has Come," *Compensation and Benefits Review* 18, no. 4 (July–August 1986), pp. 28–34.

56. See Dale Masi and Seymour Friedland, "EAP Actions & Options," *Personnel Journal* (June 1988), pp. 61–7. See also J. Hampton, "Rougher Ride at Work: Sharp Upturn in EAP

Use," *Canadian HR Reporter* (December 2, 1996), p. 25; A. Leckie, "Rapid EAP Growth Raises Quality Concerns," *Canadian HR Reporter* (May 8, 1995), p. 17.

57. Based on Masi and Friedland. See also Harry Turk, "Questions—and Answers: Avoiding Liability for EAP Services," *Employment Relations Today* (Spring 1992), pp. 111–4; See also H. LaFontaine and G. Kozdrowski "Today's Workplace: A United Nations of Needs," *Canadian HR Reporter* (July 14, 1997), p. 15–8.

58. A. Czarnecki, "Measuring the Value of an EAP," *Canadian HR Reporter* (July 15, 1996), p. 17.

59. "Employee Benefit Costs," Bureau of National Affairs, *Bulletin to Management* (January 16, 1992), pp. 12–4.

60. The Research Staff of Hewitt Associates, *Innovative Benefits*, Hewitt Associates, 160 Bloor Street East, Toronto, Ontario.

61. *Dun's Review* (July 1981), p. 49. See also Velleman, "A Benefit to Meet Changing Needs," pp. 54–62; Bureau of National Affairs, "Child Care Benefits Offered by Employers," *Bulletin to Management* (March 17, 1988), pp. 84–5. See also C. Davenport, "Child Care Solutions for a Harried Work World," *Canadian HR Reporter* (April 21, 1997), p. 16. For a discussion of other employer childcare options and the costs and problems of implementing them, see Caroline Eichman and Barbara Reisman, "How Small Employers Are Benefitting from Offering Child Care Assistance," *Employment Relations Today* (Spring 1992), pp. 51–62.

62. "Employers and Child Care: Establishing Services Through the Workplace," Women's Bureau, U.S. Department of Labor, Washington, D.C., 1982. See also BNA, "Special Survey on Child Care Assistance Programs," *Bulletin to Management* (March 26, 1987). Donald J. Peterson and Douglas Massengill, "Child Care Programs Benefit Employers, Too," *Personnel* 65, no. 5 (May 1988), pp. 58–62; and Toni A. Campbell and David E. Campbell, "Employers and Child Care," *Personnel Journal* 67, no. 4 (April 1988), pp. 84–7.

63. Lorri Johnson, "Effectiveness of an Employee-Sponsored Child Care Center," *Applied H.R.M. Research* 2, no. 1 (Summer 1991), pp. 38–67.

64. Commerce Clearing House, "As the Population Ages, There Is Growing Interest in Adding Elder Care to the Benefits Package," *Ideas and Trends* (August 21, 1987), pp. 129–31. See also "ElderCare to Eclipse Child Care, Report Says," *Canadian HR Reporter* (August 14, 1995), p. 11.

65. Kelli Earhart, R. Dennis Middlemist, and Willie Hopkins, "Elder Care: An Emerging Employee Assistance Issue," *Employee Assistance Quarterly* 8, no. 3 (1993), pp. 1–10.

66. For another example, see "Elder Care: A Maturing Benefit," *BNA Bulletin to Management* (February 20, 1992), pp. 50, 55.

67. Mary Zippo, "Subsidized Employee Transportation: A Three Way Benefit," *Personnel* 57 (May–June 1980), pp. 40–1.

68. Hewitt Associates, *Survey of Educational Reimbursement Programs*, 1984.

69. Bruce Ellig, *Executive Compensation—A Total Pay Perspective* (New York: McGraw-Hill, 1982), p. 141.

70. Lindroth, "Inflation, Taxes, and Perks," p. 939.

71. Matthew Budman, "The Persistence of Perks," *Across the Board* (February 1994), pp. 44–6.

72. J. Brad Chapman and Robert Ottermann, "Employee Preference for Various Compensation and Fringe Benefit Options" (Berea, OH: ASPA Foundation, 1975). See also, William White and James Becker, "Increasing the Motivational Impact of Employee Benefits," *Personnel* (January–February 1980), pp. 32–7; and Barney Olmsted and Suzanne Smith, "Flex for Success!" *Personnel* 66, no. 6 (June 1989), pp. 50–5.

73. Chapman and Ottermann; Albert Cole, "Flexible Benefits Are a Key to Better Employee Relations," *Personnel Journal* (January 1983), pp. 49–53. See also, Lance Tane, "Guidelines to Successful Flex Plans: Four Companies' Experiences," *Compensation and Benefits Review* 17 (July–August 1985), pp. 38–45; Peter Stonebraker, "A Three-Tier Plan for Cafeteria Benefits," *Personnel Journal* 63, no. 12 (December 1984), pp. 50–3; Commerce Clearing House, "Flexible Benefits: Will They Work for You?" Chicago, 1983; and George F. Dreher, Ronald A. Ash, and Robert D. Bretz, "Benefit Coverage and Employee Cost: Critical Factors in Explaining Compensation Satisfaction," *Personnel Psychology* 41, no. 2 (Summer 1988), pp. 237–54; and Melissa Barringer and Olivia Mitchell, "Workers' Preferences Among Company-Provided Health Insurance Plans," *Industrial and Labor Relations Review* 48, no. 1 (October 1994), pp. 141–52.

74. George Milkovich and Jerry Newman, *Compensation* (Burr Ridge, IL: Irwin, 1993), p. 405.

75. See Caroline A. Baker, "Flex Your Benefits," *Personnel Journal* 67, no. 5 (May 1988), pp. 54–8, for discussion of the pros and cons of three basic approaches to flexible benefits; and Carol Woodley, "The Benefits of Flexibility," *Personnel Management* (May 1993), pp. 36–9. See also K. Mark "Cost Management Via Flexible Plans," *Human Resources Professional* (October 1995), pp. 7–9.

76. For information about this program, contact Towers, Perrin, Forster, and Crosby, 245 Park Avenue, New York, NY 10167. Hewitt Associates similarly has a program called FlexSystem (Hewitt Associates, New York, NY). See also John Parkington, "The 'Trade-Off' Approach to Benefits Cost Containment: A Strategy to Increase Employee Satisfaction," *Compensation and Benefits Review* 19, no. 1 (January–February 1987), pp. 35–6, which explains a simple way of determining what your employees prefer in benefits.

77. J. Kauk, "The Stretch to Flex," *Benefits Canada* (December 1996), p. 61.

78. J. Tompkins, "Moving Out: A Look at Comprehensive Benefits Outsourcing," *Canadian HR Reporter* (May 5, 1997), p. 9.

79. A. Czarnecki, "Employees Show Increasing Interest in Pension Communication Systems," *Canadian HR Reporter*, July 15, 1996, p. 18.

80. D. McFarlane, "Demystifying the Pension Plan," *Canadian HR Reporter* (May 19, 1997), p. 18. See also D. McFarlane, "Errors in Pension Communication Costly," *Canadian HR Reporter* (January 27, 1997), p. 18.

81. J. Tompkins, "Benefits Technology Helps Employees Help Themselves," *Canadian HR Reporter* (July 14, 1997), p. 8.

82. This is based on Anthony Barra, "Employees Keep Informed with Interactive KIOSKs," *Personnel Journal* (October 1988), pp. 43–51.

83. C. Davenport, "Employers Twig to Value of Ongoing Pension Communication," *Canadian HR Reporter* (December 16, 1996), p. 33.

Chapter 15

Fair Treatment: The Foundation of Effective Employee Relations

Chapter Outline

◆ **Introduction**

◆ **Building Two-Way Communication**

◆ **Guaranteed Fair Treatment and Employee Discipline**

◆ **Managing Dismissals**

◆ **Managing Separations: Layoff and Retirement**

Learning Outcomes

After studying this chapter, you should be able to:

Explain in detail techniques for building two-way communications in organizations.

Discuss appropriate techniques for employee discipline.

Define wrongful dismissal and explain its importance.

Explain how employee dismissals should be handled.

List important HR considerations in adjusting to downsizings and mergers.

Describe strategies firms can use to assist their employees to adjust to retirement.

Introduction

It makes sense for employers to guarantee fair treatment of employees for several reasons. From a practical point of view, an increasingly litigious work force makes it almost a necessity that employers institute disciplinary and discharge procedures that will survive the scrutiny of arbitrators and the courts. Quite aside from legal constraints, however, it generally just makes sense for employers to show their employees that their policies and procedures are fair, since this should foster improved commitment and reduce grievances and morale problems.

While there may be no way to actually guarantee that employees are treated fairly, there are steps employers can take to move in that direction. As will be explained in this chapter, these steps include building two-way communications, implementing guaranteed fair treatment and employee discipline appeals procedures, protecting employees' privacy, and doing a better job of managing dismissals and other types of separations such as layoffs and retirements.

Building Two-Way Communication

Consider the following example of how poor communication can work against corporate objectives. Wal-Mart Canada prides itself on its open communication policy with employees. Yet their Windsor, Ontario store became the world's first unionized Wal-Mart when the Ontario Labour Relations Board certified a union, despite a large majority of employees voting against it. The Board believed that employees feared they would lose their jobs if they voted for the union, because employees who asked managers whether the store would remain open if the union was voted in were told that the company had no comment. This communication was considered by the Board to be a management threat, constituting an unfair labour practice, and thus, as will be explained in chapter 16, the union was automatically certified.[1]

Treating employees fairly begins with good listening. Managers in firms like Federal Express Canada and Saturn know that commitment is built on trust and that trust requires two-way communication. These firms thus set up programs that foster two-way communication. What follows are four examples of such programs: speak up! programs for voicing concerns and making inquiries; periodic survey-type programs for expressing opinions; various top-down programs for keeping employees informed; and guaranteed fair treatment programs for filing grievances and complaints.

"Speak Up!"-Type Programs

speak up! programs
Communication programs that allow employees to register questions, concerns, and complaints about work-related matters.

Grievance matters are the tip of the iceberg when it comes to the concerns of employees. These concerns run the gamut from malfunctioning vending machines to unlit parking lots to a manager's spending too much of the department's money on travel. IBM Canada's **Speak Up! program** aims to give employees a confidential channel for speaking their minds about such issues.[2] Anonymity makes the program unique. Employees may ask questions or make comments and get a reply without revealing their identity to anyone except the Speak Up! administrator.

The program is structured to protect the employee's identity by keeping the employee's name known only to the Speak Up! administrator. Plans are underway to put the program online for further protection of anonymity.

The investigator is usually the highest-level manager familiar with the Speak Up! concern. Answers are provided within ten working days unless the

Speak Up! requires more extensive investigation. The Speak Up! administrator first checks all responses for accuracy and completeness. He or she then personally addresses and mails the answer to the employee's home.

The program lets employees jump the normal chain of command. It enables them to express their comments, concerns, or suggestions directly to someone who is responsible for the activity in question. Employees are encouraged to write Speak Up! requests at any time but are told that they might first consider talking to their own manager, reviewing the employee handbook, or calling the department involved to get a direct answer. Similarly, the IBM Canada Suggestion Program is generally used to propose ideas that could save the company time or money.

Dofasco Inc.'s suggestion program has been a success story for decades. Employees can receive cash awards of up to $50 000, depending on the savings realized by implementing the suggestion. Another organization with a successful suggestion plan is the Royal Bank of Canada. One suggestion made in 1994, for streamlining computer backup procedures and reducing the required amount of data storage equipment, saved the bank almost $8 million over three years. Employees receive monetary rewards for suggestions that are implemented, but most of all, they say they want to improve operations and productivity for the bank and its customers.[3]

Programs like these have several benefits. They let management continuously monitor employees' feelings and concerns; they make it clear that employees have several channels through which to communicate concerns and get responses; and the net effect is that there's less chance that small problems will grow into big ones.

Employee Opinion Surveys

opinion surveys
Communication devices that use questionnaires to regularly ask employees their opinions about the company, management, and work life.

Most of these firms also administer periodic anonymous **opinion surveys.** IBM Canada's organizational effectiveness survey regularly asks employees their opinions about the company, management, and work life. The survey's purpose is to assess the morale of employees. The standard practice is to have department heads conduct feedback sessions with their department members after the survey results are compiled in order to share the results and work on solutions.

The Survey Feedback Action (SFA) program at FedEx Canada is typical. SFA includes an anonymous survey that allows employees to express feelings about the company and their managers, and to some extent about service, pay, and benefits. Each manager then has an opportunity to use the results to help design a blueprint for improving work group commitment.

SFA has three phases. First, the survey itself is a standard, anonymous questionnaire given each year to every employee. The questions are designed to gather information about what helps and hinders employees in their work environment. Sample items include:

I can tell my manager what I think.
My manager tells me what is expected.
My manager listens to my concerns.
My manager keeps me informed.
Upper management listens to ideas from my level.
FedEx does a good job for our customers.
In my environment we use safe work practices.
I am paid fairly for this kind of work.

A work group's survey results are compiled and sent to the manager. To ensure anonymity, the smaller units do not receive their own results. Instead, their results are combined with those of several other similar work units until a department head of 20 or 25 people obtains the overall group's results.

The second phase is a feedback session between the manager and his or her work group. The goal here is to identify specific concerns or problems, examine causes for these problems, and devise action plans to correct the problems. Managers are trained to ask probing questions. For example, suppose the low-scoring survey item was, "I feel free to tell my manager what I think." Managers are trained to ask their groups questions such as "What restrains you?" (timing, specific behaviours) and "What do I do that makes you feel that I'm not interested?"

The feedback meeting should lead to a third, "action plan" phase. The plan itself is a list of actions that the manager will take to address employees' concerns and boost results. Managers thus get an action planning worksheet containing four columns: What is the concern? What's your analysis? What's the cause? and What should be done? Often a follow-up session is held to review the implementation of the action plan and discuss any further action needed to fully accomplish it.

Emco Ltd. conducted an employee opinion survey with three open-ended questions:[4]

1. If you were president of the company, what would you change?
2. What does TQM mean to you?
3. Is there anything else you would like to comment on?

Management was overwhelmed with the response, and the CEO read every comment. The results showed that customer satisfaction was the top priority for most employees, and that nearly everyone was looking for methods to improve their work. The survey responses also identified some areas for improvement such as safety and TQM training.

Top-Down Communication Programs

It's hard for employees to feel committed when their boss won't tell them what's going on. Some firms, therefore, give employees extensive data on the performance of and prospects for their operations. The process builds trust.

top-down communication programs Communication activities including in-house television centres, electronic bulletin boards, and newsletters that provide continuing opportunities for the firm to update employees on important matters regarding the firm.

Employers have used a number of **top-down communication programs** over the years. Traditionally, newsletters and verbal presentations were the methods used to disseminate information from the company to employees. More recently, some organizations have utilized videos and in-house television centres for this purpose. The state of the art in the late 1990s is high-tech communication using computers[5]—email, local and wide area networks, electronic bulletin boards, intranets, and corporate home pages on the Internet.

There are a number of advantages to technology-based communication. Immediacy means that information can get to employees before it gets to the press, which is particularly important with major reorganizations, and adverse news such as downsizing. One study found that 40 percent of survivors of downsizing did not know the details of the reorganization, and 60 percent did not know what was going to happen to them.[6] The message is easily delivered straight from a keyboard without the need for presentation rehearsals or proofing printed material. A second advantage is that the message can be tailored to individual employees when it relates to personal information such as benefits. Individualized messages tell the employee that he or she matters.

Toyota's management works hard to share what it knows with every team member. There are thrice-daily five-minute team information meetings at job sites, where employees get the latest news about the plant. There are monthly "roundtable" discussions between top management and selected nonsupervisory staff, as well as a bi-monthly news bulletin reporting current events in Toyota worldwide, and a bi-weekly local newsletter. The firm's president is often in the plant, fielding questions, providing performance information, and ensuring that all in the company are "aware of Toyota's goals and where we are heading."

Guaranteed Fair Treatment and Employee Discipline

Guaranteed Fair Treatment Programs at Work

guaranteed fair treatment programs
Employer programs that are aimed at ensuring that all employees are treated fairly, generally by providing formalized, well-documented, and highly publicized vehicles through which employees can appeal any eligible issues.

The potential for grievances and discontent is always present. Just about any factor involving wages, hours, or conditions of employment has and will be used as the basis of a grievance in most firms. Discipline cases and seniority problems (including promotions, transfers, and layoffs) probably top the list. Others include grievances growing out of job evaluations and work assignments, overtime, vacations, incentive plans, and holidays.

Whatever the source, many firms today (and virtually all unionized ones) give employees channels through which to air grievances. A grievance procedure helps to ensure that every employee's grievance is heard and treated fairly, and unionized firms do not hold a monopoly on such fair treatment. Even in nonunionized firms, formal grievance procedures can help ensure effective employee-employer relations.

Programs such as Federal Express's Guaranteed Fair Treatment go beyond most grievance procedures: (1) Special, easily available forms make filing the grievance easy; (2) employees are encouraged to use the system; and (3) the highest levels of top management are routinely involved in reviewing complaints. As their employee handbook says:

> Perhaps the cornerstone of Federal Express' 'people' philosophy is the guaranteed fair treatment procedure (GFTP). This policy affirms your right to appeal any eligible issue through this process of systematic review by progressively higher levels of management. Although the outcome is not assured to be in your favour, your right to participate within the guidelines of the procedure is guaranteed. At Federal Express, where we have a 'people-first' philosophy, you have a right to discuss your complaints with management without fear of retaliation.[7]

The net effect is twofold: Complaints don't get a chance to accumulate; and all managers think twice before doing anything unfair, since their actions will likely be brought to their bosses' attention.

Eligible Concerns   GFTP is available to all permanent FedEx Canada employees. It covers all concerns regarding matters such as job promotion and discipline affecting the individual complainant. The firm's handbook points out that any recipient of discipline has access to the GFTP.

Steps   The FedEx guaranteed fair treatment procedure contains three steps. In step one, *management review,* the complainant contacts an employee representative from the HR department, who helps them to submit a written complaint to a

Employee commitment at Federal Express has been fostered by CEO Fred Smith's people-first values.

member of management (manager or senior manager of the employee's department) within seven calendar days of the occurrence of the eligible issue. Then the manager and senior manager of the employee's group review all relevant information; hold a telephone conference and/or meeting with the complainant; make a decision to either uphold, modify, or overturn management's action; and communicate their decision in writing to the complainant and the department's HR representative. All this occurs within ten calendar days of receipt of the complaint.

In step two, *officer complaint,* the complainant submits a written complaint to the managing director of his or her functional area within seven calendar days of the step one decision. The managing director then reviews all relevant information; conducts an additional investigation, when necessary; makes a decision to either uphold, overturn, or modify management's action, or initiate a review of the facts of the case; and communicates the decision in writing to the complainant with copies to the department's HR representative and the complainant's manager. As in step one, the step two review generally occurs within ten calendar days of receipt of the complaint.

Finally, in step three, *executive appeals review,* the complainant submits a written complaint within seven calendar days of the step two decision to the employee relations department. This department then investigates and prepares a GFTP case file for the international appeals board executive review. The appeals board—the VP Canada, International VP HR, and other senior executives—then reviews all relevant information; makes a decision to either uphold, overturn, or initiate a review of the facts of the case or to take other appropriate action; and generally does this within 14 calendar days of receipt of the complaint. Barring a request for a further review, the appeals board's decision is final.

IBM Canada has a similar fair treatment program called **open-door.** It gives every employee the right to appeal his or her supervisor's actions. Programs like IBM's haven't the structure and formality of FedEx's guaranteed fair treatment program. However, they do help ensure that healthy communication occurs regarding disciplinary matters and that employees' voices are heard.

open-door program
A fair treatment program that gives every employee the right to appeal the actions of his or her supervisor by taking the concern to successively higher levels of management.

Fairness in Disciplining

discipline
A procedure that corrects or punishes an employee because a rule or procedure has been violated.

The purpose of **discipline** is to encourage employees to behave sensibly at work, where being sensible is defined as adhering to rules and regulations. In an organization, rules and regulations serve about the same purpose that laws do in society; discipline is called for when one of these rules or regulations is violated.[8] A fair and just discipline process is based on three foundations: *rules and regulations; a system of progressive penalties;* and *an appeals process.*

A set of clear *rules and regulations* is the first foundation. These rules address things like theft, destruction of company property, drinking on the job, and insubordination. Examples of rules include:

> Poor performance is not acceptable. Each employee is expected to perform his or her work properly and efficiently and to meet established standards of quality.
>
> Liquor and drugs do not mix with work. The use of either during working hours and reporting for work under the influence of either are both strictly prohibited.
>
> The vending of anything in the plant without authorization is not allowed, nor is gambling in any form permitted.

The purpose of these rules is to inform employees ahead of time as to what is and is not acceptable behaviour. Employees must be told, preferably in writing, what is not permitted. This is usually done during the employee's orientation. The rules and regulations are generally listed in the employee orientation handbook.

A *system of progressive penalties* is a second foundation of effective disciplining. Penalties may range from verbal warnings to written warnings to suspension from the job to discharge. The severity of the penalty is usually a function of the type of offense and the number of times the offense has occurred. For example, most companies issue warnings for the first unexcused lateness. However, for a fourth offense, discharge is the more usual disciplinary action.

Finally, there should be an *appeals process* as part of the disciplinary process; this helps to ensure that discipline is meted out fairly and equitably. Programs like FedEx Canada's Guaranteed Fair Treatment and IBM Canada's open-door program help assure their employees a real appeals process.

Some collective agreements contain a "justice and dignity" clause that is intended to help employees "save face" in the disciplinary process.[9] These clauses prohibit management from removing an employee from active work for disciplinary reasons until a grievance with respect to the disciplinary action has been filed and resolved, except in cases where a danger to employee safety may exist.

Discipline Guidelines

Since arbitration may be a step in the discipline process (particularly in unionized firms), employers should ensure that their disciplinary actions will be viewed as fair by an independent arbitrator. Based on past disciplinary cases, here are guidelines that arbitrators may use when deciding whether there was just cause for the disciplinary action:

> *Make sure the evidence supports the charge of employee wrongdoing.* In one study, "the employer's evidence did not support the charge of employee wrongdoing" was the reason arbitrators gave most frequently for reinstating discharged employees or for reducing disciplinary suspensions. Other sample arbitrator statements included, for example, "The evidence was not persuasive against the employee."[10]

> *Ensure that the employees' due process rights are protected.* Arbitrators normally reverse discharges and suspensions that are imposed in a manner that violates basic notions of fairness or employee due process procedures.[11] Typical due process and procedural errors committed by employers include failing to follow established progressive discipline procedures, denying the employee an opportunity to tell his or her side of the story, lacking probable cause to discipline the employee; and not providing the employee a formal charge of wrongdoing.[12]

> *The discipline should be in line with the way management usually responds to similar incidents.* In one case the employer's rule stated that "leaving the plant without permission during working hours" made the worker subject to immediate discharge. A worker did leave the plant and was thus discharged. The arbitrator later found that employees frequently left the plant while they were clocked in and openly went into town for personal matters. Since the rule was not consistently applied in the past, the arbitrator ruled that the worker was wrongfully discharged.[13]

> *The employee should be adequately warned of the consequences of his or her alleged misconduct.* The person should be told of any undesirable behaviour that is noted and the consequences that may result if the employee chooses not to change that behaviour.

> *The rule that allegedly was violated should be "reasonably related" to the efficient and safe operation of the particular work environment.* Employees, in other words, are usually allowed by arbitrators to question the reason behind any rule or order.

> *Management must adequately investigate the matter before administering discipline.*

Furthermore, the investigation must be fair and objective.

The investigation should produce substantial evidence of misconduct.

Applicable rules, orders, or penalties should be applied evenhandedly and without discrimination.

The penalty should be reasonably related to the misconduct and to the employee's past history. In other words, each employee should be judged on the basis of his or her personal work record; only then should the appropriate discipline be imposed.[14]

Intensity of consequences. Moderate levels of punishment can be as effective as extreme levels.[15]

Other sensible disciplining guidelines include:

Don't rob an employee of his or her dignity.[16] Discipline the employee in private (unless he or she requests counsel) and avoid entrapment. That is, don't deliberately rig a situation that causes the employee to require disciplining.

Remember that the burden of proof is on the employer. In our society, a person is always considered innocent until proven guilty.

Get the facts. Decisions should not be based on hearsay evidence or on a "general impression."

Don't act while angry. Very few people can be objective and sensible when they are angry.

Research has shown that there are six general components of fairness relating to a disciplinary discussion between a manager and an employee. Managers should:[17]

1. Take a counselling approach to the problem
2. Exhibit a positive nonverbal demeanour
3. Provide the employee with some control over the disciplinary process and outcome
4. Provide a clear explanation of the problem behaviour
5. Ensure the discussion occurs in private
6. Ensure the discipline is not arbitrary; that is, it is consistent with other similar situations.

Discipline Without Punishment

Traditional discipline has two major potential flaws. First, although fairness guidelines like those previously mentioned can take the edge off this, no one ever feels good about being punished. Yet that is what discipline is: an employee does something wrong and is punished. There may, therefore, be residual bad feelings among all involved. A second shortcoming is that, as the saying goes, "a person convinced against his or her will is of the same opinion still." In other words, forcing the rules on employees may gain their short-term compliance but not their active cooperation when supervisors are not on hand to enforce the rules.

Discipline without punishment (or nonpunitive discipline) is aimed at avoiding these disciplinary problems. This is accomplished by gaining the employees' acceptance of the rules and by reducing the punitive nature of the discipline itself.

Here is an example. Assume there has been a breach of discipline (such as disregarding safety rules) or unsatisfactory work performance (such as carelessness in handling materials). In such a case, the following steps would constitute a typical nonpunitive approach to discipline.[18]

Step 1: First, issue an oral reminder. The supervisor's goal here is to get the employee to agree to solve the problem. Instead of warning the employee of possible disciplinary sanctions, he or she should be reminded of (1) the reason for the rule and (2) the fact that he or she has a responsibility to meet performance standards. A written record of the incident should be kept in a separate working file in the supervisor's desk rather than in the employee's HR file.

Step 2: Should another incident arise within six weeks, issue the employee a formal written reminder, a copy of which is placed in the HR file. In addition, privately hold a second discussion with the employee, again without any threats. As in step 1, the aim is to discuss the need for the rule and to obtain the employee's acceptance of the need to act responsibly at work. Make sure the person understands the rule and the explanation for why improvement is required, and express confidence in the person's ability to act responsibly at work. Should another such incident occur in the next six weeks, a follow-up meeting might be held. Here reiterate the need to act responsibly and investigate the possibility that the person is ill-suited to or bored with the job. Usually, though, the next step after the written reminder would be a paid one-day leave (step 3).

Step 3: The next step is a paid one-day "decision-making leave." If another incident occurs after the written warning in the next six weeks or so, the employee is told to take a one-day leave with pay to stay home and consider whether or not the job is right for him or her and whether or not the person wants to abide by the company's rules. The fact that the person is paid for the day is a final expression of the company's hope that the employee can and will act responsibly with respect to following the rules. When the employee returns to work, he or she meets with the supervisor and gives him or her a decision regarding whether or not the rules will be followed. At that point (assuming a positive response), the supervisor should again express confidence in the employee and, if necessary, work out a brief action plan to help the person change his or her behaviour.

Step 4: If no further incidents occur in the next year or so, the one-day paid suspension would be purged from the person's file. If the behaviour repeats itself, dismissal (see later discussion) would be required.

The process must, of course, be changed in exceptional circumstances. Criminal behaviour or in-plant fighting might be grounds for immediate dismissal, for instance. And if several incidents occurred at very close intervals, step 2—the written warning—might be skipped.

Nonpunitive discipline can be effective. Employees seem to welcome the less punitive aspects and don't seem to abuse the system by misbehaving to get a day off with pay. Grievances, sick leave usage, and disciplinary incidents all seem to drop in firms using these procedures. However, there will still be times when dismissals will be required.

Electronic Trespassing and Employee Privacy

The advent of the Internet has led to concerns about misuse of company time for visiting Web sites of personal rather than professional interest.[19] A Department of National Defence scientist was recently charged with possessing, making, and distributing child pornography over the Internet. Some employers are conducting electronic searches of employees' Web activity. Nova Corporation of Calgary has a policy that computer work must be limited to business, and the company has reserved the right to look at material employees are posting to or getting from Web sites. Nova has also blocked employees' access to newsgroups on the Web. Other companies allow employees to send personal email and surf the Net during lunch hours or breaks as a perk to increase morale.

Diversity Counts

Guaranteed Fair Treatment: *"Comparing males and females in a discipline situation."*

Watching a movie like "King Arthur" may lead viewers to the conclusion that chivalry in general and a protective attitude toward women in particular is a well-established value in many societies, but that may not be the case.[1] Not only is chivalry not necessarily a prevailing value, but there is even a competing hypothesis in the research literature. What several researchers call "The Evil Woman Thesis" certainly doesn't argue that women are evil. Instead it ". . . argues that women who commit offenses violate stereotypic assumptions about the proper behaviour of women. These women will be penalized for their inappropriate sex-role behaviour in addition to their other offenses."[2]

In other words, the unfortunately titled "Evil Woman Thesis" argues that when a woman doesn't act the way other men and women think she should act, they tend to overreact and treat her more harshly than they might if the alleged misdeed was done by a man.

While such a thesis might seem ridiculous on its face, the results of at least one careful study seem to indicate that it may in fact have considerable validity. In this study, 360 graduate and undergraduate university business school students (split about 50–50 between men and women) were asked to review a labour arbitration case. The case involved two employees, one male and one female, with similar work records and tenure with their employers. Both were discharged for violation of company rules related to alcohol and drugs. The case portrays one worker's behaviour as a more serious breach of company rules: the more culpable worker (a male in half the cases and a female in the other half) had brought the intoxicant to the work setting.

The male and female decision-maker/students were asked to express their agreement with two alternative approaches to arbitrating the dispute that arose when the culpable employee was discharged. The researchers assumed that only the male decision-maker students might come down more harshly on the culpable employee when that employee was a woman, and they were therefore surprised at their results.

In their study, they found evidence of a bias against the culpable woman employee by both the male and female students making the decisions about how to discipline the worker. In other words, the female workers in the labour case clearly received harsher treatment from the student decision-makers. And, again, at least in this study, it wasn't just the male student decision-makers that prescribed harsher penalties for the woman culpable employee. As the researchers conclude, "note that women, as decision-makers, appear to be as willing as men to impose harsher discipline on women than upon men."[3] In most respects, including the willingness to fire the culpable worker, it was the woman worker who could expect the harsher treatment, not the man.

In this study, student decision-makers were asked to come to some conclusions regarding discipline based on what they read in the case, so there is no way to conclude based solely on this study that the findings would necessarily apply in real world settings or under different conditions. However, the results of this study certainly provide food for thought regarding the fact that women just might be treated more harshly than men in a discipline situation.

1. This is based on Sandra Hartman, et al. "Males and Females in a Discipline Situation: Exploratory Research on Completing Hypotheses," *Journal of Managerial Issues* 6, no. 1 (Spring 1994), pp. 64–8.
2. Hartman, "Males and Females," p. 57.
3. Hartman, "Males and Females," p. 64.

Experts suggest that an electronic eavesdropping policy address the following issues:[20]

Offensive messages. Prohibit the use of email in ways that may be disruptive, offensive to others, or harmful to morale.

Personal messages. Ban email use to solicit or proselytize others for commercial ventures, religious or political causes, outside organizations, or other non-job-related solicitations.

Access. Employees should not be permitted to attempt to gain access to other employees' email files without permission, but management's rights to enter an employee's email files for business purposes should be reserved.[21]

Business use. The purpose of the firm's electronic message systems is to facilitate transmittal of business-related information within the organization exclusively.

Passwords. All computer pass codes and other pass codes must be available to the company, which may access them at any time.

Search authorization. Where appropriate, obtain authorizations from employees allowing the company to inspect their personal possessions and property, including email and other electronic message systems on company premises. Inform employees that searches may be conducted without advance notice, and that anyone who does not consent to inspection may be subject to discipline.

Managing Dismissals

dismissal
Involuntary termination of an employee's employment with the firm.

Dismissal is the most drastic disciplinary step that can be taken toward an employee, and one that must be handled with deliberate care. Specifically, the dismissal should be *just* in that *sufficient cause* exists for it. Furthermore, the dismissal should occur only after *all reasonable steps* to rehabilitate or salvage the employee have failed. However, there are undoubtedly times when dismissal is required, and in these instances it should be carried out forthrightly.[22]

Grounds for Dismissal

There are four bases for dismissal: unsatisfactory performance; misconduct; lack of qualifications for the job; and changed requirements of (or elimination of) the job. *Unsatisfactory performance* may be defined as a persistent failure to perform assigned duties or to meet prescribed standards on the job.[23] Specific reasons here include excessive absenteeism, tardiness, a persistent failure to meet normal job requirements, or an adverse attitude toward the company, supervisor, or fellow employees. *Misconduct* can be defined as deliberate and willful violation of the employer's rules and may include stealing, rowdyism, and insubordination. *Lack of qualifications* for the job is defined as an employee's incapability of doing the assigned work although the person is diligent. Since the employee in this case may be trying to do the job, it is especially important that every effort be made to salvage him or her. *Changed requirements of the job* may be defined as an employee's incapability of doing the work assigned after the nature of the job has been changed. Similarly, an employee may have to be dismissed when his or her job is eliminated. Here again, the employee may be industrious, so every effort should be made to retrain or transfer this person, if possible.

insubordination
Willful disregard or disobedience of the boss's authority or legitimate orders; criticizing the boss in public.

Insubordination, a form of misconduct, is sometimes the grounds for dismissal, although it may be relatively difficult to prove. Stealing, chronic tardiness, and poor-quality work are fairly concrete grounds for dismissal, while insubordination is sometimes harder to translate into words. To that end, it may be useful to remember that some acts are or should be considered insubordinate whenever and wherever they occur. These include:

1. Direct disregard of the boss's authority. At sea, this is called mutiny.
2. Flat out disobedience of, or refusal to obey, the boss's orders—particularly in front of others.
3. Deliberate defiance of clearly-stated company policies, rules, regulations, and procedures.
4. Public criticism of the boss. Contradicting or arguing with him or her is also negative and inappropriate.
5. Blatant disregard of the boss's reasonable instructions.
6. Contemptuous display of disrespect; making insolent comments, for example; and, more important, portraying these feelings in the attitude shown while on the job.
7. Disregard for the chain of command, shown by going around the immediate supervisor or manager with a complaint, suggestion, or political manoeuvre. Although the employee may be right, that may not be enough to save him or her from the charges of insubordination.
8. Participation in (or leadership of) an effort to undermine and remove the boss from power. If the effort doesn't work (and it seldom does), those involved will be "dead in the water."[24]

As in most human endeavours, it is dangerous to take the position that any of these acts should always lead to dismissal. Even at sea (as the movie *Crimson Tide* illustrates), there may be extenuating circumstances for the apparent insubordination. Cases like these should therefore be reviewed by the supervisor's boss.

For example, an Ontario millwright was fired when he pushed a company manager down the steps of a construction trailer, narrowly missing construction debris and a passing front-end loader. The manager had been reprimanding the millwright for taking a day off to go hunting, which had forced the company to hire a private electrical contractor. The millwright grieved his termination, and the arbitrator ruled that a four-month suspension would be more appropriate, as the assault was not premeditated, but the result of momentary anger in reaction to provocation by the supervisor.[25]

The Employment Contract

In Canada, the employer-employee relationship is governed by an employment contract—a formal agreement (in writing or based on mutual understanding) made between the two parties. If the contract is for a specific length of time, the contract ends at the expiration date, and the employee cannot be prematurely dismissed without just cause.

Employees are often hired under an implied contract where the understanding is that employment is for an indefinite period of time and may be terminated by either party only when reasonable notice is given.[26] Employers cannot hire and fire employees at will, as is the case in the United States. Canadian employers can only terminate an employee's employment without reasonable notice when just cause exists. If just cause is not present, then a termination without notice is considered wrongful dismissal.

Just cause is often an area of disagreement between employer and employee, but is usually considered to include disobedience, incompetence, dishonesty, insubordination, fighting, and persistent absence or lateness.[27] However, just cause cannot be assessed in isolation, and may vary depending on the possible consequences of the misconduct, the status of the employee, and the circumstances of the case. The burden of proof rests with the employer. In Canada, courts often do not accept the assertion of just cause by the employer. One Canadian researcher found that since 1980, the courts agreed with employers in only 25 percent of cases alleging incompetence, 40 percent for misconduct, 54 percent for insubordination, and 66 percent for conflict of interest/competing with the employer.[28]

In any termination where just cause is not involved, the employer must provide reasonable notice to the employee (often three to four weeks per year of service). The employee sometimes continues to work during the period of notice given, but often ceases work at the time the notice of termination is given. In the latter case, the employee receives a lump sum of money equal to his or her pay for the period of notice.

Often the amount considered reasonable is beyond the minimum notice requirements of employment/labour standards legislation. The employee can accept the notice given or can sue for wrongful dismissal if the notice is considered unacceptable. The court will review the circumstances of the dismissal, and make a final decision on the amount of notice to be provided. The courts generally award a period of notice based on their assessment of how long it will take the employee to find alternative employment, taking into account the employee's age, salary, length of service, the level of the job, and other factors. Rarely have notice periods exceeded 24 months.[29]

In some cases, employers may also be ordered to pay punitive damages for harsh and vindictive treatment of an employee, and/or damages for aggravated or mental distress if the employee suffered undue distress from not being given adequate notice of termination.[30] The employee has the responsibility to make every effort to find alternate employment as soon as possible, although not at a position inferior to the one from which he or she was terminated.

Avoiding Wrongful Dismissal Suits

wrongful dismissal
An employee dismissal that does not comply with the law or does not comply with a written or implied contractual arrangement.

With the increased likelihood that terminated employees can and will sue for **wrongful dismissal,** it behooves employers to protect themselves against wrongful dismissal suits. The time to do that is before mistakes have been made and suits have been filed. Here is what one expert recommends to avoid wrongful dismissal suits.

- Review the *employee manual* to look for and delete statements that could prejudice the employer's defense in a wrongful dismissal case. For example, delete any reference to the fact that "employees can be terminated only for just cause" (unless the company really means that). Also consider not outlining progressive discipline procedures in the manual since the employer may be obligated to stick with the rules and follow the steps exactly or be sued for failing to do so. Similarly, references to probationary periods or permanent employment may be unwise since they imply a permanence the company may not really mean to imply. Never limit the right to dismiss or list specific reasons for dismissal. Always add a sentence or paragraph that reserves for the employer the right to make changes to the handbook in the future.[31]

- Make sure that no one in a position of authority makes *promises* the company does not intend to keep, such as by saying "If you do your job here, you can't get fired."

- Have clear written rules listing infractions that may require *discipline* and *dismissal,* and then make sure to adhere to the rules. Generally, employees must be given an opportunity to correct unacceptable behaviour, and supervisors should be careful not to single out any one person.

- If a rule is broken, get the worker's side of the story in front of witnesses, and preferably get it signed. Then make sure to *check out* the story, getting both sides of the issue.

- Be sure that employees are evaluated at least annually. If an employee is showing evidence of incompetence, give that person a warning and provide a chance to improve. All evaluations should be put in writing and signed by the employee.[32]

- Keep careful records of all actions such as employee evaluations, warnings or notices, memos outlining how improvement should be accomplished, and so on. Keep all efforts at counselling or discipline confidential to avoid defamation charges.[33]

- Make sure that the company's policy about probationary periods is clear and that employees cannot infer that once they are past the probationary period their jobs are "safe."[34]

- Remember that there are a number of reasons used by the courts to protect employees from arbitrary dismissal such as whistleblowing, complaining about equal pay or wage law violations, and filing a workers' compensation claim.[35]

- Before taking any irreversible steps, *review* the person's HR file. For example, long-seniority employees may merit more opportunities to correct their actions than newly hired workers.

- Finally, consider *"buying out"* a wrongful dismissal claim with settlement pay. Do not stand in the way of a terminated employee's future employment, since a person with a new job is less likely to bring a lawsuit against the former employer than someone who remains unemployed.[36]

- In addition, firms should not:

    Discharge anyone who is about to vest in employee benefits.

    Discharge a female employee just before maternity leave.

    "Constructively discharge" employees by placing them in a lower paying job in hopes of a resignation.

    Try to induce employees to waive existing rights in exchange for gaining other rights.

    Deviate from internal complaint resolution guidelines and procedures.

    Oversell promises of job security in handbooks or oral discussions.[37]

**hr.cch.com/tips/
restruc.htm#sam**
Restructuring Tips

Constructive Dismissal Constructive dismissal can be considered to occur when the employer makes unilateral changes in the employment contract that are unacceptable to the employee, even though the employee has not been formally terminated.[38] The most common changes in employment status that are considered to constitute constructive dismissal are demotion, reduction in pay and benefits, forced resignation, forced early retirement, forced transfer, and changes in job duties and responsibilities. An employee who believes he or she has been constructively dismissed can sue the employer for wrongful dismissal. If the judge agrees that constructive dismissal occurred, he or she will determine a period of notice to be provided to the employee.

Dismissal Procedures

In the event of a dismissal, these additional steps should be followed:

Hold warning discussions before taking any final action. An employee must be made aware that he or she is not performing satisfactorily.

Get written confirmation of the final warning.

Prepare a checklist of all property that should be accounted for, including computer disks and manuals.

Change security codes and locks previously used by discharged individuals.

If the dismissal involves large numbers of employees (say, 25 or more), prepare and secure approval for a news release.

Always prepare for the possibility that the discharged individual may act irrationally or even violently, either immediately or in weeks to come.

Decide beforehand how other employees will be informed about this person's dismissal. An informal departmental meeting of those directly involved with this person is usually sufficient.

Consider having a lawyer create an employee release form. Such releases are obtained from employees who have asserted claims or who are the subject of employment actions such as discharges and layoffs. They release the employer from claims by giving the employee something of value—"consideration" in legal terms.[39] Any such release should include: (1) a general release of the employee's claims; (2) a covenant not to sue the employer; and (3) an indemnification and payback provision relating to breaches of the release and convenant-not-to-sue provisions.[40]

The Termination Interview   Dismissing an employee is one of the most difficult tasks a manager will face at work.[41] The dismissed employee, even if warned many times in the past, will often still react with total disbelief or even violence. Guidelines for the **termination interview** itself are as follows:

Step 1   Plan the interview carefully. According to experts at Hay Associates, this means:

> Schedule the meeting on a day early in the week.
>
> Make sure the employee keeps the appointment time.
>
> Never inform an employee over the phone.
>
> Allow ten minutes as sufficient time for notification in the interview.
>
> Avoid Fridays, preholidays, and vacation times when possible.
>
> Use a neutral site, never the supervisor's office.
>
> Have employee agreements, human resources file, and release announcement (internal and external) prepared in advance.
>
> Be available at a time after the interview in case questions or problems arise.
>
> Have phone numbers ready for medical or security emergencies.

Step 2   Get to the point. Do not beat around the bush by talking about the weather or making other small talk. As soon as the employee arrives, give the person a moment to get comfortable and then inform him or her of the decision.

Step 3   Describe the situation. Briefly, in three or four sentences, explain why the person is being let go. For instance, "Production in your area is down four percent, and we are continuing to have quality problems. We have talked about these problems several times in the past three months and the solutions are not being followed through. We have to make a change."[42] Remember to describe the situation rather than attacking the employee personally by saying things like "Your production is just not up to par." Also emphasize that the decision is final and irrevocable; other in-house positions were explored, management at all levels concurs, and all relevant factors—performance, workload, and so on—were considered. Don't take more than 10 to 15 minutes for the interview.

Step 4   Listen. It is important to continue the interview until the person appears to be talking freely and reasonably calmly about the reasons for his or her termination and the support package (including severance pay) he or she is to receive. Do not get into arguments; instead, actively listen and get the person to talk by using open-ended questions, restating his or her last comment, nodding, and using silence. Use the Behavioural Reaction Chart (**Figure 15.1**) to gauge the person's reaction and to decide how best to proceed.

Step 5   Next carefully review all elements of the severance package. Describe severance payments, benefits, access to office support people, and the way references will be handled. However, under no conditions should any promises or benefits

termination interview
The interview in which an employee is informed of the fact that he or she has been dismissed.

**Figure 15.1
Behavioural Reaction
to Termination and
Suggested Response**
Source: Hay Associates,
Philadelphia, Pa. 19103

Hostile and angry	Defensive and bargaining	Formal and procedural (lawsuit?)	Stoic	Crying/ sobbing
Hurt Anger Disappointment Relief	Guilt Fear Uncertainty Disbelief	Vengeful Suppressed Controlled	Shock Disbelief Numbness	Sadness Grief Worry
• Summarize the employee's response in a tentative style: "It sounds as if you are pretty angry about this." • Avoid confronting the anger or becoming defensive. • Remain objective; stick to the facts and give the employee information about the counselling process.	• Acknowledge that this is a difficult time for the employee as well as the company. • Don't get involved in any bargaining discussions. • Offer reassurance about the future and connect this to the counselling process.	• Allow the employee freedom to ask any questions as long as they pertain to his or her own case. • Try to avoid side issues and discussion of "political" motivations. • Keep the tone formal. This is a good way to lead into the role the career counsellor will play.	• Communicate to the employee that his or her shock is being recognized and say the details can be handled later if the employee prefers. • Ask if there are any specific questions for the moment. If not, tell the employee about the career counsellor and make the introduction.	• Allow the person an opportunity to cry if that occurs. Just offer some tissues. • Avoid inane comments such as "What are you crying about, it's not that important." • When the person regains composure, press on with the facts and explain the counselling process.

beyond those already in the support package be implied. Do not promise to "look into" something and get back to the employee at a later date. This will simply complicate the termination process. The termination should be complete when the person leaves.

Step 6 Identify the next step. The terminated employee may be disoriented and unsure what to do next. Explain where the employee should go upon leaving the interview. Remind the person whom to contact at the company regarding questions about the support package or references.

outplacement counselling
A systematic process by which a terminated person is trained and counselled in the techniques of self-appraisal and securing a new position.

Outplacement Counselling Outplacement counselling[43] is a systematic process by which a terminated person is trained and counselled in the techniques of conducting a self-appraisal and securing a new job that is appropriate to his or her needs and talents.[44] As the term is generally used, outplacement does not mean the employer takes responsibility for placing the terminated person in a new job. Instead it is a counselling service, the purpose of which is to provide the person with advice, instructions, and a sounding board to help formulate career goals and successfully execute a job search. Outplacement counselling thus might more accurately (but more ponderously) be called "career counselling and job search skills for terminated employees." The counselling itself is done either by the employer's in-house specialist or by outside consultants. The *outplacement* counselling is considered part of the terminated employee's support or severance package.

Outplacement counselling is usually conducted by outplacement firms such as Drake Beam Moran Inc., and Right Associates Inc. Middle- and upper-level managers who are let go will typically have office space and secretarial services they can use at local offices of such firms, in addition to the counselling services.

Exit Interviews   Many employers conduct final exit interviews with employees who are leaving the firm. These are usually conducted by the HR department. They aim at eliciting information about the job or related matters that might give the employer a better insight into what is right—or wrong—about the company. The assumption, of course, is that since the employee is leaving, he or she will be candid.

Whether the person will be candid is debatable. The person might have his or her own axe to grind, for instance, and could use the exit interview to try to retaliate against former foes. Or the person might simply not want to cause trouble that might come back to haunt him or her when in need of references for a new job.

Based on one survey, the quality of information one can expect to get from exit interviews is questionable. The researchers found that at the time of separation, 38 percent of those leaving blamed "salary and benefits," while only 4 percent blamed "supervision." Followed up 18 months later, however, 24 percent blamed supervision and only 12 percent blamed salary and benefits. Getting to the real problem during the exit interview may thus require some heavy digging.[45]

Managing Separations: Layoff and Retirement

Nondisciplinary separations are a fact of life in organizations and can be initiated by either employer or employee. For the employer, reduced sales or profits may require layoffs or downsizings, for instance, while employees may terminate their own employment to retire or to seek better jobs.

group termination laws
Laws that require an employer to notify employees in the event an employer decides to terminate a group of employees.

Group termination laws require employers who are terminating a large group of employees to give them more notice than that required upon termination of an individual employee. The laws are intended to assist employees in situations of plant closings and large downsizings. Most jurisdictions in Canada require employers who are terminating a group of employees (some specify 10 or more, some 15 or more, and some 50 or more) within a short period of time (some specify four weeks, others two months) to give advance notice to employees, and sometimes their union. The amount of notice varies by jurisdiction, and with the number of employees being terminated, but generally ranges from four weeks to 18 weeks.

The laws do not prevent the employer from closing down, nor do they require saving jobs. They simply give employees time to seek other work or retraining by giving them advance notice of the termination.

The law is not clear about how the notice to employees must be worded. However, a letter to the individual employees to be terminated might include a paragraph toward the end of the letter as follows:

As more firms relocate their manufacturing plants to foreign countries in order to minimize costs, workers protest the signing of any free trade agreements, which they think encourage such actions.

Please consider this letter to be your official notice, as required by law, that your current position with the company will end 60 days from today because of a (layoff or closing) that is now projected to take place on (date). After that day your employment with the company will be terminated, and you will no longer be carried on our payroll records or be covered by any company benefit programs. Any questions concerning this notice will be answered in the HR office.[46]

Managing Layoffs

layoff
The temporary withdrawal of employment to workers for economic or business reasons.

A **layoff**, in which workers are sent home for a time, is a situation in which three conditions are present: (1) there is no work available for the employees; (2) management expects the no-work situation to be temporary and probably short term; and (3) management intends to recall the employees when work is again available.[47] A layoff is therefore not a termination, which is a permanent severing of the employment relationship. However, some employers do use the term *layoff* as a euphemism for discharge or termination.

bumping/layoff procedures
Detailed procedures that determine who will be laid off if no work is available; generally allowing employees to use their seniority to remain on the job.

Bumping/Layoff Procedures Employers who encounter frequent business slowdowns and layoffs often have detailed procedures that allow employees to use their seniority to remain on the job. In unionized organizations, these procedures are negotiated with workers. Most such procedures have these features in common:[48]

1. For the most part, seniority is the ultimate determinant of who will work.
2. Seniority can give way to merit or ability, but usually only when none of the senior employees is qualified for a particular job.
3. Seniority is usually based on the date the employee joined the organization, not the date he or she took a particular job.
4. Because seniority is usually company-wide, an employee in one job is usually allowed to bump or displace an employee in another job provided the more senior employee is able to do the job in question without further training.

Alternatives to Layoffs

Many employers today recognize the enormous investments they have in recruiting, screening, and training their employees and in winning their commitment and loyalty. As a result, they are more hesitant to lay off employees at the first signs of business decline. Instead they are using new approaches to either blunt the effects of the layoff or eliminate the layoffs entirely.

voluntary reduction in pay plan
An alternative to layoffs in which all employees agree to reductions in pay to keep everyone working.

voluntary time off
An alternative to layoffs in which some employees agree to take time off to reduce the employer's payroll and avoid the need for a layoff.

contingent employees
Individuals hired to deal with temporary increases in an organization's workload or to perform specialized tasks for which current employees are lacking time and/or expertise.

There are several alternatives to layoff. With the **voluntary reduction in pay plan,** all employees agree to reductions in pay in order to keep everyone working. Other employers arrange to have all or most of their employees accumulate their vacation time and to concentrate their vacations during slow periods. Temporary help thus does not have to be hired for vacationing employees during peak periods, and employment automatically falls off when business declines. Other employees agree to take **voluntary time off,** which again has the effect of reducing the employer's payroll and avoiding the need for a layoff. Another way to avoid layoffs is the use of **contingent employees**. Temporary supplemental employees are hired with the understanding that their work is of a temporary nature and they may be laid off at any time. Then when layoffs come, the first group to be laid off is the cadre of contingent workers.[49] The use of contingent workers in Canada is growing, and will continue to increase, according to a 1997 Conference Board report.[50]

Adjusting to Downsizing and Mergers

downsizing
Refers to the process of reducing, usually dramatically, the number of people employed by the firm.

Downsizing—reducing, usually dramatically, the number of people employed by the firm—is used by more and more employers. The rate of workforce reduction in Canada appears to be slowing down, but one 1997 survey of over 1 000 Canadian employers found that 26 percent expected to undertake further downsizing.[51]

Although it's not clear why, most firms don't find that their operating earnings improve after major staff cuts are made. There are probably many ways to explain this anomaly but declining employee morale as a result of downsizing is one plausible candidate. Therefore, firms that are downsizing must also give attention to the employees remaining. Certainly those "downsized-out" should be treated fairly. But it is around the employees retained that the business will be built.

Dealing with the Survivors Immediately After the Downsizing One of two situations must be faced immediately following downsizing. First, if no further reductions are anticipated, workers can be reassured accordingly. However, the promise that no further reductions will occur should not be made unless it is certain that this promise can be kept.

The second situation is more difficult because it is expected that more reductions will probably take place. In this case, be honest with those remaining, explaining that while future downsizings will probably occur, they will be informed of these reductions as soon as possible. The company may well experience a transitory drop in productivity and increased attrition, but the alternative is being dishonest with all the people involved.

Specific Steps to Take A major downsizing program instituted at Duracell Canada illustrates the steps involved in a well-conceived program. The criterion used for planning decisions was employee dignity and respect—one of the company's core values. The program began with *announcement activities*. The first was a full staff meeting at the facility, where senior management announced the downsizing. This meeting was immediately followed by small group meetings between the employees who were losing their jobs, their manager, and an outplacement counsellor. Information about the support services and assistance being provided to those leaving was also made available to survivors, in order to reduce their concerns about coworkers who were leaving. The fact that employees were used to ongoing communication from the company lent credibility to this process.

Next there was an *immediate follow-up* phase during the two weeks after the announcement. Workshops were provided by outplacement counsellors to help employees begin the job search process, and one-on-one counselling was also available to those who wanted it. A career centre with internal and external job postings was set up inside the company's premises. During this period, all employees continued working, and productivity increased. Duracell attributes this result to its efforts to fully communicate all information about the downsizing to all employees, and the generous severance packages provided. Finally, a party was held for all employees on the last day of work for those leaving.

A mechanism for providing *long-term support* was also built into the program. Key managers were encouraged to meet with the remaining staff frequently and informally in order to provide them ongoing support in an open-door atmosphere.

Rebuilding employee commitment can be a key to a successful downsizing. And, as one experienced chief executive recently put it, "If companies are committed to building positive attitudes in their employees, they must actively and explicitly institute programs to achieve this during the downsizing process. This means that instead of a pure plan for cost reduction, the restructuring strategy must be broadened to achieve the additional goal of lighting a new fire of employee enthusiasm."[52]

A critical responsibility of human resources managers in any downsizing is ensuring that the bad news is delivered in a humane manner.[53] Department managers need to be trained in how to deliver unwelcome news effectively (by participating in role plays for practice), and how to listen to and observe other managers. These managers also need to identify and recognize their own personal

www.webcom.com/~garnet/labor
Employee Relations Links

www.perc.net
HR Positive Employee Relations Council

values that will anchor them during the difficult communication process. The responsibility for delivering tough news humanely, treating people with dignity and respect, and advising people of all the support services available to them must be emphasized. It helps if managers work with a partner who acts as a coach when preparing for a termination interview, and debriefs them on the experience when it is over. Finally, every effort should be made to deliver downsizing news in a one-on-one manner, and to anticipate the emotional reactions from everyone involved, including the manager.

Handling a Merger/Acquisition Dismissals and downsizings in the case of mergers or acquisitions are usually one-sided. One company essentially acquires the other, and it is often the employees of the latter who find themselves out looking for new jobs.

In such a situation the employees in the acquired firm will be hypersensitive to mistreatment of their colleagues. It thus behooves managers to ensure that those let go are treated with courtesy. Seeing former colleagues fired is bad enough for morale. Seeing them fired under conditions that look like bullying rubs salt in the wound and poisons the relationship for years to come. As a rule, therefore, managers should:[54]

- Avoid the appearance of power and domination.
- Avoid win/lose behaviour.
- Remain businesslike and professional in all dealings.
- Maintain as positive a feeling about the acquired company as possible.
- Remember that the degree to which the organization treats the acquired group with care and dignity will affect the confidence, productivity, and commitment of those remaining.

Building Employee Commitment

Long-Term Employment Without Guarantees

Two Canadian companies have retained a "no-layoff" policy throughout the downsizing fever of the 1990s.[1] Federal Express Canada and Cadet Uniform Services have outperformed the competition by lowering costs, increasing productivity, and improving customer service. Their no-layoff policies are a strategic business decision. In both companies, stable employment is part of an overall system of progressive HR practices to develop employees oriented to quality and service. Job security also seems to help employees to be receptive to change. Discretionary effort on a daily basis seems to be what makes these companies leaders in their industries. Federal Express Canada's People Manual clearly states that the company is committed to not laying off employees except in the most extreme economic conditions. Cadet's policy is not in writing, but it is a historical fact that no employee has been laid off in their 25 years of operation. In effect, these firms offer **long-term employment without guarantees**.

FedEx Canada was losing money in the early 1990s but rather than downsizing management asked employees for ideas on how to grow the business, which turned the company around. Canada is now the most profitable division in the entire company worldwide. Similarly at Cadet, employee suggestions and agreement to reduced work weeks helped them through the lean years in the early part of the 1990s.

For employers offering stable employment, careful hiring is crucial as mentioned previously. FedEx Canada fills 95 percent of positions internally. Both companies have an

long-term employment without guarantees
A commitment on the part of firms to do all that is reasonably possible to avoid layoffs and non-performance-based dismissals, while recognizing that ultimately the employment relationship is not guaranteed.

extensive interviewing process for external hiring, and look for team players with stable job backgrounds and development potential.

One way to help ensure that employment is long term is the use of temporary, part-time employees to provide the slack that helps the firm downsize without laying off permanent employees. Another approach is to have as much as 10 percent to 20 percent of compensation at risk, dropping when sales or profits plummet. Perhaps most importantly, these tactics to maintain a long-term employment strategy usually let firms stay "lean and mean" and thus more efficient and flexible than their competitors.◆

1. This is from K. Mark, "No More Pink Slips," *Human Resources Professional*, November 1996, pp. 21–3.

Retirement

retirement
The point at which a person ceases full-time work, usually between the ages of 60 to 65, but increasingly earlier today due to firms' early retirement incentive plans.

preretirement counselling
Counselling provided to employees some months, or even years before retirement, which covers matters such as benefits advice, second careers, and so on.

An employee contemplating different retirement options.

Retirement for most employees is bittersweet. For some it is the culmination of their careers, a time when they can relax and enjoy the fruits of their labour without worrying about the problems of work. For others, it is the retirement itself that is the trauma, as the once-busy employee tries to cope with suddenly being "nonproductive" and with the strange (and not entirely pleasant) experience of being home every day with nothing to do. For many retirees, in fact, maintaining a sense of identity and self-worth without a full-time job is the single most important task they'll face. And it's one that employers are increasingly trying to help their retirees cope with as a logical last step in the career management process.[55]

Preretirement Counselling   Over half (55 percent) of the employers in one survey said they had formal **preretirement counselling** aimed at easing the passage of their employees into retirement.[56] Counselling was provided in group seminars, individual meetings, and through reference material. The most common preretirement topics were:

Explanation of retirement pensions and benefits (reported by 90 percent of those with preretirement education programs)

Financial and investment counselling (84 percent)

Will and estate planning (52 percent)

Health, nutrition, and fitness counselling (49 percent)

Leisure-time counselling (49 percent)

Counselling for second careers (26 percent)

Another important trend here is that of granting part-time employment to employees as an alternative to outright retirement. Several recent surveys of blue- and white-collar employees showed that about half of all employees over age 55 would like to continue working part-time after they retire.[57]

Chapter Review

Summary

1. Managers of more progressive firms know that commitment is built on trust, and that trust requires floods of two-way communications. Firms like this therefore set up programs such as Guaranteed Fair Treatment, Speak Up!, opinion surveying, and Top-Down communication programs for keeping employees informed. Speak

Up! hotlines provide employees with anonymous channels through which they can express concerns to top management. Opinion surveys provide standardized channels through which management can take the pulse of employee attitudes. Top-down communication programs include roundtable discussions, in-house television broadcasts, and top managers continuously mingling with employees.

2. Guaranteed Fair Treatment programs, such as the one at Federal Express Canada, help to ensure that grievances are handled fairly and openly. Steps include management review, officer complaint, and executive appeals review.

3. A fair and just discipline process is based on three prerequisites: rules and regulations, a system of progressive penalties, and an appeals process. We listed a number of discipline guidelines, including that discipline should be in line with the way management usually responds to similar incidents; that management must adequately investigate the matter before administering discipline; and that managers should not rob an employee of his or her dignity.

4. One approach to discipline is called "discipline without punishment." Its basic aim is to gain an employee's acceptance of the rules by reducing the punitive nature of the discipline itself. In particular, employees are given a paid day off to consider their infraction before more punitive disciplinary steps are taken.

5. Managing dismissals is an important part of any supervisor's job. Among the reasons for dismissal are unsatisfactory performance, misconduct, lack of qualifications, changed job requirements, and insubordination. Great care should be taken to avoid wrongful dismissal suits. For example, firms should have clear written rules regarding discipline and dismissal, and avoid constructively dismiss employees by placing them in lower-paying jobs in hopes of a resignation.

6. Dismissing an employee is always difficult and the termination interview should be handled properly. Specifically, plan the interview carefully, get to the point, describe the situation, and then listen until the person has expressed his or her feelings. Then discuss the severance package and identify the next step.

7. Nondisciplinary separations such as layoffs and retirements occur all the time. Employment/labour standards laws set down requirements to be followed with regard to official notice before group termination occurs.

8. Many firms today seek alternatives to layoffs. These include voluntary reduction in pay plans, voluntary time off, and the use of contingent workers, which involves using temporary employees who are let go in adverse times.

9. Job security and employee commitment go hand in hand. That's why firms like Federal Express Canada and Cadet Uniform Services emphasize what might be called long-term employment without guarantees. On the one hand, these firms do all they can to ensure job security and, in return, they expect their employees to commit themselves to the firm and its goals.

Key Terms

bumping/layoff procedures
contingent employees
discipline
dismissal
downsizing
group termination laws
guaranteed fair treatment programs

insubordination
layoff
long-term employment without guarantees
open-door program
opinion surveys
outplacement counselling
preretirement counselling
retirement

speak up! programs
termination interview
top-down communication programs
voluntary reduction in pay plan
voluntary time off
wrongful dismissal

Discussion Questions and Exercises

1. Explain the role of communication and guaranteed fair treatment in fostering employee commitment.
2. Describe specific techniques you would use to foster top-down communication in an organization.
3. Describe the similarities and differences between a program such as Federal Express Canada's guaranteed fair treatment program and a typical union grievance procedure.
4. Explain how fairness in disciplining can be ensured, particularly the prerequisites to disciplining, disciplining guidelines, and the "discipline without punishment" approach.
5. Why is it important, in what some consider our highly litigious society, to manage dismissals properly?
6. What are the techniques which can be used as alternatives to layoffs? What do such alternatives have to do with what we refer to as long-term employment without guarantees? Why are alternatives like these important, given industry's need today for highly committed employees?
7. Working individually or in groups, interview managers or administrators in one or more workplaces in order to determine the extent to which employers build two-way communications, and the specific types of programs (such as Speak-Up programs) that are used. Do the managers think they are effective? What do the employees think of the programs?
8. Working individually or in groups, obtain copies of the student handbook for a college or university and determine to what extent there is a formal process through which students can air grievances. Would you expect the process to be effective? Why or why not? Based on contacts with students who have used the grievance process, has it been effective?
9. Working individually or in groups, determine the nature of the academic discipline process in a college or university. Does it appear to be an effective one? Based on this chapter, should any modification be made to the student discipline process?

Application Exercises

RUNNING CASE: Carter Cleaning Company

Guaranteeing Fair Treatment

Being in the laundry and cleaning business, the Carters have always felt strongly about not allowing employees to smoke, eat, or drink in their stores. Jennifer was therefore surprised to walk into a store and find two employees eating lunch at the front counter. There was a large pizza in its box, and the two of them were sipping colas and eating slices of pizza and submarine sandwiches off paper plates. Not only did it look messy, but there were also grease and cola spills on the counter and the store smelled from onions and pepperoni, even with the four-foot-wide exhaust fan pulling air out through the roof. In addition to being a turnoff to customers, the mess on the counter increased the possibility that a customer's order might actually become soiled in the store.

While this was a serious matter, neither Jennifer nor her father believe that what the counter people were doing is grounds for immediate dismissal, partly because the store manager had apparently condoned their actions. The problem is that they don't know what to do. It seems to them that the matter calls for more than just a warning but less than dismissal.

Questions

1. Should a disciplinary system be established at Carter Cleaning Centres?

2. If so, what should it cover, and how should they deal with the errant counter people?

CASE INCIDENT: Job Insecurity at IBM

For over 50 years IBM was known for its policy of job security. Throughout all those years, it had never laid off any employees, even as the company was going through wrenching changes. For example, in the late 1970s and 1980s, IBM had to close down its punch card manufacturing plants and division, but the thousands of employees who worked in those plants were simply given an opportunity to move to comparable jobs in other IBM divisions.

Unfortunately, IBM's full-employment policy eventually evaporated, and fast. As IBM's computer industry market share dropped throughout the 1980s, both its sales revenue and profits began to erode. By 1991 it had become apparent that a drastic restructuring was needed. The firm therefore accelerated its downsizing efforts, instituting various early retirement and incentive plans aimed at getting employees to leave voluntarily: Numerous imaginative schemes were introduced, including spinning off certain operations to groups of employees who then quit IBM while becoming independent consultants, doing tasks very similar to those they used to do while employees of IBM. By 1992, however, at least 40 000 more employees still had to be trimmed, and by 1993 it had become apparent that IBM's cherished long-term employment policy had to be discarded. For the first time, IBM began laying off employees, and eventually tens of thousands more employees were let go, beginning with about 300 employees of the firm's Armonk, New York headquarters.

Questions

1. What accounts for the fact that a company like IBM can have high commitment but still lose market share, sales, and profitability? In other words, why did employee commitment not translate into corporate success as well as it might have at IBM?

2. What sorts of steps should IBM have taken in order to continue to avoid layoffs? If it appears any such steps were not feasible, explain why.

3. Given IBM's experience with its long-term employment policy, what are the implications for other companies thinking of instituting similar employment policies of their own?

Human Resources Management Simulation

Exercise 18 in the simulation asks for a report recommending discipline procedures for the plant. The advantages and disadvantages of employee involvement in this exercise should be considered and included in the report. The six aspects of fairness in the disciplinary process should also be incorporated in the recommended procedures. The appropriate extent of consistency with the procedures at the existing unionized plant should also be discussed. Simulation 5 presents an opportunity to role-play a disciplinary interview. The six components of disciplinary fairness outlined in this chapter should be strictly adhered to. If possible, have some role-play teams conduct the discussion without looking at the six fairness components, and have others carry out the discussion using the fairness points as guidelines. Assess whether following the six fairness points made the interview easier and more productive.

Video Case

Corporate Contradictions

This video suggests that it is hard to understand how from 1991 to 1995 in Canada, while corporate profits increased almost 95 percent, wages increased only 10 percent, and unemployment remained between nine percent and 10 percent. Despite record corporate profits, reengineering, restructuring, and downsizing have continued, all involving job cuts. One of the effects of high unemployment is reduced purchasing power on the part of the unemployed and those who fear they will become unemployed.

The Smith family shown in the video illustrates their lifestyle changes following Mr. Smith's layoff from Nortel—grocery bills cut in half, no money for vacations, leisure time restricted to no-cost activities, constant worry about the sole remaining provider being laid off, and so on. Mr. Smith has been provided with relocation counselling and severance pay, but still feels betrayed by a company that led its employees to believe they would never be laid off. The demise of corporate loyalty is a difficult reality for his family to accept. The fact that Nortel has received taxpayer's money for research and development seems to be a particularly sore point.

Some experts believe that the unrelenting demands of global competitiveness make it necessary to pursue this relentless drive for efficiency, and that strong, globally competitive Canadian corporations will eventually strengthen the economy and result in job creation. Others believe that this behaviour on the part of corporations is a dead-end street that will result in an economic crisis. They point to the problems in the strong German and Japanese economies as evidence that these corporate actions are nonsustainable.

The experts shown in the video are divided on who, if anyone, should take responsibility for this situation, and what the solution might be. There are some new jobs in the computer and high-tech areas, but fewer than those lost in manufacturing. The expectation of job growth in Canada in organizations that become global market leaders has yet to materialize. Indeed, Nortel is one company that is considered by many to fall in that category.

Questions

1. What should Mr. Smith do now?

2. What, if anything, could Nortel do to be more fair to employees like Mr. Smith?

3. Assess the strengths and weaknesses of the arguments made by the three experts at the end of the video.

Video Resource: CBC, *The National Magazine*, "Corporate Contradictions," January 16, 1996.

Take It to the Net

Check out our Companion Website at

www.prenticehall.ca/dessler

for a multitude of practice questions, key terms and concepts, Weblinks to related sites, newsgroups, CBC video updates, and more.

Notes

1. K. Blair, "How *Not* To Foil A Union Drive," *Canadian HR Reporter* (March 10, 1997), p. 1.
2. *Think Magazine* 55, no. 6 (1989).
3. "Big Payoff For Employee Suggestions," *Canadian HR Reporter* (September 25, 1995), p. 7.
4. G. Pearson, "Employee Surveys Mean More Communication—But Be Ready To Act," *Canadian HR Reporter* (May 22, 1995), p. 15.
5. This section is based on D. McElroy, "High Tech With High Touch: A New Communication Contract," *Canadian HR Reporter* (April 7, 1997), p. G6.
6. K. Gay, "Communicating Workplace Change Is A Necessity," *Financial Post* (April 15, 1995), p. 27.
7. *The Federal Express Employee Handbook* (August 7, 1989), p. 89.
8. Lester Bittel, *What Every Supervisor Should Know* (New York: McGraw-Hill, 1974), p. 308; based on a study by the American Arbitration Association of 1 000 grievances. For a study of the variables influencing disciplinary action, see, for example, Wanda Trahan and Dirk Steiner, "Factors Affecting Supervisors' Use of Disciplinary Action Following Poor Performance," *Journal of Organizational Behavio* 15, no. 2 (March 1994), pp. 129–39.
9. E.I. Beitner, "Justice and Dignity: A New Approach to Discipline," *Labor Law Journal* (August 1984), pp. 500–5.
10. For an example of a peer review appeals process see, for example, Dawn Anfuso, "Coors Taps Employee Judgement," *Personnel Journal* (February 1994), pp. 50–9.
11. George Bohlander, "Why Arbitrators Overturn Managers in Employee Suspension and Discharge Cases," *Journal of Collective Negotiations,* Vol. 23, no. 1 (1994), pp. 76–7.
12. Bohlander, "Why Arbiters Overturn Managers," p. 82.
13. Bohlander, "Why Arbiters Overturn Managers." See also Ahmad Karim, "Arbitrator Considerations in Modifying Discharge Decisions in the Public Sector," *Journal of Collective Negotiations* 22, no. 3 (1993), pp. 245–51, and Joseph Martocchio and Timothy Judge, "When We Don't See Eye to Eye: Discrepancies Between Supervisors and Subordinates in Absence Disciplinary Decisions," *Journal of Management* 21, no. 2 (1995), pp. 251–78.
14. Commerce Clearing House, *Ideas and Trends in Personnel* (April 8, 1982), p. 88. See also Brian Klaas and Daniel Feldman, "The Impact of Appeal Systems Structure on Disciplinary Actions," *Personnel Psychology* 47 (1994), pp. 91–108.
15. J.M. Beyer and H.M. Trice, "A Field Study of the Use and Perceived Effects of Discipline in Controlling Work Performance," *Academy of Management Journal* 27 (1984), pp. 743–64.
16. Commerce Clearing House, "Non-union Employees, NLRB Rules, Have the Right to Help During Questioning by Management," *Ideas and Trends in Personnel* (August 6, 1982), p. 151.
17. G.A. Ball, *"Outcomes of Punishment Incidents: The Role of Subordinate Perceptions, Individual Differences, and Leader Behavior,"* Unpublished doctoral dissertation. The Pennsylvania State University. See also N. Cole, "Yes, Employees Can React Positively to Discipline," *Canadian HR Reporter* (November 4, 1996), p. 11; and N. D. Cole and G.P. Latham, "Effects of Training in Procedural Justice on Perceptions of Disciplinary Fairness by Unionized Employees and Disciplinary Subject Matter Experts," *Journal of Applied Psychology* 82(5), 699–705, October 1997.
18. These are based on George Odiorne, *How Managers Make Things Happen,* (Englewood Cliffs, NJ: Prentice Hall, 1961), pp. 132–43; see also Bittel, *What Every Supervisor Should Know,* pp. 285–98. See also Cynthia Fukami and David Hopkins, "The Role of Situational Factors in Disciplinary Judgments," *Journal of Organizational Behavior* 14, No. 7 (December, 1993), pp. 665–76.
19. This is based on K. Blair, "Internet Use/Abuse Gets Employers' Attention," *Canadian HR Reporter* (January 27, 1997), p. 2.
20. Deborah Jacobs, "Are You Guilty of Electronic Trespassing?" *Management Review* (April 1994), p. 22.

21. These are based on "E-Mail Raises Privacy Questions," *BNA Bulletin to Management* (February 25, 1993), p. 64.

22. Joseph Famularo, *Handbook of Modern Personnel Administration* (New York: McGraw-Hill, 1972), pp. 65.3–65.5.

23. Famularo, *Handbook of Modern Personnel Administration*.

24. Famularo, *Handbook of Modern Personnel Administration*, pp. 65.4–65.5.

25. K. Blair, "When is a Firing Justified?" *Canadian HR Reporter* (April 21, 1997), p. 5. See also K. Blair, "Just How Just Does Just Cause Have to Be?" *Canadian HR Reporter* (November 3, 1997), p. 5.

26. E.E. Mole, *Wrongful Dismissal Practice Manual*, chapter 7, (Toronto: Butterworths Canada Ltd., 1993).

27. Mole, *Wrongful Dismissal*, chapter 4.

28. T. Wagar, "Wrongful Dismissal: Perception vs. Reality," *Human Resources Professional* (June 1996), p. 10.

29. K. Blair, "Sports Editor Scores 28-Month Severance," *Canadian HR Reporter* (April 7, 1997), p. 5.

30. K. Blair, "Pay in Lieu Just the Beginning," *Canadian HR Reporter* (July 14, 1997), p. 5.

31. T. Brady, "Employee Handbooks: Contracts or Empty Promise?" *Management Review* (June 1993), pp. 33–5.

32. Kenneth Jenero, "Employers Beware: You May Be Bound by the Terms of Your Old Employee Handbooks," *Employee Relations Law Journal* 20, no. 2 (Autumn 1994), pp. 299–312.

33. Robert Paul and James Townsend, "Wrongful Termination: Balancing Employer and Employee Rights—A Summary with Recommendations," *Employee Responsibilities and Rights Journal* 6, no. 1 (1993), pp. 69–82. Wrongful termination is particularly a problem when the employee is a "whistle-blower." See for example Rosalia Costa-Clarke, "The Cost Implications of Terminating Whistle-Blowers," *Employment Relations Today* 21, No. 4 (Winter 1994), pp. 447–54.

34. Paul and Townsend, "Wrongful Termination," p. 81.

35. Paul and Townsend, "Wrongful Termination."

36. Paul and Townsend, "Wrongful Termination," p. 74.

37. Based on a speech by Peter Panken and presented in BNA, *Bulletin to Management* (June 20, 1985), pp. 11–2.

38. Mole, *Wrongful Dismissal*, chapter 3.

39. This section was based on Miriam Rothman, "Employee Termination, I: A Four-Step Procedure," *Personnel* (February 1989), pp. 31–5; and Steven Jesseph, "Employee Termination, II: Some Do's and Don'ts," *Personnel* (February 1989), pp. 36–8. For a good checklist see author Silbergeld, "Avoiding Wrongful Termination Claims: A Checklist for Employers," *Employment Relations Today* 20, no. 4 (Winter, 1993), pp. 447–54.

40. See James Coil, III and Charles Rice, "Three Steps to Creating Effective Employee Releases," *Employment Relations Today* (Spring 1994), pp. 91–4. Wrongful termination is a problem for managerial employees as well. See, for example, Clinton Longenecker and Frederick Post, "The Management Termination Trap," *Business Horizons* 37, no. 3 (May–June, 1994), pp. 71–9.

41. Based on Coil and Rice, "Three Steps," p. 92.

42. William J. Morin and Lyle York, *Outplacement Techniques* (New York: AMACOM, 1982), pp. 101–31; and F. Leigh Branham, "How to Evaluate Executive Outplacement Services," *Personnel Journal* 62 (April 1983), pp. 323–6; Sylvia Milne, "The Termination Interview," *Canadian Manager* (Spring 1994), pp. 15–6.

43. Morin and York, *Outplacement Techniques*, p. 117. See also Sonny Weide, "When You Terminate An Employee," *Employment Relations Today* (August 1994), pp. 287–93.

44. Commerce Clearing House, *Ideas and Trends in Personnel* (July 9, 1982), pp. 132–46.

45. Commerce Clearing House, *Ideas and Trends in Personnel*, p. 132.

46. Joseph Zarandona and Michael Camuso, "A Study of Exit Interviews: Does the Last Word Count?" *Personnel* 62, no. 3 (March 1985), pp. 47–8.

47. Quoted from Commerce Clearing House, *Ideas and Trends in Personnel* (August 9, 1988), p. 133.

48. Commerce Clearing House, *Personnel Practices/Communications*, p. 1402.

49. *Personnel Practices/Communications*, p. 1410.

50. Commerce Clearing House, *Contingent Work: Trends, Issues and Challenges for Employers*, Conference Board of Canada, 1997.

51. *1997 Canadian Dismissal Practices Survey*, Murray Axmith & Associates, Toronto. See also Eric Greenberg, "Upswing in Downsizings to Continue," *Management Review* (February 1993), p. 5.

52. Les Feldman, "Duracell's First Aid for Downsizing Survivors," *Personnel Journal* (August 1989), p. 94. Also based on personal communication with S. Harries-Langley, Duracell Canada, August 11, 1997. See also Daniel Feldman and Carrie Leana, "Managing Layoffs in the 90s," *B&E Review* (January–March 1993), pp. 3–13.

53. This is based on *Mossop Cornelissen Report*, August 1996.

54. James Emshoff, "How to Increase Employee Loyalty While You Downsize," *Business Horizons* (March–April 1994), pp. 49–57. See also Robert Ford and Pamela Perrewé, "After the Layoff: Closing the Barn Door Before All the Horses Are Gone," *Business Horizons* (July–August 1993), pp. 34–40.

55. Fujio Cho, "Employee Motivation by Applying the Toyota Promotion System," speech to the Asian Business Club of Harvard Business School, March 4, 1991, p. 2.

56. *1995 Canadian Dismissal Practices Survey*, Murray Axmith & Associates, Toronto.

57. "Preretirement Education Programs," *Personnel* 59 (May–June 1982), p. 47. For a discussion of why it is important for retiring employees to promote aspects of their lives aside from their careers, see Daniel Halloran, "The Retirement Identity Crisis—and How to Beat It," *Personnel Journal*. 64 (May 1985), pp. 38–40. For an example of a program aimed at training preretirees to prepare for the financial aspects of their retirement, see, for example, Silvia Odenwald, "Pre-Retirement T1raining Gathers Steam," *Training and Development Journal* 40, no. 2 (February 1986), pp. 62–3.

Chapter 16
The Dynamics of Labour Relations

Chapter Outline

- ◆ **Introduction to Labour–Management Relations**
- ◆ **The Contemporary Legal Framework**
- ◆ **The Labour Movement in Canada Today**
- ◆ **Management's Labour Relations Strategy**
- ◆ **The Labour Relations Process**
- ◆ **Union Organizing and Recognition**
- ◆ **The Impact of Unionization on HRM**

Learning Outcomes

After studying this chapter, you should be able to:

Discuss the purposes of unionization.

Summarize the common characteristics among Canadian labour relations legislation and *describe* possible unfair labour practices by unions and management.

Explain the structure and functions of Canadian labour organizations.

Describe the labour relations strategies managers can adopt.

Outline the steps in the labour relations process.

Explain why workers might desire unionization, and *describe* the union organizing and recognition processes.

Discuss the impact of unionization on HRM.

Introduction to Labour–Management Relations

labour–management relations
The ongoing economic and social interactions between labour unions and management in organizations.

collective agreement (union contract)
A signed, written agreement between an employer (or employer's organization) and the union representing a group of the organization's employees, containing provisions outlining the terms and conditions of their employment.

collective bargaining
The negotiations that take place between a labour union, collectively representing the employees of a firm or industry, and the employer or employer's association, to arrive at a mutually-acceptable collective agreement.

bargaining unit
The group of employees in a firm, plant, or industry that has been recognized by the employer and certified by a Labour Relations Board (in most cases) as appropriate for collective bargaining purposes.

The term **labour–management relations** refers to the ongoing economic and social interactions between labour unions and management in organizations. The presence of a labour union alters the relationship between employees and the organization. Managerial discretion and flexibility in dealing with employees and implementing and administering human resources policies and procedures are reduced. For example, union seniority provisions in the **collective agreement**, negotiated through **collective bargaining**, govern the selection of employees for transfers, promotions, and training programs, and specify the order in which employees can be laid off and recalled. Also, pay rates and benefits are determined and standardized through the collective bargaining process, rather than being left to management's discretion, as are many other terms and conditions of employment governing members of the **bargaining unit**.

In the context of labour–management relations, the term management refers to all individuals in positions of authority over others within the organization. As will be explained in more detail later, employees typically seek union representation because they are dissatisfied with certain aspects of the job, feel that they lack influence with management and have relatively little power in their relations with supervisors, and see unionization as a way of pursuing their interests and solving their problems.[1] If supervisors communicate effectively with employees, deal with their concerns, and treat them fairly, employees are far less likely to be interested in forming or joining a union. Conversely, in firms in which supervisors ignore employee well-being and treat employees unfairly, employees often overcome their individual lack of power and improve their quality of work life by organizing a union and bargaining with the employer collectively.

Once a union has been recognized, the industrial relations specialist in the human resources department generally assumes primary responsibility for contract negotiations and grievance arbitration. However, first-line supervisors play a critical role in shaping the labour–management relationship, because of their day-to-day involvement in administering the collective agreement.

Labour–management relations will be examined in both this chapter and the next one. Chapter 16 focuses primarily on labour unions. A **labour union (or union)** is an officially-recognized body representing a group of individuals who have joined together for the purpose of presenting a united front and collective voice in dealing with management. The aim of unions is to secure and further the social and economic interests and well-being of their members through collective bargaining, contract administration, and lobbying.

Purposes of Unionization

labour union (union)
An officially-recognized association of employees, practising a similar trade or employed in the same company or industry, who have joined together for the purpose of presenting a united front and collective voice in dealing with management.

The purposes of unionization are to:

- influence HR policies and practices, as well as conditions of employment
- achieve better pay and benefits, and influence the wage-setting process
- achieve greater control over the jobs being performed
- obtain greater job security and improved working conditions
- help employees to achieve higher job satisfaction and meet their affiliation needs
- influence the rules and procedures regarding discipline, transfers, promotions, grievances, and layoffs.

Because of their critical role in determining whether or not employees will seek unionization, and in day-to-day contract administration in unionized settings, it is essential that all supervisors and managers understand the nature of labour–management relations. They must also know how unions operate, and be thoroughly familiar with the growing body of legislation governing labour relations.

The Contemporary Legal Framework

Objectives of Canada's Labour Relations Legislation

Winnipeg General Strike

Canadian labour laws have two general purposes. The first is to provide a common set of rules for fair negotiations. Thus, labour relations legislation regulates the way in which union-management interaction is conducted, so that the parties can negotiate an agreement that is mutually satisfactory. The second objective is to ensure the protection of the public interest, by preventing the impact of labour disputes from inconveniencing the public. As a result, the labour relations laws have established a delicate balance between the rights of the public and protection of public welfare (that is, safety and security), on the one hand, and the rights of unions and management, on the other.

Protection of the public interest is an important political and social concern, and explains why police officers, hospital employees, and firefighters are denied the right to strike in most jurisdictions. Over the years, the right to strike has been extended to more and more employees—not because the services provided are less essential than they were previously, but because of increasing union pressure.

work stoppage
A neutral term used to refer to strikes and lockouts, which does not assign responsibility for the breakdown in labour–management relations.

Protection of the public interest is also occasionally used by the government as justification for intervening in a labour–management dispute in the public or quasi-public sectors, if the effect of the work stoppage (strike or lockout) is deemed to cause undue hardship. Examples include **work stoppages** involving elementary or secondary school teachers, transit workers, and postal workers.

Jurisdiction

In common with human rights legislation, primary jurisdiction for labour laws resides with the provinces and territories. Today, provincial and territorial statutes govern approximately 90 percent of labour–management relations. The remaining 10 percent, mainly federal departments, crown corporations and agencies, and businesses engaged in transportation, banking, and communications, are governed by federal labour relations legislation.

Having many separate jurisdictions within one country has several advantages over other legislative models. For one thing, it allows for some diversity in legislation to recognize cultural differences. For example, the Quebec union movement was strongly influenced by the Roman Catholic Church until after World War II, and developed within a frame of reference that was quite different due to its orientation to the culture of francophone Quebec. It also means that there is an opportunity for one jurisdiction to see whether or not a particular legislative change (such as a restriction on the use of replacement workers during a strike) is successful in another jurisdiction before enacting it in its own. This may be likened to a field experiment and can definitely lead to an improvement in the overall system.

Having many jurisdictions is not without disadvantages, however. For one thing, it can be very time consuming and costly for a multi-provincial union or company to keep track of applicable regulations, and remain current as legislation changes. Ensuring the legality of policies and procedures across multiple jurisdictions can be very complex, since it is possible for a policy, practice, or procedure to be legal in one jurisdiction, yet illegal in others.

Federal Legislation: the Canada Labour Code

Canada Labour Code
The current federal labour statute that applies to employers and employees in businesses and industries under federal jurisdiction, except federal civil servants and individuals working in federal government agencies.

The key federal statute affecting labour–management relations in Canada today is the **Canada Labour Code**, which became effective in 1971. It applies to all employees under federal jurisdiction, except federal civil servants and individuals working in federal agencies, who are covered under separate legislation.

The Code recognizes the right of employees to organize and bargain collectively through trade unions. Both employers and unions are required to bargain in good faith and to include in their collective agreement a means for resolving disputes arising during the term of the contract. The Code prohibits unfair labour practices by employers and unions, and provides for government conciliation officers and boards to help resolve differences during negotiations. The administration and enforcement of the Code is the responsibility of the Federal Minister of Labour. Some of the Minister's responsibilities—for example, the provisions regarding certification of bargaining agents—have been delegated to the Canada Labour Relations Board.

Provincial and Territorial Labour Relations Legislation

Fortunately for human resources managers, the content of the provincial and territorial laws is fairly similar to that of the federal law, and there are a number of common characteristics among the labour relations legislation in all Canadian jurisdictions, which can be summarized as follows:

- Procedures for the certification of a union to represent the employees in a particular bargaining unit. A bargaining unit may consist of all employees in a specific occupation or trade, in one or more plants, or in a branch or department of a company.
- The requirement that a collective agreement be in force for a minimum of one year.
- Procedures that must be followed by one or both parties before a strike or lockout is legal.
- The outlawing of strikes or lockouts during the life of a collective agreement.
- The requirement that disputes over matters arising from interpretation of the collective agreement be settled by final and binding arbitration.
- Prohibition of certain specified "unfair practices" on the part of labour and management.
- Establishment of a labour relations board or the equivalent to administer and enforce the provisions of the legislation.

Labour Relations Boards

Labour Relations Board
The legally recognized body, in every Canadian jurisdiction except Quebec, responsible for interpreting, administering, and enforcing the labour relations act. In Quebec, a Labour Court and 20 Commissioners perform similar functions.

There is a **Labour Relations Board** (LRB) in every Canadian jurisdiction except Quebec. The LRBs are tripartite—composed of union representatives, management representatives, and a neutral chair or a vice-chair, who is usually a representative of the government. LRBs have some degree of autonomy from the Minister of Labour, and much flexibility in their operating procedures. They are typically empowered to interpret, administer, and enforce the Act and to investigate alleged violations. In Quebec, a Labour Court and 20 Commissioners perform similar functions.

The scope of the authority of these bodies includes the power to decide whether an organization is an appropriate unit for collective bargaining purposes, and to accept or modify the unit described in the union's application to ensure that the unit accurately represents the characteristics of the employing organization. They also have the power to decide whether an individual is eligible for union membership, whether an employee is a trade union member, whether a collective agreement is in force, and whether the parties are bound by it. Other responsibilities include investigating allegations of unfair labour practices and the supervision of certification elections, topics to which we will return later.

In comparison to traditional courts of law, the LRBs are more flexible in their procedures. They can admit evidence not admissible under civil court riules of evidence, consider precedents (but don't have to rely on them), suggest a compromise, or even impose a solution. In all jurisdictions, the Board's decisions are final and binding and cannot be appealed, except on procedural matters.

Employer and Employee Rights

The labour relations legislation attempts to balance employees' statutory rights to engage in union activities with employers' proprietary and commercial rights. To protect employers' rights, employees are generally not permitted to engage in unionization activities at the work place, during working hours, unless the employer has given permission. On the other hand, the legislation also protects employees' rights. For example, employees are granted the right to join a union, as well as to refrain from joining one.

Legal Constraints on Management—Unfair Labour Practices   To prevent employers from interfering with employee rights, the law prohibits specific **unfair labour practices** by management.[2] Basically, managers are prohibited from interfering with and discriminating against employees who are exercising their rights under the labour relations legislation.

unfair labour practice
Action by the employer or union that restrains persons from exercising their lawful rights under the labour relations statutes.

blacklist
A list of persons known to be union sympathizers or union members circulated among employers to prevent their inadvertent hiring.

yellow-dog contract
A contract, initially used by the railroad companies, which each job applicant was required to sign, stating that he or she was not a union member, and would not become one.

Two practices that were common in the early years of the Canadian labour movement, but which have long been outlawed, are blacklists and yellow-dog contracts. **Blacklists** were lists of persons who were known to be union sympathizers or union members. Employers would circulate these among themselves and refuse to employ those named. **Yellow-dog contracts**, initially used by the railroad companies, were contracts that each job applicant was required to sign, stating that he or she was not a union member, and would not become one.

Other examples of prohibited unfair labour practices by employers include:

- Interference with the rights of employees to select the union of their choice for collective bargaining purposes, or discrimination against employees for union activity. This generally means that employers cannot dismiss, discipline, or threaten employees for exercising their rights under the legislation. They cannot make promises that will influence an employees' choice of a union—for example, promising better benefits should the employees select one union rather than another or vote for no union; nor can they suspend, transfer, lay off or otherwise discriminate against employees who want to unionize.

- Participating in the formation, selection, or support—financial or otherwise—of unions representing the organization's employees.

- Unilaterally changing the terms of collective agreements or changing or threatening to change the wages and working conditions during certification proceedings or during collective bargaining, if the purpose is to undermine the union. Management is compelled, as is the union negotiating team, to bargain in good faith—that is, to demonstrate a serious attempt to reach a collective agreement.

- Imposing any condition in a contract of employment that would restrict an employee's rights under the labour relations legislation.
- Suspending, discharging, or imposing any penalty on an employee for refusing to perform the duties of another employee who is participating in a legal strike.
- Intimidating or threatening an employee to compel that person to refrain from becoming, or to cease to be a member, officer, or representative of a trade union.
- Bargaining collectively with a trade union if another trade union is the **bargaining agent** for that bargaining unit.

bargaining agent
The union that is recognized as the exclusive representative for a specific group of employees for collective bargaining purposes.

Legal Constraints on Unions—Unfair Labour Practices   Canadian labour laws also place limitations on the conduct of labour unions. Unfair labour practices by unions include:

- Attempting to persuade an employee to become or continue to be a union member, at the workplace, during working hours, unless employer consent has been obtained.
- Interfering with or participating in the formation or administration of an employer's organization, or contributing financial or other support to such an organization.
- Interfering with an employer's selection of its collective bargaining representative.
- Refusing to bargain in good faith.
- Interfering with the bargaining rights of a certified union.
- Discriminating against union members or employees in the bargaining unit on grounds prohibited by human rights legislation.
- Intimidating or coercing employees to become or remain members of the union.
- Failing to provide fair representation for all employees in the bargaining unit.
- Calling or authorizing an unlawful strike, or threatening to do so.

Legislation Pertaining to the Public and Quasi-Public Sectors

Public Service Staff Relations Act (PSSRA)
Legislation passed in 1967, giving federal civil servants and individuals working in federal agencies bargaining rights similar to those granted workers in the private sector, with two key differences: The right to choose interest arbitration or strike/lockout in each set of negotiations; and denial of the right to strike to individuals performing essential services.

Public Service Staff Relations Board (PSSRB)
The body created under the PSSRA that is equivalent to the private-sector labour relations boards, but with a slightly wider range of responsibilities.

When the Federal Parliament passed the **Public Service Staff Relations Act (PSSRA)** in 1967, it generally gave federal civil servants and individuals working in federal agencies bargaining rights similar to those granted workers in the private sector—the right to join a union and bargain for wages, hours, and certain working conditions. The PSSRA also created the **Public Service Staff Relations Board (PSSRB)**, a body equivalent to the private-sector labour relations boards, but with a slightly wider range of responsibilities.

A few aspects of the PSSRA are unique, however. Bargaining agents have the right to choose compulsory interest arbitration or the right to strike in the event of a deadlock in negotiations. A different procedure can be selected for each round of collective bargaining, if so desired, but once the decision is made and the PSSRB notified, the method chosen by the union must be accepted by the employer. As in the private sector, if the strike route is selected, conciliation procedures must be followed before a strike is legal. The Act also provides for employer identification of employees who perform "essential services." Such employees are denied the right to strike.

A comparison of the federal and provincial labour relations legislation covering the public and quasi-public sectors reveals little uniformity across Canada. The Quebec Labour Code, the Saskatchewan Trade Union Act, and the British Columbia Industrial Relations Act apply to both public and private sectors. In other jurisdictions, public and quasi-public sector employees are governed by separate legislation. In Ontario, for example, seven different statutes are operative.[3]

While public-sector employees performing essential services do not have the right to strike in any jurisdiction, and all public-sector employees are still prohibited from striking in some jurisdictions, in general, the trend is toward granting public and quasi-public sector employees the same rights as those in the private sector.[4]

The Labour Movement in Canada Today

We'll now examine the labour movement as it exists in Canada today. First, we'll discuss the philosophy and goals of unions, then the types of unions, the structure and functions of union organizations, current membership trends, and contemporary challenges confronting the Canadian labour movement.

Goals and Philosophy

business unionism
The activities of labour unions focussing on economic and welfare issues, including pay and benefits, job security, and working conditions. This emphasis recognizes the fact that unions can only survive if they deliver a needed service to their members in a businesslike manner.

social (or reform) unionism
Activities of unions directed at furthering the interests of their members by influencing the social and economic policies of governments at all levels. The objectives of social unionism are often accomplished by speaking out on proposed legislative reforms.

The primary goal of the labour unions active in Canada is to obtain economic benefits and improved treatment for their members. This includes negotiating for better pay and benefits, as well as greater job security and improvements in working conditions, and ensuring that such improvements are incorporated as rights in the collective agreement. It may also involve lobbying for legislative changes pertaining to these issues, such as stricter health and safety legislation. This union philosophy, with its emphasis on economic and welfare goals has become known as **business unionism**, primarily because it recognizes that a union can only survive if it delivers a needed service to its members in a businesslike manner.[5]

Job security is one of the principal goals of business unionism. Unions strive to ensure job security for their members by providing a cushion against layoffs or terminations caused by fluctuations in economic conditions, as well as protection against unjust treatment, such as arbitrary termination. Unions provide job security by lobbying for legislative changes, such as increased notice requirements in large-scale lay-off situations; helping to establish the rules governing the work environment through collective bargaining; and resisting actions that might result in loss of members' work, such as productivity-improvement techniques (like using computers and robots), increased use of part-time workers, and subcontracting work to outside organizations.

Unions also negotiate provisions to protect those with the greatest length of service. Such seniority clauses often mean that major HR decisions, such as promotions, transfers, and layoffs, are based on seniority, at least to some degree.

Improved economic conditions for their members constitute another of the primary business goals of unions. They pursue this aim by negotiating higher wages, benefits improvements, and cost of living adjustments (COLAs) to protect their members' pay during inflationary times.

Achieving *better working conditions* is another important aim. Over the years, unions have successfully negotiated a variety of improvements in working conditions for their members, and have been instrumental in convincing politicians of the need for stricter and more comprehensive health and safety legislation. The results of such efforts include shorter work weeks, safer working conditions, longer breaks, and voluntary rather than compulsory overtime.

Many unions also choose to address broader political and social issues of concern to their members. Trying to influence economic and social policies of government at all levels is known as **social (or reform) unionism**. The objectives of social unionism are often accomplished by speaking out on proposed legislative reforms, such as the introduction of employment equity legislation or amendments to labour relations legislation.

Achieving the objectives of social and business unionism may present unions with multiple, sometimes conflicting demands. For example, negotiating a significant pay increase may result in some members being laid off. Supporting more aggressive health and safety legislation may result in improved working conditions, but significant employer costs, such that less money is available for improvements in pay or benefits.[6] Determining the appropriate course of action when confronted with such conflicting demands is a source of much intra-union debate (that is, debate among bargaining unit members).

Types of Unions

The labour unions in Canada can be divided according to (a) type of worker eligible for membership, (b) geographical scope, and (c) labour congress affiliation.

Type of Worker Eligible for Membership   Historically, unions were divided into two categories, based on the type of worker eligible for membership.

craft union
Traditionally, a labour organization representing workers practising the same craft or trade, such as carpentry or plumbing.

Craft Union   All of the early trade unions in Canada and elsewhere were **craft unions**; associations of persons performing a certain type of skill or trade—for example, carpenters or bricklayers. Examples include the United Brotherhood of Carpenters and Joiners of America and the Ontario Nurses' Association.

industrial union
Traditionally, a labour organization representing all of the unskilled and semi-skilled workers in a particular organization or industry, irrespective of the type of work performed. Over time, the term came to refer to a labour organization representing all workers eligible for union membership in a particular company or industry, including skilled tradespersons.

Industrial Union   By traditional definition, an **industrial union** is a labour organization comprising all of the semi-skilled and unskilled workers eligible for union membership in a particular company or industry, irrespective of the type of work performed. There is a long history of membership competition between craft and industrial unions. A major bone of contention was the fact that, over time, industrial unions started representing all workers eligible for union membership in a particular company or industry, including skilled tradespersons. The Canadian Union of Postal Workers is an example of an industrial union, as is the Canadian Union of United Brewery, Flour, Cereal, Soft Drink and Distillery Workers.

While the distinction between craft and industrial unions still exists, technological changes and increasing competition for members have blurred it. Although there are still some craft unions with members possessing a particular skill or "craft", many craft unions now represent all of the workers in a plant. In fact, skilled and unskilled workers, white-collar and blue-collar workers, public and private sector employees, and professional groups are now being represented by both industrial and craft unions.

Geographic Scope   Unions can also be distinguished from each other on the basis of their geographic scope.

international union
A labour union with branches and members in both Canada and the United States, the head office of which is in the United States.

International Unions   Labour unions that charter branches in both Canada and the United States are known as **international unions**. Such unions have their head office in the United States, the country in which the majority of their members works and resides. Due to their larger membership base, international unions are generally the strongest financially. For example, the merger of three international unions—the United Steelworkers of America, the United Auto Workers, and the International Association of Machinists—into the largest industrial union in North America, resulted in a strike fund of $1 billion.[7]

In recent years, Canadian membership in such unions has been declining, because Canadian branches have been breaking away from the parent unions and forming their own Canadian unions. This trend, known as **succession**, started in 1971 when the Canadian members of the Communication Workers of America separated and founded the Communication Workers of Canada. The most dramatic breakaway occurred in 1985 when the Canadian Auto Workers' Union separated from their American parent, the United Auto Workers' Union.

To retain their Canadian members, some international unions have set up separate Canadian units. Their goal in doing so is to ensure that Canadian political, economic, and social issues are given proper attention. Despite such actions, however, the number of Canadian members in international unions has been declining steadily.

National Unions   Labour unions that charter branches in Canada only and have their head office in this country are known as **national unions**. As with international unions, national unions provide a wide range of services to their branches (known as "locals"). They provide assistance with organizing activities, negotiations, grievance handling, arbitration, and strikes. Some national unions require that collective agreements bargained by their locals receive their approval prior to finalization. Others, such as the Canadian Auto Workers, actually bargain an industry-wide contract on behalf of their locals.

Other examples of national unions include the Canadian Union of Public Employees and the Canadian Union of Postal Workers. Some of the unions included in this category are actually only provincial in scope—for example, the Alberta Union of Provincial Employees.

As is illustrated in **Table 16.1**, currently about 66 percent of union members in Canada belong to national unions, and 30 percent to international unions. This is a complete reversal of the situation of about 30 years ago, when only 30 percent of union members belonged to national unions.

Local Unions   There are two types of labour unions in Canada that are purely local in geographical scope. The first is the **independent local union**. This type of local union is not affiliated with any other labour organization. As reflected in Table 16.1, membership in such unions is quite small. The second type is a **directly chartered local union**. Such unions have been organized by and received their charter (official document of recognition) directly from the Canadian Labour Congress, the major central union organization in Canada. Such locals are not part of a national or international union. As shown in Table 16.1, membership in directly chartered local unions is also relatively small.

Labour Congress Affiliation   A third way of distinguishing between labour unions is according to affiliation with one or another central labour organization. These central organizations include:

> CLC–Canadian Labour Congress
> CSN–Confédération des Syndicats Nationaux (In English CNTU–Confederation of National Trade Unions)
> AFL–CIO–American Federation of Labour and Congress of Industrial Organizations

Canadian Labour Congress (CLC)   As illustrated in **Table 16.2**, the **Canadian Labour Congress (CLC)** is the major central labour organization in Canada, and has the largest number of affiliated union members. It is headquartered in Ottawa and has regional offices across the country. Most international and national unions belong, and all directly chartered local unions, **local/district labour councils**, and **provincial/territorial federations of labour**

TABLE 16.1 Union Membership by Type of Union and Affiliation, 1997

TYPE AND AFFILIATION	NUMBER OF UNIONS	NUMBER OF LOCALS	MEMBERSHIP	
			NUMBER	PERCENT
International Unions	51	2,802	1,216,725	29.9
AFL–CIO/CLC	34	2,545	1,087,285	26.7
AFL–CIO/CFL	8	168	99,400	2.4
CLC only	2	29	6,830	0.2
AFL–CIO only	4	47	17,980	0.4
Unaffiliated unions	3	13	5,230	0.1
National Unions	233	14,488	2,662,550	65.4
CLC	55	7,320	1,575,935	38.7
CSN (CNTU)	10	2,367	251,420	6.2
CEQ	14	323	109,775	2.7
CCU	9	39	17,275	0.4
CSD	2	99	14,330	0.4
CFL	2	32	1,780	0.0†
Unaffiliated unions	141	4,308	692,035	17.0
Directly Chartered Unions	401		60,600	1.5
CSD	390		59,500	1.5
CLC	11		1,100	0.0†
Independent Local Organizations	326		134,025	3.3
Total	1,011	17,290	4,073,900	100.0

Note: Due to rounding, sums may not always equal totals. † Less than 0.1 percent.

Source: Workplace Information Directorate, *1997 Directory of Labour Organizations in Canada*, p. xxiii. Reprinted with permission from the Minister of Public Works and Government Services Canada, 1998.

are affiliated with the CLC. The CLC, the structure of which is illustrated in **Figure 16.1**, is financed through dues based on membership numbers.

The purpose of the CLC is primarily a political one: to act as the spokesperson for organized labour throughout Canada, particularly in Ottawa. When legislative changes are proposed, the CLC tries to influence the outcome by such means as extensive communication, lobbying, and making formal presentations to government bodies or other relevant groups. Another important function is to represent Canadian organized labour on the international scene.

The CLC ensures that the **provincial/territorial federations of labour** and local/district labour councils exert political influence at the provincial and local levels, respectively.

AFL-CIO The American counterpart of the CLC is the **American Federation of Labour–Congress of Industrial Organizations (AFL–CIO)**. Although the two organizations operate independently, since most international unions in the CLC are also members of the AFL–CIO, a certain degree of common interest exists.

TABLE 16.2 Union Membership by Congress Affiliation, 1997

CONGRESS AFFILIATION	MEMBERSHIP	
	NUMBER	PERCENT
CLC	**2,671,150**	**65.6**
AFL–CIO/CLC	1,087,285	26.7
CLC only	1,583,865	38.9
CSN (CNTU)	**251,420**	**6.2**
CFL	**101,180**	**2.5**
AFL–CIO/CFL	99,400	2.4
CFL only	1,780	0.0†
AFL–CIO only	**17,980**	**0.4**
CEQ	**109,775**	**2.7**
CSD	**73,830**	**1.8**
CCU	**17,275**	**0.4**
Unaffiliated International Unions	**5,230**	**0.1**
Unaffiliated Nationals Unions	**692,035**	**17.0**
Independent Local Organizations	**134,025**	**3.3**
Total	**4,073,900**	**100.0**

Note: Due to rounding, sums may not always equal totals. † Less than 0.1 percent.

Source: Workplace Information Directorate, *1997 Directory of Labour Organizations in Canada*, p.xvii, Extracted from Table 2 and reprinted with permission from the Minister of Public Works and Government Services Canada, 1998.

Figure 16.1 Structure of the Canadian Labour Congress

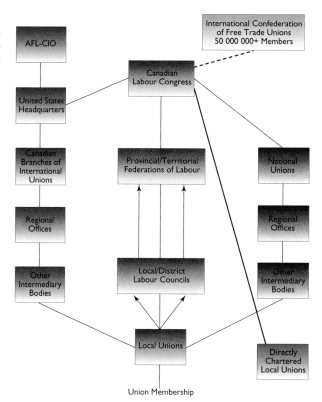

Structure and Functions

Other than those unions that are strictly local in geographic scope, most unions have central offices in each province/territory in which they have members. As well, they may have regional offices in major metropolitan centres, with various departments; as well as a number of geographically dispersed smaller branches, called "locals."

Central and Regional Offices   The central and/or regional office staff are responsible for ensuring that the locals follow the policies of the international or national union. Issues of concern include enrolment of new members, union dues, collective bargaining, and settlement of jurisdictional disputes. Staff members maintain contact with the national or international office, as well as the area branches. They assist locals with organizing activities, applications for certification, negotiations, grievance processing, arbitration, and strike activities, as the need arises.

The Union Local   The basic unit of the labour union movement in Canada is the **local**, formed in a particular plant or locality. For human resources managers, the union locals are generally the most important part of the union structure. Although the powers of the local vary considerably, overall, Canada has a system of **grass-roots unionism**, with a high degree of local autonomy or decentralization.

Each local has its own constitution, draws up its own bylaws, and has responsibility for obtaining new members, handling grievances, collective bargaining, and organizing recreational activities. An executive committee, headed by a president and vice-president, and sometimes a business agent, usually exercises power. As illustrated in **Figure 16.2**, there are generally a number of committees, each of which is assigned responsibility for specific activities. Some of the more common committees include: the organizing and membership committee, responsible for recruiting new members; the bargaining committee, which looks after negotiations; the grievance committee, responsible for processing grievances; the recreation committee, which looks after dances, parties, picnics, etc.; and the education committee, which organizes seminars and workshops and provides information about union aims and activities to both members and nonmembers.

Key players within the local are the elected officials known as **union stewards**, who are responsible for representing the interests and protecting the rights of bargaining unit employees in their department or area. Functions performed by such stewards include receiving, investigating, and attempting to resolve complaints and grievances; informing members about union policies and meetings; and recruiting new members. The senior steward for a particular area or division is known as the **chief steward**.

In smaller locals, all union executive positions are held on a voluntary part-time basis by union members working at their regular jobs, who are elected by members of the local for a specified term of office. In larger locals, there is often a full-time **business agent**, whose salary is paid by the local or the national/international office. (Some business agents are elected, others are appointed, according to the union's constitution and bylaws.)The part-time officials in smaller locals are reimbursed by the local or the employer (as specified in the collective agreement) for the time they require away from work to perform union business.

local
The basic unit of the labour union movement in Canada, formed in a particular plant or locality.

grass-roots unionism
A term referring to the fact that the Canadian labour movement tends to be driven from the bottom up. Although the powers of the locals vary considerably, most have a high degree of autonomy.

union steward
A union member elected by workers in a particular department or area of a firm to act as their union representative.

chief steward
The senior steward for a particular area or division.

business agent
A full-time, elected or appointed, paid official of a union local, whose duties involve handling grievances and helping to enforce the terms of the collective agreement.

Figure 16.2
Structure of a Typical Union Local

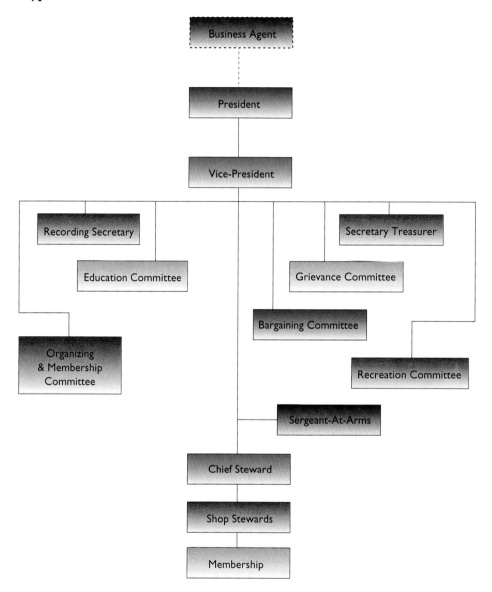

Membership Trends

As shown in **Table 16.3**, the number of persons belonging to labour unions fluctuated between 1978 and 1997, reaching an all-time high in 1992. However, the membership in unions as a percentage of the civilian labour force actually decreased fairly steadily during that period. In 1997, union membership stood at 4 074 000, representing 26.9 percent of the civilian labour force and 34.1 percent of non-agricultural paid workers.

While union membership in Canada has been declining as a percentage of both civilian labour force and non-agricultural paid workers, the drop has not been dramatic, unlike in the United States. At the present time, organized labour's share of the work force in the United States is about 16 percent and dropping. In

			TABLE 16.3 Union Membership in Canada, 1978–1997		

YEAR	UNION MEMBERSHIP IN THOUSANDS	CIVILIAN LABOUR FORCE IN THOUSANDS	TOTAL NON-AGRICULTURAL PAID WORKERS IN THOUSANDS	UNION MEMBERSHIP AS A PERCENTAGE OF CIVILIAN LABOUR FORCE	UNION MEMBERSHIP AS A PERCENTAGE OF NON-AGRICULTURAL PAID WORKERS
1978	3,278	10,860	8,840	30.2	37.1
1980	3,397	11,630	9,519	29.2	35.7
1981	3,487	11,983	9,842	29.1	35.4
1982	3,617	12,332	10,144	29.3	35.7
1983	3,563	12,398	9,786	28.7	36.4
1984	3,651	12,610	9,805	29.0	37.2
1985	3,666	12,953	10,060	28.3	36.4
1986	3,730	13,123	10,375	28.4	36.0
1987	3,782	13,378	10,744	28.3	35.2
1988	3,841	13,631	11,036	28.2	34.8
1989	3,944	13,900	11,422	28.4	34.5
1990	4,031	14,151	11,700	28.5	34.5
1991	4,068	14,329	11,733	28.4	34.7
1992	4,089	14,408	11,456	28.4	35.7
1993	4,071	14,482	11,378	28.1	35.8
1994	4,078	14,663	11,443	27.8	35.6
1995	4,003	14,832	11,668	27.0	34.3
1996	4,033	14,928	11,883	27.0	33.9
1997	4,074	15,145	11,942	26.9	34.1

Note: Labour Force and non-agricultural paid employment data shown for each year are annual averages of the preceding year; data shown for union membership are as of January of the years shown. No survey was conducted in 1979.

Source: Statistics Canada, The Labour Force Survey, Cat. No. 71-201, various years, as compiled by the Workplace Information Directorate, *1997 Directory of Labour Organizations in Canada*, p. xvi. Reprinted with permission from the Minister of Public Works and Government Services Canada, 1998.

fact, if the current trend persists, it is projected that unions will represent only 13 percent of all non-agricultural paid workers by 2000, down from a peak of about 34 percent in 1955.[8]

Various factors are responsible for the union membership trends in both Canada and the United States, including the increase in service-sector and white-collar jobs, and the decline of employment opportunities in the industries that have traditionally been highly unionized, such as manufacturing. More effective human resources practices in nonunionized firms is another contributing factor, as is the major restructuring in firms over the past ten years, which has resulted in the loss of thousands of jobs.[9] In order to offset these losses, some unions have started organizing activities in areas outside their traditional field. For instance, the United Steelworkers has organized security guards and fisheries workers; while the CAW has organized airline and railway industries.[10] Unions are also searching for new ways to meet the needs of members and potential members, a topic discussed in more detail in the Information Technology and HR box.

Information Technology and HR
Computers Assist Both Labour and Management

Labour and management leaders can benefit from the use of computers. Managers can track grievances to determine in which departments or areas and on what subjects training is needed, while union leaders may find that computers provide new ways to assist their members and potential members.

Using a computer, managers can track trends in grievances within any given time period for the whole company, a division or department, or a particular supervisor or group of supervisors. For example, it might be hypothesized that those supervisors with less than one year of experience in their positions generate more grievances than experienced supervisors. If this proves to be true, then either supervisors should be trained before starting in the position or they should be offered frequent training sessions during their first year. However, research might prove that the hypothesis is only true in some areas. Thus, if there are a number of grievances in some areas but not others, an investigation might reveal the need for (1) managerial training, probably defined by the subject of the grievances, (2) better communication on a topic (such as the importance of following safety rules), or (3) the development of a process that allows more input from employees before instituting new policies. Grievance topics can be coded for easy computer tracking, and may incorporate more than one code.

Union leaders, too, can benefit from computerization. One use of computers is to assist them to identify new strategies to meet the changing needs of members and potential members. For example, computer-based networks can be used for information sharing, providing hands-on training to maintain currency, and to assist in adjusting unemployment caused by having members with particular skills in one location and jobs requiring those skills in another. It has been suggested that unions could become "the single best source of information, training, standards, and individuals [with] specific skills and talents."[1] With the support of the international or national office, locals can be linked effectively and relatively inexpensively using telephone lines, so that there is a constant exchange of information on topics such as trends in collective bargaining, arbitration decisions, training opportunities and workshops, and job opportunities.

For union and management negotiators, it is in the area of costing that computers currently offer the most potential. As one expert put it:[2]

Access to computer data banks has significantly shortened our research time prior to negotiations. And the application of software spreadsheets has made contract cost analysis a much easier and more accurate process. In the future of collective bargaining, more development of computer skills is a necessity.

Once negotiations are under way, computers can be extremely valuable and are increasingly becoming a necessity. As demands are exchanged, negotiators can quickly estimate, using spreadsheet packages, how suggested changes may impact their costs. For example, the cost of an additional floating holiday or an increase in shift premium can quickly be estimated.◆

1. Geoffrey J. Hallet, "Unions in Our Future?" *Personnel Administration* 31, no. 4 (April 1986), pp. 40–94.
2. Michael Carrell and Christina Heavrin, *Labor Relations and Collective Bargaining* (Englewood Cliffs: Prentice Hall, 1995), p. 340.

Not all industries have the same degree of unionization. Public administration is highly unionized, as is transportation, communication, and other utilities. The agriculture, finance, and trade sectors have the lowest rates of unionization.

There are also differences in the degree of unionization in various parts of Canada. According to Statistics Canada figures, in 1997, while union membership represented 31 to 33 percent of the employed work force in Canada overall; in

www.clra.org.frameset.htm
Construction Workers

Newfoundland, 39 percent of workers belonged to a union, the highest level of unionization in the country. Quebec had the lowest level of unionization, at 22 percent.[11]

Two important developments that have had significant implications for unions are increases in the labour-force participation of women and the growth of part-time employment. Between 1962 and 1990, women accounted for 54 percent of total membership growth.[12] This increase is due largely to increasing unionization in the public and quasi-public sectors. The actual number of female union members and their percentage of total membership between 1966 and 1991 is shown in **Table 16.4**. This trend is continuing. According to a Labour Force Survey released by Statistics Canada in August 1997, during the first half of 1997, 45 percent of union members were women.[13] As female membership has increased, unions have begun to put more emphasis on issues pertaining to equity and the balancing of work and family responsibilities, such as family-related leaves, childcare, and pay and employment equity. Women are now better represented in the union hierarchy, as well as among professional staff.[14] In 1986, Shirley Carr be-

TABLE16.4 Female Union Members as a Percentage of Total Union Membership 1966–1991		
YEAR	**NUMBER OF FEMALE MEMBERS**	**% OF ALL MEMBERS**
1966	322 980	17.0
1967	407 181	19.8
1968	438 543	20.4
1969	469 235	21.2
1970	513 203	22.6
1971	558 138	23.5
1972	575 584	24.2
1973	635 861	24.6
1974	676 939	25.2
1975	711 102	26.0
1976	750 637	27.0
1977	782 282	27.7
1978	835 263	28.7
1979	890 365	29.3
1980	932 883	30.2
1981	979 862	31.0
1982	985 376	32.3
1983	1 179 000	34.8
1984	1 219 100	35.4
1985	1 264 000	36.2
1986	1 310 000	36.4
1988	1 400 000	37.5
1991	1 583 000	40.7

Source: Statistics Canada, *Annual Report of the Minister of Supply and Services Canada under the Corporations and Labour Unions Returns Act—Part II—Labour Unions*, Catalogue No. 71-202 (Ottawa: Supply and Services Canada), August 1984, p. 41 for the years 1962–1982; January 1987, p. 48 for the years 1983–1984; and December 1988, p. 31 for the years 1985–1986; and November, 1990 for the year 1988. November, 1993 for the year 1991. Reproduced by permission of the Minister of Supply and Services Canada. Adapted from Alton W.J. Craig and Norman A. Solomon, *The System of Industrial Relations in Canada*, 5th ed. (Scarborough, ON: Prentice Hall Canada Inc., 1996), p. 194.

came the first female president of the CLC, after a lengthy union career in the public sector, as a member of the Canadian Union of Public Employees.

It is interesting to note that over 73 percent of all public employees now belong to unions, as compared with 22 percent of private-sector employees,[15] and that the two largest unions in Canada represent public-sector employees. The Canadian Union of Public Employees (CUPE) is the largest union in Canada, representing 451 500 members. The second largest, representing 309 000 provincial government employees, is the National Union of Public and General Employees (NUPGE). The largest union representing employees at the federal level, and sixth largest union in Canada, is the Public Service Alliance of Canada (PSAC), with 167 800 members. **Table 16.5** lists the 25 largest unions in Canada, as of 1997.

www.psac.com
Public Service Alliance of Canada

Current Challenges to the Canadian Labour Movement

As with employers, global competition and technological advances pose challenges for the union movement. Unions also have to deal with challenges pertaining to the unionization of white-collar employees, managers, and

TABLE 16.5 The 25 Largest Unions in Canada, 1997	
LABOUR UNION	**MEMBERSHIP (000S)**
	1997
Canadian Union of Public Employees	451.5
National Union of Public and General Employees	309.0
National Automobile, Aerospace, Transportation and General Workers Union of Canada	205.0
United Steelworkers of America	200.0
United Food and Commercial Workers International Union	197.0
Public Service Alliance of Canada	167.8
Communications, Energy and Paperworkers Union of Canada	167.5
Fédération des affaires sociales inc.	97.0
International Brotherhood of Teamsters	95.0
Service Employees International Union	80.0
Fédération des enseignantes et enseignants des commissions scolaires	77.6
International Brotherhood of Electrical Workers	67.3
United Brotherhood of Carpenters and Joiners of America	56.0
Laborers' International Union of North America	54.8
International Association of Machinists and Aerospace Workers	52.9
Canadian Union of Postal Workers	51.0
Ontario Secondary School Teachers' Federation	50.6
Syndicat de la fonction publique du Québec	47.8
Fédération des infirmières et infirmiers du Québec	45.0
Industrial Wood and Allied Workers of Canada	43.0
Ontario Nurses' Association	42.0
British Columbia Teachers' Federation	42.0
Federation of Women Teachers' Associations of Ontario	41.0
International Union of Operating Engineers	36.0
Fédération des employées et employés de services Publics inc.	36.0

Source: Workplace Information Directorate, *1997 Directory of Labour Organizations in Canada*, p. xix. Adapted from Table 4 and reprinted with permission from the Minister of Public Works and Government Services Canada, 1998.

professionals; and innovative work practices that have the potential to decrease employee interest in unionization.

Global Competition and Technological Change   Increased global competition and the massive importing of steel, consumer electronics, cars, clothing, textiles, and shoes has led to job losses for Canadian union members.[16] Furthermore, foreign subsidiaries of Canadian-owned corporations, such as Northern Telecom (Nortel), have been accused by union leaders of being anti-union and of deliberately trying to decrease union membership by exporting the jobs of Canadian workers to plants offshore.[17] Canadian unions were highly opposed to the North American Free Trade Agreement (NAFTA), claiming that Canadian jobs would be lost to low-wage Mexican workers, as well as to the anti-union environment that exists in many U.S. states. To combat such fears, unions have been demanding increased government protection, which has caused lively debate in parliament between those who argue that protective trade barriers create higher prices for consumers and those who believe that such barriers are necessary to protect Canadian jobs from low-cost foreign competition.

Technological advances pose another challenge to unions.[18] Improvements in computer technology and highly automated operating systems have lowered the demand for many blue-collar workers, and resulted in a decline in union membership in the auto, steel, and other manufacturing industries. Electronic work (such as processing credit card claims) is highly portable. Modern office work can be shifted almost literally at the touch of a button from one centre to another, and even overseas. Technological advances have also decreased the effectiveness of strikes in some sectors, because highly automated organizations can remain fully operational with minimal staffing levels during work stoppages.

The Unionization of White-Collar Employees, Managers, and Professionals   In the past, many white-collar employees tended to identify more with owners or managers than with their blue-collar colleagues, often enjoying certain privileges and status symbols available to salaried employees only. Because the improvements in pay, benefits, and working conditions that were negotiated by the union representing their blue-collar coworkers were often extended to them as a matter of course, there was little perceived need to unionize. For these reasons, and because unions were more attuned to the needs and priorities of blue-collar workers (the majority of whom were males), white-collar employees have been slow to unionize. In recent years, however, the growth in the size of many public- and private-sector organizations has tended to depersonalize the work of white-collar employees and distance them from management, which has made unionization more attractive. The lack of job security related to downsizing, together with increasing difficulties in attempting to resolve grievances, has also led to increased interest in unionization among white-collar workers.[19]

In response to these changes, as well as the decline in the number of blue-collar workers, unions have been increasing their efforts to organize white-collar employees. Service-oriented organizations, such as insurance agencies, banks, retail stores, and government agencies are being targeted for organizing campaigns. Even small businesses are being organized. To attract white-collar employees, unions have changed their focus and bargaining priorities. In addition to focussing more on equity and family issues, unions are also capitalizing on the health and safety risks associated with white-collar jobs, such as the effects of working at video display terminals for long periods of time, and the potential for repetitive strain injury associated with the jobs of clerical workers and cashiers.

Another group that has been targeted for unionization is managers and professionals. Of particular appeal to these employees is the unions' desire to protect the job security of those represented, something that has been seriously threatened due to extensive downsizing in both public- and private-sector organizations.

Innovative Workplace Practices   In workplaces where employees have a high degree of autonomy and participation in decision making, little supervision, and pay linked to performance or knowledge/skills attained, there may be less perceived need for a union.[20] Some individuals argue that such innovative workplace practices as semi-autonomous work teams, skill-based pay, profit sharing, and employee stock ownership plans undermine union power by coopting employees and aligning employee interests with those of management.[21] On the other hand, in workplaces in which the unions have supported such changes, the end result may be better communication and more cooperation,[22] a win–win situation.

An example is a cooperative venture between union and management at the Shell Canada plant in Sarnia, Ontario. As the new plant was being built, members of the Energy and Chemical Workers Union executive were involved from the initial planning stages. The end result of bargaining was a collective agreement that is only a few pages in length, rather than the typical multi-paged document in which each rule and procedure is specified in detail. The plant functions as a single unit, not separate departments. Six self-managed process teams keep the plant in continuous operation. Multi-skilled workers are responsible for planning, scheduling, hiring, and training, and are paid based on the skills for which they have been certified. The results are impressive—twice the output originally expected, excellent product quality, few grievances, low turnover, and an average safety record.[23]

The Future   The labour movement in Canada is at a crossroads. Due to increasing competition and technological advances, traditional employment practices are being replaced by new forms of work organization that require a fundamental rethinking of long-established union policies and practices. The groups traditionally available for membership are declining in number. Changing demographics have caused a shift in the needs of potential union members. Progressive unions are focussing on new issues and adopting a more cooperative approach to union-management relations, as will be described in chapter 17.

Management's Labour Relations Strategy

labour relations strategy
An organization's overall plan for dealing with unions, which sets the tone for its union-management relationship.

An organization's **labour relations strategy,** one component of its HR strategy, is its overall plan for dealing with unions, which sets the tone for its union-management relationship. Based on HR goals, philosophy, and strategic plan, a firm's labour relations strategy can result in a relationship ranging from hostility (open conflict) to cooperation. The basis of an organization's labour relations strategy is the decision to accept or avoid unions.[24]

Union Acceptance Strategy

union acceptance strategy
A labour relations strategy based on management's view that the union is the legitimate representative of the firm's employees.

Managers in firms choosing a **union acceptance strategy** view the union as the legitimate representative of the firm's employees. They accept collective bargaining as an appropriate mechanism for establishing workplace rules and the terms and conditions of employment for the bargaining unit members. In such a setting, the management negotiation team strives for a mutually acceptable collective agreement, and all supervisors are (ideally) thoroughly familiar with the terms of the collective agreement and committed to abiding by them.

A union acceptance strategy is likely to result in labour–management cooperation or at least a harmonious working relationship between union and management, built on trust and communication. Ault Foods, which has seven different unions and about 38 collective agreements, has taken a number of steps to instill a stronger spirit of cooperation in its labour relations environment. These include wide dissemination of information, so that problems can be addressed in a collaborative manner; an open and constructive approach to contract administration; and a problem-solving approach to bargaining[25] (known as interest-based bargaining, which we'll describe in chapter 17).

Union Avoidance Strategy

union avoidance strategy
A labour relations strategy based on management's preference to operate in a nonunion environment. There are two possible approaches: union substitution and union suppression.

union substitution (proactive human resources management) approach
A union avoidance strategy that involves removing the incentives for unionization by ensuring that employees' needs are met.

Managers select a **union avoidance strategy** when they believe that it is preferable to operate in a nonunionized environment. This may be based on the desire for greater flexibility or fear that a union will have a disruptive influence or result in a loss of control over employees. There are two approaches that firms can adopt to avoid unionization—one is proactive and the other employs hardball tactics:[26]

Union Substitution   Also known as the **proactive human resources management approach, union substitution** involves becoming so responsive to employees' needs that there is no incentive for them to unionize. Managers ensure that the treatment employees receive, as well as their pay, benefits, and working conditions, are equal to or better than that in comparable unionized firms. For example, Dofasco, a large steel manufacturing firm in Hamilton, Ontario, which has used unionized Stelco as a frame of reference over the years, has remained nonunion by developing a reputation for fair treatment and concern for employee well-being. Management has taken numerous steps to ensure the firm lives up to its motto, "Our product is steel. Our strength is people."

Some of the strategies adopted at Dofasco and other organizations using the union substitution approach include:[27]

- designing jobs that are meaningful and satisfying
- providing job security through effective HR planning
- having objective and non-biased recruitment and selection procedures
- establishing fair, meaningful, and objective performance standards
- providing extensive training for employees and managers so that they can achieve the expected performance levels
- evaluating and rewarding employees on the basis of actual performance and adopting a promotion-from-within policy
- encouraging employee involvement and input into decision making
- establishing open communication and a fair and equitable process for resolving grievances
- sharing organizational success through profit sharing or an employee stock-ownership plan.

union suppression approach
A union avoidance strategy involving the use of hardball tactics, which may or may not be legal, to prevent a union from organizing the firm's employees, or to get rid of an existing union.

Union Suppression   Firms adopt a **union suppression approach** when there is a desire to avoid a union at all costs. "Hardball tactics," which may or may not be legal, are employed to prevent a union from organizing the firm's employees or to get rid of an existing union. This is a rather high-risk strategy that was prevalent in the early years of the union movement, but is rarely adopted today.

One legal tactic to try to prevent a union from gaining a foothold in the organization is to make it difficult for a newly-certified union to negotiate its first collective agreement, since failure to reach an agreement within a one-year period following certification can lead to automatic decertification in some jurisdictions. (It should be noted, however, that this strategy cannot be employed in jurisdictions where a breakdown in first contract negotiations can lead to a collective agreement imposed through arbitration.)

To weaken union power, employers can contract out work, thereby decreasing the number of bargaining unit positions; and/or use replacement workers during strikes or lockouts (in those jurisdictions in which this is legal).

Hardball tactics can sometimes backfire. As we will explain when describing possible management responses to a unionization attempt, in some jurisdictions, if management is found guilty of unfair labour practices a union may receive automatic certification.

The Labour Relations Process

labour relations process
A sequence of steps, beginning with the desire to unionize and ending with day-to-day contract administration.

As illustrated in **Figure 16.3**, the **labour relations process** consists of five steps:

1. Employees decide to seek collective representation
2. The union organizing campaign begins
3. If there is sufficient support, the union receives official recognition
4. Members of union and management negotiate to arrive at a mutually-satisfactory collective agreement
5. Day-to-day contract administration begins.

Figure 16.3
An Overview of the Labour Relations Process

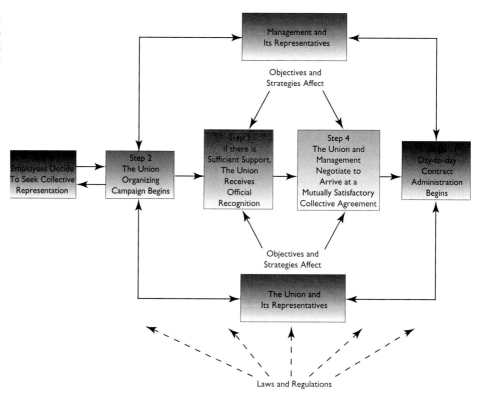

The first three steps will be described next. The last two are the focus of chapter 17.

Union Organizing and Recognition

The Desire to Unionize

A tremendous amount of time and money have been spent trying to analyze why workers unionize, and many theories have been proposed. However, there is no simple answer, partly because each individual may become interested in unionizing for very unique reasons.

Research results indicate that the desire to unionize is related to the following factors:[28]

- job dissatisfaction, especially with pay, benefits, and working conditions
- perceived inequities in pay
- unfair or biased administration of policies and practices
- lack of job security
- lack of opportunities for advancement
- lack of desired amount of influence or participation in work-related decisions
- the belief that unions can be effective in improving pay and working conditions.

Research supports the notion that dissatisfaction with wages, benefits, and working conditions provides the strongest reason to unionize. Both union members and nonmembers have their highest expectations of union performance regarding the "bread and butter" issues of collective bargaining,[29] which is quite justifiable given the fact that unionized employees in Canada receive wages 15 percent or more above those paid to nonunionized workers possessing similar attributes and employed in similar jobs. For example, the average hourly wage for union members in the first nine months of 1997 was $18.84, compared to $15.18 for nonunion members.[30]

It is quite clear, however, that dissatisfaction alone will not lead to unionization. More important seems to be the belief on the part of workers that it is only through unity that they can get a fair share of the "pie" and protect themselves from the arbitrary whims of management. In other words, it is only when workers are dissatisfied and believe that they are without the ability to change the factors causing dissatisfaction, except through collective action, that they become interested in unionizing.[31]

The Union Organizing Process

union organizing process
The steps involved when a union seeks legal recognition as the bargaining agent for a particular group of employees.

At any time, a group of nonunionized employees may come to believe that they would be better off as members of a labour union. This may be because of a newspaper article describing improvements in pay and benefits in unionized firms in the community; failure of the firm to ensure that they are offered the same treatment as unionized coworkers; or because they have been approached by members of an existing union, who convince them of the benefits of unionization. Whatever the reason, once interest in joining a union has been aroused, the **union organizing process** begins. The steps in this process typically include:

1. Employee/union contact
2. Initial organizational meeting

3. Formation of an in-house organizing committee
4. The organizing campaign
5. The outcome: certification, recognition, or rejection.

Step One: Employee/Union Contact   A formal organizing campaign may be initiated by a union organizer or by employees acting on their own behalf. Contrary to popular belief, most organizing campaigns are begun by employees who get in touch with an existing union by telephone or a visit to the union's local office.

It is true, however, that large unions, such as the Canadian Auto Workers (CAW) and the Teamsters, have formal organizing departments, the members of which are responsible for identifying organizing opportunities and launching organizing campaigns. For example, Bob White describes his early work as a **union organizer** for the CAW as follows. He and a colleague would station themselves outside the plant gate, identify individuals who "looked promising," follow them home to find out where they lived, and then return later that evening to their homes to make a "cold call" to investigate their interest in representation by the union.[32] It is important to note that no matter how large or sophisticated a union's organizing department is, the outcome of an organizing campaign depends primarily on the employees. Even the most experienced organizers find it difficult to organize a truly well-managed, successful organization.

Regardless of how the contact is initiated, the first step begins when employees and union officials make contact and explore the possibility of unionization. During these discussions, employees investigate the advantages of having union representation, and the union officials start to gather information about the employees' sources of dissatisfaction, to see if a case can be built in support of the union.

Since organizing campaigns can be expensive, union leaders carefully evaluate their chances of success and the possible benefits to be gained from their efforts. Important in this evaluation is the employer's vulnerability to unionization.[33] Union leaders also consider the effect that allowing the firm to remain nonunion might have on their union strength in the community. A nonunion employer, for example, can hinder a union's efforts to standardize employment conditions within an industry or geographic area, as well as weaken the union's bargaining power with employers it has successfully organized.

Step Two: Initial Organizational Meeting   Once he or she is convinced that the expense of an organizing campaign is justified, the union organizer generally schedules an initial meeting with the individuals who first expressed an interest in unionization and coworkers who subsequently expressed their support. The aim is to identify employees who would be willing to help the organizer direct the campaign.

Step Three: Formation of an In-House Organizing Committee   A key step in the success of an organizing campaign is the formation of an **in-house organizing committee**, a group of employees, dedicated to the goal of unionization, who are willing to assist the union organizer. The role of such volunteers is to devote the time and effort necessary to contact employees, present the case for unionization, and sign up members.

Step Four: The Organizing Campaign   Once the committee is formed, the **union organizing campaign** begins. First, the members gather together as much information as possible about the firm—its products, customers, finances,

union organizer
A full-time employee of the union, whose role is to plan and execute union membership recruitment campaigns.

in-house organizing committee
A group of employees, dedicated to the goal of unionization, who are willing to assist the union organizer.

union organizing campaign
The steps involved in a union's membership recruitment process.

production methods, employees, managers, ownership, and attitude toward employees. They also gather information about other firms in the community employing the same types of workers. Once this data has been collected, analyzed, and discussed, the committee can start to plan the next steps—particularly the most effective type of appeal to convince employees of the benefits of unionization.

Promoting the benefits of unionization.

The second step in the campaign generally involves obtaining an accurate, up-to-date list of all employees eligible to join the proposed bargaining unit. Since employers are under no obligation to provide such a list, and committee members typically want to keep the unionization campaign quiet until they have gained a lot of supporters, employee directories may be borrowed, or someone may stand at the rack near the time clock in which the employees' time cards are stored and write down employee names. Once such a list has been obtained or compiled, the committee can use it to record the responses received to membership solicitations and keep track of the level of support among the eligible employees.

The next step is for the committee members to start contacting employees. Usually, to get the campaign off to a good start, the employees who are believed to favour unionization are approached first. To avoid any suggestion of intimidation or coercion, personal contact is often made on a one-on-one basis.

When trying to organize a small firm, representatives of the organizing committee often contact individual employees on a personal basis, usually after work, just outside the company facilities or at home. To maintain confidentiality, home visits are often preferred. Because house calls are time consuming, however, even in small firms they are often restricted to those employees who are considered essential to the recruitment drive.

In a larger firm, initial contact might be made through a personalized mailing to employee homes. The aim of this contact is to have as many employees as possible sign an authorization card indicating their willingness to be represented by the union in question in collective bargaining with their employer.

The fact that the committee members making personal contact are fellow employees is very helpful in the recruitment process, since they are acquaintances, even personal friends, not strangers. They have shown by their own actions that they are in favour of the union and are requesting the person approached to follow their example. As a fellow employee, the committee representative has inside knowledge and has generally experienced similar problems or has shared concerns. He or she therefore tends to be trusted in a way that no outsider would be. It is up to the union organizer, however, to ensure that the committee members are carefully briefed on what to say. Once management becomes aware of the organizing activities, the union may switch from a policy of discreet recruitment to an all-out public campaign, although this is not a common occurrence. This tactic involves advertising the unionization campaign in the media and in handouts for distribution outside the company facilities. Today, this type of publicity tends to be used only in situations in which there has been a long history of grievances and dissatisfaction, or if a major issue has just arisen that could have a dramatic negative impact on the well-being of a large number of employees, such as the loss of a major contract or client.

authorization card
A card signed by an employee indicating his or her willingness to have the union act as his or her representative for purposes of collective bargaining.

Once a signed **authorization card** has been obtained, the union canvasser turns it over to the union office or organizer. The number of signed cards is typically kept a closely-guarded secret until a substantial number of eligible employees have been signed up.

Step Five: The Outcome There are a number of possible outcomes to a unionization campaign, including rejection by the majority of eligible employees. In order for a union to become the bargaining unit for a group of employees, it must be certified by a labour relations board or receive official recognition from the employer, processes that will be described shortly.

Signs of Organizing Activity

A firm is susceptible to unionization if there has been a sudden increase in unionization activity in the community or industry; major changes are being planned that will impact the size of the work force, such as a merger or acquisition; or there have been recent legislative changes making it easier to unionize (as happened in Ontario under the former New Democratic Party government). As mentioned earlier, however, even in these circumstances, a union rarely succeeds in organizing a well-managed firm in which employees are treated fairly. On the other hand, if the organization's wages and benefits have fallen behind industry or community averages, employees feel that their complaints have been and/or will be ignored, and there is evidence of low job satisfaction (such as high rates of absenteeism and turnover), unionization is a definite possibility.

When a number of the following signs are present, supervisors and managers have justifiable reason for suspecting that a unionization attempt may be under way:

- disappearance of employee lists or directories
- more inquiries than usual about benefits, wages, promotions, and other HR policies and procedures
- criticisms of managers and/or company policies that are more frequent and/or vocal than usual
- queries to a manager about his/her opinion of unions
- employee discussions about past or future group meetings
- the sudden popularity of certain employees (especially if they are the informal leaders)
- the sudden cessation of employee conversation when a member of management approaches
- the appearance of strangers in the parking lot
- the distribution of cards or flyers.

When such signs are present, it does not mean that an organizing campaign is definitely under way. Managers should keep their eyes and ears open to determine if their suspicions are justified, but must be extremely careful not to engage in any unfair practices. Because of his or her position of authority, even a friendly inquiry from a supervisor about unionization activities may be perceived as intimidation by an employee. For this reason, supervisors and managers should avoid asking employees any direct questions on the subject.

Employer Response to an Organizing Campaign

**www.gov.on.ca/lab/lms/lm
se.htm**
Labour Management Services
(Ontario)

Once it is evident that an organizing campaign is under way, if the employer prefers the employee group seeking unionization to retain its nonunion status, a careful campaign is generally mounted to counteract the union drive. Normally, human resources department staff are responsible for heading up such a campaign, although assistance may be obtained from outside consultants or a labour lawyer. Human resources department staff members generally play a key role in the training of supervisors, the data collection process, and information dissemination.

Absolutely critical to the success of a company's counter-campaign is the training of supervisors. They need to be informed about what they can and cannot do or say during the organizing campaign, to ensure that they do not violate labour relations legislation, and avoid actions that might inadvertently provide fuel for the union's campaign. When an unfair labour practice is committed by any member of management, it can lead to an expensive and time-consuming lawsuit, and may result in automatic union certification. Even when management actions are legal, union leaders make claim credit for any new policies or practices that are favourable to employees.

When planning a counter-campaign, data collection is essential. As much information about the union as possible should be obtained, pertaining to dues, strike record, salaries of officers, and any other relevant facts that might cause employees to question the benefits of unionization. Armed with this detailed information, communication strategies can be planned, with the aim of reminding employees about the company's good points, pointing out disadvantages of unionization, and refuting untrue union claims (if there are any). The employer's case for remaining nonunion should be presented in a factual, honest, and straightforward manner.

Answering questions is an important part of an effective counter-campaign. A good strategy is to set up an "information line," so that supervisors and employees can get quick answers to questions raised during the organizing campaign. Other communication strategies include preparing speeches outlining the benefits of remaining nonunion; writing factual articles for the company newsletter; or preparing a letter to send to the home of each employee.

Under the law, employers are granted the right to:

- Express their views and opinions regarding unions in general and the organizing union in particular.
- State their position regarding the desirability of remaining nonunion.
- Prohibit distribution of union literature on their own property on company time. (They must, however, allow solicitation on free time, subject to reasonable regulations respecting safety and proper conduct.)
- Increase wages, make promotions, and take other human resources actions, as long as they would do so in the normal course of business. In most jurisdictions, however, once an application for certification is received by the LRB, wages, benefits, and working conditions are frozen until the application is dealt with.
- Assemble employees during working hours to state the company's position, as long as employees are advised of the purpose of the meeting in advance, attendance is optional, and threats and promises are avoided. (Employers have no obligation to give the union the same opportunity.)

Employers must ensure that they do not hold "captive audience" speeches (sessions at which employee attendance is mandatory); grill employees about union activities; or increase wages and benefits in a manner that could be perceived to be a bribe for remaining nonunion.

Employers must also ensure that they do not use coercion, intimidation, threats, promises, or undue influence. The distinction between expressing one's views and exerting undue influence is not always clear, and many of the cases that come before the Labour Relations Boards pertaining to organizing campaigns revolve around this issue. When unfair practices are alleged, the LRBs look at all employer actions in the context of the employer's total response to the organizing campaign. Where there is evidence of strong anti-union propaganda, for example, what might ordinarily appear to be innocent language or actions could be viewed by the Board as less than benign.[34]

McDonald's, like Wal-Mart, has a reputation for preferring a union-free workplace.

The highly publicized Wal-Mart case provides an excellent example of the fine line that an employer must walk. Employers must not only be cautious about what they say or do during an organizing campaign, but must also ensure that legitimate employee questions are dealt with in a proper manner. Failure to answer a question may be perceived as an implied threat to job security:[35]

The case arose out of a certification drive by the United Steelworkers of America at a Wal-Mart store in Windsor, Ontario, in April of 1996. After obtaining 91 authorization cards from the 205 staff of the store, the union filed for certification. Based on the level of membership support indicated, the Board ordered that a certification vote be held. At the vote, the union was rejected by a margin of 151 to 43. The union subsequently alleged that the employer's conduct prior to the vote constituted unfair practices that unlawfully influenced the outcome of the election and was sufficiently serious to justify disregarding the results of the vote and granting automatic certification to the union.

After hearing the evidence, the LRB concluded that the union should succeed and certified the Steelworkers as the bargaining agent. Factors influencing the Board's decision included the fact that the company allowed an anti-union employee to make a speech at a company meeting, which, in the Board's opinion, contained the employee's belief that Wal-Mart would not stand for a union and that a union would harm job security. They also concluded that five managers who circulated throughout the store for a number of days exerted a subtle form of intimidation, since it appeared to be an effort to identify union supporters. Also, the LRB found that despite the company's open communication policy, management refused to answer the question as to whether the Wal-Mart store would close if it was unionized, which was perceived by the Board to be a subtle, but intentional, threat to employee job security.

Union Recognition

There are three basic ways in which a union can obtain recognition as a bargaining unit for a group of workers: 1) voluntary recognition, 2) the regular certification process, and 3) a prehearing vote. Bargaining rights can also be terminated, a topic which is discussed in the appendix to this chapter.

voluntary recognition
A situation in which an employer agrees in writing to recognize a labour union as the exclusive bargaining agent for a specific group of employees, without resorting to the formal certification procedure.

certification
The procedure whereby a labour union obtains a certificate from the relevant Labour Relations Board (or Quebec equivalent) declaring that the union is the exclusive bargaining agent for a defined group of employees in a bargaining unit that the Board considers appropriate for collective bargaining purposes.

Voluntary Recognition   An employer in every Canadian jurisdiction, except Quebec, can voluntarily recognize a union as the bargaining agent for a group of its employees, if it considers the bargaining unit to be appropriate and believes that the majority of employees, without having been subjected to undue pressure, have indicated their desire to be represented by that union. The **voluntary recognition** process is an alternative to certification and does not require the involvement of a third party. Although fairly rare, it may occur if an employer has adopted a union acceptance strategy, and believes that representation by that union is what the employees desire.

Regular Certification   While all jurisdictions differ slightly in their union **certification** procedure, the norm is for unions to present the required minimum membership evidence for a bargaining unit, which they have defined, to the appropriate Labour Relations Board, along with an application for certification. The evidence of support required to apply for certification ranges from 25 percent of bargaining unit members in Saskatchewan to 50 percent in Newfoundland and Prince Edward Island.[36] The LRB then determines whether the bargaining unit is appropriate, taking the such criteria as the following into account:

- the wishes of the employer and the trade union
- the commonality of interest among employees, considering the nature of the work performed and the skills of the employees
- the LRBs' general policy of putting office staff and production workers in separate bargaining units.

The level of membership support is then determined based on the evidence presented by the union. In every jurisdiction, signed authorization cards must be presented to the Board as evidence of membership support. In some, a receipt indicating payment of a small initiation fee is also required.

In all jurisdictions except Ontario and Alberta, labour boards can grant **automatic certification**, which means certification without a vote, if the applicant union can demonstrate by documentary evidence that it has a high enough level of support for the proposed bargaining unit (generally 50 or 55 percent).[37] Automatic certification may also be granted if the employer has engaged in unfair practices to the extent that a vote would not (or did not) reflect the true wishes of the proposed bargaining unit members, as in the Wal-Mart case.

If the level of support is not sufficient for automatic certification, but is above a specified minimum level (between 25 and 45 percent, depending on jurisdiction),[38] and the employer has not engaged in unfair practices, the board will order a **representation vote**. In some jurisdictions, there is a "quiet period" specified prior to a representation vote, during which there can be no campaigning by either side. If this prohibition is violated, then the votes may be set aside. At a representation vote, which is supervised by the LRB, eligible employees have the opportunity to cast a secret ballot, indicating whether or not they wish the union to be certified. In Newfoundland, New Brunswick, Quebec and Manitoba, to gain certification, the voting results must indicate more than *50 percent of the potential bargaining unit members* are in support of the union. In other jurisdictions, the standard is the support of *more than 50 percent of those voting*.[39] If the union loses, another election cannot be held among the same employees for at least one year.

It should be noted that the LRBs do not have to grant automatic certification in most jurisdictions, and may order a representation vote, regardless of the extent of documentary evidence. This is not common practice, however. In fact, only about 20 percent of certifications are the result of a vote—roughly four out of five certifications are the result of authorization cards alone.[40]

Prehearing Votes

automatic certification
A certification process, legally permitted in most jurisdictions, that does not require that an employee vote be held. To qualify for such certification, the applicant union must provide evidence that it has a high enough level of support for the proposed bargaining unit (usually between 50 and 55 percent). Automatic certification may also be granted if the employer has engaged in unfair practices.

representation vote
A vote conducted by the Labour Relations Board in which employees in the bargaining unit indicate, by secret ballot, whether or not they wish to be represented, or continue to be represented, by a labour union.

prehearing vote
An alternative mechanism for certification, available in most jurisdictions, used in situations in which there is evidence of irregularities early in the organizing campaign, such as unfair management practices.

In most jurisdictions, a **prehearing vote** may be conducted where there is evidence of irregularities early in an organizing campaign, such as an employer's use of unfair labour practices. In such a case, the LRB may order a vote prior to holding a hearing about the composition of the bargaining unit. The intent is to determine the level of support for the union as quickly as possible, before the employer's intimidation tactics can taint the outcome. The ballot box is then sealed until the Board determines whether the bargaining unit is appropriate and, if so, which employees are eligible for membership. Only the votes of potential bargaining unit members are counted.

If the Board determines that the bargaining unit is appropriate and, after counting the ballots, concludes that the majority of members in the bargaining unit support the union, the union is certified.

The Impact of Unionization on HRM

**www.hronline.com/forums
/index.html**
LABOR-L (Listserv)

Following the certification or voluntary recognition of a bargaining unit, both the employer and the union are legally required to bargain in good faith over the terms and conditions of employment. A collective agreement for a term of at least one year must be agreed to and signed by both parties. Once signed, the collective agreement must be administered by management and adhered to by both parties. We will describe the collective bargaining and contract administration processes in chapter 17. First, though, we'll describe the overall impact on unionization on HRM.

Organizational Structure

Once an organization is unionized, the human resources department is typically expanded by the addition of a labour relations specialist or section. In a large firm with a number of bargaining units, human resources and labour relations may form two divisions within a broader department, often called industrial relations or labour relations. In such situations, the labour relations staff specialize in negotiations and contract administration issues, while those working in the human resources section continue to look after all of the other HR functions.

Management Decision Making

Union leaders are typically involved in decisions pertaining to any issues that will affect bargaining unit members, such as subcontracting of work, productivity standards, and job content. While management continues to claim exclusive rights over certain matters, union leaders may challenge these rights.

Formulation of Policies and Procedures

In a unionized setting, management has less freedom to make unilateral changes. All HR policies must be consistent with the terms of the collective agreement. To gain the cooperation of union leaders in administering policies and procedures, union representatives are often involved in the formulation of all policies affecting bargaining unit members—such as those pertaining to disciplinary rules and regulations—or at least consulted as such policies are being drafted, a topic to which we will return in chapter 17.

Centralization of Record Keeping and Standardization of Decision Making

Unionization generally results in greater centralization of employee record keeping and standardization of decision making to ensure equity, consistency, and uniformity. More centralized coordination is typically required in the enforcement of HR policies and procedures, for example, which creates an expanded role for members of the labour relations department, as does the increased need for documentation to support decisions.

Supervisory Authority and Responsibility

The major impact of unionization is at the first-line level, since it is the supervisors who are responsible for administering the terms of the collective agreement on a day-to-day basis. Greater standardization of decision making and centralization of record keeping may lead supervisors to feel that they have lost some of their authority, which can cause resentment, especially since they inevitably find that unionization results in an increase in their responsibilities. They must ensure that all of their decisions and actions are in accordance with the terms of the collective agreement.

Even decisions that abide by the agreement may be challenged by the union. In addition, supervisors are often required to produce more written records than ever before, since documentation is critical at grievance and arbitration hearings.

Conclusion

In every organization, whether union or nonunion, ultimate responsibility for the firm's performance and the effective utilization of its human resources rests with management. While unionization does have an impact on the way in which managers perform their HR responsibilities, when the union leaders are treated as partners, they can provide a great deal of assistance with HR functions. When there is a cooperative and harmonious working relationship between management and union leaders, the result can be a win-win, a topic to which we'll return in chapter 17.

Chapter Review

Summary

1. The term labour–management relations refers to the ongoing economic and social interactions between labour unions and management in organizations.

2. Current Canadian labour laws have two general purposes: providing a common set of rules for fair negotiations, and ensuring protection of the public interest. Approximately 90 percent of labour–management relations are governed by provincial/territorial statutes. There are a number of common characteristics among the labour relations legislation in all Canadian jurisdictions, including certification procedures, a minimum duration for collective agreements of one year, procedures that must be followed by one or both parties before a strike or lockout is legal, prohibition of strikes/lockouts during the life of a collective agreement, grievance arbitration procedures, prohibition of unfair practices on the part of labour and management, and a labour relations board (or equivalent) to administer and enforce the provisions of the legislation.

3. The primary goal of labour unions active in Canada is to secure greater economic and welfare benefits for their members through negotiations, contract administration, and lobbying. This union philosophy has become known as business unionism. Many unions also choose to address broader political and social issues of concern to their members, a philosophy known as social (or reform) unionism.

4. The labour unions in Canada can be divided according to (a) type of worker eligible for membership: craft or industrial; (b) geographic scope: international, national, or local; and (c) labour congress affiliation. The Canadian Labour Congress (CLC) is the major central labour organization in Canada. Its U.S. counterpart is the American Federation of Labour—Congress of Industrial Organizations (AFL-CIO).

5. The basic unit of the labour union movement in Canada is the local, formed in a particular plant or locality. Each local has its own constitution, draws up its own bylaws, and has authority for obtaining new members, handling grievances, collective bargaining, and organizing recreational activities. There are generally elected officials, known as union stewards, who are responsible for representing the interests and protecting the rights of bargaining unit employees in their department or area. In larger locals, there is often a full-time elected or appointed business agent, whose salary is paid by the local or the national/international office.

6. The number of persons belonging to labour unions, as a percentage of non-agricultural workers, has been gradually decreasing. As with employers, unions are facing many challenges due to global competition and technological advances. Unions also have to deal with challenges pertaining to the unionization of white-

collar employees, managers and professionals, as well as innovative work practices that have the potential to decrease employee interest in unionization.

7. An organization's labour relations strategy, one component of its HR strategy, is its overall plan for dealing with unions, which sets the tone for its union-management relationship. Possible strategies include union acceptance and union avoidance. There are two avoidance strategies: union substitution and union suppression.

8. The labour relations process is a sequence of steps, beginning with the desire to unionize and ending with day-to-day contract administration. Research supports the notion that dissatisfaction with wages, benefits, and working conditions provides the strongest reason to unionize. However, it is only when workers are dissatisfied and believe that they are without the ability to change the factors causing dissatisfaction, except through collective action, that they become interested in unionizing.

9. The union organizing process involves a series of steps, which typically include: employee/union contact; an initial organizational meeting; the formation of an in-house organizing committee; an organizing campaign; and the outcome—certification, recognition, or rejection.

10. Once it is evident that an organizing campaign is under way, if the employer prefers the employee group seeking unionization to retain its nonunion status, a careful campaign is generally mounted to counteract the union drive. Care must be taken to avoid coercion, intimidation, threats, promises, or undue influence.

11. There are three basic ways in which a union can obtain recognition as a bargaining unit for a group of workers: 1) voluntary recognition, 2) the regular certification process, and 3) a prehearing vote. Bargaining rights can also be terminated, a topic which is discussed in the appendix.

12. Unions have an impact on HRM in a number of ways: 1) The human resources department is expanded by the addition of a labour relations specialist or section, 2) Unions leaders are typically involved in decisions that will affect their members. 3) Management has less freedom to make unilateral changes, 4) Unions can cause greater centralization of employee record keeping and standardization of decision making, 5) Supervisors may feel that they have lost some of their authority, while, simultaneously experiencing an increase in responsibility.

Key Terms

American Federation of Labour–Congress of Industrial Organizations (AFL-CIO)
authorization card
automatic certification
bargaining agent
bargaining unit
blacklist
business agent
business unionism
Canada Labour Code
Canadian Labour Congress (CLC)
certification
chief steward
collective agreement (union contract)
collective bargaining
craft union
decertification
directly chartered local union

grass-roots unionism
independent local union
industrial union
in-house organizing committee
international union
labour–management relations
Labour Relations Board
labour relations process
labour relations strategy
labour union (union)
local
local/district labour council
national union
prehearing vote
provincial/territorial federation of labour
Public Service Staff Relations Act (PSSRA)
Public Service Staff Relations Board PSSRB)

representation vote
social (or reform) unionism
succession
unfair labour practice
union acceptance strategy
union avoidance strategy
union organizer
union organizing campaign
union organizing process
union steward
union substitution (proactive human resources) approach
union suppression approach
voluntary recognition
work stoppage
yellow-dog contract

Discussion Questions and Exercises

1. Summarize the common characteristics among Canadian labour relations legislation.
2. Cite five examples of unfair labour practices on the part of management and five on the part of unions.
3. Explain the role of union locals and describe their structure.
4. Differentiate between business and social unionism and provide an example of a conflict that might arise between these two philosophies.
5. Describe the union acceptance, avoidance, substitution, and suppression approaches to labour relations, and explain when each might be adopted.
6. Explain why workers might desire unionization, and describe the union organizing process.
7. Describe five signs to which managers should be alert to detect an organizing campaign.
8 Working with two or three classmates, devise a management counter-campaign to a unionization attempt, ensuring that all recommended courses of action are legal.
9. Explain the three basic ways in which unions can obtain recognition.
10. Describe how you would be affected by unionization: 1) as a human resources department member, and 2) as a first-line supervisor.

Application Exercises

RUNNING CASE: Carter Cleaning Company

Unionization?

Last week something happened at one of the Carter stores that upset both Jack and Jennifer. As happens fairly regularly, one of the workers involved with cleaning and spotting had to be fired because of poor quality work. The nature of the business is such that employees are continually quitting, being fired, and being rehired somewhere else. In fact, it is not unusual for an employee in the industry to have worked in all or most of the stores in a geographic area during the period of five or so years.

Because job switching is so much a part of the industry, Jack and Jennifer were therefore taken aback when Bob, the man who was fired, reacted almost violently. He threw a bottle of chemicals to the floor, began shouting that Jack was "incompetent, unfair, and unfit to be an employer" and proceeded to warn that he was forthwith driving to the local headquarters of the textile workers' union to get them to begin organizing the Carter Cleaning Centres.

Subsequently, several of the store managers reported that employees were talking among themselves much more animatedly during lunch than they usually did, and that a man who one manager believes is a local union representative has been meeting with the employees after work, as well.

Jennifer has several questions:

Questions

1. What signs should she look for to determine if the Carter Cleaning Centre employees are in the initial stages of an organizing campaign?

2. Without violating any laws, what can she do to determine if organizing activity is under way?

3. If a unionization campaign is in progress and she and her father would prefer to remain nonunionized, what steps should she take?

CASE INCIDENT: The Organizing Campaign at Edper Furniture

Edper Furniture Manufacturing has been in existence since 1960. Its sole product line is furniture, which is sold through upscale department stores. Until recently, 30 individuals were employed in Edper's design and production department. All production employees are paid on an hourly basis.

The company is not unionized. The General Manager established a practice of monitoring wage settlements at the major unionized competitors, and ensured that Edper matched their wages. The benefits package, however, has never been as generous. For many years, despite the disparity in benefits, most of the firm's employees felt that they were slightly ahead of the workers in unionized companies, since they did not pay union dues. Edper's managers are considered to be fair, and this has contributed to a good working relationship between workers and management.

One bright sunny day during the spring of 1996, two employees, Barbara Dallas and Alex Springate, started talking about life at the company over lunch. Both agreed that although the firm has continued to match the pay rates of unionized companies, the benefits provided are not very good. Alex stated, "We do not have a pension plan, disability insurance, dental coverage, or job security. The firm can let us go tomorrow and we would not have anything to show for 20 years of service." Barbara agreed, saying, "Those facts have crossed my mind recently, and I bet other workers are thinking the same thing. This year when the company announced our wage increase I was expecting something to be done about the benefits but nothing happened."

"Obviously, if they were going to change the benefits they would have done so by now," Alex replied. After a moment, Barbara said, "If we approach management about our concerns they might think that we are trouble-makers and fire us." Lunch ended at this point and they agreed to talk to some of their close friends to get their input.

The next time Barbara and Alex met they exchanged notes. They were surprised to find out that most workers shared their concerns and felt that they should consider unionizing. Alex and Barbara initiated contact with the CAW and the sign-up process began in the summer of 1996.

During the first half of 1996, the company had suffered severe financial losses because of the recession. In fact, it lost 50 percent of its market share. The firm's financial advisors informed the management team that 30 percent was probably lost permanently due to cross-border shoppers. In July, the company decided to lay off half of its work force. Alex and Barbara were among those laid off. Workers claimed that the layoff was an intimidation tactic by management and filed an unfair labour practice charge against the company with the Labour Relations Board.

Questions

1. Why were the workers at Edper Furniture Manufacturing interested in unionizing? (Hint: Think about all possible reasons, not just those that are readily apparent).

2. Was the action by the employer an unfair labour practice? Why or why not?

3. What outcome would you predict to the employees' complaint?

Human Resource Management Simulation

Part 4 of the simulation deals with Labour Relations. Exercise 19 requires writing a report outlining recommended strategies that can be used to ensure that the nonunionized employees at the Peterborough plant don't seek union representation. Exercise 20 delves into appropriate and inappropriate strategies that management can use to keep track of rumours of unionization. Simulation 6 provides the opportunity to develop a presentation for the Peterborough Plant supervisors to teach them about the types of employee activities that might indicate that a union organizing campaign is under way, and to ensure that they are aware of what they can and cannot do once a formal application for certification has been filed.

Video Case

The New Militants

Why are young employees heading unionization drives at companies such as Wal-Mart and Starbucks Coffee? Is it simply history repeating itself or are there new issues on the table?

The video first takes viewers to a Wal-Mart store in Windsor, Ontario, for an interview with twenty-three-year-old Mary McArthur, who led the unionization drive there. As Mary explains, since retail positions are all that are available to her and many other young people, they have set out to redefine their jobs: $8.00 per hour is not enough for the rest of their working lives.

Viewers are then taken to Starbucks Coffee in Vancouver, British Columbia, where workers feel that the company has grown so fast that it has lost sight of its employees and their needs. Their drive for unionization can be depicted as a "wake-up call" for Starbucks—to start to put their focus back on valuing their employees.

As Joan Pajunen, of Retail Consultants, explains, unionization represents a way for employees to gain some control over their work lives and working conditions. However, once a union is certified, it still lacks power until a collective agreement has been signed.

The incidents shown on the video are not isolated ones: Many organizations in the retail and service sectors are facing the possibility of unionization.

Questions

1. Why are young people starting unionization drives at organizations such as Wal-Mart and Starbucks Coffee?
2. What are companies doing to avoid union certification?
3. What implications does a union have for an organization's human resources department?

Video Resource: CBC, *Venture*, "Wal-Mart (The New Militants)," February 23, 1997.

Take It to the Net

Check out our Companion Website at

www.prenticehall.ca/dessler

for a multitude of practice questions, key terms and concepts, Weblinks to related sites, newsgroups, CBC video updates, and more.

Appendix 16.1

Termination of Bargaining Rights

Just as it is possible for a labour union to become the legally certified or recognized bargaining agent for a group of employees, it is also possible for a union to lose such rights. A few of the circumstances under which bargaining rights may be terminated are described next.

Termination of A Voluntarily Recognized Union

In the case of a union that received voluntary employer recognition, bargaining rights of the union may be terminated upon application by any employee in the bargaining unit or by the labour union. The application for termination of bargaining rights must be made during the first year of the collective agreement or within one year of signing the recognition agreement if no collective agreement has been signed. If termination of such rights is the desire of the majority of bargaining unit members, the union loses its recognition status.

Employee Request for Decertification

decertification
The process whereby a union is legally deprived of its official recognition as the exclusive bargaining agent for a group of employees.

All labour relations acts provide procedures for workers to apply for the **decertification** of their unions. Generally, members may apply for decertification if the union has failed to negotiate a collective agreement within one year of certification, or if they are dissatisfied with the performance of the union. Dissatisfaction may arise because members feel that the union is weak, ineffective, or indifferent. Applications must be submitted to the appropriate Labour Relations Board, along with evidence that a significant percentage of the employees in the bargaining unit no longer wish to be represented by the union (in the form of a voluntarily-signed document). In such case, the LRB is required to satisfy itself that the majority of the employees are in favour of the termination of the union's bargaining rights by holding a secret-ballot vote. If more than fifty percent of the ballots cast (or bargaining unit members, depending on jurisdiction) are in opposition to the union, the union will be decertified.

Decertification Due to Fraud

If it is determined that the union obtained its certification through fraudulent acts, the union will be decertified immediately. Once the LRB has declared that the union no longer represents the bargaining unit employees, any collective agreement negotiated between the parties is void.

Union Request for Decertification

A labour union also has the right to notify the Labour Relations Board that it no longer wishes to continue to represent the employees in a particular bargaining unit. This is known as "termination on abandonment."

Conclusion

Although there are many different grounds on which bargaining rights may be terminated, not all of which have been described above, it should be stressed that such an event is quite unusual.

Notes

1. D.G. Gallagher and G. Strauss, "Union Membership: Attitudes a Participation," in *The State of the Unions*, G. Strauss, D. Gallagher, and J Fiorito, (eds). (Madison, Wis.: Industrial Relations Research Association, 1991), pp. v-xi.
2. The material on unfair labour practices is based on David A. Peach and Paul Bergman, *The Practice of Labour Relations*, 3rd ed. (Toronto: McGraw Hill Ryerson Limited, 1991), pp. 50–1.
3. Alton W.J. Craig and Norman A. Solomon, *The System of Industrial Relations in Canada*, 5th ed. (Toronto: Prentice Hall Canada Inc., 1996), p. 372.
4. Craig and Solomon, *Industrial Relations in Canada*, pp. 386–7.
5. P. Kumar, "Union Growth in Canada: Retrospect and Prospect" in W. C. Riddell, ed., *Canadian Labour Relations*, (Toronto: University of Toronto Press, 1986), p. 103.
6. J.W. Miller Jr., "Power, Politics and the Prospects for Collective Bargaining: An Employer's Viewpoint," in Stanley M. Jacks, ed., *Issues in Labor Policy* (Cambridge: MIT Press, 1971), pp. 3–10.
7. T.V. Alphen, "Unions Eye Blockbuster Merger Plan," *The Toronto Star* (July 29, 1995), p. A3.
8. Timothy Koeller, "Union Activity and the Decline in American Trade Union Membership," *Journal of Labor Research* 15, no. 1 (Winter 1994), pp. 19–32.
9. L. Troy, "Can Canada's Labour Policies Be A Model for the United States?" *Proceedings of the 28th Conference of the Canadian Industrial Relations Association* (Kingston, ON: Queen's University, 1991), pp. 59–64
10. Richard P. Chaykowski and Anil Verma, "Adjustment and Restructuring in Canadian Industrial Relations: Challenges to the Traditional System," *Industrial Relations in Canadian Industry* (Toronto: Dryden, 1992), pp. 1–38.
11. "Union Ranks Thinning," *Canadian HR Reporter* 11, no. 1 (January 12, 1998), p. 9.
12. John Godard, *Industrial Relations: The Economy and Society* (Toronto: McGraw-Hill Ryerson, 1994).
13. "More Women Joining Unions," *Canadian HR Reporter* 10 no. 19 (November 3, 1997), p. 7.
14. Chaykowski and Verma, "Adjustment and Restructuring," pp. 1–38.
15. "Union Ranks Thinning," p. 9.
16. Mark Partridge, "Technology, International Competitiveness, and Union Behavior," *Journal of Labor Research* 14, no. 4 (Spring, 1993) pp. 131–45.
17. Lawrence Surtees, "Unions Unite Forces Against Northern Telecom," *Globe and Mail* (October 18, 1991).
18. Dennis Chamot, "Unions Need to Confront the Results of New Technology," *Monthly Labor Review* (August 1987), p. 45.
19. Sar Levitan and Frank Gallo, "Collective Bargaining and Private Sector Employment," *Monthly Labor Review* (September 1989), pp. 24–33; Barbara Ettorre, "Will Unions Survive?" *Management Review* (August 1993) pp. 9–15.
20. Godard, *Industrial Relations*, p. 132.
21. G. Betcherman, K. McMullen, N. Leckie, and C. Caron, *The Canadian Workplace in Transition* (Kingston, ON: IRC Press, Queen's University, 1994).
22. Tom Rankin, *New Forms of Work Organization: The Challenge for North American Unions* (Toronto: University of Toronto Press, 1990), pp. 150–1
23. Rankin, *New Forms of Work Organization*, pp. 122–46.
24. T.T. Delaney, "Unions and Human Resource Policies," in K. Rowland and G. Ferris (eds.), *Research in Personnel and Human Resources Management* (Greenwich, CT: JAI Press, 1991)
25. Claudine Kapel, "Betting on "7"," *Human Resources Professional* 13, no. 1 (February/March 1996), pp. 17–9.
26. T. Kochan and H. Katz, *Collective Bargaining and Industrial Relations* (Homewood, IL: Irwin, 1988).
27. F. Foulkes, *Personnel Policies in Large Nonunion Companies* (Englewood Cliffs, NJ: Prentice Hall, 1980); J.F. Rand. "Preventive Maintenance Techniques for Staying Union Free," *Personnel Journal* (June 1980), p. 498
28. W. Clay Hamner and Frank Schmidt, "Work Attitude as Predictors of Unionization Activity," *Journal of Applied Psychology* 63, no. 4 (1978), pp. 415–521; Amos Okafor, "White Collar Unionization: Why and What to Do," *Personnel* 62, no. 8 (Aug. 1985), pp. 17–20; Jeanne Brett, "Why Employees Want Unions," *Organizational Dynamics*, (Spring 1980); John Fossum, *Labor Relations* (Dallas: Business Publications, 1982) p. 4; and Michael E. Gordon and Angelo DeNisi, "A Re-Examination of the Relationship Be-

tween Union Membership and Job Satisfaction," *Industrial and Labor Relations Review* 48, no. 2 (January 1995) pp. 222–36.

29. John A. Fossum, *Labor Relations: Development, Structure, Process*, 6th ed. (Homewood, IL: Irwin, 1995), p. 3.

30. "Union Ranks Thinning," p. 9.

31. Clive Fullager and Julian Barling, "A Longitudinal Test of a Model of the Antecedents and Consequences of Union Loyalty," *Journal of Applied Psychology* 74, no. 2 (April 1989), pp. 213–27; Adrienne Eaton, Michael Gordon, and Jeffrey Keefe, "The Impact of Quality of Work Life Programs and Grievance Systems Effectiveness on Union Commitment," *Industrial and Labor Relations Review* 45, no. 3 (April 1992), pp. 592–604.

32. Bob White, *Hard Bargains*, (Toronto, ON: McClelland and Stewart, 1987), p. 21.

33. There is an excellent discussion regarding the strategies used by union organizers in Thomas F. Reed, "Profiles of Union Organizers from Manufacturing and Service Unions," *Journal of Labor Research* 11, no. 1 (Winter 1990), pp. 73–80.

34. Peach and Bergman, *The Practice of Labour Relations* pp. 50–1.

35. Michael D. Failes, "Is Silence Really Golden?" *Human Resources Professional* 14, no. 4 (August/September 1997), pp. 33, 35.

36. Craig and Solomon, *Industrial Relations in Canada* p. 218.

37. Craig and Solomon, *Industrial Relations in Canada* p. 215.

38. Craig and Solomon, *Industrial Relations in Canada* p. 218.

39. Craig and Solomon, *Industrial Relations in Canada* p. 218

40. Craig and Solomon, *Industrial Relations in Canada* p. 216.

Chapter 17

Collective Bargaining and Contract Administration

Chapter Outline

◆ **Introduction to Collective Bargaining**

◆ **The Collective Bargaining Process**

◆ **Third-Party Assistance and Bargaining Impasses**

◆ **The Collective Agreement: Typical Provisions**

◆ **Introduction to Contract Administration**

◆ **Grievance Resolution and Rights Arbitration**

◆ **Building Effective Labour–Management Relations**

Learning Outcomes

After studying this chapter, you should be able to:

Explain the requirements of good faith bargaining.

Describe how management and union prepare for negotiations and *discuss* typical steps involved.

Differentiate between distributive, integrative, and intra-organizational bargaining, and *explain* attitudinal structuring.

Describe conciliation, mediation, strikes, lockouts, and interest arbitration as possible responses to a bargaining impasse.

Briefly *describe* typical collective agreement provisions.

Explain how grievances should be handled.

Describe strategies that can be used to build effective labour–management relations.

Introduction to Collective Bargaining

A major function of a labour union is to bargain collectively over conditions of employment on behalf of those in the bargaining unit that it has received recognition to represent. Collective bargaining is the process by which a formal collective agreement is established between labour and management, which specifies the wages, hours of work, employee benefits, provisions protecting job security, and other conditions governing the bargaining-unit members. The negotiation of a collective agreement involves discussions, concessions, and mutual trade-offs between the union negotiating team and management representatives. Negotiating is only one part of the collective bargaining process, however. As will be explained in this chapter, collective bargaining may also involve the use of third-party assistance, and economic pressure by either union (a strike) or management (a lockout) or third-party intervention. The nature of the actual bargaining process and steps required depends, to a significant extent, on the nature of the relationship between management and labour, and the relative strength of the parties.

The purposes of collective bargaining include:

**www.gov.on.ca/lab/
lms/lmsfaqe.htm#collb**
Collective Bargaining

- negotiating, in "good faith," a collective agreement that describes the scope of management and union rights and responsibilities
- arriving at an agreement that is acceptable to management, the labour union representatives, and the other bargaining unit members
- developing a framework for labour relations in the organization, including the provision of an orderly mechanism to clarify the interpretation and application of the contract and to resolve conflicts that may arise
- specifying, in writing, the manner in which management and bargaining unit members will treat each other and conduct themselves during the term of the collective agreement.

The Collective Agreement

All Canadian jurisdictions have established three essential requirements for a valid collective agreement.[1] It must:

1. Be made between an employer's organization and a trade union or council of trade unions,
2. Contain provisions regarding the terms and conditions of employment of bargaining unit members, and
3. Be in writing.[2]

The collective agreement is the cornerstone of the Canadian labour relations system. In addition to specifying terms and conditions of employment of bargaining unit members, it confirms the union's rights and responsibilities, specifies management's rights, and sets out a dispute resolution mechanism. Its provisions are also used as the basis for determining the legality or illegality of the activities of the employer, trade union, and bargaining unit members.[3]

If the terms of collective agreements meet the needs and expectations of the employees covered and are spelled out clearly, and union and management representatives share a common understanding of them, then these terms may be implemented with few difficulties. Negotiating such a contract is complex and, at times, time consuming and difficult. To try to ensure that the process is as smooth as possible, both parties are legally required to bargain in good faith.

Good Faith Bargaining

good faith bargaining
The legal requirement that the parties negotiating a collective agreement bargain honestly, fairly, and sincerely.

Good faith bargaining requires that union and management representatives communicate and negotiate, that proposals be matched with counterproposals, and that both parties make every reasonable effort to arrive at an agreement.[4] Bargaining in good faith does not mean that either party is compelled to agree to a proposal, nor does it require that either party make any specific concessions (although as a practical matter, some may be necessary).

The line between hard bargaining and bargaining in bad faith is not always clear. However, as interpreted by labour relations boards and the courts, examples of violations of the requirement for good faith bargaining generally include the following:[5]

Surface bargaining   This involves merely going through the motions of bargaining, without any real intention of reaching a mutually acceptable agreement.

surface bargaining
The term used if either party goes through the motions of collective bargaining with no intention of arriving at a mutually acceptable agreement.

dilatory tactics
Actions tending to or intended to cause delay.

Failing to make concessions or withdrawing previously granted concessions   Although neither party is required to make concessions, the definition of good faith suggests that a willingness to compromise is an essential ingredient. Withdrawing previously-granted concessions is considered to be bad-faith bargaining.

Failing to make reasonable proposals and demands   Failure to advance proposals is considered a sign of bad-faith bargaining, as is the failure to advance realistic proposals.

Dilatory tactics   The parties must meet and confer at reasonable times and intervals. Obviously, refusal to meet does not satisfy the positive duty imposed on the employer and union, nor does the use of frequent delaying tactics, such as postponement of scheduled sessions.

Imposing unreasonable conditions   Attempts to impose conditions that are so onerous or unreasonable as to indicate bad faith will be scrutinized by labour boards. Insisting that striking employees return to work before resuming negotiations would be an example of an unreasonable condition on the part of an employer.

Making unilateral changes in conditions   Such changes are viewed as a strong indication that the employer is not bargaining with the required intent of reaching an agreement.

Negotiating a collective agreement.

Bypassing the representatives   The duty to bargain in good faith is violated when either party refuses to negotiate with the selected representatives of the other party. The duty of management to bargain in good faith involves, at a minimum, accepting the fact that the legally-recognized labour union is the body with whom the employer must negotiate. Management is prohibited from overriding the bargaining process by making an offer directly to the employees. This practice, called *Boulwarism*, was named after Lemuel Boulware, vice-president of General Electric, who used this strategy in the 1950s.

Committing unfair labour practices during negotiations   Such actions may reflect upon the good faith of the guilty party.

Failing to provide information Information must be supplied to the other negotiating team, upon request, that will enable the members to understand and intelligently discuss the issues raised in bargaining. Neither party can deliberately distort information or mislead the other party.

The Collective Bargaining Process

collective bargaining process
Reaching a collective agreement, which generally involves preparation, face-to-face negotiations, and contract approval, but may also include third-party assistance and economic pressure or third-party intervention.

There are several steps that are almost always involved in the **collective bargaining process**, including preparation for bargaining, face-to-face negotiations, and obtaining approval for the proposed collective agreement. When talks do not go as smoothly as might be desired, there are two possible additional steps. First, when talks break down, third-party assistance is required by law in every jurisdiction except Saskatchewan.[6] Even when impartial third parties are brought in to assist the union and management negotiating teams, there is always the possibility of arriving at a bargaining impasse, resulting in the second additional step, a strike/lockout or interest arbitration. Each of these steps will be described next.

Preparation for Negotiations

The final outcome of the collective bargaining process is shaped, to a large extent, by the quality of pre-negotiation planning. Good preparation leads to orderly, factual collective bargaining, and a greater likelihood that desired goals will be achieved. Preparation for negotiations involves planning the bargaining strategy and process and assembling data to support bargaining proposals. Assuming that the collective agreement is not the first to be negotiated by the parties, preparations for the next round of negotiations should commence soon after the signing of the current collective agreement while the experience is still fresh in the minds of the members of both negotiating teams.

Management Strategies The organization's labour relations specialists are generally the key players in management's preparations. In addition to reviewing the strengths and weaknesses of any previous negotiating sessions, management's preparations should involve the following:[7]

Reviewing the Organization's Strategic Plan Preparation for bargaining should begin with a review of the organization's strategic plan. The firm's overall objectives, intermediate and long-term plans, upcoming changes in their product or service mix, and major technological innovations must all be taken into consideration as an initial bargaining strategy is being prepared.

Gathering Data on Economic Trends Data should be gathered on general economic conditions, cost-of-living trends and wage rates for the general geographic area. Data obtained from government sources such as the Bureau of Labour Information, HRDC, and Statistics Canada can help to support the employer's position during negotiations, as can information gleaned from local and national newspapers and reports published by the Conference Board of Canada. The unemployment rate and other economic data can also be helpful in assessing management's relative bargaining power.

Conducting Wage and Benefit Surveys and Analyzing Ability to Pay Surveys should be conducted to assess the compensation policies of competitors. Data should also be gathered that will help managers assess the organization's ability to pay. Compiling data about the wage rates and employee benefits and services offered by both union and nonunion competitors is essential. Unions generally seek to negotiate wages and benefits in line with those offered by competitors. Management must have accurate data about what is being offered elsewhere in order to anticipate likely union demands and plan their monetary proposals. The employer's ability to pay must also be taken into consideration. In order to offer effective counterproposals, the management negotiating team must be able to cite examples of the wage rates and benefits offered elsewhere, and have accurate data about the firm's financial situation.

Analyzing Other Collective Agreements   This includes a section-by-section comparison with other benchmark collective bargaining agreements, since they often provide a framework that one side or the other may seek to follow in negotiations. **Pattern bargaining** occurs when unions negotiate provisions covering wages and other benefits that are similar to those already negotiated for another bargaining unit within the region or industry. For example, the Canadian Auto Workers tries to negotiate similar contract provisions for employees at Ford, General Motors, and Chrysler.[8] Although pattern bargaining is declining, it is still quite prevalent in North America.[9] Such bargaining enables unions to provide their members with wages and benefits similar to those negotiated elsewhere, and helps to ensure that employers have labour costs comparable with those of their competitors.[10]

pattern bargaining
A collective bargaining tactic whereby a union uses a settlement negotiated with one employer as a "pattern" (or model) and seeks to secure a similar settlement from other employers in the region or industry.

Obtaining Multi-Employer Coordination   Coordination can range from the exchange of general information among loosely connected employers to the formation of a multi-employer bargaining association (where legally permissable).

Obtaining Supervisory Input   Two-way communication should be established between the labour relations specialists and first-line supervisors responsible for day-to-day contract administration, to ensure that the supervisors' interests and concerns are integrated into the planning process. Where there is an existing collective agreement, first-line supervisors are generally best equipped to identify current provisions that have proven to be difficult to implement, and to suggest possible amendments, deletions, or additions.

Reviewing the Union's Organizing-Campaign Promises or the Existing Contract   To anticipate likely union demands, the promises made during the union organizing campaign should be reviewed, or unmet demands from previous negotiations. Where there is an existing collective agreement, it should be reviewed comprehensively so that any unclear contract language that has led or could potentially lead to divergent interpretations can be identified.

Conducting an Audit and Analysis of Grievances   Such an audit provides information about grievances filed, by section of the contract, as well as the interpretation of contract provisions through grievance settlements and arbitration awards (where applicable). It often points out weaknesses in contract language or provisions.

Canvassing Relevant Arbitration Awards and LRB Rulings   Examination of such decisions often points out the need for amendments to contract language.

Costing   Management must have accurate data about the costs of any current contract provisions, as well as the costs of anticipated union demands. Often, representatives from the accounting or finance area assume major responsibility for costing. The use of computers for costing purposes is described in the Information Technology and HR box.

Information Technology and HR
Using Computers for Costing Bargaining Proposals

Students in business/management programs, whether they ultimately work for management or labour, are usually introduced to computer simulation games that require answering "what-if" questions. Some simulations require making complex strategy decisions; others are as basic as looking at cash-flow projections. These same concepts may be applied to labour–management negotiations. When labour suggests a five percent wage increase the first year, followed by three percent each of the next two years, management may counter with three, three, and five, with the understanding that their proposal will cost less over the course of the three years. However, costing out other benefits may not be as easy. Therefore, programs that rapidly calculate the dollar cost of benefits (both direct and indirect) provide the opportunity for more knowledgeable and effective bargaining.[1]

To quickly calculate the costs of offers or counterproposals, a simple table, based on (1) the percentage difference between each step in the wage range, or (2) each employee's annual pay, or (3) a particular benefit, can be created. For example, if each wage step is four percent higher than the one below, and the first step of each grade equals the middle step of the previous grade, simply changing the first step in the bottom grade in the table of the wage plan will update it. Then, by linking this table to the rate each employee is paid (keyed to that table), the new total cost is available. If an employee is paid at the rate of step four, grade three, a cell address next to that employee's name tells the company what is budgeted for that employee. If that employee has worked an average of 100 hours overtime each of the last three years, a formula would be placed next to the employee's name that includes the cell address in the wage table, plus the hourly overtime rate (if the wage plan is not in hourly figures) times 100 (to represent the 100 hours).

If the union negotiating team proposes that the benefits package be raised by seven percent to include a specified dollar amount for child care, the negotiator should have available the number of employees who have expressed an interest in this benefit and how many children are involved, as well as a range of possible costs of child care in the area. By combining this information with the current percentage of payroll assigned to benefit costs, it will be clear whether or not seven percent is a realistic estimate of probable costs. If the management negotiating team has been authorized to allocate a maximum of say five percent, the management team spokesperson may be able to negotiate a provision regarding this benefit, carefully worded in such a way that costs will remain within the authorized range (for example, by specifying a maximum yearly amount per child or per employee).

Computers, then, can help negotiators do the costing required to prepare for bargaining sessions. In addition, portable or laptop computers can provide support at the bargaining table and/or in caucus sessions, and enable negotiating team members to cost proposals and counterproposals on the spot.◆

1. M. Steven Potash, "A Scientific Approach to Bargaining," *ABA Journal* (January 1986), p. 58.

Contingency Planning The likelihood of a strike or lockout should be assessed, and contingency plans drawn up for dealing with a bargaining impasse if it is deemed to be a possibility.

Preparing an Initial Bargaining Plan and Strategy Once the above steps have been completed, an initial bargaining plan and strategy should be formulated and submitted to the senior management team (and/or board) for approval.

www.gov.on.ca/lab/lms/lmsfaqe.htm#strike
Strikes

Establishing a Bargaining Team   The composition and size of the bargaining team is generally based on industry practices and previous bargaining history (if any). Normally, union and management teams each comprise four to six representatives. Management's selection of bargaining team members should be based on an assessment of technical knowledge, experience, and personality. The chief negotiator for management is generally the vice-president or manager of labour relations. Team members typically include other representatives of the human resources or industrial relations department, especially those with expertise in such areas as compensation and benefits administration, training, and occupational health and safety; first-line supervisors; a legal expert; and a representative of the accounting or finance department.

Establishing Bargaining Guidelines   Once the team has been constituted, guidelines should be prepared and submitted for senior management approval. Such guidelines provide a framework for the negotiating team and ensure that the chief negotiator has the authority to reach a settlement. A procedure should be established to modify the guidelines, as circumstances dictate, once the negotiations are under way. The chief negotiator must know exactly how far the organization is willing to go in meeting union demands and whether or not a strike or lockout would even be considered. Generally, the guidelines established do not give the negotiating team the right to make a final decision regarding a proposed agreement. Senior management or board approval is typically required prior to the signing of a collective agreement.

Finalizing Bargaining Strategy and Proposals   Once the preliminary preparations have been completed and the bargaining team established, the plans and strategy should be refined, with input from the team members. Management's proposals should be finalized in writing and include acceptable variations to provide flexibility. At this stage, it is important that the data on which such proposals are based be rechecked for accuracy and comprehensiveness. The finalized proposals should be submitted to senior management for approval.

Establishing Communication Strategies with Senior Management   A procedure should be in place to provide the senior management team with periodic updates during negotiations. A mechanism should also be established such that the chief negotiator has ready access to the Chief Executive Officer once talks are under way.

Union Strategies   The union's preparation for negotiations involves a number of parallel steps:

Obtaining Information on Union Policy Objectives   Some of the local's demands may be shaped by the overall policy objectives of the international or national union with which the local is associated, if any.

Gathering Data on General Economic Trends   This includes data on economic conditions, cost-of-living trends, and wage rates for the general geographic area. Data obtained from government sources such as the Bureau of Labour Information, HRDC, and Statistics Canada can help to support the union's position during negotiations, as can information gleaned from local and national newspapers and reports published by the Conference Board of Canada. Data regarding unemployment rates and overall economic trends can also be helpful in assessing the union's relative bargaining power.

Obtaining Data on Collective Bargaining Trends and Settlements   The national, international, or regional office staff and business agent (if applicable) are excellent sources of information about collective bargaining trends and settlements.

Obtaining Data About the Organization's Finances   The union must gather accurate information about the financial health of the organization and its competitive position. The company's financial reports often provide valuable information. Unions recognize that despite trends elsewhere, there is a limit on each employer's ability to pay. Demanding a settlement beyond that point may result in a lengthy strike, resulting in little or no gain or even plant closure.

Analyzing Other Collective Agreements   This includes a section-by-section comparison with other benchmark collective bargaining agreements, since they often provide suggestions regarding language revisions or new provisions that could be negotiated.

Obtaining Input from Stewards and Others   People who should be consulted include stewards, chief stewards, and central or regional office staff. Since stewards and chief stewards play a key role in day-to-day contract administration, their input is valuable. Where there is an existing collective agreement, the stewards and chief stewards are generally best equipped to identify current provisions that have resulted in complaints or grievances, and to suggest possible amendments, deletions, or additions. Based on experiences with other locals, central or regional office staff often suggest demands that should be placed on the table to solve existing problems or to avoid anticipated future problems.

Obtaining Input from the Membership   Unions generally hold a meeting open to all bargaining unit members, at which individual members have the opportunity to suggest items for inclusion in the union's demands.

Gathering Data about the Bargaining Unit Members   Data about the demographic composition of the bargaining unit members is extremely helpful in assessing bargaining priorities. For example, if the majority of members are baby boomers, provisions regarding job security and pensions may be bargaining priorities. If there are a large number of women in the bargaining unit, provisions pertaining to family-friendly benefits or flexible working hours may be high on the priority list.

Reviewing Organizing-Campaign Promises or the Existing Contract
Promises made during the organizing campaign must be addressed during the negotiation of a first collective agreement. Where there is an existing collective agreement, it should be reviewed comprehensively, so that any unclear contract language that has led or could potentially lead to divergent interpretations can be identified.

Conducting an Audit and Analysis of Grievances   Such an audit provides information about grievances filed, by section of the contract, as well as the interpretation of contract provisions through grievance settlements and arbitration awards (where applicable). There may have been arbitration decisions, for example, which adversely affected the union, and which, from the union's point of view, require changes in the terms of the collective agreement or contract language.

Costing   The union must have accurate data about the costs of any current contract provisions, as well as the costs of proposed demands. Typically, financial experts from the central or regional office are responsible for the costing of monetary demands. It is not uncommon for management to indicate, towards the end of negotiations, the percentage or amount the organization is willing to commit to monetary issues. The union negotiating team must be aware of the cost of every monetary item in order to decide on the best allocation of available funds.

Contingency Planning The likelihood of a strike or lockout should be assessed, and contingency plans drawn up for dealing with a bargaining impasse if it is deemed to be a possibility.

Establishing a Bargaining Team In some situations, the union negotiating committee consists of the elected union officials, such as the president of the local, vice-president, secretary/treasurer, recording secretary, and chief stewards. In others, the bargaining unit members select individuals to serve on their negotiating team by means of a special election. The members of the union negotiating team should have detailed knowledge of the firm's operating situation and of the particular issues to be discussed at the bargaining table. They should also have a sound understanding of the collective bargaining process and labour relations, in general. If there is a business agent, he or she is almost always part of the negotiating team. He or she, or a representative of the regional or central office, often serves as the chief negotiator for the union.

Finalizing Bargaining Strategy and Proposals Once the preliminary preparations have been completed and the bargaining team established, the union's proposals should be finalized in writing and include acceptable variations to provide flexibility. At this stage, it is important that the data on which such proposals are based be rechecked for accuracy and comprehensiveness. The finalized proposals should be approved by the membership at a union meeting.

Face-to-Face Negotiations

Intention to Bargain Under labour relations legislation, representatives of either union or management can give written notice to the other party of their desire to bargain to negotiate a first collective agreement or renew an existing one, with or without modifications. Where there is an existing collective agreement, the time period is generally specified therein. For example:[11]

> *This Agreement shall be in effect from _____ and shall continue in full force and effect until _____. The agreement shall be considered to be automatically continued in all of its provisions, unless, no earlier than ninety (90) days and no later than sixty (60) days before its termination date, either party gives written notice of its intent to bargain for renewal or modification of the agreement or of any of its provisions.*

Exchange of Demands Early in the negotiating process, demands are exchanged. At the time the union bargaining team members notify the company of their intention to bargain, the union's proposals for a new or modified agreement may be submitted to the management negotiating team. Alternatively, the union's proposals may be revealed in subsequent correspondence or at the first negotiating session.

Where there is an existing contract, the company negotiating team generally also has proposals for modifications, additions, or deletions. If the union team submits the union's proposals by mail prior to the first meeting, the company team may respond in like manner. Alternatively, the company team may only notify the union team of their intent to submit proposals at that time and wait for the first or second meeting before presenting the company's proposals.

Examination and Justification of Proposals Proposals are generally submitted in writing and may either suggest precise changes or express the desire to change the meaning or content of a provision in the collective agreement without specifying exact wording. Generally included in each side's proposals are some that the negotiating team believes must be achieved, some that they would like to achieve, and some put on the table primarily for trading purposes.

Very often, after the proposals have been exchanged, each party is asked to explain to the other the intent of its proposals, to ensure proper understanding, and may also be asked for justification of its demands.

Private Assessment   At this stage, the company and union negotiating teams generally make a private assessment of the other team's demands. Usually, each team finds some items with which they can agree quite readily and others on which compromise seems likely. Tentative conclusions are also made regarding which items, if any, are potential strike or lockout issues.

Location, Frequency, and Duration of Meetings   Negotiations are generally held at a neutral, off-site location, so that there is no psychological advantage for either team. Renting a hotel meeting room or a similar facility also means that interruptions and work distractions can be kept to a minimum. There is less likelihood of emotional outbreaks or events being overheard, or witnessed and misinterpreted or taken too seriously by those not involved in the process (such as the rapid departure of a bargaining team member from a negotiating session, slamming the door behind him or her).

In addition to the room in which the negotiations are conducted, each side generally has a room in which intra-team meetings are held, known as **caucus sessions**.

The frequency and duration of negotiating sessions varies. Generally, meetings are held as often as either or both parties consider desirable, as long as the sessions are helping the parties move closer to a settlement. Meetings are typically scheduled to start at 9:30 or 10:00 a.m. so that each side can hold a caucus session first, if so desired, and generally last as long as progress is being made. A caucus session or an adjournment can be suggested by either party, when deemed appropriate.

Marathon bargaining sessions, such as those lasting all night, are not typical until conciliation has been exhausted, and the clock is ticking rapidly toward the strike/lockout deadline, a topic we will describe in detail in the section on bargaining impasses.

Some collective agreements can be negotiated relatively informally in a few hours, particularly if the contract is short and the terms are not overly complex and/or if the bargaining unit is small. For example, one of the authors negotiated a settlement with a small local of the International Union of Operating Engineers in a single day. Other collective agreements, such as those negotiated in large organizations, require months or even years of negotiation.

Initial Bargaining Session   The initial meeting of the bargaining teams is extremely important in establishing the climate that will prevail during the negotiating sessions that follow. A cordial attitude, with occasional humour, can help to relax tension and ensure a smooth set of negotiations.

Generally, the first meeting is devoted to an exchange of demands, if this has not taken place previously, and the establishment of rules and procedures that will be used during negotiations, such as length and duration of sessions, right to call a caucus session or request adjournment, and so on.

Subsequent Bargaining Sessions   In traditional approaches to bargaining, each party argues for its demands and resists those of the other at each negotiating

caucus session
A session in which only the members of one's own bargaining team are present. Such meetings are held so that team members can discuss issues among themselves and come to agreement on proposals, counterproposals, and bargaining strategies.

www.gov.on.ca/lab/lms/ lmsfaqe.htm#colla
Collective Agreements

session. At the same time, both are looking for compromise alternatives that will enable an agreement to be reached. Regardless of its degree of importance, every proposal submitted must be resolved in order to reach a settlement. A proposal may be withdrawn temporarily or permanently, accepted by the other side in its entirety, or accepted in a modified form. Ideally, both sides should come away from negotiations feeling that they have attained many of their basic bargaining goals, even if in slightly modified form; and confident that the tentative agreement reached will be acceptable to senior management and/or the board, and the members of the collective bargaining unit not involved on the negotiating team.

In order for each issue on the table to be resolved satisfactorily, the point at which agreement is reached must be within limits that the union and employer are willing to accept, often referred to as the **bargaining zone**. As illustrated in **Figure 17.1**, if the solution one party desires exceeds the limits of the other party, it is outside the bargaining zone. Unless that party modifies its demands sufficiently to bring them within the bargaining zone or the other extends its limits to accommodate such demands, a bargaining deadlock is the inevitable result.[12]

bargaining zone
The area defined by the bargaining limits (resistance points) of each side, in which compromise is possible, as is the attainment of a settlement satisfactory to both parties.

**Figure 17.1
The Bargaining Zone and Characteristics of Distributive Bargaining**

Source: Adapted from M.R. Carrell and F.E. Kuzmits, *Personnel: Human Resource Management*, 2nd ed., 1986, p. 466. Reproduced by permission of Macmillan Publishing Company.

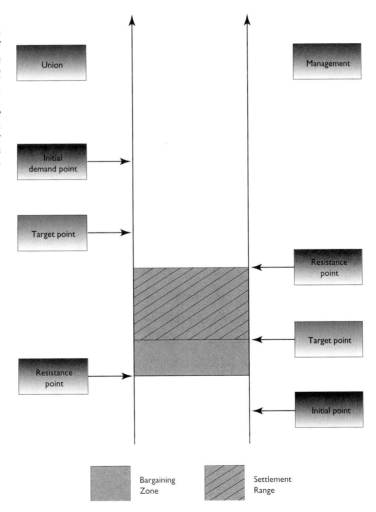

Monetary versus Non-Monetary Issues

Very often the parties separate the bargaining demands into two categories: monetary and non-monetary. **Monetary issues** include all items with direct cost implications, such as wages, overtime pay rates and shift premiums, changes in hours of work, vacation entitlement, and holidays. **Non-monetary issues** include such items as contract language, procedural matters, and administrative issues, that do not involve direct cents-per-hour cost implications. It should be noted, however, that non-monetary items may impact an employer's costs indirectly. For example, negotiated seniority provisions pertaining to layoffs can lead to situations in which a less-qualified and less-productive employee replaces an outstanding performer, thereby increasing labour costs.

Bargaining Strategies Typically, non-monetary issues are discussed first, based on the assumption that such items will be easier to resolve. Quick resolution of such items builds a pattern of give-and-take. When a deadlock subsequently occurs, the sense of past progress may increase the resolve of both sides to find a compromise.

Compromises may be achieved by offering counterproposals that take the other party's objections into account. Sometimes progress is made by simply dropping the contentious issue temporarily and moving on to other items. Further progress on other issues may lead to compromises regarding the earlier impasse.

One expert offers the following guidelines to assist those involved in the negotiating process:[13]

Set clear objectives for every bargaining item and ensure the grounds on which the objectives were established are clearly understood.

Be well prepared with firm data to support your demands and positions.

Learn to understand people and their personalities.

Be a good listener.

Don't hurry.

When in doubt, call a caucus.

Strive for flexibility in your position… don't go out on a limb.

Strive for understanding. Don't just listen to what the other party says and watch what is done, find out why. Economic motivation is not the only explanation for the other party's conduct and actions.

Respect the importance of face saving of the other party.

Be constantly alert to the real intentions of the other party with respect to both goals and priorities.

Build a reputation for being fair but firm.

Use emotions as a tool, not an obstacle. Emotions should be controlled. Don't panic.

Before making a bargaining move, make sure you understand its relationship to all other moves.

Measure each move against the team's objectives.

Pay close attention to the wording of every clause negotiated; unclear words and phrases are a source of grievances.

Remember that negotiating is, by its nature, part of a *compromise* process.

Consider the impact of present negotiations on those in future years. Negotiations are not over when the agreement is signed. The contract will be renegotiated.

Enlist the support of a conciliator if an impasse is reached and no further progress seems possible.

distributive bargaining
An approach to collective bargaining in which issues are treated in a win/lose fashion, such that one party gains at the expense of the other. This approach is often involved when dealing with fixed-sum issues, such as wage increases and benefits improvements.

As indicated by these guidelines, negotiating is a relatively complex process. In fact, it actually consists of four types of activity: distributive bargaining, integrative bargaining, attitudinal structuring and intra-organizational bargaining.

Distributive bargaining,[14] also known as forcing and competitive bargaining, is an approach often typified as "win-lose" bargaining, because the gains of one party are normally achieved at the expense of the other. It is appropriately involved when the issues being discussed pertain to the distribution of things that are available in fixed amounts, such as wage increases and benefits improvements. However, it may also be used when there is a history of distrust and adversarial relations, even when dealing with issues on which a more constructive approach is possible.

The essential characteristics of distributive bargaining are illustrated in Figure 17.1. As indicated, distributive bargaining is characterized by three distinct components: the initial point, the target point, and the resistance point. The initial point for the union is usually higher than what the union expects to receive from management. The union target point is next, and represents what the union considers a realistic assessment of what is achievable from management. The union's bargaining zone limit is its resistance point (walking-away position). This represents its minimally acceptable level.

These points are essentially reversed for management. The management team's initial point is its lowest level, which is used at the beginning of negotiations. Next is its target point, management's desired agreement level. Management's resistance point forms the other boundary of the bargaining zone. The actual settlement range generally lies in the bargaining zone, between management's target and resistance points.[15]

integrative bargaining
A negotiating strategy in which the possibility of win-win, lose-win, win-lose, and lose-lose outcomes is recognized, and there is acknowledgement that the ability to achieve a win-win outcome will depend on mutual trust and problem solving.

Integrative bargaining,[16] also known as fostering and collaborative bargaining, is an approach that assumes there is a win/win solution that can be found, but also acknowledges that one or both sides can be losers if the bargaining is not handled effectively. Integrative bargaining strategies require that both management and union negotiators adopt a genuine interest in the joint exploration of creative solutions to common problems.

Issues pertaining to work rules, job descriptions, and contract language can often be handled effectively using an integrative approach, in situations in which management negotiators are not intent on retaining management rights and both sides are committed to seeking a win-win solution. Wage rates and vacation entitlements are more likely to be fixed-sum issues handled by a distributive approach. Employers adopting a union acceptance strategy often seek to use an effective mix of integrative and distributive bargaining. When the union-management relationship is based on integrity and trust, negotiating team members are more likely to be able to identify demands that can be handled using an integrative approach and to use such an approach whenever possible.

productivity bargaining
The attempt to improve the effectiveness of the organization by eliminating work rules and inefficient work methods that have been hindering productivity, thereby resulting in increased organizational competitiveness and greater job security for bargaining unit members.

Productivity and concessionary bargaining are subcategories of integrative bargaining. One of the primary purposes of **productivity bargaining** is to improve the effectiveness of the organization by eliminating work rules and inefficient work methods that inhibit productivity. Getting the union negotiating team's agreement to do so is not always easy, since there is often a fear that this might eventually lead to the loss of union jobs and a weakening of the union's power base and strength. A union's willingness to negotiate new, improved work rules and practices, such as fewer job classifications and more generic job descriptions, is generally due to the belief that the job security of bargaining unit members will increase with improvements in the employer's ability to compete in its product or service market. In exchange for accepting such changes, unions often seek provisions restricting the transfer of work and outsourcing (subcontracting),

**concessionary
bargaining**
A strategy used when employers are experiencing severe economic problems caused by a general economic recession or financial difficulties. In return for freezes or roll-backs in wages and benefits, bargaining unit members receive greater job security, and often participate in productivity improvements through a gainsharing plan.

as well as a provision guaranteeing that members in danger of losing their jobs due to technological change will be provided with the opportunity for training and skills upgrading.

Concessionary bargaining is a special type of bargaining strategy utilized when organizations are experiencing severe economic problems that have come about as a result of general economic recession or financial difficulties. During concessionary bargaining, employers usually seek agreement from the union to freeze economic rewards such as wages and benefits. In some instances, management may seek reductions, known as "roll-backs" in wages and or benefits. While this may initially appear to be a lose situation for the union and a win for management, it is actually a win-win, if it leads to company survival and prevents layoffs. In exchange for such concessions, management usually guarantees the job security of the bargaining unit members. It should be noted that productivity and concessionary bargaining aren't necessarily mutually exclusive, since in exchange for wage concessions, management may offer a gainsharing plan (see chapter 13) that links compensation to productivity improvements and reduced operating costs. Other compensation trends linked to concessionary bargaining include profit sharing and employee stock ownership plans, both designed to gain greater employee commitment and reward performance improvements.

New Approaches to Integrative Bargaining The objective of integrative bargaining is to establish a creative negotiating relationship that benefits both labour and management. There are two relatively new bargaining techniques that involve an integrative approach, both aimed at a win-win outcome: interest-based bargaining and mutual gains bargaining.

**interest-based
bargaining**
A formal, problem-solving approach to contract negotiations. Instead of exchanging proposals and arguing positions, union and management team members find common interests and brainstorm options, compare them to standards, and reach agreement on settlements.

Interest-based bargaining[17] takes a formal, problem-solving approach to contract negotiations. Instead of exchanging proposals and arguing positions, in interest-based negotiations, union and management team members find common interests and brainstorm options, compare them to standards, and reach agreement on settlements. The end result is a mutually agreeable collective agreement in less time than usual. In recent negotiations involving The Communication, Energy and Paperworkers Union of Canada (CEP) and Inglis Limited in Cambridge, Ontario, for example, sixty issues were resolved in twelve meetings with no caucuses.[18] Other organizations that are sold on the value of this bargaining approach include Stone Consolidated, one of Canada's largest pulp, paper, and forest products companies; Bell Canada;[19] and Ault Foods.[20] The HR managers at these firms all stress that adopting an interest-based bargaining strategy requires trust, open communication, and a true win-win attitude on the part of both parties. As Bob Higgins, Manager of Organizational Design and Development at Inglis explains:[21]

I believe there are still an awful lot of companies that feel the only "win" is improved financial results. But I think companies have got to understand that in order to get the full support of the union, the goal has to be more than just improved results—it has to be improved results in the quality of the workplace, too. It has to be a win for the employees, as well as the organization.

The employees want a healthier, safer, cleaner environment where they can participate in making decisions, as well as being compensated fairly—even more than above-normal wage increases with gainsharing or pay for knowledge. If the company and union can work together, they're both going to benefit.

**mutual gains
bargaining**
A win-win approach, based on training in the fundamentals of effective problem solving and conflict resolution, in which trainees are taught to take the interests of all stakeholders into account, so the solutions developed are better and more permanent.

Mutual gains bargaining[22] also aims at seeking win-win solutions to labour relations issues and problems. As part of the mutual gains process, all key union and management negotiators are trained in the fundamentals of effective problem solving and conflict resolution. Such training is often extended to as many other employees as possible, with the aim of ensuring that the principles of mutual gains bargaining are incorporated into the organization's value system, so that promoting cooperation becomes a year-round corporate objective. According to Kevin Mahoney, Vice-President of Human Resources at SaskPower, the electric utility serving Saskatchewan, a key benefit of the mutual gains process is that it encourages people to acknowledge their common ground and to focus their attention on solving real problems. This, in turn, provides a significant edge in a highly competitive marketplace.[23] As explained by Doug Morrison, education co-ordinator with the International Brotherhood of Electrical Workers (IBEW) at SaskPower:[24]

> It doesn't take a rocket scientist to figure out that the old system of positional bargaining doesn't work as well in today's business environment. In today's climate, we need solutions that are simple and wise, and that help build relationships. And that's what mutual gains bargaining helps people do. It teaches them to take into account the interests of all stakeholders when developing solutions. So the solutions are better and more permanent.

Proponents of mutual gains bargaining at other organizations, such as Northern Telecom and Hercules Canada, point out that a joint sense of accountability is fostered among union and management representatives and that ongoing joint initiatives and activities are the result of the negotiations process. In addition, the tools that are used at the bargaining table can be applied to the resolution of all workplace issues.[25] Some of the positive results that Hercules Canada attained using a mutual gains approach are described in the HR and the Responsive Organization box.

HR and the Responsive Organization

The Mutual Gains Bargaining Approach at Hercules Canada

At Hercules Canada, it is obvious that the principles of mutual gains bargaining affect a great deal more than the approach taken at the bargaining table. In addition to their collective agreement, the company and its union, the United Steelworkers of America, have signed an "enabling agreement" that allows decisions affecting bargaining unit employees to be made outside the bargaining process, including decisions to change the contract itself—provided both sides agree on the actions to be taken.

The mutual gains approach was used to negotiate their most recent collective agreement, which set out some joint accountabilities for dealing with a number of major and complex workplace issues that could not be effectively addressed at the bargaining table: work system restructuring, job redesign, compensation and pension redesign, and productivity improvements. Thanks to their enabling agreement, Hercules management and union employees can work together to resolve these issues on an ongoing basis.

The union-management committee established at the company's plant in Burlington, Ontario, to make recommendations on how these matters should be tackled, identified employee self-direction as the key ingredient for improving the way in which work gets done. The first self-directed work team is now up and running. Hand-in-hand with the movement toward self-directed teams is a greater emphasis on cross-training and communication.

Lines of communication are much stronger at Hercules now that the principles of mutual gains bargaining have taken root. According to Marc Tigh, Human Resources Manager, "We're seeing a greater sharing of financial information with all employees. In the old days, we didn't do that." In addition, every employee at the Burlington plant has been given a great deal of information about the move toward self-directed teams.

As is obvious from the experience at Hercules, a mutual gains approach can be applied to all areas of work life, not just negotiations. If people are trained to use the mutual gains bargaining tools and apply them in day-to-day dealings, the end result may be a significant change in corporate culture.

Source: Claudine Kapel, "The Feeling's Mutual," *Human Resources Professional*, 12 no. 2, (April 1995), pp. 9–13.

Despite initial success with mutual gains bargaining, some organizations question whether such values can be sustained on a long-term basis, and wonder whether commitment will wane once the economic environment improves. SaskPower's Mahoney is optimistic that mutual gains bargaining can become a way of life for organizations—but only if they are prepared to work at it.

"There's always going to be a tendency to go back to adversarial ways, in good times or bad, because it's easier. Mutual gains is hard work. The easy out is to do it the old way," he comments. He believes, however, that the process is worth the effort, because it yields not only a better working environment, but better solutions to problems.[26]

attitudinal structuring
The shaping of such attitudes between the parties as trust or distrust, and cooperation or hostility, that have a major impact on bargaining outcomes.

As should by now be quite apparent, **attitudinal structuring**, which is the shaping of such attitudes as trust or distrust, and cooperation or hostility, has a major impact on bargaining outcomes. The organization's management and union negotiating team members need to remember that they have to work together after the bargaining sessions are over and have to live with the agreement negotiated. Bad relations outside the bargaining room can spill over into negotiations, and vice versa. If management obtains a settlement that is viewed to be unfair by the union membership, even if it is ratified by the bargaining unit members (reluctantly) and signed by the union bargaining team, supervisors may receive little cooperation once the contract goes into effect. Thus, management's bargaining strategy and philosophy, discussed in chapter 16, are critically important, as are the attitudes of the union negotiating team.

Attitudinal structuring behaviours that can assist in building the trusting relationship on which many successful negotiations are based include:[27] showing willingness to trust, checking to ensure that trusting signals being sent are being interpreted correctly by the other negotiating team, and reinforcing the other party's willingness to trust. Finally, and only if all of the previous behaviours have failed to generate a willingness to offer trust, signals should be sent regarding the adverse consequences of trust being offered and not reciprocated.

intra-organizational bargaining
This is the manoeuvring required to achieve consensus within (rather than between) the union and management organizations.

Intra-organizational bargaining also plays a major role in contract negotiations. This is the manoeuvring required to achieve consensus within (rather than between) the union and management organizations.

Within the union organization, there are many subgroups, the members of which each want their interests given adequate consideration. For example, the preferences and priorities of skilled workers, semi-skilled workers, and unskilled workers often differ; as do those of young, middle-aged, and older employees; and those of male and female members. There are also sometimes differences between the priorities of the local and those of the national or international office staff. The larger and more complex the bargaining unit, the more likely it is that desired bargaining outcomes will be divergent, perhaps even competitive, rather than common. The union negotiating team must be sensitive to internal pressures. It is often the case, for example, that the large number of demands initially submitted by the union is not just for distributive bargaining purposes, but also to demonstrate to each of its constituent groups that their preferences and priorities have been taken into consideration.

On the employer's side, there are also often conflicting points of view that have to be resolved. For example, the sales and production managers may want a settlement, regardless of cost; while the accountant emphasizes the need for a modest settlement to protect the organization's financial position. There may also be different priorities at the individual plant and overall organizational level that must be taken into account. Thus, the negotiating process is far more complex that it may appear to a casual observer. There are a number of different types of bargaining strategies involved, and there is seldom a single right answer to the economic issues in dispute. Furthermore, each side arrives at the bargaining table with political and organizational interests at stake.

The Contract Approval Process

As mentioned previously, all collective agreements must be written documents. Verbal understandings between management and labour are not collective agreements and will not be enforced as such.[28] However, parties to collective bargaining do not normally execute a formal written document until some time after the bargaining process has been completed. Instead, the terms and conditions agreed to by the parties are usually reduced to a memorandum of settlement, and submitted to the constituent groups for final approval.

ratification
Formal approval by the bargaining unit members of the agreement negotiated between union and management bargaining team members by means of a secret-ballot vote.

Generally, final approval for the employer rests with the senior management team and/or the board of directors (if applicable). In most cases, the union bargaining team submits the proposed collective agreement or memorandum of settlement to the bargaining unit members for **ratification**. In some jurisdictions, such as Ontario, ratification is required by law. All members of the bargaining unit, whether or not they are trade union members, must be given ample opportunity to cast a secret-ballot vote indicating approval or rejection of the proposed contract. A ratification vote may also be a requirement based on a union's constitution and bylaws. Even in situations in which ratification is not required by statute or by the union's constitution and bylaws, union negotiating teams often prefer to present the memorandum of settlement to the membership for a secret-ballot vote prior to finalization, to ensure that the agreement reached meets with the approval of the majority of bargaining unit members.

Whether required by statute or bylaw or voluntary, the results of a ratification vote have an impact. If the majority of bargaining unit members vote in favour of the proposal, it goes into effect, replacing any prior agreement. If the proposed collective agreement is rejected, union and management negotiators must return to the bargaining table and seek a more acceptable compromise. For example, in the fall of 1997, workers at the Wal-Mart in Windsor, Ontario, at which recognition was granted to the United Steelworkers of America in April 1996, as described in chapter 16, rejected the first contract negotiated. The United Steelworkers negotiating team was thus forced to meet with the company again in an attempt to reach a new agreement.[29] In instances such as this, third party assistance is often sought, a topic which will be discussed next.

Once approval has been received from the constituent groups, the bargaining team members sign the memorandum of settlement. Once signed, this memorandum serves as the collective agreement until the formal document is prepared, and contract administration begins.

Third-Party Assistance and Bargaining Impasses

Third-Party Assistance: Conciliation and Mediation

conciliation
The use of a neutral outside third party to assist an organization and the union representing a group of its employees to come to a mutually satisfactory collective agreement.

In their legislation, all jurisdictions provide for conciliation and mediation services. While the terms conciliation and mediation are often used interchangeably, in most Canadian jurisdictions the terms have quite distinct and different meanings.

Conciliation is usually defined as the intervention of a neutral third party whose primary purpose is to bring the parties together and keep them talking to enable them to reach a mutually-satisfactory collective agreement. The only means available to a conciliator to bring the parties to agreement is persuasion; he or she is not permitted to have any direct input into the negotiation process, nor to impose a settlement.

As illustrated in **Table 17.1**, in all jurisdictions except Saskatchewan, strikes and lockouts are prohibited until third-party assistance has been undertaken (conciliation in all but two). In every jurisdiction in which third-party assistance is

JURISDICTION	CONCILIATION OFFICER OR SIMILAR OFFICER	MEDIATOR AFTER APPOINTMENT OF CONCILIATION OFFICER	REPORT OF MEDIATOR REPLACES THAT OF CONCILIATION OFFICER	REPORT OF MEDIATOR OR SIMILAR OFFICER REPLACES REPORT OF CONCILIATION BOARD	NO. OF DAYS AFTER FIRST STAGE IF NO BOARD IS APPOINTED BEFORE STRIKE OR LOCKOUT IS PERMITTED
Federal	*	*		*a	7
British Columbia[b]	mediator				
Alberta	mediator				14
Saskatchewan	non compulsory				when contract expires
Manitoba	*				
Ontario	*	*		*	7
Quebec	*				no board provided for in legislation
New Brunswick[c]	*	*	*		7
Nova Scotia	*	*		*	14
Prince Edward Island	*		*		7
Newfoundland	*	*		*	7

TABLE 17.1 Types of Initial Third-Party Assistance

a Under the federal statute, the report of a conciliation commissioner replaces that of a conciliation board. Also, under the statute, the minister may appoint a mediator.
b The British Columbia Industrial Relations Act provides only for mediation and a strike may take place only within the three-month period after its authorization by a membership vote.
c Provides for the appointment of one or more conciliation officers.

Source: Alton W. J. Craig and Norman A. Solomon, *The System of Industrial Relations in Canada*, 5th Ed., (Scarborough, ON: Prentice Hall Canada Inc., 1996), p. 225. Used with permission.

mandatory, except British Columbia, Manitoba, and Quebec, strikes/lockouts are prohibited until conciliation efforts have failed, and a specified time period has elapsed.[30] In British Columbia, strikes are legal after a mandatory mediation process, within three months of a secret-ballot vote authorizing such action.[31] In Manitoba and Quebec, strikes/lockouts are legal during the conciliation process. In Quebec, for example, a strike or lockout is permitted 90 days after the request for the appointment of a conciliation officer has been made.[32]

A conciliator is appointed by the applicable Minister of Labour, at the request of management, union, or both parties, or at the discretion of the Minister. Conciliation is typically requested after the parties have been negotiating for some length of time to reach a first agreement or renew an existing one, and are starting to reach a deadlock, or after talks have broken down. The aim of conciliation is to try to help the parties to reach a mutually satisfactory agreement, such that the hardship of a strike or lockout can be avoided. Whether or not the conciliator will be successful depends primarily on the extent to which the parties want to settle their differences. In those jurisdictions in which conciliation is required by law, the conciliator must file a report with the Minister at the end of the process, indicating whether or not he or she was able to help the parties to reach an agreement.

Some jurisdictions have provision in their Act for a two-stage conciliation process, involving the appointment of a three-person conciliation board if the conciliation officer fails to obtain a settlement. In practice, conciliation boards are not appointed and the conciliation process involves a conciliation officer alone. In such jurisdictions, the parties are in a legal strike or lockout position following a specified number of days (ranging from seven days to two weeks)[33] after the Minister of Labour releases a "no-board report" (the report indicating that a conciliation board will not be appointed).

Mediation can also be defined as the intervention of a neutral third party whose primary purpose is to help the parties to fashion an agreement that is mutually satisfactory to both parties. As with conciliation, mediation is undertaken at the request of one or both of the parties involved or at the suggestion of the Minister of Labour. However, whereas conciliation is required by statute prior to a strike or lockout in most jurisdictions, mediation is usually a voluntary process. Typically, mediators become involved during the countdown period prior to a strike or lockout or during the existence of one. The mediator's role is an active one. It is often the case that the mediator meets with each side separately and attempts to assist them to bridge the existing gaps. He or she is allowed to have direct input into the negotiation process, but cannot impose a settlement.

www.gov.on.ca/lab/lms/
lmsfaqe.htm#conc
Conciliation

mediation
The use of an outside third party to assist an organization and the union representing its employees to reach a mutually satisfactory collective agreement. Unlike conciliation, mediation is usually voluntary.

Bargaining Impasses: Strikes, Lockouts and Interest Arbitration

When the union and management negotiating teams are unable to reach an agreement, and once the conciliation process has been undertaken (in some jurisdictions) and exhausted (in most jurisdictions), the union may exercise its right to strike or request interest arbitration, and the employer may exercise its right to lock out the bargaining unit members. Alternatively, bargaining unit members may continue to work without a collective agreement once the old one has expired, until talks resume and an agreement is reached. Mediators often play a key role if there is a decision that the bargaining unit members will continue working even after the strike or lockout deadline has been reached.

strike vote
Legally required in some jurisdictions, such a vote seeks authorization from bargaining unit members to strike if necessary. A favourable vote does not mean that a strike is inevitable.

Strikes   When talks are reaching an impasse, unions will often hold a **strike vote**. Legally required in some jurisdictions, such a vote seeks authorization from bargaining unit members to strike if necessary. A favourable vote does not mean that a strike is inevitable. A highly favourable strike vote is generally used as a bargaining ploy to gain concessions that will make a strike unnecessary. The results of a strike vote can also help the union negotiating team members to determine their relative bargaining strength. Unless strike action is supported by a substantial majority of bargaining unit members, union leaders are rarely prepared to risk a strike, and must therefore be more willing to compromise, if necessary, to avoid a work stoppage.

A **strike** can be defined as a temporary refusal by bargaining unit members to continue working for the employer. Although strikes account for only a small percentage of total workdays lost each year, they are often costly for all involved. It should be noted that approximately nine out of ten collective agreements are settled without a strike.[34]

Since a strike can have serious economic consequences for bargaining unit members, the union negotiating team must carefully analyze the prospects for its success. The members' willingness to endure the personal hardships resulting from a strike must be estimated, based in part on the results of the strike vote, particularly if the strike may be lengthy.[35] Striking union members receive no wages and often have no benefits coverage until they return to work, although they may draw some money from the union's strike fund. A long strike tends to lead to a decline in member support and sometimes exhausts the strike fund, thereby putting extreme pressure on the union negotiating team to make concessions in order to get the bargaining unit members back to work.

Another factor that must be taken into consideration is the employer's ability to continue operating in the event of a strike, through the use of supervisors and other nonstriking employees and **replacement workers** where legally permitted. (Quebec has passed "anti-scab" legislation, forbidding the use of replacement workers during a strike, as has Saskatchewan, and there are some restrictions on the use of replacement workers in British Columbia).[36] The greater the organization's ability to continue operations, the less the union's chances of gaining its demands through strike action. Other than at highly-automated workplaces, most employers cannot continue full operations during a strike, and the major costs to them relate to continuing fixed overhead expenses, and loss of customers and suppliers. Some employers, however, can arrange to outsource or subcontract enough work to avoid economic hardship.

When a union goes on strike, bargaining unit members often **picket** the employer. To ensure as many picketers as possible, the union may make strike pay contingent on picket duty. Picketers stand at business entrances, carrying signs advertising the issues in dispute, and attempt to discourage people from entering or leaving the premises. Unions cannot picket on any privately-owned property without permission, nor can they legally block entrances and exits. Even when there are a relatively small number of picketers, they may succeed in closing the entire operation, if they can convince enough people to refuse to cross the picket line. (There are many people who refuse to cross a picket line, as a matter of principle. These may include other employees who are not in the bargaining unit, customers/clients, and suppliers, who sympathize with the striking employees.) Subjecting people attempting to cross a picket line to verbal insults or physical restraint is illegal. Such actions often lead to public outrage and thus harm the union's cause. It should also be noted that when employees on the picket line become disruptive, the employer can apply to the LRB or court to have a restriction placed on the number of picketers.

Another economic weapon available to unions is a **boycott**, which is a refusal to patronize the employer. A boycott occurs when a union asks its members,

strike
The temporary refusal by bargaining unit members to continue working for the employer.

replacement workers
Individuals hired to perform the work of striking employees, often referred to as "scabs." The use of such workers is legal in all Canadian jurisdictions, except Quebec and Saskatchewan. There are some restrictions on the use of replacement workers in British Columbia.

picket
The stationing of groups of striking employees, usually carrying signs, at the entrances and exits of the struck operation. The purpose is to publicize the issues in dispute and to discourage people from entering or leaving the premises.

boycott
An organized refusal of bargaining unit members and supporters to buy the products or utilize the services of the organization whose employees are on strike, in an effort to reduce sales or service provision, and exert economic pressure on the employer.

other union members, the employer's customers/clients, and supporters in the general public, not to patronize the business involved in the labour dispute. Such action can harm the employer if the union is successful in gaining a large number of supporters. As with a strike, a boycott can have long-term consequences, if former customers/clients develop a bias against the employer's products or services or make a change in buying habits or service provider that is not easily reversed.

The duration and ultimate success of a strike depends on the relative strength of the parties. The side that experiences the most economic hardship during a strike is more likely to compromise in order to reach a settlement. Failure to achieve a desired settlement on the part of the union negotiating team may result in the union executive members being voted out of office, or even union decertification.

Once a strike is settled, striking workers are permitted to return to their job. The way in which the return to work will be handled is often a negotiated issue. Although legislation varies, in some jurisdictions, employees must submit, in writing, their intention to return to their job once the strike is over. Failure to do so means that the employer has no obligation to re-employ them.

Lockout   Although not a commonly used strategy in Canada, a **lockout** is legally permissable. This involves the employer prohibiting the bargaining unit employees involved from entering the company premises, as a means of putting pressure on the union negotiating team to agree to the terms and conditions being offered by management. Sometimes the employer chooses to close operations entirely, which means that nonstriking employees are also affected. Most employers try to avoid this option, since doing so means that the well-being of innocent parties is threatened, and often causes a great deal of damage to the organization's public image.

One problem with both strikes and lockouts is that they raise the stakes for the parties—once the work stoppage has begun, it is difficult to resolve outstanding issues without each side believing that it is "winning" something. As illustrated in **Table 17.2**, the number of days lost due to work stoppages in Canada fluctuated between 1980 and 1997, but declined significantly between 1990 and 1996, reflecting, at least in part, the impact of the economic recession.

Unlawful Strikes and Lockouts   The calling of a strike or declaration of a lockout must conform with the provisions of the labour relations legislation. An **unlawful strike** is one that contravenes one or more provisions of the relevant labour relations legislation and lays the union and its members open to charges and possible fines and/or periods of imprisonment, if found guilty. For example, it is illegal for a union to call a strike involving employees who do not have the right to strike because of the essential nature of their services, such as nurses or police officers. For example, the nurses in Quebec who went on strike several years ago were fined. In all jurisdictions, it is illegal to call a strike during the term of an existing collective agreement. In many jurisdictions, a legal strike requires a specified period of waiting time after the Minister of Labour has issued a "no-board report," following unsuccessful attempts by a conciliation officer. In Ontario, Alberta, and British Columbia, a strike vote must also have been held.[37]

A **wildcat strike** is a spontaneous walkout, not officially sanctioned by the union leaders, which may be legal or illegal, depending on its timing. Because

lockout
Temporary refusal of a company to continue providing work for bargaining unit employees involved in a labour dispute, which may also involve the temporary closure of the establishment.

unlawful strike
A strike that contravenes one or more provisions of the relevant labour relations statute and lays the union and its members open to charges and possible fines and/or periods of imprisonment, if found guilty.

wildcat strike
A spontaneous walkout, not officially sanctioned by the union leadership, which may be legal or illegal, depending on its timing.

An unlawful strike.

TABLE 17.2 Major Work Stoppages–1980-1997
person-days not worked and estimated working time

YEAR	STOPPAGES	WORKERS	% OF TOTAL PERSON-DAY	WORKING TIME
1980	135	350,350	6,899,800	0.28
1981	99	240,452	6,169,150	0.24
1982	70	410,559	3,859,810	0.16
1983	61	279,818	2,881,950	0.12
1984	67	130,852	2,331,350	0.09
1985	56	98,281	1,348,850	0.05
1986	89	430,086	5,673,310	0.21
1987	64	531,470	2,408,490	0.09
1988	54	158,888	3,393,880	0.12
1989	67	394,351	2,177,040	0.07
1990	66	226,263	3,520,150	0.12
1991	36	218,377	1,452,400	0.05
1992	44	119,791	1,145,810	0.04
1993	25	73,757	498,680	0.02
1994	29	55,283	736,470	0.03
1995	39	125,531	993,430	0.03
1996	32	256,201	2,558,696	0.09
1997	30	233,064	2,845,930	0.09

Source: Workplace Information Directorate, *Workplace Gazette* (Spring, 1998), p. 60. Reprinted with permission from the Minister of Public Works and Government Services Canada, 1998.

unlawful lockout
A lockout of employees by an employer that contravenes the applicable labour relations legislation and lays the employer open to charges and possible fines and/or periods of imprisonment.

arbitration
The use of an outside third party to investigate a dispute between an employer and union and impose a settlement.

interest dispute
A dispute arising between an organization and the union representing its employees over the terms of a first collective agreement or revisions to an existing one.

interest arbitration
The imposition of the final terms of a collective agreement.

such strikes often occur during the term of a collective agreement, they are generally illegal.

An **unlawful lockout** is one that contravenes one or more provisions of the applicable labour relations legislation. Such a lockout lays the employer open to charges and penalties similar to those involved in illegal strike situations. Locking out employees within a prescribed number of hours of a strike vote (48 to 72) is illegal in some jurisdictions.[38] It is also illegal to lock out employees during the life of a collective agreement in every jurisdiction, and prior to the exhaustion of conciliation procedures in most.

Interest Arbitration **Arbitration** involves the use of an outside third party to investigate a dispute between an employer and union, and impose a settlement (unlike conciliation and mediation). A sole arbitrator or three-person arbitration board may be involved. Arbitration decisions are final and binding and cannot be changed or revised, except in cases involving corruption, fraud, or breach of natural justice.

In some situations, arbitration may be used to settle **interest disputes**; that is, disputes arising over the terms of a first collective agreement or revisions to an existing one. This is known as **interest arbitration**, and results in the imposition of the terms of the collective agreement. The right to interest arbitration is conferred by law to those who are not permitted to strike, as is the case with hospital and nursing home employees, police officers and firefighters in most jurisdictions, and public servants in Alberta, Manitoba, Nova Scotia, and Prince

Edward Island.[39] As explained in chapter 16, federal civil servants can choose between the right to strike and interest arbitration in each set of negotiations. Public servants in New Brunswick also have the right to decide between the conciliation-strike and conciliation-arbitration routes, although unlike federal civil servants, they don't have to decide prior to negotiations, but rather, only after an impasse has been reached.[40] In some jurisdictions, the labour relations act specifies that interest arbitration may be requested to settle the terms of a first collective agreement, once the conciliation process has been exhausted.[41] Interest arbitration is also involved when special legislation is passed, ordering striking or locked-out parties back to work, due to public hardship. Because the right to strike or lockout is, in effect, removed by such legislation, any terms of the collective agreement that are still in dispute are investigated by an arbitrator, and a settlement is imposed based on his or her judgment of a fair course of action. This does not always mean an increase in wages for union members. In fact, when the Canadian Union of Postal Workers' members were legislated back to work in December of 1997, the workers received a smaller wage increase than through Bill C-24 than Canada Post had offered in the last days of negotiations prior to the strike.[42]

**www.gov.on.ca/lab/lms/
lmsfaqe.htm#arbn**
Arbitration

The Collective Agreement: Typical Provisions

The eventual outcome of collective bargaining, whether negotiated by the parties, or imposed by an arbitrator, is a formal, written, collective agreement. The length and scope of this document vary depending on organization size, type of relationship between the parties, and duration of the bargaining relationship.

The following are some of the typical provisions found in collective agreements:

- Union recognition clause
- Union security/checkoff clause
- No strike or lockout provision
- Management rights clause
- Grievance procedure
- Arbitration clause
- Disciplinary procedures
- Compensation rates and benefits
- Hours of work and overtime pay provisions
- Health and safety provisions
- Employee security/seniority provisions
- Contract expiration date

Of the twelve items listed above, five deserve closer scrutiny:

Union Recognition Clause

union recognition clause
A clause in the collective agreement, mandatory in most jurisdictions, identifying the recognized trade union, and clarifying its rights and responsibilities as the exclusive bargaining agent for the employees in the bargaining unit.

A **union recognition clause** is a mandatory collective agreement provision in most jurisdictions. It clarifies the scope of the bargaining unit by specifying the employee classifications included therein or listing those excluded. It is in this clause that the union is recognized as the exclusive bargaining agent for the employees in the bargaining unit, (even those who choose not to be union members, where such choice is permitted), as specified in the labour board's certification order or the employer's voluntary recognition notice. Even in jurisdictions in which a recognition clause is not required by law, such a clause is found in most collective agreements, since it provides a clear indication of the group to whom the document applies. For example:[43]

> *The company recognizes the union as the exclusive bargaining agent for all its employees, save and except employees charged with management and supervisory responsibilities, clerical and secretarial staff, professional and technical employees, and security staff.*

Union Security/Checkoff Clause

union security clause
The provisions in the collective agreement protecting the interests of the labour union, dealing with the issue of membership requirements and, usually, payment of union dues.

closed shop
A union security clause that specifies that only union members in good standing may be hired by the employer to perform bargaining unit work.

union shop
A type of union security arrangement in which union membership and dues payment are a mandatory condition of employment.

maintenance-of-membership
A union security arrangement that requires individuals voluntarily joining the union to remain members during the life of the collective agreement.

Rand formula (dues shop/agency shop)
A popular union security arrangement that does not require union membership, but does require all members of a bargaining unit to pay dues to the union.

open shop
The weakest type of union security arrangement, in which union membership is voluntary, and nonmembers are not required to pay dues.

checkoff
Provisions in the collective agreement requiring the employer to deduct union dues from the paycheques of bargaining unit members and forward the money to the union.

All Canadian jurisdictions permit the inclusion of a **union security clause** in the collective agreement to protect the interests of the labour union. This clause deals with the issue of membership requirements and, often, the payment of union dues. There are various forms of union security clauses, the most common of which will be described next:[44]

Closed Shop   A **closed shop** is the most restrictive form of union security. Only union members in good standing may be hired by the employer to perform bargaining unit work. (The recruitment strategy used in such cases is the union hiring hall, as described in chapter 6.) This type of security clause is common in the construction industry.

Union Shop   In a **union shop** type of security arrangement, union membership and the compulsory collection of union dues are a condition of employment. Although individuals do not have to be union members at the time they are hired, they are required to join the union on the day they commence work or on completion of probation.

Maintenance-of-Membership   Under a **maintenance-of-membership** security arrangement, individuals voluntarily joining the union must remain members during the life of the collective agreement. Membership withdrawal is typically permitted during a designated period around the time of contract expiration. Dues payment is generally mandatory for all bargaining unit members.

The Rand Formula   A setting in which the **Rand formula** is applied may also be known as a dues shop (in Canada) or agency shop (in the United States). This is a popular union security arrangement that does not require union membership but does require that all members of the bargaining unit pay dues to the union. It is a compromise arrangement, suggested by Ivan C. Rand, former Chief Justice of the Supreme Court of Canada, that recognizes the fact that the union must represent all employees in the bargaining unit and should therefore be entitled to their financial support, but also provides the choice to join or not join the union.

Open Shop   An **open shop** is a type of security arrangement that is virtually (or perhaps totally) non-existent in Canada today, in which union membership is voluntary and nonmembers are not required to pay dues.

The right of the union to enforce the security clause as a condition of employment was firmly established by the Supreme Court[45] in 1959. The normal method of enforcement is the use of the grievance and arbitration procedures outlined in the collective agreement.

The process by which union dues are collected by the employer via payroll deduction and remitted to the union is known as **checkoff**. Checkoff provisions

voluntary checkoff
An arrangement whereby the employer only deducts union dues from the paycheques of employees who authorize such deductions in writing.

voluntary revocable checkoff
An arrangement whereby an employee may sign dues over to the union but subsequently change his or her mind and revoke such assignment.

voluntary irrevocable checkoff
Once an employee has authorized deduction of union dues, such assignment cannot be revoked.

are common in collective agreements, and are not dependent upon the existence of a formal union security clause.[46] Employers in every Canadian jurisdiction must deduct union dues when authorized to do so by the employee. Where there are **voluntary checkoff** arrangements, the employer only deducts union dues from the paycheques of employees who authorize such deductions in writing. In a **voluntary revocable checkoff** arrangement, an employee may sign dues over to the union but subsequently change his or her mind and revoke such assignment. In a **voluntary irrevocable checkoff** arrangement, once an employee has authorized the deduction of union dues, such assignment cannot be revoked. Voluntary checkoff arrangements cannot exist in a union or closed shop.

Five Canadian provincial jurisdictions, (Newfoundland, Quebec, Ontario, Manitoba, and Saskatchewan) and the federal jurisdiction provide that a **compulsory checkoff** provision must be included in the collective agreement where a union so requests.[47] This means that the employer must deduct union dues from the paycheques of all employees in the bargaining unit and remit them to the union. Therefore, in these jurisdictions, the minimum union security provision in collective agreements generally involves the Rand formula.

No Strike or Lockout Provision

The statutes in all jurisdictions in Canada require that collective agreements contain a clause that forbids strikes or lockouts during their life. The intent is to guarantee some degree of stability in the employment relationship while the collective agreement is in effect, which must be at least a one-year period.

Management Rights Clause

compulsory checkoff
An arrangement whereby the employer must deduct union dues from the paycheques of all employees in the bargaining unit and remit them to the union.

management rights clause
The clause that refers to the rights of management to operate the organization, subject to the terms of the collective agreement. Any rights not limited by the clause are reserved to management.

The **management rights clause** is important because it clarifies the areas in which management may exercise its prerogatives (exclusive rights) without agreement from the union, and the issues that are not subject to collective bargaining. This clause typically refers to the rights of management to operate the organization, subject to the terms of the collective agreement. Any rights not limited by the clause are reserved to management. For example:[48]

The management of the plant and the direction of its working force is the sole responsibility of the company. These functions are broad in nature and include the right to schedule work and shift beginning and ending times, the right to schedule overtime, and the right to contract out work. The company also has the right to discipline and discharge employees for cause providing the terms of this agreement are met, and the right to determine the makeup of its work force and to transfer, layoff or demote employees. In the fulfillment of these functions, the company agrees not to violate the terms of this agreement nor to discriminate against any member of the union.

Arbitration Clause

All Canadian jurisdictions require that collective agreements contain an arbitration clause, providing for the final and binding settlement, by arbitration, of all disputes arising during the term of a collective agreement. Such disputes may relate to the application, interpretation, or administration of that agreement, as well as alleged contraventions by either party. Known as rights arbitration, this will be described in more detail later in this chapter.

Impact of Societal Changes on Contract Provisions

As with HR policies and procedures, collective agreement language and provisions change over time. As explained in chapter 16, many collective agreements now include an article protecting the job security of bargaining unit members in the event of technological innovations. Legislative issues and demographic changes can also affect contract language and provisions, as explained in the Diversity Counts box.

Introduction to Contract Administration

After a collective agreement has been negotiated and signed, the contract administration process begins. Both union and management are required to abide by the contract provisions. The contract administration and negotiation processes are highly interrelated. If there is a great deal of controversy and hostility during negotiations, a similar spirit may carry over into the administration of the contract and vice versa. Furthermore, it is in day-to-day contract administration that provisions that are difficult to implement or are poorly worded are identified, such that they can be amended or deleted at the next round of negotiations. Contract administration therefore provides negotiators with valuable feedback.

It is in day-to-day contract administration that the bulk of labour–management relations occurs. Regardless of the amount of time, effort, care, and attention put into the writing of the actual contract, it is almost inevitable that differences of opinion will arise regarding the application and interpretation of the agreement.

With the exception of the management rights clause, most provisions in the collective agreement limit the types of actions managers can take. Some of these limitations are minor and are generally included in the human resources policies of all well-managed organizations, whether unionized or not, such as providing competitive wages and benefits and safe working conditions. Other contract terms, however, may change the way that certain human resources activities are conducted, such as those regarding seniority and discipline. Because these provisions place restrictions on management, and are often subject to different interpretations, seniority and discipline issues are a major source of disagreement between union and management.

Seniority

Unions typically prefer to have employee-related decisions determined by seniority, which refers to length of service in the bargaining unit. In many collective agreements, seniority is the governing factor in layoffs and recalls (the most senior employees are the last to be laid off and the first to be recalled), and a determining factor in transfers and promotions. In some collective agreements, seniority is also the determining factor in decisions pertaining to work assignments, shift preferences, allocation of days off, and vacation time.

In a number of areas, such as the right to have first choice of vacation time, the principle of seniority has been accepted as an equitable and objective decision-making criterion, ensuring that there is no favouritism. In others, such as decisions related to transfers, promotions, and layoffs, seniority has been the source of considerable controversy. Even though both union and management may agree that length of service is an important factor in determining these matters, they may disagree about the amount of weight that should be placed on seniority as compared to ability. Managers often prefer to place greater weight on ability or merit, while unions want more emphasis placed on seniority. Thus, in some collective agreements, seniority is the sole basis for transfer, layoff, and promotion decisions; in others, seniority is the governing factor, provided that the senior applicant has sufficient ability to do the job; and in still others, seniority is the governing factor only in the case of two candidates with relatively equal skill and ability. It is very rare, in a unionized setting, to have a clause permitting the employer to have total discretion in making such decisions on the basis of merit.

Since employers are generally unwilling to accept seniority as the sole criterion for transfers and promotions, or for layoffs due to lack of work, sufficient ability and relative ability clauses are very common. Because "ability to do the job" and "relatively equal" are open to different interpretations, sufficient ability and relative ability clauses are the subject of many grievances, a topic that will be discussed shortly.

Discipline

Almost all collective agreements give the employer the right to make reasonable rules and regulations governing employees' behaviour and to take disciplinary action (impose some form of sanction or punishment) if the rules are broken. In every collective agreement, bargaining unit members are given the right to file a grievance if they feel that any disciplinary action taken was too harsh or without just cause.

Most collective agreements restrict an employer's right to discipline employees by requiring proof of just or reasonable cause for the disciplinary action imposed. Since just or reasonable cause is open to different interpretations, disciplinary action is a major source of grievances. Some unions challenge virtually all disciplinary action taken. Managers must therefore be extremely careful not only that disciplinary issues are handled in accordance with the terms of the collective agreement, but are also backed by evidence. The need for proof requires careful documentation (and thus, often, more paperwork for first-line supervisors). To satisfy this standard of proof in cases of dismissal, arbitrators have agreed that the employer must establish that, as a result of some misconduct, the grievor has demonstrated his or her incompatibility or has seriously prejudiced or injured the reputation or some other legitimate interest of the employer.[49]

Even when disciplinary action is handled carefully, the union steward representing the employee involved may argue that there were extenuating circumstances that should be taken into consideration. In resolving discipline issues in such cases, managers must be careful that they do not set a precedent. Once the rules have been altered slightly in one case, the union grievance committee may try to use the new standard in similar cases in the future. To ensure that such exceptions do not become a **precedent**, a letter of understanding can be signed indicating that the special consideration was agreed to on one occasion only, due to very specific circumstances, and cannot be used as a future standard.

When discipline cases end up at arbitration, a process that will be discussed shortly, the arbitrator or arbitration board must make two independent decisions, the first of which is whether the employee actually engaged in some form of misconduct. Then, if that question is answered in the affirmative, an assessment of whether such misconduct warrants the particular discipline imposed must be made, as well as whether such disciplinary action violated the collective agreement.

precedent
A new standard that arises based on the way in which a collective agreement provision is interpreted or administered on one occasion.

Grievance Resolution and Rights Arbitration

Grievances and the Grievance Procedure

grievance
A written allegation of the violation of the collective agreement. A grievance may be filed by an individual bargaining unit member, the union, or management.

As indicated above, **grievances**, disagreements between management and union about the application and interpretation of the contract involving an alleged violation of its terms and conditions, do not necessarily indicate bad faith on the part of either party. Instead, genuine differences of opinion may exist about the intent or interpretation of certain clauses. Differences of opinion may also arise because of misunderstandings, unclear contract language, and changing circumstances. When disagreements or problems arise in the interpretation and application of the collective agreement, they are usually handled and settled through the **grievance procedure**.

grievance procedure
The steps by which a dispute arising between an employer and bargaining unit member or between an employer and the union, during the life of the collective agreement, may be amicably settled.

A multi-step grievance procedure, the last step of which is final and binding arbitration, is found in virtually all collective agreements. Such grievance procedures have been very effective in resolving day-to-day problems arising during the life of the collective agreement, identifying areas in which contract language is unclear, highlighting areas in which supervisors need to improve and may require training, and minimizing work stoppages and sabotage.

Purposes of the Grievance Procedure

The primary purpose of the grievance procedure is to ensure the application of the contract with a degree of justice for both parties. There are a number of related, secondary purposes as well. One is to resolve issues that were not anticipated by those at the bargaining table. Since life in an organization is dynamic, issues frequently arise during the term of the collective agreement that were not anticipated and consequently were not provided for in the contract. If management takes action in dealing with such issues, with which the union disagrees, a grievance may be filed.

Grievances also provide the opportunity for the interpretation of contract language. Disagreements in interpretation of clauses, such as those pertaining to seniority in the case of layoffs, transfers, and promotions, sometimes trigger a grievance.

Another purpose of the grievance procedure is to provide a communication device through which management can become aware of employee concerns and areas of dissatisfaction. Grievances often notify management of potential trouble spots or areas of discontent requiring managerial attention.

Sometimes grievances serve an important political purpose. Stewards or other union officers may encourage bargaining unit members to file grievances, so that employees can see the important role the union plays in assisting employees to protect their rights.

Yet another purpose of the grievance procedure is to call to the attention of the union leaders, management leaders, or both, those areas of the contract requiring clarification or modification in subsequent negotiations. Contract clauses that are the subject of numerous grievances are often in need of careful examination and amendment.

Steps in the Grievance Procedure

The grievance procedure involves systematic deliberation of a complaint at progressively higher levels of authority in the company and union. The problem may be settled at any of these levels, and if not, the complaint may be submitted to an impartial outside party whose decision is final and binding. Grievances are usually filed by individual bargaining unit members. If the issue in contention is one that may affect a number of union members, either at the time or in the future, the union may file a policy grievance. Management also has the right to use the grievance procedure to process a complaint about the union, although such use is rare. All contracts contain a grievance procedure, and most provide for arbitration as a final step. While the number of steps and people involved at each vary, **Figure 17.2** illustrates a fairly typical grievance procedure.

In many collective agreements, there is provision for a complaint stage prior to filing a grievance. This is designed to provide an opportunity for employees to discuss complaints informally with their immediate supervisor prior to filing a formal, written complaint. Often, such discussion can resolve matters without resort to the actual grievance procedure. The supervisor may have been unaware of the problem, for example, or may not have realized the impact of certain decisions. Once informed, he or she may be quite willing to take immediate action to resolve the issue.

In settings in which such provisions exist, they should be used. The managers involved in the first step of the grievance procedure should not accept a written grievance until the informal complaint step has been exhausted. Informal discussion can be very beneficial in building effective relationships between employees and their supervisors. This may be particularly true with female employees, a topic discussed in the Diversity Counts box.

As illustrated in Figure 17.2, the typical first step of the grievance procedure in a collective agreement occurs when an aggrieved employee or a union steward on his or her behalf files a written complaint with the employee's immediate supervisor.

If the problem is not resolved to the satisfaction of the employee at the first step, he or she may then take the problem to the next higher managerial level designated in the contract, and so on through all of the steps available. There are generally three internal steps prior to arbitration. Time limits are typically provided for resolution at each step. Failure to respond within the specified time limit may result in the grievance being automatically processed at the next step, or deemed to have been withdrawn or resolved. Ninety percent or more of all grievances are settled, abandoned, or withdrawn prior to arbitration.

Figure 17.2
A Typical Grievance Procedure

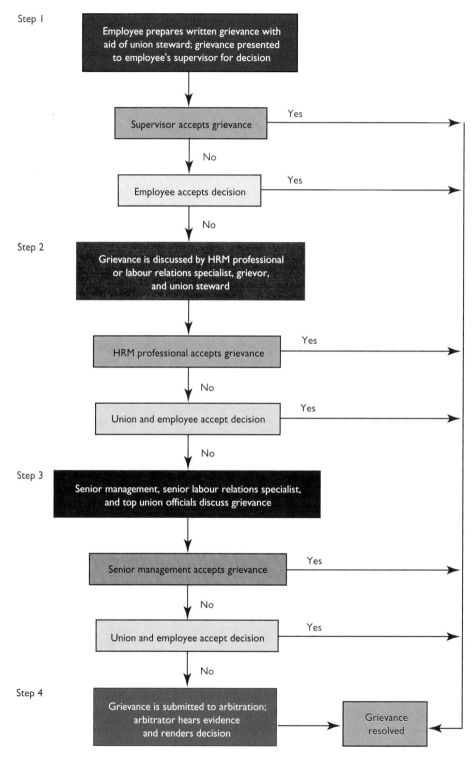

Diversity Counts
Gender Differences in Disputes and Dispute Resolution

One of the reasons for grievance processes is that problems and disputes in the workplace are normal and probably unavoidable.[1] As explained elsewhere in this chapter, disputes commonly arise over issues such as work assignments, work schedules, and discipline; once such disputes arise, it is usual for them to be addressed. They may be addressed formally (such as through union-negotiated grievance procedures) or informally, such as in face-to-face conversations.

Given the likelihood of some type of workplace dispute, the results of one recent study regarding gender differences in disputes and dispute resolution provide some useful food for thought. The study focussed on male and female clerical workers' disputes over tasks and interpersonal treatment and involved 34 in-depth interviews with 23 female and 11 male clerical workers in both unionized and nonunionized firms.[2] The researchers drew three conclusions.

First, there are gender differences in the origins of workplace problems and disputes. At least with these workers in these companies ". . . women workers displayed more sensitivity to problems associated with interpersonal relations in the workplace than men, more often voicing workplace disputes concerning personality conflicts."[3] On the other hand, the male clerical workers were relatively less likely to express concerns over personality conflicts in the workplace.[4]

Second, more women generally described how difficult it was to resolve personality conflicts through formalized channels (including grievance procedures). The reason, apparently, is that the sorts of personality conflicts sensed by the female clerical workers rarely ". . . escalate to a point that they can be labelled or proven as harassment."[5] Instead they were more subtle occurrences that "eat away at women workers" to use the researchers' phrase.[6] As a result, women were much less likely to use formal dispute resolution procedures for eliminating interpersonal conflicts, but instead were much more likely to request lateral transfers to solve the problems. In turn, such lateral transfers may reduce a woman's likelihood of receiving a raise or getting more training, since her average tenure on a job will tend to be lower.

A third conclusion is that, given the above, workplace dispute resolution procedures may actually constrain women's abilities to succeed at work. For example, suppose it is true that formal dispute resolution procedures, such as grievance processes, are unlikely to be useful forums for addressing simple interpersonal conflicts. Then women may be at a disadvantage when it comes to solving an interpersonal conflict that they may be relatively attuned to. One implication is that more formal and informal procedures should be built into an employer's dispute resolution processes in order to give both women and men a better opportunity to air interpersonal disputes and get on with their work.◆

---

[1] This feature is based on Patricia Gwartney-Gibbs and Denise Lach, "Gender Differences in Clerical Workers' Disputes over Tasks, Interpersonal Treatment, and Emotion," *Human Relations* 46, no. 6 (1994), pp. 611–639.
[2] Gwartney-Gibbs and Lach, "Gender Differences," p. 615.
[3] Gwartney-Gibbs and Lach, "Gender Differences," p. 633.
[4] Gwartney-Gibbs and Lach, "Gender Differences," p. 634.
[5] Gwartney-Gibbs and Lach, "Gender Differences," p. 634.
[6] Gwartney-Gibbs and Lach, "Gender Differences," p. 634.

Throughout the grievance process, the managers concerned ordinarily seek the advice of the labour relations expert(s) in the company's human resources department. The labour relations expert is often formally involved at step two. A Human Resources department staff member is also typically involved in the managerial decision at the final step within the organization. Many contracts also specify participation of the general manager, the chief executive officer, or the president of the company at this final internal step.

Handling Grievances

Developing the Proper Environment   The best way to handle a grievance is to develop a working environment in which grievances don't occur in the first place.[50] Constructive grievance handling depends on the ability of first-line supervisors to recognize, diagnose, and correct the causes of potential employee dissatisfaction (such as unfair appraisals, inequitable raises, or poor communications) before they become formal grievances.

Guidelines for Handling Grievances   When grievances do arise, how they are handled by first-line supervisors plays a critical role in the labour–management relationship. Such supervisors must walk a fine line, since they need to treat employees fairly, while maintaining management's rights. Walter Baer has developed a list of helpful guidelines which supervisors should keep in mind when handling grievances, some of the most critical of which follow:[51]

Do

- Investigate and handle each and every case as though it might eventually result in an arbitration hearing.
- Require the union to identify specific contractual provisions allegedly violated.
- Keep an open mind and don't presume guilt. Give the grievor a fair and thorough hearing.
- Visit the work area of the grievance issue.
- Determine whether there were any witnesses.
- Examine the grievor's HR records, especially any previous grievances.
- Treat the union steward assisting the grievor and the grievor as equals.
- Ensure grievance discussions are held in a private setting.
- Comply with the contractual time limits for handling the grievance.
- Fully inform your own supervisor about grievance matters.

Don't

- Relinquish to the union your rights as a manager.
- Allow grievances over issues that are not covered by the collective agreement. These should be handled as informal complaints.
- Discuss the case with the union steward alone; the grievor should also be present.
- Settle grievances on the basis of what seems "fair." The collective agreement should be the standard.
- Give long written answers to grievances.
- Deny grievances on the premise that your "hands have been tied by management."
- Admit to the binding effect of a past practice.
- Hold back the remedy if the company is wrong.
- Make arrangements with individual employees that are inconsistent with the collective agreement.
- Agree to informal contract amendments.
- Trade a grievance settlement for a grievance withdrawal, or try to make up for a bad decision in one grievance by bending over backward in another.

Common Difficulties with Grievance Procedures

Some employee grievances stem from perceived injustices or injured feelings rather than from actual contract violations on the part of management. When such grievances arise, the union has the difficult problem of deciding whether to process the complaint and face the possibility of rebuffs during the successive stages of the grievance procedure or whether to attempt to pacify the aggrieved employee. Management must also decide how to handle such grievances.

One author suggests that a partial solution through a "clinical approach," in contrast to a "legalistic" one, is a better device for morale and face-saving.[52] With the clinical approach, the steward and/or supervisor attempts to assess the emotional and social aspects of the complaint and deal with the problem at that level. Simply permitting the employee to vent his or her feelings may provide a partial solution. In any event, careful listening and analysis may permit the steward and/or supervisor to identify the real, underlying issue.

Another difficulty in the use of the grievance procedure is the possibility of it becoming a vehicle for the respective parties to test their relative strengths. For example, in settings in which union-management relations are poor, the union may file grievances at every opportunity to wring every possible concession from management, or a union official may decide to press a particular case as a test of strength or to "get back" at management. Similarly, management may fight every grievance in an attempt to restrict the union's rights and power.

Under such circumstances, the grievance procedure cannot possibly resolve problems at the lowest possible organizational level. On the other hand, the use of the grievance machinery, including arbitration, in such situations, may serve to clarify the limits of the contractual power of both parties.

Another difficulty may arise due to political pressures. A union steward, for example, may be subjected to considerable pressure from an aggrieved worker to push a grievance to further steps within the organization or even to arbitration. Because of a union's legal duty to provide "fair representation" to bargaining unit members, and his or her role as an elected official, the steward may feel obligated to take a case forward even if its legitimacy is somewhat questionable. Similarly, the labour relations manager may be pressured by other members of management to settle or not to settle a particular grievance. The urgency to "settle" is often dependent on the current labour relations climate within the organization.

Third Party Assistance: Rights Arbitration

rights dispute
A disagreement between an organization and the union representing its employees with regard to the interpretation or application of one or more clauses in the current collective agreement.

rights arbitration
The arbitration involved in the settlement of a rights dispute.

Grievance arbitration is an adjudicative process through which disputes arising out of the application and operation of a collective agreement are finally resolved. As such, it performs the same functions for the parties to a collective bargaining agreement as the courts do in resolving issues and disputes arising from the operation of contracts in society generally. In essence, it is a quasi-judicial system created for each collective bargaining relationship.

As mentioned previously, all jurisdictions in Canada[53] require that collective agreements include a provision for the final settlement of all differences concerning the interpretation or administration of the collective agreement, without work stoppage. Such differences are known as **rights disputes**. Thus, if the parties are unable to resolve a grievance issue themselves, it must be referred to a sole arbitrator or three-person arbitration board for a final and binding decision. The arbitration process involved in resolving such issues is known as **rights arbitration**.

In the past, most collective agreements provided for a three-person arbitration board, rather than a sole arbitrator. Many still do. In such cases, each party appoints a delegate to represent them on the board (the union and management nominees), and these two nominees are responsible for choosing a neutral chair (generally a lawyer or professor skilled in arbitration). If they cannot reach agreement on a suitable chairperson, within specified timelines, the chair is generally appointed by the applicable Minister of Labour. The advantage of using a board relates to the fact that a representative of each of the parties is directly involved in the decision-making process. The disadvantage is that boards generally take more time to reach a decision (sometimes even arranging a common meeting time is difficult), and are more costly. Arbitration costs are shared. When a three-person board is used, each party pays its nominee's expenses, and the expenses of the chair and costs involved in meeting room rental are shared.

Role of the Arbitrator/Arbitration Board

The collective agreement is recognized as the fundamental source of the subject matter that is within an arbitrator's jurisdiction.[54] Accordingly, unless the contract grants specific power to the arbitrator to "make the agreement for the parties" as opposed to "interpreting and applying the terms and conditions specified therein," arbitrators have held that they cannot make an agreement. That is, an arbitrator whose jurisdiction is to be a "rights" arbitrator under a collective agreement cannot assume jurisdiction to make an "interest" decision. This limitation is recognized and given effect when arbitrators dismiss a grievance on the basis that the subject matter of the dispute does not come within the terms of the agreement, or is premature. In the grievance-arbitration process, the arbitrator's role is generally considered quasi-judicial, that is, similar to that of a judge. He or she is expected to listen to evidence, weigh it impartially and objectively, and make a decision based on the contract language. There are some significant differences between the arbitrator's role and that of a judge, however.

First, arbitration hearings tend to be much more informal than courtroom proceedings. The parties may or may not have legal counsel present at the hearings, and the proceedings are not bound by the rules of evidence as in the court of law. However, the proceedings are expected to be conducted with dignity and fairness. They generally include the cross-examination of the parties or witnesses and the submission of documents as evidence. Secondly, the role of an arbitrator differs from that of a judge in that the arbitrator is not bound by precedents to the extent that a judge is usually held.[55] Although an arbitrator may study decisions of other arbitrators in order to further his or her understanding of the issues, and even though both parties may cite previous arbitration decisions in support of their positions, an arbitrator is not bound by such decisions. On the other hand, following precedents established in arbitration awards earlier in the relationship between the parties gives consistency to the particular relationship and may minimize unnecessary grievances.

Thirdly, both the law and court decisions have given the arbitration function considerable power and freedom. The substance or content of arbitration decisions cannot be appealed to the courts except under certain stringent circumstances. Decisions of arbitrators can become orders of the court and are thereby legally enforceable.[56]

The Arbitration Award A written arbitration award is issued at the conclusion of most rights arbitration cases, indicating that the grievance has been upheld (which means the grievor's arguments are deemed to be correct) or overturned (which means that the action(s) that launched the grievance have been deemed to be correct). In discipline cases, it is also possible for an arbitration award to substitute a penalty more or less severe than the one proposed by union or management. Responsibility for issuing an arbitration award rests with the neutral chair in the case of a three-person board. Generally, such an award includes not only the decision of the arbitrator or arbitration board, but also the rationale behind it. The rationale can provide guidance to both union and management regarding the interpretation of the collective agreement and the ways in which future disputes arising from its administration should be handled. In addition, by pointing out the merits of each party's position, the disappointment and hard feelings of the unsuccessful party can be lessened.

An arbitration award is commonly issued with one dissenting opinion, that of the nominee of the unsuccessful party. When there is a three-person arbitration board, it is possible to have an arbitration award with two dissenting opinions. In such case, both union and management nominees are dissatisfied with the decision made by the neutral chair.

Problems with Rights Arbitration   It is important that human resources managers try to resolve grievances with the union without seeking third-party assistance whenever possible. In addition to the deterioration in labour–management relations that tends to result when the majority of grievance cases end up at arbitration, and the often lengthy delay between the alleged violation and arbitration hearing date(s), there are two other potential problems with rights arbitration: the costs involved and the fact that there is the potential for an arbitration decision to drastically alter management's rights. The substitution of a lesser penalty in a discipline case, for example, means that similar future cases must be accorded the same penalty. Otherwise, a grievance is the inevitable result.

Building Effective Labour–Management Relations

In many organizations, union and management leaders recognize that an effective working relationship is in their mutual interests. When managers wish to build a more harmonious and effective relationship, there are a number of strategies that can assist:

Instituting an Open-Door Policy

When the key managers involved in labour–management relations welcome employees into their offices to discuss any problems or concerns, and employees feel comfortable in doing so, many issues can be resolved informally. For example, if the president of the local knows that he or she can approach the manager of industrial relations "off the record" and that anything discussed in such sessions will be kept strictly confidential, fewer grievances and a more trusting and harmonious relationship often results.

Extending the Courtesy of Prior Consultation

While every management decision does not require union approval, if any actions that might affect union members are discussed with the union executive first, the likelihood of grievances is greatly reduced.

Demonstrating Genuine Concern for Employee Well-Being

When managers are genuinely concerned about employee well-being, and demonstrate that concern, mutual trust and respect are often established. This involves fair treatment and communication going well above and beyond the requirements of the collective agreement.

Forming Joint Study Committees

Forming labour/management committees to investigate and resolve complex issues can lead to innovative and creative solutions, as well as a better relationship. An excellent example of a situation in which a joint study committee can be beneficial is when a quality management program is being considered, a topic which is discussed in the Building Employee Commitment box.

Building Employee Commitment

Employee Involvement Programs

Quality circles and other employee involvement programs discussed elsewhere in this book are a two-edged sword as far as unions are concerned. On the one hand, they can be the basis for building better communication and for boosting union-management harmony. On the other hand, they may build relationships between workers and management that undercut union security. Some unions are therefore a bit hesitant when it comes to the subject of commitment-building participation programs.

Based on the research, it seems that worker participation programs don't seem to be the threat some union leaders fear they may be. One study, for instance, found few differences between how quality program participants and nonparticipants viewed the performance of their unions.[1] Another researcher found that quality program participants were actually more involved in and satisfied with the union than were nonparticipants.[2]

A critical issue seems to be whether or not the union is asked to help develop and implement the program. For example, one study concluded that union officers were much less likely to view the quality program negatively when they were involved in its design and implementation.[3] Similarly, in another study, researchers found that "union members who participated in [such] programs were less likely than nonparticipants to view [them] as a threat to the union, and also remained more loyal to the union."[4]

When Inglis Limited, an appliance manufacturing firm in Cambridge, Ontario, decided to make a $38 million investment to convert to a state-of-the-art cellular manufacturing plant, based on the principles of continuous improvement, just-in-time planning, and total quality management, the Communication, Energy and Paperworkers Union of Canada (CEP) was involved from day one. The union worked hand-in-hand with management to create a flexible, cross-trained, multi-skilled work force. Now, each "cell,", a self-managed team of seven to ten members, is responsible for manufacturing a particular product and involved in all aspects of the plant operations, from goal-setting to line layout, design, tooling, and process improvements.[5]

1. Thomas Kochan, Harry Katz, and Nancy Mower, *Worker Participation and American Unions: Threat or Opportunity* (Kalamazoo, MI: W.E. Upjohn, 1984).
2. Anil Verma, "Employee Involvement Programs: Do They Alter Worker Affinity Towards Unions?" *Proceedings of the 39th Annual Meeting of the Industrial Relations Research Association* (New Or-

leans, December 1986), (Madison, WI: Industrial Relations Research Association, 1987), pp. 306–12.

3. Adrienne Eaton, "The Extent and Determinants of Local Union Control of Participative Programs," *Industrial and Labor Relations Review* 43, no. 5 (1990), pp. 604–20.

4. Adrienne Eaton, Michael Gordon, and Jeffrey Keefe, "The Impact of Quality of Work Life Programs and Grievance System Effectiveness on Union Commitment," *Industrial and Labor Relations Review* 45, no. 3 (April 1992), p. 591. See also Keith Knauss and Michael Matuszak, "An Anti-Union Corporate Culture and Quality Improvement Programs," Labor Studies Journal 1, no. 3, (Fall 1994), pp. 21–39.

5. Cynthia Davenport, "Labour Pains," *Human Resources Professional* 10, no. 11, (December 1993), pp. 13–5.

Holding Joint Training Programs

When a new collective agreement is signed, it can be beneficial to hold a joint training program to ensure that both supervisors and union stewards are familiar with the terms and conditions specified therein and understand the intent of the negotiating teams. Such training can reduce misunderstandings and the likelihood of disagreement regarding interpretation of contract language. Joint training programs can also be extremely helpful in building the cooperation necessary to deal more effectively with other employment-related issues of concern to both union and management, such as employee health and safety.

Meeting Regularly

Whether required by the collective agreement or voluntarily instituted, scheduling regular meetings, involving the union executive and the managers most involved in labour relations, can result in more effective communication and the resolution of problems/concerns before they become formal grievance issues.

Using Third-Party Assistance

To build a better relationship it is often beneficial to bring in a consultant or a government agency representative to help identify common goals and objectives and ways in which trust and communication can be strengthened.

Chapter Review

Summary

1. Collective bargaining is the process by which a formal collective agreement is established between labour and management. The purposes of collective bargaining include: negotiating a collective agreement that describes the scope of management and union rights and responsibilities; arriving at an agreement that is acceptable to management, the union representatives, and the other bargaining unit members; developing a framework for labour relations in the organization, including a mechanism to resolve conflicts that may arise; and specifying the manner in which management and bargaining unit members will treat each other and conduct themselves.

2. Good faith bargaining requires that union and management representatives communicate and negotiate, that proposals be matched with counterproposals, and that both parties make every reasonable effort to arrive at an agreement.

3. The collective bargaining process involves the following steps to arrive at a collective agreement: preparation, face-to-face negotiations, and approval of the proposed contract. The process may also include third-party assistance and the use of economic pressure by either party (strike/lockout) or third-party intervention in the form of an imposed settlement.

4. Negotiating is a relatively complex process. In fact, it actually consists of four types of activity: distributive bargaining, integrative bargaining, attitudinal structuring, and intra-organizational bargaining. Integrative strategies include productivity, concessionary, interest-based, and mutual gains bargaining.

5. Conciliation involves the use of a neutral outside third party to assist an organization and the union representing a group of its employees to come to a mutually-satisfactory collective agreement. In most Canadian jurisdictions, conciliation is mandatory when talks break down, and strikes and lockouts are prohibited until conciliation efforts have been exhausted.

6. Mediation also involves the use of an outside third party to assist union and management negotiating teams to reach a mutually-satisfactory collective agreement. Unlike conciliation, mediation is usually voluntary. Mediators play a more active role than conciliators, since they typically become involved during the countdown period prior to a strike or lockout or during the existence of one. As with conciliators, mediators do not have the power to impose a settlement.

7. When the union and management negotiating teams are unable to reach an agreement, and once the conciliation process has been undertaken (in some jurisdictions) and exhausted (in most jurisdictions), the union may exercise its right to strike or request interest arbitration, and the employer may exercise its right to lock out the bargaining unit members.

8. In some situations, arbitration may be used to settle interest disputes; that is, disputes arising over the terms of a first collective agreement or revisions to an existing one. This is known as interest arbitration, and results in the imposition of the terms of the collective agreement.

9. Typical collective agreement provisions include: a union recognition clause, a union security/checkoff clause, a no-strike or lockout provision, a management rights clause, the grievance procedure, an arbitration clause, disciplinary procedures, compensation rates and benefits, hours of work and overtime provisions, health and safety provisions, employee security/seniority provisions, and the contract expiration date.

10. After a collective agreement has been negotiated and signed, the contract administration process begins. Both union and management are required to abide by the contract provisions. It is in day-to-day contract administration that the bulk of labour–management relations occurs.

11. The grievance procedure in a collective agreement outlines the steps by which a dispute arising between an employer and bargaining unit member or between an employer and the union, during the life of the collective agreement, may be settled. It involves systematic deliberation of a complaint at progressively higher levels of authority in the company and union. The problem may be settled at any of these levels, and if not, the complaint may be submitted to an impartial outside party whose decision is final and binding, a process that is known as rights arbitration.

12. In many organizations, union and management leaders recognize that an effective working relationship is in their mutual interests. When managers wish to build a more harmonious and effective relationship, there are a number of strategies that can assist: instituting an open-door policy, prior consultation, demonstrating genuine concern for employee well-being, forming joint study committees, holding joint training programs, meeting regularly, and using third-party assistance when doing so would be beneficial.

Key Terms

attitudinal structuring
arbitration
bargaining zone
boycott
caucus session
checkoff
closed shop
collective bargaining
  process
compulsory checkoff
concessionary bargaining
conciliation
dilatory tactics
distributive bargaining
good faith bargaining
grievance
grievance procedure
integrative bargaining
interest arbitration

interest-based bargaining
interest dispute
intra-organizational
  bargaining
lockout
maintenance-of-
  membership
management rights
  clause
mediation
monetary issues
mutual gains bargaining
non-monetary issues
open shop
pattern bargaining
picket
precedent
productivity bargaining
Rand formula (dues

shop/agency shop)
ratification
replacement workers
rights arbitration
rights dispute
strike
strike vote
surface bargaining
union recognition clause
union security clause
union shop
unlawful lockout
unlawful strike
voluntary checkoff
voluntary irrevocable
  checkoff
voluntary revocable
  checkoff
wildcat strike

Discussion Questions and Exercises

1. Describe the purposes of collective bargaining and cite five examples of violations of the principle of bargaining in good faith.

2. Describe strategies used by the management and union negotiating teams to prepare for collective bargaining.

3. Explain the following terms: bargaining zone, monetary issues, and non-monetary issues. What happens if bargaining items are outside of the bargaining zone? Why are non-monetary issues normally handled first in contract negotiations?

4. Describe the typical steps and issues involved in the face-to-face negotiating process.

5. With several of your classmates, use role playing to differentiate between distributive, integrative, and intra-organizational bargaining, and explain attitudinal structuring.

6. Differentiate between conciliation and mediation and explain the role of each in the collective bargaining process.

7. Explain why strikes, lockouts, and interest arbitration may be used as possible responses to a bargaining impasse, and describe the circumstances under which each is likely to be used.

8. Obtain a copy of two collective agreements. Compare and contrast the following provisions: union recognition, management rights, union security/checkoff, grievance procedure, arbitration clause, and contract expiry date.

9. Explain why seniority and discipline are issues that cause many disagreements between union and management in the contract administration process.

10. Describe five strategies that can be used to build an effective labour–management relationship.

Application Exercises

RUNNING CASE: Carter Cleaning Company

The Grievance

On visiting one of the Carter Cleaning Centres, Jennifer was surprised to be taken aside by a long-time Carter employee, who met her as she was parking her car. "Murray (the store manager) told me I was suspended for two days without pay because I came in late last Thursday," said George. "I'm really upset, but around here the store manager's word seems to be law, and it sometimes seems like the only way anyone can file a grievance is by meeting you or your father like this in the parking lot."

Jennifer was very disturbed by this revelation and promised the employee she would look into it and discuss the situation with her father. In the car heading back to headquarters she began mulling over what alternatives there might be.

Questions

1. Do you think it is important for Carter Cleaning Centres to have a formal grievance procedure? Why or why not?

2. Based on what you know about Carter Cleaning, outline the steps that you think should be involved in the firm's grievance process, should they decide to implement one.

3. What else could Jennifer and her father do, other than implementing a grievance process, to ensure that complaints and grievances get expressed and handled?

CASE INCIDENT: Disciplinary Action

Facts: The employee, a union shop steward, was on her regularly scheduled day off at home. She was called by her supervisor and told to talk to three union members and instruct them to attend a work function called a "Quest for Quality Interaction Committee" meeting. The Quest for Quality program was a corporate initiative, a high priority with the employer (a nursing and rehabilitation facility), aimed at improving patient care. The union objected to the implementation of the program and had taken the position that employees could attend meetings if their jobs were threatened, but they should do so under protest and file a grievance afterward.

On the day in question, the union shop steward, in conversation with the employees, told them that she would not order them to attend the Quest for Quality meeting, although she had been asked by her supervisor to instruct them to do so. (Her supervisor had refused to order the employees to attend the meeting, relying on the union shop steward to do so.) When the union steward failed to order the employees to attend the meeting, the employer suspended her for two weeks, an action which she grieved.

Arguments at the Arbitration Hearing: The union's position was that the company had no authority to discipline the union shop steward on her day off for failure to give what was termed "a management direction" to perform the specified job function of attending a mandatory corporate meeting.

The union pointed out that it was unfair that the employer refused to order the employees directly to attend the meeting, but then expect the union steward to do so. The union argued that while it is not unusual to call upon a steward for assistance in problem solving, the company had no right to demand that he or she replace a supervisor or manager in giving orders and then discipline the union official for refusing to do so.

The company's position was that the opposition of the union on the Quest for Quality meetings put the employees in a position of being unable to attend without direction to do so from their union steward; that the union steward had been given a job assignment involving directing employees to attend the meeting; and that failure to carry out this assignment was insubordination and just cause for her suspension.

In its counter-argument, the union contended that the arbitrator must examine the nature of the order when deciding whether the insubordination was grounds for discipline. As to the nature of the order in this case, the employer should have to demonstrate that the order was directly related to the job classification and work assignment of the employee disciplined, and that the refusal to obey such an order posed a real challenge to supervisory authority.

The employee did not dispute the fact that she failed to follow the orders given to her by her supervisor, but pointed out that she was not on duty at the time and that the task assigned was not because of her job with the company but because of her status as a union steward.

Questions

1. If the union's opposition to the Quest for Quality program encouraged the employees not to participate, should the union be held responsible for directing the employees to attend? Why or why not?

2. As the arbitrator, do you think the employer had just cause to discipline the employee? Make a ruling and justify it.

Adapted from *Cheltenham Nursing and Rehabilitation Center*, 89 LA 361 (1987); in Michael Carrell and Christina Heavin, *Labor Relations and Collective Bargaining* (Englewood Cliffs, NJ: Prentice Hall, 1995), pp. 100–1.

Human Resources Management Simulation

There is always a possibility that an organization will become involved in a union organizing campaign. Part 4 of the simulation deals with labour relations. Since there is a desire to ensure that the Peterborough plant remains nonunionized, the focus is on avoiding unionization and ensuring that supervisors are aware of what they can and cannot do once a formal application for certification has been made. For this exercise (which is not in the simulation manual), class members are asked to assume that the CAW has just successfully organized the Peterborough plant employees. Working in small groups, each team is required to prepare a report outlining what steps should be taken to ensure that there is a harmonious labour–management relationship at the Peterborough facility, characterized by cooperation and joint problem solving.

Video Case

Fewer Union Jobs: The Key to Company Survival?

A strike at General Motors (GM) raises some serious questions. GM has been losing its market share steadily over the past decade, down to 30 percent from 50 percent. Vice-President of GM Canada, Stew Low, has stated that jobs will continue to be lost unless GM restructures its operations such that it can stay in business, which means closing plants and eliminating jobs.

The union (CAW) has retaliated by striking at one GM plant after another, virtually shutting down Canadian operations. While the union is perceived to be challenging the company's right to run the company the way management sees fit, union officials state that, in reality, the issue is a fight over jobs. It's a question of work ownership. Who owns the work—the company or the union?

The big-three automobile manufacturers (GM, Ford, and Chrysler) used to have the North American market all to themselves, but now they face fierce competition from Japanese and European car makers. The result: they're trying to stay competitive by cutting costs. Plants have been relocated to places like Mexico where wages are much lower (about one-third of those in Canada), and the companies are also outsourcing production operations that can be performed less expensively elsewhere.

Outsourcing is vehemently opposed by the CAW. Union officials believe that GM has no right to farm out work in a time of high profits. GM's position is that it needs a flexible work force in order to stay competitive, and can't afford to let the union dictate company strategies. The profits made ($1.39 billion in 1995) will be lost unless costs can be cut, and that means the loss of more jobs.

Questions

1. Briefly describe the major issue leading to the strikes depicted in the video.

2. Describe the strategies GM has used to try to cut costs and remain competitive. Why is the union opposing these strategies?

3. What type of bargaining strategy have GM and CAW negotiators been using to try to resolve their differences of opinion?

4. As a human resources professional, how would you recommend that GM and CAW negotiators resolve this issue? What actions could be taken to ensure that the relationship between union and management at GM is more harmonious in the future?

Video Resource: CBC, *The National Magazine*, "Who's Running the Company?" October 10, 1996.

Take It to the Net

Check out our Companion Website at

www.prenticehall.ca/dessler

for a multitude of practice questions, key terms and concepts, Weblinks to related sites, newsgroups, CBC video updates, and more.

Notes

1. Parts of this section are drawn from George W. Adams, *Canadian Labour Law*, (Aurora, ON: Canada Law Book Inc., 1985), pp. 670–3.
2. *Canada Labour Code*, R.S.(1985); Ontario Labour Relations Act, R.S.O.(1995). See also Adams, *Canada Labour Law*, pp. 670–3.
3. OLRB, (Ontario: Graphic Centre, 1967).
4. Dale Yoder, *Personnel Management* (Englewood Cliffs, NJ: Prentice Hall, 1972), p. 486. See also Michael Ballot, *Labour–Management Relations in a Changing Environment* (New York: John Wiley and Sons, 1992), pp. 169–425.
5. Based on Reed Richardson, *Collective Bargaining by Objectives*, (Englewood Cliffs, NJ: Prentice Hall, 1977), p. 150; adapted from Charles Morris, ed., *The Developing Labor Law*, (Washington, DC: Bureau of National Affairs, 1971), pp. 271–310.
6. Alton W.J. Craig and Norman A. Solomon, *The System of Industrial Relations in Canada*, 5th ed., (Scarborough, ON: Prentice Hall Canada Inc., 1996), p. 223.
7. Adapted from R.L. Miller, "Preparations for Negotiations," *Personnel Journal* (1978), pp. 36–9, 44.
8. Craig and Solomon, *Industrial Relations in Canada*, p. 223.
9. Peter Cappelli, "Is Pattern Bargaining Dead? A Discussion," *Industrial and Labour Relations Review* 44, no. 1 (October 1990), pp. 152–5.
10. Craig and Solomon, *Industrial Relations in Canada,* p. 263.
11. Phillip G. Day, *Industrial Relations Simulation*, (Scarborough, ON: Prentice Hall Canada Inc., 1999), p. 21.
12. Ross Stagner and Hjalmar Rosen, *Psychology of Union-Management Relations* (Belmont, CA: Wadsworth, 1965), pp. 95–7.
13. Richardson, *Collective Bargaining by Objectives*, p. 150.
14. The section on distributive bargaining is based on Richard E. Walton and Robert B. McKersie, *A Behavioral Theory of Labor Negotiations*, (New York: McGraw Hill, 1965), pp. 4–6.
15. Howard Raiff, *The Art and Science of Negotiation*, (Cambridge, MA: Belknap Harvard University Press, 1982), pp. 44–65.
16. The section on integrative bargaining is based on Walton and McKersie, *A Behavioral Theory*, pp. 4–6.
17. The section on interest-based bargaining is based on Cynthia Davenport, "Labour Pains," *Human Resources Professional* 10, no. 11 (December 1993), pp. 13–5.
18. Davenport, "Labour Pains," p. 14.
19. Davenport, "Labour Pains," pp. 14–5.
20. Claudine Kapel, "Betting on '7'," *Human Resources Professional* 13, no. 1, (February/March 1996), pp. 17–9.
21. Cited in Davenport, "Labour Pains," p. 15.
22. The section on mutual gains bargaining is based on Claudine Kapel, "The Feeling's Mutual," *Human Resources Professional* 12, no. 2, (April 1995), pp. 9–13.
23. Kapel, "The Feeling's Mutual," p. 10.
24. Cited in Kapel, "The Feeling's Mutual," p. 11.
25. Kapel, "The Feeling's Mutual," pp. 11–2.
26. Cited in Kapel, "The Feeling's Mutual," p. 13.
27. R.E. Fells, "Developing Trust in Negotiation," *Employee Relations* 14, no. 1, (1993), p. 35.
28. *Canadian LRBR*, (Donald William Movers Ltd., 1967).
29. "Wal-Mart Workers Reject Offer," *Canadian HR Reporter* 10, no. 21, (December 1, 1997), p. 6.
30. Craig and Solomon, *Industrial Relations in Canada* pp. 223–7.
31. Craig and Solomon, *Industrial Relations in Canada*, p. 225.
32. Craig and Solomon, *Industrial Relations in Canada*, p. 227.
33. Craig and Solomon, *Industrial Relations in Canada*, p. 225.
34. "Chronological Work Stoppages," Workplace Information Directorate, Labour Branch, Human Resources Development Canada, 1995.
35. Jan I. Ondrich and John F. Schnell, "Strike Duration and the Degree of Disagreement," *Industrial Relations* 32, no. 3, (Fall 1993), pp. 421–31.
36. Craig and Solomon, *Industrial Relations in Canada*, p. 231.
37. Craig and Solomon, *Industrial Relations in Canada*, p. 227.
38. Craig and Solomon, *Industrial Relations in Canada*, p. 227.
39. Craig and Solomon, *Industrial Relations in Canada*, p. 386.
40. Craig and Solomon, *Industrial Relations in Canada*, p. 382.
41. Craig and Solomon, *Industrial Relations in Canada*, pp. 235–7.
42. Chris Knight, "Time for Some Post-Strike Reckoning," *Canadian HR Reporter* 10, no. 22, (December 29, 1997), p. 4.
43. Day, *Industrial Relations Simulation*, p. 11.
44. The section on union security is based on Craig and Solomon, *Industrial Relations in Canada*, pp. 423–4.
45. Adams, *Canadian Labour Law*, p. 694.
46. Craig and Solomon, *Industrial Relations in Canada*, p. 425.
47. Craig and Solomon, *Industrial Relations in Canada*, p. 239.
48. Day, *Industrial Relations Simulation*, p. 12.
49. Donald J. M. Brown and David M. Beatty, *Canadian Labour Arbitration*, 3rd ed., (Aurora, ON: Canada Law Book Inc., 1991), p.7–22. Used by permission of Canada Law Book Inc., 240 Edward St., Aurora, Ontario. L4G 3S9.
50. See, for example, Clyde Summers, "Protecting All Employees Against Unjust Dismissal," *Harvard Business Review* 58 (January–February 1980), pp. 132–9; and George Bohlander and Harold White, "Building Bridges: Non-Union Employee Grievance Systems," *Personnel* (July 1988), pp. 62–6.
51. Walter Baer, *Grievance Handling: 101 Guides for Supervisors* (New York: American Management Association, 1970).
52. See Benjamin M. Selkam, *Labor Relations and Human Relations* (New York: McGraw-Hill, 1947).
53. Craig and Solomon, *Industrial Relations in Canada,* p. 228.
54. Brown and Beatty, *Canadian Labour Arbitration*, pp. 2-1 to 2-6.
55. See Jay E. Grenig, "Stare Decisis, Re Judicata and Collecteral Estoppel and Labour Arbitration," *Labour Law Journal* 38 (April 1987), pp. 195–205.
56. George Saunders, "Union-Management Relations: An Overview," in *Human Resources Management in Canada* (Scarborough, ON: Prentice Hall Canada Inc. 1983), p. 55 047.

Chapter 18
Occupational Health and Safety

Chapter Outline

- ◆ Why Occupational Health and Safety is Important
- ◆ Basic Facts About Occupational Health and Safety Legislation
- ◆ The Supervisor's Role in Safety
- ◆ What Causes Accidents?
- ◆ How to Prevent Accidents
- ◆ Employee Wellness: Occupational Health Issues and Challenges

Learning Outcomes

After studying this chapter, you should be able to:

Discuss Occupational Health and Safety legislation.

Explain WHMIS.

Describe the supervisor's role in safety.

Explain in detail three basic causes of accidents.

Describe how accidents at work can be prevented.

Discuss major employee wellness issues at work and *explain* how they should be handled.

Why Occupational Health and Safety Is Important

Safety and accident prevention concerns managers for several reasons, one of which is that the work-related accidents figures are staggering. According to the Association of Workers' Compensation Boards of Canada, in 1995 there were more than 749 deaths and 410 469 injuries resulting from accidents at work. These figures do not include minor injuries that do not involve lost time from work beyond the day of the accident. Furthermore, these figures don't tell the full story. They don't reflect the human suffering incurred by injured or ill workers and their families or the economic costs incurred by employers.

Workplace health concerns are also widespread. One study found that two-thirds of employed Canadian adults believed they were exposed to some sort of occupational health hazard, the most common being exposure to airborne dust and fibre, and working with a computer screen or terminal. Thirty-two percent believed that these exposures had a negative effect on their health.[1]

Basic Facts About Occupational Health and Safety Legislation

Purpose

occupational health and safety legislation
Laws intended to protect the health and safety of workers by minimizing work-related accidents and illnesses.

Occupational Health and Safety Legislation. All provinces, territories, and the federal jurisdiction have occupational health and safety legislation based on the principle of joint responsibility shared by workers and employers to maintain a hazard-free work environment and to enhance the health and safety of workers.[2] These laws fall into three categories: general health and safety rules; rules for specific industries, for example, mining; and rules related to specific hazards, for example, asbestos. In some jurisdictions, these are combined into one overall law, with regulations for specific industries and hazards, while in others they remain separate. The regulations are very complex and cover almost every conceivable hazard in great detail, as can be seen in **Figure 18.1**. Provisions of occupational health and safety legislation differ significantly across Canada, but most have certain basic features in common:

**Figure 18.1
Ontario Occupational Health and Safety Act—Construction Regulations**

Source: *Ontario Occupational Health and Safety Act.* Used with permission.

> **O.REG.213/91**
> **68. A sign used to direct traffic,**
>
> (a) shall be diamond shaped, 450 millimetres wide and 450 millimetres long, with the diamond mounted at one corner on a pole 1.2 metres long;
>
> (b) shall be made of material that has at least the rigidity of six millimetres thick plywood;
>
> (c) shall be reflective fluourescent and coloured,
>
> > (i) red-orange on one side with the corner areas coloured black, so that the red-orange area forms a regular eight-sided figure, with the word "STOP" written in legible white letters 150 millimetres high in a central position on the sign, and
> >
> > ii) chartreuse on one side, with the word "SLOW" written in legible black letters 150 millimetres high in a central position on the sign; and
>
> (d) shall be maintained in a clean condition.

Responsibilities and Rights of Employers and Employees   In all jurisdictions, employers are responsible for taking every reasonable precaution to ensure the health and safety of their workers. This is called the "due diligence" requirement. Specific duties of the employer include filing government accident reports, maintaining records, and posting safety notices and legislative information. Employees have three basic rights under the joint responsibility model: the right to know about workplace safety hazards; the right to participate in the occupational health and safety process; and the right to refuse unsafe work if they have "reasonable cause" to believe that the work is dangerous. "Reasonable cause" usually means that a complaint about a workplace hazard has not been satisfactorily resolved, or a safety problem places employees in immediate danger. If performance of a task would adversely affect health and safety, a worker cannot be disciplined for refusing to do the job. Employees are responsible for taking reasonable care to protect their own health and safety and, in most cases, that of their coworkers. Specific requirements include wearing protective clothing and equipment, and reporting any contravention of the law or regulations.

Joint Health and Safety Committees   The function of joint health and safety committees is to provide a non-adversarial atmosphere where management and labour can work together to ensure a safe and healthy workplace. Most jurisdictions require a joint health and safety committee to be established in each workplace with a minimum number of workers (usually 10 or 20). In the other jurisdictions, the government has the power to require a committee to be formed. Committees are usually required to consist of between 2 and 12 members, at least half of whom must represent workers. In small workplaces, one health and safety representative may be required. The committee is generally responsible for hazard identification by making regular inspections of the workplace to identify potential health and safety hazards. Hazard control can be achieved by addressing safety issues before an accident or injury happens; identifying ways in which a hazardous situation can be prevented from harming workers; and putting in place cleanup operations to ensure that a potential hazard will not recur.[3] Health and safety committees are also responsible for investigating employee complaints, accident investigation, development and promotion of measures to protect health and safety, and dissemination of information about health and safety laws and regulations. In Ontario, at least one management and one labour representative must be certified in occupational health and safety through a provincial training program.

www.ccohs.ca
Canada Centre for OH&S

A safety inspector visits the plant to check on reported violations of health and safety regulations.

Enforcement of Occupational Health and Safety Laws   In all Canadian jurisdictions, occupational health and safety law provides for government inspectors to periodically carry out safety inspections of workplaces. Health and safety inspectors have wide powers to conduct inspections, and employers are required to assist them.[4] Safety inspectors may enter a workplace at any time without a warrant or prior notification, and engage in any examination and inquiry they believe necessary to ascertain whether the workplace is in compliance with the law. Safety inspectors may order a variety of actions on the part of employers and employees, including orders to stop work, stop using tools, install first aid equipment, and stop emission of contaminants. Penalties across Canada consist of fines and/or jail terms. Employers have criticized the current system of penalties because workers are rarely prosecuted.[5]

Control of Toxic Substances Most occupational health and safety laws require basic precautions with respect to toxic substances, including chemicals, biohazards such as HIV/AIDS, and physical agents such as radiation, heat, and noise. An accurate inventory of these substances must be maintained, maximum exposure limits for airborne concentrations of these agents adhered to, the substances tested, and their use carefully controlled.

Workplace Hazardous Materials Information System (WHMIS) WHMIS is a Canada-wide law designed to protect workers by providing crucial information about hazardous materials or substances in the workplace. WHMIS was the outcome of a cooperative effort between the federal, provincial, and territorial governments, together with industry and organized labour. The WHMIS legislation has three components:[6]

1. Labelling of hazardous material containers to alert workers that there is a potentially hazardous product inside (see **Figure 18.2** for examples of hazard symbols)

Workplace Hazardous Materials Information System (WHMIS)
A Canada-wide law designed to protect workers by providing information about hazardous materials in the workplace.

**Figure 18.2
WHMIS Symbols**

Source: From "Occupational Health and Safety" by J. Montgomery © 1996. Reprinted with permission of ITP Nelson Canada.

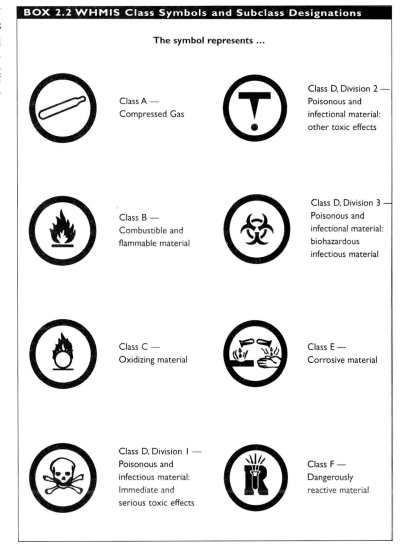

BOX 2.2 WHMIS Class Symbols and Subclass Designations

The symbol represents ...

Class A — Compressed Gas

Class B — Combustible and flammable material

Class C — Oxidizing material

Class D, Division 1 — Poisonous and infectious material: Immediate and serious toxic effects

Class D, Division 2 — Poisonous and infectional material: other toxic effects

Class D, Division 3 — Poisonous and infectional material: biohazardous infectious material

Class E — Corrosive material

Class F — Dangerously reactive material

2. Material safety data sheets (MSDS) to outline a product's potentially hazardous ingredients and the procedures for safe handling of the product (see **Figure 18.3** for a sample MSDS).

3. Employee training to ensure that employees can identify WHMIS hazard symbols, read WHMIS supplier and workplace labels, and read and apply the information on a MSDS.

Changes in Occupational Health and Safety Legislation   Occupational health and safety legislation is in the midst of considerable change in Canada today, as legislation and regulations are being reviewed in a number of jurisdictions.[7] Governments are moving away from the "command and control" model of govern-

Figure 18.3
Material Safety Data Sheet (MSDS)

Source: J. Montgomery, *Occupational Health and Safety*, (Toronto: Nelson Canada, 1996). Used with permission.

MATERIAL SAFETY DATA SHEET		Name of Product:			
SECTION I—HAZARDOUS INGREDIENTS					
Chemical Activity	Concentration	CAS Number	PIN Number	LDso Species and Route	LCso Species and Route

SECTION II—PREPARATION INFORMATION		
Prepared by (Group, Department, Etc.)	Phone Number	Date of Preparation

SECTION III—PRODUCT INFORMATION			
Product Identifier			
Manufacturer's Name		Supplier's Name	
Street Address		Street Address	
City	Province	City	Province
Postal Code	Emergency Tel. No.	Postal Code	Emergency Tel. No.
Product Use			

SECTION IV—PHYSICAL DATA			
Physical State	Odour and Appearance		Odour Threshold
Specific Gravity (water = 1)	Co-efficient of Water/Oil Distribution		Vapour Pressure
Boiling Point (°C)	Freezing Point (°C)	pH	Vapour Density (Air = 1)
Evaporation Rate (BuAc = 1)		Percent Volatile (by volume)	

(continued)

Figure 18.3 (continued)

MATERIAL SAFETY DATA SHEET	Name of Product:	

SECTION V—FIRE OR EXPLOSION HAZARD

Conditions of Flammability

Means of Extinction

Explosion Data
Sensitivity to Mechanical Impact   Sensitivity to Static Discharge

Flashpoint (°C) and Method	Upper Flammable Limit %	Lower Flammable Limit %

Autoignition Temperature (°C)	Hazardous Combustion Products	

SECTION VI—REACTIVITY DATA

Stability

Incompatible Materials

Conditions of Reactivity

Hazardous Decomposition Products

SECTION VII—TOXICOLOGICAL PROPERTIES

Route of Entry

☐ Skin Contact   ☐ Skin Absorption   ☐ Eye Contact   ☐ Inhalation   ☐ Ingestion

Effects of Acute Exposure to Product

Effects of Chronic Exposure to Product

Exposure Limits	Irritancy of Product	Synergistic Products

Evidence of Carcinogenicity, Reproductive Toxicity, Teratogenicity or Mutagenicity?		Sensitization to Product

(continued)

ment involvement to an "outcome-based" or "performance-based" model, where more responsibility is being pushed down to employers and employees. Enforcement efforts are now targeting employers with the highest accident rates rather than trying to complete as many safety inspections as possible. This shift to stronger internal responsibility is also being manifested in the trend away from government regulation to a heightened emphasis on "due diligence" by the employer. For example, Nova Scotia revised its occupational health and safety legislation in 1996 to require workplaces with as few as five employees to have a written workplace health and safety policy.[8] As well, the Nova Scotia government, together with the unions representing its workers, have agreed on a government-wide health and safety policy.[9]

Figure 18.3
(continued)

MATERIAL SAFETY DATA SHEET	Name of Product:

SECTION VIII—PREVENTIVE MEASURES

Personal Protective Equipment

Gloves (specify)	Respiratory (specify)
Eye (specify)	Footwear (specify)

Other Equipment (specify)

Engineering Controls (e.g. ventilation, enclosed process, specify)

Leak and Spill Procedure

Waste Disposal

Handling Procedures and Equipment

Storage Requirements

Special Shipping Information

SECTION IX—FIRST AID MEASURES

Inhalation

Ingestion

Eye Contact

Skin Contact

Additional Information	Sources Used

Changes are also being made in efforts to more appropriately balance accident prevention and enforcement of safety rules. Prince Edward Island, New Brunswick, and Ontario are following the lead of British Columbia and Alberta in more closely linking accident prevention and workers' compensation. Other jurisdictions are considering similar changes.

An emerging issue in the occupational health and safety field is the importance of ergonomics (defined later in this chapter) to injury prevention. British Columbia has drafted ergonomic regulations including an ergonomics code of practice, which sets out guidelines for employers to identify, assess, and control ergonomic factors in the workplace. The focus is on ergonomics as a cost-reduction issue more so than a regulatory requirement. Quebec is also running experimental ergonomics projects in several workplaces, to find simple and practical solutions to help employers rather that writing regulations telling them what to do.

Occupational Health and Safety and Other Legislation   Health and safety, human rights, labour relations, and employment standards are covered in every jurisdiction in Canada in an interlaced web of legislation. Situations arise in which it is difficult to know which law is applicable, or which one takes precedence over another.[10] For example, are the human rights of one employee to wear a ceremonial knife related to a religion more important than the safety of other employees; how much discipline is acceptable to labour arbitrators for health and safety violations; should fights in the workplace be considered a safety hazard; is sexual harassment a safety hazard; how long does an employer have to tolerate poor performance from an alcoholic employee whose attempts at treatment fail? The Saskatchewan government amended their occupational health and safety act in 1993 to include sexual harassment as a workplace hazard, in response to polls indicating that 40 percent of women in that province's workplaces claim that they have suffered health problems due to sexual harassment.[11]

Small Business Applications

A New Occupational Health and Safety Initiative for Small Business

Small businesses have often felt overburdened and underserved by health and safety agencies and workers' compensation boards.[1] A recent Canada-wide initiative is trying to improve this situation. The Safe Communities Foundation was set up on January 1, 1997 with funding from five major chartered banks, DuPont, and Noranda. The Foundation, in cooperation with workers' compensation boards, offers a safety incentive program for small businesses called the Safe Communities Incentive Program. A group of small employers in a community applies to the program as a collective, and is treated as one large employer by the Workers' Compensation Board. The employers must agree to have their employees take special small-business-oriented safety training (provided by the Foundation, in association with workers' compensation boards, safety associations, and others) and conduct a self-evaluation or safety audit of their premises to identify safety hazards.

The real payoff to the group of small businesses comes if their combined workers' compensation claims for the group are less than a target figure based on the past several years of claims for businesses in the collective. Seventy-five percent of the difference in claims is refunded to the group. This is in addition to any other workers' compensation rebates that may apply. The community benefits by being able to publicize their status as a safe place to work.

The program was piloted in the town of High River, Alberta, and has spread to other municipalities in Alberta and several in Ontario including Kingston, Peterborough, and Waterloo. It is expected to expand to other provinces after two years in operation.

1. This section is based on C. Knight, "WCB Lets Small Firms Learn and Earn Together," *Canadian HR Reporter*, November 4, 1996, pp. 1, 2. See also "Kingston the Latest Safe Community," *Canadian HR Reporter* (August 11, 1997), p. 3; "Safe Communities to Impact Bottom Line," *OH&S Canada* (November/December 1996), p. 11.

The Supervisor's Role in Safety

Most jurisdictions impose a personal duty on supervisors to ensure that workers comply with occupational health and safety regulations, and place a specific obligation on supervisors to advise and instruct workers about safety.[12] Safety-minded managers must aim to instill in their workers the desire to work safely. Minimizing hazards (by ensuring that spills are wiped up, machine guards are adequate, and so forth) is important, but no matter how safe the workplace is, there will be accidents unless workers want to and do act safely. Of course, supervisors try to watch each employee closely, but most managers know this won't work. In the final analysis, the best (and perhaps only) alternative is to get workers to want to work safely. Then, when needed, enforce safety rules.[13]

Top-Management Commitment

Most safety experts agree that safety commitment begins with top management. Historically, DuPont's accident rate worldwide has been much lower than that of the chemical industry as a whole. (In its U.S. plants, DuPont had an annual rate of 0.12 accidents per 100 workers, which was one twenty-third of the average rate for all manufacturers in that year.) If DuPont's record had been average, it would have spent more than $26 million in additional compensation and other costs, or 3.6 percent of its profits. To recover the difference, DuPont would have had to boost sales by about $500 million, given the company's 5.5 percent net return on sales at that time.[14] This good safety record is probably partly due to an organizational commitment to safety, which is evident in the following description:

> One of the best examples I know of in setting the highest possible priority for safety takes place at a DuPont Plant in Germany. Each morning at the DuPont Polyester and Nylon Plant the director and his assistants meet at 8:45 to review the past 24 hours. The first matter they discuss is not production, but safety. Only after they have examined reports of accidents and near misses and satisfied themselves that corrective action has been taken do they move on to look at output, quality, and cost matters.[15]

In summary, without the full commitment at all levels of management, any attempts to reduce unsafe acts by workers will meet with little success. The first-line supervisor is a critical link in the chain of management. If the supervisor does not take safety seriously, it's likely that those under him or her will not either.

What Causes Accidents?

The Three Basic Causes of Accidents

There are three basic causes of workplace accidents: chance occurrences, unsafe conditions, and unsafe acts on the part of employees. A 1995 accident in a subway tunnel in Toronto, which killed three passengers, provides a vivid example of all of these factors. Signal problems that had been reported by eight other drivers throughout the day had not been addressed as crews were sent to the wrong tunnel, the rookie driver ran three red signal lights, a trip alarm failed, a call for help rang 15 times and then got a voice-mail direction to call another number, emergency crews were sent to look for an "odour," the radio system didn't work in the tunnels, and the drivers had no evacuation training.[16]

Chance occurrences (such as walking past a plate-glass window just as someone hits a ball through it) contribute to accidents but are more or less beyond management's control: We will therefore focus on *unsafe conditions* and *unsafe acts*.

Unsafe Conditions and Other Work-Related Accident-Causing Factors

Unsafe conditions are one main cause of accidents. They include such factors as:

unsafe conditions
The mechanical and physical conditions that cause accidents.

- improperly guarded equipment
- defective equipment
- hazardous procedures in, on, or around machines or equipment
- unsafe storage–congestion, overloading
- improper illumination–glare, insufficient light
- improper ventilation—insufficient air change, impure air source.[17]

The basic remedy here is to eliminate or minimize the unsafe conditions. Government standards address the mechanical and physical conditions that cause accidents. Furthermore, a checklist of unsafe conditions can be used to conduct a

**Figure 18.4
Checklist for
Preventing
Compressed Air
Injuries**

Source: J.A. Ford "Safety Under Pressures," *OH&S Canada* (November/December 1996), p. 20. Used with permission.

Here is a simple checklist that you or your safety committee can use to audit how well your company scores at preventing compressed air accidents.

1) ❑ Yes ❑ No A safety rule exists that prohibits workers from blowing off clothes, skin, or hair.

2) ❑ Yes ❑ No Signs are posted to reinforce the above rule in all places where air guns are used.

3) ❑ Yes ❑ No Appropriate vacuums are available for workers to clean dust/dirt from clothes and hair.

4) ❑ Yes ❑ No Air guns are not used to blow dirt and debris off things and a safety rule prohibits this.

5) ❑ Yes ❑ No Air pressures are set for the correct amount.

6) ❑ Yes o No Filters are cleaned on a regular basis.

7) ❑ Yes ❑ No Oil in lubricators is replenished before it goes dry.

8) ❑ Yes ❑ No Air tools are not intentionally dropped on the floor.

9) ❑ Yes ❑ No Safety glasses are worn by workers using compressed air.

10) ❑ Yes ❑ No A sound level survey has been done on all jobs using compressed air.

11) ❑ Yes ❑ No Hearing protection is worn by workers using compressed air when noise levels warrant its use.

12) ❑ Yes ❑ No Compressed air feed lines come from the top of the pipe.

13) ❑ Yes ❑ No All installations have the proper filter, lubricator, and regulator, and the pressure gauge is working.

14) ❑ Yes ❑ No All compressed air equipment and components have been specifically designed for this purpose and there are no unrated, uncertified, or home-built devices.

15) ❑ Yes ❑ No Air sampling has been done to determine the amount of oil in the air in areas where there is evidence of such.

16) ❑ Yes ❑ No Lock-out procedures deal specifically with compressed air.

17) ❑ Yes ❑ No Machines using compressed air have provisions for disconnecting, bleeding stored air, and locking out the air supply.

18) ❑ Yes ❑ No Workers have had training (or review training) on the hazards of compressed air within the past three years.

job hazard analysis. One such checklist is presented in **Figure 18.4**. Common indicators of job hazards include increased numbers of accidents, employee complaints, poor product quality, employee modifications to workstations, and higher levels of absenteeism and turnover.[18]

www.safety-council.org
Safety Council

Three Other Work-Related Accident Factors   In addition to unsafe conditions, three other work-related factors contribute to accidents: the *job itself*, the *work schedule*, and *the psychological climate* of the workplace.

Certain jobs are inherently more dangerous than others. According to one study, for example, the job of crane operator results in about three times more accident-related hospital visits than does the job of supervisor. Similarly, some departments' work is inherently safer than others'. An accounting department usually has fewer accidents than a shipping department.

Work schedules and *fatigue* also affect accident rates. Accident rates usually don't increase too noticeably during the first five or six hours of the workday. But beyond that, the accident rate increases faster as the number of hours worked increases. This is due partly to fatigue. It has also been found that accidents occur more often during night shifts.

Many experts believe that the *psychological climate* of the workplace affects the accident rate. For example, accidents occur more frequently in plants with a high seasonal layoff rate and where there is hostility among employees, many garnished wages, and blighted living conditions. Temporary stress factors such as high workplace temperature, poor illumination, and a congested workplace are also related to accident rates. One writer says these findings mean that workers who work under stress, or who feel their jobs are threatened or insecure, have more accidents than those who do not.[19]

What Causes Unsafe Acts (A Second Basic Cause of Accidents)

unsafe acts
Behaviour tendencies and undesirable attitudes that cause accidents.

Most safety experts and managers know that it is impossible to eliminate accidents just by reducing unsafe conditions. People cause accidents, and no one has found a sure-fire way to eliminate unsafe employee acts such as:

- throwing materials
- operating or working at unsafe speeds—either too fast or too slow
- making safety devices inoperative by removing, adjusting, disconnecting them
- using unsafe equipment or using equipment unsafely
- using unsafe procedures in loading, placing, mixing, combining
- taking unsafe positions under suspended loads
- lifting improperly
- distracting, teasing, abusing, startling, quarreling, horseplay.

Unsafe acts such as these can undermine even the best attempts to minimize unsafe conditions. We should, therefore, discuss the causes of unsafe acts.[20]

Personal Characteristics and Accidents   A model summarizing how personal characteristics are linked to accidents is presented in **Figure 18.5**. Ernest McCormick and Joseph Tiffin say that personal characteristics (personality, motivation, and so on) serve as the basis for certain "behaviour tendencies," such as the tendency to take risks, and undesirable attitudes. These behaviour tendencies in turn result in unsafe acts, such as inattention and failure to follow procedures. In turn, such unsafe acts increase the probability of someone having an accident.

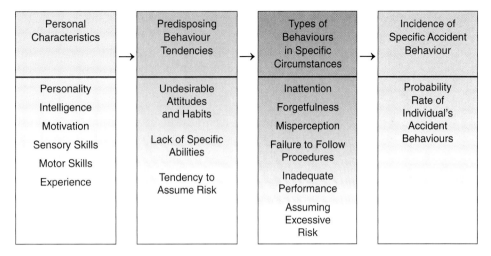

**Figure 18.5
How Personal Factors
May Influence
Employee Accident
Behaviour**

Personal Characteristics	Predisposing Behaviour Tendencies	Types of Behaviours in Specific Circumstances	Incidence of Specific Accident Behaviour
Personality

Intelligence

Motivation

Sensory Skills

Motor Skills

Experience | Undesirable Attitudes and Habits

Lack of Specific Abilities

Tendency to Assume Risk | Inattention

Forgetfulness

Misperception

Failure to Follow Procedures

Inadequate Performance

Assuming Excessive Risk | Probability Rate of Individual's Accident Behaviours |

What Traits Characterize "Accident-Prone" People?   Years of research failed to unearth any set of traits that accident repeaters seemed to have in common. Today most experts doubt that accident proneness is universal—that there are some people who will have many accidents no matter what situation they are put in. Instead the consensus is that the person who is accident prone on one job may not be on a different job—that accident proneness is situational. For example, *personality traits* (such as emotional stability) may distinguish accident-prone workers on jobs involving risk; and lack of *motor skills* may distinguish accident-prone workers on jobs involving coordination. In fact, many human traits *have* been found to be related to accident repetition *in specific situations* as the following discussion illustrates.[21]

Vision   Vision is related to accident frequency for many jobs. For example, passenger car drivers, intercity bus drivers, and machine operators who have high visual skills have fewer injuries than those who do not.[22]

Age   We also know that accidents are generally most frequent between the ages of 17 and 28, declining thereafter to reach a low in the late fifties and sixties.[23] While different patterns might be found with different jobs, this age factor seems to be a fairly general one.

Perceptual versus Motor Skills   One researcher concludes that "where [a worker's] perceptual skill is equal to, or higher than, his or her motor skill, the employee is a relatively safe worker. But where the perception level is lower than the motor level, the employee is accident-prone and his or her accident-proneness becomes greater as this difference increases."[24] This theory seems to be a twist on the "look before you leap" theme; a worker who reacts more quickly than he or she can perceive is more likely to have accidents.

Summary   In summary, these findings do not provide a complete list of the human traits that have been found to be related to higher accident rates. What the findings suggest is that for specific jobs it seems to be possible to identify accident-prone individuals and to screen them out.

How to Prevent Accidents

In practice, accident prevention boils down to two basic activities: reducing unsafe conditions and reducing unsafe acts.

Reducing Unsafe Conditions

Reducing unsafe conditions is an employer's first line of defense. Safety engineers should design jobs to remove or reduce physical hazards. In addition, supervisors and managers play a role in reducing unsafe conditions. A brief checklist like the one in Figure 18.4 can be used to identify and remove potential hazards.

Reducing Unsafe Acts Through Selection and Placement

Reducing unsafe acts is the second basic approach, and one way to do this is to screen out accident-prone persons before they are hired. Accidents are similar to other types of poor performance, and psychologists have had success in screening out individuals who might be accident prone for some specific job. The basic technique is to identify the human trait (such as visual skill) that might be related to accidents on the specific job, and then determine whether scores on this trait are related to accidents on the job.[25] For example:

> *Measures of muscular coordination.* We know that coordination is a predictor of safety for certain jobs. In one study, more than 600 employees were divided into four groups according to test scores on coordination tests. Here it was found that the poorest quarter had 51 percent more accidents than those in the better three quarters.[26]

> *Tests of visual skills.* Good vision plays a part in preventing accidents in many occupations, including driving and operating machines. In a study (in a paper mill) 52 accident-free employees were compared with 52 accident-prone employees. Here the researcher found that 63 percent of the no-accident group passed a vision test, while only 33 percent of the accident group passed it.[27]

> *Employee reliability tests.* Several studies suggest that a test such as the Employee Reliability Inventory (ERI) can help employers reduce unsafe acts at work. The ERI purportedly measures reliability dimensions such as emotional maturity, conscientiousness, safe job performance, and courteous job performance.[28] The ERI is intended to be used as a pre-interview questionnaire, in other words, one used to develop follow-up questions that can be asked during interviews and reference checks.[29] While the findings of at least one study were not definitive, the addition of the inventory to the selection process did seem to be associated with reductions in work-related accidents.[30]

Summary In summary, Professor Norman Maier concludes that:

> *Of great practical importance is the fact that there is a definite relationship between these accident-proneness tests and proficiency on the job. By selecting employees who do well—that is, score low—on accident-proneness tests, managers can reduce accidents and improve the caliber of the employees at the same time.[31]*

Canadian human rights legislation has particular relevance for safety-related screening decisions. Many employers would like to inquire about applicants' workers' compensation history prior to hiring, in part to avoid habitual workers' compensation claimants and hiring accident-prone individuals. However, inquiring about an applicant's workers' compensation injuries and claims can lead to allegations of discrimination based on disability. Similarly, applicants cannot be asked whether they have a disability nor asked to take tests that tend to screen out those with disabilities. Employers can ask each applicant whether he or she has the ability to perform the essential duties of the job and ask, "Do you know of any reason why you would not be able to perform the various functions of the job in question?"[32] Candidates can also be asked to demonstrate job-related skills, provided every applicant is required to do so.

Reducing Unsafe Acts Through Training and Education

Safety training is a third technique for reducing accidents. All employees should be required to participate in occupational health and safety training programs. The training should include instructions on safe work practices and procedures, warnings of potential hazards, the development of worker awareness about health and safety issues, and emphasis on commitment to responsible and appropriate workplace behaviour. To reinforce employee commitment, the training program should be kept up to date and closely monitored. It should include a practical evaluation process to ensure workers are applying the acquired knowledge and following recommended safety procedures. Such training is especially appropriate for new employees. This training can be delivered through a variety of mediums, including classrooms, printed material, computer, videos, intranets, and the Internet.[33]

www.hronline.com/forums/index.html
HS Canada

Safety posters can also help reduce unsafe acts. In one study, for example, their use apparently increased safe behaviour by more than 20 percent.[34] On the other hand, posters are no substitute for a comprehensive safety program; instead, they should be combined with other techniques like screening and training to reduce unsafe conditions and acts. The posters should also be changed often.[35]

Reducing Unsafe Acts Through Positive Reinforcement

Safety programs based on positive reinforcement are a fourth strategy for improving safety at work.[36] An example is a program that was instituted in a wholesale bakery that bakes, wraps, and transports pastry products to retail outlets nationwide.[37] An analysis of the safety-related conditions existing in the plant before the study suggested a number of areas that needed improvement. For example, new hires received no formal safety training, and safety was rarely mentioned on a day-to-day basis. Commercial safety posters were placed at the entrance to the work area and on a bulletin board in the dining room but were often not updated for six months. No single person was responsible for safety. Similarly, employees received little or no positive reinforcement for performing safely. Managers said little or nothing to employees who took the time to act safely. Although the accident rate had been climbing, many employees had yet to experience an injury from unsafe performance, so this "punishment" was also missing.

The Safety Program The safety program stressed positive reinforcement and training. A reasonable goal (in terms of observed incidents performed safely) was set and communicated to workers to ensure that they knew what was expected of them in terms of good performance. Next came a training phase. Here employees were presented with safety information during a 30-minute training session. Employees were shown pairs of slides (35mm transparencies) depicting scenes that were staged in the plant. In one transparency, for example, the wrapping supervisor was shown climbing over a conveyor; the parallel slide illustrated the supervisor walking around the conveyor. After viewing an unsafe act, employees were asked to describe what was wrong ("What's unsafe here?"). Then, once the problem had been aired, the same incident was again shown performed in a safe manner and the safe-conduct rule was explicitly stated ("Go around, not over or under, conveyors").

At the conclusion of the training phase, the employees were shown a graph with their pretraining safety record (in terms of observed incidents performed safely) plotted. They were encouraged to consider increasing their performance to the new safety goal for the following reasons: for their own protection, to decrease costs for the company, and to help the plant get out of last place in the safety ranking of the parent company. Then the graph and a list of safety rules (do's and don'ts) were posted in a conspicuous place in the work area.

Reinforcement and Safety The graph played a central role in the study's final, "positive reinforcement" phase. Whenever observers walked through the plant collecting safety data, they posted on the graph the percentage of incidents they had seen performed safely by the group as a whole, thus providing the workers with feedback on their safety performance. Workers could then compare their current safety performance with both their previous performance and their assigned goal. In addition, supervisors praised workers when they performed selected incidents safely. Safety in the plant subsequently improved markedly.[38]

Reducing Unsafe Acts Through Top-Management Commitment

One of the most consistent findings in the literature is that successful factory programs require a strong management commitment to safety.[39] This commitment, a fifth approach to accident reduction, manifests itself in senior managers being personally involved in safety activities on a routine basis; giving safety matters high priority in company meetings and production scheduling; giving the company safety officer high rank and status; and including safety training in new workers' training.

Summary: How to Reduce Accidents

Strict safety standards must be observed when working with asbestos.

1. Check for and *remove unsafe conditions;* use a checklist like the one presented in Figure 18.4. If the hazard cannot be removed, guard against it (for instance, with guardrails) or if necessary use personal protective equipment such as goggles or safety shoes.

2. Through *selection,* try to screen out employees who might be accident-prone for the job in question (but ensure that the requirements of human rights legislation are not violated).

3. Establish a *safety policy* emphasizing that the firm will do everything practical to eliminate or reduce accidents and injuries and the importance of accident and injury prevention at work.

4. Set specific *loss control goals.* Analyze the number of accidents and safety incidents and then set specific safety goals to be achieved, for instance, in terms of frequency of lost-time injuries per number of full-time employees.[40]

5. Encourage and *train employees* to be safety conscious; show them that senior managers and all supervisors are serious about safety.

6. Enforce *safety rules.* Discipline employees who work in a manner unsafe to themselves and others.[41]

7. Conduct *health and safety inspections* regularly. Also investigate all accidents and "near misses" and have a system in place for letting employees notify management about hazardous conditions.[42]

Controlling Workers' Compensation Costs

Employers' workers' compensation premiums are proportional to the firm's workers' compensation experience rate. Thus, the more workers' compensation claims a firm has, the more the firm will pay in premiums.

There are several factors in reducing workers' compensation claims:

Before the accident. The appropriate time to begin "controlling" workers' compensation claims is before the accident happens, not after. This involves taking all the steps previously summarized. For example, remove unsafe conditions, screen out employees who might be accident-prone for the job in question (without violating human rights legislation), and establish a safety policy and loss control goals.

After the accident. The occupational injury or illness can obviously be a traumatic event for the employee, and the way the employer handles it can influence the injured worker's reaction to it. The employee is going to have specific needs and specific questions, such as where to go for medical help and whether he or she will be paid for any time off. Employers should provide first aid and make sure the worker gets quick medical attention; make it clear that they are interested in the injured worker and his or her fears and questions; document the accident; file any required accident reports; and encourage a speedy return to work.[43]

Facilitate the employee's return to work. According to one discussion of managing workers' compensation costs:

Perhaps the most important and effective thing an employer can do to reduce costs is to develop an aggressive return-to-work program, including making light-duty work available. Surely the best solution to the current workers' compensation crisis, for both the employer and the employee, is for the worker to become a productive member of the company again instead of a helpless victim living on benefits.[44]

Specific actions to encourage early return to work can be internal and/or external to the organization. Internally, an employer can set up rehabilitation committees to identify modified work, including relevant stakeholders such as the employee and his or her colleagues, HR professionals, union representatives, and managers. Externally, the employer can work with the employee's family to ensure their support, mobilize the resources of the EAP to help the employee, ensure the availability of physical and occupational therapists, and make the family physician aware of workplace accommodation possibilities.[45] A study by consultants Sobeco, Ernst & Young found that 90 percent of companies have formal return to work programs, but only 62 percent of those are applying the program to all disabled employees.[46]

http://indie.ca/ciwa/index
.htm
Canadian Injured Workers
Alliance

The City of Toronto uses software that can develop alternative career paths for employees who are physically or psychologically unable to perform a particular job by matching their restricted abilities with jobs whose physical and psychological demands they are able to meet. The City's savings from returning employees to productivity have been estimated at \$800 000 to \$1.2 million.[47]

HR and the Responsive Organization

Employee Health and Safety

Corporate downsizings and reengineering aren't necessarily incompatible with improved worker safety, although that might at first seem the case.[1] Downsizing, for instance, strips away several of the lynch pins around which employee safety is normally built. For example, consider the downsizing program of DuPont Canada Inc. The program removed more than half the levels in manufacturing management and reduced the bureaucracy by shifting more decision-making responsibility to nonsupervisory employees. Productivity and profit levels rose, but so did lost-time injuries, which had suddenly taken an ominous upward turn.

Many of the supervisors blamed the eroding safety results on self-management. There were fewer supervisors, and those remaining had to manage more employees and manage differently—acting more like coaches in order to build commitment and teamwork. As a result, the supervisors were spending less time on the shop floor and putting less time into safety, partly on the assumption that the self-managed teams should be managing their own safety programs.

Within a year DuPont Canada had taken steps to turn the safety situation around. In the changeover to self-managed teams, authority and accountability for safety (as well as for some other matters) had unintentionally become blurred.[2] DuPont Canada's senior management responded to this by reemphasizing that each person is responsible for his or her own safety and that supervisors and managers are directly responsible for those who work for them, including their safety. And (at the risk of appearing to rescind some of the team's self-management authority) they reemphasized that violations of safety rules would not be tolerated and that discipline would be reemphasized to ensure that safety rules were followed. In this way, as one DuPont Canada executive later put it:

> Without giving up on self-management, or adding back supervision, people in the company went back to considering safety as an integral part of the job. It became accepted that to be truly world-competitive meant being excellent on all fronts. There was not a significant increase in the use of discipline for safety violations. Reemphasizing the priority of safety seemed to be enough.[3]

1. This is based on J. M. Stewart, "The Multi-Ball Juggler," *Business Quarterly* (Summer 1993), pp. 33–9.
2. Stewart, "The Multi-Ball Juggler," p. 38.
3. Stewart, "The Multi-Ball Juggler," p. 37. ◆

Employee Wellness: Occupational Health Issues and Challenges

A number of health-related issues and challenges can undermine employee performance at work.[48] These include alcoholism and substance abuse, stress, repetitive strain injuries, video display terminals, AIDS, smoking, and workplace violence.

Alcoholism and Substance Abuse

Alcoholism is a serious and widespread disease.[49] A recent Health Canada study[50] found that 85 percent of labour force participants drink, and 10 percent are heavy drinkers. More men (91 percent) and women (86 percent) in managerial and professional positions are drinkers than in any other labour force group. Eight percent of the labour force reported using illicit drugs in the year prior to the study.

The effects of alcoholism on the employee and his or her work are severe.[51] Both the quality and quantity of the work decline sharply. A form of "on-the-job absenteeism" occurs as efficiency declines. The alcoholic's on-the-job accidents do not appear to increase significantly, apparently because he or she becomes much more cautious (but his or her effectiveness suffers as well). However, the *off-the-job* accident rate is three to four times higher than for nonalcoholics. Contrary to popular opinion, turnover among alcoholics is not unusually high. The morale of other workers is affected as they have to do the work of their alcoholic peer.

Recognizing the alcoholic on the job is another problem. The early symptoms such as tardiness can be similar to those of other problems and thus hard to classify. The supervisor is not a psychiatrist, and without specialized training, identifying—and dealing with—the alcoholic is difficult.

A chart showing observable behaviour patterns that indicate alcohol-related problems is presented in **Table 18.1**. It shows that alcohol-related problems range from tardiness in the earliest stages of alcohol abuse to prolonged unpredictable absences in its later stages.[52]

Traditional Techniques The four traditional techniques for dealing with alcoholism, substance abuse, and emotional illness are disciplining, discharge,

TABLE 18.1 Observable Behaviour Patterns

STAGE	ABSENTEEISM	GENERAL BEHAVIOUR	JOB PERFORMANCE

I
Early
	Tardiness
	Quits early
	Absence from work situations
		Complaints from fellow
		  employees for not doing
		  his or her share
		Overreaction
		Complaints of not "feeling well"
			Misses deadlines
			Commits errors (frequently)
			Lower job efficiency

II
Middle
	("I drink to relieve tension")
	Frequent days off for vague
	  or implausible reasons
	
	("I feel guilty about sneaking
	  drinks"; "I have tremors")
		Makes untrue statements
		Marked changes
		Undependable statements
		Avoids fellow employees
		Borrows money from
		  fellow employees
		Exaggerates work
		  accomplishments
		Frequent hospitalization
		Minor injuries on
		  the job (repeatedly)
			Criticism from the boss
			General deterioration
			Cannot concentrate
			Occasional lapse of memory
			
			Warning from boss

III
Late
Middle
	Frequent days off; several
	  days at a time
	Does not return from lunch
	
	("I don't feel like eating";
	  "I don't want to talk
	  about it"; "I like to drink
	  alone")
		Aggressive and belligerent
		  behaviour
		Domestic problems interfere
		  with work
		Financial difficulties
		  (garnishments and so on)
		More frequent hospitalization
		Resignation: does not want
		  to discuss problems
		Problems with laws
		  in the community
			Far below expectation
			
			Punitive disciplinary action

IV
Approaching
Terminal
Stage
	Prolonged unpre-
	  dictable absences
	
	("My job interferes
	  with my drinking")
		Drinking on the job
		  (probably)
		Completely undependable
		Repeated hospitalization
		Serious financial problems
		Serious family problems: divorce
			Uneven
			
			Generally incompetent
			Faces termination or
			  hospitalization

Note: Based on content analysis of files of recovering alcoholics in five organizations. From *Managing and Employing the Handicapped: The Untapped Potential,* by Gopal C. Pati and John I. Adkins, Jr., with Glenn Morrison (Lake Forest, IL: Brace-Park, Human Resource Press, 1981).

Source: Gopal C. Pati and John I. Adkins, Jr., "The Employer's Role in Alcoholism Assistance" *Personnel Journal* 62, no. 7 (July 1983), p. 570.

in-house counselling, and referral to an outside agency. Discipline short of discharge is used more often with alcoholics than for dealing with drug problems or emotional illness. Discharge is frequently used to deal with alcoholism and drug problems after attempts at rehabilitation have failed; it is almost never used in the case of serious emotional illness.[53]

In-house counselling, often one component of an employee assistance program, can be used to assist alcoholics and those with emotional disorders. In most cases the counselling is offered by the HR department or the employer's medical staff. Immediate supervisors with special training also provide counselling in many instances.

Many companies use outside agencies such as Alcoholics Anonymous, psychiatrists, and clinics to assist employees with alcoholism and emotional illness. Outside agencies are used less often in the case of drug problems.

Trice[54] suggests a number of specific actions managers can take to deal with employee alcoholism—actions that all involve supervisory training or company policy. He says supervisors should be trained to identify the alcoholic and the problem he or she creates. Employers should also establish a company policy that recognizes alcoholism as a health problem.

Workplace Substance Abuse and the Law   Because of the seriousness of the problem, most employers are taking additional steps to deal with alcohol and substance abuse on the job.

This is difficult in Canada because employers must balance conflicting legal obligations. On the one hand, Canadian human rights and privacy laws must be respected. Alcoholism and drug addiction are generally considered disabilities under human rights legislation. On the other hand, under occupational health and safety legislation, employers are responsible for maintaining due diligence. Thus it makes sense to utilize drug testing to assess whether employees in "safety-sensitive" positions are drug and alcohol free at work. "Safety sensitive" refers to the actual functions being carried out by the employee rather than to his or her overall job. Thus, an aircraft mechanic would not be considered to be doing safety-sensitive work during an all-day training session on retirement planning.

To date, a federal tribunal has upheld the Toronto Dominion Bank's pre-employment drug testing program, but the Ontario Human Rights Commission decided that Imperial Oil's pre-employment and random drug testing discriminated against a recovering alcoholic employee because the company had not established that drug testing was relevant in assessing whether the employee could perform the job safely.[55] This conundrum is all the more important for employers because of a recent British Columbia Supreme Court decision that an employer who supplies alcohol to employees has the obligation to monitor employees' consumption of alcohol and prevent an employee from driving if he or she is likely to be impaired.[56]

Drug tests are most commonly being used to determine whether an employee is in violation of a company policy on alcohol and drug use. These tests should be conducted only in certain circumstances, including: where there are reasonable grounds based on direct observation to believe the employee is unfit for duty; as part of an accident investigation; as a condition of employment after a rule violation; to monitor an employee after drug treatment; or as a final condition for a job offer.[57]

So far, it appears that employers can have a policy forbidding drugs and alcohol in the workplace; require random drug testing for employees in drug rehabilitation; and conduct mandatory drug testing after an accident or near-accident

The use of drugs, especially in the workplace, is a growing concern for Canadian companies and has led to increased numbers of alcohol and drug abuse counselling programs.

if the employer has reasonable or probable grounds to suspect such abuse contributed to the accident.[58] Beyond that, the situation is less clear.

Guidelines for Dealing with Substance Abuse In general, a clear, well-communicated substance abuse policy that is reasonably and consistently enforced is the employer's best approach. The policy should be based on four components: employee awareness and education about substance abuse; employee access to confidential assistance programs; supervisory training; and methods to identify employees with problems.[59]

Supervisors should be the company's first line of defense in combating substance abuse in the workplace but should not try to be company detectives or medical diagnosticians. Guidelines supervisors should follow include these:

> If an employee appears to be under the influence of drugs or alcohol, ask how the employee feels and look for signs of impairment, such as slurred speech. An employee judged to be unfit for duty may be sent home but not fired on the spot.

> Make a written record of observed behaviour and follow up each incident. In addition to issuing a written reprimand, managers should inform workers of the number of warnings the company will tolerate before requiring termination.

> Troubled employees should be referred to the company's employee assistance program.

Job Stress

Overall, employers need to balance measures to control or deter substance abuse, such as drug testing, with preventive measures such as education and EAPs.

Alcoholism and drug abuse sometimes result from stress, especially *job stress*. Here job-related factors such as overwork, relocation, and problems with customers eventually put the person under such stress that a pathological reaction such as drug abuse occurs. At B.C. Tel, 20 percent of absences from work were found to be due to stress.[60]

There are two main sources of job stress: environmental and personal.[61] First, a variety of external, *environmental factors* can lead to job stress. These include work schedule, pace of work, job security, route to and from work, and the number and nature of customers or clients. Even noise, including people talking and telephones ringing, contributes to stress, with 54 percent of office workers in one recent survey reporting they were bothered often by such noise.[62] Another survey found that 46 percent of Canadian women and 36 percent of Canadian men say that "being too busy" is the main cause of work stress.[63]

However, no two people react to the same job in an identical way, since personal factors also influence stress. For example, Type A personalities—people who are workaholics and who feel driven to always be on time and meet deadlines—normally place themselves under greater stress than do others. Similarly, one's patience, tolerance for ambiguity, self-esteem, health and exercise, and work and sleep patterns can also affect how one reacts to stress. Add to job stress the stress caused by non-job problems like divorce, and many workers are problems waiting to happen.

Job stress has serious consequences for both the employee and the organization. The human consequences of job stress include anxiety, depression, anger, and various physical consequences, such as cardiovascular disease, headaches, and accidents. In some cases it can lead to other human consequences, including drug abuse, over- and undereating, and poor interpersonal relations. Stress also has serious consequences for the organization, including reductions in the quantity and quality of job performance, increased absenteeism and turnover, and increased grievances.

Yet stress is not necessarily dysfunctional. Some people, for example, work well only when under a little stress and find they are more productive as a deadline approaches. Others find that stress may result in a search that leads to a better job or to a career that makes more sense, given the person's aptitudes. A modest level of stress may even lead to more creativity if a competitive situation results in new ideas being generated.[64] As a rule, however, employers don't worry about the sorts of modest stress that lead to such positive consequences. Instead, and for obvious reasons, they focus on dysfunctional stress and its negative consequences.

Reducing Job Stress   There are a number of things a person can do to alleviate stress, ranging from commonsense remedies such as getting more sleep and eating better to more exotic remedies such as biofeedback and meditation. Finding a more suitable job, getting counselling, and planning and organizing each day's activities are other sensible responses.[65] In his book *Stress and the Manager,* Dr. Karl Albrecht suggests the following to reduce job stress.[66]

> Build rewarding, pleasant, cooperative relationships with as many colleagues and employees as possible.
>
> Don't bite off more than you can chew.
>
> Build an especially effective and supportive relationship with your boss.
>
> Understand the boss's problems and help him or her to understand yours.
>
> Negotiate for realistic deadlines on important projects. Be prepared to propose deadlines, instead of having them imposed.
>
> Study the future. Learn as much as possible about likely coming events and get as much lead time as possible to prepare for them.
>
> Find time every day for detachment and relaxation.
>
> Take a walk around the office now and then to keep refreshed and alert.
>
> Make a noise survey of the work area and find ways to reduce unnecessary noise.
>
> Get away from the work area from time to time for a change of scene and a change of mind.
>
> Reduce the amount of trivia requiring attention. Delegate routine paperwork to others whenever possible.
>
> Limit interruptions. Try to schedule certain periods of "uninterruptibility" each day and conserve other periods for personal purposes.
>
> Don't put off dealing with distasteful problems.
>
> Make a constructive "worry list." Write down the problems of concern and beside each write down what you're going to do about it, so that none of the problems will be hovering around the edges of your consciousness.

The organization and its HR specialists and supervisors can also play a role in identifying and reducing job stress. For the supervisor, this includes monitoring each employee's performance to identify symptoms of stress, and then informing the person of the organizational remedies that may be available, such as job transfers or counselling. The HR specialist's role includes using attitude surveys to identify organizational sources of stress, refining selection and placement procedures to ensure effective person–job match, and providing career planning aimed at ensuring that the employee moves toward a job that makes sense in terms of his or her aptitudes.

Managers should also be aware of probable gender differences in job stress. The evidence is far from conclusive. However, studies suggest that women competing in a male-dominated environment are subject to chronic stress, that female physicians report more stress-related problems than men, and that any such differences may be attributable to distinct stressors for women, such as harassment and particularly sexual harassment.[67] This suggests the importance of reducing gender-related potential stressors such as sexual harassment and "glass ceiling" impediments to advancement.

Based on a survey of 1 299 employees by one insurance company, the researchers suggest the following steps employers can take to reduce workplace stress:

Allow employees to talk freely with one another and to consult with colleagues about work issues.

Reduce personal conflicts on the job.

Give employees adequate control over how they do their work.

Ensure adequate staffing and expense budgets.

Have open communication between managers and employees.

Support employees' efforts, for instance, by regularly asking how they are doing.

Provide competitive personal leave and vacation benefits.

Maintain current levels of employee benefits, since benefits reductions lead to stress.

Reduce the amount of red tape for employees.

Recognize and reward employees for their accomplishments and contributions.

Ensure effective job fit, since stress overload can result when workers are mismatched with jobs.[68]

Giving employees more control over their jobs can also mediate the effects of job stress. This is illustrated by the results of a recent study,[69] in which the psychological strain caused by job stress was reduced by the amount of control employees had over their jobs. The less stressful jobs did have high demands in terms of quantitative work load, the amount of attention the employees had to pay to their work, and work pressure. But they also ranked high in task clarity, job control, supervisory support, and employee skill utilization.[70] The researchers conclude that "to achieve a balanced system, that is, to reduce psychological strain, [job] demands and [ambiguity regarding the future of the job] need to be lowered, while skill utilization, task clarity, job control, and supervisor support need to be increased."[71]

Burnout

burnout
The total depletion of physical and mental resources caused by excessive striving to reach an unrealistic work-related goal.

Dr. Herbert Freudenberger, an expert on the overachiever, says that many people may be falling victim to **burnout**—the total depletion of physical and mental resources—caused by excessive striving to reach an unrealistic work-related goal. Burnout, he contends, is often the result of too much job stress, especially when that stress is combined with a preoccupation with attaining unattainable work-related goals. Freudenberger lists other signs of possible impending burnout:[72]

You are unable to relax.

You identify so closely with your activities that when they fall apart you do too.

The positions you worked so hard to attain often seem meaningless now.

You are working more now but enjoying it less.

Your need for a particular crutch such as smoking, liquor, or tranquillizers is increasing.

You are constantly irritable, and family and friends often comment that you don't look well.

You would describe yourself as a workaholic and constantly strive to obtain your work-related goals to the exclusion of almost all outside interest.

Who Suffers from Burnout   Burnout, Freudenberger says, particularly occurs with goal-oriented individuals who are over-dedicated to what they undertake. Burnout victims often don't lead well-balanced lives; virtually all their energies are focussed on achieving their work-related goals. The burnout victim is usually a workaholic for whom the constant stress of seeking an unattainable goal, to the exclusion of other activities, can lead to physical and perhaps mental collapse. This needn't be limited to upwardly mobile executives: For instance, social-work counsellors caught up in their clients' problems are often burnout victims.

What can a burnout candidate do? Here are some suggestions:

Break patterns. First, survey how you spend your time. Are you doing a variety of things or the same one over and over? The more well-rounded your life is, the better protected you are against burnout. If you've stopped trying new activities, start them again—for instance, travel or new hobbies.

Get away from it all periodically. Schedule occasional periods of introspection during which you can get away from your usual routine, perhaps alone, to seek a perspective on where you are and where you are going.

Reassess goals in terms of their intrinsic worth. Are the goals you've set for yourself attainable? Are they really worth the sacrifices you'll have to make?

Think about work. Could you do as good a job without being so intense or by also pursuing outside interests?

Reduce stress. Organize your time more effectively, build a better relationship with your boss, negotiate realistic deadlines, find time during the day for detachment and relaxation, reduce unnecessary noise around your office, and limit interruptions.

Avoiding Stress-Related Disability Claims   As discussed in chapter 14, depression, anxiety and stress account for 20 percent to 25 percent of disability claims. Minimizing such claims usually begins with good supervision and includes, at a minimum, the following steps:

Adequately Train Supervisors   Make supervisors aware of the possible disability implications of creating stressful situations. Train them in interpersonal skills, performance evaluation, communication, discipline and discharge, and other matters like conflict management.

Open Up Communication   Let employees know that channels of communication are open and that if they have a problem it can be brought to the attention of senior managers.

Use Attitude Surveys   Use a survey to monitor attitudes and in particular supervisor-caused stress.

Hire Wisely   Make every effort to hire the right people for the right job and give them realistic previews of what the job entails. Check references carefully, and watch how the applicant acts in the interview, since the interview itself is a stressful situation.

Promote EAP Use   Encourage the use of this service and follow-up counselling.

Repetitive Strain Injuries

Repetitive strain injuries (RSIs) are fast becoming the most common occupational injury. An average RSI entails the loss of 83 working days, and costs $11 000. The physical demands of new technologies have brought a new set of RSIs, most notably carpal tunnel syndrome, a tingling or numbness in the fingers caused by the narrowing of a tunnel of bones and ligaments in the wrist. RSIs have three causes: repetitive movements, awkward postures, and forceful exertion. Pre-existing conditions such as arthritis can exacerbate RSIs. Warning signs of RSI include tightness or stiffness in the hands, elbow, wrists, shoulder, and neck; numbness and tingling in fingertips; hands falling asleep; and frequent dropping of tools. The most common symptoms are neck and shoulder strain.[73]

ergonomics
The art of fitting the workstation and work tool to the individual.

Ergonomics   Fortunately, RSIs are extremely preventable. Poorly designed workstations and bad posture are among the primary conditions leading to RSI. **Ergonomics** is the art of fitting the workstation and work tools to the individual, which is necessary because there is no such thing as an average body. **Figure 18.6** shows the difference between a conventional tool and an ergonomically designed one. The most important preventive measure is to have employees take short breaks every half hour or hour to do simple stretches at their workstations.[74] Software is now available that counts keystrokes over time and flashes a message to the employee to take a break and do the exercise shown on the screen.[75]

Ergonomically designed workstations have been found to increase productivity and efficiency as well as reducing injuries. One study found that ergonomic improvements reduced errors by 93 percent, and increased efficiency by 33 percent, while musculoskeletal problems decreased by 50 percent.[76]

**Figure 18.6
Ergonomic Hammer
Configuration**

Source: J. Montgomery, *Occupational Health and Safety*, (Toronto: Nelson Canada, 1996), p.215. Used with permission.

Hammer configurations

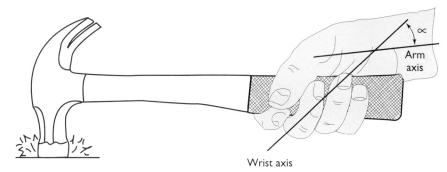

a) Conventional hammer

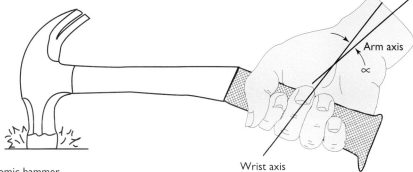

b) Ergonomic hammer

In late 1993, Canadian Tire Acceptance Corporation Ltd. in Welland, Ontario was facing increasing employee complaints of pain and stiffness, but no related lost-time injuries. A root cause analysis found that 60 percent of employees had RSI symptoms, and 50 percent had sought medical attention for them. The company launched a comprehensive RSI prevention program using internal and external community resources. The program included modification of workstations, wellness initiatives, stress management, education on risk factors, and proactive occupational therapy for RSI sufferers. Three years later, the company had no RSI-related disability claims. The success of the program was attributed to process champions, stakeholder participation, and management commitment to employees' well being.[77]

Video Display Terminals

The fact that many workers today must spend hours each day working with video display terminals (VDTs) is creating new health problems at work. A U.S. study found that short-term eye problems like burning, itching, and tearing as well as eye strain and eye soreness are common complaints among video display operators. Surveys have found that 47 percent to 76 percent of operators complain of such problems, and while no permanent vision problems have surfaced yet, long-term studies are underway. With respect to radiation, researchers conclude that "the VDT does not present a radiation hazard to the employees working at or near a terminal."[78] (However, that point remains a matter of heated debate.) Another study calmed some VDT-related fears by concluding that pregnant women who use computer monitors do not run any greater risk of having miscarriages than do women who are not exposed to VDTs.[79]

www.globalmedic.com
Online Health and Wellness Company

Backaches and neckaches are widespread among display users. These often occur because employees try to compensate for display problems like glare and immovable keyboards by manoeuving into awkward body positions. Researchers also found that employees who used VDTs and had heavy work loads were prone to psychological distress like anxiety, irritability, and fatigue. There may also be a tendency for computer users to suffer from RSI, such as carpel tunnel syndrome, caused by repetitive use of the hands and arms at uncomfortable angles.[80]

General recommendations regarding the use of VDTs can be summarized as follows:

1. Give employees rest breaks—a 15-minute rest break after two hours of continuous VDT work for operators under moderate work loads and 15-minute breaks every hour for those with heavy work loads. Some union contracts state specific break times for VDT workers.

2. Design the maximum flexibility into the work station so that it can be adapted to the individual operator. For example, use movable keyboards, adjustable chairs with midback supports, and a video display for which screen height and position are independently adjustable.

3. Reduce glare with devices such as shades over windows, terminal screen hoods properly positioned, antiglare VDT screen filters, and recessed or indirect lighting.

4. Give VDT workers a complete preplacement vision exam to ensure properly corrected vision for reduced visual strain.

Many VDT vision problems can be reduced by using the right equipment and a little common sense. The basic worker–task relationship is fairly straightforward when paperwork tasks are involved, since the light just bounces from the ceiling to the paper and then to the worker's eyes. But once a VDT is added, an employee may find himself or herself dealing with direct glare as well as reflected glare, in addition to the visual demands of watching the small screen. Therefore adjustable stands, partitions, Venetian blind–type window controls, and screen filters can help minimize VDT-caused visual problems.[81]

AIDS and the Workplace

AIDS (Acquired Immune Deficiency Syndrome) undermines the body's immune system, leaving the victim susceptible to a wide range of serious and fatal diseases.

Some of the most crucial AIDS-related questions employers must deal with concern their legal responsibilities in dealing with AIDS sufferers. While case law is only now evolving on this issue, several tentative conclusions are warranted. First, an employee cannot be singled out to be tested for AIDS, because to do so would subject the person to discriminatory treatment under human rights legislation. Similarly, while a physical exam that includes an AIDS test can be a condition of employment, refusing to hire the person because of positive test results would be a human rights code violation in most employment situations. Mandatory leave cannot be required of a person with AIDS unless work performance has deteriorated, and preemployment inquiries about AIDS (similar to inquiries about any other illnesses or disabilities) are not permitted under human rights legislation in most jurisdiction. Providing sympathy and support and making reasonable accommodations to persons with AIDS, and using education and counselling to deal with the fears of the person's coworkers, seem to be the only concrete prescriptions for dealing with the concerns AIDS will elicit at work.[82]

From a practical point of view, procedures for dealing with AIDS usually begin with a statement of the firm's AIDS policy. The purpose of the AIDS policy is twofold: to reassure employees regarding the impossibility of spreading AIDS through casual contact, and to lay out the legal rights of employees who are diagnosed with an AIDS-related condition. The policy, therefore, usually contains a medical overview of what is known about AIDS and lists a number of supervisory responsibilities, such as maintaining confidentiality of all medical conditions and records.[83] Points to be covered in an AIDS policy might include:

Discrimination or harassment will not be tolerated.

The company will reasonably accommodate employees.

Medical information will remain confidential.

HIV-positive employees (HIV is the precurser to AIDS) should be allowed to continue working as long as they can safely and effectively perform the essential functions of their jobs.

There is no medical basis for employees to refuse to work with fellow employees or customers who are HIV-positive.

The concerns of employees who fear HIV-positive coworkers and customers should be taken seriously and addressed with appropriate information and counselling.[84]

Workplace Smoking

The Nature of the Problem Smoking is a serious problem for employees and employers. Employers face higher costs deriving from higher supplementary health care and disability insurance, as smoking is associated with numerous health problems. Smoking employees have increased absenteeism and reduced productivity (which occurs when, for instance, a smoker takes a ten-minute break to finish a cigarette outside). Studies even show that for some reason smokers

Occupational health and safety legislation requires employers to file reports, monitor employee exposure to various hazards to note trends, and provide employees with information on hazards in their workplaces. Computers can assist in all three areas.

Reporting   Most government forms can be formatted and formulated on a company's computer so that only the raw data need to be entered. The computer will perform the instructed calculations and print out the results in an acceptable format. If a piece of information has been input in error, only the figure needs to be changed. Recalculations are automatic. With some forms, the inputting of results takes several hours. This task is completed in minutes with a computer.

Monitoring   Computers can track personal exposure level (PEL) for noise, particulates, vapours, or other contaminants for a given location, giving timely warnings of trigger points. A dosimeter sensor can be plugged into a personal computer to translate readings on an hourly basis. Not only does this protect, say, the hearing of workers; it can also spot equipment that needs servicing if, for example, a given decibel level indicates increased friction. Trends of various hazards can also be plotted for work redesign to make the workplace safer.

Communicating   The effectiveness of training in any area depends in part on the Hawthorne effect: the degree to which the trainee feels that the training is important and accurate. When employers communicate the hazards of a workplace, employees might not listen because they feel that they will not be exposed to those particular hazards, or that they are already careful, or that their work situation does not support those safeguards. If the supervisors push for results to the point of ignoring torn gloves, holes in respirators, inadequate ventilation, or workers who are not wearing safety glasses, then employees will ignore the training. Also, employees may not understand key parts of the training.

Interactive computers can help with some of these problems. If employees are assigned to work with a hazardous substance that was discussed with them a few weeks before, their knowledge may have become hazy. Access to a personal computer can allow the employees to refresh their memory on how to handle the substance and what to avoid doing. If there are words within the explanation that are not clear, an interactive program will allow the employees to question that word (and any words in the subsequent definition) until they are ready to return to the original explanation. How recently employees have reviewed the information correlates with the degree of retention, and computer-assisted instruction provides training any time the employees need help.◆

have a significantly greater risk of occupational accidents than do nonsmokers, as well as much higher absenteeism rates. In general, "smoking employees are less healthy than non-smokers, are absent more, make more and more expensive claims for health and disability benefits, and endanger coworkers who breathe smokey air."[85]

Smokers who are also exposed to other carcinogens in the workplace, such as asbestos, have dramatically higher rates of lung cancer, as shown in **Figure 18.7**. The effects of on-the-job exposure to radon on lung cancer rates were found to last up to 14 years, and the cancer rates were greatly increased for smokers.[86]

Smoking Policies   Governments have taken the lead in banning smoking in an increasing number of places. The Ontario, Nova Scotia, and federal governments

Figure 18.7
Smoking and Asbestos Exposure

Source: M.M. Finklestein, "Risky Business," *OH&S Canada* (September/October 1996), p. 32. Used with permission.

Age-standardized lung cancer death rates for cigarette smoking and/or occupational exposure to asbestos dust compared with no smoking and no occupational exposure to asbestos dust.*

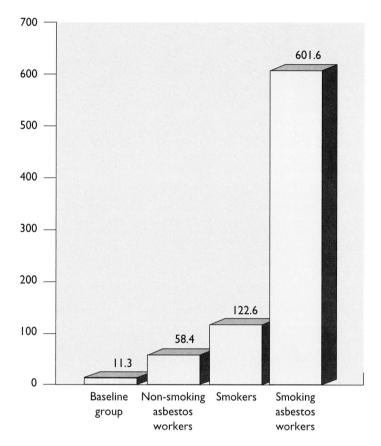

*Rates are per 100 000 persons per year

have each enacted legislation that prohibits smoking in enclosed workplaces, subject to the employer's right to designate areas where smoking is permitted (up to 20 percent of a workplace in Ontario). Alberta and Prince Edward Island have anti-smoking laws for government workplaces, and British Columbia has declared second-hand tobacco smoke to be an occupational hazard. Overall, the movement to eliminate smoking in all indoor public places appears to be gathering strength.[87]

From a practical point of view, most employers probably should be considering some smoking restrictions. As summarized in **Figure 18.8**, policies can range from total prohibitions to "Smokers and nonsmokers should courteously work out a compromise among themselves."

Violence at Work

The Nature of the Problem Violence against employees at work has become increasingly common in Canada. One EAP reported that 52 percent of traumas handled in 1993 involved violence, up from 30 percent in 1990.[88] Victims are

**Figure 18.8
Degrees of Restrictions
on Employee
Smoking—A Scale**

Source: J. Carroll Swart,
"Corporate Smoking Policies:
Today and Tomorrow,"
Personnel (August 1988), p. 62.

Policy A

It is the policy of the company to hire nonsmokers only. Smoking is prohibited off the job, and smoking is prohibited on the job.

Policy B

Smoking is prohibited in all areas on company premises.

Policy C

Smoking is prohibited in all areas in company buildings.

Policy D

Smoking is prohibited in all areas in company buildings, with few exceptions. Smoking is permitted in the smoking section of the cafeteria (or room with a similar function in the company, if there is no cafeteria); in specially designated smoking rooms (smoking lounges); and in private offices, which may be designated "smoking permitted" or "no smoking" by the occupant.

Policy E

Smoking is prohibited in all common areas except those designated "smoking permitted." Smoking is permitted in specially designated smoking rooms (smoking lounges). In open offices and in shared workspace areas where smokers and nonsmokers work together, where smokers' and nonsmokers' preferences are in conflict, employees and management will endeavour to find a satisfactory compromise. On failure to find a compromise, the preferences of the nonsmoker will prevail.

Private offices may be designated "smoking permitted" or "no smoking" by the occupant.

Policy F

It is the policy of the company to respect the preferences of both smokers and nonsmokers in company buildings. Where smokers' and nonsmokers' preferences are in conflict, employees and management will endeavour to find a satisfactory compromise. On failure to reach a compromise, the preferences of the nonsmoker will prevail.

Policy G

The company places no restrictions on employee smoking (the company does not have a smoking policy).

"Smoking Permitted" is synonymous with "Designated Smoking Area." The latter term is increasing in usage.

A basic assumption is that all companies have policies prohibiting smoking in areas where there are safety and fire hazards and where sensitive equipment may be damaged. In reference to the scale above, the term "smoking policy" refers to a written statement or statements that place restrictions on smoking and intend to accommodate health concerns.

usually women in health care professions.[89] A study of 45 000 nurses reported that 68 percent had suffered physical violence, ranging from slaps to jaw-breaking punches. One author noted that when police officers are attacked, charges of assault or resisting arrest are laid, whereas for nurses, being attacked is seen as part of the job.[90]

Workplace violence arises in three situations:

1. An employee is angry with management or a coworker
2. A customer/client is angry with the provider/denier of a product or service
3. A violent outsider attacks by chance.[91]

Workplace violence is about fear, about people losing control, and about implicit contracts between employer and employee being broken. Triggers for workplace violence include poor management relations, ambiguous work standards, inconsistent rule enforcement, ignoring cultural concerns, failure to address threats of violence, and insufficient worksite security.[92] One psychologist suggests that violence is a reaction to unbearable stress; and warns that internal threats cannot be effectively handled through standard discipline and HR procedures.[93]

Employers want to avoid such violence on humanitarian grounds, but there are legal reasons to do so as well. Employers may be found liable for the violent acts of their employees.[94] For example, an employer may be sued directly by the victim of an employee's violent act on the basis that the employer negligently hired or negligently retained someone who the employer should reasonably have known could cause the violent act. Even if the employee was not negligently hired or retained, employers may still in general be liable for employees' violent acts when the employees' actions were performed within the scope of employment. In two recent B.C. court cases relating to sexual abuse of children in government funded youth care facilities, the government was found to be vicariously liable.[95]

Prevention and Control of Workplace Violence   There are several concrete steps employers can take to reduce the incidence of workplace violence. These include instituting improved security arrangements, improving employee screening, training for violence reduction, and enhancing attention to retaining employees.

Heightened Security Measures   Heightened security measures are an employer's first line of defense against workplace violence, whether that violence derives from coworkers, customers, or outsiders. Sensible precautions for reducing the risk of workplace violence[96] include improving external lighting; using drop safes to minimize cash on hand and posting signs noting that only a limited amount of cash is on hand; installing silent alarms and surveillance cameras; increasing the number of staff on duty; providing staff training in conflict resolution and nonviolent response; and closing establishments during high-risk hours late at night and early in the morning.[97]

Improved Employee Screening   Screening out potentially explosive internal and external applicants is the employer's next line of defense. At a minimum this means instituting a sound preemployment investigation. A detailed employment application should be completed, and each applicant's employment history, education background, and references should be solicited.[98] A personal interview, job-related testing, and a review and vertification of all information provided should also be included in the selection process. Sample interview questions to ask might include, for instance, "What frustrates you?" and "Who was your worst supervisor and why?"[99]

Certain background circumstances should provide a red flag indicating the need for a more in-depth background investigation to help screen out potentially violent employees. The investigation report provides a record that everything that could have been done was done to screen out the violent employee. Red flags include:[100]

An unexplained gap in employment.

Incomplete or false information on the résumé or application.

A negative, unfavourable, or false reference.

Prior insubordinate or violent behaviour on the job.

A criminal history involving harassing or violent behaviour.

A prior termination for cause with a suspicious (or no) explanation.

Strong indications of instability in the individual's work or personal life suggested, for example, by frequent job changes or geographic moves.

Lost licences or accreditations.[101]

Workplace Violence Training   Enhanced security and screening can be supplemented with workplace violence training. Video training programs explain what workplace violence is, identify its causes and signs, and offer tips on how to prevent it and what to do when it occurs.[102] Supervisors can also be trained to identify the types of multiple clues that typically precede violent incidents. Common signs include:[103]

Verbal threats. Individuals often talk about what they may do. An employee might say, "Bad things are going to happen to so-and-so," or "That propane tank in the back could blow up easily."

Physical actions. Troubled employees may try to intimidate others, gain access to places where they do not belong, or flash a concealed weapon in the workplace to test reactions.

Frustration. Most cases do not involve a panicked individual; a more likely scenario would involve an employee who has a frustrated sense of entitlement to a promotion, for example.

Obsession. An employee may hold a grudge against a coworker or supervisor, and some cases stem from romantic interest.[104]

Enhanced Attention to Retaining Employees   Employers can also enhance their procedures for evaluating which employees should or should not be retained. Particularly given the potential liability of retaining employees who subsequently commit violent acts, circumstances to beware of in deciding whether or not to retain employees include:[105]

An act of violence on or off the job.

Erratic behaviour evidencing a loss of perception or awareness of actions.

Overly defensive, obsessive, or paranoid tendencies.

Overly confrontational or antisocial behaviour.

Sexually aggressive behaviour.

Isolationist or loner tendencies.

Insubordinate behaviour with a suggestion of violence.

Tendency to overreact to criticism.

Exaggerated interest in war, guns, violence, mass murders, catastrophes, and so on.

The commission of a serious breach of security.

Possession of weapons, guns, knives, or like items at the workplace.

Violation of privacy rights of others such as searching desks or stalking.

Chronic complaining and the raising of frequent, unreasonable grievances.

A retributory or get-even attitude.

Other Commonsense Steps to Take   Beyond these actions, there are a number of other commonsense steps an employer can take. While they should always be taken in any organization, they are repeated here for their relevance: Reduce unnecessary job stress; avoid affronts to employees' dignity (such as public condemnations); solicit and promptly address grievances; and institute employee assistance programs.[106]

Dealing with Angry Employees   What should a supervisor do when confronted by an angry, potentially explosive employee? Here are some suggestions:[107]

Diversity Counts
In Occupational Health and Safety

While there are more fatal occupational injuries to men than to women, the proportion of women who are victims of assault is much higher. Of all women who die on the job, 39 percent are the victims of assault, for instance, whereas only 18 percent of males who die at work are murdered. Violence against women in the workplace is therefore a particularly serious problem.[1]

Fatal workplace violence against women has three main sources. Of all females murdered at work, over three-fourths were victims of random criminal violence carried out by an assailant unknown to the victim, as might occur during a robbery. The remaining criminal acts were carried out either by coworkers or by family members or previous friends or acquaintances.

There's nothing "typical" about workplace violence, but research sheds some light on the typical female victim (who, remember, is often the victim of random violence). The typical female assault victim is a white female (79 percent), in her early thirties (mean age approximately 31), working as a salesperson (31 percent) in a convenience store (46 percent), and is shot by an unknown assailant (88 percent) about 11:00 p.m.[2]

While workplace violence data would be tragic under any circumstances, these "typical" figures are particularly disconcerting. As one expert notes, jobs that involve serving the public, such as convenience-store employee, fast-food server, or retail store cashier are exactly the sorts of jobs that are easily filled by women, since they offer flexible hours, require minimal training, and allow women to raise children and work their way through school.[3] It is therefore particularly ". . . shocking to think that women carry the horrible risk of being murdered while working at the very job they need to survive."[4]

Concrete security improvements including better lighting, cash drop-boxes, and similar steps are especially pertinent if such violent acts against women are to be reduced. Some firms have taken additional steps, including implementing a task force on workplace violence, training supervisors to identify which employees may be violent, and establishing an employee assistance program to which a new workplace violence prevention team refers potentially violent employees.[5]

1. This is based on Beverly Younger, "Violence Against Women in the Workplace," *Employee Assistance Quarterly* 9, no. 3/4 (1994), pp. 113–33.
2. Younger, "Violence Against Women," p. 120.
3. Younger, "Violence Against Women," p. 121.
4. Younger, "Violence Against Women."
5. Younger, "Violence Against Women," pp. 129–30.

Make eye contact.

Stop any other work and give full attention to the employee.

Speak in a calm voice and create a relaxed environment.

Be open and honest.

Let the person have his or her say.

Ask for specific examples of what the person is upset about.

Be careful to define the problem.

Ask open-ended questions and explore all sides of the issue.

Legal Constraints on Reducing Workplace Violence   As sensible as it is to try to screen out potentially violent employees, doing so incurs the risk of liability and lawsuits. As explained in chapter 7, human rights legislation limits the use of criminal records in hiring decisions. Eliminating workplace violence while safely navigating the legal shoals is, therefore, a tricky business.

Chapter Review

Summary

1. Occupational health and safety is of concern to managers at least partly because of the staggering number of deaths and accidents occurring at work. There are three reasons for safety programs: moral, legal, and economic.

2. The purpose of occupational health and safety legislation is to ensure every working person a safe and healthy workplace. Occupational health and safety standards are very complete and detailed and are enforced through a system of workplace inspections. Occupational health and safety inspectors can issue citations and recommend penalties.

3. Supervisors play a key role in monitoring workers for safety. Workers in turn have a responsibility to act safely. A commitment to safety on the part of top management that is filtered down through the management ranks is an important aspect of any safety program.

4. There are three basic causes of accidents: chance occurrences, unsafe conditions, and unsafe acts on the part of employees. In addition, three other work-related factors (the job itself, the work schedule, and the psychological climate) also contribute to accidents.

5. Unsafe acts on the part of employees are a second basic cause of accidents. Such acts are to some extent the result of certain behaviour tendencies on the part of employees, and these tendencies are possibly the result of certain personal characteristics.

6. Most experts doubt that there are accident-prone people who have accidents regardless of the job. Instead, the consensus seems to be that the person who is accident-prone in one job may not be on a different job. For example, vision is related to accident frequency for drivers and machine operators but might not be for other workers, such as accountants.

7. One approach to preventing accidents is to reduce unsafe conditions. Another approach is to reduce unsafe acts—for example, through selection and placement, education and training, positive reinforcement, and senior management commitment.

8. Alcoholism, drug addiction, and emotional illness are important and growing health problems among employees. Alcoholism is a particularly serious problem and one that can drastically lower the effectiveness of an organization. Techniques to deal with these challenges include disciplining, discharge, in-house counselling, and referrals to an outside agency.

9. Stress and burnout are other potential health problems at work. Job stress can be reduced by getting away from work for a while each day, delegating, and developing a "worry list."

10. Repetitive strain injuries, video display terminals, AIDS, and workplace smoking are other employee health issues discussed in this chapter.

11. Violence against employees is a serious problem at work. Steps that can reduce workplace violence include improved security arrangements, better employee screening, and violence-reduction training.

Key Terms

burnout
ergonomics
occupational health and
    safety legislation

unsafe acts
unsafe conditions

Workplace Hazardous
    Materials Information
    System (WHMIS)

Discussion Questions and Exercises

1. How can employers go about providing a safer environment for their employees to work in?
2. Discuss how to minimize the occurrence of unsafe acts on the part of employees.
3. Discuss the basic facts about occupational health and safety legislation—its purpose, standards, inspection, and rights and responsibilities.
4. Discuss the three requirements of the WHMIS legislation.
5. Explain the supervisor's role in safety.
6. Explain what causes unsafe acts.
7. Describe at least five techniques for reducing accidents.
8. Analyze the legal and safety issues concerning AIDS.
9. Explain how to reduce stress at work.

Application Exercises

RUNNING CASE: Carter Cleaning Company

The New Safety Program

Employee health and safety is a very important matter in the laundry and cleaning business. Each facility is a small production plant in which machines, powered by high-pressure steam and compressed air, work at high temperatures washing, cleaning, and pressing garments, often under very hot, slippery conditions. Chemical vapours are continually produced, and caustic chemicals are used in the cleaning process. High-temperature stills are almost continually "cooking down" cleaning solvents in order to remove impurities so that the solvents can be reused. If a mistake is made in this process—like injecting too much steam into the still—a boilover occurs, in which boiling chemical solvent erupts out of the still and over the floor, and on anyone who happens to be standing in its way.

As a result of these hazards and the fact that chemically hazardous waste is continually produced, government agencies have instituted strict guidelines regarding the management of dry cleaning facilities. For example, posters have to be placed in each store notifying employees of their right to be told what hazardous chemicals they are dealing with and what the proper method for handling each chemical is. Special waste-management firms must be used to pick up and properly dispose of the hazardous waste.

A chronic problem the Carters (and most other laundry owners) have is the unwillingness on the part of the cleaning–spotting workers to wear safety goggles. Not all the chemicals they use require safety goggles, but some—like the hydrofluorous acid used to remove rust stains from garments—are very dangerous. The latter is kept in special plastic containers, since it dissolves glass. The problem is that wearing safety goggles can be troublesome. They are somewhat uncomfortable, and they also become smudged easily and thus cut down on visibility. As a result, Jack has always found it almost impossible to get these employees to wear their goggles.

Questions

1. How should the firm go about identifying hazardous conditions that should be rectified?

2. Would it be advisable for the firm to set up a procedure for screening out accident-prone individuals?

3. How would you suggest the Carters get all employees to behave more safely at work? Also how would you advise them to get those who should be wearing goggles to do so?

CASE INCIDENT: Hartley Corporation

The Hartley Corporation is composed of ten autonomous divisions and corporate headquarters. The case focuses on the Bien Works. Its organization is illustrated in **Figure 18.9**. Bien Works is housed in a five-story building erected in 1904. The top two floors are not used, since they are too dangerous. The second and third floors have holes and rotted places in them.

Figure 18.9
Organization Chart: Bien Works

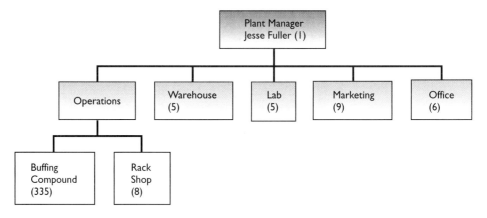

The third floor holds the rack shop, lab, and marketing departments. The second floor contains the office, some warehousing, and some buffing compound production lines. The first floor contains the warehousing for heavier materials and the rest of the manufacturing lines. The main operation is manufacturing. The rack shop is a support unit to make racks for drying chemicals. The work is nonunion.

Jesse Fuller has been with Hartley for 20 years, all of it in conjunction with the Bien Works. He holds a B.Sc. in chemistry from Northern University. He worked his way through school. He's done almost everything at Bien. He started as a supervisor in the manufacturing unit. He's run the rack shop, supervised the warehouse for two years, and sold the compounds. The office and lab are white-collar or technical jobs, so he hasn't worked there. His employees like him, although they are a bit afraid of him, too. He has a terrible temper, which he loses about once a month. When this happens, everyone tries to get out of his way.

Jesse is now 53 years old. He's happy with the Bien Works. He likes the town and wouldn't move. Bien is like his own firm, since he's isolated geographically from Hartley. Since Bien makes more money for Hartley than his budget calls for, it lets Jesse alone. He has lower turnover than expected. Absenteeism is also low. All in all, Hartley and Jesse are happy with the Bien Works.

Except for health and safety. For some reason, the health and safety inspector came around Bien often. The local inspector was James Munsey. In April, he came to Bien when Jesse was at a meeting at Hartley. He determined that the buffing manufacturing was producing unsafe gases. As is his right, he shut the plant down that day. Jesse flew back and modified the gas filters. James passed the filters, and Bien started production again.

In May, James came back and shut the plant again when Jesse was at a Rotary meeting. Again, the filters were cleaned and modified. This time Jesse was really angry. After the plant was reopened and James gone, Jesse held a meeting of all employees. At the meeting, he said: "Look, this inspector is killing us. This is an old works. We can't afford to be shut down. At my recent meeting at corporate headquarters, I tried to make the case that we needed a new building here. The sharp pencil boys pointed out that we are profitable now but not if we have to build a new plant. The industry is overcrowded, and Hartley will close this plant rather than spend money on it. If we get shut down or have to buy a lot of antipollution garbage, they could shut us down. That inspector is the enemy—just like a traffic cop. We've got to pull together, or we could all sink together."
The employees had never seen Jesse so angry before, and they feared for their jobs now more than ever. There was a lot of unemployment in the area.

Questions

1. What do you think of Jesse's approach to safety?
2. What changes, if any, would you recommend? Explain why.

Source: William F. Glueck and George Stevens, *Cases and Exercises in Personnel/Human Resources Management,* 3rd ed. (Plano, TX: Business Publications, 1983), pp. 145–6. Copyright 1983, Business Publications, Inc. Reprinted by permission.

Human Resources Management Simulation

Exercise 15 in the simulations and exercises manual provides an opportunity to prepare a policy manual on occupational health and safety. It should be indicated that all policies required by law are being included, and that in addition, further policies are being included due to the employer's concern for the health and safety of their employees. In this situation, where the employer wants to maintain a nonunion plant, some indication of the costs that would be incurred by the employer in maintaining these employee safety policies should be given. Exercise 16 requires a report in support of the establishment of an EAP. Try to include some estimates of return on investment. Consider carefully the labour relations implications of implementing the program in the nonunion plant only.

Video Case

Stress

Stress is something all employees have in common. Stressors are everywhere in today's organizations, where employees are asked to do more with less, under the constant threat of downsizing. Stress is estimated to cost Canadian business $30 billion per year through decreased productivity, absenteeism, disability claims, and death. Disability claims for depression topped $300 million in 1994, and the total costs related to depression are estimated at $3 billion per year.

Corporations have taken a number of steps to try to reduce these costs. Disability management consultants provided by insurance companies can help businesses to cut the costs of stress-related disability claims by finding where the stress points are in the client's organizations. Many companies have established employee assistance programs (EAPs), which provide outsourced confidential counselling to help employees deal with problems that create stress, such as divorce and substance abuse. Others have implemented wellness programs to try to prevent stress. These include flexible hours, on-site fitness facilities, and daycare.

With profit margins slipping due to global competition, many companies are trying to gain a competitive advantage through their human resources. Thus it is imperative to avoid the increased costs and decreased productivity resulting from stress-related problems. As there is no end in sight to the ongoing reality of stress at work, stress management has become a growth industry.

Questions

1. What proactive measures, other than those discussed in the video, can be taken by companies to prevent stress-related problems among their employees? What proactive measures can employees take?

2. The video provides the example of Nortel's 700 percent return on investment in their EAP. Contact three companies with EAPs and gather whatever data they have on the cost-effectiveness of their EAPs.

3. Why are some companies not interested in establishing wellness programs? What arguments might be used to try to persuade them to reconsider?

Video Resource: CBC, *Venture*, "Stress," March 3, 1996.

Take It to the Net

Check out our Companion Website at

http://www.prenticehall.ca/dessler

for a multitude of practice questions, key terms and concepts, Weblinks to related sites, newsgroups, CBC video updates, and more.

Notes

1. Statistics Canada, *Health Status of Canadians*, chapter 6, 1994.
2. This section is based on T.A. Opie and L. Bates, *1997 Canadian Master Labour Guide* (CCH Canada Inc.), pp. 1015–34.
3. J. Montgomery, *Occupational Health and Safety* (Toronto: Nelson Canada, 1996), p. 97.
4. J.E. Canto-Thaler, "Employers Should be Ready for Inspectors' Visits," *Canadian HR Reporter* (April 10, 1995), p. 8.
5. J.E. Canto-Thaler, "Ontario H&S Policy Omits Worker Accountability," *Canadian HR Reporter* (July 15, 1996), p. 12.
6. J. Montgomery, *Occupational Health and Safety*, p. 34.
7. This section is based on C. Bryson, "From Sea to Legislative Sea," *OH&S Canada* (March/April 1996), pp. 56–66.
8. C. Knight, "New Nova Scotia OHS Act," *Canadian HR Reporter* (July 15, 1996), pp. 1, 3.
9. S. Lebrun, "Government-Wide OH&S Policy," *Canadian HR Reporter* (July 14, 1997), p. 7.
10. P. Strahlendorf, "Tug of War," *OH&S Canada* (March 1997), pp. 36–54.
11. K. Prisciak, "Health, Safety & Harassment?" *OH&S Canada* (April/May 1997), pp. 20–1.
12. P. Strahlendorf, "What Supervisors Need to Know," *OH&S Canada* (January/February 1996), pp. 38–40.
13. Lester Bittel, *What Every Supervisor Should Know* (New York: McGraw-Hill, 1974), p. 25. For an example of an effective safety training program, see Michael Pennacchia, "Interactive Training Sets the Pace," *Safety and Health* 135, no. 1 (January 1987), pp. 24–7, and Philip Poynter and David Stevens, "How to Secure an Effective Health and Safety Program at Work," *Professional Safety 32*, no. 1 (January 1987), pp. 32–41. Appointing a safety committee can also be useful. See for example, Neville Tompkins, "Getting the Best Help from your Safety Committee," *H R Magazine* 40, no. 4 (April 1995), p. 76.
14. David S. Thelan, Donna Ledgerwood, and Charles F. Walters, "Health and Safety in the Workplace: A New Challenge for Business Schools," *Personnel Administrator* 30, no. 10 (October 1985), p. 44.
15. Hammer, *Occupational Safety Management and Engineering.*
16. L. Jack, "Tunnel Vision," *OH&S Canada* (January/February 1997), pp. 31–7.
17. *A Safety Committee Man's Guide*, Aetna Life and Casualty Insurance Company, Catalog 872684.
18. J. Roughton, "Job Hazard Analysis," *OH&S Canada* (January/February 1996), pp. 41–4.
19. Willard Kerr, "Complementary Theories of Safety Psychology," in Edwin Fleishman and Alan Bass, *Industrial Psychology* (Homewood, IL: Dorsey Press, 1974), pp. 493–500. See also Alan Fowler, "How to Make the Workplace Safer," *People Management* 1, no. 2 (January, 1995), pp. 38–9.
20. List of unsafe acts from *A Safety Committee Man's Guide*, Aetna Life and Casualty Insurance Company.
21. Ernest McCormick and Joseph Tiffin, *Industrial Psychology* (Englewood Cliffs, NJ: Prentice Hall, 1974), pp. 522–3; Norman Maier, *Psychology and Industrial Organization*

(Boston: Houghton-Mifflin, 1965), pp. 458–62; Milton Blum and James Nayler, *Industrial Psychology* (New York: Harper & Row, 1968), pp. 519–31. For example, David DeJoy, "Attributional Processes and Hazard Control Management in Industry," *Journal of Safety Research* 16 (Summer 1985), pp. 61–71.
22. McCormick and Tiffin, *Industrial Psychology,* p. 523.
23. John Miner and J. Frank Brewer, "Management of Ineffective Performance," in Marvin Dunnette, ed., *Handbook of Industrial and Organizational Psychology* (Chicago: Rand McNally, 1976), pp. 995–1031; McCormick and Tiffin, *Industrial Psychology,* pp. 524–5. Younger employees probably have more accidents also, at least in part because they fail to perceive specific situations as being as risky as do older employees. See, for example, Peter Finn and Barry Bragg, "Perceptions of the Risk of an Accident by Young and Older Drivers," *Accident Analysis and Prevention* 18, no. 4 (August 1986). See also Olivia Mitchell, "The Relation of Age to Workplace Injuries," *Monthly Labor Review* 111, no. 7 (July 1988), pp. 8–13.
24. Blum and Nayler, *Industrial Psychology,* p. 522.
25. Miner and Brewer, "Management of Ineffective Performance," in Dunnette, ed., *Handbook of Industrial and Organizational Psychology,* pp. 1004–5.
26. Maier, *Psychology and Industrial Organization,* p. 463.
27. S.E. Wirt and H.E. Leedkee, "Skillful Eyes Prevent Accidents," Annual Newsletter, National Safety Council, Industrial Nursing Section (November 1945), pp. 10–2, quoted in Maier, *Psychology and Industrial Organization,* p. 466.
28. Gerald Borofsky, Michelle Bielema, and James Hoffman, "Accidents, Turnover, and Use of a Pre-employment Screening Interview," *Psychological Reports* (1993), pp. 1067–76.
29. Borofsky, Bielema and Hoffman, "Accidents, Turnover," p. 1069.
30. Borofsky, Bielema and Hoffman, "Accidents, Turnover," p. 1072.
31. Maier, *Psychology and Industrial Organization,* p. 464.
32. *Workers' Compensation Manual for Managers and Supervisors,* pp. 22–3.
33. B. Broadbent, "The Training Alternative," *OH&S Canada* (July–August 1996), pp. 36–41.
34. S. Laner and R. J. Sell, "An Experiment on the Effect of Specially Designed Safety Posters," *Occupational Psychology* 34 (1960), pp. 153–69, in McCormick and Tiffin, *Industrial Psychology,* p. 536.
35. McCormick and Tiffin, *Industrial Psychology,* p. 537. A group of international experts met in Belgium in 1986 and concluded that a successful safety poster must be simple and specific and reinforce safe behaviour rather than negative behaviour. See "What Makes an Effective Safety Poster," *National Safety and Health News* 134, no. 6 (December 1986), pp. 32–4.
36. J. Surry, "Industrial Accident Research: Human Engineering Approach" (Toronto: University of Toronto, Department of Industrial Engineering, June 1968), Chapter 4, quoted in McCormick and Tiffin, *Industrial Psychology,* p.

534. For an example of a very successful incentive program aimed at boosting safety at Campbell Soup Company, see Frederick Wahl, Jr., "Soups on for Safety," *National Safety and Health News* 134, no. 6 (December 1986), pp. 49–53. For a discussion of how employee involvement can impact job re-design and employee safety, see Douglas May and Catherine Schwoerer, "Employee Health by Design: Using Employee Involvement Teams in Ergonomics Job Redesign," *Personnel Psychology* 47, no. 4 (Winter, 1994), pp. 861–876.

37. Judi Komaki, Kenneth Barwick, and Lawrence Scott, "A Behavioral Approach to Occupational Safety: Pinpointing and Reinforcing Safe Performance in a Food Manufacturing Plant," *Journal of Applied Psycholog* 63 (August 1978), pp. 434–45. See also Robert Reber, Jerry Wallin, and David Duhon, "Preventing Occupational Injuries Through Performance Management," *Public Personnel Management* 22, no. 2 (Summer 1993), pp. 301–11, Anat Arkin, "Incentives to Work Safely," *Personnel Managemen* 26, no. 9 (September 1994), pp. 48–52, and Peter Makin and Valerie Sutherland, "Reducing Accidents Using a Behavioral Approach," *Leadership & Organizational Development Journal* 15, no. 5 (1994), pp. 5–10.

38. Judi Komaki, Arlene Heinzmann, and Lorealie Lawson, "Effect of Training and Feedback: Component Analysis of a Behavioral Safety Program," *Journal of Applied Psychology* 65 (June 1980), pp. 261–70. See also Jorma Sari, "When Does Behavior Modification Prevent Accidents?" *Leadership & Organizational Development Journal* 15, no. 5 (1994), pp. 11–15.

39. Dove Zohar, "Safety Climate in Industrial Organization: Theoretical and Implied Implications,"*Journal of Applied Psychology* 65 (February 1980), p. 97. For a discussion of the importance of getting employees involved in managing their own safety program, see John Lutness, "Self-managed Safety Program Gets Workers Involved," *Safety and Health* 135, no. 4 (April 1987), pp. 42–5. See also Frederick Streff, Michael Kalsher, and E. Scott Geller, "Developing Efficient Workplace Safety Programs: Observations of Response Co-Variations," *Journal of Organizational Behavior Managemen* 13, no. 2 (1993), pp. 3–14.

40. *Workers' Compensation Manual for Managers and Supervisors,* p. 24. James Frierson, "An Analysis of ADA Provisions on Denying Employment Because of a Risk of Future Injury," *Employee Relations Law Journal* 17, no. 4 (Spring 1992), pp. 603–22.

41. W.S. Cook, "Unsafe Practices Require Discipline," *Canadian HR Reporter* (September 25, 1995), p. 15.

42. Bureau of National Affairs, "Workplace Safety: Improving Management Practices," *Bulletin to Management (*February 9, 1989), pp. 42, 47; see also Marlene Morgenstern, "Workers' Compensation: Managing Costs," *Compensation and Benefits Review* (September–October 1992), pp. 30–8. See also Linda Johnson, "Preventing Injuries: The Big Payoff," *Personnel Journal* (April 1994), pp. 61–4; and David Webb, "The Bathtub Effect: Why Safety Programs Fail," *Management Review* (February 1994), pp. 51–4.

43. *Workers' Compensation Manual for Managers and Supervisors,* pp. 36–9.

44. *Workers' Compensation Manual for Managers and Supervisors*, p. 51.

45. A. Bierbier, "Controlling Sky-High Absenteeism," *OH&S Canada* (January–February 1996), pp. 54–63.

46. Sobeco, Ernst & Young, *OH&S Canada* (January–February 1996), p. 10.

47. S. Ritcey, "Psychological Job Matching," *OH&S Canada* (September–October 1996), pp. 50–6.

48. This section based largely on Miner and Brewer, "Management of Ineffective Performance," pp. 1005–23.

49. James Schreir, "Survey Supports Perceptions: Work-Site Drug Use Is on the Rise," *Personnel Journal* (October 1987), pp. 114–8. Pallassana Balgopal, "Combating Alcoholism in Industries: Implications for Occupational Social Work," *Management and Labor Studies* 17, no. 1 (January 1992), pp. 33–42. For a review of the background factors possibly leading to drug abuse, see for example, Richard Clayton et al., "Risk and Protective Factors: A Brief Review," *Drugs & Society, a Journal of Contemporary Issues* 8, no. 3–4 (1995), pp. 7–14.

50. B. Butler, "Alcohol and Drug Testing in Canada," *OH&S Canada* (January/February 1997), pp. 28–31.

52. Harrison Trice, "Alcoholism and the Work World," *Sloan Management Review,* no. 2 (Fall 1970), pp. 67–75, reprinted in W. Clay Hamner and Frank Schmidt, *Contemporary Problems in Personnel,* rev. ed., (Chicago: St. Clair Press, 1977), pp. 496–502. Note also that dependence on ordinary substances can be as devastating as hard drug problems. See, for example, Peter Minetos, "Are You Addicted to Legal Drugs?" *Safety and Health* 136, no. 2 (August 1987), pp. 46–9. For a discussion of substance abuse in the small business see, for example, Harry Lasher and John Grashof, "Substance Abuse in Small Business: Business Owner Perceptions and Reactions," *Journal of Small Business Management* (January 1993), pp. 63–72.

52. Pati and Adkins, "Employer's Role in Alcoholism Assistance." See also Commerce Clearing House, "How Should Employers Respond to Indications an Employee May Have an Alcohol or Drug Problem?" *Ideas and Trends (*April 6, 1989), pp. 53–7.

53. Based on Miner and Brewer, "Management of Ineffective Performance." The survey was conducted jointly by the American Society for Personnel Administration and the Bureau of National Affairs. The results were based on an analysis of the questionnaire data made by Professors Miner and Brewer, who acknowledge the assistance of John B. Schappi, associate editor of the Bureau of National Affairs, and Mary Green Miner, director of *BNA Surveys,* in making this information available.

54. Trice, "Alcoholism and the Work World." See also Larry A. Pace and Stanley J. Smits, "Substance Abuse: A Proactive Approach," *Personnel Journal* 68, no. 4 (April 1989), pp. 84–90, and Commerce Clearing House, "Typical Behavior Changes in an Employee with a Drinking Problem," *Ideas and Trends (*April 6, 1989), p. 56.

55. B. Butler, "Drug Tests May Not Constitute Impairment Tests," *Canadian HR Reporter* (October 7, 1996), p. 8.

56. D.P. Church and S.D. Matthews, "Providing Alcohol at Work," *OH&S Canada* (July/August 1996), pp. 46–8.

57. Butler, "Drug Tests."

58. J.E. Canto-Thaler, "Drug Testing Remains a Murky Legal Issue," *Canadian HR Reporter* (September 9, 1996), p. 8.

59. Butler, "Drug Tests."

60. S. Lebrun, "Safety in Numbers," *Canadian HR Reporter* (April 7, 1997), p. G19.

61. This is based on Terry Beehr and John Newman, "Organizational Stress, Employer Health, and Organizational Effectiveness: A Factor Analysis, Model, and Literature Review," *Personnel Psychology* 31 (Winter 1978), pp. 665–99. See also Stephan Motowizlo, John Packard, and Michael Manning, "Occupational Stress: Its Causes and Consequences for Job Performance," *Journal of Applied Psychology* 71, no. 4 (November 1986), pp. 618–29.

62. Eric Sundstrom, et al., "Office Noise, Satisfaction, and Performance," *Environment and Behavior* 26, no. 2 (March 1994), pp. 195–222.

63. R. Scotland, "Canadians Totally Stressed Out at Work, Survey Says," *Financial Post* (November 15, 1994), p. 15.

64. Andre DuBrin, *Human Relations: A Job Oriented Approach* (Reston, VA: Reston, 1978), pp. 66–7.

65. John Newman and Terry Beehr, "Personal and Organizational Strategies for Handling Job Stress: A Review of Research and Opinion," *Personnel Psychology* (Spring 1979), pp. 1–43. See also Bureau of National Affairs, "Work Place Stress: How to Curb Claims," *Bulletin to Management* (April 14, 1988), p. 120.

66. Karl Albrecht, *Stress and the Manager* (Englewood Cliffs, NJ: Spectrum, 1979). For a discussion of the related symptoms of depression see James Krohe, Jr., "An Epidemic of Depression?" *Across-the-Board* 31, no. 8 (September 1994), pp. 23–7.

67. Michael Leiter, David Clark, and Josette Durup, "Distinct Models of Burnout and Commitment Among Men and Women in the Military," *Journal of Applied Behavioral Science* 30, no. 1 (March 1994), pp. 63–4.

68. "Solutions to Workplace Stress," *BNA Bulletin to Management* (February 11, 1993), p. 48. See also Christopher Bachler, "Workers Take Leave of Job Stress," *Personnel Journal* 74, no. 1 (January, 1995) p. 38.

69. Pascale Carayon, "Stressful Jobs and Non-Stressful Jobs: A Cluster Analysis of Office Jobs," *Ergonomics* 37, no. 2 (1994), pp. 311–23.

70. Carayon, "Stressful Jobs."

71. Carayon, "Stressful Jobs." pp. 319–20.

72. Herbert Freudenberger, *Burn-Out* (Toronto: Bantam Books, 1980). See also Susan Jackson, Richard Schwab, and Randall Schuler, "Toward an Understanding of the Burnout Phenomenon," *Journal of Applied Psychology* 71, no. 4 (November 1986), pp. 630–40, and James R. Redeker and Jonathan Seagal, "Profits Low? Your Employees May Be High!" *Personnel* 66, no. 6 (June 1989), pp. 72–6. See also Cary Cherniss, "Long Term Consequences of Burnout: An Exploratory Study," *Journal of Organizational Behavior* 13, no. 1 (January 1992), pp. 1–11; and Raymond Lee and Blake Ashforth, "A Further Examination of Managerial Burnout: Toward an Integrated Model," *Journal of Organizational Behavior* 14 (1993), pp. 3–20.

73. J. Hampton, "RSIs: The Biggest Strain is on the Bottom Line," *Canadian HR Reporter* (February 10, 1997), pp. 15,

19. See also G. Harrington, "Pushing Ergonomics Into Place," *Canadian HR Reporter* (April 24, 1995), pp. 11–2.

74. S.B. Hood, "Repetitive Strain Injury," *Human Resources Professional* (June/July 1997), pp. 29–34.

75. C. Knight, "Computer Tells Employees to Take a Break," *Canadian HR Reporter* (April 7, 1997), p. 9.

76. J. Purdie, "Better Offices Mean Greater Productivity," *Financial Post* (November 26, 1990), p. 35.

77. N.J. Gowan, "The Case for Integration," *OH&S Canada Buyer's Guide 1997*, pp. 68–77.

78. See, for example, Michael Smith and others, "An Investigation of Health Complaints and Job Stress in Video Display Operations," *Human Factors* (August 1981), pp. 387–400; see also Bureau of National Affairs, "How to Protect Workers from Reproductive Hazards," *Fair Employment Practices* (July 23, 1987), pp. 89–90. See also Commerce Clearing House, "Suffolk County New York Passes Law Covering Employers with Twenty Terminals or More Regarding VDT Regulation," *Ideas and Trends* (1988), p. 48.

79. Bureau of National Affairs, "No Link Found Between VDTs and Miscarriages," *Bulletin to Management* (March 21, 1991), p. 81.

80. J.A. Savage, "Are Computer Terminals Zapping Workers' Health?" *Business and Society Review* (1994).

81. Bureau of National Affairs, "Solutions to VDT Viewing Problems," *Bulletin to Management* (November 5, 1987), pp. 356–7.

82. Bureau of National Affairs, "AIDS and the Workplace: Issues, Advice, and Answers," *Bulletin to Management* (November 14, 1985), pp. 1–6. See also David Ritter and Ronald Turner, "AIDS: Employer Concerns and Options," *Labor Law Journal* 38, no. 2 (February 1987), pp. 67–83; and Bureau of National Affairs, "How Employers Are Responding to AIDS in the Workplace," *Fair Employment Practices* (February 18, 1988), pp. 21–2. For a complete guide to services and information regarding "The Work Place and AIDS," see *Personnel Journal* 66, no. 10 (October 1987), pp. 65–80. See also William H. Wager, "AIDS: Setting Policy, Educating Employees at Bank of America," *Personnel* 65, no. 8 (August 1988), pp. 4–10. See also Margaret Magnus, "AIDS: Fear and Ignorance," *Personnel Journal* 67, no. 2 (February 1988), pp. 28–32, for poll regarding major workplace comments associated with AIDS. See also "AIDS/HIV in the Workplace: A Fact Sheet for Employees," *BNA Bulletin to Management,* October 6, 1994.

83. Commerce Clearing House, "The Wells Fargo AIDS Policy," *Ideas and Trends* (April 5, 1988), pp. 52–3.

84. Quoted or paraphrased from Michael Esposito and Jeffrey Myers, "Managing AIDS in the Workplace," *Employee Relations Law Journal* 19, no. 1 (Summer 1993), p. 68.

85. Daniel Warner, "'We Do Not Hire Smokers': May Employers Discriminate Against Smokers?" *Employee Responsibilities and Rights Journal* 7, no. 2 (1994), p. 129.

86. M.M. Finklestein, "Risky Business," *OH&S Canada* (September/October 1996), pp. 32–4.

87. R.G. Wyckham, "Regulating the Marketing of Tobacco Products in Controlling Smoking in Canada," *Canadian Journal of Administrative Sciences*, 14(2), June 1997, pp.

141–65. See also "Cigarettes a B.C. Workplace Hazard," *Canadian HR Reporter* (November 7, 1997), p. 11.

88. M. Hancock, "Violence in the Retail Workplace," *Accident Prevention* (May/June 1995), pp. 15–21.

89. "Looking Out for Trouble," *OH&S Canada* (March/April 1995), pp. 34–7.

90. J. Montgomery, *Occupational Health and Safety*, p. 297.

91. S.A. Baron, *Violence in the Workplace,* (Ventura CA: Pathfinder Publishing, 1993), p. 98.

92. E. Newton, "Clear Policy, Active Ear Can Reduce Violence," *Canadian HR Reporter* (February 26, 1996), pp. 16–7.

93. "Violence Caused by Workplace Failures," *OH&S Canada* (September/October 1996), p. 15.

94. Alfred Feliu, "Workplace Violence and the Duty of Care: The Scope of an Employer's Obligation to Protect Against the Violent Employee," *Employee Relations Law Journal* 20, no. 3 (Winter 1994/95), pp. 381–406.

95. K. Blair, "Employers on the Hook for Sexual Assault," *Canadian HR Reporter* (June 16, 1997), p. 5.

96. "Workplace Violence: Sources and Solutions," *BNA Bulletin to Management(* November 4), 1993, p. 345.

97. Workplace Violence: Sources and Solutions.

98. Feliu, "Workplace Violence and the Duty of Care," p. 395.

99. Dawn Anfuso, "Workplace Violence," *Personnel Journal* (October 1994), pp. 66–77.

100. Feliu, "Workplace Violence and the Duty of Care," p. 395.

101. Quoted from Feliu, "Workplace Violence and the Duty of Care," p. 395.

102. Anfuso, "Workplace Violence," p. 71.

103. "Preventing Workplace Violence," *BNA Bulletin to Management* (June 10, 1993), p. 177. See also Jenny McCune, "Companies Grapple with Workplace Violence," *Management Review* 83, No. 3 (March 1994), pp. 52–7.

104. Quoted or paraphrased from "Preventing Workplace Violence," p. 177.

105. Feliu, "Workplace Violence and the Duty of Care," pp. 401–2.

106. See, for example, Feliu, "Workplace Violence and the Duty of Care," p. 402.

107. Donna Rosato, "New Industry Helps Managers Fight Violence," *USA Today* (August 8, 1995), p. 1.

Chapter 19

Managing Human Resources in an International Business

Chapter Outline

♦ **The Internationalization of Business**

♦ **How Intercountry Differences Affect HRM**

♦ **Improving International Assignments Through Selection**

♦ **Training and Maintaining International Employees**

Learning Outcomes

After studying this chapter, you should be able to:

Explain how to improve international assignments through employee selection.

Answer the question, "What sort of special training do overseas candidates need?"

Discuss the major considerations in formulating a compensation plan for overseas employees.

Describe the main considerations in repatriating employees from abroad.

The Internationalization of Business

The Growth of International Business

It is clear that international business is important to companies here and abroad. In 1996, Canadian direct investment abroad stood at $170.8 billion, an increase of more than $55 billion over 1993. In the same year, $180.4 billion of direct investment came into Canada from abroad. Also, Canada's exports increased by 47 percent from 1993 to 1996. [1]

This rapid export growth reflects the fact that more Canadian-based companies are focussing their marketing efforts not just here but also abroad. Huge global companies like Noranda, Labatt's, and Molson's have long had extensive overseas operations. But with the European market unification that occurred in 1992, the opening of Eastern Europe, and the rapid development of demand in the Pacific Rim and other areas of the world, more and more companies are finding their success depends on their ability to market and manage overseas. And, of course, to foreign companies like Toyota, Canada is "overseas," and thousands of foreign firms already have thriving operations in Canada.

As a result of this internationalization, companies must increasingly be managed globally, but globalization confronts managers with some Herculean challenges. Market, product, and production plans must be coordinated on a worldwide basis, for instance, and organization structures capable of balancing centralized home-office control with adequate local autonomy must be created. We'll see in this chapter that some of the most pressing challenges concern globalization's impact on an employer's HR management system, and specifically the techniques used to recruit, select, train, compensate, and maintain the quality of work life of employees who are based abroad.

Types of International Businesses

Companies have many alternatives when it comes to extending their operations abroad. Most companies don't initially "go international" by making substantial investments in foreign countries. Instead initial international operations usually focus on either exporting, licensing, or franchising.[2]

Exporting is often the first choice when manufacturers decide to expand overseas. *Exporting* means selling abroad, either directly to target customers or indirectly by retaining foreign sales agents and distributors. Either way, the impact on the firm's HR management is usually minimal since few (if any) of its employees are expected to be posted overseas.

Licensing is another way to start international operations. *International licensing* is an arrangement whereby a firm (the licensor) grants a foreign firm the right to use intangible ("intellectual") property such as patents, copyrights, manufacturing processes, or trade names for a specific period of time, usually in return for a royalty.[3] *Franchising* is a similar option and is defined as a parent company's granting another firm the right to do business in a prescribed manner. The main difference between the two is that franchising usually requires the franchisee to follow much stricter guidelines in running the business than does licensing; licensing also tends to be limited to manufacturers, while franchising is more popular with service firms such as restaurants, hotels, and rental services.

Many internationally aspiring firms find that exporting, licensing, and franchising can get them only so far.[4] At some point, they find that to take full advantage of foreign opportunities, they have to make a substantial, direct investment of their own funds in another country. In general, *foreign direct investment* refers to operations in one country that are controlled by entities in a foreign country. This might mean building new facilities in another country, as Honda Canada did when it built its Camry manufacturing plant in Alliston, Ontario. Strictly speaking, a foreign direct investment means acquiring control by owning more than 50 percent of the operation. But in practice, it is possible for any firm (including a foreign firm) to gain effective control by owning less. In any event, a foreign direct investment turns a firm into a multinational enterprise. A *multinational enterprise* is one that controls operations in more than one country.

Joint ventures and wholly-owned subsidiaries are two examples of foreign direct investments. A *joint venture* is defined as "the participation of two or more companies jointly in an enterprise in which each party contributes assets, owns the entity to some degree, and shares risk."[5] In contrast, a *wholly-owned subsidiary* is owned 100 percent by the foreign firm. Thus, in Canada today, Honda Canada Inc. and its facility in Alliston, Ontario make up a wholly-owned subsidiary of Honda Motor Corporation, which is based in Japan. A joint venture, a wholly-owned subsidiary, or simply the need to staff one or more company offices abroad requires a considerable international effort by a company's HR managers.

Companies obviously differ in their degree of international involvement. An *international business* is any firm that engages in international trade or investment.[6] *International trade* refers to the export or import of goods or services to consumers in another country. Similarly, *international investment* refers to the investment of resources in business activities outside a firm's home country.

The multinational corporation is one type of international business enterprise. A *multinational corporation* (MNC) can be defined as "an internationally integrated production system over which equity-based control is exercised by a parent corporation that is owned and managed essentially by the nationals of the country in which it is [situated]."[7] (Equity-based control means the parent owns a large share of the foreign operation). In other words, the multinational corporation operates manufacturing and marketing facilities in several countries; these operations are coordinated by a parent firm, whose owners are mostly based in the firm's home country.

Canadian firms like Alcan and Dominion Textile have long been multinational corporations, but marketing expert Theodore Levitt contends that the MNC's reign as the preeminent international trade vehicle is nearing its end. It is being replaced, he says, by a new type of international enterprise he calls the global corporation. Whereas the multinational corporation operates in a number of countries and adjusts its products and practices to each, the *global corporation* operates as if the entire world (or major regions of it) were a single entity. They sell essentially the same things in the same way everywhere, much as Sony sells a standardized product such as Walkman throughout the world with components that may be made or designed in different countries.[8]

HRM and International Business

Consistent with these international business options, international HR management takes several forms. First, it can mean formulating and implementing HR policies and activities in the home-office headquarters of multinational companies like Coca-Cola and IBM.[9] HR responsibilities include selecting, training, and transferring parent-company staff abroad, and formulating HR policies for the firm as a whole and for its foreign operations. Some firms just apply parent-country HR policies to subsidiaries abroad, but most adapt their home-office HR practices to those common in the host countries, as we'll see.

Conducting HR activities in the foreign subsidiary of an MNC is a second form of international HRM. For example, Sumitomo Bank and Sony conduct HR operations in their Canadian subsidiaries. Again, local HR practices are often based on the parent firm's HR policies, albeit fine tuned for local-country practices and legal constraints.

International HR management is important in smaller firms, too. For example, Canadian companies may sell abroad exclusively by exporting through sales agents in Europe. Managers then have many international HR decisions to make. Someone may have to be sent abroad to help train the independent European sales agents; international HR policies will then have to be created to provide guidelines for paying these home-office employees' travel and living expenses and possibly for posting them abroad for several months. And, as European sales rise, a decision may have to be made to hire one or more engineers in the home office who are fluent in the language of one or more European countries.

How Intercountry Differences Affect HRM

While vacationers like these in Luxembourg are legally entitled to five weeks' holiday, standards vary widely even within Europe.

To a large extent, companies operating only within Canada's borders have the luxury of dealing with a relatively limited set of economic, cultural, and legal variables. Notwithstanding the range from liberal to conservative, for instance, Canada is basically a capitalist competitive society. And while a multitude of cultural and ethnic backgrounds are represented in the Canadian work force, various shared values (such as an appreciation for democracy) help to blur the otherwise sharp cultural differences.

A company operating multiple units abroad is generally not blessed with such relative homogeneity. For example, minimum legally mandated holidays may range from none in the United Kingdom to five weeks per year in Luxembourg. And while there are no formal requirements for employee participation in Italy, employee representatives on boards of directors are required in companies with more than 30 employees in Denmark. The point is that the management of the HR function in multinational companies is complicated enormously by the need to adapt HR policies and procedures to the differences among countries in which each subsidiary is based. The following are some intercountry differences that demand such adaptation.[10]

Cultural Factors

Wide-ranging cultural differences from country to country demand corresponding differences in HR practices among a company's foreign subsidiaries. We might generalize, for instance, that the cultural norms of the Far East and the importance there of the patriarchal system will mould the typical Japanese worker's view of his or her relationship to an employer as well as influence how that person works. Japanese workers have often come to expect lifetime employment in return for their loyalty, for instance. And incentive plans in Japan tend to focus on the work group, while in the West the more usual prescription is still to focus on individual worker incentives.[11] Similarly, in a recent study of about 330 managers from Hong Kong, the People's Republic of China, and the United States, U.S. managers tended to be most concerned with getting the job done while Chinese managers were most concerned with maintaining a harmonious environment; Hong Kong managers fell between these two extremes.[12]

A well-known study by Professor Geert Hofstede underscores other international cultural differences. Hofstede says societies differ first in *power distance;* in other words, the extent to which the less powerful members of institutions accept and expect that power will be distributed unequally.[13] He concluded that the institutionalization of such an inequality is higher in some countries (such as Mexico) than in others (such as Sweden).

His findings identified several other cultural differences. *Individualism versus collectivism* refers to the degree to which ties between individuals are normally loose rather than close. In more individualistic countries, "all members are expected to look after themselves and their immediate families."[14] Individualistic countries include Canada and the United States. Collectivist countries include Indonesia and Pakistan. *Masculinity versus femininity* refers, said Hofstede, to the extent to which society values assertiveness ("masculinity") versus caring (what he called "femininity"). Japan and Austria ranked high in masculinity; Denmark and Chile ranked low.

Such intracountry cultural differences have several HR implications. First, they suggest the need for adapting HR practices such as testing and pay plans to local cultural norms. They also suggest that HR staff members in a foreign subsidiary are best drawn from host-country citizens. A high degree of sensitivity and empathy for the cultural and attitudinal demands of coworkers is always important when selecting employees to staff overseas operations. However, such sensitivity is especially important when the job is HRM and the work involves "human" jobs like interviewing, testing, orienting, training, counselling, and (if need be) terminating. As one expert puts it, "An HR staff member who shares the employee's cultural background is more likely to be sensitive to the employee's needs and expectations in the workplace—and is thus more likely to manage the company successfully."[15]

www.shrm.org/hrlinks/intl. htm
HR Links

Economic Factors

Differences in economic systems among countries also translate into intercountry differences in HR practices. In free enterprise systems, for instance, the need for efficiency tends to favour HR policies that value productivity, efficient workers, and staff cutting where market forces dictate. Moving along the scale toward more socialist systems, HR practices tend to shift toward preventing unemployment, even at the expense of sacrificing efficiency.

Labour Cost Factors

Differences in labour costs may also produce differences in HR practices. High labour costs can require a focus on efficiency, for instance, and on HR practices (like pay-for-performance) aimed at improving employee performance.

Intercountry differences in labour costs are substantial. For example, hourly compensation costs in U.S. dollars for production workers in manufacturing recently ranged from $2.65 in Mexico and $4.31 in Hong Kong to $16.79 in the United States and a high of $25.56 in Germany. Other illustrative rates were: Italy, $15.97; France, $16.31; Singapore, $5.38; Japan, $19.20; and Canada, $16.36.[16]

There are other comparative labour costs to consider. For example, wide gaps exist in hours worked. Thus, workers in Portugal average about 1 980 hours of work annually, while workers in Germany average 1 648 hours. Employees in Europe generally receive four weeks of vacation as compared with two or three weeks in Canada. And several European countries including the United Kingdom and Germany require substantial severance pay to departing employees, usually equal to at least two year's service in the United Kingdom and one year in Germany.[17]

Industrial Relations Factors

Industrial relations, and specifically the relationship between the worker, the union, and the employer, vary dramatically from country to country and have an enormous impact on HRM practices. In Germany, for instance, *codetermination* is the rule. Here employees have the legal right to a voice in setting company policies. In this and several other countries workers elect their own representatives to the supervisory board of the employer, and there is also a vice president for labour at the top-management level.[18] On the other hand, in many other countries the state interferes little in the relations between employers and unions. In Canada for instance, HR policies on most matters such as wages and benefits are set not by the government but by the employer, or by the employer in negotiations with its labour unions. In Germany, on the other hand, the various laws on codetermination including the Works Constitution Act (1972), the Co-Determination Act (1976), and the ECSC Co-Determination Act (1951) largely determine the nature of HR policies in many German firms.

The European Community (EC)

In 1992 the 12 separate countries of the European community (EC) were unified into a common market for goods, services, capital, and even labour.[19] Generally speaking, tariffs for goods moving across borders from one EC country to another no longer exist, and employees (with some exceptions) find it easier to move relatively freely between jobs in various EC countries.

However, differences remain. Many countries have minimum wages while others do not, and maximum hours permitted in the workday and workweek vary. Other differences are apparent in matters like minimum annual holidays, minimum notice to be given by employer, termination formalities, and employee participation.

The impact of the European Community will be to gradually reduce these sorts of differences. Social legislation and examinations by the union's European Parliament and its administrative European Commission are slowly reducing some. However, even if all the differences are eventually eliminated, HR practices will still differ from country to country; cultural differences will require that, no doubt. Even into the near future, in other words, and even just within Europe, managing human resources multinationally will present tricky problems for HR managers.

In Summary: The Impact of Intercountry Differences on HRM

HR managers must consider the potential impact of intercountry differences on HR operations conducted globally. For example, differences in culture, economic systems, labour costs, and legal and industrial relations systems complicate the task of training employees who will have to work together. Such intercountry differences also mean there will be corresponding differences in management styles and practices from country to country, and such differences ". . . may strain relations between headquarters and subsidiary personnel or make a manager less effective when working abroad than at home."20 International assignments thus run a relatively high risk of failing unless special steps are taken to select, train, and compensate international assignees.

Improving International Assignments Through Selection

Why International Assignments Fail

Canadian companies have reported low failure rates for employees on foreign assignments relative to other countries, particularly the United States.[21] Failure is defined as the premature return of employees to their home country or the inability of expatriates to achieve their business goals. Although the exact number of failures is understandably difficult to quantify, one survey of U.S., European, and Japanese multinationals concluded that three-quarters of U.S. multinational companies experience expatriate assignment failure rates of 10 percent or more.[22] European and Japanese multinationals reported lower failure rates, with only about one-sixth of Japanese multinationals and three percent of European multinationals reporting more than a 10 percent expatriate recall rate.

The reasons reported for expatriate failure differed between the U.S., European, and Japanese multinationals.[23] For U.S. multinationals, the reasons in descending order of importance were inability of spouse to adjust, managers' inability to adjust, other family problems, managers' personal or emotional immaturity, and inability to cope with larger overseas responsibility. Managers of European firms emphasized only the inability of the manager's spouse to adjust as an explanation for the expatriate's failed assignment. Japanese firms emphasized (in descending order) inability to cope with larger overseas responsibility, difficulties with new assignment, personal or emotional problems, lack of technical competence, and finally, inability of spouse to adjust.

These findings underscore a truism regarding selection for international assignments, namely, that it's usually not inadequate technical competence but family and personal problems that undermine the international assignee. As one expert puts it:

> The selection process is fundamentally flawed…. Expatriate assignments rarely fail because the person cannot accommodate to the technical demands of the job. The expatriate selections are made by line managers based on technical competence. They fail because of family and personal issues and lack of cultural skills that haven't been part of the process.[24]

The Canadian experience is more unique.[25] Factors identified by Canadian firms as important to expatriate success include flexibility, language ability, and family adjustment. However, these factors were not identified by Canadian companies as having been part of the selection and training process for expatriates. There are three potential explanations for this result. First, Canadians may be more culturally adaptable than their foreign counterparts because they are already familiar with bilingualism and multiculturalism. Second, Canadian expatriates are so few in number that they can be dealt with on an individual basis. Thus their firms may be doing more to prepare and support them than they report, because their systems are not formalized. Third, Canadian expatriate assignments have tended to be in culturally similar situations, which make successful adaptation more likely.

International Staffing: Sources of Managers

There are several ways to classify international managers. *Locals* are citizens of the countries where they are working. *Expatriates* are noncitizens of the countries in which they are working.[26] *Home-country nationals* are the citizens of the country in which the multinational company's headquarters is based.[27] *Third-country nationals* are citizens of a country other than the parent or the host country—for example, a British executive working in a Tokyo subsidiary of a Canadian multinational bank.[28]

Expatriates represent a minority of managers. Thus, "most managerial positions are filled by locals rather than expatriates in both headquarters or foreign subsidiary operations."[29]

There are several reasons to rely on local, host-country management talent for filling the foreign subsidiary's management ranks. Many people simply prefer not working in a foreign country, and in general the cost of using expatriates is far greater than the cost of using local management talent.[30] The MNC may be viewed locally as a "better citizen" if it uses local management talent, and indeed some governments actually press for the "nativization" of local management.[31] There may also be a fear that expatriates, knowing they're posted to the foreign subsidiary for only a few years, may overemphasize short-term projects rather than focus on perhaps more necessary long-term tasks.[32]

There are also several reasons for using expatriates—either home-country or third-country nationals—for staffing subsidiaries. The major reason is reportedly technical competence: in other words, employers can't find local candidates with the required technical qualifications.[33] Multinationals also increasingly view a successful stint abroad as a required step in developing top managers. For instance, the head of General Electric's Asia-Pacific region was transferred back to a top executive position of vice-chair at GE in 1995. Control is another important reason. Multinationals sometimes assign home-country nationals from their headquarters staffs abroad on the assumption that these managers are more steeped in the firm's policies and culture and more likely to unquestioningly implement headquarters' instructions.

International Staffing Policy

Multinational firms' top executives are often classified as either ethnocentric, polycentric, or geocentric.[34] In an ethnocentric corporation, "... the prevailing attitude is that home country attitudes, management style, knowledge, evaluation criteria, and managers are superior to anything the host country might have to offer."[35] In the polycentric corporation, "there is a conscious belief that only host country managers can ever really understand the culture and behaviour of the host country market; therefore, the foreign subsidiary should be managed by local people."[36] Geocentrism, rarely seen, assumes that management candidates must be searched for on a global basis, on the assumption that the best manager for any specific position anywhere on the globe may be found in any of the countries in which the firm operates.

These three multinational attitudes translate into three international staffing policies. An ethnocentric staffing policy is one in which all key management positions are filled by parent-country nationals.[37] At Royal Dutch Shell, for instance, virtually all financial controllers around the world are Dutch nationals. Reasons given for ethnocentric staffing policies include lack of qualified host-country senior management talent, a desire to maintain a unified corporate culture and tighter control, and the desire to transfer the parent firm's core competencies (for instance, a specialized manufacturing skill) to a foreign subsidiary more expeditiously.[38]

A polycentric-oriented firm would staff foreign subsidiaries with host-country nationals and its home-office headquarters with parent-country nationals. This may reduce the local cultural misunderstandings that expatriate managers may exhibit. It will also almost undoubtedly be less expensive. One expert estimates that an expatriate executive can cost a firm up to three times as much as a domestic executive because of transfer expenses and other expenses such as schooling for children, annual home leave, and the need to pay income taxes in two countries.[39]

A geocentric staffing policy "seeks the best people for key jobs throughout the organization, regardless of nationality."[40] This may allow the global firm to use its human resources more efficiently by transferring the best person to the open job, wherever he or she may be. It can also help build a stronger and more consistent culture and set of values among the entire global management team. Team members here are continually interacting and networking with each other as they move from assignment to assignment around the globe and participate in global development activities.

Selecting International Managers

There are common traits that managers to be assigned domestically and overseas will obviously share. Wherever a person is to be posted, he or she will need the technical knowledge and skills to do the job and the intelligence and people skills to be a successful manager, for instance.[41]

However, as discussed earlier in this chapter, foreign assignments make demands on expatriate assignees that are different from what the manager would face if simply assigned to a management post in his or her home country. There is the need to cope with a work force and management colleagues whose cultural inclinations may be drastically different from one's own, and the considerable stress that being alone in a foreign land can bring to bear on the single manager. And, of course, if spouse and children will share the assignment, there are the complexities and pressures that the family will have to confront, from learning a new language, to shopping in strange surroundings, to finding new friends and attending new schools.

Selecting managers for expatriate assignments, therefore, means screening them for traits that predict success in adapting to what may be dramatically new environments. A list of such expatriate selection traits would include:[42]

Adaptability and flexibility: ability to adapt to new circumstances and situations and to respond flexibly to different and often novel ideas and viewpoints.[43]

Cultural toughness: the ability to succeed in an alien culture.

Self-orientation: self-esteem, self-confidence, and mental well-being.

Others orientation: the ability to interact effectively with host-country nationals and more generally to develop long-lasting friendships.[44]

Perceptual ability: the ability to understand why people behave as they do and to empathize with them.

Family adaptability: the ability of the manager's spouse and children to adapt to and be happy in the foreign environment.

A recent study identified five factors perceived by international assignees to contribute to success in a foreign assignment. They were job knowledge and motivation, relational skills, flexibility/adaptability, extracultural openness, and family situation. (Some of the specific items that constitute each of these five factors are presented in **Figure 19.1**).[45] In this study 338 international assignees from many countries and organizations completed questionnaires; they were asked to

**Figure 19–1
Five Factors Important
in International
Assignee Success**

Source: Adapted from Arthur
Winfred Jr. and Winston
Bennett, Jr., "The
International Assignee: The
Relative Importance of Factors
Perceived to Contribute to
Success,"*Personnel Psychology*
48 (1995), pp. 106-7.

I) **Job Knowledge and Motivation**
Managerial ability
Organizational ability
Imagination
Creativity
Administrative skills
Alertness
Responsibility
Industriousness
Initiative & energy
High motivation
Frankness
Belief in mission & job
Perseverance
II) **Relational Skills**
Respect
Courtesy & tact
Display of respect
Kindness
Empathy
Being nonjudgmental
Integrity
Confidence

III) **Flexibility/Adaptability**
Resourcefulness
Ability to deal with stress
Flexibility
Emotional stability
Willingness to change
Tolerance for ambiguity
Adaptability
Independence
Dependability
Political sensitivity
Positive self-image
IV) **Extra-Cultural Openness**
Variety of outside interests
Interest in foreign cultures
Openness
Knowledge of local language(s)
Outgoingness & extraversion
Overseas experience
V) **Family Situation**
Adaptability of spouse & family
Spouse's positive opinion
Willingness of spouse to live abroad
Stable marriage

indicate which of various listed managerial traits were important for the success of managers on foreign assignment. Various reported items including managerial ability, organizational ability, administrative skills, and creativity were then statistically combined into a single "job knowledge and motivation" factor. Respect, courtesy and tact, display of respect, and kindness were some of the items comprising the "relational skills" factor. "Flexibility/adaptability" included such items as resourcefulness, ability to deal with stress, flexibility, and emotional stability. "Extracultural openness" included variety of outside interests, interest in foreign countries, and openness. Finally, several items including adaptability of spouse and family, spouse's positive opinion, willingness of spouse to live abroad, and stable marriage comprise the "family situation" factor.[46]

The five factors were not equally important in the foreign assignee's success, according to the responding managers. As the researchers conclude, "Family situation was generally found to be the most important factor, a finding consistent with other research on international assignments and transfers."[47] Therefore, while all five factors were perceived as important to the foreign assignee's success, the company that ignores the candidate's family situation does so at its peril.

Adaptability Screening   This being the case, *adaptability screening* is generally recommended as an integral part of the expatriate screening process. Generally conducted by a professional psychologist or psychiatrist, adaptability screening aims to assess the family's probable success in handling the foreign transfer and to alert the couple to personal issues (such as the impact on children) the foreign move may involve.[48]

Past experience is often the best predictor of future success. Companies like Colgate-Palmolive, therefore, look for overseas candidates whose work and nonwork experience, education, and language skills already demonstrate a commitment to and facility in living and working with different cultures.[49] Even several successful summers spent travelling overseas or participating in foreign student programs would seem to provide some concrete basis for believing that the potential transferee can accomplish the required adaptation when he or she arrives overseas.

Diversity Counts
Sending Female Managers Abroad

While the number and proportion of female managers working domestically has climbed fairly quickly in the past few years, the same apparently can't be said about sending female managers abroad. One recent estimate states that women filled only about 6 percent of the overseas international management positions at major companies, for instance, compared with about 37 percent of domestic U.S. management positions.[1]

This raises the interesting question of why more firms don't send female managers abroad, and the answer seems to come down to several erroneous assumptions. One myth is that women are reluctant to transfer overseas and/or simply do not want to be international managers. International management expert Nancy Adler points out that this myth seems to be based in part on research that has shown that when men are assigned overseas and are accompanied by their non-working spouses, the wife's inability to adjust is a major reason that the assignments fail. However, findings like these certainly do not necessarily extend to working career women. For example, surveys of more than one thousand MBAs revealed no significant difference between female and male MBAs in pursuing international careers. In fact, "more than four out of five MBAs—both women and men—wanted international assignment at some time during their career."[2] Yet the erroneous myth that women don't want to serve overseas remains a problem: In one series of interviews most women said that they found that it had never occurred to their employers to consider women for overseas posts.[3]

The fact that dual-career marriages make sending female managers abroad impossible is a second erroneous assumption limiting their access to positions abroad. For example, in one survey, more than three-fourths of the HR executives sighted dual-career marriages as a reason for not sending female managers abroad, yet responses of female international managers in a separate interview indicated that dual-career couples' career problems can indeed be ironed out.[4]

Perhaps the most persistent impediment to sending female managers abroad is the assumption that they would face so much foreign prejudice that they could not succeed if sent. The assumption here is that foreigners in general (and foreign men in particular) in many societies are so unduly prejudiced against female managers that the latter could not do their jobs effectively. Yet, here also, the evidence belies the assumption: In one survey, all the female managers (97 percent) reported that their international assignments were successful.[5] Even in a historically patriarchal society like Hong Kong's, another study found that ". . . problems associated with their gender in conjunction with that specific cultural environment did not materialize and did not engender any significant impediment to effective managerial performance in ways that might have been anticipated."[6] In other words, here too, as these researchers conclude, "the excuse used by some companies for not sending women on overseas assignments—that local values are antithetical to such female participation—appeared to be unfounded."[7]

1. Nancy Adler, "Women Managers in a Global Economy," *Training & Development,* April 1994, p. 31.
2. Adler, "Women Managers," p. 32.
3. Adler, "Women Managers," p. 32.
4. Adler, "Women Managers," p. 32.
5. Adler, "Women Managers," p. 32–3.
6. R.I. Westwood and S.M. Leung, "The Female Expatriate Manager Experience: Coping with Gender and Culture," *International Studies of Management & Organization* 24, no. 3, Fall 1994, pp. 64–85.
7. Westwood and Leung, "The Female Expatriate Manager Experience," p. 81.

Realistic job previews at this point are also crucial. Again, both the potential assignee and his or her family require all the information that can be provided on the problems to expect in the new job (such as mandatory private schooling for the children) as well as any information obtainable about the cultural benefits, problems, and idiosyncrasies of the country in question. International human resources managers speak about avoiding culture shock in much the same way as we discussed using realistic job previews to avoid reality shock among new employees. In any case, the rule here is to spell it out ahead of time, as firms like Ciba-Geigy do for their international transferees.[50]

There are also paper-and-pencil tests that can be used to more effectively select employees for overseas assignments. Generally speaking, of course, any such test should be company specific and validated as a tool for placing candidates overseas. However, experts have developed and validated general-purpose tests that focus on the aptitudes and personality characteristics of successful overseas candidates. The Overseas Assignment Inventory is one such assessment tool. Based on 12 years of research with more than 7 000 candidates, the test's publisher contends that it is useful in identifying characteristics and attitudes such candidates should have.[51]

Training and Maintaining International Employees

Painstaking screening is just the first step in ensuring the foreign assignee's success. The employee may then require special training and, in addition, international HR policies must be formulated for compensating the firm's overseas managers and maintaining healthy labour relations.

Orienting and Training Employees for International Assignments

When it comes to providing the orientation and training required for success overseas, the practices of most North American firms reflect more form than substance. One consultant says that despite many companies' claims, there is generally little or no systematic selection and training for assignments overseas. One relevant survey concluded that a sample of company presidents and chairpersons agreed that international business was growing in importance and required employees firmly grounded in the economics and practices of foreign countries. However, few of their companies actually provided such overseas-oriented training to their employees.[52]

Orientation and training for international assignments can help employees (and their families) avoid "culture shock" and better adjust to their new surroundings.

What sort of special training do overseas candidates need? One firm specializing in such programs prescribes a four-step approach.[53] Level 1 training focuses on the impact of cultural differences, and on raising trainees' awareness of such differences and their impact on business outcomes. Level 2 focuses on attitudes and aims at getting participants to understand how attitudes (both negative and positive) are formed and how they influence behaviour. (For example, unfavourable stereotypes may subconsciously influence how a new manager responds to and treats his or her new foreign employees.) Finally, level 3 training provides factual knowledge about the target country, while level 4 provides skill building in areas like language and adjustment and adaptation skills. (Additional guidelines for developing international executives—such as "Brief candidates fully and clearly on all relocation policies," and "Provide all relocating executives with a mentor to monitor their overseas careers and help them secure appropriate jobs with the company when they repatriate"—were discussed in chapter 9.)

Beyond these special training practices, there is also the need for more traditional training and development of overseas employees. At IBM, for instance, such development includes using a series of rotating assignments that permits overseas IBM managers to grow professionally. At the same time, IBM and other major firms have established management development centres around the world where executives can come to hone their skills. Beyond that, classroom programs (such as those at the London Business School, or at INSEAD in Fountainebleu, France) provide overseas executives the opportunities they need to hone their functional skills.

In addition to honing functional skills, international management development often aims to foster improved control of global operations by building a unifying corporate culture. The assumption here is that the firm should bring together managers from its far-flung subsidiaries and steep them for a week or two in the firm's cherished values and current strategy and policies. The managers should then be more likely to consistently adhere to these values, policies, and aims once they return to their assignments abroad.

International Compensation

The whole area of international compensation management presents some tricky problems. On the one hand, there is a certain logic in maintaining company-wide pay scales and policies so that, for instance, divisional marketing directors throughout the world are all paid within the same narrow range. This reduces the risk of perceived inequities and dramatically simplifies the job of keeping track of disparate country-by-country wage rates.

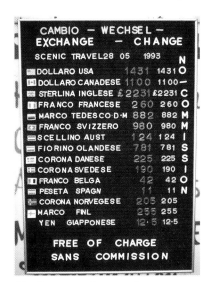

The European Community unites 12 countries with many common bonds and many differences.

Yet not adapting pay scales to local markets can present an HR manager with more problems than it solves. The fact is that it can be enormously more expensive to live in some countries (like Japan) than others (like Greece); if these cost-of-living differences aren't considered, it may be almost impossible to get managers to take "high-cost" assignments.

However, the answer is usually not just to pay, say, marketing directors more in one country than in another. For one thing, the firm could thereby elicit resistance when telling a marketing director in Tokyo who's earning $3 000 per week to move to a division in Spain, where his or her pay for the same job (cost of living notwithstanding) will drop by half. One way to handle the problem is to pay a similar base salary company-wide and then add on various allowances according to individual market conditions.[54]

Determining equitable wage rates in many countries is no simple matter. There is a wealth of "packaged" compensation survey data already available in North America, but such data are not so easy to come by overseas. As a result, "one of the greatest difficulties in managing total compensation on a multinational level is establishing a consistent compensation measure between countries that builds credibility both at home and abroad."[55]

Some multinational companies deal with this problem for local managers by conducting their own annual compensation surveys. For example, Kraft conducts an annual study of total compensation in Belgium, Germany, Italy, Spain, and the United Kingdom. Kraft tries to maintain a fairly constant sample group of study participants (companies) in its survey. It then focusses on the total compensation paid to each of ten senior management positions held by local nationals in these firms. The survey covers all forms of compensation, including cash, short- and long-term incentives, retirement plans, medical benefits, and perquisites.[56] Kraft then uses these data to establish a competitive value for each element of pay. This information in turn becomes the input for annual salary increases and proposed changes in the benefit package.

The most common approach to formulating expatriate pay is to equalize purchasing power across countries, a technique known as the balance sheet approach.[57] The basic idea is that each expatriate should enjoy the same standard of living he or she would have had at home. With the balance sheet approach, four main home-country groups of expenses—income taxes, housing, goods and services, and reserve—are the focus of attention. The employer estimates what each of these four expenses is for the expatriate's home country and also what each is expected to be in the expatriate's host country. Any differences—such as additional income taxes or housing expenses—are then paid by the employer.

In practice this usually boils down to building the expatriate's total compensation around five or six separate components. For example, *base salary* will normally be in the same range as the manager's home-country salary. In addition, however, there might be an overseas or foreign service premium. This is paid as a percentage of the executive's base salary,[58] in part to compensate the manager for the cultural and physical adjustments he or she will have to make. There may also be several allowances, including a housing allowance and an education allowance for the expatriate's children. Income taxes represent another area of concern. In many cases a Canadian manager posted abroad may have to pay not only Canadian taxes, but income taxes to the country to which he or she is posted as well.

One international compensation trend awards long-term incentive pay to overseas managers. While it may not seem particularly logical, many multinationals only permit the top managers at corporate headquarters to participate in long-term incentive programs like stock option plans.[59] Equally problematic is the fact that many of the multinationals that do offer overseas managers long-term incentives (32 of 40 in one survey) use only overall corporate performance criteria when awarding incentive pay. Since the performance of the company's stock on a Canadian stock market may have little relevance to, say, a manager in a German subsidiary, the incentive value of such a reward is highly suspect. This is particularly so because, regardless of size, a foreign subsidiary's influence on its parent company's stock price is more likely to result from exchange rate movements than from management action.[60]

The answer here, more multinationals are finding, is to formulate new long-term incentives specifically for overseas executives. Multinationals are thus devising performance-based long-term incentive plans that are tied more closely to performance at the subsidiary level. These can help build a sense of ownership among key local managers while providing the financial incentives needed to attract and keep the people required for overseas operations.

www.cancham.com.hk
Canadian Chamber of
Commerce in Hong Kong

Performance Appraisal of International Managers

Several things complicate the task of appraising an expatriate's performance.[61] For one thing, the question of who actually appraises the expatriate is a crucial issue. Obviously local management must have some input in the appraisal, but the appraisals may then be distorted by cultural differences. Thus, an expatriate manager in India may be evaluated somewhat negatively by his host-country bosses who find his use of participative decision making inappropriate in their culture. On the other hand, home-office managers may be so geographically distanced from the expatriate that they can't provide valid appraisals because they're not fully aware of the situation the manager actually faces. This can be problematic: The expatriate may be measured by objective criteria such as profits and market share, but local events such as political instability may undermine the manager's performance while remaining "invisible" to home-office staff.[62]

Two experts make five suggestions for improving the expatriate appraisal process:

1. Stipulate the assignment's difficulty level. For example, being an expatriate manager in China is generally considered more difficult than working in England, and the appraisal should take such difficulty-level differences into account.

2. Weight the evaluation more toward the on-site manager's appraisal than toward the home-site manager's distant perceptions of the employee's performance.

3. If, however (as is usually the case), the home-site manager does the actual written appraisal, he or she should use a former expatriate from the same overseas location to provide background advice during the appraisal process. This can help ensure that unique local issues are considered during the appraisal process.

4. Modify the normal performance criteria used for that particular position to fit the overseas position and characteristics of that particular locale. For example, "maintaining positive labour relations" might be more important in Chile, where labour instability is more common, than it would be in Canada.

5. Attempt to give the expatriate manager credit for relevant insights into the functioning of the operation and specifically the interdependencies of the domestic and foreign operations. In other words, don't just appraise the expatriate manager in terms of quantifiable criteria like profits or market share. His or her recommendations regarding how home office/foreign subsidiary communication might be enhanced, and other useful insights, should also affect the appraisal.

International Labour Relations

www.ilo.org/
International Labour
Organization

Firms opening subsidiaries abroad will find substantial differences in labour relations practices among the world's countries and regions. The following synopsis illustrates some of these differences by focusing on Europe. However, keep in mind that similarly significant differences would exist in South and Central America, and Asia. Some important differences between labour relations practices in Europe and North America include:[63]

Centralization. In general, collective bargaining in Western Europe is likely to be industry-wide or regionally oriented, whereas North American collective bargaining generally occurs at the enterprise or plant level.

Union structure. Because collective bargaining is relatively centralized in most European countries, local unions in Europe tend to have much less autonomy and decision-making power than in North America, and they basically concentrate on administrative and service functions.

Employer organization. Due to the prevalence of industry-wide bargaining, the employer's collective bargaining role tends to be performed primarily by employer associations in Europe; individual employers in North America generally (but not always) represent their own interests when bargaining collectively with unions.

Union recognition. Union recognition for collective bargaining in Western Europe is much less formal than in North America. For example, in Europe there is no legal mechanism requiring an employer to recognize a particular union; even if a union claims to represent 80 percent of an employer's workers, another union can try to organize and bargain for the other 20 percent.

Union security. Union security in the form of formal closed-shop agreements is largely absent in continental Western Europe.

Labour–management contracts. As in North America, most European labour–management agreements are legally binding documents, except in Great Britain where such collective agreements are viewed as "gentlemen's agreements" existing outside the law.

Content and scope of bargaining. North American labour–management agreements tend to focus on wages, hours, and working conditions. European agreements, on the other hand, tend to be brief and simple and to specify minimum wages and employment conditions, with employers free to institute more generous terms. The relative brevity of the European agreements is a function of two things: industry-wide bargaining makes it difficult to write detailed contracts applicable to individual enterprises, and in Europe the government is much more heavily involved in setting terms of employment such as vacations and working conditions.

Grievance handling. In Western Europe, grievances occur much less frequently than in North America; when raised, they are usually handled by a legislated machinery outside the union's formal control.

Strikes. Generally speaking, strikes occur less frequently in Europe. This is probably due to industry-wide bargaining, which generally elicits less management resistance than in North America, where demands "… cut deeper into the individual enterprise's revenues."[64]

Government's role. In Europe, governments generally do not regulate the bargaining process but are much more interested in directly setting the actual terms of employment than is the case in North America.

Worker participation. Worker participation has a long and relatively extensive history in Western Europe where it tends to go far beyond matters such as pay and working conditions. The aim is to create a system by which workers can participate in a meaningful way in the direct management of the enterprise. Determining wages, hours, and working conditions is not enough; employees should participate in formulating all management decisions. In many countries in Western Europe works councils are required. A *works council* is a committee in which plant workers consult with management about certain issues or share in the governance of the workplace.[65] Codetermination is a second form of worker participation in Europe. *Codetermination* means that there is mandatory worker representation on an enterprise's board of directors. It is especially prevalent in Germany.

Repatriation: Problems and Solutions

Repatriation is often a bittersweet experience for the returning expatriate. *Repatriation,* the process of moving back to the parent company and country from the foreign assignment, means returning one's family to familiar surroundings and old friends.[66] But the returning employee all too often discovers that in many respects his or her employer has ignored the manager's career and personal needs.

Several repatriation problems are very common. One is the expatriate's fear that he or she has been "out of sight, out of mind" during an extended foreign stay and thus lost touch with the parent firm's culture, top executives, and those responsible for the firm's management selection processes. Indeed, such fears can be well-founded: Many repatriates are temporarily placed in mediocre or make-shift jobs.[67] Many are shocked to find that the executive trappings of the overseas job (private schools for the children and a company car and driver, for instance) are lost upon return, and that the executive again is just a small fish in a big pond. Perhaps more exasperating is the discovery that some of the expatriate's former colleagues have been more rapidly promoted while he or she was overseas. Even the expatriate's family may undergo a sort of reverse culture shock, as spouse and children face the often daunting task of picking up old friendships and habits or starting schools anew upon their return.

Progressive multinationals anticipate and avoid these problems by taking a number of sensible steps. These can be summarized as follows:[68]

Write repatriation agreements. Many firms use repatriation agreements. These guarantee in writing that the international assignee will not be kept abroad longer than some period (such as five years), and that on return he or she will be given a mutually-acceptable job.

Assign a sponsor. The employee should be assigned a sponsor (such as a senior manager at the parent firm's home office). This person's role is to look after the expatriate while he or she is away. This includes keeping the person apprised of significant company events and changes back home, monitoring his or her career interests, and putting the person's name into consideration for key openings when the expatriate is ready to come home.

Provide career counselling. Provide formal career counselling sessions to ensure the repatriate's job assignments upon return meet his or her needs.[69]

Keep communications open. Keep the expatriate "plugged in" to home-office business affairs through management meetings around the world, frequent home leave combined with stays at headquarters to work on specific problems, and regularly scheduled meetings at headquarters.[70]

Offer financial support. Many firms pay real estate and legal fees and help the expatriate to rent or in some other way to maintain his or her residence, so that the repatriate and his or her family can actually return "home."

Develop reorientation programs. Finally, provide the repatriate and his or her family with a reorientation program to facilitate their adjustment back into the home culture.

Chapter Review

Summary

1. Companies must increasingly be managed globally. Among the alternatives for extending operations abroad are exporting, licensing, franchising, and foreign direct investment. Joint ventures and wholly-owned subsidiaries are two examples of foreign direct investments. A multinational enterprise is one that controls operations in more than one country. A multinational corporation (MNC) is an internationally-integrated production system over which equity-based control is exercised by a parent corporation that is owned and managed essentially by the nationals of the country in which it is domiciled.

2. International HRM can take several forms. It can mean formulating and implementing HR policies in the home-office headquarters of multinational companies, conducting HR activities in the foreign subsidiary of a multinational company, or implementing internationally-related HR activities in relatively small firms that don't have a major presence abroad.

3. Intercountry differences impact a company's HRM processes. Cultural factors such as Hofstede's power distance, individualism versus collectivism, and masculinity versus femininity suggest differences in values, attitudes, and therefore behaviours and reactions of people from country to country. Economic factors and labour cost factors help determine whether the human resources emphasis should be on efficiency, commitment building, or some other approach. Industrial relations and specifically the relationship between the worker, the union, and the employer manifest themselves in concepts such as Germany's codetermination; these in turn influence the nature of a company's specific HR policies from country to country. Even within the relatively unified European Community, substantial differences in matters like minimum wage laws and length of work day exist between member countries.

4. A large percentage of expatriate assignments fail, but the results can be improved through careful international assignee selection. First, there are various sources HR departments can use to staff domestic and foreign subsidiaries. Most managerial positions are filled by locals rather than expatriates. This is not always the case, though. In the ethnocentric corporation the prevailing attitude is that home-country managers are superior; in polycentric firms host-country managers predominate; and in geocentric firms the best manager for any specific position is chosen from among the firm's global work force.

5. Selecting managers for expatriate assignments means screening them for traits that predict success in adapting to dramatically new environments. Such expatriate traits include adaptability and flexibility, cultural toughness, self-orientation,

job knowledge and motivation, relational skills, extracultural openness, and family situation. Adaptability screening focussing on the family's probable success in handling the foreign transfer can be an especially important step in the expatriate selection process.

6. Prior to assignment, training for overseas managers typically focusses on cultural differences, on how attitudes influence behaviour, and on factual knowledge about the target country. The most common approach to formulating expatriate pay is to equalize purchasing power across countries, a technique known as the balance sheet approach. With this approach the employer estimates expenses for income taxes, housing, goods and services, and reserve, and pays supplements to the expatriate in such a way as to maintain the same standard of living he or she would have had at home.

7. The expatriate appraisal process can be complicated by the need to have both local and home-office supervisors provide input into the expatriate's performance review. Suggestions for improving the expatriate appraisal process include stipulating difficulty level, weighing the on-site manager's appraisal more heavily, and having the home site manager get background advice from managers familiar with the location abroad before completing the expatriate's appraisal.

8. Firms opening subsidiaries abroad find substantial differences in labour relations practices among the world's countries and regions. For example, even within Europe, differences exist with respect to centralization of collective bargaining, local union autonomy, use of employer associations, procedures for gaining union recognition, and grievance handling.

9. Repatriation problems are very common but can be minimized. They include the often well-founded fear that the expatriate is "out of sight, out of mind" and difficulties in reassimilating the expatriate's family back into home-country culture. Suggestions for avoiding these problems include using repatriation agreements, assigning a sponsor, offering career counselling, keeping the expatriate plugged in to home-office business, providing financial support to maintain the expatriate's home-country residence, and offering reorientation programs to the expatriate and his or her family.

Discussion Questions and Exercises

1. What are the main ways in which to extend the operations of a small business abroad? Which generally makes the most sense for a small business, and why?

2. What is a multinational corporation? Give three specific examples of such corporations. Check in the library, on the Internet, or with each firm to determine in what countries these firms have operations and explain the nature of some of their operations.

3. What forms can international HRM take? What are some of the specific activities each type of international HR manager typically engages in?

4. What intercountry differences affect HRM? Give several examples of how each may specifically affect HRM.

5. A firm is about to send its first employees overseas to staff a new subsidiary. The president asks why such assignments fail, and what can be done to avoid such failures. Write a memo in response to these questions.

6. Choose three traits useful for selecting international assignees, and create a straightforward test (not pencil and paper) to screen candidates for these traits.

7. What special training do overseas candidates need? In what ways is such training similar to and different from traditional diversity training?

8. Describe the most common approach to formulating expatriate pay. Use a library source to determine the relative cost of living in five countries as of this year, and explain the implications of such differences for drafting a pay plan for managers being sent to each country.

9. How does appraising an expatriate's performance differ from appraising that of a home-office manager? How can some of the unique problems of appraising the expatriate's performance be avoided?

10. What accounts for the fact that worker participation has a long and relatively extensive history in Europe? How has this relatively extensive participation affected the labour relations process?

11. What program could be established to reduce repatriation problems of returning expatriates?

Application Exercises

RUNNING CASE: Carter Cleaning Company

Going Abroad

With Jennifer gradually taking the reigns of Carter Cleaning Company, Jack decided to take his first long vacation in years and go to Mexico for a month in January, 1998. What he found surprised him: While he spent much of the time basking in the sun in Acapulco, he also spent considerable time in Mexico City and was surprised at the dearth of cleaning stores, particularly considering the amount of air pollution in the area. Travelling north, he passed through Juarez, Mexico and was similarly surprised at the relatively few cleaning stores he found there. As he flew home, he began to think about whether the NAFTA Agreement might not be enough of a boost to the Mexican economy to actually make it advisable to consider expanding his chain of stores into Mexico.

Quite aside from the possible economic benefits, he liked what he had seen of the lifestyle in Mexico and was also attracted by the idea of possibly facing the sort of exciting challenge he had experienced years ago when he started Carter Cleaning in Canada: "I guess entrepreneurship is in my blood," is the way he put it.

As he drove home from the airport to have dinner with Jennifer, he began to formulate the questions he would have to ask before deciding whether or not to expand abroad.

Questions

1. Assuming they began by opening just one or two stores in Mexico, what are the main HR-related challenges he and Jennifer would have to address?

2. How should Jack and Jennifer go about choosing a manager for their new store? For instance, should they hire someone locally or send someone from one of the existing stores? Why?

3. The cost of living in Mexico is substantially below that of Ontario where Carter is now located: How can they go about developing a pay plan for their new manager if they decided to send an expatriate to Mexico?

4. Present a detailed explanation of the factors Jack and Jennifer should look for in a candidate for an expatriate management position in Mexico.

Video Case

Burma Primer

The country of Myanmar (formerly known as Burma) is a nation of 45 million people ruled by an oppressive military regime, who took power from a democratically elected government, and placed the democratic leader under house arrest. They have carried out brutal repression of any opposition, including civil wars with several ethnic groups. The Myanmar people are considered conservative even by Asian standards, and they do not want their culture to be "polluted" by others. However, after three decades of isolation, they want to join in on the economic boom in Asia and are actively seeking more foreign investment in Myanmar. Their Asian neighbours are particularly interested as they are not concerned with human rights issues to the extent that Western countries are.

Dozens of hotels are being built to house foreign tourists, even though the transportation systems are poor and power is often interrupted. The newly privatized banking system is disorganized and inefficient. A number of practices on the part of the Myanmar government are considered to be a violation of human rights by Western standards. For example, the "national work tax" is the use of unpaid forced labour to build hotels and other projects. These and other problems have led to calls for an international boycott of Myanmar.

Questions

1. What problems might Canadian companies have in hiring workers in Myanmar?
2. What problems might Canadian managers working in Myanmar face? What kind of training, if any, might be advisable for these managers prior to leaving Canada?
3. Should Canadian business boycott countries like Myanmar with oppressive military regimes and poor human rights records? Why or why not?

Video Resource: CBC, *Venture,* "Burma," March 12, 1995.

Take It to the Net

Check out our Companion Website at

http://www.prenticehall.ca/dessler

for a multitude of practice questions, key terms and concepts, Weblinks to related sites, newsgroups, CBC video updates, and more.

Notes

1. *Statistics Canada Report 11-010-XPB,* October 1997.
2. Gary Dessler, *Managing Organizations in an Era of Change,* (Ft. Worth, TX: Dryden, 1995), chapter 2.
3. See, for example, John Daniels and Lee Radebaugh, *International Business* (Reading, MA: Addison-Wesley, 1994), p. 544.
4. Dessler, *Managing Organizations in an Era of Change,* pp. 45–6.
5. Katherine Rudie Harrigan, "Joint Ventures and Global Strategies," *Columbia Journal of World Business* 19 (Summer 1984), pp. 7–16; Michael Czinkota et al., *International Business,* (Ft. Worth, TX: Dryden Press, 1992), p. 278.
6. Charles Hill, *International Business,* (Burr Ridge, IL: Irwin, 1994), p. 4.
7. Richard Robinson, *Internationalization of Business: An Introduction,* (Hindsdale, IL: Dryden, 1984), pp. 271–2.
8. Theodore Levitt, "The Globalization of Markets," *Harvard Business Review* (May–June 1983), pp. 92–102.
9. For a discussion, see Dennis Briscoe, *International Human Resource Management* (Englewood Cliffs, NJ: Prentice-Hall, 1995), pp. 6–8.
10. These are based on Eduard Gaugler, "HR Management: An International Comparison," *Personnel* (August 1988), pp. 24–30. See also Yasuol Kuwahara, "New Developments in Human Resource Management in Japan," *Asia Pacific Journal of Human Resources* 31, no. 2 (1993), pp. 3–11; and Charlene Marmer Solomon, "How Does Your Global Talent Measure Up," *Personnel Journal* (October 1994), pp. 96–108.
11. For a discussion of this, see Gaugler, "HR Management," p. 26; see also George Palmer, "Transferred to Tokyo–A Guide to Etiquette in the Land of the Rising Sun," *Multinational Business* no. 4 (1990/1991), pp. 36–44.
12. David Ralston, Priscilla Elsass, David Gustafson, Fannie Cheung, and Robert Terpstra, "Eastern Values: A Comparison of Managers in the United States, Hong Kong, and the People's Republic of China," *Journal of Applied Psychology* 71, no. 5 (1992), pp. 664–71.
13. Geert Hofstede, "Cultural Dimensions in People Management," in Vladimir Pucik, Noel Tishy, and Carole Barnett (Eds.), *Globalizing Management,* (New York: John Wiley & Sons, Inc., 1992), p. 143.
14. Hofstede, "Cultural Dimensions."
15. Gaugler, "HR Management," p. 27. See also Simcha Ronen and Oded Shenkar, "Using Employee Attitudes to Establish MNC Regional Divisions," *Personnel* (August 1988), pp. 32–9.
16. "Labor Costs in Manufacturing by Nation," *BNA Bulletin to Management* (August 4, 1994), pp. 244–5.
17. "Comparing Employment Practices," *BNA Bulletin to Management* (April 22, 1993), p. 1.
18. This is discussed in Gaugler, "HR Management," p. 28.
19. This is based on Rae Sedel, "Europe 1992: HR Implications of the European Unification," *Personnel* (October 1989), pp. 19–24. See also Chris Brewster and Ariane Hegewish, "A Continent of Diversity," *Personnel Management* (January 1993), pp. 36–9.
20. Daniels and Radebaugh, *International Business,* p. 764.
21. Based on B.J. Punnett, "International Human Resources Management," in A.M. Rugman (ed.), *International Business in Canada: Strategies for Management* (Scarborough, Ontario: Prentice Hall Canada, 1989), pp. 330–46).
22. R.L. Tung, "Selection and Training Procedures of U.S., European, and Japanese Multinationals," *California Management Review* 25 (1982), pp. 51–71.
23. Discussed in Charles Hill, *International Business,* pp. 511–5.
24. Michael Schell, quoted in Charlene Marmer Solomon, "Success Abroad Depends on More than Job Skills," *Personnel Journal* (April, 1994), p. 52.
25. Punnett, "International Human Resources Management," pp. 334–5.
26. Daniels and Radebaugh, *International Business,* p. 767.
27. Arvind Phatak, *International Dimensions of Management,* (Boston: PWS-Kent, 1989), pp. 106–7.
28. Phatak, *International Dimensions of Management,* p. 106.
29. Daniels and Radebaugh, *International Business,* p. 767.
30. Daniels and Radebaugh, *International Business,* p. 768; Phatak, *International Dimensions of Management,* p. 106.
31. Phatak, *International Dimensions of Management,* p. 108.
32. Daniels and Radebaugh, *International Business,* p. 769.
33. Daniels and Radebaugh, *International Business,* p. 769; Phatak, *International Dimensions of Management,* p. 106.
34. Howard Perlmutter, "The Torturous Evolution of the Multinational Corporation," *Columbia Journal of World Business* 3, no. 1 (January–February 1969), pp. 11–4, discussed in Phatak, *International Dimensions of Management,* p. 129.
35. Phatak, *International Dimensions of Management,* p. 129.
36. Phatak *International Dimensions of Management.*
37. Hill, *International Business,* p. 507.
38. Hill, *International Business,* pp. 507–10.
39. Hill, *International Business,* p. 509.
40. Hill *International Business.*
41. Phatak, *International Dimensions of Management,* p. 113; and Charlene Marmer Solomon, "Staff Selection Impacts Global Success," *Personnel Journal* (January 1994), pp. 88–101. For another view, see Anne Harzing, "The Persistent Myth of High Expatriate Failure Rates," *International Journal of Human Resource Management* 6, no. 2 (May 1995), pp. 457–74.
42. These are based on Hill, *International Business,* pp. 513–6; Phatak, *International Dimensions of Management,* pp. 113–6; Daniels and Radebaugh, *International Business,* pp. 770–6; and Michael Czinkota, Pietra Rivoli, and Ilkka Ronkainen, *International Business* (Ft. Worth, TX: Dryden, 1992), pp. 514–6.
43. Phatak, *International Dimensions of Management,* p. 114.
44. Several of these are based on M. Mendenhall and G. Oddou, "The Dimensions of Expatriate Acculturation: A Review," *Academy of Management Review* 10 (1985), pp. 39–47.
45. Winfred Arthur, Jr. and Winston Bennett, Jr., "The International Assignee: The Relative Importance of Factors Perceived to Contribute to Success," *Personnel Psychology* 48 (1995), pp. 99–114; table on pp. 106–7. See also Davison and Betty Punnett, "International Assignments: Is There a

Role for Gender and Race in Decisions?" *International Journal of Human Resource Management* 6, no. 2 (May 1995), pp. 411–41.

46. Arthur and Bennett, "International Assignments," pp. 105–8.
47. Arthur and Bennett, "International Assignments," p. 110.
48. Phatak, *International Dimensions of Management*, p. 119.
49. See, for example, Blocklyn, "Developing the International Executive," p. 45.
50. Blocklyn, "Developing the International Executive," p. 45.
51. Discussed in Madelyn Callahan, "Preparing the New Global Manager," *Training and Development Journal* (March 1989), p. 30. The publisher of the inventory is the New York consulting firm Moran, Stahl & Boyer; see also Jennifer Laabs, "The Global Talent Search," *Personnel Journal* (August 1991), pp. 38–44 for a discussion of how firms such as Coca-Cola recruit and develop international managers, and T.S. Chan, "Developing International Managers: A Partnership Approach," *Journal of Management Development* 13 no. 3, (1994), pp. 38–46.
52. Callahan, "Preparing the New Global Manager," pp. 29–30. See also Charlene Marmer Solomon, "Global Operations Demand that HR Rethink Diversity," *Personnel Journal* (July 1994), pp. 40–50.
53. This is based on Callahan, "Preparing the New Global Manager," p. 30. See also Daniel Feldman, "Repatriate Moves as Career Transitions," *Human Resource Management Review* 1, no. 3 (Fall 1991), pp. 163–78; and John Yanouzas and Sotos Boukis, "Transporting Management Training into Poland: Some Surprises and Disappointments," *Journal of Management Development* 12, no. 1 (1993), pp. 64–71. See also Jennifer Laabs, "How Gilette Grooms Global Talent," *Personnel Journal* (August 1993), pp. 64–76, and Charlene Marmer Solomon, "Transplanting Corporate Cultures Globally," *Personnel Journal* (October 1993), pp. 78–88.
54. James Stoner and R. Edward Freeman, *Management,* 4th ed. (Englewood Cliffs, NJ: Prentice Hall, 1989), p. 783. See also John Cartland, "Reward Policies in a Global Corporation," *Business Quarterly,* (Autumn 1993), pp. 93–6; and Laura Mazur, "Europay,"*Across-the-Board* (January 1995), pp. 40–3.
55. Hewitt Associates, "On Compensation," (May 1989), p. 1 (Hewitt Associates, 86–87 East Via De Ventura, Scottsdale, Arizona 85258).
56. Hewitt Associates, "On Compensation," p. 2.
57. Hill, *International Business*, pp. 519–520.
58. Phatak, *International Dimensions of Management*, p. 134.
59. This is based on Brian Brooks, "Long-Term Incentives: International Executives Need Them, Too," *Personnel* (August 1988), pp. 40–2. See also James Ward and Mark Blumenthal, "Localization: A Study in Cost Containment," *Innovations in International Compensation* 17, no. 4, (November, 1991), pp. 3–4. See also Laura Mazur, "Europay," *Across the Board* 32, no. 1, (January 1995), pp. 40–3.
60. Brooks, "Long-Term Incentives," p. 41.
61. Except as noted, this is based on Gary Addou and Mark Mendenhall, "Expatriate Performance Appraisal: Problems and Solutions," in Mark Mendenhall and Gary Addou, *International Human Resource Management,* (Boston: PWS-Kent Publishing Co., 1991), pp. 364–74.
62. Addou and Mendenhall, "Expatriate Performance Appraisal," p. 366. See also Maddy Janssens, "Evaluating International Managers' Performance: Parent Company Standards as Control Mechanism," *The International Journal of Human Resource Management* 5, no. 4, (December 1994), pp. 853–73.
63. Robert Sauer and Keith Voelker, *Labor Relations: Structure and Process* (New York: Macmillan, 1993), pp. 510–25.
64. Sauer and Voelker, *Labour Relations*, p. 516. See also Marino Regini, "Human Resource Management and Industrial Relations in European Companies," *The International Journal of Human Resource Management* 4, no. 3, (September 1993), pp. 555–68.
65. Quoted from Sauer and Voelker, *Labour Relations*, p. 519.
66. Definition based on Dennis Briscoe, *International Human Resource Management,* p. 65. See also Linda Stroh, "Predicting Turnover Among Repatriates: Can Organizations Affect Retention Rates?" *International Journal of Human Resource Management* 6, no. 2, (May 1995), pp. 443–56.
67. Phatak, *International Dimensions of Management*, p. 124. See also Reyer Swaak, "Today's Expatriate Families: Dual Careers and Other Obstacles," *Compensation and Benefits Review* 27, no. 3, (May 1995), pp. 21–6.
68. These are based on Briscoe, *International Human Resource Management*, p. 66; Phatak, *International Dimensions of Management*, p. 124; and Daniels and Radebaugh, *International Business*, p. 772.
69. Briscoe, *International Human Resource Management*, p. 66.
70. Phatak, *International Dimensions of Management*, p. 126.

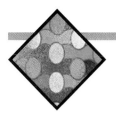

Index

Name and Organization

Subject

Note: Key terms are boldface.